FOURTH EDITION

Criminal Law and Procedure

JOHN M. SCHEB, J.D., LL.M.

Judge, Florida Court of Appeal, Second District (Ret.)
Distinguished Professorial Lecturer, Stetson University College of Law

JOHN M. SCHEB II, Ph.D.

Professor of Political Science
University of Tennessee

WADSWORTH

THOMSON LEARNING™

Australia • Canada • Mexico • Singapore • Spain • United Kingdom • United States

WADSWORTH

★
™

THOMSON LEARNING

DISCLAIMER

In this textbook the authors have attempted to present the general principles of substantive and procedural criminal law. However, because of the variance in statutes and court decisions from state to state, it is recommended that students and officers conduct their own research or consult with their legal advisors and not assume that principles of law applicable in other states apply in their state.

Executive Editor, Criminal Justice: Sabra Horne
Criminal Justice Editor: Shelley Murphy
Development Editor: Terri Edwards
Assistant Editor: Dawn Mesa
Editorial Assistant: Lee McCracken
Marketing Manager: Jennifer Somerville
Marketing Assistant: Karyl Davis
Project Manager, Editorial Production: Jennie Redwitz
Print/Media Buyer: Robert King
Technology Project Manager: Susan DeVanna

Permissions Editor: Stephanie Keough-Hedges
Production Service: Matrix Productions
Text Designer: Adriane Bosworth
Copy Editor: Donald Pharr
Cover Designer: Bill Stanton
Cover Image: Arrest scene: Stone/Rex Viak; Scales: Corbis
Cover Printer: R. R. Donnelley, Willard
Compositor: ColorType, San Diego
Printer: R. R. Donnelley, Willard

ExamView® and ExamView Pro® are registered trademarks of FSCreations, Inc. Windows is a registered trademark of the Microsoft Corporation used herein under license. Macintosh and Power Macintosh are registered trademarks of Apple Computer, Inc. Used herein under license.

Library of Congress Cataloging-in-Publication Data
Scheb, John M. (John Malcolm), [date]
   Criminal Law and procedure / John M. Scheb, John M. Scheb II.—4th ed.
      p. cm.
   Includes index
   ISBN 0-534-57259-6
   1. Criminal law—United States. 2. Criminal procedure—United States. I. Scheb. John M., [date] II. Title.
KF9219 .S34 2002
345.73—dc21

Wadsworth/Thomson Learning
10 Davis Drive
Belmont, CA 94002-3098
USA

For information about our products, contact us:
Thomson Learning Academic Resource Center
1-800-423-0563
http://www.wadsworth.com

International Headquarters
Thomson Learning
International Division
290 Harbor Drive, 2nd Floor
Stamford, CT 06902-7477
USA

UK/Europe/Middle East/South Africa
Thomson Learning
Berkshire House
168-173 High Holborn
London WC1V 7AA
United Kingdom

Asia
Thomson Learning
60 Albert Street #15-01
Albert Complex
Singapore 189969

Canada
Nelson Thomson Learning
1120 Birchmount Road
Toronto, Ontario M1K 5G4
Canada

00-068607

This Book Is Dedicated to
Ryan Patrick Scheb and John M. Scheb III

About the Authors

JOHN M. SCHEB was born in Orlando, Florida, in 1926. He entered the practice of law in 1950. He served as municipal judge in Sarasota, Florida, from 1957 to 1959. From 1959 to 1970, he served as City Attorney for the city of Sarasota. In 1974 he was appointed to the Florida District Court of Appeal, second district, a position he held until his retirement in 1992. Judge Scheb is now a Senior Judge for the Florida Court System and Distinguished Professorial Lecturer at Stetson University College of Law in St. Petersburg. He holds the B.A. from Florida Southern College, the J.D. from the University of Florida, and the LL.M. from the University of Virginia.

JOHN M. SCHEB II was born in Sarasota, Florida, in 1955. He attended the University of Florida from 1974 to 1982, receiving the B.A., M.A., and Ph.D. in political science. He is now Professor of Political Science at the University of Tennessee, where he teaches courses in criminal law, constitutional law, administrative law, judicial process, and law in society. Professor Scheb has authored numerous articles in professional journals and is coauthor, with Otis H. Stephens Jr., of *American Constitutional Law*, Second Edition (West/Wadsworth, 1999).

Contents

Preface to the Fourth Edition

This textbook is intended to furnish students in criminology, criminal justice, pre-law, political science, and paralegal studies a concise yet comprehensive introduction to substantive and procedural criminal law. The book is also an appropriate reference for the criminal justice professional who needs to better understand the legal environment in which he or she must function. Of course, laws vary substantially across jurisdictions, and this text is not intended to be a substitute for independent legal research or competent legal advice.

Criminal law is among the most dynamic fields of American law. In this Fourth Edition of *Criminal Law and Procedure*, we have tried to capture some of the important developments that have taken place in the three years since the Third Edition was completed. All of the chapters have been thoroughly updated, and several new excerpts from judicial decisions have been added. Some chapters have been substantially reorganized to make them more coherent and reader-friendly.

To enhance the book's pedagogical utility, we have expanded the use of examples and the "Case-in-Point" feature, which has proved popular in previous editions. We have also incorporated a new feature, "Supreme Court Perspective," that appears in a number of chapters and highlights recent decisions of the U.S. Supreme Court dealing with issues of criminal law and procedure.

Recognizing the increasing importance of the Internet in legal research, we have expanded our treatment of web-based research in our appendix on legal research methods. We have also incorporated "web-based research activities" into each of the chapters. We hope these changes make this book even more useful to students, instructors, and professionals.

Acknowledgments

We would like to thank Donna Buchholz, Esq., who recently received her J.D. degree from Stetson University College of Law; David Grammar Jr., Esq., who has retired from a successful practice of law in Albuquerque, New Mexico; and Sarah Palmer, Esq., staff attorney, Second District Court of Appeal, Lakeland, Florida. Each has contributed by reviewing manuscripts of various chapters. Sally G. Waters, Esq., research librarian at Stetson University College of Law, St. Petersburg, Florida, reviewed our appendix on legal research and added up-to-date information on computerized legal research and use of the Internet.

We also wish to express our gratitude to Keith Clement and John Barbrey, political science graduate students at the University of Tennessee, who provided helpful research assistance in the area of sentencing laws.

As always, we wish to thank the team at Wadsworth Publishing—in particular, Sabra Horne, Shelley Murphy, Terri Edwards, Jennifer Somerville, and Dawn Mesa—for their excellent assistance throughout this project. We also wish to thank the reviewers of this edition.

Finally, we thank our wives, Mary Burns Scheb and Sherilyn Claytor Scheb, for their patience and support, without which the project could not have been undertaken, much less completed.

Naturally, we assume full responsibility for any errors contained herein. We welcome comments and suggestions from our readers.

John M. Scheb
judgescheb@aol.com

John M. Scheb II
scheb@utk.edu

PART I

Legal Foundations of Criminal Justice

CHAPTER

1

Fundamentals of Criminal Law and Procedure

CHAPTER OUTLINE

Introduction

One of the fundamental problems facing any society is how to achieve social control—protecting people's lives and property and establishing socially desirable levels of order, harmony, safety, and decency. Societies have developed several informal means of achieving this control, including family structures, social norms, and religious precepts. In contrast, law is a formal means of social control. Law can be defined as a body of rules prescribed and enforced by government for the regulation and protection of society. Criminal law is that branch of the law prohibiting certain forms of conduct and imposing penalties on those who engage in prohibited behavior.

All modern societies have developed systems for administering criminal justice. In democratic societies such as ours, a person cannot be convicted of a crime unless he or she has committed a specific offense against a law that provides for a penalty. This principle is expressed in the maxim *nullen crimen, nulla poena, sine lege,* a Latin saying that means "there is no crime, there is no punishment, without law." In the United States, formal law governs every aspect of criminal justice, from the enactment of criminal prohibitions to the enforcement of those prohibitions and the imposition of punishment.

Our criminal law prescribes both substantive and procedural rules governing the everyday operation of the criminal justice system. **Substantive criminal law** prohibits certain forms of conduct by defining crimes and establishing the parameters of penalties. **Procedural criminal law** regulates the enforcement of the substantive law, the determination of guilt, and the punishment of those found guilty of crimes. For example, although substantive law makes the possession of heroin a crime, the procedural law regulates the police search and seizure that produce the incriminating evidence. The substantive law makes premeditated murder a crime; the procedural law determines the procedures to be observed at trial and, if a conviction ensues, at sentencing.

Figure 1.1 provides an overview of the system of criminal law and procedure that exists in this country. The figure suggests three fundamental principles at work:

1. **Constitutional supremacy.** In keeping with the ideal of the **rule of law,** the entire system of criminal law and procedure is subordinate to the principles and provisions of the United States Constitution. The Constitution sets forth the powers of government, the limits of those powers, and the rights of individuals. The Constitution thus limits government's power to make and enforce criminal sanctions in several important ways. These limitations are enforced by **judicial review,** which is the power of courts of law to invalidate substantive laws and procedures that are determined to be contrary to the Constitution.

2. **Federalism.** There is a fundamental division of authority between the national government in Washington, D.C., and the fifty state governments. Although both levels of government have authority and responsibility in the realm of criminal justice, most of the day-to-day peacekeeping function is exercised by the states and their political subdivisions (primarily counties and cities). Each of the states has its own machinery of government as well as its own constitution that empowers and limits that government. Each state constitution imposes limits on the criminal justice system within that state. Of course, the provisions of the state constitutions, as well as the statutes adopted by the state legislatures, are subordinate to the provisions of the U.S. Constitution and the laws adopted by Congress.

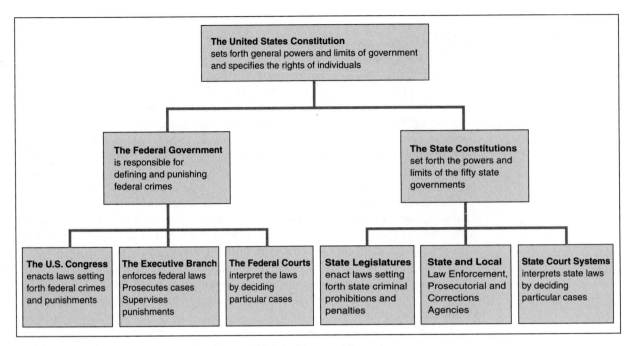

FIGURE 1.1 Overview of the American System of Criminal Law and Procedure

3. **Separation of powers.** The national government and each of the fifty state governments are constructed on the principle that legislative, executive, and judicial powers must be separated into independent branches of government. Thus, the federal government and the states have their own legislative branches, their own executive branches, and their own system of courts. The legislative branch is responsible for enacting laws that specify crimes and punishments. The executive branch is responsible for enforcing those prohibitions and for carrying out the punishments imposed by the judicial branch, but it is the judicial branch that interprets the laws and ensures that persons charged with crimes receive fair treatment by the criminal justice system.

What Is a Crime?

Every crime involves a wrongful act (***actus reus***) specifically prohibited by the criminal law. For example, in the crime of battery, the *actus reus* is the striking or offensive touching of another person. Even the failure to take action can be considered a wrongful act if the law imposes a duty to take action in a certain situation. For example, a person who fails to file a federal income tax return is guilty of a federal offense.

In most cases, the law requires that the wrongful act be accompanied by criminal intent (***mens rea***). Criminal intent does not refer to a person's motive or reason for acting, but merely to having formed a mental purpose to act. To convict a person of a crime, it is not necessary to know why a person committed a crime. It is only necessary to show that the individual intentionally committed a prohibited act. An unintentional act is usually not a crime although, as we will discover, there are exceptions to this principle. Moreover, in certain instances, one may be held criminally responsible irrespective of intent. Crimes of this latter nature are classified as **strict liability**

offenses. A good example of a strict liability offense is selling liquor to a minor. (Strict liability offenses and general elements of crimes are discussed in Chapter 4.)

Felonies and Misdemeanors

Criminal law distinguishes between serious crimes, known as **felonies,** and less serious offenses, called **misdemeanors.** Generally speaking, felonies are offenses for which the offender can be imprisoned for more than one year; misdemeanors carry jail terms of less than one year. Common examples of felonies include murder, rape, kidnapping, arson, assault with a deadly weapon, robbery, and grand larceny. Typical misdemeanors include petit theft, simple assault and battery, public drunkenness, disorderly conduct, prostitution, gambling, and various motor vehicle infractions.

Societal Interests Served by the Criminal Law

We can distinguish among types of crimes by the underlying societal interests that give rise to criminal prohibitions. Obviously, government has a duty to protect the lives and property of citizens—this is the essence of the social contract on which democratic government is based. But society also has an interest in protecting the public peace, order, and safety. Traditionally, the preservation of public morality has been regarded as an important function of the criminal law, although recently this notion has come under attack. Increasingly, the protection of the public health and the preservation of the natural environment are being recognized as societal interests that should be furthered by the criminal law. Finally, society has an interest in efficient and honest public administration and, in particular, the administration of justice. Table 1.1 lists the societal interests served by the criminal law and shows some particular crimes that relate to each interest. The table also indicates the chapters in

Table 1.1 An Overview of Types of Crimes and the Societal Interests Involved		
Societal Interest Being Served	**Examples of Crimes**	**Discussed in**
Protection of Persons Against Violence	Assault and Battery, Rape and Sexual Battery, Murder, Manslaughter, Spousal and Child Abuse, Kidnapping, Stalking	Chapter 6, "Offenses Against Persons"
Protection of Private Property	Vandalism, Theft, Burglary, Arson, Extortion, Forgery, Larceny, Fraud, Embezzlement	Chapter 7, "Crimes Against Property and Habitation" (See also Chapter 10, "White Collar and Organized Crime")
Maintenance of Traditional Morality	Prostitution, Sodomy, Obscenity, Incest, Bigamy, Indecent Exposure, Lewd and Lascivious Conduct, Illegal Gambling, Alcohol and Drug Offenses	Chapter 8, "Offenses Against Public Morality" (see also Chapter 9, "Drug and Alcohol Offenses")
Public Health and the Natural Environment	Fishing and Hunting Violations, Smoking Violations, Illegal Toxic Waste Disposal, Illegal Air Pollution	Chapter 11, "Offenses Against Public Health and the Environment"
Public Peace, Order, and Safety	Disorderly Conduct, Incitement to Riot, Motor Vehicle Offenses, Loitering, Weapons Violations, Alcohol and Drug Offenses	Chapter 12, "Offenses Against Public Order and Safety" (see also Chapter 9, "Drug and Alcohol Offenses")
Honest and Efficient Public Administration and the Administration of Justice	Resisting Arrest, Bribery, Perjury, Obstruction of Justice, Contempt of Court, Escape	Chapter 13, "Offenses Against Justice and Public Administration"

this book that deal with the different types of crimes. Note that some of the crimes relate to more than one societal interest.

Crime: An Injury Against Society

As suggested by the previous discussion of the societal interests served by the criminal law, our legal system regards crimes not merely as wrongs against particular victims but as offenses against the entire society. Indeed, there does not have to be an individual victim for there to be a crime. For example, it is a crime to possess cocaine, even though it is unlikely that a particular individual will claim to have been victimized by another person's use of the drug. This is a crime because society, through its governing institutions, has made a collective judgment that cocaine use is inimical to the public welfare. Similarly, certain consensual sexual acts (for example, sodomy) remain crimes in some jurisdictions because communities continue to regard such actions as contrary to public morality. Of course, as society evolves and its standards change, behaviors that were once defined as crimes (for example, fornication) are no longer subject to criminal sanction. Over time, the particular prohibitions of the criminal law more or less reflect an evolving social consensus about both what is right and wrong and what is public and private. When a particular criminal prohibition is no longer supported by societal consensus (for example, adultery), it is apt to be unenforced or be stricken from the laws.

Because crime is an injury against society, government, as society's legal representative, brings charges against persons accused of committing crimes. In the United States, we have a federal system—that is, a division of power and responsibility between the national and state governments. Both the national government and the states enact their own criminal laws. Thus, both the national government and the state governments may prosecute persons accused of crimes. The national government initiates a prosecution when a federal (national) law has been violated; a state brings charges against someone who is believed to have violated one of its laws. (Chapter 2 discusses the organization of courts and the various actors in the criminal justice system.)

Criminal Responsibility

The criminal law, indeed our entire legal system, rests on the idea that individuals are responsible for their actions and must be accountable for them. This is the essential justification and rationale for imposing punishments on persons convicted of crimes. On the other hand, society recognizes that certain individuals (for example, young children) lack the capacity to appreciate the wrongfulness of their conduct. Similarly, factors beyond individuals' control can lead them to commit criminal acts. In such instances the law exempts individuals from responsibility. Moreover, there are situations in which acts that would otherwise be crimes might be justified. The best example of this is committing a homicide in self-defense. Individuals can invoke a host of defenses beyond a simple denial of guilt. Indeed, a substantial body of law is devoted to the topic of **criminal responsibility** and defenses. We examine this topic in some detail in Chapter 14.

The Role of the Crime Victim

Because the government prosecutes criminals on behalf of society, the **victim** of a crime is not a party to the criminal prosecution. By filing a complaint with a law enforcement agency, a victim initiates the process that leads to prosecution, but once the prosecution begins, the victim's participation is primarily that of being a witness. Quite often, victims feel lost in the shuffle of the criminal process. They sometimes feel that the system is insensitive or even hostile to their interests in seeing justice done. Some states are now taking steps to address victims' concerns. Despite some measures being proposed and others that have been adopted, crime victims remain secondary players in the criminal justice system. The principal parties in a criminal case are the prosecution (that is, the government) and the defendant (that is, the accused person). In some situations, however, the victim might have another remedy: a civil suit to recover damages for losses or injuries suffered.

Civil and Criminal Law

The criminal law is not the only body of law that regulates the conduct of persons. The civil law provides remedies for essentially private wrongs, offenses in which the state has a less direct interest. Most civil wrongs are classified as **breaches of contract** or **torts.** A breach of contract occurs when a party to a contract violates the terms of the agreement. A tort, on the other hand, is a wrongful act that does not violate any enforceable agreement but nevertheless violates a legal right of the injured party. Common examples of torts include wrongful death, intentional or negligent infliction of personal injury, wrongful destruction of property, trespass, and defamation of character. A crime normally entails intentional conduct; thus, a driver whose car accidentally hits and kills another person would not necessarily be guilty of a crime, depending on the circumstances (see discussions of manslaughter and vehicular homicide in Chapter 6). If the accident resulted from the driver's negligence, the driver would have committed the tort of wrongful death and would be subject to a civil suit for damages.

The criminal law and the civil law often overlap. Conduct that constitutes a crime can also involve a tort. For example, suppose Randy Wrecker intentionally damages a house belonging to Harvey Homeowner. Wrecker's act might well result in both criminal and civil actions being brought against him. Wrecker may be prosecuted by the state for the crime of willful destruction of property and may also be sued by Homeowner for the tort of wrongful destruction of property. The state would be seeking to punish Wrecker for his antisocial conduct, whereas Homeowner would be seeking compensation for the damage to his property. The criminal case would be designated *State v. Wrecker* (or *People v. Wrecker,* or even *Commonwealth v. Wrecker,* depending on the state); the civil suit would be styled *Homeowner v. Wrecker.*

The Origins and Sources of the Criminal Law

Many antisocial acts classified as crimes have their origin in the norms of primitive societies. Humanity has universally condemned certain types of behavior since ancient times. Acts such as murder, rape, robbery, and arson are considered ***mala in se,*** or inherent wrongs. Other acts that the modern criminal law regards as offenses are merely ***mala prohibita;*** they are offenses only because they are so defined by the law. Many so-called victimless crimes, such as gambling or possession of marijuana, are generally not regarded as offensive to universal principles of morality. Rather, they are wrong simply because the law declares them wrong. In the case of *mala prohibita* offenses, society has made a collective judgment that certain conduct, although not contrary to universal moral principles, is nevertheless incompatible with the public good.

Development of Law in the Western World

The general consensus is that law developed in Western civilization as leaders began formalizing and enforcing customs that had evolved among their peoples. Eventually, informal norms and customs came to be formalized as codes of law. The Code of Hammurabi regulated conduct in ancient Babylonia some two thousand years before Christ. In the seventh century B.C., Draco developed a very strict code of laws for the Athenian city-states. Even today, one hears strict rules or penalties characterized as being "Draconian." These developments influenced the Romans in their development of the Twelve Tables in the fifth century B.C. And, of course, long before the time of Jesus, the Hebrews had developed very elaborate substantive and procedural laws.

In the sixth century A.D., the Emperor Justinian presided over a codification of the Roman law that would prove to be very influential in the evolution of law on the European continent. The Napoleonic Code, promulgated under Napoleon Bonaparte in 1804 as a codification of all the civil and criminal laws of France, was based largely on the Code of Justinian. The Napoleonic Code became a model for a uniform system of law for Western European nations. This is why the legal systems of Western Europe are often said to be "Roman law" systems. Roman law systems are based on the primacy of statutes enacted by the legislature. These statutes are integrated into a comprehensive code designed to be applied by the courts with a minimum of judicial interpretation.

Development of the English Common Law

American criminal law is derived largely from the **English common law,** which dates from the eleventh century. Before the Norman Conquest of 1066, English law was a patchwork of local laws and customs, often applied by feudal courts. William the Conqueror, the first Norman king of England, dispatched royal judges who traveled the country settling disputes based on the common customs of the people (hence the term common law). By 1300, the decisions of the royal judges were being recorded to serve as precedents to guide judges in future similar cases. The common-law doctrine of following precedent, known as ***stare decisis,*** remains an important component of both the English and American legal systems. As the centuries passed, coherent principles of law and definitions of crimes emerged from the judges' decisions. Thus, in contrast with Roman law systems, which are based on legal codes, the common law developed primarily through judicial decisions.

By 1600, the common-law judges had defined as felonies the crimes of murder, manslaughter, mayhem, robbery, burglary, arson, larceny, rape, suicide, and sodomy. They had also begun to define a number of lesser offenses as misdemeanors. In contrast with the criminal law that was developing on the continent, England developed trial by jury and trained barristers to argue cases on an adversarial basis. A "barrister" is a lawyer permitted to cross the "bar" in the courtroom that separates the bench from the spectators. Thus, in England, a barrister is a trial lawyer. Although we do not use the term barrister in the United States, we do refer to licensed attorneys as having been "admitted to the bar."

As representative government developed in England, the dominance of the common-law courts diminished. Parliament came to play a significant role in the formation of the criminal law by adopting **statutes** that revised and supplemented the common law. The adversarial system of justice continued, however, and the basic English felonies remain today defined essentially as they were by the common-law judges centuries ago.

Development of the American Criminal Law

Our criminal laws are basically derived from the common law as it existed when America proclaimed its independence from England in 1776. After independence, the new American states adopted the English common law to the extent that it did not conflict with the new state and federal constitutions. However, the federal government did not adopt the common law of crimes. From the outset, statutes passed by Congress defined federal crimes. Of the fifty states, Louisiana is the only one whose legal system is not based essentially on the common law. Rather, it is based primarily on the Napoleonic Code.

The new American judges and lawyers were greatly aided by Blackstone's *Commentaries on the Laws of England,* published in 1769, in which Sir William Blackstone, a professor at Oxford, codified the principles of the common law. Blackstone's seminal effort was a noble undertaking, but it demystified English law. Consequently, Blackstone's encyclopedic treatment of the law was less than popular among English barristers, who by this time had developed a close fraternity and took great pride in offering their services to "discover the law." In America, however, **Blackstone's Commentaries** became something of a "legal bible."

State and Local Authority to Enact Criminal Prohibitions

At the time of the American Revolution, the English common law constituted the criminal law of the new United States. As new states entered the Union, their legislatures usually enacted "reception statutes" adopting the common law to the extent that it did not conflict with the federal or their respective state constitutions. Eventually, most common-law definitions of crimes were superseded by legislatively defined offenses in the form of statutes adopted by the state legislatures. Today, the state legislatures are the principal actors in defining crimes and punishments. Persons who violate state criminal statutes are prosecuted in the state courts (see Chapter 2).

For the most part, modern state statutes retain the *mala in se* offenses defined by the common law, but many of the old common-law crime definitions have been modified to account for social and economic changes. For example, the offense of rape originated under English common law, but the offense is defined much differently under modern state statutes. Today, under most state laws, the offender and victim may be of either sex, and the offense encompasses anal and oral as well as vaginal penetrations by a sex organ or by another object. Indeed, the broader modern offense of sexual battery embraces all types of sexual impositions (see Chapter 6).

As we shall see, modern criminal statutes often go far beyond the common law in prohibiting offenses that are *mala prohibita.* Drug and alcohol offenses, environmental crimes, offenses against public health, and traffic violations fall into this category.

When authorized by state constitutions or acts of state legislatures, cities and counties may adopt **ordinances** that define certain criminal violations. Local ordinances typically deal with traffic offenses, animal control, land use, building codes, licensing of businesses, and so forth. Usually these offenses are prosecuted in courts of limited jurisdiction, such as municipal or county courts (see Chapter 2).

Federal Authority to Define Crimes

As we have seen, the common law of crimes was more or less adopted by the various state legislatures. The U.S. Congress never adopted the common law, as there was no need for it to do so. The national government's responsibility in the criminal justice area has always been more limited than that of the states. Unlike the state legislatures, Congress does not possess **police power,** which is the broad authority to enact prohibitions to protect public order, safety, decency, welfare, etc. Yet Congress does possess authority to enact criminal statutes that relate to Congress's particular legislative powers and responsibilities. Thus, there are federal criminal laws that relate to military service, immigration and naturalization, use of the mail, civil rights, and so forth. In particular, Congress has used its broad power to regulate interstate commerce to criminalize a wide range of offenses, including carjacking, loan sharking, kidnapping, illicit drug dealing, wire fraud, and a variety of environmental crimes (see Chapter 3). Of course, persons who commit federal crimes are subject to prosecution in the federal courts (see Chapter 2).

The Model Penal Code (MPC)

The American Law Institute (ALI) is an organization of distinguished judges, lawyers, and academics that have a strong professional interest in drafting model codes of laws. In 1962, after a decade of work that produced several tentative drafts, the ALI published its Proposed Official Draft of the **Model Penal Code** (MPC). The MPC consists of general provisions concerning criminal liability, definitions of specific crimes, defenses, and sentences. The MPC is not law; rather, it is designed as a model code

SUPREME COURT PERSPECTIVE

United States v. Morrison, 529 U.S. 598, 120 S.Ct. 1578, 146 L.Ed.2d 477 (2000)

In this case, which stemmed from an alleged rape by football players at Virginia Tech University, the Supreme Court declared unconstitutional a federal statute that provided a federal civil remedy to victims of "gender-motivated violence." The Court found that the law exceeded Congress's authority to enact legislation regulating interstate commerce. In his opinion for the Court, Chief Justice William Rehnquist stated the following:

"Under our written Constitution . . . the limitation of congressional authority is not solely a matter of legislative grace. . . . We accordingly reject the argument that Congress may regulate noneconomic, violent criminal conduct based solely on that conduct's aggregate effect on interstate commerce. The Constitution requires a distinction between what is truly national and what is truly local. . . . In recognizing this fact we preserve one of the few principles that has been consistent since the [Commerce] Clause was adopted. The regulation and punishment of intrastate violence that is not directed at the instrumentalities, channels, or goods involved in interstate commerce has always been the province of the States. . . . Indeed, we can think of no better example of the police power, which the Founders denied the National Government and reposed in the States, than the suppression of violent crime and vindication of its victims."

The Court's decision in *Morrison* reinforced the traditional notion that Congressional authority to enact criminal law is much more limited than that of the states.

of criminal law for all states. It has had a significant impact on legislative drafting of criminal statutes, particularly during the 1970s, when the majority of the states accomplished substantial reforms in their criminal codes. In addition, the MPC has been influential in judicial interpretation of criminal statutes and doctrines, thereby making a contribution to the continuing development of the decisional law. In this text, we illustrate many principles of law by selected statutes from federal and state jurisdictions; however, in some instances where the MPC is particularly influential, the reader will find references to specific provisions of the MPC.

Sources of Procedural Law

The procedural criminal law is promulgated by legislative bodies, through enactment of statutes, and by the courts, through judicial decisions and the development of rules of court procedure. The U.S. Supreme Court prescribes rules of procedure for the federal courts. Generally, the highest court of each state, usually called the state supreme court, is empowered to promulgate rules of procedure for all the courts of that state.

In addition to the common law, statutes, regulations, and ordinances, the federal and state constitutions contribute to the body of substantive and procedural law. For example, the U.S. Constitution defines the crime of treason, U.S. Const. Art. III, Sec. 3. The Constitution has much to say about criminal procedure, most notably as it relates to search and seizure, U.S. Const. Amend. IV; the protection against compulsory self-incrimination, U.S. Const. Amend. V; the right to counsel, U.S. Const. Amend. VI; and the right to trial by an impartial jury, U.S. Const. Amend. VI. Of course, the courts are primarily responsible for "fleshing out" the general principles of criminal procedure contained in the federal and state constitutions by deciding specific cases presented to them. Also, by adopting statutes, the Congress and the state legislatures provide more detailed rules in this area.

The Role of Courts in Developing the Criminal Law

Although substantive law and procedural criminal law are often modified by federal and state statutes, courts play an equally important role in the development of law. Trial courts exist primarily to make factual determinations, apply settled law to established facts, and impose sanctions. In reviewing the decisions of trial courts, appellate courts must interpret the federal and state constitutions and statutes. The federal and state constitutions are replete with majestic phrases such as "equal protection of the laws" and "privileges and immunities" that require interpretation. That is, courts must define exactly what these grand phrases mean within the context of particular legal disputes. Likewise, federal and state statutes often use vague language like "affecting commerce" or "reasonable likelihood." Courts must assign meaning to these and a multitude of other terms. Although most states have abolished all, or nearly all, common-law crimes and replaced them by statutorily defined offenses, the common law remains a valuable source of statutory interpretation. This is because legislatures frequently use terms known to the common law without defining such terms. For example, in proscribing burglary, the legislature might use the term "curtilage" without defining it. In such an instance, a court would look to the common law, which defined the term to mean "an enclosed space surrounding a dwelling."

In rendering interpretations of the law, appellate courts generally follow precedent, in keeping with the common-law doctrine of *stare decisis*. In our rapidly changing society, however, courts often encounter situations to which precedent arguably does not or should not apply. In such situations, courts will sometimes deviate from or even overturn precedent. Moreover, there are situations in which there is no applicable precedent. When this occurs, the appellate courts will have the opportunity to make new law. Thus, appellate courts perform an important **lawmaking function** as well as an **error correction function.** Therefore, any serious student of criminal law must follow developments in the **decisional law**—that is, law as developed by courts in deciding cases.

Reflecting the central importance of court decisions in the development of the law, this book contains a number of edited court decisions at the end of each chapter (beginning with Chapter 3). We selected these cases to illustrate concepts, principles, and reasoning processes that are central to criminal law and procedure.

Constitutional Limitations on the Criminal Justice System

The prohibitions of the criminal and civil law are subject to limitations contained in the federal and state constitutions. For example, the United States Constitution (Article I, Sections 9 and 10) prohibits Congress and the state legislatures from enacting *ex post facto* **laws.** In essence, an act cannot be made a crime retroactively. To be criminal, an act must be illegal at the time it was committed (see Chapter 3 for more discussion).

The Bill of Rights

Many of the most important constitutional provisions relative to criminal justice are found in the **Bill of Rights** (the first ten amendments to the Constitution adopted by Congress in 1789 and ratified by the states in 1791). For example, the First Amendment to the U.S. Constitution prohibits government from using the civil or criminal law to abridge freedom of speech. To illustrate, a person cannot be punished merely for advocating violence unless there is "imminent lawless action." *Brandenburg v. Ohio*, 395 U.S. 444, 89 S.Ct. 1827, 23 L.Ed.2d 430 (1969). The First Amendment also has important implications for the crimes of obscenity and public indecency. Other provisions and principles of the Bill of Rights limit the authority of government to define certain conduct as criminal. These limitations will be discussed in some detail in Chapter 3.

In addition to limitations on the enactment of criminal laws, the Bill of Rights has much to say about the enforcement of these laws. These provisions, which constitute much of the basis of criminal procedure, include the Fourth Amendment prohibition of unreasonable searches and seizures, the Fifth Amendment injunction against compulsory self-incrimination, and the Sixth Amendment right to trial by jury. Finally, the Eighth Amendment prohibition of "cruel and unusual punishments" protects citizens against criminal penalties that are barbaric or excessive.

Virtually all the provisions of the Bill of Rights have been held to apply with equal force to the states and to the national government. *Duncan v. Louisiana*, 391 U.S. 145, 88 S.Ct. 1444, 20 L.Ed.2d 491 (1968). Thus, the Bill of Rights limits the adoption of criminal laws, whether by Congress, the state legislatures, or the myriad city and county legislative bodies. The Bill of Rights also limits the actions of police, prosecutors, judges, and corrections officers at the local, state, and national levels.

Due Process of Law

By far the broadest, and probably the most important, constitutional principle relating to criminal procedure is found in the due process clauses of the Fifth and Fourteenth amendments to the Constitution. The same principle can be found in similar provisions of every state constitution. Reflecting a legacy that can be traced to the Magna Charta (1215), such provisions forbid the government from taking a person's life, liberty, or property, whether as punishment for a crime or any other reason, without **due process of law.** Due process refers to those procedural safeguards necessary to ensure the fundamental fairness of a legal proceeding. Most fundamentally, due process requires **fair notice** and a **fair hearing.** That is, persons accused of crimes must have ample opportunity to learn of the charges and evidence being brought against them as well as the opportunity to contest those charges and that evidence in open court.

The Presumption of Innocence

One of the most basic tenets of due process in a criminal case is that the defendant is presumed innocent and that the prosecution must establish the defendant's guilt beyond a reasonable doubt. *In re Winship,* 397 U.S. 358, 90 S.Ct. 1068, 25 L.Ed.2d 368 (1970). A classic statement of the **presumption of innocence** and the closely related **reasonable doubt standard** was given by the Massachusetts Supreme Court more than a century ago:

> The burden of proof is upon the prosecutor. All the presumptions of law independent of evidence are in favor of innocence; and every person is presumed to be innocent until he is proved guilty. If upon such proof there is reasonable doubt remaining, the accused is entitled to the benefit of it by an acquittal. For it is not sufficient to establish a probability, though a strong one arising from the doctrine of chances, that the fact charged is more likely to be true than the contrary, but the evidence must establish the truth of the fact to a reasonable and moral certainty; a certainty that convinces and directs the understanding, and satisfies the reason and judgment, of those who are bound to act conscientiously upon it. *Commonwealth v. Webster,* 59 Mass. 295, 320 (1850).

The reasonable doubt standard that applies in criminal prosecutions differs markedly from the preponderance of evidence standard that applies to civil cases. In a civil trial, the judge or jury must find only that the weight of the evidence favors the plaintiff or the defendant. In a criminal case, the fact finder must achieve the "moral certainty" that arises from eliminating "reasonable doubt" as to the defendant's guilt. Of course, it is difficult to define with precision the term "reasonable." Ultimately, this is a judgment call left to the individual judge or juror.

Stages in the Criminal Process

Certain basic procedural steps are common to all criminal prosecutions, although specific procedures vary greatly among jurisdictions. As cases move through the system from arrest through adjudication and, in many instances, toward the imposition of punishment, there is considerable attrition. Of any one hundred felony arrests, perhaps as few as twenty-five will result in convictions. This "sieve effect" occurs for many reasons, including insufficient evidence, police misconduct, procedural errors, and the transfer of young offenders to juvenile courts.

Search and Seizure

Searches are directed at locating evidence of crime; seizures occur when searches are fruitful. Like all activities of law enforcement, **search and seizure** are subject to constitutional limitations. The Fourth Amendment to the U.S. Constitution, enforceable against the states through the Due Process Clause of the Fourteenth Amendment, explicitly protects citizens from unreasonable searches and seizures. *Mapp v. Ohio,* 367 U.S. 643, 81 S.Ct. 1684, 6 L.Ed.2d 1081 (1961). The Supreme Court has interpreted this protection as requiring law enforcement officers to have specific grounds for conducting searches: either probable cause or, in some instances, the less stringent standard of reasonable suspicion. *Terry v. Ohio,* 392 U.S. 1, 88 S.Ct. 1868, 20 L.Ed.2d 889 (1968). Furthermore, the Court has held that officers must obtain warrants authorizing searches unless exigent circumstances make it impracticable to obtain a warrant and also preserve evidence of crime. *Carroll v. United States,* 267 U.S. 132, 45 S.Ct. 280, 69 L.Ed. 543 (1925). There are several well-defined types of searches, each subject to a distinct set of constitutional rules. The limited investigatory detention, the stop-and-frisk, the border search, the search incident to a lawful arrest, and electronic eavesdropping are some types of searches that have been addressed by the courts.

To enforce the protections of the Fourth Amendment, the Supreme Court has fashioned a broad **exclusionary rule** that bars the fruits of illegal searches and seizures from being used as evidence in criminal trials. *Weeks v. United States,* 232 U.S. 383, 34 S.Ct. 341, 58 L.Ed. 652 (1914); *Mapp v. Ohio,* 367 U.S. 643, 81 S.Ct. 1684, 6 L.Ed.2d 1081 (1961). Recent decisions by the Court have somewhat narrowed the scope of this exclusionary rule. See, for example, *United States v. Leon,* 468 U.S. 897, 104 S.Ct. 3405, 82 L.Ed.2d 677 (1984). Nevertheless, because it excludes from many cases evidence that is both reliable and probative, the exclusionary rule remains controversial. (Search and seizure are discussed thoroughly in Chapter 15.)

Arrest and Interrogation

Arrest consists of taking into custody a person whom the police have probable cause to believe committed a crime. Arrests can be made on the basis of warrants issued by magistrates or indictments handed down by grand juries. More commonly, arrests are made by police who observe commission of a crime or have probable cause to believe a crime has been committed, but face exigent circumstances that prevent them from obtaining an arrest warrant. When an officer restricts a person from leaving the officer's presence or formally places that person under arrest, several constitutional protections come into play. These include the well-known *Miranda* warnings given to suspects in custody advising them of their constitutional rights. *Miranda v. Arizona,* 384 U.S. 436, 86 S.Ct. 1602, 16 L.Ed.2d 694 (1966).

The investigative tool of **police interrogation** takes many forms—from direct questioning to the use of subtle psychological techniques. Subject to narrow exceptions, custodial interrogation is not permitted until the suspect has been issued the *Miranda* warnings and has either waived those rights or has obtained counsel. A Fifth Amendment analogue of the Fourth Amendment exclusionary rule requires that confessions obtained by police through custodial interrogation must be excluded from evidence unless they meet these constitutional criteria. *Miranda v. Arizona,* supra.

Generally, an individual arrested for a minor misdemeanor is released from police custody and ordered to appear in court at a later date to answer the charge. If the arrest is for a major misdemeanor or felony, the individual is usually held in custody pending an initial appearance before a judge or magistrate. (Arrest and interrogation are discussed thoroughly in Chapter 16.)

Initial Appearance

Under the Constitution, a person accused of a crime has the right to a **speedy and public trial.** U.S. Const., Amend. VI. This includes the right to be brought before a judge to be formally apprised of the charges. In addition to reading the charges, the judge at the first appearance attempts to ascertain whether the defendant is represented by an attorney. If not, and the defendant is indigent, the judge generally appoints counsel. Finally, the judge determines whether the accused is to be released from custody pending further proceedings. A defendant who is granted **pretrial release** can be released either on bail or on his or her own promise to appear in court. In deciding whether to grant pretrial release, and whether to require that the defendant post a bond to assure the court the defendant will appear to answer the charges, a judge must weigh the seriousness of the alleged crime as well as the defendant's prior record and ties to the community.

Summary Trials for Minor Offenses

For minor misdemeanors, including many traffic violations, trials are often held in a summary fashion without the use of a jury, usually at the defendant's first appearance in court. The U.S. Supreme Court has held that a jury trial is not constitutionally required unless the defendant is subject to incarceration for more than six months. *Duncan v. Louisiana,* 391 U.S. 145, 88 S.Ct. 1444, 20 L.Ed.2d 491 (1968). In such cases, we might question whether the traditional presumption of innocence readily applies. In a **summary trial** the charges are read, the defendant is asked to plead to the charges, and a verdict is reached, often within a few minutes. In most such cases, defendants do in fact plead guilty, but even when they proclaim their innocence, they are seldom acquitted. This is largely because judges are more inclined to take the word of the arresting officer than that of the accused, and rarely are there any additional witnesses. Although a person charged with any criminal offense has the right to retain counsel, most defendants charged with minor misdemeanors are not represented by counsel. A principal reason is the expense of retaining a lawyer, which can exceed the fine imposed. The Supreme Court has said that indigent persons do not have a right to counsel at public expense unless they are actually sentenced to more than six months in jail. *Scott v. Illinois,* 440 U.S. 367, 99 S.Ct. 1158, 59 L.Ed.2d 383 (1979).

The Grand Jury Indictment

According to the Constitution, "no person shall be held to answer for a capital, or other infamous crime, unless on a presentment of indictment of a Grand Jury. . . ." U.S. Const. Amend. V. The **grand jury,** not to be confused with the **trial jury,** is a body that considers evidence obtained by the prosecutor to determine whether there is probable cause to hold a trial. Grand juries also have the power to conduct investigations on their own initiative. As a mechanism designed to prevent unwarranted prosecutions, the grand jury dates back to twelfth-century England.

Each federal judicial district maintains a grand jury. These grand juries comprise twenty-three jurors. Grand juries are also maintained in many state jurisdictions, although the Supreme Court has held that states are not required to use grand juries in charging criminal defendants. *Hurtado v. California,* 110 U.S. 516, 4 S.Ct. 111, 28 L.Ed. 232 (1884).

Grand jury proceedings are typically closed to the public. The prosecutor appears before the grand jury with a series of cases he or she has built against various defendants. Witnesses are called, and physical evidence is presented. If the grand jury believes that a given case is substantial, it hands down an **indictment,** or true bill. In the overwhelming majority of cases, grand juries hand down indictments against persons as requested by prosecutors, leading some to question the utility of the grand jury procedure as a means of guarding against arbitrary or unwarranted prosecution.

The Preliminary Hearing

About half of the states, especially those that entered the Union later, have dispensed with or limited the functions of grand juries. These states have opted instead for charging defendants in a fashion that is less cumbersome and arguably more protective of the innocent. Under the more modern approach, the prosecutor files an accusatorial document called an **information** containing the charge against the accused. A **preliminary hearing** is then held in which a judge or magistrate must determine whether there is probable cause to hold the defendant for trial. At the preliminary hearing, the prosecutor presents physical evidence and testimony designed to persuade the judge that probable cause exists. The defense attorney, whose client is also usually present, generally exercises the right to cross-examine the prosecution's witnesses. In addition, the defense may, but seldom does, present evidence on behalf of the defendant at that time.

Several states—for example, Tennessee and Georgia—use the grand jury mechanism, supplemented by an optional preliminary hearing. This hybrid model provides a double check against the possibility of unwarranted prosecution. In other states, the grand jury is retained for capital cases; lesser felonies are charged via an information.

Arraignment

The **arraignment** is the defendant's first appearance before the court that has the authority to conduct a trial. At this stage the defendant must plead to the charges that have been brought. The defendant has four options: (1) to plead guilty, in which case guilt will be pronounced and a date set for sentencing; (2) to plead not guilty, in which case a trial date will be set; (3) to plead *nolo contendere,* or no contest (with the approval of the court), which is tantamount to a plea of guilty; (4) to remain silent, in which case the court enters a plea of not guilty on behalf of the accused.

Plea Bargaining

Only a small proportion (perhaps five percent) of felony cases ever reach the trial stage. Many cases are dropped by the prosecutor for lack of evidence. Some cases are dropped because of obvious police misconduct. Others are dismissed by judges at preliminary hearings, usually for similar reasons. Of the cases that reach the arraignment stage, only a fraction result in trials. In most cases, defendants enter pleas of guilty, often in exchange for concessions from the prosecution. To avoid trial, which is characterized by both delay and uncertainty, the prosecutor often attempts to persuade the defendant to plead guilty, either by reducing the number or severity of charges, or by promising not to seek the maximum penalty allowed by law.

Under a **plea bargain,** a charge of possession of cocaine with intent to distribute might be reduced to simple possession. First-degree murder, which may carry a death sentence, might be reduced to second-degree murder, which carries a term of imprisonment. A series of misdemeanor charges stemming from an altercation in a bar might be reduced to a single charge of disorderly conduct.

The U.S. Supreme Court has upheld the practice of plea bargaining against claims that it violates the due process clauses of the Fifth and Fourteenth amendments. *Brady v. United States,* 397 U.S. 742, 90 S.Ct. 1463, 25 L.Ed.2d 747 (1970); *North Carolina v. Alford,* 400 U.S. 25, 91 S.Ct. 160, 27 L.Ed.2d 162 (1970). However, because there is always a danger of coerced guilty pleas, especially when defendants are ignorant of the law, it is the judge's responsibility to ascertain whether the defendant's guilty plea is voluntarily and knowingly entered and that there is some factual basis for the offense charged. *Boykin v. Alabama,* 395 U.S. 238, 89 S.Ct. 1709, 23 L.Ed.2d 274 (1969).

Pretrial Motions

Typically, a number of **pretrial motions** are available to both the defense and prosecution in a criminal case. Of particular importance are these motions:

1. To dismiss the charges against the accused
2. To inspect evidence in the hands of the prosecution
3. To request suppression of evidence because of alleged illegalities in gathering the evidence
4. To request a change of venue (location) of a trial to protect the accused from prejudicial pretrial publicity
5. To request a continuance (postponement) of the trial
6. To inspect the minutes of grand jury proceedings
7. To request psychiatric evaluation of the accused
8. To request closure of pretrial proceedings (again, to protect the right of the accused to a fair trial)

Pretrial motions are important vehicles in the adversary process. They enable the prosecution and defense to explore areas of concern and determine the strength of the prosecution's case. Thus, the rulings on these motions often lead to dismissal of a case or to plea negotiations, all part of the "sieve effect" we mentioned earlier. When the pretrial processes do not lead to a resolution of a case, they frame the issues and organize the evidence, thereby setting the stage for the formal adversarial presentation that occurs in a criminal trial. (Pretrial procedures from initial appearance through pretrial motions are discussed in greater detail in Chapter 17.)

Jury Selection

The Supreme Court has held that defendants in both state and federal prosecutions have the right to a jury trial if they are subject to more than six months' incarceration. *Duncan v. Louisiana,* supra. Potential trial jurors (referred to collectively as the venire) are selected typically, but not universally, from the rolls of registered voters. The actual process of jury selection, known as *voir dire,* consists of questioning potential jurors to determine their suitability for jury duty. In the federal courts, *voir dire* is conducted primarily by the judge; in the states, it is typically conducted by the attorneys for both sides. In all jurisdictions, attorneys may challenge jurors they find to be unsuitable. Attorneys may exercise a limited number of **peremptory challenges,** which are generally granted as a matter of course. However, peremptory challenges may not be based solely on the race or gender of a prospective juror. *Batson v. Kentucky,* 476 U.S. 79, 106 S.Ct. 1712, 90 L.Ed.2d 69 (1986); *J.E.B. v. Alabama ex rel. T.B.,* 511 U.S. 127, 114 S.Ct. 1419, 128 L.Ed.2d 89 (1994).

Unlike peremptory challenges, **challenges for cause** must be supported by reasons acceptable to the court. The attorney making the challenge must articulate a reason that the prospective juror is unsuitable. However, there is considerable discretion in the court's allowance of such challenges. Although peremptory challenges are limited in number, there is no set limit to the number of challenges for cause.

Trial Procedures and Adjudication

The **criminal trial** is a formal and complex adversarial encounter between the government and the accused. The trial is governed by **rules of evidence** and procedure that are designed to develop the case in an orderly fashion and assist the fact finder (judge or jury) in reaching the correct result. After opening statements by counsel, the prosecution, by introducing testimony and physical evidence, attempts to prove the guilt of the accused beyond a reasonable doubt. The defense's goal is to create reasonable doubt about the government's case. In some cases, the defense relies solely on cross-examination of the prosecution's witnesses to establish doubt. In most cases, the defense introduces evidence to contradict the evidence against the defendant or to discredit the government's witnesses. Witnesses called by each side are subject to cross-examination, and physical evidence is subject to inspection and challenge. During closing arguments, counsel attempt to persuade juries of the merits of their positions. Following this, the trial judge instructs the jury about the relevant points of law and the jurors' responsibilities in reaching a verdict. When a jury returns a verdict of guilty, defense counsel frequently moves for a new trial or other relief. (Trial procedures are discussed at length in Chapter 18.)

Sentencing

After an accused person has been convicted, the process moves into the **sentencing** phase. Frequently, a separate court appearance is scheduled to allow a presentence investigation before sentence is imposed. In imposing sentences, judges generally must follow statutory requirements governing the type and severity of sentence for particular crimes. Types of sentences include probation, incarceration, work release, monetary fines, community service, and, of course, death. Different statutory approaches govern the length of prison sentences that courts may impose. Indeterminate sentencing occurs when individuals are incarcerated for periods of time to be determined by correctional agencies. Determinate sentencing occurs when statutes specify prison terms for particular crimes. In most jurisdictions, judges can impose particular sentences within broad parameters defined by statutes. In recent years, we have witnessed two trends away from broad judicial discretion in sentencing. First is the tendency for legislatures to require flat or mandatory sentences for the most serious crimes. Second, some jurisdictions have developed sentencing guidelines to address the problem of sentencing disparity.

Congress enacted the Sentencing Reform Act of 1984 to "provide certainty and fairness in meeting the purposes of sentencing, avoiding unwarranted sentencing disparities among defendants with similar records who have been found guilty of similar criminal conduct while maintaining sufficient flexibility to permit individualized sentences also warranted by mitigating or aggravating factors. . . ." 28 U.S.C.A. § 992(b)(1)(B). Where unusual circumstances exist, federal appellate courts have permitted district courts to exercise wide discretion in determining upward or downward departures from the recommended sentences.

Even before the federal government adopted sentencing guidelines, Minnesota, in 1980—followed by a number of other states—adopted its own guidelines through legislation. Over the past few years, the experience of these states, along with that of the federal courts, has encouraged several state efforts in enacting similar guidelines. (Sentencing is discussed in Chapter 19.)

Appeal and Discretionary Review

Federal law and the laws of every state provide those convicted of crimes a limited right to **appeal** their convictions to higher tribunals. Appellate courts generally confine their review of convictions to legal, as distinct from factual, issues. Even though appellate courts review the legal sufficiency of evidence, they do not attempt to second-guess the factual determinations of trial judges and juries. Rather, appellate courts review such procedural issues as denial of fair trial, denial of counsel, admission of illegal evidence, and improper jury instructions. Appellate courts focus on errors of consequence, often overlooking so-called harmless errors.

When convictions are upheld on appeal, defendants may petition higher appellate courts for further review. Such review is available at the discretion of the higher court. The Supreme Court receives thousands of petitions each year from defendants whose convictions have been affirmed by the United States Courts of Appeals or the highest appellate tribunals of the states. Of course, the Supreme Court can review only a small percentage of these cases. These tend to be the most difficult cases involving the most significant legal questions.

Postconviction Relief

A person who has been convicted of a crime, has exhausted all normal appellate remedies, and is confined to prison may still challenge his or her conviction, sentence, or conditions of confinement by filing a petition for a **writ of habeas corpus.** Habeas corpus is an ancient common-law device that permits judges to review the legality of someone's confinement. In modern American criminal procedure, habeas corpus has become a way for prisoners who have exhausted all other avenues of appeal to obtain judicial review. A federal prisoner petitions the appropriate federal district court for habeas corpus relief. Under most state statutes, state prisoners may file habeas corpus petitions or other similar petitions for **postconviction relief** with the appropriate state courts.

Under federal law, a state prisoner who wants to raise a federal constitutional issue—for example, the alleged denial of the Sixth Amendment right to be represented by counsel—may petition a federal district court for habeas corpus relief. The power of federal courts to issue habeas corpus in state cases can be traced to an act

Table 1.2 Elements of Criminal Procedure Discussed in This Book

Elements of Criminal Procedure	Discussed in Chapter(s)
Search for and seizure of evidence by police	15
Arrest, interrogation, and identification of suspects	16
Processes prior to the commencement of trial	17
Jury selection, evidence, and trial procedures	18
Sentencing and the administration of punishments	19
Appellate procedures	20

of Congress adopted just after the Civil War. See *Ex parte McCardle,* 74 U.S. (7 Wall.) 506, 19 L.Ed. 264 (1869).

The denial or grant of habeas corpus relief by a federal district court is subject to appeal in the U.S. Court of Appeals. The circuit court's ruling is subject to review by the Supreme Court on a discretionary basis. Thus, it can take several years to finally resolve one federal habeas corpus petition, especially if the petition raises difficult constitutional claims where the law is not yet fully settled. If a state prisoner were permitted to raise each of many issues in separate federal habeas corpus petitions, it could take decades to resolve all the claims. This is why the Supreme Court has moved recently to require prisoners to raise all claims in their first habeas corpus petition. The Court has said that, unless there are exceptional circumstances, failure to do so constitutes an abuse of the writ of habeas corpus. *McCleskey v. Zant,* 499 U.S. 467, 111 S.Ct. 1454, 113 L.Ed.2d 517 (1991). (The appellate process is discussed in detail in Chapter 20.)

Criminal Punishment

Another factor that differentiates criminal prosecutions from civil cases is the nature of the sanctions that can be applied. A defendant in a civil trial who is found liable for a tort or breach of contract may be ordered to pay monetary damages to the plaintiff. In a criminal case, however, a defendant faces a variety of punishments, depending on the nature and severity of the crime. These punishments are designed to meet one or more of the basic goals of the criminal justice system: retribution, deterrence, incapacitation, and rehabilitation.

1. **Retribution.** Literally, this term refers to something demanded as payment. In criminal justice, retribution is the idea that the criminal must pay for wrongs perpetrated against society. The biblical phrase "an eye for an eye" is often invoked in this regard. Another oft-used phrase is that criminals must be given their "just deserts."
2. **Deterrence.** This is the idea that punishing persons who commit crimes will prevent other similarly disposed individuals from committing like offenses.
3. **Incapacitation.** One goal of punishment is to incapacitate the offender—that is, prevent that person from committing additional crimes.

4. **Rehabilitation.** Perhaps the loftiest goal of the criminal justice system, rehabilitation means reforming the offender so that the offender can function in civil society without resorting to criminal behavior.

Each of these goals or justifications of punishment is somewhat controversial, and there is no consensus about which goal should be paramount. As we examine particular punishments, you should reflect on which of these goals is being served. The following discussion provides a brief overview of criminal punishments.

The Death Penalty

During the colonial period of American history, and indeed well into the nineteenth century, the **death penalty** was often inflicted for a variety of felonies, including rape, arson, and horse theft. Today, the death penalty is reserved for only the most aggravated forms of murder. Although the Supreme Court's decision in *Furman v. Georgia,* 408 U.S. 238, 92 S.Ct. 2726, 33 L.Ed.2d 346 (1972), temporarily halted the imposition of the death penalty, capital punishment returned in 1977, when the state of Utah placed convicted murderer Gary Gilmore in front of a firing squad. Since then, the administration of the death penalty has become more common. Currently, thirty-nine states as well as the federal government have statutes providing for capital punishment by electrocution, the gas chamber, the firing squad, or lethal injection. Although the public largely supports the death penalty for the crime of premeditated murder, the penalty remains controversial among criminologists. The evidence to support the hypothesis that capital punishment is a general deterrent to murder is tenuous at best.

Incarceration

Incarceration is the conventional mode of punishment prescribed for persons convicted of felonies. Under federal and state law, felonies are classified by their seriousness, and convicted felons may be imprisoned for periods ranging from one year to life. Incarceration is usually available as a punishment for those convicted of the more serious misdemeanors, but only as long as one year in most jurisdictions. Although it was originally thought to be an effective means of rehabilitation, most criminologists now view incarceration simply as a means of isolating those persons who pose a serious threat to society.

In 1999 the U.S. Department of Justice reported that the number of inmates in federal and state prisons had surpassed 1.2 million and that another 600,000 persons were confined in local jails. Between 1990 and 1999, the rate of incarceration (state and federal) increased from 1 in every 218 U.S. residents to 1 in every 147 residents. This tremendous increase reflects the fact that during the 1980s and 1990s, federal and state sentencing laws were made more punitive. Unfortunately, many prisons are now seriously overcrowded to the point that courts must limit the number of inmates who can be confined.

Monetary Fines

Monetary fines are by far the most common punishment for those convicted of misdemeanors. Felons are likewise often subject to fines in addition to, or instead of, incarceration. Usually, the law allows the sentencing judge to impose a fine, a jail term, or some combination of the two. A number of felonies, especially serious economic crimes, now carry very heavy fines. For example, violations of federal banking and securities laws are punishable by fines running into the millions of dollars.

Probation

This alternative to incarceration is common for first-time offenders, except in cases involving the most serious crimes. **Probation** is usually conditioned on restrictions on the probationer's everyday conduct. The most extreme limitations on conduct and movement take the form of house arrest. Arguably, probation has the advantage of placing the probationer in the supervision of the government but away from the possibly crime-inducing environment of the prison. Unfortunately, the success of probation has often been hindered by inadequate staffing, resulting in inadequate supervision of probationers. Increasingly, probationers are being monitored through the use of electronic ankle bracelets that allow officials to track probationers' whereabouts.

Restitution

As society becomes more cognizant of the rights of crime victims, courts are increasingly likely to require that persons convicted of crimes pay sums of money to their victims by way of **restitution.** Typically, requirements to make restitution are imposed in property crime cases where victims have suffered some sort of economic loss. Very often, the requirement to pay restitution is one of several conditions that must be met before the offender gains release via probation. The term "restitution" should not be confused with the term "retribution," which, as we noted earlier, is one of the classic justifications for imposing criminal punishments.

Community Service

The requirement that an offender perform community service is becoming more attractive as a punishment for less serious crimes, especially for juveniles and first-time offenders. **Community service** is generally regarded as a more meaningful sanction than the imposition of a fine. It is also viewed as less likely than incarceration to promote future criminal behavior. The theory underlying community service is that an offender will become aware of obligations to the community and how his or her criminal conduct violated those obligations. Community service is often imposed as a condition of probation or as part of a **pretrial diversion program** in which first-time nonviolent offenders are offered the opportunity to avoid prosecution by completing a program of counseling or service.

Loss of Civil Rights

Federal and state statutes subject convicted felons to the **loss of civil rights,** most notably the rights to vote and to hold public office. In recent years, however, the courts have held that incarcerated criminals do retain certain fundamental constitutional rights, such as the right to freely exercise their religious beliefs. *Cruz v. Beto,* 405 U.S. 319, 92 S.Ct. 1079, 31 L.Ed.2d 263 (1972). Even where courts have recognized the constitutional rights of prisoners, they have generally restricted the scope of these rights because of the overriding necessity for security and discipline in the prison environment. *Bell v. Wolfish,* 441 U.S. 520, 99 S.Ct. 1861, 60 L.Ed.2d 447

(1979). The issue of which rights prisoners and other convicted felons forfeit and which rights they retain will be litigated for some time to come.

Conclusion

The American system of criminal justice is deeply rooted in the common law, but the specifics of criminal law and procedure have evolved substantially from their medieval English origins. Today, American criminal law is largely codified in statutes adopted by Congress and the state legislatures, as interpreted by the courts in specific cases.

One of the more tragic aspects of the crime problem is that many Americans are losing faith in the ability of their government to protect them from criminals. Indeed, in some areas of the country, victims are unlikely even to report crimes to the police. Some victims are unwilling to endure the ordeal of being a witness. Others simply believe that the perpetrator will not be apprehended or, if so, will not be punished.

Our state and federal governments are severely constrained both by legalities and practicalities in their efforts to fight crime. Not only is the specter of "a cop on every corner" distasteful to most Americans, but it is impossible to achieve even with unlimited public resources, let alone in this age of fiscal retrenchment.

Currently, the nation's prison system is filled beyond capacity, but the public is demanding that more convicted criminals be incarcerated and for longer periods of time. Yet the public appears unwilling to provide the revenues needed to build the additional prisons necessary to house these inmates.

Finally, society must confront the problem of the constitutional limitations on crime definition and law enforcement. Judges do have considerable discretion in interpreting the state and federal constitutions. Yet, if these documents are to be viable protections of our cherished liberties, we must accept that they place significant constraints on our efforts to control crime. For instance, to what degree is the public willing to allow the constitutional protection against unreasonable searches and seizures to be eroded? To what degree are we willing to sacrifice our constitutionally protected privacy and liberty to aid the ferreting out of crime? These are the fundamental questions of criminal law and procedure in a society that prides itself on preserving the rights of the individual.

Key Terms

nullen crimen, nulla poena, sine lege
substantive criminal law
procedural criminal law
constitutional supremacy
rule of law
judicial review
federalism
separation of powers
actus reus
mens rea

strict liability offenses
felonies
misdemeanors
criminal responsibility
victim
breaches of contract
torts
mala in se
mala prohibita
English common law

stare decisis
statutes
Blackstone's *Commentaries*
ordinances
police power
Model Penal Code
lawmaking function
error correction function
decisional law
ex post facto laws
Bill of Rights
due process of law
fair notice
fair hearing
presumption of innocence
reasonable doubt standard
search and seizure
exclusionary rule
arrest
police interrogation
speedy and public trial
pretrial release
summary trial
grand jury
trial jury
indictment

information
preliminary hearing
arraignment
plea bargain
pretrial motions
voir dire
peremptory challenges
challenges for cause
criminal trial
rules of evidence
sentencing
appeal
writ of habeas corpus
postconviction relief
retribution
deterrence
incapacitation
rehabilitation
death penalty
incarceration
monetary fines
probation
restitution
community service
pretrial diversion program
loss of civil rights

Web-Based Research Activity

1. Go to the web. Log on to **www.findlaw.com**.
2. Go to the following page: **http://www.findlaw.com/casecode/supreme.html**.
3. Use this page to locate the Supreme Court's decision in *Mapp v. Ohio* (1961).
4. Read the decision. Identify the key issue and the Court's holding. What is the rationale for the Court's decision? What counter-arguments are made by the dissenting opinion?

Questions for Thought and Discussion

1. Should morality, in and of itself, be considered a sufficient basis for defining particular conduct as criminal?
2. What are the chief distinctions between the civil and criminal law? Why do the criminal and civil law sometimes overlap?
3. To what extent is the English common law significant in contemporary American criminal law?

4. What is the essential difference between substantive criminal law and procedural criminal law? Can you give examples of each?

5. What means of punishment for criminal offenses exist in your state? Is capital punishment available for persons convicted of first-degree murder? Which punishments, if any, do you think are most effective in controlling crime?

6. What civil rights should convicted felons forfeit? What rights should they retain? What about prisoners confined to maximum security institutions? What rights, if any, should they retain?

Organization of the Criminal Justice System

Introduction

In every modern country, criminal justice is a complex process involving a plethora of agencies and officials. In the United States, criminal justice is particularly complex, largely because of **federalism,** the constitutional division of authority between the national and state governments. Under this scheme of federalism, the national government operates one criminal justice system to enforce federal criminal laws, and each state has a justice system to apply its own criminal laws. As a result of this structural complexity, it is difficult to provide a coherent overview of criminal justice in America. Each system is to some extent different in both substantive and procedural law.

Despite the differences that exist between federal and state criminal justice systems, there are certain similarities. All fifty-one criminal justice systems in the United States involve legislative bodies, law enforcement agencies, prosecutors, defense attorneys, courts of law, and corrections agencies. All follow certain general procedures beginning with arrest and, in some cases, ending in punishment (see Chapter 1). Finally, all systems are subject to the limitations of the United States Constitution, as interpreted by the courts (see Chapter 3). In this chapter we present an overview of the roles played by the institutions that make up the criminal justice system in the United States.

Legislatures

The governmental institution with primary responsibility for enacting laws is the **legislature.** Because the United States is organized on the principle of federalism, there are fifty-one legislatures in this country—the **United States Congress** and the fifty state legislatures. Each of these bodies has the power to enact **statutes** that apply within its respective jurisdiction. The U.S. Congress adopts statutes that apply throughout the United States and its territories, whereas the Illinois General Assembly, for example, adopts laws that apply only within the state of Illinois. For the most part, federal and state statutes complement one another. When there is a conflict, the federal statute prevails.

Legislative Powers of Congress

Congress's legislative authority may be divided into two broad categories: **enumerated powers** and **implied powers.** Enumerated powers are those that are mentioned specifically in Article I, Section 8 of the Constitution, such as the power to tax and the power to borrow money on the credit of the United States. Among the constitutionally enumerated powers of Congress, there are only two direct references to criminal justice. Congress is explicitly authorized to "provide for the Punishment of counterfeiting the Securities and current Coin of the United States" and to "define and punish Piracies and Felonies committed on the high Seas, and Offenses against the Law of Nations." Of course, Congress's power to define federal crimes is much more extensive than these two clauses suggest.

The enumerated power to "regulate commerce among the states" has provided Congress with a vast reservoir of legislative power. Many of the criminal statutes enacted by Congress in recent decades have been justified on the basis of the Commerce Clause of Article I, Section 8 (see Chapter 3).

Congress's implied powers are those that are deemed to be "necessary and proper for carrying into Execution the foregoing Powers, and all other Powers vested . . . in the Government of the United States, or in any Department or Officer thereof." As long as Congress's policy goal is permissible, any legislative means that are "plainly adapted" to that goal are likewise permissible. *McCulloch v. Maryland,* 17 U.S. (4 Wheat.) 316, 4 L.Ed. 579 (1819). Under the doctrine of implied powers, scarcely any area exists over which Congress is absolutely barred from legislating, because most social and economic problems have a conceivable relationship to the broad powers and objectives contained in the Constitution.

As the nation expanded and evolved, Congress became more active in passing social and economic legislation. In the twentieth century, and especially the last several decades, Congress established a host of federal crimes. There is now an elaborate body of criminal law. Of course, Congress may not enact laws that violate constitutional limitations such as those found in the Bill of Rights (see Chapter 3).

PUBLICATION OF FEDERAL STATUTES

Federal statutes are published in *United States Statutes at Large,* an annual publication dating from 1789 in which federal statutes are arranged in order of their adoption. Statutes are not arranged by subject matter, nor is there any indication of how they affect existing laws. Because the body of federal statutes is quite voluminous, and because new statutes often repeal or amend their predecessors, it is essential that new statutes be merged into legal codes that systematically arrange the statutes by subject. To find federal law as it currently stands, arranged by subject matter, one must consult the latest edition of the *Official Code of the Laws of the United States,* generally known as the **U.S. Code.** The U.S. Code is broken down into fifty subjects, called "titles." Title 18, "Crimes and Criminal Procedure," contains many of the federal crimes established by Congress.

The most popular compilation of the federal law, used by lawyers, judges, and criminal justice professionals, is the *United States Code Annotated* (U.S.C.A.). Published by West Group, the U.S.C.A. contains the entire current U.S. Code, but each section of statutory law in U.S.C.A. is followed by a series of annotations consisting of court decisions interpreting the particular statute along with historical notes, cross-references, and other editorial features (for more discussion, see Appendix A).

State Legislatures

Under the U.S. Constitution, each state must have a democratically elected legislature because that is the most fundamental element of a "republican form of government." State legislatures for the most part resemble the U.S. Congress. Each is composed of representatives chosen by the citizens of their respective states. All of them, except Nebraska, are bicameral (i.e., two-house) institutions. In adopting statutes, they all follow the same basic procedures. When state legislatures adopt statutes, they are published in volumes known as **session laws.** Then statutes are integrated into state codes. Annotated versions of most state codes are available to anyone who wishes to see how state statutes have been interpreted and applied by the state courts.

As we noted in Chapter 1, after the American Revolution, states adopted the English common law as their own state law. (Congress, on the other hand, never did.) Eventually, however, state legislatures codified much of the common law by enacting statutes, which in turn have been developed into comprehensive state codes. Periodically, states revise portions of their codes to make sure they remain relevant to a constantly changing society. For example, in 1989 the Tennessee General Assembly undertook a modernization of its criminal code. Old offenses that were no longer being enforced were repealed, other offenses were redefined, and sentencing laws were completely overhauled.

Statutory Interpretation

Statutes are necessarily written in general language, so legislation often requires judicial interpretation. Because legislative bodies have enacted vast numbers of laws defining offenses that are *mala prohibita,* such interpretation assumes an importance largely unknown to the English common law. Courts have responded by developing certain techniques to apply when a statute appears unclear as related to a specific factual scenario. These techniques are generally referred to as **rules of statutory interpretation** and over the years have given rise to various maxims that courts apply in attempting to determine the legislature's intention in enacting a statute.

Courts recognize that it is the legislative bodies and not the courts that exercise the power to define crimes and penalties. It follows that the most frequent maxim applied by courts in determining legislative intention is the **plain meaning rule.** As the U.S. Supreme Court observed early in the twentieth century, "Where the language [of a statutory law] is plain and admits of no more than one meaning the duty of interpretation does not arise. . . ." *Caminetti v. United States,* 242 U.S. 470, 37 S.Ct. 192, 61 L.Ed. 442 (1917). The Court's dictum seems self-evident, yet even learned judges often disagree as to whether the language of a given statute is plain. This gives rise to certain **canons of construction** applied by courts to determine the **legislative intent** behind a statutory definition of a crime.

A primary canon of construction is that criminal statutes must be strictly construed. The rule originated at common law, when death was the penalty for committing a felony, but the rule has remained. However, it is now based on the rationale that every criminal statute should be sufficiently precise to give fair warning of its meaning. Today we see the rule applied most frequently in a constitutional context when courts determine a criminal statute to be **void for vagueness.** We address this aspect in more detail in the following chapter. Another canon of construction provides for an **implied exception** to a statute. For example, courts have ruled that there is an implied exception to a law imposing speed limits on the highway in instances where police or other emergency vehicles violate the literal text of the law. Would a court apply a statute that makes it an offense for any person to sleep in a bus terminal and thereby find a ticketed passenger guilty who fell asleep while waiting for a bus that was overdue? The implied exception doctrine seems to simply reflect a commonsense approach in determining the meaning of a statute.

Often a statute uses a term that has a definite meaning at common law. In general, courts interpret such terms according to their common-law meaning. Recall that in Chapter 1 we observed that in defining the crime of burglary a legislature might use the term "curtilage" without defining it. In such an instance, we noted that a court would ordinarily look to the common law, which defined the term to mean "an enclosed space surrounding a dwelling."

But this rule does not always apply when dealing with modern statutes, particularly at the federal level, where there is generally considerable legislative history in the form of committee reports and floor debates recorded in the *Congressional Record* that can aid in determining the true intent of a statute. Thus, in *Perrin v. United States,* 444 U.S. 37, 100 S.Ct. 311, 62 L.Ed.2d 199 (1979), the Supreme Court determined that the word "bribery" in a federal statute was not limited to its common-law definition because the legislative history revealed an intent to deal with bribery in organized crime beyond its common-law definition. In general, there is considerably less legislative history available at the state legislative level. However, at times courts seek to determine legislative intent based on available resources.

Law Enforcement Agencies

Law enforcement agencies are charged with enforcing the criminal law. They have the power to investigate suspected criminal activity, to arrest suspected criminals, and to detain arrested persons until their cases come before the appropriate courts of law. Society expects law enforcement agencies not only to arrest those suspected of crimes but also to take steps to prevent crimes from occurring.

Historical Development

Before the Norman Conquest in 1066, there were no organized police in England, but by the thirteenth century constables and justices of the peace came to symbolize enforcement of the rule of law in England. Large communities, somewhat similar to counties in America, were called "shires." The king would send a royal officer called a "reeve" to each shire to keep order and to exercise broad powers within the shire. The onset of the Industrial Revolution led to the development of large cities. Industrialists and merchants began to establish patrols to protect their goods and buildings. But the need for more effective policing became evident. In 1829 Sir Robert Peel, the British Home Secretary, organized a uniformed, but unarmed, police force for London. The name "Bobbies" is still applied to police officers in England in honor of Peel. In later years, Parliament required counties and boroughs to establish police departments modeled along the lines of the London force.

Colonial America basically followed the English system, with local constables and county sheriffs following the English concept of constables and shire reeves. These early law officers were often aided by local vigilante groups of citizens known as "posses." Once America became a nation, states and local communities began to follow the Peel model, and by the mid-1800s, Boston, New York, and Philadelphia had developed professional police departments. By the twentieth century, police were aided by technological developments, and by the 1930s, many departments were equipped with motorcycles and patrol cars. Detectives were soon added to the force, police became equipped with modern communications equipment, and police were trained in ballistics and the scientific analysis of blood samples and handwriting.

Policing in Modern Times

In the United States nearly 20,000 federal, state, and local agencies are involved in law enforcement and crime prevention. Collectively, these agencies employ nearly 800,000 **sworn officers.** Increasingly, law enforcement officers are trained professionals who must acquire a good working knowledge of the criminal law. At the local level, the typical police recruit now completes about 1,000 hours of training before being sworn in. Except in the smallest communities, law enforcement agencies are equipped with computers, sophisticated communications technology, and scientific crime detection equipment.

POLICING AT THE NATIONAL LEVEL

At the national level, the **Federal Bureau of Investigation** (FBI) is the primary agency empowered to investigate violations of federal criminal laws. Located in the **Department of Justice,** the FBI is by far the most powerful of the federal law enforcement agencies, with broad powers to enforce the many criminal laws adopted by the Congress. The FBI currently employs nearly 25,000 people, including more than 10,000 **special agents** spread out over fifty-six field offices in the United States and twenty-one foreign offices. With an annual budget exceeding two billion dollars, the FBI uses the most sophisticated methods in crime prevention and investigation. Its crime laboratory figures prominently in the investigation and prosecution of numerous state and federal crimes.

The **United States Marshals** is the oldest unit of federal law enforcement, dating back to 1790. The marshals execute orders of federal courts and serve as custodians for the transfer of prisoners. U.S. Marshals played a prominent role in the crises in school integration during the civil rights struggles of the 1950s and early 1960s.

Nearly fifty other federal agencies have law enforcement authority in specific areas. Among them are the Bureau of Alcohol, Tobacco, and Firearms; the Internal Revenue Service; the Bureau of Indian Affairs; the Drug Enforcement Administration; the Customs Service; the Immigration and Naturalization Service; the Bureau of Postal Inspection; the Tennessee Valley Authority; the National Park Service; the Forest Service; the U.S. Capitol Police; the U.S. Mint; and the Secret Service.

STATE AND LOCAL POLICING

All states have law enforcement agencies that patrol the highways, investigate crimes, and furnish skilled technical support to local law enforcement agencies. Similarly, every state has a number of state agencies responsible for enforcing specific areas of the law, ranging from agricultural importation to food processing and from casino gambling to dispensing alcoholic beverages. Probably among the best known to all citizens are the state highway patrol and the fish and game warden. Generally, cases developed by state officers are processed through local law enforcement and prosecution agencies.

At the local level, we find both county and municipal law enforcement agencies. Nearly every county in America (more than three thousand of them) has a **sheriff.** In most states, sheriffs are elected to office and exercise broad powers as the chief law enforcement officers of their respective counties. They are usually dependent on funding provided by a local governing body, generally the county commission. In some areas, particularly the urban Northeast, many powers traditionally exercised by sheriffs have been assumed by state or metropolitan police forces. In the rest of the country, however, especially in the rural areas, sheriffs (and their deputies) are the principal law enforcement agents at the county level.

Nearly 15,000 cities and towns have their own **police departments.** Local police are charged with enforcing the criminal laws of their states, as well as of their municipalities. Although the county sheriff usually has jurisdiction within the municipalities of the county, he or she generally concentrates enforcement efforts on those areas outside municipal boundaries.

In addition to city and county law enforcement agencies, there are numerous special districts and authorities that have their own police forces. Most state universities have their own police departments, as do many airports and seaports.

Besides providing law enforcement in the strictest sense of the term, local law enforcement agencies initiate the criminal justice process and assist prosecutors in preparation of cases. Sheriffs in many larger counties and many metropolitan police departments have developed SWAT (special weapons and tactics) teams to assist in the rescue of victims of catastrophes and persons taken hostage. They are also heavily involved in **order maintenance** or "keeping the peace," hence the term "peace officers." Often, keeping the peace involves more of a process of judgment and discretion rather than merely applying the criminal law.

Some of the newer and innovative policing responsibilities include community relations departments that seek to foster better relations among groups of citizens, especially minorities and juveniles, and to assist social agencies in efforts to rehabilitate drug and alcohol abusers. Finally, the public looks to the police to prevent crime through their presence in the community and through education of the public on crime prevention measures. Under the rubric of **community policing,** police agencies are making an effort to become actively involved in their communities in order to earn the trust and confidence of the citizens they serve. Most police departments in cities of 50,000 people or more now have specialized community policing divisions.

Prosecutorial Agencies

Although law enforcement agencies are the "gatekeepers" of the criminal justice system, prosecutors are central to the administration of criminal justice. It is the **prosecutors** who determine whether to bring charges against suspected criminals. They have enormous discretion, not only in determining whether to prosecute but also in determining what charges to file. Moreover, prosecutors frequently set the tone for **plea bargaining** and have a powerful voice in determining the severity of sanctions imposed on persons convicted of crimes. Accordingly, prosecutors play a crucial role in the criminal justice system.

Historical Background

The early English common law considered many crimes to be private matters between individuals; however, the role of the public prosecutor evolved as early as the thirteenth century, when the King's counsel would pursue crimes considered to be offenses against the Crown and, in some instances, when injured victims declined to prosecute. Today in England, a public prosecutor prosecutes crimes that have great significance to the government, but the majority of offenses are handled by police agencies that hire barristers to prosecute charges. Unlike American prosecutors, the English barrister may represent the police in one case and in the next case represent the defendant.

The office of public prosecutor in England became the prototype for the office of attorney general in this country at the national and state levels. In Colonial days, an attorney general's assistants handled local prosecutions. However, as states became independent, the practice ceased. The state attorneys general assumed the role of chief legal officers, and local governments began electing their own prosecuting attorneys.

Federal Prosecutors

In the United States, the chief prosecutor at the federal level is the **Attorney General,** who is the head of the Department of Justice. Below the Attorney General are several **United States Attorneys,** each responsible for prosecuting crimes within a particular federal district. The United States Attorneys, in turn, have a number of assistants who handle most of the day-to-day criminal cases brought by the federal government. The President, subject to the consent of the Senate, appoints the Attorney General and the United States Attorneys. Assistant U.S. Attorneys are federal civil service employees.

In addition to the regular federal prosecutors, Congress has provided for the appointment of **independent counsel** (special prosecutors) in cases involving alleged misconduct by high government officials. By far, the most infamous such case was "Watergate," which resulted in the convictions of several high-ranking officials and led to the resignation of President Nixon in 1974. But there have been numerous cases where, under congressional direction, a special prosecutor has been appointed. The best-known recent example of this was Kenneth Starr's appointment to investigate the Whitewater scandal that involved close associates of President Bill Clinton and First Lady Hillary Rodham Clinton, an investigation that eventually culminated in President Clinton's impeachment and his subsequent acquittal by the U.S. Senate in February 1999.

State and Local Prosecutors

Each state likewise has its own attorney general, who acts as the state's chief legal officer, and a number of assistant attorneys general, plus a number of district or **state's attorneys** at the local level. Generally speaking, local prosecutors are elected for set terms of office and have the responsibility for the prosecution of crimes within the jurisdiction for which they are elected. In most states, local prosecutors act autonomously and possess broad discretionary powers. Many local prosecutors function on a part-time basis, but in the larger offices the emphasis is for the prosecutor and assistant prosecutors to serve on a full-time basis. Larger offices are establishing educational programs and developing specially trained assistants or units to handle specific categories of crime—for example, white collar and governmental corruption, narcotics offenses, and consumer fraud.

Cities and counties also have their own attorneys. These attorneys, generally appointed by the governing bodies they represent, sometimes prosecute violations of city and county ordinances, but increasingly their function is limited to representing their cities or counties in civil suits and giving legal advice to local councils and officials.

The Prosecutor's Broad Discretion

Federal and state prosecutors (whether known as district attorney, state attorney, or county prosecutor) play a vital role in the criminal justice system in the United States. As mentioned, a politically appointed U.S. Attorney supervises prosecutors at the federal level whereas state and local prosecutors generally come into office by election in partisan contests. Thus, prosecutors become sensitive to the community norms while exercising the broad discretion that the law vests in prosecutorial decision making.

Prosecutors not only determine the level of offense to be charged; in exercise of their very broad discretion they exercise the power of ***nolle prosequi,*** usually called *nol pros,* which allows a prosecutor not to proceed in a given case, irrespective of the factual basis for prosecution. Prosecutors sometimes *nol pros* cases to secure cooperation of a defendant in furthering other prosecution; in other instances, a prosecutor may allow a defendant to participate in some diversionary program of rehabilitation. In recent years, completion of a prescribed program in a drug court has often resulted in a case being *nol prossed* by a prosecutor. (See the discussion of drug courts in Chapter 9.)

Defense Attorneys

In American criminal law, individuals accused of any crime, no matter how minor the offense, have the right to employ counsel for their defense. U.S. Const. Amend. VI. Indeed, the U.S. Supreme Court has held that a defendant has the right to be represented by an attorney at "every stage of a criminal proceeding when substantial rights of a criminal accused may be affected." *Mempa v. Ray,* 389 U.S. 128, 88 S.Ct. 254, 19 L.Ed.2d 336 (1967).

In this country, many lawyers specialize in criminal defense work. Of course, defendants are free to employ an attorney of their choice at their own expense. Some well-known attorneys, such as Johnnie Cochran, Alan Dershowitz, and F. Lee Bailey, are national celebrities who specialize in representing defendants in high-profile trials like the O. J. Simpson case. However, most criminal defendants are not wealthy, and few people accused of crimes can afford to hire such "dream teams" to represent them.

Many attorneys are highly skilled in handling criminal cases and are available for employment in federal and state criminal proceedings. In fact, it is not uncommon for attorneys who start their careers as prosecutors to eventually enter private practice in criminal matters. Today some state bar associations grant special recognition to lawyers who qualify by virtue of experience and examination as "certified criminal defense attorneys."

Representation of Indigent Defendants

Beginning in the 1960s, the United States Supreme Court greatly expanded the right to counsel by requiring states to provide attorneys to **indigent defendants.** *Gideon v. Wainwright,* 372 U.S. 335, 83 S.Ct. 792, 9 L.Ed.2d 799 (1963); *Argersinger v. Hamlin,* 407 U.S. 25, 92 S.Ct. 2006, 32 L.Ed.2d 530 (1972). In some states, courts appoint attorneys from the private bar to represent indigent defendants. However, most states have chosen to handle the problem of indigent defense by establishing the office of public defender. Like public prosecutors, **public defenders** are generally elected to set terms of office. Because of their constant contact with criminal cases, public defenders acquire considerable expertise in representing defendants. Moreover, because they are public officials who, like prosecutors, are provided budgets, public defenders are often able to hire investigators to aid their staff of assistant public defenders in their representation of indigent defendants. We discuss the right to appointed counsel and the right to self-representation in detail in Chapter 17.

The Role of Defense Attorneys

The role of the **defense attorney** is perhaps the most misunderstood in the criminal justice system. First and foremost, a defense attorney is charged with zealously representing his or her client and ensuring that the defendant's constitutional rights are fully protected. To anyone who has watched *Perry Mason* or a similar television program, the defense attorney's most visible role is that of vigorously cross-examining prosecution witnesses or passionately pleading for a client before a jury. The defense attorney's role is far greater than being a courtroom advocate. As a counselor, defense attorneys must evaluate the alternative courses of action that may be available to a defendant. They must attempt to gauge the strength of the prosecution's case, advise on the feasibility of entering a plea of guilty, and attempt to negotiate a fair and constructive sentence. In instances where a defendant elects to plead not guilty, defense attorneys challenge the police and prosecution. Many observers point out that these efforts by defense attorneys "keep the system honest" by causing police and prosecuting authorities to be scrupulous in their adherence to constitutional standards.

Perhaps the most frequently voiced reservation concerning defense attorneys relates to representation of a defendant who, from all facts available, is believed to be guilty. Defense attorneys are quick to point out that it is not their function to make a judgment of the defendant's guilt or innocence; there are other functionaries in the system charged with that responsibility. The answer does not easily satisfy critics. Nevertheless, in our system of adversarial justice the defense attorney is required to represent a defendant with fidelity, to protect the defendant's constitutional rights, to assert all defenses available under the law of the land, and to make sure before a defendant is found guilty that the prosecution has sustained its burden of proving the defendant guilty beyond a reasonable doubt. A defense attorney must make sufficient objections and other tactical moves to preserve any contention of error for review by a higher court. If the defendant is convicted, the duty continues to ensure imposition of a fair sentence, advise as to the right to appeal to a higher court, and, in some instances, seek postconviction relief if an appeal fails.

Juries

The **jury** is one of the great contributions of the English common law. After the Norman Conquest in 1066, juries began to function in England, but not as we know juries today. Rather, these early juries comprised men who had knowledge of the disputes they were to decide, but eventually juries began to hear evidence and make their verdicts accordingly. By the eighteenth century, juries occupied a prominent role in the English common-law system and served as a buffer between the Crown and the citizenry. The colonists brought the concept to the New World.

There are two types of juries: the **grand jury** and the **petit (trial) jury.** The juries derive their names based on the number of persons who serve, the grand jury consisting of a larger number than the petit jury.

Grand Juries

Grand juries essentially serve to consider whether there is sufficient evidence to bring charges against a person; petit or trial juries sit to hear evidence at a trial and render a verdict accordingly. The Fifth Amendment to the U.S. Constitution stipulates that "[n]o person shall be held to answer for a capital, or otherwise infamous crime, unless on a presentment or indictment of a grand jury." The constitutional requirement binds all federal courts; however, the Supreme Court has held that states are not bound to abide by the grand jury requirement. *Hurtado v. California,* 110 U.S. 516, 4 S.Ct. 111, 28 L. Ed.232 (1884).

Sixteen to twenty-three persons serve on a federal grand jury. The number varies according to each state but usually consists of between twelve and twenty-three citizens. Grand jurors serve for a limited time to hear evidence and to determine whether to hand down an indictment, sometimes referred to as a **true bill,** or to refuse to indict when the jury determines there is insufficient evidence of a crime by returning a **no bill.** Twelve must vote to return an indictment in federal court, and states usually require at least a majority of grand jurors to return an indictment. Courts have broad authority to call a grand jury into session, and grand juries are authorized to make wide-ranging inquiries and investigations into public matters. Grand juries may make accusations called *presentments* independently of a prosecutor.

Although the English common law system gave birth to the grand jury, England abolished grand juries in the 1930s, having found that the return of **indictments** was almost automatic and that the use of grand juries tended to delay the criminal process. Today, critics argue that grand juries are so dominated by the prosecutors who appear before them that they cease to serve as an independent body to evaluate evidence. Indeed, many states have eliminated the requirement that a grand jury hand down indictments and have substituted a **prosecutor's information,** an accusatorial document charging a crime. Yet many reformers would retain the grand jury as an institution for investigation of corruption in government. We discuss grand juries in more detail in Chapter 17.

Trial Juries

Article III, Section 2 of the U.S. Constitution establishes the right to trial by jury in criminal cases. The Sixth Amendment guarantees "the right to a **speedy and public trial** by an impartial jury." The Seventh Amendment grants a right to a trial by jury in civil suits at common law. All state constitutions confer the right of trial by jury in criminal cases; however, the federal constitutional right to a jury trial applies to the states, thereby guaranteeing a defendant a right to a jury trial in a state criminal prosecution if such a right would exist in a federal prosecution. *Duncan v. Louisiana,* 391 U.S. 145, 88 S.Ct. 1444, 20 L. Ed.2d 491 (1968). A common-law jury consisted of twelve men. Today, twelve persons are required in federal juries; however, the number varies in states, although all states require twelve-person juries in capital cases. The Supreme Court has approved the use of six-person juries in noncapital felony prosecutions. *Williams v. Florida,* 399 U.S. 78, 90 S.Ct. 1893, 25 L.Ed. 2d 446 (1970).

Even though trial juries function in a relatively small number of criminal cases, their availability to serve has a considerable impact on the criminal justice system. In Chapter 18 we discuss in detail the various requirements concerning the right to trial by jury, the right to a public trial, the composition of trial juries, the selection of juries, and proposals for jury reforms.

The Courts

Courts of law are the centerpieces of the federal and state criminal justice systems. Courts of law are responsible for determining both the factual basis and legal sufficiency of criminal charges and for ensuring that criminal defendants are provided due process of law. Basically, there are two kinds of courts: trial and appellate courts. **Trial courts** conduct criminal trials and various pretrial and post-trial proceedings. **Appellate courts** hear appeals from the decisions of the trial courts. Trial courts are primarily concerned with ascertaining facts, determining guilt or innocence, and imposing punishments, whereas appellate courts are primarily concerned with matters

Jurisdiction Over Crimes Committed by Native Americans on Reservations

Article I, Section 8 of the U.S. Constitution mentions Indian tribes as being subject to Congressional legislation. Congress has provided that federal courts have jurisdiction over specified offenses committed by Native Americans on Indian reservations. 18 U.S.C.A. § 1153. At the same time, Congress has permitted certain states to exercise jurisdiction over such offenses. 18 U.S.C.A. § 1162. Furthermore, offenses committed by one Native American against another on a reservation are generally subject to the jurisdiction of tribal courts, unless the crime charged has been expressly made subject to federal jurisdiction. *Keeble v. United States,* 412 U.S. 205, 93 S.Ct. 1993, 36 L.Ed.2d 844 (1973).

Courts of the state where a Native American reservation is located have jurisdiction over crimes on the reservation when the offense is perpetrated by a non-Indian against a non-Indian, but non-Indian defendants charged with committing a crime on a reservation are subject to federal jurisdiction if the victim is a member of the tribe. *United States v. Antelope,* 430 U.S. 641, 97 S.Ct. 1395, 51 L.Ed.2d 701 (1977).

of law. Appellate courts correct legal errors made by trial courts and develop law when new legal questions arise.

Jurisdiction

The first question facing a court in any criminal prosecution is that of **jurisdiction,** the legal authority to hear and decide the case. A court must have jurisdiction, over both the subject matter of a case and the parties to a case, before it may proceed to adjudicate that controversy. The jurisdiction of the federal courts is determined by both the language of Article III of the Constitution and the statutes enacted by Congress. The respective state constitutions and statutes determine the jurisdiction of the state courts.

Essentially, the federal courts adjudicate criminal cases where defendants are charged with violating federal criminal laws; state courts adjudicate alleged violations of state laws.

The Federal Court System

Article III of the U.S. Constitution provides that "[t]he judicial Power of the United States shall be vested in one supreme Court, and in such inferior Courts as the Congress may from time to time ordain and establish." Under this authority Congress enacted the Judiciary Act of 1789, creating the federal court system. After passage of the Judiciary Act of 1801 the Supreme Court justices were required to "ride circuit," a practice that had its roots in English legal history. The circuit courts then consisted of district court judges who heard appeals alongside "circuit riding" Supreme Court justices. In 1891 Congress created separate appellate courts, and since then Supreme Court justices have remained as reviewing justices.

United States District Courts handle prosecutions for violations of federal statutes. In addition, federal courts sometimes review convictions from state courts when defendants raise issues arising under the U.S. Constitution. Appeals are heard by United States Courts of Appeals, and, of course, the Supreme Court is at the apex of the judicial system.

UNITED STATES DISTRICT COURTS

The principal trial court in the federal system is the United States District Court. There are district courts in ninety-four federal judicial districts around the country. A criminal trial in the district court is presided over by a judge appointed for life by the President with the consent of the Senate. Federal magistrate judges, who are appointed by federal district judges, often handle pretrial proceedings in the district courts and trials of misdemeanors. In 1998 there were 57,023 criminal cases filed in U.S. District Court (Administrative Office of the United States Courts, *Annual Report of the Director, 1998* [Washington, D.C., Administrative Office of the United States Courts, pp. 210–212]). Congress created the district courts by the Judiciary Act of 1789. Since then, Congress has created specialized courts to handle specific kinds of cases (for example, the United States Court of International Trade and the United States Claims Court).

THE UNITED STATES COURTS OF APPEALS

The **intermediate appellate courts** in the federal system are the **United States Courts of Appeals** (also known as circuit courts). Twelve geographical circuits (and one "federal circuit") cover the United States and its possessions. Figure 2.1 indicates the geographical distribution of the circuit courts. The circuit courts hear both criminal and civil appeals from the district courts and from quasi-judicial tribunals in the

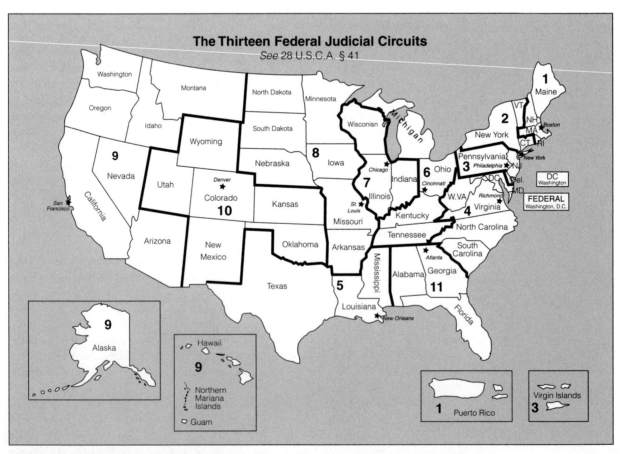

FIGURE 2.1 The Federal Judicial Circuits.
Source: Federal Reporter, 2d Series (West Publishing Company).

independent regulatory agencies. Generally, decisions of the courts of appeals are rendered by panels of three judges who vote to affirm, reverse, or modify the lower-court decisions under review. Of the 53,805 appeals filed in the U.S. Courts of Appeal in 1998, 10,535 were criminal cases (Administrative Office of the United States Courts, *Annual Report of the Director, 1998* [Washington, D.C., Administrative Office of the United States Courts, 1999, p. 18, pp. 126–130]). There is a procedure by which the circuit courts provide *en banc* **hearings,** where all judges assigned to the court (or a substantial number of them) participate in a decision. Like their counterparts in the district courts, federal appeals court judges are appointed to life terms by the President with the consent of the Senate.

MILITARY TRIBUNALS

Crimes committed by persons in military service are ordinarily prosecuted in proceedings before **courts-martial.** Only under conditions of martial law do military tribunals have the authority to try civilians. *Ex parte Milligan*, 71 U.S. (4 Wall.) 2, 18 L.Ed. 281 (1866). Article 1, Section 8 of the U.S. Constitution grants Congress the authority to regulate the armed forces. Under this authority, Congress has enacted the **Uniform Code of Military Justice** (UCMJ), 10 U.S.C.A. §§ 801–940. The UCMJ gives courts-martial jurisdiction to try all offenses under the code committed by military personnel. Notwithstanding this grant of authority, the United States Supreme Court held in 1969 that military jurisdiction was limited to offenses that were service connected. *O'Callahan v. Parker*, 395 U.S. 258, 89 S.Ct. 1683, 23 L.Ed.2d 291 (1969). The *O'Callahan* decision greatly narrowed military jurisdiction over offenses committed by servicepersons. In 1987 the Court, in a 5–4 decision, overruled *O'Callahan* and said that military jurisdiction depends solely on whether an accused is a military member. *Solorio v. United States*, 483 U.S. 435, 107 S.Ct. 2924, 97 L.Ed.2d 364 (1987). Thus, courts-martial may now try all offenses committed by servicepersons in violation of the UCMJ.

Commanders of various military units convene court-martial proceedings and appoint those who sit similar to a civilian jury. These commanders are called the convening authorities and are assisted by military lawyers designated as staff judge advocates. There are three classes of court-martial: summary, special, and general. The summary court-martial is somewhat analogous to trial by a civilian magistrate whereas special and general court-martial proceedings are more analogous to civilian criminal courts of record. Only the most serious offenses are tried by a general court-martial. Military trial procedures and rules of evidence are similar to the rules applied in federal district courts. A trial counsel serves as prosecutor, and a defendant is furnished legal counsel by the government unless the accused chooses to employ private defense counsel. A military judge presides at special and general courts-martial. The extent of punishment that may be imposed varies according to the offense and the authority of the type of court-martial convened.

Decisions of courts-martial are reviewed by military courts of review in each branch of the armed forces. In specified instances, appeals are heard by the United States **Court of Appeals for the Armed Forces.** This court is staffed by civilian judges who are appointed to fifteen-year terms by the President with the consent of the Senate.

THE UNITED STATES SUPREME COURT

The highest appellate court in the federal judicial system is the **United States Supreme Court.** The Supreme Court has jurisdiction to review, either on appeal or by **writ of certiorari** (discretionary review), all the decisions of the lower federal courts and many decisions of the highest state courts. The Supreme Court comprises nine justices who, like district and circuit judges, are appointed for life by the President with the consent of the Senate. These nine individuals have the final word in determining what the U.S. Constitution requires, permits, and prohibits in the areas of law enforcement, prosecution, adjudication, and punishment. The Supreme Court also promulgates **rules of procedure** for the lower federal courts to follow in both criminal and civil cases.

As of December 31, 2000, William H. Rehnquist was the chief justice of the Supreme Court, and the associate justices were John Paul Stevens, Sandra Day O'Connor, Antonin Scalia, Anthony M. Kennedy, David H. Souter, Clarence Thomas, Ruth Bader Ginsburg, and Stephen G. Breyer.

In the twelve months ending September 30, 1999, the Court received 5,518 petitions for certiorari and granted review in 137 (about 2.5%) of these cases. (See Administrative Office of the United States Courts, "Judicial Business of the United States Courts: 1999 Annual Report of the Director.") During its 1999 term, the Court issued ninety-two full-opinion decisions.

Supreme Court opinions are officially reported in the *United States Reports* (abbreviated U.S.) and in private publications, *Supreme Court Reporter* (abbreviated S.Ct.) and *Lawyers Edition, 2d* (abbreviated L.Ed.2d). Immediate access to a recently issued opinion may be obtained by logging on to **www.findlaw.com**.

State Court Systems

Each state has its own independent judicial system. These courts handle more than 90 percent of criminal prosecutions in the United States. State judicial systems are characterized by variations in structure, jurisdiction, and procedure but have certain commonalities. Every state has one or more levels of trial courts and at least one appellate court. Most states have **courts of general jurisdiction,** which conduct trials in felony and major misdemeanor cases, and **courts of limited jurisdiction,** which handle pretrial matters and conduct trials in minor misdemeanor cases. Most states also have some form of intermediate appellate courts that relieve the **state supreme court** (known as the Court of Appeals in New York and Maryland) from hearing routine appeals. Many states also have separate **juvenile courts,** which operate in ways that differ significantly from the criminal courts for adults.

Some states, like North Carolina, have adopted tidy, streamlined court systems (see Figure 2.2). Other states' court systems are extremely complex, as is the case in Texas (see Figure 2.3). In structural complexity, most states' systems fall somewhere between the two extremes.

Contrasting Judicial Functions and Environments

As we noted in Chapter 1, trial courts primarily make factual determinations, often assisted by juries; apply settled law to established facts; and impose sanctions. Appellate courts, on the other hand, interpret the federal and state constitutions and statutes, correct errors in law made by trial courts, and develop the law by "filling in the gaps" that often become apparent in the application of statutory laws.

The difference in the roles of trial and appellate courts is also evident in the environment where trial and appellate judges perform their functions. A trial court usually sits in a county courthouse or other county judicial building. Trial judges preside over courtrooms where there is considerable daily activity with the impaneling of juries, testimony of witnesses, and attorneys making objections and pleas for their

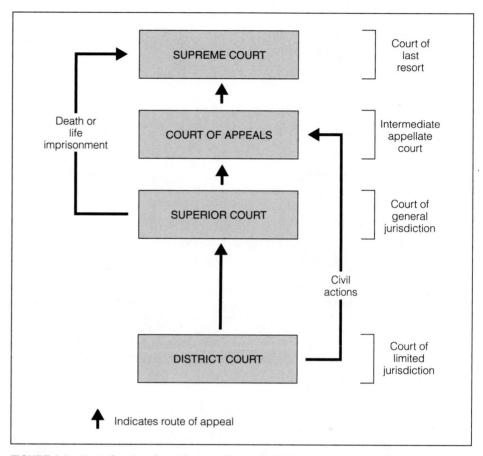

FIGURE 2.2 North Carolina Court System. Source: U.S. Department of Justice/National Center for State Courts.

clients. At other times the judges are busy hearing arguments in their chambers. In short, the trial scene is one of high visibility and is often attended by the comings and goings of numerous spectators and, where a high-profile case is being tried, by print and television media. In short, the trial court setting is a venue of daily interaction between court personnel and the citizens of the community.

In contrast, appellate courts are often described as "invisible courts" because their public proceedings are generally limited to hearing legal arguments by attorneys on prescribed oral argument days. Few clients and even fewer spectators are generally in attendance. Media representatives usually attend only when some high-profile appeal is being argued. Many of the documents arrive by mail to a staff of clerks. Proceedings are resolved primarily by review of records from the lower court or administrative agency, by study of the law briefs submitted by counsel, and by discussion among the panel of judges assigned a particular case, often supplemented by independent research by judges and their staff attorneys.

Unlike the busy atmosphere that normally characterizes a trial court, an appellate court often sits in the state capitol building or in its own facility, usually with a complete law library. The décor in the buildings that house appellate courts is usually quite formal, often with portraits of former judges regarded as oracles of the law. When a panel of judges sits to hear oral arguments, they normally emerge from behind a velvet curtain on a precise schedule and to the cry of the court's marshal. When

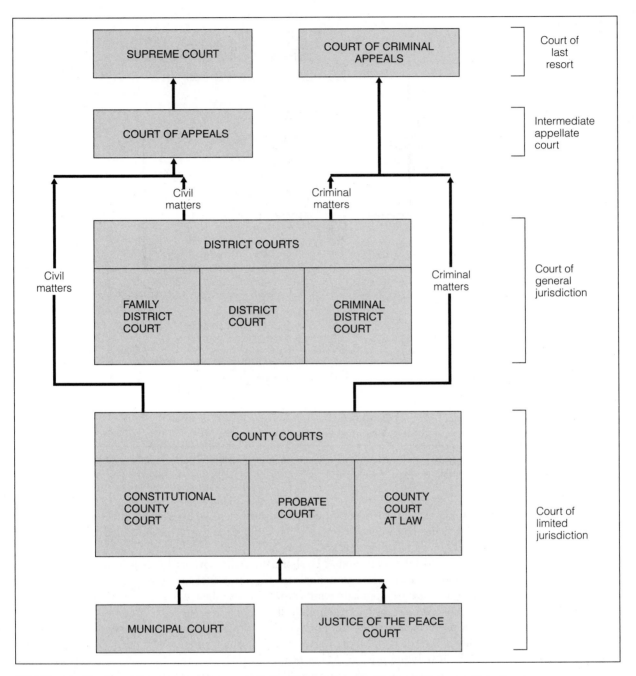

FIGURE 2.3 The Texas Court System. Source: U.S. Department of Justice/National Center for State Courts.

not hearing oral arguments, appellate judges usually occupy a suite of offices with their secretaries and law clerks. It is in these individual chambers that appellate judges study and write their opinions on cases assigned to them.

The United States Supreme Court occupies a majestic building in Washington, D.C., with spacious office suites and impressive corridors and library facilities. With enhanced attributes similar to those mentioned for appellate courts, the elegance and dignity of the facilities comport with the significant role of the Court as final arbiter in the nation's judicial system. Unlike the sparse attendance at most state and intermediate federal appellate courts, parties interested in the decisions that will result from arguments, a coterie of media persons, and many spectators will fill the courtroom to hear arguments that often significantly affect the economic, social, and political life of the nation. Photography is not allowed, and the arguments and dialogue between the counsel and the justices are observed silently and respectfully by those who attend. There is sometimes a contrasting scene outside the Supreme Court building, where demonstrators sometimes gather to give visibility to the causes they represent.

The Juvenile Justice System

The juvenile justice system includes specialized courts, law enforcement agencies, social services agencies, and corrections facilities designed to address problems of **juvenile delinquency** as well as child neglect and abuse. "Delinquency" refers to conduct that would be criminal if committed by an adult. In addition to being charged with delinquency, young people may be subjected to the jurisdiction of a juvenile court for engaging in conduct that is prohibited only for minors. Such behaviors, which include truancy (chronic absence from school) and incorrigibility, are often called **status offenses,** because they are peculiar to the status of children.

Historical Basis

The common law treated all persons above the age of fourteen as adults for purposes of criminal responsibility (see Chapter 14). Because the American legal system was based on English common law, American courts followed the common-law rules for the treatment of juveniles. Young teenagers were treated essentially as adults for the purposes of criminal justice. During the colonial period of American history, it was not uncommon for teenagers to be hanged, flogged, or placed in the public pillory as punishment for their crimes. Later, as state penitentiaries were established, it was not unusual for 20 percent of prison populations to be juveniles.

In the late nineteenth century, public outcry against treating juveniles like adults led to the establishment of a separate juvenile justice system in the United States. Reformers were convinced that the existing system of criminal justice was inappropriate for young offenders who were more in need of reform than punishment. Reformers proposed specialized courts to deal with young offenders not as hardened criminals, but as misguided youth in need of special care. This special treatment was justified legally by the concept of *parens patriae,* the power of the state to act to protect the interests of those who cannot protect themselves.

The first state to act in this area was Illinois in 1899. By the 1920s, many states had followed suit, and by 1945, juvenile court legislation had been enacted by Congress and all state legislatures. The newly created juvenile courts were usually separate from the regular tribunals; often, the judges or referees presiding over these courts did not have formal legal training. The proceedings were generally nonadversarial, and there was little in the way of procedural regularity or even the opportunity for the juvenile offender to confront his or her accusers. In fact, juvenile delinquency proceedings were conceived as civil, as opposed to criminal, proceedings. Dispositions of cases were usually nonpunitive in character; therefore, accused juvenile offenders were not afforded most of the rights of criminal defendants.

Because the juvenile justice system emphasized rehabilitation (rather than retribution, incapacitation, or deterrence), juveniles who were found delinquent were often placed in reformatories for indeterminate periods, sometimes until they reached the age of majority. Juvenile courts often suffered from lack of trained staff and adequate facilities, and by the 1960s, a system that was conceived by reformers was itself under attack by a new generation of reformers.

The Constitutional Reform of Juvenile Justice

The abuses that came to be associated with juvenile courts were addressed by the Supreme Court in the landmark case of *In re Gault*, 387 U.S. 1, 87 S.Ct. 1428, 18 L.Ed.2d 527 (1967). In *Gault*, the Court essentially required that juvenile courts adhere to standards of due process, applying most of the basic procedural safeguards enjoyed by adults accused of crimes. Moreover, *Gault* held that juvenile courts must respect the right to counsel, the freedom from compulsory self-incrimination, and the right to confront (cross-examine) hostile witnesses. Writing for a nearly unanimous bench, Justice Fortas observed that "under our Constitution, the condition of being a boy does not justify a kangaroo court." 387 U.S. at 28, 87 S.Ct. at 1444, 18 L.Ed.2d at 546. Four years later in *McKeiver v. Pennsylvania*, 403 U.S. 528, 91 S.Ct. 1976, 29 L.Ed.2d 647 (1971), the Court refused to extend the right to trial by jury to juvenile proceedings. In *Schall v. Martin*, 467 U.S. 253, 104 S.Ct. 2403, 81 L.Ed.2d 207 (1984), the Court upheld a pretrial detention program for juveniles that might well have been found violative of due process had it applied to adults. Writing for the Court, Justice Rehnquist stressed that "the Constitution does not mandate elimination of all differences in the treatment of juveniles." 467 U.S. at 263, 104 S.Ct. at 2409, 81 L.Ed.2d at 216.

In the wake of *Gault*, a number of states revised their juvenile codes to reflect the requirements of those decisions and to increase the qualifications of persons serving as juvenile judges and to transform juvenile courts into courts of record. Today it is common for the juvenile court to simply be a division of a court of general jurisdiction, such as a circuit or a superior court. Nevertheless, juvenile courts retain their distinctive character. For example, juvenile court proceedings are not subject to the constitutional "public trial" requirement. The Federal Juvenile Delinquency Act, 18 U.S.C.A. §§ 5031–5042, gives the court discretion on the issue of whether to close proceedings involving a child and whether to grant public access to the records of the proceedings. State laws vary, often allowing the presiding judge to exercise discretion in these matters.

There are significant differences in the adjudication of juvenile cases and adult criminal proceedings as well as the punishments imposed. We discuss some of the aspects of adjudication of juveniles in Chapter 18 and the distinctions between the punishments of juveniles and of adults in Chapter 19.

The Corrections System

The **corrections system** is designed to fulfill the criminal justice system's objective of providing punishment and rehabilitation of offenders. As with the court system, corrections facilities are operated at the federal and state levels. The system includes prisons and jails as well as a variety of programs that include probation, parole, and supervised community service.

Historical Background

Punishments inflicted under the English common law were quite severe—the death penalty was prescribed for most felonies, and those convicted of misdemeanors were generally subjected to such corporal punishment as flogging in the public square. The new American colonies generally followed common-law practice; by the time of the American Revolution, the death penalty was in wide use for a variety of felonies, and corporal punishment, primarily flogging, was widely used for a variety of crimes.

The American **Bill of Rights,** ratified in 1791, prohibited the imposition of "cruel and unusual punishments." The Framers sought to prevent the use of torture, which had been common in Europe as late as the eighteenth century; however, they did not intend to outlaw the death penalty or abolish all forms of corporal punishment.

During the nineteenth century, reformers introduced the concept of the **penitentiary**—literally, "a place to do penance." The idea was that criminals could be reformed through isolation, Bible study, and hard labor. This gave rise to the notion of rehabilitation, the idea that the criminal justice system could reform criminals and reintegrate them into society. Many of the educational, occupational training, and psychological programs found in modern prisons are based on this theory.

Contemporary Developments in Criminal Punishment

By the twentieth century, incarceration largely replaced corporal punishment as the states, as well as the federal government, constructed prisons to house persons convicted of felonies. Even cities and counties constructed jails for the confinement of persons convicted of misdemeanors. The **death penalty,** an intensely controversial penalty, remains in effect today in more than half the states, although its use is now limited to the most aggravated cases of murder. Today, the focus of criminal punishment is on the goal of incapacitation to prevent commission of further crimes.

There are procedural as well as substantive issues in the area of sentencing and punishment. Sharp disagreements exist regarding the roles that legislatures, judges, and corrections officials should play in determining punishments. Specifically, criminal punishment is limited by the Eighth Amendment prohibition of **cruel and unusual punishments,** the due process clauses of the Fifth and Fourteenth amendments, and by similar provisions in all fifty state constitutions. Today the criminal law provides for a variety of criminal punishments, including monetary **fines, incarceration, probation, community service,** and, of course, the death penalty.

As with courts, there is a federal corrections system and fifty separate state corrections systems. Each of these systems is responsible for supervising those persons sentenced to prison by courts of law. Originally, prisons were conceived as places for criminals to reflect on their misdeeds and repent, hence the term "penitentiary." In the twentieth century, the emphasis shifted to rehabilitation through psychological and sociopsychological methods. Unfortunately, these efforts were less than successful. Ironically, prisons appear to "criminalize" individuals more than to rehabilitate them. Inmates are exposed to an insular society with norms of conduct antithetical to those of civil society. As essentially totalitarian institutions, prisons do not encourage individuals to behave responsibly; furthermore, prisons provide an excellent venue for the spreading of criminal techniques. It is probably unrealistic to expect rehabilitation programs to succeed in such an environment. Today, prisons are generally regarded as little more than a way to punish and isolate those persons deemed unfit to live in civil society.

The Burgeoning Prison Population

Federal and state prison populations have experienced extremely rapid growth in recent years. In 1999 state and federal prisons held more than 1.2 million inmates. During the 1990s, state and federal prison populations grew at an average rate of nearly 6% per year. Between June 30, 1998, and June 30, 1999, the federal prison population rose by nearly 10%, the largest 12-month gain ever (U.S. Department of Justice, Office of Justice Programs, Bureau of Justice Statistics Bulletin, "Prison and Jail Inmates at Midyear 1999," April 2000, NCJ 181643). For more information, log on to the BJS website at **http://www.ojp.usdoj.gov/bjs/**.

The dramatic increases in state and federal prison populations were not attributable to rising crime rates. In fact, both violent crime and property crime declined sharply in the 1990s. Rather, burgeoning prison populations resulted from the adoption of more punitive sentencing policies in the 1980s and 1990s. These policy changes included the elimination or curtailment of **parole** and the adoption of **"truth in sentencing" laws, "three strikes" laws,** and **mandatory minimum sentences** (see Chapter 19). As a result of these changes in policy, the nationwide incarceration rate nearly doubled, from approximately 300 to 600 inmates per 100,000 residents between 1985 and 1995 (U.S. Department of Justice, Office of Justice Programs, Bureau of Justice Statistics Bulletin, "Prison and Jail Inmates, 1995," August 1996, NCJ–161132).

In any event, the proliferation of prison inmates has produced a crisis in many jurisdictions where there is simply not enough space to house prisoners. According to the Bureau of Justice Statistics, at the end of 1998, the federal prison system was operating at 27% above capacity while state prison populations varied between 13% and 22% beyond capacity.

The Future Outlook

The public continues to demand harsh sentences for convicted felons, but legislators (and taxpayers) are often unwilling to pay the price of constructing more prisons. Moreover, local residents often object to prisons being built in their "backyards." Even those states that have been aggressive in prison construction have found that demand for cell space continues to exceed supply. In many instances, federal courts have ordered prison officials to reduce overcrowding to comply with the U.S. Constitution's prohibition against "cruel and unusual punishments."

In many state prisons, cells originally designed for one or two inmates now house three or four prisoners. Increasingly, state prison systems must rely on local jails to house inmates, a situation that presents its own set of problems relating both to security and to conditions of confinement. Aside from the threat of federal judicial intervention, overcrowded prisons are more likely to produce inmate violence and even riots.

In addition to prisons, corrections systems include agencies that supervise probation, parole, community service, and other forms of alternative sentences. With burgeoning prison populations, these alternatives to incarceration are assuming more importance and consuming more resources, especially at the state level.

Conclusion

The American system of criminal justice is extremely complicated. The primary reason for this complexity is the principle of federalism, which refers to the division of political and legal authority in this country between one national government and fifty state governments. The United States Congress on behalf of the national government and each state legislature on behalf of its respective state enact their own criminal laws. The national government and each state government has its own law enforcement agencies, prosecutors, courts, and prison systems. No two systems are exactly alike. Indeed, there is tremendous variation from one jurisdiction to the next, both in the substantive criminal law and in the practices and procedures used by the various components of the criminal process. Yet, despite their substantive and procedural differences, all jurisdictions share two basic goals: to protect society from crime and, at the same time, to protect the rights of the individuals suspected of having committed offenses. Much of the conflict and inefficiency inherent in our criminal justice system stems from the need to balance these two competing objectives.

Key Terms

federalism
legislature
United States Congress
statutes
enumerated powers
implied powers
U.S. Code
session laws
mala prohibita
rules of statutory interpretation
plain meaning rule
canons of construction
legislative intent
void for vagueness
implied exception
sworn officers
Federal Bureau of Investigation
Department of Justice
special agents
United States Marshals
sheriff
police departments
order maintenance
community policing
prosecutors
plea bargaining
Attorney General
United States Attorneys

independent counsel
state's attorneys
nolle prosequi
indigent defendants
public defenders
defense attorney
jury
grand jury
petit (trial) jury
true bill
no bill
indictments
prosecutor's information
speedy and public trial
trial courts
appellate courts
jurisdiction
United States District Courts
intermediate appellate courts
United States Courts of Appeals
en banc hearings
courts-martial
Uniform Code of Military Justice
Court of Appeals for the Armed
    Forces
United States Supreme Court
writ of certiorari
rules of procedure

courts of general jurisdiction
courts of limited jurisdiction
state supreme court
juvenile courts
juvenile delinquency
status offenses
parens patriae
corrections system
Bill of Rights
penitentiary

death penalty
cruel and unusual punishments
fines
incarceration
probation
community service
parole
"truth in sentencing" laws
"three strikes" laws
mandatory minimum sentences

 # Web-Based Research Activity

1. Go to the Web.
2. Locate the United States Code. Hint: Try the "Legal Information Institute."
3. Locate Title 18, "Crimes and Criminal Procedure."
4. Locate Chapter 115, "Treason, Sedition, and Subversive Activities."
5. What is the offense of "seditious conspiracy"?

Questions for Thought and Discussion

1. How does the concept of federalism complicate the administration of criminal justice in the United States?

2. Describe the functions of federal and state law enforcement agencies.

3. Compare and contrast the functions of trial and appellate courts. How are they similar? How are they different?

4. What function does a grand jury serve? Does replacement of the indictment function of grand juries at the state level with prosecutors authorized to charge crimes by filing a sworn information impair the rights of citizens charged with crimes?

5. Is there a justification for the broad discretion vested in a prosecutor?

6. To what extent does the United States Constitution protect the right to trial by jury in a criminal case?

7. What are the arguments for and against allowing trial judges broad discretion in criminal sentencing?

8. What factors do you think a prosecutor should take into consideration in determining whether to prosecute an individual the police have arrested for possession of illegal drugs?

9. What chief characteristics distinguish the military justice system under the Uniform Code of Military Justice from civilian criminal prosecutions?

10. Under what circumstances, if any, is prison not an appropriate sanction for the commission of a felony?

PART II

The Substantive Criminal Law

Constitutional Limitations on the Prohibition of Criminal Conduct

CHAPTER OUTLINE

Introduction

In most democratic countries, legislative bodies are supreme in enacting statutes defining crimes and providing penalties. The only overarching authority is the will of the people manifested through the ballot box, where permitted, or through revolution. Being very familiar with the English monarchy and its parliamentary system, the framers of the United States Constitution understood that unbridled power to make and enforce criminal prohibitions constitutes a serious threat to liberty. Thus, they framed a Constitution that delimits the power of Congress and state legislatures to enact criminal statutes. Although federal and state legislative bodies have authority to enact statutes defining crimes and setting penalties, various provisions of the U.S. Constitution and state constitutions limit that power.

Being aware of the abusive prosecutions for treason, the Framers sought to prohibit the federal government from using that offense to punish political dissenters. Thus, they specifically defined **treason** against the United States in Article III, Section 3, saying it "shall consist only in levying War against them, or in adhering to their Enemies, giving them Aid and Comfort." The Bill of Rights, consisting of the first ten amendments to the Constitution, was ratified in 1791 to further restrict the power of the federal government in its relationship to the people. The Fourteenth Amendment (1868), adopted after the Civil War, ensures that the rights and liberties of the people are protected from encroachment by the states.

Our goal in this chapter is to provide an overview of the various constitutional provisions that limit legislative authority in defining conduct as criminal and prescribing penalties for violations or offenses. We discuss the effect of judicial interpretations of criminal statutes and the power of courts to declare void laws that violate the constitutional principles.

The Importance of Judicial Review

Constitutional limits on the enactment and enforcement of criminal statutes do not depend for their vitality only on the voluntary compliance of legislators, prosecutors, and police officers. Under the doctrine of **judicial review,** courts are empowered to declare null and void laws that violate constitutional principles. In a landmark decision in 1803, the Supreme Court first asserted the power to invalidate legislation that is in conflict with the Constitution. *Marbury v. Madison,* 5 U.S. (1 Cranch) 137, 2 L.Ed. 60 (1803). Speaking for the Court in *Marbury,* Chief Justice John Marshall said, "It is emphatically the province and duty of the judicial department to say what the law is." 5 U.S. (1 Cranch) at 177, 2 L.Ed. at 175. Although the power of judicial review is generally associated with the Supreme Court, all courts of record, whether state or federal, can exercise the power to strike down unconstitutional legislation. It is doubtful whether constitutional limitations on governmental power would be meaningful in the absence of judicial review.

Throughout this textbook, we will be discussing constitutional limitations on the criminal justice system. Many of these principles are procedural in nature, imposing restrictions and obligations on law enforcement, prosecution, adjudication, and sentencing. In this chapter we are concerned only with those constitutional provisions that place limits on the substantive criminal law, both in the types of laws that legislatures are barred from enacting and the situations in which police and prosecutors are barred from enforcing existing statutes.

SIDEBAR   **A Note on Briefing Cases**

Beginning with this chapter, each chapter in this book includes a number of excerpts from appellate court decisions. We have chosen these decisions to illustrate some of the important concepts and principles described in the chapters. Some instructors might want their students to "brief" some or all of these cases. Whether or not the instructor assigns it, students might find briefing cases useful in learning material and preparing for examinations.

A case brief is simply a summary of a court decision, usually in outline format. Typically, a case brief contains the following elements:

- The name of the case, the court deciding the case, and the date of the decision.

- The essential facts of the case.
- The key issue(s) of law involved.
- The holding of the court.
- A brief summary of the court's opinion.
- Summaries of concurring and dissenting opinions, if any.
- A brief comment on the impact of the decision on law or public policy.

Students might also want to make a note of any questions or comments they have at the end of the brief.

Unconstitutional Per Se and Unconstitutional as Applied

In addressing constitutional assaults on criminal statutes, courts are sometimes asked to declare that a statute is unconstitutional under any circumstances, whereas in other instances a court might simply be asked to rule that the statute cannot constitutionally apply to certain conduct. A statute may be declared **unconstitutional per se** in that it inherently trenches on some constitutionally protected liberty or exceeds the constitutional powers of government. Alternatively, a law that is facially valid, such as an ordinance prohibiting disorderly conduct, may be declared **unconstitutional as applied** if it is enforced in a way that impermissibly restricts or punishes the exercise of constitutional rights.

The Power to Enact Criminal Laws

The **police power** of government is the authority to enact legislation to protect the public health, safety, order, welfare, and morality. Under our system of federalism, the police power of government is vested primarily in the state legislatures. State legislatures have comprehensive power to adopt statutes regulating the activities of individuals and corporations as long as these statutes do not violate limitations contained in the state and federal constitutions. State legislatures, in turn, may delegate some of this power to local governments, which enact ordinances defining criminal offenses within their jurisdictions.

Federal Lawmaking Power

Unlike the state legislatures, the United States Congress does not possess plenary legislative authority (except over the District of Columbia and federal territories). As James Madison observed in 1788,

> The powers delegated by the proposed Constitution to the federal government are few and defined. Those which are to remain in the State governments are numerous and indefinite. (*The Federalist* No. 45, pp. 292–293 (C. Rossiter ed., 1961)

Article I, Section 8 of the U.S. Constitution enumerates Congress's legislative powers. Several of these **enumerated powers** allow Congress to enact criminal laws in certain areas. These include the power to establish rules governing immigration and naturalization, to "define and punish piracies and felonies committed on the high seas," and to "provide for the punishment of counterfeiting the securities and current coin of the United States."

Congress also possesses a reservoir of **implied powers,** which are justified by the Necessary and Proper Clause of Article I, Section 8. The doctrine of implied powers was established by the Supreme Court in *McCulloch v. Maryland,* 17 U.S. (4 Wheat.) 316, 4 L.Ed. 579 (1819). Writing for the Court, Chief Justice John Marshall articulated the doctrine as follows:

> Let the end be legitimate, let it be within the scope of the Constitution, and all means which are plainly adapted to that end, which are not prohibited, but consist with the letter and spirit of the Constitution, are constitutional. 17 U.S. (4 Wheat.) at 421, 4 L.Ed. at 605.

The doctrine of implied powers expands the legislative capabilities of Congress but by no means confers on Congress the plenary legislative authority possessed by state legislatures. To qualify as a valid expression of implied powers, federal legislation must be "plainly adapted" to the goal of furthering one or more of Congress's enumerated powers.

THE COMMERCE CLAUSE

In terms of the criminal law, by far the most significant of Congress's enumerated powers is power to regulate **interstate commerce.** For example, Congress is not empowered to prohibit prostitution per se, but Congress may make it a crime to transport persons across state lines for "immoral purposes" by drawing on its broad power to regulate interstate commerce. *Hoke v. United States,* 227 U.S. 308, 33 S.Ct. 281, 57 L.Ed. 523 (1913). Congress has relied on the Commerce Clause to enact a wide variety of criminal laws, including prohibitions against the following:

- interstate transportation of kidnapped persons (see 18 U.S.C.A. Sec. 1201)

- interstate transportation of stolen automobiles (see 18 U.S.C.A. Sec. 2312)

- manufacture, sale, distribution, and possession of controlled substances (see 21 U.S.C.A. § 801 et seq.)

- carjacking (see 18 U.S.C.A. § 2119)

- fraudulent schemes that use interstate television, radio, or wire communications (see 18 U.S.C.A. § 1343)

- conspiracies to restrain trade (see 15 U.S.C.A. § 1 et seq.)

- loan sharking (see 18 U.S.C.A. 891 et seq.)

- "computer crimes" (see 18 U.S.C.A. § 1030)

- racketeering and organized crime (see 18 U.S.C.A. §§ 1961–1963)

- various "environmental crimes" (see Chapter 11)

In the modern era, Congress has stretched the concept of interstate commerce to justify broader authority to enact criminal statutes. For the most part, the courts have been willing to accommodate this expansion of federal legislative power. See, e.g., *Perez v. United States,* 402 U.S. 146, 91 S.Ct. 1357, 28 L.Ed.2d 686 (1971). However, in recent years the Supreme Court has attempted to circumscribe this authority. For example, in *United States v. Lopez,* 514 U.S. 549, 115 S.Ct. 1624, 131 L.Ed.2d 626 (1995), the Court struck down the Gun-Free School Zones Act of 1990, which made it a federal crime for any person to knowingly possess a firearm while close to a school. Writing for the Court, Chief Justice Rehnquist observed that the challenged statute

> has nothing to do with "commerce" or any sort of economic enterprise, however broadly one might define those terms. [The law] is not an essential part of a larger regulation of economic activity, in which the regulatory scheme could be undercut unless the intrastate activity were regulated. It cannot, therefore, be sustained under our cases upholding regulations of activities that arise out of or are connected with a commercial transaction, which viewed in the aggregate, substantially affects interstate commerce.

The Court's *Lopez* decision was reinforced by its decision in *United States v. Morrison,* 529 U.S. 598, 120 S.Ct. 1578, 146 L.Ed.2d 477 (2000), where the Court struck down a provision of the Violence Against Women Act of 1994 that provided a federal civil remedy to victims of gender-motivated violence. Together, *Lopez* and *Morrison* call into question a number of the criminal statutes enacted by Congress under the Commerce Clause. At the very least, these decisions send a signal to Congress that it must tread lightly when relying on the Commerce Clause as a source of police power.

Bills of Attainder and *Ex Post Facto* Laws

Two historic abuses of the English Parliament that the Framers of the Constitution sought to correct were bills of attainder and *ex post facto* laws. A **bill of attainder** is a legislative act inflicting punishment on an individual or on a group of easily identifiable individuals. *United States v. Brown,* 381 U.S. 437, 85 S.Ct. 1707, 14 L.Ed.2d 484 (1965). Laws of this character are antithetical to the basic principle that a person accused of wrongdoing is entitled to a fair trial in a court of law.

An *ex post facto* **law** retroactively (1) makes an innocent act illegal, (2) increases the punishment for a criminal act, or (3) decreases the standard of proof required to convict a defendant of a crime. *Calder v. Bull,* 3 U.S. (3 Dall.) 386, 1 L.Ed. 648 (1798). Because the essence of the *ex post facto* law is retroactivity, it is flatly inconsistent with the principle of legality, which holds that individuals are entitled to know in advance if particular contemplated conduct is illegal.

Article I, Section 9 of the Constitution prohibits Congress from adopting bills of attainder and *ex post facto* laws. Article I, Section 10 extends these same prohibitions to the state legislatures. These categorical injunctions probably account for the fact that there have been relatively few judicial decisions striking down laws on these grounds.

SUPREME COURT PERSPECTIVE

Carmell v. Texas, 529 U.S. 513, 120 S.Ct. 1620, 46 L.Ed.2d 577 (2000)

In 1997 Scott Leslie Carmell was convicted in a Texas court of sexual assault, aggravated sexual assault, and indecency with a child. Evidence showed that between 1991 and 1995, Carmell committed various sex acts with his stepdaughter, starting when she was only twelve years old. Carmell was sentenced to life in prison on two convictions for aggravated sexual assault and twenty years in prison on thirteen other counts.

On May 1, 2000, the U.S. Supreme Court reversed four of Carmell's convictions by a vote of 5–4. These convictions were for sexual assaults that were alleged to have occurred in 1991 and 1992, when Texas law provided that a defendant could not be convicted merely on the testimony of the victim unless she was under fourteen. At the time of the alleged assaults in question, the victim was fourteen or fifteen. The law was later amended to extend the "child victim exception" to victims under eighteen years old. Carmell was convicted under the amended law, which the Supreme Court held to be an unconstitutional *ex post facto* law as defined by *Calder v. Bull*, 3 U.S. (3 Dall.) 386, 1 L.Ed. 648 (1798).

Writing for the Court, Justice Stevens observed that "[u]nder the law in effect at the time the acts were committed, the prosecution's case was legally insufficient and [Carmell] was entitled to a judgment of acquittal, unless the State could produce both the victim's testimony *and* corroborative evidence."

In dissent, Justice Ruth Bader Ginsburg argued that the provision of Texas law at issue in the case "does nothing more than accord to certain victims of sexual offenses full testimonial stature, giving them the same undiminished competency to testify that Texas extends to witnesses generally in the State's judicial proceedings." In Ginsburg's view, the Court's "precedents make clear that such a witness competency rule validly may be applied to offenses committed before its enactment."

In 2000 the United States Supreme Court handed down a decision invoking the prohibition against *ex post facto* laws (see the Supreme Court Perspective above).

The Bill of Rights

Although the original Constitution contained few express limitations on legislative power, the Bill of Rights ratified in 1791 added several important constraints on Congress. For criminal law, the most significant of these are the First Amendment freedoms of expression, religion, and assembly; the Second Amendment protection of "the right to keep and bear arms"; the Fifth Amendment Due Process Clause; the Eighth Amendment Cruel and Unusual Punishments Clause; and the Ninth Amendment guarantee of "rights retained by the people."

The Bill of Rights begins with the injunction that "*Congress* shall make no law . . ." [emphasis added]. Unlike certain provisions in the original, unamended Constitution, the Bill of Rights makes no mention of limitations on the state and local governments. Throughout much of the nineteenth century, the Bill of Rights was viewed as imposing limitations only on Congress, having no effect on state legislatures or local governing bodies. The Supreme Court officially adopted this view in *Barron v. Baltimore*, 32 U.S. (7 Pet.) 243, 8 L.Ed. 672 (1833). Under this interpretation of the Bill of Rights, citizens had to look to their state constitutions and state courts for protection against state and local actions that infringed on their rights and liberties.

Application of the Bill of Rights to State and Local Laws

The ratification of the Fourteenth Amendment in 1868 provided a justification for extending the scope of the Bill of Rights to apply against the states. Section 1 of the Fourteenth Amendment enjoins the states from depriving "any person of life, liberty, or property, without due process of law." It also prohibits states from adopting laws that "abridge the privileges and immunities of citizens of the United States."

In a series of decisions, the Supreme Court has held that the Due Process Clause of the Fourteenth Amendment makes enforceable against the states those provisions of the Bill of Rights that are "implicit in the concept of ordered liberty." *Palko v. Connecticut,* 302 U.S. 319, 58 S.Ct. 149, 82 L.Ed. 288 (1937). This **doctrine of incorporation** has been employed by the Court to enforce the procedural guarantees of the Bill of Rights in state criminal prosecutions. For example, in *Wolf v. Colorado,* 338 U.S. 25, 69 S.Ct. 1359, 93 L.Ed. 1782 (1949), the Court said that the Fourth Amendment protection against unreasonable searches and seizures is applicable to state and local, as well as federal, law enforcement authorities. Similarly, in *Duncan v. Louisiana,* 391 U.S. 145, 88 S.Ct. 1444, 20 L.Ed.2d 491 (1968), the Court held that the Fourteenth Amendment requires states to observe the jury trial requirement of the Sixth Amendment.

In addition to incorporating the procedural protections of the Bill of Rights into the Fourteenth Amendment, the Court has extended the substantive limitations of the Bill of Rights to the states. In 1925 the Supreme Court recognized that the First Amendment protections of free speech and free press apply to state as well as federal laws. *Gitlow v. New York,* 268 U.S. 652, 45 S.Ct. 625, 69 L.Ed. 1138 (1925). Likewise, in 1934 the Court said that the First Amendment guarantee of free exercise of religion is enforceable against state and local governments. *Hamilton v. Regents of the University of California,* 293 U.S. 245, 55 S.Ct. 197, 79 L.Ed. 343 (1934).

The Supreme Court has incorporated virtually all the provisions of the Bill of Rights into the Fourteenth Amendment, making them applicable to the state and local governments. The Federal Constitution, and in particular the Bill of Rights, now stands as a barrier to unreasonable or oppressive criminal laws, whether they are enacted by Congress, a state legislature, or a local governing body.

The First Amendment Freedom of Expression

Perhaps the most treasured of our liberties, and the rights most essential to maintaining a democratic polity, are the First Amendment freedoms of speech and press. Often, freedom of speech and freedom of the press are referred to jointly as freedom of expression. Although the concept of free expression is fundamental to our democratic society, the Supreme Court has said that the First Amendment has "never been thought to give absolute protection to every individual to speak whenever or wherever he pleases, or to use any form of address in any circumstances that he chooses." *Cohen v. California,* 403 U.S. 15, 19, 91 S.Ct. 1780, 1785, 29 L.Ed.2d 284, 290 (1971). The task of the courts, of course, is to strike a reasonable balance between the right of expression and the legitimate interests of society in maintaining security, order, peace, safety, and decency. In what has become a classic phrase, Justice Oliver Wendell Holmes, Jr., observed that the "most stringent protection of free speech would not protect a man in falsely shouting fire in a theater, and causing a panic."

Schenck v. United States, 249 U.S. 47, 51, 39 S.Ct. 247, 249, 63 L.Ed. 470, 473 (1919). Moreover, the Supreme Court has said that certain types of speech are so inherently lacking in value as not to merit any First Amendment protection:

> There are certain well defined and narrowly limited classes of speech, the prevention and punishment of which have never been thought to raise any constitutional problem. These include the lewd and obscene, the profane, the libelous, and the insulting or "fighting" words—those which by their very utterance inflict injury or tend to incite an immediate breach of the peace. It has been well observed that such utterances are no essential part of any exposition of ideas, and are of such slight social value as a step to truth that any benefit that may be derived from them is clearly outweighed by the social interest in order and morality. *Chaplinsky v. New Hampshire,* 315 U.S. 568, 571, 62 S.Ct. 766, 769, 86 L.Ed. 1031, 1035 (1942).

Advocacy of Unlawful Conduct

One of the most basic problems posed by the First Amendment is whether speech advocating unlawful conduct might itself be made unlawful. The Supreme Court first encountered this problem in *Schenck v. United States,* supra, where an official of the Socialist Party appealed from a conviction under the Espionage Act of 1917, 40 Stat. at L. 217, 219. Charles T. Schenck had been convicted of participating in a conspiracy to cause insubordination in the military services and to obstruct military recruitment at a time when the United States was at war. The "conspiracy" consisted of activities surrounding the mailing of a leaflet to draftees urging them to resist induction into the military. The Supreme Court upheld Schenck's conviction, saying that

> the question in every case is whether the words used are used in such circumstances and are of such a nature as to create clear and present danger that they will bring about the substantive evils that Congress has a right to prevent. It is a question of proximity and degree. When a nation is at war many things that might be said in time of peace are such a hindrance to its effort that their utterance will not be endured so long as men fight, and that no court could regard them as protected by any constitutional right. 249 U.S. at 52, 39 S.Ct. at 249, 63 L.Ed. at 473.

The Supreme Court first invoked the **clear and present danger doctrine** to reverse a criminal conviction in a case involving a Georgia man who had been prosecuted under a state law prohibiting "any attempt, by persuasion or otherwise" to incite insurrection. *Herndon v. Lowry,* 301 U.S. 242, 57 S.Ct. 732, 81 L.Ed. 1066 (1937). Since then, the doctrine has been used by state and federal courts to reverse numerous convictions where persons have been prosecuted for merely advocating illegal acts.

The modern Supreme Court has refined the clear and present danger doctrine so that public advocacy may be prohibited only in situations when there is **imminent lawless action.** *Brandenburg v. Ohio,* 395 U.S. 444, 89 S.Ct. 1827, 23 L.Ed.2d 430 (1969). Today, it is questionable whether the courts would uphold a conviction in circumstances similar to those in the *Schenck* case. The courts might find that mailing a leaflet or standing on a street corner urging resistance to the draft—activities that were fairly common during the Vietnam War—are not fraught with imminent lawless action and therefore do not constitute a clear and present danger.

An excerpt from *Brandenburg v. Ohio* appears at the end of the chapter.

Symbolic Speech and Expressive Conduct

Freedom of expression is a broad concept embracing speech, publication, performances, and demonstrations. Even wearing symbols is considered to be constitutionally protected **symbolic speech.** *Tinker v. Des Moines Independent Community*

School District, 393 U.S. 503, 89 S.Ct. 733, 21 L.Ed.2d 731 (1969). The Supreme Court has recognized a wide variety of conduct as possessing "sufficient communicative elements to bring the First Amendment to play." *Texas v. Johnson*, 491 U.S. 397, 404, 109 S.Ct. 2533, 2539, 105 L.Ed.2d 342, 353 (1989). The Court has accorded First Amendment protection to, among other things, "sit-ins" to protest racial segregation, *Brown v. Louisiana*, 383 U.S. 131, 86 S.Ct. 719, 15 L.Ed.2d 637 (1966); civilians wearing American military uniforms to protest the Vietnam War, *Schacht v. United States*, 398 U.S. 58, 90 S.Ct. 1555, 26 L.Ed.2d 44 (1970); and "picketing" over a variety of issues, *Amalgamated Food Employees Union v. Logan Valley Plaza, Inc.*, 391 U.S. 308, 88 S.Ct. 1601, 20 L.Ed.2d 603 (1968).

Without question, the most controversial applications of the concept of expressive conduct have been the Supreme Court's decisions holding that the public burning of the American flag is protected by the First Amendment. In *Texas v. Johnson*, supra, the Court invalidated a Texas statute banning flag desecration. Gregory Johnson had been arrested after he publicly burned an American flag outside the Republican National Convention in Dallas in 1984. The Supreme Court's decision to reverse Johnson's conviction and strike down the Texas law resulted in a firestorm of public criticism of the Court as well as the enactment of a new federal statute. The Flag Protection Act of 1989, amending 18 U.S.C.A. § 700, imposed criminal penalties on anyone who knowingly "mutilates, defaces, physically defiles, burns, maintains upon the floor or ground, or tramples upon" the American flag. In *United States v. Eichman*, 496 U.S. 310, 110 S.Ct. 2404, 110 L.Ed.2d 287 (1990), the Supreme Court invalidated this federal statute as well, saying that "punishing desecration of the flag dilutes the very freedom that makes this emblem so revered, and worth revering." 496 U.S. at 319, 110 S.Ct. at 2410, 110 L.Ed.2d at 296.

Free Expression Versus Maintenance of the Public Order

One type of expression that sometimes transgresses the criminal law is public speech that threatens the public peace and order. Numerous state and local laws prohibit incitement to riot and disturbing the peace. The Supreme Court has said, "[w]hen clear and present danger of riot, disorder, interference with traffic upon the public streets, or other immediate threat to public safety, peace, or order appears, the power of the State to prevent and punish is obvious." *Cantwell v. Connecticut*, 310 U.S. 296, 308, 60 S.Ct. 900, 905, 84 L.Ed. 1213, 1220 (1940). Moreover, the Court has held that so-called **fighting words** are unprotected by the Constitution. *Chaplinsky v. New Hampshire*, supra. Fighting words are "those personally abusive epithets which, when addressed to the ordinary citizen, are, as a matter of common knowledge, inherently likely to provoke violent reaction." *Cohen v. California*, 403 U.S. at 20, 91 S.Ct. at 1785, 29 L.Ed.2d at 291.

Although government must have the authority to maintain order, it may not under the guise of preserving public peace unduly suppress free communication of views. Again, the problem for courts is to strike a reasonable balance between legitimate competing interests in the context of the particular facts in the case at hand.

Hate Speech

In recent years, legislatures and courts have become concerned with the problem of **hate speech.** Hate speech refers to any instance of hateful expression, whether verbal, written, or symbolic, that is based on racial, ethnic, or religious prejudice or some other similar animus. Because it constitutes expression, hate speech is generally protected by the Constitution unless it falls within one of the recognized exceptions to the First Amendment. Would a public cross burning by the Ku Klux Klan in a black neighborhood qualify as fighting words, or would it be considered expressive conduct protected by the First Amendment? What about the display of swastikas by Nazis parading through the streets of a predominantly Jewish city? Would police be justified in these instances to make arrests for incitement to riot? These questions became more real than hypothetical during the 1980s, when the country witnessed a resurgence of racist organizations, and cities and states countered with laws proscribing hate speech. One such law, a St. Paul, Minnesota, ordinance, provided the following:

> Whoever places on public or private property a symbol, object, appellation, characterization or graffiti, including, but not limited to, a burning cross or Nazi swastika, which one knows or has reasonable grounds to know arouses anger, alarm or resentment in others on the basis of race, color, creed, religion or gender commits disorderly conduct and shall be guilty of a misdemeanor.

In *R.A.V. v. City of St. Paul*, 505 U.S. 377, 112 S.Ct. 2538, 120 L.Ed.2d 305 (1992), the Supreme Court declared this ordinance unconstitutional in the context of a criminal prosecution of a white teenager who burned a cross on the front lawn of a black family's home. Lest the public be tempted to conclude that the Supreme Court condoned racially motivated cross burnings, the Court stated the following:

> Let there be no mistake about our belief that burning a cross in someone's front yard is reprehensible. But St. Paul has sufficient means at its disposal to prevent such behavior without adding the First Amendment to the fire. 505 U.S. at 396, 112 S.Ct. at 2550, 120 L.Ed.2d at 326.

Obscenity

Traditionally, state and local governments have proscribed speech, pictures, films, and performances regarded as obscene, generally classifying these as misdemeanor offenses. Despite challenges to the constitutionality of such obscenity laws, the Supreme Court has held that **obscenity** is beyond the pale of the First Amendment and thus subject to criminal prosecution. *Roth v. United States*, 354 U.S. 476, 77 S.Ct. 1304, 1 L.Ed.2d 1498 (1957).

The problem for the legislatures, police, prosecutors, and courts is to determine what is obscene and therefore unprotected by the First Amendment. The Supreme Court has held that for expression to be obscene, it must (1) appeal to a prurient interest in sex; (2) depict sexual conduct in a patently offensive way; and (3) lack serious literary, artistic, political, or scientific value. *Miller v. California*, 413 U.S. 15, 93 S.Ct. 2607, 37 L.Ed.2d 419 (1973). Despite this test, the concept of obscenity remains somewhat vague. Nevertheless, the Supreme Court has made it clear that obscenity refers only to "hard-core" pornography. *Jenkins v. Georgia*, 418 U.S. 153, 94 S.Ct. 2750, 41 L.Ed.2d 642 (1974). (The "intractable obscenity problem," as it has been called, is dealt with more fully in Chapter 8.)

An excerpt from the Supreme Court's decision in *Miller v. California* appears at the end of the chapter.

Nude Dancing

Every state has a prohibition against indecent exposure. Generally, these statutes are applied in situations where individuals expose themselves in public or in private to unwilling viewers. But what if the exposure takes place by mutual consent, such as in a nightclub that features nude dancing? The Supreme Court has recognized that this form of entertainment is entitled to First Amendment protection under certain circumstances, but has also expressed a willingness to uphold reasonable regulations, especially involving establishments that serve alcoholic beverages. *Doran v. Salem Inn,* 422 U.S. 922, 95 S.Ct. 2561, 45 L.Ed.2d 648 (1975). In *Barnes v. Glen Theatre, Inc.,* 501 U.S. 560, 111 S.Ct. 2456, 115 L.Ed.2d 504 (1991), the Court upheld an Indiana statute requiring that night club dancers wear "pasties" and "G-strings" when they dance. In an opinion expressing the view of three justices, Chief Justice Rehnquist observed that "Indiana's requirement that the dancers wear at least pasties and a G-string is modest, and the bare minimum necessary to achieve the state's purpose. . . ." 501 U.S. at 571, 111 S.Ct. at 2463, 115 L.Ed.2d at 515.

After the Supreme Court's decision in *Barnes v. Glen Theatre,* the city of Erie, Pennsylvania, adopted an ordinance making it an offense for anyone to "knowingly or intentionally appear in public in a state of nudity." To comply with the ordinance, erotic dancers were required to wear pasties and G-strings. The owners of Kandyland, a club that featured all-nude erotic dancers, filed suit in a state court to challenge the constitutionality of the new ordinance. The Court of Common Pleas declared the ordinance unconstitutional under the First Amendment, and the Pennsylvania Supreme Court agreed, concluding that the unstated purpose of the ordinance was the suppression of expression. On certiorari, the United States Supreme Court reversed and upheld the ordinance. Writing for a plurality of justices, Justice Sandra Day O'Connor concluded that the requirement that dancers wear pasties and G-strings was "a minimal restriction" that left dancers "ample capacity" to convey their erotic messages. *City of Erie et al. v. Pap's A. M.,* 529 U.S. 277, 120 5.ct.1382, 146 L.Ed 2d 265 (2000).

Profanity

Although in *Chaplinsky v. New Hampshire,* supra, the Supreme Court specifically enumerated profanity as being among those categories of speech so lacking in value as not to merit First Amendment protection, this view no longer prevails. In *Cohen v. California,* supra, the Supreme Court invalidated the "offensive conduct" conviction of a man who entered a courthouse wearing a jacket emblazoned with the slogan "Fuck the Draft." Writing for the Court, Justice Harlan opined that

> while the particular four-letter-word being litigated here is perhaps more distasteful than others of its genre, it is nevertheless often true that one man's vulgarity is another's lyric. Indeed, we think it is largely because government officials cannot make principled distinctions in this area that the Constitution leaves matters of taste and style so largely to the individual. 403 U.S. at 25, 91 S.Ct. at 1788, 29 L.Ed.2d at 294.

Despite the Supreme Court's decision in *Cohen v. California,* most states and many cities retain laws proscribing profanity. These laws are seldom enforced and rarely challenged in court.

Freedom of Assembly

The First Amendment specifically protects the "right of the people peaceably to assemble." Yet, as we have seen, one of the most important purposes of the criminal law is to maintain public peace and order. Sometimes these values conflict, as in the civil rights struggle of the 1960s, when public demonstrations became an important part of a powerful political movement. See, for example, *Cox v. Louisiana,* 379 U.S. 559, 85 S.Ct. 476, 13 L.Ed.2d 487 (1965); *Adderley v. Florida,* 385 U.S. 39, 87 S.Ct. 242, 17 L.Ed.2d 149 (1966); *Walker v. City of Birmingham,* 388 U.S. 307, 87 S.Ct. 1824, 18 L.Ed.2d 1210 (1967).

Governments may not ban assemblies in the **public forum** as long as they are peaceful and do not impede the operations of government or the activities of other citizens. Yet, to promote the interests of safety, order, and peace, governments may impose reasonable **time, place, and manner regulations** on public assemblies. The character of a given place and the pattern of its normal activities determine the type of time, place, and manner regulations that the courts consider reasonable. *Grayned v. City of Rockford,* 408 U.S. 104, 92 S.Ct. 2294, 33 L.Ed.2d 222 (1972). For example, a restriction against the use of sound amplifiers near a courthouse or library might well be judged reasonable, whereas a ban on "picketing" on the steps of the same buildings would not. In imposing time, place, and manner regulations, governments must be careful not to deprive demonstrations or protests of their essential content by imposing excessive or unnecessarily burdensome regulations. *United States v. Grace,* 461 U.S. 171, 103 S.Ct. 1702, 75 L.Ed.2d 736 (1983).

Free Exercise of Religion

The value of **freedom of religion** is so deeply rooted in American culture that rarely have legislatures sought to impinge directly on that right. Yet from time to time lawmakers have sought to prevent certain unpopular religious groups from proselytizing. The Supreme Court has been quick to invalidate such efforts. In one leading case, the Court struck down a state statute that made it a misdemeanor for any person to solicit door-to-door for religious or philanthropic reasons without prior approval from local officials, who were authorized to make determinations as to whether solicitors represented bona fide religions. The law was successfully challenged by a member of the Jehovah's Witnesses sect who was prosecuted for engaging in door-to-door proselytizing without a permit. *Cantwell v. Connecticut,* supra.

Much more problematic are government attempts to enforce criminal statutes designed to protect the public health, safety, and welfare against religious practices deemed inimical to these interests. Does the right to freely exercise one's religion permit a person to violate an otherwise valid criminal statute? In 1878 the Supreme Court answered this question in the negative by upholding the prosecution of a polygamist. *Reynolds v. United States,* 98 U.S. (8 Otto) 145, 25 L.Ed. 244 (1878). More recently, however, the Supreme Court granted to members of the Old Order Amish sect an exemption to the Wisconsin compulsory education law. The Court found that the law significantly interfered with the Amish way of life and thus violated their right to freely exercise their religion. *Wisconsin v. Yoder,* 406 U.S. 205, 92 S.Ct. 1526, 32 L.Ed.2d 15 (1972).

Unusual Religious Practices

Several state courts have decided cases arising from unusual forms of worship. The Tennessee Supreme Court upheld the validity of a statute making it a crime to handle poisonous snakes in religious ceremonies against the claim that the law violated the right to free exercise of religion guaranteed by the state constitution. *Harden v. State,* 216 S.W.2d 708 (Tenn. 1949).

In a decision that cuts the other way, the California Supreme Court reversed the convictions of several members of the Native American Church for possession of peyote, which contains an illegal hallucinogen. *People v. Woody,* 394 P.2d 813 (Cal. 1964). In the court's view, the sacramental use of peyote was central to the worship by members of the Native American Church and thus protected by the First Amendment. In 1990, however, the U.S. Supreme Court held that the sacramental use of peyote by members of the Native American Church was not protected by the Free Exercise Clause of the First Amendment. *Employment Division v. Smith,* 494 U.S. 872, 110 S.Ct. 1595, 108 L.Ed.2d 876 (1990). This decision by the nation's highest court means that state courts that have granted such protection might want to reconsider their positions. In our federal system, however, state courts are free to provide greater levels of protection to individual rights under the terms of their state constitutions than those provided by the federal constitution.

The principle that underlies *Employment Division v. Smith* is that the Free Exercise Clause does not provide the basis for an exemption to a generally applicable criminal statute. A law aimed specifically at the practices of one religious group is another matter, as the Supreme Court made clear in striking down a Hialeah, Florida, ordinance prohibiting animal sacrifices. *Church of the Lukumi Babalu Aye, Inc. v. City of Hialeah,* 508 U.S. 520, 113 S.Ct. 2217, 124 L.Ed.2d 472 (1993).

Refusal of Medical Treatment

One of the more troubling and tragic situations in which the Free Exercise Clause potentially conflicts with the criminal law involves the refusal of medical treatment. Certain religious groups, such as the Christian Scientists, believe that physical healing is to be achieved through spiritual power. Thus, when faced with an illness or injury, they are likely to refuse medical treatment. Other groups—for example, the Jehovah's Witnesses—believe that blood transfusions are specifically enjoined by Scripture.

The courts have recognized the right of a competent adult to refuse medical treatment on religious grounds, even if the refusal results in death. See, for example, *In re Estate of Brooks,* 205 N.E.2d 435 (Ill. 1965); *In re Milton,* 505 N.E.2d 255 (Ohio 1987). It is another matter entirely when parents refuse to allow medical treatment for their children. The Supreme Court has recognized that

> parents may be free to become martyrs themselves. But it does not follow that they are free in identical circumstances to make martyrs of their children before they have reached the age of full legal discretion when they can make that choice for themselves. *Prince v. Massachusetts,* 321 U.S. 158, 170, 64 S.Ct. 438, 444, 88 L.Ed. 645, 654 (1944).

Accordingly, courts seldom allow freedom of religion as a defense to a criminal charge stemming from a situation in which parents refused to seek or allow medical treatment for their children. In one recent case, a member of the Christian Scientist faith was prosecuted for involuntary manslaughter after failing to seek medical treatment of her daughter's meningitis, which turned out to be fatal. The California Supreme Court rejected the defendant's free exercise of religion defense, saying that "parents have no right to free exercise of religion at the price of a child's life." *Walker v. Superior Court,* 763 P.2d 852 (Cal. 1988).

The Right to Keep and Bear Arms

There are numerous criminal prohibitions—at the federal, state, and local levels—against the sale, possession, and use of certain types of firearms. "Gun control" laws are seen by many as antithetical to the **right to keep and bear arms.** The Second Amendment to the U.S. Constitution provides as follows:

> A well regulated Militia, being necessary to the security of a free state, the right of the people to keep and bear arms shall not be infringed.

In *United States v. Miller,* 307 U.S. 174, 59 S.Ct. 816, 83 L.Ed. 1206 (1939), the Supreme Court upheld a federal law criminalizing the interstate shipment of sawed-off shotguns, saying that "the right to keep and bear arms" had to be interpreted in relation to the "well regulated militia." The Court concluded that possession of sawed-off shotguns had no reasonable relationship to serving in the militia. In reaffirming *Miller,* the Court said that "the Second Amendment guarantees no right to keep and bear a firearm that does not have some reasonable relationship to the preservation or efficiency of a well regulated militia." *Lewis v. United States,* 445 U.S. 55, 65 n.8, 100 S.Ct. 915, 921 n.8, 63 L.Ed.2d 198, 209 n.8 (1980). Like the federal constitution, many state constitutions contain language dealing with the right to keep and bear arms. Yet state courts tend to give wide latitude to state and local gun control laws.

The Doctrines of Vagueness and Overbreadth

The Fifth Amendment to the U.S. Constitution provides that "no person . . . shall be deprived of life, liberty or property without due process of law." The two fundamental aspects of due process are **fair notice** and **fair hearing.** The principle of fair notice implies that a person has a right to know whether particular contemplated conduct is illegal. Indeed, the Supreme Court has emphatically stated that "[n]o one may be required at peril of life, liberty or property to speculate as to the meaning of penal statutes." *Lanzetta v. New Jersey,* 306 U.S. 451, 453, 59 S.Ct. 618, 619, 83 L.Ed. 888, 890 (1939).

A criminal law that is excessively vague in its proscriptions offends this principle and is thus invalid under the Due Process Clause of the Fifth or Fourteenth Amendments (depending on whether it is a federal or state statute). However, we must realize that the **vagueness doctrine** is "designed more to limit the discretion of police and prosecutors than to ensure that statutes are intelligible to persons pondering criminal activity." *United States v. White,* 882 F.2d 250, 252 (7th Cir. 1989). Accordingly, the Supreme Court has held that the requisite specificity of criminal statutes may be achieved through judicial interpretation. *Rose v. Locke,* 423 U.S. 48, 96 S.Ct. 243, 46 L.Ed.2d 185 (1975). As interpreted by the Seventh Circuit Court of Appeals in *United States v. White,* "provided that conduct is of a sort widely known among the lay public to be criminal. . . , a person is not entitled to clear notice that the conduct violates a particular criminal statute." *United States v. White,* supra at 252.

In a landmark decision, the Supreme Court struck down a Jacksonville, Florida, ordinance that prohibited various forms of vagrancy, including loitering and "prowling by auto." *Papachristou v. City of Jacksonville,* 405 U.S. 156, 92 S.Ct. 839, 31 L.Ed.2d 110 (1972). Writing for the Court in *Papachristou,* Justice Douglas objected to the "unfettered discretion" the ordinance placed in the hands of the police, allowing for "arbitrary and discriminatory enforcement of the law." (For further discussion of the vagueness doctrine as it relates to the crimes of vagrancy and loitering, see Chapter 12.)

Closely related to the concept of vagueness, the **doctrine of overbreadth** was developed exclusively in the context of the First Amendment and concerns the precision of a criminal law that potentially infringes First Amendment freedoms. The evil of overbreadth of a law is that it may permit police to make arrests for constitutionally protected conduct, such as political speech, as well as for unprotected activity, such as inciting people to violence through use of fighting words.

Coates v. City of Cincinnati, 402 U.S. 611, 91 S.Ct. 1686, 29 L.Ed.2d 214 (1971), illustrates both the vagueness doctrine and the doctrine of overbreadth. In *Coates* the Supreme Court reviewed a Cincinnati ordinance that made it unlawful for "three or more persons to assemble . . . on any sidewalks and there conduct themselves in a manner annoying to persons passing by. . . ." In striking the ordinance, the Court first addressed the vagueness issue:

> Conduct that annoys some people does not annoy others. Thus, the ordinance is vague, not in the sense that it requires a person to conform his conduct to an imprecise but comprehensible normative standard, but rather in the sense that no standard of conduct is specified at all. As a result, "men of common intelligence must necessarily guess at its meaning."

Then, addressing the overbreadth of the ordinance, the Court observed the following:

> The ordinance also violates the constitutional right of free assembly and association. Our decisions establish that mere public intolerance or animosity cannot be the basis for abridgment of these constitutional freedoms. . . . The First and Fourteenth Amendments do not permit a State to make criminal the exercise of the right of assembly simply because its exercise may be "annoying" to some people. . . . And such a prohibition . . . contains an obvious invitation to discriminatory enforcement against those whose association together is "annoying" because their ideas, their lifestyle, or their physical appearance is resented by the majority of their fellow citizens.

As the Court points out, the overbreadth of the law may permit police to make arrests for constitutionally protected conduct, such as political speech, as well as for unprotected activity, such as fighting words. Ordinarily a person can contest only a law that has been directed against him or her. However, the doctrine of overbreadth enables a person to contest a law imposing restrictions on First Amendment freedoms even when that person has not been charged with violating the law. This doctrine was designed to bring to the courts' attention laws that have a "chilling effect" on the exercise of First Amendment rights.

In the 1980s, the Supreme Court appeared to be retreating somewhat from the overbreadth doctrine. In *New York v. Ferber,* 458 U.S. 747, 102 S.Ct. 3348, 73 L.Ed.2d 1113 (1982), for example, the Court rejected an overbreadth challenge to a child pornography statute that criminalized child pornography well beyond the legal test of obscenity delineated in *Miller v. California,* supra. Although expressing concern that the statute might possibly be applied to punish constitutionally protected artistic expression, the Court concluded that the law was not "substantially overbroad" and that impermissible applications of the statute should be addressed on a case-by-case basis. According to the *Ferber* Court, a statute should not be invalidated for overbreadth if its legitimate reach "dwarfs its arguably impermissible applications." 458 U.S. at 773, 102 S.Ct. at 3363, 73 L.Ed.2d at 1133.

The overbreadth doctrine was given new life by the Supreme Court in 1997, when the Court struck down provisions of the Communications Decency Act (CDA) of 1996, 47 U.S.C.A. §§ 223(a), 223(d) (Supp. 1997). Under the CDA, Congress had attempted to ban "indecent" as well as "obscene" speech from the Internet. Criminal penalties were provided for persons who transmitted such messages in a fashion that they could be received by children. The Court found that the law swept within its ambit constitutionally protected speech as well as obscenity. *Reno v. American Civil Liberties Union,* 521 U.S. 844, 117 S.Ct. 2329, 138 L.Ed.2d 874 (1997).

The Prohibition Against Cruel and Unusual Punishments

The Eighth Amendment prohibits the imposition of **cruel and unusual punishments.** This principle applies both to the procedures by which criminal sentences are imposed, *Furman v. Georgia,* 408 U.S. 238, 92 S.Ct. 2726, 33 L.Ed.2d 346 (1972), and to the substantive laws that define punishments. For example, in *Coker v. Georgia,* 433 U.S. 584, 97 S.Ct. 2861, 53 L.Ed.2d 982 (1977), the Supreme Court invalidated a provision of a state death penalty law that allowed capital punishment in cases of rape.

Writing for the plurality, Justice White concluded that "the death penalty, which is 'unique in its severity and its irrevocability,' is an excessive penalty for the rapist who, as such, does not take human life." 433 U.S. at 598, 97 S.Ct. at 2869, 53 L.Ed.2d at 993. Generally, however, in Eighth Amendment cases the Supreme Court does not rule on the validity of a statute, but rather confines its inquiry to the constitutionality of a particular sentence. For example, in *Solem v. Helm,* 463 U.S. 277, 103 S.Ct. 3001, 77 L.Ed.2d 637 (1983), the Supreme Court vacated a life sentence without possibility of parole imposed under a state habitual offender law. The Court found that life imprisonment without parole was significantly disproportionate to the defendant's crimes, all of which were nonviolent in nature.

On occasion, the Eighth Amendment has even been employed to limit the definition of crimes. In *Robinson v. California,* 370 U.S. 660, 82 S.Ct. 1417, 8 L.Ed.2d 758 (1962), the Supreme Court, relying on the Cruel and Unusual Punishments Clause, struck down a state law that made it a crime for a person to be "addicted to the use of narcotics." The Court found it unacceptable that an individual could be punished merely for a "status" without regard to any specific criminal conduct. In effect, the Court "constitutionalized" the traditional requirement that a crime involve a specific *actus reus.*

The Constitutional Right of Privacy

Although there is no mention of "privacy" in the text of the Constitution, the Supreme Court has held that a sphere of intimate personal conduct is immune from legislative interference. In its first explicit recognition of this **constitutional right of**

An excerpt from *Griswold v. Connecticut* appears at the end of the chapter.

privacy, *Griswold v. Connecticut,* 381 U.S. 479, 85 S.Ct. 1678, 14 L.Ed.2d 510 (1965), the Court relied in part on the Ninth Amendment, which provides that

> [t]he enumeration in the Constitution, of certain rights, shall not be construed to deny or disparage others retained by the people.

In the *Griswold* case, the Supreme Court invalidated a state law proscribing the use of birth control devices as applied to married couples. In *Eisenstadt v. Baird,* 405 U.S. 438, 92 S.Ct. 1029, 31 L.Ed.2d 349 (1972), the Court extended the principle to protect single individuals from a similar anti-contraception statute. Writing for the Court in *Eisenstadt,* Justice Brennan stated that the right of privacy is "the right of the individual, married or single, to be free from unwarranted governmental intrusion into matters so fundamentally affecting a person as the decision whether or not to beget a child." 405 U.S. at 453, 92 S.Ct. at 1038, 31 L.Ed.2d at 362.

Abortion

The Supreme Court's *Griswold* and *Eisenstadt* decisions paved the way for its landmark abortion decision in *Roe v. Wade,* 410 U.S. 113, 93 S.Ct. 705, 35 L.Ed.2d 147 (1973). In *Roe,* the Court held that the right of privacy was broad enough to include a woman's decision to terminate her pregnancy. This 7–2 decision invalidated the Texas anti-abortion statute and rendered unenforceable similar laws in most states. The essential holding in *Roe v. Wade* has been reaffirmed by the Supreme Court on several occasions, most recently in 2000 when it struck down a Nebraska law banning a procedure commonly described as "partial-birth abortion." *Stenberg v. Carhart,* 530 U.S. 914, 120 S.Ct. 1736, 146 L.Ed.2d 640 (2000).

The continuing "pro-life" and "pro-choice" demonstrations around the country attest to the extremely controversial nature of legal abortion. (The abortion issue is discussed more thoroughly in Chapter 6.) Few questions today have greater philosophical, religious, ethical, medical, and political saliency than the issue of abortion. Seemingly irreconcilable views on the subject of abortion exist, and the issue continues to spawn legislative and judicial attention. The continuing clashes between demonstrators resulting in injuries and even death have caused some states to respond by restricting the proximity of demonstrators to clinics. In *Madsen v. Women's Health Center,* 512 U.S. 753, 114 S.Ct. 2516, 129 L.Ed.2d 593 (1994), the U.S. Supreme Court attempted to balance the constitutional rights of those seeking access to abortion clinics against the First Amendment rights of the protesters. In a 6–3 decision, the Court upheld the basic provisions of a state court injunction intended to keep disruptive protesters from blocking access to the clinics.

On May 26, 1994, President Clinton signed the Freedom of Access to Clinic Entrances Act (FACE), 18 U.S.C.A. § 248. This federal law was prompted by the 1993 killing of an abortion doctor outside a Pensacola, Florida, clinic as well as by numerous episodes around the country in which persons working at or seeking access to abortion clinics had been harassed and threatened by anti-abortion activists. The new act provides civil and criminal remedies against whoever

> (1) by force or threat of force or by physical obstruction, intentionally injures, intimidates or interferes with or attempts to injure, intimidate or interfere with any person because that person is or has been, or in order to intimidate such person or any other person or any class of persons from, obtaining or providing reproductive health services. 18 U.S.C.A. § 248(a).

An initial interpretation by a U.S. District Court for the Eastern District of Virginia in June 1994 held that the new act was within the power delegated to Congress under the Commerce Clause of the U.S. Constitution. Further, the court declared that the act does not violate the freedoms of speech and religion protected by the First Amendment. *American Life League, Inc. v. Reno*, 855 F. Supp. 137 (E.D. Va. 1994).

Privacy and Sexual Conduct

In 1986 the Supreme Court declined to extend the right of privacy to protect homosexual conduct between consenting adults. In *Bowers v. Hardwick*, 478 U.S. 186, 106 S.Ct. 2841, 92 L.Ed.2d 140 (1986), the Court upheld a Georgia statute making sodomy a crime. However, the Court did not address the question of whether the state could enforce its sodomy law against private heterosexual activity between consenting adults. Since the decision in *Bowers v. Hardwick*, however, a number of state courts have invalidated sodomy laws on state constitutional grounds (see Chapter 8).

Under a strict interpretation of the right of privacy, sexual relations between consenting adults would not be subject to governmental prohibition. Such a principle could, of course, invalidate long-standing (if seldom enforced) proscriptions against sodomy, adultery, fornication, and seduction. It might also raise serious questions about the validity of statutes proscribing incest, bigamy, and prostitution, which are nearly universal among the American states (see Chapter 8).

The Right to Die

A competent adult with a terminal illness has the **right to refuse medical treatment** that would unnaturally prolong his or her life. See, for example, *Satz v. Perlmutter*, 379 So.2d 359 (Fla. 1980). Under certain circumstances courts have allowed the family of a comatose individual to direct removal of extraordinary means of life support. See, for example, *In re Quinlan*, 355 A.2d 647 (N.J. 1976).

The so-called **right to die,** if extended beyond the right of a terminally ill person to refuse artificial means of life support, runs headlong into criminal prohibitions against suicide and, potentially, homicide. As yet, courts have been unwilling to extend the right of privacy this far. For example, in *Gilbert v. State*, 487 So.2d 1185 (Fla. App. 1986), a Florida appeals court rejected Roswell Gilbert's "euthanasia" defense to the charge that he committed premeditated murder against his wife, who suffered from osteoporosis and Alzheimer's disease. More recently, the United States Supreme Court upheld state laws criminalizing doctor-assisted suicide against constitutional attack. *Washington v. Glucksberg*, 521 U.S. 702, 117 S.Ct. 2258, 138 L.Ed.2d 772 (1997).

Equal Protection of the Laws

The Fourteenth Amendment of the U.S. Constitution forbids states from denying persons **equal protection of the laws.** The Due Process Clause of the Fifth Amendment has been interpreted to impose a similar prohibition on the federal government. *Bolling v. Sharpe*, 347 U.S. 497, 74 S.Ct. 693, 98 L.Ed. 884 (1954). Most state constitutions contain similar requirements. On occasion, the concept of equal protection has been used to challenge the validity of criminal statutes. For example, in *Loving v. Virginia*, 388 U.S. 1, 87 S.Ct. 1817, 18 L.Ed.2d 1010 (1967), the Supreme Court relied on the Equal Protection Clause of the Fourteenth Amendment in striking down a state statute that criminalized interracial marriage. The effect of *Loving* was that any law that criminalized conduct solely on the basis of the race of the parties was rendered null and void. In *Eisenstadt v. Baird,* supra, the Court invoked the Equal Protection Clause in striking a Massachusetts law that criminalized the use of birth control devices by single persons, but not by married couples. And in *Craig v. Boren,* 429 U.S. 190, 97 S.Ct. 451, 50 L.Ed.2d 397 (1976), the Court invalidated an Oklahoma law that forbade the sale of beer containing 3.2 percent alcohol to females under the age of eighteen and males under the age of twenty-one. The Court concluded that the state lacked a sufficient justification for discriminating between the sexes regarding the legal availability of the contested beverage.

Standards of Judicial Review

At a minimum, a criminal law prohibition that touches on a constitutionally protected interest must be "rationally related to furthering a legitimate government interest." *Massachusetts Board of Retirement v. Murgia,* 427 U.S. 307, 96 S.Ct. 2562, 49 L.Ed.2d 520 (1976). For example, a state law that makes it a crime for a person to perform surgery without a license is obviously a rational means of advancing the state's legitimate interests in public health and safety. Thus, even though the law deprives lay persons of their right to make contracts freely and discriminates against those unable to obtain a license, there is little doubt it would withstand judicial review under the **rational basis test.**

Criminal laws that infringe **fundamental rights** such as the First Amendment freedoms of speech and press are judged by a more stringent standard of review. Such laws are subject to **strict judicial scrutiny,** which means, in effect, that they are presumed to be unconstitutional. To survive judicial review, government must show that the challenged law furthers a **compelling government interest** and is narrowly tailored to that purpose. *Shapiro v. Thompson,* 394 U.S. 618, 89 S.Ct. 1322, 22 L.Ed.2d 600 (1969). This is a heavy burden for the government to carry. Consequently, most laws subjected to strict judicial scrutiny are declared unconstitutional. However, the application of strict scrutiny is not necessarily equivalent to a declaration of unconstitutionality. For example, in *New York v. Ferber,* supra, the Supreme Court upheld a child pornography law that impinged on the First Amendment freedom of expression because, in the view of the Court, the law served a compelling interest in protecting children from the abuse typically associated with the pornography industry.

The Importance of State Constitutions

Under our federal system of government, the highest court of each state possesses the authority to interpret with finality its state constitution and statutes. A decision by a state court is not subject to review by the United States Supreme Court, except insofar as the state law on which it is based is being challenged as a violation of the federal constitution or statutes. Because every state constitution contains language protecting individual rights and liberties, many state court decisions implicate both state and federal constitutional provisions. Under the relevant language of their constitutions and statutes, state courts are free to recognize greater (but not lesser) protections of individual rights than are provided by the U.S. Constitution as interpreted by the federal courts. As a result of the increased conservatism of the federal judiciary, and in particular the Supreme Court, over the last two decades, there has been a resurgence of interest in state constitutional law as it relates to civil rights and liberties.

In *Michigan v. Long,* 463 U.S. 1032, 1040, 103 S.Ct. 3469, 3476, 77 L.Ed.2d 1201, 1214 (1983), the U.S. Supreme Court said that "when a state court decision fairly appears to rest primarily on federal law, or to be interwoven with the federal law, and when the adequacy and independence of any possible state law ground is not clear from the face of the opinion, we will accept as the most reasonable explanation that the state court decided the case the way it did because it believed that federal law required it to do so." However, the Court also indicated that "if the state court decision indicates clearly and expressly that it is alternatively based on bona fide separate, adequate, and independent grounds, we, of course, will not undertake to review the decision." 463 U.S. at 1041, 103 S.Ct. at 3476, 77 L.Ed.2d at 1214 (1983).

Michigan v. Long effectively invited the state courts to consider the parallel provisions of their state constitutions independently. Some state courts have accepted the invitation. For example, in *In re T.W.,* 551 So.2d 1186 (Fla. 1989), the Florida Supreme Court struck down as a violation of the right of privacy a statute that required parental consent in cases where minors sought abortions. The constitutionality of a similar law had been upheld on federal grounds by the U.S. Supreme Court in *Planned Parenthood v. Ashcroft,* 462 U.S. 476, 103 S.Ct. 2517, 76 L.Ed.2d 733 (1983). In *T.W.,* the Florida Supreme Court made it clear that it was basing its decision on an amendment to the Florida Constitution that (unlike the federal constitution) explicitly protects the right of privacy. Similarly, in *State v. Kam,* 748 P.2d 372 (Hawaii 1988), the Hawaii Supreme Court adopted an interpretation of its state constitution that affords considerably broader protection to pornography than that provided by the U.S. Constitution. Finally, in *Williams v. City of Fort Worth,* 782 S.W.2d 290 (Tex. App. 1989), a Texas appellate court struck down as a violation of the state's equal rights amendment a city ordinance prohibiting females, but not males, from publicly exposing their breasts in nightclub performances. These decisions, and many others like them, mean that a person interested in constitutional limitations on the prohibition of criminal conduct must not ignore the provisions of state constitutions that parallel the U.S. Constitution.

Conclusion

Enacting laws defining crimes and specifying punishments is a legislative function carried out by Congress and by state legislatures. The power to exercise that function is subject to the limitations in various provisions of the U.S. Constitution and state constitutions. Criminal laws must be rationally related to a legitimate public interest and must be specific to avoid being declared void for vagueness. Moreover, laws that restrict such fundamental rights as First Amendment freedoms are subject to strict judicial scrutiny. As you read later chapters, you will find these constitutional restraints are especially evident in the definition of offenses against public morality, discussed in Chapter 8, where the constitutional right of privacy has assumed increasing importance, and in the definition of offenses against public order, discussed in Chapter 12, where courts are scrupulous in upholding the freedoms of expression and assembly. Courts address not only definitions of crimes, but also the application of those definitions to specific conduct. These serious constraints on the definition of criminal conduct and the enforcement of the criminal law are sustained through the well-established power of judicial review. This protects the constitutional rights of the individual and ensures that the rule of law will prevail in the nation.

Key Terms

treason
judicial review
unconstitutional per se
unconstitutional as applied
police power
enumerated powers
implied powers
interstate commerce
bill of attainder
ex post facto law
doctrine of incorporation
clear and present danger doctrine
imminent lawless action
freedom of expression
symbolic speech
fighting words
hate speech
obscenity

public forum
time, place, and manner regulations
freedom of religion
right to keep and bear arms
fair notice
fair hearing
vagueness doctrine
doctrine of overbreadth
cruel and unusual punishments
constitutional right of privacy
right to refuse medical treatment
right to die
equal protection of the laws
rational basis test
fundamental rights
strict judicial scrutiny
compelling government interest

Web-Based Research Activity

1. Go to the web. Log on to Findlaw's Constitutional Law Center at **http://supreme.findlaw.com/**.
2. Examine the pending cases on the Supreme Court's docket.
3. Do any of these cases involve constitutional limitations on criminal law?

Questions for Thought and Discussion

1. Can you think of an example of an *ex post facto* law?

2. Is it possible for the criminal law to define the crime of obscenity precisely enough to avoid the "vice of vagueness" or the problem of overbreadth?

3. Can a municipality enforce an ordinance totally banning religious organizations from canvassing neighborhoods in search of new members? What about an ordinance that prohibits such canvassing between the hours of 8 P.M. and 8 A.M.?

4. Should the constitutional right of privacy invalidate criminal statutes that proscribe homosexual conduct between consenting adults?

5. Would the constitutional right of privacy provide a defense to a charge of possession of obscene materials where videotapes were viewed only by the defendant in the privacy of his or her home?

6. Could a father who, without judicial approval, unplugs the respirator sustaining the breathing of his comatose, terminally ill child be prosecuted for murder?

7. Would a law making it an offense for a person to carry prescription medicine in other than the original labeled container meet the test of being rationally related to a legitimate government interest?

8. How does the doctrine of judicial review affect the power of a state legislature to define criminal conduct? Would the constitutional limitations on legislative power be as stringent without the power of courts to declare laws unconstitutional?

9. Give an example of a law that would be constitutional per se, and point out how such a law may be unconstitutional in its application to a specific conduct.

10. Give an example of a law defining a crime that, although held constitutional by the U.S. Supreme Court, has been declared unconstitutional by some state courts. Why can such a result occur in our federal system?

Problems for Discussion and Solution

1. Amelia Eyeland has been arrested for trespass, disorderly conduct, and resisting arrest. The charges stem from an incident in which Amelia and other members of the Green Warriors staged a raucous protest in a privately owned shopping mall during regular business hours. The protest was aimed at the decision of the mall's owners to expand the parking lot into a wetlands area known to be a habitat for a number of animals. Amelia's attorney is considering a defense based on the First Amendment freedoms of speech and assembly. What chance does the attorney have at being successful with this defense?

2. John Masters, a licensed psychotherapist, has been charged with violating a new state statute making it a crime for "any licensed psychologist, psychiatrist, or psychotherapist to have sexual intercourse with a patient during the existence of the professional relationship." Masters is challenging the constitutionality of the statute on two principal grounds: (a) that it intrudes on his right of privacy and (b) that it violates the Equal Protection Clause of the Fourteenth Amendment in that it fails to apply the same prohibition to other health care professionals. Do you think Masters is likely to prevail in his challenge to the statute? If you were a judge faced with these constitutional questions, how would you be inclined to rule? What additional information would you need to render your decision?

Brandenburg v. Ohio

Supreme Court of the United States, 1969.
395 U.S. 444, 89 S.Ct. 1827, 23 L.Ed.2d 430.

[In this landmark case, the U.S. Supreme Court considers whether, and under what circumstances, the advocacy of unlawful conduct is protected by the First Amendment.]

PER CURIAM.

The appellant, a leader of a Ku Klux Klan group, was convicted under the Ohio Criminal Syndicalism statute for "advocat[ing] . . . the duty, necessity, or propriety of crime, sabotage, violence, or unlawful methods of terrorism as a means of accomplishing industrial or political reform" and for "voluntarily assembl[ing] with any society, group, or assemblage of persons formed to teach or advocate the doctrines of criminal syndicalism." . . . He was fined $1,000 and sentenced to one to 10 years' imprisonment. The appellant challenged the constitutionality of the criminal syndicalism statute under the First and Fourteenth Amendments to the United States Constitution, but the intermediate appellate court of Ohio affirmed his conviction without opinion. The Supreme Court of Ohio dismissed his appeal, sua sponte, "for the reason that no substantial constitutional question exists herein." It did not file an opinion or explain its conclusions. Appeal was taken to this Court, and we noted probable jurisdiction. . . .

The record shows that a man, identified at trial as the appellant, telephoned an announcer-reporter on the staff of a Cincinnati television station and invited him to come to a Ku Klux Klan "rally" to be held at a farm in Hamilton County. With the cooperation of the organizers, the reporter and a cameraman attended the meeting and filmed the events. Portions of the films were later broadcast on the local station and on a national network.

The prosecution's case rested on the films and on testimony identifying the appellant as the person who communicated with the reporter and who spoke at the rally. The State also introduced into evidence several articles appearing in the film, including a pistol, a rifle, a shotgun, ammunition, a Bible, and a red hood worn by the speaker in the films.

One film showed 12 hooded figures, some of whom carried firearms. They were gathered around a large wooden cross, which they burned. No one was present other than the participants and the newsmen who made the film. Most of the words uttered during the scene were incomprehensible when the film was projected, but scattered phrases could be understood that were derogatory of Negroes and, in one instance, of Jews. Another scene on the same film showed the appellant, in Klan regalia, making a speech. The speech, in full, was as follows:

> This is an organizers' meeting. We have had quite a few members here today which are—we have hundreds, hundreds of members throughout the State of Ohio. I can quote from a newspaper clipping from the Columbus, Ohio, Dispatch, five weeks ago Sunday morning. The Klan has more members in the State of Ohio than does any other organization. We're not a revengent organization, but if our President, our Congress, our Supreme Court, continues to suppress the white, Caucasian race, it's possible that there might have to be some revengeance taken.
>
> We are marching on Congress July the Fourth, four hundred thousand strong. From there we are dividing into two groups, one group to march on St. Augustine, Florida, the other group to march into Mississippi. Thank you.

The second film showed six hooded figures, one of whom, later identified as the appellant, repeated a speech very similar to that recorded on the first film. The reference to the possibility of "revengeance" was omitted, and one sentence was added: "Personally, I believe the nigger should be returned to Africa, the Jew returned to Israel." Though some of the figures in the films carried weapons, the speaker did not.

The Ohio Criminal Syndicalism Statute was enacted in 1919. From 1917 to 1920, identical or quite similar laws were adopted by 20 States and two territories. In 1927, this Court sustained the constitutionality of California's Criminal Syndicalism Act, the text of which is quite similar to that of the laws of Ohio. . . . The Court upheld the statute on the ground that, without more, "advocating" violent means to effect political and economic change involves such danger to the security of the State that the State may outlaw it. But [this view] has been thoroughly discredited by later decisions. . . . These later decisions have fashioned the principle that the constitutional guarantees of free speech and free press do not permit a State to forbid advocacy . . . [unless it] is directed to inciting or producing imminent lawless action and is likely to incite or produce such action. . . . A statute which fails to draw this distinction impermissibly intrudes upon the freedoms guaranteed by the First and Fourteenth Amendments. It sweeps within its condemnation speech which our Constitution has immunized from governmental control. . . .

Measured by this test, Ohio's Criminal Syndicalism Act cannot be sustained. The Act punishes persons who "advocate or teach the duty, necessity, or propriety" of violence "as a means of accomplishing industrial or political reform"; or who publish or circulate or display any book or paper containing such advocacy; or who "justify" the commission of violent acts "with intent to exemplify, spread or advocate the propriety of the doctrines of criminal syndicalism"; or who "voluntarily assemble" with a group formed "to teach or advocate the doctrines of criminal syndicalism." Neither the indictment nor the trial judge's instructions to the jury in any way refined the statute's bald definition of the crime in terms of mere advocacy not distinguished from incitement to imminent lawless action.

Accordingly, we are here confronted with a statute which, by its own words and as applied, purports to punish mere advocacy and to forbid, on pain of criminal punishment, assembly with others merely to advocate the described type of action. Such a statute falls within the condemnation of the First and Fourteenth Amendments. The contrary teaching of *Whitney v. California* [1927] . . . cannot be supported and that decision is therefore overruled.

Reversed.

Mr. Justice BLACK, concurring . . .

Mr. Justice DOUGLAS, concurring . . .

●　　●　　●　　●　　●　　●　　●　　　　●　　●　　●　　●　　●　　●　　●

Miller v. California

Supreme Court of the United States, 1973.
413 U.S. 15, 93 S.Ct. 2607, 37 L.Ed.2d 419.

[In this case the Supreme Court sets forth the constitutional standards for determining obscenity. The defendant, Miller, was convicted in the Orange County Superior Court of "knowingly distributing obscene matter," a misdemeanor under California law. The appellate court affirmed his conviction without opinion.]

Mr. Chief Justice BURGER delivered the opinion of the Court.

This case involves the application of a State's criminal obscenity statute to a situation in which sexually explicit materials have been thrust by aggressive sales action upon unwilling recipients who had in no way indicated any desire to receive such materials. . . . It is in this context that we are called on to define the standards which must be used to identify obscene material that a State may regulate without infringing the First Amendment as applicable to the States through the Fourteenth Amendment. . . .

This much has been categorically settled by the Court, that obscene material is unprotected by the First Amendment. . . . We acknowledge, however, the inherent dangers of undertaking to regulate any form of expression. State statutes designed to regulate obscene materials must be carefully limited. . . . As a result, we now confine the permissible scope of such regulation to works which depict or describe sexual conduct. That conduct must be specifically defined by the applicable state law, as written or authoritatively construed. A state offense must also be limited to works which, taken as a whole, appeal to the prurient interest in sex, which portray sexual conduct in a patently offensive way, and which, taken as a whole, do not have serious literary, artistic, political, or scientific value.

The basic guidelines for the trier of fact must be: (a) whether "the average person, applying contemporary community standards" would find that the work, taken as a whole, appeals to the prurient interest, . . . (b) whether the work depicts or describes, in a patently offensive way, sexual conduct specifically defined by the applicable state law, and (c) whether the work, taken as a whole, lacks serious literary, artistic, political, or scientific value. . . .

We emphasize that it is not our function to propose regulatory schemes for the States. That must await their concrete legislative efforts. It is possible, however, to give a few plain examples of what a state statute could define for regulation. . . .

(a) Patently offensive representations or descriptions of ultimate sexual acts, normal or perverted, actual or simulated.

(b) Patently offensive representations or descriptions of masturbation, excretory functions, and lewd exhibition of the genitals.

Sex and nudity may not be exploited without limit by films or pictures exhibited or sold in places of public accommodation any more than live sex and nudity can be exhibited or sold without limit in such public places. At a minimum, prurient, patently offensive depiction or description of sexual conduct must have serious literary, artistic, political, or scientific value to merit First Amendment protection. . . .

Under the holdings announced today, no one will be subject to prosecution for the sale or exposure of obscene materials unless these materials depict or describe patently offensive "hard core" sexual conduct specifically defined by the regulating state law, as written or construed. We are satisfied that these specific prerequisites will provide fair notice to a dealer in such materials that his public and commercial activities may bring prosecution. . . .

Under a national Constitution, fundamental First Amendment limitations on the powers of the States do not vary from community to community, but this does not mean that there are, or should or can be, fixed, uniform national standards of precisely what appeals to the "prurient interest" or is "patently offensive." These are essentially questions of fact, and our nation is simply too big and too diverse for this Court to reasonably expect that such standards could be articulated for all 50 States in a single formulation, even assuming the prerequisite consensus exists. When triers of fact are asked to decide whether "the average person, applying contemporary community standards" would consider certain materials "prurient," it would be unrealistic to require that the answer be based on some abstract formulation. . . . To require a State to structure obscenity proceedings around evidence of a national community standard would be an exercise in futility. . . .

. . . The First Amendment protects works which, taken as a whole, have serious literary, artistic, political or scientific value, regardless of whether the government or a majority of the people approve the ideas these works represent. . . . But the public portrayal of hard core sexual conduct for its own sake, and for the ensuing commercial gain, is a different matter. . . .

Mr. Justice DOUGLAS, dissenting.

. . . The idea that the First Amendment permits punishment for ideas that are "offensive" to the particular judge or jury sitting in judgment is astounding. No greater leveler of speech or literature has ever been designed. To give the power to the censor, as we do today, is to make a sharp and radical break with the traditions of a free society. . . . The use of the standard "offensive" gives authority to government that cuts the very vitals out of the First Amendment. As is intimated by the Court's opinion, the materials before us may be garbage. But so is much of what is said in political campaigns, in the daily press, on TV or over the radio. By reason of the First Amendment—and solely because of it—speakers and publishers have not been threatened or subdued because their thoughts and ideas may be "offensive" to some. . . .

Mr. Justice BRENNAN, with whom Mr. Justice STEWART and Mr. Justice MARSHALL join, dissenting. . . .

Griswold v. Connecticut

Supreme Court of the United States, 1965.
381 U.S. 479, 85 S.Ct. 1678, 14 L.Ed.2d 510.

[In this case the U.S. Supreme Court reviews a state law making it a crime, even for married couples, to use birth control devices.]

Mr. Justice DOUGLAS delivered the opinion of the Court.

Appellant Griswold is Executive Director of the Planned Parenthood League of Connecticut. Appellant Buxton is a licensed physician and a professor at the Yale Medical School who served as Medical Director for the League at its Center in New Haven—a center open and operating from November 1 to November 10, 1961, when appellants were arrested.

They gave information, instruction and medical advice to married persons as to the means of preventing conception. They examined the wife and prescribed the best contraceptive device or material for her use. Fees were usually charged, although some couples were serviced free. . . .

The appellants were found guilty as accessories and fined $100 each, against the claim that the accessory statute as so applied violated the Fourteenth Amendment. The Appellate Division of the Circuit Court affirmed. The Supreme Court of Errors affirmed that judgment. . . .

. . . We do not sit as a super-legislature to determine the wisdom, need and propriety of laws that touch economic problems, business affairs, or social conditions. This law, however, operates directly on an intimate relation of husband and wife and their physician's role in one aspect of that relation. . . .

[Previous] . . . cases suggest that specific guarantees in the Bill of Rights have penumbras, formed by emanations from those guarantees that help give them life and substance. Various guarantees create zones of privacy. The right of association continued in the penumbra of the First Amendment is one, as we have seen. The Third Amendment in its prohibition against the quartering of soldiers "in any house" in time of peace without the consent of the owner is another facet of that privacy. The Fourth Amendment explicitly affirms the "right of the people to be secure in their persons, houses, papers, and effects, against unreasonable searches and seizures." The Fifth Amendment in its Self-Incrimination Clause enables the citizen to create a zone of privacy which government may not force him to surrender to his detriment. The Ninth Amendment provides: "The enumeration in the Constitution, of certain rights, shall not be construed to deny or disparage others retained by the people."

The Fourth and Fifth Amendments [provide] . . . protection against all governmental invasions "of the sanctity of a man's home and the privacies of life." We recently referred in *Mapp v. Ohio* . . . to the Fourth Amendment as creating a "right to privacy, no less important than any other right carefully and particularly reserved to the people." . . .

We have had many controversies over these penumbral rights of "privacy and repose." . . . These cases bear witness that the right of privacy which presses for recognition here is a legitimate one.

The present case, then, concerns a relationship lying within the zone of privacy created by several fundamental constitutional guarantees. And it concerns a law which, in forbidding the use of contraceptives rather than regulating their manufacture or sale, seeks to achieve its goals by means having a maximum destructive impact upon that relationship. Such a law cannot stand in light of the familiar principle, so often applied by this Court, that a "governmental purpose to control or prevent activities constitutionally subject to state regulation may not be achieved by means which sweep unnecessarily broadly and thereby invade the area of protected freedoms." . . . Would we allow the police to search the sacred precincts of marital bedrooms for telltale signs of the use of contraceptives? The very idea is repulsive to the notions of privacy surrounding the marriage relationship. . . .

Mr. Justice BLACK, with whom Mr. Justice STEWART joins, dissenting. . . .

Mr. Justice STEWART, whom Mr. Justice BLACK joins, dissenting.

Since 1879 Connecticut has had on its books a law which forbids the use of contraceptives by anyone. I think this is an uncommonly silly law. As a practical matter, the law is obviously unenforceable, except in the oblique context of the present case. As a philosophical matter, I believe the use of contraceptives in the relationship of marriage should be left to personal and private choice, based upon each individual's moral, ethical, and religious beliefs. As a matter of social policy, I think professional counsel about methods of birth control should be available to all, so that each individual's choice can be meaningfully made. But we are not asked in this case to say whether we think this law is unwise, or even asinine. We are asked to hold that it violates the United States Constitution. And that I cannot do. . . .

Elements of Crimes and Parties to Crimes

Introduction

The essential elements of a crime are a physical act, often referred to as the ***actus reus*** (wrongful act), and the intent or state of mind, frequently called the ***mens rea*** (guilty mind). To establish that a defendant is guilty of a crime, the prosecution must prove the defendant committed some legally proscribed act or failed to act when the law required certain action. The prosecution must also prove that such act or failure to act occurred with a simultaneous criminal intent. It would be contrary to our common-law heritage to punish someone who accidentally or unwittingly committed a wrongful act without any intent to commit a crime. Likewise, a person cannot be punished for a mere intention, however wrongful that intention may be.

Certain offenses, primarily regulatory and public-welfare-type offenses, are classified as strict liability crimes and are exceptions to the common-law concept of requiring proof of a defendant's criminal intent. They came into prominence during the Industrial Revolution, and today they form a significant part of the substantive criminal law, particularly in the so-called "public welfare offenses" such as food and drug laws and traffic offenses.

In addition to the basic requirement of establishing a physical act and intent, in some instances the prosecution must establish that certain circumstances existed at the time the act was committed. For example, in some sexual battery offenses the prosecution must establish that the defendant's acts occurred without the victim's consent. Moreover, in other situations the prosecution must establish that that defendant's acts caused specific results. For instance, in homicide cases the prosecution must prove a causal relationship between the defendant's act and the victim's death.

At common law, parties to crimes were classified as **principals, accessories before the fact,** and **accessories after the fact;** crimes were classified as **felonies** and **misdemeanors.** An awareness of the history of these terms leads to a better understanding of their function in contemporary American criminal law and the procedure of federal and state court systems. In this chapter we first explain the elements of a crime; then we discuss parties to crimes.

The *Actus Reus* (The Act Requirement)

The term *actus reus* means "the act of a criminal." But simply committing a wrongful act does not mean that one has committed a crime. To fulfill the requirements of the criminal law, the actor must willfully commit a proscribed physical act or intentionally fail to act where the law requires a person to act. The rationale for the *actus reus* requirement is to prevent a person from being guilty of an offense based on thoughts or intent alone. Common-law crimes required commission of an act or omission and not merely an evil state of a person's mind. Of course, in the United States, a law that made it a criminal offense simply to entertain an evil thought would be patently unconstitutional.

What Is an Act?

Probably the most complete definition of an "act" as contemplated by the criminal law is found in the Model Penal Code (MPC), which we introduced in Chapter 1. In

§ 1.13(2) the MPC defines "act" as a "bodily movement whether voluntary or involuntary"; however, § 2.01(1) states that "a person is not guilty of an offense unless his liability is based on conduct that includes a voluntary act or the omission to perform an act of which he is capable." Indeed, courts have generally held that some outward manifestation of voluntary conduct must occur to constitute the physical act necessary in criminal law. The rationale for the requirement of a voluntary act is simple: Only those persons whose acts result from free choice should be criminally punished. Most acts are voluntary. For example, when you raise your hand, it is considered a voluntary act, but when your hand moves as a result of a muscle spasm, it is not a voluntary act. Likewise, movements committed by a person who is unconscious, or acts by someone having an epileptic seizure or sleepwalking, are not regarded as voluntary acts. On the other hand, a driver who takes sleeping pills before beginning to operate an automobile and then falls asleep at the wheel would generally be held criminally responsible for a traffic accident because the driver voluntarily committed the act of taking the pills. Consider the following examples:

- A enters B's house or strikes B. A has quite obviously committed an "act."
- A picks up a pistol and fires it in the direction of B. A, by pulling the trigger of the gun, has committed an "act."
- A hands B a glass of liquid to be given to C. Unknown to B, A added poison to the glass of liquid before handing it to B. B gives the liquid to C, who drinks it and dies. Here A has acted through B, an innocent agent; thus, A has committed the "act."
- While riding as a passenger on a bus, A suffers an unexpected attack of epilepsy. As a consequence, A violently kicks his leg, inflicting an injury on B, a fellow passenger. A would not be criminally responsible for the injury to B.

When Does Failure to Act Constitute an Act?

The requirement for an act is usually fulfilled by an affirmative act. But even a person's failure to act—that is, an **act of omission**—can satisfy the requirements of a physical act in the criminal law. To be guilty of a crime for failure to act, there must have been a legal duty to act in the first place. Such a duty can arise in one of three ways: (1) by relationship of the actor to the victim, for example, parent–child or husband–wife; (2) by a statutory duty; or (3) by contract between the actor and the victim. Consider these examples:

- A, an expert swimmer, while lying on the beach sees a young girl, unrelated to him, struggling to stay afloat and crying for help. A disregards her cries, and she drowns. Is A criminally liable? The answer is no, for although we might agree that A had a strong moral obligation to attempt to save the child, there was no legal obligation to do so. If, on the other hand, A were the child's parent or guardian, or a lifeguard on duty, then A's failure to act would most likely qualify as a criminal act.
- B receives an annual income of $50,000 from operation of her business. She fails to file a federal income tax return as required by the laws of the United States. Is B's omission a criminal act? Clearly it is, for she has violated a statutory obligation, the breach of which is punishable by law.
- C, a surgeon, undertakes to perform an operation on a patient for a fee. Before completing the operation, C decides to cease his efforts. As a result of such inattention, the patient dies. Would C's failure to complete what he undertook

professionally qualify as an act within the meaning of the criminal law? Yes, because C had a contractual relationship with his patient.

In some instances, failure to perform an **administrative-type act** required by law might not be a crime. In *Lambert v. California*, 355 U.S. 225, 78 S.Ct. 240, 2 L.Ed.2d 228 (1957), the U.S. Supreme Court reviewed a case where the defendant, a convicted felon, was charged with failing to register with authorities as required by a Los Angeles city ordinance. The Court held that as applied to one who has no actual knowledge of a duty to register, and where no showing is made of the probability of such knowledge, the ordinance violates the Due Process Clause of the Fourteenth Amendment to the U.S. Constitution.

Possession as a Criminal Act

In certain crimes, **possession** alone is considered to be the wrongful act. For example, in the offense of carrying a concealed weapon, the possession of the weapon concealed from ordinary observation is the wrongful act. Likewise, possession of contraband such as illegal drugs or untaxed liquors constitutes the wrongful act element of certain offenses. Possession is not usually defined in criminal statutes, however, the law recognizes two classes of possession: actual and constructive. **Actual possession** exists when a person has something under his or her direct physical control. An example of actual possession would be when an item is on your person, within your reach, or located in a place where you alone have access. **Constructive possession,** on the other hand, is a more difficult concept because it is based on a legal fiction. A person who has the power and intention to control something either directly or through another person is said to be in constructive possession. The exact meaning of these terms is usually determined by the context of the situation. The difficulty is exacerbated when two or more persons are in joint possession of the premises or vehicle where an object is found. Consider the following examples:

- A and B rent and jointly share an apartment. A police search yields contraband drugs found on the coffee table in the living room used by both A and B. Can both be charged with possession of the contraband? They probably can: Possession by both A and B can be inferred because the drugs are in plain view and located in a place to which both have access.

- Under the same circumstances of a shared apartment, drugs are found in a privately owned, closed container in a dresser drawer where only A keeps clothing and valuables. Because B has no access to this area, the law does not infer that B has constructive possession of the contents in the drawer. Of course, there might be circumstances under which the prosecution could prove that B actually had rights to the drugs, knowledge of their whereabouts, and access to them. Then the prosecution could establish that B was in constructive possession of the contraband.

People v. Valot, a 1971 Michigan appellate decision excerpted at the end of this chapter, illustrates divergent views of constructive possession.

Status as a Criminal Act

"**Status**" refers to a person's state of being, and ordinarily the state cannot criminalize a person's status. For example, a person's race or gender represents a status. But is addiction to narcotics a status that cannot be criminalized? In *Robinson v. California*, 370 U.S. 660, 82 S.Ct. 1417, 8 L.Ed.2d 758 (1962), the U.S. Supreme Court declared

The *Actus Reus* Requirement

Law officers found two whiskey stills and all the paraphernalia for making liquor on the defendant's land. Seeing no activity, they drove away. As they did, they met a car driven by the defendant heading toward the property. The car contained a quantity of sugar and other indicators of the illegal activity the officers suspected. The defendant committed no act of making liquor in the presence of the officers, but on the basis of what they observed, they arrested the defendant, and he was convicted of making liquor unlawfully.

On appeal, the South Carolina Supreme Court reversed the conviction, observing that "the evidence overwhelmingly tends to show an intention to manufacture liquor. . . . But intent alone, not coupled with some overt act . . . is not cognizable by the court. [T]he act must always amount to more than mere preparation, and move directly toward the commission of the crime." Citing respectable textbook authority, the court explained that the law does not concern itself with mere guilty intention, unconnected with any overt act.

State v. Quick, 19 S.E.2d 101 (S.C. 1942).

unconstitutional a California statute that made it an offense for a person "to be addicted to the use of narcotics." The Court observed that

> we deal with a statute which makes the "status" of narcotic addiction a criminal offense, for which the offender may be prosecuted "at any time before he reforms." . . . We hold that a state law which imprisons a person thus afflicted as a criminal, even though he has never touched any narcotic drug within the State or been guilty of any irregular behavior there, inflicts a cruel and unusual punishment in violation of the Fourteenth Amendment. 370 U.S. at 666–667, 82 S.Ct. at 1420, 8 L.Ed.2d at 762–763.

The issue of when a criminal statute proscribes status, as opposed to conduct, can be very close. This is illustrated by the Supreme Court's decision in *Powell v. Texas,* 392 U.S. 514, 88 S.Ct. 2145, 20 L.Ed.2d 1254 (1968). Powell was a chronic alcoholic who was convicted of public intoxication. Four justices held that Powell had been punished for being in a public place on a particular occasion while intoxicated, rather than for his status as a chronic alcoholic. A fifth justice concurred in affirming Powell's conviction. But the four dissenting justices thought the case was indistinguishable from *Robinson v. California,* supra. In their view, both cases involved defendants who were prosecuted for being in a condition that they had no capacity to alter or avoid.

Excerpts from the Supreme Court's decisions in *Robinson v. California* and *Powell v. Texas* appear in Chapter 9, "Alcohol and Drug Offenses."

The *Mens Rea* (The Criminal Intent Requirement)

The common law developed the doctrine that there should be no crime without a *mens rea,* or "guilty mind." This element is customarily referred to as the criminal intent. To constitute a crime, there must be a concurrence of the *actus reus* with a

The *Mens Rea* Requirement

The defendant was convicted under a statute that made it an offense to fondle or caress the body of a child less than sixteen years "with the intent to gratify the sexual desires or appetites of the offending person or . . . to frighten or excite such child." On appeal, the Indiana Supreme Court noted that the strongest evidence in favor of the prosecution was that both the defendant's daughters admitted that during playfulness the father touched and came in contact with the breasts of one of his daughters. However, there was no evidence that this was done with the intent to gratify the sexual desires of the defendant or to frighten the child.

In reversing the defendant's conviction, the court observed that "[a] crime has two components—an evil intent coupled with an overt act. The act alone does not constitute the crime unless it is done with a specific intent declared unlawful by the statute in this state. . . . There must also be proved beyond a reasonable doubt, the specific intent at the time of touching to gratify sexual desires or to frighten the child as stated in the statute."

Markiton v. State, 139 N.E.2d 440 (Ind. 1957).

---

person's criminal intent. Strict liability offenses, discussed later, are an exception to this principle.

Criminal intent must be distinguished from **motive.** To obtain a conviction, a prosecutor must establish the defendant's criminal intent, but not necessarily the defendant's motive for committing a crime. A person's motive often equates with an impulse, an incentive, or a reason for certain behavior, and proof of one's motive can assist in establishing criminal intent. To illustrate, if the prosecution relies on circumstantial evidence to establish the defendant's guilt in a homicide case, the fact that the defendant had vowed "to get even" with the victim might be a relevant factor in the proof. Yet the failure to establish a defendant's motive is not fatal to proving guilt. On the other hand, good motives do not exonerate a person from a crime. Thus, one who steals food simply to give it to a poor, hungry family might have a noble motive. Nevertheless, such a person would be guilty of a crime because of his or her act and intent.

The basic reason that the law requires proof of a criminal intent as well as an act or omission is to distinguish those acts or omissions that occur accidentally from those committed by a person with a "guilty mind." As the California Supreme Court observed in *In re Hayes*, 442 P.2d 366, 369 (Cal. 1968), "an essential element of every orthodox crime is a wrongful or blameworthy mental state of some kind."

General and Specific Intent

At common law, crimes were generally classified as either "general intent" or "specific intent" crimes. American courts followed that tradition. **General intent** is the intent to do an act but not necessarily to cause the results that occur from that act. Historically, many trial judges would instruct a jury "the law presumes that a person intends the ordinary consequences of his voluntary acts." In 1979, in *Sandstrom v. Montana*, 442 U.S. 510, 99 S.Ct. 2450, 61 L.Ed.2d 39, the Supreme Court ruled that it is unconstitutional for a judge to so instruct the jury. The Court held that such a presumption conflicts with the presumption of innocence of the accused and violates the Due Process Clause of the Fourteenth Amendment, which requires that the state prove every element of a criminal offense beyond a reasonable doubt.

Where a crime requires only proof of a general intent, the fact finder (that is, the judge or jury) may infer the defendant's intent from the defendant's acts and the circumstances surrounding those acts. Thus, the prosecution does not have to prove that the defendant had any specific intent to cause a particular result when the act was committed: "General intent exists when from the circumstances the prohibited result may reasonably be expected to follow from the offender's voluntary act, irrespective of a subjective desire to have accomplished such result." *Myers v. State,* 422 N.E.2d 745, 750 (Ind. App. 1981).

Criminal statutes that prohibit particular voluntary acts are generally classified as **general-intent statutes.** See *State v. Poss,* 298 N.W.2d 80 (S.D. 1980). Statutory words such as "willfully" or "intentionally" generally indicate that the offender must have only intended to do the act and not to accomplish any particular result. Thus, a statute making it the crime of arson to "willfully and unlawfully" set fire to a building is generally viewed as defining a general-intent crime. *Linehan v. State,* 476 So.2d 1262 (Fla. 1985).

On the other hand, **specific intent** refers to an actor's mental purpose to accomplish a particular result beyond the act itself. Again, in the context of the crime of arson, suppose the statute read that it was an offense for any person "to willfully and with the intent to injure or defraud an insurance company to set fire to any building." In this instance the prosecution would be required to prove that the defendant had the specific intent to injure or defraud an insurance company when the proscribed act was perpetrated. Again, a statute defining murder that includes the language "premeditated killing of a human being" requires the prosecution to prove the defendant's specific intent. Courts have consistently said that a **specific-intent statute** designates "a special mental element which is required above and beyond any mental state required with respect to the *actus reus* of the crime." See, for example, *State v. Bridgeforth,* 750 P.2d 3, 5 (Ariz. 1988).

Assume that State X charged a defendant with burglary of a dwelling under a specific-intent statute that defines the offense as "the unauthorized entry of a dwelling by a person with the intent to commit theft therein." Three basic elements must be established to convict the defendant. First, the state must prove the defendant made an unauthorized entry. Second, it must prove that the entry was into a dwelling house. Finally, it must establish that the defendant made such unauthorized entry with the intent to commit a theft. Intent, of course, is a state of mind, but it can be (and almost always is) inferred from the defendant's actions and surrounding circumstances. Therefore, if some of the dwelling owner's property had been moved and other items left in disarray, the inference would be that the defendant who made an unauthorized entry intended to commit theft from the dwelling. And this would be true whether the defendant did in fact commit a theft within the dwelling.

In a situation where the defendant might not have had a specific intent to cause a particular result but there was a substantial likelihood of the result occurring, courts have developed the concept of **constructive intent** as a substitute for the defendant's specific intent.

The Model Penal Code Approach to Intent

Over the years, the common-law classifications of general and specific intent have become subject to many variations in court decisions in the various jurisdictions. In the chapters of this text that discuss substantive offenses, the reader will find a variety of terms that legislatures and courts have used to describe the *mens rea* requirements of various crimes. Such terms include "unlawfully," "feloniously," "willfully," "maliciously," "wrongfully," "deliberately," "recklessly," "negligently," "with premeditated intent," "with culpable negligence," "with gross negligence," and numerous others.

The wide variety of terms used to describe the mental element of crimes and the dichotomy between general and specific intent have led to considerable difficulty in determining intent requirements in statutory crimes. In 1980 the Supreme Court recognized the common-law classification of crimes as requiring either "general intent" or "specific intent." Nevertheless, the Court pointed out that this distinction has been a continuing source of confusion. The Court suggested the merits of the Model Penal Code classification (referring to the 1962 tentative draft of the M.P.C.) that replaces the term "intent" with a hierarchy of culpable states in a descending order as purpose, knowledge, recklessness, and negligence. *United States v. Bailey,* 444 U.S. 394, 100 S.Ct. 624, 62 L.Ed.2d 575 (1980). However, courts must deal with the intent requirement that legislative bodies include when defining statutory crimes. Thus, in its recent decision in *Holloway v. United States,* 526 U.S. 1, 119 S.Ct. 966, 143 L.Ed.2d 1 (1999), the Court referred to a federal statute in 18 U.S.C.A. § 2119 defining carjacking as "tak[ing] a motor vehicle . . . from . . . another by force and violence or by intimidation . . . with the intent to cause death or serious bodily harm" as a law including a specific-intent element.

Today, almost all crimes are statutory, and in 1985 the American Law Institute published the Official Draft of the **Model Penal Code (MPC),** with some revisions of the earlier tentative draft published in 1962. The MPC rejects the common-law terms for intent. Instead, it simplifies the terms describing culpability and proposes four states of mind: purposely, knowingly, recklessly, and negligently. M.P.C. § 2.02(2). Section 2.02(4) states that the prescribed culpability requirement applies to all material elements of an offense. (The term "purposely" seems to roughly correspond to the common-law specific-intent requirement while other MPC categories seem to fall within the general-intent category.)

Several recent legislative revisions of state criminal codes have followed the MPC in setting standards of culpability. For example, in 1977 Alabama adopted § 13A–2–2 of its Criminal Code to provide as follows:

The following definitions apply to this Criminal Code:

1. **Intentionally.** A person acts intentionally with respect to a result or to conduct described by a statute defining an offense, when his purpose is to cause that result or to engage in that conduct.

2. **Knowingly.** A person acts knowingly with respect to conduct or to a circumstance described by a statute defining an offense when he is aware that his conduct is of that nature or that the circumstance exists.

3. **Recklessly.** A person acts recklessly with respect to a result or to a circumstance described by a statute defining an offense when he is aware of and consciously disregards a substantial and unjustifiable risk that the result will occur or that the circumstance exists. The risk must be of such nature and degree that disregard thereof constitutes a gross deviation from the standard of conduct that a reasonable person would observe in the situation. A person who creates a risk but is unaware thereof solely by reason of voluntary intoxication, as defined in subdivision (e)(2) of Section 13A–3–2, acts recklessly with respect thereto.

4. **Criminal negligence.** A person acts with criminal negligence with respect to a result or to a circumstance which is defined by statute as an offense when he fails to perceive a substantial and unjustifiable risk that the result will occur or

that the circumstance exists. The risk must be of such nature and degree that the failure to perceive it constitutes a gross deviation from the standard of care that a reasonable person would observe in the situation. A court or jury may consider statutes or ordinances regulating the defendant's conduct as bearing upon the question of criminal negligence.

Commentary following § 13A–2–2 points out that this section "is derived principally from Michigan Revised Criminal Code § 305, which followed New York Penal Law § 15.05, which in turn is based on the Model Penal Code § 2.02." Some other states have essentially adopted the MPC proposals, but, like Alabama, several have opted to use the term "intentionally" instead of the MPC term "purposely." This difference appears to be only one of terminology.

Section 13A–6–3 of Alabama's Criminal Code now begins defining manslaughter by stating, in part, that "[a] person commits the crime of manslaughter if (1) He recklessly causes the death of another person . . ." whereas a state that has not adopted the MPC classifications might define manslaughter in terms of "an unlawful killing of a person by culpable negligence" or "a killing of a human being without malice aforethought."

In addition to understanding traditional concepts of general and specific intent, a student should become acquainted with previously quoted sections of the MPC that define "act" and relate to levels of culpability. While these are among the most widely relied-on provisions of the MPC, in later chapters dealing with substantive crimes we refer to instances where the MPC has been influential in the revision of criminal statutes.

The Doctrine of Transferred Intent

When a person intends to commit one criminal act but accomplishes another, the law implies that the necessary criminal intent for the second wrongful act is present. This is the **doctrine of transferred intent,** in which the defendant's original intent is transferred from one against whom it was directed to the one who suffered the consequences. The doctrine does not require one fact to be presumed based on the finding of another fact. Rather, under this concept it becomes immaterial whether the accused intended to injure a person who is actually harmed. If the accused acted with the required intent toward someone, that intent suffices as the required element of intent for the crime charged. *State v. Locklear,* 415 S.E.2d 726 (N.C. 1992).

The doctrine of transferred intent is designed to hold a person who is committing a dangerous illegal act responsible for the consequences to the innocent victim. The doctrine links the perpetrator's mental state toward an intended victim with the resulting harm to another person who inadvertently becomes the victim. The doctrine is most frequently applied in homicide cases. In the classic illustration, A aims a gun at B intending to kill B. A misses and instead kills C. A's mental state directed against B is said to be transferred to C, the unintended victim.

Applying the doctrine of transferred intent seems to achieve just results, and, perhaps more important from the viewpoint of the prosecution, it obviates the need to establish that it was predictable that A's actions directed against B would result in injury to C, an innocent victim. Of course, the actor must have had a criminal intent in the first place. Thus, if a parent lawfully administering punishment to a child accidentally strikes an innocent bystander, there is no criminal intent to transfer.

In *Ford v. State,* 625 A.2d 984 (Md. 1993), Maryland's highest court recognized that the doctrine applies to both general- and specific-intent crimes, but the court distinguished its applicability to two types of specific-intent offenses. The first requires a specific intent to cause somebody a specific type of harm, and the doctrine is applicable. The second includes only those offenses that, by statutory definition, require a specific intent to cause a specific type of harm to a specified person—that is, where the statute requires that the defendant's intent be directed toward the actual victim. Thus, if a defendant charged with an attempt to commit premeditated murder had shot at but missed the intended victim, the defendant may be convicted of attempted murder, but the premeditated intent to kill a specific victim would not apply to an unintended victim who was killed. Of course, such a killing of an unintended victim could be prosecuted as a homicidal crime, but not one that required the defendant's specific intent to commit premeditated murder. A similar rationale was adopted earlier by a California appellate court. See *People v. Birreuta*, 208 Cal. Reptr. 635 (Cal. App. 1984).

The Importance of Determining the Intent Required

There are two reasons why it is essential to determine whether a particular offense is a general-intent or a specific-intent crime or, in some recent statutory revisions, meets the MPC culpability requirements. First, the intent requirement in a criminal statute determines the extent of proof that must be offered by the prosecution. Second, as we will explain in later chapters, in certain crimes the intent required to be proven determines whether particular defenses are available to the defendant.

The Strict Liability Offenses

As we previously noted, common-law crimes consist of a criminal act or omission known as the *actus reus* and the mental element known as the *mens rea*. However, legislative bodies have the power to dispense with the necessity for the mental element and authorize punishment of particular acts without regard to the actor's intent.

As we pointed out in Chapter 1, **mala in se offenses** are inherent wrongs whereas **mala prohibita offenses** are considered wrongs because they are so defined by the law. In such common-law felonies as murder, rape, robbery, and larceny, the proscribed conduct is considered *mala in se*, and the intent is deemed inherent in the offense. This holds true today even if the statute proscribing such conduct fails to specify intent as an element of the offense.

Mala prohibita offenses are commonly referred to as **strict liability offenses.** For the most part, they include "regulatory" or "public welfare" types of offenses often tailored to address unique problems created by the Industrial Revolution and present-day technology. We see some of the earliest examples of strict liability in cases involving sale of liquor and adulterated milk. Examples of strict liability laws today include traffic regulations, food and drug laws, and laws prohibiting the sale of liquor and cigarettes to minors. Strict liability offenses now constitute a substantial part of the criminal law.

The fact that a statute is silent on the matter of criminal intent does not necessarily mean that it defines a strict liability offense. If the prohibited conduct falls within a traditional common-law crime category, courts may interpret such statutes to contain a *mens rea* requirement. For example, in *Morissette v. United States*, 342 U.S. 246, 72 S.Ct. 240, 96 L.Ed. 288 (1952), the defendant had been convicted of violating federal law by taking some old bomb casings from a government bombing range. At trial, the district court had refused to instruct the jury on the issue of intent, in

An excerpt from the Supreme Court's opinion in *Morissette v. United States* appears at the end of this chapter.

effect holding that the government was only required to prove the defendant's act, not his intent, because the statute only required proof of the prohibited act. The Supreme Court reversed Morissette's conviction. The Court held that the crime for which he was prosecuted was a variant of the common-law offense of larceny and that failure to include the intent requirement in the statute did not eliminate the element of intent.

Critics of strict liability offenses argue that they run counter to the standards of criminal culpability. Others argue that it is desirable to classify these offenses as regulatory or administrative, thereby removing the "criminal" stigma. Still others counter that to remove the criminal aspect from these offenses would remove their deterrent factor. One thing seems certain: In a rapidly urbanizing, technological society, with increased awareness of the necessity to protect the public health, safety, and environment, strict liability offenses will become even more prominent.

In the chapters that follow, note that as penalties for statutory offenses become heavier, courts are reluctant to dispense with proof of intent. This is true in environmental crimes (see Chapter 11) and in some serious motor vehicle violations. For example, many state courts have addressed the issue of whether proof of a criminal intent is necessary to convict someone of the statutory crime of driving with a revoked or suspended license. In *Jeffcoat v. State*, 639 P.2d 308 (Alaska App. 1982), the Alaska Court of Appeals held that even though the statute is silent, the element of *mens rea* must be read into it by implication. In *State v. Keihn*, 542 N.E.2d 963 (Ind. 1989), the Indiana Supreme Court agreed that in a prosecution for driving with a suspended license, the State was required to prove the defendant's knowledge of the suspension. But the Indiana court pointed out that several state courts hold that criminal liability can be affixed without regard to knowledge or intent. See, for example, *People v. Morrison*, 500 N.E.2d 442 (Ill. App. 1987).

The Causation Requirement

When an offense is defined in a manner that a specific result must occur, the concept of **causation** becomes important. This is most commonly associated with homicide offenses. For example, the various degrees of homicide require that to be guilty of murder or manslaughter, the accused's conduct must have resulted in the death of a human being. Sometimes lawyers refer to legal causation as **proximate cause,** defined as "a cause that in a natural, continuous sequence, unbroken by any intervening causes, produces the consequences that occur." Proximate cause is satisfied if the result that occurs was foreseeable. Sometimes the "but for" test is employed here, meaning that "but for" the accused's actions, the harm would not have occurred. This can be illustrated by an instance where but for the accused's firing a pistol, the victim would not have been killed. But suppose the victim was only slightly injured by the accused's having fired a pistol and later taken to a hospital, where through the negligence of health care providers the victim died. If the victim's death occurred from such an intervening cause, it would likely result in the perpetrator being charged with a lesser offense such as assault with a dangerous weapon, a crime not requiring the infliction of death.

Although causation is important in many crimes to link the elements of the accused's act and intent, in Chapter 5 we will study the incomplete offenses of attempt, solicitation, and conspiracy, which are classified as inchoate (incomplete) offenses. These offenses, among others that we will later study, do not require that certain specified results occur.

Parties to a Crime

Historically, the common law classified parties to crimes as either principals or accessories. Principals were persons whose conduct involved direct participation in a crime; accessories were **accomplices** or those who gave aid and comfort to principals. The common law classified crimes other than treason as felonies and misdemeanors. Felonies were very serious; in fact, at times, a person found guilty of a felony could be deprived of all worldly possessions and suffer either death or lengthy imprisonment. Because of the serious nature of felonious conduct and because all persons involved might not be equally guilty, the common law developed several technical distinctions among the various participants.

Common-Law Distinctions Among Participants in Crime

To comprehend present criminal law regarding participants in a crime, a basic knowledge of the common-law scheme is essential. At common law, a person directly involved in committing a felony was classified as a principal; a person whose conduct did not involve direct participation was classified as an accessory. Principals were further classified by the degree of their participation. A person who directly or through the acts of an innocent agent actually committed the crime was a principal in the first degree. A principal in the second degree was a person not directly involved but actually or constructively present at the commission of the crime who aided and abetted the perpetrator. To be constructively present, one had to be sufficiently close to render assistance to the perpetrator. For example, suppose a man led a woman's escort away from her so that another man could sexually attack the woman. The man who led the escort away would probably be constructively present and would be classified as a principal in the second degree because he was **aiding and abetting** a crime. Aiding and abetting another in the commission of a crime means assenting to an act or lending countenance or approval, either by active participation in it or by encouraging it in some other manner.

An accessory at common law was classified as either an accessory before or after the fact. An accessory before the fact was one who procured or counseled another to commit a felony, but was not actually or constructively present at commission of the offense. An accessory after the fact knowingly assisted or gave aid or comfort to a person who had committed a felony.

Because misdemeanors were far less serious than felonies, the common law found it unnecessary to distinguish between participants. As with treason, all participants in misdemeanor offenses were regarded as principals.

Accessories to felonies were not regarded as being as culpable as the principals, so they were punished less severely at common law. Moreover, under the common law a party had to be charged as a principal or as an accessory. The principal had to be tried first, and if the principal was found not guilty, the accessory could not be tried for the offense.

The Modern American Approach

The American approach has been to abolish both the substantive and procedural distinctions between principals and accessories before the fact. Federal law stipulates that "[w]hoever commits an offense against the United States or aids, abets, counsels, commands, induces, or procures its commission, is punishable as a principal. . . ." 18 U.S.C.A. § 2(a). The federal statute reflects the law of most of the states insofar as it abolishes the distinction between principals and accessories before the fact. As early as 1872, California enacted a statute defining principals as "all persons concerned in the commission of a crime, whether it be felony or misdemeanor, and whether they directly commit the act constituting the offense, or aid and abet in its commission, or, not being present, have advised and encouraged its commission." West's Ann. Cal. Penal Code § 31. As explained by the Supreme Court of Appeals of West Virginia in *State v. Fortner,* 387 S.E.2d 812, 822 (W.Va. 1989),

> Being an accessory before the fact or a principal in the second degree is not, of itself, a separate crime, but is a basis for finding liability for the underlying crime. . . .
> In essence, evidence of such complicity simply establishes an alternative theory of criminal liability, i.e., another way of committing the underlying substantive offense.

The common-law distinction between principals and accessories before the fact has been largely abolished, but the concept of accessory after the fact as a separate offense has been retained by many jurisdictions. Modern statutes view an accessory after the fact as less culpable than someone who plans, assists, or commits a crime. Thus, statutes generally define accessory after the fact as a separate offense and provide for a less severe punishment. See, for example, West's Ann. Cal. Penal Code § 33. In most states, a lawful conviction as an accessory after the fact requires proof that a person knew that the person he or she aided or assisted had committed a felony. The gist of being an accessory after the fact lies essentially in obstructing justice, and a person is guilty who knows that an offense has been committed and receives, relieves, comforts, or assists the offender to hinder his or her apprehension, trial, or punishment. *United States v. Barlow,* 470 F.2d 1245 (D.C. Cir. 1972). However, federal law does not distinguish whether the person assisted has committed a felony or a misdemeanor. 18 U.S.C.A. § 3.

Because of a wife's duty at common law to obey her husband, a woman who gave aid and comfort to her husband was exempt from the law governing accessories after the fact. Although this exemption no longer prevails, some state statutes exempt spouses and other classes of relatives from penalty for being accessories after the fact.

CASE-IN-POINT ## Aiding and Abetting

Both Walter Godinez and Julio Montes were indicted for murder, attempted armed robbery, and armed violence. Montes's case was tried separately before a judge. The evidence revealed that Eduardo Soto was shot to death on April 28, 1986, in Chicago, Illinois. Montes confessed that Walter Godinez attempted to rob Soto and shot him while the defendant Montes acted as a lookout. Montes was convicted.

On appeal, Montes argued several points, including his contention that the evidence failed to establish his guilt on the basis of accountability. The court rejected his contention, stating that "the defendant said that he knew that Godinez intended to rob Soto two days before the shooting and again on the night of the shooting. On both occasions he agreed to act as lookout; and he knew that Godinez was armed with a revolver. Acting as a lookout is an act aiding and abetting the commission of the offense."

People v. Montes, 549 N.E.2d 700, 707 (Ill. App. 1989).

For example, Florida law has long prevented the prosecution as an accessory after the fact of any person standing in the relation of husband or wife, parent or grandparent, child or grandchild, brother or sister, either by blood or marriage. West's Fla. Stat. Ann. § 777.03(1)(a). In 1999 the legislature amended the statute to add that, regardless of relation to the offender, a person who maintains or assists a principal or accessory before the fact knowing the offender has committed child abuse or a related offense is subject to prosecution unless the court finds that such person is a victim of domestic violence. West's Fla. Stat. Ann. § 777.03(1)(b).

Conclusion

The concepts discussed in this chapter, though technical, are basic to an understanding of the criminal law in the United States. At this stage, such fundamental concepts as the *actus reus* and the *mens rea* seem abstract; however, they will become more concrete as we relate them to the various offenses discussed in later chapters.

Common-law crimes were considered *mala in se,* or wrongs in themselves, and required proof of a general or specific intent. In some criminal code revisions today, these traditional categories of intent are being replaced by categories of culpability recommended by the Model Penal Code. In contrast, many modern statutory offenses are classified as *mala prohibita*—that is, they are offenses simply because a legislative body has classified them as wrongs, and they are considered strict liability crimes. Yet even where a statute describes a strict liability crime, courts will imply an intent requirement if the crime is basically of common-law origin or imposes a heavy punishment.

The elements of crimes discussed in this chapter will be relevant throughout the text. In contrast, the background concerning the designation of parties to crimes is largely of historical importance. Modern criminal law treats parties to crimes as principals, whether perpetrators or accomplices. This approach can be debated, but society has found it necessary, and this principle has become firmly ingrained in modern criminal law.

Key Terms

actus reus	motive
mens rea	general intent
principals	general-intent statutes
accessories before the fact	specific intent
accessories after the fact	specific-intent statute
felonies	constructive intent
misdemeanors	Model Penal Code (MPC)
act of omission	intentionally
administrative-type act	knowingly
possession	recklessly
actual possession	criminal negligence
constructive possession	doctrine of transferred intent
status	*mala in se* offenses

mala prohibita offenses   proximate cause
strict liability offenses   accomplices
causation   aiding and abetting

Web-Based Research Activity

1. Go to the web. Locate your state's criminal statutes (or another state's if yours are not available on line).
2. Determine whether your state uses Model Penal Code terminology ("purposely," "knowingly," "recklessly," and "negligently") in defining criminal intent.
3. Download examples of crime definitions using the MPC terminology.

Questions for Thought and Discussion

1. Distinguish between the concepts of motive and intent in the criminal law. Can you cite an instance where, despite good motives, a person would be guilty of a crime?
2. What justifies the criminal law making mere possession of contraband articles illegal? Would this rationale extend to criminalizing the mere possession of such innocent items as a screwdriver, a pair of pliers, or an ice pick that could be used to commit burglary?
3. Does the proliferation of strict liability crimes offend the basic principles of criminal liability outlined in Chapter 1?
4. Should the criminal law punish a person whose mere carelessness, as opposed to willfulness, causes harm to another?
5. Is there a justification for the criminal law not punishing a person for failing to act when there is a clear moral duty to act?
6. Has the moral integrity of the criminal law been jeopardized by the increasing number of offenses for which a person can be convicted without proof of any criminal intent?
7. Why has the common-law doctrine distinguishing between principals and accessories before the fact diminished in importance in contemporary criminal law?
8. Contrast an offense that requires proof of causation with one that does not.
9. Is it fair to assess the same degree of fault and impose the same punishment on an accomplice as on a perpetrator?
10. Is there a valid reason to exempt close family relatives from punishment as accessories after the fact to felonious conduct?

Problems for Discussion and Solution

1. Sol Toolmaker visited his long-time friend, I. N. Mate, a prisoner in a state institution. Mate had previously told Toolmaker how much he wanted to escape from the prison. So on this occasion, Toolmaker brought Mate two small saws. Mate hid the saws in a place where he thought the prison guards would not find them, but the

guards promptly discovered and confiscated the saws. The warden turned this evidence over to the prison's legal counsel with a request that charges be prepared against Mate for attempting to escape from prison. Assuming Mate intended to escape from prison, did his conduct constitute a criminal act?

2. Alice Alpha had a long-standing grievance against Benjamin Beta and had threatened to kill him. When Alpha saw Beta standing on a street corner amidst a crowd of people, Alpha pulled a gun and fired a shot. The bullet grazed Beta's arm, injuring him slightly. But it struck and killed Gerry Gamma, who was unknown to Alpha. Considering the concepts discussed in this chapter, what crime or crimes has Alpha committed?

● ● ● ● ● ● ● ● ● ● ● ● ● ●

EXCERPTS FROM JUDICIAL DECISIONS

People v. Valot

Michigan Court of Appeals, 1971.
33 Mich. App. 49, 189 N.W.2d 873.

[In the excerpts that follow from the opinion and dissent, the Michigan Court of Appeals illustrates the disagreement in judicial views about what constitutes constructive possession of contraband.]

CHURCHILL, Judge

Defendant, Harold Valot, was charged with having had possession and control of marijuana contrary to the provisions of M.C.L.A. § 335.153 (Stat. Ann. 1957 Rev. § 18.1123). He was convicted by a non-jury trial. The judgment of sentence refers to possession of marijuana. The trial judge's recited findings at the conclusion of the trial make it clear that the conviction was based on findings of control. Possession and control are separate offenses under the statute. *People v. Harper* (1962), 365 Mich. 494, 113 N.W.2d 808. . . .

The legislature used the words "possession" and "control" in the narcotics statute in their commonly understood sense, and not in a restricted, technical sense. *People v. Harper, supra.* The trial judge conceded the possibility that someone, unbeknownst to Defendant, brought the marijuana into the room, but nevertheless did not have a reasonable or fair doubt as to the Defendant's control thereof. It was a fact question. There was strong circumstantial evidence to support the Court's finding. Defendant's control of the marijuana in the room as a fact reasonably inferred from the evidence.

His conviction is affirmed.

LEVIN, Judge (dissenting).

I dissent because it is not a crime to be in control of a room where marijuana is found and because the People failed to prove that the defendant, Harold Eugene Valot, Jr., was in possession or control of marijuana. . . . [To] infer from the fact that a person is in control of a room that he is in control of marijuana in the possession of other persons in the room is not a reasonable inference.

● ● ● ● ● ● ● ● ● ● ● ● ● ●

Morissette v. United States

Supreme Court of the United States, 1952.
342 U.S. 246, 72 S.Ct. 240, 96 L.Ed. 288.

[The U.S. Supreme Court holds that the absence of statutory language denoting an intent requirement will not necessarily be construed as eliminating that element.]

Mr. Justice JACKSON delivered the opinion of the Court.

. . . On a large tract of uninhabited and untilled land in a wooded and sparsely populated area of

Michigan, the government established a practice bombing range over which the Air Force dropped simulated bombs at ground targets. These bombs consisted of a metal cylinder about 40 inches long and eight inches across, filled with sand and enough black powder to cause a smoke puff by which the strike could be located. At various places the range signs read "Danger—Keep Out—Bombing Range." Nevertheless, the range was known as good deer country and was extensively hunted.

Spent bomb casings were cleared from the targets and thrown into piles "so that they will be out of the way." They were not stacked or piled in any order but were dumped in heaps, some of which had been accumulating for four years or upwards, were exposed to the weather and rusting away.

Morissette, in December of 1948, went hunting in this area but did not get a deer. He thought to meet expenses of the trip by salvaging some of these casings. He loaded three tons of them on his truck and took them to a nearby farm, where they were flattened by driving a tractor over them. After expending this labor and trucking them to market in Flint, he realized $84. Morissette, by occupation, is a fruit stand operator in summer and a trucker and scrap iron collector in winter. An honorably discharged veteran of World War II, he enjoys a good name among his neighbors and has no blemish on his record more disreputable than a conviction for reckless driving.

. . . He was indicted, however, on the charge that he "did unlawfully, willfully and knowingly steal and convert" property of the United States of the value of $84, in violation of 18 U.S.C. § 641. . . . Morissette was convicted and sentenced to imprisonment for two months or to pay a fine of $200. The Court of Appeals affirmed, one judge dissenting.

On his trial, Morissette, as he had at all times told investigating officers, testified that from appearances he believed the casings were cast-off and abandoned, that he did not intend to steal the property, and took it with no wrongful or criminal intent. The trial court, however, was unimpressed, and . . . refused to submit or to allow counsel to argue to the jury whether Morissette acted with innocent intention. It charged:

> And I instruct you that if you believe the testimony of the government in this case, he intended to take it. . . . He had no right to take this property. [A]nd it is no defense to claim that it was abandoned, because it was on private property. . . . And I instruct

you to this effect: That if this young man took this property (and he says he did), without any permission (he says he did), that was on the property of the United States Government (he says it was), that it was of the value of one cent or more (and evidently it was), that he is guilty of the offense charged here. If you believe the government, he is guilty. . . . The question on intent is whether or not he intended to take the property. He says he did. Therefore, if you believe either side, he is guilty.

Petitioner's counsel contended, "But the taking must have been with a felonious intent." The court ruled, however, "That is presumed by his own act."

The Court of Appeals . . . affirmed the conviction because "[a]s we have interpreted the statute, appellant was guilty of its violation beyond a shadow of doubt, as evidenced even by his own admissions." Its construction of the statute is that it creates several separate and distinct offenses, one being knowing conversion of government property. The court ruled that this particular offense requires no element of criminal intent. This conclusion was thought to be required by the failure of Congress to express such a requisite.

. . . Stealing, larceny, and its variants and equivalents, were among the earliest offenses known to the law that existed before legislation; they are invasions of rights of property which stir a sense of insecurity in the whole community and arouse public demand for retribution, the penalty is high and, when a sufficient amount is involved, the infamy is that of a felony, which, says Maitland, is ". . . as bad a word as you can give to man or thing." State courts of last resort, on whom fall the heaviest burden of interpreting criminal law in this country, have consistently retained the requirement of intent in larceny-type offenses.

. . . Congress, therefore, omitted any express prescription of criminal intent from the enactment before us in the light of an unbroken course of judicial decision in all constituent states of the Union holding intent inherent in this class of offense, even when not expressed in a statute. Congressional silence as to mental elements in an act merely adopting into federal statutory law a concept of crime already so well defined in common law and statutory interpretation by the states [does not mean that intent is not required as an element of the crime].

. . . The government asks us by a feat of construction radically to change the weights and balances in the scales of justice. The purpose and obvious effect of doing away with the requirement of a guilty intent is to ease the prosecution's path to conviction, to strip the defendant of such benefit as he derived at common law from innocence of evil purpose, and to circumscribe the freedom heretofore allowed juries. Such a manifest impairment of the immunities of the individual should not be extended to common-law crimes on judicial initiative. . . .

We hold that mere omission from § 641 of any mention of intent will not be construed as eliminating that element from the crimes denounced. . . .

We find no grounds for inferring any affirmative instruction from Congress to eliminate intent from any offense with which this defendant was charged.

As we read the record, this case was tried on the theory that even if criminal intent were essential its presence (i) should be decided by the court (ii) as a presumption of law, apparently conclusive, (iii) predicated upon the isolated act of taking rather than upon all of the circumstances. In each of these respects we believe the trial court was in error. . . .

Reversed.

CHAPTER

5

Inchoate Offenses

Introduction

The word *inchoate* means "underdeveloped" or "unripened." Thus, an **inchoate offense** is one involving activity or steps directed toward the completion of a crime. There are three such offenses: attempt, solicitation, and conspiracy. Although preparatory to commission of other offenses, they are separate and distinct crimes. During the 1800s each was recognized as a misdemeanor at common law, too late to become a part of the common law under the reception statutes adopted by most new American states. Most American jurisdictions now define these offenses by statute, frequently classifying them as felonies.

Inchoate offenses were originally created by the courts in response to the need to prevent commission of serious crimes. The development of the law in this area has been primarily through the courts. Frequently the courts have found difficulty in determining when mere noncriminal activity has reached the stage of criminal conduct. Yet, by recognizing an actor's design toward commission of an offense, the law permits police to apprehend dangerous persons who have not yet accomplished their criminal objectives. Consequently, by making certain inchoate conduct illegal, the law affords law enforcement officers an opportunity to terminate such conduct at an early stage.

Attempt

Attempt is the most frequently charged of the inchoate crimes. Attempt, of course, means an effort to accomplish a particular purpose. A criminal attempt consists of an intent to commit a specific offense coupled with an act that goes beyond mere preparation toward the commission of that offense. *People v. Tuczynski,* 378 N.E.2d 1200 (Ill. App. 1978). Thus, as explained in an early New York opinion, whether an attempt to commit a crime has been made depends on both the actor's mind and conduct. *People v. Moran,* 25 N.E. 412 (N.Y. 1890).

No particular federal statute proscribes the offense of attempt. In general, federal courts have recognized the requisite elements of attempt as (1) an intent to engage in criminal conduct, and (2) the performance of an act that constitutes a substantial step toward the completion of the substantive offense. See *United States v. Manley,* 632 F.2d 978 (2d Cir. 1980).

State penal codes often specifically provide for attempts to commit the most serious crimes, such as murder. The remaining offenses are then covered by a general attempt statute. A typical statute that covers all attempts provides that "[w]hoever attempts to commit an offense prohibited by law and in such attempt does any act toward the commission of such an offense, but fails in the perpetration or is intercepted or prevented in the execution of the same, commits the offense of criminal attempt." West's Fla. Stat. Ann. § 777.04(1). The "act" requirement contemplates an **overt act** that constitutes a **substantial step** toward commission of an offense. Although the quoted statute makes no distinction between felony or misdemeanor offenses, statutes in some states limit the crime of attempt to attempts to commit felonies or certain specified crimes.

The Act Requirement

As we have noted, the "act" element in the crime of attempt requires an act that constitutes a substantial step toward the commission of an offense. The Model Penal

CASE-IN-POINT

What Constitutes an Overt Act?

Defendant was found guilty of attempting to escape from prison. He appealed, contending the state failed to prove beyond a reasonable doubt that he had committed an overt act as required by law. He characterized his actions as preparatory steps indicative only of an intention to attempt an escape.

The Supreme Judicial Court of Maine rejected his contention and affirmed his conviction: "[T]here was undisputed evidence that a dummy was found in defendant's cell; that defendant was in an unauthorized area attempting to conceal his presence; and that a rope ladder was found in a paper bag close to where he was concealed. [Defendant] had gone far beyond the preparation stage."

State v. Charbonneau, 374 A.2d 321, 322 (Me. 1977).

In *Bucklew v. State,* reprinted at the end of the chapter, the Mississippi Supreme Court interprets a statute that defines attempt as an endeavor to commit a crime coupled with the commission of an overt act.

Code distinguishes **preparatory conduct** from an attempt. It allows conviction for the crime of attempt, where the actor engages in "an act or omission constituting a substantial step in a course of conduct planned to culminate in the commission of the crime." M.P.C. § 501 (1)(c). Federal courts apply this test. *United States v. Mandujano,* 499 F.2d 370, 376 (5th Cir. 1974). It is possible that where multiple intentions underlie an act, that one act may establish several different criminal attempts. For example, in *State v. Walters,* 804 P.2d 1164 (Or. 1991), the court held that the defendant's conduct established an attempt to commit kidnapping, rape, and sodomy.

Many state statutes also include the term "substantial step" in defining the act requirement. Where they do not, courts usually imply that the act must constitute a substantial step toward commission of a substantive offense. In either instance, it becomes necessary to distinguish between mere preparatory acts of planning or arranging means to commit a crime and those acts that constitute a direct movement toward commission of an offense. The question is how close that act must be to accomplishment of the intended crime. Appellate courts have taken various approaches. This issue frequently turns on the specific factual situation involved. An early, and demanding, test held that an actor must have engaged in the "last proximate act necessary to accomplish the intended crime," but most courts have now rejected that test. See, for example, *People v. Parrish,* 197 P.2d 804, 806 (Cal. App. 1948). Some courts apply a more realistic test that holds that the actor's conduct must be "within dangerous proximity to success." New York courts have summed it up in a practical manner, opining simply that an accused's conduct must be "very near" to the completion of the intended crime. *People v. Mahboubian,* 543 N.E 2d 34 (N.Y. 1989).

The Requisite Criminal Intent

To find a defendant guilty of the crime of attempt, most courts require the prosecution to prove that the defendant had a specific intent to commit the intended offense, frequently referred to as the **target crime.** Most courts reason that one cannot attempt to do something without first forming the specific intent to accomplish that particular act. See, for example, *Thacker v. Commonwealth,* 114 S.E. 504 (Va. 1922). The rationale for this majority view seems to be that an attempt involves the concept of intended consequences by the actor. In any event, courts require at least the level of intent that must be established in proof of the target crime.

Attempts in Relation to Substantive Crimes

When a criminal attempt completes a substantive crime, the attempt usually merges into the target offense. The actor is then guilty of the substantive crime, rather than merely an attempt to commit it. Thus, a person who is successful in an attempt to commit murder is guilty of murder. However, there can be no attempt to commit certain crimes because some substantive offenses by definition embrace an attempt. To illustrate, consider the statutory crime of uttering a forged instrument. Statutes usually define the crime as including an attempt to pass a forged instrument to someone to obtain something of value. Therefore, one who makes such an attempt would be guilty of uttering a forged instrument, not merely an attempt to do so. In effect, the attempt is subsumed by the very definition of the substantive crime. Needless to say, it would be redundant to charge someone with attempting to attempt to commit a given crime.

Defenses to the Crime of Attempt

The Model Penal Code proposes that an accused who "purposely engages in conduct that would constitute the crime if the attendant circumstances were as he believed them to be" is guilty of an attempt. M.P.C. § 5.01(1)(a). Although many state statutes track this Model Penal Code language, it raises the issue of whether the law should pursue a conviction for an attempt to commit a crime that is impossible to commit.

The rule developed in most jurisdictions is that **legal impossibility** is a defense to the crime of attempt but that **factual impossibility** is not. The distinction can be very close. For example, attempted rape requires a human victim. Therefore, a man who assaults a mannequin dressed as a woman would not be guilty of attempted rape because it would be legally impossible to commit that offense. Yet this example must be distinguished from the classic illustration in *State v. Mitchell,* 71 S.W. 175 (Mo. 1902). There a man was held responsible for attempted murder when he shot into the room in which his target usually slept, but who fortuitously, was sleeping elsewhere in the house at the time of the shooting. Although the bullet struck the target's customary pillow, attainment of the criminal objective was factually impossible. Likewise, a person who picks another's pocket intending to steal money may be found guilty of attempted theft, even if the victim's pocket is empty. In these instances courts have said that although it was factually impossible to commit the crime, it was legally possible to do so.

New York law currently provides that it is no defense to a prosecution for attempt that the crime charged to have been attempted was either factually or legally impossible to commit, if it could have been committed had the circumstances been what the defendant believed them to be. McKinney's N.Y. Penal Law § 110.10; *People v. Davis,* 526 N.E.2d 20 (N.Y. 1988). The trend is toward finding an attempt to commit a crime in instances where the actor's intent has been frustrated merely because of some factor unknown at the time. Thus, if the accused believed a victim was alive when the accused shot at the victim, it follows that such an attempt to kill a dead person would constitute an attempt under New York law. *People v. Dlugash,* 363 N.E.2d 1155 (N.Y. 1977).

Some jurisdictions have laws providing that it is a defense to the crime of attempt if the defendant abandons an attempt to commit an offense or otherwise prevents its consummation. See, for example, Vernon's Tex. Ann. Penal Code § 15.04(a). If recognized as a defense, abandonment must be wholly voluntary. It cannot be the result of any outside cause such as the appearance of the police on the scene. See, for example, *People v. Walker,* 191 P.2d 10 (Cal. 1948).

Solicitation

By the 1800s, the common law specified that a person who counseled, incited, or solicited another to commit either a felony or a misdemeanor involving breach of the peace committed the offense of **solicitation.** A person who solicited another to commit a crime was guilty of solicitation even if the crime counseled, incited, or solicited was not committed. The offense of solicitation is now defined by statute in most American jurisdictions. In explaining why its penal code makes solicitation an offense, a California appellate court offered two reasons: first, to protect individuals from being exposed to inducement to commit or join in the commission of crime; and second, to prevent solicitation from resulting in the commission of the crime solicited. *People v. Cook,* 199 Cal. Rptr. 269 (Cal. App. 1984).

The statutory definition of solicitation in Illinois is typical: "A person commits solicitation when, with intent that an offense be committed, other than first-degree murder, he commands, encourages, or requests another to commit the offense." Illinois S.H.A. 720 ILCS 5/8–1. The gist of the offense remains the solicitation, so the offender may be found guilty irrespective of whether the solicited crime is ever committed. Conviction under federal law requires the solicitation to be of a federal offense. *United States v. Korab,* 893 F.2d 2122 (9th Cir. 1989).

Commission of the crime of solicitation does not require direct solicitation of another; it may be perpetrated through an intermediary. In *State v. Cotton,* 790 P.2d 1050 (N.M. App. 1990), the court reversed a defendant's conviction of criminal solicitation because there was no evidence that the defendant ever communicated the

CASE-IN-POINT

When Is the Crime of Solicitation Committed?

Defendant Roger Gardner, an alleged contract killer, subcontracted the killing of Alvin Blum to a man named Tim McDonald for a fee of $10,000. Gardner met with McDonald and gave him some expense money, a gun, and ammunition. In talking with McDonald, Gardner said that he (Gardner) would first kill a man named Hollander, and if this did not create the desired result, then McDonald would be directed to kill Blum. Gardner's attempts were foiled when he was arrested and charged with solicitation to murder. It turned out that McDonald was a police informant whose assistance led to Gardner's arrest.

On appeal, Gardner argued that he did not commit the crime of solicitation because he did not actually direct McDonald to proceed with the murder of Blum or pay him all of the money he had promised. In affirming Gardner's conviction, the Maryland Court of Appeals said "the crime of solicitation was committed when he asked McDonald to commit the murder." The Court explained that "[n]either a final direction to proceed nor fulfillment of conditions precedent (paying of the money) was required." In holding that the crime of solicitation was committed, the Court observed that "[t]he gist of the offense is incitement."

Gardner v. State, 408 A.2d 1317, 1322 (Md. 1979).

solicitation to the person he intended to solicit to commit a crime. However, the court recognized that solicitation could be perpetrated through an intermediary. Thus, if Abel solicits Barnes to solicit Cummings to commit a crime, Abel would be liable even where he did not directly contact Cummings because Abel's solicitation of Barnes itself involves the commission of the offense.

Under some state statutes, there must be communication between the solicitor and the person to be solicited for the crime of solicitation to take place, although some jurisdictions permit a solicitor to be charged with attempted solicitation when no communication has occurred. See *State v. Cotton,* supra. In contrast, as the Model Penal Code proposal states, "It is immaterial . . . that the actor fails to communicate with the person he solicits to commit a crime if his conduct was designed to effect such communication." M.P.C. § 5.02(2). Under the Model Penal Code and state laws based upon it, the intent to solicit combined with an effort to solicit is enough to constitute the crime.

The Requisite Criminal Intent

The statutory language making solicitation a crime might not seem to require the prosecution to establish the defendant's specific intent. However, most courts hold that to commit solicitation, the solicitor must have specifically intended to induce or entice the person solicited to commit the target offense. See, for example, *Kimbrough v. State,* 544 So.2d 177 (Ala. Crim. App. 1989). The prosecution should at least establish that the actor who solicits someone to commit a crime had the requisite intent for the crime solicited.

Solicitation Distinguished from Other Inchoate Crimes

The offenses of solicitation and attempt are different crimes, analytically distinct in their elements. Although each is an inchoate offense, solicitation is complete when the request or enticement to complete the intended offense is made, and it is immaterial if the solicitee agrees, if the offense is carried out, or if no steps were taken toward consummation of the offense. Mere solicitation is generally not sufficient to constitute an attempt because attempt requires proof of an overt act to commit the intended criminal act. This principle was succinctly explained by the Idaho Supreme Court: "The solicitation of another, assuming neither the solicitor nor solicitee proximately acts toward the crime's commission, cannot be held for an attempt." *State v. Otto,* 629 P.2d 646, 650 (Idaho 1981).

Solicitation is distinguished from conspiracy because although solicitation requires an enticement, conspiracy requires an agreement. Sometimes a solicitation results in a conspiracy, and some courts have regarded the offense as "an offer to enter into a conspiracy." See, for example, *Commonwealth v. Carey,* 439 A.2d 151, 155 (Pa. Super. 1981).

Most students of the criminal law would concede that solicitation should be a criminal offense. But, you might ask, is it more serious than the inchoate crime of attempt? The Tennessee Supreme Court has suggested that it is not, stating, "There is not the same degree of heinousness in solicitation as in attempts, nor is solicitation as likely to result in a completed crime, there not being the same dangerous proximity to success as found in attempts." *Gervin v. State,* 371 S.W.2d 449, 451 (Tenn. 1963). The Connecticut Supreme Court took the contrary point of view:

> The solicitation to another to [commit] a crime is as a rule far more dangerous to society than the attempt to commit the same crime. For the solicitation has behind

In *State v. Keen,* reprinted at the end of the chapter, the North Carolina Court of Appeals explains that the crime of solicitation to commit a felony is complete with the solicitation and does not require acquiescence in the scheme by the one solicited.

it an evil purpose, coupled with the pressure of a stronger intellect upon the weak and criminally inclined. *State v. Schleifer,* 121 A. 805, 809 (Conn. 1923).

Defenses to the Crime of Solicitation

Generally, the fact that the solicitor countermands the solicitation is not a defense to the crime of solicitation. Nor is it a defense that it was impossible for the person solicited to commit the crime. The Model Penal Code provides that a complete and voluntary renunciation of the accused's criminal purpose is a defense to a charge of solicitation. M.P.C. § 5.02 (3). Some states have adopted this position. Kentucky law agrees; however, Section 506.060 of the Kentucky Statutes stipulates the following:

> A renunciation is not "voluntary and complete" ... when it is motivated in whole or in part by: (a) A belief that circumstances exist which pose a particular threat of apprehension or detection of the accused or another participant in the criminal enterprise or which render more difficult the accomplishment of the criminal purpose; or (b) A decision to postpone the criminal conduct until another time or to transfer the criminal effort to another victim or another but similar object.

....

Conspiracy

At common law, **conspiracy** consisted of an agreement by two or more persons to accomplish a criminal act or to use unlawful means to accomplish a noncriminal objective. The gist of the offense was the unlawful agreement between the parties, and no overt act was required.

The common law regarded a husband and wife as one person for most purposes; therefore, a husband and wife could not be guilty of conspiring with each other. Since the trend of the law in recent years has been to recognize the separate identities of the spouses, there appears to be no valid reason to continue the common-law approach. See, for example, *People v. Pierce,* 395 P.2d 893 (Cal. 1964).

Today the offense of conspiracy is defined by statute in all jurisdictions. Most state laws define the elements of the offense along the lines of the common law. Typically, as the Florida law states, "A person who agrees, conspires, combines, or confederates with another person or persons to commit any offense commits the offense of criminal conspiracy." West's Fla. Stat. Ann. § 777.04(3). Thus, under Florida law, both an agreement and an intention to commit an offense are necessary elements to support a conviction for conspiracy. *Webster v. State,* 646 So.2d 752 (Fla. App. 1994). On the other hand, federal law (with some exceptions) requires an overt act in a conspiracy to commit an offense or to defraud the United States. 18 U.S.C.A. § 371. Several states also require proof of an overt act to convict someone for conspiracy. For example, Texas law provides that "[a] person commits criminal conspiracy if, with intent that a felony be committed, (1) he agrees with one or more persons they or one or more of them engage in conduct that would constitute the offense, and (2) he or one or more of them performs an overt act in pursuance of the agreement." Vernon's Tex. Penal Code Ann. § 15.02(a). Note that the Texas statute also requires an intent that a felony be committed, whereas in many states it is necessary only to prove an intent to commit a criminal offense.

Because of the variations encountered in statutory language, in reviewing any statute defining conspiracy it is necessary to determine at the outset (1) the type of the offense or unlawful activity the statute proscribes, (2) whether it requires proof of an overt act in furtherance of the parties' agreement, and if so, what constitutes such an overt act.

Justification for the Offense of Conspiracy

Why is conspiracy considered an offense distinct from the substantive offense the conspirators agree to commit? Perhaps the late U.S. Supreme Court Justice Felix Frankfurter articulated one of the most cogent responses to this question. In *Callanan v. United States,* 364 U.S. 587, 593–594, 81 S.Ct. 321, 325, 5 L.Ed.2d 312, 317 (1961), Frankfurter observed the following:

> Concerted action both increases the likelihood that the criminal object will be successfully attained and decreases the probability that the individuals involved will depart from their path of criminality. Group association for criminal purposes often, if not normally, makes possible the attainment of ends more complex than those which one criminal could accomplish. . . . Combination in crime makes more likely the commission of crimes unrelated to the original purpose for which the group was formed. In sum, the danger that a conspiracy generates is not confined to the substantive offense that is the immediate aim of the enterprise.

The Range of Conspiracies in Society

The range of conspiracies cuts across socioeconomic classes in society. Traditionally, state prosecutions for conspiracy have been directed at criminal offenses such as homicide, arson, perjury, kidnapping, and various offenses against property. In recent years an increasing number of both state and federal conspiracy prosecutions have been related to illicit drug trafficking. In addition to the numerous narcotics violations, federal prosecutions include a variety of conspiracies not found under state laws. Among these are customs violations, counterfeiting of currency, copyright violations, mail fraud, lotteries, and violations of antitrust laws and laws governing interstate commerce and other areas of federal regulation. Recently, several federal prosecutions have involved conspiracies to deprive persons of their civil rights secured by the Constitution or laws of the United States. See 18 U.S.C.A. § 241.

The Act Element in Conspiracy

In general, the *actus reus* of the crime of conspiracy is the unlawful agreement. Where an overt act is required, such act need not be a substantial movement toward the target offense. For example, in California, where the law requires an overt act, the courts have said that an overt act tending to effect a conspiracy may merely be a part of preliminary arrangements for commission of the ultimate crime. *People v. Buono,* 12 Cal. Rptr. 604 (Cal. App. 1961). In fact, a single act such as a telephone conversation arranging a meeting has been held to be sufficient proof of an overt act. *United States v. Civella,* 648 F.2d 1167 (8th Cir. 1981).

In *State v. Dent,* 869 P.2d 392 (Wash. 1994), the Supreme Court of Washington articulated the difference between the *actus reus* requirement in the crimes of attempt and conspiracy. Washington statutes include definitions of these two inchoate offenses. Attempt is defined as follows:

> A person is guilty of an attempt to commit a crime if, with intent to commit a specific crime, he does any act which is a substantial step toward the commission of that crime. RCW 9A.28.020(1).

CASE-IN-POINT

Conspiracy to Deliver Controlled Substances

On February 16, 1988, Corporal Cook, working undercover, agreed to purchase fifty doses of LSD from Bruce Erickson at a park in the City of Snohomish, Washington. Erickson asked Smith for a ride to go there, ostensibly to meet David Hensler (who owed Smith $600, a sum Smith very much wanted to collect). When Smith and Erickson arrived in Smith's vehicle, the officer approached the car and asked Erickson if he had LSD. When Erickson produced a bag of LSD, the officer asked Smith if he had tried it. Smith replied that "he was going to college . . . and couldn't afford to get messed up, but that his wife had taken some of it, and . . . 'it really [messed] her up.'" At that point Corporal Cook agreed to purchase the LSD, handed the money to Erickson, and arrested both Smith and Erickson. Smith was found guilty of conspiracy to deliver lysergic acid diethylamide (LSD).

On appeal, Smith argued that the evidence was insufficient to support his conviction because there was no proof beyond a reasonable doubt (1) that he agreed to engage in delivery of LSD and (2) that he intended that it be delivered. The appellate court rejected both contentions and affirmed Smith's conviction. The appellate court first pointed out that "a formal agreement is not necessary to the formation of a conspiracy." Then the court observed that although Smith's primary purpose in giving Erickson a ride to the park was to meet Hensler, his secondary purpose was to assist in delivering LSD. In finding the evidence sufficient to show that Smith intended to assist Erickson, the court opined that "there was evidence not only of knowledge of Erickson's unlawful purpose, but an agreement to assist with the plan by providing the necessary transportation. . . . Here there were two overt acts: first, that Smith drove Erickson to Snohomish knowing, according to Corporal Cook, Erickson's purpose for the trip; and second, that Smith provided encouragement for the sale by assuring the officer of the potency of the drug. . . ."

State v. Smith, 828 P.2d 654, 656, 657 (Wash. App. 1992).

In contrast, conspiracy is defined as follows:

> A person is guilty of criminal conspiracy when, with intent that conduct constituting crime be performed, he agrees with one or more persons to engage in or cause the performance of such conduct, and *any one of them takes a substantial step in pursuance of such agreement* [emphasis added]. RCW 9A.28.040(1).

The Washington Supreme Court observed that the two crimes differ in the nature of the conduct sought to be prohibited and in the significance of the "substantial step" requirement (known as the "overt act" requirement in some jurisdictions) in each context. "A substantial step," the court noted, "is required in the context of attempt to prevent the imposition of punishment based on intent alone." But the court explained that the purpose of the substantial step or overt act requirement is different in the context of conspiracy: "The purpose of the 'substantial step' requirement is, therefore, to manifest that the conspiracy is at work, and is neither a project still resting solely in the minds of the conspirators nor a fully completed operation no longer in existence." 869 P.2d at 397. For these reasons, the court concluded that the state's conspiracy statute requires only an act that is a substantial step.

The Requisite Criminal Intent

Statutes frequently fail to encompass the intent requirement in the offense of conspiracy. This difficulty is compounded by failure of the courts to clearly define the intent required for a conviction. In general, the prosecution must prove that a defendant intended to further the unlawful object of the conspiracy, and such intent must exist in the minds of at least two of the parties to the alleged conspiracy. *People v. Cohn*, 193 N.E. 150 (Ill. 1934). Many courts refer to the crime as requiring a specific intent. See, for example, *People v. Marsh*, 376 P.2d 300 (Cal. 1962). As previously noted relative to attempts, such intent may be inferable from the conduct of the parties and the surrounding circumstances. Although many federal court decisions have not required proof of a specific intent, the U.S. Supreme Court has said that in federal prosecutions there must be proof of at least the criminal intent necessary for the requirements of the substantive offense. *United States v. Feola*, 420 U.S. 671, 95 S.Ct. 1255, 43 L.Ed.2d 541 (1975).

Contrary to some popular views, the participants in a conspiracy need not even know or see one another as long as they otherwise participate in common deeds. The essence of the offense is the mutual agreement of the parties to the conspiracy, not the acts done to accomplish its object. Moreover, the agreement need not be explicit. In fact, it seldom is. In most instances, the agreement is implied from the acts of the parties and the circumstances surrounding their activities. Furthermore, all the conspirators do not have to join in the conspiracy at the same time.

Conspiracy Distinguished from Aiding and Abetting and Attempt

As we noted in Chapter 4, aiding and abetting someone in the commission of a crime makes a person either a principal or an accessory before the fact. Conspiracy is a separate offense and must be distinguished from aiding and abetting. Conspiracy involves proof of an agreement between two or more persons, an element often present, but not essential, in proving that a defendant aided and abetted a crime. On the other hand, aiding and abetting requires some actual participation. Conspiracy differs from the crime of attempt in that it focuses on intent, whereas attempt places more emphasis on the defendant's actions.

The *Pinkerton* Rule

In *Pinkerton v. United States*, 328 U.S. 640, 66 S.Ct. 1180, 90 L.Ed 1489 (1946), Pinkerton was charged with conspiring with his brother for tax evasion, including some offenses allegedly committed by his brother during times that Pinkerton was incarcerated. The trial court instructed the jury that it could find Pinkerton guilty if it found he was a party to a conspiracy and that the offenses were in furtherance of the conspiracy. Pinkerton was convicted, and on review the U.S. Supreme Court upheld his conviction, stating that a member of a conspiracy is liable for all offenses committed in furtherance of the conspiracy. The Court did indicate that a different result may occur if the offenses were not reasonably foreseeable as a natural consequence of the unlawful agreement of the conspirators. This has come to be known as the **Pinkerton Rule.** It is based on the theory that conspirators are agents of one another, and just as principals are bound by the acts of their agents within the scope of the agency relationship, so too conspirators are bound by the acts of their co-conspirators. *United States v. Troop*, 890 F.2d 1393 (7th Cir. 1989).

The *Pinkerton* doctrine has broad implications, and not all courts have accepted it. For example, in *People v. McGee*, 399 N.E.2d 1177 (N.Y. 1979), the court rejected the *Pinkerton* doctrine and observed that "[i]t is not offensive to permit a conviction of conspiracy to stand on the overt act committed by another, for the act merely provides corroboration of the existence of the agreement and indicates that the agreement has reached a point where it poses a sufficient threat to society to impose sanctions. . . . But it is repugnant to our system of jurisprudence, where guilt is generally personal to the defendant . . . to impose punishment, not for the socially harmful agreement to which the defendant is a party, but for substantive offenses in which he did not participate."

Some Unique Aspects of the Offense of Conspiracy

When the courts view each conspirator as an agent of the others, it follows that each will be held responsible for the acts of the others within the context of their common design. *Commonwealth v. Thomas,* 189 A.2d 255 (Pa. 1963). This principle permits an exception to the rule of evidence that ordinarily excludes hearsay statements from being used in a trial over the defendant's objection. Indeed, statements by a co-conspirator in furtherance of the conspiracy made during the pendency of the conspiracy may be admitted into evidence. Statements that have been found to be "in furtherance of" the conspiracy include statements to inform other conspirators of the activities or status of the conspiracy and those identifying other conspirators. Federal courts have upheld the use of statements as to the sources or purchaser of controlled substances. See, for example, *United States v. Patton,* 594 F.2d 444 (5th Cir. 1979). Before receiving this type of evidence, a court must receive independent evidence that a conspiracy has been committed. In some instances, courts receive the hearsay evidence subject to it being tied into the offense by independent evidence of the conspiracy. Court procedures in this area are very technical because the court must determine the scope of the conspiracy and the inception of the conspirator's participation.

The Supreme Court of Hawaii properly characterized the judicial approach to conspiracy:

> In the eyes of the law conspirators are one man, they breathe one breath, they speak one voice, they wield one arm, and the law says that the acts, words, and declarations of each, while in the pursuit of the common design, are the words and declarations of all. *Territory v. Goto,* 27 Hawaii 65 (1923).

Courts have held that once formed, a conspiracy continues to exist until consummated, abandoned, or otherwise terminated by some affirmative act. *Cline v. State,* 319 S.W.2d 227 (Tenn. 1958).

These unique aspects are significant. They assist the prosecution in proof of cases that might be otherwise unprovable. Perhaps the law has established these exceptions in recognition of the difficulties of prosecuting persons involved in conspiracies, which are generally formed in secret.

Conspiracy Does Not Merge into the Target Crime

In *Gomez v. People,* reprinted at the end of the chapter, the Colorado Supreme Court details the evidence it found to be sufficient to support a conviction for conspiracy.

Conspiracy is regarded as a separate and distinct crime; therefore, it usually does not merge into the target offense. As the New Jersey Supreme Court has pointed out, a conspiracy may be an evil in itself, independent of any other evil it seeks to accomplish. *State v. Lennon,* 70 A.2d 154 (N.J. 1949). A pragmatic consideration is that by not merging conspiracy into the target offense, the law can more effectively deter efforts of organized crime.

The Wharton's Rule Exception

Wharton's Rule, named after Francis Wharton, a well-known commentator on criminal law, provides an exception to the principle that conspiracy does not merge into the target crime. Wharton's Rule holds that two people cannot conspire to commit a crime such as adultery, incest, or bigamy because these offenses require only two participants. The rationale is that, unlike the usual conspiracy (often viewed as a wheel with many spokes or as a chain of circumstances), the offenses named do not endanger the public generally. Wharton's Rule has been applied in many state and federal courts, but it has its limitations. In holding the rule inapplicable to various federal gambling offenses under the Organized Crime Control Act of 1970, the Supreme Court pointed out that the rule itself is simply an aid to determination of legislative intent and must defer to a discernible legislative judgment. *Iannelli v. United States*, 420 U.S. 770, 786, 95 S.Ct. 1284, 1294, 43 L.Ed.2d 616, 628 (1975).

Criticism of the Conspiracy Laws

There has been an increased tendency in recent years to prosecute defendants for conspiracies as well as target crimes. The offense of conspiracy is a potent weapon for prosecutors, particularly as they try to cope with the problem of organized crime. Because the intent requirement and the form of agreement required are somewhat imprecise, a conspiracy is easier to prove than specific substantive crimes. On this basis, some critics argue that prosecutors, judges, and juries are given too much latitude in finding a defendant guilty. Other critics claim that conspiracy prosecutions may inhibit or effectively abolish First Amendment rights of free expression.

Defenses to the Charge of Conspiracy

In some states, statutes specifically provide for a defense of withdrawal from and renunciation of a conspiracy. As an illustration, Missouri law specifies that "[n]o one shall be convicted of conspiracy if, after conspiring to commit the offense, he prevented the accomplishment of the objectives of the conspiracy under circumstances manifesting a renunciation of his criminal purpose." Vernon's Mo. Ann. Stat. § 564.016(5)(1). In the absence of statutory authority, courts have been reluctant to approve a person's withdrawal as a defense. One difficulty in approving withdrawal as a defense is that even though a conspirator withdraws, the criminal objective of the conspiracy may proceed. Therefore, it seems reasonable to require that a person who would rely on such defense not only renounce any criminal purpose but also take the necessary steps to thwart the objective of the conspiracy. To accomplish this result, the conspirator would probably have to notify law enforcement authorities of the pertinent details of the conspiracy. In any event, if an accused is allowed to offer such a defense, the defendant has the burden of establishing his or her withdrawal from the conspiracy.

Entrapment, a defense to be examined in Chapter 14, may under some circumstances be a defense to conspiracy. For example, in *Stripling v. State*, 349 So. 2d 187 (Fla. App. 1977), the court found reversible error in the trial judge having instructed the jury that the defense of entrapment was not available to a defendant if the officer acted in good faith and merely furnished an opportunity for commission of a crime by one who already had the intent to commit the crime. As the appellate court said, "A defendant could deny being a party to a conspiracy and yet raise the issue that any overt acts done by him or her were done because of entrapment; that rationale

Salinas v. United States, 522 U.S. 52, 118 S.Ct. 469, 139 L.Ed.2d 352 (1997)

In this case, the Supreme Court upheld a conviction for conspiracy to violate the federal racketeering laws (see discussion of the "RICO" statute in Chapter 10). Writing for a unanimous Court, Justice Anthony Kennedy discussed the characteristics of the offense of conspiracy:

"A conspiracy may exist even if a conspirator does not agree to commit or facilitate each and every part of the substantive offense. . . . The partners in the criminal plan must agree to pursue the same criminal objective and may divide up the work, yet each is responsible for the acts of each other. . . . If conspirators have a plan which calls for some conspirators to perpetrate the crime and others to provide support, the supporters are as guilty as the perpetrators. As Justice Holmes observed: '[P]lainly a person may conspire for the commission of a crime by a third person.' . . . A person, moreover, may be liable for conspiracy even though he was incapable of committing the substantive offense. . . .'"

being that inconsistencies in defenses in criminal cases are allowable so long as the proof of one does not necessarily disprove the other." Id at 191.

....

Conclusion

By criminalizing attempt, solicitation, and conspiracy, the law endeavors to prevent the occurrence of criminal acts that pose prospective harm to persons. These inchoate offenses often pose substantial problems for law enforcement agencies, courts, and legislative bodies. Police and courts experience difficulty determining the stage at which an act tends toward commission of a crime such that it qualifies as criminal attempt. Moreover, there are difficulties in distinguishing between what is legally impossible and what is factually impossible. Solicitation poses a major problem because the solicitor often exerts power by manipulating the solicitee to commit a crime. There remains controversy whether it should be a criminal offense to solicit another person to commit a crime, irrespective of whether the solicited offense is a felony or a misdemeanor. In conspiracy, group action can accomplish criminal purposes not otherwise likely from individual efforts. But conspiracy is also problematic. Some statutes extend criminal liability beyond legislatively defined crimes to include injuries to the public health and morals, making the offense of conspiracy vulnerable to the criticism that the law is converting civil wrongs into criminal conduct. And in some instances, prosecution of conspiracy might chill the exercise of First Amendment freedoms.

Despite the problems associated with inchoate offenses, there is strong public support for criminalizing conduct directed toward future injuries to society. Criminalizing such conduct permits timely intervention of law enforcement agencies to restrain dangerous persons and prevent intended crimes.

....

Key Terms

inchoate offense	substantial step
attempt	preparatory conduct
overt act	target crime

legal impossibility   conspiracy
factual impossibility   *Pinkerton* Rule
solicitation   Wharton's Rule

Web-Based Research Activity

1. Go to the web. Locate your state's statutes on line.
2. Does your state have a generic statute defining attempt, solicitation, and conspiracy? If not, find a state that does have such a statute.
3. Download the statutory definitions of the three inchoate offenses. How do they compare with the definitions offered in this text?

Questions for Thought and Discussion

1. What justifies criminalizing attempt, solicitation, and conspiracy?
2. How does the criminal law distinguish between mere preparatory conduct and the overt act required for a criminal attempt? Can you think of a situation in which preparatory conduct might have the appearance of prospective criminal conduct but would not constitute a criminal attempt?
3. Should it be a defense to a charge of attempt that the accused voluntarily abandoned the attempt?
4. Describe a scenario where an attempt would not merge into a target crime.
5. What is the rationale for making solicitation a crime even where a solicitor's requests are completely unheeded?
6. Which do you think poses a more serious threat to society: an attempt or a solicitation to commit murder? Why?
7. Should statutes defining conspiracy require proof of an overt act in furtherance of the conspirators' agreement? Why or why not?
8. Given the First Amendment protections of freedom of expression and association, can members of a revolutionary political organization be prosecuted for conspiring to overthrow the government of the United States?
9. What evil is the offense of conspiracy designed to combat?
10. What distinguishes the offense of conspiracy from the crime of aiding and abetting, discussed in Chapter 4?

Problems for Discussion and Solution

1. Leo Lothario was having an affair with Lucy Slarom, a woman separated from her husband, Joe. One night while Lothario and Lucy were playing tennis in her backyard, Joe appeared on the scene. Lothario demanded that Joe leave, but he declined and sat in one of the yard chairs. Lothario went to the garage, picked up a rifle, pointed it at Joe, and from a distance of approximately seventy-five feet, fired a shot

in the direction of Joe. The bullet missed Joe by about eighteen inches. Lothario explained to the police that he was simply trying to scare Lucy's estranged husband so he would not bother her. On the strength of these facts, do you think there is a basis to charge Lothario with attempted murder?

2. John and Jane were running a student loan "scam." They were convicted of soliciting several students to make false applications in exchange for a "cut" of the loan proceeds and also for aiding and abetting those same students in making false applications for loans. On appeal, they argue that the solicitation charges merged into their convictions for aiding and abetting the making of the false applications. The state responds that John and Jane were guilty of both crimes because the solicitation offenses were completed before John and Jane assisted the students in making the false applications. How should the appellate court rule on this appeal? Why?

3. A state statute makes it a criminal offense for "three or more persons to conduct, direct, or own a gambling business." Several defendants were convicted of "conspiring to violate the statute." In addition, each was convicted of the substantive offense of gambling. On appeal, each defendant argues that the conspiracy offense merged into the substantive offense of gambling because the offense of gambling required participation of a number of persons. The state counters that the harm attendant upon commission of the offense of gambling is not limited to the parties to the conspiracy. Moreover, it points out that those prosecuted for the conspiracy would not necessarily be identical to those who are prosecuted for the substantive offense of gambling. How do you think an appellate court should rule in this instance? Why?

● ● ● ● ● ● ● ● ● ● ● ●

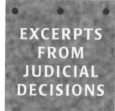

EXCERPTS FROM JUDICIAL DECISIONS

Bucklew v. State

Supreme Court of Mississippi, 1968.
206 So.2d 200.

[The appellant here was convicted of attempt under a Mississippi statute that defined an attempt as an endeavor to commit a crime coupled with commission of an overt act.]

ROGERS, Justice:

This is an appeal from a judgment of conviction of attempted embezzlement from the Circuit Court of Jones County, Mississippi, wherein the mayor of the City of Laurel was fined in the amount of $816.05. The testimony in this case shows that sometime in the summer of 1965, Henry Bucklew, the mayor of Laurel, Mississippi, called a representative of Kelly-Lowe Dodge, Inc., an automobile repair shop, advised them that he had a jeep which belonged to the Pest Control Department of the City of Laurel, and asked whether or not they could repair it. Kelly-Lowe Dodge, Inc., repaired the jeep and purchased tires and chains for it. The repair bill, including labor and parts, amounted to $816.05. Kelly-Lowe submitted its bill by mail to the City of Laurel on November 25, 1965. When the clerk saw the bill he recognized that it was not an obligation of the city and took it to the mayor. The mayor advised the clerk that he would "take care of it." Some time later, John Jacobs, who was in charge of what is known as the Pest Control Department of the City of Laurel, was requested by the mayor to sign the bill which had been submitted by Kelly-Lowe. In the meantime, the city clerk had requested a copy of this bill from the repair shop "for the files" of the City of Laurel. Later, the mayor was indicted by the grand jury of Jones County for the crime of an attempt to commit embezzlement. The bill for repairs to the jeep was never finally submitted to the city for payment by the mayor or anyone else. The testimony shows that the city clerk had an understanding with the mayor and city commissioners that before bills could be paid by the city it was necessary for the heads of the various departments to approve the payment before they were submitted to the clerk for payment. Thereafter, the mayor or commissioner to whom the bill had been referred would indicate his approval of the bill by signing his name to the approval sheet attached to the bill. The city clerk would then prepare a check in the payment of the amount indicated and return it to the mayor for his signature. Before the check could be cashed it required the signature of the clerk. In the absence of the mayor it was necessary for one of the commissioners to sign checks with the clerk before they could be paid.

The testimony showing the approval of Mr. Jacobs by affixing his signature on the bill is the only testimony showing the intention of the mayor after the bill had been turned over to him by the clerk, except that an auditor testified that the mayor told him that he approved the bill by mistake. The original bill was not offered in evidence.

The defendant, Henry Bucklew, was indicted under section 2122, Mississippi Code 1942 Annotated (1956).

When the State had concluded its testimony, the defendant made a motion to exclude the evidence offered on behalf of the State and requested the court to direct the jury to find the defendant not guilty, for the reason that the State had not shown that the defendant had committed an overt act toward the commission of the crime of embezzlement as charged in the indictment. The court overruled this motion and defendant rested his case, without introducing testimony in his behalf and without having testified in his own defense. The issue is, therefore, clearly defined: Did the State show that the defendant committed an overt act in an attempt to commit the crime of embezzlement?

Under the general law it has been pointed out that an attempt to commit a crime consists of three elements: (1) an intent to commit a particular crime; (2) a direct ineffectual act done toward its commission; and (3) the failure to consummate its commission. . . . Our statutory law requires proof of an overt act in order to sustain a conviction of an attempt to commit a crime.

The pertinent part of section 2017, Mississippi Code 1942 Annotated (1956), is as follows:

> Every person who shall design and endeavor to commit an offense, and shall do any overt act toward the commission thereof, but shall fail therein,

or shall be prevented from committing the same, on conviction thereof, . . .

This Court is in accord with the general law as to the essential elements of the crime of "attempt to commit a crime." We have held that the law requires that the State establish criminal intent as an element to the crime of attempt "to commit a crime." . . .

We have also held that there must be an overt act done toward the commission of the crime in order to establish the crime of "attempt to commit a crime." . . .

We have held that the mere intention to commit a crime is not punishable. . . . The intention must therefore be coupled with an overt act. But, what is meant by the requirement that the State prove "an overt act"? . . .

In *Williams v. State,* 209 Miss. 902, 48 So.2d 598 (1950), the defendant was convicted of attempting to commit larceny by the "pigeon dropping" game. The Court there said:

> The necessary elements of an attempt are the intent to commit, and the overt act toward its commission. . . . The rule is well recognized that "whenever the design of a person to commit crime is clearly shown, slight acts done in furtherance of this design will constitute an attempt." . . .

In that case, however, the testimony showed that the various acts of preparation had been concluded and that the defendant then went to the place to receive the money. This Court held that this was a sufficient overt act to establish an attempt.

In the case of *Stokes v. State,* 92 Miss. 415, 46 So. 627 (1908), this Court pointed out that where one attempted to procure another to kill a third party, and in furtherance of his design took a gun, loaded it and went with the party to a point where the killing was to occur, but was arrested, his act was sufficient to establish an attempt to commit a crime.

The records in the foregoing cases indicate that the defendants had reached a point in the proceedings to commit a crime beyond mere preparation, so that they had actually begun to commit the alleged crime. In *Williams* the defendant had done everything necessary to commit a crime except receive the money, and in *Stokes* the defendant had performed his part in the crime of murder and there was nothing left for him to do in furtherance of the crime.

It is contended by the State in the instant case that the appellant, defendant in the court below, accomplished the required overt act by having the department head of the Pest Control Department sign the bill submitted by Kelly-Lowe Dodge, Inc. An examination of the testimony in this case, however, shows that if all the State attempted to prove was true, the acts done by the defendant were mere acts in preparation to the submission of the bill to the clerk for payment. The testimony shows that it was necessary for the mayor to sign the bill before submitting it to the clerk for payment, and the proof shows that the mayor did not submit the bill to the clerk for payment. Moreover, there is nothing in the record to show that there was any extraneous cause that prevented the mayor from attempting to collect the amount due to the automobile company. Moreover, the record shows that the mayor told the auditor that the bill had been signed through a mistake. Therefore, if the mayor had intended to defraud the

City, the record shows that he had abandoned his purpose before attempting to collect the funds from the city treasury. . . .

Inasmuch as the law does not punish for the mere appearance of evil, we conclude that the testimony in this case does not establish an attempt to commit a crime, for the reason that it does not show an overt act on the part of the appellant to commit the crime charged, before it is shown that he abandoned his alleged purpose. We are, therefore, constrained to hold that the judgment of the trial court must be reversed, and the appellant, Henry Bucklew, discharged. . . .

ETHRIDGE, C.J., and JONES, INZER and SMITH, JJ., concur.

● ● ● ● ● ● ●   ● ● ● ● ● ● ●

State v. Keen

North Carolina Court of Appeals, 1975.
214 S.E.2d 242.

[This case deals with solicitation to commit murder.]

VAUGHN, Judge.

Defendant was charged in a bill of indictment with soliciting Blaine Bacon and Ben Wade to kill and murder Susan Page Keen, wife of defendant. Evidence for the State is summarized as follows. Blaine Bacon first saw Patrick Alan Keen, the defendant, on the afternoon of 12 September 1973. Defendant brought his Volkswagen bus into Bacon's garage to be repaired. Bacon examined the vehicle, told defendant that he did not have the necessary parts, and suggested that defendant return the next day. Defendant returned the next day and Bacon proceeded to repair the vehicle. Defendant asked Bacon if he knew "someone with few scruples and in need of some money." Defendant replied that he wanted his wife killed so that he could collect the proceeds from an insurance policy in her name. He agreed to pay Bacon $5,000.00 from the proceeds of policy.

Defendant told Bacon the death of his wife must occur before 1 October since that was the expiration date of her life insurance policy. At the close of the conversation Bacon asked the defendant to give him a few days to consider the proposition and to contact him the following Monday.

Defendant had purchased a $100,000.00 policy on his wife's life dated 1 July 1973, and was the named beneficiary. Defendant paid the quarterly premium for the months of July, August, and September but did not pay the premium due 1 October 1973, and the policy lapsed on 31 October.

Bacon immediately attempted to contact several law enforcement officers with whom he had become acquainted when he had worked as an informer or undercover agent. He finally reached a U.S. Treasury agent and informed him of what defendant had said. The agent advised him to keep in contact. Bacon's actions thereafter were generally directed by law enforcement officers. On Friday, the defendant again visited Bacon, told him of the urgency of the time factor, and sought a definite answer as to whether Bacon would kill Mrs. Keen. Defendant informed Bacon that she was in Fayetteville and said he could go there and "blow her brains out." Bacon again told the defendant to wait until Monday for an answer.

The following Monday afternoon, defendant met Bacon at his garage. Ben Wade, an agent of the State Bureau of Investigation, was concealed in Bacon's rear office so that he could overhear their conversation. At this meeting defendant again stressed the importance of time and asked Bacon when he was going to kill Mrs. Keen. Bacon replied that accidents were not his style but that he had discussed the matter with a friend who was a professional killer. Bacon told the defendant that his friend was an expert at making deaths appear accidental and that he would be in Asheville the following Friday. On Wednesday defendant visited Bacon again. The two established Friday morning as their meeting time, and defendant was asked to bring a picture of his wife.

On that Friday the two men drove in defendant's van to a motel in Asheville. They went to a room where Wade, posing as a professional killer, was waiting. A wireless transmitter was taped to Wade's back for the purpose of recording the conversation. Tapes of the conversation were introduced at trial for the purpose of corroboration.

At the motel defendant told Wade that his wife was in Fayetteville and gave him her address. He also gave him a photograph and physical description of her. He told Wade that his wife's death must appear accidental and must occur prior to the cancellation of her life insurance policy on the first of October. Defendant volunteered to raise the fee for the killing to $6,000.00 and the method of payment was discussed. With respect to "front money," defendant said that he had no cash but did have a motorcycle, a Volkswagen bus, and a five-acre tract of land to which titles could be signed over to Bacon who, in turn, could transfer them to Wade. Wade replied that he wanted the titles transferred that day and instructed defendant to put the vehicles in Bacon's name and the property in Wade's name. He told defendant he would wait at the motel until 2:30 that afternoon.

At the conclusion of the conversation, defendant left the room. Police immediately placed him under arrest. Upon being arrested defendant replied, "Oh my God how did you find out about it so fast?"

Defendant testified, in substance, as follows. He did not originally intend to have his wife killed but Bacon implanted the idea in his mind. After he and Bacon discussed the life insurance policy in Mrs. Keen's name, Bacon suggested that defendant "knock her off" and collect on the policy. Bacon volunteered to kill Mrs. Keen for $5,000.00. When Bacon tele-

phoned and told him that his friend had arrived, defendant indicated to Bacon that he wanted to call off the thing and did not care to visit Bacon's friend. Bacon responded that his friend had come all the way to Asheville, would be very upset if defendant did not at least talk with him and might seek vengeance on defendant. Defendant, although he had no intention of following through with the plan, proceeded to the motel in order to talk the other men out of it. He was frightened and answered Wade's questions because of his fear.

The jury found defendant guilty. . . .

Defendant argues that there could have been no completion of the crime since all parties with whom he spoke were connected with law enforcement. The answer is that the interposition of a resisting will, by a law enforcement officer or anyone else, between the solicitation and the proposed felony is of no consequence. This is so "because the solicitation was complete before the resisting will of another had refused its assent and cooperation." . . . Defendant was not charged with the crime of conspiracy, a crime which was not completed because of the failure of Bacon, in fact, to concur in defendant's scheme to murder defendant's wife. The crime of solicitation to commit a felony is complete with the solicitation even though there could never have been an acquiescence in the scheme by the one solicited. . . .

The crime of which defendant was convicted is but one step away from conspiracy to murder—and that step is not one defendant could have taken. If Bacon had concurred in defendant's scheme to murder the latter's wife, the conspiracy would have been complete. Bacon's rejection of defendant's atrocious scheme does not render defendant's conduct any less "infamous" than it would have been if his offer had been accepted. We hold that the punishment imposed does not exceed that authorized by law.

We have considered the other contentions made in defendant's brief and find them to be without merit. . . .

MARTIN and ARNOLD, JJ., concur.

● ● ● ● ● ● ● ● ● ● ● ● ● ●

Gomez v. People

Colorado Supreme Court, 1963.
381 P.2d 816.

[This case involves conspiracy to commit larceny.]

McWILLIAMS, Justice.

Joyce Gomez and Roberta Taylor were jointly tried and convicted by a jury of conspiring on November 1, 1960, to commit the crime of larceny from the person of one Edward Cook. By the present writ of error Gomez alone seeks reversal of the judgment and sentence entered pursuant to the verdict of the jury.

The only assignment of error pertains to the sufficiency of the evidence, Gomez contending that the trial court erred in refusing to direct a verdict in her favor and, *a fortiori,* that the evidence does not support the subsequent determination by the jury that she is guilty of the crime of conspiracy. From a careful review of the record we conclude that her contention is without merit. However, inasmuch as the legal sufficiency of the evidence has been challenged, it becomes necessary to review the record before us in some detail in order to give meaning to our conclusion that there is evidence to support the verdict.

The evidence adduced by the People established the following:

1. That Cook, a locomotive engineer, got off work at about midnight on November 1, 1960, and he was going via automobile from the roundhouse at 40th Avenue and Williams Street in Denver to his home in southwest Denver when he encountered Gomez and Taylor at 26th Avenue and Welton Street;

2. That Cook at this time had approximately $340 in his wallet, $75 of which was secreted in an inside compartment of the wallet, the balance of the currency being in the wallet proper;

3. That Cook had this comparatively large amount of money on his person because this was his pay day, and he had cashed his pay check, getting "paid in ten dollar bills";

4. That while Cook was stopped for a traffic light at 26th Avenue and Welton Street, Gomez and Taylor with no invitation opened the right-hand door of his car and proceeded to deposit themselves on the front seat;

5. That Gomez, who was seated immediately next to Cook, asked or "ordered" him to drive on, stating: "Help us out; this girl's [Taylor's] husband is going to kill her," and that one of the two women stated that Taylor's husband was armed with a gun;

6. That Cook promptly proceeded to drive for several blocks, but when he got over his "surprise" stopped the car and ordered the two women to leave his car;

7. That the two refused to leave, whereupon Cook got out of his car, went around it and opened the right-hand door, and with only little difficulty succeeded in getting Taylor out of the automobile;

8. That with his back turned to Taylor he then proceeded to forcibly evict Gomez from his car, that she initially resisted, but after considerable struggle he was able to pull her out of his car by the coat collar;

9. That about this time he realized for the first time that his wallet which he carried in his left rear trousers pocket was missing;

10. That Gomez and Taylor then broke and ran, whereupon he gave hot pursuit, and after a four-to-five-block chase espied the two crouching down on the floor of the front seat of an abandoned automobile;

11. That he opened the left-hand front door of this auto and saw Taylor and Gomez "down on the floor board attempting to hide";

12. That as he was in the act of pulling Taylor out of the car as the police arrived, whereupon Gomez got out of the front door on the right-hand side of the vehicle, crying "rape";

13. That a subsequent search of this auto by the police revealed 26 ten-dollar bills under the front seat in such a position that they could not have been accidentally "dropped there," because they were a foot or so back under the seat;

14. That search of Cook's automobile by the police thereafter disclosed that his wallet was "pushed

down in the crack on the [front] seat quite a ways"; and

15. That though Cook's wallet still contained the $75 hidden in the inside compartment, the remainder of his currency was missing.

The foregoing resume demonstrates quite clearly to us that the trial court did not commit error in submitting the case to the jury, and that actually there is ample evidence to support the jury's verdict.

True, there was evidence to the contrary. Although Taylor elected not to testify, Gomez did testify in her own behalf, and her testimony was radically different from that of Cook in virtually all particulars, as under the circumstances might well be expected. However, no good purpose would be served by detailing Gomez's testimony, as it did no more than create a conflict in the evidence and thereby pose a disputed issue of fact properly to be resolved by the jury. . . . There being competent evidence, both of a direct and circumstantial nature, to support the jury's determination, we are not at liberty to set it aside.

In support of the general proposition that a conspiracy "need not be proved directly, but may be inferred by the jury from the facts proved." . . .

The judgment is affirmed.

FRANTZ, C.J. and DAY, J., concur.

CHAPTER

6

Offenses Against Persons

Introduction

Every civilized society attempts to protect its members from injury or death at the hands of wrongdoers. As the English common law developed, the judges created criminal offenses to protect individuals from conduct that society deemed wrongful and injurious. These basic offenses as defined by English common law were inherited by the American colonists. Since then, many social changes have occurred in America, and federal and state statutes have redefined many of these offenses and have created new ones. In this chapter, we examine the common-law crimes against persons and discuss their statutory development in the United States. We also explore some representative statutes defining present-day offenses against persons.

The Common-Law Background

By the time of the English colonization in America, the common law had identified four basic groups of offenses against persons. These consisted of (1) the assaultive crimes—that is, assault, battery, and mayhem; (2) the homicidal crimes of murder, manslaughter, and suicide; (3) sex-related offenses of rape, sodomy, and abortion; and (4) offenses known as false imprisonment and kidnapping. Murder, manslaughter, suicide, rape, and sodomy were common-law felonies; the remaining offenses named were classified as misdemeanors.

The American Development

Early substantive criminal law in America was essentially a continuation of the English common law of crimes. By the 1800s, however, America's quest for representative government and its penchant for definiteness and certainty, combined with the standards of written constitutions, resulted in legislative definition of crimes. Defining offenses against persons became primarily a state rather than a federal legislative function, and the new states basically followed the common-law themes with variations deemed necessary in the new social and political environment.

As the United States became urbanized, more densely populated, and increasingly mobile, the areas of conduct statutorily defined as criminal offenses against persons required revision and, in many instances, enlargement. Under modern statutes, assault and battery have been classified according to their seriousness, the character of the victim, and the environment in which these crimes are committed. More recently, legislatures have enacted statutes proscribing a new offense, stalking. Conduct that constituted the offense of mayhem at common law is often prosecuted under other criminal statutes. Murder has been classified based on the degree of the offender's culpability, and a new offense of vehicular homicide has been created to cope with the dangers inherent in motor vehicle traffic. At early common law, suicide was punished by causing the forfeiture of the decedent's goods and chattels to the king. Suicide statutes are now designed primarily to punish those who assist others in committing suicide.

In recent years, contemporary moral standards have caused the offense of rape to be expanded into a more comprehensive offense of sexual battery, with new emphasis on the victim's age and vulnerability. At the same time, enforcement of laws proscribing consensual sodomy has declined, and in many jurisdictions sodomy laws have been repealed or invalidated by the courts. Abortion, a common-law crime, has become a woman's constitutional right. Laws prohibiting doctor-assisted suicide have become controversial, and statutes now address such conduct as child and spousal abuse. The offense of false imprisonment is essentially the same as at common law, but the crime of kidnapping serves a much different role in American society than it did under the English common law. Finally, there is a new emphasis on enforcement of civil rights laws that originated in the post-Civil War environment and have been supplemented by modern enactments.

Assaultive Offenses

Assault and battery, though commonly referred to together, were separate offenses at common law. An assault was basically an attempted battery consisting of an offer to do bodily harm to another by using force and violence; a battery was a completed or consummated assault. Although an actual touching was not required, words alone did not constitute an assault. The common law made no distinction between classes or degrees of assault and battery but dealt more severely with aggravated cases.

Modern Statutory Development

Today all jurisdictions make **assault** an offense, and most make **battery** a crime as well. Assault is defined by statute, as is battery, and sometimes the term "assault and battery" is used to indicate one offense. Simple assaults and batteries generally remain misdemeanors, whereas those perpetrated against public officers (for example, fire and police personnel) are frequently classified as felonies. Legislatures commonly classify as felonies more egregious assaultive conduct such as **aggravated assault, aggravated battery,** and assault with intent to commit other serious crimes.

The California Penal Code defines an assault as "an unlawful attempt, coupled with a present ability, to commit a violent injury on the person of another." West's Ann. Cal. Penal Code § 240. It imposes increased penalties for an assault committed on a person engaged in performing the duties of a peace officer, fire fighter, lifeguard, process server, paramedic, physician, or nurse. West's Ann. Cal. Penal Code § 241(b). Like most states, California makes it a felony to commit an assault with a deadly weapon or with force likely to produce great bodily injury. West's Ann. Cal. Penal Code § 245. Many states classify this latter offense as aggravated assault. For example, under Florida law, a person who commits an assault with a deadly weapon without intent to kill or an assault with intent to commit a felony is guilty of aggravated assault, a felony offense. West's Fla. Stat. Ann. § 784.021.

The California Penal Code defines as battery "any willful and unlawful use of force or violence upon the person or another." West's Ann. Cal. Penal Code § 242. The code also specifies increased punishment for batteries committed against specific classes of officers, West's Ann. Cal. Penal Code § 243.6, or when committed on school property, park property, or hospital grounds, West's Ann. Cal. Penal Code § 243.2. Consistent with its handling of aggravated assaults, Florida law classifies a battery resulting in great bodily harm, permanent disability, or permanent disfigurement or one committed with a deadly weapon as an aggravated battery, an even more serious felony than aggravated assault. West's Fla. Stat. Ann. § 784.045.

Although most assault and battery prosecutions occur under state laws, the federal government also has a role in this area. Federal statutes proscribe assault within the

CASE-IN-POINT

Assault with a Deadly Weapon

Rasor, a police officer, stopped a vehicle and attempted to arrest the driver, Jackson, for driving while intoxicated. As he did, a fight broke out between the officer and Jackson. At that point the defendant, Lloyd Gary, a passenger in Jackson's car, approached the two combatants, removed the officer's pistol, and pointed it at Rasor and Jackson. Gary was convicted of assault with a deadly weapon. On appeal, he argued that the trial judge erred in not directing the jury to return a verdict of not guilty because the evidence showed no attempt to commit a physical injury. The Arizona Supreme Court rejected Gary's argument, saying that "[t]he pointing of a gun may constitute 'an assault' . . . and it is not necessary to show in addition that there was an intent to do physical harm to the victim."

State v. Gary, 543 P.2d 782, 783 (Ariz. 1975).

maritime and territorial jurisdiction of the United States. 18 U.S.C.A. § 113. Federal courts have held that the statute covers the entire range of assaults, *United States v. Eades*, 615 F.2d 617 (4th Cir. 1980), and that the word "assault" includes acts that would constitute batteries under most state laws. *United States v. Chaussee*, 536 F.2d 637 (7th Cir. 1976). Additional federal statutes proscribe assaults on federal officers, including members of the uniformed services, engaged in the performance of official duties, 18 U.S.C.A. § 111, and assaults of foreign diplomatic and other official personnel, 18 U.S.C.A. § 112.

Common Illustrations of Assault and Battery

Statutory definitions vary, but under most statutes a simple assault would include a threat to strike someone with the fist, or a missed punch. Firing a shot in the direction of a person, throwing a rock at someone but not hitting the person, or threatening someone with a weapon would probably all qualify as aggravated assaults.

A battery, on the other hand, involves some physical contact with the victim. Some common illustrations of a simple battery would include hitting or pushing someone, a male hugging and kissing a female—or even an offensive touching—if against her will, using excessive force in breaking up a fight, intentionally tripping another individual, or using excessive force (by a parent or teacher) in disciplining a child. The acts referred to above as constituting aggravated assault, if completed, would most likely be prosecuted as aggravated batteries.

A frequently litigated issue in prosecutions for aggravated assault and aggravated battery is whether the instrument used by the defendant is a dangerous weapon capable of producing death or great bodily harm. An air pistol, a hammer, a club, or an ice pick—and under some circumstances, even a person's fist—have been found to qualify. Courts generally reason that the test is not whether great bodily harm resulted, but whether the instrument used was capable of producing such harm. In December 1995, the press reported that a father in New Mexico pled no contest to conspiring to commit aggravated assault with a deadly weapon. The unique aspect of the charge was that the father allegedly had sharpened the chinstrap on his son's football helmet, and the razor-edged buckle hurt several opposing players during a game.

The Burden of the Prosecution

The proof required to establish assaultive offenses depends on the statutory language of the offense. To convict a defendant of simple assault or battery, the prosecution generally needs only prove the act and the defendant's general, not specific, intent. In aggravated assault and aggravated battery prosecutions, courts have arrived at different interpretations of the intent requirement, but proof of the defendant's general intent is usually sufficient. In contrast, if a defendant is prosecuted for committing an assault or battery "with the intent to do great bodily harm" or "with the intent to commit a specific felony, for example, murder," courts generally require the prosecution to prove the defendant's specific intent to accomplish those results.

Defenses to Charges of Assault and Battery

Many forms of conduct involving intentional use of physical force do not constitute batteries. In many instances, there is an express or implied consent of the person against whom the physical force is exerted. Reasonableness is the test applied in sports contests and friendly physical encounters. Everyday examples include such contact sports as football, in which the participants obviously consent to forceful bodily contact. The physician who performs surgery with consent of the patient provides another example of physical contact that, if properly applied, does not constitute a battery. Reasonableness is also the test applied to interpersonal relationships. Thus, although a person might imply consent to a friendly kiss or caress, seldom could a person imply consent to an act of violence, even when done under the guise of affection.

A teacher may discipline a pupil, and a police officer or prison guard may use reasonable force to effect an arrest or preserve order. Often, statutory law regulates the degree of force used by teachers, police officers, and correction officials, and an excessive use of force may constitute a battery. Likewise, parents and guardians and those standing *in loco parentis* have a right to impose reasonable punishment when disciplining a child, but must consider the child's age, health, size, and all other relevant circumstances. Parents who inflict injury on a child or who impose excessive punishment may be guilty of committing a simple or even an aggravated battery. They may also be subject to prosecution under modern statutes proscribing child abuse.

A person charged with battery may defend by showing that the touching or hitting was unintentional, that the physical force used was reasonable, or that the action was taken in **self-defense.** Self-defense is subject to qualifications, as we will explain in Chapter 14. Defenses applicable to the offense of battery generally apply as well to a charge of assault. The theory is that a person who fails to make physical contact with another can defend on the same basis of reasonableness or self-defense as a person who successfully commits a battery.

State v. Towers (1973), in which the Maine Supreme Court upholds a conviction for aggravated assault and battery, is excerpted at the end of the chapter.

Stalking

By the late 1980s, police were receiving complaints from persons who were being continually followed, threatened, or harassed by others. Most frequently the complainants were women who were targeted by men. Law enforcement officers began to refer to this type of behavior as *stalking.* Many prosecutors felt that the traditional protections of the criminal law were not always sufficient to protect victims from the needless torment caused by this type of conduct. They urged legislators to adopt appropriate statutes to combat the problem.

By 1993, most states responded by enacting laws defining **stalking** and making it a crime. These laws generally stipulate that a person who willfully, maliciously, and repeatedly follows or harasses another and makes a credible threat against that person is guilty of stalking. In the wake of litigation over what constitutes a "credible threat," this term has been eliminated from some statutes.

In what is often considered to be one of the toughest laws, the Illinois Criminal Code makes stalking another person a felony and provides that one guilty of aggravated stalking commits a more serious felony. 720 ILCS 5/12–7.3 provides the following:

> (a) A person commits stalking when he or she, knowingly and without lawful justification, on at least 2 separate occasions follows another person or places the person under surveillance or combination thereof and:
>
> > (1) at any time transmits a threat to that person of immediate or future bodily harm, sexual assault, confinement or restraint and the threat is directed towards that person or a family member; or
> >
> > (2) places that person in reasonable apprehension of immediate or future bodily harm, sexual assault, confinement or restraint.

Subsection (d) states that a defendant "places a person under surveillance" by remaining present outside the person's school, place of employment, vehicle, other place occupied by the person, or residence other than the residence of the defendant. Subsection (e) stipulates that the words "follows another person" mean (i) to move in relative proximity to a person as that person moves from place to place or (ii) to remain in relative proximity to a person who is stationary or whose movements are confined to a small area. However, subsection (e) points out that to follow another person does not include a following within the residence of the defendant. Subsection (h) broadly defines "family member."

720 ILCS 5/12–7.4(a) provides the following:

> A person commits aggravated stalking when he or she, in conjunction with committing the offense of stalking, also does any of the following:
>
> (1) causes bodily harm to the victim;
>
> (2) confines or restrains the victim; or
>
> (3) violates a temporary restraining order, an order of protection, or an injunction prohibiting the behavior described in subsection (b)(1) of Section 214 of the Illinois Domestic Violence Act of 1986.

The Illinois Supreme Court has upheld these stalking laws against challenges that the statutes are unconstitutionally vague, overbroad, and intrude on the right to freedom of speech. *People v. Bailey,* 657 N.E.2d 953 (Ill. 1995). In 1999 the Colorado Supreme Court noted that at least forty-eight states have enacted stalking laws and that the majority of courts in those states have upheld stalking statutes against overbreadth attacks. *People v. Baer,* 973 P.2d 1225 (Colo. 1999). In the same year a California appellate court held that a stalking statute that prohibited harassing another person is not unconstitutionally vague. *People v. Ewing,* 90 Cal. Rptr.2d 177 (Cal. App. 1999).

An interesting legal question arose in Georgia concerning whether *attempted* stalking is a criminal offense. In *Rooks v. State,* 458 S.E.2d 667 (Ga. App. 1995), a Georgia appellate court ruled that an indictment charging a defendant with an attempt to stalk did not allege a crime. But the State of Georgia challenged that ruling, and in April 1996 the Georgia Supreme Court reversed the appellate court's decision. The state's highest court reasoned that stalking is not merely an assault, which requires proof of an immediate fear of injury. Rather, it is an intentional act designed to cause emotional distress by inducing fear in the victim or the victim's family, but contains no immediacy requirement. The court concluded that attempted stalking is an offense because such conduct constitutes an attempt to follow, place under surveillance, or contact another person. *State v. Rooks,* 468 S.E.2d 354 (Ga. 1996).

In some instances a stalker's intent may simply be amorous, but to the victim it may strike terror. Recently some women have complained that they are becoming victims of relentless e-mail messages. In May 2000 the Georgia Legislature responded by broadening its statute proscribing stalking to prohibit certain "contacts" by telephone, mail, computer, or other electronic device. O.C.G.A. § 16–5–90.

Mayhem

At common law, **mayhem** consisted of willfully and maliciously injuring another so as to render the victim less able in fighting. Mayhem became a statutory crime in most states, with some statutes extending the common-law definition to include injuries that disfigure a person. In most instances it is a general-intent offense; however, some statutes require proof of the actor's specific intent to maim or disfigure the victim.

Mayhem statutes are less common today because many of the acts formerly prosecuted under these laws are now prosecuted under such statutory crimes as aggravated battery and attempted murder.

Homicide

The word **homicide** means the taking of the life of one human being by another. The English common law recognized both criminal and noncriminal homicides. Criminal homicide embraced the crime of murder and manslaughter; noncriminal homicide included those killings of humans deemed either justifiable or excusable. The killing of a human being was the common factor in all classes of homicide; however, the perpetrator's state of mind was significant in determining whether an offense had been committed and, if so, the category of that offense.

At common law, murder was the unlawful killing of one person by another with **malice aforethought.** The required malice could be either express or implied. There were no degrees of murder. **Manslaughter** was the unlawful killing of one human being by another when no malice was involved. There were two categories: voluntary and involuntary. Voluntary manslaughter consisted of an intentional, unlawful killing that occurred in the heat of passion as a result of some adequate provocation. Involuntary manslaughter was the unintentional killing of another by the accused's gross or wanton negligence. Simply stated, the difference between the two was that the former was intentional whereas the latter was unintentional.

At common law, homicide was justifiable if performed by the command or permission of the law; it could be excusable if it occurred through accident or when committed for necessary self-protection.

With some variations, the basic scheme of common-law homicide has been carried over into the statutory law of American jurisdictions. However, most states classify murder as either first or second degree. First-degree murder is usually defined as requiring either malice aforethought or premeditation. Second-degree murder commonly requires proof that the accused was guilty of imminently dangerous or outrageous conduct, albeit not malicious in the common-law sense of malice aforethought.

All states make manslaughter a crime, although some statutes abolish the distinction between **voluntary manslaughter** and **involuntary manslaughter.** Moreover, modern statutes extend the offense of manslaughter to embrace a person's responsibility for death resulting from an omission to act where the law imposes a duty to act.

Modern criminal codes generally provide that it is justifiable homicide for one to take another's life by authority of the law (for example, an executioner performing a duty). It is usually considered excusable homicide if death results from the inadvertent taking of another's life when the actor is not guilty of criminal negligence (for example, death occurring from an unavoidable traffic accident).

The overwhelming majority of homicide prosecutions are brought under state laws. However, federal statutes provide jurisdiction over the killing of certain officers and employees of the United States engaged in performance of their official duties, 18 U.S.C.A. § 1114, as well as certain foreign officials, 18 U.S.C.A. § 1116. Federal statutes classify criminal homicide as murder in the first degree, felony murder, and manslaughter. 18 U.S.C.A. § 1111–1112.

First-Degree Murder

The California Penal Code illustrates a modern statutory approach to homicide. It defines murder as the "unlawful killing of a human being, or a fetus, with malice aforethought" but stipulates that death of the fetus is not murder when an abortion is performed by a physician when the mother's life is endangered or with the mother's consent. West's Ann. Cal. Penal Code § 187. The malice required by the code may be either express or implied. When a deliberate intention is manifested to take a person's life unlawfully, the malice is considered express; it may be implied when no considerable **provocation** appears or under other circumstances indicating malice. West's Ann. Cal. Penal Code § 188.

In defining degrees of murder, the California code states that

> all murder which is perpetrated by means of a destructive device or explosive, knowing use of ammunition designed primarily to penetrate metal or armor, poison, lying in wait, torture, or by any other kind of willful, deliberate, and premeditated killing, or which is committed in the perpetration of, or attempt to perpetrate, arson, rape, carjacking, robbery, burglary, mayhem, kidnapping . . . is murder of the first degree; and all other kinds of murder are of the second degree. West's Ann. Cal. Penal Code § 189.

The penalties in California and other jurisdictions for **first-degree murder** are the most severe, with decreasing penalties provided for second-degree murder and manslaughter.

First-degree murder is the highest classification of homicide. It contemplates a true "intent to kill" and, as noted, usually requires proof of either malice aforethought or **premeditation.** Thus, to obtain a conviction, the prosecution must establish the defendant's specific intent to take another's life.

The California Supreme Court has said that "when a defendant with a wanton disregard for human life, does an act that involves a high degree of probability that it will result in death, he acts with malice aforethought." Moreover, the court has opined that "willful, deliberate, and premeditated" as used in the statute indicates its

First-Degree Murder: Evidence of Premeditation

Defendant Phillip Lee Young suggested to his two companions that they rob and kill John Cooke in order to obtain money to buy liquor. After the three men used a ruse to gain entry to Cooke's house, Young stabbed Cooke twice in the chest, and one of the companions stabbed the victim several times in the back. Cooke died as a result of the injuries. A jury found Young guilty of first-degree murder, and he appealed. After explaining that first-degree murder is the unlawful killing of a person with malice and with premeditation and deliberation, the North Carolina Supreme Court rejected Young's contention that the evidence was insufficient to support a conviction.

State v. Young, 325 S.E.2d 181 (N.C. 1985).

intent to require as an essential element of first-degree murder substantially more reflection "than the mere amount of thought necessary to form the intention to kill." *People v. Cruz*, 605 P.2d 830, 834 (Cal. 1980). The Pennsylvania Supreme Court has defined malice aforethought more elaborately, saying it is "not only a particular ill will, but a hardness of heart, cruelty, recklessness of consequences, and a mind regardless of social duty." *Commonwealth v. Buzard*, 76 A.2d 394, 396 (Pa. 1950). Such malice may be expressed or may be implied from the circumstances under which a homicidal act is performed.

Many jurisdictions define first-degree murder based on the "premeditated intent" of the offender. For example, Florida classifies a homicide as a first-degree murder if the unlawful killing of a human being is "perpetrated from a premeditated design to effect the death of the person killed or any human being." West's Fla. Stat. Ann. § 782.04. Initially, one might be inclined to think of a premeditated act as requiring a lengthy period of deliberation. Indeed, dictionaries commonly define *premeditation* as a conscious and deliberate preplanning over a period of time. However, judicial decisions defining premeditation emphasize that although it requires thought beforehand, no particular length of time is required. The length of time necessary to deliberate, or to form a specific intent to kill, need only be time enough to form the required intent before the killing. It matters not how short that time may be, as long as the process of premeditation occurs at any point before the killing. See, for example, *State v. Corn*, 278 S.E.2d 221(N.C. 1981).

The prosecution may establish either malice aforethought or premeditation by a variety of evidentiary facts and circumstances. These include threats, quarrels, and expressions of ill will, as well as the nature of the weapon used, and the presence or absence of adequate provocation. Courts also consider any previous difficulties between the parties, the manner in which the homicide was committed, the nature of the wound inflicted, and the manner in which it was inflicted.

State v. Corder (S.D. 1990), illustrates the factors a court considers in determining if the evidence is sufficient to establish a defendant's premeditated design to effect death of a victim. An excerpt from the South Dakota Supreme Court's opinion appears at the end of the chapter.

Felony Murder

The common law developed a doctrine that where an accused was engaged in the commission of a felony and a homicide occurred, the felonious act was regarded as a substitute for the proof of malice aforethought required to find the defendant guilty of murder. Thus, it became **felony murder** when an accused unintentionally killed a human being while committing, or attempting to commit, such common-law felonies as burglary, arson, rape, or robbery. The theory was that if a killing resulted, even though unintentional or accidental, the required malice was carried over from the original felony. Consequently, the felon would be found guilty of murder.

Although of dubious ancestry, the felony murder doctrine has been incorporated into most criminal codes in the United States. See *People v. Aaron*, 229 N.W.2d 304 (Mich. 1980). With the proliferation of crimes classified as felonies, legislatures have generally limited the applicability of felony murder to felonies involving violence or posing great threat to life or limb (for example, rape, robbery, kidnapping, arson, and burglary). See, for example, West's Ann. Cal. Penal Code § 189. Recently, some have sought to equate certain felonious drug offenses with violent felonies. Some statutes provide for degrees of felony murder depending on the seriousness of the felony attempted or perpetrated by the accused, whether the killing occurred by a person other than the person perpetrating or attempting to perpetrate the felony, and whether the accused was present at the scene when the killing occurred. See, for example, West's Fla. Stat. Ann. § 782.04. Felony murder statutes have produced much litigation in the criminal courts. Some of the pertinent questions raised include the following:

- Can a felon who perpetrates an offense be guilty of felony murder where the victim of the intended offense kills a co-felon?
- Should the felon committing a crime such as robbery be guilty of felony murder if a police officer mistakenly kills the felon's intended victim?
- Can a felon be guilty of felony murder when a co-felon accidentally kills a bystander or a police officer?

Most courts have held that the doctrine of felony murder does not extend to a killing stemming from the commission of the felony if it is directly attributable to the act of someone other than the defendant or those actively participating with the defendant in the unlawful enterprise. Nevertheless, courts have arrived at different solutions to these and other problems arising under felony murder laws.

Perhaps questions such as these led the Michigan Supreme Court in 1980 to abrogate the felony murder doctrine. After commenting on how its prior decisions had already significantly restricted the doctrine, the court concluded that the rule that substitutes the intent to commit the underlying felony for the malice element of murder had to be abolished. Its abrogation of the doctrine does not make irrelevant the fact that a death occurred in the course of a felony. Rather, the court noted that a jury could properly infer malice from evidence that a defendant intentionally set in motion a force likely to cause death or great bodily harm. However, Michigan juries are no longer instructed to find malice if they are satisfied from all the evidence that it does not exist. *People v. Aaron*, supra.

A cogent argument can be made that the felony murder rule violates the basic requirement of moral culpability in the criminal law. Moreover, critics point out that under the early common law, conviction of a felony was punishable by death. Consequently, they note, when a death occurred in the commission of a felony and the accused was guilty of felony murder, no additional consequences resulted. This is not so today because no felony except murder (and certain federal offenses recently made capital offenses) committed under aggravating circumstances is punishable by death. Nevertheless, the felony murder doctrine is well established in most jurisdictions. With legislatures perceiving the need to take a "hard line" on crime, it is doubtful that many states will be motivated to repeal felony murder statutes. Therefore, courts will likely become increasingly conscious of the need to strictly interpret such statutes. Observing that it is the commission of a specified felony that supplants the requirement of premeditation for first-degree murder, the Florida Supreme Court declared that for the felon to be guilty of felony murder there must be some causal connection between the homicide and the underlying felony. *Bryant v. State,* 412 So.2d 347 (Fla. 1982).

Second-Degree Murder

In many jurisdictions, **second-degree murder** is a residual classification applied to unlawful homicides not evidenced by malice aforethought or premeditation, not occurring in conjunction with other felonies, and not falling within the statutory definition of manslaughter. More commonly, second-degree murder is defined as the defendant having a **depraved mind or heart.** Florida statutes define second-degree murder as a killing "perpetrated by any act **imminently dangerous** to another and evincing a depraved mind regardless of human life, although without any premeditated design to effect the death of any particular individual." West's Fla. Stat. Ann. § 782.04. Florida courts have said that an act is imminently dangerous to another and evinces a depraved mind if a person of ordinary judgment would know it is reasonably certain to kill or cause serious bodily injury to another and is done from ill will, hatred, spite, or an evil intent, so as to indicate an indifference to human life. See, for example, *Marasa v. State,* 394 So.2d 544 (Fla. App. 1981). Second-degree murder is usually a general-intent crime. *Gentry v. State,* 437 So.2d 1097 (Fla. 1983).

In practice, convictions for second-degree murder often reflect a **jury pardon.** A classic example is when the state prosecutes a defendant for first-degree murder

---

CASE-IN-POINT

Second-Degree Murder: Evidence of Depraved Indifference

The state charged a fifteen-and-a-half-year-old boy with murder in the second degree under Section 125.25(2) of the New York–McKinney's Penal Law, which provides as follows: "A person is guilty of murder in the second degree when: . . . (2) Under circumstances evincing a depraved indifference to human life, he recklessly engages in conduct which creates a grave risk of death to another person, and thereby causes the death of another person." The evidence at trial revealed the defendant loaded a mix of "live" and "dummy" shells at random into the magazine of a 12-gauge shotgun and then pumped a shell into the firing chamber, not knowing whether it was a "dummy" or "live" round. He next raised the gun to his shoulder and pointing it directly at the victim exclaimed, "Let's play Polish roulette," and asked,

"Who is first?" Then the defendant pulled the trigger, discharging a live round into a thirteen-year-old victim's chest, resulting in the eventual death of the victim.

On appeal, the court first distinguished the crime of second-degree murder by depraved indifference from manslaughter, by saying that it must be shown that the actor's reckless conduct is imminently dangerous and presents a grave risk of death, whereas in manslaughter the conduct need only present the lesser "substantial risk" of death. Then pointing out that the defendant had an intense interest in and a detailed knowledge of weapons and analogizing the incident to a macabre game of chance, the New York Court of Appeals held the evidence was legally sufficient to support the defendant's conviction of second-degree murder.

People v. Roe, 542 N.E.2d 610 (N.Y. 1989).

and the jury determines that the circumstances surrounding the killing do not show malice aforethought or premeditation, or simply do not justify the penalty, often death. In such an instance a jury sometimes returns a verdict for the lesser offense of second-degree murder, always a noncapital felony. We might generalize that second-degree murder convictions often occur when a jury is convinced the defendant acted recklessly or even outrageously, but with no intent to take the victim's life.

Manslaughter

As we have noted, there were two classes of manslaughter at common law: voluntary and involuntary. California, like many states, preserves that distinction and defines manslaughter as the "unlawful killing of a human being without malice." California law enumerates three categories: voluntary, involuntary, and vehicular. Voluntary manslaughter refers to instances where death of the victim occurs in a sudden quarrel or in the heat of passion. Involuntary manslaughter occurs where a death results from the commission of a lawful act that might produce death, in an unlawful manner, or without due caution and circumspection. The third category, vehicular homicide, involves death resulting from the perpetrator driving a vehicle while in the commission of an unlawful act not amounting to a felony, and not with gross negligence, or driving a vehicle in the commission of a lawful act that might produce death in an unlawful manner, and with gross negligence. West's Ann. Cal. Penal Code § 192.

Many other states define manslaughter without categorizing it as voluntary or involuntary. Still other state legislatures have defined manslaughter by degrees. For example, New York law provides that a person who recklessly causes the death of another person, commits an unlawful abortion on a female that causes her death, or intentionally causes or aids another to commit suicide commits manslaughter in the second degree. McKinney's N.Y. Penal Law § 125.15. However, a person who inflicts certain intentional serious injuries that cause the death of another under circumstances that do not constitute murder may be guilty of the more serious offense of manslaughter in the first degree if he or she (1) acts under the influence of extreme emotional disturbance or (2) commits an unlawful abortional act that causes the death of a female pregnant for more than twenty-four weeks unless it is an abortional act deemed justifiable by statutory exceptions. McKinney's N.Y. Penal Law § 125.20. Irrespective of whether a statute classifies manslaughter as voluntary, involuntary, or by degree, certain situations generally fall within the definition of the offense. Common examples include a death resulting from mutual combat or killing someone by use of excessive force while defending oneself or a family member or acting in defense of property.

The intent that must be established to obtain a conviction of manslaughter may depend on the nature of the charge. To establish voluntary manslaughter, the prosecution may have to establish the defendant's specific intent. On the other hand, in a prosecution for involuntary manslaughter, the defendant's intent need only be general and may be inferred from the defendant's act and surrounding circumstances.

Often a charge of involuntary manslaughter is based on allegations of criminal negligence. A highly publicized example of this arose from a tragic accident occurring in the film industry. In 1982 some Hollywood moviemakers shooting a scene for the movie *The Twilight Zone* used a helicopter that crashed on the set, decapitating an actor and a child and crushing another child. The state prosecuted the director and four of his associates for involuntary manslaughter, claiming they were guilty of criminal negligence. The defendants argued that the tragic deaths resulted from an unforeseeable accident. In May 1987, after a dramatic five-month trial, a jury found them all not guilty.

Provocation is frequently a factor in manslaughter trials. Provocation that would cause a reasonable person to lose control may be sufficient to convert an otherwise intentional killing of another to manslaughter. Mere words, however gross or insulting, are not sufficient to constitute provocation. Rather, to reduce a homicide from murder to manslaughter, it must generally be shown that there was sufficient provocation to excite in the defendant's mind such anger, rage, or terror as would obscure an ordinary person's reasoning and render the person incapable of cool reflection. See, for example, *Hardin v. State,* 404 N.E.2d 1354 (Ind. 1980). A classic example is discovering one's spouse in an act of adultery with significant sexual contact taking place. See, for example, *Tripp v. State,* 374 A.2d 384 (Md. App. 1977).

Modern statutes often define manslaughter as consisting of the negligent performance of a legal duty or the doing of a lawful act in an unlawful manner. In addition to the more common instances, courts have upheld manslaughter convictions under such statutes for death occurring because of criminal negligence of medical practitioners or because of parental failure to provide medical attention or adequate nourishment for their children. See, for example, *People v. Ogg,* 182 N.W.2d 570 (Mich. App. 1970). The California Supreme Court held that a parent of a seriously ill child who makes only provision for prayer may be guilty of such criminal negligence that the parent can be found guilty of involuntary manslaughter or child endangerment. *Walker v. Superior Court,* 763 P.2d 852 (Cal. 1988).

In a high-profile case, in October 1997, a Massachusetts jury found Louise Woodward, a young British *au pair* serving an American family, guilty of second-degree murder in the death of an eight-month-old child under her care. The child died a few days after receiving a severe head trauma while in Ms. Woodward's care. There was no evidence the defendant had ever abused or injured the child prior to the fatal injury. Fearing a compromise verdict, Ms. Woodward's counsel requested the court not instruct the jury on the offense of manslaughter. After the verdict, the trial judge found the defendant's actions "were characterized by confusion, inexperience, frustration, immaturity and some anger, but not malice (in the legal sense) supporting a conviction for second degree murder" and reduced the defendant's conviction to manslaughter. The prosecution challenged the trial judge's action; however,

In *Manuel v. State* (1977), reprinted at the end of the chapter, a Florida appellate court distinguishes second-degree murder from the offense of manslaughter.

CASE-IN-POINT ### Manslaughter by Culpable Negligence

William Burge and Juanita Calloway became involved in an argument over the fact that Calloway was apparently sleeping with one of her sons. When Calloway displayed a knife, Burge pulled a gun that he carried to kill snakes that lurked in the walls of his house. Burge pointed the gun at Calloway and cocked it. Burge then pushed Calloway in an attempt to get her into his car. When he did, Calloway's hand hit the gun and it went off, severely wounding Calloway. While driving her to the hospital, Burge ran out of gas and called an ambulance. Calloway died en route to the hospital.

Despite his plea of self-defense, a jury found Burge guilty of manslaughter by culpable negligence. In affirming the conviction, the Mississippi Supreme Court rejected the defendant's contentions of self-defense and excusable and justifiable homicide. The court observed that the jury could reasonably have determined that although the victim was holding a knife the defendant was not in danger of great personal injury.

Burge v. State, 472 So.2d 392 (Miss. 1985).

CASE-IN-POINT

Vehicular Homicide: Criminal Liability for Second Accident

On the evening of February 14, 1987, Gary Dawson was a passenger in a car driven by Richard Peaslee, Jr., on a snow-packed, icy road in Maine. As a result of Peaslee's intentional "fishtailing," the car went out of control and overturned, throwing Dawson onto the road. Dawson, unable to move, lay on the road where he was run over by another vehicle several minutes later. Dawson died before help arrived on the scene. A jury found Peaslee guilty of vehicular manslaughter, and he appealed.

In affirming Peaslee's conviction, the Maine Supreme Court rejected his contention that he was not criminally responsible for the second accident. "The separate accidents were not independent of each other," said the court, "because Dawson would not have been lying immobile on the road in the path of the other car were it not for Peaslee's conduct." Moreover, the court concluded that "[w]hether Dawson was killed by the first or second impact makes no difference."

State v. Peaslee, 571 A.2d 825 (Me. 1990).

the Massachusetts Supreme Judicial Court concluded that the trial judge did not abuse his discretion. *Commonwealth v. Woodward,* 694 N.E.2d 1277 (Mass. 1998).

Vehicular Homicide

The carnage on American highways has prompted many states to enact statutes making **vehicular homicide** a specific felony, rather than opting to rely on prosecutors charging a defendant with manslaughter for causing a traffic death. The Florida statute is typical:

> "Vehicular homicide" is the killing of a human being or the killing of a viable fetus by any injury to the mother caused by the operation of a motor vehicle by another in a reckless manner likely to cause the death of, or great bodily harm to, another. West's Fla. Stat. Ann. § 782.071.

The Florida Supreme Court has said that in enacting the statute the legislature created a separate offense with a lesser standard of proof than is required for conviction under the state's manslaughter statute. Thus, the statute enables the prosecution to secure a conviction where the state is unable to meet the level of proof otherwise required in establishing manslaughter. Therefore, the court said the state could charge a defendant with manslaughter for operating a motor vehicle in a culpably negligent manner that causes the death of a human being or could proceed under vehicular homicide, a lesser included offense. *State v. Young,* 371 So.2d 1029 (Fla. 1979).

Justifiable and Excusable Homicide

As in most jurisdictions, California classifies nonculpable homicide as excusable or justifiable. It is excusable "when committed by accident or misfortune or in doing any other lawful act by lawful means, with usual and ordinary caution, and without any unlawful intent." It may also be excusable "when committed in the heat of passion, or on sudden and sufficient provocation, or on sudden combat where no undue advantage is taken nor any dangerous weapon is used and the killing is not done in a cruel or unusual manner." West's Ann. Cal. Penal Code § 195. Examples of **excusable**

homicide include killing someone when resisting attempts to murder or to inflict great bodily injury upon a person; or when in defense of a person's home under certain circumstances; or in some instances of self-defense where there is a reasonable ground to apprehend imminent danger of great bodily harm to a person's self or spouse, parent, or child. See West's Ann Cal. Penal Code § 196; *People v. Collins,* 11 Cal. Rptr. 504 (Cal. App. 1961).

When death is inflicted by public officers in obedience to a court judgment or in discharge of certain other legal duties, or when necessarily committed in apprehending felons, it is considered **justifiable homicide.** West's Ann. Cal. Penal Code § 196; *People v. Young,* 29 Cal. Rptr. 595 (Cal. App. 1963).

Removal of Life-Support Systems

Another area of contemporary concern has resulted from technological advances in medicine that have enabled physicians to use sophisticated life-support systems to prolong life for indefinite periods. In a landmark case involving Karen Quinlan, the New Jersey Supreme Court in 1976 reviewed the request of Karen's parents to remove the life-support systems sustaining the life of their daughter, who lay in a comatose state with no reasonable medical probability of regaining a sapient existence. The court ruled that withdrawal of such life-support systems, under the circumstances, would not constitute a criminal homicide. *In re Quinlan,* 355 A.2d 647 (N.J. 1976).

A significant body of decisional law has now developed on the issue of when life-sustaining measures should be initiated and when they may be removed. Generally, a competent adult who is terminally ill may decide to forgo such extraordinary measures or may order such measures discontinued. However, there are varying judicial opinions as to when, under what circumstances, and by whom discontinuance may be ordered for minors and incompetents. Statutes in several states now address many of the problems in this area, yet there is no statutory or judicial consensus on the procedures to effect discontinuance. Moreover, the issue of whether removal of life-support systems extends to discontinuance of hydration and nourishment as well as respirators and similar life-prolonging devices has surfaced. These problems involve moral, ethical, and religious concerns that legislators and judges must consider when developing viable policy in this area. Courts have been cautious not to allow criminal prosecutions where life-sustaining medical procedures have been discontinued in good faith based on competent medical advice and consent of a competent patient and the patient's family. See, for example, *Barber v. Superior Court,* 195 Cal. Rptr. 484 (Cal. App. 1983).

Prosecutorial Burdens in Homicide Cases

To obtain a conviction in a homicide case, the prosecution bears several burdens peculiar to homicide cases. The victim of the crime must have been alive, the defendant's actions must be the cause of the victim's death, and, in some jurisdictions, death of the victim must occur within a stated period of time. Although these may appear to be matters easily proven, sometimes they pose problems for prosecutors.

REQUIREMENT THAT VICTIM WAS "ALIVE" BEFORE THE HOMICIDAL ACT

By definition, a criminal homicide consists of someone taking another person's life. It follows that before the accused can be found guilty of a homicidal crime, the prosecution must establish that the victim was alive before the accused's criminal act. In most instances this is not too difficult, but consider, for example, the killing of a fetus. Under common law a child was not considered born until the umbilical cord had been severed, and the child's circulation became independent of its mother's.

In the highly publicized case of *Keeler v. Superior Court*, 470 P.2d 617 (Cal. 1970), the California Supreme Court held that in enacting its homicide statute, the legislature intended it to have the settled common-law meaning that to be the subject of homicide a fetus must be "born alive." Consequently, the court overturned a murder conviction where the defendant stomped on a pregnant woman's abdomen, thereby causing the death of her fetus. As a result, California amended section 187 of its penal code that defines murder to include the present language, *"the unlawful killing of a human being, or a fetus, with malice aforethought* [emphasis added]."

Absent legislative reform, many courts today would probably follow the view taken by the California court before the legislative amendment to section 187.

THE *CORPUS DELICTI* REQUIREMENT

In addition to establishing that a human being was alive before a killing took place, the prosecution must always establish the **corpus delicti,** or body of the crime. The *corpus delicti* consists of the fact that a human being is dead and that the death was caused by the criminal act or agency of another person. *State v. Feuillerat,* 292 N.W.2d 326 (S.D. 1980). Some argue that the *corpus delicti* requirement is simply a technicality that impedes the search for truth. Others contend that by requiring some independent evidence to link a defendant to the crime charged ensures that no one is convicted based on a mistake or fabricated confession. This rule is firmly implanted in American law. To prove the *corpus delicti,* the prosecution must show by either direct or circumstantial evidence, independent of the accused's statements, that the victim died as a result of a criminal act. Usually, the victim's body is available for medical examination, and a physician can testify about the cause of death. If the deceased's body is not recovered and the victim's death cannot be determined to have resulted from a criminal act, a conviction cannot be lawfully obtained. Consider the case of *Ex parte Flodstrom,* 277 P.2d 101 (Cal. 1954). There, it could not be determined if a baby died from the mother's alleged homicidal act or whether death occurred as a result of natural causes. Consequently, since there was no evidence available to establish the *corpus delicti,* the appellate court discharged the accused mother from custody on the ground that she was being held to answer charges of murder without probable cause.

THE PROXIMATE CAUSE OF THE VICTIM'S DEATH

To hold a defendant responsible for the death of a victim, the prosecution must establish that the defendant's act was the **proximate cause** of the victim's death. This means that the victim's death must have been the natural and probable consequence of the defendant's unlawful conduct.

Where A shoots or physically beats B, or A pushes B out of a window or overboard from a boat, or A administers poison to B, medical evidence can usually establish the cause of the victim's death. However, killings can be accomplished in hundreds of ways. For example, death can be precipitated by fright or shock or by other means not involving physical contact with the victim. The accused's acts or omissions need not be the immediate cause of the victim's death as long as the death results naturally from the accused's conduct.

Some situations present perplexing issues for medical experts and courts. For example, a defendant fired a shot into the water about six feet from a boat occupied by two boys. When a second shot struck nearer to the boat than the first, one of the boys leaped out of the boat into the water. The boat capsized with the remaining boy in it. Both boys drowned. The defendant argued that he could not be guilty of causing the death of the boy who drowned when the boat overturned. The Tennessee Supreme Court rejected his contention and upheld the defendant's conviction for involuntary manslaughter, concluding that it was his shots, not the act of the boy who caused the boat to capsize, that caused the decedent's death. *Letner v. State*, 299 S.W. 1049 (Tenn. 1927).

In another instance, a wife who had been severely beaten by her husband in the past was impelled by fear of another beating at his hands to jump from a moving automobile. She died from injuries sustained. Her husband was charged with her murder and was found guilty of the lesser offense of manslaughter. On appeal, the Florida Supreme Court upheld the conviction. *Whaley v. State*, 26 So.2d 656 (Fla. 1946).

In a recent prosecution for several counts of attempted murder, the evidence revealed that the defendant was aware that he had tested positive for human immunodeficiency virus (HIV). The defendant's probation officer had even informed him that if he passed HIV to another person, "he would be killing someone." Nevertheless, he repeatedly and intentionally engaged in sexual activity with multiple partners and refused to take "safe sex" precautions. The defendant was convicted, and he appealed. He argued that he meant only to satisfy himself sexually and such was insufficient to prove intent to cause death. The Oregon Court of Appeals rejected his appeal and held that the defendant did not act impulsively merely to satisfy his sexual desire; rather, he acted deliberately to cause his victims serious bodily injury and death. *State v. Hinkhouse*, 912 P.2d 921 (Or. App. 1996).

WHEN DEATH OCCURS

Just as it is necessary to determine that a homicide victim was alive before the injury that caused death, it is also necessary to establish that death has, in fact, occurred. In most instances, the classic definition will suffice: Death occurs when the heart stops beating and respiration ends. However, technological advances have rendered this definition obsolete as the sole means of determining when death occurs. Many state legislatures have now adopted a definition of **brain death** that specifies that irreversible cessation of total brain functions constitutes death. In other instances, courts have adopted the new definition. See, for example, *In re Bowman*, 617 P.2d 731 (Wash. 1980).

THE "ONE YEAR AND A DAY" RULE

Another obstacle to the prosecution of homicide cases can be the common-law **one year and a day rule.** Under this ancient common-law doctrine, if more than a year and a day intervened between the injury inflicted by the accused and the victim's death, the person who caused the injury could not be held criminally responsible for the victim's death. *State v. Moore*, 199 So. 661 (La. 1940). This inflexible rule continued because of uncertainties of medical science in establishing the cause of a victim's death after a lengthy period had elapsed. But in an age of advancing medical technology, the "one year and a day" rule has little relevance.

In 1984 the North Carolina Supreme Court observed that to remain oblivious to advances in medical science when considering whether to apply such an ancient common-law rule would be "folly." *State v. Hefler*, 310 S.E.2d 310 (N.C. 1984). Many states have since abolished the rule by statute; other states have modified it. California law, which formerly provided that to make a killing either murder or manslaughter the victim must die within three years, amended its statute in 1996 to stipulate that "[i]f death occurs beyond the time of three years and a day, there shall be a rebuttal presumption that the killing was not criminal." West's Ann. Cal. Penal Code § 194. In other states, courts have abolished the rule by judicial decision. Nevertheless, where such temporal requirements have not been abrogated, the prosecution must establish that the victim's death occurred within the prescribed common-law or statutory period.

Defenses to Homicidal Crimes

Defendants charged with murder or manslaughter frequently plead either self-defense or insanity. These defenses are discussed in detail in Chapter 14. Where an accused defends against a charge of murder, the **heat of passion** defense discussed earlier may be available in some instances, as would be the defense of reasonable care or accidental killing in others.

....

Suicide

The early English common law defined the offense of **suicide** as the intentional taking of a person's life by self-destruction. Suicide was not only regarded as being contrary to nature; it was regarded as an offense against the biblical commandment "Thou shalt not kill." Suicide was a species of felony punishable by forfeiture of the decedent's goods and chattels because it deprived the king of one of his subjects.

In the United States, the thrust of the criminal law has been to make it an offense to cause or aid another person to commit suicide, with many states making **assisted suicide** a crime. New York law provides that a person who "intentionally causes or aids another person to commit suicide" is guilty of manslaughter in the second degree. McKinney's N.Y. Penal Law § 125.15. In Texas, a person who, with intent to promote or assist in the commission of suicide, aids or attempts to aid another to commit suicide is guilty of a misdemeanor. If the actor's conduct causes a suicide or an attempted suicide that results in serious bodily injury, the offense becomes a felony. Vernon's Tex. Penal Code Ann. § 22.08. Until recently, the validity of laws of this character went unchallenged. As we explain in the following sections, this is no longer the case.

On November 8, 1994, Oregon voters adopted a Death with Dignity Act that allows terminally ill adult patients to obtain a physician's prescription for a lethal dose of medication. Two doctors must determine that the patient has less than six months to live and is mentally competent. The patient must request a lethal dose of medicine both orally and in writing and must wait at least fifteen days to obtain it. Although a federal district court originally enjoined the enforcement of the act, the injunction was vacated by the U.S. Court of Appeals. *Lee v. State of Oregon,* 107 F.3d 1382 (9th Cir. 1997). The U.S. Supreme Court declined to review the case. 522 U.S. 927, 118 S.Ct. 328, 139 L.Ed.2d 254 (1997).

The Michigan Experience

Over the past several years, a series of judicial decisions have held that physicians may withhold or withdraw medical treatment at a patient's request. But the courts recognized a sharp distinction between such activity and administering drugs to assist a person to take his or her own life. Michigan, and several other states, had no laws against assisted suicide. This was dramatized on June 4, 1990, when a fifty-four-year-old woman suffering from Alzheimer's disease took her life by pressing a button that injected a lethal substance into her system through use of a suicide machine developed by Dr. Jack Kevorkian, a retired Michigan pathologist. Murder charges filed against the doctor were dismissed on the grounds that Michigan had no law against assisted suicide and that the prosecutors failed to show that the doctor tripped the device used to effect the death. After additional instances of assisted suicide of terminally ill patients, the Michigan legislature enacted a bill banning assisted suicide effective on April 1, 1993.

In succeeding years, the press reported numerous instances of alleged participation by Dr. Kevorkian in assisting terminally ill persons to commit suicide. After several unsuccessful attempts to prosecute Kevorkian, in 1999 a Michigan jury found him guilty of second-degree murder in the death of a man suffering from Lou Gehrig's disease. The court sentenced him to serve 10–25 years in prison. In February 2000, the media reported that he had been denied release on bond pending his appeal from his conviction and sentence.

During the 1990s, state laws that prohibit assisted suicide were challenged on constitutional grounds in instances where terminally ill patients sought to end their lives with the aid of a physician. Soon the state of Washington became the venue for a direct challenge to a state statute prohibiting assisted suicide, a challenge that would eventually lead to a seminal decision by the United States Supreme Court.

The Washington Experience

To prevent assisted suicide in the state of Washington, the legislature enacted a law providing that "[a] person is guilty of promoting a suicide attempt when he knowingly causes or aids another person to attempt suicide." Wash. Rev. Code § 9A.36.060(1) (1994). "Promoting a suicide attempt" is a felony, punishable by up to five years' imprisonment and up to a $10,000 fine. §§ 9A.36.060(2) and 9A.20.021(1)(c). However, Washington's Natural Death Act, enacted in 1979, states that the "withholding or withdrawal of life sustaining treatment" at a patient's direction "shall not, for any purpose, constitute a suicide." Wash. Rev. Code § 70.122.070(1).

In 1994 the U.S. District Court for the Western District of Washington ruled that Washington's statute banning assisted suicide was unconstitutional. *Compassion in Dying v. Washington,* 850 F. Supp. 1454, 1459 (W.D. Wash. 1994). A panel of the Court of Appeals for the Ninth Circuit reversed, emphasizing that "[i]n the two hundred and five years of our existence no constitutional right to aid in killing oneself has ever been asserted and upheld by a court of final jurisdiction." *Compassion in Dying v. Washington,* 49 F. 3d 586, 591 (1995). Following the reversal by the three-judge appellate panel, the Ninth Circuit reheard the case *en banc,* reversed the panel's decision, and affirmed the District Court. *Compassion in Dying v. Washington,* 79 F. 3d 790, 798 (1996). In its *en banc* decision the Ninth Circuit concluded that "the Constitution encompasses a due process liberty interest in controlling the time and manner of one's death—that there is, in short, a constitutionally recognized 'right to die.'" 79 F.3d at 816. After "[w]eighing and then balancing" this interest against Washington's various interests, the court held that the State's assisted suicide ban was unconstitutional "as applied to terminally ill competent adults who wish to hasten their deaths with medication prescribed by their physicians." 79 F.3d 836, 837.

The U.S. Supreme Court granted certiorari and on June 26, 1997, in *Washington v. Glucksberg,* 521 U.S. 844, 117 S.Ct. 2258, 138 L.Ed.2d 772 (1997), reversed the Ninth Circuit's decision. Writing for a unanimous Court, Chief Justice Rehnquist discussed the historical and cultural background of laws prohibiting assisted suicide.

He pointed out that in almost every state it is a crime to assist in a suicide and that the statutes banning assisted suicide are long-standing expressions of the states' commitment to the protection and preservation of all human life.

The Court's opinion analyzed the interests that come into play in determining whether a statute banning assisted suicide passes constitutional muster. In doing so, the Court rejected any parallel between a person's right to terminate medical treatment and the "right" to have assistance in committing suicide. As the Court opined,

> We need not weigh exactingly the relative strengths of these various interests. They are unquestionably important and legitimate, and Washington's ban on assisted suicide is at least reasonably related to their promotion and protection. We therefore hold that Wash. Rev. Code § 9A.36.060(1) (1994) does not violate the Fourteenth Amendment, either on its face or "as applied to competent, terminally ill adults who wish to hasten their deaths by obtaining medication prescribed by their doctors." 521 U.S. at 844, 117 S.Ct. at 2275, 138 L.Ed.2d at 797.

Following its recent deference to the lawmaking role of the states, the Court left the issue somewhat ajar:

> Throughout the Nation, Americans are engaged in an earnest and profound debate about the morality, legality, and practicality of physician assisted suicide. Our holding permits this debate to continue, as it should in a democratic society. 521 U.S. at 844, 117 S.Ct. at 2275, 138 L.Ed.2d at 797.

Competing Values in Suicide Laws

Laws against assisted suicide bring into play significant policy issues and require legislatures to carefully balance competing claims of individual liberty, ethics, and the interest of society. Some proponents of allowing assisted suicide argue that it simply

CASE-IN-POINT   **Assisted Suicide**

In 1997 Charles E. Hall, a mentally competent, but terminally ill, patient, and his physician, Cecil McIver, M.D., sought to have a Florida court declare that section 782.08, Florida Statutes, which prohibits assisted suicide, violated the Privacy Clause of the Florida Constitution and the Due Process and Equal Protection Clauses of the Fourteenth Amendment to the United States Constitution. They sought an injunction against the state attorney from prosecuting the physician for giving deliberate assistance to Mr. Hall in committing suicide. Basing its conclusion on Florida's privacy provision and the federal Equal Protection Clause, the trial court held that the Florida law could not be constitutionally enforced against Mr. Hall and Dr. McIver. The

Florida Supreme Court granted an expedited review. By the time it rendered its decision on July 17, 1997, the U.S. Supreme Court had ruled that state laws prohibiting assisted suicide pass muster under the federal constitution. On basis of that decision the Florida Supreme Court summarily disposed of the contention that the Florida law violated the U.S. Constitution. The court then proceeded to find that neither was the explicit privacy provision in the Florida constitution offended by the state's 129-year old statute prohibiting assisted suicide. In concluding its opinion, the court opted to leave "social policy" to the state legislature when it observed that "[w]e do not hold that a carefully crafted statute authorizing assisted suicide would be unconstitutional."

Krischer v. McIver, 697 So.2d 97 (Fla. 1997).

enables a person who has a rational capacity to make a choice. Those who reject this view urge that the state has an interest in the preservation of life and argue that some individuals may elect to die needlessly as a result of misdiagnosis. Moreover, opponents of legalizing assistable suicide argue that allowing assisted suicide leads to an indifference to the value of life. As a result of the Supreme Court's 1997 decision in *Washington v. Glucksberg,* supra, the states may enforce statutory bans on assisted suicide with more assurance, yet as the terminally ill population continues to increase, the debate is destined to continue. The Supreme Court's decision places that debate in the state legislatures and the state judicial tribunals. Less than one month after the Court's eagerly awaited decision was announced, the Florida Supreme Court ruled that the state statute prohibiting assisted suicide did not offend the state constitution. *Krischer v. McIver,* 697 So.2d 97 (Fla. 1997).

Rape and Sexual Battery

There are early biblical accounts of the offense of rape; however, the law of rape, as it exists today, has its roots in the early English common law. It was a felony for a male to have unlawful **carnal knowledge** (that is, sexual intercourse) of a female by force and against her will. This is usually referred to as **common-law rape** or **forcible rape.** In later stages of the English law, it became a statutory offense for a man to have carnal knowledge of a female child less than ten years of age with or without the child's consent. This latter offense came to be known as **statutory rape.**

The common-law offenses required penetration, however slight, of the female's sexual organ by the male sexual organ; no emission of seed was required. At common law, there was a conclusive presumption that a male under age fourteen could not commit the crime of rape.

Common-law rape contemplated unlawful intercourse; therefore, a husband could not be guilty of raping his wife. Although this **marital exception** is of somewhat dubious judicial origin, it is generally credited to the writings of Sir Matthew Hale, who served as Lord Chief Justice in England from 1671 to 1676. Of course, in egregious cases the husband could be charged with assault or battery of his wife. Furthermore, a husband or even another woman could be charged as an aider or abettor if he or she assisted or procured another man to rape his wife.

More than two centuries after Hale's demise, in March 1991, England's Court of Appeal dismissed an appeal by a man who was convicted of an attempted rape of his estranged wife. In delivering the opinion of the five-judge court, the Lord Chief Justice observed that a rapist remains a rapist irrespective of his relationship with his victim. Further, the court observed the centuries-old legal doctrine that a husband could not be guilty of raping his wife no longer represented the law, considering the position of a wife in contemporary society.

The American Approach

The new American states followed the common-law scheme in statutorily defining rape; however, two principal changes soon occurred. First, many states explicitly rejected the common-law presumption that males under age fourteen could not commit the offense. Second, legislatures in most states made consensual intercourse with a young female an offense (statutory rape) if the female was younger than sixteen or

Does Asking an Attacker to Wear a Condom Constitute Consent to Sex?

In May 1993, in Travis County, Texas, Joel Valdez, a twenty-eight-year-old defendant who was charged with rape, claimed that the female with whom he admittedly had sexual intercourse had asked him to wear a condom. Valdez testified that he complied with the woman's request and that accordingly they were simply "making love." But the twenty-six-year-old complainant explained that she pleaded with her attacker to wear a condom only to protect herself from AIDS. The jury in Austin, Texas, found Valdez guilty of rape, implicitly finding that asking the attacker to wear a condom does not constitute consent to sexual intercourse.

eighteen, rather than ten. Some, however, added the qualification that the female must have been "of previous chaste character."

American courts disagreed on the intent required for a defendant to be guilty of rape. Some held that no intent other than that evidenced by the doing of the act of intercourse was needed. See, for example, *Walden v. State,* 156 S.W.2d 385 (Tenn. 1941). Others required proof of the defendant's specific intent. See, for example, *Thomas v. State,* 95 P.2d 658 (Okl. Crim. App. 1939).

Courts in American jurisdictions struggled with the requirements of **force** and **consent** in the law of forcible rape. Some judges instructed juries that "for the defendant to be found guilty of rape, you must find that the woman resisted to her utmost." Later cases recognized that it was not necessary for a female victim to resist to the utmost; rather, the degree of resistance came to be regarded as a relative matter dependent on all the circumstances surrounding the incident. Yet courts continued to recognize that resistance generally had to be more than a mere negative verbal response by a female.

All courts recognized that to constitute common-law rape, sexual intercourse had to be without the female's consent. However, there could be no valid consent by a woman who was asleep, unconscious, or mentally incapable. Likewise, consent obtained by fraud or impersonation or through pretext was invalid. Thus, if a man impersonated a woman's husband and caused her to submit to sexual intercourse, he would be guilty of rape. Likewise, a physician who had intercourse with female patients who were not conscious of the nature of the doctor's acts because of the treatments being administered was properly found guilty of rape. *People v. Minkowski,* 23 Cal. Rptr. 92 (Cal. App. 1962).

Statutory Rape Laws

In America, state legislatures enacted laws to protect young women from acts of sexual intercourse. These statutory rape laws usually stipulate that carnal knowledge (sexual intercourse) with a female under age sixteen, seventeen, or eighteen is a crime. In contrast with common-law rape, the elements of force and consent are irrelevant in statutory rape laws. In effect, underage females are deemed unable to validly consent to sexual relations. A few states have allowed a male to defend against a charge of statutory rape on the basis that he was mistaken about the female's age, but most hold a male defendant strictly liable even if he made a reasonable inquiry in good faith to determine the victim's age. We discuss this concept of a "strict liability" in Chapter 4.

A California law making statutory rape a crime was challenged on the basis of gender discrimination because only males could be prosecuted for the offense. The United States Supreme Court rejected the challenge. *Michael M. v. Superior Court,* 450 U.S. 464, 101 S.Ct. 1200, 67 L.Ed.2d 437 (1981). Notwithstanding, the trend is for newer statutory rape laws to be phrased in gender-neutral terms.

Statutory rape laws are now gender-neutral in most states, and some impose penalties only if there is at least a two-to five-year disparity between the ages of the perpetrator and the underage party. Obviously, it would be inconceivable to prosecute every minor who has a consensual sexual relationship. The original concept of statutory rape laws was to protect the chastity of young females; however, those who support these laws now emphasize both the psychological effects and threat of disease that accompany sexual encounters involving minors. They also point out that it is adult males who impregnate most teenage mothers and that, when vigorously enforced, statutory rape laws that focus on sexual relationships involving age discrepancies of several years are one solution to the problem of teenage pregnancy. In 1996 the Florida legislature made it a second-degree felony for a person age twenty-four or older to engage in sex with a person age sixteen or seventeen. West's Fla. Stat. Ann. § 794.05.

There is universal agreement that very young children should be protected from sexual predators, but there is considerable opposition to statutory rape laws. Opponents argue that these laws are out of touch with present-day sexual mores. Some see statutory rape laws as depriving women in their late teens of exercising a personal choice; others point out that these laws are largely unobserved and lend themselves to selective enforcement along the lines of race and social class. Despite the conflict in views, it appears that for the foreseeable future statutory rape laws, now often termed "voluntary sexual assault or battery" laws, will remain on the American legal scene.

Reform in the American Law of Rape

During the late 1970s and the 1980s, protests led to several statutory and judicial reforms in the law of rape. Initially, many such protests were by women's groups who complained of traumatic encounters between female victims and police, prosecutors, defense attorneys, and courts. In all too many instances, women's groups contended, a female rape victim was degraded and made to feel ashamed for the assault she suffered. As societal awareness increased, significant changes in the law occurred. Before examining a modern criminal code proscribing sexual offenses, we will examine the more significant legislative and judicial reforms in this area.

LEGISLATIVE REFORMS

Legislative reforms focused on making rape a **gender-neutral offense,** dividing the offense into categories, and adopting rape shield laws. The denomination of rape as sexual battery and making it a gender-neutral offense became a basic reform. No longer was the offense limited to the common-law concept of vaginal rape of a female. The offender and victim may be of either sex, and newer statutes embrace all types of sexual impositions, including anal, oral, or vaginal penetrations by a sex organ or by another object, excepting acts performed for *bona fide* medical purposes. In many states, either statutes or judicial decisions now provide that a husband may be charged with rape of his wife.

The trend of the newer statutes has been to divide the offense of sexual battery into various classifications. Punishment varies according to the type of sexual conduct or contact, the character and extent of force used, and the age and vulnerability of the victim. Those who commit sexual batteries against the helpless, and those who take advantage of their position of familial or supervisory authority, can be singled out for special punishment. These reforms have achieved more just results in punishing offenders. Furthermore, proper classification of offenses has led to convictions where merited by the evidence.

One of the most significant legal reforms concerning rape has been the enactment of **rape shield laws.** In a prosecution for rape (or sexual battery), these laws preclude presentation of evidence of a victim's prior sexual activity with anyone other than the defendant. Even where the defendant seeks to introduce evidence of prior relations with a victim, statutes often require such evidence to be first presented to the court *in camera* for a determination as to whether the evidence of the defendant's prior relationship with the victim is relevant to the victim's consent.

Rape shield laws are based on the theory that a victim's prior sexual activity is not probative of whether the victim has been violated in the instance for which the defendant stands accused. Thus, in *State v. Madsen,* 772 S.W.2d 656 (Mo. 1989), the Missouri Supreme Court held that neither evidence of a victim having a "live-in" boyfriend or having two illegitimate children was relevant in a prosecution for rape. But can a female victim offer testimony of a prior rape to explain her conduct in failing to resist an attacker? In *Raines v. State,* 382 S.E.2d 738 (Ga. App. 1989), the appellate court found this to be appropriate.

In interpreting the applicability of rape shield laws to some unusual factual situations, courts have faced some difficult judgments. In a Massachusetts decision, the court ruled that a defendant charged with rape should have been allowed to question the complainant as to whether she had sexual intercourse with anyone else on the night of the attack. The court concluded that such evidence would not constitute an attack on the complainant's credibility. Rather, the court held that such evidence tended to support the defendant's theory that someone else had attacked the complainant and that she had wrongly accused him. *Commonwealth v. Fitzgerald,* 590 N.E.2d 1151 (Mass. 1992).

A Virginia appellate court ruled that evidence that a victim did not report the alleged rape until a month after the incident, when she learned that she had contracted gonorrhea, was admissible to show ill will of the complainant. The court found that such evidence did not relate to the sexual conduct of the victim and was therefore not barred by the Virginia rape shield statute. *Evans v. Commonwealth,* 415 S.E.2d 851 (Va. App. 1992).

JUDICIAL REFORMS

Significant judicial reforms have also occurred in the law of rape. For example, for many years courts have not insisted that a woman must "resist to the utmost" to establish that her sexual privacy has been violated. This is consistent with the advice of law enforcement officers, who frequently caution women that violent resistance to a rapist's attack can result in the victim's serious injury or death. In considering whether a victim's resistance has been overcome, courts find it appropriate to consider several factors. The extent of the offender's force and violence remains important. So, too, is the psychological and emotional stress of a female victim whose sensibilities are outraged by fear of violation of her bodily integrity.

Courts have also come to realize that there is no unique reason to single out the testimony of a sexual battery victim and instruct juries that it deserves more scrutiny

In *State v. Studham,* reprinted at the end of the chapter, the Utah Supreme Court (1977) explains how force can be psychological as well as physical and how this relates to sexual assault.

than the testimony of other crime victims. The low conviction rate for rape defendants belies the need for special scrutiny for the uncorroborated testimony of a rape victim. In fact, data compiled several years ago by the Federal Bureau of Investigation revealed that of the FBI's four violent crimes (murder, forcible rape, robbery, and aggravated assault), rape had the highest rate of acquittal or dismissal. See *People v. Rincon-Pineda*, 538 P.2d 247 (Cal. 1975).

A Contemporary Statutory Treatment of Sexual Offenses

Michigan has modern, comprehensive laws that classify criminal sexual conduct by various degrees, depending on whether it involves sexual penetration or sexual contact with another person as well as other factors. It defines **sexual penetration** as sexual intercourse, cunnilingus, fellatio, anal intercourse, or any other intrusion, however slight, of any part of a person's body or of any object into the genital or anal openings of another person's body, but emission of seed is not required. Sexual contact is defined as including the intentional touching of the victim's intimate parts or the intentional touching of the clothing covering the immediate area of the victim's intimate parts, if that intentional touching can reasonably be construed as being for the purpose of sexual arousal or gratification. Mich. Comp. Laws Ann. § 750.520a(k)(l).

Section 720.520(b) deals with first-degree criminal sexual conduct and provides the following:

1. A person is guilty of criminal sexual conduct in the first degree if he or she engages in sexual penetration with another person and if any of the following circumstances exists:

    (a) That other person is under 13 years of age.

    (b) That other person is at least 13 but less than 16 years of age and any of the following:

    (i) The actor is a member of the same household as the victim.

    (ii) The actor is related to the victim by blood or affinity to the fourth degree.

    (iii) The actor is in a position of authority over the victim and used this authority to coerce the victim to submit.

    (c) Sexual penetration occurs under circumstances involving the commission of any other felony.

    (d) The actor is aided or abetted by 1 or more other persons and either of the following circumstances exists:

    (i) The actor knows or has reason to know that the victim is mentally incapable, mentally incapacitated, or physically helpless.

    (ii) The actor uses force or coercion to accomplish the sexual penetration. Force or coercion includes but is not limited to any of the circumstances listed in subdivision (f)(i) to (v).

    (e) The actor is armed with a weapon or any article used or fashioned in a manner to lead the victim to reasonably believe it to be a weapon.

    (f) The actor causes personal injury to the victim and force or coercion is used to accomplish sexual penetration. Force or coercion includes but is not limited to any of the following circumstances:

    (i) When the actor overcomes the victim through the actual application of physical force or physical violence.

(ii) When the actor coerces the victim to submit by threatening to use force or violence on the victim, and the victim believes that the actor has the present ability to execute these threats.

(iii) When the actor coerces the victim to submit by threatening to retaliate in the future against the victim, or any other person, and the victim believes that the actor has the ability to execute this threat. As used in this subdivision, "to retaliate" includes threats of physical punishment, kidnapping, or extortion.

(iv) When the actor engages in the medical treatment or examination of the victim in a manner or for purposes which are medically recognized as unethical or unacceptable.

(v) When the actor, through concealment or by the element of surprise, is able to overcome the victim.

(g) The actor causes personal injury to the victim, and the actor knows or has reason to know that the victim is mentally incapable, mentally incapacitated, or physically helpless.

(h) The other person is mentally incapable, mentally disabled, mentally incapacitated, or physically helpless, and any of the following:

(i) The actor is related to the victim by blood or affinity to the fourth degree.

(ii) The actor is in a position of authority over the victim and uses this authority to coerce the victim to submit.

2. Criminal sexual conduct in the first degree is a felony of the first degree.... Mich. Comp. Laws Ann. § 520(b).

Second-degree criminal sexual conduct follows substantially along the lines of the preceding section, but instead of penetration it makes sexual contact with a victim unlawful. Violation is a second-degree felony. Mich. Comp. Laws Ann. § 750.520(c).

Third-degree criminal sexual conduct includes two of the same elements as a first-degree offense (that is, penetration and use of force or coercion) but does not include the element that the defendant was aided or abetted in the act by one or more persons. Mich. Comp. Laws Ann. § 750.520(d).

Fourth-degree criminal sexual conduct involves **sexual contact** with another person involving force or coercion, or where the actor knows or has reason to know that the victim is mentally incapable, mentally incapacitated, or physically helpless, or the victim is under jurisdiction of the department of corrections and the actor is associated with that department. It is a serious misdemeanor. Mich. Comp. Laws Ann. § 750(e).

Note that the Michigan law makes no distinction as to the sex of the actor or victim—in other words, it is gender-neutral. It broadly defines sexual penetration and sexual contact and divides the offense of criminal sexual conduct into degrees considering the conduct of the actor and the vulnerability of the victim. Thus, it embodies many of the reforms discussed earlier.

Demise of the Marital Exception

As noted, Lord Hale, the seventeenth-century English jurist, wrote that a husband could not be guilty of the rape of his wife. To support this rationale, the common-law courts offered three reasons. First, the wife is a chattel belonging to her husband; second, a husband and wife are "one," and obviously a husband cannot rape himself; and finally, by marriage the wife irrevocably consents to intercourse with her husband on a continuing basis. Until the late 1970s, American courts almost universally accepted Hale's Rule.

The 1980s witnessed the erosion of **Hale's Rule.** Today courts tend to disavow the unity concept of marriage. In 1981 the New Jersey Supreme Court held that the state's rape statute that used the language "any person who has carnal knowledge of a woman forcibly against her will" did not except from its operation a husband who was living apart from his wife. *State v. Smith,* 426 A.2d 38 (N.J. 1981).

The marital exception has been abrogated in a number of ways. Pending adoption of gender-neutral sexual battery statutes, some courts addressed challenges to traditional rape statutes on constitutional grounds. For example, in *People v. Liberta,* 474 N.E.2d 567 (N.Y. 1984), New York's highest court termed the notion of a wife's implied consent to intercourse as "irrational and absurd" and emphasized that a married woman should have the same right to bodily autonomy as a single woman. It dismissed any idea of the wife being property of the husband because the state recognizes that wives and husbands are separate legal entities. In rejecting any distinction between marital and nonmarital rape, appellate courts in other states began to rely on constitutional arguments similar to those expounded by the New York court. See, for example, *Shunn v. State,* 742 P.2d 775 (Wyo. 1987).

Many state legislatures have now enacted statutes either redefining "rape" or defining "sexual battery" as gender-neutral offenses. For example, in 1990 Louisiana made rape a gender-neutral offense by redefining it as "the act of anal or vaginal sexual intercourse with a male or female person committed without the person's lawful consent." West's L.S.A.–R.S. 14:41. In other instances, states have enacted statutes specifically excluding marriage as a defense to rape or sexual battery. Several states now criminalize forced sexual relations between spouses or cohabitors. For example, Connecticut law now defines "sexual intercourse" very broadly:

> No spouse or cohabitor shall compel the other spouse or cohabitor to engage in sexual intercourse by the use of force against such other spouse or cohabitor, or by the threat of the use of force against such other spouse or cohabitor which reasonably causes such other spouse or cohabitor to fear physical injury. C.G.S.A. § 53a–70b.

Some argue that prosecution of a husband for rape might make reconciliation of marital differences impossible. Furthermore, they contend that proof of guilt will be difficult to obtain because of the usual lack of corroborating evidence of the incident. Nevertheless, legislatures and courts have come to realize that marriage in contemporary society is regarded as a partnership and should not be deemed a license to enjoy sex on demand by a forcible encounter with one's spouse.

Prosecutorial Burdens

As in all criminal cases, the prosecution must prove the *corpus delicti*—that is, the fact that the crime has been committed. Proof that an act of sexual intercourse has taken place with the victim is usually sufficient in a rape case. In addition, in a statutory rape case, proof must be offered of the age of the victim (usually the female) and, in some instances, age of the offender (usually the male). In sexual battery prosecutions, proof of the defendant's general intent is usually sufficient, absent a statute requiring proof of specific intent.

One common problem in sexual battery prosecutions is the lack of independent eyewitness testimony. Consequently, it frequently becomes the victim's word against the defendant's word. Thus, police and prosecutors place paramount importance on

In *State v. Rothenberg* (1985), the Connecticut Supreme Court examines the sufficiency of evidence to support a conviction for sexual assault. An excerpt from the court's decision appears at the end of the chapter.

a "fresh complaint" by a victim. Preservation of semen, photographs of bruises, torn clothing, and even pubic hairs become valuable evidence to corroborate a victim's testimony. Seldom is the credibility of a complaining witness as vital as in sexual battery prosecutions. To appear in court and testify concerning a sexual assault is a traumatic experience for a victim of sexual assault. This is particularly true for young children. To assist youngsters, many courts permit them to illustrate their testimony through the use of anatomically detailed dolls.

Rape Trauma Syndrome

In 1974, to describe a recurring pattern of physical and emotional symptoms experienced by rape victims, psychiatrists coined the term **rape trauma syndrome.** Since then, prosecutors have sought to introduce expert testimony at rape trials to establish that a victim's symptoms are consistent with that of the syndrome. This type of evidence has particular relevance to prosecutions where the defendant claims consent of the victim as a defense. On review of convictions, appellate courts have disagreed on whether such evidence is admissible. Very early, the Kansas Supreme Court allowed the introduction of psychiatric testimony that a rape victim suffered from rape trauma syndrome, noting that such expert evidence is relevant where the defendant claims consent. *State v. Marks,* 647 P.2d 1292 (Kan. 1982). Other state supreme courts have reached a similar conclusion. *State v. Liddell,* 685 P.2d 918 (Mont. 1984); *State v. Huey,* 699 P.2d 1290 (Ariz. 1985). An Ohio appellate court held that such expert psychiatric testimony is admissible but only where its value outweighs its prejudicial impact. The court noted that expert opinion of this type assists laypersons in interpreting reactions of a victim, especially in child rape cases. *State v. Whitman,* 475 N.E.2d 486 (Ohio App. 1984).

There is respectable judicial authority to the contrary. In 1982 the Minnesota Supreme Court ruled that the rape trauma syndrome is not a fact-finding tool but rather a therapeutic tool and that admission of expert testimony on the subject at a rape trial is erroneous. *State v. Saldana,* 324 N.W.2d 227 (Minn. 1982). Several other appellate courts have held that expert testimony concerning the syndrome is not admissible to prove that a rape in fact occurred. For example, in *People v. Pullins,* 378 N.W.2d 502 (Mich. App. 1985), the court held evidence of rape trauma syndrome inadmissible to establish that a rape in fact occurred. This came the year after the Missouri Supreme Court in *State v. Taylor,* 663 S.W.2d 235 (Mo. 1984), concluded that such testimony was beyond that proper basis of expert opinion. The subject remains controversial, and there is much to be written yet.

In 1990 New York's highest court concluded that the scientific community has now generally accepted that rape is a highly traumatic event that triggers the onset of certain identifiable symptoms. The court agreed that expert testimony of the rape trauma syndrome may be admitted to aid the jury's understanding of the victim's behavior after the assault. Nevertheless, the court observed that identifiable symptoms in rape victims do not indicate whether an incident did or did not occur; thus, trial judges cannot allow such testimony to be introduced for this purpose. *People v. Taylor,* 552 N.E.2d 131 (N.Y. 1990). In 1995 the Kansas Supreme Court, noting that it was the first high court to allow introduction of qualified expert psychiatric testimony regarding the existence of rape trauma syndrome, ruled that a social worker was not qualified to testify on the subject. *State v. Willis,* 888 P.2d 839 (Kan. 1995).

Can a defendant charged with rape introduce expert testimony concerning the rape trauma syndrome to establish that a rape did not occur? In *Henson v. State,* 535 N.E.2d 1189 (Ind. 1989), the defense presented a witness who testified to seeing the victim dancing and drinking at a bar on the evening after the alleged rape. The defense then sought to introduce expert testimony on the subject, but the trial judge would not allow it. The state supreme court ruled that the testimony must be permitted because it would be unfair to allow the prosecution to present expert testimony on rape trauma syndrome but deny a defendant the same opportunity.

Sex Offender Registration Laws

On June 20, 1997, a Trenton, New Jersey, court sentenced Jesse Timmendequas to death for the rape and murder of seven-year-old Megan Kanka in 1994. The case attracted national attention after it was revealed that Timmendequas had a record of committing sex offenses against children. Public outrage led the New Jersey legislature to enact a law requiring convicted sex offenders who are released from prison, move into the state, or simply change their addresses to register with local law enforcement agencies. This statute became widely known as **Megan's Law** in memory of Megan Kanka. Failure to comply with the registration requirement is itself a criminal offense. These agencies in turn must make this information available to the public. After fifteen years with no violations, an offender may request a court to terminate sex offender status. See, generally, N.J.S.A. 2C: 7–1 et seq.

Similar laws have been enacted in most states, and most of these laws have survived constitutional attack (see the Case-in-Point below). In 1996 Congress enacted a federal version of Megan's Law. 42 U.S.C.A. § 14071. The federal statute sets forth guidelines for state programs and encourages states to adopt such programs by threatening them with the loss of federal funds. It remains to be seen how effective the various versions of Megan's Law will be in protecting children from sexual predators. There is also concern that these laws may be too inclusive in that persons convicted in the past of minor sexual offenses are subjected to undeserved community scorn. This appears to have been especially problematic in California, where officials searched court records going back decades to identify and locate sex offenders. Megan's Law is also subject to the criticism that it imposes penalties based on status rather than on wrongful acts. However, the public has demanded that the justice system do more to protect people from sexual predators, and such individuals often remain a serious threat to the community even after they have paid their debt to society.

CASE-IN-POINT ## Constitutionality of Sex Offender Registration Laws

In 1990 Arthur Cutshall pled guilty to aggravated sexual battery of a five-year-old child and was sentenced to prison. When he learned that his name and address would be forever placed on the state's sex offender registry upon his release from prison, he brought suit in federal district court to challenge the constitutionality of Tennessee's version of Megan's Law. See Tenn. Code § 40–39–106. Among other things,

Cutshall argued that the law constituted double jeopardy. A federal district judge rejected the challenge, as did the U.S. Court of Appeals for the Sixth Circuit. In upholding the statute, the appellate court observed that "the focus of the act is not on circumscribing the conduct of the offender, but on the protection of the public. . . ." The United States Supreme Court denied certiorari, leaving the Sixth Circuit's decision intact.

Cutshall v. Sundquist, 193 F.3d 466 (6th Cir. 1999).

Defenses to Charges of Sexual Battery

Beyond a general denial of the charges, the most common defense asserted in a rape case is that the victim consented. For consent to be a defense, it must be voluntarily given before the sexual act. As we pointed out previously, the defense of consent is not available where the victim is unconscious, asleep, or mentally deficient.

The defense of consent would not be valid in a case of voluntary sexual battery (that is, statutory rape) because persons under a certain age are legally incapable of consent. Moreover, it is usually not a defense to a charge of voluntary sexual battery that the defendant believed the victim was older than the prohibited age. Most courts hold this to be true despite the victim's appearance or if the victim misrepresented his or her age.

Impotency (that is, the inability to engage in sexual intercourse) can be asserted as a defense to a charge of rape. The majority of cases where the defense of impotency is asserted involve charges against young males and men of an advanced age. However, this defense is seldom successful. Modern laws have so broadened the definition of sexual battery as to render impotency irrelevant in many sexual impositions.

Finally, if the statute under which the defendant is prosecuted requires proof of a specific intent, the defendant may show an inability to form such intent due to voluntary intoxication (see Chapter 14).

Sodomy

Consensual **sodomy** is not a crime against a person, but in the jurisdictions that retain this offense, it is considered an offense against morality (for further discussion, see Chapter 8). Nonconsensual sodomy, on the other hand, is very definitely a crime against a person, often falling under the category of rape or sexual battery. In some jurisdictions, sodomy is charged in addition to sexual battery in instances of rape involving forcible oral or anal intercourse.

Abortion

Abortion has been legally defined as the willful bringing about of the miscarriage of a pregnant woman. It was a common-law misdemeanor for a woman who was "quick" with child to have an abortion. The stage of "quickening" referred to the point during a woman's pregnancy when the fetus stirred in the womb.

Most American jurisdictions adopted statutes proscribing abortion, but many made abortion criminal throughout pregnancy. However, there was a tendency to spell out that an abortion was justified if physicians found it essential to save the mother's life. More liberal statutes allowed abortions to be performed when one or two physicians advised that it was necessary to preserve the life or health of the mother. By 1970, a few states had even repealed criminal penalties for abortions where they were performed under medical supervision in the very early stages of a woman's pregnancy.

The 1960s and 1970s, a period of liberalized views on sexual practices, witnessed a clamor for liberalization of abortion laws. But before significant reforms occurred in most states, the U.S. Supreme Court entertained a challenge to the constitutionality of a Texas law that permitted abortion only on medical advice that it was necessary to save the mother's life. In a landmark 7–2 decision in 1973, the Court in *Roe v. Wade*, 410 U.S. 113, 93 S.Ct. 705, 35 L.Ed.2d 147 (1973), held that a fetus was not a "person" within the meaning of the Fourteenth Amendment to the United States Constitution. Therefore, the fetus was not entitled to the constitutional protection of the law granted persons. The Court then extended its views on privacy by holding that a woman's personal right of privacy was involved in the decision whether to abort a fetus. The Court's decision had the effect of invalidating most state laws proscribing or regulating abortions. A decision whether to abort during the first trimester of a pregnancy, the Court said, was a matter between the woman and her physician without state regulation. After the first trimester, procedures for abortion could be regulated when "necessarily related to maternal health." In the final trimester, when the fetus has become "viable," the state may prohibit abortion except "when it is necessary, in appropriate medical judgment, to preserve the life or health of the mother."

The controversial issue of abortion has philosophical, religious, ethical, medical, and political dimensions. As part of the national debate, Congress in the early 1980s considered but rejected a constitutional amendment to restrict abortions. A more conservative Supreme Court has modified *Roe* to allow states greater leeway in regulating abortions in such areas as waiting periods and required counseling. In the wake of one of these decisions, *Planned Parenthood v. Casey*, 505 U.S. 833, 112 S.Ct. 2791, 120 L.Ed.2d 674 (1992), supporters of abortion rights clamored for Congress to adopt a statute that would codify the holding in *Roe v. Wade*. Although Congress has not done this, President Clinton in 1993 issued an executive order eliminating several restrictions on abortion counseling in federally funded clinics that had been imposed by the previous administration.

The Conflict Over Partial-Birth Abortion

In 1997 Congress passed a bill making it a crime for a physician to perform an infrequently used procedure commonly known as **partial birth abortion.** President Clinton vetoed the bill, preventing it from becoming law. However, several states have enacted similar laws, several of which have been declared unconstitutional.

On June 28, 2000, the United States Supreme Court struck down a Nebraska statute banning partial birth abortion. *Stenberg v. Carhart*, 530 U.S. 914, 120 S.Ct. 2597, 147 L.Ed.2d 743 (2000). The statute defined partial birth abortion as "an abortion procedure in which the person performing the abortion partially delivers vaginally a living unborn child before killing the unborn child and completing the delivery." Neb. Rev. Stat. Ann. § 28–326(9) (Supp. 1999). The Supreme Court, dividing five-to-four, invalidated the law because it lacked an exception for the preservation of the health of the mother and imposed an undue burden on a woman's right to choose abortion.

Writing for the Court, Justice Breyer recognized that millions of Americans believe that abortion is akin to causing the death of an innocent child while millions of others fear that a law that forbids abortion would condemn many American women to lives that lack dignity and would lead to illegal abortions with the attendant risk of death and suffering. He observed that under the Nebraska law,

> some present prosecutors and future Attorneys General may choose to pursue physicians who use . . . the most commonly used method for performing previability second trimester abortions. All those who perform abortion procedures using that method must fear prosecution, conviction, and imprisonment. The result is an undue burden upon a woman's right to make an abortion decision. 530 U.S. at 934, 120 S.Ct. at 2617, 147 L.Ed.2d at 745.

Dissenting, Justice Kennedy observed the following:

> The decision nullifies a law expressing the will of the people of Nebraska that medical procedures must be governed by moral principles having their foundation in the intrinsic value of human life, including life of the unborn. Through their law the people of Nebraska were forthright in confronting an issue of immense moral consequence. The State chose to forbid a procedure many decent and civilized people find so abhorrent as to be among the most serious of crimes against human life, while the State still protected the woman's autonomous right of choice. . . . The Court closes its eyes to these profound concerns. 530 U.S. at 952, 120 S.Ct. at 2635, 147 L.Ed.2d at 795.

These excerpts from the Court's lengthy decision reflect the wide chasm in the debate over abortion. Because of the irreconcilable points of views on the subject, the debate will likely continue for decades.

Abusive Offenses

Laws proscribing abuse of one person by another are modern concepts. Many of these laws have been proposed by social agencies that bear the responsibility of coping with problems of members of society who require protection from abusive behavior. Increasingly, legislatures, and even more recently, Congress, have responded by enacting laws designed to protect children, spouses and other intimate partners, and, in some instances, the elderly.

Child Abuse

Since the 1980s, complaints of **child abuse** have increased dramatically. Many cases involve commission of assault, battery (or aggravated categories thereof), or some category of sexual assault or sexual battery and are prosecuted under one or more of such statutes. Nevertheless, with the rise of neglect, abuse, and violence against children, many states have enacted specific child abuse laws to cover a broader range of abusive behavior. These laws often refer to **endangering the welfare of a child,** and they hold parent or guardian responsible for abuse of a child regardless of the source of the mistreatment. These concerns appear to be reflected in McKinney's N.Y. Penal Law § 260.10. That law makes endangering the welfare of a child a misdemeanor and provides that a person is guilty of endangering the welfare of a child when

(1) He knowingly acts in a manner likely to be injurious to the physical, mental or moral welfare of a child less than seventeen years old or directs or authorizes such child to engage in an occupation involving a substantial risk of danger to his life or health; or

(2) Being a parent, guardian or other person legally charged with the care or custody of a child less than eighteen years old, he fails or refuses to exercise reasonable diligence in the control of such child to prevent him from becoming an "abused child," a "neglected child," a "juvenile delinquent," or a "person in need of supervision," as those terms are defined in articles ten, three and seven of the family court act.

Because of the age and vulnerability of minors, statutes proscribing child abuse are strict liability crimes in many states. In addition to conduct that is commonly understood to constitute abuse, the press has reported numerous instances of a parent being charged with having allowed a child to be locked in a closed car while the parent was shopping. In other instances a parent has been charged with endangering a child's welfare by transporting a child in an auto while the parent was driving while under the influence of intoxicating beverages.

Statutes now commonly require medical professionals and social workers to report instances of suspected child abuse to the enforcement authorities. When such cases of child abuse reach the courts, they often involve legal issues as to whether parents, social workers, and others who discuss these matters with an abused child are to be permitted to testify in court concerning communications with the child. Moreover, expert testimony of physicians, psychologists, and social workers is often relied on to explain a child's sometimes-curious behavior that might be a result of certain types of abuse.

The widespread drug problem has led to prosecutions of women for child abuse when expectant mothers ingested cocaine and demonstrable medical effects were present in their children at birth. Courts have generally declined to hold that such action constitutes child abuse. For example, Kentucky Revised Statute § 508.110 criminalizes abuse of "another person of whom [the offender] has actual custody" which "places him in a situation that may cause him serious physical injury." In 1993 the Kentucky Supreme Court held the statute does not apply to a mother whose baby suffered injuries as the result of the mother's ingestion of drugs during her pregnancy. *Commonwealth v. Welch,* 864 S.W.2d 280 (Ky. 1993). In reaching its decision, the court cited *Johnson v. State,* 602 So.2d 1288 (Fla. 1992). There, the Florida Supreme Court held that cocaine passing through a baby's umbilical cord after birth, but before the cord was cut, did not violate a Florida law making it a crime for an adult to deliver a controlled substance to a minor.

Spousal Abuse

In recent years, legislatures and courts have given increased attention to **spousal abuse.** Many of these abuses constitute criminal violations of one or more traditional statutes previously discussed. Nevertheless, laws have been enacted in many states to provide for issuance of court injunctions to protect spouses from domestic violence and provide for arrest of those who violate these orders. In many instances, courts issue protective orders of this character during litigation. In *Cole v. Cole,* 556 N.Y.S.2d 217 (Fam. Ct. 1990), a wife petitioned the court to have her husband held in contempt for violating such an order. A question arose about the effectiveness of such an order when the wife voluntarily seeks reconciliation with her husband. The court explained that a victim of domestic violence who has procured such an order is entitled to the court's protection from violence throughout the duration of the order, even if the victim is desirous of pursuing a goal of voluntary reconciliation with the offending spouse.

Prosecutions for spousal abuses are sometimes hindered by the difficulty of showing which instances of domestic violence have occurred in which legal jurisdiction. Recognizing this, Congress included in the Violent Crime Control and Law Enforcement Act of 1994 (commonly referred to as "the federal Crime Bill") an offense of "interstate domestic violence." Section 40221 of the Act inserts a new chapter titled Domestic Violence after Chapter 110 in 18 U.S.C.A. It makes it a crime for a person who

> travels across a State line or enters or leaves Indian country with the intent to injure, harass, or intimidate that person's spouse or intimate partner, and who, in the

course of or as a result of such travel, intentionally commits a crime of violence and thereby causes bodily injury to such spouse or intimate partner;

or who causes a spouse or intimate partner to cross a State line or to enter or leave Indian country by force, coercion, duress, or fraud and, in the course or as a result of that conduct, intentionally commits a crime of violence and thereby causes bodily injury to such spouse or intimate partner.

Shortly after the new act took effect, Christopher Bailey was charged with violating it for assaulting his spouse and driving her around West Virginia and Kentucky until he finally carried her into an emergency room. On May 23, 1995, Bailey was the first person to be convicted under the new act.

Abuse of the Elderly

Abuse of the elderly is often defined as physical abuse, neglect, fiduciary abuse, abandonment, isolation, or other treatment resulting in physical harm, pain, or mental suffering, or in the deprivation of goods or services necessary to avoid physical harm or mental suffering. Abuse of the elderly is generally handled through regulatory agencies. Frequently, this can require resort to civil court processes. In other instances, abuse of the elderly is reported to law enforcement agencies, and prosecution may occur for violation of one or more traditional criminal statutes. In some instances, legislatures have provided for enhanced penalties for those who commit crimes of violence against elderly persons.

In New York, § 260.32 of the Penal Law now provides that a person is guilty of endangering the welfare of a vulnerable elderly person when a caregiver for a vulnerable elderly person intentionally or recklessly causes serious physical injury to that person. Section 260.32 of the Penal Law makes it an offense for a caregiver to subject a vulnerable elderly person "to sexual contact without the latter's consent."

False Imprisonment and Kidnapping

In recognition of the need to protect an individual's freedom of movement, the common law developed two misdemeanor offenses: **false imprisonment** and **kidnapping.** False imprisonment consisted of confining someone against the person's will, whereas kidnapping involved forcibly abducting and taking a person to another country.

The Statutory Offense of False Imprisonment

Not all states have adopted statutes making false imprisonment an offense. Those that have generally classify it as a misdemeanor and define it much as did the common law. Typically, the Texas statute states that "[a] person commits an offense if he intentionally and knowingly restrains another person." Vernon's Tex. Penal Code Ann. § 20.02(a). Texas law declares the offense to be a misdemeanor but provides that if the offender recklessly exposes the victim to a substantial risk of serious bodily injury, it becomes a felony. Vernon's Tex. Penal Code Ann. § 20.02(c). Usually, a prosecution for false imprisonment requires only proof of a defendant's general intent, although this depends on the language of the particular statute.

SOME COMMON SCENARIOS OF FALSE IMPRISONMENT

Four hypothetical situations illustrate the crime of false imprisonment:

- A police officer takes a person into custody under an unlawful arrest.
- A prison warden fails to release a prisoner who has served his or her term.
- A storekeeper detains a customer when the storekeeper has a hunch the customer has shoplifted but has no reasonable basis for such suspicion.
- An overzealous male suitor refuses to allow his female companion to leave his apartment without yielding to his sexual demands.

FALSE IMPRISONMENT NOT A COMMONLY CHARGED OFFENSE

In *State v. Snider* (1991), the Court of Appeal of Iowa reversed a defendant's conviction for false imprisonment on the ground the facts did not show the victim's freedom was substantially restricted. An excerpt appears at the end of the chapter.

In recent years, false imprisonment has not been a commonly charged offense. Three reasons chiefly account for this: (1) serious charges involving restraint of a person frequently reveal elements constituting the statutory offense of kidnapping; (2) persons claiming to have been falsely imprisoned often seek to recover damages in a civil suit, rather than press criminal charges; and (3) on close investigation, many restraints undoubtedly are determined to have been imposed based on authority, or at least a reasonable belief that there was authority to have restrained the complaining party.

Modern Statutory Treatment of Kidnapping

Unlike false imprisonment, the crime of kidnapping is a serious felony universally proscribed by state and federal jurisdictions. It plays a far greater role in our society than it did at common law.

Under modern legislation it is not necessary, as it was at common law, that the victim of kidnapping be taken to another country. The elements of the crime necessarily depend on the precise wording of the statute in a particular jurisdiction, but in general, to constitute kidnapping there must be an unlawful taking and forcible carrying away (sometimes called **asportation**) of a victim without that person's consent. Intimidation and coercion can substitute for the required force, and even where consent has been given, a person who has the capacity to consent must have voluntarily given it. Therefore, young children and incompetent persons cannot legally consent to an act of asportation.

Most states classify kidnapping as **simple kidnapping** and **kidnapping for ransom.** Others classify the offense by degrees. In New York, kidnapping in the second degree is a felony that merely involves the abduction of another person. McKinney's N.Y. Penal Code § 135.20. Kidnapping in the first degree is a more serious felony, and the statute proscribing it states the following:

A person is guilty of kidnapping in the first degree when he abducts another person and when:

1. His intent is to compel a third person to pay or deliver money or property as ransom, or to engage in other particular conduct, or to refrain from engaging in particular conduct; or

2. He restrains the person abducted for a period of more than twelve hours with intent to:

(a) Inflict physical injury upon him or violate or abuse him sexually; or

(b) Accomplish or advance the commission of a felony; or

(c) Terrorize him or a third person; or

(d) Interfere with the performance of a governmental or political function; or

3. The person abducted dies during the abduction or before he is able to return or to be returned to safety. McKinney's N.Y. Penal Code § 135.25.

The Requirement of Asportation in Kidnapping

The asportation or movement of the victim distinguishes the crime of kidnapping from the offense of false imprisonment. One of the more commonly litigated issues in kidnapping prosecutions concerns the extent of movement of the victim required to meet this element of the crime. In recent years, courts have tended to limit the scope of kidnapping statutes by deciding that the required movement of a victim must be something more than that inherent in or incidental to the commission of another felony. The proliferation of court decisions on this subject might be the result of prosecutors' tendencies to levy multiple charges against a criminal defendant for conduct arising from a single criminal episode.

When is the offender's movement of a victim in conjunction with an independent offense such as assault, rape, or robbery sufficient to constitute an independent offense of kidnapping? If the movement is merely incidental to a crime and does not involve an additional significant risk to the victim, courts generally will not sustain a conviction for kidnapping in addition to the other offense. Appellate court decisions are instructive. The New Hampshire Supreme Court has held that a defendant was properly convicted for kidnapping as an accomplice of a defendant who forced a woman into a car and drove her to an apartment where the principal defendant assaulted her. *State v. Goodwin,* 395 A.2d 1234 (N.H. 1978). In the same vein, two years later, the North Carolina Supreme Court sustained a kidnapping conviction where a handyman forced a woman off the street and into her home for purposes of sexually assaulting her. *State v. Adams,* 264 S.E.2d 46 (N.C. 1980).

Two 1983 appellate court decisions addressed the problem, expounding a somewhat different approach. The Florida Supreme Court held that the statutory requirement of "confining, abducting, or imprisoning another person . . . with intent to commit or facilitate commission of any felony" does not include movement or confinement that is inconsequential or inherent in the nature of the felony. *Faison v. State,* 426 So.2d 963 (Fla. 1983). In applying this rationale, a California appellate court held that moving a robber's victim across a room or from one room to another was an insufficient movement to meet the requirement for kidnapping. *People v. John,* 197 Cal. Rptr. 340 (Cal. App. 1983).

Federal Kidnapping Laws

Perhaps the most notorious kidnapping to have occurred in the United States was the abduction of the infant son of Charles A. Lindbergh, the "Lone Eagle" who, in 1927, made the first nonstop solo flight across the Atlantic Ocean. The Lindbergh baby was abducted from the family home in New Jersey in 1932. Bruno Richard Hauptmann was convicted of the crime after a spectacular trial and was executed in 1936. The Lindbergh kidnapping led to a demand for federal laws to enable the Federal Bureau of Investigation to become involved in apprehending kidnappers. This, in turn, led to sweeping changes in state and federal laws on kidnapping. The Federal Kidnapping Act, commonly called the Lindbergh Law, provides the following:

> Whoever unlawfully seizes, confines, inveigles, decoys, kidnaps, abducts, or carries away and holds for ransom or reward or otherwise any person, except in the case of

a minor by a parent thereof . . . shall be punished by imprisonment. . . . 18 U.S.C.A. § 1201(a).

Subsection (b) of the statute raises a presumption that if the kidnapped victim is not returned within twenty-four hours after the taking, then the defendant did, in fact, take the victim across state lines. This presumption effectively allows the federal government to act promptly to bring federal agents into the investigation of an alleged kidnapping.

A recent federal statute makes **hostage taking** an offense. 18 U.S.C.A. § 1203. Other federal statutes make it a crime to knowingly receive, possess, or dispose of any money or property that has been delivered as ransom for a victim of a kidnapping, 18 U.S.C.A. § 1202, or for a bank robber to avoid apprehension by forcing someone to accompany him, 18 U.S.C.A. § 2113(e).

Defenses to Charges of False Imprisonment and Kidnapping

It is not false imprisonment for a person to detain another under authority of the law. Thus, an officer, or even a private citizen, who makes a lawful arrest or a jailer who detains a prisoner lawfully committed to custody is not guilty of an offense. Likewise, a parent who reasonably disciplines a child or a teacher who reasonably restrains a pupil would not be guilty of false imprisonment.

Consent can also be a defense to false imprisonment or kidnapping. Of course, the consent must not have been induced by threat, coercion, or misrepresentation and must have been given by a person competent to give consent. A person who relies on consent as a defense has the burden of establishing the validity of such consent.

Finally, as we have noted, a defendant may challenge whether there was sufficient movement of the victim to constitute the asportation element of kidnapping.

CASE-IN-POINT

Rape and Kidnapping: Required Resistance in Face of Threats

Late one night after leaving work, a woman responded to a request by two men to assist them in getting their car off the road. When she began to leave, both men grabbed her, ordered her into the back seat of the car, and threatened to kill her unless she cooperated. The men told her that they had escaped from prison and were holding her as a hostage. They then drove their victim to a tent, disrobed her, and forced her to submit to sexual acts with each of them. When they drove her back to her car the next morning, they told her that they would kill her if she reported the incident to the police.

The defendants were convicted of rape, kidnapping, and several other offenses. On appeal, they argued that the victim had cooperated in their endeavors; hence, they were not guilty of either rape or kidnapping. The Indiana Supreme Court rejected their contentions and explained that the resistance necessary to protect against sexual attack is dependent on all circumstances. Further, the court noted that a victim need not physically resist after being confronted with threats and being in fear of injury.

Ballard v. State, 385 N.E.2d 1126 (Ind. 1979).

Child Snatching

In recent years, marital disputes have given rise to many serious problems concerning the custody of children of divorced or separated parents. It has been estimated that in excess of 300,000 children are abducted by family members each year. The term **child snatching** is now commonly applied to situations in which one parent deliberately retains or conceals a child from the other parent. The problem has resulted partly from the ability of one parent to seize a child from the custodial parent, travel to another state, and petition the court in the latter state for custody of the child.

In 1995 the Supreme Judicial Court of Maine affirmed a conviction of a father who took his children from their home where their mother had equal legal custody rights. The evidence revealed the defendant's purpose was to keep the children away from their mother, to secrete them, and to hold them in a place where they were not likely to be found. The court found this evidence sufficient to support conviction of the father for violating a statute defining criminal restraint to include taking a child "from the custody of his other parent." *State v. Butt,* 656 A.2d 1225 (Me. 1995).

Most states have made child snatching a felony, thereby subjecting violators to extradition for prosecution in the state where the offense occurs. In addition, child snatching is now being curbed by several approaches:

- In many states, trial judges include a provision in a divorce judgment requiring court approval to remove a child from the state where the divorce is granted. Violation may subject the offending party to being held in contempt of court or, in some states, to be prosecuted for a felony.

- The **Uniform Child Custody Jurisdiction Act (UCCJA),** proposed in 1968 and now in force in all fifty states, generally continues jurisdiction for custody in the home or resident state of the child. Cooperation between the courts in the different states is becoming increasingly effective in preventing "judge shopping."

- In 1980 Congress enacted the **Parental Kidnapping Prevention Act (PKPA),** 28 U.S.C.A. § 1738A. The federal act is designed to prevent jurisdictional conflicts over child custody, and it takes precedence over any state law, including the UCCJA. Its primary goal is to reduce any incentive for parental child snatching.

- Federal and state governments, as well as religious and civic organizations and the media, have initiated programs for identifying children and for collecting and disseminating information on missing children.

Civil Rights Offenses

A category of offenses unknown to the common law involves injuries to the **civil rights** of individuals. After the Civil War, Congress adopted a series of laws designed to protect the civil rights of the newly freed former slaves. Today, these statutes as amended can be used to initiate federal prosecutions against individuals who conspire or use their official positions to deprive persons of rights guaranteed by the U.S. Constitution or the laws of the United States. The relevant provisions are as follows:

18 U.S.C.A. § 241. Conspiracy against rights

If two or more persons conspire to injure, oppress, threaten, or intimidate any inhabitant of any State, Territory, Commonwealth, Possession, or District in the free exercise or enjoyment of any right or privilege secured to him by the Constitution or laws of the United States, or because of his having so exercised the same; or

If two or more persons go in disguise on the highway, or on the premises of another, with intent to prevent or hinder his free exercise or enjoyment of any right or privilege so secured—

They shall be fined under this title or imprisoned not more than ten years, or both; and if death results from the acts committed in violation of this section or if such acts include kidnapping or an attempt to kidnap, aggravated sexual abuse or an attempt to commit aggravated sexual abuse, or an attempt to kill, they shall be fined under this title or imprisoned for any term of years or for life, or both, or may be sentenced to death.

18 U.S.C.A. § 242. Deprivation of rights under color of law

Whoever, under color of any law, statute, ordinance, regulation, or custom, willfully subjects any person in any State, Territory, or District to the deprivation of any rights, privileges, or immunities secured or protected by the Constitution or laws of the United States, or to different punishments, pains, or penalties, on account of such person being an alien, or by reason of his color, or race, than are prescribed for the punishment of citizens, shall be fined under this title or imprisoned not more than one year, or both; and if bodily injury results from the acts committed in violation of this section or if such acts include the use, attempted use, or threatened use of a dangerous weapon, explosives, or fire, shall be fined under this title or imprisoned not more than ten years, or both; and if death results from the acts committed in violation of this section or if such acts include kidnapping or an attempt to kidnap, aggravated sexual abuse, or an attempt to commit aggravated sexual abuse, or an attempt to kill, shall be fined under this title, or imprisoned for any term of years or for life, or both, or may be sentenced to death.

These statutes are used most frequently to prosecute in federal court individuals who engage in criminal acts that are racially motivated. Thus, although a conspiracy to commit arson may be prosecuted as such under state law, if it is racially motivated, it may also constitute a federal civil rights violation under 18 U.S.C.A. § 241. Instances of police brutality are sometimes prosecuted under 18 U.S.C.A. § 242. Readers will recall the highly publicized case of the Los Angeles police officers who were charged with various state-law offenses stemming from the arrest and beating of suspect Rodney King, an African American. Subsequent to their acquittal in state court,

CASE-IN-POINT

When Is Sexual Assault a Deprivation of Constitutional Rights?

In 1992 a Tennessee state judge was charged with violating the constitutional rights of five women by sexually assaulting them in his chambers. In a somewhat novel theory of the scope of 18 U.S.C.A. § 242, the federal indictment alleged that the judge, acting willfully and under color of state law, had deprived his victims of their federal constitutional right to be free from willful sexual assault. The jury returned verdicts of guilty on seven counts, and Lanier was sentenced to twenty-five years in federal prison. The court of appeals reversed the conviction, but the United States Supreme Court in turn reversed that decision.

United States v. Lanier, 520 U.S. 259, 117 S.Ct. 1219, 137 L.Ed.2d 432 (1997).

two of these officers were convicted in federal court under Section 242 and sentenced to prison.

Increasingly, Section 242 is being used to prosecute state officials who engage in other types of egregious conduct. To be guilty of willfully depriving a person of constitutional rights under this section, the defendant's actions must be done under color of law; where use of force is involved, the force used must be unreasonable and unnecessary. *United States v. Stokes,* 506 F.2d 771 (5th Cir. 1975).

As a result of judicial interpretation, federal civil rights laws now protect individuals from a wide range of injurious conduct by public officials or other persons acting under the authority of the government.

Hate Crimes

Hate crimes are offenses motivated by bias against a person's race, religion, nationality, gender, disability, or sexual orientation. Hate crimes can be offenses against property—for example, an instance of synagogue vandalism that is motivated by anti-Semitism. But most hate crimes are violent crimes against persons. In recent years there have been a number of highly publicized homicides where the only apparent motive was animus based on the victim's race, religion, gender, or sexual orientation. One of the most grisly such crimes was the racially motivated murder of James Byrd, Jr., in Jasper, Texas, in 1998. Byrd, who was African American, was chained by his ankles to the back of a pickup truck and dragged for three miles. He died when he was decapitated when his body struck a culvert. Two of three white men convicted of Byrd's murder were sentenced to death by a Texas court; the third was sentenced to life in prison.

Concerned about an apparent rise in hate crimes, Congress in 1990 enacted the Hate Crime Statistics Act, 28 U.S.C. § 534, which requires the Justice Department to acquire data on such offenses. In 1997 the Justice Department recorded 9,861 hate crimes nationwide, 7,017 of which were crimes against persons largely involving assaults and instances of intimidation (*Sourcebook of Criminal Justice Statistics, 1998,* U.S. Department of Justice, Bureau of Justice Statistics, Washington, DC: U.S.G.P.O., 1999, Table 3.125, p. 285).

Federal law currently limits federal prosecution of hate crimes to civil rights offenses, 18 U.S.C. § 245, which criminalizes interference with "federally protected activities" such as voting. Advocates of a stronger federal role in this area have called on Congress to enact the Hate Crimes Prevention Act, which was introduced in Congress in 1999. The proposed legislation would criminalize willful acts of violence involving guns, explosives, or fire directed at individuals because of their actual or perceived race, color, nationality, religion, gender, disability, or sexual orientation. On June 20, 2000, the Senate voted to pass this legislation, but as of the time this book went to press the House had not adopted the bill.

Some opponents of the Hate Crimes Prevention Act based their objections on what they perceived to be a federal usurpation of state and local law enforcement responsibilities. Others questioned the very concept of the hate crime. Not everyone agrees that a crime should be punished more severely because the perpetrator was motivated by racial hatred rather than greed, lust, or any other motive. Others argue that existing criminal sanctions are adequate to punish hate crimes. On the other hand, criminalizing hate crimes clearly communicates society's strong aversion to bigotry.

Most states now have laws permitting courts to enhance criminal penalties when defendants are convicted of hate crimes. For example, New Jersey law provides for enhanced penalties where the perpetrator "acted with a purpose to intimidate an individual or group of individuals because of race, color, gender, handicap, religion, sexual orientation or ethnicity." N.J. Stat. Ann. § 2C: 44–3(e) (West Supp. 2000). The Supreme Court has upheld hate crime laws of the penalty enhancement variety—see *Wisconsin v. Mitchell,* 508 U.S. 476, 113 S.Ct. 2194, 124 L.Ed.2d 436 (1993)—but it has also said that the factual question of whether a crime was motivated by animus against a particular group is an element of the crime that must be proved beyond a reasonable doubt. In a jury trial, this question must be submitted to the jury. *Apprendi v. New Jersey,* 530 U.S. 466, 120 S.Ct. 2348, 147 L.Ed.2d 435 (2000). For further discussion of the penalty enhancement approach to hate crimes, see Chapter 19, "Sentencing and Punishment."

Conclusion

Crimes against persons usually result in either death or injury to the victim. Surviving victims of violent personal crimes often suffer emotional and psychological damage, as well as physical injury. In addition, offenses resulting in death or injury frequently have long-lasting social and economic effects on the victim. Consider the economic plight of a family in which a working parent is disabled by a penniless assailant, or the strains imposed on a marital union in which the young bride has been sexually assaulted or kidnapped and ravished.

Over the centuries the assaultive, homicidal, sexual, and detention crimes have been a stable base for prosecuting persons whose antisocial conduct offended the basic norms of civilized people. Yet laws must change to cope with the needs of a dynamic society. In this chapter we have attempted to broaden the scope of the usual coverage of crimes against persons. New offenses against stalking, abuse of children and spouses, and child snatching, as well as federal laws concerning violations of civil rights, have become integral parts of the criminal justice system.

Key Terms

assault	premeditation
battery	felony murder
aggravated assault	second-degree murder
aggravated battery	depraved mind or heart
self-defense	imminently dangerous
stalking	jury pardon
mayhem	vehicular homicide
homicide	excusable homicide
malice aforethought	justifiable homicide
manslaughter	*corpus delicti*
voluntary manslaughter	proximate cause
involuntary manslaughter	brain death
provocation	one year and a day rule
first-degree murder	heat of passion

suicide
assisted suicide
carnal knowledge
common-law rape
forcible rape
statutory rape
marital exception
force
consent
gender-neutral offense
rape shield laws
sexual penetration
sexual contact
Hale's Rule
rape trauma syndrome
Megan's Law
impotency
sodomy
abortion

partial birth abortion
child abuse
endangering the welfare of a child
spousal abuse
abuse of the elderly
false imprisonment
kidnapping
asportation
simple kidnapping
kidnapping for ransom
hostage taking
child snatching
Uniform Child Custody Jurisdiction
  Act (UCCJA)
Parental Kidnapping Prevention Act
  (PKPA)
civil rights
hate crimes

Web-Based Research Activity

1. Go to the web. Locate your state's statutes on line.
2. Find the statute defining homicidal crimes. How does your state define the various gradations of homicide?
3. Locate the on-line statutes for a nearby state. How does that state's homicide statute differ from your own state's laws in this area?

Questions for Thought and Discussion

1. What elements, in addition to those required for assault or battery, must be proven to convict a defendant of aggravated assault or battery?
2. Is it legitimate for a jury to find a defendant guilty of manslaughter in a case where there is evidence of premeditation, simply because members of the jury feel that the defendant was somewhat justified in taking the life of the victim?
3. How can the prosecution establish the *corpus delicti* in a murder case when the body of the victim cannot be found?
4. Compare the U.S. Supreme Court's 1997 opinion holding that there is no constitutional right to have assistance in committing suicide with the constitutional right of privacy discussed in Chapter 3.
5. Why has the common-law doctrine of felony murder become controversial among courts and legal scholars in recent years?
6. Is a state law making it a crime to kill a viable fetus constitutional, notwithstanding the Supreme Court's decision in *Roe v. Wade*?
7. A male who has been diagnosed with acquired immune deficiency syndrome (AIDS) engages in sexual intercourse with a female. He does not inform the

female that he has AIDS. As a result, the female contracts AIDS and dies from the disease some two years later. Under the laws of your state, could the male be convicted of a homicidal act?

8. What interests does the law seek to protect in proscribing (a) forcible rape and (b) statutory rape?

9. Which statutory and judicial reforms of the 1970s and 1980s in the law of rape were the most significant from a female victim's standpoint? Are there other biases against female victims of sexual assault that should be addressed?

10. Does "Hale's Rule," which creates a "marital exception" in the law of rape, apply in your state?

11. What role do the Uniform Child Custody Jurisdiction Act (UCCJA) and the Parental Kidnapping Prevention Act (PKPA) play in controlling child snatching?

12. Do the federal statutes making it unlawful to deprive persons of their civil rights under color of law have a significant deterrent effect on misconduct of law enforcement personnel? Or do these statutes hamper effective police action?

Problems for Discussion and Solution

1. Shortly before midnight, a man is driving through a residential area in an attempt to get his wife, who is in labor, to the hospital. The posted speed limit is 30 mph, but the anxious husband is driving 50 mph. In a dark area, the car strikes and kills a ten-year-old boy who is playing in the middle of the street. Can the driver be convicted of (a) manslaughter or (b) vehicular homicide?

2. A store manager observes Lucy Grabit stuffing a pair of nylon hose into her purse before going through the checkout counter in a supermarket. The manager detains her and promptly directs his employee to call the police. Is the store manager guilty of false imprisonment? Why or why not?

3. Several college freshmen enter the dean's private office and remain there for several hours. They refuse to let the dean leave until he yields to their demands to allow unrestricted visitation in all dormitories. Under contemporary criminal statutes, what offense, if any, have the students committed? Explain.

4. An intoxicated driver recklessly drove his vehicle into a car being driven by a woman who was seven months pregnant. As a result of the accident, the woman's baby was born prematurely, suffered from extensive brain damage, and died two days later. The state law defines a person as an individual "who has been born and is alive." Nevertheless, the state prosecuted the intoxicated driver, and a jury found him guilty of manslaughter. Do you think an appellate court should uphold the defendant's conviction? Why or why not?

5. The defendant was convicted of battery under a statute that provides "A person commits a battery when he either intentionally or knowingly, and without legal justification, makes physical contact of an insulting or provoking nature with an individual." The evidence disclosed that one morning the male defendant picked up a female friend whom he had invited to have breakfast with him. En route to the restaurant he unbuttoned her blouse and placed his hand on her breast; after she removed his hand and asked him to stop, he again placed his hand on her breast. On appeal, the defendant argues that his conviction should be reversed because his acts were not insulting, there was no struggle, and the female did not testify that she was traumatized or disturbed by his acts. Moreover, he points out that the evidence disclosed

that after the incident the female complainant accompanied him to a restaurant where they had breakfast together. Should the appellate court reverse this conviction on the ground that the evidence is insufficient? Why or why not?

6. The defendant and her husband have two sons, ages five and three. Without notifying her husband, she left the family home with both children while no court proceedings were pending concerning either their marriage or custody of their children. Two weeks later, and without the wife's knowledge, the husband obtained a court order granting him custody of the two children. An arrest warrant was eventually issued for the wife. She was arrested in another state and brought back to her home state, where she now faces prosecution under a statute that provides "Whoever, being a relative of a child . . . without lawful authority, holds or intends to hold such a child permanently or for a protracted period, or takes or entices a child from his lawful custodian . . . shall be guilty of a felony." The wife's attorney stipulates that the facts are correct as stated, but contends the wife cannot be convicted of parental kidnapping under the quoted statute. What result do you think should occur? Why?

7. A nineteen-year-old woman returns home from an evening at the beach. She tells her mother that she has been raped and sodomized by an attacker she doesn't know. Some hours later, the woman identifies her attacker to her mother, and they notify the police. At trial, the prosecution seeks to admit expert testimony on rape trauma syndrome to explain the victim's reticence in promptly identifying her attacker. The defense objects. Should the court allow expert testimony on this subject to explain the reactions of the female victim in the hours following her attack and to explain why she may initially have been unwilling to report the defendant who attacked her? Why or why not?

EXCERPTS FROM JUDICIAL DECISIONS

State v. Towers

Supreme Court of Maine, 1973.
304 A.2d 75.

[Here the Supreme Court of Maine upholds the defendant's conviction for aggravated assault and battery.]

WERNICK, Justice.

Defendant has appealed from a judgment of the Superior Court (Penobscot County) embodying his conviction, on October 15, 1971, of the offense of assault and battery, high and aggravated in degree. . . .

Evidence produced at the trial, jury-waived, warranted the following factual conclusions.

Defendant had visited a friend's house to return a car bed. The complaining witness, a thirteen year old girl, was in the house "babysitting" for a child two years of age and an infant of six months. She had known defendant as a neighbor for approximately half a year, and in all of her prior contacts with him he had always acted toward her as a gentleman. Defendant and the complaining witness engaged in conversation for about fifteen minutes. Then, while complainant was holding the six months old infant, who was crying, under her right arm, defendant took hold of her and kissed her on the cheek and lips. She immediately asked him "to leave me alone," but defendant continued to hold her and proceeded to touch her breasts and place one of his hands between her legs in contact with her "private part" from outside her clothing. The complainant told defendant to "stop," whereupon defendant did stop and with the remark to complainant: "Don't tell anybody," he left the house. The complainant did not mention the incident until the following morning, almost twenty-four hours later, when she told her mother. The complainant waited because when she had returned home, she found that "everybody was around."

Defendant's single contention on appeal is that, within the legal meaning of "high and aggravated," the finding of an aggravated degree of assault and battery may not here stand as a matter of law. Defendant points to the fleeting nature of the incident insofar as he ceased his actions upon the second request by complainant. He further mentions that there were no physical injuries inflicted and maintains that the psychological impact upon the girl must have been minimal since she waited almost twenty-four hours before she reported what had transpired.

In *State v. Bey,* 161 Me. 23, 206 A. 2d 413 (1965) this Court observed that assault and battery may become "high and aggravated in nature" by the presence of "circumstances of aggravation, such as . . . great disparity between the ages and physical conditions of the parties, a difference in the sexes, inde-

cent liberties or familiarities with a female, the purposeful infliction of shame and disgrace. . . ." . . .

State v. Rand, 156 Me. 81, 161 A. 2d 852 (1960) involved a factual situation so remarkably similar to the instant case that, for purposes of the appropriate application of controlling legal principles, the cases must be held indistinguishable. Sustaining a conviction of assault and battery, high and aggravated in nature, we said in Rand: "What intention could the respondent have had other than an evil intention to indulge his own lustful desires? By his indecent acts he violated the person and dignity of the child in a manner abhorrent to society." . . .

Under the combined import of *State v. Bey* and *State v. Rand* the present adjudication that defendant had committed an assault and battery, high and aggravated in degree was legally warranted. . . .

● ● ● ● ● ● ● ● ● ● ● ● ● ●

State v. Corder

Supreme Court of South Dakota, 1990.
460 N.W.2d 733.

[In affirming a conviction for first-degree murder, the Supreme Court of South Dakota discusses the sufficiency of evidence of the defendant's premeditation.]

HENDERSON, Justice
. . . At the conclusion of the trial on May 2, 1989, the jury returned a verdict of guilty against Corder for Premeditated First Degree Murder. On May 9, 1989, Corder was sentenced to life in prison. On appeal, Corder argues that . . . [h]is motion for judgment of acquittal should have been granted. . . .

On the morning of December 4, 1988, the bludgeoned and lifeless body of Clifford Hirocke was found by two hunters, 3 miles south of Vermillion. Due to the injuries inflicted on the body, authorities began investigating the case as a homicide.

Law enforcement authorities received information that Corder and Ernst had been with the victim at approximately 2:15 A.M. on December 4, 1988, at a local bar and subsequently a pizza establishment in Vermillion. Since Corder and Ernst were apparently the last persons to have seen Hirocke alive, a determination was made by law enforcement officials to interview Corder and Ernst. . . .

At the end of the State's case-in-chief and at the end of all the evidence, Corder moved for a judgment of acquittal. Those motions, however, were denied by the trial court and the case was thereafter submitted to the jury. Corder now argues on appeal that the trial court erred in denying said motions.

In reviewing a motion for judgment of acquittal, the trial court, must view the evidence in a light most favorable to the nonmovant. . . .

Corder argues that the trial court erred in denying his motion for a directed verdict of acquittal on the grounds that the State failed to establish the prima facie showing of premeditation. There is abundant case law to the effect that the fact of premeditation may be inferred from the facts and circumstances surrounding the killing. The question of Corder's premeditation in the killing of Hirocke was a question of fact for the jury. On appeal, the jury's finding of premeditation will not be disturbed unless there is an absence of evidence which would support a reasonable inference thereof.

In determining the sufficiency of evidence to establish a premeditated design to effect death in murder cases, the courts generally consider the following factors of importance: the use of a lethal or deadly weapon; the manner of the killing; the accused's conduct before and after the killing; and a determination of the presence or absence of provocation.

The testimony adduced at trial pertaining to Corder's deliberation and premeditation may be capsulized as follows:

Hirocke was beaten repeatedly about the head and chest areas. According to the pathologist who performed the autopsy, the cause of death was listed as multiple head and abdominal trauma. Hirocke suffered a laceration to his liver and had multiple rib fractures. The pathologist testified that any one of these injuries could have easily resulted in the victim's death.

The record also shows that Ernst stated that they "had to make sure he was dead, they had to kill him." With that in mind, Corder went to where Hirocke was lying and picked up a log. After striking Hirocke in the head with the log, Corder threw it into the river. Surely there was sufficient time for Corder to form the intent to kill and an opportunity for him to reconsider the matter and not strike Hirocke with the log. Further, in an apparent attempt to conceal evidence, Corder removed Hirocke's shirt and jacket and tried to burn them in order to destroy any fingerprints. Attempting to remove any remaining fingerprints, Corder dragged Hirocke's body along the ground.

While there was no evidence of a highly structured plan to kill Hirocke, we are persuaded that sufficient evidence was produced to support a reasonable inference of premeditation and that, therefore, the jury's finding of this fact should not be disturbed. Murder has no tongue, yet it speaks by direct and circumstantial evidence, through the organ of law, demanding justice.

Conviction of premeditated first-degree murder and sentence of life in prison, in all things, affirmed. . . .

● ● ● ● ● ● ● ● ● ● ● ● ● ●

Manuel v. State

District Court of Appeal of Florida, Second District, 1977.
344 So.2d 1317.

[In this case a Florida appellate court discusses the distinction between second-degree murder and manslaughter.]

OTT, Judge.

Appellant was convicted of second-degree murder. We reverse and remand for the imposition of a sentence of manslaughter for reasons hereinafter stated.

On the night of March 26, 1976, Robert Jackson, 10, was playing with Wendell Elliott, 13, in the vicinity of Janie Mae Hayes' house. The house fronted on Ohio Street in Lake Wales. The boys were playing "chase"—a game which rewards silence and stealth. They were playing so quietly and the night was so dark that a woman sitting on a nearby porch was unaware of their presence.

Earlier that night, Louise Manuel, wife of the appellant, had come to Ms. Hayes' house and accused a lodger, Ella Mae Kindrick, of having an affair with her husband. An argument ensued, after which Mrs. Manuel left the area.

The appellant was in a bar when he heard that his wife had been involved in a tiff. He obtained his .32 caliber pistol and began walking down Ohio Street toward the Hayes house. Upon reaching the area in front of the Dunlap house—two doors from the Hayes house—Manuel stopped walking when he saw Ella Mae Kindrick on the Dunlap front porch. He said to her, "Who's doing this to my wife?" . . . "Who's that messing with my wife?" He then fired a single shot into the ground.

After firing the first shot, Manuel proceeded to a lightpost (the light was broken) in front of the house between the Dunlap and Hayes houses. At this point, Wendell Elliott, having heard the shot, ran from the rear of the Hayes house to a point about three feet from Manuel. Once there, Wendell called for Robert, but received no answer. The record contains no indication that Wendell attempted to warn Manuel that Robert was in the area.

About three minutes after firing the first shot, Manuel fired another shot. According to Ms. Kindrick, from her vantage point on the Dunlap porch she could not tell exactly in which direction Manuel had pointed the pistol when he fired the second shot. On direct examination, Wendell Elliott testified that he could not tell at what, if anything, Manuel was aiming. On cross-examination, however, Wendell testified that the gun was pointed in the general direction of an area on the far side of Ms. Hayes' front yard where a trash barrel and other garbage containers were located. Nothing in his testimony indicated he could actually see the trash barrel and other garbage containers. Nothing in his testimony indicated he knew where Robert Jackson was at the time the second shot was fired.

The deputy sheriff who took Manuel into custody testified that Manuel asked about Jackson's condition and stated that he had not intended to hit the boy and was sorry about it. According to this deputy, Manuel did not indicate whether or not he knew the boy was in the area, but did say that "he knew he hit the boy when he shot" and that "the boy got in the way."

The testimony was uncontradicted that Ohio Street was very badly lit, especially in the area where the boys were playing. A police photographer who arrived soon after the shooting testified that one could not see where to walk without a flashlight.

The record is somewhat sparse with regard to Manuel's mental state. The deputy who took Manuel into custody testified that Manuel stated that "he had got his pistol to try to protect his wife, stop the fight, keep anybody from hurting her."

The statute governing murder in the second degree, Section 782.04(2), Florida Statutes, provides in relevant part:

The unlawful killing of a human being, when perpetrated by any act imminently dangerous to another and evincing a depraved mind regardless of human life, although without any premeditated design to effect the death of any particular individual, shall be murder in the second degree.

The Florida Standard Jury Instruction for murder in the second degree provides as follows:

An act is one imminently dangerous to another and evincing a depraved mind regardless of human life if it is an act (or a series of acts) which

1. a person of ordinary judgment would know is reasonably certain to kill or do serious bodily injury to another;

2. is done from ill will, hatred, spite or an evil intent, and

3. is of such a nature that the act itself indicates an indifference to human life.

Number 2 above amounts to what is frequently termed malice. The depravity of mind required in second degree murder has been equated with malice in the commonly understood sense of ill will, hatred, spite or evil intent. . . .

Within the category of second degree murder there exist varying gradations of cases. The reason for this is that some acts are simply more depraved than others. . . .

[In] the instant case . . .Manuel pointed his gun in a direction (toward the garbage area) where one would think a shot could not result in harm to any person. In addition, the lack of any substantial evidence of malevolence directed toward any person strongly suggests to this court that Manuel's conduct, while certainly culpable and inexcusable, falls far short of malice.

The statute governing manslaughter, Section 782.07, Florida Statutes, provides in relevant part:

The killing of a human being by the . . . culpable negligence of another, without lawful justification . . . shall be deemed manslaughter.

The Florida Standard Jury Instruction for manslaughter defines culpable negligence as follows:

Culpable negligence is negligence of a gross and flagrant nature and consists of more than a mere failure to use ordinary care. Culpable negligence is consciously doing an act or following a course of conduct which any reasonable person would know would likely result in death or great bodily injury to some other person, even though done without the intent to injure any person but with utter disregard for the safety of another.

In *Savage v. State,* 152 Fla. 367, 11 So.2d 778, 779 (1943), the court defined culpable negligence as that conduct which showed a

. . . gross and flagrant character, evincing reckless disregard of human life or of the safety of persons exposed to its dangerous effects; or that entire want of care which would raise the presumption of indifference to consequences; or such wantonness or recklessness or grossly careless disregard of the safety and welfare of the public, or that reckless indifference to the rights of others, which is equivalent to an intentional violation of them.

In the manslaughter area, one distinct line of cases involves accidental shootings in which manslaughter convictions were not upheld. As with the second degree murder cases, these "accident" cases are not all alike; some illustrate more serious and reprehensible conduct than do others. . . .

It is submitted that the facts in the instant case, although clearly indicating more culpable conduct than the facts of the non-manslaughter "accident" cases, supra, are not sufficient to warrant a conviction for second degree murder. . . . In the instant case there was no evidence that the appellant either observed the victim or had any notice (actual or constructive) of his possible presence.

Thus, the noiseless playing of the victim, the inky blackness of the night and the lack of demonstrated ill will on the part of the appellant point more toward culpable negligence than the evincing of a depraved mind regardless of human life.

REVERSED and REMANDED.

● ● ● ● ● ● ● ● ● ● ● ● ● ● ● ●

State v. Studham

Supreme Court of Utah, 1977.
572 P.2d 700.

[In this opinion the Supreme Court of Utah discusses some of the more modern judicial concepts concerning trials in rape cases.]

CROCKETT, Justice:

Defendant, Clyde Lloyd Studham, appeals from a jury conviction of rape. . . .

The prosecutrix, Janis ———, had lived with defendant in a meretricious relationship beginning in November, 1972. A son, Chad ———, was born on September 14, 1973. The relationship between Janis and the defendant had terminated in December of 1974 and the defendant was under a court order not to annoy or visit her.

At approximately 4:00 A.M. on the morning of March 5, 1976, Janis was awakened at her apartment by a knocking and ringing of her doorbell. Defendant, who had been drinking, was at the door and he said he wanted to talk to her, but she refused to let him in. He kicked the door open and entered; and he remained in the apartment for about two hours, during which there was some kissing and amorous advances.

The prosecutrix testified that in his efforts to force sexual intercourse upon her defendant threatened her, pinned her to the floor during a struggle, put his hand over her mouth so that she had difficulty breathing, and forced intercourse upon her against her will. She did not scream or attempt to run from her apartment, which she said was due to its futility and the fact that her young son was asleep in the adjoining room.

After the defendant left, she called her mother, who reported the incident to the police. Deputy Lester Newren of the Salt Lake County Sheriff's office came to investigate. Janis's only visible injuries were a bruised face and cut lip; and there were blood stains on her bathrobe. Pursuant to his questioning and investigation, he took the prosecutrix to St. Mark's Hospital where she was examined by Dr. John Corkrey. Later in the day the defendant was arrested and charged with this offense.

Defendant's argument that the evidence is not sufficient to prove his guilt beyond a reasonable doubt is that it rests almost solely upon her own self-interested testimony; that it is inherently improbable and inconsistent because, though she claims force, and denies consent, she did not scream, or try to escape from the apartment even though during the time he was there she had opportunity to do so.

Most crimes are committed in such secrecy as can be effected; and that is particularly so of this type of offense. Therefore, the question of guilt or innocence often depends upon the weighing of the credibility of the victim against that of the accused. Accordingly, the rule is that if there is nothing so inherently incredible about the victim's story that reasonable minds would reject it, a conviction may rest upon her testimony alone.

In regard to the failure of the victim to make an outcry, this is to be said: Whether an outcry was made, or should have been made, depends upon how practical and effective it might have been. It is evidence which may be received and it is one of the circumstances to be considered as bearing upon the critical issue of consent. But mere failure to make such an outcry does not render a conviction unsupportable.

The essential element in rape is the forcing of intercourse upon a woman "without her consent" and "against her will." It is sometimes said that those terms mean essentially the same thing, but this is not true because such an act might occur in circumstances which would be "without her consent" but which would not necessarily involve overcoming her will and her resistance, both of which must be proved. In that regard there has often been much preoccupation with and stress placed upon the matter of the physical confrontation between the accused and the victim; and it has sometimes been said that she "must resist to the utmost" or other expressions of that import. But that view no longer obtains. Even though it is necessary that the rape be against the victim's will, manifest by a determined effort on her part to resist, it is not necessary that it be shown that she engaged in any heroics which subjected her to great brutality or that she suffered or risked serious wounds or injuries.

What we think is a sounder view recognizes that the bruising and terrorizing of the senses and sensibilities can be just as real and just as wrong as the beating and bruising of the flesh; and that the law should afford a woman protection, not only from physical violence, but from having her feelings and sensibilities outraged by force or fear in violation of what she is entitled to regard and protect as the integrity of her person. Accordingly, in determining whether the victim's will and resistance were overcome, it is appropriate to consider that this may be accomplished by either physical force and violence,

or by psychological or emotional stress imposed upon her, or by a combination of them. As to the degree of resistance required: The victim need do not more than her age and her strength of body and mind make it reasonable for her to do under the circumstances to resist. In this case there is a reasonable basis in the evidence upon which the jury could believe beyond a reasonable doubt that that test was met.

In urging that the court committed error in refusing to instruct the jury that rape is easy to charge and difficult to defend against, defendant asserts that it was particularly applicable here because, in addition to the lack of corroboration, and their prior difficulties, there existed the possibility of malice behind the charge. We are aware that such an instruction in abstract terms and not focused upon the particular evidence in the case has been given without it being prejudicial error. Nevertheless, such an instruction is not looked upon with favor since it is in the nature of a directive to the jury as to how they should evaluate evidence, rather than a statement of law. Under our procedure the judging of the evidence should be left exclusively to the jury and the trial judge should neither comment thereon nor give any indication as to what he may or may not think as to the quality of the evidence. In any event, we see no reason to believe that the failure to give such an instruction in this case was error. . . .

•   •   •   •   •   •   •   •   •   •   •   •   •   •   •

State v. Rothenberg

Supreme Court of Connecticut, 1985.
195 Conn. 253, 487 A.2d 545.

[This case examines the sufficiency of the evidence to support Rothenberg's conviction for sexual assault and unlawful restraint.]

PETERS, Chief Justice.
. . . After a trial to the court, the defendant was found guilty . . . and judgment was rendered accordingly. The defendant appeals from the judgment against him.

The trial court reasonably found the following facts. The defendant and the complainant met at a bar in Southbury during the early morning hours of Au-

gust 23, 1981. The complainant recognized the defendant as someone she had met there previously. They danced. The defendant asked the complainant to accompany him to a party at a friend's condominium in Woodbury. Somewhat reluctantly, the complainant agreed and drove to the condominium in her own car.

When the couple arrived at the condominium, it appeared to be empty. In fact, however, the two bedrooms, although their doors were closed, were occupied throughout the events that then transpired. The owner of the condominium was in one bedroom and two guests were in the other.

After a brief tour of the condominium, the complainant and the defendant sat on a couch in the living room. They kissed and the defendant gave the fully clothed complainant a back rub. The complainant, at the defendant's request, gave him a back rub while he was clad only in his undershorts.

The complainant then told the defendant that she wanted to leave, but he told her that she could not go. On the pretext of wanting to use the bathroom, the complainant ran to and partially opened the front door of the condominium. The defendant closed the door and forcibly prevented her from leaving by holding her arms. The complainant could not persuade the defendant to let her leave the condominium but was allowed to use the bathroom, where she remained for approximately thirty minutes until she looked for a way to escape or a weapon. During this time, the defendant alternately promised that he would let the complainant leave and threatened to wake up his friend to join the harassment of the complainant if she did not leave the bathroom.

As the complainant emerged from the bathroom, the defendant took her by the arms and pulled her, struggling, to the living room couch. Fearing injury if she were to resist further, the complainant then submitted. The defendant sexually assaulted the complainant several times before finally releasing her.

The unseen occupants of the bedrooms in the condominium remained there throughout the night. One did not hear either the defendant or the complainant at all. The others heard sounds of conversation when the defendant and complainant first entered the condominium, but soon thereafter fell asleep and heard nothing further.

The defendant does not deny the occurrence of the sexual activity but contends that the state failed to prove that it was anything other than consensual. . . .

The defendant claims that the evidence adduced at trial to support his conviction was insufficient in two respects. First, the defendant argues that the complainant's testimony that the defendant restrained and sexually assaulted her was unbelievable as a matter of law in light of the totality of the evidence at the trial. Second, the defendant claims that the evidence showed that he lacked the criminal intent necessary to a finding of guilt. We find neither assertion persuasive.

. . . [T]he defendant claims that the complainant's account of the events at the condominium is fatally undermined by the evidence given by the occupants of the bedrooms. The complainant testified that the defendant had "slammed" the front door during her escape attempt and had "yelled" at her while she was in the bathroom. The other people in the condominium testified that they had heard nothing beyond normal conversation and had slept throughout the incident. According to the defendant, the juxtaposition of this evidence necessarily validates his contention that the complainant's continued presence in the condominium and participation in the sexual activity was consensual.

"The trier of the facts determines with finality the credibility of witnesses and the weight to be accorded their testimony." . . . The trial court could have believed the complainant's testimony that the defendant prevented her from leaving, and forcibly imposed himself upon her, without giving significant weight to her account of how loudly the defendant spoke or how noisily he closed the door. Alternatively, the court could have disbelieved the testimony of the occupants of the bedrooms. Viewing the evidence, as we must, in the light most favorable to sustaining the judgment of the trial court, . . . we conclude that the trial court could reasonably have found that the evidence established the defendant's guilt beyond a reasonable doubt. . . .

The defendant's second claim of insufficiency of the evidence relies upon the trial court's own finding that the complainant's conduct was ill-advised and subject to misconstruction. The trial court did find that the complainant "committed a serious error in judgment when she accompanied the defendant, a young man whom she knew only slightly, to an unknown location, where she really had no idea what might confront her. And once there, she compounded her error in judgment by her voluntary conduct in engaging in intimate physical contact with the defendant, who was almost completely unclothed. In the Court's view, this was a foolhardy act of very poor judgment that was subject to misinterpretation by a young man, such as the defendant, as indicative of a willingness to engage in more explicit sexual conduct. I am satisfied in my own mind that this is essentially what happened. The defendant did misconstrue the complainant's conduct and concluded that she would, in fact, be a willing participant in further sexual activity." According to the defendant, this finding proves that he was mistaken about the complainant's consent and therefore lacked the mental state necessary to commit the charged offenses.

This argument would be compelling had the trial court's opinion ended where the defendant's quotation stops. The trial court went on, however, to find that "[w]hen the complainant sought to withdraw from the situation, a situation that was developing beyond her expectations, the defendant was unwilling to permit her to do so. And he thereafter forced his attentions on the complainant and compelled her to engage in sexual intercourse against her will. The defendant failed to recognize that consensual sexual relations are one thing, forced sexual intercourse is something altogether different. The term 'consensual sexual relations' means full consent, and that clearly implies that a party should always be free to decline to go beyond a certain point. This the complainant tried to do. The defendant refused to honor this decision of the complainant and permit her to leave. For this he must be and is found guilty of both offenses as charged in the information." The trial court's finding in its totality makes it clear that the complainant's unambiguous request to leave the condominium disabused the defendant of any misinterpretation of her wishes. The defendant's conduct thereafter was knowingly coercive. A temporary misunderstanding about consent does not give irreversible license to compel sexual intercourse. There was ample evidence to support the trial court's finding and the defendant's conviction.

The defendant's second claim of error is that the trial court should have excluded testimony about his prior sexual history, just as the court upheld objections to similar questions asked of the complainant on her cross-examination. Under General Statutes Section 54–861, evidence of the sexual history of a sexual assault victim is now admissible only in clearly and narrowly defined circumstances established in a separate hearing. The defendant urges us to hold that the policy represented by that statute is as applicable to defendants as it is to complaining witnesses. In either case, he maintains, the prejudicial effect of evidence of prior sexual conduct, in the absence of special circumstances, far outweighs its probative value.

On this record, it would be improper to find error. We recognize that the defendant's argument has much to commend it; especially in light of the recent enactment of General Statutes Section 54–86f. . . . We therefore agree that defendants, like sex crime victims, should be shielded from unnecessarily prejudicial evidence of their prior sexual conduct. Appellate review of evidentiary rulings of the trial court is, however, limited to the specific legal issue raised by the objection of trial counsel. . . . In the absence of an objection in the trial court on the grounds of prejudice, we find no error in the admission of the challenged evidence. . . .

● ● ● ● ● ● ● ● ● ● ● ● ● ● ●

State v. Snider

Court of Appeal of Iowa, 1991.
479 N.W.2d 622.

[In this case the Iowa Court of Appeals considers whether there is sufficient evidence to support the defendant's conviction for false imprisonment. Note the contrasting views of the majority opinion and the dissent.]

SACKETT, Judge.
. . . Iowa Code section 710.7 (1989), False Imprisonment, states:

> A person commits false imprisonment when, having no reasonable belief that the person has any right or authority to do so, the person intentionally confines another against the other's will. A person is confined when the person's freedom to move about is substantially restricted by force, threat or deception.

. . . The facts, taking the evidence in light most favorable to the verdict, are that the defendant had been drinking for a considerable period in a bar where the victim worked as a bartender. The defendant and the victim were the last people in the bar when the victim told the defendant her boyfriend was coming. She asked the defendant to finish his drink so she could close the bar. The defendant went behind the bar, grabbed the victim by the arms, took her from behind the bar and pushed her about ten feet to a pool table. Once at the pool table, he pushed her backward against the table and held her against her will for no more than fifteen minutes. He then left the bar. Her boyfriend arrived two minutes later and called the police. The defendant was arrested.

The essential elements of false imprisonment are (1) detention or restraint against one's will, and (2) the unlawfulness of such detention or restraint. . . .

The term "confines or removes" in defining kidnapping under section 710.1 requires no minimum period of confinement or distance of removal, but does require more than the confinement or removal that is an inherent incident of commission of the crime. . . .

Section 710.7 specifies a person is confined when the person's freedom to move about is substantially restricted. The words "substantially restricted" do not appear in the kidnapping statute. . . .

We first look to whether the period of confinement or distance of removal exceeded that which would normally be incidental to an assault. . . . To do so, we assess whether the confinement or removal was significantly independent from the assault because it either (1) substantially increased the risk of harm to the victim, (2) lessened the risk of detection, or (3) significantly facilitated the defendant's escape following the assault.

Holding the victim against the pool table did not lessen defendant's risk of detection or facilitate his escape. The defendant had been at the bar for some time. He was known by the victim. The bar area where the victim was held was open to the public. The victim had told the defendant her boyfriend was coming to help her close up. Consequently, the longer the defendant stayed in the bar and held the victim down, the more likely he would be detected.

A pivotal question is whether holding the victim against the pool table substantially increased her risk of harm. The victim was harmed by the assault. The defendant was convicted of assault. He has not appealed that conviction. The State has the burden to show the confinement or movement was not merely incidental to the assault. . . . In [*State v.*] *Rich*, 305 N.W.2d at 745, the court determined a defendant's movement of a victim a short distance from a mall into a restroom was not in and of itself sufficient confinement or removal within the meaning of Iowa Code section 710.1. The factors that raised the defendant's actions to a removal and confinement in *Rich*, are not present here. The facts of this case do not show the victim's freedom was substantially restricted. We reverse the conviction for false imprisonment.

REVERSED AND DISMISSED.

HABHAB, Judge (dissenting).

I respectfully dissent from the majority's reversal and dismissal of Snider's conviction for false imprisonment. I believe the evidence was sufficient to generate a jury question on the issue. . . .

Forcible confinement for almost fifteen minutes is not merely incidental to the initial assault. Additionally, the facts show the confinement was separate from the assault. . . . The confinement itself was substantial. . . . Unlike the majority, I do not find the confinement against the victim's will merged into the assault charge. I believe both offenses were separate.

The evidence supports submission of both assault and false imprisonment charges to the jury. I would find the trial court did not err in denying the motion for directed verdict on the false imprisonment charge.

I would affirm.

CHAPTER

7

Crimes Against Property

Introduction

Private property is a basic value of American society; hence, it is a fundamental tenet of American law. In early America, property interests beyond raw land were often meager, consisting primarily of those possessions necessary for survival. Dwellings for most people were modest. At that time, enforcement of the law largely depended on "self-help." As the nation developed, property interests became a vital part of the American economy, and professional law enforcement became the rule rather than the exception. The public law recognized the need to deter people from infringing on the property interests of others and to punish transgressors. In today's affluent society and with the rapid technological advances of the past few decades, crimes against property have assumed even greater significance. In this chapter we examine the background of basic common-law property and habitation offenses and provide a sampling of the present-day statutory crimes in this area.

The Common-Law Background

When the common law emerged, England was an agrarian country with relatively little commercial activity. Possession of private property was an important concept, but beyond the right to occupy a dwelling, the property interests of most people consisted largely of what the law refers to as "tangible" property (that is, such things as animals, cooking implements, and tools). In contrast, a majority of households today own some intangible property, such as stocks, bonds, or notes. Thus, in contrast to the early common–law period, intangible assets are now of great economic importance.

The common-law offenses involving property reflect the environment in which they matured. It was a very serious offense for someone to permanently deprive another of the possession of personal property, whether through stealth or through force, violence, or intimidation. However, it was of far less consequence to cheat someone by the use of false tokens or false weights and measures. When it came to such breaches of ethics as misrepresentations and violations of trust, the common law generally left victims to their civil remedies. This view gave rise to such early maxims as *caveat emptor*, meaning "let the buyer beware." Because commercial transactions were not a major concern, forgery remained a misdemeanor. Likewise, extortion and malicious mischief were also misdemeanors because the conduct involved in these offenses did not qualify for the severe punishment meted out for felonies. Finally, offenses concerning the rights of landholders were dealt with largely through the civil law.

The Common-Law Theft Offenses

The early common law recognized two offenses dealing with theft: **larceny** and **receiving stolen property.** The theft offenses of **false pretenses** and **embezzlement** were later created by statutes passed by the English Parliament.

Larceny

The basic common-law offense against infringement of another's personal property was larceny, the crime from which all other property offenses developed. Larceny was a felony that consisted of (1) the wrongful taking and carrying away of (2) the personal property of another (3) with the intent to permanently deprive the other person of the property. Many terms used in reference to larceny are not commonly used today. The taking was called the "caption," the carrying away was called the "asportation," and the personal property had to have a "corporeal" (that is, a physical) existence. The wrongful act of taking was described as a "trespass," and the intent to permanently deprive the victim of the property was known as the *animus furundi*.

To constitute common-law larceny, the taking had to be a deprivation of the owner's or possessor's interest in personal property. Real estate and the property attached to it were not subject to larceny; neither were trees nor crops wrongfully severed from the land. But if the owner of property had already severed crops and a thief carried them away, it was larceny because the thief was carrying away personal property rather than merely infringing on the owner's real property.

These distinctions are difficult to appreciate today, but they were significant in the development of the common law, where wrongs concerning a person's land gave rise to civil, as opposed to criminal, remedies. Also, at common law, anyone wrongfully deprived of possession of personal property was entitled to recover damages based on the tort (civil wrong) of conversion. Thus, there was overlap between the crime of larceny and the tort of conversion.

As the common law developed, personal property consisted largely of tools, household items, and domestic animals. Items such as promissory notes were not subject to larceny because they represented intangible legal rights; however, coins and bills were, because they had a physical existence.

A taking by a person who had a lawful right to possession was not larceny. As we will discuss later, this led Parliament to enact the crime of embezzlement. Because the property had to be taken from another, a co-owner or partner did not commit larceny by taking jointly owned property. Nor did a spouse commit larceny by taking the other spouse's property because at common law, spouses were considered one.

To find an accused guilty of larceny, it was necessary to prove that the taker carried the property away. This element was usually satisfied by even a slight removal of the property. It was also essential to prove the taker's intent to permanently deprive the owner or possessor of the property. A person could not be convicted for just borrowing or using property under a reasonable belief of a right of possession. Consequently, a person who temporarily took another's horse would not be guilty of larceny because there was no intent to permanently deprive the owner of the horse. Furthermore, had someone taken a horse that reasonably appeared to be the taker's own, the taker would likely have been acting under a bona fide mistake of fact, hence not guilty of larceny. (See Chapter 14 for a discussion of the mistake of fact defense.) Yet a person who secured possession of goods through trickery could be found guilty of larceny if there was proof that the trickster intended to permanently deprive the owner of the goods.

Receiving Stolen Property

The common-law offense of receiving stolen property was a misdemeanor consisting of knowingly receiving possession and control of personal property belonging to another with the intent to permanently deprive the owner of possession of such property.

CASE-IN-POINT

Receiving Stolen Property: Sufficient Evidence to Convict

Defendant Lynn Belt was convicted of receiving stolen property in violation of Utah Code Ann. 76–6–408(1) (Supp. 1989), which makes it a crime for a person to receive property of another "knowing that it has been stolen or believing that it probably has been stolen . . . with a purpose to deprive the owner thereof." Belt appealed, contending the evidence was legally insufficient to support his conviction.

The evidence revealed that the defendant purchased videocassette recorders from Sgt. Illsley of the Metro Major Felony Unit during an undercover operation involving purchase and sale of

stolen property. Defendant met Illsley at an empty parking lot, where Illsley offered the new recorders to the defendant at a very low price, explaining that the store name and serial numbers had been cut off. Defendant replied, "I don't want to hear about the serial number or store names—just do our business." Illsley testified that at one point the defendant said, "I wish you wouldn't cut the serial numbers off. That makes it look hot." The Court of Appeals of Utah held that the evidence was sufficient for the jury to have found that the defendant believed the goods he purchased were stolen and affirmed Belt's conviction.

State v. Belt, 780 P.2d 1271 (Utah App. 1989).

In contrast, the crime of larceny was a common-law felony, except where property of a very minor value was involved.

False Pretenses and Embezzlement

Many technical and often subtle distinctions developed in the common-law crime of larceny. Perhaps one reason for this was the reluctance of courts to find a thief guilty of larceny because the penalty at early common law was death. As commerce became more significant in England, the crime of larceny was not adequate either to deal with those who obtained financial advantage through false pretenses or to deter or punish servants who fraudulently appropriated property that rightfully came into their possession. Consequently, by the late 1700s, the English Parliament created two supplemental misdemeanor offenses: false pretenses and embezzlement. The offense of false pretenses came into being in 1757, before the American Revolution. The offense thereby became a part of the common law of those states that adopted it with the statutory modifications made by Parliament before the American Revolution. Embezzlement, on the other hand, did not become a statutory crime until 1799, too late to become part of the common law adopted by the new American states. By subsequent enactments, the English Parliament broadened the scope of embezzlement.

False pretenses (actually "obtaining property by false pretenses") was usually directed at a seller who obtained someone else's property by (1) the accused obtaining wares or merchandise of another (2) by false pretenses and (3) with the intent to cheat or defraud the other person. Parliament's enactment of the offense of false pretenses during the Industrial Revolution represented an important development in the English criminal law. Because false pretenses became an offense just before the American Revolution, few English court decisions interpreting these offenses became a part of the common law adopted by the new American states. Yet the English law in this area influenced both American legislation and judicial decisions.

In contrast with larceny, embezzlement occurred where an accused who had lawful possession of another's property (for example, a servant or employee) wrongfully appropriated the property. A series of enactments by the English Parliament brought not only servants and employees but also brokers, bankers, lawyers, and trustees within the scope of embezzlement. Thus, an embezzlement occurred when someone occupying a position of trust converted another's property to his or her own use, whereas larceny required proof of a wrongful taking and carrying away of the personal property of another. Nevertheless, to convict a defendant of embezzlement, it was necessary to prove that the accused intended to defraud the victim.

The Modern Approach to Theft Offenses

A review of the various technical distinctions that developed in the common-law offenses of larceny, receiving stolen property, false pretenses, and the early statutory offense of embezzlement makes it obvious that significant reforms were needed. A redefinition of these basic property offenses was required to cope with the various aspects of theft in American society. Modern theft ranges from the theft of vehicles, shoplifting, and looting to such sophisticated forms of theft as credit card frauds, various scams, theft of trade secrets, and computer-related crimes. Indeed, theft is a nationwide problem that must be dealt with by both state and federal authorities.

Federal Approaches

Congress has enacted a series of statutes comprehensively proscribing theft and embezzlement. The first, 18 U.S.C.A. § 641, provides the following:

> Whoever embezzles, steals, purloins, or knowingly converts to his use or the use of another, or without authority, sells, conveys or disposes of any record, voucher, money, or thing of value of the United States or any department or agency thereof, or any property made or being made under contract for the United States or any department or agency thereof; or
> Whoever receives, conceals, or retains the same with intent to convert it to his use or gain, knowing it to have been embezzled, stolen, purloined or converted;
> Shall be fined. . . .

The purpose of 18 U.S.C.A. § 641 is to place in one part of the criminal code crimes so kindred as to belong in one category. The Supreme Court has said that despite the failure of Congress to have expressly included the common-law intent requirement for larceny, Section 641 should not be construed to eliminate that intent requirement. The statute has been held to apply not only to larceny and embezzlement but also to all instances in which a person may obtain wrongful advantage from another's property. *Morissette v. United States,* 342 U.S. 246, 72 S.Ct. 240, 96 L.Ed. 288 (1952). Another federal statute, 18 U.S.C.A. § 659, provides penalties for embezzling or unlawfully taking the contents of any vehicle moving in interstate or foreign commerce or from any passenger therein. Federal appellate courts have characterized the intent requirement under this statute as the intent to appropriate or convert the property of the owner. Furthermore, the federal appellate courts have said that a simultaneous intent to return the property or make restitution does not make the offense any less embezzlement. See, for example, *United States v. Waronek,* 582 F.2d 1158 (7th Cir. 1978).

Larceny Committed Through a Phony Night-Deposit Box

A Massachusetts jury convicted Brian Donovan and Robert Grant of larceny. Evidence introduced at trial showed that they had constructed a phony night-deposit box and attached it to the wall of a bank building. The box was constructed of heavy-gauge steel just like a real depository. Seven depositors lost an estimated $37,000 by making deposits to the phony box. Although the phony box was never recovered, a witness testified that he overheard de-fendants in a bar talking about the phony deposit box as "a helluva'n idea." Another witness stated that Grant had admitted to her that he had robbed a bank using a phony deposit box. On appeal, the Massachusetts Supreme Court rejected defendants' contentions that certain testimony had been improperly admitted into evidence and that the evidence produced at trial was legally insufficient to prove the crime of larceny.

Commonwealth v. Donovan, 478 N.E.2d 727 (Mass. 1985).

A variety of other federal statutes concern embezzlement and theft by public officers or employees of the United States and custodians of federal funds, bank examiners, and bank officers and employees. See 18 U.S.C.A. §§ 641–665.

State Approaches

All states have enacted statutes expanding the common-law concept of larceny to include all types of tangible and intangible property. Historically, the states maintained numerous statutes basically adopting the concepts of common-law larceny, receiving stolen property, false pretenses, and embezzlement. As new problems developed, legislative bodies attempted to fill the gaps by creating new offenses. As a result, legislatures enacted numerous statutory offenses proscribing various forms of stealing and dishonest dealings. Often, these statutes have been confusing; in some instances, they have been contradictory.

In recent years, many states have replaced their various statutes with a consolidated theft statute that proscribes stealing in very broad terms. These new statutes make it unlawful for a person to commit any of the common-law theft offenses mentioned as well as other crimes, and penalties are based on the amount and character of the property stolen.

Florida, for example, passed the Florida Anti-Fencing Act in 1977. Despite its narrow title, the act defines theft as including all the common-law theft offenses, several former statutory offenses, possession of property with altered or removed identifying features, and dealing in stolen property (that is, fencing). As do other modern theft statutes, the statute defines theft by degrees based on the seriousness of the offender's conduct. West's Fla. Stat. Ann. § 812.012–037.

Section 812.014(1) provides the following:

> A person commits theft if he or she knowingly obtains or uses, or endeavors to obtain or to use, the property of another with intent to, either temporarily or permanently: (a) Deprive the other person of a right to the property or a benefit from the property. (b) Appropriate the property to his or her own use or to the use of any person not entitled to the use of the property.

Under the comprehensive Florida theft statute, the phrase "obtains or uses" replaces the old common-law requirement of "taking and carrying away." This statute defines "obtains or uses" as "any manner of (a) taking or exercising control over property; (b) making any unauthorized use, disposition, or transfer of property; (c) obtaining property by fraud, willful misrepresentation of a future act, or false promise; or (d) by conduct previously known as stealing, larceny, purloining, abstracting, embezzlement, misapplication, misappropriation, conversion, obtaining money or property by false pretense, fraud, or deception; or (e) other conduct similar in nature." § 812.012(1)(2).

"Property" is broadly defined to include "(a) Real property, including things growing on, affixed to, and found in land; (b) Tangible or intangible personal property, including rights, privileges, interests, and claims; and (c) Services." § 812.012(3). "Property of another" means "property in which a person has an interest upon which another person is not privileged to infringe without consent, whether or not the other person has an interest in the property." § 812.012(4).

The value and type of property stolen categorize the seriousness of the offense. **Grand theft** in the first degree is the most serious felony. It involves stealing property valued at $100,000 or more, or if the offender commits any grand theft and in the course of committing the offense uses a motor vehicle as an instrumentality, other than merely as a getaway vehicle, to assist in committing the offense and thereby damages the real property of another; or causes damage to the real or personal property of another in excess of $1,000. § 812.014(2)(a).

Grand theft in the second degree, a somewhat less serious felony, involves theft of property valued at $20,000 or more, but less than $100,000. § 812.014(2)(b). It is grand theft of the third degree and a lesser felony if the property stolen is valued at $300 or more, but less than $20,000; or if the property stolen is a will, codicil, or other testamentary instrument, firearm, motor vehicle, livestock, fire extinguisher; or 2,000 or more pieces of citrus fruit, a stop sign, or property taken from an identified construction site. § 812.014(2)(c). If the property stolen is valued at $100 or more, but less than $300 and is taken from a dwelling or from the unenclosed curtilage of a dwelling, the offense is also classified as a third-degree felony. § 812.014(2)(d). Otherwise, except for the specified articles, theft of property having a value under $300 is petit theft, a misdemeanor. § 812.014 (2)(e). Finally, a person previously convicted of theft who commits **petit theft** is guilty of a more serious misdemeanor, § 812.014(3)(b), though one who has been convicted of theft two or more times commits a felony of the third degree. § 812.014(3)(c).

Theft remains a specific-intent crime, but like many newer theft statutes, the Florida statute simply refers to the **intent to deprive.** The Florida Supreme Court has said this simply means the "intent to steal" and not necessarily the intent to permanently deprive the owner of the property. *State v. Dunmann,* 427 So. 2d 166 (Fla. 1983). Because the statutory definition of theft includes an endeavor to commit theft, the crime is fully proved when an attempt, along with the requisite intent, is established. *State v. Sykes,* 434 So.2d 325 (Fla. 1983) (see Chapter 5).

An excerpt from *State v. Richard,* a decision of the Nebraska Supreme Court dealing with shoplifting, appears at the end of the chapter.

Computer Crime: New Offenses to Cope with High-Tech Crime

Once computers became common in society, criminals began to employ them to commit a variety of offenses. Indeed, the pervasiveness of computers poses some unique challenges to law enforcement agencies and prosecutors. Most computer crimes violate laws defining theft, fraud, or embezzlement at the state level and, often, mail fraud at the federal level. Nevertheless, since 1978 nearly every state has enacted laws specifically defining computer crimes. These laws define *access, computer program, software, database, hacking, financial instrument,* and other terms used in modern computer parlance, and address such activities as computer manipulation, theft of intellectual property, telecommunications crimes, and software piracy. They also create such offenses as **theft of computer services, computer fraud,** and **computer trespass.** The Virginia legislature has addressed each of these offenses by enacting the Virginia Computer Crimes Act.

Section 18.2–152.3 provides the following:

Any person who uses a computer or computer network without authority and with the intent to:

1. Obtain property or services by false pretenses;

2. Embezzle or commit larceny; or

3. Convert the property of another shall be guilty of the crime of computer fraud.

Depending on the value of property or services actually obtained, the offense is either a felony or a serious misdemeanor.

Section 18.2–152.4 provides the following:

Any person who uses a computer or computer network without authority and with the intent to:

1. Temporarily or permanently remove, halt or otherwise disable any computer data, computer programs, or computer software from a computer or computer network;

2. Cause a computer to malfunction regardless of how long the malfunction persists;

3. Alter or erase any computer data, computer programs, or computer software;

4. Effect the creation or alteration of a financial instrument or of an electronic transfer of funds;

5. Cause physical injury to the property of another, or

6. Make or cause to be made an unauthorized copy, in any form, including, but not limited to, any printed or electronic form of computer data, computer programs, or computer software residing in, communicated by, or produced by a computer or computer network shall be guilty of the crime of computer trespass.

7. Falsify or forge electronic mail transmission information or other routing information in any manner in connection with the transmission of unsolicited bulk electronic mail through or into the computer network of an electronic mail service provider or its subscribers.

Depending on the value of property damaged and whether the act is done maliciously, the offense is either a misdemeanor or felony.

A Unique Prosecutorial Burden in Theft Offenses

Except where statutorily specified articles are stolen, theft offenses are usually classified as grand theft or petit theft. Statutes commonly grade the felony and misdemeanor offenses based on ranges of market value of goods stolen. Therefore, the prosecution must establish the market value of goods or services stolen. The determining factor

CASE-IN-POINT

Unauthorized Access to a Voice Mail Box

Andrea M. Gerulis was convicted in a bench trial of two counts of unlawful use of a computer and two counts of violating a statute that criminalized intentionally obtaining various electronic services "available only for compensation" by deception, unauthorized connection, etc. Defendant was ordered to make restitution. The evidence revealed that the defendant deposited and retrieved information from voice mailboxes (VMBs) of a hospital and a telephone message company without authority from either to do so. By altering passwords she thereby prevented authorized users from using their VMBs. The defendant appealed, contending the evidence was insufficient to sustain her convictions.

The appellate court found that VMBs are "computers" within the meaning of the statute, and the defendant's disruption of normal use of the

VMBs violated the statute. The court then addressed the defendant's convictions for theft of services. The court observed that the prosecution had charged the defendant under a statute that makes it an offense if a person "intentionally obtains services for himself or for another which he knows are available only for compensation." Because the evidence revealed that the VMBs the defendant accessed were provided by the hospital and message company without charge for their employees, the court found that the defendant's mere intent to obtain free services did not violate that statute. Accordingly, the court affirmed the defendant's convictions for unlawful use of a computer, reversed her convictions for theft of services, and remanded the case to the trial court to modify the restitution order imposed as defendant's sentence.

Commonwealth v. Gerulis, 616 A.2d 686 (Pa. Super. 1992).

is generally the market value at the time and in the locality of the theft. *State v. Kimbel,* 620 P.2d 515 (Utah 1980). This may be shown by proof of the original market cost, the manner in which the property stolen has been used, and its general condition and quality. *Negron v. State,* 306 So.2d 104 (Fla. 1974). Judges customarily instruct juries that if the value of the property cannot be ascertained, they must find the value to be less than that required for grand theft. But consider the theft of a credit card. Usually, holders of these cards have set credit limits available to them on proper signature. Therefore, a credit card has no market value in lawful channels for a third person. In *Miller v. People,* 566 P.2d 1059 (Colo. 1977), the Colorado Supreme Court held that the amount that could be purchased on the stolen card in the "illegitimate" market could be considered in determining whether a defendant was guilty of felony theft.

Proof of value is very important in a theft case because it can often mean the difference between the defendant being convicted of a misdemeanor or a felony, or even of a felony of various degrees. For this reason, courts often receive expert testimony on this issue.

Robbery

At common law, **robbery** was a felony that consisted of (1) a taking of another's personal property of value (2) from the other person's possession or presence (3) by force or placing the person in fear and (4) with the intent to permanently deprive the other person of that property. In reality, robbery was an aggravated form of larceny where the taking was accomplished by force or threats of force with the same specific-intent requirement as in common-law larceny. To constitute robbery, the violence or intimidation had to overcome the victim's resistance and precede or accompany the actual taking of property. Property in the victim's dwelling or vicinity was regarded as being in the victim's possession. To illustrate a significant difference between larceny and robbery, a person who spirited a person's wallet from his pocket would be guilty of larceny, but if the victim resisted and the thief took the wallet by force or violence, the offense constituted robbery.

Statutory Approaches to Robbery

In some respects, robbery is an offense against the person because it usually involves an assault or battery. See, for example, *State v. Shoemake*, 618 P.2d 1201 (Kan. 1980). Yet it also involves a taking of property and is generally classified as an offense against property.

FEDERAL LAW

A federal statute makes it an offense to take, or attempt to take, by force and violence or intimidation from the person or presence of another, any property or money belonging to or in the care of a bank, credit union, or savings and loan association. 18 U.S.C.A. § 2113(a).

Federal jurisdiction is established where the bank is a federally chartered institution or where its deposits are federally insured. *United States v. Harris*, 530 F.2d 576 (4th Cir. 1976). The statutory offense varies from the common-law crime of robbery in that the government need only establish the defendant's general intent. *United States v. Klare*, 545 F.2d 93 (9th Cir. 1976).

STATE LAWS

Robbery is an offense in every state. Many states have enacted statutes simply defining it as did the common law, a practice sometimes referred to as codifying the common law. Other states classify robbery according to degree, with the seriousness of the offense usually based on whether the assailant is armed, the degree of force used, and, in some instances, on the vulnerability of the victim. The value of the property taken does not usually affect the degree of the crime of robbery, as it does that of theft.

The Colorado Criminal Code provides a good illustration of classification of robbery offenses: "A person who knowingly takes anything of value from the person or presence of another by the use of force, threats, or intimidation commits robbery." West's Colo. Rev. Stat. Ann. § 18–4–301(1). This is "simple robbery," in contrast with the statutory offense of **aggravated robbery.** The Colorado statute further provides as follows:

(1) A person who commits robbery is guilty of aggravated robbery if during the act of robbery or immediate flight therefrom:

(a) He is armed with a deadly weapon with intent, if resisted, to kill, maim, or wound the person robbed or any other person; or

(b) He knowingly wounds or strikes the person robbed or any other person with a deadly weapon or by the use of force, threats, or intimidation with a deadly weapon knowingly puts the person robbed or any other person in reasonable fear of death or bodily injury; or

(c) He has present a confederate, aiding or abetting the perpetration of the robbery, armed with a deadly weapon, with the intent, either on the part of the defendant or confederate, if resistance is offered, to kill, maim, or wound the person robbed or any other person, or by the use of force, threats, or intimidation puts the person robbed or any other person in reasonable fear of death or bodily injury; or

(d) He possesses any article used or fashioned in a manner to lead any person who is present reasonably to believe it to be a deadly weapon or represents verbally or otherwise that he is then and there so armed. West's Colo. Rev. Stat. Ann. § 18–4–302.

Under Colorado law, robbery of the elderly or handicapped is punishable the same as the offense of aggravated robbery. West's Colo. Rev. Stat. Ann. § 18–4–304. The Colorado Supreme Court has said that the gist of the crime of robbery under the Colorado statutes is "the putting in fear and taking of property of another by force or intimidation." *People v. Small*, 493 P.2d 15 (Colo. 1972). Aggravated robbery is distinguished from simple robbery by the fact that an accomplice or confederate is armed with a dangerous weapon with intent, if resisted, to maim, wound, or kill. The court said that simple and aggravated robbery are but two degrees of the same offense. *Atwood v. People*, 489 P.2d 1305 (Colo. 1971). The prosecution is simply required to prove the perpetrator's intent to force the victim to give up something of value. *People v. Bridges*, 612 P.2d 1110 (Colo. 1980). Property is taken from the "presence of another" under Colorado law when it is so within the victim's reach, inspection, or observation that he or she would be able to retain control over the property but for the force, threats, or intimidation directed by the perpetrator. *People v. Bartowsheski*, 661 P.2d 235 (Colo. 1983).

In the margin:

> In *Jones v. Commonwealth*, reprinted at the end of the chapter, the Virginia Court of Appeals considers the sufficiency of the evidence to support the defendant's conviction for robbery.

The Temporal Relationship of Force to the Taking

Is it essential that the element of violence or intimidation occur before or at the same time as the taking of the victim's property? State appellate courts are divided on this issue, often based on the specific statutory language. Note that the Colorado statute in addressing aggravated robbery includes the language "if during the act of robbery or immediate flight therefrom." The Colorado Supreme Court has said that force used in robbery need not occur simultaneously with the taking. *People v. Bartowsheski*, supra. Other courts have agreed. In *Hermann v. State*, 123 So.2d 846 (Miss. 1960), a defendant, after stealthily obtaining gasoline, made a getaway from a filling station by pointing a deadly weapon at the attendant. The attendant stuck his hand through the window of the vehicle but was pushed away by the offender. The Mississippi Supreme Court held that this act of pushing the victim away constituted the force element of robbery. Again, in *People v. Kennedy*, 294 N.E.2d 788 (Ill. App. 1973), the court held that while the taking may be without force, the offense is robbery if the departure with the property is accomplished by the use of force.

In 1986 the Florida Supreme Court held that defendants who used force while fleeing a retail store after committing theft in the store could not be convicted of robbery. The court followed the traditional common-law view that the use of force must occur before or at the same time as the taking of property. *Royal v. State*, 490 So.2d 44 (Fla. 1986). The state legislature promptly amended the statutory definition of robbery to add "an act shall be deemed 'in the course of committing the robbery' if it occurs in an attempt to commit robbery or in flight after the attempt or commission." West's Fla. Stat. Ann. § 812.13(3)(a). The statute also added that "an act shall

CASE-IN-POINT

Armed Robbery: Is an Unloaded Gun a "Dangerous Weapon"?

On the morning of July 26, 1984, Lamont Julius McLaughlin and a companion, both wearing masks, entered a bank in Baltimore. McLaughlin brandished a handgun and told those in the bank to put up their hands and not to move. While McLaughlin held the gun, his companion leaped over the counter and stuffed several thousand dollars into a brown paper bag. Police officers were waiting outside and promptly arrested the pair. It was then determined that McLaughlin's gun was not loaded.

McLaughlin was found guilty in federal court of bank robbery "by the use of a dangerous weapon." 18 U.S.C.A. § 2113(d). On appeal, McLaughlin argued that his unloaded gun did not qualify as a "dangerous weapon" under the federal bank rob-

bery statute. The United States Supreme Court rejected the argument and upheld McLaughlin's conviction:

"Three reasons, each independently sufficient, support the conclusion that an unloaded gun is a "dangerous weapon." First, a gun is an article that is typically and characteristically dangerous; the use for which it is manufactured and sold is a dangerous one, and the law reasonably may presume that such an article is always dangerous even though it may not be armed at a particular time or place. In addition, the display of a gun instills fear in the average citizen; as a consequence, it creates an immediate danger that a violent response will ensue. Finally, a gun can cause harm when used as a bludgeon."

McLaughlin v. United States, 476 U.S. 16, 106 S.Ct. 1677, 90 L.Ed.2d 15 (1986).

be deemed 'in the course of taking' if it occurs either prior to, contemporaneous with, or subsequent to the taking of the property and if it and the act of taking constitute a continuous series of acts and events." § 812.13(3)(b).

A New Statutory Offense: Carjacking

Depending on the circumstances, a person who forcibly takes another's vehicle is subject to prosecution under various state statutes. Recognizing the serious national threat that forcible auto theft poses to persons and their motor vehicles, and after a nationwide spree of **carjacking,** in 1992 Congress enacted the Anti-Car Theft Act of 1992. 18 U.S.C.A. § 2119. As originally enacted, the statute made it a crime for anyone who "takes a motor vehicle that has been transported, shipped, or received in interstate or foreign commerce from the person or presence of another by force and violence or by intimidation, or attempt to do so." The Ninth Circuit interpreted the 1992 statute as creating a general-intent offense. *United States v. Martinzez,* 49 F.3d 1398 (9th Cir. 1995).

In 1994 Congress amended Section 2119 to provide the following:

> Whoever, *with the intent to cause death or serious bodily harm* [emphasis added] takes a motor vehicle that has been transported, shipped, or received in interstate or foreign commerce from the person or presence of another by force and violence or by intimidation or attempts to so shall be [fined or imprisoned].

In *United States v. Randolph,* 93 F.3rd 656 (9th Cir. 1996), the Ninth Circuit viewed the amended statute as defining a specific-intent offense that requires proof of more than the brandishing of a weapon or a mere threat or conditional threat to harm. The following year, the Third Circuit, in *United States v. Anderson,* 108 F.3d 478 (3d Cir. 1997), disagreed with *Randolph,* supra. The Third Circuit explained that the "intent to cause death or serious bodily harm" provision of the statute is satisfied once the government establishes that the defendant intended to cause death or serious bodily harm if the victim refused to relinquish the vehicle. This is sometimes referred to as establishing the defendant's "conditional intent." In 1999 the Supreme Court adopted the Third Circuit's view, holding that Section 2119 merely requires proof of an intent to seriously harm or kill the driver if necessary, rather than an unconditional intent to harm or kill, to effect a carjacking. *Holloway aka Ali v. United States,* 526 U.S. 1, 119 S.Ct. 966, 143 L.Ed.2d 1 (1999).

The Supreme Court's decision in *Holloway aka Ali v. United States* is excerpted at the end of the chapter.

Federal courts upheld the constitutionality of the act as a valid expression of Congressional power under the Commerce Clause of the Constitution, most recently in *United States v. Coleman,* 78 F.3d 154 (11th Cir. 1996). In recent years, however, the Supreme Court has indicated that there are limits to congressional authority to create new federal crimes under the auspices of the Commerce Clause. See *United States v. Lopez,* 514 U.S. 549, 115 S.Ct. 1624, 131 L.Ed.2d 626 (1995). Some critics have suggested that the Court might also invalidate the federal carjacking statute, but this seems unlikely inasmuch as the automobile is a major article of interstate commerce and a primary vehicle of interstate transportation.

Forgery and Uttering a Forged Instrument

Blackstone defined common-law **forgery** as "the fraudulent making or alteration of a writing to the prejudice of another man's right." The early cases reveal that such writings as wills, receipts, and physicians' certificates were subject to forgery. To convict a defendant of forgery under common law, it was essential to establish the accused's intent to defraud. **Uttering a forged instrument** was also a common-law offense, but one separate and distinct from forgery. "Utter," a term of art synonymous with "publish," distinguishes the actual forgery from the act of passing a forged instrument to someone. As an indication of the lesser importance of commercial matters in early English society, the common law classified both forgery and uttering a forged instrument as misdemeanors.

Statutory Expansion of Forgery Offenses

Unlike the common law, federal and state statutes generally classify forgery as a felony. Reflecting the importance of written and printed documentation in our modern economy, statutes in all American jurisdictions have extended the crime of forgery to almost every type of public or private legal instrument.

Federal Statutes

Under federal law, "[w]hoever, with intent to defraud, falsely makes, forges, counterfeits, or alters any obligation or other security of the United States" commits the crime of forgery. 18 U.S.C.A. § 471. Federal courts have stated that the manifest purpose of these laws is to protect all currency and obligations of the United States, *United States v. LeMon,* 622 F.2d 1022 (10th Cir. 1980), and that the prosecution must prove not only the passing, but also the defendant's "intent to pass the bad money," *United States v. Lorenzo,* 570 F.2d 294, 299 (9th Cir. 1978).

Several other federal statutes relate to forgery and the **counterfeiting** of federal securities, postage stamps, postage meters, money orders, public records, judges' signatures, and court documents. See 18 U.S.C.A. §§ 472–509. Many prosecutions are brought under 18 U.S.C.A. § 495, which makes it unlawful to forge and utter forged United States Treasury checks. To convict someone under this statute, the government must establish the defendant's specific fraudulent intent. *United States v. Sullivan,* 406 F.2d 180 (2d Cir. 1969).

State Statutes

Most states have substantially adopted the common-law definition of forgery, but have expanded the number of instruments that can be forged to include a lengthy list of public and private documents. For example, the Arizona Criminal Code makes forgery a felony and provides the following:

> a. A person commits forgery if, with intent to defraud, such person:
>
> 1. Falsely makes, completes or alters a written instrument; or
>
> 2. Knowingly possesses a forged instrument; or
>
> 3. Offers or presents, whether accepted or not, a forged instrument or one which contains false information. Ariz. Rev. Stat. § 13–2002.

Under this section, the offenses of forgery and uttering have been coupled under the term *forgery,* but the distinction as separate offenses must still be observed because the elements of the offenses are not the same and the proof required can differ. *State v. Reyes,* 458 P.2d 960 (Ariz. 1969). Thus, under Arizona law the crime of forgery has three elements: (1) signing the name of another person, (2) intending to defraud, and (3) knowing that there is no authority to sign. *State v. Nettz,* 560 P.2d 814 (Ariz. App. 1977). On the other hand, uttering is the passing or publishing of a false, altered, or counterfeited paper or document. *State v. Reyes,* supra. Proof of the intent to defraud is essential to obtain a conviction of forgery, *State v. Maxwell,* 445 P.2d 837 (Ariz. 1968), but such intent may be inferred from circumstances in which the false instrument is executed or issued, *State v. Gomez,* 553 P.2d 1233 (Ariz. App. 1976). Note that based on the wording of the Arizona statute proscribing forgery, a conviction for "attempt to pass" is a conviction of forgery, not of an attempt. *Ponds v. State,* 438 P.2d 423 (Ariz. App. 1968) (see Chapter 5).

The Arizona Court of Appeals' opinion in *State v. Gomez* is reprinted at the end of the chapter.

Common Examples of Forgery and Uttering a Forged Instrument

Among the more common examples of forgery today are the following:

- Signing another's name to an application for a driver's license
- Printing bogus tickets to a concert or sports event
- Signing another's name to a check on his or her bank account without authority
- Altering the amount of a check or note
- Signing another's name without authority to a certificate transferring shares of stock
- Signing a deed transferring someone's real estate without authorization
- Making an unauthorized change in the legal description of property being conveyed under a deed
- Altering the grades or credits on a college transcript.

CASE-IN-POINT

Forgery

The state prosecuted defendant Donald E. Hicks for forgery. At trial, the evidence revealed that on August 4, 1984, defendant Hicks went to see Edmond Brown to make a payment on a debt. Hicks told Brown that he could pay him $100 on his debt if Brown could cash a two-party check for him. Hicks presented Brown with a check for $349 made out to Hicks on the account of Gott, Young, and Bogle, P.A., a Wichita law firm. The check was signed "Gott Young." The defendant told Brown that the check was a partial payment of a settlement of a claim stemming from an automobile accident. Hicks assured Brown that the check was good and endorsed it over to him. Brown accepted the check and returned $249 to Hicks. When the check was returned by the bank, Brown contacted the law firm. He was told that there was no one by the name of "Gott Young" at the firm and that the firm had never represented Hicks. He further learned that some twenty-five checks from the firm's petty cash account were missing. Hicks was found guilty by a jury, and his conviction was affirmed on appeal.

State v. Hicks, 714 P.2d 105 (Kan. App. 1986).

Uttering a forged instrument commonly occurs when a person knowingly delivers a forged check to someone in exchange for cash or merchandise, knowingly sells bogus tickets for an event, or submits a deed with forged signatures for official recording.

Falsification of computerized records such as college credits and financial records poses new challenges to laws proscribing forgery. The increasing use of computers gives rise to the need for new applications of statutes proscribing forgery and uttering a forged instrument.

Worthless Checks

As commercial banking developed, the passing of "bad checks" became a serious problem. A person who writes a worthless check on his or her bank account does not commit a forgery. In early cases, some courts referred to issuance of checks without funds in the bank as use of a "false token." These cases were prosecuted under statutes making it unlawful to use false pretenses to obtain property.

States have now enacted a variety of statutes making it unlawful to issue checks with insufficient funds to cover payment. Earlier statutes often provided that to be guilty of false pretenses for issuing a worthless check, a person had to fraudulently obtain goods. This proved to be an impracticable method to control issuance of checks by depositors who misgauged their checking account balances. The widespread use of commercial and personal banking led legislatures to enact **worthless check statutes** to cope with the problem. These statutes usually classify such an offense as a misdemeanor, and legislatures have increasingly opted to allow offenders to make restitution of losses caused by worthless checks. For example, the Texas law that makes issuance of bad checks a misdemeanor stipulates the following:

> A person commits an offense if he issues or passes a check or similar sight order for the payment of money knowing that the issuer does not have sufficient funds in or on deposit with the bank or other drawee for the payment in full of the check or order as well as all other checks or orders outstanding at the time of issuance. Vernon's Tex. Penal Code Ann., § 32.41(a).

The Texas Penal Code presumes the issuer knows that there are insufficient funds if he or she had no account with the bank or other drawee when the check was issued, or if payment is refused by the bank on presentation within thirty days after issue and the person who wrote the check failed to pay the holder in full within ten days after receiving notice of such refusal. Vernon's Tex. Penal Code Ann., § 32.41(b)(1–2). A person charged with an offense under Section 32.41 is permitted to make restitution under certain conditions. Vernon's Tex. Penal Code Ann., § 32.41(e).

Access Device Fraud

Until this edition of the text, this topic was called "Credit Card Fraud." But debit cards, automated teller machine (ATM) cards, account numbers, personal identification numbers (PINs), and other means are now commonly available to named persons who assume the obligation of their use. Because of their widespread use, state legislatures have realized the necessity to enact comprehensive statutes proscribing the fraudulent use of devices to secure cash, goods, and services through means beyond the traditional credit card.

In 1998 Pennsylvania rewrote its statute titled "Credit Card Fraud" to proscribe a variety of means of gaining fraudulent access to money, goods, and services. As amended, the revised section of Purdon's Pennsylvania Consolidated Statutes Annotated now provides as follows:

Section 4106. Access device fraud

(a) Offense defined.—A person commits an offense if he:

(1) uses an access device to obtain or in an attempt to obtain property or services with knowledge that:

(i) the access device is counterfeit, altered or incomplete;

(ii) the access device was issued to another person who has not authorized its use;

(iii) the access device has been revoked or canceled; or

(iv) for any other reason his use of the access device is unauthorized by the issuer or the device holder; or

(2) publishes, makes, sells, gives, or otherwise transfers to another, or offers or advertises, or aids and abets any other person to use an access device knowing that the access device is counterfeit, altered or incomplete, belongs to another person who has not authorized its use, has been revoked or canceled or for any reason is unauthorized by the issuer or the device holder; or

(3) possesses an access device knowing that it is counterfeit, altered, incomplete or belongs to another person who has not authorized its possession.

(a.1) Presumptions.—For the purpose of this section as well as in any prosecution for theft committed by the means specified in this section:

(1) An actor is presumed to know an access device is counterfeit, altered or incomplete if he has in his possession or under his control two or more counterfeit, altered or incomplete access devices.

(2) Knowledge of revocation or cancellation shall be presumed to have been received by an access device holder seven days after it has been mailed to him at the address set forth on the access device application or at a new address if a change of address has been provided to the issuer.

(b) Defenses.—It is a defense to a prosecution under subsection (a)(1)(iv) if the actor proves by a preponderance of the evidence that he had the intent and ability to meet all obligations to the issuer arising out of his use of the access device.

Subsection (c) stipulates that if the value involved is $500 or more, the offense constitutes a felony; if less than $500, the offense constitutes a misdemeanor. The degree of felony or misdemeanor depends on the value involved.

Subsection (d) includes the following definitions:

- "Access device." Any card, including, but not limited to, a credit card, debit card and automated teller machine card, plate, code, account number, personal identification number or other means of account access that can be used alone or in conjunction with another access device to obtain money, goods, services or anything else of value or that can be used to transfer funds.

- "Altered access device." A validly issued access device which after issue is changed in any way.

- "Counterfeit access device." An access device not issued by an issuer in the ordinary course of business.

- "Device holder." The person or organization named on the access device to whom or for whose benefit the access device is issued by an issuer.

Many of the offenses proscribed by the above statute could likely be prosecuted under a modern comprehensive theft or larceny statute; however, because of the widespread use of access devices, other states have or will likely adopt statutes similar to the quoted Pennsylvania law.

Habitation Offenses

Two felonies developed at common law reflect the value of privacy and the need to protect the security of a person's dwelling. The offenses of **burglary** and **arson** gave credence to the old English saying "A man's home is his castle." These offenses were created to protect not only the dwelling house but also the buildings within the **curtilage,** an enclosed area around the dwelling that typically included the cookhouse and other outbuildings. In England the enclosure had to be formed by a stone fence or wall; however, this custom has not been established in the United States. *State v. Bugg,* 72 P. 236 (Kan. 1903). Rather, American courts tend to define curtilage as the ground surrounding a dwelling that is used for domestic purposes or for the convenience of the family.

Both burglary and arson became felonies in the United States. Modern statutes have greatly broadened the scope of the common-law crimes of burglary and arson, and extended the protection of the criminal law far beyond the traditional concept of offenses against habitation. Nevertheless, to understand their historic development, it is helpful to classify them as offenses against habitation.

Burglary at Common Law

According to Blackstone, common-law burglary consisted of (1) breaking and entering of (2) a dwelling of another (3) during the nighttime (4) with intent to commit a felony therein. The "breaking" at common law could be either "actual" or "constructive." An actual breaking could be merely technical, such as pushing open a door or opening a window. An entry gained through fraud or deception was considered a "constructive" breaking. Even the slightest entry was deemed sufficient; for instance, a hand, a foot, or even a finger within the dwelling was regarded as a sufficient entry. Proof of the defendant's intent to commit a felony was essential: A breaking and entering did not constitute burglary at common law unless the perpetrator had a specific intent to commit a felony (for example, murder, rape, or larceny); however, it was not necessary to prove that any felony was committed. *Dwelling* was defined as the house or place of habitation used by the occupier or member of the family "as a place to sleep in." Finally, to constitute burglary at common law, it was essential that the offense be committed at nighttime, generally defined as the period between sunset and sunrise.

In *State v. Feldt,* reprinted at the end of the chapter, the Supreme Court of Montana considers an appeal by a convenience store employee who was convicted of burglary.

Statutory Revisions of Burglary

Many states have enacted statutes proscribing **breaking and entering,** thereby placing a new label on the common-law crime of burglary. At a minimum, these statutes expand the offense of burglary beyond dwelling houses and eliminate the requirement that the offense take place in the nighttime. Most states retain the common-law requirement that the accused break and enter with intent to commit a felony, and others include the language "or theft." Even where the offense is still labeled burglary, legislatures have made significant changes in the common-law definition. In addition to eliminating the nighttime requirement, they have broadened the offense to include buildings and structures of all types. Today, most criminal codes include vehicles, aircraft, and vessels either in the definition of burglary or by a separate statute. Finally, modern statutes frequently provide that a person who enters a structure with consent, but who remains therein with intent to commit a felony, may be found guilty of burglary notwithstanding an original lawful entry. An example of this would be someone intentionally remaining in a department store intending to commit an offense therein after the store closes for the day. Michigan law illustrates a modern statutory approach and specifies the following:

> Any person who breaks and enters with intent to commit any felony, or any larceny therein, a tent, hotel, office, store, shop, warehouse, barn, granary, factory or other building, structure, boat or ship, or railroad car shall be guilty of a felony. Mich. Comp. Laws Ann. § 750.110.

The Michigan statute states that if the dwelling is occupied, the offender shall be punished more severely. Mich. Comp. Laws Ann. § 750.110. Another Michigan statute makes it an offense for a person to enter without breaking into any of the structures or vehicles enumerated in the breaking and entering statute. Mich. Comp. Laws Ann. § 750.111.

Courts tend to liberally construe the terms "breaking" and "entering" commonly found in burglary statutes. In *State v. Jaynes,* 464 S.E. 2d 448 (N.C. 1995), the North Carolina Supreme Court said that for purposes of burglary, "any force, however slight, employed to effect entrance through any usual or unusual place of ingress, whether open, partly open, or closed . . . by any use of force, however slight, . . . will suffice as the 'breaking' required for burglary." A New York appellate court has said that a defendant "enters" a building within the meaning of that state's burglary statute when a defendant's person or any part of defendant's body intrudes. *People v. Jackson,* 638 N.Y.S. 2d 140 (1996), appeal denied, 672 N.E. 2d 620 (1996).

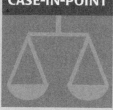

Evidence Sufficient to Establish Burglary

In the morning of October 18, 1981, Philadelphia police were called to Cramer's Kiddy Shop. Entering the store, they heard footsteps on the roof. They went up to the second floor, where they discovered a two-foot hole in a wall with access to the roof. One of the officers went through the hole and found himself covered with plaster dust. He then observed two males climbing down an exterior wall. One of them was apprehended. His hands were dirty, and

his clothes were covered with plaster dust. In the alley behind the store, police located several items of children's clothing that had been taken from the store along with a crowbar. Patrick Carpenter, who was apprehended, was found guilty of burglary and other offenses. On appeal, Carpenter argued that the evidence was insufficient to warrant a conviction for burglary. The appellate court rejected the contention and upheld defendant's conviction.

Commonwealth v. Carpenter, 479 A.2d 603 (Pa. Super. 1984).

Possession of Burglar's Tools

Michigan, like most states, makes **possession of burglar's tools** a felony if the possessor has the intent to use the tools for burglarious purposes. Michigan law provides the following:

> Any person who shall knowingly have in his possession any nitroglycerine, or other explosive, thermite, engine, machine, tool or implement, device, chemical or substance, adapted and designed for cutting or burning through, forcing or breaking open any building, room, vault, safe or other depository, in order to steal therefrom any money or other property, knowing the same to be adapted and designed for the purpose aforesaid, with intent to use or employ the same for the purpose aforesaid, shall be guilty of a felony. Mich. Comp. Laws Ann. § 750.116.

Many years ago, the Michigan Supreme Court emphasized that to obtain a conviction the state must prove the accused knowingly had possession of burglar's tools, knew the tools could be used for a criminal purpose, and intended to use them for such purpose. *People v. Jefferson,* 126 N.W. 829 (Mich. 1910).

Arson at Common Law

Like burglary, arson was a felony at common law designed to protect the security of the dwelling place. The crime consisted of (1) the willful and malicious burning (2) of a dwelling (3) of another. There was no requirement that the dwelling be destroyed or even that it be damaged to a significant degree. In fact, a mere charring was sufficient, but scorching or smoke damage did not constitute arson at common law. The common law defined the term "dwelling" the same as in burglary. Consequently, the burning of buildings within the curtilage constituted arson. The common law regarded arson as a general-intent crime, with the required malice being presumed from an intentional burning of someone's dwelling. However, setting fire to one's own home was not arson at common law. Yet some early English cases indicate that under circumstances where burning one's own house posed a danger to others, "houseburning" was a misdemeanor offense.

Statutory Revision of Arson

Modern statutes have extended the offense of arson to include the intentional burning of buildings, structures, and vehicles of all types. Frequently, this even includes a person's own property. Several states have enacted statutes that provide that use of explosives to damage a structure constitutes arson. As in burglary, the modern offense of arson is designed to protect many forms of property. Therefore, arson can no longer be considered strictly a habitation offense. By categorizing arson, legislatures can make appropriate distinctions and provide penalties accordingly.

Michigan law embraces four categories of arson. Mich. Comp. Laws Ann. § 750.72 provides as follows:

> Any person who wilfully or maliciously burns any dwelling house, either occupied or unoccupied, or the contents thereof, whether owned by himself or another, or any building within the curtilage of such dwelling house, or the contents thereof, shall be guilty of a felony.

In *People v. Williams*, 318 N.W.2d 671 (Mich. App. 1982), the court held that to establish the *corpus delicti* (see Chapter 6) of arson of a dwelling house, the state must show not only a burning of the house but also that it resulted from an intentional criminal act. The court explained that where only a burning is shown, a presumption arises that it was accidentally caused.

Section 750.73 makes it a lesser felony for anyone to willfully or maliciously burn any building or other real property, or contents thereof, while Section 750.74 makes it a misdemeanor to willfully and maliciously burn personal property worth less than $50 and a felony if the value is greater. For a fire to be "willfully" set by the accused requires that the defendant commit such act stubbornly and for an unlawful purpose. Mere proof of carelessness or accident is not sufficient to establish guilt. *People v. McCarty*, 6 N.W.2d 919 (Mich. 1942).

In contrast with Michigan, many state statutes broaden the scope of the offense by referring to "damage caused by fire" rather than "burning." And in contrast with the common law, under many modern statutes proof of damage by smoke or

---

CASE-IN-POINT

Proving the Crime of Arson

Early on the morning of September 23, 1981, a fire destroyed a log cabin belonging to Henry Xavier Kennedy. Investigators determined the fire was incendiary in origin. A hot plate with its switch in the "on" position was found in the most heavily burned area of the cabin. Investigators also determined that kerosene poured around the area of the hot plate had accelerated the fire.

Five days before the fire, Kennedy had renewed a $40,000 insurance policy on the cabin. Evidence was also presented that Kennedy's building business was slow. Kennedy introduced evidence of an alibi from midnight until 4:00 A.M. Although the fire was reported at 3:42 A.M., investigators testified that the incendiary device could have been set before midnight.

Kennedy was convicted of arson, and his conviction was upheld on appeal.

Kennedy v. State, 323 S.E.2d 169 (Ga. App. 1984).

scorching is sufficient to constitute arson. See, for example, *State v. McVeigh*, 516 P.2d 918 (Kan. 1973).

Most jurisdictions have enacted statutes making it a crime to burn any property with the intent to defraud an insurance company, usually requiring the prosecution to prove the defendant's specific intent to defraud. In this respect, Mich. Comp. Laws Ann. § 750.75 stipulates the following:

> Any person who shall wilfully burn any building or personal property which shall be at the time insured against loss or damage by fire with intent to injure and defraud the insurer, whether such person be the owner of the property or not, shall be guilty of a felony.

Malicious Mischief

A mere trespass to land or personal property was not a crime at common law unless it was committed forcibly or maliciously. However, it was a common-law misdemeanor called **malicious mischief** for a person to damage another's real or personal property. Modern statutes usually define the offense much as did the common law, often referring to the offense as **vandalism** and imposing penalties based on the extent of damage inflicted on the victim's property. For example, Section 594(a) of the California Penal Code states the following:

> Every person who maliciously commits any of the following acts with respect to any real or personal property not his or her own, in cases other than those specified by state law, is guilty of vandalism:
>
> (1) Defaces with graffiti or other inscribed material.
>
> (2) Damages.
>
> (3) Destroys.

In *State v. Tonnisen,* reprinted at the end of the chapter, the Appellate Division of the New Jersey Superior Court rejects an appeal by a defendant who was found guilty of malicious mischief.

The California statute sets the penalty based on the amount of defacement, damage, or destruction.

Extortion

In describing common-law **extortion,** Blackstone said it was "the taking by color of an office of money or other thing of value, that is not due, before it is due, or more than is due." Under most modern statutes, extortion has been extended beyond acts by public officers. As the California law provides,

> Extortion is the obtaining of property from another, with his consent, or the obtaining of an official act of a public officer, induced by a wrongful use of force or fear, or under color of official right. West's Ann. Cal. Penal Code § 518.

It further stipulates the following:

> Fear, such as will constitute extortion, may be induced by a threat, either:
>
> 1. to do an unlawful injury to the person or property of the individual threatened or of a third person; or,

2. to accuse the individual threatened, or any relative of his, or member of his family, of any crime; or,

3. to expose, or to impute to him or them any deformity, disgrace or crime, or,

4. to expose any secret affecting him or them. West's Ann. Cal. Penal Code § 519.

In many instances, the statutory offense of extortion has become synonymous with the common understanding of **blackmail.** In fact, 18 U.S.C.A. § 873—a federal statute that provides "Whoever, under a threat of informing, or as a consideration for not informing, against any violation of any law of the United States, demands, or receives any money or other valuable thing, shall be fined . . ."—is often referred to as the "blackmail statute." Another federal statute, 18 U.S.C.A. § 876, makes it a crime to mail through the Postal Service a demand for ransom or threat to injure a person's property or reputation. The only specific intent required to support a conviction under § 876 is that the defendant knowingly deposited a threatening letter in the mail, not that he or she intended to carry out the threat. *United States v. Chatman,* 584 F.2d 1358 (4th Cir. 1978).

Defenses to Property Crimes

At common law, the offenses of larceny and robbery were specific-intent crimes. This intent requirement has been carried over in statutes proscribing theft, either comprehensively or in various descriptive crimes, but the intent requirement in modern robbery statutes varies. Therefore, in a prosecution for theft, a defendant may raise the defense of mistake of fact (but this does not necessarily follow when defending a charge of robbery—see Chapter 14). This means that a defendant who took items of property from another person in the good-faith belief that they belonged to the taker may have a defense. A classic example: Sherry leaves a coat on a coat rack, and later Mary does also. The jackets are similar, and Sherry mistakenly walks away with Mary's jacket. The problem becomes more acute if Mary has left a wallet in her jacket with hundreds of dollars of currency in it. These mistakes justify requiring the prosecution to prove a defendant's specific intent in theft offenses. Have you ever opened the door of a car like yours in a shopping center parking lot, thinking the car was your own?

In some theft prosecutions, mistake of law has been held to be a defense. This is limited to situations where there are exceedingly technical questions concerning ownership rights (see Chapter 14).

In a prosecution for forgery, an accused can defend by proving that he or she was authorized to sign another's name. Under certain circumstances, a person accused of forgery can also assert the defense of "mistake of fact" (see Chapter 14).

In some instances, a person charged with burglary can also assert mistake of fact as a defense. For example, an intoxicated person who enters a "row-house" identical to his or her own may have a defense. And, of course, the requirement that the prosecution prove "an intent to commit a felony" would make it difficult to prove that a person who took refuge from a storm on the porch of an unoccupied dwelling did so with intent to commit a felony therein (see Chapter 14). Arson, on the other hand, is usually a general-intent crime. This imposes a limitation on defenses beyond consent, where a person intentionally commits the proscribed acts. Because statutes proscribing the commission of arson with the intent to defraud an insurer usually require proof of the defendant's specific intent to defraud, the lack of such intent can be shown in defense.

Conclusion

Most statutory property crimes parallel the basic common-law scheme but have been broadened to meet the demands of our changing society. Although the common-law crimes against property and habitation provide a good starting point for legislating against offenses involving property, there is a need for continuing statutory revision to consolidate the laws proscribing certain property offenses that have proliferated over the years.

Statutes that proscribe various forms of theft and forgery need to be updated, particularly because of computer and credit card crimes, which increasingly create serious problems in both the public and private sectors. Definitions must be reviewed to ensure adequate protection against those who willfully take computer data or access computer systems without authority.

Consumers are no longer willing to acquiesce in outmoded doctrines such as *caveat emptor.* Thus, laws concerning representations made in commercial transactions assume a role of importance in today's society. Consumer fraud, intentional false advertising, credit card fraud, and a variety of other scams need to be specifically proscribed or included in omnibus definitions of theft and forgery statutes.

The laws proscribing burglary and arson must protect more than homes. These offenses pose serious threats to lives and property, regardless of whether they are committed in a residential or business property, whether the structure involved is private or public, and whether it is a vehicle, vessel, building, or other structure. These offenses have moved from being crimes against habitation to being crimes against property. Modern statutes tend to make these offenses crimes against persons as well. With the almost universal dependence on insurance to protect against casualty losses, the need for a close look at statutes proscribing insurance fraud is also essential.

Key Terms

larceny
receiving stolen property
false pretenses
embezzlement
grand theft
petit theft
intent to deprive
theft of computer services
computer fraud
computer trespass
robbery
aggravated robbery
carjacking

forgery
uttering a forged instrument
counterfeiting
worthless check statutes
burglary
arson
curtilage
breaking and entering
possession of burglar's tools
malicious mischief
vandalism
extortion
blackmail

Web-Based Research Activity

1. Go to the web. Locate the decisions of your state's highest appellate court.
2. Find a recent decision in which the court discussed the definition of one of the crimes covered in this chapter. If you cannot locate such a decision from your state's highest court, try another state.

Questions for Thought and Discussion

1. What advantages do you see in a state adopting a comprehensive theft statute?

2. How does the crime of burglary as it is typically defined under modern statutes differ from the definition of this offense under English common law?

3. Is it more important for theft offenses than robbery to be classified as specific-intent crimes? Why?

4. What provisions would you include in a model statute making arson a crime? Would you provide for separate degrees of the offense?

5. Should the offense of forgery be divided into degrees based on the importance of the forged documents? If so, what criteria would you propose for the various degrees of the crime?

6. Give some examples of actions that would probably fall within the conduct proscribed by (a) extortion and (b) vandalism or malicious mischief statutes.

7. What offense would a person commit who destroyed or damaged data in someone's computer? If a person electronically accessed another's computer without permission, would this constitute a criminal offense?

Problems for Discussion and Solution

1. A. H. Hacker is a skilled computer operator at a business office. Through stealthful operation of his computer, he successfully obtains a list of names and addresses of a competitor's customers without the knowledge or consent of the competitor. For what offense would Hacker most likely be prosecuted in your state?

2. Lefty Lightfingers steals a ham with a price tag of $19.50 from the meat counter in a supermarket. As he leaves the store, he is approached by a security guard. Lightfingers injures the security guard in his attempt to leave with the ham he has stolen. In your state, would Lightfingers be charged with petit theft, grand theft, or robbery? Why?

3. Sally Spendthrift has an established bank account at a local bank. She gives a check to a merchant for purchase of a new stereo. Her bank returns the check to the merchant because Ms. Spendthrift's account has insufficient funds to cover payment. Do you think Ms. Spendthrift should face criminal charges or simply be required to compensate the bank and anyone who suffered a loss?

State v. Richard

Supreme Court of Nebraska, 1984.
216 Neb. 832, 346 N.W.2d 399.

[This case deals with the offense of larceny.]

PER CURIAM.

Defendant was convicted in the county court for Scotts Bluff County of violation of Scottsbluff city ordinance § 13–201, which provided in part: "It is hereby declared unlawful for any person within the city to steal any money, goods or chattels of any kind whatever." Defendant appealed to the district court, in which his conviction and fine of $100 were affirmed. Defendant appeals to this court. For the reasons hereinafter stated we reverse and dismiss.

The evidence on behalf of the State showed that defendant entered Alexander's Super Market on March 25, 1983, between 7 and 8 A.M. He examined the bacon displayed for sale, picked up a 1-pound package, and walked by the meat counter. Alexander's meat manager followed defendant, and by demonstration at trial showed that defendant thrust his hand into his coat, went toward the express lane, and "didn't have the bacon [in his hand] anymore." The meat manager told the checker to call "service 50," which indicated that "shoplifting" was going on.

Other Alexander employees then came up, and the meat manager saw nothing further. On cross-examination the meat manager testified that he followed and watched defendant "[b]ecause he looked suspicious, in that when he picked up the bacon he moved his head from side to side."

The manager of Alexander's testified that he responded to the "service 50" call and first saw defendant halfway down one of the aisles, approached him and talked to him about the bacon, and defendant took the pound of bacon from his coat. The bacon was priced at $1.89. This witness could not remember whether defendant told him that he was going to pay for the bacon, but did remember that defendant handed the bacon to the witness and walked out of the store after the confrontation.

A Scottsbluff policeman testified that the manager of the store told the police officer that defendant told them he was going to pay for the bacon,

gave the bacon back, informed the store personnel that "they were not going to hold him for the police," and left.

Defendant testified that he had examined different types of bacon, selected one pound, did not put it in his coat, was stopped by the store personnel, showed them his wallet with "seventy-some" dollars in it, offered to pay, and when that offer was refused told the store personnel that he was not trying to steal the bacon; and said "either you're going to take my money or . . . I'm going to walk back, . . . I'm going to put it down, I'm going to walk out of here."

It is clear from the evidence considered in the light most favorable to the State that the bacon was not removed from the store by defendant. Counsel for the parties agree that to constitute the crime of "stealing" there must be a taking and "asportation" with intent to steal. The State contends that in a self-service store, "The elements of a taking and asportation are satisfied where the evidence shows that the property was taken from the owner and was concealed or put in a convenient place for removal. The fact that the possession was brief or that the person was detected before the goods could be removed from the owner's premises is immaterial." . . .

We cannot agree. With the changes in merchandising and the enactment of new and different statutes affecting a shopper's conduct, we have gone beyond the law cited by the State that to take an article feloniously is accomplished by simply laying hold of, grasping, or seizing it *animo furundi*, with the hands or otherwise, and that the very least removal of it by the thief from the place where found is an asportation or carrying away. . . . To constitute larceny the object stolen must be removed from the premises of the owner, with intent to steal, before the larceny is complete. In so stating we reiterate what we said in *State v. Hauck*, 190 Neb. 534, 537, 209 N.W.2d 580, 583 (1973): "The determination of what constitutes a taking and carrying away of property with the intent to permanently deprive the owner of possession and whether that taking is with or without the consent of the owner involves issues of intent which are often difficult of determination. Where merchandise in a store is involved, those issues are vitally affected if the store is operated on a self-service basis. The cases appear to be in agreement that in a self-service store, where customers select and pick up articles to be paid for at the checkout counter, the mere picking up of an article in the display area does not constitute asportation." . . . In *Durphy v. United States,* 235 A.2d 326, 327 (D.C. 1967), the court stated that "the normal procedure in this type of market is for customers to circulate through the sales area, taking from the shelves any items they wish to buy but not paying for their selections until they pass through the check-out counter. . . . The fact that appellant placed the goods in a shopping bag provided no valid reason for the trial court to infer a criminal intent or a possession clearly adverse to the interest of the store."

Our holding is not to be read that defendant's conduct might not have warranted conviction on other charges, such as attempted stealing (Neb. Rev. Stat. § 28–201 (Reissue 1979), or violation of Neb. Rev. Stat. § 28–551.01(1) (Cum. Supp. 1982), which provides that a person commits the crime of theft by shoplifting when, with intent to appropriate property without paying for it, he "(a) Conceals or takes possession of the goods or merchandise of any store or retail establishment."

In this difficult area of the law regarding self-service stores, precision in charging and proving offenses will result in clarity in determining what conduct is, or is not, criminal.

Reversed and dismissed.

● ● ● ● ● ● ● ● ● ● ● ● ● ●

Jones v. Commonwealth

Court of Appeals of Virginia, 1992.
13 Va. App. 566, 414 S.E.2d 193.

[In this case the Virginia Court of Appeals considers the sufficiency of the evidence to support the appellant's conviction for robbery.]

BRAY, Judge.

Jerry Earl Jones (defendant) was convicted in a jury trial of robbery and sentenced in accordance with the verdict to twenty years imprisonment. He contends that the evidence was insufficient to sustain the verdict. We disagree and affirm the conviction.

The evidence disclosed that, on the morning of March 17, 1989, Deputy John Stanton (Stanton) of the Williamsburg Sheriff's Department was transporting defendant from the "Richmond Penitentiary" to Williamsburg. Defendant was manacled in "leg chains and . . . a waist chain that ha[d] a handcuff attached to each side." Stanton was the operator of the "unmarked" vehicle, defendant was seated in the rear and no "divider" separated the two.

In route, defendant suddenly stated, "Sheriff, don't make me blow your damn brains out." Stanton was "startled" and "scared" and "jerked" his "head to the right to see what was going on." He observed defendant with "an object . . . something metal that appeared to be the barrel of a pistol," which Stanton "assumed it was." The vehicle was then traveling "approximately 65 [mph]," and Stanton lost control for "10 or 15 seconds," until it came to rest in the grassy median.

Stanton immediately began to "look and feel for [his] gun," which was missing and had been "in [his] holster at the time . . . the car went out of control." Unarmed, the deputy "was fearful for [his] life" and, when defendant demanded that Stanton "get the car back on the road," he "decided . . . that [he] wasn't going with" defendant. In an effort to "wreck" the car and "bail out," Stanton "cut . . . toward the guardrail" and "jumped out on the grass." Defendant, however, "got to the wheel and got it straightened out" and escaped in the vehicle.

The car was discovered in downtown Richmond later the same day with its two radio antennae and several hubcaps removed and in the trunk. A "fake gun" was found on the rear seat. Defendant was arrested shortly thereafter on a Richmond street and Stanton's stolen pistol was found in the "waistband" of his trousers. He was indicted on March 20, 1989. . . .

. . . When the sufficiency of the evidence is challenged on appeal, it is well established that we must view the evidence in the light most favorable to the Commonwealth, granting to it all reasonable inferences fairly deducible therefrom. The conviction will be disturbed only if plainly wrong or without evidence to support it. . . .

The elements of robbery, a common law offense in Virginia, include a "taking, with intent to steal, of the personal property of another, from his person or in his presence, against his will, by violence or intimidation" which precedes or is "concomitant with the taking." . . .

Defendant threatened Stanton's life while brandishing an object which appeared to be a weapon. As a result, Stanton was fearful and surrendered the vehicle to defendant. Defendant then escaped with both the automobile and Stanton's pistol, apparently taken by defendant while Stanton was in extremity. These circumstances amply support a robbery conviction.

Accordingly, the judgment of conviction is affirmed.

● ● ● ● ● ● ● ● ● ● ● ● ● ●

Holloway a.k.a. Ali v. United States

United States Supreme Court, 1999.
526 U.S. 1, 119 S.Ct. 966, 143 L.Ed.2d 1.

[Here the Court examines the question of the intent required to establish a violation of the federal carjacking statute. The petitioner was charged with three counts of carjacking in violation of 18 U.S.C. § 2119. In each of the crimes, petitioner and an armed accomplice approached the driver, produced a gun, and threatened to shoot unless the driver turned over the car keys. At trial, the accomplice testified that the plan was to steal the cars without harming the victims, but that he would have used his gun if any of the drivers had given him "a hard time." The trial judge instructed the jury that the intent requisite under § 2119 may be "conditional," and that this element of the offense is met as long as the defendant intended to cause death or serious bodily harm if the victims refused to surrender their automobiles. The conviction was upheld by the Court of Appeals, which rejected petitioner's view that the trial judge misconceived the mens rea requirement under § 2119.]

JUSTICE STEVENS delivered the opinion of the Court.

. . . The specific issue in this case is what sort of evil motive Congress intended to describe when it used the words "with the intent to cause death or serious bodily harm" in the 1994 amendment to the carjacking statute. More precisely, the question is whether a person who points a gun at a driver, having decided to pull the trigger if the driver does not comply with a demand for the car keys, possesses the intent, at that moment, to seriously harm the driver. In our view, the answer to that question does not depend on whether the driver immediately hands over the keys or what the offender decides to do after he gains control over the car. At the relevant moment, the offender plainly does have the forbidden intent.

The opinions that have addressed this issue accurately point out that a carjacker's intent to harm his victim may be either "conditional" or "unconditional." The statutory phrase at issue theoretically might describe (1) the former, (2) the latter, or (3) both species of intent. Petitioner argues that the "plain text" of the statute "unequivocally" describes only the latter: that the defendant must possess a specific and unconditional intent to kill or harm in order to complete the proscribed offense. To that end, he insists that Congress would have had to insert the words "if necessary" into the disputed text in order to include the conditional species of intent within the scope of the statute. . . . Because Congress did not include those words, petitioner contends that we must assume that Congress meant to provide a federal penalty for only those carjackings in which the offender actually attempted to harm or kill the driver (or at least intended to do so whether or not the driver resisted).

We believe, however, that a commonsense reading of the carjacking statute counsels that Congress intended to criminalize a broader scope of conduct than attempts to assault or kill in the course of automobile robberies. . . .

This interpretation of the statute's specific intent element does not, as petitioner suggests, render superfluous the statute's "by force and violence or by intimidation" element. While an empty threat, or intimidating bluff, would be sufficient to satisfy the latter element, such conduct, standing on its own, is not enough to satisfy § 2119's specific intent element. In a carjacking case in which the driver surrendered or otherwise lost control over his car without the defendant attempting to inflict, or actually inflicting, serious bodily harm, Congress' inclusion of the intent element requires the Government to prove beyond a reasonable doubt that the defendant would have at least attempted to seriously harm or kill the driver if that action had been necessary to complete the taking of the car.

In short, we disagree with petitioner's reading of the text of the Act and think it unreasonable to assume that Congress intended to enact such a truncated version of an important criminal statute. The intent requirement of § 2119 is satisfied when the Government proves that at the moment the defendant demanded or took control over the driver's automobile the defendant possessed the intent to seriously harm or kill the driver if necessary to steal the car (or, alternatively, if unnecessary to steal the car). Accordingly, we affirm the judgment of the Court of Appeals.

JUSTICE SCALIA, dissenting.

. . . This seems to me not a difficult case. The issue before us is not whether the "intent" element of some common-law crime developed by the courts themselves—or even the "intent" element of a statute that replicates the common-law definition—includes, or should include, conditional intent. Rather, it is whether the English term "intent" used in a statute defining a brand new crime bears a meaning that contradicts normal usage. Since it is quite impossible to say that longstanding, agreed-upon legal usage has converted this word into a term of art, the answer has to be no. And it would be no even if the question were doubtful. I think it particularly inadvisable to introduce the new possibility of "conditional-intent" prosecutions into a modern federal criminal-law system characterized by plea bargaining, where they will predictably be used for *in terrorem* effect. I respectfully dissent.

JUSTICE THOMAS, dissenting.

I cannot accept the majority's interpretation of the term "intent" in 18 U.S.C. § 2119 to include the concept of conditional intent. The central difficulty in this case is that the text is silent as to the meaning of "intent"—the carjacking statute does not define that word, and Title 18 of the United States Code, unlike some state codes, lacks a general section defining intent to include conditional intent. . . . As the majority notes, there is some authority to support its view that the specific intent to commit an act may be conditional. In my view, that authority does not demonstrate that such a usage was part of a well-established historical tradition. Absent a more settled tradition, it cannot be presumed that Congress was familiar with this usage when it enacted the statute. For these reasons, I agree with Justice Scalia the statute cannot be read to include the concept of conditional intent and, therefore, respectfully dissent.

● ● ● ● ● ● ● ● ● ● ● ● ● ●

State v. Gomez

Court of Appeals of Arizona, 1976.
27 Ariz. App. 248, 553 P.2d 1233.

[This case involves the crimes of forgery and embezzlement.]

KRUCKER, Judge.

This is an appeal from convictions of forgery, A.R.S. 13–421, and theft by embezzlement, A.R.S. 13–682, and concurrent sentences thereon of not less than eight nor more than ten years on the forgery charge and not less than eight nor more than ten years on the embezzlement charge. . . .

The pertinent facts are as follows. On June 3, 1975, Emma Cisneros purchased a 1964 Volkswagen van bus from one Chris Powers. A certificate of title was conveyed to Ms. Cisneros and testimony revealed that Gerald Wager, a notary public, notarized the signature of Chris Powers, which assigned the title to Ms. Cisneros. The record reflects that Ms. Cisneros came in contact with appellant, Bobby Gomez, while dining at the Coronado Inn in Nogales on the evening of June 7, 1975. Appellant expressed interest in purchasing the 1964 VW microbus for $500, predicated upon a one-hour test drive. Ms. Cisneros agreed and when appellant failed to return after one and a half hours, she left the restaurant. For the next three months she was unsuccessful in her attempts to locate either the vehicle or appellant.

On September 17, 1975, Ms. Cisneros observed her VW microbus at the Diaz Garage in Nogales, Arizona. Mr. Diaz, a mechanic, testified that in mid-June, 1975, the vehicle was delivered for repairs to his garage in Mexico by Mr. Rodolfo Gomez, appellant's uncle. Although the record is not completely clear, apparently at a later date Diaz contacted Gomez to inform him that the repairs were complete. Diaz was directed to bring the microbus to the garage in Nogales, Arizona, which was owned by his uncle. The vehicle was delivered at noon on September 17, 1975. After observing the microbus, Ms. Cisneros removed the ignition keys and told Mr. Diaz to send the person who claimed the van to her office at the Wager Insurance Agency in Nogales, Arizona. That same day appellant appeared at the Wager Insurance Agency to pick up the keys to the vehicle. Upon Ms. Cisneros' refusal to give up the keys, appellant left the agency but later returned with the certificate of title. Claiming that he did not want to have anything else to do with the car, Gomez gave the title to Ms. Cisneros.

The name and address of Ms. Cisneros had been removed from the certificate and replaced with the name and address of Bobby Gomez. Testimony revealed that the document was on the sun visor of the microbus when it was loaned to appellant on June 7, 1975. On October 22, 1975, a preliminary hearing was held in the Santa Cruz County Justice Court. On January 14, 1976, verdicts of guilty were returned against appellant after a trial by jury on the aforementioned counts. . . .

Appellant's . . . contention on appeal is that the State failed to present sufficient evidence to convict him of the crime of forgery. A.R.S. 13–421 (A) (1). Specifically, he complains that there was no showing that he actually did forge his name upon the document in question or of the requisite intent to defraud.

We have held that intent to defraud is an essential element of forgery. . . . However, intent to defraud may be, and often must be, inferred from the circumstances in which the false instrument is executed or issued. . . . We do not require direct evidence of appellant physically obscuring or obliterating Ms. Cisneros' name and address with liquid paper and inserting his own. To do so would place a virtually impossible burden on the State. It is not within the best interests of justice to grant a special status to covert activities by rendering immune from prosecution those individuals performing actions outside the public view.

In the case at bench, a certificate of title was transferred to Ms. Cisneros and the signature of the transferor, Chris Powers, was notarized. Ms. Cisneros testified that the title was inside the microbus when appellant took the vehicle on June 7, 1975. She further testified that she next saw this document on September 17, 1975, when appellant produced it from his wallet at her place of work and returned it to her. Her name and address, which had appeared on the document, were replaced by that of appellant.

We have no difficulty in concluding that the circumstances of the disappearance and recovery of the vehicle, along with appellant's physical possession of the altered document, provided sufficient evidence to support the jury's determination that appellant altered the document with intent to defraud or aided and abetted the alteration with the same intent.

Appellant also contends that the State never showed "that the appellant ever embezzled anything" in violation of A.R.S. 13–682. We have stated that the gist of the crime of embezzlement is a breach of trust. . . . The elements necessary to establish embezzlement are a trust relation, possession or control of property by virtue of the trust relation, and a fraudulent appropriation of the property to a use or purpose not in the due and lawful execution of the trust. . . .

We believe there is ample evidence to support appellant's conviction of embezzlement. The record reflects that during a discussion of the possibility of appellant's purchase of Ms. Cisneros' VW microbus, appellant requested possession and control of the vehicle for the purpose of a test drive and stated that he would return "in about an hour or so." Ms. Cisneros waited for approximately one and a half hours before leaving the restaurant where she had met appellant. From early June until the discovery of the van in mid-September she attempted to locate both appellant and the vehicle.

The foregoing certainly reflects that possession and control of the microbus was entrusted to appellant for the express and limited purpose of a one-hour test drive as a condition of purchase. The vehicle was never returned and at no time did appellant tender payment for it or notify Ms. Cisneros of its whereabouts. Instead, from June 7 until its discovery on September 17, the microbus was apparently converted to appellant's own use. . . . The requisite intent is inferred from the circumstances. . . .

● ● ● ● ● ● ● ● ● ● ● ● ● ●

State v. Feldt

Supreme Court of Montana, 1989.
239 Mont. 398, 781 P.2d 255.

[Charles Matthew Feldt was convicted of burglary and theft and was sentenced to concurrent five-year prison terms for each offense. In this case the Montana Supreme Court considers an appeal of the burglary conviction.]

SHEEHY, Justice.

. . . The issue on appeal is stated as follows: (1) Whether the trial court erred in finding that the defendant entered his employer's premises "unlawfully," thereby committing burglary under 45–6–204(1), MCA.

On the morning of April 27, 1987, the manager of T.C. Foods, a convenience store in Great Falls, Montana, was called to the store by the morning clerk. Upon arrival, the manager found a set of keys in the door, subsequently determined to have been issued to defendant, Feldt, an employee at T.C. Foods. The manager discovered $1,459 was missing from the safe. In addition, the manager found a note posted on the cash register which stated, "I know you trusted me, but I couldn't handle it at home. I am sorry. If you want, you can try and get the money out of my car or bike. Chuck."

On April 28, 1987, the defendant turned himself in to the Great Falls police department. He gave the police a bag containing $1,219 at the time of his surrender. He confessed to entering the store after hours by means of his keys, taking the money and leaving the note on the cash register.

At trial, the manager testified that all employees were given keys to the store and access to the store safe. The defendant testified that he was required to open and close the store and he was permitted access to the store's safe. According to both the man-

ager and the defendant, the manager allowed employees to enter the store after business hours for any proper purposes. The evidence fails to disclose, from the State or from the defendant, that when the store key was delivered to Feldt, any limitation, written or oral, was placed upon his use of it, or upon his access to the safe. . . .

Section 45–6–204(1), MCA, defines burglary as follows:

A person commits the offense of burglary if he knowingly enters or remains unlawfully in an occupied structure with the purpose to commit an offense therein. . . .

"Enters or remains unlawfully" is defined in 45–6–201, MCA, which reads in pertinent part:

A person enters or remains unlawfully . . . when he is not licensed, invited, or otherwise privileged to do so.

"There is no breaking in or entering a house or room and therefore, no burglary, if the person who enters has a right to do so." . . . To constitute a burglary the nature of the entry must itself be a trespass. . . .

The defendant Feldt was given permission to enter T.C. Foods where he was employed. As an employee of T.C. Foods, the manager gave Feldt a set of keys to enter the store and provided Feldt with access to the safe. In issuing the keys, the manager provided Feldt with authority to enter the premises at any time. The record reveals no limitations to the defendant's right to enter the store. However, the manager did testify at trial that Feldt could only enter the store after it was closed for proper purposes. Despite the manager's testimony, Feldt could enter T.C. Foods at any time day or night.

. . . [T]he defendant can not be convicted of burglary. He lawfully entered the building after closing hours with keys provided by the manager of T.C. Foods. Feldt did not trespass when he entered T.C. Foods. His keys granted him authority to enter T.C. Foods after hours.

The State argues that Feldt abused his privilege to enter T.C. Foods after hours, when he entered for the improper purpose to steal the money from the safe. The State further contends that Feldt's improper entry into T.C. Foods after hours transforms his original permissible entry into a trespass that can form the basis of a burglary charge. . . . While Feldt acted improperly in taking the money from the safe, his entry into T.C. Foods was authorized by management. Feldt was properly charged and convicted for theft, but the State failed to meet the "unlawful entry" element of the burglary statute. . . .

The defendant had access to T.C. Foods and did not "enter or remain unlawfully" as defined in 45–6–201, MCA. Since there was no unlawful entry, the defendant's actions do not constitute a burglary as defined in 45–6–204, MCA. We reverse the burglary conviction. The theft conviction was not appealed. The sentence imposed upon Feldt for the District Court is modified to strike therefrom the penalty assessed for burglary, and as modified, the sentence is affirmed.

GULBRANDSON, Justice, dissenting.

I respectfully dissent. The trial judge . . . found [that] T.C. Foods store was closed for business when the defendant entered said store and took the money. Defendant did not have permission to enter the store at that time and he did not have permission to take the money.

. . . The record as a whole supports the trial judge's verdict that the defendant was guilty of burglary. . . .

● ● ● ● ● ● ●   ● ● ● ● ● ● ●

State v. Tonnisen

Superior Court of New Jersey, Appellate Division, 1966.
92 N.J. Super. 452, 224 A.2d 21.

[This case involves an appeal from a defendant's conviction for malicious mischief.]

The opinion of the court was delivered by SULLIVAN, S.J.A.D.

After a trial by jury, defendant was convicted of malicious mischief. The statute involved is N.J.S. 2A: 122–1, N.J.S.A., which provides:

> Any person who willfully or maliciously destroys, damages, injures or spoils any real or personal property of another, either of a public or private nature, for which no punishment is otherwise provided by statute, is guilty of a misdemeanor.

The State produced evidence that the employees of the Peter J. Schweitzer Plant were on strike and some of the employees were on a picket line across the entrance to the plant. Defendant was one of the employees at or near the plant entrance at the time of the incident in question.

A tank trailer truck loaded with caustic soda arrived at the plant entrance but was blocked by the pickets. A police officer on duty proceeded to clear a path for the truck through the picket line. Defendant was then seen by the officer and other persons to go over to the side of the truck and stick his hand in between the tractor and the trailer. When he withdrew his hand there was grease on it. The officer attempted to tell the driver "to hold it" but before his warning could be heard, the tractor pulled ahead and separated from the trailer which fell down on the road causing the bottom of the tank to crack and the contents thereof to begin to leak out on the road. Examination of the vehicle showed that the safety mechanism of the coupling between the tractor and trailer had been pulled. The dollar amount of the damage resulting from the incident was not shown by the State.

Defendant, who testified in his own defense, denied that he had put his hand "anywhere in the vicinity of the coupling between the truck and the trailer."

On this appeal defendant argues that the State failed to prove criminal willfullness or malice on defendant's part. We disagree. These elements are rarely if ever susceptible of direct proof. In the usual case they are inferred from the totality of the State's case. Here we find ample credible evidence from which a jury could have found that beyond a reasonable doubt defendant pulled the safety mechanism and did so willfully or maliciously within the intent of the statute. . . .

Affirmed.

CHAPTER

8

Offenses Against Public Morality

··

Introduction

Traditionally, one of the functions of the law has been to express and reinforce the prevailing morality of the society. In this chapter we discuss a number of crimes traditionally classified as offenses against public morality. These offenses include various forms of sexual misconduct as well as several forms of **public indecency.** Some of the offenses discussed in this chapter, notably **gambling, prostitution,** and **obscenity,** are often classified as **vice crimes.** All of these offenses have evolved substantially in recent decades, reflecting tremendous changes in society.

Offenses involving alcohol and drugs, although they can be viewed as crimes against morality, can also be seen as offenses against public order and safety. Given the importance of these offenses in contemporary society, we have chosen to place them in a separate chapter (Chapter 9).

The Common-Law Background

The common-law crimes developed largely because of society's demands for security of persons and property, the need to maintain public order, and the judges' perceptions of society's concepts of morality. Many ideas of morality were based on the Bible and church doctrine; others were simply the product of the shared experiences of the people. These concepts became the foundation for the criminal laws in this country in the pre-Revolutionary days, when early settlers tended to equate sin with crime. Later, as legislative bodies defined crimes, the statutes more closely reflected the moral standards of the new American society. Eventually, the equation of crime with sin gave way to a more secular approach to crime.

Religious Influences

The contemporary criminal law still reflects to a great extent the morality of the Bible and church doctrine. In fact, it has been said that organized religion is the greatest single moral force in our society. Conflicts sometimes surface because this pluralistic nation has a constitutional prohibition against the establishment of religion and a guarantee of the free exercise thereof. Therefore, questions arise concerning whether a law with a religious origin can be enforced without offending these basic constitutional guarantees. The short answer is that most criminal laws that proscribe behavior forbidden by the Bible have also been found to serve a recognized secular purpose. Obviously, certain moral principles must be enforced for the protection of society. No one suggests that murder should not be regarded as criminal simply because of the biblical injunction "Thou shall not kill." Historically, some of our ancestors imposed severe criminal sanctions for taking the name of the Lord in vain. Today, however, even those who regard such an act as a serious sin would not support criminal sanctions for violation of this commandment.

Is Morality a Legitimate Basis for Legislation?

An essential characteristic of a sovereign state is its **police power,** the power to legislate in pursuit of public health, safety, welfare, and morality. More than a century ago the United States Supreme Court assumed that regulation of morality was among the purposes of government:

> Whatever differences of opinion may exist as to the extent and boundaries of the police power, and however difficult it may be to render a satisfactory definition of it, there seems to be no doubt that it does extend to . . . the preservation of good order and the public morals. *Boston Beer Co. v. Massachusetts,* 97 U.S. (7 Otto) 25, 33, 24 L.Ed. 989 (1878).

Today this assumption is often questioned by those who believe that morality, like religion, is a personal matter. Persons of a libertarian persuasion generally believe that the state should be neutral in matters of morality, much as it is with respect to religion. Others, stressing the practical aspect of the problem, cite the aphorism "you can't legislate morality." However, critics must realize that the moral basis of the law extends far beyond prohibitions of sexual conduct. Many proscriptions of the criminal law, from animal cruelty to insider stock trading, are based on collective societal judgments about what is right and what is wrong.

Constitutional Limitations

In the United States, legislative bodies have broad authority to define conduct as criminal and to set the punishment to be meted out to violators. Of course, there are restrictions. As noted in Chapter 3, the U.S. Constitution and the constitutions of every state impose limitations on government efforts to criminalize certain forms of conduct. For example, in *Griswold v. Connecticut,* 381 U.S. 479, 85 S.Ct. 1678, 14 L.Ed.2d 510 (1965), the U.S. Supreme Court struck down a state law that made it a crime for all persons, even married couples, to use birth control devices. The Court said that the law violated the right of privacy that inheres in the Bill of Rights and is imposed on the states via the Fourteenth Amendment. Some would argue that this right of privacy ought to be interpreted to prohibit government from "legislating morality" altogether. However, the Supreme Court has never accepted this view. Writing for the Court in *Bowers v. Hardwick,* 478 U.S. 186, 106 S.Ct. 2841, 92 L.Ed.2d 140 (1986), Justice Byron White observed that "the law . . . is constantly based on notions of morality, and if all laws representing essentially moral choices are to be invalidated . . . , the courts will be very busy indeed." 478 U.S. at 196, 106 S.Ct. at 2846, 92 L.Ed. at 149.

Police Power and the Social Consensus

It has long been assumed that legislative bodies have the authority to criminalize conduct they determine to be contrary to the health, safety, and morals of the people, as long as such prohibitions do not infringe on rights protected by the state and federal constitutions. The problem is primarily one of legislative perception of the standards that society requires and is willing to accept. Historically, enforcement of the criminal law has largely depended on community acceptance of certain conduct being forbidden by law. But public opinion about law changes. A societal consensus resulted in a constitutional amendment in 1919 prohibiting the sale of intoxicating liquors. It proved unworkable, and after a strong consensus developed against Prohibition, the amendment was repealed in 1933. See U.S. Const. amendments XVIII and XXI.

Today, there are varying attitudes about whether certain forms of conduct should be illegal. For example, public opinion is divided on the need for laws making it a crime to engage in certain forms of gambling. Consequently, the criminal prohibitions against gambling vary considerably throughout the United States. Since the sexual revolution of the 1960s, the consensus supporting laws prohibiting sexual activities between consenting adults has eroded. This decline in consensus has led many legislatures to revise their criminal codes to remove prohibitions against certain sexual conduct. As with gambling laws, statutes governing sexual conduct now vary from state to state.

Criminal Prohibitions of Sexual Conduct

Debate concerning offenses against public morality usually focuses primarily on the statutory prohibitions against fornication, adultery, seduction, sodomy, prostitution, and, to a lesser degree, incest. Many people today believe that such behavior is, or at least ought to be, private in character and thus beyond the reach of the criminal law. In contrast, many still subscribe to the classical conservative view that such prohibitions are necessary to maintain a proper moral climate.

Fornication, Adultery, and Seduction

Fornication is sexual intercourse between unmarried persons. **Adultery** is generally defined as sexual intercourse between a male and female, at least one of whom is married to someone else. Fornication and adultery were regarded as offenses against morality and were punishable in the ecclesiastical courts in England. Neither was a common-law crime unless committed openly. In such instances the act was prosecuted as a public nuisance. Historically, the rationale for criminalizing these acts was threefold: (1) to avoid disharmony in family relationships, (2) to prevent illegitimate births, and (3) to prevent the spread of sexually transmitted diseases.

Because of changing societal attitudes, these offenses are rarely prosecuted today. Indeed, many states have eliminated these offenses altogether. Adultery and fornication might be widespread, but they generally occur under the most private of circumstances. Consequently, complaints about these sexual encounters are seldom reported to the authorities. In instances where sexual conduct is the subject of a complaint by a participant, it may fall under the classification of sexual battery (see Chapter 6).

Seduction was not a crime at common law; hence, it exists only by statute. The essence of the offense is that a male obtains sexual intercourse with a virtuous female on the unfulfilled promise of marriage. Historically, prosecution for seduction served the role of persuading a recalcitrant suitor to marry the woman he seduced. Most states have repealed their seduction statutes, and where such laws remain on the books, prosecution is rare.

Incest

Incest is sexual intercourse within or outside the bonds of marriage between persons related within certain prohibited degrees. *Haller v. State*, 232 S.W. 2d 829 (Ark. 1950). Incest was not a crime at common law but was punishable by the ecclesiastical courts.

There are strong religious and moral taboos against incest. Furthermore, it has been almost universally believed that incest not only disrupts family relationships but also leads to genetically defective offspring. For these reasons, all states prohibit marriage or sexual relations between certain close relatives.

Statutes that prohibit intermarriage or sexual relations between persons within certain degrees of kinship usually refer to relationship by consanguinity (that is, blood relationships). Typically, Florida law provides as follows:

> Whoever knowingly marries or has sexual intercourse with a person to whom he is related by lineal consanguinity, or a brother, sister, uncle, aunt, nephew, or niece, commits incest, which constitutes a felony of the third degree. West's Fla. Stat. Ann. § 826.04.

Statutes do not usually distinguish between relationships of half-blood and full-blood. However, some go further than the Florida statute and classify as incestuous close relationships between persons related by affinity (that is, marriage) as well as relationships by the bloodline. For example, South Dakota law provides the following:

> Any person, fourteen years of age or older, who knowingly engages in sexual contact with another person, other than his spouse, if that person is under the age of twenty-one and is within the degree of consanguinity or affinity within which marriages are by the laws of this state declared void . . . is guilty of a felony. South Dakota Codified Laws, § 22–22–19.1.

Once the prosecution establishes the defendant's knowledge of the prohibited relationship, proof of the act of sexual intercourse is sufficient to show violation of the statute.

Bigamy

Like most sexual offenses, **bigamy** was originally a canonical offense punishable by the ecclesiastical courts in England; later it became a common-law offense. All American jurisdictions prohibit bigamy (that is, marriage between two persons when one is already legally married to another). Usually these statutes require the prosecution to prove that the defendant had knowledge of the prior marital status of the person whom he or she married. Since everyone is presumed to know the consequences of his or her acts, no further intent need be shown.

Before the turn of the century, arguments were advanced that polygamy—the practice of one person being married to several spouses at the same time—was a religious practice protected by the First Amendment. These contentions were soundly rejected by the United States Supreme Court when it held that a religious belief cannot be made a justification for commission of an overt act made criminal by the state. *Reynolds v. United States*, 98 U.S. (8 Otto) 145, 25 L.Ed. 244 (1878).

Sodomy

The word **sodomy** is derived from the biblical account of Sodom, the city that was destroyed because of its vices. Sodomy consists of committing acts that were once commonly referred to as "crimes against nature." Sodomy was originally an ecclesiastical offense but became a felony in the later stages of the common law. In his *Commentaries on the Laws of England*, Blackstone described sodomy as an offense "the very mention of which is a disgrace to human nature" and "a crime not fit to be named." In general, the offense includes oral or anal sex between humans and sexual intercourse between humans and animals (the latter is often termed "bestiality"). Until 1961, all states had statutes outlawing sodomy. Today, less than half the states retain this offense, and enforcement is rare. When a person is prosecuted for sodomy, it is generally incident to a charge of rape or sexual battery. When sodomy is nonconsensual, it is considered a crime against a person, not as an offense against morality.

CASE-IN-POINT

Invalidity of Sodomy Law Under the New York Constitution

Ronald Onofre was charged with violating New York's consensual sodomy statute. Before his trial, Onofre moved for a dismissal of the indictment on the ground that enforcement of the statute invaded his constitutional right to privacy. After the motion was denied, Onofre admitted to having had "deviate sexual intercourse" with another male and was convicted. On appeal, the Appellate Division reversed the conviction and declared the sodomy law unconstitutional. The New York Court of Appeals affirmed, saying that the constitutional right of privacy included the freedom "to seek sexual gratification from what at least once was commonly regarded as 'deviant' conduct, so long as the decisions [to engage in such conduct] are voluntarily made by adults. . . ."

People v. Onofre, 415 N.E.2d 936, 940 (N.Y. 1980).

An excerpt from the Supreme Court's decision in *Bowers v. Hardwick* appears at the end of the chapter.

In the mid-1980s, sodomy became the subject of public discussion when a federal appeals court in Georgia struck down that state's sodomy law on the ground that it violated the constitutional right of privacy. The decision came in a civil case brought by an adult male who was arrested (but not prosecuted) for committing sodomy with another adult male in the privacy of his bedroom. In a 5–4 decision, the U.S. Supreme Court overturned the ruling and upheld Georgia's sodomy law. *Bowers v. Hardwick*, supra. Writing for the Court in *Hardwick*, Justice White concluded that the Constitution did not confer "a fundamental right to homosexuals to engage in acts of consensual sodomy." 478 U.S. at 192, 106 S.Ct. at 2844, 92 L.Ed.2d at 146. Dissenting, Justice Blackmun, joined by three other members of the Court, insisted that the case was not about the right to engage in homosexual sodomy but, rather, about "the right to be let alone." 478 U.S. at 199, 106 S.Ct. at 2848, 92 L.Ed.2d at 151. Indeed, the Court's decision left open the question of whether sodomy laws would be enforceable against acts of heterosexual sodomy, whether within or without the bounds of marriage.

As an apparent moral statement, the *Hardwick* decision engendered considerable controversy. But the impact of the decision has been, and will continue to be, quite limited. First, many jurisdictions have repealed their prohibitions against sodomy. Second, because most acts of sodomy are performed in private by consenting adults, they tend to be beyond the effective reach of the criminal law.

An excerpt from *Campbell v. Sundquist*, in which the Tennessee Court of Appeals struck down a state law forbidding homosexual sodomy, appears at the end of the chapter.

As we noted in Chapter 3, a state constitution may afford more protection to its citizens than does the federal constitution. Thus, in 1998 the Georgia Supreme Court struck down the same sodomy law upheld by the U.S. Supreme Court in *Bowers v. Hardwick*. Writing for the court, Chief Justice Robert Benham found that the sodomy statute, "insofar as it criminalizes the performance of private, non-commercial acts of sexual intimacy between persons legally able to consent, 'manifestly infringes upon a constitutional provision' . . . which guarantees to the citizens of Georgia the right of privacy." *Powell v. State*, 510 S.E.3d 18, 26 (Ga. 1998).

Prostitution

Although prostitution was not a crime at common law, statutes proscribing prostitution have been part of the laws directed against public immorality since the early history of the United States. Lawmakers have officially deplored the existence of

Table 8.1 Prostitution Arrests in the United States by Gender of Arrestee, 1990 and 1997				
Gender	Arrests in 1990	Percentage*	Arrests in 1997	Percentage*
Male	32,770	36	28,785	40
Female	58,323	64	43,600	60
Total	91,093	100	72,385	100

*Percentages have been rounded to nearest whole number.

Sources: Data for 1990 were obtained from the *Sourcebook of Criminal Justice Statistics 1991*, U.S. Department of Justice, Bureau of Justice Statistics, Washington, DC: U.S. Government Printing Office, 1992. Data for 1997 were obtained from *Sourcebook of Criminal Justice Statistics 1998*, U.S. Department of Justice, Bureau of Justice Statistics, Washington, DC: U.S. Government Printing Office, 1999.

prostitution, and law enforcement authorities have long linked the activity with vice, narcotics offenses, and the exploitation of women.

A prostitute is a person who indulges in indiscriminate sexual activity for hire. Today, prostitution is illegal in all states except Nevada, where it exists by local option in some counties, although it is strictly regulated by law. See Nev. Rev. Stat. §§ 201.380, 201.430, 201.440. Historically, statutes prohibiting prostitution have been directed at females who have sexual intercourse with males for compensation, but in recent years, as prostitution by males has increased, enforcement has come to be directed at males as well (see Table 8.1).

Previously, enforcement was directed almost exclusively at the prostitute. However, newer statutes provide for conviction of customers as well as prostitutes. Indeed, if the statutes are not so construed, they might be vulnerable to constitutional attack as a denial of equal protection under the law.

In addition to making prostitution an offense, most states make it an offense to solicit for a prostitute or to live off the earnings of a person engaged in prostitution. Statutes also commonly declare brothels and houses of prostitution as public nuisances.

Texas statutes provide that a person who offers or agrees to engage, or engages in sexual conduct for a fee, or who solicits another in a public place to engage in such conduct commits the misdemeanor offense of prostitution. Vernon's Tex. Penal Code Ann. § 43.02. Texas also makes promotion of prostitution a misdemeanor offense, Vernon's Tex. Penal Code Ann. §§ 43.03–43.04, and makes it a serious felony for a person to cause another by force, threat, or fraud to commit prostitution or to cause by any means a person younger than seventeen years to commit prostitution, Vernon's Tex. Penal Code Ann. § 43.05. Prostitution has been dealt with primarily at the state and local level, but the federal government has also shown an interest in coping with the problem. The Mann Act, 18 U.S.C.A. § 2421 et seq., prohibits interstate transportation of an individual for purposes of prostitution or with the intent to compel an individual to become a prostitute or to engage in any other immoral practice. The Supreme Court has held that the act applies to transporting persons for immoral purposes even if commercial vice is not involved. *Cleveland v. United States*, 329 U.S. 14, 67 S.Ct. 13, 91 L.Ed. 12 (1946).

An excerpt from *Austin v. State*, a 1990 Texas Court of Appeals decision dealing with prostitution, appears at the end of the chapter.

Criticism of Laws Regulating Sexual Conduct

Considerable criticism is leveled at laws that proscribe sexual conduct between consenting adults. Those who advocate the repeal of statutes making fornication, adultery, and seduction crimes argue that sexual conduct between consenting adults is essentially a matter of private moral concern. They believe such behavior should be left to the discretion of the participants. Furthermore, they contend that the resources needed to fight serious crime should not be wasted in attempts to apprehend violators of sexual mores. Moreover, they argue that because laws against these activities are largely unenforced, they lend themselves to charges of arbitrary enforcement against persons whose lifestyles are socially unacceptable. Finally, many critics contend that the very fact that these laws are not enforced breeds disrespect and encourages violation of laws that society regards as essential.

There is considerably less support for repeal of laws forbidding incest. Some who do advocate the repeal of these laws advance the same arguments as for decriminalizing fornication, adultery, and seduction. In addition, many who see incest as a genuine concern urge that government should approach the problem through counseling and by furnishing psychiatric assistance to transgressors, rather than by making incest a penal offense.

Those who oppose the prostitution laws now extant in the United States point to the fact that the so-called oldest profession has survived many centuries of condemnation yet exists as a cultural institution. Thus, they argue, it fulfills a socially desirable function because it furnishes an outlet for certain sexual impulses and tends to lessen the incidence of forcible sexual attacks on women. In addition to the need to conserve scarce resources to fight serious crime and the futility of trying to eradicate an ingrained institution, reformers contend that legalization of prostitution would lead to needed regulation. This, they point out, could provide for medical inspections to diminish the spread of sexually transmitted diseases. Finally, many critics of the present laws concerning prostitution contend that legalization would allow the police to take this activity from the grips of organized crime and control more effectively many of the vices that now accompany prostitution.

Bigamy and polygamy are still practiced in some areas. Given that such marriages are considered null and void, some argue that criminalizing such conduct is unnecessary. However, there is no great movement to abolish such laws, and any such effort would probably be to little avail.

The Prognosis for Reform

The repeal of laws prohibiting fornication is not a priority item for legislators. When criminal codes are revised, however, such laws often disappear. In our monogamous society, laws proscribing adultery will most likely remain as a public statement on morality, but they will be largely unenforced. Seduction has been mostly relegated to civil suits for breach of promise to marry, but even this type of action has been outlawed in many jurisdictions.

The practice of incest among those related by consanguinity is widely condemned in Western civilization, and laws forbidding it will undoubtedly remain. However, one area for limited reform is statutes that forbid marriage among certain persons related by affinity. For example, changing the incest statutes that prohibit such practices as a brother marrying his deceased brother's wife would be inoffensive to most and welcomed by many. In some cultures, such a practice is regarded as an obligation.

Monogamy is an ingrained institution in contemporary American culture, and it seems safe to predict that scattered efforts to revise laws prohibiting bigamy will continue to be ignored by legislators.

The prognosis on prostitution is a difficult one. One certainty is that increasingly, buyers as well as sellers of sexual services will be prosecuted. Despite the cries for reform, any decriminalization of prostitution will most likely be in selected locations only and will confine activities to prescribed areas. The inherent privacy of the scene of offenses makes it very difficult to apprehend prostitutes and their customers. Therefore, enforcement should focus on those who are the procurers of prostitutes and solicitors for their services and not merely on those who render their services.

Indecent Exposure

At common law, it was a misdemeanor for persons to intentionally expose their "private parts" in a public place. Today, statutes and local ordinances in most jurisdictions make it a misdemeanor to expose one's private parts to the view of another under offensive circumstances. Several state courts have upheld laws criminalizing **indecent exposure** against a variety of constitutional challenges. See, for example, *Keller v. State*, 738 P. 2d 186 (Okl. Crim. App. 1987); *State v. Ludwig*, 468 So.2d 1151 (La. 1985). However, such laws have been generally interpreted not to prohibit public exposure of the buttocks. See, for example, *Duvallon v. District of Columbia*, 515 A.2d 724 (D.C. App. 1986).

Frequently, the offense of indecent exposure is termed **lewd and lascivious conduct.** Because a person can expose himself or herself either accidentally or of necessity, laws generally provide that indecent exposure must be done willfully and in an offensive manner. See, for example, *People v. Randall*, 711 P.2d 689 (Colo. 1985). Often, statutes require that offensive exposure must be in the "presence" of another person. Interpreting the term *presence*, the Florida Supreme Court has ruled that it "encompasses sensory awareness as well as physical proximity." Consequently, the court reversed the conviction of a man who admitted to masturbating in the presence of his thirteen-month-old child. In the court's view, the child did not have "sensory awareness" of the act in question. *State v. Werner*, 609 So.2d 585 (Fla. 1992).

Nude Dancing in Places of Public Accommodation

Is nude dancing for entertainment in a bar or theater a form of indecent exposure? Or is it a form of expression protected by the First Amendment? In *Barnes v. Glen Theatre, Inc.*, 501 U.S. 560, 111 S.Ct. 2456, 115 L.Ed.2d 504 (1991), the U.S. Supreme Court upheld an Indiana law that prohibited totally nude dancing. Writing

---

CASE-IN-POINT **Indecent Exposure**

A man exposing himself in a second-story apartment in New Orleans was seen from below by persons in the apartment parking lot. He was prosecuted for indecent exposure under a statute that had been interpreted as criminalizing indecent exposure if it was viewable from any location open to the public. In upholding his conviction, the Louisiana Supreme Court noted that the parking lot from which the victims observed the man exposing himself was not enclosed, nor was it posted as private property, and was open to any visitors to the apartment complex.

State v. Clark, 372 So.2d 1218 (La. 1979).

for a plurality of justices, Chief Justice Rehnquist observed that "the governmental interest served by the text of the prohibition is societal disapproval of nudity in public places and among strangers." 501 U.S. at 572, 111 S.Ct. at 2463, 115 L.Ed.2d at 515. In Rehnquist's view, "Indiana's requirement that the dancers wear at least pasties and a G-string is modest, and the bare minimum necessary to achieve the state's purpose." 501 U.S. at 572, 111 S.Ct. at 2463, 115 L.Ed.2d at 515.

In 2000 the Supreme Court reaffirmed its decision in *Barnes v. Glen Theatre*. The Court upheld an Erie, Pennsylvania, ordinance that was interpreted to require dancers in clubs to wear pasties and G-strings. *City of Erie v. Pap's A.M.*, 529 U.S. 277, 120 S.Ct. 1382, 146 L.Ed.2d 265 (2000). Writing for a plurality, Justice Sandra Day O'Connor concluded that "Erie's asserted interest in combating the negative secondary effects associated with adult entertainment establishments . . . is unrelated to the suppression of the erotic message conveyed by nude dancing." 529 U.S. at 296, 120 S.Ct. at 1394, 146 L.Ed.2d at 282.

Nudity and Seminudity on Public Beaches

Historically, public nudity has been taboo in Western societies. Yet only a few states have imposed outright bans. Many states maintain that public nudity on beaches and other recreational areas violates laws proscribing lewd and lascivious conduct or indecent exposure. For example, in Florida, where public beaches are popular attractions, signs are commonly posted notifying beachgoers that nude sunbathing is a violation of Florida Statute Section 877.03. Actually, that law prohibits "such acts as are of a nature to corrupt the public morals, or outrage the sense of public decency, or affect the peace and quiet of persons who may witness them." In 1976 the Florida Supreme Court held that the legislative intent of the statute prohibits adult females from openly exposing their breasts on public beaches. *Moffett v. State*, 340 So.2d 1155 (Fla. 1976). Arrests under this provision are not common. In fact, Miami Beach and other Florida cities that attract large numbers of tourists have set aside specified areas where topless or nude sunbathing is permitted.

Obscenity

At common law, vulgar and obscene language and indecent public exhibitions were considered public nuisances, punishable as misdemeanors. Historically, federal and state governments in the United States passed laws banning various forms of obscenity. By the late 1800s, Congress had made it an offense to mail any "obscene, lewd or lascivious paper or writing" and provided that the word *obscene* should be given fully as broad a significance as it had at common law. *Knowles v. United States*, 170 F. 409 (8th Cir. 1909). The states also passed laws making sale or distribution of obscene materials a crime. Typically, Section 6567 of the Connecticut General Statutes (1949 Revision) provided that "[b]uying, selling, giving or showing any obscene, indecent or impure book, paper or picture is a crime." Likewise, most municipalities adopted ordinances proscribing various forms of obscenity.

Historically, statutes and ordinances making obscenity an offense seldom defined it. Thus, they were vulnerable to contentions that they were vague and did not provide an ascertainable standard of guilt. As questions arose, the courts tended to define obscenity as sexual or erotic speech or conduct. The word "obscene" came to mean something offensive to the senses—that is, repulsive, disgusting, foul, or filthy.

The Emerging Constitutional Standards

As mass communications developed, laws banning obscene speech, materials, and performances became subject to scrutiny under the First Amendment. The Supreme Court's first direct encounter with regulating obscenity came in *Roth v. United States,* 354 U.S. 476, 77 S.Ct. 1304, 1 L.Ed.2d 1498 (1957). Roth was found guilty of sending erotic materials through the mail, and his conviction was affirmed on appeal. The Supreme Court granted review and announced that the dispositive issue was "whether obscenity is utterance within the area of protected speech and press." The Court held that obscenity was not constitutionally protected; rather, the Court viewed it as "utterly without redeeming social importance." After observing that "sex and obscenity are not synonymous," Justice Brennan, writing for the Court, said the test for determining obscenity was "whether to the average person applying contemporary community standards, the dominant theme of the material taken as a whole, appeals to the prurient interest." 354 U.S. at 489, 77 S.Ct. at 1311, 1 L.Ed.2d at 1509 (1957).

By the late 1950s, there was a flood of erotic materials on the market. Whether particular materials were obscene had become an increasingly important issue. *Roth* effectively made the definition of obscenity a matter of federal constitutional law. It also evidenced the Court's concern for First Amendment freedoms and for protecting the free flow of expression from local interpretations of what constituted obscenity. Because of the problems in determining whether materials were obscene under the *Roth* standards, law enforcement officers experienced great difficulty in enforcing obscenity laws.

From 1957 to 1973, the Supreme Court granted review of several lower court decisions determining that particular books, plays, and movies were obscene, often explicating due process guidelines to be followed by lower courts in determining what constitutes obscenity. During this period the Court found the French film *The Lovers* not to be obscene and implied that national standards would govern in determining whether materials were obscene. There Justice Stewart, in expressing the view that obscenity is limited to **hard-core pornography,** made his oft-quoted remark on obscenity: "I know it when I see it." *Jacobellis v. Ohio,* 378 U.S. 184, 197, 84 S.Ct. 1676, 1683, 12 L.Ed.2d 793 (1964) (Stewart, J. concurring).

As the 1970s approached, observers speculated that the Supreme Court was taking a more liberal approach. In *Stanley v. Georgia,* 394 U.S. 557, 89 S.Ct. 1243, 22 L.Ed.2d 542 (1969), the Court reviewed a defendant's conviction for violating a statute making knowing possession of obscene materials a crime. In *Stanley,* the police had seized materials (which the Court assumed to be obscene) from the defendant's home. In reversing the defendant's conviction, the Court held that "the State may no more prohibit mere possession of obscene matter on the ground that it may lead to antisocial conduct than it may prohibit possession of chemistry books on the ground that they may lead to the manufacture of homemade spirits." 394 U.S. at 567, 89 S.Ct. at 1248, 22 L.Ed.2d at 551. Some read *Stanley* as an indication the Court was relaxing its standards on regulating obscenity. They were mistaken.

The Intractable Obscenity Problem

When the Supreme Court decided the seminal case of *Miller v. California,* 413 U.S. 15, 93 S.Ct. 2607, 37 L.Ed.2d 419 (1973), it referred to "the intractable obscenity problem." 413 U.S. at 16, 93 S.Ct. at 2610, 37 L.Ed.2d at 426. In *Miller,* the defendant had mailed unsolicited material containing explicit sexual drawings in violation of a California law. A jury found him guilty, and an appellate court upheld the judgment without opinion. At the outset, Chief Justice Burger reiterated that obscene materials were unprotected by the Constitution. Then the Court suggested that local juries could base their judgments on local and not national standards. Most significantly, the Court redefined the standards for determining obscenity, saying that the

> basic guidelines for the trier of fact must be: (1) whether "the average person, applying contemporary community standards" would find that the work, taken as a whole, appeals to the **prurient interest;** (b) whether the work depicts or describes, in a **patently offensive** way, sexual conduct specifically defined by the applicable state law; and (c) whether the work, taken as a whole, lacks serious literary, artistic, political, or scientific value. 413 U.S. at 24, 93 S.Ct. 2614, 37 L.Ed.2d at 431.

Finally, the Court expressly rejected any requirement that the challenged materials be found to be "utterly without redeeming social importance." 413 U.S. at 24, 93 S.Ct. at 2614, 37 L.Ed.2d at 431. The Court gave examples of "patently offensive" by saying it meant "representations or descriptions of ultimate sexual acts, normal or perverted, actual or simulated . . . representations or descriptions of masturbation, excretory functions, and lewd exhibition of genitals." 413 U.S. at 25, 93 S.Ct. at 2615, 37 L.Ed.2d at 431. The Court made it clear that no one would be subject to prosecution unless the materials alleged to be obscene described patently offensive "hardcore" sexual conduct.

In a companion case, *Paris Adult Theatre I v. Slaton,* 413 U.S. 49, 93 S.Ct. 2628, 37 L.Ed.2d 446 (1973), the Court observed that the states have a right to "maintain a decent society" and may challenge obscene material even if it is shown only to consenting adults.

These decisions indicated an increasing concern over the issue of obscenity and allowed local juries to make judgments based on more explicit standards. These decisions also tended to eliminate the practice of using expert witnesses to testify on such issues as contemporary community standards and whether materials were "utterly without redeeming social value."

Significant Post-*Miller* Developments

Miller may have clarified the tests for obscenity, but it did not satisfy those who sought to ban pornographic materials. For example, *Carnal Knowledge,* a very successful movie in the early 1970s, was held not obscene under the *Miller* test. There were scenes in which "ultimate sexual acts" were understood to be taking place; however, the camera did not focus on the bodies of the actors, nor was there any exhibition of genitals during such scenes. The Court said that the film was not a "portrayal of hard core sexual conduct for its own sake, and for the ensuing commercial gain" and did not depict sexual conduct in a patently offensive way. *Jenkins v. Georgia,* 418 U.S. 153, 161, 94 S.Ct. 2750, 2755, 41 L.Ed.2d 642, 650 (1974).

The 1980s witnessed two significant developments in the laws concerning obscenity. First, in *New York v. Ferber,* 458 U.S. 747, 102 S.Ct. 3348, 73 L.Ed.2d 1113 (1982), the Supreme Court unanimously held that **child pornography,** like obscenity, is unprotected by the First Amendment to the Constitution. The Court upheld a New York law prohibiting persons from distributing materials that depict children engaging in lewd sex. The Court found such laws valid even if the material does not appeal to the prurient interest of the average person and is not portrayed in a patently offensive manner. The Court found a compelling state interest in protecting the well-being of children and perceived no value in permitting performances and photo reproductions of children engaged in lewd sexual conduct.

The second significant development was a refinement of the Court's decision in *Miller*. In *Pope v. Illinois*, 481 U.S. 497, 107 S.Ct. 1918, 95 L.Ed.2d 439 (1987), the Court said that application of "contemporary community standards" is appropriate in evaluating the first two prongs of the *Miller* test for obscenity—that is, the work's appeal to the prurient interest and its patent offensiveness. However, the Court concluded that the third prong concerning the work's value cannot be tested by "community standards." The Court said the third prong must be determined on an objective basis, with the proper inquiry being

> not whether an ordinary member of any given community would find serious literary, artistic, political, or scientific value in allegedly obscene material, but whether a reasonable person would find such value in the material, taken as a whole. 481 U.S. at 500, 107 S.Ct. at 1921, 95 L.Ed.2d at 445.

State and Local Regulation of Obscenity

States, of course, may interpret their own constitutions to allow greater freedom of expression than is allowed under the current federal constitutional interpretations. In that vein, in 1987 the Oregon Supreme Court held that "any person can write, print, read, say, show or sell anything to a consenting adult even though that expression may be generally or universally condemned as 'obscene.'" *State v. Henry,* 732 P.2d 9, 18 (Or. 1987).

Some states classify violations of their obscenity statutes by degree. For example, in New York a person is guilty of obscenity in the third degree when, knowing its content and character, he or she

1. Promotes, or possesses with intent to promote, any obscene material; or

2. Produces, presents or directs an obscene performance or participates in a portion thereof which is obscene or which contributes to its obscenity. McKinney's N.Y. Penal Law § 235.05.

A person is guilty of obscenity in the second degree "when he commits the crime of obscenity in the third degree . . . and has been previously convicted of obscenity in the third degree." McKinney's N.Y. Penal Law § 235.06. A person is guilty of obscenity in the first degree "when, knowing its content and character, he wholesale promotes or possesses with intent to wholesale promote, any obscene material." McKinney's N.Y. Penal Law § 235.07. New York law makes third-degree obscenity a misdemeanor, whereas second-degree or first-degree obscenity is a felony.

CASE-IN-POINT

Obscenity

In the first federal appeals court decision applying the *Miller v. California* obscenity test to a musical composition, the Eleventh Circuit Court of Appeals ruled that the recording *As Nasty as They Wanna Be* by 2 Live Crew was not obscene. The Eleventh Circuit ruled that even assuming the work was "patently offensive" and appealed to a "prurient interest," the trial judge erred in concluding, simply on the basis of his own listening to a tape recording, that the work lacked "serious artistic value."

Luke Records, Inc. v. Navarro, 960 F.2d 134 (11th Cir. 1992).

States generally set higher penalties for exposing juveniles to pictures or shows where obscenity or even pornography is involved. In New York, disseminating indecent material to minors is a felony. McKinney's N.Y. Penal Law § 235.22.

Defenses to Charges of Obscenity

New York law provides a defense for those charged with obscenity if they can establish that the allegedly obscene material was disseminated to or performed for an audience of persons having scientific, educational, governmental, or other similar justification for possessing or viewing the material. McKinney's N.Y. Penal Law § 235.15. Moreover, it is a defense for disseminating indecent material to minors if the defendant had reasonable cause to believe that the minor involved was seventeen years old or older and exhibited official documentation to the defendant to establish that fact. McKinney's N.Y. Penal Law § 235.23. This latter provision was undoubtedly inserted to protect theater personnel from conviction on a strict liability basis.

Problems of Enforcement

Police and prosecutors often experience difficulty in determining what is to be considered obscene based on "contemporary community standards." Juries in most instances now determine the issue of obscenity simply by reviewing the material. As a result, it is not unusual for a given work to be determined obscene by a jury in one locality and not obscene by another jury in a different locality. For example, the rock musical stage production *Hair* was found not to be obscene by a federal court in Georgia. *Southeastern Promotions, Ltd. v. Atlanta,* 334 F. Supp. 634 (N.D. Ga. 1971). The following year, it was found to be obscene by another federal court in Tennessee, but this decision was reversed by the Supreme Court. *Southeastern Promotions, Inc. v. Conrad,* 341 F. Supp. 465 (E.D. Tenn. 1972), aff'd., 486 F.2d 894 (6th Cir. 1973), rev'd., 420 U.S. 546, 95 S.Ct. 1239, 43 L.Ed.2d 448 (1975).

Legal problems incident to searches and seizures of allegedly obscene materials can be very technical. Because books, movies, and even live performances are presumptively protected by the First Amendment, the Supreme Court has held that police must obtain a search warrant before searches and seizures of such materials. *Roaden v. Kentucky,* 413 U.S. 496, 93 S.Ct. 2796, 37 L.Ed.2d 757 (1973). However, the Court has explained that the Fourth Amendment does not prohibit undercover police officers from purchasing allegedly obscene materials because such a purchase would not constitute a "seizure." *Maryland v. Macon,* 472 U.S. 463, 105 S.Ct. 2778, 86 L.Ed.2d 370 (1985).

An excerpt from *Radey v. State,* a 1989 Ohio Court of Appeals decision dealing with obscenity, appears at the end of the chapter.

Pornography on the Internet

Amid growing public concerns about the prevalence of sexually explicit material on the Internet, and especially the relatively easy access of children to such material, Congress enacted the Communications Decency Act of 1996 (CDA). The CDA contained two provisions aimed at pornography on the Internet. The "indecent transmission" provision, codified at 47 U.S.C.A. § 223(a) (Supp. 2000), prohibited the knowing transmission of obscene or indecent messages to any recipient under eighteen years of age. The "patently offensive display" provision, codified at 47 U.S.C.A. § 223(d) (Supp. 1997), prohibited the knowing sending or displaying of patently offensive messages in a manner that is available to a person under eighteen years of age. Immediately after the CDA was signed into law by President Clinton, twenty plaintiffs, including the American Civil Liberties Union, brought suit challenging its constitutionality. In *Reno v. American Civil Liberties Union*, 521 U.S. 844, 117 S.Ct. 2329, 138 L.Ed.2d 874 (1997), the Supreme Court struck down the CDA on First Amendment grounds. Focusing on the statute's proscription of "indecent" transmissions, the Court concluded that the CDA presented a real threat of censoring expression entitled to First Amendment protection. Thus, the Court held that the statute was unconstitutionally overbroad. However, the Court left open the possibility that a more carefully drafted statute might pass constitutional muster. A statute limited to the prohibition of "obscene," as distinct from merely "indecent," material might survive constitutional scrutiny.

Profanity

Many states and local communities have enacted statutes and ordinances making it an offense to use loud and profane language in public places. In recent years, courts have frequently struck down such laws for vagueness. In other instances, courts have upheld their validity but ruled that such laws can be applied only where the defendant's language consisted of "fighting words" or the defendant's conduct threatened a breach of the peace (see Chapter 12). In *Cohen v. California*, 403 U.S. 15, 19, 91 S.Ct. 1780, 1785, 29 L.Ed.2d 284, 290 (1971), the Supreme Court invalidated the "offensive conduct" conviction of a man who entered a courthouse wearing a jacket emblazoned with the slogan "Fuck the Draft." Writing for the Court, Justice Harlan noted that "while the particular four-letter-word being litigated here is perhaps more distasteful than others of its genre, it is nevertheless often true that one man's vulgarity is another's lyric." 403 U.S. at 25, 91 S.Ct. at 1788, 29 L.Ed.2d at 294. Despite the Supreme Court's decision in *Cohen v. California*, most states and many cities retain laws proscribing **profanity.** These laws are seldom enforced and even more rarely challenged in court. A notable exception occurred in 1999 in the widely publicized case of the "cussing canoeist" (see the Case-in-Point below).

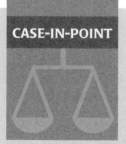

CASE-IN-POINT

The Case of the Cussing Canoeist

When Timothy Boomer, age twenty-five, fell out of his canoe and into the Rifle River in Michigan, he let loose a three-minute tirade of profanity. Two sheriff's deputies patrolling the river heard Boomer and ticketed him. Boomer was charged with violating an 1897 Michigan statute that prohibits uttering profanity in the presence of women and children. Standing before the Arenac County Circuit Court, Boomer said, ". . . [I]f my words offended anyone, I'm sorry. I've said from the beginning that I did not know that there were children in the area and I would not have said what I said if I had known there were children around." After a jury found Boomer guilty, Judge Alan Yenoir sentenced him to four days' community service and a $75 fine. With assistance from the American Civil Liberties Union, Boomer appealed his conviction on First Amendment grounds. Kary Moss, Executive Director of the ACLU of Michigan, said, "From the start the police had other laws at its disposal it could use to deal with noise problems on the river. That they chose not to suggests a broader ambition—to censor speech."

Table 8.2 Legalized Gambling by State	
Alabama	Parimutuel betting, bingo, tribal gaming
Alaska	Bingo only
Arizona	Parimutuel betting, lottery, bingo, tribal gaming
Arkansas	Parimutuel betting only
California	Parimutuel betting, lottery, card rooms, bingo, tribal gaming
Colorado	Parimutuel betting, lottery, casinos, bingo, tribal gaming
Connecticut	Parimutuel betting, lottery, bingo, tribal gaming, jai alai
Delaware	Parimutuel betting, lottery, bingo
District of Columbia	Lottery, bingo
Florida	Parimutuel betting, lottery, bingo, tribal gaming, jai alai
Georgia	Bingo only
Hawaii	None
Idaho	Parimutuel betting, lottery, tribal gaming
Illinois	Parimutuel betting, lottery, bingo, riverboat casinos
Indiana	Lottery, bingo
Iowa	Parimutuel betting, lottery, riverboat casinos, bingo, tribal gaming
Kansas	Parimutuel betting, lottery, bingo, tribal gaming
Kentucky	Parimutuel betting, lottery, bingo
Louisiana	Parimutuel betting, lottery, bingo, tribal gaming, one casino (New Orleans)
Maine	Parimutuel betting, lottery, bingo
Maryland	Parimutuel betting, lottery, casinos, bingo
Massachusetts	Parimutuel betting, lottery, bingo
Michigan	Lottery, bingo, parimutuel betting, tribal gaming
Minnesota	Lottery, bingo, parimutuel betting, tribal gaming
Mississippi	Bingo, riverboat casinos
Missouri	Lottery, bingo, tribal gaming

Gambling

Traditionally, to gamble has meant to risk money on an event, chance, or contingency in the hope of realizing a gain. See *State v. Stripling*, 21 So. 409 (Ala. 1897). The common law did not regard gambling as an offense. However, many of the new American states, either by constitution or statute, made all or certain forms of gambling illegal. Today, federal laws and a variety of state statutes and local ordinances prohibit gambling (see Table 8.2). Laws regulating gambling come under the police power of the state, and the United States Supreme Court has recognized that there is no constitutional right to gamble. *Lewis v. United States*, 348 U.S. 419, 75 S.Ct. 415, 99 L.Ed. 475 (1955).

Bingo, craps, baccarat, poker, raffles, bookmaking, and slot machines are just a few common forms of gambling. Gambling also includes betting on sports events and card games. Many forms of gambling are legal; therefore, when considering gambling,

Table 8.2 *(Continued)*	
Montana	Lottery, bingo, casinos, parimutuel betting, tribal gaming
Nebraska	Lottery, bingo, parimutuel betting, jai alai
Nevada	Bingo, casinos, parimutuel betting, sports betting
New Hampshire	Lottery, bingo, parimutuel betting
New Jersey	Lottery, bingo, parimutuel betting, casino gambling (Atlantic City only)
New Mexico	Bingo, parimutuel betting, tribal gaming
New York	Lottery, bingo, parimutuel betting, tribal gaming
North Carolina	Bingo, jai alai
North Dakota	Bingo, parimutuel betting, tribal gaming
Ohio	Lottery, bingo, parimutuel betting
Oklahoma	Bingo, parimutuel betting, tribal gaming
Oregon	Lottery, bingo, parimutuel betting, jai alai, tribal gaming
Pennsylvania	Lottery, bingo, parimutuel betting
Rhode Island	Lottery, bingo, parimutuel betting
South Carolina	Bingo, jai alai
South Dakota	Lottery, bingo, parimutuel betting, tribal gaming
Tennessee	Parimutuel betting only
Texas	Bingo, parimutuel betting
Utah	None
Vermont	Lottery, bingo, parimutuel betting
Virginia	Lottery, bingo, parimutuel betting
Washington	Lottery, bingo, parimutuel betting, tribal gaming
West Virginia	Lottery, bingo, parimutuel betting
Wisconsin	Lottery, bingo, parimutuel betting, tribal gaming
Wyoming	Bingo, parimutuel betting

Source: Authors' research.

we must separate the legal from the illegal. For example, those who pay something of value to take a chance to win a prize in a **lottery** are gambling. In many jurisdictions, this is a criminal offense. Yet in several states, lotteries are not only legal; they are an important source of public revenue. In effect, it is unregulated gambling that is illegal. A common form of unregulated gambling is "numbers." To play, you place a bet on a number with the hope that it will correspond to a preselected number. The **numbers racket** is widespread and, along with prostitution, is a major source of income for organized crime.

What Constitutes Gambling?

To constitute gambling, gaming activity must generally include these three elements: (1) a **consideration,** (2) a **prize,** and (3) a **chance.** Retail stores conduct a variety of promotional schemes; local carnivals and fairs offer opportunities to play a variety of games for prizes. When are they gambling, and when are they games of skill? And if games of skill, are they exempt from laws prohibiting gambling? Some statutes regulating gambling provide the answer. In other instances, courts may be called on to determine whether a particular activity offends a statutory prohibition against gambling.

Most statutes prohibiting gambling are interpreted to exclude athletics or other contests in which participants pit their physical or mental skills against one another for a prize. Courts tend to be practical in their interpretations. For example, an Ohio appellate court found that a pinball machine that allowed the outcome of its operation to be determined largely by the skill of the user was not "a game of chance," and the pinball operators were not in violation of the Ohio gambling statute. *Progress Vending, Inc. v. Department of Liquor Control*, 394 N.E.2d 324 (Ohio App. 1978).

Statutory Regulation of Gambling

A federal statute called the Travel Act, 18 U.S.C.A. § 1952, prohibits interstate travel in aid of gambling. The act is not aimed at local criminal activity; rather, its purpose is to attack crime that has a definite interstate aspect. *United States v. O'Dell*, 671 F.2d 191 (6th Cir. 1982).

Many states broadly proscribe gambling much the same as Florida law, which provides the following:

> Whoever plays or engages in any game at cards, keno, roulette, faro or other game of chance, at any place, by any device whatever, for money or other thing of value, shall be guilty of a misdemeanor of the second degree. West's Fla. Stat. Ann. § 849.08.

Typically, Florida law creates certain exemptions. Nonprofit organizations are permitted to conduct bingo games under strict regulations, West's Fla. Stat. Ann. § 849.0931, and charitable and nonprofit organizations are allowed to conduct certain drawings by chance, West's Fla. Stat. Ann. § 849.0935. Subject to specific restrictions, certain retail merchandising promotions with prizes awarded to persons selected by lot are permitted. West's Fla. Stat. Ann. § 849.092. Another exception allows penny-ante card games with participants age eighteen or older provided that the games are conducted in a dwelling in which the winnings of any player in a single round or game do not exceed $10 in value. West's Fla. Stat. Ann. § 849.085.

Where gambling is prohibited, states customarily make it unlawful to possess gambling devices and provide for their confiscation. See, for example, West's Fla. Stat. Ann. §§ 849.231, 849.232.

An excerpt from *United States v. Pinelli*, a federal circuit court decision dealing with gambling, appears at the end of the chapter.

Prosecutorial Problems and Defenses

The problems encountered in enforcing prostitution and sexual laws are also obstacles to enforcing gambling statutes. Because of the consensual nature of gambling, apprehension of violators largely depends on the use of informants by police. Procedures for obtaining search and arrest warrants are technical and require close adherence to Fourth Amendment standards. The prosecution, of course, must prove all elements of the offense. In most instances, this requires proof of a consideration, a prize, and a chance; however, some statutes have eliminated the consideration requirement. If the statute prohibiting gambling makes intent an element of the offense, the prosecution must prove the defendant's intent; otherwise, it is sufficient merely to prove the act of gambling.

What Constitutes an Illegal Gaming Machine?

The Michigan Liquor Control Commission imposed a $250 fine on the Sanford Eagles Club for having a "video poker" machine on its premises. The machine had five windows, and when a quarter was deposited, a playing card appeared in each window. Essentially, the contestant played a game of five-card draw against the machine. A "winner" could gain credits entitling the player to free replays based on a random "reshuffling" of the cards. After administrative and judicial hearings, the court of appeals held that the machine was not an illegal gaming device, since there was no monetary payoff. The Michigan Supreme Court reversed. The court based its decision on a provision of the statute addressing gambling devices that exempted mechanical amusement devices that reward a player with replays as long as the device is not allowed to accumulate more than fourteen replays at one time. Because the video poker machine at issue in this case permitted the player to accumulate more than fourteen replays, it did not fall within the statutory exemption.

Automatic Music and Vending Corp. v. Liquor Control Comm., 396 N.W. 204 (Mich. 1986).

Texas law makes it an offense to bet on results of games, contests, political nominations, or elections or to play games with cards and dice. See Vernon's Tex. Penal Code Ann. § 47.02(a). The state legislature has taken a pragmatic approach by providing that it is a defense to prosecution under that section of the statute if

> (1) the actor engaged in gambling in a private place; (2) no person received any economic benefit other than personal winnings; and (3) except for the advantage of skill or luck, the risks of losing and the chances of winning were the same for all participants. Vernon's Tex. Penal Code Ann. § 47.02(b).

Section 47.02(c) provides that it is a defense to prosecution if the actor reasonably believed that the gambling conduct was permitted under bingo or a charitable raffle, or occurred under a lottery approved by a parks and wilderness agency for determination of hunting privileges.

In some instances a defendant charged with gambling might succeed in establishing entrapment, a defense discussed in Chapter 14.

The Paradox of Gambling Laws

The law on gambling seems paradoxical. Some laws authorize nonprofit organizations to conduct certain forms of gambling that are otherwise forbidden. In some states, people can legally bet at dog tracks and horse tracks yet may still be prosecuted for betting in their own homes on the World Series or the Kentucky Derby. Many reformers contend that present laws are ineffective to suppress gambling. Instead, they claim these laws actually lend support to the activities of organized crime.

Certain forms of legalized gambling, particularly state lotteries and state-franchised dog and horse tracks, have become increasingly acceptable. Yet unregulated forms of gambling will most likely continue to be prohibited in most instances. In any event, if inroads are to be made in controlling unregulated gambling, enforcement efforts must be directed primarily toward gambling activity that is under control of organized crime syndicates.

Conclusion

In addition to defining crimes against persons and property and establishing rules necessary to preserve public order, the law proscribes certain forms of conduct simply because they offend societal morality. Chief among these prohibitions are the laws prohibiting certain forms of sexual activity, public indecency, obscenity, profanity, and gambling. Offenses involving the use of alcohol and drugs, although sometimes categorized as offenses against public morality, can also be seen as threats to public order, safety, and peace. Thus, we have dealt with them in a separate chapter.

Most offenses against morality, it should be remembered, are ecclesiastical in origin. Many now question whether the criminal law ought to be a vehicle for enforcing moral standards that originated from religious sources. However, the courts have not rejected morality as a proper basis for the criminal law. Clearly, the fact that a form of conduct was or is proscribed by one or more religious traditions is not a sufficient basis for criminalizing that activity. But if an act violates societal consensus, even if that consensus derives from religious traditions, it may be legitimately prohibited by the criminal law. As societal consensus changes—as it surely has with respect to sexual activities, pornography, and gambling—the prohibitions of the criminal law must, and do, change as well. Thus, the offenses against public morality constitute a particularly dynamic area of the criminal law.

Key Terms

public indecency	sodomy
gambling	indecent exposure
prostitution	lewd and lascivious conduct
obscenity	hard-core pornography
vice crimes	prurient interest
police power	patently offensive
fornication	child pornography
adultery	profanity
seduction	lottery
incest	numbers racket
bigamy	consideration, prize, and chance

 # Web-Based Research Activity

1. Go to the web. Locate your state's criminal statutes online.
2. Does your state maintain a proscription against sodomy or a related offense? Using your state's on-line judicial resources, try to determine whether the offense has been recently addressed in the appellate courts.

Questions for Thought and Discussion

1. Is there a rational basis for the law to extend the crime of incest to prohibit intermarriage between persons related by affinity?

2. Should it be a defense to a charge of bigamy that both persons in the alleged bigamous union are adherents to a religious faith that sanctions polygamy?

3. Can the criminalization of sexual conduct such as prostitution and sodomy be reconciled with the constitutional right of privacy discussed in Chapter 3?

4. Would prostitution be more injurious or less injurious to the public health, welfare, and morality if it were legalized and regulated?

5. Would it be more desirable to regulate obscenity by criminalizing it or by using zoning to restrict its dissemination to certain locations?

6. How are laws proscribing obscenity susceptible to the overbreadth and vagueness challenges discussed in Chapter 3?

7. What, if any, constitutional objections could be raised against a city ordinance making it a criminal offense "to use profane language in a public place"?

8. What forms of gambling are legal and illegal in your state? Are there any particular games that fall into a gray area between permitted and prohibited activity? Is church bingo legal in your state?

Problems for Discussion and Solution

1. Tanya Thong has been convicted of indecent exposure stemming from an incident in which she appeared topless on a public beach. On appeal, Thong argues that the indecent exposure statute amounts to unconstitutional sex discrimination because it prohibits women, but not men, from baring their breasts in public. Does Thong have a valid argument?

2. Gerald N. runs a video game arcade. One of his most popular games is called Video Blackjack. Essentially, the game is a computerized form of blackjack in which the contestant plays against the computer. The cost of playing the game is fifty cents. The contestant who wins the game is issued a token that can be used to play any other game in the arcade. Suppose your state gambling statute prohibits all "games involving valuable consideration, chance, and a possible prize." If you were the prosecutor, would you be concerned about the legality of this game?

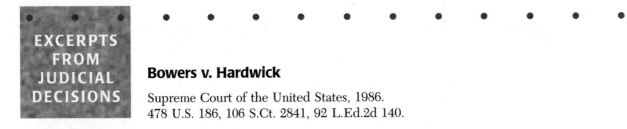

Bowers v. Hardwick

Supreme Court of the United States, 1986.
478 U.S. 186, 106 S.Ct. 2841, 92 L.Ed.2d 140.

[In this case the Supreme Court considers a challenge to the constitutionality of a Georgia sodomy law as applied to homosexual conduct.]

Justice WHITE delivered the opinion of the Court.

In August 1982, respondent was charged with violating the Georgia statute criminalizing sodomy by committing that act with another adult male in the bedroom of respondent's home. After a preliminary hearing, the District Attorney decided not to present the matter to grand jury unless further evidence developed.

Respondent then brought suit in the Federal District Court, challenging the constitutionality of the statute insofar as it criminalized consensual sodomy. He asserted that he was a practicing homosexual, that the Georgia sodomy statute, as administered by the defendants, placed him in imminent danger of arrest, and that the statute for several reasons violates the Federal Constitution. The District Court granted the defendants' motion to dismiss. . . .

A divided panel of the Court of Appeals for the Eleventh Circuit reversed. . . . Relying on our decisions in *Griswold v. Connecticut* . . . [1965], *Eisenstadt v. Baird* . . . [1972], *Stanley v. Georgia* . . . [1969], and *Roe v. Wade* . . . [1969], the court went on to hold that the Georgia statute violated respondent's fundamental rights because his homosexual activity is a private and intimate association that is beyond the reach of the state regulation by reason of the Ninth Amendment and the Due Process Clause of the Fourteenth Amendment. The case was remanded for trial, at which, to prevail, the State would have to prove that the statute is supported by a compelling interest and is the most narrowly drawn means of achieving that end.

Because other Courts of Appeals have arrived at judgments contrary to that of the Eleventh Circuit in this case, we granted the State's petition for certiorari. . . .

This case does not require a judgment on whether laws against sodomy between consenting adults in general, or between homosexuals in particular, are wise or desirable. It raises no question about the right or propriety of state legislative decisions to repeal their laws that criminalize homosexual sodomy, or of state court decisions invalidating those laws on state constitutional grounds. The issue presented is whether the Federal Constitution confers a fundamental right upon homosexuals to engage in sodomy and hence invalidates the laws of the many States that still make such conduct illegal and have done so for a very long time. . . .

We first register our disagreement with the Court of Appeals . . . that the Court's prior cases have construed the Constitution to confer a right of privacy that extends to homosexual sodomy and for all intents and purposes have decided this case. . . .

Accepting the decisions in these cases and the above description of them, we think it evident that none of the rights announced in those cases bears any resemblance to the claimed constitutional right of homosexuals to engage in acts of sodomy that is asserted in this case. No connection between family, marriage, or procreation on the one hand and homosexual activity on the other has been demonstrated, either by the Court of Appeals or by respondent. Moreover, any claim that these cases nevertheless stand for the proposition that any kind of private sexual conduct between consenting adults is constitutionally insulated from state proscription is insupportable. . . .

Precedent aside, however, respondent would have us announce, as the Court of Appeals did, a fundamental right to engage in homosexual sodomy. This we are quite unwilling to do. . . .

. . . Sodomy was a criminal offense at common law and was forbidden by the laws of the original thirteen States when they ratified the Bill of Rights. In 1868, when the Fourteenth Amendment was ratified, all but 5 of the 37 States in the Union had criminal sodomy laws. In fact, until 1961, all States outlawed sodomy, and today, 24 States and the District of Columbia continue to provide criminal penalties for sodomy performed in private and between consenting adults. . . . Against this background, to claim that a right to engage in such conduct is "deeply rooted in this Nation's history and tradition" or "implicit in the concept of ordered liberty" is, at best, facetious. . . .

Nor are we inclined to take a more expansive view of our authority to discover new fundamental rights imbedded in the Due Process Clause. The Court is most vulnerable and comes nearest to illegitimacy when it deals with judge-made constitutional law having little or no recognizable roots in the language or design of the Constitution. . . .

Respondent, however, asserts that the result should be different where the homosexual conduct occurs in the privacy of the home. . . . Plainly enough, otherwise illegal conduct is not always immunized whenever it occurs in the home. Victimless crimes, such as the possession and use of illegal drugs, do not escape the law where they are committed at home. . . . And if respondent's submission is limited to the voluntary sexual conduct between consenting adults, it would be difficult, except by fiat, to limit the claimed right to homosexual conduct while leaving exposed to prosecution adultery, incest, and other sexual crimes even though they are committed in the home. We are unwilling to start down that road.

Even if the conduct at issue here is not a fundamental right, respondent asserts that there must be a rational basis for the law and there is none in this case other than the presumed belief of a majority of the electorate in Georgia that homosexual sodomy is immoral and unacceptable. This is said to be an inadequate rationale to support the law. The law, however, is constantly based on notions of morality, and if all laws representing essentially moral choices are to be invalidated under the Due Process Clause, the courts will be very busy indeed. Even respondent makes no such claim, but insists that majority sentiments about the morality of homosexuality should be declared inadequate. We do not agree, and are unpersuaded that the sodomy laws of some 25 States should be invalidated on this basis. . . .

Accordingly, the judgment of the Court of Appeals is reversed.

Chief Justice BURGER, concurring. . . .

I join the Court's opinion, but I write separately to underscore my view that in constitutional terms there is no such thing as a fundamental right to commit homosexual sodomy.

As the Court notes, . . . the proscriptions against sodomy have very "ancient roots." Decisions of individuals relating to homosexual conduct have been subject to state intervention throughout the history of Western Civilization. Condemnation of those practices is firmly rooted in Judeao–Christian moral and ethical standards. Homosexual sodomy was a capital crime under Roman law. . . . During the English Reformation when powers of the ecclesiastical courts were transferred to the King's Courts, the first English statute criminalizing sodomy was passed. . . . Blackstone described "the infamous crime against nature" as an offense of "deeper malignity" than rape, an heinous act "the very mention of which is a disgrace to human nature," and "a crime not fit to be named." . . . The common law of England, including its prohibition of sodomy, became the received law of Georgia and the other Colonies. In 1816 the Georgia Legislature passed the statute at issue here, and that statute has been continuously in force in one form or another since that time. To hold that the act of homosexual sodomy is somehow protected as a fundamental right would be to cast aside millennia of moral teaching. . . .

Justice POWELL, concurring. . . .

Justice BLACKMUN, with whom Justice BRENNAN, Justice MARSHALL, and Justice STEVENS join, dissenting.

. . . The Court concludes today that none of our prior cases dealing with various decisions that individuals are entitled to make free of governmental interference "bears any resemblance to the claimed constitutional right of homosexuals to engage in acts of sodomy that is asserted in this case." . . . We protect . . . rights not because they contribute, in some direct and material way, to the general public welfare, but because they form so central a part of an individual's life. "[T]he concept of privacy embodies the 'moral fact that a person belongs to himself and not others nor to society as a whole.'" . . .

The behavior for which Hardwick faces prosecution occurred in his own home, a place to which the Fourth Amendment attaches special significance. The Court's treatment of this aspect of this case is symptomatic of its overall refusal to consider the broad principles that have informed our treatment of privacy in specific cases. Just as the right to privacy is more than the mere aggregation of a number of entitlements to engage in specific behavior, so too, protecting the physical integrity of the home is more than merely a means of protecting specific activities that often take place there. . . . [T]he essence of a Fourth Amendment violation is "not the breaking of [a person's] doors, and the rummaging of his drawers," but rather is "the invasion of his indefeasible right of personal security, personal liberty and private property." . . .

. . . [T]he right of an individual to conduct intimate relationships in the intimacy of his or her own home

seems to me to be the heart of the Constitution's protection of privacy. . . .

Justice STEVENS, with whom Justice BRENNAN and Justice MARSHALL join, dissenting. . . .

● ● ● ● ● ● ● ● ● ● ● ● ● ● ●

Campbell v. Sundquist

Tennessee Court of Appeals, 1996.
926 S.W.2d 250.

[In this case the Tennessee Court of Appeals considers a constitutional challenge to a state statute criminalizing homosexual sodomy. Students should compare and contrast this decision with the U.S. Supreme Court's decision in Bowers v. Hardwick, reprinted above.]

CRAWFORD, J.:

This appeal involves a constitutional challenge under the Tennessee Constitution to Tennessee's Homosexual Practices Act, T.C.A. § 39–13–510 (1991). . . . The complaint, as amended, seeks a declaratory judgment . . . that the Homosexual Practices Act (HPA), a criminal law, violates plaintiffs' right to privacy under . . . the Tennessee Constitution and their right to equal protection of the laws under Article I, Section 8 of the Tennessee Constitution. Plaintiffs also seek to enjoin the enforcement of the HPA.

Each of the plaintiffs admitted that they have violated the HPA in the past, and that they intend to continue violating the HPA in the future. Plaintiffs allege that they are each harmed by the HPA because it criminalizes their private, intimate conduct, and that each of them believe they are threatened with prosecution for violations of the statute, which could result in plaintiffs losing their jobs, professional licenses, and/or housing should they be convicted. . . .

T.C.A. § 39–13–510 (1991) provides:

Homosexual acts—It is a Class C misdemeanor for any person to engage in consensual sexual penetration, as defined in § 39–13–501(7), with a person of the same gender.

T.C.A. § 39–13–501(7) (1991) provides:

"Sexual penetration" means sexual intercourse, cunnilingus, fellatio, anal intercourse, or any other intrusion, however slight, of any part of a person's body or of any object into the genital or anal openings of the victim's, the defendant's, or any other person's body, but emission of semen is not required. . . .

We note at the outset that in determining the parameters of the right to privacy under the Tennessee Constitution, neither this Court nor the Tennessee Supreme Court is bound by the United States Supreme Court's decision in *Bowers v. Hardwick*. It is settled constitutional law that where the Tennessee Constitution and the federal constitution contain similar or identical provisions, the Tennessee Supreme Court may "impose higher standards and stronger protection than those set by the federal constitution.". . .

The right to privacy, or personal autonomy ("the right to be let alone"), while not mentioned explicitly in our state constitution, is nevertheless reflected in several sections of the Tennessee Declaration of Rights. . . .

. . . Based on both the language and the development of our state constitution, we have no hesitation in drawing the conclusion that there is a right of individual privacy guaranteed under and protected by the liberty clauses of the Tennessee Declaration of Rights. . . .

Undoubtedly, that right to privacy incorporates some of the attributes of the federal constitutional right to privacy and, in any given fact situation, may also share some of its contours. As with other state constitutional rights having counterparts in the federal bill of rights, however, there is no reason to assume that there is a complete congruency. . . .

The Homosexual Practices Act prohibits sexual contact between individuals of the same gender regardless of the location of the contact. That is, as written, the statute is sufficiently broad to prohibit private sexual activity which takes place behind closed doors in an individual's home. The sanctity of the home has long been recognized by both federal law and Tennessee law, and both bodies of law have drawn distinctions between actions which are committed in the privacy of the home and those committed in public. We think it is consistent with this State's Constitution and constitutional jurisprudence to hold that an adult's right to engage in consensual and noncommercial sexual activities in the privacy of that adult's home is a matter of intimate personal concern which is at the heart of Tennessee's protection of the right to privacy, and that this right should not be diminished or afforded less constitutional protection when the adults engaging in that private activity are of the same gender.

Since we have determined that the Homosexual Practices Act constitutes a governmental intrusion into the plaintiffs' right to privacy, we must next address the question of whether this intrusion is unwarranted and therefore, unconstitutional. Since the right to privacy is protected by the Tennessee Constitution, it is therefore a fundamental right. . . . Legislation which regulates the exercise of a fundamental right will be reviewed under a strict scrutiny analysis. . . . To withstand strict scrutiny, the legislation must be justified by a "compelling state interest" and must be narrowly drawn to advance that interest. . . .

The appellants offer essentially five state interests that are allegedly advanced by the Homosexual Practices Act. First, the Act discourages activities which cannot lead to procreation. Second, the Act discourages citizens from choosing a lifestyle which is socially stigmatized and leads to higher rates of suicide, depression, and drug and alcohol abuse. Third, the Act discourages homosexual relationships which are "short lived," shallow, and initiated for the purpose of sexual gratification. Fourth, the Act prevents the spread of infectious disease, and fifth, the Act promotes the moral values of Tennesseans.

None of the foregoing asserted State interests are sufficient to save the Homosexual Practices Act under strict scrutiny analysis, because either the asserted interest is not a compelling one, or the Act is not narrowly drawn to advance that interest. The first asserted interest, that the statute discourages activity which cannot lead to procreation, is neither a compelling nor even a constitutionally valid justification for the Act. The United States Supreme Court's decision in *Griswold v. Connecticut* (1965), establishes that the State cannot outlaw certain intimate sexual activities of its citizens simply because those activities do not or cannot lead to procreation. . . .

The second justification for the statute, that it discourages a socially stigmatized lifestyle which leads to higher rates of suicide, depression, and substance abuse, also fails to save the statute under strict scrutiny analysis. We think there is little doubt that the State's attempt to rescue homosexuals from a socially unpopular lifestyle does not provide a compelling reason or even a valid reason for infringement of the fundamental right of adults to engage in private, noncommercial, consensual sex. . . . While we agree that the State has a compelling interest in preventing substance abuse and suicide among its citizens, there is insufficient evidence in the record before us to demonstrate that the Homosexual Practices Act advances this interest. Moreover, even if we assume that the State can punish a "lifestyle," the record before us indicates that there is no one "homosexual lifestyle" in which all or even a majority of homosexuals engage; thus, with respect to this justification, the statute is overly broad by infringing upon the privacy rights of homosexuals who do not engage in a lifestyle encompassing alcoholism, drug abuse, and suicide.

The State's third justification for the statute is that it prevents homosexuals from entering into short lived, shallow, and promiscuous relationships which weaken the "fabric" of the community at large. The appellants argue that homosexual relationships are instable and that this instability has consequences for others in society. We think this justification also fails to rescue the Homosexual Practices Act under strict scrutiny analysis, because there is insufficient evidence in the record to prove that homosexual relationships are short lived and shallow and thereby weaken the "fabric" of the community.

The State's fourth asserted justification for the statute is that it prevents the spread of infectious disease. We agree that the State certainly has a compelling interest in preventing the spread of infectious disease among its citizens, however, the Homosexual Practices Act is not narrowly tailored to advance this interest. The statute prohibits all sexual contact between people of the same gender even if the people involved are disease free, practicing "safe sex," or engaging in sexual contact which does not contribute to the spread of disease. Moreover, the appellees and the American Public Health Association, as *amicus curiae,* forward a compelling argument that the statute is actually counterproductive to public health goals. The appellees introduced evidence that due to fear of prosecution, some homosexual individuals infected with sexually transmitted diseases do not seek medical treatment for the infection or report the infection, and that others are reluctant to be tested to determine if they are infected.

The final asserted justification for the Homosexual Practices Act is that the Act advances the morals of Tennessee citizens. The appellants assert that by criminalizing homosexual acts, the citizens of this State, through their elected representatives, have indicated that they "find the practice of homosexuality offensive and violative of their own moral standards, whether those standards are founded in religious conviction or are derived from a system of secular moral philosophy." The appellants argue that it is axiomatic that our State's laws may constitutionally reflect the moral values and standards of its citizens and may prohibit conduct which is violative of those moral values and standards. . . .

In reviewing these arguments we note that the propriety of the infusion of majoritarian morality into our laws has been debated since the inception of this Nation, and this debate has resulted in judicial conclusions that are as vastly different as the contexts in which these debates have arisen. In this case, both the appellants and the appellees present compelling arguments regarding the extent to which our laws may reflect majoritarian morality. We recognize that many of the laws of this State reflect "moral choices" regarding the standard of conduct by which the citizens of this State must conduct themselves. However, we also recognize that when these "moral choices" are transformed into law, they have constitutional limits. In this case, since the law in question infringes upon the plaintiffs' right to privacy, a fundamental right, the law must be justified by a compelling state interest and must be narrowly drawn to advance that interest. Even if we assume that the Homosexual Practices Act represents a moral choice of the people of this State, we are unconvinced that the advancement of this moral choice is so compelling as to justify the regulation of private, noncommercial, sexual choices between consenting adults simply because those adults happen to be of the same gender. . . .

Pursuant to this state's constitution and constitutional jurisprudence, we conclude that our citizens' fundamental right to privacy ("the right to be let alone") encompasses the right of the plaintiffs to engage in consensual, private, non-commercial, sexual conduct, because that activity "involv[es] intimate questions of personal and family concern." Therefore, we hold that the Homosexual Practices Act, T.C.A. § 39–13–510, which criminalizes such conduct, is unconstitutional. . . .

CANTRELL, J., dissenting in part. . . .

●　　●　　●　　●　　●　　●　　●　　●　　●　　●　　●　　●　　●　　●

Austin v. State

Court of Appeals of Texas, 1990.
794 S.W.2d 408.

[In this case a Texas appellate court determines whether there was sufficient evidence to support the appellant's conviction for prostitution.]

JOHN F. ONION, Jr., Assigned Justice.

This is an appeal from a conviction for prostitution. Tex. Pen. Code Ann. § 43.02(a)(1) (1989). At the conclusion of the bench trial, the trial court assessed appellant's punishment at sixty (60) days confinement in the county jail, and at a fine of $200.00. The imposition of the sentence was suspended, and the appellant was placed on probation of 180 days subject to certain conditions of probation. . . .

. . . [A]ppellant contends the evidence was insufficient to support her conviction. The elements of the offense under § 43.03(a)(1) are: (1) A person (2) knowingly (3) offers or agrees to engage in sexual conduct (4) in return for a fee payable to the actor. . . .

The complaint and information in the instant case alleged in pertinent part that the appellant on or about April 30, 1988, "did then and there knowingly agree to engage in sexual conduct for a fee, to wit: the said Kimberli Austin agreed to have sexual intercourse with J. Hutto for a fee."

Thus, the State had the burden to prove beyond a reasonable doubt that (1) Kimberli Austin (2) did knowingly (3) agree to engage in sexual conduct, to wit: sexual intercourse with J. Hutto (4) for a fee.

In the instant bench trial there was only one witness—Officer John Hutto of the Austin Police Department. He related that on April 20, 1988, he and other officers were in the process of investigating massage parlors and modeling studios; that on that date he went to the Satin Spa in Travis County. Hutto entered a living room area where there was a male and two females. The male told Hutto to select one of the females, and Hutto selected the appellant Austin. She led him down a hall to a room where there was a sign or signs as to the prices for "Basic Body Rub" and "Swedish Deep Muscle Rub." The appellant informed Hutto the "Basic Rub" was a "fingertip" massage, and the "Swedish Deep Muscle Rub" was a "more thorough and stimulating rub." The highest cost of the former was $60.00 for 60 minutes, and the highest cost of the latter was $130.00 for 60 minutes. Hutto, a veteran of several years with the Austin Police Department, had experience with the terminology and understood that "Swedish Deep Muscle Rub" was "a catch phrase" or "key words" for prostitution. Hutto gave appellant $140.00 for the highest price "Swedish" rub. Appellant left the room and returned with his change of $10.00. They both then disrobed. The nude appellant laid face down on the bed and asked Hutto to massage her back, which he did for ten minutes. Then the appellant gave Hutto massage on his back, legs, and buttocks for ten minutes. Appellant then asked Hutto if he would "like to end the session." He pretended not to understand, protesting that he had only been there twenty minutes, and had paid for an hour. Appellant repeated her inquiry. Hutto then asked if they ended the session could he "get more than just a rub." Appellant said "yes," and Hutto inquired whether he needed to pay her more money or give her a tip. Appellant replied "no, it's all taken care of."

The record then reflects on redirect examination:

a. And after she said it was taken care of I asked her what I could get. And she asked me what did I want. And I told her a blow job or maybe a f__k. And she said "Choose one. It's one or the other."

Q. Was that—was either the blow job or the f__k included in the $130.00?

a. That was my understanding. Because she said that it was taken care of when I asked her if I needed to pay more. . . .

a. Well, we agreed on sexual intercourse and she—she—I asked her if she had some protection I could use, and she said "Yes" and got a condom out of her purse.

Q. Did the defendant agree to engage in sexual conduct with you for a fee?

a. Yes.

Q. And specifically what was that sexual conduct?

a. Sexual intercourse.

The trial judge in a bench trial is the sole trier of the facts, the credibility of the witnesses and the weight to be given to their testimony, and may accept any part of or all the testimony given by the witnesses. . . .

Appellant agrees that the prosecution established all the elements of the offense except one. Appellant acknowledges the proof showed she agreed to engage in sexual intercourse, but argues the evidence does not show that she did so "for a fee." She contends the $130.00 "session" ended before she agreed to the sexual intercourse, that she "was no longer being compensated for her personal services, and that she made no effort to obtain compensation for any sexual activity." The State counters that the evidence showed that Hutto agreed to end the 20-minute "session" only after he determined from the appellant that he could get "more than a rub" and that it was "all taken care of," and that the parties agreed to sexual intercourse. There was certainly evidence to this effect, and the trial court was the trier of the facts." . . .

The judgment is affirmed.

POWERS, Justice, dissenting.

. . . I believe the evidence insufficient to establish . . . that Austin "knowingly" agreed to sexual intercourse for a fee. . . .

In the present case, there was no initial agreement for conduct on Austin's part that was explicitly sexual. Instead, the officer paid $130 for a "massage" described as a "Swedish Deep Muscle Rub." If that meant sexual conduct, it was only by innuendo or suspicion. "Swedish Deep Muscle Rub" was ambiguous at best as to what it meant; nominally at least it was a "massage." Thus, the evidence does not show, without more, a link between the fee paid by the officer and Austin's subsequent agreement for sexual relations, reached after the fee was paid and the massage begun. . . .

● ● ● ● ● ● ● ● ● ● ● ● ● ●

Radey v. State

Court of Appeals of Ohio, 1989.
54 Ohio App. 3d 18, 560 N.E. 2d 247.

[In this case an Ohio appellate court discusses the operational definition of obscenity. The appellant was charged with pandering obscenity in violation of Ohio law. He was tried before a jury and convicted.]

REECE, Judge.

Defendant-appellant, Richard A. Radey, was arrested by members of the Medina Police Department after he had sold ten greeting cards to two Medina police officers. . . . All of the cards have photographic depictions that are either sexually suggestive or explicit. . . . The photographs often show nude male or female figures and in most cases show one or the other's genitals. In none of the cards is penetration, however slight, depicted. Nor is there a showing of contact between a mouth or tongue and a penis, vagina or anus. . . .

This court is obligated to make an independent, *de novo* judgment as to whether the material involved is constitutionally protected. . . .

In *Miller* [*v. California* (1973)], the Supreme Court set forth the current test for determining whether challenged materials are obscene. *Miller* stated the test for judging whether material is obscene as follows:

The basic guidelines for the trier of fact must be: (a) whether 'the average person, applying contemporary community standards' would find that the work, taken as a whole, appeals to the prurient interest . . . , (b) whether the work depicts or describes, in a patently offensive way, sexual conduct specifically defined by the applicable state law; and (c) whether the work, taken as a whole, lacks serious literary, artistic, political, or scientific value. . . .

In *Pope v. Illinois* . . . (1987), the Supreme Court reiterated that parts (a) and (b) of the *Miller* tripartite test should be determined with reference to contemporary community standards. The court held that the proper inquiry for part (c) is whether a reasonable person would find value in the material taken as a whole.

The Supreme Court has characterized the second part of the *Miller* test as a two-step inquiry. . . . The threshold or substantive question is whether the materials depicted "hard core" sexual conduct. The second part of the test is whether, as a matter of fact, the materials were patently offensive under contemporary community standards. Moreover, *Miller* requires that this court review the jury finding under part (c). . . .

The Supreme Court of Ohio has found [the Ohio obscenity statute] to be constitutional when read in *pari materia* with the *Miller* guidelines. . . . Therefore, the *Miller* test for defining obscenity was incorporated into the statute by an authoritative state court construction specifically sanctioned by *Miller*. . . . Therefore, when the Ohio statutes are read to incorporate the guidelines prescribed in *Miller*, the material:

(a) must depict conduct which is expressly set forth by the definition of "sexual conduct" . . . and (b) the sexual conduct depicted must be "obscene," . . . and (c) the material must meet the three guidelines of *Miller*.

In this case, the purchased articles are not obscene as a matter of law. The items do not, in and of themselves, describe or depict "hard core sexual conduct" as defined in the Ohio statutes and as required by *Miller* . . .

Accordingly, . . . the judgment of conviction is reversed and appellant is discharged.

• • • • • • • • • • • • • • •

United States v. Pinelli

United States Court of Appeals, Tenth Circuit, 1989.
890 F.2d 1461.

*[In this case the U.S. Court of Appeals for the Tenth
Circuit reviews the sufficiency of the evidence against
seven defendants convicted of several federal gambling offenses.]*

PHILLIPS, District Judge, sitting by designation.

This gambling prosecution stems from a thirty-
five (35) count indictment returned by a federal
grand jury sitting in Colorado on February 5, 1986.
The indictment charged fourteen defendants, including the seven appellants here, with violating several
federal criminal statutes. The pertinent statutes on
appeal are 18 U.S.C. § 1955 (operating an illegal gambling business in violation of the laws of Colorado, involving five or more persons, with gross wagers in
excess of $2,000 on any single day), 18 U.S.C. § 1952
(interstate use of a telephone to facilitate the gambling business), 26 U.S.C. § 7201 (income tax evasion), 26 U.S.C. § 7262 (failure to pay gambling
occupation tax), and 26 U.S.C. § 7203 (failure to file
requisite tax forms).

Four defendants entered pleas of guilty prior to
trial. Three defendants were acquitted on all charges
by the jury. The remaining seven defendants, appellants here, suffered convictions on the counts. . . .

Appellants have raised numerous issues on appeal. . . . We find that there was abundant evidence
from which a reasonable jury could find the defendants guilty of the offense for which they were convicted, and further find no reversible error in the
record of this case. Accordingly, we affirm the convictions of all seven appellants. . . .

In a challenge based upon the sufficiency of the
evidence, we must affirm the judgment of conviction
if there is record evidence which would allow a rational trier-of-fact to find the appellants guilty of the
crimes charged in the indictment. . . . Moreover, this
Court must view the evidence in the light most favorable to the government. . . . Viewed in that light,
we conclude that the evidence, both direct and circumstantial, satisfies the test.

The government's evidence at trial focused on appellant's gambling activities from September through
December, 1984. The evidence consisted of the testimony of thirty-six (36) witnesses, including numerous bettor witnesses, the introduction of several
hundred tape recordings of telephone conversations
intercepted pursuant to court-authorized electronic
surveillance, documentary evidence seized pursuant
to search warrants executed on December 9, 1984
after the termination of the wiretap, and expert testimony by an FBI agent on the roles played by the
various defendants in the gambling operation.

The electronic surveillance in this case was active for approximately twenty-four days in November
and December, 1984. The government's wiretap evidence and seized records in this case indicated the
gambling business in question accepted wagers in
excess of $2,300,000 in November and December,
1984. . . .

Special Agent William Holmes of the Federal
Bureau of Investigation testified as an expert witness
for the government as to the roles of each of the
participants in the gambling activity in question. His
opinions were based on review of the electronic surveillance and search evidence. . . . He did not rely on
and was not privy to the testimony of the bettor witnesses. . . . At the outset of his testimony, Holmes explained some basic gambling terminology. . . .

Holmes described the "point spread" or "line" as
having the purpose of attracting equal amounts of betting on each side of a contest. Bookmakers change the
line on a particular game to attract betting on the other
team. A line of "Denver minus six" means Denver is
favored by six points and to win a bet on Denver,
Denver must win by seven or more points. The term
"vig" or "vigorish" represents a ten percent commission charged to losing bets, which compensates the
bookmaker for the privilege of placing bets. In other
words, a $100 losing bet would require payment of
$110, which payment includes a $10 "vig." According
to Holmes, a bookmaker theoretically strives to accept
the same amount of bets on each side of a contest, or
balance his books, and take the "vig" as profit.

Agent Holmes explained the concept of "lay-off
wagering" as that which allows a bookmaker "to get

rid of wagers that he feels he is not financially able to handle and reduce the risk of great financial loss by having to pay off on large sums of money." . . . The following example of lay-off wagering was provided by Holmes during his testimony: Suppose Bookmaker X has wagers of $1,500 on team A and $1,000 on team B. Bookmaker X would lay-off the $500 excess on team A with Bookmaker Y. If team A wins, Bookmaker X would collect $1,000 from those who bet on team B, plus the 10% vig for a total of $1,100. Bookmaker X would collect his $500 lay-off wager from Bookmaker Y, which would make the total amount collected $1,600. From this amount, he would have to pay his bettors who had bet $1,500 on team A. Bookmaker X would thus make a profit of $100 without risking any of his own money. If Bookmaker X had not laid-off his excess wagers and team A had won, then he would have collected $1,100 from the losers ($1,100 + 10% vig) and had to pay out $1,500 to the winners for a net loss of $400. . . . As will be shown, the concept of lay-off wagering played a central role in the successful prosecution of appellants.

Viewing the evidence in the light most favorable to the government, as we must, a brief summary of the evidence pertaining to each appellant is set forth below. . . . [The Court summarizes the evidence against all seven appellants. Only the summaries pertaining to Phil Pinelli and David Pinelli are retained here.]

. . . The evidence introduced by the government established that defendant Phil Pinelli was in the business of accepting wagers on sporting events. Specifically, the evidence indicated that Phil Pinelli accepted over $800,000 in wagers during November and December, 1984. . . .

Evidence consisting of taped conversations between Phil Pinelli and his brother David Pinelli demonstrated a mutuality of risk between the two brothers in their wagering activities, . . . and indicated the brothers had mutual financial interests. . . . Further, wiretapped telephone conversations demonstrated that Phil Pinelli accepted wagers from, and placed wagers with, other bookmakers.

For instance, from taped conversations introduced by the government it was evident that Phil Pinelli accepted wagers from another bookmaker, Aaron Mosko, and placed bets by telephone with Ralph Lackey. . . . In particular, the government introduced a taped conversation between Aaron Mosko and Phil Pinelli in which Mosko told Pinelli that he

"needed" certain amounts on various games. . . . In another telephone conversation introduced by the government between Pinelli and a person identified as "Doc," Pinelli told Doc that he had "about five or six bookmakers and they unload their, like Aaron and them guys, they load all their shit on me."

The evidence introduced by the government also indicated that Phil Pinelli kept his gambling records in such a way as to obfuscate their true meaning. For instance, a review of seized records indicates that none of his accounts were identified by recognizable names, but rather by entries such as "K" and "PB." . . . Moreover, the government introduced a taped conversation between Pinelli and Aaron Mosko in which Pinelli explained to Mosko that he kept his books in a certain manner so "if they ever pick up my book, they'll say twenty to twenty, you know, they can't say what they are." . . . Phil Pinelli received line formation for his gambling activities by placing telephone calls to Las Vegas. . . .

FBI Agent Holmes testified that in his opinion Phil Pinelli was in the business of accepting sports wagering activity and David Pinelli was his partner and assisted Phil in accepting wagers, setting line, and deciding lay-off policy. . . .

Tape recorded conversations between the two brothers demonstrated the mutuality of financial interests between the two. . . . For instance, in one conversation the Pinellis discussed what they collectively had on Denver and how much they wanted to "lay-off." . . . In another conversation David and Phil Pinelli went over the day's wagering activity. . . .

Agent Holmes described David Pinelli as a partner of Phil Pinelli in his gambling business who assisted Phil in accepting wagers, setting line, and deciding lay-off policy. . . .

Central to appellants' challenge to the sufficiency of the evidence is their claim that the government did not prove the jurisdictional elements of 18 U.S.C. § 1955. Section 1955 makes it a crime to operate an illegal gambling business in violation of the laws of the State of Colorado involving five or more persons which was in substantially continuous operation in excess of thirty days, or which had gross wagers in excess of $2,000 on any single day. Here, the multiple telephone calls on particular days, as well as the coordination among appellants which was evident in many conversations, together with the generated revenues, which were substantially in excess of $2,000 per day, amply provide a basis for the jury's findings.

The remaining charges may be briefly summarized. Title 18 U.S.C. § 1952 prohibits interstate telephone calls which facilitate a gambling business. Title 26 U.S. § 7203 makes it a misdemeanor for willful attempts to evade the 2% excise tax on wagers accepted. Title 26 U.S.C. § 7203 makes it a misdemeanor for willful failure to file a tax return, while 26 U.S.C. § 7262 is a misdemeanor offense arising out of the failure to pay the gambling occupation tax.

We are convinced that the evidence collectively, both direct and circumstantial, when viewed in the light most favorable to the government, satisfies each of the essential elements of Section 1955 and the other counts of conviction, and demonstrates appellants' participation in a substantial and continuous bookmaking business conducted by multiple bookmakers and others linked through lay-off wagering, exchange and the use of line formation and ancillary activities.

JUDGMENT AFFIRMED.

CHAPTER 9

Alcohol and Drug Offenses

Introduction

In this chapter we examine several offenses involving the misuse of drugs and alcohol. Because the English common law had little to say about the abuse of alcohol, and nothing to say about illicit drugs, these offenses are based on statutory enactments. These prohibitions reflect the modern awareness of the adverse social consequences of drug and alcohol abuse. Although drug and alcohol offenses can be, and often are, classified as crimes against public morality, they are sufficiently distinctive in character and frequent in their occurrence to warrant separate treatment in a study of criminal law.

Drug Offenses

The misuse of drugs is among the oldest vices in society. Some believe that illicit drug use should be strictly a moral question, where each person is free to decide his or her own limits. Yet drug abuse affects more than just the individual user. Drug abuse creates many dramatic economic, social, and health problems in our society. Illegal trafficking in drugs has led to many violent crimes as well as to instances of official corruption. Moreover, many violent crimes are committed by people under the influence of illicit drugs. The correlation between drug abuse and crime is demonstrated by the fact that in twenty-three of the larger cities in the United States, between 50 and 77 percent of male arrestees test positive for drugs. (See National Institute of Justice, *Drug Use Forecasting: 1999 Annual Report on Adult and Juvenile Arrestees.*)

Since the 1980s, the focus of the drug problem has been the widespread use of cocaine and, in particular, "crack," an inexpensive form of cocaine that is ingested through smoking. The prevalence of cocaine and the destructive consequences of its use led political leaders to declare a "war on drugs" in the late 1980s. Even though the national war on drugs has attained only limited results, evidence indicates that it has had a positive impact. For example, in 1985, 13.1 percent of high school seniors reported that they had used cocaine within the last twelve months; by 1996, the figure had declined to 2.2 percent (U.S. Department of Justice, Bureau of Justice Statistics, *Sourcebook of Criminal Justice Statistics 1996*, p. 259).

Some commentators, believing that the national "war on drugs" has failed, have argued for the legalization of such drugs as marijuana, cocaine, and heroin. These commentators would prefer to see use of these drugs legalized, although highly regulated, with increased efforts directed toward educational and treatment programs. Advocates of legalization contend that drug use is a moral issue. They point out that criminal prohibition of drug use has led to a vast underground economy, and that the war on drugs has debased the rule of law by ineffective attempts to alter personal conduct and by curtailment of individual rights through relaxed standards of procedures for searches and seizures. And although the attitude toward legalization appears to be more favorable toward marijuana than other drugs, in 1998 only 28 percent of Americans thought its use should be made legal (U.S. Department of Justice, Bureau of Justice Statistics, *Sourcebook of Criminal Justice Statistics 1998*, p. 147).

Federal Laws

In the United States, the 1960s saw a resurgence of drug abuse, a problem that had caused great concern in the early twentieth century when it was legal to market products containing opium and cocaine. As attention focused on the illegal use of drugs as a national problem, Congress enacted the Comprehensive Drug Abuse Prevention and Control Act of 1970. 21 U.S.C.A. § 801 et seq. The act, commonly referred to as the **Controlled Substances Act,** establishes the criteria for classification of substances and lists controlled substances according to their potential for abuse. Offenses involving the manufacture, sale, distribution, and possession with intent to distribute are defined and the penalties are prescribed in 21 U.S.C.A. § 841. Penalties for simple possession of controlled substances are prescribed in 21 U.S.C.A. § 844. Provision is made for registered practitioners to dispense narcotics for approved purposes in 21 U.S.C.A. § 823.

In 1972 the Uniform Controlled Substances Act was drafted by the Commission on Uniform Laws. Its purpose was to achieve uniformity among state and federal laws. There are three versions of the Uniform Controlled Substances Act: 1970, 1990, and 1994. Provisions within each version are similar. All fifty states and the Virgin Islands have adopted one of the three versions. Like the federal statute, the uniform act classifies controlled substances according to their potential for abuse. For example, opiates are included in Schedule I because they are unsafe for use even under medical treatment, whereas Schedule II includes drugs that have a high potential for abuse but may be medically acceptable under certain conditions. The remaining schedules include controlled substances that have lesser potential for abuse and dependency. The range of controlled substances includes such well-known drugs as cocaine, amphetamines, tranquilizers, and barbiturates.

State Statutes

An excerpt from the U.S. Supreme Court's decision in *Robinson v. California* appears at the end of the chapter.

All states make the manufacture, sale, and possession of **controlled substances** illegal. Offenses involving drugs that have a high potential for abuse (for example, heroin and cocaine) are usually very serious felonies. Although it is constitutionally permissible to enact such laws, the U.S. Supreme Court has ruled that states may not criminalize the mere status of being addicted to such drugs. *Robinson v. California,* 370 U.S. 660, 82 S.Ct. 1417, 8 L.Ed.2d 758 (1962).

The following California statute is fairly typical of state drug laws:

> (a) Except as otherwise provided in this division, every person who transports, imports into this state, sells, furnishes, administers, or gives away, or offers to transport, import into this state, sell, furnish, administer, or give away . . . any controlled substance . . . shall be punished by imprisonment in the state prison for three, four, or five years. West's Annotated California Codes, Health and Safety Code, § 11352 (a) (1989).

Offenses involving the mere possession of less harmful substances are often classified as lesser-degree felonies or, where a very small quantity of marijuana is involved, are frequently classified as misdemeanors. In Nebraska, for example, possession of more than one ounce but less than one pound of marijuana is a misdemeanor; possession of more than one pound is a felony. Rev. Stat. Neb. § 28–416 (6)(7) (1989).

During the 1970s, several states decriminalized their anti-marijuana laws by removing the threat of a jail sentence for possession offenses. In Nebraska, possession of less than one ounce of marijuana is considered an "infraction" for which a first-time offender may be fined no more than one hundred dollars and made to attend a drug education course. Rev. Stat. Neb. § 28–416 (8)(a) (1989).

Despite the attempts at enforcement, marijuana remains widely available and exemplifies the difficulty of enforcing a law that has less than universal public support. Nevertheless, courts have generally declined to reassess legislative judgments in this area, and statutes making it a criminal offense to possess marijuana have withstood numerous constitutional challenges. Three decisions from state appellate courts are illustrative. In *State v. Smith,* 610 P.2d 869 (Wash. 1980), the Supreme Court of Washington held that criminal penalties for possession of marijuana did not violate the constitutional prohibition against cruel and unusual punishments. Judicial attitudes apparently have not changed in the 1990s. In *State v. Harland,* 556 So.2d 256 (La. App. 1990), the court rejected the contention that such penalties violated a state constitutional provision protecting the right of privacy. Alaskan courts have taken a more liberal view toward laws restricting the private use of marijuana. See, for example, *Ravin v. State,* 537 P.2d 494 (Alaska 1975). Yet the court of appeal held that a state law that decriminalizes possession of up to four ounces of marijuana for a person over age eighteen does not deny equal protection of the law to a person under eighteen who may be criminally punished for the same conduct. *Allan v. State,* 830 P.2d 435 (Alaska App. 1992).

Prohibition of Drug Paraphernalia

Possession of paraphernalia associated with illicit drug use is also commonly a criminal offense. Controlled substances and **drug paraphernalia** are declared **contraband** and are subject to confiscation. Likewise, vehicles and aircraft involved in trafficking of controlled substances may be seized and declared forfeited under various federal and state statutes. See, for example, 21 U.S.C.A. § 881.

Forfeiture of Property

In 1984 Congress enacted a law providing for **forfeiture** of real estate used in illegal drug trafficking. 21 U.S.C.A. § 881(a). However, in *United States v. A Parcel of Land,* 507 U.S. 111, 113 S.Ct. 1126, 122 L.Ed.2d 469 (1993), the Supreme Court ruled that although proceeds traceable to an unlawful drug transaction are subject to forfeiture, an owner's lack of knowledge that her home had been purchased with proceeds of illegal drug transactions constitutes a defense to a forfeiture proceeding under federal law. Moreover, the Court has set a theoretical limit on the amount of property that may be seized by government through forfeiture. In *Austin v. United States,* 509 U.S. 602, 113 S.Ct. 2801, 125 L.Ed.2d 488 (1993), the Court remanded for reconsideration a case where the federal government seized a business and a mobile home from a man who sold two grams of cocaine to an undercover agent. The Court ruled that forfeitures, although not technically criminal proceedings, are subject to the Excessive Fines Clause of the Eighth Amendment.

Problems of Enforcement

Federal and state laws on controlled substances mirror one another in many respects. Federal enforcement is usually directed against major interstate or international drug traffickers; states usually concentrate on those who possess or distribute controlled substances. Many drug-trafficking violations of federal law involve prosecution for conspiracy. Unlike many state laws, the federal law on conspiracy to violate the Controlled Substances Act does not require proof of an overt act. 21 U.S.C.A. § 846; *United States v. Pulido*, 69 F.3d 192 (7th Cir. 1995); *United States v. Wilson*, 657 F.2d 755 (5th Cir. 1981).

Because those involved in narcotics transactions are usually willing participants, enforcement often depends on use of confidential informants by police. Obtaining search warrants and making arrests based on probable cause often present difficult Fourth Amendment problems.

Prosecutorial Problems

The level of intent that the prosecution must establish in contraband cases can vary according to the particular statutory offense (see Chapter 4). However, courts have generally held that statutes making possession, distribution, or trafficking in contraband unlawful require the prosecution to prove only the defendant's general intent. See, for example, *State v. Williams*, 352 So. 2d 1295 (La. 1977); *State v. Bender*, 579 P.2d 796 (N.M. 1978).

In drug possession cases, a critical problem is proving that the defendant was in possession of a controlled substance. The prosecution may prove either actual or constructive possession of contraband to satisfy the possession requirement. Proof of **actual possession** is established by evidence that the contraband was found on the accused's person or that the accused was in exclusive possession of the premises or vehicle where the contraband was discovered. Where the accused is not in actual possession, however, or where the accused and another person jointly occupy a dwelling

CASE-IN-POINT

Constructive Possession of Drugs

After Minneapolis police obtained a tip that crack cocaine was being sold out of cars parked in front of a certain duplex, an officer observed a blue Cadillac parked in front of the building. A female later identified as the defendant, Nina Knox, made several trips between the car and the duplex. At one point she drove the car from the scene but returned shortly and sat in the car for a period of time as a number of men approached the car and walked away after brief encounters. The officer, who was experienced in dealing with drug offenses, believed the activities he witnessed to be drug transactions, although he was unable to observe money and drugs being exchanged. Knox was arrested, and a search of the car produced 14.3 grams of crack cocaine and $2,200 in cash. A search of Knox's purse produced a large amount of money and food stamps. Knox was convicted in federal court of possession with intent to distribute a controlled substance.

On appeal, Knox argued that the evidence failed to establish that she was in physical control of the cocaine and was intending to sell it. The U.S. Court of Appeals rejected Knox's contention, concluding that the evidence supported a finding that Knox had exercised "dominion over the premises in which the contraband [was] concealed," since she was observed driving the car, sitting in the car, and entering it on several occasions. The court further concluded that intent to distribute could be inferred from the fact that sizable amounts of cash and cocaine were found at the scene. Knox's conviction was affirmed.

United States v. Knox, 888 F.2d 585 (8th Cir. 1989).

or automobile where contraband is discovered, the prosecution must attempt to prove what the law calls **constructive possession.**

A person has constructive possession of contraband if he or she has ownership, dominion, or control over the contraband itself, or over the premises in which it is concealed. *United States v. Schubel,* 912 F.2d 952 (8th Cir. 1990). The prosecution usually attempts to establish constructive possession by evidence of incriminating statements and circumstances from which the defendant's ability to control the contraband may be inferred. This can pose a formidable difficulty.

In *State v. Somerville,* 572 A.2d 944 (Conn. 1990), the defendant appealed his conviction for possession of cocaine with intent to sell sixty-nine vials of crack cocaine. He argued that no evidence was presented at his trial to establish that he possessed the drugs in question. He pointed to the fact that no drugs and no large sums of money were found on his person. The evidence revealed that the police found the sixty-nine vials of cocaine underneath a garbage can at the defendant's neighbor's house. Witnesses had seen the defendant selling crack cocaine in small vials before his arrest. They testified that he had been stooping near the garbage can under which the police found the vials of cocaine. The Connecticut Supreme Court rejected the defendant's contention and found the evidence sufficient to establish that the defendant had dominion and control over the cocaine and had knowledge of the character of the contraband and its presence.

> In *Embry v. State,* an excerpt of which appears at the end of the chapter, the Arkansas Supreme Court discusses constructive possession.

Defenses

Defendants on trial for drug offenses sometimes assert that they were entrapped by the police, a defense discussed in Chapter 14. More frequently, defense counsel attempt to suppress the contraband seized by police on the ground that it was obtained in violation of the Fourth Amendment prohibition against unreasonable searches and seizures. In some instances, a defendant presents an expert witness to contest the type of contraband introduced in evidence, and frequently defendants challenge the chain of custody of the contraband from the time it was seized until the time it was introduced into evidence. Because the gravity of the offense is often based on the amount of contraband seized, defendants sometimes challenge the weight of the contraband being introduced into evidence. Possession with intent to deliver drugs within a certain proximity of a school is a more serious offense that can carry severe penalties. Defendants charged with this offense often challenge the measurement of the distance between the school and the place where the offense allegedly occurred.

In a number of cases, courts have rejected such defenses as economic coercion and duress, but in some instances courts have accepted the defense of "medical necessity" in possession of marijuana cases (see Chapter 14).

Drug Courts: A New Approach

In response to the effects of increasing use of illegal drugs, legislatures in the 1980s adopted tougher laws and communities demanded stricter law enforcement. Court dockets became overloaded with drug prosecutions. By the late 1980s, judges began to recognize that traditional court processes were neither deterring substance abusers nor addressing the medical, social, and economic problems associated with drug abuse. In an effort to use the court's authority to divert certain offenders to closely monitored programs, courts began to develop the concept of a **drug court.** Rather than sending nonviolent defendants to jail, a drug court, in collaboration with prosecutors, defense counsel, and other professionals, would monitor their progress through status hearings and prescribe sanctions and rewards.

Development of the Drug Court Concept

Between 1989 and 1994, forty-two drug court programs were established. The Violent Crime Control and Law Enforcement Act of 1994 (**Violent Crime Act**) authorized federal grants for drug court programs that include court-supervised drug treatment. By March 31, 1997, 161 drug court programs were operating in thirty-eight states, the District of Columbia, and Puerto Rico, with about 40 percent of the programs in California and Florida (*Drug Court: Overview of Growth, Characteristics, and Results*, U.S. General Accounting Office, July 1997, pp. 5–6, 35).

Methodology of Drug Court Programs

The methodology of processing defendants who might be eligible for participation in a drug court program varies from standard post-arrest processes. After an individual who has not committed a violent crime is arrested for possession of a controlled substance, a background check is made. If the arrestee meets the drug court eligibility requirements and the prosecuting attorney agrees, the defendant may opt to be diverted to a drug court program. Prosecution is deferred as long as the participant progresses. Once in the program, the participant must obtain a sponsor, attend certain meetings and counseling sessions, give frequent urine samples, and attend required court status hearings. The participant signs a "contract" to complete the program within a specified period, usually twelve months. The treatment phases consist of detoxification, counseling sessions, and often assistance in job training or employment. In some programs a participant who agrees is given acupuncture treatments to aid in detoxification and to make the participant more receptive to counseling sessions.

The status hearings before the drug court are central to the program. They are held in open court with all participants present. The judge may begin with a short orientation emphasizing the need for sobriety and gainful employment. The judge then reviews each participant's progress file and commends those whose urine samples are "clean" and who are in complete compliance with their contract. Participants applaud those with outstanding records of performance. The judge encourages those who have minor deviations in their performance and admonishes those who have relapsed. Often the court prescribes additional counseling, treatment, community service, or a short stay in jail for those who have seriously relapsed in their efforts.

Most programs countenance some relapse; however, positive urine tests, additional arrests, and/or failure to attend status hearings or treatment sessions may cause a participant to be terminated and prosecution resumed. Successful completion of a drug court program usually results in the charges against the participant being dropped or the plea of guilty being stricken from the record.

Evaluation of Drug Courts

Although the preceding topics provide a general outline of drug court programs, many variations exist. Some focus on women or juveniles; others handle both male and female adults. Some provide support services such as health and housing assistance and job placement; others do not. Some operate with a professional staff; in other instances, the assigned judge might have minimal professional assistance. These factors, along with the relative newness of the programs and the problem of comparing a given group of drug court participants with a control group of those whose offenses are handled in the traditional manner, make it difficult to evaluate the success of the drug court program. Nevertheless, the relapse rate of the participants and the frequency of new arrests are criteria that can be used to assess the program's effectiveness. And, though still a new and innovative institution, drug courts appear to hold considerable promise to deter repetitive criminal behavior of drug abusers. They also hold a promise to relieve courts and other functionaries in the criminal justice system of the burden of repetitive arrests and overloaded trial and sentencing dockets of criminal cases where drugs play an important role.

Intoxication Offenses

By the turn of the twentieth century, a substantial segment of the population perceived alcohol as an evil that had to be eradicated. In response to growing, but far from unanimous, public sentiment, Congress enacted the Eighteenth Amendment, which was ratified by the states in 1919. This amendment, widely referred to as "Prohibition," made unlawful the "manufacture, sale, or transportation of intoxicating liquors" within the United States. The national prohibition of alcohol was widely violated and contributed greatly to the development of organized crime syndicates in this country. Ultimately, Prohibition was repealed by the Twenty-First Amendment, ratified in 1933. Under the Twenty-First Amendment, however, state and local governments retain the authority to ban or regulate the manufacture, sale, and use of alcohol within their borders. Indeed, even though the sale of alcohol is widespread today, there are still a number of so-called "dry counties" throughout the United States, mainly in the South and Midwest, where the sale of all or some alcoholic beverages is prohibited. Although no state has chosen to ban the sale of alcohol altogether, all states regulate the sale and use of alcoholic beverages and retain a number of alcohol-related offenses.

Two offenses of statutory origin in the United States are directed at those who consume excessive amounts of alcoholic beverages. They are **public drunkenness** and **driving under the influence (DUI)** of intoxicants. These are sometimes regarded as offenses against public morality, but they are primarily designed to protect the safety of the public, as well as of the offender.

Public Drunkenness Laws

Laws and ordinances making public drunkenness an offense have long been enforced by all jurisdictions, with most states and municipalities simply providing that whoever shall become intoxicated from the voluntary use of intoxicating liquors shall be punished. The offense merely involves a person being found in a public place in a state of intoxication. This offense is usually classified as a minor misdemeanor. A common police practice has been to take offenders into custody and release them once they have "sobered up," a practice sometimes described as a "revolving door."

There is a growing awareness that alcoholism is a disease, and many have urged that the criminal law is an inappropriate mechanism to deal with it. In addition, some reformers have contended that criminalizing the public presence of an intoxicated

An excerpt from *Powell v. Texas* appears at the end of the chapter.

person is contrary to the Eighth Amendment's prohibition of cruel and unusual punishments. However, the Supreme Court has declined to accept such a view. Instead, in *Powell v. Texas,* 392 U.S. 514, 88 S.Ct. 2145, 20 L.Ed.2d 1254 (1968), the Court upheld a public intoxication law. In effect, the Court ruled that the defendant, Powell, was not being punished for his status as an alcoholic, but rather for his presence in a public place in an inebriated condition.

In recent years, some states have enacted statutes directing police officers to take persons found intoxicated in public places to treatment facilities rather than to incarcerate them. Consistent with this approach, many statutes now criminalize only **disorderly intoxication.** This newer offense involves the offender being intoxicated in a public place or on a public conveyance and endangering the safety of others, not merely being in a state of intoxication in public. See, for example, West's Texas Stat. Ann. § 49.02. In 1992 a Texas appellate court ruled that a police officer had sufficient probable cause for a warrantless arrest for public intoxication. The officer believed that the defendant could have fled from the scene, posing a danger to himself and others. Witnesses testified that the defendant ran into a parked car while intoxicated. *Segura v. State,* 826 S.W. 2d 178 (Tex. App. 1992).

Driving Under the Influence of Alcohol or Drugs

The carnage on the American highways attests to the urgent need for states to take stern measures to keep drunk drivers off the road, and all states have enacted laws attempting to accomplish this goal. Perhaps these measures have contributed to the decline from 1,503,000 arrests for driving while under the influence of intoxicants in 1985 to 986,000 such arrests in 1997, a decrease of 35 percent (U.S. Department of Justice, Bureau of Justice Statistics, *Sourcebook of Criminal Justice Statistics 1998*, p. 366).

The "classical" offense in this area is **driving while intoxicated (DWI)** or, more accurately, operating a motor vehicle while intoxicated. In the 1960s and 1970s, many jurisdictions expanded the offense to prohibit driving while under the influence of intoxicating liquors or drugs (DUI). DWI and DUI laws sometimes allowed a defendant to avoid conviction because of the ambiguity of his or her subjective behavior. In response to this problem, most states have modified their statutes to prohibit **driving with an unlawful blood-alcohol level (DUBAL),** usually defined as 0.10 percent or more alcohol in the bloodstream. By 2000, eighteen states and the District of Columbia had adopted an even stricter standard, prohibiting a 0.08 percent blood-alcohol level. This nationwide movement was promoted by Congress's enactment of the Transportation Equity Act for the 21st Century, Public Law 105–178, in the summer of 1998. The act created a 500-million-dollar incentive program under which states receive lucrative federal grants for lowering the prohibited blood-alcohol level to .08.

In 1996 Kentucky enacted a "zero tolerance law," also known as the "juvenile D.U.I. law," which makes it an offense for a person under age 21 to drive with a blood alcohol content of .02 percent or higher. In *Commonwealth v. Howard,* 969 S.W.2d 700 (Ky. 1998), the Kentucky Supreme Court upheld the law as being rationally related to a legitimate legislative purpose of reducing teenage traffic fatalities and protecting all members of the public. Therefore, the court held that it does not violate the equal protection rights of those who are prosecuted. By January 2000, most states had followed Kentucky's lead in establishing a lower permissible blood-alcohol level for juveniles (in most cases, .02 percent).

Prosecution and Defense of DWI, DUI, and DUBAL Charges

To obtain a conviction for DWI, DUI, or DUBAL, the prosecution must first establish that the defendant charged with driving while intoxicated or driving under the influence was operating the vehicle. This may be accomplished by either eyewitness testimony or circumstantial evidence. In *State v. Harrison*, 846 P.2d 1082 (N.M. App. 1992), the court reviewed a DUI conviction where the defendant's only contention was that the prosecution failed to prove he was driving a vehicle. Evidence at the defendant's trial revealed that he was found asleep behind the steering wheel of his car parked on the roadway with the key in the ignition, the motor running, and the transmission in drive. The court determined that this evidence established that the defendant was in actual physical control of the vehicle and therefore was sufficient to prove that the defendant was driving the automobile.

Next, the prosecution must establish the intoxication. Statutes, it should be noted, often refer to intoxication occurring as a result of alcohol or from ingestion of contraband substances. Intoxication is often a difficult state to articulate. Therefore, police often use such field sobriety techniques as the touching-finger-to-nose, walking-the-line, and counting-backwards tests to corroborate their testimony concerning the defendant's condition at the time of arrest.

In *Berkemer v. McCarty*, 468 U.S. 420, 104 S.Ct. 3138, 82 L.Ed.2d 317 (1984), the U.S. Supreme Court held that an officer's roadside questioning and administration of a **field sobriety test** to an individual stopped for irregular driving was not a "custodial interrogation" that required giving the suspect the *Miranda* warnings. However, the Court cautioned that the *Miranda* warnings apply once the suspect is under arrest. (For more discussion of field sobriety tests, see Chapter 16.)

Evidence indicates that field sobriety tests can be somewhat unreliable, and courts are beginning to scrutinize cases that rely solely on field sobriety tests without supporting chemical testing of the blood, urine, or breath of the suspect. Still, most courts permit persons to be convicted of DUI without chemical tests, especially when multiple sobriety tests have been performed by more than one officer.

Increasingly, police videotape suspects' performance on field sobriety tests and make audiotape recordings of suspects' speech. Many police agencies today have mobile blood-alcohol testing units ("Batmobiles") equipped with **breathalyzer** testing machines, videotape equipment, and voice recorders. These vans, available at the call of the arresting officer, give the police the opportunity to promptly collect evidence at or near the scene of the arrest.

One of the most sophisticated methods of alcohol detection is by measuring the grams of alcohol in a volume of breath by use of a spectrophotometer, which measures the absorption of infrared light by a sample of a gas. The sampled gas is human breath, and the absorption of infrared light by a sample of the gas is affected by the concentration of alcohol in the gas. A formula can be used to determine the concentration of alcohol. An instrument called the Intoxilyzer 5000 is increasingly used to perform this calculation electronically and provide a printout of the results.

Although generally regarded as superior to field sobriety tests from an evidentiary standpoint, chemical tests are not devoid of problems. When prosecutors rely solely on chemical evidence, defense counsel often challenge the reliability and validity of chemical testing equipment and the operator's level of competence. Ideally, to obtain a conviction, a prosecutor would like to have evidence that the defendant was driving abnormally, smelled of alcohol, exhibited slurred speech, failed a battery

An excerpt from *People v. Randolph*, a 1989 California appeals court decision involving DUI, appears at the end of the chapter.

of field sobriety tests administered by several officers, and registered an impermissibly high blood-alcohol level on one or more chemical tests performed by a trained technician. Of course, in the real world of law enforcement, such thorough evidence is seldom obtained.

Implied Consent Statutes

To facilitate chemical testing in DWI, DUI, and DUBAL cases, California and most other jurisdictions have enacted **implied consent statutes.** Under these laws, a person who drives a motor vehicle is deemed to have given consent to a urine test for drugs and to blood, breath, or urine testing to determine blood-alcohol content. The testing is made incident to a lawful arrest of a driver. See, for example, West's Ann. Cal. Vehicle Code § 23157. In most instances, refusal to submit to the tests required by an implied consent law will result in an administrative suspension of licensing privileges. The Supreme Court has upheld the validity of the Massachusetts implied consent law providing for suspension of the driver's license of a person who refuses to take a breathalyzer test. *Mackey v. Montrym,* 443 U.S. 1, 99 S.Ct. 2612, 61 L.Ed.2d 321 (1979).

Conclusion

The widespread abuse of drugs and alcohol is a serious social problem with many undesirable consequences. Society has responded to this problem largely through the criminal justice system. However, there are those who believe that criminalizing drug possession is undesirable public policy. At this time, the public appears to be strongly committed to maintaining the criminal sanctions against the manufacture, sale, and possession of drugs. Nevertheless, the public seems receptive to efforts to deter drug abuse by nonviolent offenders through treatments administered by drug courts. The public is equally committed to strengthening criminal penalties and stepping up enforcement for drunk driving, an area where results are being achieved. Clearly, these undesirable behaviors will remain criminal offenses and, accordingly, major problems for police, prosecutors, courts, and prison officials.

Key Terms

Controlled Substances Act
controlled substances
drug paraphernalia
contraband
forfeiture
actual possession
constructive possession
drug court
Violent Crime Act

public drunkenness
driving under the influence (DUI)
disorderly intoxication
driving while intoxicated (DWI)
driving with an unlawful blood-alcohol
   level (DUBAL)
field sobriety test
breathalyzer
implied consent statutes

🌐 Web-Based Research Activity

1. Go to the web. Locate your state's criminal statutes.
2. Determine whether possession of small amounts of marijuana is a felony, a misdemeanor, or a noncriminal infraction in your state.

Questions for Thought and Discussion

1. Is it sensible to maintain the criminal prohibitions against illicit drugs, or should these substances be legalized, carefully regulated, and their abuse dealt with through other means?

2. What are the typical difficulties facing prosecutors in drug possession cases?

3. Why, according to *Robinson v. California,* may a person not be held criminally liable for being addicted to illicit narcotics? Is this decision distinguishable from *Powell v. Texas*?

4. Is the drug court method of dealing with nonviolent drug offenders superior to the traditional methods of imposing a fine, jail term, or placing the defendant on probation? Should drug courts limit eligibility to participate to first-time offenders?

5. Should chronic alcoholism be a defense to intoxication offenses such as public drunkenness or driving under the influence?

6. Is requiring a person suspected of driving while intoxicated to submit to a blood-alcohol test a violation of the Fifth Amendment prohibition against compulsory self-incrimination?

7. In November 1998, the District of Columbia passed ballot initiative 59, legalizing marijuana for medicinal purposes. Since physicians who prescribe marijuana are violating federal law, Initiative 59 allows marijuana use if the individual has a physician's written or oral recommendation. In addition, the initiative allows for other "caregivers" to "cultivate, distribute and possess marijuana for the purpose of supplying an individual with marijuana for medicinal purposes." The U.S. Drug Enforcement Administration (DEA) counters that using marijuana for "medicinal" purposes may damage the immune system, causing more harm than good. Is Initiative 59 a cleverly disguised first step toward drug legalization or a genuine effort to help alleviate the symptoms of diseases such as cancer, glaucoma, and AIDS? If this initiative is truly a humanitarian effort, why don't we ask voters to approve other cancer treatments?

Problems for Discussion and Solution

1. During the late afternoon, police were called to quell a disturbance at a motel where the management had reported some disorderly conduct and apparent drug use. Outside the motel, the police observed Henry Egad standing by a tree. About

eighteen inches from Egad's feet, the police discovered a matchbox on the ground. Their examination revealed that the matchbox contained a substance that later proved to be PCP, an illegal drug. Police placed Egad under arrest and charged him with possession of a controlled substance. Based on these facts alone, do you think the prosecutor can establish that Egad was in possession of the PCP?

2. Late one night, a deputy sheriff found Ronald Rico in his car parked on the side of a road in a rural area of the county. Rico was at the wheel, the headlights were on, and the radio was playing at a loud volume. The motor was not running. No one else was in the vehicle. A field sobriety test and a later chemical test indicated that Rico had 0.14 blood alcohol concentration level. Under these circumstances, should Rico be prosecuted for driving under the influence of alcohol? If you were representing Rico, what defense would you raise?

● ● ● ● ● ● ● ● ● ● ● ● ● ●

EXCERPTS FROM JUDICIAL DECISIONS

Robinson v. California

Supreme Court of the United States, 1962.
370 U.S. 660, 82 S.Ct. 1417, 8 L.Ed.2d 758.

[Robinson was convicted in a California court of violating a state statute that made it a criminal offense to "be addicted to the use of narcotics." In this appeal to the U.S. Supreme Court, Robinson challenges the constitutionality of that statute, as it had been interpreted by the California courts, as violative of the Cruel and Unusual Punishments Clause of the Eighth Amendment to the U.S. Constitution.]

Mr. Justice STEWART delivered the opinion of the Court.

. . . This statute . . . is not one which punishes a person for the use of narcotics, for their purchase, sale or possession, or for anti-social or disorderly behavior resulting from their administration. It is not a law which even purports to provide or require medical treatment. Rather, we deal with a statute which makes the "status" of narcotic addiction a criminal offense, for which the offender may be prosecuted "at any time before he reforms." California has said that a person can be continuously guilty of this offense, whether or not he has ever used or possessed any narcotics within the state, and whether or not he has been guilty of any anti-social behavior there.

It is unlikely that any state at this moment in history would attempt to make it a criminal offense for a person to be mentally ill, or a leper, or to be afflicted with a venereal disease. A state might determine that the general health and welfare require that the victims of these and other human afflictions be dealt with by compulsory treatment, involving quarantine, confinement, or sequestration. But, in the light of contemporary human knowledge, a law which made a criminal offense of such a disease would doubtless be universally thought to be an infliction of cruel and unusual punishment in violation of the Eighth and Fourteenth amendments.

We cannot but consider the statute before us as of the same category. In this Court counsel for the state recognized that narcotic addiction is an illness. Indeed, it is apparently an illness which may be contracted innocently or involuntarily. We hold that a state law which imprisons a person thus afflicted as a criminal, even though he has never touched any narcotic drug within the state or been guilty of any irregular behavior there, inflicts a cruel and unusual punishment in violation of the Fourteenth Amendment. To be sure, imprisonment for 90 days is not, in the abstract, a punishment which is either cruel or unusual. But the question cannot be considered in the abstract. Even one day in prison would be a cruel and unusual punishment for the "crime" of having a common cold. . . .

Mr. Justice FRANKFURTER took no part in the consideration or decision of this case.

Mr. Justice DOUGLAS, concurring.

. . . [T]he addict is a sick person. He may, of course, be confined for treatment or for the protection of society. Cruel and unusual punishment results not from confinement, but from convicting the addict of a crime. A prosecution for addiction, with its resulting stigma and irreparable damage to the good name of the accused, cannot be justified as a means of protecting society, where a civil commitment would do as well.

Mr. Justice CLARK, dissenting. . . .

Mr. Justice WHITE, dissenting. . . .

• • • • • • • • • • • • • • •

Embry v. State

Supreme Court of Arkansas, 1990.
302 Ark. 608, 792 S.W.2d 318.

[In this case the Arkansas Supreme Court considers the sufficiency of the evidence to support the convictions of two individuals for possession of illegal drugs with intent to deliver.]

TURNER, Justice.

Sammie Lee Embry and John Wesley Phillips, a.k.a. Ibraheem Shabazz, were each convicted of possession of cocaine with intent to deliver and possession of marijuana with intent to deliver. Embry was sentenced to twenty years on the cocaine charge and five years on the marijuana charge. Phillips was found to be an habitual offender, previously convicted of four or more felonies and was thus sentenced to life imprisonment on the cocaine charge and to 20 years on the marijuana charge. Both defendants appeal the convictions. We find the appeal of Embry to be meritorious and reverse and dismiss his convictions. Phillips's appeal, however, is without merit, and we therefore affirm.

Embry and Patricia Booker had an off-and-on relationship; consequently, Embry spent considerable amounts of time at Booker's residence at 1414 May Avenue in Fort Smith. Embry, who was the father of Booker's child, kept clothing at Booker's house and frequently stayed there.

Law enforcement authorities placed the house under surveillance as a probable outlet for drugs and gave identifiable currency to a confidential informant who was to make a drug buy at that address. When the informant returned, he delivered a quantity of crack cocaine to the authorities. The police obtained a search warrant, and at 2:50 P.M. the officers conducted a search of the Booker residence. They found illicit controlled substances and arrested Booker, Phillips, and others at the scene. Embry was not at the house at the time of the search and arrests. About

an hour later, after leaving work, he arrived at the residence and was taken into custody. . . .

It is well established that the state need not prove the accused had actual possession of a controlled substance; constructive possession is sufficient. . . . Constructive possession, which is the control or right to control the contraband, can be implied where the contraband is found in a place immediately and exclusively accessible to the accused and subject to his control. . . .

Where there is joint occupancy of the premises where the contraband is seized, some additional factor must be found to link the accused to the contraband. . . . In such instances, the state must prove that the accused exercised care, control, and management over the contraband and also that the accused knew that the matter possessed was contraband. . . .

The appellant Embry was not present when the house was entered and searched and had no controlled substance on his person at the time of the arrest. He had no ownership interest in the house or furnishings, though he was a frequent (if not full-time) occupant and kept personal clothing there. It cannot be said that he had a superior or an equal right to the control of the house. He made no effort to dispose of any incriminating matter and made no incriminating statement. . . .

. . . [Embry] possessed no contraband, and the state failed to prove that he constructively possessed either the marijuana or cocaine found at the residence. His conviction must therefore be reversed.

Considering next the challenge by the appellant Phillips/Shabazz to the sufficiency of the evidence, the record reveals an entirely different scenario under the same facts. Though Phillips had no possessory interest in the house or furnishings, he had sold marijuana, according to testimony, and another substance thought to be cocaine inside the Booker house and at the front door; he was present at the time of the search and attempted to flee from the officer entering the front door; then, when confronted by officers entering through the back door, he tossed away a cigarette package later determined to contain marijuana cigarettes. During the search, the officers discovered a .25 caliber semi-automatic pistol in a closet which had been brought to the Booker house by Phillips and was later found to belong to Phillips's girlfriend.

All of the recited evidence was sufficient to support the jury's finding of guilt....

•   •   •   •   •   •   •   •   •   •   •   •   •   •

Powell v. Texas

Supreme Court of the United States, 1968.
392 U.S. 514, 88 S.Ct. 2145, 20 L.Ed.2d 1254.

[In this case the U.S. Supreme Court considers whether it is cruel and unusual punishment under the Eighth Amendment to convict a person suffering from chronic alcoholism of the crime of public drunkenness.]

Mr. Justice MARSHALL announced the judgment of the Court and delivered an opinion in which The CHIEF JUSTICE, Mr. Justice BLACK, and Mr. Justice HARLAN join.

In late December 1966, appellant [Leroy Powell] was arrested and charged with being found in a state of intoxication in a public place....

... [Powell's] counsel urged that appellant was "afflicted with the disease of chronic alcoholism," that "his appearance in public [while drunk was] not of his own volition," and therefore that to punish him criminally for that conduct would be cruel and unusual, in violation of the Eighth and Fourteenth Amendments to the United States Constitution.

The trial judge in the county court, sitting without a jury, made certain findings of fact, but ruled as a matter of law that chronic alcoholism was not a defense to the charge. He found appellant guilty, and fined him $50....

Appellant ... seeks to come within the application of the Cruel and Unusual Punishment Clause announced in *Robinson v. California* ... (1962), which ... held ... that "a state statute which imprisons a person thus afflicted [with narcotic addiction] as a criminal, even though he has never touched any narcotic drug within the State or been guilty of any irregular behavior there, inflicts a cruel and unusual punishment."...

On its face the present case does not fall within that holding, since appellant was convicted, not for being a chronic alcoholic, but for being in public while drunk on a particular occasion. The State of Texas thus has not sought to punish a mere status, as California did in *Robinson,* nor has it attempted to regulate appellant's criminal sanction for public behavior which may create substantial health and safety hazards, both for appellant and for members of the general public, and which offends the moral and aesthetic sensibilities of a large segment of the community. This seems a far cry from convicting one for being an addict, being a chronic alcoholic, being "mentally ill, or a leper."...

... [T]he most troubling aspects of this case, were *Robinson* to be extended to meet it, would be the scope and content of what could only be a constitutional doctrine of criminal responsibility. In dissent it is urged that the decision could be limited to conduct which is "a characteristic and involuntary part of the pattern of the disease as it afflicts" the particular individual, and that "[i]t is not foreseeable" that it would be applied "in the case of offenses such as driving a car while intoxicated, assault, theft, or robbery."... That is limitation by fiat. In the first place, nothing in the logic of the dissent would limit its application to chronic alcoholics. If Leroy Powell cannot be convicted of public intoxication, it is difficult to see how a State can convict an individual for murder, if that individual, while exhibiting normal behavior in all other respects, suffers from a "compulsion" to kill, which is an "exceedingly strong influence," but "not completely overpowering." Even if we limit our consideration to chronic alcoholics, it would seem impossible to confine the principle within the arbitrary bounds which the dissent seems to envision.

It is not difficult to imagine a case involving psychiatric testimony to the effect that an individual suffers from some aggressive neurosis which he is able to control when sober; that very little alcohol suffices to remove the inhibitions which normally contain these aggressions, with the result that the individual engages in assaultive behavior without becoming actually intoxicated; and that the individual suffers from a very strong desire to drink, which is an "exceedingly strong influence" but "not completely overpowering." Without being untrue to the rationale of this case, should the principles advanced in dissent be accepted here, the Court could not avoid holding such an individual constitutionally unaccountable for his assaultive behavior.

Traditional common-law concepts of personal accountability and essential considerations of federalism lead us to disagree with appellant. We are unable to conclude, on the state of this record or on the current state of medical knowledge, that chronic alcoholics in general, and Leroy Powell in particular, suffer from such an irresistible compulsion to drink and to get drunk in public that they are utterly unable to control their performance of either or both of these acts and thus cannot be deterred at all from public intoxication. And in any event this Court has never articulated a general constitutional doctrine of *mens rea.*

We cannot cast aside the centuries-long evolution of the collection of interlocking and overlapping concepts which the common law has utilized to assess the moral accountability of an individual for his antisocial deeds. The doctrines of *actus reus, mens rea,* insanity, mistake, justification, and duress have historically provided the tools for a constantly shifting adjustment of the tension between the medical views of the nature of man. This process of adjustment has always been thought to be the province of the States.

Nothing could be less fruitful than for this Court to be impelled into defining some sort of insanity test in constitutional terms. . . . It is simply not yet the time to write into the Constitution formulas cast in terms whose meaning, let alone relevance, is not yet clear either to doctors or to lawyers.

Mr. Justice BLACK, whom Mr. Justice HARLAN joins, concurring. . . .

Mr. Justice WHITE, concurring in the result.
. . . I cannot say that the chronic alcoholic who proves his disease and a compulsion to drink is shielded from conviction when he has knowingly failed to take feasible precautions against committing a criminal act, here the act of going to or remaining in a public place. On such facts the alcoholic is like a person with smallpox, who could be convicted for being on the street but not for being ill, or, like the epileptic, who would be punished for driving a car but not for his disease. . . .

Mr. Justice FORTAS, with whom Mr. Justice DOUGLAS, Mr. Justice BRENNAN, and Mr. Justice STEWART join, dissenting.
. . . [T]he essential constitutional defect here is the same as in *Robinson,* for in both cases the particular defendant was accused of being in a condition which he had no capacity to change or avoid. The trial judge . . . found . . . that Powell is a "chronic alcoholic." . . . I read these findings to mean that appellant was powerless to avoid drinking; that having taken his first drink, he had "an uncontrollable compulsion to drink" to the point of intoxication; and that, once intoxicated, he could not prevent himself from appearing in public places. . . .

The findings in this case . . . compel the conclusion that the infliction upon appellant of a criminal penalty for being intoxicated in a public place would be "cruel and inhuman punishment" within the prohibition of the Eighth Amendment. This conclusion follows because appellant is a "chronic alcoholic" who, according to the trier of fact, cannot resist the "constant excessive consumption of alcohol" and does not appear in public by his own volition but under a "compulsion" which is part of his condition.

I would reverse the judgment below.

People v. Randolph

Appellate Department, Superior Court of Ventura County, California, 1989.
262 Cal. Rptr. 378.

[*Kerry Don Randolph was charged with violating the California Vehicle Code Section 23152, subdivision (a), driving while under the influence of alcohol, and section 23152, subdivision (b), driving with 0.10 percent or more of alcohol in his blood. He admitted a prior similar conviction. Randolph was convicted by a jury and sentenced to probation. He appealed, challenging the sufficiency of the evidence introduced against him at trial.*]

OSBORNE, Judge.

. . . We have reviewed the detailed 31-page engrossed settled statement on appeal to determine whether it discloses substantial evidence such that any reasonable trier of fact could find appellant guilty beyond a reasonable doubt.

At the trial the witnesses were an experienced traffic officer and an experienced criminalist. . . .

The officer testified to the driving, arrest, and tests. At 11:55 P.M., the officer saw two cars southbound on Victoria Avenue on the Santa Clara River bridge. He later ascertained that appellant was driving the first car. The first car hit its brakes, causing the second to come nearly to a complete stop. Appellant then accelerated, began drifting over the double line, slowed down, and accelerated again. At the next curve, both cars slowed, and the second tried to pass appellant on the right shoulder. Appellant abruptly cut the second car off to the right. There could have been a collision. The second car then tried to pass on the left, and appellant pulled into the oncoming lane and cut off the second car again. The officer stopped both cars.

He approached the first car. Appellant . . . began yelling that someone had been tailgating him. After appellant calmed down, he was cooperative. The officer smelled the odor of an alcoholic beverage on his breath, and noted appellant's eyes were bloodshot and glassy.

Appellant said he had two burritos to eat at 6 P.M., and drank from 9 to 10:15 that evening at a party. He said he felt the effects of the alcohol "a little bit."

The officer had appellant perform several field sobriety tests. Appellant's performance on some was unremarkable.

The officer asked appellant to select one leg and stand on it for 15 seconds. Defendant held his leg up one second, put his foot down, lifted it for a second, put it down, stood staring into space, lifted it for two seconds, put it down, then lifted it for about ten seconds while hopping on his foot, eventually losing his balance.

Defendant was instructed to walk heel-to-toe nine steps out and seven steps back. Appellant walked seven steps heel-to-toe, then stated, "Oh, yeah, you wanted me to walk nine." He then took three more steps which were not heel-to-toe, turned and walked back eight steps heel-to-toe.

The officer instructed appellant to write numbers backwards from 99 to 69. He transposed two numbers.

After being arrested, appellant selected a breath test which was administered to him at the Ventura County jail by the officer. The officer used a checklist as he had in administering the test 150 to 200 times before. The tests were taken at 12:31 and 12:33 A.M. the day after appellant was stopped. The results were 0.10 and 0.10 percent.

In the opinion of the officer, appellant was under the influence of alcohol. . . .

The criminalist testified to his education and experience, the license held by the laboratory, the operation of the Intoxilyzer, and the training of the officer to operate the Intoxilyzer.

If a subject gives an adequate deep-lung air sample, the Intoxilyzer will record an accurate blood-alcohol percent. If the subject provides an inadequate sample, the result shown on the machine will be lower than the subject's actual blood-alcohol percent. The relationship between blood-alcohol and breath-alcohol is good, that is, usually within 0.01 percent, in a healthy subject in the elimination phase.

As a person's alcohol level increases, the probability of causing an accident increases. Mental factors, including judgment and the ability to gather and process information, are affected. The ability to concentrate on a task and one's attitude toward driving change. Inhibitions are one of the first things affected. If the alcohol level gets high enough, balance and coordination are affected. One can be under the influence of alcohol for driving at 0.05 BAL. All persons are impaired and cannot drive safely at 0.10 BAL. Drunk people have more alcohol in their systems than people who are merely impaired. From 0.15 BAL and up, where the physical impairment is more obvious, you see staggering and slurred speech as opposed to just the mental factors. Given defendant's weight, he explained the relationship between blood-alcohol concentration and how much alcohol he must have drunk. Alcohol is metabolized at a "pretty predictable rate" of 0.015 percent per hour.

The manufacturer of the Intoxilyzer states the machine's accuracy is better than plus or minus 0.01 percent.

Because the statute is expressed in terms of blood-alcohol level, breath-alcohol results must be converted to equivalent blood-alcohol results. The ratio between breath alcohol and blood alcohol varies to some degree among individuals. The state requires breath testing machines, such as the Intoxilyzer, to be constructed to use a specified conversion ratio. He referred to the writings of Dr. DeBowski, an expert whose opinion is that the actual ratio for approximately 85 percent of the population is such that a breath test underestimates the actual blood-alcohol level by 0.01 percent. . . .

The jury had evidence of appellant's driving, his performance on field sobriety tests, his behavior, his breath test results, and the time elapsed from drinking and driving to the breath tests. A reasonable trier of fact could have found beyond a reasonable doubt that appellant drove a vehicle while having a blood-alcohol level of 0.10 percent or more. There was sufficient evidence to sustain the conviction. . . .

Finding no error, the judgment is affirmed.

JONES, P.J., and LANE, J., concur.

CHAPTER

10

White-Collar and Organized Crime

Introduction

Criminologists often classify offenses committed by persons in the upper socioeconomic strata of society as **white-collar crimes.** These are offenses often committed in the course of the occupation or profession of such persons and include many crimes discussed in other chapters—for example, bribery, forgery, extortion, embezzlement, and obtaining property by false pretenses. This classification excludes many crimes—for example, assaultive and homicidal offenses—discussed in other chapters, even though they too are sometimes committed by "white-collar persons."

White-collar crimes are frequently defined to include prostitution, gambling, and obscenity (discussed in Chapter 8) and offenses relating to the importation, manufacture, and supply of illegal drugs and alcohol (discussed in Chapter 9). Environmental crimes and violations of the federal food and drug acts (discussed in Chapter 11) are likewise often included in the white-collar crime category, as are obstruction of justice and other offenses against the administration of justice (see Chapter 13). Sometimes, violations of civil rights (see Chapter 6) are categorized as white-collar crimes as well. In addition, several federal statutes (and to a lesser extent various state statutes) proscribe acts uniquely referred to as white-collar crimes. These include **antitrust violations, bid rigging, price fixing, money laundering, insider trading, tax fraud,** and various other offenses discussed in this chapter. Essentially, these offenses involve the use of deceit and concealment (as opposed to force or violence) to obtain economic benefits or advantages.

Organized crime involves offenses committed by persons or groups who conduct their business through illegal enterprises. Organized crime figures often attempt to gain political influence through graft and corruption, and they frequently resort to threats and acts of violence in commission of white-collar offenses. Organized crime gained its greatest foothold during the Prohibition era, when the Eighteenth Amendment to the U.S. Constitution prohibiting the sale and distribution of alcoholic beverages was in effect. By the time Prohibition was repealed in 1933, organized crime had become involved in many phases of our economy, often pursuing its interests through such illegal activities as loansharking, gambling, prostitution, and drug trafficking. Protection rackets and other forms of racketeering have become the methodology of organized crime as it has infiltrated many legitimate business operations. Although white-collar crime and organized crime often overlap, this chapter will first address white-collar crime, followed by organized crime.

Legal Principles Governing White-Collar Crimes

The principles discussed in relation to the elements of crimes and parties generally also apply to white-collar offenses. Requirements under both state and federal laws for an *actus reus, mens rea,* and causation of harm, as well as the definition of principals and accessories, are explained in Chapter 4. In prosecuting white-collar crimes in federal court, the government is usually required to prove that the accused committed the prohibited act "knowingly and willfully." Frequently, federal prosecutors charge white-collar defendants with conspiracy, either under 18 U.S.C.A. § 371 or under one of the conspiracy provisions pertaining to substantive offenses. As pointed out in Chapter 5, the prosecution enjoys certain procedural advantages in using conspiracy as a basis for criminal charges.

Most white-collar crimes prosecuted as federal violations are based on statutes enacted by Congress under the authority of Article I, Section 8 of the U.S. Constitution, which grants Congress power over postal, bankruptcy, and taxing matters and authority to regulate domestic and foreign commerce. Although many prosecutions involve large corporate frauds, federal and state white-collar offenses frequently involve telephone and mail solicitations by those who commit frauds and swindles as they furnish their victims "opportunities" to buy unregistered securities, obtain undeserved diplomas, participate in phony contests, or a variety of scams involving home improvement schemes and fraudulent land sales.

Many statutes defining offenses that have become known as white-collar crimes also provide civil remedies designed to compensate those who have suffered pecuniary losses as a result of a defendant's activities. These laws provide an example of the overlap between the civil and criminal law discussed in Chapter 1. In instances where a civil proceeding and a criminal proceeding are conducted at the same time, courts often stay the civil proceeding pending resolution of the criminal action.

Prosecution of Corporate Defendants

Under common law, a corporation was not held criminally responsible for its acts. This was because a corporation is an artificial being that cannot form the mental element necessary for imposition of criminal liability and cannot be imprisoned. However, its members could be held responsible. As strict liability offenses not requiring proof of a *mens rea* developed, corporations were held criminally responsible. Eventually, courts began to interpret the words *person* and *whoever* in criminal statutes to include corporations. Where statutes prescribed punishment other than death or incarceration, courts began to impose criminal liability based on acts of the corporation's agents and to punish corporations by imposing fines. In some jurisdictions, however, a corporation cannot be held criminally liable for crimes against persons unless the offense is based on the corporation's negligence rather than on a crime based on specific intent. The rationale for this is that the corporation cannot form the necessary *mens rea*.

Acts by Corporate Agents

Today, prosecutions of white-collar crime are frequently directed against corporate defendants, and corporations are held criminally liable for the acts of their agents committed within the scope of an agent's authority. Courts tend to broadly define what constitutes **scope of authority,** but generally the agent's acts must be to benefit the corporation in some way.

A few states have adopted Section 2.07 of the Model Penal Code or some version of it. Section 2.07(1) provides that a corporation may be convicted of an offense under the following guidelines:

> (a) the offense is a violation defined by a statute in which a legislative purpose to impose liability on corporations plainly appears and the conduct is performed by an agent of the corporation acting in behalf of the corporation within the scope of his office or employment, except that if the law defining the offense designates the agents for whose conduct the corporation is accountable or the circumstances under which it is accountable, such provisions shall apply; or

(b) the offense consists of an omission to discharge a specific duty of affirmative performance imposed on corporations by law; or

(c) the commission of the offense was authorized, requested, commanded, performed or recklessly tolerated by the board of directors or by a high managerial agent acting in behalf of the corporation within the scope of his office or employment.

In other jurisdictions, courts simply seek to determine whether the corporate agent or employee was acting within the scope of his or her authority. If so, the courts impute that action to the corporation. Although a corporation may be prosecuted for crimes, that does not exonerate individuals committing an unlawful act. In fact, in prosecutions for white-collar crimes committed by or on behalf of a corporation, it is not uncommon for corporate executives to be individually punished, generally by the imposition of large fines.

Common Federal White-Collar Crimes

In addition to those categories of offenses mentioned earlier and those discussed in other chapters, among the more common federal white-collar crimes are those committed in the following areas.

Antitrust Violations

The **Sherman Antitrust Act,** 15 U.S.C.A. § 1 et seq., makes it a crime to enter any contract or engage in any combination or conspiracy in restraint of trade. The act is designed to protect and preserve a system of free and open competition. Its scope is broad and reaches individuals and entities in profit and nonprofit activities as well as local governments and educational institutions. The act includes civil remedies as well as criminal sanctions.

To prove a criminal violation of the act, the government must establish that (1) two or more entities formed a combination or conspiracy; (2) the combination or conspiracy produces, or potentially produces, an unreasonable restraint of trade or commerce; (3) the restrained trade or commerce is interstate in nature; and (4) the defendant's general intent is to violate the law.

Principles outlined in Chapter 5 concerning conspiracies come into play in prosecutions for antitrust violations. The antitrust statutes are unclear whether intent must be proven to convict a defendant; however, in *United States v. U.S. Gypsum Co.,* 438 U.S. 422, 98 S.Ct. 2864, 57 L.Ed.2d 854 (1978), a case involving alleged price fixing, the Supreme Court rejected any idea that criminal violations of the act were intended to be strict liability crimes. Rather, the Court observed that "intent is an indispensable element of a criminal antitrust case as in any other criminal offense." 438 U.S. at 443, 98 S.Ct. at 2876, 57 L.Ed.2d at 873.

The essence of a Sherman Antitrust Act violation is a combination and conspiracy in restraint of trade. Among the more common violations are price fixing and bid rigging. Bid rigging involves interference with competitive bidding for award of a contract. Illustrative convictions are the following:

- An agreement not to bid competitively at a bankruptcy auction and to hold a later auction and then split the profits. *United States v. Seville Industrial Machinery Corp.,* 696 F. Supp. 986 (D.N.J. 1988).

- A conspiracy to submit collusive noncompetitive bids on a project. *United States v. Mobile Materials, Inc.*, 881 F.2d 866 (10th Cir. 1989).

The Justice Department alone is authorized to enforce the criminal sanctions of the act. Criminal violations are felonies. Corporations may be fined as much as $10,000,000. Individuals may be fined as much as $350,000, sentenced to three years' imprisonment, or both. Corporate defendants often seek to avoid liability for violations committed by their agents. However, courts have generally held that as long as an agent acts within the scope of employment or apparent authority, the corporation may be held legally responsible.

Most state legislatures have enacted statutes under which intrastate violations of securities laws are prosecuted. The text of state statutes and their judicial interpretations often parallel the federal views.

Computer Crimes

Under the **Computer Abuse Amendments Act** of 1994, 18 U.S.C.A. § 1030(a) 5(A), it is a crime to "knowingly cause the transmission of a program, information, code, or command" in interstate commerce with an intent to cause damage to a computer exclusively used by a financial institution or the U.S. government. In addition, the act prohibits "knowingly and with intent to defraud, trafficking in passwords to permit unauthorized access to a government computer, or to affect interstate or foreign commerce." 18 U.S.C.A. § 1030(a) 6(A)(B). It is also a federal crime to "knowingly with intent to defraud" produce, use, or traffic in counterfeit access devices. 18 U.S.C.A. § 1029(a). **Access devices** include cards, plates, codes and electronic serial numbers, mobile identification numbers, personal identification numbers, telecommunications services, equipment, or instrument identifiers or other means that can be used to obtain goods or services. 18 U.S.C.A. § 1029(e).

Despite the federal laws addressing computer crimes, the improper use of personal computers by white-collar criminals as well as by organized crime groups has led to a new kind of fraud in counterfeiting checks. In May 1997, the Secret Service and FBI warned Congress of the growing threat posed by fraudulent use of computers. Computers are now producing checks; formerly, technical skills were required in order to use offset printing equipment. To cope with the problem, some banks began demanding that noncustomers affix thumbprints to checks.

Most states have enacted computer crimes statutes, some of which are discussed in Chapter 7. Often these statutes expand the traditional definitions of "property" to include computer technologies and make it a criminal offense to alter, delete, or destroy computer programs or files; to access computer programs or files without consent; or to contaminate computers with viruses. Other state statutes prohibit accessing or using computer systems without the consent of the owner or rightful possessor. States are also beginning to address the need to enact laws to prosecute child pornographers who abuse the Internet or who use it to arrange meetings with potential victims.

False Statements and Bankruptcy Fraud

Making a false statement to obtain some government benefit or in connection with performing work for the government is a classic instance where the federal government prosecutes violators. When proceeding under the **False Statements Act,**

18 U.S.C.A. § 1001, the government must prove that the accused knowingly and willfully submitted to a government agency or department a statement that was false and material. The issue of materiality is one for the court to consider. *United States v. Rodgers,* 466 U.S. 475, 104 S.Ct. 1942, 80 L.Ed.2d 492 (1984).

Federal statutes criminalize **bankruptcy fraud,** which is defined as the knowing and fraudulent concealment of assets, avoiding distribution of nonexempt assets, taking false oaths, and related conduct in connection with bankruptcy proceedings. 18 U.S.C.A. § 152. To convict, the government must prove the defendant acted willfully; however, one who acts with willful blindness can be found to have acted with the requisite criminal intent.

The False Claims Act

Medicare and Medicaid provide health care benefits to millions of Americans. Medicare is designed to provide medical care primarily to older citizens whereas Medicaid is a program that furnishes health care services to the needy. Historically, criminal violations of the federal statutes providing these benefits, as well as other false claims to federal entitlements, have been prosecuted under the **False Claims Act,** 18 U.S.C.A. § 287, and the False Statements Act. To prove Medicare or Medicaid fraud under the False Claims Act, the government must prove that (1) the defendant presented a claim seeking reimbursement from the government for medical services or goods, (2) the claim was false or fraudulent, and (3) the accused knew of the claim's falsity.

In *United States v. Catena,* 500 F.2d 1319 (3d Cir. 1974), the evidence at trial disclosed that the defendant had submitted false claims to Pennsylvania Blue Shield and the Travelers Insurance Company, but not to any federal agency or official. These insurance companies processed and paid the claims and were reimbursed by the federal government for their payments and costs of processing the claims. The defendant was convicted and appealed. A question arose whether the insurance carriers could be considered "agencies" of the United States for purposes of criminal prosecution. The court doubted that the insurance carriers were agencies of the United States; however, it cited another federal statute, 18 U.S.C.A. § 2(b), which provides that "[w]hoever willfully causes an act to be done which if directly performed by him or another would be an offense against the United States, is punishable as a principal." Finding the proof established that the defendant "caused" the private carriers to submit false claims to the government, the court affirmed the defendant's conviction.

On August 21, 1996, President Clinton signed into law the Health Insurance Portability and Accountability Act of 1996, Public Law 104–191. Section 244 of the act establishes a new false statement offense that prohibits making material false or fraudulent statements or entries in connection with delivery of or payment for health care benefits. This new section covers statements and concealments made to private insurers that could not be prosecuted under the False Statements Act.

The new act also includes several other criminal provisions. Section 242 makes it an offense to knowingly and willfully execute or attempt to execute a scheme or artifice to defraud any health care benefit program or to fraudulently obtain money or property of such programs in connection with the delivery of or payment for health care benefits, items, or services. Section 243 proscribes knowingly and willfully embezzling assets of a health care benefit program. Section 245 creates a new crime that prohibits willfully obstructing, misleading, or delaying communication of information or records to a criminal investigator relating to a violation of a federal health care offense.

Mail Fraud

A used car distributor engaged in purchasing used cars, rolling back their odometers, and then selling them to retail dealers at inflated prices. The dealers, in turn, mailed the title applications to the state transportation department. Finding that the mailings by the dealers were essential to the defendant distributor's fraudulent acts, the Supreme Court upheld the defendant's conviction. The Court said the mailings were "part of the execution of the scheme as conceived by the perpetrator at the time."

Schmuck v. United States, 489 U.S. 705, 109 S.Ct. 1443, 103 L.Ed.2d (1989).

The Federal Mail Fraud and Wire Fraud Statutes

The Federal Mail Fraud Statute, 18 U.S.C.A. § 1341, makes it a crime to use the mail to defraud. **Mail fraud** consists of (1) a scheme devised or intended to defraud or to obtain money or property by fraudulent means and (2) the use or causing to use the mails in furtherance of the fraudulent scheme. Courts have held that to obtain a conviction, the government must prove a scheme committed by the defendant with a specific intent to defraud the government through use of the U.S. mail or some other interstate commercial carrier.

A companion statute, the Federal Wire Fraud Statute, 18 U.S.C.A. § 1343, parallels the mail fraud statute and makes fraudulent schemes that use interstate television, radio, or wire communications a crime. Although the U.S. Constitution grants Congress jurisdiction over the postal service, Congress enacted the **wire fraud** statute under its authority to regulate interstate commerce. U.S. Const., Art. I, § 8. Therefore, a violation of this statute exists only if the communication crosses state lines.

Money Laundering and Currency Reporting

The process of disguising illegal income to make it appear legitimate is known as "money laundering" and is prohibited by the **Money Laundering Control Act** of 1986, 18 U.S.C.A. 1956, 1957. Section 1956 (a) (1) provides as follows:

> Whoever, knowing that the property involved in a financial transaction represents the proceeds of some form of unlawful activity, conducts, or attempts to conduct such a financial transaction which in fact involves the proceeds of specified unlawful activity
>
> (A)(i) with the intent to promote the carrying on of specified unlawful activity; or (ii) with intent to engage in conduct constituting a violation of section 7201 or § 7206 of the Internal Revenue Code of 1986; or
>
> (B) knowing that the transaction is designed in whole or in part (i) to conceal or disguise the nature, the location, the source, the ownership, or the control of the proceeds of specified unlawful activity; or (ii) to avoid a transaction reporting requirement under State or Federal law, shall be sentenced to a fine of not more than $500,000 or twice the value of the property involved in the transaction, whichever is greater, or imprisonment for not more than twenty years, or both.

Thus, crimes under Section 1956 fall into three categories: (1) acts committed with intent to promote unlawful activity; (2) those committed with knowledge that a transaction is to conceal ownership, control, or source of funds; and (3) those designed to avoid certain currency reporting laws.

Section 1957 makes it a crime to engage in or attempt to engage in a transaction involving criminally derived property. To convict a defendant of money laundering, the government must show that (1) the defendant took part in a financial transaction and knew that the property in the transaction involved proceeds of illegal activity; (2) that the property involved was in fact proceeds of illegal activity; and (3) that the defendant knew that the transaction was designed in whole or part to conceal or disguise the nature, source, location, ownership, or control of illegal proceeds. The government bears a heavy burden to establish that a defendant is guilty of money laundering. It must show the accused has "actual knowledge" or is guilty of "willful blindness" to the criminal acts; simply showing that a defendant "should have known" is insufficient to establish guilt.

Often, federal appellate courts have had to determine whether certain acts constitute a financial transaction within the meaning of the statute. In *United States v. Jackson,* 935 F.2d 832 (7th Cir. 1991), the defendant appealed his conviction on three counts of money laundering in violation of Section 1956(a) and other violations. The evidence revealed the defendant had deposited funds derived from both legitimate and illegal activities in a local savings and loan institution and had written checks on the account. After first pointing out that writing a check on an account in a financial institution is a "transaction" within the money laundering statute, the court of appeals rejected the defendant's argument that the prosecution failed to establish that the financial transactions involved the proceeds of unlawful activity within the meaning of the statute because the checks involved were written on an account that contained both legitimate funds and drug profits. The court held it was sufficient for the government to show that the transaction in question involved the proceeds of one of the

---

CASE-IN-POINT

Structuring Financial Transactions: When Is Structuring to Avoid Currency Reporting Requirements Not a Crime?

When Ratzlaf offered to pay $100,000 on a gambling debt to a Reno casino, the casino informed him that payment by a check in that amount would trigger the currency reporting requirements under federal law. Ratzlaf then proceeded to obtain a series of $10,000 cashier's checks from various banks to pay his debt. The government charged him with "structuring transactions" in violation of 31 U.S.C.A. § 5322 and § 5324. A jury found him guilty; he was convicted and sentenced in U.S. District Court, and his conviction was upheld by the United States Court of Appeals for the Ninth Circuit. Ratzlaf petitioned, and the Supreme Court granted review. He pointed to the fact that the trial judge had instructed the jury

that the government had only to prove Ratzlaf's knowledge and intent to evade the statutory reporting requirement, but not that Ratzlaf knew the structuring was unlawful. He argued that he could not be convicted "solely on the basis of his knowledge that a financial institution must report currency transactions in excess of $10,000 and his intention to avoid such reporting." In a 5–4 decision, the Court interpreted "willfully" in the statute to require the Government to prove that a "defendant acted with knowledge that his conduct was unlawful." Accordingly, the Court reversed Ratzlaf's conviction.

Ratzlaf v. United States, 510 U.S. 135, 114 S.Ct. 655, 126 L.Ed.2d 615 (1994).

types of criminal conduct specified. Federal courts have also held that the term "financial transaction" includes making a deposit into an account. See *United States v. Reynolds,* 64 F.3d 292 (7th Cir. 1995).

Federal statutes require financial institutions to file currency transaction reports with the Secretary of the Treasury for cash transactions in excess of $10,000. 31 U.S.C.A. § 5313. A related provision, 31 U.S.C.A. § 5324, prohibits a person from **structuring** or assisting in structuring a transaction with one or more institutions to evade the requirement and provides penalties for persons who willfully conduct a transaction to evade this structuring requirement.

Securities Fraud

A variety of federal and state statutes criminalize conduct involving misrepresentations, omissions, insider trading, and other aspects of fraud in securities dealing. The most significant federal acts are the Securities Act of 1933, 15 U.S.C.A. § 77a et seq., and the **Securities and Exchange Act** of 1934, 15 U.S.C.A. § 78a et seq. Again, these statutes provide for civil remedies as well as criminal sanctions. The Securities and Exchange Commission (SEC) refers most criminal prosecutions to the Department of Justice. Convictions can result in fines in millions of dollars and imprisonment.

Not all misrepresentations or omissions involving securities give rise to criminal violations. Rather, the government must prove the accused's willful intent to commit a substantive fraud in connection with the purchase or sale of a security or in the offering or sale of a security involving interstate commerce or through use of the mails. Courts uniformly hold that to sustain a conviction, the omission or misrepresentation must be material and be made in reckless disregard for the truth or falsity of the information provided. See, for example, *United States v. Farris,* 614 F.2d 634 (9th Cir. 1979). The specific intent that must be proven to sustain a criminal prosecution can be found in a defendant's deliberate and intentional acts or reckless disregard for the facts. *United States v. Boyer,* 694 F.2d 58 (3d Cir. 1982).

Churning and Insider Trading

In recent years, many financial executives and securities brokers have been prosecuted under the Securities and Exchange Act for fraudulent conduct known as **churning** and insider trading. "Churning" is a term applied to transactions in a customer's account without regard to the customer's investment objectives, simply to generate commissions for the broker. When determining whether a broker is guilty of churning, courts often focus on whether the trading by a broker was disproportionate to the size of the customer's account. Insider trading usually occurs when a person who operates "inside" a corporation has access to material nonpublic information and uses that information to trade securities without first disclosing that information to the public.

Securities and Exchange Commission Rule 10(b) proscribes (1) using any "deceptive device" (2) "in connection with the purchase or sale of any security," in contravention of rules promulgated by the Securities Exchange Commission. Insider trading qualifies as a "deceptive device" because the insider occupies a position of trust and confidence with regard to the corporation's shareholders. This position of trust requires the insider to abstain from trading based on information he or she has acquired by virtue of the insider status. *Chiarella v. United States,* 445 U.S. 222, 228 229, 100 S.Ct. 1108, 63 L.Ed.2d 348 (1980).

CASE-IN-POINT

Is Anyone Who Profits from Inside Information an Insider?

During 1975–76, Vincent Chiarella worked as a "markup man" for a company that printed announcements of corporate takeover bids. From the copy submitted for printing, he discerned information that enabled him to purchase stock in companies targeted for takeover before this information was disclosed to the general public. Chiarella made a profit in excess of $30,000 from the purchase, and later sale, of stock in the targeted companies. He was convicted in the U.S. District Court for violating Section 10(b) of the Securities Exchange Act of 1934, 15 U.S.C.A. §§ 78b, 78j(b). In 1978 the U.S. Court of Appeals for the Second Circuit affirmed his conviction.

On review, the Supreme Court recognized that a corporate insider must not trade in shares of a corporation without having first disclosed all material insider information. But the Court ruled that the obligation to disclose is based on having the "duty to disclose arising from a relationship of trust and confidence between parties to a transaction." Thus, the Court held that the trial court erred when, in effect, it instructed the jury that Chiarella owed a duty to everyone, to all sellers—indeed, to the market as a whole. Accordingly, the Court reversed his conviction.

Chiarella v. United States, 445 U.S. 222, 100 S.Ct. 1108, 63 L.Ed.2d 348 (1980).

The late 1980s witnessed sensational cases involving insider trading by prominent Wall Street financiers. Since then, the SEC has secured indictments under Rule 10(b) against numerous prominent individuals and corporations for securities violations.

The Hobbs Act

Congress enacted the Anti-Racketeering Act of 1934 in an effort to control racketeering activities. However, the act did not specifically mention racketeering, and as a result of certain judicial interpretations, in 1946 Congress enacted the **Hobbs Act,** 18 U.S.C.A. § 1951. Subsection (a) provides as follows:

> Whoever in any way or degree obstructs, delays, or affects commerce or the movement of any article or commodity in commerce, by robbery or extortion or attempts or conspires so to do, or commits or threatens physical violence to any person or property in furtherance of a plan or purpose to do anything in violation of this section shall be fined not more than $10,000 or imprisoned not more than twenty years, or both.

Note that the act includes the inchoate offenses of attempt and conspiracy. Other subsections define "robbery," "extortion," and "commerce." The Hobbs Act was enacted under the power of Congress to regulate interstate commerce; however, the courts have held that it is sufficient if the government simply proves that an act has an effect on interstate commerce. Courts allow this to be established by proof of an actual impact, however small, or in the absence of actual impact, by proof of a probable or potential impact.

Originally, most prosecutions under the Hobbs Act were based on extortion by public officials using force, violence, or fear. Now prosecutors frequently rely on the act as a basis to prosecute state and local officials based on extortion "under color of official rights."

CASE-IN-POINT

An Unusual Prosecution Under the Hobbs Act

Defendants were convicted of violating the Hobbs Act after they committed butyric acid attacks on two abortion clinics in New York. On appeal, the U.S. Court of Appeals for the Second Circuit held that the federal court had jurisdiction over the offense. The court reasoned that because the evidence revealed that some of the patients came from out of state and the clinics used supplies from out-of-state manufacturers, the requisite impact on interstate commerce was sufficient to vest federal courts with jurisdiction. Second, the court addressed whether "property" was involved within the meaning of the Hobbs Act. On this issue, the court determined that the butyric acid attacks were not isolated instances of vandalism, but were part of a strategy to cause abortion providers to give up their property rights to engage in the business of providing abortion services for fear of future attacks.

United States v. Arena, 180 F.3d 380 (2d Cir. 1999).

An excerpt from *Evans v. United States* appears at the end of the chapter.

In *Evans v. United States,* 504 U.S. 255, 112 S.Ct. 1881, 119 L.Ed.2d 57 (1992), Evans, a DeKalb County, Georgia, commissioner was approached by an undercover FBI agent who posed as a real estate developer seeking assistance in a rezoning petition. The agent gave Evans a $1,000 check payable to a campaign fund and $7,000 in cash. Evans reported a $1,000 campaign contribution but failed to report the cash payment of $7,000 on either his campaign disclosure form or his income tax return. In upholding his conviction for extortion under the Hobbs Act, the United States Supreme Court stated that "[w]e hold today the Government need only show that a public official has obtained a payment to which he was not entitled, knowing that the payment was made in return for official acts." 504 U.S. at 268, 112 S.Ct. at 1889, 119 L.Ed.2d at 72. The Court's view has given federal prosecutors broad authority in prosecutions of public officials at all levels who accept "gratuities" and "kickbacks" in exchange for official acts.

Tax Fraud

Prosecutions for white-collar crime often include charges of violating federal tax statutes. Although the government can employ a wide variety of federal criminal statutes to prosecute those who commit tax fraud, most prosecutions are based on the Internal Revenue Code, 26 U.S.C.A. § 7201 et seq. Whether violations are felonies or misdemeanors, to obtain a conviction the government must prove the defendant's willfulness to commit the proscribed act. *United States v. Bishop,* 412 U.S. 346, 93 S.Ct. 2008, 36 L.Ed.2d 941 (1973). To establish "willfulness," the government must prove the defendant's "intentional violation of a known legal duty." *United States v. Pomponio,* 429 U.S. 10, 97 S.Ct. 22, 50 L.Ed.2d 12 (1976). In reaffirming this standard of proof, the Supreme Court observed in *Cheek v. United States,* 498 U.S. 192, 111 S.Ct. 604, 112 L.Ed.2d 617 (1991), that the term "willfully" as used in federal criminal tax statutes serves to "carve out an exception to the traditional rule that ignorance of the law or mistake of law is no defense to prosecution." 498 U.S. at 200, 111 S.Ct. at 609, 112 L.Ed.2d at 628.

Many prosecutions for tax evasion occur under Section 7201, which makes it a felony to willfully attempt to evade or to evade federal taxes. A successful prosecution requires that the government prove willfulness, the existence of a tax deficiency, and an affirmative act of evasion or attempted evasion of the tax. *Sansone v. United States*, 380 U.S. 343, 85 S.Ct. 1004, 13 L.Ed.2d 882 (1965).

Section 7202 also makes it a crime to willfully fail to collect taxes, account truthfully for taxes, and pay over taxes. Although most employers do not fail to collect taxes, a more common violation is the employer's failure to pay over those taxes to the Internal Revenue Service (IRS).

Section 7203 makes it a misdemeanor to willfully fail to pay an estimated tax, file a tax return, keep records, or supply information required by law. To successfully prosecute an accused, the government must establish that the accused had knowledge of a duty to file a return and willfully failed to file.

Section 7206 makes it a felony to commit fraud or make false statements in conjunction with tax obligations. To convict a person of "tax perjury," the government must prove the defendant acted willfully and (1) filed a return containing a written declaration, (2) made under penalty of perjury, and (3) did not believe that the return was true and correct as to every material matter. The defendant's willfulness may be inferred from the existence of unreported or misreported tax information. The court must determine the issue of "materiality" as a matter of law. A second provision of Section 7206 makes it a felony to willfully aid and assist another in a material falsity. Tax preparers are sometimes prosecuted under this provision of the statute.

Additional sections of 26 U.S.C.A. criminalize the furnishing of false and fraudulent statements to the IRS, interfering with the administration of the tax laws, and delivering a fraudulent tax return.

Organized Crime

During the Prohibition era, organized gangs trafficked in liquor and became involved in prostitution and other vices. After repeal of the Eighteenth Amendment in 1933, these **crime syndicates** expanded into **loansharking,** gambling, narcotics, and extortion. As they did, they infiltrated legitimate businesses and conducted widespread illegal operations through their own complex and secretive structures.

As we have pointed out in other chapters, the common-law development of crimes and the legislative acts defining crimes focused on particular acts of wrongdoing and on inchoate activities. This approach did not cover the ongoing criminal activity by organized groups. To that extent, the traditional definitions of crime left a void in the criminal justice system.

In 1961 Congress enacted three statutes to combat the growing problem of organized crime. These acts gave the FBI jurisdiction over gambling violations and interstate and foreign travel or transportation in aid of racketeering, 18 U.S.C.A. 1952; interstate transportation of wagering paraphernalia, 18 U.S.C.A. 1953; and prohibition of illegal gambling, 8 U.S.C.A. § 1955. In 1968 Congress passed the Omnibus Crime Control and Safe Streets Act. This act provided for the conduct of court-authorized electronic surveillance. 18 U.S.C.A. §§ 2510–2521.

The Omnibus Crime Control Act of 1970

Notwithstanding the FBI's increased attention to organized crime, the problem continued to grow. Based on congressional findings that organized crime had weakened the stability of the nation's economy through infiltration of legitimate businesses and labor unions and threatened to subvert and corrupt our democratic processes, under its power to regulate foreign and interstate commerce, Congress enacted the **Organized Crime Control Act** of 1970. Title IX of the act, titled "Racketeer Influenced and Corrupt Organizations," is commonly referred to by the acronym **RICO** and prohibits infiltration of legitimate organizations by racketeers where foreign or interstate commerce is affected. 18 U.S.C.A. §§ 1961–1963. In addition to increased criminal penalties, the new RICO statute provided for forfeiture of property used in criminal enterprises and permitted the government to bring civil actions against such enterprises.

RICO created new crimes and a new approach to criminal prosecution. First, it makes it a crime for any person "who has received any income derived, directly or indirectly, from a **pattern of racketeering** activity or through collection of an unlawful debt . . . to use or invest [in] any enterprise which is engaged in interstate or foreign commerce." 18 U.S.C.A. § 1962(a). Second, RICO makes it unlawful for any such person to participate, directly or indirectly, in the conduct of the enterprise's affairs through a "pattern of racketeering." 18 U.S.C.A. § 1962(b). Third, it is a crime for any person "employed by or associated with any enterprise engaged in, or the activities of which affect, interstate or foreign commerce, to conduct or participate, directly or indirectly, in the conduct of such enterprise's affairs through a pattern of racketeering activity or collection of unlawful debt." 18 U.S.C.A. § 1962(c). This latter subsection has become the most frequently used provision by prosecutors. Finally, the act prohibits conspiracies to violate any of these proscriptions. 18 U.S.C.A. § 1962(d).

The Expanded Scope of RICO

RICO broadly defines racketeering activity to include a variety of federal offenses as well as nine state crimes that are characteristically felonies. 18 U.S.C.A. § 1961(1). To establish a "pattern of racketeering activity" requires proof of at least two of these acts of racketeering having occurred within a period of ten years, excluding any period of imprisonment. 18 U.S.C.A. § 1961(5). Courts frequently refer to these acts as **predicate acts,** and any combination of two or more can constitute a pattern of racketeering. To obtain a conviction under RICO, the government must establish the defendant's involvement in a "pattern of racketeering or collection of an unlawful debt." See, for example, *United States v. Dozier,* 672 F.2d 531 (5th Cir. 1982). There is no requirement that a state conviction be obtained before the state offense can be used as a predicate act of the racketeering activity charged. *United States v. Malatesta,* 583 F.2d 748 (5th Cir. 1978). RICO provides for a maximum of twenty years' imprisonment, a heavier penalty than many of the predicate offenses on which a RICO conviction can be based.

What Constitutes an Enterprise?

In RICO, Congress has defined **enterprise** broadly to include "any individual, partnership, corporation, association, or other legal entity, and any union or group of individuals associated in fact although not a legal entity." 18 U.S.C.A. § 1961(4). The Supreme Court has said that the term encompasses both legitimate and illegitimate entities and groups. *United States v. Turkette,* 452 U.S. 576, 101 S.Ct. 2524, 69 L.Ed.2d 246 (1981). Lower federal courts have held the term includes both private and public entities such as corporations, banks, and decedents' estates, as well as state agencies, police departments, traffic courts, and prostitution rings.

But does an enterprise have to have an economic motive? In *National Organization for Women v. Scheidler,* 510 U.S. 249, 114 S.Ct. 798, 127 L.Ed.2d 99

(1994), the Supreme Court resolved a conflict on this point between decisions from different circuits of the United States Courts of Appeals. The Court examined the definition of "enterprise" in RICO and concluded that the term was broadly defined and did not require that an enterprise have an economic motive. Although *Scheidler* was based on a civil RICO action, the decision drew heavily from criminal precedents and raises the issue of whether the federal government can use RICO as a basis to prosecute unruly anti-abortion demonstrators whose motives are social and religious rather than economic.

RICO does not criminalize a person for being a racketeer—it criminalizes that person's conduct of an enterprise through a pattern of racketeering. Therefore, a jury that finds a defendant has committed the required predicate acts must still find that these acts were committed in connection with a pattern of racketeering or collection of an unlawful debt. A RICO violation involves a separate criminal proceeding; therefore, the Double Jeopardy Clause of the United States Constitution does not prohibit the government from prosecuting a defendant for a RICO charge where the defendant has been previously prosecuted for a substantive offense used as one of the predicate crimes. *United States v. Smith*, 574 F.2d 308 (5th Cir. 1978).

RICO was conceived as a weapon for prosecution of organized crime, but it has become the basis of prosecution against white-collar criminals as well. Prosecutors have long experienced difficulty in securing convictions of organized crime leaders for violating specific criminal statutes. In part, this occurs because the evidence of a specific statutory violation might be unconvincing to a judge or jury. The reaction of a judge or jury is likely to be different when the prosecution parades before the court evidence of a series of violations that reveal a pattern of criminal behavior.

RICO has been justified because the harm that organized crime inflicts on society is far greater than the harm inflicted by those who commit statutory crimes. It can be an effective tool to help prosecutors fight against crime syndicates. Yet membership in organized crime is not a necessary element for a conviction under RICO. Unlike criminal statutes that historically have been narrowly construed, Congress provided that RICO is to be liberally interpreted to effect its remedial purposes. The liberal construction of the enterprise requirement and the fact that the pattern requirement of racketeering activity is cast in numerical terms have engendered some criticism. Critics contend that RICO is a "catch-all" statute that gives prosecutors too much discretion to expand the range of indictable offenses. Examples of RICO prosecutions include the following:

- Several members of the Outlaws Motorcycle Club were prosecuted for a RICO violation based on narcotics and prostitution offenses. *United States v. Watchmaker*, 761 F.2d 1459 (11th Cir. 1985).

- Vogt, a U.S. Customs Services Officer, accepted payment for information that was used to facilitate a drug smuggling operation. The bribe money was invested in foreign bank accounts, thus constituting a money laundering enterprise. *United States v. Vogt*, 910 F.2d 1184 (4th Cir. 1990).

- A gambler and a police officer were convicted for their involvement in a police protection racket. *United States v. Sanders*, 962 F.2d 660 (7th Cir. 1992).

- Gang members were convicted of racketeering offenses for extorting protection money from local Chinese businesses, committing robberies, and kidnapping and murdering rival gang members, potential witnesses, and business owners who refused to pay protection money. *United States v. Wong*, 40 F.3d 1347 (2d Cir. 1994).

RICO, Predicate Offenses, and Double Jeopardy

Sixty members of the Nicodemo Scarfo crime family allegedly controlled Mafia operations in parts of Pennsylvania and New Jersey. The government alleged that over the course of eleven years the family's activities included a number of felony offenses. All the defendants were found guilty of conspiring to participate and participating in an enterprise through a pattern of racketeering in violation of 18 U.S.C.A. § 1962.

On appeal, Scarfo contended that the use of his former convictions as predicate offenses on which to base the RICO prosecution violated his constitutional right not to be placed in jeopardy twice for the same offense. In rejecting Scarfo's claims, the U.S. Court of Appeals pointed out the following: (1) As to state convictions used as predicate offenses, there could be no double jeopardy because different sovereigns were involved; and (2) that as to federal convictions used as predicate offenses, the court in previous cases has ruled that a RICO offense "is not, in a literal sense, the 'same' offense as one of the predicate offenses" because a RICO violation requires proof of a "pattern of racketeering" and is intended to deter continuous criminal conduct whereas the predicate offenses are intended to deter discrete criminal acts. Accordingly, the court rejected Scarfo's contentions.

United States v. Pungitore, 910 F.2d 1084 (3d Cir. 1990).

- An attorney was convicted of violating RICO based on participating in a scheme involving bribery of judges where evidence revealed that the defendant had agreed to seek to corruptly use the court system by bribing judges to appoint attorneys as special assistant public defenders. *United States v. Massey*, 89 F.3d 1433 (11th Cir. 1996).

Extension of RICO Beyond Its Original Scope

RICO has been extended beyond its original purpose to target such nonorganized crime as white-collar criminals and corrupt government officials. Thus, through RICO a prosecutor can circumvent statutes of limitation and seek to inflict multiple punishments for the same offenses.

Most states have adopted RICO-type statutes. Some closely parallel the federal act, whereas others have varying provisions concerning prohibited acts, sanctions, forfeitures of property, and the procedures involved.

Despite criticism, RICO is firmly established as a weapon in the arsenal of federal and, in many instances, state prosecutors. It has proved to be a useful tool in the war against racketeering and corruption, both private and public, whether organized or not.

Two RICO cases are excerpted at the end of the chapter. *United States v. Gambino* provides a good example of a traditional RICO prosecution. *United States v. Lewis* illustrates a more contemporary application of the statute.

Defenses in White-Collar and Organized Crime Cases

Defenses available to defendants charged with white-collar and organized crime offenses are similar to those available to defendants generally; however, the defenses of entrapment, double jeopardy, and selective prosecution appear more frequently in these cases than in other situations. Moreover, the complexities involved in many federal statutes aimed at organized crime raise more issues of statutory construction and legislative intent than do the more traditionally defined crimes.

Conclusion

Unlike transactional criminal offenses, white-collar crime and organized crime are not easily defined, and the conduct involved is often elusive. We lack the accurate data and statistical information that is available on the traditional defined offenses; hence, the extent of white-collar offenses and organized crime is not readily quantifiable. Some conduct criminalized today as white-collar crimes might have passed as simply unethical business practices in our earlier history. Other behavior, although long recognized as offensive, did not fit into the molds developed at common law and has become statutorily forbidden only in recent years. In today's society, so dependent on electronic transactions, the computer criminal might become as significant a danger to our well-being as is the street criminal who robs, burglarizes, and steals.

Organized crime is a phenomenon of our modern social and economic institutions. Through a variety of coercive and illegal tactics, it has infiltrated legitimate business operations. White-collar and underworld figures cater to people's desire for goods and services that cannot be legally supplied but that can be made available to them at minimal risks to the providers. On the positive side, there is an increased awareness of organized crime operations and an increased emphasis, particularly at the federal level, on investigation and prosecution. RICO and other measures have provided the legal system with effective tools to prosecute criminal enterprise activity and those who engage in racketeering. If the public demands increased efforts in this area, we should see considerable progress in ferreting out and punishing those who threaten the safety and economic well-being of society.

Key Terms

white-collar crimes
antitrust violations
bid rigging
price fixing
money laundering
insider trading
tax fraud
organized crime
scope of authority
Sherman Antitrust Act
Computer Abuse Amendments Act
access devices
False Statements Act
bankruptcy fraud
False Claims Act

mail fraud
wire fraud
Money Laundering Control Act
structuring
Securities and Exchange Act
churning
Hobbs Act
crime syndicates
loansharking
Organized Crime Control Act
RICO
pattern of racketeering
predicate acts
enterprise

Web-Based Research Activity

1. Go to the web. Locate your state's criminal statutes.
2. Determine whether your state has its own laws against racketeering or other forms of organized crime.
3. Use your state government's Internet resources to determine whether your state attorney general's office has an active criminal enforcement effort under way in the area of organized crime or in some other area of white-collar crime.

Questions for Thought and Discussion

1. Is it appropriate to define "white-collar offenses" by focusing on the offender's social and economic status?
2. What is the federal constitutional authority for enacting (a) antitrust and wire fraud laws? (b) postal offenses? (c) securities laws? (d) bankruptcy laws?
3. Why do federal criminal statutes figure so prominently in the context of white-collar offenses?
4. Under what circumstances can a corporation be held legally responsible for a white-collar offense committed by one of its agents or employees?
5. Why does the rationale for federal antitrust and securities laws require the availability of both civil and criminal sanctions?
6. What criminal offenses described in Chapters 5 through 9 can be committed by using a computer?
7. Describe a factual scenario that could occur in the operation of a municipal or county government in your state that could likely result in a person being prosecuted under the Hobbs Act.
8. What led Congress to the realization that the traditional common-law transactional approach to crime was inadequate to deal with organized crime?
9. What is required to establish a "pattern of racketeering activity" under RICO?
10. How does RICO define "enterprise," and what is its significance in prosecution of RICO offenses?

Problems for Discussion and Solution

1. An elderly widow whose income was derived primarily from Social Security and a small pension owned $100,000 in government bonds that she inherited from her late husband. Other than her home and a modest checking account, her bonds constituted her estate. On advice of A. Brokero, a licensed securities broker, she converted the bonds into cash and deposited the proceeds with Mr. Brokero to manage. She explained her financial situation and investment objectives. She and Brokero agreed that her funds should be invested in conservative, income-producing investments. Instead, Brokero, who had trading authorization from the widow, bought and sold numerous issues of aggressive stocks for the account, and at the end of two years

the account had dwindled to $28,500. During the two-year period, Brokero had earned thousands of dollars in commissions for buying and selling the investments. What, if any, criminal violation is suggested by this scenario?

2. At a state peace officers' convention, two police officers from Sedateville, a small rural community, developed a friendship with two officers from Trendville, a metropolitan city. Gambling, except for a state lottery, was prohibited in the state. As their friendship developed, they enjoyed "a friendly game of poker" with modest betting. They all agreed that "after all, gambling is really not all bad" and probably should not be prohibited. As the rural officers began to lament their modest salaries, the Trendville officers introduced them to some "prominent businessmen." They all agreed that "it would hurt no one" to allow these businessmen to conduct some private gambling operations in Sedateville. But, of course, the operation would require some protection by the local police. With cooperation of the officers, the businessmen opened a bar where gambling was conducted in a back room. The new operation also accommodated male patrons seeking prostitutes by transporting the men to Trendville for a weekend "sports event." Through the cooperation of the officers, the new operation was "overlooked" by the Sedateville police. In turn, the officers from Trendville and Sedateville participated in the profits from the gambling and prostitution activities. The four officers' gains eventually exceeded their salaries as police officers, and as they later said, "No one was hurt in this operation—people were just allowed to have a good time." Under what circumstances would this scenario present a basis for a RICO prosecution?

EXCERPTS FROM JUDICIAL DECISIONS

Evans v. United States

United States Supreme Court, 1992.
504 U.S. 255, 112 S.Ct. 1881, 119 L.Ed.2d 57.

[A jury convicted Evans, a local official, of extortion in violation of the Hobbs Act, 18 U.S.C.A. § 1951.]

JUSTICE STEVENS delivered the opinion of the Court.

. . . At common law, extortion was an offense committed by a public official who took "by colour of his office" money that was not due to him for the performance of his official duties. A demand, or request, by the public official was not an element of the offense. Extortion by the public official was the rough equivalent of what we would now describe as "taking a bribe." It is clear that petitioner committed that offense. The question is whether the federal statute, insofar as it applies to official extortion, has narrowed the common law definition.

Congress has unquestionably expanded the common law definition of extortion to include acts by private individuals pursuant to which property is ob-

tained by means of force, fear, or threats. It did so by implication in the Travel Act, 18 U.S.C.A. § 1952 . . . and expressly in the Hobbs Act. The portion of the Hobbs Act that is relevant to our decision today provides:

(a) Whoever in any way or degree obstructs, delays, or affects commerce or the movement of any article or commodity in commerce, by robbery or extortion or attempts or conspires so to do, or commits or threatens physical violence to any person or property in furtherance of a plan or purpose to do anything in violation of this section shall be fined not more than $10,000 or imprisoned not more than twenty years, or both.
(b) As used in this section—
(2) The term 'extortion' means the obtaining of property from another, with his consent, induced by wrongful use of actual or threatened force, violence, or fear, or under color of official right. 18 U.S.C.A. § 1951.

The present form of the statute is a codification of a 1946 enactment, the Hobbs Act, which amended the federal Anti-Racketeering Act. In crafting the 1934 Act, Congress was careful not to interfere with legitimate activities between employers and employees. . . . The 1946 Amendment was intended to encompass the conduct held to be beyond the reach of the 1934 Act by our decision in *United States v. Teamsters,* 315 U.S. 521 (1942). The Amendment did not make any significant change in the section referring to obtaining property "under color of official right" that had been prohibited by the 1934 Act. Rather, Congress intended to broaden the scope of the Anti-Racketeering Act and was concerned primarily with distinguishing between "legitimate" labor activity and labor "racketeering," so as to prohibit the latter while permitting the former. . . .

Although the present statutory text is much broader than the common law definition of extortion because it encompasses conduct by a private individual as well as conduct by a public official, the portion of the statute that refers to official misconduct continues to mirror the common law definition. There is nothing in either the statutory text or the legislative history that could fairly be described as a "contrary direction," *Morissette v. United States,* 342 U.S., at 263, from Congress to narrow the scope of the offense. . . .

Petitioner argues that the jury charge with respect to extortion . . . allowed the jury to convict him on the basis of the "passive acceptance of a contribution." . . . He contends that the [trial judge's] instruction did not require the jury to find "an element of duress such as a demand," . . . and it did not properly describe the *quid pro quo* requirement for conviction if the jury found that the payment was a campaign contribution.

We reject petitioner's criticism of the instruction, and conclude that it satisfies the *quid pro quo* requirement of *McCormick v. United States,* 500 U.S. 257 (1991), because the offense is completed at the time when the public official receives a payment in return for his agreement to perform specific official acts; fulfillment of the *quid pro quo* is not an element of the offense. We also reject petitioner's contention that an affirmative step is an element of the offense of extortion "under color of official right" and need be included in the instruction. As we explained above, our construction of the statute is informed by the common law tradition from which the term of art was drawn and understood. We hold today that the Government need only show that a public official has obtained a payment to which he was not entitled, knowing that the payment was made in return for official acts.

Our conclusion is buttressed by the fact that so many other courts that have considered the issue over the last 20 years have interpreted the statute in the same way. Moreover, given the number of appellate court decisions, together with the fact that many of them have involved prosecutions of important officials well known in the political community, it is obvious that Congress is aware of the prevailing view that common law extortion is proscribed by the Hobbs Act. . . .

The judgment is affirmed.

JUSTICE O'CONNOR, concurring in part and concurring in the judgment. . . .

JUSTICE KENNEDY, concurring in part and concurring in the judgment. . . .

JUSTICE THOMAS, with whom THE CHIEF JUSTICE and JUSTICE SCALIA join, dissenting. . . .

● ● ● ● ● ● ● ● ● ● ● ● ● ● ●

United States v. Gambino

United States Court of Appeals, Second Circuit, 1977.
566 F.2d 414.

*[The appellants, Gambino and Conti, were convicted
of a number of offenses, including violations of the
federal RICO statute.]*

GURFEIN, Circuit Judge.

. . . The appellants contend that there was insufficient evidence to prove a conspiracy to acquire and maintain control of the private sanitation industry in the Coop City area of the Bronx through a pattern of racketeering activity. They argue that there was insufficient evidence to warrant a conviction under Count Four, which charged that Gambino and Conti used threats and violence in order to collect an extension of credit for Peter Darminio. Specifically, they point to an alleged lack of corroboration of Darminio's testimony.

The general outline of the case indicates that Gambino and Conti had controlled certain stops for private garbage collection in the Bronx but were unable to get a carting license from the City. They arranged for Terminal Sanitation, a licensed private sanitation firm, owned by Peter and Anthony Darminio, to collect at all of the stops which Gambino had previously acquired in the Bronx. The Darminios were required to kick back to Gambino one-third of all the moneys they received from servicing the stops.

[The trial court] . . . found that Gambino and Conti maintained control of garbage collection in Coop City and other areas of the Bronx by threatening to kill competitors and by administering beatings. This activity included an assault on an undercover agent of the FBI who was posing as a cart man and who had solicited a stop in Coop City. [The trial court] also found that Gambino engaged in extensive loansharking activities, lending a total of $90,000 to Peter and Anthony Darminio in 1970 and 1971 and $75,000 to Peter in 1972. These loans were collected by Gambino and Conti through the use of threats and violence.

The court carefully reviewed the evidence. Ralph Torres, an employee of Gambino and Conti, was found to be a credible witness by . . . [the trial court]. Although the credibility of Peter Darminio was in

question, his testimony concerning the defendant's extortionate extensions of credit was corroborated by an exhibit in evidence bearing Gambino's handwriting, headed with the word "Peter" and containing a column of figures and certain calculations. [The trial court] . . . further found that Conti, who was collecting the payments, threatened and beat Darminio from time to time when he was late in making payments.

In July of 1973 one Bernard Ettinger, who had sold Terminal to the Darminios in 1968 and who had not been paid in full in connection with the sale, complained in writing to the New York City Department of Consumer Affairs, requesting that the Department see to it that the Darminios fulfilled their obligations to him before the department approved any sale of stops registered to Terminal. Shortly thereafter, Conti visited Ettinger at his office, slapped Mr. Ettinger on the face, and told him that he had better not complain to the department.

On an earlier occasion when Ettinger had threatened to foreclose on Anthony Darminio's home, on which he held a mortgage, Mr. and Mrs. Darminio had asked Mr. Gambino for assistance, and Gambino replied, "Don't worry about it. I'll send Carlo Conti to straighten it out." In 1974, Ettinger pressed Darminio for payment, which was then a balance of $90,000. A meeting was arranged. Gambino came with Darminio. Gambino said that if Ettinger would settle, Darminio could sell some stops and there would be some stops left over so that Peter Darminio could continue his route. Ettinger agreed to settle for $40,000. One Joseph Perillo, who was also present at the meeting, indicated that he was prepared to purchase some stops from Terminal but did not have money with him for a down payment. Gambino gave Perillo $5,000, which Perillo, in turn, gave to Ettinger. The court found Ettinger to be a highly credible witness.

In November 1975, Terminal entered into a contract with P & S Sanitation, a newly organized company, to take over Terminal's stops. The court found that Gambino was active in P & S. . . .

In the Fall of 1976, the FBI incorporated American Automated Refuse & Waste Removal, Inc., and set up an office in the Bronx. They bought trucks and a winch, the winch being shipped from Texas, and arranged to dump the garbage in New Jersey. They then began soliciting garbage collection accounts, including Harry's Service Station which they knew was being serviced by P & S Sanitation. On December 1, 1976, Harry's entered into an agreement with American Automated, the Government company. American Automated arranged to drop off a container at Harry's to store garbage which would be collected by Automated. Shortly thereafter, Conti telephoned American Automated and came to the office. He threatened to kill the person seated at the desk, who called himself Wayne Dacon but who was in fact an agent of the FBI named Walter Wayne Orrell. Conti's statement to Orrell included a threat to throw the agent out of the window. This conversation was tape-recorded and the tape was received in evidence. Conti indicated that anything new that opened up in Coop City was his. There were two places on the tape where a crunching sound was audible. Agent Orrell testified that Conti punched him. The evidence established that Conti acted frequently at the behest of Gambino, that both men conspired to acquire and maintain control of the private sanitation industry in Coop City and other areas of the Bronx through a pattern of racketeering activity and they in fact carried out the purpose of the conspiracy, that both men obstructed commerce by extorting payments from Terminal Sanitation and its principals, and that Conti attempted to obstruct commerce by assaulting and threatening to kill persons associated with American Automated, Inc.

These findings . . . cannot lightly be set aside. Nor do we see any reason for so doing. We hold that there was sufficient evidence to sustain the conviction. . . .

● ● ● ● ● ● ● ● ● ● ● ● ● ● ●

United States v. Lewis

U.S. Circuit Court of Appeals, Eighth Circuit, 1995.
70 F.3d 1507.

[In this case seven defendants were convicted of conducting a criminal racketeering enterprise in violation of 18 U.S.C.A. Section(s) 1962(c) (1988). Six of the seven were also convicted of conspiring to conduct and participate in the same criminal racketeering enterprise in violation of 18 U.S.C.A. Section(s) 1962(d). All seven were sentenced to life in prison. Here the U.S. Court of Appeals considers the sufficiency of the evidence supporting their convictions.]

BOWMAN, Circuit Judge.

The United States presented evidence at the appellants' trial tending to show that Jerry Lee Lewis participated in and became the leader of a powerful criminal racketeering enterprise that for over ten years controlled a large percentage of the market for T's and Blues (a heroin substitute), heroin, and cocaine in north St. Louis. Lewis obtained and maintained his position by murdering competitors and others who threatened his organization (the Jerry Lewis Organization or JLO).

The profitable but bloody activities of the appellants in this case, all members of the JLO, were described by other JLO members who eventually cooperated with the government. . . . In essence, the investigation and prosecution of Jerry Lee Lewis and his associates produced evidence of a long-term, violent drug-trafficking enterprise operating behind a facade known as Subordinate Temple No. 1 of the Moorish Science Temple of America (MSTA). Jerry Lee Lewis held the position of Grand Sheik in the MSTA, and the membership of the JLO and the MSTA overlapped. A large number of MSTA/JLO members were arrested when a grand jury handed down the initial indictment in this case in January 1991. A superseding indictment was handed down in September 1992, and the trial of the seven appellants in this case and two other defendants began on October 28, 1992.

. . . All of the appellants argue that the District Court should have granted their motions for a judgment of acquittal . . . because the evidence does not support the jury's verdicts. When evaluating a claim of insufficient evidence, this Court considers "the evidence in the light most favorable to the guilty verdict, giving the government the benefit of all reasonable inferences that might be drawn from the evidence." . . . We will reverse a conviction for insufficient evidence and order the entry of a judgment of acquittal only if no construction of the evidence exists to support the jury's verdict. . . .

To establish the elements of a substantive RICO offense (Count I), the government must prove (1) that an enterprise existed; (2) that the enterprise affected interstate or foreign commerce; (3) that the defendant associated with the enterprise; (4) that the defendant participated, directly or indirectly, in the conduct of the affairs of the enterprise; and (5) that the defendant participated in the enterprise through a pattern of racketeering activity by committing at least two racketeering (predicate) acts. . . . To establish the charge of conspiracy to violate the RICO statute (Count II), the government must prove, in addition to elements one, two, and three described immediately above, that the defendant "objectively manifested an agreement to participate in the affairs of [the] enterprise." . . . Proof of an express agreement is not required; "the government need only establish a tacit understanding between the parties, and this may be shown wholly through the circumstantial evidence of [each defendant's] actions." . . .

Appellants argue that the evidence was insufficient to prove (1) the single enterprise charged by the government and (2) an enterprise with a structure distinct from the structure necessary to commit the predicate acts charged. . . .

A. Evidence of a Single Enterprise

Appellants argue that the evidence failed to establish the single enterprise charged in the indictment but instead established two parallel enterprises that eventually merged into a third enterprise. The government, on the other hand, argues that the JLO existed throughout the time frame alleged in the indictment and that other individuals . . . associated with the JLO for specific, short-term criminal activities. The government concedes that during part of the time frame alleged in the indictment [one of the appellants] headed his own criminal enterprise. After [his] enterprise failed, however, its members, including [the appellant], joined the JLO. To determine whether multiple conspiracies exist when a single large conspiracy has been charged by the government, this Court considers the totality of the circumstances, "including the nature of the activities involved, the location where the alleged events of the conspiracy took place, the identity of the conspirators involved, and the time frame in which the acts

occurred." . . . We conclude that the evidence overwhelmingly supports the conclusion that only one conspiracy existed throughout the time frame alleged in the indictment, although personnel varied.

The indictment in this case alleged that twenty-four named individuals (nine defendants, including the seven appellants, and fifteen unindicted co-conspirators) had associated in fact for the purpose of (1) obtaining an income from the distribution of cocaine, heroin, and marijuana; (2) protecting and preserving the distribution enterprise from competition and interference from law enforcement; and (3) promoting the enterprise and its activities. . . . The indictment alleged that these individuals "committed acts of criminal racketeering" while engaging in interstate commerce and other activities affecting interstate commerce. These acts of racketeering included "(i) murder and acts and threats involving murder; (ii) [felony] act(s) involving dealing in narcotic and other dangerous drugs chargeable under state law; and (iii) felonious dealing in narcotic and other dangerous drugs, punishable under any law of the United States."

. . . [T]he indictment also alleged that the enterprise achieved its purposes through (1) the possession and distribution of controlled substances; (2) the "possession, transfer, concealment and use of one or more firearms"; (3) the commission of murder, "act(s) involving murder, threat(s) involving murder," and attempts to conceal such acts and the identities of the responsible individuals from law enforcement officers; (4) "utilization of motels, digital paging devices, telephones, [and] two-way radios to facilitate (i) the distribution of [controlled substances]; (ii) the commission [and concealment] of murder or acts or threats involving murder; and (iii) the attempt to use, or the use of intimidation," to prevent a witness from testifying or "to hinder or prevent the communication to a law enforcement officer or judge of the United States of information relating to the commission or possible commission of a federal offense."

At trial, the government offered the testimony of several participants in the events alleged in the indictment to establish that the JLO constituted a single enterprise and that members of the Bennett enterprise joined the JLO during the time frame alleged in the indictment. . . .

The testimony of [these participants and] several other witnesses tends to prove that the JLO was a single enterprise throughout the time frame of the indictment and that the members of the Bennett organization joined the JLO to continue to profit from the sale of drugs after the Bennett organization was no longer viable. A narcotics investigator described the organizations as "intertwined" and "commingled extensively." . . .

Viewing the evidence in the light most favorable to the government, as we must, we conclude that sufficient evidence was presented at trial to show that the JLO was a single enterprise throughout the time frame alleged in the indictment. "A single conspiracy may be found when the defendants share a common overall goal, even if the actors are not always the same." The evidence, including the reasonable inferences that can be drawn from the evidence, overwhelmingly supports the jury's verdict on this issue.

B. Distinct Structure of the Enterprise

[Three] appellants . . . argue that the government failed to prove the existence of an enterprise distinct from the structure necessary to commit the various predicate acts. The government argues that the evidence presented at trial sufficiently establishes the enterprise element of the RICO offenses charged in the indictment.

To prove the existence of an enterprise, the government must offer proof of (1) a common purpose; (2) a formal or informal organization of the participants in which they function as a unit ("some continuity of both structure and personality"); and (3) "an ascertainable structure distinct from that inherent in the conduct of a pattern of racketeering activity." . . . Appellants apparently concede that the first two elements were established as they argue only that the government failed to prove a distinct, ascertainable structure. . . . The government argues that, based on the evidence at trial, a reasonable jury could easily ascertain that the JLO had a distinct structure. We agree with the government. The evidence of the JLO's distinct structure is overwhelming.

To prove an ascertainable structure, the government need not introduce the enterprise's by-laws or certificate of incorporation. "Common sense suggests that the existence of an association-in-fact is oftentimes more readily proven by what it does, rather than by abstract analysis of its structure." . . .

While the government must prove both the pattern and enterprise elements, "the same piece of evidence may . . . help to establish both." . . . It is not necessary to show that the enterprise has some function wholly unrelated to the racketeering activity (such as a legitimate line of business), but rather that it has an existence beyond that which is necessary merely to commit each of the acts charged as predicate racketeering offenses. The function of overseeing and coordinating the commission of several different predicate offenses and other activities on an ongoing basis is adequate to satisfy the separate existence requirement.

As noted above, . . . the Superseding Indictment charged the appellants with engaging in a pattern of racketeering that included three types of predicate acts: murders and attempted murders; dealing drugs in violation of state law; and dealing drugs in violation of federal law. In addition to proof of these acts, the government offered evidence of oversight and coordination activities sufficient to establish an ascertainable structure distinct from the structure needed to commit the predicate acts or to engage in the pattern of racketeering activities. Co-conspirators . . . testified that members of the JLO shared information to protect their drug trade, avoid apprehension, and defeat competitors. JLO leaders believed that this would help their members sell drugs more effectively. [One co-conspirator] also testified that the JLO would hold post-shooting reviews to improve the techniques it employed to snuff out rivals and informants. Additionally, the evidence established that Jerry Lewis directed and oversaw the affairs of the JLO from the late 1970s until (and perhaps after) his incarceration in 1991. The government's evidence clearly establishes the ascertainable and distinct structure element of the RICO charges, and the jury's verdict on this element is thus supported by sufficient evidence. . . .

Offenses Against Public Health and the Environment

Introduction

Although developed by the courts, common-law crimes were revised and expanded by legislative bodies for our evolving society. In contrast, crimes against the public health and the environment originated directly from federal and state legislatures in response to the needs of a changing society. Many offenses relating to public health developed during the Industrial Revolution as a result of the widespread distribution of food, drugs, and cosmetics and the need to control communicable diseases. By the early 1900s, municipalities perceived the need for zoning to control nuisances and to regulate land use. Since the middle of this century, pollution of the ground, water, and air has been recognized as a major threat to the health and welfare of the people and, indeed, to the ecological balance of the earth.

Enforcing regulations in these fields is accomplished largely through regulatory agencies and measures imposing civil liability. Nevertheless, legislatures have found it necessary to impose criminal sanctions to effectively enforce standards and to deter violators. Although not faced with the severe environmental problems of our age, the common law did regard wildlife, game, and fish as resources to be preserved. In the United States, the state and federal governments have for many years enacted regulations and imposed criminal sanctions on poachers to protect these resources for the benefit of the public.

In contrast with the typical common-law crimes, many offenses against the public health and environment consist of an offender's neglect to comply with required standards or failure to take action required by law. These offenses are *mala prohibita,* and statutes criminalizing conduct in these areas generally contemplate a lower level of intent, frequently imposing a standard of strict liability. For example, in *State v. Budd Co.,* 425 N.E.2d 935 (Ohio App. 1980), the defendant was convicted under a state law that made it a criminal offense to dispose of garbage or other pollutants in any ditch, pond, stream, or other watercourse. On appeal, the court rejected the appellant's argument that it was necessary for the state to prove his criminal intent. The court observed that the law did not require proof of intent and that "the destruction of wildlife through pollution, will occur whenever the waterways are intentionally or accidentally polluted." 425 N.E.2d at 938.

Public Health Legislation

The authority of government to enact laws to protect the public health is a basic function of the police power of the state. Statutes delegating to public health agencies the power to declare quarantines, and later to require inoculations to control communicable diseases, were among the earliest application of this police power. At the turn of the century, the Supreme Court reviewed a defendant's sentence to pay a fine for refusing to be vaccinated for smallpox as required by a Cambridge, Massachusetts, ordinance. The defendant argued that a compulsory vaccination law invaded his liberty secured by the Constitution. Rejecting this contention, the Court observed that "persons and property are subjected to all kinds of restraints and burdens in order to secure the general comfort, health, and prosperity of the state." *Jacobson v. Massachusetts,* 197 U.S. 11, 26, 25 S.Ct. 358, 361, 49 L.Ed. 643, 650 (1905).

Today, numerous federal, state, and local laws address health concerns, providing criminal penalties for serious violations. Modern statutes address a variety of contemporary problems. California, like other states, has a comprehensive collection of laws concerning prevention and control of communicable disease and sexually transmitted disease. Section 120600 of the California Health and Safety Code stipulates the following:

> Any person who refuses to give any information to make any report, to comply with any proper control measure or examination, or to perform any other duty or act required by this chapter, or who violates any provision of this chapter or any rule or regulation of the state board issued pursuant to this chapter, or who exposes any person to or infects any person with any venereal disease; or any person infected with a venereal disease in an infectious state who knows of the condition and who marries or has sexual intercourse, is guilty of a misdemeanor.

In *Reynolds v. McNichols*, 488 F.2d 1378 (10th Cir. 1973), a federal appeals court upheld a Denver, Colorado, "hold and treat" ordinance authorizing detention and treatment, if necessary, of a woman arrested for prostitution who was reasonably suspected of having a venereal disease. Indeed, many states now have statutes imposing criminal penalties on health care professionals who fail to report communicable diseases. See, for example, West's Colo. Stat. Ann. §§ 25–4–402–407. A California appellate court has held that under the "special needs" doctrine, the state, without individualized suspicion, may require that a person convicted of prostitution be tested for acquired immune deficiency syndrome (AIDS). *Love v. Superior Court*, 276 Cal. Rptr. 660 (Cal. App. 1990). Florida has enacted laws criminalizing intentional sexual transmission of HIV without a partner's consent, and making it a felony for a person who is HIV-positive to donate blood or organs. West's Fla. Stat. Ann. §§ 381.004; 384.24. In Nevada, a licensed prostitute who practices with knowledge of a positive HIV test result is guilty of a felony. Nev. Rev. Stat. § 201.358. Most public health laws that impose criminal penalties do not include any intent requirement. In those instances the government need only prove the defendant violated the statute. Offenses of this type are known as **strict liability offenses,** a concept we introduced in Chapter 4.

The Federal Pure Food, Drug, and Cosmetic Act

In 1848 Congress first enacted legislation to prevent the importation of adulterated drugs and medicines. Today, numerous federal acts relate to foods and drugs, but the basic **Pure Food, Drug, and Cosmetic Act** dates back to 1906. It was comprehensively amended in 1938 and subsequently amended many times. 21 U.S.C.A. §§ 301–392. The present law prohibits traffic in food, drugs, and cosmetics being prepared or handled under unsanitary circumstances or under conditions that render them injurious to health. Included in its broad sweep are prohibitions against misbranding and adulteration of food, drugs, and cosmetics, as well as requirements for truthful labeling. The act provides substantial fines and imprisonment for violators. Among other prohibitions, Section 331(k) proscribes the following:

> The alteration, mutilation, destruction, obliteration, or removal of the whole or any part of the labeling of, or the doing of any other act with respect to, a food, drug, device, or cosmetic, if such act is done while such article is held for sale (whether or not the first sale) after shipment in interstate commerce and results in such article being adulterated or misbranded.

21 U.S.C.A § 453 (g) states that a food shall be deemed to be adulterated

(3) if it consists in whole or in part of any filthy, putrid, or decomposed substance or is for any other reason unsound, unhealthful, unwholesome, or otherwise unfit for human food;

(4) if it has been prepared, packed, or held under insanitary conditions whereby it may have become contaminated with filth, or whereby it may have been rendered injurious to health;

(5) if it is, in whole or in part, the product of any poultry which has died otherwise than by slaughter;

(6) if its container is composed, in whole or in part, of any poisonous or deleterious substance which may render the contents injurious to health;

(7) if it has been intentionally subjected to radiation, unless the use of the radiation was in conformity with a regulation or exemption in effect pursuant to section 348 of this title;

(8) if any valuable constituent has been in whole or in part omitted or abstracted therefrom; or if any substance has been substituted, wholly or in part therefore; or if damage or inferiority has been concealed in any manner; or if any substance has been added thereto or mixed or packed therewith so as to increase its bulk or weight, or reduce its quality or strength, or make it appear better or of greater value than it is.

Like most public health laws, food and drug laws fall in the category of **regulatory offenses.** Therefore, unless the statute criminalizing conduct or failure to act requires an intent element, criminal liability can attach without proof of the defendant's intent. *United States v. Park,* 421 U.S. 658, 670, 95 S.Ct. 1903, 1910, 44 L.Ed.2d 489, 500 (1975).

Criminal Liability of Responsible Corporate Officers

Food, drugs, and cosmetics are usually produced and distributed by corporate enterprises. To effectively enforce regulatory laws imposing criminal sanctions in these areas, government agencies must be able to affix responsibility on individuals in supervisory positions as well as on corporate entities. The Supreme Court first recognized the concept of a **responsible corporate officer** in *United States v. Dotterweich,* 320 U.S. 277, 64 S.Ct. 134, 88 L.Ed. 48 (1943), but before 1975 there were conflicting federal court decisions about whether a corporate officer who failed to take measures to prevent violations of the food and drug laws from occurring could be held criminally liable. Noting a conflict in decisions among the courts of appeal, the Supreme Court addressed the standard of liability of corporate officers under the Pure Food, Drug, and Cosmetic Act in *United States v. Park,* supra. There, a national retail food chain and its president and chief executive officer were charged with causing food shipped in interstate commerce to be held in a building accessible to rodents and exposed to contamination. The food chain pled guilty, but its president contested the charges against him. He contended that although he retained authority over corporate affairs, he delegated "normal operating duties," including sanitation, to lower-level personnel. In rejecting his contention as a basis of nonliability, the Court held that the prosecution established a *prima facie* case of the guilt of the accused when it established that "the defendant had, by reason of his position in the corporation, responsibility and authority either to prevent in the first instance or promptly to correct, the violation complained of, and that he failed to do so." 421 U.S. at 673, 95 S.Ct. at 1912, 44 L.Ed.2d at 502.

CASE-IN-POINT

Responsibility Follows Authority

Starr, secretary-treasurer of Cheney Brothers Food Corporation, was convicted of violating the Federal Food, Drug, and Cosmetic Act, 21 U.S.C.A. §§ 301–391, for allowing contamination of food stored in a company warehouse over which he had operational responsibility. After an inspector from the Food and Drug Administration (FDA) pointed out the problem, the janitor for the warehouse was instructed to make corrections, but no action was taken. A month later, a second inspection by the FDA disclosed that the problem had not been corrected. On appeal, Starr contended that he was not responsible because the janitor in charge had failed to comply with instructions to clean up the warehouse. The court rejected his argument, noting that Mr. Starr was aware of the problem after the first inspection and had ample time to remedy the situation. In affirming his conviction, the court also observed that supervisory officers have a duty to anticipate the shortcomings of their delegees.

United States v. Starr, 535 F.2d 512 (9th Cir. 1976).

Criticism of Strict Liability Public Health Laws

Many legal scholars criticize the imposition of strict liability in regulatory offenses, such as food, drug, and health laws. They contend that it brands as criminals people who are without moral fault. Arguing against making violation of such laws punishable by incarceration, critics suggest decriminalization, liability predicated on a **negligence standard** rather than on strict liability, or punishment by only a monetary fine. These criticisms notwithstanding, Congress has determined that the interest of society requires a high standard of care and has been unwilling to eliminate either the strict liability standard or incarceration. The courts hold that a corporate agent who bears a responsible relationship to the operation of the enterprise, and has power to take measures necessary to ensure compliance, can be found guilty of violating such regulatory statutes.

Planning and Zoning Laws

Although sometimes used interchangeably, the terms *zoning* and *planning* are not synonymous. Zoning is primarily concerned with the use and regulation of buildings and structures, whereas planning is a broader term embracing the systematic and orderly development of a community. *State ex rel. Kearns v. Ohio Power Co.,* 127 N.E.2d 394, 399 (Ohio 1955). In *Village of Euclid, Ohio v. Ambler Realty Co.,* 272 U.S. 365, 47 S.Ct. 114, 71 L.Ed. 303 (1926), the Supreme Court first upheld the concept of comprehensive zoning, which allows local governments to divide areas of the community and to designate the permitted and prohibited land uses in the respective districts. Since then, zoning has become both widespread and sophisticated. Building codes are generally encompassed within the overall local zoning requirements. Today, **comprehensive planning** guides the development of a community, and that planning is implemented to a large degree by local **zoning ordinances** (their enactment usually preceded by studies and recommendations of professional consultants). In addition, local citizens are enlisted to sit on planning and zoning boards that make recommendations to the governing body. Any comprehensive zoning ordinance must provide for a board of adjustment to act in a quasi-judicial capacity. The board must have the power to grant variances where strict enforcement of an ordinance would cause an undue hardship to property owners. It may also be empowered to approve special exceptions based on the landowner's compliance with specified criteria.

As with other regulatory measures, enforcement of local zoning codes is accomplished administratively in most instances. Failing this, local governments often resort to civil court actions, commonly seeking injunctive relief against violators. Most zoning ordinances classify violations as misdemeanors and provide for a fine and a jail term on conviction. Zoning ordinances, like most health regulations, generally do not include an intent requirement. Prosecution of violators is usually undertaken only as a last resort. But once a state or local government commences prosecution of a defendant for violation of a zoning ordinance, it must meet all burdens placed on the prosecution in criminal proceedings. *People v. St. Agatha Home for Children*, 389 N.E.2d 1098 (N.Y. 1979).

The Scope of Federal and State Environmental Statutes

Numerous federal statutes and agencies play a part in regulating and enforcing the laws affecting our environment. Among the older agencies are the Army Corps of Engineers, the Coast Guard, and the departments of the Interior, Commerce, Transportation, and Justice. A newer agency, the **Environmental Protection Agency** **(EPA)**, acts under the authority of some twenty-nine major congressional enactments and has significant responsibilities in numerous areas, including hazardous wastes, toxic substances, and air and water pollution. State environmental agencies became active in the 1970s, and planning and coordinating councils now function at state, regional, and local levels. They play an important part in environmental regulation by establishing pollution controls, water management programs, and wastewater and solid-waste disposal programs.

CASE-IN-POINT **The *Exxon Valdez* Prosecution**

In March 1989, the supertanker *Exxon Valdez* ran aground and ruptured, spilling more than 240,000 barrels of oil into Alaska's Prince William Sound and wreaking havoc on the natural environment. Subsequently, the federal government brought criminal charges against the Exxon Shipping Co. and its parent, Exxon Corporation, under the Clean Water Act and several other federal environmental statutes.

In October 1991, one week before the case was scheduled to go to trial, Exxon accepted a plea bargain under which it agreed to pay $25 million in federal fines and another $100 million in restitution, split between the federal and state governments. The $125 million fine was the largest environmental criminal fine in U.S. history.

Source: Stephen Raucher, "Raising the Stakes for Environmental Polluters: The *Exxon Valdez* Criminal Prosecution." *Ecology Law Quarterly* 147 (1993).

Environmental regulation at the federal and state levels has become a vast undertaking. During the 1970s, government agencies relied almost exclusively on civil penalties as an enforcement tool. The concept changed in the 1980s, when criminal enforcement of environmental laws became prominent, particularly in instances of egregious violations involving hazardous waste disposal, water pollution, and air pollution. These enforcement policies were in effect long before the *Exxon Valdez* supertanker spilled millions of gallons of crude oil in Alaskan waters in 1989, destroying wildlife and despoiling beaches.

Some environmental crimes require only proof that the defendant committed a proscribed act or failed to comply with a required standard. In prosecutions of these strict liability offenses, the government may establish the defendant's guilt in a manner similar to prosecuting many crimes against the public health. Other statutes require the government to establish the defendant's negligent conduct or a willful or knowing violation, and many court decisions in environmental prosecutions turn on whether the evidence is sufficient to meet the required statutory standard.

Major Federal Environmental Legislation Providing Criminal Sanctions

Congress enacted its first major environmental law, the **Rivers and Harbors Act,** in 1899. 33 U.S.C.A. §§ 401–467. This act makes it a misdemeanor to discharge refuse into the navigable waters of the United States. Notwithstanding the act's provisions for criminal enforcement, the federal government traditionally sought enforcement through the civil courts. In recent years, the following acts of Congress have provided significant means to enforce criminal violations of environmental laws and regulations:

- **Clean Air Act** of 1970, 42 U.S.C.A. §§ 7401–7642.
- Federal Water Pollution Control Act of 1972 (**Clean Water Act**), 33 U.S.C.A. §§ 1251–1376.
- **Resource Conservation and Recovery Act** of 1976 (RCRA), 42 U.S.C.A. §§ 6901–6992.
- **Toxic Substances Control Act** of 1976 (TSCA), 15 U.S.C.A. §§ 2601–2692.
- **Comprehensive Environmental Response, Compensation and Liability Act** of 1980 (CERCLA), 42 U.S.C.A. §§ 9601–9675.

The Clean Air Act

The Clean Air Act sets federal standards designed to enhance the quality of the air by deterring air polluters. In 1977 Congress passed a series of amendments establishing stricter standards for air quality. As amended, the act provides criminal sanctions for violation of any provisions for which civil penalties apply, and for any person who knowingly makes any false representation in a document filed under the act. Enforcement may be delegated to the states pursuant to the State Implementation Plan (SIP), 42 U.S.C.A. § 7410, but the states are not required to enact minimum criminal provisions to receive EPA approval of their implementation plans. Nevertheless, states are increasingly toughening criminal penalties in this area. For example, a violation of Oklahoma's Clean Air Act entails a fine of $25,000 per day of violation, imprisonment for no more than ten years, or both. 27A Okl. Stats. Ann. § 2–5–116.

Two reasons have been advanced for the relatively few criminal prosecutions for air pollution as compared with prosecutions for violations of hazardous waste and water pollution laws. First, the cost of criminal enforcement in this area is apparently great; second, the problems of enforcement are made exceedingly difficult for states because air pollution is a less stationary category of pollution.

The Clean Water Act

The Federal Water Pollution Control Act of 1972 (Clean Water Act), 33 U.S.C.A. §§ 1251–1376, is designed to control water pollution and regulate industrial and other discharges into navigable waters. Although the Clean Water Act is enforced primarily through civil means, criminal sanctions have been imposed for willful or negligent violations of certain provisions concerning permits and the making of false statements. Amendments in 1987 eliminated the "willful" requirement and imposed more stringent penalties for negligent violations and even more severe penalties for knowing violations of the act's criminal provisions. 33 U.S.C.A. § 1319(c)(2).

A majority of the states have programs approved by the EPA. Although states vary somewhat in their approaches, many provide penalties similar to those in the federal act for either willful or negligent violations of water pollution provisions.

Courts tend to construe the penal provisions of the Clean Water Act broadly and generally hold supervisory personnel vested with authority to a high standard of compliance. The trend in the federal courts is to hold responsible corporate officers criminally liable in environmental offenses despite their lack of "consciousness of wrongdoing." See, for example, *United States v. Brittain,* 931 F.2d 1413, 1419 (10th Cir. 1991).

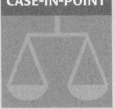

CASE-IN-POINT

Criminal Prosecution Under the Clean Water Act

David W. Boldt was Chemical Engineering Manager for Astro Circuit Corporation, a Massachusetts company that manufactured circuit boards using an electroplating process. Boldt's duties included supervising the company's pretreatment process, a part of the pollution control system. He was charged with six counts of violating the Clean Water Act. He was convicted on two counts: one for knowingly aiding and abetting the discharge of pollutants into a municipal sewer in 1987, when the copper level in Astro's effluent greatly exceeded the federal standards; another for ordering a subordinate in 1988 to dump 3,100 gallons of partially treated industrial wastewater containing excessive metals into the municipal sewer. At trial, Boldt asserted the defense of impossibility to the first incident, arguing he was only a mid-level manager who was not responsible for the discharge. Boldt acknowledged

responsibility for the second discharge, but pleaded the defense of necessity, arguing it was necessary to authorize the discharge to avoid a worse harm.

In upholding both convictions, the appellate court observed that the evidence showed that pollution control was part of Boldt's area of responsibility and that, regarding the 1987 violation, he was aware of the practice of bypassing the pollution control system and had condoned it on the occasion at issue. Regarding the 1988 incident, the court found the evidence undisputed that Boldt directly ordered his subordinate to dump the copper wastewater, a conclusion bolstered by his subordinate's testimony that Boldt attempted to cover up the incident. Finally, the appellate court observed that the record of the trial disclosed that the president of Astro testified that Boldt was authorized to shut down the plant.

United States v. Boldt, 929 F.2d 35 (1st Cir. 1991).

The Resource Conservation and Recovery Act (RCRA)

The enactment of RCRA in 1976 was a significant step in environmental control. Its objective is to encourage the states—through grants, technical assistance, and advice—to establish standards and provide for civil and criminal enforcement of state regulations. The EPA sets minimum standards requiring the states to enact criminal penalties against any person who knowingly stores or transports any hazardous waste to an unpermitted facility, who treats such waste without a permit, or who makes false representations to secure a permit. All states have enacted criminal statutes pursuant to the criteria specified in RCRA.

RCRA proscribes a comprehensive list of illegal actions and imposes criminal penalties on any person who

1. knowingly transports or causes to be transported any hazardous waste to an unpermitted facility, 42 U.S.C.A. § 6928(d)(1);

2. knowingly treats, stores, or disposes of any hazardous waste without a permit, in knowing violation of any material condition or requirement of the interim status regulations, 42 U.S.C.A. § 6928(d)(2)(A)–(C); or one who

3. knowingly omits material information or makes any false statement or representation in any record or document required to be maintained under the regulations or submitted to the [EPA] or any state which is authorized to run RCRA programs. 42 U.S.C.A. § 6928(d)(3).

In addition, Section 6928(e) makes it a criminal offense to knowingly place another person in imminent danger of death or serious bodily injury in conjunction with the transportation, storage, or disposal of hazardous wastes.

RCRA has become an important tool for enforcement, and prosecutors frequently rely on RCRA when prosecuting persons who illegally dispose of hazardous wastes. In *United States v. Johnson & Towers, Inc.*, 741 F.2d 662, 664 (3d Cir. 1984), the court held that the term "person" in RCRA Section 6928(d) includes employees as well as owners and operators and that proof of the knowledge element required may be inferred for those individuals holding responsible corporate positions.

In *United States v. Hayes International Corp.*, 786 F.2d 1499, 1503 (11th Cir. 1986), the court affirmed a conviction under Section 6928(d)(1) for unlawfully transporting hazardous waste materials to an unpermitted facility and ruled that neither a lack of knowledge that paint waste was a hazardous material nor ignorance of the permit requirement was a defense. Conviction for the treatment, storage, or disposal of hazardous waste without an RCRA permit has been more problematic. In *United States v. Hoflin*, 880 F.2d 1033 (9th Cir. 1989), the court held that the government is not required to prove the defendant's knowledge of the lack of a permit to secure a conviction in either transport or storage cases; nevertheless, a person who does not know that the waste material he or she is disposing of is hazardous cannot be guilty of violating Section 6928(d)(2)(a).

One of the most serious cases brought under the RCRA involved Section 6928(e), which makes it a criminal violation to knowingly place employees "in imminent danger of death or serious bodily injury." *United States v. Protex Industries, Inc.*, 874 F.2d 740, 742 (10th Cir. 1989), involved a company that operated a drum-recycling facility and in connection with its business purchased drums that previously contained toxic chemicals. The evidence revealed that the company's safety provisions were inadequate to protect its employees and that, as a result, certain company employees suffered from solvent poisoning and exhibited serious maladies. The court upheld a

In *United States v. Sellers,* the U.S. Court of Appeals for the Fifth Circuit upholds a conviction under RCRA. An excerpt from the decision appears at the end of the chapter.

conviction of Protex for placing employees in an industrial environment without sufficient protection against exposure to toxic chemicals.

The Toxic Substances Control Act (TSCA)

The Toxic Substances Control Act of 1976 authorizes the EPA to require testing and to prohibit the manufacture, distribution, or use of certain chemical substances that present an unreasonable risk of injury to health or the environment, and to regulate their disposal. Although the act depends primarily on civil penalties, a person who knowingly or willfully fails to maintain records or submit reports as required violates the criminal provisions of the act. 15 U.S.C.A. §§ 2614; 2615(b). In 1982 a court upheld the conviction of Robert Earl Ward Jr., the chairman of the board of Ward Transformer Company, on eight counts of the unlawful disposal of toxic substances (PCB-containing oils from used transformers) and willfully aiding and abetting the unlawful disposal of toxic substances. The evidence at trial revealed that although the defendant himself did not dispose of the toxic substances, the company's employees performed the task while he was kept advised of the progress. *United States v. Ward,* 676 F. 2d 94 (4th Cir. 1982).

The Comprehensive Environmental Response, Compensation, and Liability Act (CERCLA)

In 1980 Congress enacted the Comprehensive Environmental Response, Compensation, and Liability Act (CERCLA), commonly known as the Superfund Law. Its purpose is to finance cleanup and provide for civil suits by citizens. As revised in 1986, the act requires notice to federal and state agencies of any "release" of a "reportable quantity" of a listed hazardous substance. *Release* is broadly defined, and *reportable quantity* is related to each of the several hundred "hazardous substances." CERCLA also allows the EPA to promulgate regulations for the collection and disposal of solid wastes. The act imposes criminal sanctions against those who fail to report as required, or who destroy or falsify records. 42 U.S.C.A. § 9603(d)(2).

Standard of Liability of Corporate Officers

Many violations in the public health area are caused by corporate entities; therefore, courts often focus on whether an accused, by reason of his or her position in the corporate enterprise, had sufficient responsibility and authority to either prevent or correct the violation charged. The same legal doctrine is being applied by the courts to environmental crimes. In fact, Congress has adopted the "responsible corporate officer" doctrine in the Clean Air Act, 42 U.S.C.A. § 7413(c)(6), and the Clean Water Act, 33 U.S.C.A. § 1319(c)(3)(6). And the doctrine has been upheld in CERCLA cases by federal appeals courts. For example, in *United States v. Carr,* 880 F.2d 1550 (2d Cir. 1989), the court rejected a maintenance supervisor's argument that he could not be guilty because he was a relatively low-level employee. The court explained that CERCLA imposes criminal responsibility on a person "even of relatively low rank" who acts in a supervisory capacity and is "in a position to detect, prevent, and abate a release of hazardous substances." 880 F.2d at 1554. Thus, a responsible corporate officer not only cannot avoid criminal liability by delegating tasks to others but also must remedy any violations that occur. At the state level, corporate executives have been charged with criminally negligent homicide and manslaughter where employees' deaths have resulted from the improper use of hazardous substances. See, for example, *People v. Hegedus,* 443 N.W.2d 127 (Mich. 1989); *State ex rel. Cornellier v. Black,* 425 N.W.2d 21 (Wis. App. 1988).

Lack of Uniformity in Environmental Laws

Disparate environmental standards, enforcement policies, and sanctions in the areas of water and air pollution and disposal of hazardous wastes can lead to "shopping" by industry to secure locations that will enable them to be more competitive by not having to comply with stringent environmental standards. Significant differences exist among the fifty states in the standards of proof required and in the sanctions imposed for criminal violations of hazardous waste, water pollution, and air pollution laws.

Compare the differences between the statutory language in the Kentucky and Vermont offenses set out in Table 11.1. What level of proof should be required for establishing a defendant's guilt under the "knowingly" standard of the Kentucky laws? Would a different standard of proof be required under Vermont's laws concerning hazardous wastes and air pollution?

Unfortunately, fines imposed on violators of environmental laws are too often regarded as "costs of doing business" because in reality these costs can be passed on to the ultimate consumer. The threat of imprisonment, on the other hand, is one cost that cannot be passed on to a consumer; therefore, it is a powerful deterrent to those who would pollute the environment. As states more aggressively prosecute environmental crimes, more uniformity of criminal sanctions will undoubtedly develop, much as it has for the more common criminal offenses.

Noise Pollution

Congress enacted the **Quiet Communities Act** of 1978, 42 U.S.C.A. §§ 4901–4918, to protect the environment against noise pollution, which has become perceived as a growing danger to the health and welfare of the population. Section 4909 details prohibited acts, and § 4910 provides criminal penalties for those who knowingly or willfully import, manufacture, or distribute products that fail to comply with noise standards specified in the statute. However, the act recognizes that the primary responsibility for protecting communities against noise pollution lies with state and local governments.

Historically, local governments have adopted ordinances that prohibit excessive noise. In the twentieth century, ordinances have reflected concern about amplified sound equipment. The following ordinance was enacted by the city of Ithaca, New York:

> No person shall play, operate or use, or cause to be played, operated or used, any mechanical instrument, radio or wireless, speaker or horn, or any other instrument, device or thing in the city so as to disturb the peace and quiet of any neighborhood.
> The Code of Ordinances of the City of Ithaca, N.Y., Art. 16, § 16–12, subdivision (b).

Ordinances of this type can be used to prohibit the use of loud stereo equipment in an apartment building where residents live in close quarters, or to disband loud late-night parties that are disturbing neighbors. Such an ordinance might be enforced against a person whose car stereo is played so loudly as to be an annoyance or even a safety hazard.

Table 11.1   Kentucky and Vermont Environmental Laws Imposing Criminal Penalties Concerning Hazardous Wastes, Water Pollution, and Air Pollution

Kentucky Revised Statutes Annotated

HAZARDOUS WASTES

Unlawful acts: Knowingly engaging in the generation, treatment, storage, transportation, or disposal of hazardous wastes in violation of this chapter, or contrary to a permit, order, or administrative regulation issued or promulgated under the chapter; or knowingly making a false statement, representation, or certification in an application for, or form pertaining to, a permit, or in a notice or report required by the terms and conditions of an issued permit. Ky. Rev. Stat. Ann. § 224.99–010(6).

Penalties: Felony; imprisonment between one and five years or a fine up to $25,000 per day of violation, or both. § 224.99–010(6).

WATER POLLUTION

Unlawful acts: Knowingly, or with criminal negligence, violating any of the following:

§ 224.71–110 (water pollution)

§ 224.73–120 (monitoring and reporting)

§ 224.40–100 (waste disposal)

§ 224.50–545 (oil pollution)

§ 224.40–305 (unpermitted waste disposal facilities)

Any determination, permit, administrative regulation, or order of the Cabinet promulgated pursuant to those sections which have become final; or knowingly providing false information in any document filed or required to be maintained under this chapter; or knowingly rendering inaccurate any monitoring device or method required to be maintained. § 224.99–010(4).

Penalties: Misdemeanor; imprisonment up to one year or a fine between $1,000 and $15,000 per day of violation, or both. § 224.99–010(4).

AIR POLLUTION

Unlawful acts: Knowingly, or with criminal negligence, violating § 224.20–110 (air pollution), or any determination, permit, administrative regulation, or order of the Cabinet promulgated pursuant to those sections which have become final; or knowingly providing false information in any document filed or required to be maintained under this chapter; or knowingly rendering inaccurate any monitoring device or method required to be maintained. § 224.99–010(4).

Penalties: Misdemeanor; imprisonment up to one year or a fine between $1,000 and $15,000 per day of violation, or both. § 224.99–010(4).

Vermont Statutes Annotated

HAZARDOUS WASTES

Unlawful acts: Violating any provision of the waste management chapter (transportation, storage, disposal, or treatment of hazardous waste: permit and manifest requirements), rules promulgated therein, or terms or conditions of any order of certification. Vt. Stat. Ann., Title 10, § 6612(a) (1991).

Penalties: Imprisonment up to six months or a fine up to $25,000 per day of violation, or both. Title 10, § 6612(a).

WATER POLLUTION

Unlawful acts: Violating any provision of the water pollution control subchapter, or failing, neglecting, or refusing to obey or comply with any order or the terms of any permit issued under this subchapter. Title 10, § 1275(a).

Penalties: Imprisonment up to six months or a fine up to $25,000 per day of violation, or both. Title 10, § 1275(a).

Unlawful acts: Knowingly making any false statement, representation, or certification in any document filed or required to be maintained under the water pollution control subchapter, or by any permit, rule, regulation, or order issued thereunder; or falsifying, tampering with, or knowingly rendering inaccurate any monitoring device or method required to be maintained under this subchapter, or by any permit, rule, regulation, or order issued thereunder. Title 10, § 1275(b).

Penalties: Imprisonment up to six months or a fine up to $10,000 or both. § 1275(b).

AIR POLLUTION

Unlawful acts: Violating a provision of the air pollution control chapter (discharge of air contaminants without a permit or in violation of pollution standards) except § 563 and § 567 (relating to motor vehicles and confidential records), or any rule issued thereunder. Title 10, § 568.

Penalties: Imprisonment up to five years, a fine up to $100,000 per violation, or both. Title 10, § 568.

Antismoking Legislation

As society has become more aware of the ill effects of smoking and, in particular, the hazards of "secondhand smoke," governments have restricted smoking in public buildings and places of public accommodation and transportation. Perhaps the best-known example is the Federal Aviation Administration regulation prohibiting all smoking on domestic passenger airline flights. Most **antismoking laws** carry minor civil penalties analogous to parking fines. However, some jurisdictions have experimented with criminal sanctions. As amended in 1998, § 144.414 of Minnesota's Clean Indoor Air Act now provides the following: "No person shall smoke in a public place or at a public meeting except in designated smoking areas." In addition, the law prohibits smoking in "a day care center or a hospital, health care clinic, doctor's office, or other health care-related facility." Section 144.417 provides that "[a]ny person who violates section 144.414 is guilty of a petty misdemeanor." Because people have become more aware of the dangers of secondhand smoke, the use of criminal sanctions against smokers is apt to increase.

Wildlife Protection Laws

Since the early common law, fish and game have been viewed as animals *ferae naturae,* meaning that the state as sovereign owns them in trust for the people. *Bayside Fish Flour Co. v. Gentry,* 297 U.S. 422, 56 S.Ct. 513, 80 L. Ed. 772 (1936). As trustee, the state has the duty to preserve and protect wildlife by regulating fishing in public and private streams and by controlling the taking of game. *Shively v. Bowlby,* 152 U.S. 1, 14 S.Ct. 548, 38 L.Ed. 331 (1894). Owners of private property retain a qualified interest, so those seeking to take fish or game from the confines of private property must secure the owner's permission.

Although it is generally within the jurisdiction of the states to regulate wildlife, fish, and game, the federal government has jurisdiction to enact statutes to carry out treaties for migratory birds. The jealous regard that the states have over wildlife within their borders led Missouri to challenge the constitutionality of the **Migratory Bird Conservation Act,** a statute passed by Congress to enforce the provisions of the Migratory Bird Treaty entered into by the United States in 1916. Missouri claimed the federal statute infringed rights reserved to the states by the Tenth Amendment to the United States Constitution. The Supreme Court rejected that challenge, thereby settling the issue of federal control. The Court held that Article II, Section 2 of the Constitution grants the president the power to make treaties, and Article I, Section 8 gives Congress the power to enact legislation to enforce those treaties. *Missouri v. Holland,* 252 U.S. 416, 40 S.Ct. 382, 64 L.Ed. 641 (1920). Of course, the federal government retains jurisdiction to protect all wildlife, game, and fish within national game preserves. *Hunt v. United States,* 278 U.S. 96, 49 S.Ct. 38, 73 L. Ed. 200 (1928). Enforcement of the Migratory Bird Act (MBA), 16 U.S.C.A. §§ 703–712, remains a viable part of the federal environmental enforcement program. Following conflicting court decisions about whether the penal provisions of MBA imposed strict liability for both misdemeanor and felony violations, Congress inserted the word "knowingly" into the section of the act providing criminal sanctions, thus requiring the prosecution to prove the defendant's *mens rea* as well as *actus reus* to establish a violation (see Chapter 4).

The Endangered Species Act

Modern efforts of the federal government to preserve the environment through protection of wildlife is illustrated by the Federal **Endangered Species Act** of 1973, 16 U.S.C.A. §§ 1531–1544. This act is designed to conserve ecosystems by preserving wildlife, fish, and plants. And although enforcement is largely through civil penalties, criminal liability is imposed against any person who knowingly violates regulations issued under the act. 16 U.S.C.A. § 1540(b). In *United States v. Billie*, 667 F. Supp. 1485 (S.D. Fla. 1987), the defendant was charged with killing a Florida panther, an endangered species. He argued that the prosecution had to prove his specific intent—that is, that he knew the animal he shot was a Florida panther, as opposed to a species of panther not on the list of "endangered species." The U.S. District Court rejected his argument and held that the government "need prove only that the defendant acted with general intent when he shot the animal in question." 667 F. Supp. at 1493. The court discussed the fact that the defendant was charged with violating a regulatory statute enacted to conserve and protect endangered species, and that its purposes would be eviscerated if the government had to prove that a hunter who killed an animal recognized the particular subspecies as being protected under the act. 667 F. Supp. at 1492–1493.

Despite the existence of criminal penalties for violation of environmental laws, often the most effective means of enforcement is to secure an injunction against actual or threatened violations. This is illustrated by an action against Volusia County, Florida, filed under the citizen-suit provision of the Endangered Species Act (ESA), 16 U.S.C.A. § 1540(g)(1)(A), discussed in the following Case-in-Point.

CASE-IN-POINT

A Federal Appellate Court Grants Protection to Nesting Sea Turtles

In 1978 the U.S. Fish and Wildlife Service listed the loggerhead sea turtle as a threatened species and the green sea turtle as an endangered species. In the spring, the female sea turtles come ashore on the beaches in Volusia County, Florida, and deposit their eggs in the sand and return to the ocean. Nesting females avoid bright lights. Months later, the hatchlings break out of their shells at night and instinctively crawl toward the brightest light on the horizon, which on an undeveloped beach is the moon's reflection off the surf. But on a developed beach, the brightest light can be artificial and can lead to disorientation of the turtles. Citizens acting on behalf of the endangered turtles sought an injunction against the county's refusal to ban beach driving and beachfront artificial light sources that adversely impact sea turtles during sea turtle nesting season, arguing that the county had violated the "take" prohibition

of 16 U.S.C.A. § 1538(a)(1)(B). The county responded that it had implied permission to "take" federally protected sea turtles through artificial beachfront lighting because it had a federal permit conditioned on its implementation of detailed lighting-related mitigatory measures. The district court enjoined the county from permitting beach driving during the nesting season but denied relief as to the beachfront lighting. The turtles appealed.

In a case of first impression, the U.S. Court of Appeals for the Eleventh Circuit held that the Endangered Species Act's incidental take permit exception to its "take prohibition" did not apply to an activity performed as a purely mitigatory measure upon which the permit is conditioned and thus did not authorize the county to take protected sea turtles through measures associated with artificial beachfront lighting.

Turtles v. Volusia County, 148 F.3d 1231 (11th Cir. 1998).

Legislatures may make it a strict liability offense to take or possess fish and game in violation of regulations. *Cummings v. Commonwealth,* 255 S.W. 2d 997 (Ky. 1953). Most states have done so, usually imposing strict liability for taking quantities of game or fish in excess of permitted allowances and for hunting and fishing during closed seasons. But it can be quite difficult to determine whether a given law that imposes a criminal penalty for violating a fishing or game regulation is a strict liability statute. If a wildlife penal statute includes language incorporating a *mens rea* requirement, it is clear that the prosecution must prove the defendant's intent. Although it is difficult to generalize, if a wildlife penal law does not explicitly require intent by including such words as "willfully" or "knowingly," only proof of the *actus reus* of the offense is required. The courts have tended to make an exception to imposing strict liability where the offense is of a more serious criminal character (for example, smuggling and chemical trafficking) or where the offense is designated as a felony or otherwise carries a severe punishment.

In *State v. Rice,* 626 P.2d 104 (Alaska 1981), the court considered a game regulation that lacked any requirement for criminal intent. As we have noted, this type of regulation is generally treated much like a traffic law. The Alaska Supreme Court took a different approach, saying that "strict liability is an exception to the rule that requires criminal intent" and that criminal statutes will be "strictly construed to require some degree of *mens rea* absent a clear legislative intent to the contrary." 626 P.2d at 108.

Statutes also commonly make it a strict liability offense to use improper types of fishing nets, to hunt with artificial lights, and to shoot over baited fields. In addition, statutes provide for forfeiture of illegal equipment used to hunt or fish in violation of laws. See, for example, *State v. Billiot,* 229 So.2d 72 (La. 1969), where the Louisiana Supreme Court upheld the forfeiture of seines and other devices used in trawling for shrimp during a closed season.

Irrespective of whether a penal statute imposes strict liability or requires proof of intent, the prosecution is not required to establish that a person accused of fishing in a closed season actually caught fish, *State v. Parker,* 167 A. 854, 855 (Me. 1933), nor is it a defense that a hunter has failed to kill any game, *Key v. State,* 384 S.W.2d 22 (Tenn. 1964).

Conclusion

Imposing strict criminal liability on responsible corporate officers has proven to be successful in deterring violations of laws protecting the purity and safety of food and drugs. Moreover, the concept of strict liability is firm relative to traditional public health statutes. Strict liability is also applied to transgressors of wildlife regulations, although—whenever a violation rises to the level of a felony—courts are inclined to require proof of the defendant's intent before upholding a conviction that visits serious consequences on the offender.

Until recently, governmental agencies relied almost exclusively on civil penalties to punish violators of environmental laws, but the regulatory climate is changing. This new decade will continue to witness an increased reliance by federal and state authorities on criminal sanctions, often with greatly increased penalties. As this trend continues, legislatures (or, in their absence, courts of law) will most likely include a *mens rea* requirement in regulatory statutes that subject violators to severe punishment.

Noise pollution and smoking in public places are increasingly viewed by society as detrimental. It is reasonable to expect that criminal sanctions—which, after all, mirror societal norms—will be increasingly applied to these problems.

Key Terms

strict liability offenses
Pure Food, Drug, and Cosmetic Act
regulatory offenses
responsible corporate officer
negligence standard
comprehensive planning
zoning ordinances
Environmental Protection Agency
Rivers and Harbors Act
Clean Air Act
Clean Water Act

Resource Conservation and Recovery Act
Toxic Substances Control Act
Comprehensive Environmental Response, Compensation and Liability Act
Quiet Communities Act
antismoking laws
Migratory Bird Conservation Act
Endangered Species Act

Web-Based Research Activity

1. Go to the web. Locate your state's statutes.
2. Search your state's environmental laws. Determine which, if any, prohibitions involve criminal sanctions.
3. What, if any, additional criminal sanctions would you support if you were elected to your state legislature?

Questions for Thought and Discussion

1. Are criminal sanctions essential to the effective enforcement of food, drug, and cosmetic laws?
2. Should the term "responsible corporate officer" be explicitly defined by statute, or should courts make this determination on a case-by-case basis?
3. Does your community impose criminal penalties for violations of zoning regulations? If so, are violations treated as strict liability offenses?
4. Should efforts be made to formulate a model state code of environmental regulations?
5. Should smoking be prohibited in all public places? Why or why not? If so, should violations be treated as civil or criminal infractions?
6. Do you think hunting and fishing violations should be decriminalized and treated as civil infractions in the way that many states treat traffic offenses?
7. Should environmental crimes that carry major penalties be strict liability offenses, or should prosecutors be required to prove that a defendant knowingly or willfully committed an offense?

8. Can you describe some instances where it is advisable to seek injunctive relief rather imposing criminal penalties for violations of environmental laws?

··

Problems for Discussion and Solution

1. Two boys died of asphyxiation after playing in a dumpster in which a toxic solvent was disposed of improperly. The solvent was placed in the dumpster by workers at a nearby industrial plant. Under which, if any, federal statute can the plant manager be prosecuted?

2. Hoss Tile is arrested after police are called to the scene of a private social club where Mr. Tile is a member. The police are called because Tile refuses to extinguish his cigarette in the dining room and is becoming belligerent. He is charged with a misdemeanor under a new ordinance that prohibits smoking in "restaurants and other places of public accommodation other than those in which alcoholic beverages are sold for consumption on the premises." The club in which he was arrested does not sell or serve alcohol. How might Mr. Tile defend himself in this case?

● ● ● ● ● ● ● ● ● ● ● ● ●

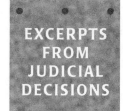

EXCERPTS
FROM
JUDICIAL
DECISIONS

United States v. Sellers

United States Court of Appeals, Fifth Circuit, 1991.
926 F.2d 410.

[In this case the U.S. Court of Appeals for the Fifth Circuit reviews a criminal conviction under the Resource Conservation and Recovery Act. The appellant, James Ralph Sellers, was convicted of sixteen counts of knowingly and willfully disposing of a hazardous waste without obtaining a permit, as required by RCRA.]

KING, Circuit Judge:

On March 5, 1989, residents in rural Jones County, Mississippi discovered sixteen 55-gallon drums of hazardous paint waste on an embankment of the Camp Branch Creek, which flows into the Leaf River. These drums were later determined to contain paint waste and methylethylketone (M.E.K.), a paint solvent, and one of the drums was found to be leaking. Sellers was indicted on October 16, 1989 on sixteen counts of violating 42 U.S.C. § 6928(d)(2)(A) for disposing of sixteen drums of hazardous waste without a permit on or about March 4 or 5, 1989. Sellers was tried January 8 through 11, 1990 in front of a jury. On the issue of guilt or innocence, the jury heard testimony from 14 government witnesses and

two defense witnesses. The government witnesses testified about the discovery of the drums, the circumstances surrounding the waste's origin in Port Violet, Louisiana, and the fact that Sellers had been paid $45 per drum to dispose of the waste. In addition, the government called James William Ward (Ward), who testified that he had assisted Sellers in loading the 55-gallon drums in Louisiana and transporting them to Jones County, Mississippi where Ward and Sellers unloaded them. Ward testified that Sellers did not tell him what was in the drums, but did tell Ward that it was flammable. Subsequently, Ward voluntarily came forward and told the police about his involvement in dumping the drums. Testimony by other witnesses established that Sellers did not have a permit as required for disposing of hazardous waste, nor did he take the waste to a licensed disposal area. The government's last witness in its case in chief, Douglas E. Bourgeois (Bourgeois), was allowed to testify over Sellers's objection. Bourgeois testified that he had a conversation with Sellers in late April or sometime in May in which Sellers stated that he had been hauling waste chemicals and discarding them in a rural area outside Petal, Mississippi. During the conversation, Sellers referred to M.E.K., which he knew was a solvent used primarily to clean paint equipment.

The crux of Sellers's defense was that he denied dumping the paint waste in question. He testified that it was Ward alone who had dumped the drums into Camp Branch Creek, although he admitted that his family owned property in Jones County near the site of the dumping.

After deliberation, the jury found Sellers guilty of all sixteen counts of the indictment. On March 14, 1990, Sellers was sentenced to 41 months imprisonment on each count, with the sentences to run concurrently. In addition, Sellers was sentenced to three years of supervised release and was ordered to make restitution to the State of Mississippi of $6,130.70, the amount required to clean up the hazardous waste site. Sellers also received a special assessment of $800. Sellers filed a timely notice of appeal. . . .

The applicable statute [R.C.R.A.] . . . provides criminal penalties for "[a]ny person who . . . knowingly treats, stores, or disposes of any hazardous waste identified or listed under this subchapter . . . without a permit under this subchapter. . . ."

On appeal, Sellers argues that the jury charge should have required the government to prove that Sellers knew that the paint waste could be hazardous or harmful to persons or the environment. Sellers argues that a "reading of the statute involved . . . leads to the conclusion that Congress intended to punish only knowing violations."

At trial, Sellers requested an instruction that the government must prove that "the Defendant knew or reasonably should have known that the substance was waste." This instruction was not necessary as the district court's instruction explicitly required the government to prove that "the Defendants knew what the wastes were . . . paint and paint solvent waste."

In the alternative, Sellers requested that the trial court instruct the jury that "the Defendant knew or reasonably should have known that the substance was waste and that the waste could be harmful to persons or the environment if . . . improperly disposed of." Although the district judge did not give his reason for rejecting this instruction, it is clear that this instruction is incorrect. There is no requirement that the defendant must know that the waste would be harmful "if improperly disposed of." Under Sellers's construction, arguably he would not be liable if he disposed of the harmful waste in what he considered to be proper containers. Because this alternative instruction suggested by Sellers is legally deficient, the district court was correct in rejecting it. . . .

Based on the foregoing, we affirm the conviction and sentence. . . .

CHAPTER

12

Offenses Against Public Order and Safety

Introduction

Without question, government has a fundamental obligation to protect the public order and safety, much as it has to protect public health and the environment. The criminal law is one way government performs this function—by criminalizing acts that threaten society's interests in order and safety. As with most basic criminal offenses, the crimes against public order and safety are rooted in the common law.

The common law recognized the right of the people to assemble peaceably for lawful purposes. Nevertheless, maintaining public order was given a high priority. To maintain order, the common law developed three misdemeanors: **unlawful assembly, rout,** and **riot.** If three or more persons met together with the intention of cooperating to disturb the public peace by doing an unlawful act, their gathering was considered an unlawful assembly. If they took steps to achieve their purpose, it was a rout, and if they actually executed their plans, they committed a riot.

Modern statutes have modified these common-law crimes somewhat. Today, the category of offenses known as **breaches of the peace** includes unlawful assembly, riot, **inciting a riot,** and **disorderly conduct,** as well as violations of **noise ordinances.** While these offenses are very important in carrying out the day-to-day peacekeeping function of the police, they do raise constitutional problems in certain instances. The First Amendment guarantees the rights of free expression and assembly. Of course, the exercise of these freedoms sometimes poses a threat to public order and safety. The line between what the Constitution protects and what the criminal law legitimately forbids can sometimes be difficult to perceive (see Chapter 3).

To discourage idleness, the common law also developed the offense of **vagrancy,** which was the crime of "going about without visible means of support." Historically, this offense allowed the police tremendous discretion in dealing with suspicious persons. Accordingly, it has been the subject of considerable controversy. Today, the offense of vagrancy has been largely supplanted by the modern offense of **loitering,** although it too is subject to criticism. Numerous vagrancy and loitering laws have been attacked as being excessively vague and therefore in violation of the constitutional requirement that criminal laws provide fair notice as to what specific conduct is prohibited.

Offenses against public order and safety also include **motor vehicle violations** and **weapons offenses,** which, while unknown to the common law, exist by virtue of modern legislation aimed at protecting the public safety. While there is little constitutional debate over traffic safety laws, weapons offenses are sometimes challenged under the Second Amendment to the Constitution, which protects the right to keep and bear arms. Today, there is a strident political debate taking place in this country on both the desirability and constitutionality of **gun control laws.**

Breaches of the Peace

In the United States, the responsibility for maintaining public order and peace rests primarily with state and local governments, although the federal government has a significant role as well. A variety of state statutes and local ordinances prohibit unlawful assemblies, riots, and disorderly conduct. Control of unlawful assemblies and riots is aimed at group behavior, whereas laws proscribing disorderly conduct are aimed at both group and individual behavior. By enforcing laws prohibiting disorderly conduct, state and local governments attempt to prevent such undesirable conduct as violent and tumultuous behavior, excessive noise, offensive language and gestures, actions impeding movement of persons on public sidewalks and roads, and disturbances of lawfully conducted meetings.

Unlawful Assembly and Riot

Most states have enacted statutes proscribing unlawful assemblies and riots. For example, the Indiana Code defines unlawful assembly as "an assembly of five or more persons whose common object is to commit an unlawful act, or a lawful act by unlawful means." West's Ann. Ind. Code § 35–45–1–1. It further defines tumultuous conduct as "conduct that results in, or is likely to result in, serious bodily injury to a person or substantial damage to property." West's Ann. Ind. Code § 35–45–1–1. Under the Indiana Code, a person who is a "member of an unlawful assembly who recklessly, knowingly, or intentionally engages in tumultuous conduct commits rioting." Under Indiana law, the offense is punishable as a misdemeanor unless committed while armed with a deadly weapon, in which case it becomes a felony. West's Ann. Ind. Code § 35–45–1–2.

Historically, federal statutes have made it a crime to riot. However, the controversy over the Vietnam War, racial unrest, poverty, and a host of other social ills during the 1960s became catalysts for riotous behavior beyond proportions previously experienced. To better cope with riots, Congress enacted the **Federal Anti-Riot Act** of 1968. The act applies to persons who travel in or use any facility of interstate and foreign commerce. It proscribes interstate travel and use of the mail, telegraph, telephone, radio, or television with intent to incite, encourage, participate in, or carry on a riot; or to aid or abet any person in inciting or participating in a riot or committing any act of violence in furtherance of a riot. 18 U.S.C.A. § 2101(a). The act comprehensively defines riot by stating that

> the term "riot" means a public disturbance involving (1) an act or acts of violence by one or more persons part of an assemblage of three or more persons, which act or acts shall constitute a clear and present danger of, or shall result in, damage or injury to the property of any other person or to the person of any other individual or (2) a threat or threats of the commission of an act or acts of violence by one or more persons part of an assemblage of three or more persons having, individually or collectively, the ability of immediate execution of such threat or threats, where the performance of the threatened act or acts of violence would constitute a clear and present danger of, or would result in, damage or injury to the property of any other person or to the person of any other individual. 18 U.S.C.A. § 2102(a).

It defines to "incite a riot" by explaining that

> the term "to incite a riot," or "to organize, promote, encourage, participate in, or carry on a riot," includes, but is not limited to, urging or instigating other persons to riot, but shall not be deemed to mean the mere oral or written (1) advocacy of ideas or (2) expression of belief, not involving advocacy of any act or acts of violence or assertion of the rightness of, or the right to commit, any such act or acts. 18 U.S.C.A. § 2102(b).

In 1972 the United States Court of Appeals for the Seventh Circuit held that the Anti-Riot Act is not unconstitutionally vague or overbroad in relation to the First Amendment. *United States v. Dellinger,* 472 F.2d 340 (7th Cir. 1972).

CASE-IN-POINT

Evidence Sustaining a Conviction for Inciting to Riot

A jury convicted Powell of inciting a riot. He appealed, challenging the sufficiency of the evidence. The jury heard evidence that after Anderson rejected Powell's request to have sex with him, he threatened to have his girlfriend, Johnson, beat her. As Anderson and her friends Lattimore and Faust walked down the street, Johnson cursed them, and at Powell's direction, Johnson jumped on Lattimore's back and began pulling her hair and punching her. When Lattimore's sister attempted to break up the fight, Powell insisted on keeping the fight going and shoved away everyone who tried to stop it. Before Faust returned with Lattimore's mother and uncle, who ended the fight, between twenty-five and sixty onlookers had gathered.

In affirming Powell's conviction, the Georgia Court of Appeals noted that the essential elements of inciting to riot are (1) engaging in conduct which urges, counsels, or advises others to riot; (2) with intent to riot; and (3) at a time and place and under circumstances which produce a clear and present danger of a riot. OCGA § 16–11–31(a). The court observed that Powell encouraged Johnson to confront Anderson, that after Johnson attacked Lattimore, Powell directed Johnson's moves and yelled "you ought to be beating this bitch" and "don't stop the fight, the bitch got too much mouth." Further, Powell shoved and bullied several people in the gathering crowd in order to prevent any interference with the fight.

Powell v. State, 462 S.E.2d 447 (Ga. App. 1995).

Disorderly Conduct

Closely related to statutes prohibiting unlawful assembly and riot are laws making disorderly conduct an offense. The Indiana Code concisely, yet comprehensively, proscribes disorderly conduct by providing that

> [a] person who recklessly, knowingly or intentionally: (1) engages in fighting or in tumultuous conduct; (2) makes unreasonable noise and continues to do so after being asked to stop; (3) disrupts a lawful assembly of persons; commits disorderly conduct. . . . West's Ann. Ind. Code § 35–45–1–3.

Statutes and ordinances similar to those in Indiana are found in virtually every state. There is no constitutional problem when such laws are applied to conduct that is violent or threatens to produce **imminent lawless action.** *Brandenburg v. Ohio,* 395 U.S. 444, 89 S.Ct. 1827, 23 L.Ed.2d 430 (1969). Nor is there any constitutional barrier against applying such statutes to the utterance of **fighting words.** *Chaplinsky v. New Hampshire,* 315 U.S. 568, 571, 62 S.Ct. 766, 769, 86 L.Ed. 1031, 1035 (1942). However, the Constitution "does not permit a State to make criminal the peaceful expression of unpopular views." *Edwards v. South Carolina,* 372 U.S. 229, 237, 83 S.Ct. 680, 684, 9 L.Ed.2d 697, 703 (1963). (For more discussion of these First Amendment concepts, see Chapter 3.)

In *Edwards v. South Carolina,* supra, the Supreme Court reviewed a set of convictions that stemmed from a civil rights protest. On the morning of March 2, 1961, a large group of black students congregated on the lawn of the statehouse in Columbia, South Carolina, to protest the state's segregation laws. Speeches were made; songs were sung. The students responded by clapping and stamping their feet. A large crowd of onlookers gathered nearby. Nobody among the crowd caused or threatened any trouble, and there was no obstruction of pedestrian or vehicular traffic. A contingent of thirty or more police officers was present to meet any foreseeable possibility of disorder. After refusing to obey a police order to disperse, many of the students were arrested and found guilty of breach of the peace. In reversing their convictions, the United States Supreme Court said the following:

> These petitioners were convicted of an offense as to be, in the words of the South Carolina Supreme Court, "not susceptible of exact definition." And they were convicted upon evidence which showed no more than that the opinions which they were peaceably expressing were sufficiently opposed to the views of the majority of the community to attract a crowd and necessitate police protection. . . . The Fourteenth Amendment does not permit a State to make criminal the peaceful expression of unpopular views. 372 U.S. at 237, 83 S.Ct. at 684, 9 L.Ed.2d at 703.

It is instructive to compare and contrast *Edwards* with a case in the 1970s in which the Supreme Court upheld a conviction for disorderly conduct arising from a confrontation between a police officer and a student protester. After conducting a political demonstration, several students got into their cars and formed an entourage. A police officer stopped one of the vehicles after noting that its license plate had expired. The other cars in the group also pulled over. One of the students approached the officer to find out what was wrong. After explaining the situation, the officer asked the student to leave. After refusing to do so, the student was arrested for violating Section 437.016(1)(f) of the Kentucky Revised Statutes, which provided that a person was guilty of disorderly conduct "if, with intent to cause public inconvenience, annoyance or alarm, or recklessly creating a risk thereof," he "congregates with other persons in a public place and refuses to comply with a lawful order of the police to disperse." A conviction for disorderly conduct was upheld by the Kentucky Court of Appeals. *Colten v. Commonwealth*, 467 S.W.2d 374 (Ky. 1971). In upholding the state court, the U.S. Supreme Court said this:

> As the Kentucky statute was construed by the state court, . . . a crime is committed only where there is no *bona fide* intention to exercise a constitutional right—in which event, by definition, the statute infringes no protected speech or conduct— or where the interest so clearly outweighs the collective interest sought to be asserted that the latter must be deemed to be insubstantial. . . . Individuals may not be convicted under the Kentucky statute merely for expressing unpopular or annoying ideas. The statute comes into operation only when the individual's interest in expression, judged in the light of all relevant factors, is "minuscule" compared to a particular public interest in preventing that expression or conduct at that time and place. *Colten v. Kentucky*, 407 U.S. 104, 111, 92 S.Ct. 1953, 1958, 32 L.Ed.2d 584, 590 (1972).

In *Cavazos v. State*, 455 N.E.2d 618 (Ind. App. 1983), an Indiana appellate court found that a defendant calling a police officer an "asshole" and continuing to debate with him about the arrest of her brother was insufficient to support her conviction for disorderly conduct. The court reasoned that the defendant's words to the police officer did not constitute fighting words or fall within any of the other unprotected classes of speech.

In 1999 a Georgia appellate court reversed a defendant's conviction for disorderly conduct. The court held that although the defendant's statement to a female medic that she had "nice tits" was crude and socially unacceptable, such words were not such as to incite a breach of the peace. *Lundgren v. State*, 518 So.2d 908 (Ga. App. 1999). But vulgar language, when combined with physical action, may constitute disorderly conduct. In 1999 the Supreme Judicial Court of Maine affirmed a

In *Commonwealth v. Young,* reprinted at the end of the chapter, the Superior Court of Pennsylvania upholds a defendant's conviction for disorderly conduct.

defendant's conviction for disorderly conduct where, in addition to the use of foul and vulgar language, the defendant, an emergency room patient, "head butted" a physician. *State v. McKenzie,* 605 A.2d 72 (Me. 1999).

Excessive Noise

Local governments often use disorderly conduct ordinances to control **excessive noise.** To sustain a conviction based on unreasonable noise, the prosecution must show that the speech at issue infringed on the peace and tranquility enjoyed by others. *Hooks v. State,* 660 N.E. 1076 (Ind. App. 1996). For example, the noise produced by a late-night party with a live band might be actionable under a breach of the peace ordinance, but only if the party is in fact disturbing the peace of the neighborhood. Courts are inclined to uphold the application of ordinances that proscribe making excessive noise in areas such as hospitals and nursing homes. Police officers responding to complaints about excessive noise usually first request that the offending party "turn it down." If this fails, the offender may be charged with a breach of the peace.

Vagrancy, Loitering, and Curfews

Elites in feudal England placed great emphasis on able-bodied serfs performing labor and not straying from their assigned tasks. This was motivated by both the need for laborers and the desire to prevent idle persons from becoming public charges. With the breakup of feudal estates, England found it necessary to prevent workers from moving from one area to another in search of improved working conditions. Thus, to regulate the economics of the populace, the common law developed the misdemeanor offense of vagrancy. The offense comprised three elements: (1) being without visible means of support, (2) being without employment, and (3) being able to work but refusing to do so. *Fenster v. Leary,* 229 N.E.2d 426 (N.Y. 1967). In sixteenth-century England, persons who loitered idly for three days were subject to punishment under the Enslavement Acts.

Eventually the emphasis shifted from merely punishing idleness toward the prevention of crime, as England enacted statutes defining vagrancy. The objective then became to protect the people and their property from persons considered potential criminals or simply regarded as undesirables. Thus, by the time the American colonists settled in their new environment, the concept of punishing vagrants had become firmly implanted, and the colonists found it to be a desirable way to prevent idleness and to outlaw conduct offensive to their social mores.

The American Approach to Vagrancy

During the 1800s, virtually all American states and most cities enacted statutes and ordinances punishing a wide variety of conduct as vagrancy. Statutory language was intentionally rather vague, presumably to allow police broad discretion to arrest persons they deemed undesirable to the community. Vagrancy laws not only proscribed such acts as disorderly conduct, begging, and loitering; they also criminalized the condition of being poor, idle, of bad reputation, or simply "wandering around without any lawful purpose." By 1865, Alabama's vagrancy statute included "runaway" and "stubborn servants." By making a person's status an offense, these laws ran counter to the historical concept that a crime consisted of the commission of an unlawful act or the failure to perform a required act. Frequently, vagrancy laws were directed against persons without the means to contest their validity or to challenge the application of such laws to them. Moreover, the United States Supreme Court had sanctioned them in 1837 by saying that

> [w]e think it [is] as competent and as necessary for a state to provide precautionary measures against the moral pestilence of paupers, vagabonds, and possibly convicts; as it is to guard against . . . physical pestilence. . . . *City of New York v. Miln,* 36 U.S. (11 Pet.) 102, 142, 9 L.Ed. 648, 664 (1837).

In the first half of the 1900s, arrests and convictions for vagrancy were common, as were appellate court decisions upholding convictions in a variety of circumstances. For example, in Minnesota a defendant's conviction was affirmed for wandering about the streets with no place of abode and without giving a good account of himself. *State v. Woods,* 163 N.W. 518 (Minn. 1917). In Virginia, an appellate court held that a defendant's conduct in consorting with gamblers and idlers constituted the offense of vagrancy. *Morgan v. Commonwealth,* 191 S.E. 791 (Va. 1937). Even a defendant's conduct as part of "a group of 4 or 5 suspicious men" at a saloon was, under the particular circumstances, held to be vagrancy. *State v. Carroll,* 30 A.2d 54 (N.J. 1943).

The wide range of vaguely proscribed conduct in vagrancy laws made them susceptible to arbitrary enforcement by law enforcement agencies. In their efforts to prevent crime and control "undesirables," these laws became somewhat of a catchall of the criminal justice system. Police commonly used them as a basis to arrest a suspect, who was then held pending investigation, or as a method of getting the suspect to confess. Vagrancy laws also furnished a convenient basis for police to justify a search incident to arrest as an exception to the warrant requirement of the Fourth Amendment.

By the 1950s, the vagrancy laws were enforced primarily against loafers, alcoholics, derelicts, and tramps when they left the environs of "skid row" and ventured into the more "respectable" neighborhoods, where residents found their presence offensive. The constitutionality of the vagrancy laws was frequently being challenged on grounds that they were vague, violated due process of law requirements, and exceeded the police power of the states. But such challenges were rejected by state and federal courts, which generally upheld the right of the legislature to define what constitutes being a vagrant. During the 1960s, however, a number of statutes defining a vagrant as a person "without visible means of support" or who "wanders around the streets at late hours" or who "fails to give account of himself" were declared unconstitutional.

The Death Knell of Vagrancy Laws

In 1972 the United States Supreme Court issued an opinion that had a profound effect on the enforcement of vagrancy laws in the United States. *Papachristou v. City of Jacksonville,* 405 U.S. 156, 92 S.Ct. 839, 31 L.Ed.2d 110 (1972).

In Jacksonville, Florida, eight defendants were convicted under a municipal ordinance that broadly defined vagrancy and levied criminal penalties on violators of as many as ninety days' imprisonment, a $500 fine, or both. The ordinance included language common to many of the statutes and ordinances extant at the time:

> Rogues and vagabonds, or dissolute persons who go about begging, common gamblers, persons who use juggling or unlawful games or plays, common drunkards, common night walkers, thieves, pilferers or pickpockets, traders in stolen property, lewd, wanton and lascivious persons, keepers of gambling places, common railers and brawlers, persons wandering or strolling around from place to place without

any lawful purpose or object, habitual loafers, disorderly persons, persons neglecting all lawful business and habitually spending their time by frequenting houses of ill fame, gaming houses, or places where alcoholic beverages are sold or served, persons able to work but habitually living upon the earnings of their wives or minor children shall be deemed vagrants. . . . Quoted in *Papachristou,* 405 U.S. at 158–159, n. 1, 92 S.Ct. at 840, 31 L.Ed.2d at 112.

Speaking for a unanimous Supreme Court, Justice William O. Douglas said that the Jacksonville ordinance was void for vagueness, both in the sense that it "fails to give a person of ordinary intelligence fair notice that his contemplated conduct is forbidden by the statute and because it encourages arbitrary and erratic arrests and convictions." 405 U.S. at 162, 92 S.Ct. at 843, 31 L.Ed.2d at 115.

Despite the Supreme Court's ruling in *Papachristou v. City of Jacksonville,* the effects of the vagrancy ordinances lingered on. In 1968 a Nevada police officer arrested Lloyd Powell under a Henderson, Nevada, vagrancy ordinance. In a search incident to the arrest, the officer discovered a .38-caliber revolver with six spent cartridges in the cylinder. Laboratory analysis determined that the weapon was used in a recent murder. Powell was convicted of second-degree murder, and although a federal court later declared the vagrancy ordinance unconstitutional, the use of the evidence against Powell, and his conviction for murder, were ultimately sustained. *Stone v. Powell,* 428 U.S. 465, 96 S.Ct 3037, 49 L.Ed.2d 1067 (1976).

State legislatures and local governments continued to enact ordinances in an attempt to control conduct they deemed objectionable; however, courts have invalidated such laws when they criminalize a person's status (for example, homelessness or intoxication) as opposed to proscribing a person's actions, frequently on the ground that such laws are vague and lead to arbitrary enforcement. One state supreme court took the view that a vagrancy statute that made it an offense to be a habitual drunkard violated the constitutional prohibition against cruel and unusual punishment for punishing a person's status. *State v. Pugh,* 369 So.2d 1308 (La. 1979).

Loitering

After the Supreme Court's decision in *Papachristou,* a new generation of laws making loitering a crime came on the scene. These new laws are narrower and often focus on preventing such crimes as prostitution and drug dealing. Courts scrutinize these ordinances carefully because they often prohibit or restrict constitutionally protected activities. Some have met the same fate as the traditional vagrancy ordinances.

One such ordinance enacted by Akron, Ohio, made it an offense to loiter "for the purpose of engaging in drug-related activity." The ordinance then listed eleven factors that may be considered in determining whether such purpose is manifested. The Ohio Supreme Court found the ordinance to be unconstitutionally vague under both the federal and state constitutions because it did not give persons of ordinary intelligence a reasonable opportunity to know what conduct was prohibited. Moreover, the court held that the enumerated factors to be considered—for example, looking like a drug user, being in an area known for unlawful drug use, and so on—could well be innocent and constitutionally protected conduct. Finally, the court pointed out that the ordinance was flawed because it delegated matters to enforcement authorities without providing necessary objective standards. *Akron v. Rowland,* 618 N.E.2d 138 (Ohio 1993).

In 1992 the Nevada Supreme Court held that the Nevada statute and Las Vegas Municipal Code provision criminalizing "loitering" on private property when the person has "no lawful business with owners or occupant thereof" lacked guidelines to avoid arbitrary and discriminatory enforcement and were unconstitutionally vague under the due process clauses of the federal and state constitutions. *State v. Richard,* 836 P.2d 622 (Nev. 1992).

Any ordinance that proscribes loitering without clearly defining the activities prohibited and without providing objective guidelines for enforcement is vulnerable to constitutional objections; however, courts have upheld loitering ordinances with a more narrow scope. For example, in 1989 the Oregon Supreme Court rejected a defendant's argument that the phrase "loiter in a manner and under circumstances manifesting the purpose of soliciting prostitution" did not meet the required constitutional standard of certainty. *City of Portland v. Levi,* 779 P.2d 192 (1989).

Police often use loitering ordinances and statutes to remove suspected drug dealers from the streets. At least one appellate court has approved this approach. See *Griffin v. State,* 479 S.E. 2d 21 (Ga. App. 1996), where the court held that the sale of drugs on the streets violated a state loitering statute.

CHICAGO'S GANG LOITERING ORDINANCE

In a major decision of the 1996–1997 term, the U.S. Supreme Court held unconstitutional the "Gang Congregation Ordinance" enacted by the Chicago City Council in 1992. The ordinance made it a criminal offense for gang members to loiter with one another in any public place "with no apparent purpose." It required police to order a group of people who were standing around "with no apparent purpose" to move along if an officer believed that at least one of them belonged to a street gang. Those who disregarded an order to disperse were subject to arrest. Some 45,000 people were arrested in the three years the ordinance was enforced before the Illinois Supreme Court struck down the ordinance as violating due process of law by giving the police too much discretion and impermissibly restricting personal liberty. *City of Chicago v. Morales,* 687 N.E.2d 53 (Ill. 1997).

On review, the Supreme Court agreed with the Illinois Supreme Court. Writing for a divided Court, Justice John Paul Stevens criticized the ordinance for telling people to move on without inquiring about their purpose for standing around. He wrote that the ordinance "affords too much discretion to the police and too little notice to citizens who wish to use the public streets." *City of Chicago v. Morales,* 527 U.S. 41, 119 S.Ct. 1849, 144 L.Ed.2d 67 (1999).

To withstand constitutional attack, it appears that any ordinance proscribing loitering must, at a minimum, focus on a person's conduct and not a person's status or association, give fair notice as to what is proscribed, and afford a person an opportunity to explain his or her presence before being ordered to disperse.

An excerpt from the Supreme Court's decision in City of Chicago v. Morales *appears at the end of the chapter.*

Curfews

In an attempt to combat juvenile crime and protect children by keeping them off the streets at night, most large cities and many counties have enacted **curfew ordinances.** While restrictions vary considerably, most curfew laws define juveniles as unmarried persons under age eighteen and prohibit them from being on public streets or in other public places from midnight to 6:00 A.M. unless accompanied by a parent or guardian or another adult approved by the juvenile's parent or guardian. Many curfew ordinances provide that parents and guardians violate the ordinance if they knowingly allow their child to commit a violation. Curfew laws often provide exceptions concerning work, school and civic events, travel, and emergencies.

Considerable litigation has ensued concerning the validity of curfews. Those who seek to sustain them argue that a juvenile curfew is a valid exercise of the government's police power. They liken the curfew regulations to requirements that minors are required to attend school and are prohibited from purchasing alcoholic beverages, and are subject to restrictions on operation of motor vehicles. Challengers contend that curfew regulations are vague and violate First Amendment rights of association, abridge Fourth Amendment rights to be free from unreasonable detention, deny juveniles the equal protection of the law, and interfere with parental rights.

In *City of Wadsworth v. Owens,* 536 N.E.2d 67 (Ohio 1987), a city ordinance prohibited anyone under age eighteen from being on the streets, sidewalks, or other public places during certain nighttime hours, unless accompanied by a parent or some other responsible adult having the parent's permission. The court found the ordinance unconstitutionally overbroad, pointing out that it contained no exceptions, thereby restricting a minor's church, school, and work activities. Courts in New Jersey, Ohio, Hawaii, and the state of Washington have also found curfew ordinances unconstitutional. On the other hand, in *Panora v. Simmons,* 445 N.W.2d 363 (Iowa 1989), the Iowa Supreme Court upheld an ordinance making it unlawful for any minor to be or remain upon any street or in any public place between 10:00 P.M. and 5:00 A.M. The ordinance provided exceptions for a minor accompanied by a parent or other adult custodian and for a minor traveling between home and places of employment, and to church, civic, or school functions.

More recent curfew ordinances that have been upheld have included an expanded number of exceptions. For example, in May 1997, Pinellas Park, Florida, adopted a curfew ordinance along the lines described above. In addition to permitting a juvenile to be accompanied by a parent or adult when authorized by a custodial parent, the ordinance includes numerous exceptions such as when a juvenile is exercising First Amendment rights to attend religious, political, and governmental meetings or events sponsored by civic and governmental groups, during or going to and from lawful employment and school-sponsored or theme-park events, when on the sidewalk at home or at a neighbor's home with the neighbor's permission, or when involved in interstate travel. The trial court, applying a strict scrutiny test (see Chapter 3), invalidated the ordinance on the basis that it violates a juvenile's parents' fundamental right to raise their children without governmental intrusion. On appeal, the court applied a "heightened scrutiny" test and reversed the trial court, noting that the ordinance includes adequate exceptions to limit the scope of the curfew. *State v. T.M.,* 761 So.2d 1140 (Fla. App. 2000). A few months later, the same appellate court upheld the juvenile curfew ordinance of Tampa, Florida, pointing out that the ordinance substantially relates to important governmental interests, provides adequate exceptions that limit the scope of the curfew, and focuses enforcement on the prevention of juvenile crime and victimization. *J.P. v. State,* 775 So.2d 324 (Fla. App. 2000). Courts in Texas, Virginia, and Washington, D.C., have also upheld curfew ordinances.

Those who oppose curfews recognize the authority of parents to impose the restrictions, but they claim the government should not intrude into the parental sphere. They also point to studies showing no correlation between arrests for curfew violations (which are quite common) and the incidence of juvenile crime. The American Civil Liberties Union has been very active in attacking curfew laws in the courts. In a September 1999 press release, ACLU of New Jersey Legal Director Lenora Lapidus observed that "police already have the ability to arrest juvenile criminals; the curfew adds nothing more than the discretion to arrest the innocent as well." In her view, "The proper response to juvenile crime is to arrest the criminals, not to place thousands of law-abiding young people under house arrest."

Despite the controversial nature of juvenile curfews, law enforcement officials and local governing bodies overwhelmingly support these measures. They are likely to remain on the scene as long as juvenile crime continues to plague our nation's cities, although to be upheld the ordinances must recognize reasonable exceptions.

Motor Vehicle Violations

States, and often municipalities, have adopted laws defining a wide range of motor vehicle violations. These are generally strict liability offenses; therefore, there is generally no requirement to prove criminal intent to find a defendant guilty of a traffic violation (see Chapter 4). Among other offenses, these laws proscribe speeding; failing to yield the right-of-way; failing to observe traffic officers, signs, and signals; and driving without required equipment. By the 1980s, many states adopted a number of "model" laws, providing legal uniformity to the **rules of the road.** Such uniformity is highly desirable given the mobility of today's populace and the volume of traffic on the nation's highways. People driving along the nation's highways, often passing through several states on a single trip, would be ill served by variance in state traffic laws.

When a driver is stopped for a traffic violation, police may observe conduct or evidence that gives rise to probable cause to conduct a search or make an arrest. Frequently drugs, alcohol, and weapons are discovered by police officers stopping automobiles for routine traffic violations. (We discuss these aspects further in Chapters 15 and 16.)

Decriminalization of Traffic Offenses

Historically, traffic offenders were treated like persons committing other misdemeanors; they were arrested and required to post bond to avoid confinement pending the adjudication of their cases. Since the 1960s, most states and municipalities have decriminalized minor traffic offenses, which means that these offenses are now considered **civil infractions** rather than misdemeanors. For example, consider the following excerpt from the Maine Revised Statutes, Title 29–A:

§ 103. Traffic infraction

1. Traffic infraction. A traffic infraction is not a crime. The penalty for a traffic infraction may not be deemed for any purpose a penal or criminal punishment.

2. Jury trial. There is no right to trial by jury for a traffic infraction.

3. Exclusive penalty. The exclusive penalty for a traffic infraction is a fine of not less than $25 nor more than $500, unless specifically authorized, or suspension of a license, or both.

In Maine and most other states, traffic violators are now commonly issued citations or "tickets" instead of being subject to arrest. Offenders may avoid a court appearance by simply paying a fine according to a predetermined schedule of fines. Of course, offenders may elect to contest the charge by appearing in the appropriate court, often a municipal court or **traffic court.** In addition to fines, most states assess "points" against a driver for traffic violations, and an accumulation of points can lead to suspension or revocation of a driver's license.

The **decriminalization of routine traffic offenses** has proved to be an expeditious and efficient means of maintaining discipline and order on the public thoroughfares. Under most traffic codes, however, the more serious motor vehicle offenses,

In *State v. Young* (1988), excerpted at the end of the chapter, the Court of Appeals of Ohio reviews a man's conviction for failing to yield to oncoming traffic.

such as driving while intoxicated, eluding a police officer, and reckless driving, are still defined as misdemeanors, and offenders are subject to arrest.

Weapons Offenses

The Second Amendment to the United States Constitution provides that "a well regulated Militia, being necessary to the security of a free state, the right of the people to keep and bear Arms, shall not be infringed." Nevertheless, there are numerous state and federal statutory prohibitions against the manufacture, sale, possession, and use of firearms and other weapons. For example, federal law prohibits the sale, possession, and use of machine guns and other automatic weapons. The Supreme Court has said that federal gun control laws do not violate the Second Amendment because the amendment only protects the keeping and bearing of arms in the context of a **well-regulated militia.** See *United States v. Miller*, 307 U.S. 174, 59 S.Ct. 816, 83 L.Ed. 1206 (1939); *Lewis v. United States*, 445 U.S. 55, 100 S.Ct. 915, 63 L.Ed.2d 198 (1980).

The Illinois weapons statute, S.H.A. 720 ILCS 5/24, is fairly typical of state laws proscribing the unlawful use of weapons. It prohibits the manufacture, sale, and possession of various types of weapons that have no value for hunting, archery, or marksmanship, or for the protection of a person's home from intruders. Explosives, gaseous devices, machine guns, and gun silencers are among the particular weapons banned. The law also prohibits carrying a wide variety of weapons, including "stun guns," "dangerous knives," and "billy clubs," with the intent of unlawfully using the weapon against another.

The Illinois statute also prohibits the manufacture, sale, transfer, possession, or discharge of metal-piercing bullets or bullets represented to be metal-piercing. S.H.A. 720 ILCS 5/24–2.1, 24–2.2, 24–3.2. In addition, the law proscribes the sale or delivery of firearms on any school premises, S.H.A. 720 ILCS 5/24–3.3, carrying concealed weapons, S.H.A. 720 ILCS 5/24–1, or carrying weapons while a person's face is masked or hooded to conceal the person's identity, S.H.A. 720 ILCS 5/24–1. Like most states, Illinois exempts police officers and various other public officials, as well as licensed private investigators and security personnel, from the statutory prohibitions regarding possession and use of firearms. S.H.A. 720 ILCS 5/24.

Concealed Weapons

States commonly enact statutes making it unlawful to carry a **concealed weapon.** Most define a concealed weapon as one being carried on or about a person in such a manner as to conceal it from the ordinary sight of another person. It follows that a defendant was properly convicted of carrying a concealed weapon in her purse when it was disclosed by a metal detector at a courthouse. *Schaaf v. Commonwealth*, 258 S.E.2d 574 (Va. 1979). But more often, litigation involves less than absolute concealment. For example, a Georgia appellate court ruled that even though the handle of a pistol tucked in a defendant's pants was visible to some extent through a slit in his shirt, the weapon was concealed. *Marshall v. State*, 200 S.E.2d 902 (Ga. App. 1973). Similarly, in *People v. Charron*, 220 N.W.2d 216 (Mich. App. 1974), a Michigan appellate court held that a knife slightly protruding from a defendant's rear pocket was a concealed weapon.

CASE-IN-POINT

Unlawful Possession of a Firearm

South Carolina law provides that it is unlawful for any person to carry a pistol about his or her person, regardless of whether the pistol is concealed. S.C. Code § 16–23–20. The statute provides twelve exceptions to the prohibition. Barry Clarke was convicted of violating the statute after he was stopped for a traffic violation and the police officer noticed a gun in a holster next to the driver's seat. On appeal, Clarke argued that the burden of proof should have been on the prosecution to show that he did not qualify under any of the twelve exceptions to the prohibition. The South Carolina Supreme Court disagreed, saying that "[t]he general rule, when dealing with statutory crimes to which there are exceptions, is that the defendant 'has the burden of excusing or justifying his act; and hence the burden may be on him to bring himself within an exception in the statute or to prove the issuance of a license or permit.'"

State v. Clarke, 396 S.E. 2d 827 (S.C. 1990).

Many concealed-weapons statutes also make it an offense to carry a concealed weapon in a vehicle, and in numerous cases courts have been asked to rule on the application of these laws. For example, a defendant reached into his automobile and withdrew a revolver from a shelf behind the driver's seat. In affirming the defendant's conviction, the Wisconsin Supreme Court said that "[i]f the weapon is hidden from ordinary observation, it is concealed." The court noted that "absolute invisibility to other persons" was not "indispensable to concealment." The question was this: "Was [the weapon] carried so as not to be discernible by ordinary observation?" *Mularkey v. State,* 230 N.W. 76, 77 (Wis. 1930). More recently, an Illinois appellate court observed that "[i]t is well settled . . . that a weapon is 'concealed' . . . even though there is some notice of its presence to an alert police officer who can see part of the gun when he approaches the vehicle." *People v. Williams,* 350 N.E. 2d 81, 83 (Ill. App. 1976).

Federal Gun Control Laws

The **Federal Gun Control Act** of 1968, 18 U.S.C.A. § 921 et seq., established a fairly comprehensive regime governing the distribution of firearms. The statute prohibits firearms dealers from transferring handguns to persons who are under twenty-one, nonresidents of the dealer's state, or those who are otherwise prohibited by state or local laws from purchasing or possessing firearms. 18 U.S.C.A. § 922(b). The law also forbids possession of a firearm by, and transfer of a firearm to, persons in several categories, including convicted felons, users of controlled substances, persons adjudicated as incompetent or committed to mental institutions, illegal aliens, persons dishonorably discharged from the military, persons who have renounced their citizenship, and fugitives from justice. 18 U.S.C.A. §§ 922(d) and (g).

In the early 1990s, Congress enacted three important gun control statutes. The **Gun-Free School Zones Act** of 1990, 18 U.S.C.A. § 922, made it unlawful for any individual knowingly to possess a firearm in a school zone, regardless of whether the school is in session. The 1993 **Brady Bill,** also codified at 18 U.S.C.A. § 922, requires a five-working-day waiting period for the purchase of a handgun. And the 1994 Crime Bill banned the manufacture, transfer, or possession of firearms classified as "assault weapons." 18 U.S.C.A. § 922(v)(1).

The Supreme Court's *Lopez* decision is excerpted at the end of the chapter.

In *United States v. Evans*, reprinted at the end of the chapter, the United States Court of Appeals for the Ninth Circuit considers the constitutionality of the federal statute that prohibits possession of unregistered machine guns. Students should consider whether this decision can be reconciled with the Supreme Court's opinion in *United States v. Lopez*.

In 1995 the U.S. Supreme Court struck down the Gun-Free School Zones Act of 1990 and reversed a student's conviction for carrying a handgun to school. The Court found that the law, in its full reach, was beyond the power of Congress to regulate interstate commerce. *United States v. Lopez,* 514 U.S. 549, 115 S.Ct. 1624, 131 L.Ed.2d 626 (1995).

In 1997 the Court dealt another blow to federal gun control efforts when it invalidated a section of the Brady Bill requiring local law enforcement officers to conduct background checks of prospective gun purchasers. *Printz v. United States,* 521 U.S. 98, 117 S.Ct. 2365, 138 L.Ed.2d 914 (1997). Despite the Supreme Court's decisions in *Lopez* and *Printz,* the extensive regime of federal gun control legislation remains essentially intact.

The New York Gun Safety Law of 2000

After several catastrophic incidents involving firearms, state legislatures have begun to focus on gun safety legislation. Perhaps none has been more significant than the New York statute that Governor George Pataki signed into law in August 2000. The new law requires criminal background checks on persons who buy guns at gun shows. It also mandates child safety trigger locks, raises the legal age to acquire a permit to buy a handgun from eighteen to twenty-one, creates criminal penalties for attempting to illegally buy guns or failing to report a lost or stolen gun, and establishes a statewide ban on assault weapons. (1999 A.B. 11535 [SN]).

The New York law comes on the heels of several other state legislative enactments. Maryland's Gun Safety Act of 2000 requires built-in safety locks on all new handguns sold after 2003. MD Code Art.27, Sec.442C. Rhode Island and New Jersey have also been active in enacting gun safety legislation.

....

Conclusion

Offenses against public order and safety present a picture of the dynamic development of the common law in a constitutional democracy. The need to maintain order, protect the public safety, and prevent crime are high-priority items for any organized society. Yet the United States Constitution mandates that government maintain a delicate balance between these interests and the rights of citizens. Of particular relevance to offenses against public order are the protections of the First Amendment.

In studying offenses against public order and safety, indeed the criminal law generally, we should realize that the law must be viewed from a sociological, political, and philosophical perspective and not merely as a set of objective rules of conduct. The offenses against public order have been shaped to a great extent by social change and political events. They have also been sculpted by the values of freedom of speech and assembly that are held within the broader legal and political culture.

....

Key Terms

unlawful assembly	breaches of the peace
rout	inciting a riot
riot	disorderly conduct

noise ordinances
vagrancy
loitering
motor vehicle violations
weapons offenses
gun control laws
Federal Anti-Riot Act
imminent lawless action
fighting words
excessive noise
curfew ordinances

rules of the road
civil infractions
traffic court
decriminalization of routine traffic
   offenses
well-regulated militia
concealed weapon
Federal Gun Control Act
Gun-Free School Zones Act
Brady Bill

Web-Based Research Activity

1. Go to the web. Locate your state's criminal statutes.
2. Examine your state's gun control laws. In your judgment, are these laws too permissive or too restrictive?
3. Are any of these statutes susceptible to challenge under your state constitution?
4. If you were in the state legislature, what changes would you propose to your state's weapons laws?

Questions for Thought and Discussion

1. Why has it been necessary for American courts to interpret laws proscribing breach of peace and vagrancy more strictly than did the English common-law courts?

2. How does the Federal Anti-Riot Act seek to prevent the definition of "to incite a riot" from being applied in such a way that it violates First Amendment guarantees of freedom of expression?

3. Is an ordinance that defines "disturbing the peace" simply as "tumultuous or offensive conduct" sufficiently precise to meet the constitutional standard of giving a person of ordinary intelligence fair notice of what conduct is forbidden?

4. Why did the English common-law concept of making vagrancy a crime take root in America? What purposes did it serve in the early history of the United States?

5. How did the Jacksonville, Florida, vagrancy ordinance invalidated by the Supreme Court in the *Papachristou* case offend the Constitution of the United States? Have the reforms in vagrancy laws at the state and local levels sufficiently removed the threat of criminalizing a person's status? Are they now written with the precision necessary to protect citizens from arbitrary enforcement of the law?

6. Based on the ruling of the Supreme Court in *City of Chicago v. Morales*, what protections to the individual do you think must be included in an ordinance proscribing loitering?

7. Why are most traffic violations strict liability offenses?

8. Have traffic offenses been decriminalized in your state? To what extent? What procedures are available to contest a traffic ticket?

9. Why have the courts refused to interpret the Second Amendment's protection of the "right to keep and bear arms" to prohibit gun control legislation?

10. On what bases other than the Second Amendment can one make constitutional attacks on federal gun control laws?

Problems for Discussion and Solution

1. Consider the following hypothetical case: Members of the American Nazi Party announced a demonstration to be held in Pleasant Ridge, a predominantly Jewish suburb of Metropolis. The Pleasant Ridge City Council quickly adopted an ordinance requiring groups planning demonstrations to obtain a permit from the police department. Under the ordinance, to hold a demonstration without a permit was a misdemeanor, punishable by a $1,000 fine and 60 days in jail. The Nazis applied for a permit and were denied on the grounds that their presence in Pleasant Ridge constituted a "clear and present danger to the public order." The Nazis held their demonstration anyway. Approximately one hundred demonstrators congregated on the city square. Many were dressed in Nazi uniforms, others carried banners emblazoned with swastikas, and others held signs on which were printed anti-Semitic slogans. Pleasant Ridge police arrived at the scene and asked the demonstrators to disperse. When they refused, police arrested demonstrators; others ran to avoid arrest. The leader of the Nazi group, Asa Houle, was convicted of a number of offenses, including violation of the new ordinance. On appeal, Houle is challenging the constitutionality of the ordinance. What do you think the court's ruling should be? Explain your reasoning.

2. The city of Dystopia experienced difficulties with groups of rowdy individuals congregating on downtown sidewalks and harassing passersby. When the local police were unable to control the situation by enforcing the disorderly conduct statute, the city council enacted the following ordinance:

> Sec. 1. It shall be unlawful for three or more persons to assemble on any public sidewalk or walkway within the city while conducting themselves in a manner that is annoying or bothersome to surrounding persons.

> Sec. 2. Anyone found guilty of violating this ordinance shall be punished as provided in the city charter.

After the ordinance went into effect, three college students congregated on a public sidewalk and made loud, obnoxious remarks to passersby. The police arrested the students and charged them under the ordinance. The students admit that they were rowdy but argue that the ordinance unduly restricts their First Amendment rights. What constitutional arguments could they, or their counsel, present to a court in an effort to reverse their conviction? Do you think they would prevail?

Commonwealth v. Young

Superior Court of Pennsylvania, 1988.
370 Pa. Super. 42, 535 A.2d 1141.

[This decision examines the offense of disorderly conduct.]

HESTER, Judge.

On September 24, 1986, appellant was found guilty of the summary offense of disorderly conduct by a district justice. On appeal to the Court of Common Pleas of Erie County, he was again found guilty of the same offense following a *de novo* hearing held on December 4, 1986. This appeal followed the January 8, 1987, judgment of sentence of thirty days imprisonment, a fine, and costs. We affirm.

The evidence introduced at trial establishes the following. On August 28, 1986, at approximately 2:45 A.M., appellant and Quincy Barnes were on the campus at Behrend College. They went to Perry Hall, a co-ed dormitory. The women's section of the dormitory consists of two floors on the right side of the building. The two sides are separated by a lobby. To enter the right side, which is locked, a nonresident must be accompanied by a resident with a key. The first-floor women's restroom, located in the middle of the hall, serves approximately fifty dormitory residents and has six stalls containing toilets, six shower stalls, and sinks.

An unidentified resident admitted appellant and Barnes into the first floor women's section, and accompanied them to the room of a dormitory resident the two men knew. They visited briefly with that resident, and on their way out of the dormitory, the two men walked into the women's restroom. Appellant walked over to the stall, which did not lock, opened the door and said: "Hey baby, what you doing." . . . The woman screamed, pulled up her pants and chased the men out of the dormitory. She testified that she was extremely frightened by the incident as she was not sure of the men's intentions when they opened the stall door.

In his defense, appellant testified that while he had gone to Perry Hall and visited with the resident he knew, he did not enter the restroom.

He argues that the evidence was insufficient to support his conviction for disorderly conduct. The test we apply in this situation is as follows:

In testing the sufficiency of the evidence, we must view the evidence in a light most favorable to the Commonwealth as the verdict winner and draw all reasonable inferences upon which the fact finder could have properly based its verdict. . . . A determination must be made as to whether there exists sufficient evidence to enable the trier of fact to find, beyond a reasonable doubt, every element of the crime for which the appellant has been convicted. . . .

Disorderly conduct is defined in relevant part as follows:

§ 5503. Disorderly Conduct

(a) Offense defined.—A person is guilty of disorderly conduct if, with intent to cause public inconvenience, annoyance or alarm, or recklessly creating a risk thereof, he: . . . creates a hazardous or physically offensive condition by any act which serves no legitimate purpose of the actor. . . .

(c) Definition.—As used in this section the word "public" means affecting or likely to affect persons in a place to which the public or a substantial group has access; among the places included are highways, transport facilities, schools, prisons, apartment houses, places of business or amusement, any neighborhood, or any premises which are open to the public.

We reject appellant's argument that since his conduct affected only a single individual, he did not have the *mens rea* to cause "public" inconvenience, annoyance or alarm as defined by the statute. The statute specifically states that "recklessly creating a risk" of public annoyance or alarm is sufficient. The evidence viewed in the light most favorable to the Commonwealth establishes that appellant deliberately entered a women's public restroom without justification.

Under the statutory definition, the restroom was a public place. The term includes a place to which the public or a "substantial group" has access. . . . The restroom serves the fifty women who reside in the dormitory. Moreover, any female visitor can freely gain access to the area. Thus, the restroom is accessible to a substantial group. The size of the restroom supports this conclusion: It has six toilet stalls and six shower stalls, which is larger than public restrooms in most department stores and restaurants. . . .

When appellant entered the public restroom, he recklessly created a risk of public annoyance or alarm. The fortuitous fact that only one individual was in the area does not vitiate the risk he created. Any number of women, in various states of undress, could have been using the showers, sinks and toilets in the area.

We have held that one who exhibits disorderly behavior in a public place is guilty of disorderly conduct even if that behavior is directed at a single individual. . . .

Appellant did not know the victim and was not searching for her. In this context, she was a member of the general public, and appellant deliberately entered the women's restroom solely to find anyone in her position or in a similarly embarrassing situation. He thereby created a risk of public annoyance or alarm, even if only one individual was alarmed and annoyed.

Further, the evidence establishes that appellant's conduct created a physically offensive condition to the victim. She was performing a private bodily function. She feared that appellant and his companion were going to assault her. Any reasonable woman in her situation would have been offended by appellant's actions. . . .

In *Commonwealth v. Greene*, 410 Pa. 111, 115–16, 189 A.2d 141, 144 (1963) which is still authoritative on this subject, Justice Musmanno . . . emphasized that the touchstone of disorderly conduct is an activity that does not form "an integral part of the movement of a civilized community." . . . Appellant's behavior fits those descriptions.

. . . We therefore affirm the judgment of sentence.

BECK, J., files a dissenting opinion. . . .

● ● ● ● ● ● ● ● ● ● ● ● ● ●

City of Chicago v. Morales

Supreme Court of the United States, 1999.
527 U.S. 41, 119 S.Ct. 1849, 144 L.Ed.2d 67.

[Chicago's Gangland Congregation Ordinance prohibited criminal "street gang members" from loitering in public places. The Illinois Supreme Court held that the ordinance violated due process of law in that it was impermissibly vague and was an arbitrary restriction on personal liberties. The city of Chicago sought review, and the U.S. Supreme Court affirmed.]

JUSTICE STEVENS announced the judgment of the Court. . . .

. . . The ordinance creates a criminal offense punishable by a fine of up to $500, imprisonment for not more than six months, and a requirement to perform up to 120 hours of community service. Commission of the offense involves four predicates. First, the police officer must reasonably believe that at least one of the two or more persons present in a "public place" is a "criminal street gang membe[r]." Second, the persons must be "loitering," which the ordinance defines as "remain[ing] in any one place with no apparent purpose." Third, the officer must then order

"all" of the persons to disperse and remove themselves "from the area." Fourth, a person must disobey the officer's order. If any person, whether a gang member or not, disobeys the officer's order, that person is guilty of violating the ordinance. . . .

The basic factual predicate for the city's ordinance is not in dispute. As the city argues in its brief, "the very presence of a large collection of obviously brazen, insistent, and lawless gang members and hangers-on on the public ways intimidates residents, who become afraid even to leave their homes and go about their business. That, in turn, imperils community residents' sense of safety and security, detracts from property values, and can ultimately destabilize entire neighborhoods." The findings in the ordinance explain that it was motivated by these concerns. We have no doubt that a law that directly prohibited such intimidating conduct would be constitutional, but this ordinance broadly covers a significant amount of additional activity. Uncertainty about the scope of that additional coverage provides the basis for respondents' claim that the ordinance is too vague. . . .

Vagueness may invalidate a criminal law for either of two independent reasons. First, it may fail to provide the kind of notice that will enable ordinary people to understand what conduct it prohibits; second, it may authorize and even encourage arbitrary and discriminatory enforcement. . . .

"It is established that a law fails to meet the requirements of the Due Process Clause if it is so vague and standardless that it leaves the public uncertain as to the conduct it prohibits. . . ." The Illinois Supreme Court recognized that the term "loiter" may have a common and accepted meaning, . . . but the definition of that term in this ordinance—"to remain in any one place with no apparent purpose"—does not. It is difficult to imagine how any citizen of the city of Chicago standing in a public place with a group of people would know if he or she had an "apparent purpose." If she were talking to another person, would she have an apparent purpose? If she were frequently checking her watch and looking expectantly down the street, would she have an apparent purpose?

Since the city cannot conceivably have meant to criminalize each instance a citizen stands in public with a gang member, the vagueness that dooms this ordinance is not the product of uncertainty about the normal meaning of "loitering," but rather about what loitering is covered by the ordinance and what is not. The Illinois Supreme Court emphasized the law's failure to distinguish between innocent conduct and conduct threatening harm. Its decision followed the precedent set by a number of state courts that have upheld ordinances that criminalize loitering combined with some other overt act or evidence of criminal intent. However, state courts have uniformly invalidated laws that do not join the term "loitering" with a second specific element of the crime.

The city's principal response to this concern about adequate notice is that loiterers are not subject to sanction until after they have failed to comply with an officer's order to disperse. . . . We find this response unpersuasive for at least two reasons.

First, the purpose of the fair notice requirement is to enable the ordinary citizen to conform his or her conduct to the law. "No one may be required at peril of life, liberty or property to speculate as to the meaning of penal statutes." . . . Although it is true that a loiterer is not subject to criminal sanctions un-

less he or she disobeys a dispersal order, the loitering is the conduct that the ordinance is designed to prohibit. If the loitering is in fact harmless and innocent, the dispersal order itself is an unjustified impairment of liberty. . . . Because an officer may issue an order only after prohibited conduct has already occurred, it cannot provide the kind of advance notice that will protect the putative loiterer from being ordered to disperse. Such an order cannot retroactively give adequate warning of the boundary between the permissible and the impermissible applications of the law.

Second, the terms of the dispersal order compound the inadequacy of the notice afforded by the ordinance. It provides that the officer "shall order all such persons to disperse and remove themselves from the area." . . . This vague phrasing raises a host of questions. After such an order issues, how long must the loiterers remain apart? How far must they move? If each loiterer walks around the block and they meet again at the same location, are they subject to arrest or merely to being ordered to disperse again? As we do here, we have found vagueness in a criminal statute exacerbated by the use of the standards of "neighborhood" and "locality." . . .

Lack of clarity in the description of the loiterer's duty to obey a dispersal order might not render the ordinance unconstitutionally vague if the definition of the forbidden conduct were clear, but it does buttress our conclusion that the entire ordinance fails to give the ordinary citizen adequate notice of what is forbidden and what is permitted. The Constitution does not permit a legislature to "set a net large enough to catch all possible offenders, and leave it to the courts to step inside and say who could be rightfully detained, and who should be set at large." . . . This ordinance is therefore vague "not in the sense that it requires a person to conform his conduct to an imprecise but comprehensible normative standard, but rather in the sense that no standard of conduct is specified at all." . . .

The broad sweep of the ordinance also violates "the requirement that a legislature establish minimal guidelines to govern law enforcement." . . . There are no such guidelines in the ordinance. In any public place in the city of Chicago, persons who stand or sit in the company of a gang member may be ordered to disperse unless their purpose is apparent. The mandatory language in the enactment directs the police to issue an order without first making any inquiry about their possible purposes. It matters not whether the reason that a gang member and his father, for example, might loiter near Wrigley Field is to rob an unsuspecting fan or just to get a glimpse of Sammy Sosa leaving the ballpark; in either event, if their purpose is not apparent to a nearby police officer, she may—indeed, she "shall"—order them to disperse.

Recognizing that the ordinance does reach a substantial amount of innocent conduct, we turn, then, to its language to determine if it "necessarily entrusts lawmaking to the moment-to-moment judgment of the policeman on his beat." . . . As we discussed in the context of fair notice, . . . the principal source of the vast discretion conferred on the police in this case is the definition of loitering as "to remain in any one place with no apparent purpose."

As the Illinois Supreme Court interprets that definition, it "provides absolute discretion to police officers to determine what activities constitute loitering." . . . We have no authority to construe the language of a state statute more narrowly than the construction given by that State's highest court. "The power to determine the meaning of a statute carries with it the power to prescribe its extent and limitations as well as the method by which they shall be determined." . . .

Nevertheless, the city disputes the Illinois Supreme Court's interpretation, arguing that the text of the ordinance limits the officer's discretion in three ways. First, it does not permit the officer to issue a dispersal order to anyone who is moving along or who has an apparent purpose. Second, it does not permit an arrest if individuals obey a dispersal order. Third, no order can issue unless the officer reasonably believes that one of the loiterers is a member of a criminal street gang.

Even putting to one side our duty to defer to a state court's construction of the scope of a local enactment, we find each of these limitations insufficient. That the ordinance does not apply to people who are moving—that is, to activity that would not constitute loitering under any possible definition of the term—does not even address the question of how much discretion the police enjoy in deciding which stationary persons to disperse under the ordinance. Similarly, that the ordinance does not permit an arrest until after a dispersal order has been disobeyed does not provide any guidance to the officer deciding whether such an order should issue. The "no apparent purpose" standard for making that decision is

inherently subjective because its application depends on whether some purpose is "apparent" to the officer on the scene.

Presumably an officer would have discretion to treat some purposes—perhaps a purpose to engage in idle conversation or simply to enjoy a cool breeze on a warm evening—as too frivolous to be apparent if he suspected a different ulterior motive. Moreover, an officer conscious of the city council's reasons for enacting the ordinance might well ignore its text and issue a dispersal order, even though an illicit purpose is actually apparent.

It is true, as the city argues, that the requirement that the officer reasonably believe that a group of loiterers contains a gang member does place a limit on the authority to order dispersal. That limitation would no doubt be sufficient if the ordinance only applied to loitering that had an apparently harmful purpose or effect, or possibly if it only applied to loitering by persons reasonably believed to be criminal gang members. But this ordinance, for reasons that are not explained in the findings of the city council, requires no harmful purpose and applies to non-gang members as well as suspected gang members. It applies to everyone in the city who may remain in one place with one suspected gang member as long as their purpose is not apparent to an officer observing them. Friends, relatives, teachers, counselors, or even total strangers might unwittingly engage in forbidden loitering if they happen to engage in idle conversation with a gang member.

Ironically, the definition of loitering in the Chicago ordinance not only extends its scope to encompass harmless conduct, but also has the perverse consequence of excluding from its coverage much of the intimidating conduct that motivated its enactment. As the city council's findings demonstrate, the most harmful gang loitering is motivated either by an apparent purpose to publicize the gang's dominance of certain territory, thereby intimidating nonmembers, or by an equally apparent purpose to conceal ongoing commerce in illegal drugs. As the Illinois Supreme Court has not placed any limiting construction on the language in the ordinance, we must assume that the ordinance means what it says and that it has no application to loiterers whose purpose is apparent. The relative importance of its application to harmless loitering is magnified by its inapplicability to loitering that has an obviously threatening or illicit purpose. . . .

In our judgment, the Illinois Supreme Court correctly concluded that the ordinance does not provide sufficiently specific limits on the enforcement discretion of the police "to meet constitutional standards for definiteness and clarity." We recognize the serious and difficult problems testified to by the citizens of Chicago that led to the enactment of this ordinance. "We are mindful that the preservation of liberty depends in part on the maintenance of social order." However, in this instance the city has enacted an ordinance that affords too much discretion to the police and too little notice to citizens who wish to use the public streets.

Accordingly, the judgment of the Supreme Court of Illinois is Affirmed.

JUSTICE O'CONNOR, with whom JUSTICE BREYER joins, concurring in part and concurring in the judgment. . . .

JUSTICE KENNEDY, concurring in part and concurring in the judgment. . . .

JUSTICE BREYER, concurring in part and concurring in the judgment. . . .

JUSTICE SCALIA, dissenting. . . .

JUSTICE THOMAS, with whom THE CHIEF JUSTICE and JUSTICE SCALIA join, dissenting.

The duly elected members of the Chicago City Council enacted the ordinance at issue as part of a larger effort to prevent gangs from establishing dominion over the public streets. By invalidating Chicago's ordinance, I fear that the Court has unnecessarily sentenced law-abiding citizens to lives of terror and misery. The ordinance is not vague. "[A]ny fool would know that a particular category of conduct would be within [its] reach." . . .

The human costs exacted by criminal street gangs are inestimable. In many of our Nation's cities, gangs have "[v]irtually overtak[en] certain neighborhoods, contributing to the economic and social decline of these areas and causing fear and lifestyle changes among law-abiding residents." . . . Gangs fill the daily lives of many of our poorest and most vulnerable citizens with a terror that the Court does not give sufficient consideration, often relegating them to the status of prisoners in their own homes. . . .

In order to perform their peace-keeping responsibilities satisfactorily, the police inevitably must exercise discretion. Indeed, by empowering them to act as peace officers, the law assumes that the police will exercise that discretion responsibly and with sound judgment. That is not to say that the law should not provide objective guidelines for the police, but simply that it cannot rigidly constrain their every action. By directing a police officer not to issue a dispersal order unless he "observes a person whom he reasonably believes to be a criminal street gang member loitering in any public place," . . . Chicago's ordinance strikes an appropriate balance between those two extremes. . . .

The . . . conclusion that the ordinance "fails to give the ordinary citizen adequate notice of what is forbidden and what is permitted," . . . is similarly untenable. There is nothing "vague" about an order to disperse. While "we can never expect mathematical certainty from our language," . . . it is safe to assume that the vast majority of people who are ordered by the police to "disperse and remove themselves from the area" will have little difficulty understanding how to comply. . . .

. . . Today, the Court focuses extensively on the "rights" of gang members and their companions. It can safely do so—the people who will have to live with the consequences of today's opinion do not live in our neighborhoods. Rather, the people who will suffer from our lofty pronouncements are people . . . who have seen their neighborhoods literally destroyed by gangs and violence and drugs. They are good, decent people who must struggle to overcome their desperate situation, against all odds, in order to raise their families, earn a living, and remain good citizens. . . . By focusing exclusively on the imagined "rights" of the two percent, the Court today has denied our most vulnerable citizens the very thing that it elevates above all else—the "freedom of movement." And that is a shame. I respectfully dissent.

● ● ● ● ● ● ● ● ● ● ● ● ● ●

State v. Young

Court of Appeals of Ohio, 1988.
50 Ohio App. 3d 17, 552 N.E.2d 226.

[Kevin W. Young was convicted of violating Ohio R.C. 4511.44 by failing to yield to approaching traffic. In this appeal to the Ohio Court of Appeals, Young claims the trial judge erred in interpreting the statute under which he was convicted.]

McCORMAC, Judge.

. . . On April 10, 1987, defendant was driving southbound on U.S. Route 33 through Nelsonville when he noted a traffic jam caused by an accident. To avoid the traffic jam, Young pulled into a private driveway leading to the Nelsonville Sewage Treatment Plant and turned around.

At this point, U.S. Route 33 has three lanes—a southbound, a northbound, and a center lane, which is a turning lane only.

Young wanted to turn north onto U.S. 33. He waited in the private driveway until a car in the southbound lane of U.S. 33 motioned for him to go. Young drove across the southbound lane before he turned north. He testified that he looked to see if there was any traffic coming but he could not see anything until he got to the center lane because his vision was blocked by stopped traffic.

Officer Waggoner was traveling southbound on U.S. 33 in the center turn lane going thirty miles an hour. He testified that he was trying to get to a car accident and that he could not travel in the normal lane because it was backed up. Officer Waggoner had on his warning lights, but not his siren. He testified that he was trying to turn on his siren, which is located on the floor. When he looked up, Young's car was across the center lane. The two cars collided.

Defendant argues that the trial court erred in interpreting R.C. 4511.44 to require motorists to yield the right-of-way to illegally operated oncoming traffic.

R.C. 4511.44 specifies that a driver entering or crossing a highway from any place other than another roadway shall "yield the right-of-way to all traffic approaching on the roadway to be entered or crossed." R.C. 4511.01(UU) states that:

"Right of way" means the right of a vehicle . . . to proceed uninterruptedly in a lawful manner in the direction in which it or he is moving in preference to another vehicle . . . approaching from a different direction into its or his path.

This definition of right-of-way must be used in conjunction with R.C. 4511.44. . . . Thus, in order to find a defendant guilty of the criminal violation of R.C. 4511.44, it is necessary to find that defendant failed to yield to a vehicle proceeding uninterruptedly in a lawful manner because those are the elements of the offense. It is not sufficient simply to find that defendant was negligent, careless or at fault, partially or totally, in causing the accident.

The issue then is whether the police officer proceeding in the turn-only lane at thirty miles an hour displaying warning lights, but not using his siren, was proceeding in a lawful manner. That question must be answered in the negative. An operator of a public safety vehicle may drive in a turn-only lane lawfully only if he uses at least one flashing, rotating, or oscillating light visible under normal atmospheric conditions from a condition of five hundred feet from the front of the vehicle and he gives an audible signal by siren, exhaust whistle, or bell. . . . The evidence is clear that the police officer failed to give an audible signal and that, therefore, he lost his preferential status as the driver of an emergency vehicle by operating his vehicle unlawfully. . . . Moreover, there was not due regard for the safety of all persons and property on the highway when the police officer drove thirty miles an hour in a turn-only lane, particularly when he failed to use his siren.

Appellant's assignment of error is sustained. The judgment of the trial court is reversed, and the cause is remanded to the trial court with instructions to enter final judgment for defendant. . . .

GREY, P.J., and STEPHENSON, J., concur.

●   ●   ●   ●   ●   ●   ●   ●   ●   ●   ●   ●   ●   ●

United States v. Evans

United States Court of Appeals, Ninth Circuit, 1991.
928 F.2d 858.

[In this case the Ninth Circuit Court of Appeals considers the constitutionality of the federal statute that prohibits possession of unregistered machine guns, 26 U.S.C.A. Sec. 5861(d) (1982). The appellant, Creed M. Evans, was convicted in U.S. District Court of making false statements to the Bureau of Alcohol, Tobacco, and Firearms. In his appeal, Evans argues that the mere possession of machine guns is not sufficiently related to interstate commerce to permit Congress to make it a criminal offense. A question to ponder: Does the Ninth Circuit's reasoning here square with the Supreme Court's decision in United States v. Lopez, reprinted below?]

WIGGINS, Circuit Judge:
. . . Evans contends that Congress lacks the power to prohibit the mere possession of unregistered machine guns without requiring proof of a nexus with interstate commerce. The general standard by which a statute that is said to violate the Commerce Clause is to be measured is firmly established. Although we independently review the validity of an act that is said to violate the Commerce Clause, . . . our review is conducted in a highly deferential manner. We consider whether a reasonable Congress could find that the class of activity regulated affects interstate commerce. . . . Congress need not make specific findings of fact to support its conclusion that a class of activity affects interstate commerce. . . . However, if Congress does make such findings, they carry great weight in this court's analysis. . . .

The statutes at issue in this case easily meet this standard. Congress specifically found that at least 750,000 people had been killed in the United States by firearms between the turn of the century and the time of the Act's enactment. It was thus reasonable for Congress to conclude that the possession of firearms affects the national economy, if only through the insurance industry. Since Evans does not contend that any specific Constitutional rights are implicated, this rather tenuous nexus between the activity regulated and interstate commerce is sufficient. . . .

We AFFIRM the judgment of the District Court.

●   ●   ●   ●   ●   ●   ●   ●   ●   ●   ●   ●   ●   ●

United States v. Lopez

Supreme Court of the United States, 1995.
514 U.S. 549, 115 S.Ct. 1624, 131 L.Ed.2d 626.

[In enacting the Gun-Free School Zones Act of 1990, Congress made it a federal offense "for any individual knowingly to possess a firearm at a place that the individual knows, or has reasonable cause to believe, is a school zone." A twelfth-grade student in San Antonio, Texas, was convicted under the statute after he was found to be carrying a concealed .38 caliber handgun and five bullets at school. The Court of Appeals for the Fifth Circuit reversed the respondent's conviction, holding that the act was invalid because Congress had exceeded its authority under the Commerce Clause. The Supreme Court granted certiorari.]

CHIEF JUSTICE REHNQUIST delivered the opinion of the Court.
. . . [The challenged statute] is a criminal statute that by its terms has nothing to do with "commerce" or any sort of economic enterprise, however broadly one might define those terms. [It] is not an essential part of a larger regulation of economic activity, in which the regulatory scheme could be undercut unless the intrastate activity were regulated. It cannot, therefore, be sustained under our cases upholding regulations of activities that arise out of or are connected with a commercial transaction, which, viewed in the aggregate, substantially affects interstate commerce. . . .

The Government's essential contention . . . is that we may determine here that [the challenged statute] is valid because possession of a firearm in a local school zone does indeed substantially affect interstate commerce. . . . The Government argues that possession of a firearm in a school zone may result in violent crime and that violent crime can be expected to affect the functioning of the national economy in two ways. First, the costs of violent crime are substantial, and, through the mechanism of insurance, those costs are spread throughout the population. . . . Second, violent crime reduces the willingness of individuals to travel to areas within the country that are perceived to be unsafe. . . . The Government also argues that the presence of guns in schools poses a substantial threat to the educational process by threatening the learning environment. A handicapped educational process, in turn, will result in a less productive citizenry. That, in turn, would have an adverse effect on the Nation's economic well-being. As a result, the Government argues that Congress could rationally have concluded that [the challenged statute] substantially affects interstate commerce.

We pause to consider the implications of the Government's arguments. The Government admits, under its "costs of crime" reasoning, that Congress could regulate not only all violent crime, but all activities that might lead to violent crime, regardless of how tenuously they relate to interstate commerce. . . . Similarly, under the Government's "national productivity" reasoning, Congress could regulate any activity that it found was related to the economic productivity of individual citizens: family law (including marriage, divorce, and child custody), for example. Under the theories that the Government presents in support of [the challenged statute], it is difficult to perceive any limitation on federal power, even in areas such as criminal law enforcement or education where States historically have been sovereign. Thus, if we were to accept the Government's arguments, we are hard-pressed to posit any activity by an individual that Congress is without power to regulate. . . .

To uphold the Government's contentions here, we would have to pile inference upon inference in a manner that would bid fair to convert congressional authority under the Commerce Clause to a general police power of the sort retained by the States. . . . This we are unwilling to do. . . .

JUSTICE KENNEDY, with whom JUSTICE O'CONNOR joins, concurring. . . .

JUSTICE THOMAS, concurring. . . .

JUSTICE STEVENS, dissenting.

. . . Guns are both articles of commerce and articles that can be used to restrain commerce. Their possession is the consequence, either directly or indirectly, of commercial activity. In my judgment, Congress' power to regulate commerce in firearms includes the power to prohibit possession of guns at any location because of their potentially harmful use; it necessarily follows that Congress may also prohibit their possession in particular markets. The market for the possession of handguns by school-age children is, distressingly, substantial. Whether or not the national interest in eliminating that market would have justified federal legislation in 1789, it surely does today.

JUSTICE SOUTER, dissenting. . . .

CHAPTER

13

Offenses Against Justice and Public Administration

Introduction

The English common-law judges found it essential to create certain offenses to maintain the integrity of the law and the administration of justice. Principally, these offenses were **bribery, perjury** and **subornation of perjury, resisting arrest, obstruction of justice, compounding a crime,** and **escape.** At common law, these offenses were misdemeanors. In addition, the common law developed the concept of **criminal contempt** to enable judges to maintain the dignity and authority of the courts and the respect due judicial officers. All of these common-law crimes remain an important part of contemporary criminal law in the United States, although they have been expanded and augmented by a variety of modern statutes. The offenses against public administration and the administration of justice in particular serve as a means to punish those who breach the public trust and whose actions corrupt the orderly processes of government and the justice system.

Bribery

The concept of bribery dates back to biblical times, when it was regarded as sinful to attempt to influence the judge with a gift because the judge represented the divine. Thus, when the common law developed the crime of bribery, it sought to penalize only persons whose actions were designed to improperly influence those identified with the administration of justice. Later, it was considered bribery for anyone to give or receive anything of value or any valuable service or promise with the intent to influence any public officer in the discharge of a legal duty. Bribery is generally a felony under modern law.

The Modern Statutory Offense of Bribery

Today, a variety of federal statutes proscribe bribery of specific public officers and witnesses as well as of jurors and government employees and functionaries. The most prominent among these is 18 U.S.C.A. § 201. To convict an accused of violating Section 201(b)(1), the government is required to prove that something of value was requested, offered, or given to a federal public official with a corrupt intent to influence some official act. Other subsections of the statute make it a crime to offer a bribe to a witness or for a witness to solicit or accept a bribe.

State statutes generally define bribery in broad terms and frequently address specific situations as well. The trend has been to enlarge the common-law approach by extending the offense to new categories of persons and conduct and by making the punishment more severe. The broad statutory definition of bribery is illustrated in a Florida law that makes bribery a felony and provides as follows:

> "Bribery" means corruptly to give, offer, or promise to any public servant, or, if a public servant, corruptly to request, solicit, accept, or agree to accept for himself or another, any pecuniary or other benefit with an intent or purpose to influence the performance of any act or omission which the person believes to be, or the public servant represents as being, within the official discretion of a public servant, in violation of a public duty, or in performance of a public duty. West's Fla. Stat. Ann. § 838.015(1).

Section 838.015(2) makes explicit that the person sought to be bribed need not have authority to accomplish the act sought or represented.

Generally, courts broadly construe such terms as "public servant" and "benefit" to accomplish the intended legislative purpose of statutes defining bribery.

Arizona law adds the term "party officer" to its statute proscribing bribery. It defines that term as "a person who holds any position or office in a political party, whether by election, appointment or otherwise." Ariz. Rev. Stat. § 13–2601.

Section 13–2602 of the Revised Arizona Statutes provides the following:

A. A person commits bribery of a public servant or party officer if with corrupt intent:

1. Such person offers, confers or agrees to confer any benefit upon a public servant or party officer with the intent to influence the public servant's or party officer's vote, opinion, judgment, exercise of discretion or other action in his official capacity as a public servant or party officer; or

2. While a public servant or party officer, such person solicits, accepts or agrees to accept any benefit upon an agreement or understanding that his vote, opinion, judgment, exercise of discretion or other action as a public servant or party officer may thereby be influenced.

B. It is no defense to a prosecution under this section that a person sought to be influenced was not qualified to act in the desired way because such person had not yet assumed office, lacked jurisdiction or for any other reason.

C. Bribery of a public servant or party officer is a class 4 felony.

Although the Arizona statute is explicit on the subject, irrespective of statutes, courts generally hold that where the act intended to be influenced is connected with a person's public duty, it is immaterial whether the person bribed has the authority to do a specific act. See, for example, *State v. Hendricks*, 186 P.2d 943 (Ariz. 1947).

The Range of Bribery Offenses

Acts sought to be accomplished by bribes cover a wide range of conduct, and as we pointed out in Chapter 10, the offense of bribery is frequently present in white-collar and organized crime situations. Common examples of bribery include obtaining the release or acquittal of an arrestee, securing an award of a government contract, and even obtaining a favorable vote by a legislator on a pending bill. The Arizona statute just quoted expands the traditional concept of "public servant" by recognizing the potential for bribery within the ranks of political parties. Although we commonly think of money being offered or requested as a bribe, a variety of other things are offered, sought, or exchanged. These include not only cash or its equivalent but also such tangible and intangible benefits as price advantages, use of vehicles, vacation homes, and even sexual favors. Bribes often occur in subtle or disguised ways. For example, a sale of property for less than its true value would likely be considered bribery if the seller's real purpose was to benefit the purchaser to influence his or her official governmental action. See, for example, *State v. Sawyer*, 63 N.W.2d 749 (Wis. 1954).

The Burden of the Prosecution

The gist of the crime of bribery is the unlawful offer or agreement to do something under color of office. Ordinarily, the prosecution must prove not only the offer or agreement or the request or acceptance of a benefit but also that the defendant had

CASE-IN-POINT

Bribery: What Constitutes a Thing of Value?

Defendant was convicted of bribery under an Alabama statute that provided that it was bribery for any public official to accept "any gift, gratuity, or other thing of value." On appeal, defendant argued that "sexual intercourse, or the promise of sexual intercourse, or the promise of other sexual favors or relationship" did not meet the test of being a "thing of value" under the bribery statute. The Alabama Court of Criminal Appeals rejected the defendant's contention, saying that "[t]he word 'thing' does not necessarily mean a substance. . . . [I]t includes an act, or action."

McDonald v. State, 329 So.2d 583 (Ala. Crim. App. 1975).

---

a false or corrupt intent. One difficulty encountered in prosecuting a bribery charge is establishing the corrupt intent element. For example, it can be extremely difficult to prove that a person received employment or was granted a contract as a result of a bribe. The difficulty is compounded because, not infrequently, bribes are disguised as gifts or even as political or charitable contributions.

Offenses Extending the Concept of Bribery

Many states have enacted statutes to extend the offense of bribery to encompass the conduct of persons other than public officials and employees. The two principal areas of extension have been commerce and sports.

Commercial Bribery

Section 224.8 of the Model Penal Code outlines an offense known as **commercial bribery.** Some states have classified certain corrupt business practices—for example, fraudulent acts of purchasing agents—as commercial bribery. The New Jersey law making commercial bribery a crime includes many of the provisions outlined in the Model Penal Code. As amended in 1986, the statute provides as follows:

a. A person commits a crime if he solicits, accepts or agrees to accept any benefit as consideration for knowingly violating or agreeing to violate a duty of fidelity to which he is subject as:

(1) An agent, partner or employee of another;

(2) A trustee, guardian, or other fiduciary;

(3) A lawyer, physician, accountant, appraiser, or other professional adviser or informant;

(4) An officer, director, manager or other participant in the direction of the affairs of an incorporated or unincorporated association;

(5) A labor official, including any duly appointed representative of a labor organization or any duly appointed trustee or representative of an employee welfare trust fund; or

(6) An arbitrator or other purportedly disinterested adjudicator or referee.

b. A person who holds himself out to the public as being engaged in the business of making disinterested selection, appraisal, or criticism of commodities, real properties or services commits a crime if he solicits, accepts or agrees to accept any benefit to influence his selection, appraisal or criticism.

c. A person commits a crime if he confers, or offers or agrees to confer, any benefit the acceptance of which would be criminal under this section. N.J. Stat. Ann. § 2C: 21–10.

Under the New Jersey statute, the benefit offered, conferred, agreed to be conferred, solicited, accepted, or agreed to determines the degree of the crime and the penalty.

Sports Bribery

Because of the increased role of both professional and amateur sports in society, most states now have made **sports bribery** a crime. Sports bribery statutes generally make it an offense for a person to offer anything of value to a participant or an official in an amateur or professional athletic contest to vary his or her performance. Likewise, it is a crime for a participant or an official in a sports event to accept a bribe under such circumstances. See, for example, Iowa Code Ann. § 722.3; *State v. Di Paglia,* 71 N.W.2d 601 (Iowa 1955).

Defenses to the Crime of Bribery

An excerpt from *State v. Gustafson,* in which a Minnesota appeals court addresses the offenses of bribery and conspiracy to commit perjury, appears at the end of the chapter.

Of course, the fact that an offer to bribe is not legally enforceable is no defense. The only recognized defense to a charge of bribery, other than denial, is entrapment. See *State v. Harrington,* 332 So.2d 764 (La. 1976). We discuss the defense of entrapment in Chapter 14.

Perjury

Like bribery, the crime of perjury has its roots in biblical times. The Mosaic Code included an admonition against the bearing of false witness. At common law, perjury came to consist of willfully giving under oath in a judicial proceeding false testimony that was material to the issue. Because of the narrow scope of the offense, it was eventually supplemented by the common-law offense of false swearing, a crime committed when an oath was taken in other than a judicial proceeding.

Elements of the Offense of Perjury

The general common-law offenses of perjury have been codified by federal law, 18 U.S.C.A. § 1621, which provides as follows:

> Whoever (1) having taken an oath before a competent tribunal, officer, or person, in any case in which a law of the United States authorizes an oath to be administered, that he will testify, declare, depose, or certify truly, or that any written testimony, declaration, deposition, or certificate by him subscribed, is true, willfully and contrary to such oath states or subscribes any material matter which he does not believe to be true; or (2) in any declaration, certificate, verification, or statement under penalty of perjury as permitted under section 1746 of title 28, United States Code, willfully subscribes as true any material matter which he does not believe to be true; is guilty of perjury. . . .

All states have laws making perjury a criminal offense. For example, the California perjury statute provides that a person who has taken an oath to tell the truth and who "willfully and contrary to the oath, states as true any material matter which he or she knows to be false" is guilty of perjury. West's Ann. Cal. Penal Code § 118. Although Section 118 relates to oaths in administrative and judicial proceedings, Section 118a makes it perjury for a person to give a false affidavit to be used in those proceedings. As in other jurisdictions, additional California statutes make it unlawful for anyone to give a false statement under oath in various applications, certificates, and reports. Courts have ruled that a grant of immunity (discussed in Chapter 14) will not protect a witness from prosecution for perjury if the witness testifies falsely. The courts reason that although a witness may be compelled to testify, the witness is not compelled to testify falsely. See, for example, *DeMan v. State,* 677 P.2d 903 (Alaska App. 1984).

The Burden of the Prosecution

To convict a defendant of perjury, the prosecution must establish that the defendant took an oath to tell the truth and knowingly made a false statement of fact. Statutes usually permit anyone with scruples against taking an oath to affirm that a statement is true. In either event, a person cannot be lawfully convicted of perjury unless there is proof that he or she was administered the oath by or made an affirmation before someone with legal authority. *Whitaker v. Commonwealth,* 367 S.W.2d 831 (Ky. 1963). Furthermore, the defendant's statement must have been material. This means that the testimony given by the defendant must have been capable of influencing the tribunal on the issues before it. *United States v. Jackson,* 640 F.2d 614 (8th Cir. 1981).

SUPREME COURT PERSPECTIVE

United States v. Gaudin, 515 U.S. 506, 115 S.Ct. 2310, 132 L.Ed.2d 444 (1995)

Michael E. Gaudin was charged with making false statements on Department of Housing and Urban Development (HUD) loan documents in violation of 18 U.S.C. § 1001. At trial, the judge instructed the jury that the prosecution had to prove that the alleged false statements were material to HUD's decision with regard to the loans. The question of materiality, the court ruled, was an issue to be determined by the court and not by the jury. Gaudin was convicted, but the Court of Appeals reversed. The Ninth Circuit held that the trial judge erred in withholding the question of materiality from the jury and that Gaudin's right to due process and trial by jury were infringed. Reviewing the case on certiorari, the Supreme Court agreed. The following are excerpts from Justice Antonin Scalia's opinion for a unanimous Court:

"The Fifth Amendment to the United States Constitution guarantees that no one will be deprived of liberty without 'due process of law'; and the Sixth, that '[i]n all criminal prosecutions, the accused shall enjoy the right to a speedy and public trial, by an impartial jury.' We have held that these provisions require criminal convictions to rest upon a jury determination that the defendant is guilty of every element of the crime with which he is charged, beyond a reasonable doubt. . . ."

"[O]ne of the elements in the present case is materiality; respondent therefore had a right to have the jury decide materiality."

"[W]e find nothing like a consistent historical tradition supporting the proposition that the element of materiality in perjury prosecutions is to be decided by the judge. Since that proposition is contrary to the uniform general understanding (and we think the only understanding consistent with principle) that the Fifth and Sixth Amendments require conviction by a jury of all elements of the crime, we must reject those cases that have embraced it."

Historically, courts in many jurisdictions held that the question of whether a witness's statement was material was a matter to be decided by the judge. In the 1990s, however, some courts reasoned that because materiality is an element of the crime of perjury, a jury must determine that such element has been proved beyond a reasonable doubt. See, e.g., *State v. Anderson*, 603 A.2d 928 (N.J. 1992). Their view prevailed in 1995, for as pointed out in the Supreme Court Perspective (p. 318), the Constitution requires that in a perjury prosecution the materiality of the defendant's statements, like all other elements of a crime, be a jury question.

Some statutes that define perjury require the prosecution to prove that the defendant's statement was made with the "intent to deceive." See, for example, Vernon's Tex. Penal Code Ann. § 37.02(a). Irrespective of statutory requirements, most jurisdictions require the prosecution to prove that the defendant's false statement was made "willfully and corruptly" because at common law, perjury was a specific-intent crime. Requiring the prosecution to prove the defendant's specific intent generally eliminates the likelihood of a defendant being convicted for simply having made a careless or offhand statement.

Perjury is one of the most difficult crimes to prove. The inherent difficulty of convicting a defendant of this offense is exacerbated by the **two-witness rule** that prevails in most jurisdictions. Under this rule, the prosecution must prove the falsity of a defendant's statements either by two witnesses or by one witness and corroborating documents or circumstances. See, for example, McKinney's N.Y. Penal Law § 210.50.

Perjury by Contradictory Statements

An excerpt from *United States v. Scott,* in which the U.S. Court of Appeals for the Eighth Circuit discusses perjury by contradictory statements, appears at the end of the chapter.

Early American cases followed the common-law principle that a defendant could not be convicted of **perjury by contradictory statements** unless the prosecution established which one of the statements was false. Modern statutes make it unnecessary for the prosecution to establish which of two contradictory statements is false. See, for example, McKinney's N.Y. Penal Law § 210.20.

Subornation of Perjury

At common law, subornation of perjury consisted of instigating or procuring another person to commit perjury. Statutes now generally define subornation of perjury much as did the common law. To convict a defendant of the offense, the prosecution must first establish that the defendant induced another to testify falsely and that an actual perjury was committed. *State v. Devers*, 272 A.2d 794 (Md. 1971). Thus, the Tennessee Supreme Court upheld a subornation of perjury conviction of an attorney for counseling four men charged with illegally selling whiskey to commit perjury. However, the attorney was prosecuted only after his four clients were convicted. *Grant v. State*, 374 S.W.2d 391 (Tenn. 1964).

Defenses to the Crime of Perjury

Truth, of course, is a complete defense to a charge of perjury; therefore, a defendant who while under oath gives an answer that is "literally accurate, technically responsive or legally truthful" cannot lawfully be convicted of perjury. *United States v. Wall*, 371 F.2d 398, 400 (6th Cir. 1967).

After making a false statement under oath, a witness sometimes recants and tells the truth. Federal law provides for a **recantation** defense to a prosecution for perjury if the perjured testimony has not substantially affected the proceedings, or if it has

Perjury: The Truth Must Be Unequivocal

A police officer was convicted of committing perjury on the basis of his denial of having received money from certain persons while in performance of his police duties. On appeal, he argued that his answer, "No sir. Not for my duties," to the prosecutor's question whether he received any money from any persons while on official duty as a Chicago police officer was literally true and therefore formed no basis for his conviction. The United States Court of Appeals, Seventh Circuit, rejected his contention. The court explained that his initial response, "No sir," was directly responsive and false, so his nonresponsive attempted hedge that followed was not effective.

United States v. Nickels, 502 F.2d 1173 (7th Cir. 1974).

not become manifest that such falsity has been or will be exposed. 18 U.S.C.A. § 1623(d). To assert this defense, a defendant must unequivocally repudiate his or her prior testimony. *United States v. Tobias,* 863 F.2d 685 (9th Cir. 1988).

In reviewing a state statute similar to the federal statute, in *Nelson v. State,* 500 So.2d 1308 (Ala. Cr. App. 1986), the court held that retraction of a false statement is a defense if the retraction occurs in the same proceeding and the statement is retracted before it becomes manifest that the fabrication is or will be exposed.

New York courts have held that recantation is a defense, provided it occurs promptly, before the body conducting the inquiry (for example, a grand jury) has been deceived or any prejudice has occurred, and before the defendant's perjury has most likely become known to the authorities. *People v. Ezaugi,* 141 N.E.2d 580 (N.Y. 1957). The rationale for the recantation defense is that the object of judicial investigations and trials is to ascertain the truth. It follows that the law should encourage a witness to correct a false statement without fear of perjury charges as long as the false statement has prejudiced no one.

Obstruction of Justice

At common law, it was a crime to commit an act obstructing or tending to obstruct public justice. Any act that prevented, obstructed, impeded, or hindered the administration of justice was considered a common-law misdemeanor. This included a host of acts such as obstructing an officer, tampering with jurors or witnesses, preparing false evidence, and secreting or destroying evidence. As statutory law came into being, some offenses that had been prosecuted as obstructions of justice—for example, escape and rescue and, later, resisting arrest—were dealt with as distinct crimes.

Modern Statutory Developments

Federal statutes proscribe a lengthy list of actions that constitute obstruction of justice. Among the actions made unlawful are assault on a process server; theft or alteration of process; endeavoring to influence or impede grand or petit jurors; obstructing proceedings before departments, agencies, and committees; tampering with or retaliating against a witness, a victim, or an informant; and obstructing court orders. 18 U.S.C.A. 1501–1518. Postal laws make it an offense to willfully and knowingly obstruct or retard the passage of the mail. 18 U.S.C.A. § 1701. Thus, in *United States v. Upshaw*, 895 F.2d 109 (3d Cir. 1990), a federal appeals court upheld a defendant's conviction for obstructing mail where a postal truck driver took home a package after he signed out from work.

All jurisdictions have statutes proscribing interference with officers in the performance of their duties. Some laws define obstruction to embrace many forms of conduct. Common examples include statutes making it unlawful to

- Give false information to an officer with the intent to interfere with the officer's lawful performance of duties
- Knowingly give a false fire or emergency alarm
- Impersonate an officer
- Intimidate a victim or witness
- Tamper with a juror
- Destroy or tamper with public records or physical evidence to be offered in official proceedings.

The Citizen's Duty to Assist Law Enforcement Officers

The common law imposed a duty on citizens to assist the sheriff and, on request, to keep the peace and apprehend wrongdoers. Modern statutes impose on citizens the duty to come to the assistance of law enforcement officers on request. Rather typical is the Ohio law that makes it a misdemeanor to fail to aid a law enforcement officer. Ohio Rev. Code Ann. § 2921.23(a) states the following:

> No person shall negligently fail or refuse to aid a law enforcement officer, when
> called upon for assistance in preventing or halting the commission of an offense,
> or in apprehending or detaining an offender, when such aid can be given without
> a substantial risk of physical harm to the person giving it.

Many states also have comprehensive statutes making it an offense to prevent, hinder, or delay the discovery or apprehension of persons sought by law enforcement.

....

Resisting Arrest

All jurisdictions make resisting arrest a crime. The common law did not permit a person to resist a lawful arrest by an authorized officer of the law. However, it did permit a person to use force to resist an unlawful arrest. *United States v. Heliczer*, 373 F.2d 241 (2d Cir. 1967). Until recently, this rule of law was applied in most American jurisdictions, but the functioning of the rule in modern society brought about the need to change it. The legality of an arrest may frequently be a close call, and because officers will normally overcome resistance with necessary force, there is a great danger of escalating violence between the officer and the arrestee. Thus, in recent years many courts have reexamined this common-law doctrine and have held that there is no longer authority to use physical force to resist an arrest by a police officer, whether such arrest is legal or illegal. See *Miller v. State*, 462 P.2d 421 (Alaska 1969).

Legislatures have also reexamined the issue of using physical force in resisting arrest. In 1980 the New York legislature amended its penal law to provide as follows:

> A person may not use physical force to resist an arrest, whether authorized or un-
> authorized, which is being effected or attempted by a police officer or peace officer

when it would reasonably appear that the latter is a police officer or peace officer. McKinney's N.Y. Penal Law § 35.27.

Oregon law now provides that "[a] person commits the crime of resisting arrest if the person intentionally resists a person known by the person to be a peace officer in making an arrest." Or. Rev. Stat. § 162.315(1). In *State v. Wright*, 799 P.2d 642 (Or. 1990), the Oregon Supreme Court held that a person may not lawfully resist arrest, even if the arresting officer lacked the legal authority to make the arrest, provided that the officer was acting under color of official authority. In addition, the court observed that if a police officer uses excessive force in making an arrest, the arrestee may use only such physical force as is reasonably necessary to defend against such excessive force.

The modern statutory and judicial revisions to the common-law approach make sense. It is not too great a burden today for a person who believes that he or she has been unlawfully arrested to submit to the officer and seek legal remedies in court. The circumstances surrounding an arrest are completely different from those that prevailed at common law. An arrestee today must be promptly taken before a magistrate, and legal counsel is readily available. Moreover, today's detention facilities do not resemble the crude dungeons where arrestees were incarcerated for lengthy periods before trial under the early English common law. The abandonment of the common-law rule is another example of a rule of law ceasing to exist when the rationale for it has ceased to exist.

An excerpt from *State v. Blanton,* a New Jersey case that involves resisting arrest and other offenses, appears at the end of the chapter.

Compounding a Crime

At common law, a person who accepted money or something else of value in exchange for agreeing not to prosecute a felony was guilty of compounding a felony. In the later history of the common law, it became a misdemeanor to compound a misdemeanor, if the conduct constituted an offense against public justice and was dangerous to society. To conceal a felony was also a common-law offense, known as **misprision of felony,** which was based on the common-law duty to inform authorities about any felony of which a person had knowledge. A person who saw someone commit a felony and used no means to prevent the felony or apprehend the felon committed the offense of misprision of felony.

The Modern Statutory Approach

The legal theory underlying making it an offense to compound a crime is that justice is debased when an offender bargains to escape the consequences of his or her crime. Most states have enacted statutes making it a crime to compound a felony, but some have expanded the common-law rule by making it a crime to compound any offense. To illustrate, New Hampshire law provides that a person is guilty of a misdemeanor who

1. Solicits, accepts, or agrees to accept any benefit as consideration for his refraining from initiating or aiding in a criminal prosecution; or

2. Confers, offers, or agrees to confer any benefit upon another as consideration for such person refraining from initiating or aiding in a criminal prosecution.

3. It is an affirmative defense that the value of the benefit did not exceed an amount which the actor believed to be due as restitution or indemnification for the loss caused, or to be caused by the offense. N.H. Rev. Stat. Ann. § 642: 5.

Most states have not made misprision of felony a statutory crime, probably relying on enforcement of statutes making it an offense to become an accessory after the fact to an offense (see Chapter 4). However, the federal criminal code specifically makes misprision of felony a crime, the gist of the offense being concealment and not merely the failure to report a felony. 18 U.S.C.A. § 4. The U.S. Court of Appeals for the Second Circuit has held that the elements of misprision of felony are that the defendant had full knowledge that the principal committed and completed an alleged felony, that the defendant failed to notify authorities, and that the defendant took steps to conceal the crime. *United States v. Cefalu*, 85 F.3d 964 (2d Cir. 1996).

A Common Scenario of Compounding a Crime

The offense of compounding a crime often appears where a crime victim whose goods have been stolen agrees with the thief to take back the goods in exchange for not prosecuting. Such an action would ordinarily constitute an offense by the victim. But the New Hampshire statute makes it an affirmative defense that the value of the benefit did not exceed that which the actor believed due as restitution for a loss. In some instances, courts will approve dismissal of a prosecution based on an agreement for restitution to the victim, but persons should not reach such an agreement without prior court approval.

··

Escape

At common law, a person who departed from lawful custody committed the crime of escape. Where the prisoner used force, the offense came to be known as prison break. Finally, a person who forcibly freed another from lawful custody was guilty of the offense of rescue.

Modern Statutory Approaches to Escape

Statutes proscribing escape are generally broad enough to embrace all three common-law offenses relating to escape. Often the punishment is more severe when force has been used. Federal statutes prohibit a person who has been lawfully arrested or confined from escaping or attempting to escape from custody, 18 U.S.C.A. § 751, or from rescuing or attempting to rescue a federal prisoner, 18 U.S.C.A. § 752.

Most state statutes define escape in rather simple terms. For example, Texas law provides that a person commits the offense of escape "if he escapes from custody when he is: (1) under arrest for, charged with, or convicted of an offense; or (2) in custody pursuant to a lawful order of court." Vernon's Tex. Penal Code Ann. § 38.06.

The Elements of the Offense of Escape

The gist of the offense of escape is the prisoner's unauthorized departure from lawful custody. Lawful custody is generally presumed once the prosecutor establishes that the escapee was confined to an institution specified by law. In other instances it may be essential for the prosecutor to establish proof of lawful custody; however, those who escape from a jail, juvenile detention home, penal institution, or reformatory are usually presumed to have been in lawful custody. Likewise, a person who fails to return to detention following a temporary release or furlough generally falls within the ambit of escape statutes.

Absent an explicit statutory requirement, courts differ on whether the prosecution must prove the defendant's specific intent to avoid lawful confinement. Of course, if a statute requires specific intent, the prosecution must establish this before a conviction can be lawfully obtained. The Supreme Court has held that under the federal statute, the government need prove only that the escapee knew that his or her actions would result in leaving confinement without permission. *United States v. Bailey,* 444 U.S. 394, 100 S.Ct. 624, 62 L.Ed.2d 575 (1980).

State appellate courts differ on whether the prosecution must prove that the escapee intended to leave or be absent from lawful custody. Recognizing that a slim majority of jurisdictions hold that intent is not an element of the crime, a Florida appellate court in 1975 held that the state must prove that a defendant intended to leave or be absent from lawful custody. Despite the lack of such a statutory requirement in Florida law, the court justified its position by raising some interesting "horribles" under which a defendant charged with escape could be improperly convicted if the state were not required to establish the escapee's specific intent to avoid lawful confinement. In one scenario, the court hypothesized that a road gang member had fallen asleep under a tree and was left behind by a negligent guard. The prisoner awakened only to find the guards and work detail had returned to the prison. Because of such possibilities, the court opted for requiring the prosecution to establish the defendant's specific intent to escape. *Helton v. State,* 311 So.2d 381 (Fla. App. 1975).

Defenses to the Charge of Escape

Occasionally, an innocent person is unlawfully confined. Nevertheless, if custody was lawful, the fact that a person was innocent is not generally recognized as a defense to a charge of escape. See *Woods v. Commonwealth,* 152 S.W.2d 997 (Ky. 1941). Of course, a person who escapes can always assert the defense of unlawful confinement or custody. *State v. Dickson,* 288 N.W.2d 48 (Neb. 1980).

During the 1970s, there was considerable focus on the conditions of our prisons. This is illustrated by a landmark 1974 California decision. Defendant Marsha Lovercamp was attacked by other inmates demanding sex. Prison authorities failed to provide Lovercamp with adequate protection, and she escaped. She was found guilty of escape, but an appellate court awarded her a new trial because the trial judge had denied her the opportunity to submit evidence of her plight as a justification for her escape. In reversing Lovercamp's conviction, the appellate court enumerated guidelines for asserting the defense of duress or necessity in these situations. *People v. Lovercamp,* 118 Cal. Rptr. 110 (Cal. App. 1974). The court opined that a limited defense is available if the following conditions exist:

(1) The prisoner is faced with a specific threat of death, forcible sexual attack or substantial bodily injury in the immediate future;

(2) There is no time for a complaint to the authorities or there exists a history of futile complaints which make any result from such complaints illusory;

(3) There is no time or opportunity to resort to the courts;

(4) There is no evidence of force or violence used toward prison personnel or other "innocent" persons in the escape; and

(5) The prisoner immediately reports to the proper authorities when he has attained a position of safety from the immediate threat.

In 1991 the Kansas Court of Appeals observed that the great majority of courts now follow the principles outlined in *Lovercamp. State v. Pichon,* 811 P.2d 517 (Kan.

App. 1991). See, for example, *People v. Unger*, 338 N.E.2d 442 (Ill. App. 1975), aff'd., 362 N.E.2d 319 (Ill. 1977); *State v. Alcantaro*, 407 So.2d 922 (Fla. App. 1981).

In 1980 the United States Supreme Court recognized the defense of necessity as being valid in the context of the crime of escape. To sustain the defense, the Court said a prisoner must demonstrate (1) that because of an imminent threat of harm, escape was the prisoner's only reasonable alternative, and (2) that the prisoner made a *bona fide* effort to surrender or return to custody as soon as the duress or necessity lost its coercive force. *United States v. Bailey*, supra.

An excerpt from the Maine Supreme Court's decision in *State v. Ring*, which illustrates the offense of attempted escape, appears at the end of the chapter.

Legislatures respond to public opinion, and improvement of prison conditions is not a high priority for most voters. Because courts tend to focus on issues where the legislative process affords no relief, they will undoubtedly continue to give attention to complaints concerning prison conditions. As they do, prisoners will most likely seek to extend the defense of necessity to justify an escape based on the inadequacy of prison conditions. Some have already argued that the denial of needed medical care should be recognized as a defense to escape. Courts have generally refused to accept such a defense. See, for example, *Commonwealth v. Stanley*, 446 A.2d 583 (Pa. 1982).

Contempt

Early in the history of the common law, judges began to exercise the power to punish persons whose conduct interfered with the orderly functioning of the courts in the administration of justice. Federal and state courts exercise the power to hold an offender—sometimes called a **contemnor**—in either civil or criminal contempt.

Civil contempt is beyond the scope of this text. Briefly, it is a sanction imposed to coerce a recalcitrant person to obey a court order. For example, a court may hold someone in civil contempt for failing to pay court-ordered support for dependents.

The power of the federal courts to hold persons in criminal contempt is recognized by statute. 18 U.S.C.A. § 401. However, even in the absence of statutory recognition, the courts are deemed to have broad inherent powers to hold persons in contempt. See, for example, *Martin v. Waters*, 259 S.E.2d 153 (Ga. App. 1979); *United States v. Wendy*, 575 F.2d 1025 (2d Cir. 1978).

A court imposes criminal contempt to punish an offender whose deliberate conduct is calculated to obstruct or embarrass the court or to degrade a judicial officer in the role of administering justice. Intent is always an element in criminal contempt proceedings.

Direct and Indirect Criminal Contempt

Criminal contempt is classified as either direct or indirect. **Direct contempt** is contemptuous behavior committed in the presence of the court or so close to the court as to interrupt or hinder the judicial proceedings. Disruptions of the examination of a witness or an assault on a judge or juror are examples of direct contempt. **Indirect contempt,** sometimes called constructive contempt, refers to acts that occur outside the court's presence that tend to degrade the court or hinder the proceedings of the court. Illustrations of indirect contempt are an attorney charged with responsibility of a case who is willfully absent from the courtroom or a juror discussing the facts of a case with a news reporter before the trial of a case has been completed.

One reason for classifying contempt as "direct" or "indirect" is to determine the processes that must be followed. Direct criminal contempt proceedings are usually

CASE-IN-POINT

Direct Criminal Contempt

Attorney Terrence M. Spears represented Gary Kaeding in an indirect criminal contempt proceeding. During the Kaeding proceeding, the judge stated that he would give Spears five days to file a motion for substitution of judge. Thereafter, the following exchange took place between the court and counsel for the parties:

THE COURT: Also I am going to *sua sponte* enter an order ordering Mr. Kaeding to be examined by a psychiatrist of the choice of the Court, because I do not know whether he is competent to stand trial.

MR. SPEARS: You cannot rule since there has been a Motion for Leave—

THE COURT: (Interrupting) I can; anybody can request a psychiatric examination. I am going to do that.

MR. SPEARS: I will be asking for one for you, Judge; have that on the record.

MR. SCHARF: Judge, I would ask he be found in contempt for that.

THE COURT: I am going to hold you in contempt, $500 fine.

MR. SPEARS: Praise God, praise the Lord Almighty God. May you—

MR. SCHARF: (Interrupting) I ask for jail.

MR. SPEARS: May you reap what you sow, Judge, by the good book.

THE COURT: You have 24 hours to pay the fine, or you are going to jail.

In affirming the trial court's finding that attorney Spears was in contempt, the appellate court noted that "Direct criminal contempt is contemptuous conduct occurring in the very presence of the judge, making all the elements of the offense matters within his own personal knowledge. Direct criminal contempt may be found and punished summarily without the usual procedural due process rights being followed. Criminal contempt is conduct which is calculated to embarrass, hinder, or obstruct a court in its administration of justice or derogate from its authority or dignity, thereby bringing the administration of law into disrepute.

"We find that Spears' comments were calculated to embarrass the court and to derogate from the court's authority and dignity. Accordingly, we hold that based on this conduct, the trial court's finding of direct criminal contempt was proper."

People v. Kaeding, 607 N.E.2d 580 (Ill. App. 1993).

handled summarily. The judge must inform the contemnor of the accusation and ask if he or she can show any cause to preclude the court from entering a judgment of contempt. The court then proceeds to enter its judgment accordingly. Courts justify the summary character of these proceedings because the contemptuous act has occurred in the presence of the judge.

The process is more formal in indirect contempt proceedings. The judge is required to issue a written order to the contemnor to show cause as to why he or she should not be held in contempt of court. The order must set forth the essential facts of the charge and allow the contemnor a reasonable time to prepare a defense. The judge tries all issues of law and fact, but the contemnor has the right to counsel, to the compulsory process to secure witnesses, and to refuse to testify.

United States Supreme Court decisions have established basic due process rights that must be accorded contemnors in these proceedings. Of course, if there are statutes or court rules in a particular jurisdiction that prescribe the method of processing criminal contempt, the judge must not deviate from those rules to the prejudice of the contemnor's rights. In any contempt proceeding, if the contemnor is to be sentenced to a term of imprisonment for more than six months, he or she is entitled to a jury trial. *Baldwin v. New York*, 399 U.S. 66, 90 S.Ct. 1886, 26 L.Ed.2d 437 (1970).

Is Criminal Contempt Really a Crime?

Until the 1960s, there was considerable division of thinking on this subject. In 1968 the United States Supreme Court in *Bloom v. Illinois*, 391 U.S. 194, 88 S.Ct. 1477, 20 L.Ed.2d 522 (1968), held that criminal contempt is a crime in the ordinary sense and may be punished by fine, imprisonment, or both. A person charged with criminal contempt is presumed innocent and must be afforded the procedural and substantive benefits of due process of law. Consequently, a contemnor must be proven guilty beyond a reasonable doubt before being held in criminal contempt. In some states, criminal contempt has been made a statutory crime. See, for example, McKinney's N.Y. Penal Law § 215.50–51.

Legislative Contempt

Legislative bodies also have the power to punish those persons whose deliberate acts impede legislative activities. Some states have enacted statutes to cover specific instances of criminal contempt in respect to legislative functions. For example, New York makes criminal contempt of the legislature a misdemeanor. McKinney's N.Y. Penal Law § 215.60 provides as follows:

> A person is guilty of criminal contempt of the legislature when, having been duly subpoenaed to attend as a witness before either house of the legislature or before any committee thereof he:
>
> 1. Fails or refuses to attend without lawful excuse; or
>
> 2. Refuses to be sworn; or
>
> 3. Refuses to answer any material and proper questions; or
>
> 4. Refuses, after reasonable notice, to produce books, papers, or documents in his possession or under his control which constitute material and proper evidence.

Courts have been zealous in ensuring that legislative bodies afford contemnors due process of law before adjudging them to be in contempt. See, for example, *Watkins v. United States*, 354 U.S. 178, 77 S.Ct. 1173, 1 L.Ed.2d 1273 (1957). In practice, the Congress and state legislative bodies frequently make citations for contempt and then turn the matter over to the courts to handle.

....

Conclusion

The fair and impartial administration of justice and the orderly processes of democratic government depend on the honesty and integrity of those who occupy positions of authority. Hence, the basic common-law offenses described in this chapter have endured over the centuries. The offense of bribery seeks to avoid corruption of those in positions of trust, whereas the crime of perjury seeks to maintain the integrity of the judicial system and agencies of government.

To safeguard the security and effectiveness of law enforcement personnel, all jurisdictions make it a crime to resist arrest, even if the arrest is later declared to be unlawful. Society must ensure confinement of those it has chosen to incarcerate, so it is essential to maintain the offense of escape. With increased awareness of inhumane prison conditions and the rights of prisoners, however, courts have recognized that under some circumstances necessity can be a defense to a charge of escape. The abandonment of the common-law principle that allowed a person to forcibly resist an unlawful arrest and the recognition of the necessity defense in the law of escape both demonstrate the dynamic nature of the criminal law in response to societal change.

Finally, to maintain the effectiveness and the dignity of the judicial and legislative processes, courts and legislatures must have the authority to hold persons in contempt, although that authority must be exercised with due regard for the constitutional rights of contemnors.

Key Terms

bribery	sports bribery
perjury	two-witness rule
subornation of perjury	perjury by contradictory statements
resisting arrest	recantation
obstruction of justice	misprision of felony
compounding a crime	contemnor
escape	direct contempt
criminal contempt	indirect contempt
commercial bribery	

Web-Based Research Activity

1. Go to the web. Locate the decisions of your state's highest appellate court.
2. Search the court's recent decisions for references to any of the offenses discussed in this chapter.
3. Find the most recent of these decisions, and write a synopsis of the decision.

Questions for Thought and Discussion

1. Why have contemporary legislative bodies expanded the scope of bribery and extended it to cover classes of persons beyond public officials?
2. How does the requirement that the prosecution prove a defendant's specific intent to deceive protect citizens from unwarranted prosecutions for perjury?
3. Contrast the common-law rule allowing a person to resist an unlawful arrest with the modern trend of requiring citizens to submit to unlawful arrests by police officers. Which approach makes more sense in today's society?

4. Is a state statute that makes it a criminal offense "to hinder or delay a law enforcement officer in the performance of his or her duties" likely to be held void for vagueness under the tests outlined in Chapter 3?

5. Would a person who accepts the return of stolen goods from a thief without agreeing to refrain from filing a criminal complaint be guilty of compounding a crime?

6. Name some acts that would likely be considered obstruction of justice under federal and state statutes.

7. Despite the wording of most statutes proscribing the offense of escape, courts increasingly require the prosecution to prove the defendant's specific intent to avoid lawful confinement. Are courts justified in imposing such a requirement on the statutory law?

8. Have courts aided society by allowing escapees from prison to defend their actions on the basis of intolerable prison conditions? Are such conditions likely to be remedied by the legislative process?

9. Describe some specific acts that a trial judge could justifiably consider to be direct contempts of court.

10. Why does the law require more formal proceedings in cases of indirect contempt than in cases of direct criminal contempt?

Problems for Discussion and Solution

1. The state charged Larcen Inmatio with escape from prison. The court appointed the public defender to represent him. You are assigned to investigate the case and report your findings to the public defender. Your investigation reveals that Inmatio was convicted of burglary of a dwelling and was serving the second year of a five-year sentence in the state prison. He complained to the warden that another inmate had sexually molested him and requested transfer to another prison or at least another cell block. After confirming that an inmate in Inmatio's cell block had molested him on one occasion, the warden told Inmatio that he would place him in another cell block. During the next three days, the warden took no action. On the fourth day, while Inmatio and other prisoners were on a work detail picking up trash from the roadside outside the prison, Inmatio left without permission and caught a ride to a nearby city, where he obtained a construction job. He had no contact with the prison until two weeks later, when the local police apprehended him and returned him to prison. Based on your investigation, do you think the public defender can successfully establish the defense of necessity on behalf of Inmatio?

2. Early one evening, Alden Dancio was sitting at a table in a tavern with his girlfriend and two other couples. They had been drinking beer and were talking and laughing. A local uniformed police officer, who was patrolling the area, stopped in to have a sandwich. Annoyed by the loud talking and laughing, the officer walked over to the table. There he saw Angela Mellow, a female he occasionally dated, sitting with her arm around Dancio. No one at the table was intoxicated. The officer demanded that Dancio produce some identification, and when Dancio refused, the officer told him he was under arrest for disorderly conduct and ordered him to get in the patrol car. Dancio refused, and after an altercation between the two, the officer handcuffed Dancio and placed him in the patrol car. After reviewing the police file, the

prosecutor acknowledged that Dancio should not have been arrested for disorderly conduct. He dismissed that charge. Nevertheless, the prosecutor decided to file an information against Dancio for resisting arrest. Is there a basis for charging Dancio with resisting arrest in the state where you live?

● ● ● ● ● ● ● ● ● ● ●

EXCERPTS FROM JUDICIAL DECISIONS

State v. Gustafson

Court of Appeals of Minnesota, 1986.
396 N.W.2d 583.

[The appellant, Gustafson, was convicted of bribery and conspiracy to commit perjury.]

FOLEY, Judge.

. . . On October 2, 1984, appellant was on a motorcycle talking to someone in a parked car. After ignoring several requests by a police officer to move the motorcycle, which was obstructing traffic, appellant was given a citation. Appellant was placed in the rear of the squad car after failing to have identification and giving a false name; he was patted down pursuant to police department rules. The police officer felt a hard object inside appellant's leather jacket and pulled out a beeper. Two plastic bags were also seized from the jacket; one containing a white powdery substance, the other containing folded pieces of paper. Money totaling $1,330 was also taken from appellant. The bags were later tested and found to contain cocaine. Appellant was charged with possession of cocaine and was released from jail. Upon his release, he picked up a vest and gloves, part of the property taken the night of the arrest. The leather coat, beeper and money were held for evidence. Appellant never claimed that the leather coat or gloves were not his.

Appellant's cocaine possession trial was scheduled for March 12, 1985. In mid-February 1985, appellant called an acquaintance, Andrew Beggs, and offered to give him a car worth $200 to $300 if Beggs would tell appellant's lawyer, Joe Kaminsky, that Beggs owned the leather jacket. Appellant told Beggs that his brother had done something similar and had gotten away with it.

Appellant later told Beggs that if he [Gustafson] were convicted he would go to jail. Appellant explained the circumstances surrounding his arrest and told Beggs to say that he had won the cocaine in a

pool game. Appellant then drove Beggs to a street in North Minneapolis to show him the car he had promised, gave Beggs the keys and assured him that he would provide title to the vehicle "in time." Appellant further told Beggs that since Beggs had a clean record the most he would get was probation.

A few days later appellant drove Beggs to Kaminsky's office where Beggs told Kaminsky the jacket and cocaine were his. When Kaminsky asked Beggs where the jacket was, he responded that he had it for the past two weeks. Kaminsky then informed Beggs that the police still had the jacket.

Appellant told Beggs that another witness was needed to corroborate the story since Beggs had mistakenly claimed possession of the jacket. Appellant then asked Brian Guyant to claim that he had observed Beggs give appellant the jacket. Guyant agreed and met with Beggs to make their stories consistent. A few days later, Beggs met with appellant, appellant's girlfriend and appellant's mother to discuss the story again. Beggs took notes at the meeting.

Beggs and Guyant went to Kaminsky's office on March 11, 1985. Minneapolis Police Officer Wayne Brademan and Hennepin County Attorney's Office Investigator Paul Stanton were also present at the meeting. Beggs was asked to identify the jacket but had difficulty locating the pocket in which the cocaine was found. Stanton testified that Beggs seemed nervous and confused. Beggs testified that Brademan and Stanton laughed when he could not find the inside pocket and he suspected that they did not believe his story that he had loaned appellant the jacket when appellant was about to test drive a motorcycle he had planned to purchase. Beggs was arrested. A search of his pockets produced a marijuana cigarette and two sheets of paper containing notes relating to the story he had just told.

After Beggs was in jail for three hours, he called Stanton and the next day said that he had lied about the cocaine and ownership of the jacket. Beggs explained that appellant had asked him to take the rap and gave a statement. The investigators then decided to set up a taped conversation between Beggs and appellant to determine who actually owned the cocaine. Beggs was released from jail and a "body bug" was placed on his back. Beggs was also given a phony complaint which stated that he was charged with possession of cocaine and possession of cocaine with intent to sell.

Beggs met appellant at a North Minneapolis home owned by Beggs' brother. Stanton and another police officer were in the basement during this meeting. In the tape recording, appellant makes numerous incriminating statements.

During the conversation, appellant referred to the cocaine as "my stash." He did not disagree when Beggs referred to their fabricated story nor did he disagree when Beggs said that Kaminsky knew he was lying. Appellant did show concern over the crib sheets found in Beggs' pocket, however, and reassured Beggs that at most he would serve 30 days in the workhouse. Appellant disagreed with the description of the seized cocaine in the phony complaint being in a baggie and said it was in a zip lock bag and also said that he had "two white papers" and "three rocks." When Beggs asked for title to the car,

appellant said that he forgot it. Subsequently, appellant's brother and Guyant brought the title card to Beggs who then turned it over to the investigators.

On April 18, 1985, a complaint was filed charging appellant with one count of conspiracy to commit perjury and one count of bribery. Both complaints (cocaine possession and conspiracy to commit perjury/bribery) were set for trial and were severed at appellant's request. At the first trial for cocaine possession, appellant did not testify. He was eventually acquitted.

At the second trial, appellant testified in his own defense, claiming that Beggs gave him the jacket and gloves to wear and denying ownership of the cocaine found in the jacket. Appellant stated that he did not tell anyone earlier that the jacket and cocaine belonged to Beggs because he was not a "snitch." He further testified that he sold the car to Beggs for $100 and that Beggs still owed him $50. Appellant was convicted of bribery and conspiracy to commit perjury and this appeal followed. . . .

We . . . conclude that the evidence was sufficient for the jury to convict appellant of bribery and conspiracy to commit perjury. Beggs' testimony was amply corroborated by evidence that appellant gave Beggs a car, by the crib notes found on Beggs at his arrest and by appellant's statements during the taped conversation. . . .

●　●　●　●　●　●　●　●　●　●　●　●　●　●

United States v. Scott

United States Court of Appeals, Eighth Circuit, 1982. 682 F.2d 695.

[This case deals with perjury by contradictory statements. The appellant, Teresa Ann Scott, was convicted in the U.S. District Court for the Western District of Missouri of three counts of making inconsistent material declarations while under oath.]

McMILLAN, Circuit Judge.

. . . On July 20, 1980, FBI Agent Robert Callahan went to Scott's residence to question her about the November 1979 robbery of the Blue Valley Federal Savings & Loan (Blue Valley) and the January 1980 robbery of the Rockhill Federal Savings & Loan

(Rockhill). Scott was not at home so Callahan left a message for her to contact him. The following Monday, July 14, Scott voluntarily went to the FBI office located in Kansas City, Missouri, and met with Agents Callahan and Parnell Miles. Callahan told Scott that he had a government witness who was going to testify in such a way as to implicate Scott in numerous crimes if she did not cooperate in the FBI's investigation of the robberies. Scott agreed and examined three bank surveillance photographs taken during the two robberies. Scott identified Bobby McNeal, her present boyfriend, and George Brown, a former boyfriend, as the individuals in the Blue Valley photograph and McNeal and Olie Ealom, her half-brother, as the individuals in the Rockhill photographs.

At some point Scott made statements implicating herself as an accessory to the robberies. An understanding was reached whereby Scott would not be indicted in exchange for her cooperation with the government. On December 30, 1980, Scott was deposed in connection with the government's case against McNeal for the Blue Valley robbery. She was shown the same bank surveillance photographs, exhibits C, D, and E, and again identified the individuals in exhibit C, the Blue Valley robbery, as Brown and McNeal and the individuals in exhibit E, the Rockhill robbery, as Ealom and McNeal. The face of the person identified as McNeal was not identifiable in the photographs. However, Scott stated that the striped coat worn by that person during both robberies belonged to her and that she had lent it to McNeal on the morning of the Blue Valley robbery. In addition, exhibit D was a front shot of that person and showed that he was made up to appear as a woman during the Blue Valley robbery. Scott stated that she had applied McNeal's makeup on the morning of the Blue Valley robbery.

On January 20, 1981, Scott was called to testify at McNeal's trial. On direct examination she was again shown exhibits C, D, and E. However, she testified that she could not identify the striped coat worn by one of the individuals in exhibit C, that she could not identify the individual in exhibit D whom she had previously identified as McNeal, and that she could not identify the individuals in exhibit E whom she had previously identified as McNeal and Ealom. The jury found McNeal not guilty and shortly thereafter the government dismissed its case against McNeal and Ealom for the Rockhill robbery.

The government subsequently charged Scott with three counts of making irreconcilably contradictory declarations under oath in violation of 18 U.S.C. § 1623. At her trial Scott testified that her deposition testimony was false and that she had recanted at McNeal's trial. Scott also testified that the reason she lied during the deposition was Callahan's threat that she could be sent to prison and lose custody of her children if she did not cooperate with the investigation. Scott further testified that before she made the July 20, 1980, statement to Callahan he had told her that he already knew the identities of the individuals in the bank surveillance photographs and also

knew that the striped coat belonged to Scott. On cross-examination Scott admitted that she had visited McNeal at the Wyandotte County Jail on January 14, 1981, signed the deposition on January 15, and visited McNeal again on January 16. The jury found Scott guilty on all three counts.

On appeal Scott first argues that her prosecution was barred by the "recant" provision of 18 U.S.C. § 1623(d) which provides:

> Where, in the same continuous court or grand jury proceeding in which a declaration is made, the person making the declaration admits such declaration to be false, such admission shall bar prosecution under this section if, at the time the admission is made the declaration has not substantially affected the proceeding, or it has not become manifest that such falsity has been or will be exposed.

Alternatively, Scott argues that, in light of this section, there was insufficient evidence to support her conviction. We reject these arguments.

Scott did not raise the recantation argument by pretrial motion. Rather, she attempted to convince the jury that her deposition testimony was false and that she had recanted at McNeal's trial. The recantation section of the statute was included in the jury instructions and referred to in her counsel's closing argument. Because Scott chose to submit the issue to the jury the question before us is whether there is substantial evidence, taking the view most favorable to the government to support the verdict. See *Glasser v. United States*, 315 U.S. 60, 80, 62 S.Ct., 457, 469, 86 L.Ed. 680 (1942). Viewed in this light, the evidence shows that the government agreed not to indict Scott as an accomplice in the robberies in exchange for her testimony at McNeal's trial, that her deposition testimony was consistent with earlier statements made to the FBI and finally, that she was romantically involved with McNeal and visited him the day before and after signing the deposition. The jury could reasonably have found from the evidence that Scott was truthful in the deposition and lied at McNeal's trial.

Scott next argues that neither the indictment nor the jury instruction defining the elements of the offense included all the essential elements of the offense. Specifically, Scott asserts that the ancillary nature of her deposition had to be alleged in the indictment and that the instruction should have required the jury to make a finding that the deposition was an ancillary proceeding. There is no merit to this argument.

Title 18 U.S.C. § 1623 applies to inconsistent declarations made "in any proceeding before or ancillary to any court or grand jury of the United States." The term "ancillary" proceedings has been construed to include depositions and exclude "statements given in less formal contexts than depositions." *Dunn v.*

United States, 442 U.S. 100, 111, 99 S.Ct. 2190, 2196, 60 L.Ed.2d 743 (1979). Therefore, the terms "deposition" and "ancillary proceeding" are synonymous under the statute and requiring the indictment to specifically allege the ancillary nature of the deposition or requiring the jury to find that a deposition is an ancillary proceeding would be redundant. . . .

The judgment of the district court is affirmed.

• • • • • • • • • • • • • • • •

State v. Blanton

Superior Court of New Jersey, Appellate Division, 1979.
166 N.J. Super. 62, 398 A.2d 1328.

[This case involves the offenses of assault and battery upon a police officer, "atrocious assault and battery," and resisting arrest.]

CONFORD, P. J. A. D., Retired (temporarily assigned).

These are consolidated appeals by defendant Elijah Blanton, Sr. ("Elijah") and his son, John Blanton ("John"). Elijah was convicted of assault and battery upon a police officer and John of atrocious assault and battery and resisting arrest. The events giving rise to the charges resulting in these convictions occurred in the course of a disturbance on May 28, 1976, at a playground near a low-income housing project in Long Branch.

The police were originally dispatched to the playground after Elijah's wife called to report an argument between another of her sons and a third person she thought to be in possession of a gun. No gun was found. However, Elijah was carrying on in a loud manner, yelling at and chasing children and arguing with the purported possessor of the gun. There was other testimony that Elijah was simply trying to restore peace to the area. The police soon withdrew from the scene.

Within a short time the police returned to the scene on the order of a superior officer to arrest Elijah if he was found to be causing trouble. The return of the police developed into a melee either witnessed or participated in by a large number of people, mostly juveniles. According to the State's evidence, Officers Wettermark and Brown accosted

Elijah and informed him he was under arrest. He pulled away from them, and sticks and other objects were thrown at the officers, Officer Wettermark being struck by some of them. Officer Brown embraced Elijah in a full nelson and in return was bitten by Elijah on his arm. This action was the basis of the charge against Elijah of assault and battery against a police officer.

The charges against John arose out of the attempt of Officer DeFillipo to go to the aid of the officers seeking to arrest Elijah. DeFillipo testified that as he approached the officers and Elijah he noticed an individual wearing an orange tee shirt to his right at a distance of between six and ten feet and immediately thereafter sustained a blow to the top of his head. The man in the orange shirt was John. DeFillipo at once turned around and confronted John, the latter looking directly at him, about three feet away. John had a stick or pipe in his hand of a cylindrical shape and about 2 feet long. There were no other people in the immediate area. John turned and ran toward his apartment with DeFillipo and Officer Richards in pursuit, the former yelling, "I want him. He hit me." John ran into one door and out another, whereupon he was tackled by one of the officers. There was testimony that John was resisting the officers' efforts to subdue him, "moving his arms about" and attempting to arise from the ground. DeFillipo was bleeding profusely from his scalp. There was other testimony that prior to the assault on Officer DeFillipo, John had run into Officer May and had struck him on the arm with a stick and then continued running. However, he was acquitted of a separate charge of assault on Officer May.

John's testimonial version of the events was that he was in the playground practicing for a state championship relay meet to be held the next day and that he was in possession of a relay baton about 12 inches long. When the police came upon the scene they began spraying mace. John saw his father surrounded by police officers and others and asked the officers to let his father alone. One of the officers angrily reached for his gun and John ran away in fear, alleging, before an objection by the State was sustained, that he recalled a former local incident involving the shooting of a juvenile by police. He did not strike anyone but remembered bumping into someone while running away. No one told him he was under arrest at any time. He was assaulted by the police after he emerged from his home. . . .

Defendant [John Blanton] argues that the trial judge's instructions to the jury with respect to the charge of resisting arrest were defective because they permitted the jury to conclude that John's flight from the pursuing officers constituted guilt of the offense of resisting arrest. The specific portion of the charge to the jury objected to consisted of the instruction that among the elements of the crime required to be proven by the State was one that defendant "did know that he was under arrest or that the officer was attempting to arrest him and . . . that with that knowledge the defendant John Blanton intentionally sought to avoid or frustrate that arrest."

Our examination of the relevant authorities satisfies us that there was no error in the charge even if the jurors could understand therefrom that flight from a police officer with knowledge by the fugitive that the officer was attempting to arrest him and with the purpose of avoiding or frustrating that arrest, constituted guilt of the common-law offense of resisting arrest.

Resisting arrest is an integral part of the common-law crime of "obstruction of or resistance to a public officer in the performance of his duties." . . . [T]he use of actual force is not always necessary to constitute the offense so long as there is some overt act of obstruction. . . . In many jurisdictions this crime has been codified, and the statutes have generally been construed as permitting a determination of guilt without a finding of the use of force or violence against the officer. . . .

In formulating § 2C: 29–2 of The New Jersey Penal Code . . . the New Jersey Criminal Law Revision Commission stated: "We reject the MPC [Model Penal Code] view that mere nonsubmission should not be an offense, believing an affirmative policy of submission to be appropriate as now seems to be our law." . . . The cited section of the Code, both as proposed and adopted, provides for guilt of resisting arrest if the person "purposely prevents a law enforcement officer from effecting a lawful arrest." . . . [W]hile mere flight from an intending arresting officer may, depending upon other circumstances, be regarded under the new statute as only a disorderly persons offense, the general offense of resisting arrest may be found to have been committed short of use of force or risk of causing injury so long as the accused has purposely sought to prevent the police officer from effecting an arrest. Our view of the common law . . . is, accordingly, that flight knowingly intended to prevent a police officer from effecting an arrest of the fugitive constitutes guilt of the common-law crime of resisting arrest.

The circumstances given in evidence clearly permitted the jury to find that John knew the police were seeking to arrest him. Office DeFillipo testified that while pursuing John he yelled out, "I want him. He hit me." John admitted, in effect, that he was seeking to elude the police, although his explanation of his flight was consistent with innocence of the crime of assault. Nevertheless, knowing that a uniformed police officer was seeking to apprehend him, it was his duty to submit and not resist. . . .

We consequently find no error in the trial judge's instructions to the jury in the respect complained of. . . .

State v. Ring

Supreme Court of Maine, 1978.
387 A.2d 241.

[This case involves the offense of attempted escape.]

PER CURIAM.

Appellants Donald Ring and Ricky Waugh bring this appeal from judgments entered following a jury trial in the Knox County Superior Court. Appellants were tried jointly for attempted escape . . . from the Maine State Prison.

Appellants assert two issues on appeal. They . . . challenge the sufficiency of the evidence to demonstrate that there were the overt acts or intent necessary to constitute the offense of attempted escape. . . .

We deny the appeal.

The record shows that on July 28, 1976, the date of the alleged attempted escape, both appellants were incarcerated in the Maine State Prison where they were serving sentences imposed for prior crimes. They had no official permission to be absent on that day. A prison guard testified at trial that he had seen appellants walking together in the prison yard around 1:00 P.M. One appellant was observed carrying an unconcealed "rope" and a hammer.

When it later appeared that neither appellant had showed up for the 4:00 P.M. cell count, a search of the prison was undertaken. Eventually both appellants were discovered in the "steam cage," a dark, enclosed unused portion of the prison. Subsequent searches revealed the presence of the "rope" and hammer hidden in crevices in the room.

Appellant Ring chose to testify on his own behalf. He basically contended that he and some other inmates had been drinking "homebrew" and had decided to hide in the steam cage so that their intoxication would not be discovered. While this story was corroborated by another inmate, the bag out of which appellants had been drinking was never discovered. Appellant Waugh decided not to testify.

Appellants first contend that the evidence was insufficient to prove that they intended to escape. They further claim that the evidence demonstrated, at most, mere preparation for an escape, not the requisite overt act.

We disagree.

As appellants contend, intent to "leave[s] official custody" or to "fail[s] to return to official custody following temporary leave" must be proven in order to establish a violation. . . . Moreover, appellants are correct when they argue that in proving an "attempt," the State must prove more than mere preparation; it must prove "a positive action . . . directed towards the execution of the crime." . . .

Our task in assessing the sufficiency of the evidence on these two points, however, is not to retry the case or to substitute our impressions of the facts for those of the jurors. Our function is merely to ascertain if the jury was warranted in finding for the State. . . . A witness' credibility is a jury matter. . . .

The jury here was justified in rejecting the testimony that appellants were in the "steam cage" solely to avoid detection of their intoxication. The fact of being hidden and the fact of their possession of "rope" and a hammer would have demonstrated to the jury that appellants had an intent to escape and that they had taken actions "directed toward the execution of the crime." This was a justified finding despite the fact that the actual escape might have been difficult to execute under the facts presented in this case. . . .

Judgments affirmed.

CHAPTER

14

Criminal Responsibility and Defenses

Introduction

As the English common law developed, the concept of **criminal responsibility** became a significant consideration. As it did, various defenses to criminal conduct emerged. Incapacity to commit a crime because of **infancy, insanity,** or, under some circumstances, **intoxication** came to be recognized as defenses. **Self-defense, defense of others,** and **defense of habitation and other property** were also recognized as defenses because of justification for a defendant's use of force in those instances. Moreover, the common law allowed a defendant to assert certain matters as an excuse or justification for having committed a criminal act. **Mistake of fact** that occurred honestly, **necessity, duress,** and—under limited circumstances—**consent** were recognized as defenses.

Essentially these defenses have been recognized in the various jurisdictions in the United States, although they have been modified over the years. The Fifth Amendment to the United States Constitution and corresponding provisions of the state constitutions furnish defendants two additional defenses: **immunity** and **double jeopardy.** Legislatures initiated the concept of a **statute of limitations** on the prosecution of most crimes. Through judicial development, **entrapment** has become a recognized defense where improper governmental conduct has induced an otherwise innocent person to commit a crime. In rare instances, defendants have successfully asserted the defense of **selective prosecution**—that is, being singled out for prosecution.

In previous chapters, we have mentioned some defenses applicable to specific substantive crimes. We revisit some of those defenses in this chapter, further examining the scope of common-law, constitutional, and statutory defenses to criminal charges.

Defenses in General

Defendants who plead not guilty to a criminal charge may not only rely on their general denial; they may also offer any defense (sometimes called a **negative defense**) not required to be specifically pled. A defendant merely has the burden of raising some evidence of a negative defense. This is sometimes referred to as the defendant's **burden of production of evidence;** in some instances, however, the prosecution's own evidence might raise the issue. Once such evidence is produced, the prosecution usually has the burden to overcome it. For example, Henry Homeowner is charged with the manslaughter of a person who forced entry into his home one night after Homeowner had gone to bed. Homeowner claims to have acted in self-defense by using deadly force to defend his home. If any evidence discloses that he acted in self-defense, then to establish that Homeowner is guilty of manslaughter, the prosecution must ordinarily prove that he did not act reasonably. But in some jurisdictions, depending on the specific defense, the defendant not only must be required to produce evidence but must also carry the burden of proving the defense by the greater weight of the evidence, usually referred to as the **preponderance of the evidence.**

A defense that must be specifically pled is classified as an **affirmative defense**—that is, one that does not simply negate an element of the crime but, rather, consists of new matters relied on as an excuse or justification for the defendant's otherwise illegal conduct. To illustrate, suppose Larry Boatman is charged with burglary of a vacant beach cottage. He pleads not guilty, raising the affirmative defense of necessity. He argues that although he entered the cottage with the intent to take food from within, it was an act of necessity because he and his starving companions were shipwrecked in a desolate area without other means of obtaining food or drinking water. Ordinarily, a defendant has the **burden to prove** the matters offered as an affirmative defense. Therefore, it is up to Boatman to prove by the preponderance of the evidence that he acted out of necessity. Courts sometimes vary in their views about whether a defense is a negative or affirmative one.

For purposes of analysis and study, we have divided defenses to crimes (beyond simply negative defenses) into five categories:

1. Those asserting lack of capacity (infancy, intoxication, insanity, automatism)
2. Those asserting excuse or justification (duress, necessity, consent, mistake of law or of fact)
3. Those justifying the use of force (self-defense, defense of others, defense of property and habitation, and using force to resist an arrest)
4. Those relying on constitutional or statutory rights (immunity, double jeopardy, statutes of limitation)
5. Those assailing governmental conduct (entrapment, selective prosecution)

It is difficult to generalize whether a specific defense is or is not an affirmative one. The defenses we categorized are generally classified as affirmative defenses, but this is not always true. The prosecution is always required to prove the defendant guilty beyond any reasonable doubt. Still, the law may constitutionally place the burden on a defendant to establish an affirmative defense as long as that defense is not one that simply negates an element of the crime the prosecution must prove to convict the defendant. *Patterson v. New York*, 432 U.S. 197, 97 S.Ct. 2319, 53 L.Ed.2d 281 (1977). Defenses authorized by statute are often styled as affirmative defenses, but merely labeling a defense an affirmative defense is not sufficient. Courts look to the substance to make certain that an affirmative defense is one that alleges lack of capacity to commit a crime or seeks to excuse or justify conduct that would otherwise lead to criminal responsibility, rather than one that simply negates an element of the crime.

Defenses Asserting Lack of Capacity to Commit a Crime

Four defenses assert the lack of capacity to commit a crime: infancy, intoxication, insanity, and automatism.

Infancy

The common law regarded a child under age seven as incapable of forming criminal intent. Thus, infancy gave rise to a conclusive presumption of incapacity for a child younger than seven. This presumption of incapacity was rebuttable regarding a child between seven and fourteen years old, with the prosecution having the burden to demonstrate that a child younger than fourteen was capable of comprehending the wrongdoing involved in commission of an offense. Children over age fourteen were treated as adults. *Commonwealth v. Cavalier*, 131 A. 229 (Pa. 1925).

The rationale for these common-law presumptions was that young children require protection from the harshness of the adversarial processes of the law. Some jurisdictions have abolished these presumptions because legislatures have provided that children under certain ages, usually sixteen to eighteen, are subject to the jurisdiction of the juvenile courts, where the procedures are tailored toward less mature offenders. In establishing juvenile courts, the legislatures frequently intend to eliminate the common-law presumption of incapacity of infants. See *People v. Miller,* 334 N.E.2d 421 (Ill. App. 1975), for the court's perception of legislative intent under Illinois law. Under federal law, a juvenile is a person who has not attained age eighteen at the time of the commission of an offense. 18 U.S.C.A. § 5031.

Starting with Illinois in 1899, all states developed juvenile court systems. These courts traditionally handled juvenile offenders separately from adults in nonadversarial proceedings. The theory was that the state acted as **parens patriae,** taking a clinical and rehabilitative, rather than an adversarial or punitive, approach to youthful offenders. Nevertheless, the system suffered from many deficiencies, such as inadequate staffing and substandard facilities, and the results were disappointing. Many youthful offenders were not rehabilitated, nor were they afforded even the most basic constitutional rights accorded adults in the criminal justice system. In the words of the United States Supreme Court, "[T]he child receives the worst of both worlds: that he gets neither the protections accorded to adults nor the solicitous care and regenerative treatment postulated for children." *Kent v. United States,* 383 U.S. 541, 556, 86 S.Ct. 1045, 1054, 16 L. Ed. 2d 84, 94 (1966). Although juvenile courts remain as part of the judicial scene, statutes commonly provide that for certain offenses a juvenile may be tried as an adult.

Intoxication

Intoxication can result from ingestion of alcohol or drugs. The common law did not excuse from responsibility for criminal conduct a person who voluntarily became intoxicated. In an early English case, the court approved a death sentence for a homicide committed by an extremely intoxicated defendant. *Regina v. Fogossa,* 75 Eng. Rep. 1 (1550).

In evaluating whether intoxication is a defense, **voluntary intoxication** must first be distinguished from **involuntary intoxication.** In most jurisdictions, voluntary intoxication may be considered in determining whether a defendant can formulate the specific intent the prosecution must establish in such crimes as larceny, burglary, and premeditated murder. Most courts reject the defense of voluntary intoxication for general-intent crimes. See, for example, *United States v. Hanson,* 618 F.2d 1261 (8th Cir. 1980) (assault on a federal officer); *Commonwealth v. Bridge,* 435 A.2d 151 (Pa. 1981) (voluntary manslaughter); *State v. Keaten,* 390 A.2d 1043 (Me. 1978) (gross sexual misconduct). These decisions are grounded in the public policy of not excusing conduct by those who voluntarily impair their own judgment. In Indiana, however, a different rule prevails: A defendant can offer a defense of voluntary intoxication to any crime. *Johnson v. State,* 584 N.E.2d 1092 (Ind. 1992).

In 1996 the U.S. Supreme Court, in a 5–4 decision, upheld a Montana law that does not allow a jury to consider a defendant's voluntary intoxication in determining whether the defendant possessed the mental state necessary for commission of a crime. *Montana v. Egelhoff,* 518 U.S. 37, 116 S.Ct. 2013, 135 L.Ed.2d 361 (1996). In 1999 the Florida Legislature enacted a statute that eliminates voluntary intoxication as a defense. The new law specifies that evidence of voluntary intoxication is not admissible to show a lack of specific intent or to show insanity at the time of the

In *Latimore v. State,* an excerpt from which appears at the end of the chapter, an Alabama appellate court addresses a defendant's contention that his voluntary intoxication should be accepted as a defense to a charge of murder.

offense. However, the statute makes an exception for controlled substances taken pursuant to a doctor's prescription. West's Fla. Stat. Ann. § 775.051.

Involuntary intoxication rarely occurs, but when it does, it relieves the criminality of an act committed under its influence if, as a result of intoxication, the defendant no longer knows right from wrong. *State v. Mriglot,* 564 P.2d 784 (Wash. 1977). A person can become involuntarily intoxicated through the trickery or fraud of another person—see, for example, *Johnson v. Commonwealth,* 115 S.E. 673 (Va. 1923)—or through inadvertent ingestion of medicine. See *People v. Carlo,* 361 N.Y.S.2d 168 (N.Y. App. Div. 1974). The New Hampshire Supreme Court summarized the law in this area:

> Generally the defense of involuntary intoxication will only be considered when it is shown that the intoxication was the product of external pressures such as fraud, force, or coercion, or when intoxication resulted from a medical prescription. *State v. Plummer,* 374 A.2d 431, 435 (N.H. 1977).

Intoxication as a defense to criminal liability has been codified in some jurisdictions. Section 939.42 of the Wisconsin Statutes is rather typical:

> An intoxicated or a drugged condition of the actor is a defense only if such condition:
>
> (1) Is involuntarily produced and renders the actor incapable of distinguishing between right and wrong in regard to the alleged criminal act at the time the act is committed; or
>
> (2) Negatives the existence of a state of mind essential to the crime *except as provided in § 939.24(3).* Wis. Stat. Ann. § 939.42.

The Wisconsin legislature inserted the italicized exception in 1987 to ensure that a voluntarily produced intoxicated or drugged condition is not a defense to liability for criminal recklessness.

Wisconsin courts have said that to establish the defense of involuntary intoxication, the accused must show the inability to tell right from wrong at the time of the offense. To establish voluntary intoxication, the defendant must show that the defendant's condition negated the existence of the state of mind necessary to commit the crime. *State v. Repp,* 342 N.W.2d 771 (Wis. App. 1983), aff'd. 362 N.W.2d 415 (Wis. 1985).

Insanity

All persons are presumed sane unless previously adjudicated insane. Even a person who has been adjudicated legally insane may still be found guilty of a criminal act if it was committed during a lucid interval. Insanity is a legal concept and is defined differently in various jurisdictions in the United States. A person who meets the requirements of the definition at the time of commission of an offense may plead insanity as a defense to criminal conduct.

Few cases have caused as great a concern about how the criminal justice system functions as did the verdict of **not guilty by reason of insanity** in John Hinckley's federal court trial for the 1981 shooting of President Ronald Reagan, his press secretary, and two law officers. The defense of insanity has never been popular with the public. It has sometimes been called "a rich person's defense" because defendants who invoke it frequently expend considerable financial resources to present psychiatric testimony. The Hinckley verdict motivated Congress and several state legislatures to review the status of insanity defenses.

HISTORICAL ROOTS OF THE INSANITY PLEA

The concept of mental responsibility has deep roots in Anglo-American law—the common-law crimes included a *mens rea,* the mental element. Nevertheless, the common law was slow to develop any standard for a mental condition that would excuse a person from criminal responsibility. By the eighteenth century, some English courts applied what has sometimes been called a "wild beast" test. For example, one English judge opined that "a man . . . totally deprived of his understanding and memory, . . . and doth not know what he is doing, no more than an infant, than a brute, or a wild beast . . . is never the object of punishment." *Rex v. Arnold,* 16 Howell's State Trials 695 (Eng. 1724).

THE *M'NAGHTEN* RULE

Little progress occurred in the development of the defense of insanity until 1843, when an event in England caused even greater consternation than the Hinckley verdict caused in the United States. Suffering from delusions that he was being persecuted by government officials, Daniel M'Naghten decided to kill Sir Robert Peel, the British Home Secretary. (Peel was the founder of the British Police System; hence, the term "bobbies" is still applied to British law officers.) From outside Peel's home, M'Naghten saw Peel's secretary, Edward Drummond, leave the house. Believing Drummond to be Peel, M'Naghten shot and killed him. At trial, M'Naghten's barristers argued that he was insane at the time of the shooting and therefore should be found not guilty. The jury agreed. Enraged by the verdict, Queen Victoria insisted that the law provide a yardstick for the defense of insanity. The House of Lords responded, and the test they developed is still referred to as the **M'Naghten rule.** It provides that "at the time of committing the act, the party accused as labouring under such a defect of reason, from disease of the mind, as not to know the nature and quality of the act he was doing; or, if he did know it, that he did not know what he was doing was wrong." *M'Naghten's Case,* 8 Eng. Rep. 718 (1843).

The *M'Naghten* rule became the test for insanity used in both federal and state courts in the United States. As psychology and psychiatry developed new theories of mental capacity, critics attacked the rule as being based solely on cognition (that is, a process of the intellect) and ignoring a person's emotions. In response, some courts accepted the **irresistible impulse** test that stressed volition (that is, self-control) as a supplement to the *M'Naghten* rule. See *Parsons v. State,* 2 So. 854 (Ala. 1887). This allowed a person who knew an act was wrong but who acted under an uncontrollable desire or the duress of mental disease to be excused from a criminal act.

THE *DURHAM* TEST

Another test for insanity evolved from *Durham v. United States,* where the United States Court of Appeals for the District of Columbia held that an accused is not criminally responsible if that person's unlawful act was "the product of mental disease or defect." 214 F.2d 862, 876 (D.C. Cir. 1954). Many psychiatrists applauded the **Durham test,** but it gained little judicial support outside of the District of Columbia. It was eventually discarded even there. *United States v. Brawner,* 471 F.2d 969 (D.C. Cir. 1972).

THE ALI STANDARD

In 1962 the American Law Institute (ALI), an association of distinguished lawyers and judges, proposed a new standard combining both cognitive and volitional capacities as a test for insanity. It is sometimes referred to as the **ALI Standard** or **substantial capacity test** and reads as follows:

> A person is not responsible for criminal conduct if at the time of such conduct, as a result of mental disease or defect, a person lacks substantial capacity either to appreciate the wrongfulness of his conduct or to conform his conduct to the requirements of the law.

The ALI Standard was adopted by most federal courts and has sometimes been referred to as the *Freeman* rule, stemming from an endorsement of the test by the United States Court of Appeals for the Second Circuit in *United States v. Freeman*, 357 F.2d 606 (2d Cir. 1966). This substantial capacity concept was applied as the test for insanity in the Hinckley case.

State courts, however, divided in their approaches to the defense of insanity. Many opted to follow the new substantial capacity test; the remainder adhered to the basic *M'Naghten* **right from wrong test.** Under the ALI criteria, a showing of substantial impairment of a person's mental faculties is enough to meet the test of insanity. In contrast, establishing insanity under a strict *M'Naghten* approach requires a showing of total incapacity, and evidence that does not tend to prove or disprove the defendant's ability to distinguish right from wrong is irrelevant.

THE CURRENT FEDERAL STANDARD

Dissatisfied with the ALI test, Congress decided to eliminate the volitional prong in the federal test for insanity and to revert substantially to the *M'Naghten* rule when it enacted the **Insanity Defense Reform Act of 1984.** This act provides that in federal courts:

> It is an affirmative defense to a prosecution under any federal statute that, at the time of the commission of the acts constituting the offense, the defendant, as a result of a severe mental disease or defect, was unable to appreciate the nature and quality or the wrongfulness of his acts. Mental disease or defect does not otherwise constitute a defense. 18 U.S.C.A. § 17(a).

In addition, the act stipulates that "[t]he defendant has the burden of proving the defense of insanity by clear and convincing evidence." 18 U.S.C.A. § 17(b). The **clear and convincing evidence standard** is higher than the usual civil evidentiary standard of preponderance of the evidence but somewhat lower than the standard of **beyond a reasonable doubt,** the evidentiary standard required for criminal convictions. Although there has been some controversy concerning the legitimacy of placing the burden of proof of insanity on the defendant, the United States Supreme Court has held that this type of "burden shifting" does not violate the defendant's right of due process of law under the U.S. Constitution. *Patterson v. New York*, supra. Moreover, federal appellate court decisions in 1986 affirmed the constitutionality of this burden shifting under the 1984 federal act. *United States v. Freeman*, 804 F.2d 1574 (11th Cir. 1986); *United States v. Amos*, 803 F.2d 419 (8th Cir. 1986).

On April 4, 1995, a federal jury found Francisco Martin Duran guilty of attempting to assassinate President Bill Clinton. Duran pleaded insanity. His counsel argued that Duran was a paranoid schizophrenic who was shooting at the White House as a symbol of a government he hated. Unlike the John Hinckley trial, the new federal standard for insanity applied in Duran's trial. The jury rejected Duran's plea of insanity and found him guilty of attempting to assassinate the president, as well as guilty of several other charges.

An excerpt from the Eleventh Circuit's opinion in *United States v. Freeman*, in which the court addresses the Insanity Defense Reform Act, appears at the end of the chapter.

THE INSANITY DEFENSE REFORM ACT:
THE EFFECT ON THE USE OF PSYCHIATRIC EVIDENCE

Under the Insanity Defense Reform Act, psychiatric evidence of impaired volitional control is inadmissible to support an insanity defense. After passage of the new law, a question arose as to whether Congress also intended to prohibit the use of psychiatric evidence to negate a defendant's specific intent to commit an offense. In 1990 the United States Court of Appeals for the Eleventh Circuit addressed the issue: "Both Congress and the courts have recognized the crucial distinction between evidence of psychological impairment that supports an 'affirmative defense,' and psychological evidence that negates an element of the offense charged." The court ruled that the language of the new federal act does not bar the use of psychiatric evidence to negate specific intent where that level of intent is an element of the offense charged by the government. *United States v. Cameron,* 907 F.2d 1051, 1063 (11th Cir. 1990).

CONTEMPORARY STATE DEVELOPMENTS

Although Congress has placed the burden on defendants who plead insanity in federal courts to prove their defense, state courts are divided on the issue. In some states, where insanity is classified as an affirmative defense, the defendant bears the burden of proof of insanity, usually by a preponderance of the evidence. See, for example, *Clark v. State,* 588 P.2d 1027 (Nev. 1979). In other states, when a defendant pleads insanity and introduces some evidence of insanity, the state must then establish the defendant's sanity, usually by proof beyond a reasonable doubt, the standard required for establishing a defendant's guilt. See, for example, *Parkin v. State,* 238 So.2d 817 (Fla. 1970). Courts usually permit laypersons as well as expert witnesses to testify about a defendant's sanity.

Unlike a defendant who is simply found not guilty, a defendant who is found not guilty by reason of insanity is exposed to institutionalization and may, in some circumstances, be committed to a mental institution. *Jones v. United States,* 463 U.S. 354, 103 S.Ct. 3043, 77 L.Ed.2d 694 (1983). This is generally accomplished subsequent to the verdict by the trial judge, who determines whether the protection of the public requires that the defendant be confined.

On the premise that a person should not be found not guilty on the basis of insanity, some states have recently resorted to verdicts of **guilty but mentally ill** in cases where the defendant's insanity has been established. For example, in *People v. Sorna,* the court explained that this category of verdict deals with situations "where a defendant's mental illness does not deprive him of substantial capacity sufficient to satisfy the insanity test but does warrant treatment in addition to incarceration." 276 N.W.2d 892, 896 (Mich. App. 1979).

Kansas became the fourth state to abolish the defense of insanity when it enacted Kan. Stat. Ann. § 22–3220, effective January 1, 1996. Montana, Idaho, and Utah had previously abolished insanity as a defense. In *State v. Cowan,* 861 P.2d 884 (Mont. 1993), the Montana Supreme Court held that its state law abolishing insanity as a defense did not violate the federal constitution. The defendant, asserting a constitutional right to plead the defense, asked the U.S. Supreme Court to review his case. In March 1994, the Court refused to review the *Cowan* decision. *Cowan v. Montana,* 511 U.S. 1005, 114 S.Ct. 1371, 128 L.Ed.2d 48 (1994). Although the Court declined to definitively settle the issue, its action suggests that the federal constitution does not require that states allow a defendant to plead insanity.

It is sometimes difficult to classify the results that occur from a plea of insanity when a jury acquits the defendant. For example, in 1994 Lorena Bobbit was charged

CASE-IN-POINT

Insanity Defense

Joy Ann Robey was charged with involuntary manslaughter and child abuse in connection with the death of her ten-month-old daughter, Christina. At trial, Robey admitted to beating the child severely and repeatedly over a two-month period but pleaded not guilty by reason of insanity. The trial court found that the defendant was temporarily insane each time she beat the child but that she returned to sanity thereafter. Accordingly, the defendant could

not be held criminally liable for the beatings but was responsible for her failure to seek medical care for her child. Robey was convicted of involuntary manslaughter and child abuse and sentenced to three concurrent ten-year terms in prison. Her conviction was upheld on appeal over her contention that the trial court erred in holding her criminally responsible after acknowledging that she was insane at the time of the beatings.

Robey v. State, 456 A.2d 953 (Md. App. 1983).

with severing her husband's penis, a fact that was not in controversy. She relied on insanity as a defense but in a novel way. She testified about her husband's alleged cruel and abusive behavior toward her and characterized herself as a victim. A jury in Manassas, Virginia, acquitted her. Some observers have characterized her acquittal as a jury nullification rather than a finding of not guilty by reason of insanity.

Automatism

Older cases treated defendants who claimed that their unlawful acts were committed because of an involuntary condition such as somnambulism (that is, sleepwalking) within the context of the insanity defense. Newer cases tend to classify such involuntary actions as **automatism** and view them as a basis for an affirmative defense independent from insanity. The defense is usually limited to a situation where criminal conduct is beyond a person's knowledge and control. *Sellers v. State,* 809 P.2d 676 (Okla. Cr. App. 1991). In *Fulcher v. State,* 633 P.2d 142 (Wyo. 1981), the court explained that one reason for regarding automatism as a separate defense is that there are generally no follow-up consequences such as institutionalization, which usually occurs in an acquittal by reason of insanity. The defense of sleepwalking is infrequently pled. In November 1994, a defendant in Butler, Pennsylvania, contended that his sleep apnea disorder depleted his oxygen and caused him to shoot his wife. The prosecution countered by arguing the man shot his wife because she had planned to leave him. The jury rejected the defendant's claim and found him guilty of murder.

Defenses Asserting Excuse or Justification

A defendant who asserts an excuse admits the offense but claims that under the circumstances his or her conduct should not result in punishment. A defendant who asserts a justification for conduct says, in effect, that it was justified under the circumstances. Five principal defenses are based on a defendant asserting an excuse or justification: duress, necessity, consent, mistake of law, and mistake of fact. For convenience, we also discuss **alibi** under this topic although, rather than offering an excuse, a defendant who pleads alibi simply says that he or she was elsewhere when an offense was committed.

Duress

The common law recognized that duress can be a defense to criminal charges if the coercion exerted involved the use of threats of harm that were "present, imminent and pending" and "of such nature as to include well-grounded apprehensions of death or serious bodily harm if the act was not done." Nevertheless, no form of duress, even the threat of imminent death, was sufficient to excuse the intentional killing of an innocent human being. American courts have generally followed this approach, with both federal and state courts having made it clear that threats of future harm are not sufficient to constitute duress. See, for example, *United States v. Agard*, 605 F.2d 665 (2d Cir. 1979); *State v. Clay*, 264 N.W. 77 (Iowa 1935).

The defense of duress, sometimes referred to as coercion, compulsion, or duress, is recognized today by either statute or decisional law. Duress has been asserted most frequently by defendants who have committed robberies and thefts and by prisoners who have escaped from custody. Some courts look on duress as negating an element of the offense charged and classify it as a negative defense. See *People v. Graham*, 129 Cal. Rptr. 31 (Cal. App. 1976). However, most courts classify duress as an affirmative defense and require the defendant to prove the defense by the preponderance of the evidence.

The common-law presumption was that if a wife committed a felony other than murder or treason in her husband's presence, she did so under coercion of her husband. That presumption has little significance in modern America and has been abolished in some jurisdictions either by statute—see, for example, Wis. Stat. Ann. § 939.46(2)—or by judicial decision—see *People v. Statley*, 206 P.2d 76 (Cal. App. 1949).

In November 1992, a California appellate court announced a new development in the law of duress. The court held that evidence of the **battered woman syndrome** (BWS) is admissible to support a woman's defense that she committed robbery offenses because she was afraid the man she lived with would kill her if she did not do as he demanded. *People v. Romero*, 13 Cal. Rptr. 2d 332 (Cal. App. 1992). The court compared the situation to California decisions allowing evidence of BWS when a woman is accused of killing a man she lives with who batters her (see the later discussion of self-defense in this chapter).

In *People v. Merhige*, 180 N.W. 418 (Mich. 1920), the defendant, a cab driver, transported passengers to a bank, knowing they planned to commit a robbery. It was established at trial that the passengers held a gun to the defendant's head and that he believed he would be killed if he attempted to escape or render his cab inoperable. On the basis of the defendant having acted under duress, the Michigan Supreme Court reversed the cab driver's conviction.

Prisoners who escape custody frequently plead duress. As pointed out in Chapter 13, the requirement for establishing duress as a defense to escape requires the defendant to show that a *bona fide* effort was made to surrender or return to custody as soon as the claimed duress had ended or lost its coercive force. See *United States v. Bailey*, 444 U.S. 394, 100 S.Ct. 624, 62 L.Ed.2d 575 (1980).

There is a conflict among jurisdictions about whether a threat against persons other than the defendant is a sufficient basis for a defendant to invoke the defense

CASE-IN-POINT

Rejecting Economic Duress as a Defense

Defendant was arrested on board a boat in the Gulf of Mexico just off the coast of Florida and was charged with trafficking in cannabis in excess of ten thousand pounds. He pled not guilty and asserted the defense of duress. At trial, the defendant and his wife testified that economic reasons forced him to participate in trafficking in cannabis by piloting the boat. The trial judge declined to instruct the jury on duress, and the defendant was convicted. On appeal, the court affirmed the conviction and said that such claim of economic coercion was insufficient to call for a jury instruction on duress.

Corujo v. State, 424 So.2d 43 (Fla. App. 1982), rev. denied, 434 So.2d 886 (Fla. 1983).

of duress. Kansas allows a person to plead duress as a defense to crimes other than murder where the threat is against one's spouse, parent, child, brother, or sister. Kan. Stat. Ann. § 21–3209. Some courts have adhered to this view irrespective of statute; others have concluded that threats against other persons are not sufficient to constitute duress. For example, in *Jackson v. State,* 504 S.W.2d 488 (Tex. Crim. App. 1974), the court said that because the statute defining duress did not include threats concerning third parties, the court would not permit threats against members of the defendant's family to be considered as a basis to assert the defense of duress.

Necessity

Whereas in duress the situation has its source in the actions of others, in the defense of necessity, forces beyond the actor's control are said to have required a person's choice of the lesser of two evils. Early common-law cases recognized that "a man may break the words of the law . . . through necessity." *Regina v. Fogossa,* supra. Contemporary American judicial authorities hold that if there is a reasonable legal alternative to violating the law, the defense of necessity fails.

Suppose several people are shipwrecked on a cold night. One person swims to shore, breaks into an unoccupied beach cottage, and takes food and blankets to assist the injured until help can be secured. Prosecution in such an event would be unlikely, but if prosecuted, the defendant would properly plead the defense of necessity.

Is the defense of necessity applicable to a person with a suspended license driving a motor vehicle? In South Carolina, a defendant admitted to the offense but justified his actions on the ground that he needed to get help for his pregnant wife, who was suffering. He had no telephone, and his neighbor who did was not at home. The defendant drove to the nearest phone booth to request a relative to take his wife to the hospital. As he left, the police stopped him for having a broken tail light. He was then arrested for driving with a suspended license. At his trial, the judge refused his request to instruct the jury on the defense of necessity. The jury found him guilty, and he appealed. In a 3–2 decision, the Supreme Court of South Carolina ruled that under the circumstances the defendant was entitled to plead the defense of necessity. *State v. Cole,* 403 S.E.2d 117 (S.C. 1991).

In 1991 a Florida court of appeal allowed a husband and wife who contracted acquired immune deficiency syndrome (AIDS) to assert the defense of necessity to charges of possession and cultivation of marijuana. *Jenks v. State,* 582 So.2d 676 (Fla. App. 1991).

A number of defendants have attempted to justify actions involving "civil disobedience" on the ground of necessity in instances where they have forcefully asserted their personal or political beliefs. One of the most dramatic of these incidents occurred in 1980 when a group of antinuclear activists entered a factory in Pennsylvania, damaged components of nuclear bombs, and poured human blood on the premises. An appellate court approved of the defendants entering a defense of necessity; however, the Pennsylvania Supreme Court reversed the decision. *Commonwealth v. Berrigan*, 501 A.2d 226 (Pa. 1985). Other attempts to plead the necessity defense by antinuclear activists have also failed.

In most, but not all cases, the necessity defense has been unavailing to defendants espousing other social and political causes. In another instance, several defendants were charged with criminal trespass when they refused to leave an abortion clinic in Anchorage, Alaska. They claimed their actions were necessary to avert the imminent peril to human life that would result from abortions being performed. They were convicted, and on appeal they argued that the trial court erred in refusing to instruct the jury on their claim of necessity as a defense. In rejecting their contention, the Alaska Supreme Court outlined three requirements that must be met by a person who pleads the defense of necessity: (1) the act charged must have been done to prevent a significant evil, (2) there must have been no adequate alternative, and (3) the harm caused must not have been disproportionate to the harm avoided. *Cleveland v. Municipality of Anchorage*, 631 P.2d 1073, 1078 (Alaska 1981).

A Wisconsin statute codifies the defense of necessity by providing that

> [p]ressure of natural physical forces which causes the actor reasonably to believe that his or her act is the only means of preventing imminent public disaster, or imminent death or great bodily harm to the actor or another and which causes him or her so to act, is a defense to a prosecution for any crime based on that act, except that if the prosecution is for first-degree intentional homicide, the degree of the crime is reduced to second-degree intentional homicide. Wis. Stat. Ann. § 939.47.

Consent

Because in most instances a victim may not excuse a criminal act, American courts have said that consent is not a defense to a criminal prosecution. See, e.g., *State v. West*, 57 S.W. 1071 (Mo. 1900). Yet there are exceptions to this general statement. For example, where lack of consent is an element of the offense, as in larceny, consent is a defense. This can also be true today in a prosecution for rape, but only where competent adults freely consent before having sexual relations. Thus consent would not be a defense to a charge of statutory rape (the strict liability offense of having sexual intercourse with a minor).

Consent is commonly given to physicians who perform surgery. In contact sports, such as football and boxing, consent is implied and may be a defense to reasonable instances of physical contact that may otherwise be regarded as batteries.

Of course, a valid consent presupposes that it is voluntarily given by a person legally competent to do so and is not induced by force, duress, or deception. Moreover, a victim cannot ratify a criminal act by giving consent after the offense has been committed. *State v. Martinez*, 613 P.2d 974 (Mont. 1980).

Mistake of Law

One of the oft-quoted maxims of the law is that "ignorance of the law is no excuse." The safety and welfare of society demand that persons not be excused from commission of criminal acts on the basis of their claims of not knowing that they committed crimes. Although this is the generally accepted view, in some instances a defendant's honest, but mistaken, view of the law may be accepted as a defense. One example is where such a mistake negates the specific-intent element of a crime. Thus, a **mistake of law** may be asserted as a defense in a larceny case where there is a technical question of who has legal title to an asset. *State v. Abbey*, 474 P.2d 62 (Ariz. App. 1970). Likewise, a defendant's good-faith, but mistaken, trust in the validity of a divorce has been held to be a defense to a charge of bigamy. *Long v. State*, 65 A.2d 489 (Del. 1949).

The Illinois Criminal Code lists four exceptions to the general rule that a person's ignorance of the law does not excuse unlawful conduct:

> A person's reasonable belief that certain conduct does not constitute a criminal offense is a defense if:
>
> (1) The offense is defined by an administrative regulation which is not known to him and has not been published or otherwise made reasonably available to him, and he could not have acquired such knowledge by the exercise of due diligence pursuant to facts known to him; or
>
> (2) He acts in reliance upon a statute which later is determined to be invalid; or
>
> (3) He acts in reliance upon an order or opinion of an Illinois Appellate or Supreme Court, or a United States appellate court later overruled or reversed; or
>
> (4) He acts in reliance upon an official interpretation of the statute, regulation or order defining the offense, made by a public officer or agency legally authorized to interpret such statute. Smith-Hurd Ann. 720 ILCS 5/4–8(b).

Citing the preceding statutory exceptions, the Illinois Supreme Court held that a taxpayer who contended that she reasonably believed that she would be subject only to civil penalties, not to criminal sanctions, for failure to file an occupational tax return did not present a "mistake of law" defense. *People v. Sevilla*, 547 N.E.2d 117 (Ill. 1989).

In *United States v. Moore*, 627 F.2d 830 (7th Cir. 1980), the court said that "the mistake of law defense is extremely limited and the mistake must be objectively reasonable." 627 F.2d at 833. Furthermore, a court will never recognize a dishonest pretense of ignorance of the law as a defense. *State v. Carroll*, 60 S.W. 1087 (Mo. 1901).

CASE-IN-POINT

When a Penalty Is Imposed for Failure to Act, Reasonable Notice of a Local Ordinance May Be Required

A Los Angeles, California, ordinance made it unlawful for any "convicted persons" to remain in the city for more than five days without registering with the police, or if they lived outside of the city, to enter the city on five or more occasions during a thirty-day period without registering. Virginia Lambert, a convicted felon, was found guilty of failing to register, fined $250, and placed on probation for three years.

On appeal to the United States Supreme Court, Lambert's conviction was reversed. Writing for the Court was Justice Douglas: "Enshrined in our concept of due process is the requirement of notice. Notice is sometimes essential so that the citizen has the chance to defend charges. . . . Notice is required in a myriad of situations where a penalty or forfeiture might be suffered from mere failure to act."

Lambert v. California, 355 U.S. 225, 78 S.Ct 240, 2 L.Ed.2d 228 (1957).

A defendant can always raise the unconstitutionality of a statute as a defense to a prosecution for its violation. But a person who violates a statute thinking it unconstitutional does so at his or her peril; courts have said that a person's belief that a statute is unconstitutional, even if based on advice of counsel, does not constitute a valid defense for violating the law. *State v. Thorstad*, 261 N.W.2d 899 (N.D. 1978).

Mistake of Fact

In contrast with the ancient common-law maxim that "ignorance of the law is no excuse," at common law, ignorance or mistake of fact, guarded by an honest purpose, afforded a defendant a sufficient excuse for a supposed criminal act. American courts have agreed but have generally said that a mistake of fact will not be recognized as a defense to a general-intent crime unless the mistake is a reasonable one for a person to make under the circumstances. However, even an unreasonable mistake may be asserted as a defense to a crime that requires a specific intent. The decisions in recent years have indicated that a mistake of fact may be a defense as long as it negates the existence of the mental state essential to the crime charged. See, for example, *State v. Fuentes,* 577 P.2d 452 (N.M. App. 1978). Some jurisdictions have codified the mistake-of-fact defense. In Indiana, for example, mistake of fact is an affirmative defense by statute:

> It is a defense that the person who engaged in the prohibited conduct was reasonably mistaken about a matter of fact if the mistake negates the culpability required for commission of the offense. West's Ind. Code Ann. § 35–41–3–7.

In strict liability offenses, the defense of mistake of fact is unavailing because these offenses are not based on intent (see Chapter 4). In pointing out that this view represents the weight of authority, the Montana Supreme Court held that ignorance or even a *bona fide* belief that a minor was of legal age did not constitute a defense to prosecution for selling intoxicating liquor to a minor, unless expressly made so by the statute. *State v. Parr,* 283 P.2d 1086 (Mont. 1955). Likewise, because having consensual sexual relations with a minor is generally considered a strict liability offense, a mistake of fact as to a minor's age is generally not a defense to a charge of statutory rape. Even if a court finds that a statutory rape statute requires proof of a general criminal intent to convict, a defendant's reasonable mistake of fact concerning a female's age is generally not available as a defense. *State v. Stiffler,* 788 P.2d 220 (Idaho 1990). In 1964, however, the California Supreme Court departed from this almost universally accepted rule and held that an accused's good-faith, reasonable belief that a female had reached the age of consent would be a defense to statutory rape. *People v. Hernandez,* 393 P.2d 673 (Cal. 1964).

Other state courts have noted, but not followed, the view of the Supreme Court of California. In 1993 the Court of Appeals in Maryland held that a rape statute prohibiting sexual intercourse with underage persons defines a strict liability offense. The court explained that the statute does not require the prosecution to prove *mens rea* and makes no allowance for a mistake-of-fact defense. *Garnett v. State,* 632 A.2d 797 (Md. App. 1993). A dissenting judge acknowledged the rationale for protecting very young females but challenged such statutes that protect young, mature women: "But when age limits are raised to sixteen, eighteen, and twenty-one, when the young girl becomes a young woman, when adolescent boys as well as young men are attracted to her, the sexual act begins to lose its quality of abnormality and physical danger to the victim. Bona fide mistakes in the age of girls can be made by men and boys who are no more dangerous than others of their social, economic and educational level." Id. at 815.

In the past few years, in cases of statutory rape, some trial courts have heard arguments based on a minor's right to privacy. The contention is that because a minor female can consent to an abortion, she should be able to consent to sexual intercourse. Although this argument has generally fallen on deaf ears, some trial judges have questioned the need to continue to employ a strict liability standard in consensual sexual relationships where the female is a minor and appears to be an adult and represents herself as such.

In *State v. Freeman* (1990), the Supreme Court of Iowa considers the defense of mistake of fact in context of a conviction for "delivering a simulated controlled substance." An excerpt from this decision appears at the end of the chapter.

Alibi

Alibi means "elsewhere," and the defense of alibi may be interposed by a defendant who claims to have been at a place other than where the crime allegedly occurred. A criminal defendant who relies on an alibi as a defense does not deny that a crime was committed. Rather, he or she denies the ability to have perpetrated such crime because of having been elsewhere at the time.

The Colorado Supreme Court has pointed out that most jurisdictions have concluded that an alibi is not an affirmative defense. *People v. Huckleberry,* 768 P.2d 1235 (Colo. 1989). A few, however, characterize the defense as an affirmative one requiring proof of alibi by the defendant. Generally, a defendant who asserts an affirmative defense essentially admits the conduct charged and seeks to excuse or justify it. One who claims an alibi does not so admit. Therefore, it seems logical not to classify alibi as an affirmative defense. As explained by the Missouri Supreme Court,

> The theory of alibi is that the fact of defendant's presence elsewhere is essentially inconsistent with his presence at the place where the alleged offense was committed and, therefore, defendant could not have personally participated. Although the defense is not an affirmative one, the fact of defendant's presence elsewhere is an affirmative fact logically operating to negative his presence at the time and place. *State v. Armstead,* 283 S.W.2d 577, 581 (Mo. 1955).

Statutes or court rules commonly require that to assert alibi as a defense, a defendant must notify the prosecution in advance of trial and furnish the names of witnesses the defendant intends to use to support the alibi. The Supreme Court has said that this requirement does not violate the defendant's right to due process of law. *Williams v. Florida,* 399 U.S. 78, 90 S.Ct. 1893, 26 L.Ed.2d 446 (1970). In 1973, however, the Court held that when the state requires such information, the prosecution must make similar disclosures to the defendant concerning refutation of the evidence that the defendant furnishes. *Wardius v. Oregon,* 412 U.S. 470, 93 S.Ct. 2208, 37 L.Ed.2d 82 (1973). Alibi-notice statutes and court rules now commonly require disclosure by both defense and the prosecution.

Defenses Justifying the Use of Force

When offering a defense justifying the use of force, a defendant admits to an offense but claims that his or her conduct was justified under the circumstances. The use of force may be a defense to a criminal charge that the defendant caused injury or death to another. Therefore, the defense of **justifiable use of force** applies to the assaultive and homicidal offenses.

As a starting point, the use of **deadly force** (that is, force likely to cause death or serious bodily injury) must be distinguished from the use of **nondeadly force.** In general, the use of deadly force in self-defense requires that the person using such force (1) be in a place where he or she has a right to be, (2) act without fault, and (3) act in reasonable fear or apprehension of death or great bodily harm. *Lilly v. State,* 506 N.E.2d 23 (Ind. 1987). In evaluating whether the use of deadly force is reasonable, courts consider numerous factors. Among these are the sizes, ages, and physical abilities of the parties, whether the attacker was armed, and the attacker's reputation for violence. Ordinarily, a person may use whatever nondeadly force appears reasonably necessary under the circumstances. *State v. Clay,* 256 S.E.2d 176 (N.C. 1979).

Self-Defense

Defendants frequently admit the commission of acts that constitute an assaultive or homicidal offense but claim to have acted in self-defense. Generally, when a defendant raises the issue of self-defense, the prosecution must prove beyond a reasonable doubt that the accused did not act in self-defense. *Wash v. State,* 456 N.E.2d 1009 (Ind. 1983). Variations exist in the law on the permitted degree of force that can be used in self-defense, but the test of reasonableness appears common to all views. In determining the lawfulness of force used in self-defense, courts first look to see if the force used by the aggressor was unlawful. If so, the defender must show there was a necessity to use force for self-protection and that the degree of force used by the defender was reasonable considering the parties and circumstances.

At common law, a person attacked had a duty "to retreat to the wall" before using deadly force in self-defense. *State v. Sipes,* 209 N.W. 458 (Iowa 1926). In *Scott v. State,* 34 So.2d 718 (Miss. 1948), the court explained that to justify the slaying of another in self-defense at common law, there must have been actual danger of loss of life or suffering of great bodily harm. But the court said that the American approach has been that the danger need not be actual but must be "reasonably apparent and imminent."

Most courts reject the common-law doctrine of requiring a person to retreat to the greatest extent possible before meeting force with force. Rather, they say that a person attacked or threatened may stand his or her ground and use any force reasonably necessary to prevent harm. Courts that take this view often state it in positive terms, as did the Oklahoma Court of Criminal Appeals when citing one of its 1912 precedents: "The law in Oklahoma is clear: There is no duty to retreat if one is threatened with bodily harm." *Neal v. State,* 597 P.2d 334, 337 (Okl. Crim. App. 1979).

A substantial minority of courts, however, have adopted the principle that a person who can safely retreat must do so before using deadly force. But courts that follow the **retreat rule** have generally adopted the principle that a person does not have to retreat in his or her own dwelling. *State v. Bennett,* 105 N.W. 324 (Iowa 1905).

The Wisconsin Statutes codify the general law on use of force in self-defense:

> A person is privileged to threaten or intentionally use force against another for the purpose of preventing or terminating what the actor reasonably believes to be an unlawful interference with his or her person by such other person. The actor may intentionally use only such force or threat thereof as he reasonably believes is necessary to prevent or terminate the interference. The actor may not intentionally use force which is intended or likely to cause death or great bodily harm unless the actor reasonably believes that such force is necessary to prevent imminent death or great bodily harm to himself or herself. Wis. Stat. Ann. § 939.48(1).

CASE-IN-POINT

The Law of Self-Defense

Defendant Ernest Young was distributing religious literature on the street when he was approached by George Coleman, who began to harass and swear at him. Later, Coleman again accosted Young, this time at a table in a fast-food restaurant. Coleman began swearing at Young and grabbed his arm. Young pulled out a handgun and shot Coleman three times, killing him. Young was charged with and tried for murder.

Notwithstanding his plea of self-defense, the jury returned a verdict of guilty of voluntary manslaughter. As the appellate court reviewing the conviction said, "The jury heard appellant's story and it determined that he acted in the heat of the moment rather than in self-defense. There is ample evidence to support its verdict." The defendant's conviction was affirmed.

Young v. State, 451 N.E.2d 91 (Ind. App. 1983).

The use of deadly force presents the greatest issue in self-defense. As we noted earlier, deadly force may be used only where it reasonably appears necessary to use such force to prevent death or serious injury. In considering whether a defendant is justified in using deadly force, the law has traditionally applied an **objective test for the use of deadly force.** See, for example, *State v. Bess,* 247 A.2d 669 (N.J. 1968). Today, however, there is a conflict in the decisional law. Some courts apply a **subjective standard of reasonableness** to determine if circumstances are sufficient to induce in the defendant an honest and reasonable belief that force must be used. See, for example, *State v. Wanrow,* 559 P.2d 548 (Wash. 1977). Although the objective test requires the jury to place itself in the shoes of a hypothetical "reasonable and prudent person," the subjective test permits a jury "to place itself in the defendant's own shoes."

Much of the impetus for courts applying the subjective test to determine whether the use of deadly force is reasonable has resulted from cases where women charged with committing assaultive or homicidal offenses against men have defended their use of force. In *State v. Wanrow,* supra, a woman on crutches was convicted of second-degree murder and first-degree assault in her fatal shooting of a large, intoxicated man who refused to leave her home. In reversing her convictions, the Washington Supreme Court held that the trial judge erred by giving instructions to the jury that did not make it clear that Ms. Wanrow's actions were to be judged against her own subjective impressions and not those that the jury might determine to be objectively reasonable.

THE BATTERED WOMAN SYNDROME

Beyond the subjective standard of self-defense, in recent years the concept of self-defense by women has been expanded where a woman claims to have been continually battered by a man. The "battered spouse syndrome" soon became the "battered woman syndrome" (BWS). It describes a pattern of psychological and behavioral symptoms of a woman living with a male in a battering relationship. Some jurisdictions now permit a female in that situation who is charged with assaulting or killing a man to show that even though she did not face immediate harm, her plea of self-defense should be recognized because her actions were her response to constant battering by the man with whom she lived.

Decisional law is in the developing stage on the admissibility of expert testimony concerning the battered woman syndrome, with the trend being to hold that when a woman kills her batterer and pleads self-defense, expert testimony about BWS is admissible to explain how her particular experiences as a battered woman affected her perceptions of danger and her honest belief in its imminence. *State v. Hill,* 339 S.E.2d 121 (S.C. 1986); *People v. Aris,* 264 Cal. Rptr. 167 (Cal. App. 1989); *State v. Hickson,* 630 So.2d 172 (Fla. 1994).

In some instances, legislatures have enacted statutes to provide for admission of such evidence. See, for example, Section 563 of the Missouri Statutes Annotated: "Evidence that the actor was suffering from the battered spouse syndrome shall be admissible upon the issue of whether the actor lawfully acted in self-defense or defense of another."

THE BATTERED CHILD SYNDROME (BCS)

Following the same rationale, where there is evidence that a child has been abused continually over an extended period, there is a movement now to assert the **battered child syndrome** (BCS) in defense of a child accused of assaulting or killing a parent. Many prosecutors claim that the use of BCS is undermining the law of self-defense, yet there are experts who claim that a child's perceptions of the need to use force are shaped by his or her experience of constant abuse by a parent. These experts argue that when juries hear such evidence, they may be persuaded that a child acted in self-defense and not out of retribution.

In the state of Washington, a boy who killed his stepfather was convicted of second-degree murder and two counts of second-degree assault. At his trial, the court held that evidence of the battered child syndrome could not, as a matter of law, support a finding of self-defense because there was no "imminent threat" to the defendant. In a much-discussed opinion, the appellate court held that this ruling was in error: "Neither law nor logic suggest any reason to limit to women recognition of the impact a battering relationship may have on the victim's actions or perceptions. . . . [T]he rationale underlying the admissibility of testimony regarding the battered women syndrome is at least as compelling, if not more so, when applied to children." *State v. Janes,* 822 P.2d 1238, 1243 (Wash. App. 1992).

In 1993 California charged Erik and Lyle Menendez, ages eighteen and twenty-one, respectively, with the murder of their parents. Although the defendants admitted killing their parents, they claimed to have been victims of parental abuse. Their first two trials ended in mistrials because the jurors could not agree on a verdict. In March 1996, the Menendez brothers were convicted and sentenced to life in prison without the possibility of parole.

In *People v. Greene,* an Illinois appellate court upholds a trial court's rejection of the defendant's claim of self-defense to a charge of homicide. An excerpt from the court's opinion appears at the end of the chapter.

Defense of Others

At common law, a defender had the right to use reasonable force to prevent commission of a felony or to protect members of the household who were endangered, a principle that was codified in many jurisdictions. See, for example, *State v. Fair,* 211 A.2d 359 (N.J. 1965). The trend in American jurisdictions is to allow a person "to stand in the shoes of the victim" and to use such **reasonable force** as is necessary to defend anyone, irrespective of relationship, from harm. As the court noted in *State v. Grier,* "What one may do for himself, he may do for another." 609 S.W.2d 201, 203 (Mo. App. 1980). Today a number of states have statutes that permit a person to assert force on behalf of another. To illustrate, the Wisconsin statute provides as follows:

A person is privileged to defend a third person from real or apparent unlawful interference by another under the same conditions and by the same means as those under and by which the person is privileged to defend himself or herself from real or apparent unlawful interference, provided that the person reasonably believes that the facts are such that the third person would be privileged to act in self-defense and that the person's intervention is necessary for the protection of the third person. Wis. Stat. Ann. § 939.48(4).

Like the quoted Wisconsin statute, statutes in many other states limit a person's right to defend another individual from harm to those persons who "reasonably believe" that force is necessary to protect another. Some courts take a more restrictive view and hold that an intervenor is justified in using force to defend another only if the party being defended would have been justified in using the same force in self-defense. Under either standard, however, the right to go to the defense of another does not authorize a person to resort to retaliatory force.

Defense of Habitation

The common law placed great emphasis on the security of a person's dwelling and permitted the use of deadly force against an intruder. *Russell v. State,* 122 So. 683 (Ala. 1929). This historical view was chronicled by the Illinois Supreme Court in *People v. Eatman:*

> As a matter of history the defense of habitation has been the most favored branch of self-defense from the earliest times. Lord Coke, in his Commentaries, says: "A man's home is his castle—for where shall a man be safe if it be not in his house?" 91 N.E.2d 387, 390 (Ill. 1950).

Referring to a person's defense of habitation, the *Eatman* court opined that "he may use all of the force apparently necessary to repel any invasion of his home." 91 N.E. 2d at 390. This is sometimes referred to as the **castle doctrine.** Even though

---

CASE-IN-POINT

Defense of Habitation

Defendant Raines was charged with murder in connection with the death of Ricky Stinson. Stinson was the passenger in a car driven by James Neese. The evidence showed that Neese had threatened to kill Raines and that Neese had driven past Raines's trailer and fired some shots out the window of his car. Raines was not home at the time, but when he returned, his live-in companion, Sharon Quates, told him what had happened. A few minutes later they heard a car approaching and went outside. Quates identified the car as the same one from which the shots had been fired. As the car drove away, Raines fired five shots from a semiautomatic rifle. Quates testified that Raines said that "he'd just shoot the tire out and stop it and we'd go get the law and find out who it was." However, one of the bullets struck Ricky Stinson in the head, killing him. Despite his plea that he acted in self-defense and defense of his habitation, Raines was convicted of manslaughter.

The conviction was upheld on appeal, the appellate court saying that "although Raines may well have been in fear of danger when the . . . car approached, such fear alone did not justify his firing at the car as it drove down the public road past his trailer." As the court further observed, "One assaulted in his house need not flee therefrom. But his house is his castle only for the purposes of defense. It cannot be turned into an arsenal for the purpose of offensive effort against the lives of others."

Raines v. State, 455 So.2d 967, 972–3 (Ala. Crim. App. 1984).

a householder may, under some circumstances, be justified in using deadly force, the householder would not be justified in taking a life to repel a mere trespass.

In *State v. McCombs*, 253 S.E.2d 906 (N.C. 1979), the North Carolina Supreme Court addressed the issue of using deadly force to protect one's home. The court said that the use of deadly force is generally justified to prevent a forcible entry into the habitation in circumstances such as threats or where the occupant reasonably apprehends death or great bodily harm to self or other occupants or reasonably believes the assailant intends to commit a felony. Although this states the law generally applied by the courts, some statutory and decisional variations exist.

Courts have generally applied the castle doctrine against trespassers, but a minority of courts have refused to apply the doctrine where co-occupants legally occupy the same residence. Florida courts followed this minority position, but in 1999 the state supreme court receded from such a view and held there is no duty to retreat from a residence before resorting to deadly force against a co-occupant if such force is necessary to prevent death or great bodily harm. In joining the majority of jurisdictions that apply the castle doctrine to co-occupants, the court expressed considerable concern about domestic violence against women and pointed out that those who retreat from their residence when attacked by a co-occupant spouse or boyfriend may increase the danger of harm to themselves. *State v. Weiand*, 732 So.2d 1044 (Fla. 1999).

Defense of Property

The right to defend your property is more limited than the right to defend your homeplace or yourself. The common law allowed a person in lawful possession of property to use reasonable, but not deadly, force to protect it. *Russell v. State*, supra. Today, the use of force to protect a person's property is often defined by statute. Typically, Iowa law provides that "[a] person is justified in the use of reasonable force to prevent or terminate criminal interference with his or her possession or other right to property." Iowa Code Ann. § 704.4. The quoted statutory language generally represents contemporary decisional law even in absence of a statute.

Some older court decisions hold that a person may oppose force with force, even to the extent of taking a life in defense of his or her person, family, or property against a person attempting to commit a violent felony such as murder, robbery, or rape. However, these decisions focus on preventing a dangerous felony rather than simply on protecting or recapturing property. The prevailing view of the courts is that, in the absence of the felonious use of force by an aggressor, a person must not inflict deadly harm simply for the protection or recapture of property. *State v. McCombs*, supra. This is because the law places higher value on preserving the life of the wrongdoer than on protecting someone's property.

One method of defending property has been through the use of a mechanical device commonly known as a "spring gun" that is set to go off when someone trips a wire or opens a door. In the earlier history of the country, these devices were used on farms, in unoccupied structures, and sometimes in a residence at night to wound or kill an intruder. Some early court decisions said that use of a spring gun that resulted in the death of an intruder into a person's home was justified in instances where a homeowner, if present, would have been authorized to use deadly force.

Today, if someone is killed or injured as a result of a spring gun or similar mechanical device, the party who set it (and anyone who caused it to be set) generally will be held criminally responsible for any resulting death or injury. This is true even if the intruder's conduct would ordinarily cause a party to believe that the intrusion threatened death or serious bodily injury, conditions that might justify the use of deadly force.

The Model Penal Code § 3.06(5) takes the position that a device for protection of property may be used only if

(a) the device is not designed to cause or known to create a substantial risk of causing death or serious bodily harm; and

(b) the use of the particular device to protect the property from entry or trespass is reasonable under the circumstances, as the actor believes them to be; and

(c) the device is one customarily used for such a purpose or reasonable care is taken to make known to probable intruders the fact that it is used.

Even courts in jurisdictions that have not adopted the MPC view take a harsh view of the use of such mechanical devices, reasoning that to allow persons to use them can imperil the lives of innocent persons such as firefighters, police officers, and even children at play. Finally, some courts point to another reason: Although a deadly mechanical device acts without mercy or discretion, there is always the possibility that a human being protecting property would avoid taking a human life or injuring someone. See *People v. Ceballos,* 526 P.2d 241 (Cal. 1974).

Defense to Being Arrested

At common law, a person had the right to use such force as reasonably necessary, short of killing, to resist an unlawful arrest. The common-law rule developed at a time when bail was largely unavailable, arraignments were delayed for months until a royal judge arrived, and conditions in English jails were deplorable. Most American courts followed the English view. See, for example, *State v. Small,* 169 N.W. 116 (Iowa 1918). In some states a person may still forcibly resist an unlawful arrest.

As pointed out in Chapter 13, however, the rationale for the rule has substantially eroded. Increasingly, legislatures and courts recognize that resisting an arrest exposes both the officer and the arrestee to escalating violence. Moreover, defendants are now promptly arraigned, and counsel is generally available to debate the legality of an arrest in court. See *United States v. Ferrone,* 438 F.2d 381 (3d Cir. 1971).

Use of Force by Police

Most states have statutes or police regulations that specify the degree of force that may be used to apprehend violators. Officers are usually permitted to use such force as is reasonably necessary to effect an arrest and are not required to retreat from an aggressor. In practice, deadly force is seldom used by modern police forces, yet many states have statutes that authorize the use of deadly force by police in apprehending felons.

An excerpt from *Tennessee v. Garner* appears at the end of Chapter 16.

The Supreme Court's decision in *Tennessee v. Garner,* 471 U.S. 1, 105 S.Ct. 1694, 85 L.Ed.2d 1 (1985), limits an officer's use of deadly force to situations where it is necessary to prevent the escape of a suspect who poses a significant threat of death or serious injury to the officer or others.

A law enforcement officer who injures or kills a person or damages someone's property in the line of duty is sometimes charged with a criminal offense. As long as the officer acted reasonably and not in violation of the Fourth Amendment, a statute, or valid police regulations, the defense of having performed a public function is available to the officer.

Defenses Based on Constitutional and Statutory Authority

In earlier chapters we mentioned that, subject to certain exceptions, the First Amendment to the Constitution provides a defense for legitimate speech, press, assembly, and religious activities. We also discussed how the due process clauses of the Fifth and Fourteenth amendments permit one to defend against criminal charges based on statutes that are void for vagueness.

In this section we discuss two significant constitutional defenses asserted by defendants in criminal cases: immunity and double jeopardy. In addition, we mention here the defense provided by statutes of limitations, which are legislative enactments establishing time limits for prosecution of most offenses.

Constitutional Immunity

Everyone is familiar with the scenario of the witness who invokes the constitutional privilege against self-incrimination based on the Fifth Amendment to the Constitution, which provides that "no person . . . shall be compelled in any criminal case to be a witness against himself." The privilege against self-incrimination is applicable to the states through the Fourteenth Amendment, *Malloy v. Hogan,* 378 U.S. 1, 84 S.Ct. 1489, 12 L.Ed.2d 653 (1964), although states have similar protections in their constitutions.

The privilege against self-incrimination guaranteed by the federal constitution is a personal one that applies only to natural persons and not corporations. *United States v. White,* 322 U.S. 694, 64 S.Ct. 1248, 88 L.Ed. 1542 (1944). A strict reading of the clause would limit the privilege to testimony given in a criminal trial. However, the Supreme Court has held that an individual may refuse "to answer official questions put to him in any . . . proceeding, civil or criminal, formal or informal, where the answers might incriminate him in future criminal proceedings." *Lefkowitz v. Turley,* 414 U.S. 70, 77, 94 S.Ct. 316, 322, 38 L.Ed.2d 274, 281 (1973). A classic example is the privilege of suspects in police custody to invoke their *Miranda* rights.

Frequently, when a witness invokes the Fifth Amendment and refuses to testify, the court is requested to compel the witness's testimony. This may be accomplished by conferring immunity on the witness, which is a grant of amnesty to protect the witness from prosecution through the use of compelled testimony. A witness compelled to give incriminating testimony thus receives **use immunity** (that is, the testimony given cannot be used against the witness). This form of immunity (sometimes referred to as "derivative immunity") is coextensive with the scope of the privilege against self-incrimination and meets the demands of the Constitution. *Kastigar v. United States,* 406 U.S. 441, 92 S.Ct. 1653, 32 L.Ed.2d 212 (1972).

In some states a witness who testifies under a grant of immunity is given **transactional immunity,** a broader protection than is required under the federal constitution. Transactional immunity protects a witness from prosecution for any activity mentioned in the witness's testimony. An example of requiring broader protection occurred in 1993 when the Alaska Supreme Court ruled that its state constitution requires that witnesses who are compelled to testify be given the more-protective transactional immunity from prosecution, not just use immunity or derivative immunity as required by the federal constitution. *State v. Gonzalez,* 853 P.2d 526 (Alaska 1993). A defendant may assert the defense of immunity by a pretrial motion. Despite a grant of immunity, a witness may be prosecuted for making material false statements under oath. *United States v. Apfelbaum,* 445 U.S. 115, 100 S.Ct. 948, 63 L.Ed.2d 250 (1980) (see Chapter 13).

Other Forms of Immunity

Sometimes a prosecutor, with approval of the court, grants a witness **contractual immunity.** The purpose is to induce a suspect to testify against someone and thereby enable the prosecution to obtain a conviction not otherwise obtainable because of constitutional protection against self-incrimination. This type of immunity is rarely granted if other available evidence will lead to a conviction. The authority to grant immunity in federal courts is vested in the United States Attorney with approval of the Attorney General or certain authorized assistants. 18 U.S.C.A. § 6003. At the state level, such authority is generally vested in the chief prosecuting officer (that is, the district or state attorney).

Under international law, a person who has diplomatic status and serves as part of a diplomatic mission, as well as members of the diplomat's staff and household, is immune from arrest and prosecution, thus enjoying **diplomatic immunity.** The expectation, of course, is that American diplomats and their dependents and staff members will enjoy like immunity in foreign nations.

Double Jeopardy

The concept of forbidding retrial of a defendant who has been found not guilty developed from the common law. *Ex parte Lange,* 85 U.S. (18 Wall.) 163, 21 L.Ed. 872 (1873). The Fifth Amendment to the United States Constitution embodies this principle: "[N]or shall any person be subject for the same offence to be twice put in jeopardy of life or limb." The Double Jeopardy Clause was made applicable to the states through the Fourteenth Amendment in *Benton v. Maryland,* 395 U.S. 784, 89 S.Ct. 2056, 23 L.Ed.2d 707 (1969). Even before that, all states provided essentially the same protection through their constitutions, statutes, or judicial decisions recognizing common-law principles.

Justice Black expressed the rationale underlying the Double Jeopardy Clause:

> The underlying idea, one that is deeply ingrained in at least the Anglo-American system of jurisprudence, is that the State with all its resources and power should not be allowed to make repeated attempts to convict an individual for an alleged offense, thereby subjecting him to embarrassment, expense and ordeal and compelling him to live in a continuing state of anxiety and insecurity, as well as enhancing the possibility that even though innocent he may be found guilty. *Green v. United States,* 355 U.S. 184, 187–188, 78 S.Ct. 221, 223, 2 L.Ed.2d 199, 204 (1957).

The subject of double jeopardy is very complex, but certain principles seem clear. Jeopardy attaches once the jury is sworn in, *Crist v. Bretz,* 437 U.S. 28, 98 S.Ct. 2156, 57 L.Ed.2d 24 (1978), or when the first witness is sworn in to testify in a nonjury trial, *Serfass v. United States,* 420 U.S. 377, 95 S.Ct. 1055, 43 L.Ed.2d 265 (1975). The defense of double jeopardy may be asserted by pretrial motion.

The Double Jeopardy Clause forbids a second prosecution for the same offense after a defendant has been acquitted. *Ball v. United States,* 163 U.S. 662, 16 S.Ct. 1192, 41 L.Ed. 300 (1896). In recent years, this principle has been applied even after a conviction. *United States v. Wilson,* 420 U.S. 332, 95 S.Ct. 1013, 43 L.Ed.2d 232 (1975). But if a defendant appeals from a conviction and prevails, it is not double jeopardy for the prosecution to retry the defendant, unless the appellate court rules that there was insufficient evidence to sustain the defendant's conviction. *Burks v.*

United States, 437 U.S. 1, 98 S.Ct. 2141, 57 L.Ed.2d 1 (1978). Note the distinction between a conviction reversed by a higher court on basis of **insufficient evidence** and a defendant's conviction being vacated and a new trial ordered based on the **weight of the evidence.** In the latter case, a retrial of the defendant would not constitute double jeopardy. *Tibbs v. Florida,* 457 U.S. 31, 102 S.Ct. 2211, 72 L.Ed.2d 652 (1982). Nor is it double jeopardy to retry a defendant if the trial court, at the defendant's request, has declared a mistrial. *Oregon v. Kennedy,* 456 U.S. 667, 102 S.Ct. 2083, 72 L.Ed.2d 416 (1982). If, however, the government moves for a mistrial, the defendant objects, and the court grants the mistrial, the prosecution must establish a **manifest necessity** for the mistrial in order for a retrial to be permitted. An example of a manifest necessity might be a highly improper opening statement by the defendant's counsel. *Arizona v. Washington,* 434 U.S. 497, 98 S.Ct. 824, 54 L.Ed.2d 717 (1978).

Some offenses are crimes against both the federal and state governments. The policy, and in some instances state law, forbids a second prosecution once an offender has been prosecuted in a different jurisdiction. Nevertheless, because separate sovereigns are involved, under our federal system the Double Jeopardy Clause does not preclude a prosecution by both the federal and state governments. *Bartkus v. Illinois,* 359 U.S. 121, 79 S.Ct. 676, 3 L.Ed.2d 684 (1959). Yet this principle does not allow two courts within a state to try an accused for the same offense. Therefore, a person who has been prosecuted in a city or county court cannot be tried again in any court in the state for the same offense. *Waller v. Florida,* 397 U.S. 387, 90 S.Ct. 1184, 25 L.Ed.2d 435 (1970). In addition to protecting against a second prosecution for the same offense after conviction or acquittal, the Double Jeopardy Clause protects against multiple punishments for the same offense. *North Carolina v. Pearce,* 395 U.S. 711, 89 S.Ct. 2072, 23 L.Ed.2d 656 (1969). However, the Constitution does not define "same offense." In 1932 the Supreme Court said the following:

> The applicable rule is that, where the same act or transaction constitutes a violation of two distinct statutory provisions, the test to be applied to determine whether there are two offenses or only one is whether each provision requires proof of an additional fact which the other does not. *Blockburger v. United States,* 284 U.S. 299, 304, 52 S.Ct. 180, 182, 76 L.Ed. 306, 309 (1932).

The ***Blockburger* test** compares the elements of the crimes in question. It is a tool of interpretation and creates a presumption of legislative intent, but it is not designed to contravene such intent. Rather, the Supreme Court has said that the "legislative intent," if clear, determines the scope of what constitutes "same offenses." *Missouri v. Hunter,* 459 U.S. 359, 103 S.Ct. 673, 74 L.Ed.2d 535 (1983); *Albernaz v. United States,* 450 U.S. 333, 101 S.Ct. 1137, 67 L.Ed.2d 275 (1981). In 1980 the Supreme Court reviewed a case where the defendant was first convicted of failing to slow down to avoid an accident with his car. Later he was charged with manslaughter arising from the same incident. After reciting the "elements" test in *Blockburger,* the Court stated that

> if in the pending manslaughter prosecution Illinois relies on and proves a failure to slow to avoid an accident as the reckless act necessary to prove manslaughter, Vitale [the defendant] would have a substantial claim of double jeopardy under the Fifth and Fourteenth Amendments of the United States Constitution. *Illinois v. Vitale,* 447 U.S. 410, 420, 100 S.Ct. 2260, 2267, 65 L.Ed.2d 228, 238 (1980).

The *Blockburger* test examines the elements, not the facts. Since the Supreme Court's decision in *Illinois v. Vitale,* supra, not all courts have regarded *Blockburger* as the exclusive method of determining whether successive prosecutions violate the principle of double jeopardy. Indeed, some courts look also to the evidence to be presented to prove those crimes. For example, the Connecticut Supreme Court, citing *Vitale*, held that prosecution of a defendant for operating a vehicle under the influence of intoxicants after prior acquittal for manslaughter with a motor vehicle while intoxicated was barred by principle of double jeopardy. Even though the offenses were not the same under the *Blockburger* test, the evidence offered to prove a violation of the offense charged in the first prosecution was to be the sole evidence offered to prove an element of the offense charged in the second prosecution. Thus, the court held the second prosecution barred by the principle of double jeopardy. *State v. Lonergan*, 566 A.2d 677 (Conn. 1989). Other courts continue to determine the issue of double jeopardy by applying the *Blockburger* test. See, for example, *Butler v. State*, 816 S.W.2d 124 (Tex. App. 1991).

In *Grady v. Corbin*, 495 U.S. 508, 110 S.Ct. 2084, 109 L.Ed.2d 548 (1990), the Supreme Court, by a 5–4 vote, continued to follow the approach in *Illinois v. Vitale*. The Court said that "if to establish an essential element of an offense charged in that prosecution, the government will prove conduct that constitutes an offense for which the defendant has already been prosecuted," a second prosecution may not be undertaken. 495 U.S. at 510, 110 S.Ct. at 2087, 109 L.Ed.2d at 557. This became known as the **same evidence test** and barred a second prosecution based on the same conduct by the defendant that was at issue in the first prosecution. In June 1993, however, in *United States v. Dixon*, 509 U.S. 688, 113 S.Ct. 2849, 125 L.Ed.2d 556 (1993), by a 5–4 margin, the Court overruled *Grady v. Corbin*, replacing the same evidence test for double jeopardy analysis by a return to the **same elements test** from *Blockburger v. United States*, which bars punishment for offenses that have the same elements, or when one offense includes or is included in another offense. In *Dixon*, the Court also ruled that a criminal contempt conviction represents a "jeopardy" that triggers the bar against a second prosecution for the same offense.

In 1994 the U.S. Supreme Court invalidated a Montana tax on the possession of illegal drugs, imposed on a party already convicted of possession of illegal drugs. The Court ruled that the added tax was punishment in violation of the Double Jeopardy Clause. *Dept. of Revenue of Montana v. Kurth Ranch*, 511 U.S. 767, 114 S.Ct. 1937, 128 L.Ed.2d 767 (1994). After a defendant won dismissal of DUI-related charges in

CASE-IN-POINT **Double Jeopardy**

In a high-profile case in 1992, four Los Angeles police officers were tried by jury in a California state court on charges arising out of the beating of Rodney King, an African American motorist stopped by the police for traffic infractions. The event was videotaped by an onlooker and televised nationally. The jury's verdict finding them not guilty was followed by considerable outrage and large-scale rioting in Los Angeles. Despite the acquittal on state charges, the federal government brought new charges against the officers for violating King's civil rights. Their pleas that the new federal charges were barred by the Double Jeopardy Clause of the Fifth Amendment were rejected by the United States District Court, and in April 1993 two of the four officers were convicted after a jury trial. 833 F.Supp. 769. On appeal, the Ninth Circuit said that "there is no evidence that the federal prosecution was a 'sham' or a 'cover' for the state prosecution."

United States v. Koon, 34 F.3d 1416 (9th Cir. 1994).

Colorado on the basis that his driver's license had already been revoked because of the offense, defense attorneys began to assert a double jeopardy defense to DUI prosecutions. They argued that, on the basis of *Montana v. Kurth Ranch,* an administrative revocation of the accused's driver's license constituted "punishment" that barred a subsequent prosecution for DUI. In July 1996, the Colorado Supreme Court unanimously held that "imposition of criminal sanctions, subsequent to an administrative driver's license revocation proceeding does not constitute the imposition of multiple punishments and does not violate the Double Jeopardy Clause." *Deutschendorf v. People,* 920 P.2d 53, 61 (Colo. 1996). The court's opinion appears to be in accord with the opinion of most courts that have addressed this issue.

As we noted earlier, the dual sovereignty of the federal government and the states allow separate trials of a defendant for the same offense. In the past, this has not been a major problem because it has been governmental policy not to cause duplicate prosecutions. Some deviations from this policy have occurred in recent years, however.

Statutes of Limitation

A statute of limitations is a legislative enactment that places a time limit on the prosecution of a crime. Common law placed no time limits on prosecution. There is no federal constitutional basis to limit the time in which a prosecution can be initiated. Nonetheless, the federal government and almost all states have laws that prescribe certain time limits for prosecution of most offenses, except murder. There are two primary public policy reasons for enacting statutes of limitations on the prosecution of crimes. First, it is generally accepted that a person should not be under threat of prosecution for too long a period. Second, after a prolonged period, proof is either unavailable or, if available, perhaps not credible.

Statutes of limitations seldom place time limits on prosecutions for murder and other very serious offenses. This was dramatized in 1994, when Byron De La Beckwith was convicted for the June 1963 murder of Medgar Evers. Evers was an official of the National Association for the Advancement of Colored People, and his death galvanized support for the enactment of civil rights laws in the 1960s. Two trials in 1964 ended in deadlocked juries. But after extended litigation, and a lapse of more than thirty years since the victim's death, a Mississippi jury found Beckwith guilty of killing Evers. On December 22, 1997, the Mississippi Supreme Court affirmed Beckwith's conviction. *Beckwith v. State,* 707 So. 2d 547 (Miss. 1997).

Under most statutes of limitations, the period for prosecution begins when a crime is committed, rather than when it is discovered. The period ends when an arrest warrant is issued, an indictment is returned, or an information is filed. The period of limitations is interrupted while a perpetrator is a fugitive or conceals himself or herself from authorities. This cessation of the statute of limitations is often referred to as the **tolling** of the statutory period.

Federal statutes of limitations provide a five-year limitation on prosecution of noncapital crimes. 18 U.S.C.A. § 3282 et seq. Although limitation periods vary among the states, the Ohio law appears representative:

> Except as otherwise provided in this section, a prosecution shall be barred unless it is commenced within the following periods after an offense is committed:
>
> (1) For a felony other than aggravated murder or murder, six years;
>
> (2) For a misdemeanor other than a minor misdemeanor, two years;
>
> (3) For a minor misdemeanor, six months. Page's Ohio Rev. Code Ann. § 2901.13(A).

There is a conflict among the various jurisdictions as to whether a statute of limitations in a criminal action is an affirmative defense. An affirmative defense that is not pled is ordinarily deemed waived, but some courts have said that such a waiver must be knowing and voluntary. In *State v. Pearson*, 858 S.W.2d (Tenn. 1993), the Tennessee Supreme Court treated the statute of limitations as waivable by a defendant when it is about to run out, indicating that a defendant may wish to waive the protection of the statute. The court cited an instance where a defendant needs to gain time for plea bargaining, and another instance where a defendant who is charged with a more serious offense that is not time-barred might want to waive the statute of limitations on a lesser included offense. But, as the court pointed out, any waiver of the statute of limitations must be knowingly and voluntarily entered. Other courts follow the rule that the statute of limitations is jurisdictional and that if the state's information or indictment discloses that the prosecution is initiated beyond the period allowed by the applicable statute of limitations, the prosecution is barred.

Defenses Based on Improper Government Conduct

There are two defenses that are based on improper government conduct. The defense of entrapment aims to prevent the government from manufacturing crime. This defense is widely asserted in prosecution for narcotics violations, for these cases are frequently based on undercover police operations. The defense of selective prosecution is infrequently imposed and has achieved very limited success. Nevertheless, it is designed to prevent the government from singling out an individual for prosecution based on impermissible grounds.

Entrapment

Law enforcement officers may provide an opportunity for a predisposed person to commit a crime, but they are not permitted to "manufacture" crime by implanting criminal ideas into innocent minds. Therefore, a person who has been induced to commit an offense under these latter circumstances may plead the defense of entrapment. A defendant who claims to have committed an offense as a result of inducement by an undercover police officer or a confidential police informant often asserts the defense of entrapment. It is not available to a defendant who has been entrapped by a person not associated with the government or police. See *Henderson v. United States*, 237 F.2d 169 (5th Cir. 1956).

Entrapment was not a defense under the common law, and, strictly speaking, it is not based on the Constitution. Nevertheless, it has long been recognized in federal and state courts in the United States. In 1980 the Tennessee Supreme Court acknowledged that Tennessee was the only state in the Union that did not allow entrapment as a defense and proceeded to remedy the situation by declaring, "From this day forward entrapment is a defense to a Tennessee criminal prosecution." *State v. Jones*, 598 S.W.2d 209, 212 (Tenn. 1980).

In a landmark case arising during Prohibition days, the United States Supreme Court held that a federal officer had entrapped a defendant by using improper inducements to cause him to buy illegal liquor for the officer. The Court observed that the evidence revealed that the defendant, Sorrells, had not been predisposed to commit a crime but had been induced by the government agent to do so. The Court opined that entrapment occurs when criminal conduct involved is "the product of the creative activity of [law enforcement officers]." *Sorrells v. United States,* 287 U.S. 435, 451, 53 S.Ct. 210, 216, 77 L.Ed. 413, 422 (1932).

In *Sorrells,* the majority of the justices viewed entrapment as an issue of whether the defendant's criminal intent originated in the mind of the officer or whether the defendant was predisposed to commit the offense. This focus on the predisposition of the defendant has come to be known as the **subjective test of entrapment.** A minority of justices in *Sorrells* would have applied what is now known as the **objective test of entrapment.** Under this view, the court would simply determine whether the police methods were so improper that they likely induced or ensnared a person into committing a crime.

In the past, the majority of federal and state courts followed the subjective view. Thus, a person who pled entrapment was held to have admitted commission of the offense. See, for example, *United States v. Sedigh,* 658 F.2d 1010 (5th Cir. 1981); *State v. Amodei,* 563 P.2d 440 (Kan. 1977). A jury would then proceed to determine whether the defendant committed the crime because of predisposition or was improperly induced to do so by the police. To sustain the defense of entrapment, it is usually sufficient for the defendant to show that the police used methods of persuasion likely to cause a normally law-abiding person to commit the offense. See, for example, *State v. Mullen,* 216 N.W. 2d 375 (Iowa 1974).

The subjective approach to entrapment has the disadvantage of not providing the police with any bright lines for enforcement. Moreover, in proving predisposition, the prosecutor often brings in evidence of a defendant's past conduct that may be otherwise inadmissible. This can prejudice the jury with respect to arriving at a verdict on the principal offense charged.

The traditional view of courts has been that a defendant who asserts entrapment as a defense admits the offense charged. There have been conflicting decisions in the federal courts between this view and the more modern view, which holds that a defendant may assert entrapment without being required to concede commission of the crime or any element thereof. The U.S. Supreme Court resolved the issue in *Mathews v. United States,* 485 U.S. 58, 108 St. 883, 99 L.Ed.2d 54 (1988). The Court ruled that a defendant who pleads entrapment does not necessarily admit to the crime charged or any element thereof. The Court's decision affects only the federal courts; state courts vary in their approach as to whether a defendant who pleads entrapment admits the crime charged, their views sometimes being based on state laws providing for the defense of entrapment.

Where courts follow the objective view, the judge, not the jury, determines whether the police methods were so improper as to constitute entrapment. See, for example, *People v. D'Angelo,* 257 N.W.2d 655 (Mich. 1977). Some federal courts have simply said that where police conduct is outrageous, it becomes a question of law for the judge to determine if governmental misconduct is so shocking as to be a due process of law violation. See, for example, *United States v. Wylie,* 625 F.2d 1371 (9th Cir. 1980). In courts that strictly follow the objective view, the defendant's predisposition to commit an offense is irrelevant. The objective approach has the advantage of enabling the courts to scrutinize governmental action to ensure that outrageous methods are not employed in seeking to ferret out crime.

In 1993 the Wyoming Supreme Court declined to adopt the objective theory of entrapment. Nevertheless, it indicated that a defendant can rely on "outrageous government conduct" as a defense if the circumstances reveal police conduct that violates fundamental fairness and is shocking to the universal sense of justice mandated by the due process clauses of the Fifth and Fourteenth amendments. *Rivera v. State*, 846 P.2d 1 (Wyo. 1993).

Recent decisions indicate that the subjective and objective tests can coexist. Some state courts now first determine whether a defendant who pleads entrapment has been ensnared by outrageous police methods. If so, the judge dismisses the charges against the ensnared defendant. If not, the court then allows the defendant to attempt to establish the defense of entrapment by proving improper inducement. The prosecution usually counters with evidence showing the defendant's prior criminal activity and ready acquiescence in committing the crime charged. The court then instructs the jury to determine whether the defendant committed the crime because of his or her predisposition or through inducement by the police. At least two states have adopted this general approach. *Cruz v. State*, 465 So.2d 516 (Fla. 1985); *State v. Talbot*, 364 A.2d 9 (N.J. 1976).

Two principal reasons account for the increased assertion of the defense of entrapment in recent years. First, numerous violations of narcotics laws have been prosecuted on the basis of undercover police activity and evidence given by confidential police informants. Second, there has been increased attention to prosecuting corruption involving government officials.

One of the most highly publicized cases resulted from the 1980 Abscam operation, in which FBI agents posed as wealthy Arab businessmen and attempted to buy influence from members of Congress. Despite their claims of entrapment, several members of Congress were found guilty of offenses involving misuse of office. See, for example, *United States v. Jenrette*, 744 F.2d 817 (D.C. Cir. 1984).

In 1987 Keith Jacobson was indicted for violating the Child Protection Act of 1984, 18 U.S.C.A. § 2252(a)(2)(A), which criminalizes the knowing receipt through the mails of a "visual depiction [that] involves the use of a minor engaging in sexually explicit conduct." At trial, Jacobson contended the government entrapped him into committing the crime. A jury found him guilty, and his conviction was affirmed by the court of appeals. The United States Supreme Court granted review.

In evaluating the evidence at Jacobson's trial, the Supreme Court found that when it was still legal to do so, Jacobson ordered some magazines containing photos of nude boys. After Congress enacted the Child Protection Act, making this illegal, two government agencies learned that Jacobson had ordered the magazines. The agencies sent mail to Jacobson through fictitious organizations to explore his willingness to break the law. He was literally bombarded with solicitations, which included communications decrying censorship and questioning the legitimacy and constitutionality of the government's efforts to restrict availability of sexually explicit materials. He finally responded to an undercover solicitation to order child pornography and was arrested after a controlled delivery of the explicit sexual materials.

After pointing out that for twenty-six months government agents had made Jacobson the target of repeated mailings, the Court held that the prosecution failed to produce evidence that Jacobson was predisposed to break the law before the government directed its efforts toward him. Adding that government agents may not implant a criminal design in an innocent person's mind and then induce commission of a crime, the Court reversed his conviction, observing that Congress had not intended for government officials to instigate crime by luring persons otherwise innocent to commit offenses. *Jacobson v. United States*, 503 U.S. 540, 112 S.Ct. 1535, 118 L.Ed.2d 174 (1992).

In 1994 the U.S. Court of Appeals for the Seventh Circuit rendered an *en banc* decision holding that when a defendant pleads entrapment, the government must prove that the defendant was not only "willing" to commit the offense charged, but

An excerpt from *Cruz v. State* appears at the end of the chapter.

A Promise of Sex–Entrapment as a Matter of Law

Law enforcement officers told a female that she might not be prosecuted for possession of cocaine if she would become a confidential informant. She agreed and met with the defendant, James Banks, a suspected drug dealer, on two nights. The meetings included "kissing and hugging," after which she told Banks that if he "could get her something [they] would get together for the weekend, fool around and party." Defendant obtained some cocaine for her, and as a result, he was arrested. The trial judge dismissed the charges because the uncontested facts

established that the officers used a method with a substantial risk of persuading or inducing the defendant to commit a criminal offense.

The state appealed the dismissal. The appellate court affirmed: "When law enforcement agencies utilize confidential informants who use sex, or the express or implied promise thereof, to obtain contraband the defendant did not already possess, there is no way for the courts or anyone else to determine whether such inducement served only to uncover an existing propensity or created a new one. This violates the threshold objective test."

State v. Banks, 499 So.2d 894 (Fla. App. 1986).

also that he or she was "ready" to commit the offense in absence of official encouragement. *United States v. Hollingsworth*, 9 F.3d 593 (7th Cir. 1994).

Because the Supreme Court's decision in *Jacobson v. United States* is not grounded on constitutional principles, it affects only federal law enforcement activities. Nonetheless, it signals state enforcement authorities not to play on the weaknesses of innocent parties to beguile them into committing crimes.

Selective Prosecution

Selective enforcement of the criminal law is not itself a constitutional violation; therefore, without more, it does not constitute a defense. *Oyler v. Boles*, 368 U.S. 448, 82 S.Ct. 501, 7 L.Ed.2d 446 (1962). There are many cases rejecting the defense of selective prosecution. To prevail, a defendant must ordinarily demonstrate that other similarly situated persons have not been prosecuted for similar conduct and that the defendant's selection for prosecution was based on some impermissible ground such as race, religion, or exercise of the First Amendment rights of free speech. *United States v. Arias*, 575 F.2d 253 (9th Cir. 1978).

In 1996 the Supreme Court reviewed a case where defendants indicted for federal narcotics violations filed a pretrial motion for discovery of information they contended would show that they were being selectively prosecuted because of their race. The Court held that the defendants failed to establish an entitlement to discovery based on their claim because they failed to produce any credible evidence that similarly situated defendants of other races could have been prosecuted but were not. *United States v. Armstrong*, 517 U.S. 456, 116 S.Ct. 1480, 134 L.Ed.2d 687 (1996).

In *United States v. Eagleboy*, 200 F.3d 1137 (8th Cir. 1999), the defendant, who was not a member of a federally recognized Indian tribe, was charged with possessing hawk parts in violation of the Migratory Bird Treaty Act (MBTA). Had the defendant been a member of a federally recognized Indian tribe, he would not have been charged with a violation of the MBTA. Pointing to this policy, the defendant moved to dismiss on the ground of selective prosecution. The U.S. Court of Appeals for the Eighth Circuit held that Eagleboy was not selectively prosecuted. The court

CASE-IN-POINT

Rejecting the Defense of Selective Prosecution

In 1982 David Alan Wayte was indicted for willfully failing to register under the Military Selective Service Act. Wayte sought dismissal of the indictment on the ground of selective prosecution. He contended that he and the others being prosecuted had been singled out of an estimated 674,000 nonregistrants because they had voiced opposition to the Selective Service requirements. The district court dismissed the indictment on the ground that the government

had failed to rebut Wayte's *prima facie* showing of selective prosecution. The case was eventually heard by the United States Supreme Court. The Court held that the government's passive enforcement policy, under which it prosecuted only those nonregistrants who reported themselves or were reported by others, did not violate the First or Fifth amendments to the Constitution.

Wayte v. United States, 470 U.S. 598, 105 S.Ct. 1524, 84 L.Ed.2d 547 (1985).

said that the government's policy of not enforcing the act against recognized Indian tribes distinguished between persons on the basis of membership in a federally recognized Indian tribe, not on the basis of race.

Nontraditional Defenses

Although they are seldom successful, defendants sometimes employ **novel and innovative defenses.** We previously discussed the status of the battered women and battered children defenses, which, though not traditional, can no longer be considered novel. In this section, we discuss the assertion of religious beliefs and practices usually based on sincerely held religious beliefs. In addition, we offer some of the more interesting novel defenses. These involve the victim's negligence, premenstrual syndrome (PMS), compulsive gambling, post-traumatic stress syndrome (PTSS), the junk food defense, television intoxication, and pornographic intoxication. In instances where a novel defense leads to an acquittal, appellate courts do not have an opportunity to evaluate the legal basis of the defense. This is because the prosecution is not permitted to appeal an acquittal.

Unusual Religious Beliefs and Practices

The courts have long rejected contentions by defendants that they have been commanded by God or the Scriptures to commit illegal acts. See *Hotema v. United States,* 186 U.S. 413, 22 S.Ct. 895, 46 L.Ed. 1225 (1902). Moreover, laws prohibiting religious rites that endanger the lives, health, or safety of the participants or others are customarily upheld by the courts. This is illustrated by the Kentucky Court of Appeals' decision in *Lawson v. Commonwealth,* 164 S.W.2d 972 (Ky. 1942). There, despite the defendants' contentions that their constitutional guarantees of freedom of religion were violated, the court upheld the constitutionality of a statute making it a misdemeanor for anyone to handle snakes or reptiles in connection with any religious service.

Courts have traditionally upheld the right of parents to raise their children by their own religious beliefs, ruling that the state's interest must yield to the parents' religious beliefs that preclude medical treatment when the child's life is not immediately imperiled. See, for example, *In re Green,* 292 A.2d 387 (Pa. 1972). Nevertheless, the courts have held that where a child's life is imperiled, the parents have an affirmative duty to provide medical care that will protect the child's life. Thus, an appellate court upheld a conviction of parents for manslaughter when it found that a child's death was directly caused by the parents' failure to secure needed medical care. *Commonwealth v. Barnhart,* 497 A.2d 616 (Pa. Super. 1985). In about half of the states, child abuse and criminal neglect statutes permit parents to choose spiritual means or prayer as a response to illness without regard to a child's medical condition. In *State v. McKown,* 461 N.W.2d 720 (Minn. App. 1990), the court upheld dismissal of manslaughter charges against a parent and stepparent who relied on spiritual means and failed to secure medical treatment for an eleven-year-old boy. The child died allegedly as a result of medical problems resulting from diabetes.

The need to furnish medical care to children poses a problem of balancing the parents' interests in bringing up their offspring in accordance with their religious beliefs against the interest of the state in preservation of life. In January 1988, the press reported that the American Academy of Pediatrics urged repeal of laws allowing parents to reject medical treatment for their children on religious grounds. The academy pointed out that about three-fourths of the states have laws that permit some rejection of medical care on religious or philosophical grounds. However, the academy noted that courts have frequently intervened to order certain treatments for minors.

Victim's Negligence

Federal and state courts hold that a victim's negligence, credulity, or wrongdoing is not a defense to a prosecution. *United States v. Kreimer,* 609 F.2d 126 (5th Cir. 1980); *State v. Lunz,* 273 N.W.2d 767 (Wis. 1979). Likewise, because a crime is an offense against society as well as against the victim, it follows that a victim's forgiveness or condoning does not relieve an actor of criminal responsibility.

Premenstrual Syndrome

Premenstrual syndrome (PMS) refers to certain physiological changes that occur in some women, usually in the days close to onset of menstruation. This results from hormonal imbalance and can cause serious depression and irritability. In certain cases, medical treatment is required. Some argue that a woman so affected should be allowed to assert PMS as a defense to criminal conduct because some physicians say that PMS directly affects behavior. Nevertheless, PMS has not been accepted as a defense in the United States. In England, it has been recognized as a basis to mitigate punishment.

Compulsive Gambling

Evidence of compulsive gambling is generally not considered as a defense unless it rises to the level of insanity. For example, a defendant was convicted of entering a bank with intent to commit larceny and robbery. On appeal, he argued that the trial court erred in instructing the jury that "as a matter of law pathological gambling disorder is not a disease or defect within the meaning of the American Law Institute test for insanity." The United States Court of Appeals, while still applying the former ALI standard, rejected his contention. *United States v. Gould*, 741 F.2d 45 (4th Cir. 1984).

Post-Traumatic Stress Syndrome

Post-traumatic stress syndrome (PTSS) commonly refers to the unique stresses suffered during combat, often manifesting such symptoms as flashbacks, outbursts of anger, and blocked-out memories. After World War I, these conditions were usually referred to as "shell shock." Following World War II, the term "combat fatigue" was often used to describe such anxiety disorders. Present generations have heard these conditions described as "post-traumatic stress syndrome." Because of the bizarre type of warfare that service personnel endured in Vietnam, the unpopularity of the war, the availability of drugs, and the difficulties encountered in adjusting to civilian life, many veterans suffered severe psychological reactions. To a lesser extent, the stress of combat in Operation Desert Storm also caused delayed traumatic stress syndrome.

Although not a legal defense in itself, in some instances PTSS may affect a defendant's understanding to the point of allowing a plea of insanity. More frequently, PTSS will be introduced as evidence bearing on a defendant's intent or offered at a sentencing hearing in an effort to mitigate punishment.

The "Junk Food" Defense

Dan White, a former city supervisor, shot and killed the mayor of San Francisco in 1978. Following this, he killed another supervisor, who was a leader of the local gay community. In defense to charges of first-degree murder, White's counsel sought to establish that his client was depressed by having gorged himself on junk food. White was convicted of manslaughter instead of murder, giving some credence to reports that the jury may have accepted White's defense. This was jury action, so it set no precedent to establish any such defense.

Television Intoxication

An adolescent boy was tried in Miami for the first-degree murder of an elderly woman. He attempted to establish insanity on the basis of psychiatric testimony concerning the effects of "involuntary subliminal television intoxication." The trial court rejected his claim. An appellate court, stating that the trial judge correctly limited the evidence to the requirements of the *M'Naghten* rule, found no difficulty in upholding the trial court's decision. *Zamora v. State*, 361 So.2d 776 (Fla. App. 1978).

Pornographic Intoxication

There is a lively academic debate over the effect of pornography on the psyche. Does it stimulate sexual violence? Some defendants have attempted to employ a "pornography intoxication defense," but with little success. For example, in *Schiro v. Clark*, 963 F.2d 962 (7th Cir. 1992), a federal appellate court held that acting under the influence of pornography could not be used to mitigate the defendant's death sentence for rape and murder.

XYY Chromosome Abnormality

Growing evidence indicates that a person's genes influence behavior, and there has been speculation in media reports that people accused of violent crimes might find a medical basis to assert a "my genes made me do it" defense. While this is not recognized as a specific defense, there is some medical evidence that indicates presence of an extra Y chromosome may lead to physical and mental problems that cause an affected person to act aggressively. Some defendants have used evidence of this abnormality as a basis for the insanity defense.

Multiple Personality Defense

One who asserts a multiple personality argues that he or she did not commit the offense alleged; rather, another personality over which the defendant has no memory of and no control over committed the crime. In October 2000, the press reported that a woman named Mary in Kansas City, Missouri, who pled not guilty by reason of insanity to several offenses, contended that her multiple personalities were responsible for the deaths of her two young sons in 1999. Her lawyers and expert witnesses said she had severe psychosis and a personality named "Sharon" who controlled her actions. Notwithstanding her claim, the defendant was found guilty of murder and a series of child abuse charges.

Other Novel Defenses

Other novel defenses that have been asserted include urban survival syndrome and black rage. Like the other nontraditional defenses above, these are based on claims that could develop over the years in response to perceptions of social needs.

Conclusion

Despite the fact that the prosecution has met its burden of proving the elements of a crime, a defendant has the opportunity to not only dispute such proof, but also to affirmatively assert defenses to the conduct charged. A defendant may assert the incapacity to commit a crime. The law does not hold an insane person responsible, but as we have pointed out, legislatures and courts continue to struggle with the definition of insanity and the disposition of persons found to be insane. Young children are not held responsible, but, here again, the law encounters problems in determining at what age a child should be held responsible for crime. The use of alcohol and drugs now plagues the courts, as evidenced by the various approaches now taken to defenses asserting voluntary intoxication.

A person's right to use reasonable force in self-defense and defense of habitation and property has always been regarded as basic in Anglo-American jurisprudence, yet in modern society it becomes increasingly difficult to determine the extent of force that may be used in other situations. The use of force by police and the use of force by parents and by guardians and teachers who serve *in loco parentis* often present difficult questions. To what extent should police be permitted to use force in making arrests? When does the legitimate use of disciplinary force cease and child abuse begin? And what about the battered woman who seeks to justify her use of force against a charge of homicide or assault on the man she lives with? Or the abused child who assaults his or her parent?

Mistake of fact and mistake of law are merely expository of the commonsense foundation of the criminal law. They are a part of the civilized application of law. So too are the defenses of necessity and duress. However, courts have not been receptive to claims of necessity based on sociopolitical claims. Nor have they been receptive to claims of duress on the ground of economic coercion.

The defenses of immunity and double jeopardy are based squarely on the Constitution. The statute of limitations defense emerged from our penchant for certainty and our distrust of prosecutions resting on stale testimony. Our inherent distaste for "frame-ups" and outrageous conduct by the police has caused entrapment to become a viable defense to admitted criminal conduct.

The concepts of criminal responsibility and of criminal defenses will continue to evolve in response to our increased knowledge of human behavior and society's balance of the rights of the individual against society's legitimate demand for protection. Some nontraditional defenses could become viable, given new social science and medical research. In some instances, a nontraditional defense may result in the defendant's acquittal, may lead to a conviction for a lesser offense, or may be a mitigating factor in sentencing.

Key Terms

criminal responsibility
infancy
insanity
intoxication
self-defense
defense of others
defense of habitation and other
   property
mistake of fact
necessity
duress
consent
immunity
double jeopardy
statute of limitations
entrapment
selective prosecution
negative defense
burden of production of evidence
preponderance of the evidence
affirmative defense
burden to prove
parens patriae
voluntary intoxication
involuntary intoxication
not guilty by reason of insanity

M'Naghten rule
irresistible impulse
Durham test
ALI Standard
substantial capacity test
right from wrong test
Insanity Defense Reform Act of 1984
clear and convincing evidence
   standard
beyond a reasonable doubt
guilty but mentally ill
automatism
alibi
battered woman syndrome
mistake of law
justifiable use of force
deadly force
nondeadly force
retreat rule
objective test for use of deadly force
subjective standard of reasonableness
battered child syndrome
reasonable force
castle doctrine
use immunity
transactional immunity

contractual immunity
diplomatic immunity
insufficient evidence
weight of the evidence
manifest necessity
Blockburger test

same evidence test
same elements test
tolling
subjective test of entrapment
objective test of entrapment
novel and innovative defenses

Web-Based Research Activity

1. Use the Internet to examine your state statute dealing with the insanity defense and any judicial decisions interpreting the statute.
2. What is the test for determining insanity in your state?
3. Who bears the burden of proof? What is the standard of proof?
4. What are the rules governing the introduction of psychiatric testimony?

Questions for Thought and Discussion

1. In general, courts permit intoxication evidence only to the extent that it negates the *mens rea* of a specific-intent crime. Should evidence of voluntary intoxication be allowed for both general-intent and specific-intent crimes? Alternatively, should courts bar such evidence for both general-intent and specific-intent crimes? What position have the courts of your state taken?

2. What is the test for insanity in your state? Who has the burden of proof once the defendant introduces some evidence of insanity? Do you think the test in your state adequately protects (a) the public and (b) the defendant's rights?

3. Should the courts recognize battered woman syndrome (BWS) as a defense to assaultive and homicidal crimes by a woman living with a man who continually batters her? What position does your state take on this issue?

4. Explain the difference between the objective and subjective approaches to the defense of entrapment. Which approach is more just? Why?

5. Should the law require a person to retreat when attacked in his or her own home? Should the law make a distinction between co-occupants? Explain the justification for your view.

6. The Fifth Amendment to the U.S. Constitution requires the court to grant "use immunity" to a witness who is required to testify over a legitimately invoked right of self-incrimination. In some states, a witness who testifies under a grant of immunity is given "transactional immunity," a broader protection than the federal constitution requires. Explain the difference between the two categories of immunity.

7. To what extent, if at all, do you think the courts should interfere with the right of a parent to opt for spiritual, as opposed to medical, healing for a child who suffers from a curable disease?

8. Can one make a credible argument that any one of the nontraditional defenses outlined in the chapter should be accepted as a defense to criminal conduct?

··

Problems for Discussion and Solution

1. While taking his nightly walk, Charley Goodneighbor saw Joe Macho commit a battery on Charlene Loverly, a fourteen-year-old girl. Goodneighbor came to Charlene's defense and struck Macho so hard it fractured his skull. The police arrested both Macho and Goodneighbor. Goodneighbor explained to the police that he came to Charlene's aid to prevent her from being injured by Macho. What factors will the prosecutor probably consider in determining whether to file charges against Goodneighbor?

2. Nathan Ninja, who holds a black belt in karate, arrives at his home to find an intruder fleeing from the garage. Ninja pursues the intruder across the front yard and catches him in the street. An exchange of blows renders the intruder unconscious. A medical examination reveals substantial brain damage to the intruder as a result of the blows inflicted by Ninja. In a prosecution for aggravated battery, can Ninja successfully assert as a defense his use of force to protect his habitation?

3. Sally Shopper drives a 1995 gray Honda Accord. She parks it in a shopping center lot while she shops. Two hours later, Sally enters a car parked nearby that is almost identical to hers. As she drives away, the owner spots her and demands that a nearby police officer stop her. Just as the officer approaches her, Sally realizes that she is in someone else's vehicle. Had she looked at the vehicle more carefully, she would have observed that it had a license tag from a different state and some unique bumper stickers. On complaint of the owner, the officer arrests Sally and charges her with theft. What is Sally likely to assert in her defense?

4. A destitute homeless man steals food from a convenience market. When prosecuted for theft, he pleads the defense of necessity. The prosecutor urges the trial judge to strike the defense on the ground that the defendant could have qualified for assistance from local welfare organizations. Should the defendant be allowed to present his defense to the jury? Do you think he has a credible defense? Why or why not?

5. A defendant was found guilty of having forcible sexual intercourse with a fifteen-year-old female of previous chaste character. He is charged, convicted, and sentenced for violating two statutes: (a) common-law rape involving force and lack of consent, and (b) statutory rape involving intercourse with a minor of previous chaste character. On appeal, the defendant contends that his sentence violates the Double Jeopardy Clause of the Fifth Amendment. What arguments are his counsel likely to present to the appellate court? What should be the appellate court's decision?

6. The police suspect Mary Jane Hemphill of having sold marijuana at the Sibanac Bar. An undercover agent approaches her and asks her to go out with him. After a movie, the agent says that he would like to buy some marijuana for his close friend. At first, Mary Jane makes no response. They make another date, and after a very pleasant evening together, the undercover agent pleads with Mary Jane to help him find marijuana for his friend. She agrees, and the next day she delivers a quantity of the contraband to the agent, who gives her $200. As he concludes his purchase, the undercover agent arrests Mary Jane and charges her with the sale of contraband. Mary Jane's attorney pleads entrapment at her trial. Do you think her defense will be successful? Why or why not?

7. Boris Bottlemore has just finished celebrating his new job promotion by consuming ten double shots of bourbon in a bar near his home. He staggers from the bar to his home, which is one of twenty identical row houses on his block. In his ine-

briated state, Boris mistakes his neighbor's home for his own. Finding the door unlocked, he enters and promptly raids the refrigerator. He then collapses on a couch in the living room and passes out. The next morning, Patty Purebred is shocked to find a stranger sleeping in her living room and her refrigerator standing open, with food strewn across the kitchen floor. She telephones the police, who arrive and take Bottlemore into custody, charging him with burglary. What defense or defenses are available to Bottlemore? How would you assess his chances before a jury?

EXCERPTS FROM JUDICIAL DECISIONS

Latimore v. State

Court of Criminal Appeals of Alabama, 1988.
534 So.2d 665.

[Among the points the court addresses is the defendant's contention that his voluntary intoxication is a defense to murder.]

McMILLAN, Judge.

The appellant was transferred from Juvenile Court to the Circuit Court of Pike County, where he was found guilty of intentional murder. He was sentenced to 50 years' imprisonment in the penitentiary.

Patricia Pennington testified that she was present at the Cookie Jar, a lounge, on the night of March 15, 1986. She testified that, as she was dancing, she witnessed the appellant shooting Eddie Dwayne Jones. She testified that a woman grabbed the appellant around the waist and he began to struggle. When he had freed himself he shot again toward the victim, Eddie Dwayne Jones.

Juan Howard testified that he was present at the Cookie Jar on the night in question and heard a shot. He then saw the appellant with the gun. He further testified that he made a statement to the appellant indicating that the appellant should put down the gun and that the appellant threatened to shoot him. He further testified that a young woman was struggling with him and eventually pulled him out of the lounge.

Arthur Jones testified that he was also present at the Cookie Jar on the night in question. He testified that he heard a shot and observed the appellant pointing a gun at the victim, who was lying on the floor. He testified that a girl and another man were struggling with the appellant, who was still firing the gun. He testified that the girl and the man pushed the appellant out of the lounge. Jones then went to the police station for help.

James Alex Neal testified that he was present at the Cookie Jar on the night in question and heard a gunshot. He testified that he then observed people running from one side of the lounge and then heard two more gunshots. He observed a female struggling with the appellant, who was holding a gun. He then heard Juan Howard tell the appellant to stop shooting his gun and heard the appellant threaten to shoot Howard. The appellant continued to struggle with the female as they left the lounge. Neal followed them outside and asked the appellant for his gun. The appellant replied that he had not shot anyone and did not have a gun. Neal then asked the female for the gun and, as she was handing it to Neal, the appellant grabbed the gun and two more shots were fired. Thereafter, Neal got the gun from the appellant and gave it to Officer Freddie Brooks of the City of Troy Police Department.

The appellant testified that he had smoked some marijuana and consumed some alcohol prior to going to the Cookie Jar. The appellant testified that, as he was walking to his table, Eddie Dwayne Jones "stuck his hand out" and stopped the appellant. He testified that Jones was talking to him, but that he was unable to hear what was being said. The appellant further testified that Jones then pushed him back toward the door and that the appellant fell into a table. The appellant stated that he was afraid and pulled out his pistol and pointed it at Jones. The appellant said that Jones was walking toward appellant and the appellant pulled the trigger. The appellant testified that he was 17 years old and was carrying a gun because he knew that the Cookie Jar had a reputation for being a violent and dangerous place. . . .

The appellant argues that the evidence at trial was sufficient to establish that he acted in self-defense. . . .

The only evidence of self-defense . . . was the appellant's testimony. "Self-defense evidence, like all other conflicting evidence, is a matter to be left to the jury to decide, and it is the province of the jury to decide how much weight and credibility to give such evidence or testimony." . . .

The appellant argues that there was sufficient evidence to establish that he was intoxicated to such an extent as to create a reasonable doubt of his ability to form a specific intent. Voluntary intoxication can never justify or excuse the commission of a crime. . . . However, excessive intoxication may render an individual incapable of forming a specific intent. . . . However, although the appellant testified that he had smoked part of two marijuana cigarettes and had drunk over a pint of whiskey and several beers, there was no evidence to show as a matter of law that the appellant was intoxicated to such an extent as to render him incapable of forming the requisite intent. "The intoxication must be of such character and extent as to render the accused incapable of consciousness that he is committing a crime, incapable of discriminating between right and wrong—stupefaction of the reasoning faculty." . . . Whether appellant's intoxicated condition rendered him incapable of harboring the special intent was a question for the jury. . . .

● ● ● ● ● ● ● ● ● ● ● ● ● ●

United States v. Freeman

United States Court of Appeals, Eleventh Circuit, 1986.
804 F.2d 1574.

[This case examines the insanity defense in federal court as modified by the Insanity Defense Reform Act of 1984.]

HILL, Circuit Judge.

Appellant Dwayne Freeman challenges his conviction of bank robbery under 18 U.S.C. § 2113(b), (d) (1982). At trial, the facts surrounding the robbery and the defendant's guilt were never at issue. Freeman merely contests the trial court's determination that [he] was sane at the time of the offense. Freeman bases his appeal on two grounds. First, he challenges the constitutionality of the Insanity Defense Reform Act of 1984, Pub.L.No. 98–473, § 402, 98 Stat. 1837, 2057 (codified at 18 U.S.C. § 20 (Supp. 1986); Fed.R.Evid. 704(b). Second, Freeman asserts that as a matter of law, he has established his insanity by clear and convincing evidence. We reject both of the defendant's arguments. The Insanity Defense Reform Act produced three principal changes to the insanity defense in federal courts. First, the definition of insanity was restricted so that a valid defense only exists where the defendant was "unable to appreciate the nature of the wrongfulness of his acts" at the time of the offense. The amendment thus eliminated the volitional prong of the defense; prior to the Act, a defendant could assert a valid defense if he were unable to appreciate the nature of his act or unable to conform his conduct to the law. . . . The second change produced by the Act resulted in a shifting of the burden of proof from the government to the defendant. Prior to the Act, the government was required to prove beyond a reasonable doubt that the defendant was sane at the time of the offense. . . . Under the current act, the defendant must prove his insanity by clear and convincing evidence. . . . The third change prohibits experts for either the government or defendant from testifying as to the ultimate issue of the accused's sanity. . . .

The defendant's principal contention concerning the constitutionality of the act pertains to the burden of proof being placed on the defendant. . . . *Davis v. United States,* 160 U.S. 469, 16 S.Ct. 353, 40 L.Ed. 499 (1895), established that the prosecution must prove the defendant's sanity beyond a reasonable doubt in federal cases. The Supreme Court, however, has pointed out that *Davis* is not a constitutional ruling, but an exercise of the Supreme

Court's supervisory power over prosecutions in federal court. *Leland v. Oregon,* 343 U.S. 790, 72 S.Ct. 1002, 96 L.Ed. 1302 (1952); *Patterson v. New York,* 432 U.S. 197, 97 S.Ct. 2319, 53 L.Ed.2d 281 (1977).

In *Leland,* the Court held that a state could constitutionally require a defendant to prove insanity beyond a reasonable doubt. . . . The Supreme Court . . . has repeatedly reaffirmed the *Leland* holding. . . . The United States Constitution does not draw meaningless distinctions. Therefore, *Leland* compels a holding that the aspect of the Insanity Reform Act of 1984 requiring a defendant to prove insanity by clear and convincing evidence is constitutional. Additionally, we hold that the Act's restriction against opinion testimony as to the ultimate issue of insanity does not restrict the defendant in the preparation of his defense in violation of the Fifth Amendment. . . . The defendant is not prohibited from introducing evidence which would assist the jury in making this determination. Furthermore, the restriction . . . is applicable to the government, as well as the defendant. There is no constitutional violation. . . .

Freeman additionally contends that he has established his insanity by clear and convincing evidence. [At trial,] Dwayne Freeman asserted that he was an enthusiastic volunteer for the "Save the Children" campaign to feed starving children in drought-stricken Ethiopia. Freeman's evidence was that he degenerated to the point of obsession. He then became depressed about not raising enough money for the children. On February 26, 1985, Freeman robbed a bank, allegedly to obtain money for the Ethiopia fund.

The district court found that the defendant had failed to prove by clear and convincing evidence that he was unable to appreciate the nature and quality of his acts at the time of the offense. . . .

A psychiatric team from the federal institute at Springfield, Missouri, did conclude that Freeman was suffering from severe mental illness and was manic depressive or possibly schizophrenic. Additionally, Freeman presented evidence showing that he had been hearing noises and was experiencing severe depression prior to the robbery. Ample evidence exists, however, indicating that Freeman knew his conduct was wrongful. The evidence shows Freeman changed his clothes after robbing the bank to avoid identification. Freeman employed a mask, handgun and satchel to execute the robbery and avoid apprehension. He informed bank personnel that if the police were called, he would come back and kill everyone. When spotted by the police, Freeman ran to avoid apprehension. . . . Finally, Freeman's probation officer observed Freeman's demeanor as being entirely appropriate following his arrest. The district court's decision was not clearly erroneous.

We therefore AFFIRM the district court's decision.

● ● ● ● ● ● ● ● ● ● ● ● ● ●

State v. Freeman

Supreme Court of Iowa, 1990.
450 N.W.2d 826.

[In this case the Iowa Supreme Court considers the defense of mistake of fact in the context of a conviction for "delivering a simulated controlled substance."]

McGIVERIN, Chief Justice.

The facts of this case are not disputed. The defendant, Robert Eric Freeman, agreed to sell a controlled substance, cocaine, to Keith Hatcher. Unfortunately for Freeman, Hatcher was cooperating with the government. Hatcher gave Freeman $200, and Freeman gave Hatcher approximately two grams of what was supposed to be cocaine. To everyone's surprise, the "cocaine" turned out to be acetaminophen. Acetaminophen is not a controlled substance.

Freeman was convicted at a bench trial of delivering a simulated controlled substance with respect to a substance represented to be cocaine, in violation of Iowa Code section 204.410(2)(a) (1987). The sole question presented by Freeman's appeal is whether he can be convicted of delivering a simulated controlled substance when, in fact, he believed he was delivering and intended to deliver cocaine.

Our review is to determine whether any error of law occurred. Iowa R.App.P. 4. Finding no error, we affirm the conviction.

I. The statutory framework.

Iowa Code section 204.410(2) provides, in relevant part:

> [I]t is unlawful for a person to create, deliver, or possess with intent to deliver . . . a simulated controlled substance. . . .

The term "simulated controlled substance" is defined by Iowa Code section 204.10(27):

> "Simulated controlled substance" means a substance which is not a controlled substance but which is expressly represented to be a controlled substance, or a substance which is not a controlled substance but which is impliedly represented to be a controlled substance and which because of its nature, packaging, or appearance would lead a reasonable person to believe it to be a controlled substance.

Violation of section 204.401(2) with respect to a simulated controlled substance represented to be cocaine is a class "C" felony. . . .

II. Scienter and the offense of delivery of a simulated controlled substance.

Our cases indicate that knowledge of the nature of the substance delivered is an imputed element of section 204.401(1) offenses. . . . Proof of such knowledge has been required to separate those persons who innocently commit the overt acts of the offense from those persons who commit the overt acts of the offense with scienter, or criminal intent. . . . In general, only the latter are criminally responsible for their acts. . . .

The Iowa Code prohibits delivery of controlled substances and imitation controlled substances, as well as delivery of counterfeit substances, in language nearly identical to that prohibiting delivery of simulated controlled substances. . . . The distinctions between these statutory classifications are not relevant to this case.

Seizing upon the similarity of the statutory prohibitions, Freeman argues that he cannot be convicted of delivering a simulated controlled substance because he mistakenly believed he was delivering and intended to deliver an actual controlled substance.

We disagree. Freeman's construction of section 204.401(2) would convert the offense of delivery of a simulated controlled substance into one requiring knowing misrepresentation of the nature of the substance delivered. The statute clearly does not require knowing misrepresentation of the nature of the substance delivered.

Reading sections 204.401(2) and 204.10(27) together shows that the gist of this offense is knowing representation of a substance to be a controlled substance and delivery of a noncontrolled substance rather than knowing misrepresentation and delivery. As one court explained under similar circumstances, statutes like section 204.401(2) are designed "to discourage anyone from engaging or appearing to engage in the narcotics traffic rather than to define the contractual rights of the pusher and his victim. . . ."

Freeman's mistaken belief regarding the substance he delivered cannot save him from conviction. Mistake of fact is a defense to a crime of scienter or criminal intent only where the mistake precludes the existence of the mental state necessary to commit the crime. . . . In this case, Freeman would not be innocent of wrongdoing had the situation been as he supposed; rather he would be guilty of delivering a controlled substance. His mistake is no defense. The scienter required to hold him criminally responsible for committing the overt acts of the charged offense is present regardless of the mistake. Freeman knowingly represented to Hatcher that the substance he delivered was cocaine.

In conclusion, we hold that a person who delivers a substance that is not a controlled substance, but who knowingly represents the substance to be a controlled substance, commits the offense of delivery of a simulated controlled substance regardless of whether the person believed that the substance was controlled or not controlled. . . .

Affirmed.

People v. Greene

Appellate Court of Illinois, 1987.
160 Ill. App. 3d 1089, 112 Ill. Dec. 483, 513 N.E.2d 1092.

[This case examines, among other things, self-defense as a defense to a homicide charge.]

Justice MANNING delivered the opinion of the court.

Defendant, James Greene, was charged by indictment with the murder of Rickey Baldwin. Following a bench trial in the circuit court of Cook County, the defendant was found guilty of murder (Ill. Rev.Stat. 1985, ch. 38, par. 9–1), and sentenced to 27 years imprisonment. . . .

The defendant . . . contends that the weight of the evidence showed that he acted in self-defense when he shot the victim and that his conviction for murder should be reversed. Alternatively, the defendant argues that his murder conviction should be reduced to voluntary manslaughter since he had a reasonable belief that he was acting in self-defense. Whether a homicide is murder or manslaughter, or whether it is justified as self-defense, is a question to be determined by the trier of fact. . . .

The defendant relies upon the following factors to support his contention that he acted in self-defense. The victim was: (1) a convicted felon; (2) a member of a rival gang; (3) armed with a chain; (4) older than the defendant; (5) accompanied by two companions while the defendant was alone; and (6) the victim had accompanied other individuals, one of whom had shot the defendant the previous year.

The general rule regarding justifiable use of force provides:

> A person is justified in the use of force against another when and to the extent that he reasonably believes that such conduct is necessary to defend himself or another against such other's imminent use of unlawful force. However, he is justified in the use of force which is intended or likely to cause death or great bodily harm only if he reasonably believes that such force is necessary to prevent imminent death or great bodily harm to himself or another, or the commission of a forceable felony. . . .

The use of force in defense of the person is justified where (1) that force is threatened against the person; (2) the person threatened is not the aggres-

sor; (3) the danger of harm is imminent; (4) the force threatened is unlawful; and (5) the person threatened must actually believe that a danger exists, that the use of force is necessary and that such beliefs are reasonable. . . .

The issue of self-defense is an affirmative defense based upon satisfaction of the above elements. . . . This defense is raised only if the defendant presents some evidence regarding each element. . . . Once the issue is raised, the State must prove beyond a reasonable doubt that the defendant did not act in self-defense. . . .

This issue of self-defense is determined by the trier of fact. If the trier of fact has determined that the State has negated beyond a reasonable doubt any one of the elements justifying the use of force, then the State has carried its burden of proof. . . . The trier of fact's decision on the issue of self-defense will not be disturbed on review unless the decision is so improbable or unsatisfactory as to raise a reasonable doubt of the defendant's guilt. . . .

The State argues that in the instant case there was no evidence to support self-defense. We agree. The defendant became the aggressor when he fired a warning shot at the three individuals approaching him who withdrew when defendant fired the weapon. Defendant then proceeded to chase only the victim and shot him in the back. Therefore, he can not claim that he was in imminent fear of death or great bodily harm. If the defendant is the aggressor, the use of deadly force is justified only if:

> (1) Such force is so great that he reasonably believes that he is in imminent danger of death or great bodily harm, and that he has exhausted every reasonable means to escape such danger other than the use of force which is likely to cause death or great bodily harm to the assailant; or (2) In good faith, he withdraws from physical contact with the assailant and indicates clearly to the assailant that he desires to withdraw and terminate the use of force. . . .

The defendant as the aggressor never attempted to escape the danger, if such danger existed. Moreover, he never withdrew nor terminated the use of force. In fact, he accelerated his use of force by pursuing the victim and firing a second shot, although the victim had retreated.

A reading of the record fails to reveal any evidence which tends to show that force was threatened against the defendant. Although it is undisputed that the victim was carrying a 30-inch chain, there is no evidence that the victim used the chain to threaten the defendant. Moreover, by the defendant's own testimony he admitted to shooting the victim in the back from a distance of 10 feet.

Even if the victim had been the initial aggressor, the right of self-defense does not permit the pursuit and killing in retaliation or revenge of an initial aggressor after he retreats. . . .

Clearly, the evidence supports the trial court's decision to reject defendant's claim of self-defense. After a review of the record, we must conclude that the trial court's decision was not so improbable or unsatisfactory as to suggest reasonable doubt of the defendant's guilt.

Alternatively, the defendant contends that the evidence supports a finding of voluntary manslaughter. A person commits voluntary manslaughter if he kills an individual without lawful justification under a sudden and intense passion resulting from serious provocation, or if he intentionally or knowingly kills an individual believing the circumstances would justify or exonerate the killing, but his belief is unreasonable. . . .

The record in the instant case revealed that the defendant did not act under a "sudden and intense passion resulting from serious provocation." Defendant testified that no verbal exchange occurred between the defendant and victim nor did the victim physically threaten him with the chain. The defendant deliberately chased and shot the victim after the latter fell.

In regards to the defendant's unreasonable belief that the circumstances would justify the killing, defendant points out that he was "scared" and "panicked" when Thompson, Adams and the victim began to walk towards him. However, we fail to see how the defendant could have been in fear of harm from these individuals when they ran after the first shot was fired. We believe that the evidence supports a finding that the defendant had no subjective belief that the force he used was necessary, which is consistent with the finding of murder, not voluntary manslaughter.

A person commits murder if he either intends to kill or do great bodily harm to that individual or another or if he knows that such acts create a strong probability of death or great bodily harm. . . . It is not necessary to prove that the defendant had the intent to commit murder, only that he voluntarily and willfully committed an act, the natural consequences of which was to cause death or great bodily harm. . . . Although the defendant asserts that he did not intentionally kill the victim, he knew or should have known that the natural and probable consequences of shooting the victim in the back would cause death or do great bodily harm.

The reviewing court's power to reduce a murder conviction to manslaughter . . . should be cautiously exercised. . . . Based on the facts of this case we will not substitute our judgment for that of the trier of fact. We find no reason to disturb the trial court's finding upon review. . . .

JUDGMENT AFFIRMED.

CAMPBELL and O'CONNOR, JJ., concurring.

Cruz v. State

Supreme Court of Florida, 1985.
465 So.2d 516.

[In this case the Florida Supreme Court provides the trial courts with a two-prong threshold test of police activity to determine whether entrapment has occurred as a matter of law.]

EHRLICH, Justice.

This case is before us on appeal from a decision of the Second District Court of Appeal, *State v. Cruz,* 426 So.2d 1308 (Fla. 2d DCA 1983). The decision directly and expressly conflicts with *State v. Casper,* 417 So.2d 263 (Fla. 1st DCA), review denied, 418 So.2d 1280 (Fla. 1982). We take jurisdiction pursuant to article V. section 3(b)(3), Florida Constitution. We disapprove the district court's decision.

Tampa police undertook a decoy operation in a high-crime area. An officer posed as an inebriated indigent, smelling of alcohol and pretending to drink wine from a bottle. The officer leaned against a building near an alleyway, his face to the wall. Plainly displayed from a rear pants pocket was $150 in currency, paper-clipped together. Defendant Cruz and a woman happened upon the scene as passersby some time after 10 P.M. Cruz approached the decoy officer, may have attempted to say something to him, then continued on his way. Ten to fifteen minutes later, the defendant and his companion returned to the scene and Cruz took the money from the decoy's pocket without harming him in any way. Officers then arrested Cruz as he walked from the scene. The decoy situation did not involve the same *modus operandi* as any of the unsolved crimes which had occurred in the area. Police were not seeking a particular individual, nor were they aware of any prior criminal acts by the defendant.

Cruz was charged by information with grand theft. Pursuant to Florida Rule of Criminal Procedure 3.190(c)(4), Cruz moved to dismiss the information, arguing that the arrest constituted entrapment as a matter of law. The trial court granted the motion to dismiss on the authority of *State v. Casper.* . . . On appeal, the Second District court of appeal reversed, acknowledging its decision was in conflict with *Casper.*

The entrapment defense arises from a recognition that sometimes police activity will induce an otherwise innocent individual to commit the criminal act the police activity seeks to produce. . . .

The entrapment defense . . . normally focuses on the predisposition of the defendant. We adopted this view in *State v. Dickinson,* 370 So.2d 762 (Fla. 1979). The First District, in *State v. Casper,* . . . focused on predisposition when it found the "drunken bum" decoy at issue here to constitute entrapment as a matter of law. In *Casper,* Jacksonville police set up a decoy situation legally indistinguishable from the scenario in this case. The *Casper* court held that the state must prove the defendant was predisposed to steal from the decoy and that predisposition can be found under four circumstances: (1) the defendant has prior convictions for similar crimes; (2) the defendant has a reputation for committing similar crimes; (3) police have a reasonable suspicion the defendant was engaged in similar crimes; or (4) the defendant showed ready acquiescence to commit the crime suggested by police. . . . The *Casper* court found no evidence of the first two elements in that case. The third element is irrelevant in the type of random expedition at issue here. The question thus boiled down to whether *Casper* "readily acquiesced" to the criminal scenario. The *Casper* court found that an otherwise unpredisposed passerby who chose to take the money did not acquiesce, but "succumbed to temptation . . . to the lure of the bait." . . . The *Casper* court therefore distinguished between "succumbing to temptation" and "readily acquiescing," and found that this is a question of law: where a trial judge finds the defendant succumbed to temptation, the matter shall not be put to a jury. The Second District, in the case now before us, rejected this position. The *Cruz* court found that such a judgment is one for the jury to make. "[W]here, as here, a defendant's intent or state of mind (i.e., predisposition) is an issue, that issue should not be decided on a motion to dismiss." . . . Petitioner would have this court hold that where the only evidence of predisposition is the commission of the crime the police scenario was designed to elicit, there is an insufficient showing of predisposition, as a matter of law. We do not agree.

We agree with the Second District that the question of predisposition will always be a question of fact for the jury. However, we also believe that the First District's concern for entrapment scenarios in which the innocent will succumb to temptation is well founded. To protect against such abuse, we turn to another aspect of entrapment.

Entrapment is a potentially dangerous tool given to police to fight crime. "Society is at war with the criminal classes, and courts have uniformly held that in waging this warfare the forces of prevention and detection may use traps, decoys, and deception to obtain evidence of crime." . . . "The appropriate object of this permitted activity, frequently essential to the enforcement of the law, is to reveal the criminal design; to expose the illicit traffic, the prohibited publication, the fraudulent use of the mails, the illegal conspiracy, or other offenses, and thus to disclose the would-be violators of the law. A different question is presented when the criminal design originates with the officials of the Government, and they implant in the mind of an innocent person the disposition to commit the alleged offense and induce its commission in order that they may prosecute." . . . "Such a gross abuse of authority given for the purpose of detecting and punishing crime, and not for the making of criminals, deserves the severest condemnation, but the question whether it precludes prosecution or affords a ground of defense, and, if so, upon what theory, has given rise to conflicting opinions." . . .

To guide the trial courts, we propound the following threshold test of an entrapment defense: Entrapment has not occurred as a matter of law where police activity (1) has as its end the interruption of a specific ongoing criminal activity; and (2) utilizes means reasonably tailored to apprehend those involved in the ongoing criminal activity.

The first prong of this test addresses the problem of police "virtue testing," that is, police activity seeking to prosecute crime where no such crime exists but for the police activity engendering the crime. As Justice Roberts wrote . . . , "society is at war with the criminal classes." . . . Police must fight this war, not engage in the manufacture of new hostilities.

The second prong of the threshold test addresses the problem of inappropriate techniques. Consider-

ations in deciding whether police activity is permissible under this prong include whether a government agent "induces or encourages another person to engage in conduct constituting such offense by either: (a) making knowingly false representations designed to induce the belief that such conduct is not prohibited: or (b) employing methods of persuasion or inducement which create a substantial risk that such an offense will be committed by persons other than those who are ready to commit it." . . .

Applying this test to the case before us, we find that the drunken bum decoy operation fails. In Cruz's motion to dismiss, one of the undisputed facts was that "none of the unsolved crimes occurring near this location involved the same *modus operandi* as the simulated situation created by the officers." . . . The record thus implies police were apparently attempting to interrupt some kind of ongoing criminal activity. However, the record does not show what specific activity was targeted. This lack of focus is sufficient for the scenario to fail the first prong of the test. However, even if the police were seeking to catch persons who had been "rolling" drunks in the area, the criminal scenario here, with $150 (paper-clipped to ensure more than $100 was taken, making the offense a felony) enticingly protruding from the back pocket of a person seemingly incapable of noticing its removal, carries with it the "substantial risk that such an offense will be committed by persons other than those who are ready to commit it." . . . This sufficiently addresses the *Casper* court's proper recognition that entrapment has occurred where "the decoy simply provided the opportunity to commit a crime to anyone who succumbed to the lure of the bait." . . . This test also recognizes, as the *Cruz* court did, that the considerations inherent in our threshold test are not properly addressed in the context of the predisposition element of the second, subjective test.

For the reasons discussed, we hold that the police activity in the instant case constituted entrapment as a matter of law under the threshold test adopted here. Accordingly, we quash the district court decision.

It is so ordered. . . .

ALDERMAN, Justice, dissenting. . . .

Law Enforcement and Criminal Procedure

CHAPTER

15

Search and Seizure

CHAPTER OUTLINE

Introduction

Search and seizure are essential tools of law enforcement. A **search** occurs when government agents look for evidence in a manner that intrudes into a person's legally protected zone of privacy. A **seizure** takes place when agents take possession or control of property or persons. Because search and seizure often entail serious invasions of privacy, the power of law enforcement agencies to conduct searches and seizures is limited by the federal and state constitutions and by a number of federal and state statutes. Most important among these legal limitations is the Fourth Amendment to the United States Constitution:

> The right of the people to be secure in their persons, houses, papers and effects, against unreasonable searches and seizures, shall not be violated, and no Warrants shall issue but upon probable cause, supported by Oath or affirmation, and particularly describing the place to be searched and the persons or things to be seized.

As a general rule, the Fourth Amendment requires law enforcement officers to obtain a **warrant** before conducting searches and seizures. Although some warrantless searches and seizures are permissible, they all must conform to a standard of reasonableness. Law enforcement officers are not permitted to conduct searches and seizures arbitrarily, or even based on their hunches about criminal activity. For a search to be reasonable under the Fourth Amendment, police generally must have **probable cause** to believe that a search will produce evidence of crime. In certain instances, police may conduct limited searches based on the lesser standard of **reasonable suspicion.** Subject to certain exceptions, evidence obtained through unreasonable searches and seizures is not admissible in criminal prosecutions.

Historical Background

Before the late seventeenth century, there was very little protection at common law against invasions of privacy by unreasonable searches and seizures. Although a system of warrants had long been in place to provide legal authority for arrests, searches, and seizures, executive as well as judicial authorities could issue warrants. Moreover, there was no requirement that a search warrant specify the location to be searched or the items to be seized. For hundreds of years, English subjects (and, later, American colonists) were subjected to the abuse of the **general warrant**—that is, a warrant authorizing searches of unspecified persons and places.

In the wake of the Glorious Revolution of 1688, English courts began to place more stringent and effective limitations on the Crown's power. The power of search and seizure was one area in which courts moved to limit royal authority.

By far the most significant English case in the area of search and seizure before the American Revolution was *Entick v. Carrington*, 95 Eng.Rep. 807 (1765). John Entick, who edited a newspaper highly critical of the government, was arrested on a charge of seditious libel. A warrant was issued calling for the seizure of all his books, letters, and papers. Entick successfully sued for trespass. On appeal, the judgment was upheld and the practice of general warrants declared illegal. The opinion in *Entick v. Carrington* proved to be very influential. The next year, Parliament declared the notorious general warrant invalid. Addressing the House of Commons, William Pitt declared that

> [t]he poorest man may, in his cottage, bid defiance to all the forces of the Crown. It may be frail; its roof may shake; the wind may blow through it; the storm may enter; but the King of England may not enter; all his force dares not cross the threshold of the ruined tenement.

Adoption of the Fourth Amendment

Although the common law provided some protection against general warrants, the framers of the Bill of Rights adopted a more explicit, and more thorough, proscription of unreasonable searches and seizures. To a great extent they were motivated by a distaste for the Writs of Assistance, which gave customs officials in the American colonies unlimited powers to search for smuggled goods. In a famous debate in 1761, James Otis called the Writs of Assistance "the worst instrument of arbitrary power, the most destructive of English liberty and the fundamental principles of law, that ever was found in an English law book." Quoted in *Boyd v. United States,* 116 U.S. 616, 625, 6 S.Ct. 524, 529, 29 L.Ed. 746, 749 (1886). The Fourth Amendment was adopted to ensure that officials of the United States government would never be able to exercise such unlimited powers of search and seizure.

Their distaste for general warrants led the framers of the Bill of Rights to write a particularity requirement into the Warrant Clause of the Fourth Amendment. The Supreme Court has recognized that "limiting the authorization to search to the specific areas and things for which there is probable cause to search . . . ensures that the search will be carefully tailored to its justifications, and will not take on the character of the wide-ranging exploratory searches the Framers intended to prohibit." *Maryland v. Garrison,* 480 U.S. 79, 84, 107 S.Ct. 1013, 1016, 94 L.Ed.2d 72, 80 (1987).

Extension of the Fourth Amendment to Apply to State and Local Action

The Fourth Amendment, like all the protections of the Bill of Rights, was originally conceived as a limitation on the powers of the newly created national government. Under the original conception of the Bill of Rights, citizens seeking legal protection against actions of state and local governments had to look to their state constitutions and state courts for relief. *Barron v. Baltimore,* 32 U.S. (7 Pet.) 243, 8 L.Ed. 672 (1833). However, the protection of the Fourth Amendment, along with most of the protections contained in the Bill of Rights, has been extended to defendants in state criminal prosecutions on the basis of the Fourteenth Amendment's limitations on state action. In 1949 the Supreme Court held that the freedom from unreasonable searches and seizures is "implicit in 'the concept of ordered liberty' and as such enforceable against the States through the Due Process Clause [of the Fourteenth Amendment]." *Wolf v. Colorado,* 338 U.S. 25, 27–28, 69 S.Ct. 1359, 1361, 93 L.Ed. 1782, 1785 (1949). The judicial extension of the Fourth Amendment and other protections of the Bill of Rights to limit the actions of the state and local governments is referred to as the **doctrine of incorporation.** Under this doctrine, provisions of the Bill of Rights deemed to be essential to a scheme of ordered liberty are incorporated into the Fourteenth Amendment's broad limitations on state and local authority. *Palko v. Connecticut,* 302 U.S. 319, 58 S.Ct. 149, 82 L.Ed. 288 (1937).

When, Where, and to Whom the Fourth Amendment Applies

As a result of *Wolf v. Colorado,* supra, and subsequent court decisions, the Fourth Amendment limits search and seizure activities by law enforcement agencies at all levels of government, whether federal, state, or local. The application of the Fourth Amendment to state prosecutions ensures a minimal national standard governing search and seizure. Under our system of federalism, state courts are free to provide higher levels of protection for individuals under applicable provisions of their state constitutions than are provided by the Fourth Amendment. But they cannot provide less protection to the individual without running afoul of the Fourteenth Amendment. *Mapp v. Ohio,* 367 U.S. 643, 81 S.Ct. 1684, 6 L.Ed.2d 1081 (1961).

In an attempt to reduce confusion and unnecessary complexity owing to different federal and state standards of search and seizure, at least one state has amended its constitution. In 1982 the Florida Constitution was amended to render its prohibition of unreasonable searches and seizures coextensive with that of the Fourth Amendment. West's Fla. Const. Art. 1, § 12 (as amended 1982). Interpreting this novel amendment, the Florida Supreme Court has held that, in effect, the Florida constitution incorporates all decisions of the United States Supreme Court interpreting the Fourth Amendment, regardless of when they were rendered. *Bernie v. State,* 524 So.2d 988 (Fla. 1988).

The Fourth Amendment Does Not Apply to Private Actors

Because the Constitution limits government action, the Fourth Amendment protects a person's rights against the police and other government agents, but not against searches and seizures conducted by private individuals. The Supreme Court has said that the Fourth Amendment "is wholly inapplicable to a search or seizure, even an unreasonable one, effected by a private individual not acting as an agent of the Government or with the participation or knowledge of any government official." *United States v. Jacobsen,* 466 U.S. 109, 113, 104 S.Ct. 1652, 1656, 80 L.Ed.2d 85, 94 (1984). In determining whether a private citizen has acted as an agent of the government, the court must consider (1) whether the government knew of and acquiesced in the activity, and (2) whether the citizen was motivated on the basis of assisting the government. *United States v. Feffer,* 831 F.2d 734, 739 (7th Cir. 1987). Thus, a search by a privately employed security guard is ordinarily considered a search by a private citizen. Likewise, a search of a package by an employee of a common carrier is not considered a violation of the Fourth Amendment unless the search was instigated by government action. *United States v. Monroe,* 943 F. 2d 884 (8th Cir. 1991).

Border Searches and Searches Outside the United States

Travelers crossing the borders of the United States are routinely subjected to searches even when they are not the targets of suspicion. Suspicionless **border searches** are justified by the view that persons crossing the national border are not entitled to the protections of the Fourth Amendment. *United States v. Ramsey,* 431 U.S. 606, 97 S.Ct. 1972, 52 L.Ed.2d 617 (1977). This is not to say that agents conducting border searches are beyond the law. Regardless of the applicability of the Fourth Amendment, methods of search and seizure may not be so severe or extreme as to "shock the conscience." *Rochin v. California*, 342 U.S. 165, 72 S.Ct. 205, 96 L.Ed. 183 (1952).

The border search exception to the Fourth Amendment extends to searches conducted at established stations near the border or other functional equivalents of a border search. An example would be the search of a ship when it first docks after entering the territorial waters of the United States. *United States v. Prince*, 491 F.2d 655 (5th Cir. 1974). On the other hand, in *Almeida-Sanchez v. United States*, 413 U.S. 266, 93 S.Ct. 2535, 37 L.Ed.2d 596 (1973), the Supreme Court invalidated a search by a roving patrol some twenty-five miles within the border because agents lacked probable cause.

The Fourth Amendment does not apply to searches and seizures conducted by United States agents outside the territory of the United States. The purpose of the amendment is to restrict only those searches and seizures conducted domestically. *United States v. Verdugo-Urquidez,* 494 U.S. 259, 110 S.Ct. 1056, 108 L.Ed.2d 222 (1990).

The Home, Its Curtilage, and the Open Fields Doctrine

The English common law held that "a man's home is his castle," and it sought to protect persons in their homes by, among other things, creating the crime of burglary. The Fourth Amendment specifically mentions the right of the people to be secure in their houses. Of course, it also mentions their persons, papers, and effects. But it is fair to say that when a person is in his or her home, the protection afforded by the Fourth Amendment is at its maximum.

At common law, the concept of **curtilage** was developed to afford the area immediately surrounding a house the same protection under the law of burglary as afforded the house itself. The term "curtilage" refers to the enclosed space of ground surrounding a dwelling. The Supreme Court has held that the Fourth Amendment provides the same protection to the curtilage as to the house itself. On the other hand, the open fields surrounding the house and curtilage are not entitled to Fourth Amendment protection. *Hester v. United States*, 265 U.S. 57, 44 S.Ct. 445, 68 L.Ed. 898 (1924). Writing for the Supreme Court in *Hester*, Justice Oliver Wendell Holmes noted that

> the special protection accorded by the Fourth Amendment to the people in their "persons, houses, papers and effects," is not extended to the open fields. The distinction between the latter and the house is as old as the common law. 265 U.S. at 59, 44 S.Ct. at 446, 68 L.Ed. at 900.

The **open fields doctrine** was reaffirmed by the Supreme Court in *Oliver v. United States,* 466 U.S. 170, 104 S.Ct. 1735, 80 L.Ed.2d 214 (1984). In *Oliver,* narcotics officers entered the defendant's land by going around a locked gate and ignoring "No Trespassing" signs. When they observed a field of marijuana, they arrested the owner of the property for manufacturing contraband. The Court upheld the search because it concluded that the Fourth Amendment did not apply to the open fields around his home, despite his attempt to protect it by posting signs.

State courts are divided on whether to provide greater protection under their state constitutions. In *People v. Scott*, 593 N.E.2d 1328 (N.Y. 1992), New York's highest court ruled that where property owners fence or post "No Trespassing" signs on their private property or, by some other means, indicate that entry is not permitted, they have a reasonable expectation of privacy that must be respected. The New York decision illustrates that a state is free to provide greater protection under its state constitution than the U.S. Supreme Court determines is required under the federal constitution. A New Jersey appellate court was unwilling to grant greater protection than afforded by the federal constitution when it excused a warrantless entry onto private lands by conservation officers investigating suspected violation of fish and game law. *State v. Gates,* 703 A.2d 696 (N.J. Super. 1997)

Applicability of the Fourth Amendment to Administrative Searches

Although the Fourth Amendment refers to "houses," its protections are extended to stores, offices, and places of business. *See v. City of Seattle,* 387 U.S. 541, 87 S.Ct. 1737, 18 L.Ed.2d 943 (1967). However, an exception is made for those areas of commercial properties that carry an implied invitation for the public to enter. *Maryland v. Macon,* 472 U.S. 463, 105 S.Ct. 2778, 86 L.Ed.2d 370 (1985). Moreover, various statutes provide for unannounced inspections of "pervasively regulated businesses," such as establishments that sell alcoholic beverages. In 1998 the Michigan Supreme Court considered a massage parlor to be a pervasively regulated business and on that basis upheld a warrantless search of the premises. *Gora v. City of Ferndale,* 376 N.W.2d 141 (Mich. 1998).

Local ordinances also allow routine inspections to enforce building codes and other regulations. The Supreme Court has recognized these **administrative searches** as exceptions to normal Fourth Amendment protections. *Colonnade Catering Corp. v. United States,* 397 U.S. 72, 90 S.Ct. 774, 25 L.Ed.2d 60 (1970). The Fourth Amendment applies, but the standard is one of "reasonableness" rather than the more stringent test required of searches conducted by the police. *Camara v. Municipal Court,* 387 U.S. 523, 87 S.Ct. 1727, 18 L.Ed.2d 930 (1967). To determine whether an administrative search meets the reasonableness requirement, courts balance the need to search against the invasion that such search entails. *United States v. Bulacan,* 156 F.3d 963 (9th Cir. 1998).

Searches of Abandoned Property

Because it mentions "effects," the Fourth Amendment applies to items of personal property as well as to real estate. However, it should be noted that the Fourth Amendment does not apply to property that has been abandoned. Therefore, police may search

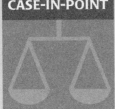

CASE-IN-POINT

Does the Fourth Amendment Apply to Garbage Placed by the Curb?

A police officer requested a trash collector to turn over bags of garbage collected from the Greenwood home in Laguna Beach, California. The officer searched the garbage bags and found evidence indicating illicit drug use. She used this evidence as a basis for obtaining a warrant to search the Greenwood home. During the search, the police discovered cocaine and hashish. As a result, the police charged the defendants with possession of contraband. The trial court dismissed the charges on the ground the warrantless trash search violated the Fourth Amendment, and the California appellate court affirmed.

The United States Supreme Court granted review and reversed on the ground that the defendants, by placing their garbage outside the curtilage, had exposed their garbage to the public, and regardless whether they may have had an expectation of privacy in their garbage, it was not an expectation that society is prepared to accept as being objectively reasonable.

California v. Greenwood, 486 U.S. 35, 108 S.Ct. 1625, 100 L.Ed. 2d 30 (1988).

abandoned premises and seize **abandoned property** without the necessity of legally justifying their actions. *Abel v. United States,* 362 U.S. 217, 80 S.Ct. 683, 4 L.Ed.2d 668 (1960).

Automobile Inventory Searches

Most law enforcement agencies that impound automobiles for parking violations or abandonment, or pursuant to the arrest of a motorist, routinely conduct an inventory of the contents and remove any valuables for safekeeping. When conducted according to standard police procedures, an **inventory search** is generally regarded as an administrative search not subject to ordinary Fourth Amendment requirements. Inventory searches are justified by the need for protection of the owner's property while the vehicle remains in police custody, protection of the police from claims of lost property, and protection of the police from potential dangers that might be lurking inside closed automobiles. Of course, if a routine inventory search yields evidence of crime, it may be seized and admitted into evidence without violating the Fourth Amendment. *South Dakota v. Opperman,* 428 U.S. 364, 96 S.Ct. 3092, 49 L.Ed.2d 1000 (1976).

It should be recognized that police are not permitted to use an inventory search as a pretext for a criminal investigation. *Colorado v. Bertine,* 479 U.S. 367, 107 S.Ct. 738, 93 L.Ed.2d 739 (1987). Nevertheless, once the police have legitimately taken a vehicle into custody, they are not required to overlook contraband articles discovered during a valid inventory search, and such items may be used as evidence. Lower federal and state courts have emphasized that an inventory search must be in accordance with established inventory procedures. See, for example, *United States v. Velarde,* 903 F. 2d 1163 (7th Cir. 1990). In 1998 the Arkansas Supreme Court held that the fact that defendant lacked a valid driver's license constituted good cause to justify a police officer's impounding his vehicle and completing a warrantless inventory of its contents pursuant to the police department's standards. *Thompson v. State,* 966 S.W.2d 901 (Ark. 1998).

Searches Based on Consent

Constitutional rights may be waived, and Fourth Amendment rights are no exception. Voluntary cooperation with police officers often results in fruitful searches and seizures. The Supreme Court has refused to require law officers to inform suspects of their right to refuse to **consent to a search.** *Schneckloth v. Bustamonte,* 412 U.S. 218, 93 S.Ct. 2041, 36 L.Ed.2d 854 (1973). More recently, the Court held that police are not required to inform motorists who are stopped for other reasons that they are "free to go" before asking them to consent to a search of their automobile. *Ohio v. Robinette,* 519 U.S. 33, 117 S.Ct. 417, 136 L.Ed.2d 347 (1996).

THE VOLUNTARINESS REQUIREMENT

To be valid, consent must be truly voluntary. If a person actually assists the police in conducting a search, or consents after having been advised that consent is not required, courts have little difficulty in finding that consent was voluntary. Yet consent has to involve more than mere acquiescence to the authority of the police. Thus, in *Bumper v. North Carolina,* 391 U.S. 543, 88 S.Ct. 1788, 20 L.Ed.2d 797 (1968), the Court held that a claim of police authority based on a nonexistent warrant was so coercive as to invalidate the defendant's consent. Similarly, a Georgia appellate court invalidated an automobile search where the defendant and a companion were surprised by six heavily armed law officers, were searched at gunpoint, and were then asked to consent to a search of their automobile. *Love v. State,* 242 S.E.2d 278 (Ga. App. 1978).

When a person summons the police to the home to investigate crime that has allegedly taken place there, there is an **implied consent** to a search of the premises related to the routine investigation of the offense. Of course, once police are lawfully on the premises, any evidence of crime that is in their plain view may be seized, even if the person who initially summoned the police may be ultimately prosecuted as a result of such evidence.

THIRD-PARTY CONSENT

A perennial problem in the area of consent searches is that of **third-party consent.** The problem is especially acute in situations where several persons share a single dwelling, as is common among college students. For example, may an apartment dweller consent to the search of his or her roommate's bedroom? The Supreme Court has said that the consent of a third party is valid only when there is mutual use of the property by persons generally having joint access or control. Thus, any of the co-occupants has the right to permit the inspection. The others have assumed the risk that one of their number might permit the common area to be searched. *United States v. Matlock,* 415 U.S. 164, 94 S.Ct. 988, 39 L.Ed.2d 242 (1974). *Matlock* stands for the principle that the validity of third-party consent is tested by the degree of dominion and control exercised by the third party over the searched premises and that a joint occupant may provide valid consent only if the other party is not present.

In *Illinois v. Rodriguez,* 497 U.S. 177, 110 S.Ct. 2793, 111 L.Ed.2d 148 (1990), the Supreme Court shifted the focus from the dominion and control of the third party to the police officer's subjective belief that the third party has the authority to grant consent to a search of the premises. Writing for the Court, Justice Scalia opined that a warrantless entry is valid when based on the consent of a third party whom the police reasonably believe to possess common authority over the premises, even if the third party does not in fact have such authority.

There are a number of well-established situations in which third-party consent is not valid. Tenancy arrangements are a good example. A landlord does not have the implied authority to consent to the search of a tenant's premises. *Chapman v. United States,* 365 U.S. 610, 81 S.Ct. 776, 5 L.Ed.2d 828 (1961). Likewise, a hotel manager or clerk does not have the right to consent to the search of a guest's room during the time the guest has a legal right to occupy the room. *Stoner v. California,* 376 U.S. 483, 84 S.Ct. 889, 11 L.Ed.2d 856 (1964).

Courts have taken different approaches to searches of college dormitory rooms, often depending on the regulations the student agrees to when occupying a dormitory room. A search routinely performed by college officials for reasons of health or safety that reveals incriminating evidence in plain view would probably not be in violation of the Fourth Amendment. On the other hand, a search of a dormitory room by police would ordinarily require a search warrant issued on basis of probable cause. In *Commonwealth v. McCloskey,* 272 A. 2d 271 (Pa. Super. 1970), the court held that absent **exigent circumstances,** police entry into a college dormitory room by means of a pass key possessed by the head resident was improper. Even though the university had reserved the right to check the room for damage and use of unauthorized appliances, the court found that the university did not have authority to consent to a governmental search of the student's room.

Some current problems in the area of third-party consent involve parental consent to searches of premises occupied by their adult children and spousal consent to searches of the other spouse's property, such as an automobile. But again, the Supreme

Court has shifted the focus to the police officer's subjective belief regarding the authority of third parties. In general, state courts have followed the *Matlock* approach. The Louisiana Supreme Court did that in 1999 by holding that a warrantless search may be valid even if consent was given by one without authority, if the facts available to officers at the time of entry justified the officers' reasonable, albeit erroneous, belief that the one consenting to the search had authority over the premises. *State v. Edwards,* 750 So.2d 893 (La. 1999). But not all state courts have been willing to follow *Matlock;* some provide more protection to their citizens. For example, Oregon courts have ruled that the state constitution requires that consent by a third party must be based on actual authority. See *State v. Will,* 885 P.2d 715 (Or. App. 1994).

The Scope of Privacy Protected by the Fourth Amendment

The term "seizure" refers to the taking into custody of physical evidence, property, or even a person. What constitutes a "search"? The answer is not so clear. Originally, the protection of the Fourth Amendment was limited to physical intrusions to one's person or property. *Olmstead v. United States,* 277 U.S. 438, 48 S.Ct. 564, 72 L.Ed. 944 (1928). Historically, courts looked at whether a trespass had taken place in deciding whether the Fourth Amendment was implicated. Thus, surveillance without physical contact with the suspect or the suspect's property was deemed to fall outside the protections of the Fourth Amendment. Accordingly, the Fourth Amendment was not deemed applicable to **wiretapping** or **electronic eavesdropping.**

In *Katz v. United States,* 389 U.S. 347, 88 S.Ct. 507, 19 L.Ed.2d 576 (1967), the Supreme Court overruled *Olmstead* and abandoned the trespass doctrine, saying "the Fourth Amendment protects people, not places." 389 U.S. at 361, 88 S.Ct. at 516, 19 L.Ed.2d at 582. The contemporary approach to determining the scope of protected privacy under the Fourth Amendment is nicely stated in Justice Harlan's concurring opinion in *Katz:*

An excerpt from the Supreme Court's opinion in *Katz v. United States* appears at the end of the chapter.

> My understanding of the rule as it has emerged from prior decisions is that there is a twofold requirement, first that a person have exhibited an actual (subjective)

CASE-IN-POINT

No Reasonable Expectation of Privacy for Commercial Visitors to Homes

A police officer peered into an apartment through a gap in a closed blind. Inside, he observed three people bagging cocaine. One person resided in the apartment while the other two were there only to help package the cocaine. The Minnesota Supreme Court held that the visitors to the apartment had a legitimate expectation of privacy and that the officer's peering through the closed blind constituted an unreasonable search. *State v. Carter,* 569 N.W.2d 695 (1997). The United States Supreme Court reversed, finding the visitors had no legitimate expectation of privacy as they were "essentially present for a business transaction and were only in the home a matter of hours to conduct a commercial transaction for a short period of time."

Minnesota v. Carter, 525 U.S. 83, 119 S.Ct. 469, 142 L.Ed.2d 373 (1998).

Bond v. United States, 529 U.S. 334, 120 S.Ct. 1462, 146 L.Ed.2d 365 (2000)

Steven D. Bond was traveling on a Greyhound bus from California to Little Rock, Arkansas. When the bus stopped at a border patrol checkpoint in Texas, an agent boarded the bus to check for undocumented aliens. During the course of the inspection the agent squeezed the soft luggage in the overhead storage space above the seats. In squeezing a canvas bag belonging to Bond, the agent detected a "brick-like" object that aroused his suspicions. Upon the agent's request, Bond consented to a search of the bag, which produced a brick of methamphetamine wrapped in duct tape.

After his motion to suppress the contraband was denied, Bond was convicted of possession with intent to distribute methamphetamine and was sentenced to 57 months in prison. The Court of Appeals upheld the denial of the suppression motion, holding that the agent's action in squeezing the canvas bag was not a search within the meaning of the Fourth Amendment. On certiorari, the Supreme Court reversed, dividing 7–2.

The key issue in the case was whether Mr. Bond had a reasonable expectation of privacy that was violated by the agent's physical contact with the canvas bag in which the contraband was sequestered. Writing for the Court, Chief Justice Rehnquist opined as follows:

"When a bus passenger places a bag in an overhead bin, he expects that other passengers or bus employees may move it for one reason or another. Thus, a bus passenger clearly expects that his bag may be handled. He does not expect that other passengers or bus employees will, as a matter of course, feel the bag in an exploratory manner. But this is exactly what the agent did here. We therefore hold that the agent's physical manipulation of petitioner's bag violated the Fourth Amendment."

In dissent, Justice Breyer, joined by Justice Scalia, observed that "the traveler who wants to place a bag in a shared overhead bin and yet safeguard its contents from public touch should plan to pack those contents in a suitcase with hard sides, irrespective of the Court's decision today."

expectation of privacy and, second, that the expectation be one that society is prepared to recognize as "reasonable." 389 U.S. at 361, 88 S.Ct. at 516, 19 L.Ed.2d at 587.

Reasonable Expectations of Privacy

Potentially, the term "search" applies to any official invasion of a person's reasonable expectation of privacy as to one's person, house, papers, or effects. In *Katz,* the Court held that a suspected bookie who was using a public telephone allegedly in conduct of a gambling business enjoyed a **reasonable expectation of privacy,** and that a police wiretap of the phone booth was a search within the meaning of the Fourth Amendment. This decision brought wiretapping and other forms of electronic eavesdropping within the limitations of the Fourth Amendment. Currently, any means of invading a person's "reasonable expectation of privacy" is considered a "search" for Fourth Amendment purposes. The critical question that courts must address in reviewing cases where police conduct surveillance or eavesdropping without probable cause or prior judicial authorization is whether such surveillance intruded on a suspect's reasonable expectation of privacy.

The issue of what constitutes a reasonable expectation of privacy has been litigated in hundreds of cases in federal and state courts. Police techniques such as canine sniffs are considered among the least intrusive means of government investigation. Thus, police were allowed to conduct a "sniff test" of a passenger's luggage at an airport without reasonable suspicion because it did not violate a person's reasonable expectation of privacy. *United States v. Place,* 462 U.S. 696, 106 S.Ct. 2637, 77

L.Ed.2d 110 (1983). However, the uniqueness of individual situations has resulted in disparate views, with police frequently complaining that judicial decisions fail to furnish any "bright line" rules. In a number of well-defined situations, however, courts have upheld minimally intrusive suspicionless searches on the assumption that people's privacy expectations are reduced in such situations.

With increased concern over airplane hijacking and terrorism has come increased security at the nation's airports. Passengers attempting to board aircraft routinely pass through metal detectors; their carry-on baggage and checked luggage are routinely subjected to X-ray scans. Should these procedures suggest the presence of suspicious objects, physical searches are conducted to determine what the objects are. There is little question that such searches are reasonable, given their minimal intrusiveness, the gravity of the safety interests involved, and the reduced privacy expectations associated with airline travel. Indeed, travelers are often notified through airport public address systems and signs that "all bags are subject to search." Such announcements place passengers on notice that ordinary Fourth Amendment protections do not apply.

Sobriety Checkpoints

Society has also become incensed about the problem of drunk driving and the resulting carnage on the nation's highways. One device increasingly used by law enforcement to combat this problem is **sobriety checkpoints,** in which all drivers passing a certain point are stopped briefly and observed for signs of intoxication. To the extent that police officers at these checkpoints visually inspect the passenger compartments of stopped automobiles, these brief encounters involve searches, although in most instances these procedures entail only minor intrusion and inconvenience. Critics of sobriety checkpoints object to the fact that police temporarily detain and visually search cars without any particular suspicion. Yet the courts have generally approved such measures. See, for example, *Michigan Dept. of State Police v. Sitz,* 496 U.S. 444, 110 S.Ct. 2481, 110 L.Ed.2d 412 (1990). (This topic is explored further in the next chapter.)

Jail and Prison Searches and Strip Searches

Obviously, anyone lawfully incarcerated in a prison or jail has no reasonable expectation of privacy. Jail and prison cells are routinely "swept" for weapons and other contraband, and inmates are routinely subjected to searches of their persons. The Supreme Court in *Bell v. Wolfish,* 441 U.S. 520, 99 S.Ct. 1861, 60 L.Ed.2d 447 (1979), upheld strip searches of prison inmates because of the demands for institutional security. But the Court did not give prison officials carte blanche. Rather, the Court held that the Fourth Amendment requires balancing the need for the particular search against the invasion of personal rights. Thus, courts must consider the justification and scope of the intrusion, and the manner and place in which it is conducted.

Absent cause for suspicion, visitors to a prison may be subjected to reasonable searches—for example, a pat-down search or a metal detector sweep. However, before conducting a strip search of a visitor, prison authorities must have at least a reasonable suspicion that the visitor is bearing contraband. *Spear v. Sowders,* 71 F.3d 626 (6th Cir. 1995).

Courts have generally disapproved of blanket policies that allow **strip searches** of all persons who have been arrested, particularly where traffic violators are concerned. Some courts hold that strip searches are violative of Fourth Amendment rights unless there is probable cause to believe the arrestee is concealing weapons or

Is There a Reasonable Expectation of Privacy from Aerial Observation?

Police received a tip that defendant, Ciraolo, was growing marijuana in his backyard. The backyard was not visible from the street due to a privacy fence that surrounded the property. The police then obtained an aircraft that was flown above the suspect's home at 1,000 feet. From that altitude, they observed marijuana plants visible to the naked eye. Police then obtained a warrant, conducted a search, and seized the contraband. The defendant objected to the search on the grounds that the aerial observation on which it was predicated was an unreasonable invasion of his privacy.

The Supreme Court disagreed and upheld the aerial observation, the search warrant, and the seizure of the contraband. The Court concluded that simply because Ciraolo's backyard was within the curtilage did not bar any and all forms of police observation. As the Court said, "[W]e readily conclude that [Ciraolo's] expectation that his garden was protected from [aerial] observation is unreasonable and is not an expectation that society is prepared to honor."

California v. Ciraolo, 476 U.S. 207, 106 S. Ct. 1809, 90 L.Ed.2d 210 (1986).

contraband. See, for example, *Mary Beth G. v. Chicago*, 723 F.2d 1263 (7th Cir. 1983). Other courts have permitted such searches where there is a reasonable suspicion that the arrestee is concealing weapons or contraband. See, for example, *Weber v. Dell*, 804 F.2d 796 (2d Cir. 1986).

Strip searches can also have civil consequences. For example, in *Jones v. Edwards*, 770 F.2d 739 (8th Cir. 1985), Marlin E. Jones was arrested and taken into custody for failing to sign a summons and complaint on an animal leash law violation. He was subjected to a visual strip search of his anal and genital area. The court ruled that such a search, under these circumstances, subjected the police and jail personnel to liability for violation of the arrestee's civil rights. The court emphasized that the police had no reason to suspect that Jones was harboring weapons or contraband on his person.

The Warrant Requirement

As pointed out, when searches are challenged as being unreasonable, courts must first determine if the Fourth Amendment is applicable. The Fourth Amendment does not apply to border searches or searches conducted outside the United States, nor does it apply to open fields or abandoned property. Indeed, the Fourth Amendment does not apply to any situation where a person lacks a reasonable expectation of privacy. Where it does apply, the Fourth Amendment expresses a decided preference for searches and seizures to be conducted pursuant to a warrant. The warrant requirement is designed to ensure that the impartial judgment of a judge or a magistrate is interposed between the citizen and the state. The right of privacy is "too precious to entrust to the discretion of those whose job is the detection of crime and the arrest of criminals." *McDonald v. United States*, 335 U.S. 451, 455–456, 69 S.Ct. 191, 195–96, 93 L.Ed. 153, 158 (1948).

The Probable Cause Requirement

With the exception of warrants permitting administrative searches, search warrants must be based on probable cause. Like many legal terms, "probable cause" is not susceptible to precise definition. Probable cause exists when prudent and cautious police officers have trustworthy information leading them to believe that evidence of crime might be obtained through a particular search. See *Brinegar v. United States*, 338 U.S. 160, 69 S.Ct. 1302, 93 L.Ed. 1879 (1949); *Carroll v. United States*, 267 U.S. 132, 45 S.Ct. 280, 69 L.Ed. 543 (1925).

An excerpt from the Supreme Court's opinion in *Illinois v. Gates* appears at the end of the chapter.

The Supreme Court has said that courts should view the determination of probable cause as a "commonsense, practical question" that must be decided in light of the **totality of circumstances** in a given case. *Illinois v. Gates*, 462 U.S. 213, 230, 103 S.Ct. 2317, 2328, 76 L.Ed.2d 527, 543 (1983). This approach has been amplified by lower federal courts, which have observed that even though an innocent explanation might be consistent with the facts alleged in an affidavit seeking a search warrant, this does not negate probable cause. See, for example, *United States v. Fama*, 758 F. 2d 834 (2d Cir. 1985).

Although state courts are free to impose a higher standard, most have followed this approach. For example, the Ohio Supreme Court ruled that an affidavit by a police agent saying that he observed a tall marijuana plant growing in an enclosed backyard furnished probable cause for a magistrate to conclude there was marijuana or related paraphernalia in the residence. *State v. George*, 544 N.E.2d 640 (Ohio 1989). Some state courts have declined to follow the *Gates* approach and have opted to provide their citizens more protection than allowed by the federal view. In some instances, these state views result from linguistic variations in state constitutional counterparts to the Fourth Amendment. See, for example, *Commonwealth v. Upton*, 476 N.E.2d 548 (Mass. 1985).

Issuance of the Search Warrant

Under normal circumstances, a police officer with probable cause to believe that evidence of a crime is located in a specific place must submit under oath an application for a search warrant to the appropriate judge or magistrate. Rule 41(a) of the Federal Rules of Criminal Procedure allows a federal agent to obtain a search warrant from a federal magistrate or a judge of a state court of record within the district wherein the property or person sought is located. Whether by statute or judicial rules, states usually provide similar authorization.

In *Coolidge v. New Hampshire*, 403 U.S. 443, 91 S.Ct. 2022, 29 L.Ed.2d 564 (1971), the Supreme Court invalidated a warrant issued by the state attorney general. The Court said that a warrant must be issued by a neutral and detached magistrate and certainly not by an official responsible for criminal prosecutions. Similarly, in *United States v. United States District Court*, 407 U.S. 297, 92 S.Ct. 2125, 32 L.Ed.2d 752 (1972), the Court invalidated a statute that permitted electronic eavesdropping to be authorized solely by the U.S. Attorney General in cases involving national security. Writing for the Court, Justice Powell observed that "unreviewed executive discretion may yield too readily to pressures to obtain incriminating evidence and overlook potential invasions of privacy . . . ." 407 U.S. at 317, 92 S.Ct. at 2136, 32 L.Ed.2d at 766.

The Supporting Affidavit

An **affidavit** is a signed document attesting under oath to certain facts of which the **affiant** (the person submitting the affidavit) has knowledge (see Figure 15.1). Generally, an affidavit by a law enforcement officer requesting issuance of a search warrant is

ACODC NO. 29

Commonwealth of Massachusetts

Middlesex_____ , ss.   Concord District Court
                                                    Court

AFFIDAVIT IN SUPPORT OF APPLICATION FOR SEARCH WARRANT*
G.L. c. 276, ss. 1 to 7; St. 1964, c. 557 As Amended

I, __Sam Buckley_____ , being duly sworn, depose and say: _____21_____June_____ , 19_80_
            Name of applicant

1. I am ____Police Chief of Concord, Massachusetts_____
            (Describe position, assignment, office, etc.)

2. I have information based upon (describe sources, facts indicating reliability of source and nature of information; if based on personal knowledge and belief, so state) (If space is insufficient, attach affidavit or affidavits hereto)

   Based on information from a Federal Drug Enforcement Officer, the above has reason to belive at 123 Smith Street, one-story red brick house, with garage, 2 bedrooms, kitchen, living room, and bathroom, there is a small brown suitcase containing a controlled substance believed to be heroin.

*3. Based upon the foregoing reliable information - and upon my personal knowledge and belief - and ~~searched affidavits~~ - there is probable cause to believe that the property hereinafter described - has been stolen - or is being concealed, etc.
   and may be found in the possession of ___Miss Francine Taggart_____
                                                Name or person or persons

   at premises _____123 Smith Street, Concord_____
                    (Identify number, street, place, etc.)

4. The property for which I seek the issuance of a search warrant is the following (here describe the property as particularly as possible).

   One small brown suitcase taken from a station locker by Francine Taggart on June 19, 1980, containing heroin.

WHEREFORE, I respectfully request that the court issue a warrant and order of seizure, authorizing the search of (identify premises and the person or persons to be searched)

and directing that if such property or evidence or any part thereof be found that it be seized and brought before the court; together with such other and further relief that the court may deem proper.

                                    Police Chief Sam Buckley
                                        Signature of applicant

Then personally appeared the above named __Chief Buckley_____
and made oath that the foregoing affidavit by him subscribed is true.

                    Before me this ___21___ day of __June__ 19 _80_
                        J.P. Jones - Special Justice
                    Justice of Special Justice
                    Clerk or Assistant Clerk of the Muninclpal Court.
                                                      District

* Strike inapplicable clauses

            REVISED JULY 1965   APPROVED BY THE CHIEF JUSTICE OF THE DISTRICT COURTS

FIGURE 15.1 Application for a Search Warrant

presented to a judge or magistrate. The manner in which the affidavit is recorded and transmitted may vary. For example, the Idaho Supreme Court, finding that electronically recorded testimony is no less reliable than a sworn, written statement, held that the word "affidavit" under the Idaho constitution was sufficiently broad to include tape recording of oral testimony. *State v. Yoder*, 534 P.2d 771 (Idaho 1975).

Rule 41(c)(2) of the Federal Rules of Criminal Procedure provides that a federal magistrate judge may issue a warrant based upon sworn oral testimony communicated by phone or other appropriate means, including facsimile transmission. Some states follow this approach—for example, California law permits police officers to complete affidavits using the telephone to expedite the issuance of a warrant. West's Ann. Cal. Pen. Code. § 1526(b).

The officer's affidavit in support of a search warrant must always contain a rather precise description of the place(s) or person(s) to be searched and the things to be seized. Moreover, the affidavit must attest to specific facts that establish probable cause to justify a search. An affidavit cannot establish probable cause for issuance of a search warrant if it is based merely on the affiant's suspicion or belief without stating the facts and circumstances that the belief is based on.

The information on which an affidavit is based must be sufficiently fresh to ensure that the items to be seized are probably located on the premises to be searched. The issue of when a search warrant becomes invalid because the information the affidavit is based on is stale has been litigated in many cases, with varying results. No set rule can be formulated. For example, in *State v. Pulgini*, 366 A.2d 1198 (Del. Super. 1976), the court invalidated a search warrant where there was an unexplained delay of twenty-three days between the last alleged fact and the issuance of the warrant. On the other hand, in *United States v. Rosenbarger*, 536 F.2d 715 (6th Cir. 1976), a twenty-one-day time lapse between observation of the receipt of stolen property and issuance of the warrant did not invalidate the warrant because the magistrate could determine there was a reasonable probability that the stolen goods were still in the defendant's home.

In *State v. Carlson*, 4 P.3d 1122 (Idaho App. 2000), an Idaho appellate court held that a warrant to search a defendant's residence was not based upon stale information even though there was a lapse of twenty-four days between the informant's initial observations and the issuance of the search warrant. The court considered the fact that the information was supplemented by a second report regarding observation of a marijuana plant three days prior to the issuance of the warrant, and the implication that a marijuana operation continued in the interim period.

Tips from Police Informants

A magistrate's finding of probable cause may be based on hearsay evidence. See, for example, Fed. R. Crim. P. 41(c)(1). This rule permits police to obtain search warrants based on tips from anonymous or **confidential informants.** Confidential informants, or "CIs," are often persons who have been involved with the police and are seeking favorable consideration in respect to their own offenses. Because their motivation may be suspect, their reliability is checked carefully. For many years the Supreme Court required magistrates to apply a rigorous two-pronged test to determine probable cause. See *Aguilar v. Texas*, 378 U.S. 108, 84 S.Ct. 1509, 12 L.Ed.2d 723 (1964); *Spinelli v. United States*, 393 U.S. 410, 89 S.Ct. 584, 21 L.Ed.2d 637 (1969). The *Aguilar–Spinelli* test required that the officer's affidavit satisfy two criteria: (1) it had to demonstrate that the informant was both credible and reliable, and (2) it had to reveal the informant's basis of knowledge.

The *Aguilar–Spinelli* test made it very difficult for police to use anonymous tips. In 1983 the Supreme Court relaxed the test and permitted magistrates to consider the totality of circumstances when evaluating applications based on hearsay evidence. *Illinois v. Gates,* supra. The following year, the Court held that the standard for determining probable cause announced in the *Gates* decision was to be given a broad interpretation by lower courts. *Massachusetts v. Upton,* 466 U.S. 727, 104 S.Ct. 2085, 80 L.Ed.2d 721 (1984).

Despite the Supreme Court's relaxed standard for determining probable cause based on tips from informants, some states have chosen to follow the stricter standards formerly imposed by the *Aguilar* and *Spinelli* decisions. This, of course, is the prerogative of the states. In a comprehensive opinion in *State v. Cordova,* 784 P. 2d 30 (N.M. 1989), the New Mexico Supreme Court reviewed an affidavit for a search warrant that recited that Cordova had brought heroin into town and was selling it at the house in question. However, the affidavit was devoid of explanation about how the informant gathered this information. Further, although the affidavit stated the informant had personal knowledge that "heroin users" had been at the residence in question, there was nothing to indicate the source of the informant's knowledge and no explanation of how the informant knew the persons in question were heroin users. Because the affidavit did not establish that the informant was both credible and reliable, the court found it did not provide a substantial basis for believing the informant and for concluding that the informant gathered the information in a reliable manner. Further, the affidavit did not adequately state the informant's basis of knowledge that the defendant was selling heroin. In rejecting the state's appeal, the New Mexico Supreme Court declined to follow the *Gates* totality of circumstances rule and found the affidavit did not meet the requirements of the New Mexico Constitution and its rules of criminal procedure.

In 1985 the Connecticut Supreme Court criticized the "totality of the circumstances" test as being "too amorphous" and an inadequate safeguard against unjustified police intrusions. That court has recently held that if the information supplied by a CI fails the *Aguilar–Spinelli* test, probable cause may still be found if the affidavit sets forth other circumstances that bolster any deficiencies. *State v. Barton,* 594 A.2d 917 (Conn. 1991). Four years later, the Tennessee Supreme Court held that the two-pronged standard for probable cause inquiries incident to the issuance of a search warrant announced in the *Aguilar* and *Spinelli* cases, if not measured hypertechnically, is the standard to measure whether there is probable cause to issue a warrant. *State v. Jacumin,* 778 S.W.2d 430 (Tenn. 1989).

When a defendant demands to know the identity of the informant who provided the police with information on which they based their affidavit for a search warrant, courts face a delicate problem. There is a limited privilege to withhold identity of the confidential informant. In determining whether to require disclosure, the court balances the interest of the public in preserving the anonymity of the informant against the defendant's need to have this information to prepare a defense, and where the questioned identity "is relevant and helpful to the defense of an accused, or is essential to a fair determination of a cause, the privilege must give way." *Roviaro v. United States,* 353 U.S. 53, 77 S.Ct. 623, 1 L.Ed.2d 639 (1957).

Required Specificity of a Search Warrant

The Fourth Amendment mandates that "no warrants shall issue" except those "particularly describing the place to be searched and the persons or things to be seized." Thus, the scope of a search and seizure is bound by the terms of the warrant (see

CASE-IN-POINT

Required Specificity of a Search Warrant

A police officer was executing a search warrant that specified a particular copyrighted software program and gave its serial number and added "all other computer related software." The officer was unable to find a floppy disk containing the program, but did locate the program on the hard drive of the defendant's computer. In affirming the defendant's conviction for an offense involving intellectual property, the court held that the hard drive was properly seized even though not specifically listed in the warrant.

State v. Tanner, 534 So. 2d 535 (La. App. 1988).

Figure 15.2). Likewise, a warrant that described property to be seized as "various long play phonographic albums, and miscellaneous vases and glassware" was held insufficient. Nevertheless, in 1999 the Maine Supreme Judicial Court upheld a search warrant that authorized seizure of all computer-related equipment in the defendant's house. The police knew only that images of minors allegedly sexually exploited were taken by digital camera and downloaded on a computer. *State v. Lehman,* 736 A.2d 256 (Me. 1999).

Courts tend to be less strict when it comes to the description of contraband (such as heroin), since it is illegal per se, but stricter in cases involving First Amendment rights. For example, a federal appeals court invalidated a warrant authorizing the seizure of "a quantity of obscene materials, including books, pamphlets, magazines, newspapers, films and prints." *United States v. Guarino,* 729 F.2d 864, 865 (1st Cir. 1984).

Anticipatory Search Warrants

The dramatic increase in drug trafficking over the last decade has given rise to a countermeasure known as the **anticipatory search warrant.** Traditionally, police wait until a suspect receives contraband and then prepare an affidavit to obtain a search warrant. If the magistrate finds that probable cause exists at that time, a search warrant is issued. In the case of an anticipatory warrant, probable cause does not have to exist until the warrant is executed and the search conducted.

During the 1980s, several state appellate courts approved anticipatory search warrants. See, for example, *State v. Coker,* 746 S.W.2d 167 (Tenn. 1987). In one of these cases, *Bernie v. State,* supra, a freight delivery service notified police that a package that broke in transit revealed a suspicious substance that later proved to be cocaine. An anticipatory warrant was issued to search the residence to which the package was addressed. Police were on the scene when the freight company delivered the package. The warrant was served, the cocaine seized, and the defendant taken into custody. On appeal, the search was upheld by the state supreme court, which observed that neither the federal nor the state constitution prohibited issuance of a search warrant to be served at a future date in anticipation of the delivery of contraband.

The Alaska Supreme Court has cautioned that a magistrate issuing an anticipatory warrant should make its execution contingent on the occurrence of an event that evidences probable cause that the items to be seized are in the place to be searched, rather than directing that the warrant be executed forthwith. *Johnson v. State,* 617 P.2d 1117 (Alaska 1980).

ACODC NO. 30

Commonwealth of Massachusetts

Middlesex , ss.

Concord District
Court

(Search Warrant)

TO THE SHERIFFS OF OUR SEVERAL COUNTIES, OR THEIR DEPUTIES, ANY STATE POLICE OFFICER, OR ANY CONSTABLE OR POLICE OFFICER OF ANY CITY OR TOWN, WITHIN OUR SAID COMMONWEALTH:

Proof by affidavit having been made this day before   Special Justic J.Q. Jones
                                                                                     (Name of person issuing warrant)

by   Police Chief Sam Buckley
                                                (Name of person or persons signing affidavit)

*that there is probable cause for believing that certain property has been stolen, embezzled, or obtained by false pretenses — certain property is intended for use or has been used as the means of committing a crime — certain property has been concealed to prevent a crime from being discovered — certain property is unlawfully possessed or kept or concealed for an unlawful purpose.

WE THEREFORE COMMAND YOU in the daytime (or at any time of the day or night) to make an immediate search of   123 Smith Street, Concord
                                                          (Identify premises)

(occupied by   Francine Taggart   ) and of the person of
                              (Name of occupant)

_____, and of any person present who may
                  (Name of person)

be found to have such property in his possession or under his control or to whom such property may have been delivered, for the following property:

_____

(Description of property)

One small brown suitcase believed to contain heroin.

and if you find any such property or any part therof to bring it and the persons in who possession it is found before the   Concord District Court
                                          (Name of Court)

at   Concord, Massachusetts
                        (Court location)

in said County and Commonwealth, as soon as it has been served and in any event not later than seven days of issuance thereof. (Officer to make return on reverse side)

Witness _J.Q. Jones_ , Esquire, Justice, at _Concord_ ,

Dist Court

_____ aforesaid, this __21__ day of __June__

in the year of our Lord one thousand nine hundred and __80__

_____ P.L. Norman

* Strike inapplicable clauses

Justice
~~Clerk~~
Assistant Clerk

G.L. c. 276, ss. 1 to 7; St. 1964, c. 557

APPROVED BY THE CHIEF JUSTICE OF THE DISTRICT COURTS

FIGURE 15.2 A Typical Search Warrant

The United States Supreme Court has not yet addressed the issue of whether a search based on an anticipatory warrant passes muster under the Fourth Amendment. However, while there is a split of authority, the majority of federal appellate courts have upheld the basic concept that contraband does not have to be currently located at the place described in a search warrant if there is probable cause to believe it will be there when the warrant is executed. In 1986 the Ninth Circuit Court of Appeals held that an anticipatory search warrant is permissible "where the contraband to be seized is on a sure course to its destination." *United States v. Hale,* 784 F.2d 1465, 1468 (9th Cir. 1986). Two years later, the U.S. Court of Appeals for the Fourth Circuit upheld an anticipatory search warrant permitting an inspector to search an apartment for child pornography where the issuing magistrate conditioned the validity of the warrant on the contraband being placed in the mail. Thus, when the mailing was accomplished, the contraband was on a certain course to its destination. *United States v. Dornhofer,* 859 F.2d 1195 (4th Cir. 1988).

In January 2000, a Michigan appellate court first addressed the issue; following the trend of appellate courts, it concluded that an anticipatory search warrant does not violate the federal and state constitutional prohibitions against unreasonable searches and seizures. *People v. Kasalowski,* 608 N.W.2d 539 (Mich. App. 2000).

Execution of a Search Warrant

Applicable federal and state laws and rules of criminal procedure govern the manner and time in which warrants are executed. Rule 41(c)(1) of the Federal Rules of Criminal Procedure provides that the warrant

> shall command the officer to search, within a specified period of time not to exceed 10 days, the person or place named or the property or person specified. The warrant shall be served in the daytime, unless the issuing authority . . . authorizes its execution at times other than daytime.

Rule 41(h) defines daytime as between 6:00 A.M. and 10:00 P.M. according to local time. States have varying provisions governing the period of time within which a search warrant may be executed. Texas allows three days, excluding the date of issuance and the date of execution, Vernon's Tex. Code Crim. P. art. 18.06(a), whereas California allows ten, West's Ann. Cal. Penal Code § 1534. Likewise, state laws vary on the hours during which a search warrant may be executed. California law permits a warrant to be executed between the hours of 7:00 A.M. and 10:00 P.M. West's Ann. Cal. Penal Code § 1533. Some states, including Texas, do not impose restrictions on the hours when a warrant may be executed; others allow nighttime searches under special circumstances.

The Knock-and-Announce Rule

At the time the Constitution was adopted, the common law indicated that law enforcement officers should ordinarily announce their presence and authority before entering a residence to conduct a search or make an arrest pursuant to a warrant. Under federal law an officer is required to **knock and announce** on arrival at the place to be searched. 18 U.S.C.A. § 3109. Most states have similar knock-and-announce requirements, but courts have created some exceptions to protect officers and to prevent the destruction of evidence. In *Wilson v. Arkansas,* 514 U.S. 927, 115 S.Ct. 1914. 131 L.Ed.2d 976 (1995), the U.S. Supreme Court elevated the knock-and-announce rule to constitutional status under the Fourth Amendment. However, the Court did recognize that exigent circumstances may render the knock-and-announce requirement unnecessary.

The purpose of the knock-and-announce requirement is to reduce the potential for violence and to protect the right of privacy of the occupants. Courts have generally ruled that there are no rigid limits as to the time that must elapse between the announcement and the officers' entry. A few seconds may even suffice. Moreover, courts frequently excuse compliance when to require it would endanger the lives of the officers or simply provide an occasion for occupants to dispose of evidence. The most common example of disposing of evidence after police have announced their presence is the flushing of contraband down a toilet. See, for example, *State v. Stalbert*, 783 P. 2d 1005 (Or. App. 1989).

Testing the Sufficiency of the Basis for Issuing a Search Warrant

In ***Franks v. Delaware,*** 438 U.S. 154, 98 S.Ct. 2674, 57 L.Ed.2d 667 (1978), the Supreme Court was faced with the issue of whether a defendant can challenge the affidavit for a search warrant in a pretrial proceeding. The Delaware Supreme Court had ruled that a defendant could not challenge the veracity of the statements made by the police to obtain their search warrant. The United States Supreme Court reversed and held that the Fourth Amendment requires an evidentiary hearing (called a ***Franks* hearing**) into the truthfulness of allegations in an affidavit in support of an application for a search warrant "where the defendant makes a substantial preliminary showing that a false statement knowingly and intentionally, or with reckless disregard for the truth, was included by the affiant in the warrant affidavit, and if the allegedly false statement is necessary to the finding of probable cause." 439 U.S. 154, 155–156, 98 S.Ct. 2674, 2676, 57 L.Ed.2d 667 (1978).

Return of Seized Property

Illegally seized property must be returned to the owner; however, the government may retain property lawfully seized as long as the government has a legitimate interest in its retention. Whether seized legally or illegally, contraband or property subject to forfeiture is not subject to being returned. See *United States v. Carter*, 859 F. Supp. 202 (E.D. Va. 1994). The return of seized property is generally handled expeditiously based on a motion of the party seeking return. See, for example, Fed. R. Crim. P. 41(e).

Exceptions to the Warrant Requirement

Courts have recognized that an absolute warrant requirement would be impractical. Consequently, they have upheld the reasonableness of **warrantless searches** under so-called exigent circumstances. Yet, despite a number of exceptions, the warrant requirement remains a central feature of Fourth Amendment law. Whenever possible, police officers should obtain warrants because their failure to do so can jeopardize the fruits of a successful search. The following are well-defined exceptions to the warrant requirement. However, it is important to understand that all these exceptions assume that police officers have probable cause to believe that a given search is likely to produce evidence of crime.

Evidence in Plain View

The Supreme Court has said that evidence in plain view of a police officer is not subject to the warrant requirement. *Harris v. United States,* 390 U.S. 234, 88 S.Ct. 992, 19 L.Ed.2d 1067 (1968). Police officers are not required to close their eyes or wear blinders in the face of evidence of a crime. Police officers have long been permitted to seize evidence that comes to their attention inadvertently, provided that (1) the officer has a legal justification to be in a constitutionally protected area when the seizure occurs, (2) the evidence seized is in the plain view of the officer who comes across it, and (3) it is apparent that the object constitutes evidence of a crime. *Coolidge v. New Hampshire,* supra. An officer may not seize anything and everything in plain view—the officer must have probable cause.

The "inadvertent discovery" requirement announced in *Coolidge v. New Hampshire* remained in effect for more than a decade. However, in *Horton v. California,* 496 U.S. 128, 110 S.Ct. 2301, 110 L.Ed.2d 112 (1990), the Supreme Court noted that the inadvertence requirement was not an essential part of the plurality opinion in *Coolidge v. New Hampshire.* As the Court observed in 1983, "There is no reason [the police officer] should be precluded from observing as an officer what would be entirely visible to him as a private citizen." *Texas v. Brown,* 460 U.S. 730, 740, 103 S.Ct. 1535, 1542, 75 L.Ed.2d 502 (1983). Notwithstanding, some state courts have continued to insist that the inadvertence requirement is a limitation on the plain-view exception to the warrant requirement. See, for example, *State v. Halczyszak,* 496 N.E.2d 925 (Ohio 1986).

The **plain-view doctrine** may apply both where the item seized is in plain view before the commencement of a search and where it comes into the plain view of an officer conducting an otherwise valid search or entry. For example, in *United States v. Pacelli,* 470 F.2d 67 (2d Cir. 1972), the court invoked the plain-view doctrine to uphold the seizure of illegal chemicals found during a search based on a warrant to search for heroin. The search warrant gave police officers the right to enter and search the premises; other items of contraband found in plain view during the search were deemed properly seized.

In contrast with *Pacelli,* consider the case of *Arizona v. Hicks,* 480 U.S. 321, 107 S.Ct. 1149, 94 L.Ed.2d 347 (1987). There, police who had lawfully entered an apartment to search for weapons noticed stereo equipment that seemed out of place, given the squalid condition of the apartment. His suspicion aroused, an officer moved the stereo equipment to locate the serial numbers. A check of the numbers indicated that the equipment was stolen. The Supreme Court disallowed the "search" of the serial numbers because they were not in plain view when the police entered the apartment.

Emergency Searches

Police frequently must respond to emergencies involving reports of crime or injuries. In other instances, they accompany firefighters to the scene of a fire. Increasingly, law enforcement authorities are called to investigate bomb threats where explosive devices are possibly sequestered inside buildings. Although these are among the most dramatic emergencies, in many other situations police are called to conduct emergency searches. The law recognizes that police do not have the time to obtain search warrants in such instances. Of course, police must possess probable cause to make warrantless **emergency searches** of dwellings. While they are on premises in response to an emergency, police may seize evidence in plain view during the course of their legitimate emergency activities. *Michigan v. Tyler,* 436 U.S. 499, 98 S.Ct. 1942, 56 L.Ed.2d 486 (1978).

Even when investigating a crime scene, police are not permitted to search anything and everything found. In *Flippo v. West Virginia,* 528 U.S. 11, 120 S.Ct. 7, 145 L.Ed.2d 16 (1999), the police responded to a 911 call reporting that a man and his wife had been attacked in a cabin at a state park. When they arrived, the police found the woman fatally wounded. While investigating the crime scene, they discovered a briefcase. They opened it and an envelope within it, and found photographs that tended to incriminate the husband. The prosecutor attempted to justify the seizure based on a "crime scene" exception to the warrant requirement. While recognizing that police may make warrantless searches for perpetrators and victims at a crime scene, the Supreme Court rejected the contention that there is a "crime scene exception" to the Warrant Clause of the Fourth Amendment. In remanding the case to the lower court, the Court allowed that the police might have secured the evidence by consent, under the plain-view doctrine or inventory exception to the warrant requirement, but not on the basis of a claimed "crime scene exception."

Police do not violate the Fourth Amendment if they stop a vehicle when they have adequate grounds to believe the driver is ill or falling asleep. *State v. Pinkham,* 565 A.2d 318 (Me. 1989). Likewise, police who make warrantless entries and searches when they reasonably believe that a person within is in need of immediate aid do not violate the protections against unreasonable search and seizure. Once inside, the police may justifiably seize evidence in plain view. See *Mincey v. Arizona,* 437 U.S. 385, 392, 98 S.Ct. 2408, 2413, 57 L.Ed.2d 290, 300 (1978). An officer's belief that an emergency exists must be reasonable, however; former Chief Justice (then judge) Burger in *Wayne v. United States,* 318 F.2d 205, 212 (D.C. Cir. 1963), opined that "the need to protect or preserve life or avoid serious injury is justification for what would be otherwise illegal absent an exigency or emergency." In *United States v. Al-Azzawy,* 784 F.2d 890 (9th Cir. 1985), the court upheld a warrantless search where a suspect was believed to be in possession of explosives and in such an agitated state as to create a risk of endangering the lives of others.

Preservation of Evidence

A frequently invoked justification for a warrantless search and seizure is the preservation of **evanescent evidence**—evidence that might be lost or destroyed. Where there is a reasonable belief that loss or destruction of evidence is imminent, a warrantless entry of premises may be justified, *United States v. Gonzalez,* 967 F.2d 1032 (4th Cir. 1992), but a mere possibility of such is insufficient, *United States v. Hayes,* 518 F.2d 675, 678 (6th Cir. 1975). The leading case in this area is *Schmerber v. California,* 384 U.S. 757, 86 S.Ct. 1826, 16 L.Ed.2d 908 (1966), where the Supreme Court upheld a warrantless blood-alcohol test of a person who appeared to be intoxicated. The Court characterized the forcible blood test as a "minor intrusion" and noted that the test was performed by qualified medical personnel. However, the most significant fact of the case was that the suspect's blood-alcohol level was rapidly diminishing, and the time required for police to obtain a search warrant could well have changed the results of the test.

In 1984 the Supreme Court narrowed the doctrine, saying that destruction of evidence does not constitute exigent circumstances if the underlying offense is relatively minor. *Welsh v. Wisconsin,* 466 U.S. 740, 104 S.Ct. 2091, 80 L.Ed.2d 732 (1984). Since then, lower courts have disagreed over what constitutes a "relatively minor" offense. In particular, drug offenses, many of which are felonies or misdemeanors depending on the quantity of contraband involved, have proven vexing to police and courts trying to apply the "relatively minor" standard. In 1993 the Idaho Supreme

Court said that a minor offense is one that is nonviolent; thus, drug possession offenses, even if felonies, are "minor offenses." The court announced its decision in a case where police, acting with probable cause but without a warrant, entered a home and seized marijuana they believed was about to be destroyed. *State v. Curl,* 869 P.2d 224 (Idaho 1993). It remains to be seen whether other states will take the position adopted by the Idaho Supreme Court.

Roadside Searches of Motor Vehicles

Police frequently stop automobiles based on probable cause to believe that criminal activity is taking place. Quite often, such stops involve warrantless roadside searches and seizures. The Supreme Court has long recognized the validity of the so-called **automobile exception,** assuming that the police officer has probable cause to believe the vehicle contains contraband or evidence of crime, on the premise that the mobile character of a motor vehicle creates a practical necessity for an immediate search. *Carroll v. United States,* supra. The Court has held that once begun under exigent circumstances, a warrantless search of an automobile may continue after the vehicle has been taken to the police station. *Chambers v. Maroney,* 399 U.S. 42, 90 S.Ct. 1975, 26 L.Ed.2d 419 (1970).

Several state supreme courts have refused to go along with *Chambers v. Maroney.* See, for example, *State v. Kock,* 725 P.2d 1285 (Ore. 1986); *State v. Larocco,* 592 P.2d 460 (Utah 1990). In August 1993, the Connecticut Supreme Court refused to adopt *Chambers v. Maroney* as a matter of state constitutional law. In *State v. Miller,* 630 A.2d 1315 (Conn. 1993), the court noted that any exigent circumstances that might justify a roadside automobile search disappear once the vehicle has been impounded. Writing for the court was Chief Justice Peters:

> We tolerate the warrantless on-the-scene automobile search only because obtaining a warrant would be impracticable in light of the inherent mobility of automobiles and the latent exigency that that mobility creates. The balance between law enforcement interests and individuals' privacy interests thus tips in favor of law enforcement in the context of an on-the-scene automobile search. If the impracticability of obtaining a warrant no longer exists, however, our state constitutional preference for warrants regains its dominant place in that balance, and a warrant is required. 630 A.2d at 1325.

One perennial problem associated with warrantless automobile searches is how closed containers, such as suitcases, found inside automobiles should be treated. In 1982 the U.S. Supreme Court held that a police officer having probable cause to believe that evidence of crime is concealed within an automobile may conduct a search as broad as one that could be authorized by a magistrate issuing a warrant. *United States v. Ross,* 456 U.S. 798, 102 S.Ct. 2157, 72 L.Ed.2d 572 (1982). This ruling effectively allowed police officers to search closed containers found during the course of an automobile search without first having to obtain a warrant. In *United States v. Johns,* 469 U.S. 478, 105 S.Ct. 881, 83 L.Ed.2d 890 (1985), the Court upheld the warrantless search of plastic containers seized during an automobile search, even though the police had waited several days before opening the containers. The Court reasoned that since police legitimately seized the containers during the original search of the automobile, no reasonable expectation of privacy could be maintained once the containers came under police control. The search of the containers, which produced a substantial quantity of marijuana, was therefore not unreasonable simply because it was delayed.

An excerpt from the Supreme Court's decision in *United States v. Ross* appears at the end of the chapter.

In 1998 a highway patrol officer in Wyoming stopped a speeding car. While speaking to the driver, the officer noticed a syringe in the driver's pocket. The driver admitted using the syringe to inject drugs. Having probable cause to search the car, the officer then opened a passenger's purse on the back seat and found contraband. The Wyoming Supreme Court ruled that the search that yielded the contraband was not within the permissible scope of search of the vehicle. *Houghton v. Wyoming*, 956 P.2d 363 (1998). On review, the U.S. Supreme Court held that police officers who have probable cause to search a vehicle may search the belongings of passengers who are capable of concealing objects of the search. *Wyoming v. Houghton*, 526 U.S. 295, 119 S.Ct. 1297, 140 L.Ed.2d 408 (1999).

Search Incident to a Lawful Arrest

A **search incident to a lawful arrest** is an exception to the warrant requirement in order that the police may disarm an arrestee and preserve evidence. It has long been recognized that such a search is permissible. *Weeks v. United States*, 232 U.S. 383, 34 S.Ct. 341, 58 L.Ed. 652 (1914). For many years, this rule was interpreted quite broadly. For example, in *United States v. Rabinowitz*, 339 U.S. 56, 70 S.Ct. 430, 94 L.Ed. 653 (1950), the Supreme Court upheld a warrantless search of an entire home incident to a lawful arrest that occurred there. In 1969 the Supreme Court narrowed the permissible scope of searches incident to lawful arrests. *Chimel v. California*, 395 U.S. 752, 89 S.Ct. 2034, 23 L.Ed.2d 685 (1969). Under *Chimel*, police may search the body of an arrestee and the area within that person's immediate control. The area of immediate control is often defined as the area within the "grasp" or "lunge" of the arrestee. To conduct a more extensive search, police must generally obtain a search warrant.

Even if a formal arrest is not made until after a search, the search will be upheld as one incident to arrest if there was probable cause for the arrest before the search was begun. *Bailey v. United States,* 389 F.2d 305 (D.C. Cir. 1967). On the other hand, courts will not uphold a search where it is shown that the arrest was a mere pretext to conduct a warrantless search. See, for example, *United States v. Jones,* 452 F.2d 884 (8th Cir. 1971).

There are definite limitations on police conducting a search incident to arrest. Despite the existence of probable cause, absent extraordinary circumstances, the police have no right to search a dwelling when an arrest occurs outside it. As the Supreme Court observed in *Payton v. New York,* 445 U.S. 573, 591, 100 S.Ct. 1371, 1382, 63 L.Ed.2d 639, 653 (1980), "The Fourth Amendment has drawn a firm line at the entrance to the house. Absent exigent circumstances, that threshold may not reasonably be crossed without a warrant." Exigent circumstances would most likely include a situation where, after an arrest, the officers have a reasonable basis to suspect there may be others on the premises who pose a danger to the police or who may destroy evidence. See *Vale v. Louisiana,* 399 U.S. 30, 90 S.Ct. 1969, 26 L.Ed.2d 409 (1970). Thus, police who made an arrest outside a residence and had knowledge regarding cocaine trafficking taking place inside were not barred from entering the house to conduct a "protective sweep" for other persons who might pose a threat to their safety. *United States v. Hoyos,* 892 F.2d 1387 (9th Cir. 1989). Nevertheless, once a person is arrested and in custody, searching that person's car at another location is not a search incident to arrest. *Preston v. United States,* 376 U.S. 364, 84 S.Ct. 881, 11 L.Ed.2d 777 (1964).

In *New York v. Belton,* 453 U.S. 454, 101 S.Ct. 2860, 69 L.Ed.2d 768 (1981), the Supreme Court held that a police officer who makes a valid arrest of an occupant of an automobile may search the passenger compartment of the car even in the absence of probable cause to believe there is evidence located there. This search incident to arrest is justified on the assumption that the arrestee could reach into the passenger compartment to destroy evidence or obtain a weapon. Of course, if a person is in handcuffs or otherwise under the control of the police, it would seem unlikely that he or she could exercise any control over the passenger compartment of the car. Thus, *Belton* has been criticized as moving beyond the rationale of *Chimel.* Most state courts have followed the *Belton* approach, but several have not. For example, in *People v. Blasich,* 432 N.E.2d 745 (N.Y. 1982), the New York Court of Appeals declined to adopt *Belton* as a matter of state constitutional law. Likewise, in *State v. Brown,* 588 N.E.2d 113 (Ohio 1992), the Ohio Supreme Court rejected *Belton,* which it characterized as allowing police "to search every nook and cranny of an automobile just because the driver is arrested for a traffic violation." 588 N.E.2d at 115. Of course, if a driver is taken into custody and there is no one else legally able to take control of the car, police may impound the vehicle and conduct an inventory search. Moreover, if police who have legitimately stopped an automobile have probable cause to believe that it contains evidence of crime, they may conduct a full-blown roadside search in the absence of a warrant. *United States v. Ross,* supra.

As interpreted by the state supreme court, Iowa law allowed an officer to conduct a full-blown search of an automobile and its driver when the officer stopped a motorist for speeding and issued a traffic citation. An officer stopped a vehicle, issued a traffic citation for speeding, and searched the vehicle without consent or probable cause. The search revealed a bag of marijuana and a "pot pipe." The search was upheld by the Iowa Supreme Court. *State v. Knowles,* 569 N.W.2d 601 (Iowa 1997). But the U.S. Supreme Court granted review and the following year held that a search under these circumstances violates the Fourth Amendment. *Knowles v. Iowa,* 525 U.S. 113, 119 S.Ct. 484, 142 L.Ed. 2d 492 (1998).

Hot Pursuit

Officers in **hot pursuit** of a fleeing suspect already have probable cause to make an arrest. The Supreme Court has long recognized that police may pursue the suspect into a protected place, such as a home, without having to abandon their pursuit until a warrant can be obtained. *Warden v. Hayden,* 387 U.S. 294, 87 S.Ct. 1642, 18 L.Ed.2d 782 (1967). As the police enter a building and look for a suspect therein, they are by definition engaged in a search. If they find the suspect and make an arrest, they have in effect made a seizure. Once the suspect is in custody, police may engage in a warrantless search of the immediate area, which might produce evidence such as discarded weapons or contraband.

Exceptions to the Probable Cause Requirement

Warrantless searches are now well established in the law, and although reasonable people might disagree about specific cases, there is consensus that warrantless searches are often necessary and proper. The same cannot be said for the next category of searches—those based on something less than probable cause. In these special situations, courts permit limited searches based on the lesser standard of reasonable suspicion. Reasonable suspicion is the belief, based on articulable circumstances, that criminal activity might be afoot. The classic application of the reasonable suspicion standard is to the so-called "stop-and-frisk."

Stop-and-Frisk

The **stop-and-frisk** is a routine law enforcement technique whereby police officers stop, question, and sometimes search suspicious persons. In *Terry v. Ohio,* 392 U.S. 1, 88 S.Ct. 1868, 20 L.Ed.2d 889 (1968), the Supreme Court upheld the authority of police officers to detain and conduct a limited "pat-down" search of several men who were acting suspiciously. Given the limited intrusiveness of the pat-down, and the compelling need to protect officers in the field, the Court allowed the warrantless search for weapons on a reasonable suspicion standard, instead of imposing the traditional probable cause requirement. Subsequently, the Court stressed the narrow scope of the stop-and-frisk exception by saying that "nothing in *Terry* can be understood to allow . . . any search whatever for anything but weapons." *Ybarra v. Illinois,* 444 U.S. 85, 93–94, 100 S.Ct. 338, 343, 62 L.Ed.2d 238, 247 (1979).

In *Michigan v. Long,* 463 U.S. 1032, 103 S.Ct. 3469, 77 L.Ed.2d 1201 (1983), the Supreme Court held that seizure of contraband other than weapons during a lawfully conducted *Terry* search was justified under the "plain-view" doctrine. Going a step further in *Minnesota v. Dickerson,* 508 U.S. 366, 113 S.Ct. 2130, 124 L.Ed.2d 334 (1993), the Court said that police may seize nonthreatening contraband detected through their sense of touch during a protective patdown search as long as that search stays within the bounds of a *Terry* search. This extension of *Terry* is sometimes referred to as a "plain feel" exception to the warrant requirement of the Fourth Amendment. Nevertheless, in *Dickerson* the Court found the search and seizure of contraband invalid because the officer conducting the search determined that the item he seized was contraband only after searching beyond the scope authorized in *Terry*. (More attention is given to the so-called *Terry*-stop in Chapter 16.)

Drug Courier Profiles

In attempting to identify and to apprehend drug smugglers, law enforcement agencies have developed **drug courier profiles.** These profiles are sets of characteristics that typify drug couriers, such as paying for airline tickets in cash, appearing nervous,

---

CASE-IN-POINT   ## Detention and Search of a Suspected Drug Courier

A suspected drug courier was held incommunicado in an airport security room for sixteen hours while officers obtained a court order permitting an X-ray and rectal examination. During the examination a plastic balloon containing cocaine was retrieved. Over the next several days, the defendant passed some eighty-eight cocaine-filled balloons. The Supreme Court upheld the protracted detention and search, despite the lack of probable cause. The Court said that in such circumstances the lesser standard of reasonable suspicion was sufficient.

United States v. Montoya de Hernandez, 473 U.S. 531, 105 S. Ct. 3304, 87 L.Ed.2d 381 (1985).

carrying certain types of luggage, and so forth. In *Reid v. Georgia*, 448 U.S. 438, 100 S.Ct. 2752, 65 L.Ed.2d 890 (1980), the Supreme Court suggested that fitting a drug courier profile was not in itself sufficient to constitute the reasonable suspicion necessary to allow police to detain an airline passenger. Therefore, the stopping of an airline passenger on that basis violated the Fourth Amendment.

School Searches

In the First Amendment context, the Supreme Court has said that students in public schools do not "shed their constitutional rights . . . at the schoolhouse gate." *Tinker v. Des Moines Independent Community School District*, 393 U.S. 503, 506, 89 S.Ct. 733, 736, 21 L.Ed.2d 731, 737 (1969). Following this premise, the Court has held that the Fourth Amendment protects children in the public schools from unreasonable searches and seizures. However, the Court has said that such searches are to be judged by a reasonableness standard and are not subject to the requirement of probable cause. Moreover, the Court has said that the warrant requirement is particularly unsuited to the unique circumstances of the school environment. *New Jersey v. T.L.O.*, 469 U.S. 325, 105 S.Ct. 733, 83 L.Ed.2d 720 (1985).

Drug Testing

The illicit use of drugs has become a national concern. Because of the paramount interest in ensuring the public safety, courts have recently upheld the constitutionality of regulations permitting supervisory personnel to order urinalysis testing of public safety officers based on reasonable suspicion of drug abuse. See, for example, *Turner v. Fraternal Order of Police*, 500 A.2d 1005 (D.C. App. 1985). In 1989 the United States Supreme Court upheld federal regulations requiring drug and alcohol testing of railroad employees involved in train accidents. *Skinner v. Railway Labor Executives' Association*, 489 U.S. 602, 109 S.Ct. 1402, 1411, 103 L.Ed.2d 639 (1989). The Court has also sustained a Customs Service policy requiring drug tests for persons seeking positions as customs inspectors. *National Treasury Employees Union v. Von Raab*, 489 U.S. 656, 109 S.Ct. 1384, 103 L.Ed.2d 685 (1989). As yet, the Supreme Court has not addressed the issue of general, random drug testing of public employees. However, it has invalidated a policy under which all political candidates were required to submit to drug testing as a condition of qualifying for the ballot. *Chandler v. Miller*, 520 U.S. 305, 117 S.Ct. 1295, 137 L.Ed.2d 513 (1997).

In 1995 the U.S. Supreme Court stated that a public school district's student athlete drug policy, which authorized random urinalysis drug testing of students who participated in athletic programs, did not violate a student's right to be free from unreasonable searches. While mandatory drug testing is a search, Justice Scalia, writing for an 6–3 majority of the Court, pointed out that, given the decreased expectation of privacy of a public school student, the relative unobtrusiveness of the search, and the severity of the need, such a search was not unreasonable. *Veronica School District v. Acton*, 515 U.S. 646, 115 S.Ct. 2386, 132 L.Ed.2d 564 (1995).

Several state courts have addressed the question of random drug testing of public employees, and at least one state appellate court has found such a policy to be unconstitutional. *City of Palm Bay v. Bauman*, 475 So.2d 1322 (Fla. App. 1985). Given the scope of the drug problem, and the governmental resolve to do something about it, the issue of random drug testing is certain to be litigated for some time to come.

Technology and the Fourth Amendment

The drafters of the Fourth Amendment obviously did not contemplate present-day technology. Yet, in framing the Bill of Rights, they used simple, straightforward language that has endured through the centuries—language capable of being adapted to the needs of the people. Today's technology makes possible silent and invisible intrusions on the privacy of the individual, and the courts are responding to these new, innovative means of surveillance, always cognizant that the touchstone of the Fourth Amendment is its prohibition of "unreasonable" searches and seizures. In this section, we present a sampling of some of these technological advances.

Electronic Surveillance

Electronic surveillance refers to a variety of technological means of gaining information about a suspect that is unavailable to the ordinary senses. Generally speaking, eavesdropping through the use of wiretaps, highly sensitive microphones, and other electronic devices implicates the protections of the Fourth Amendment. However, merely using technology to augment the senses does not necessarily implicate the Fourth Amendment. For example, the Supreme Court has approved the use of searchlights, field glasses, aerial photography, and various other means of enhancing the police's powers of observation. *United States v. Lee,* 274 U.S. 559, 47 S.Ct. 746, 71 L.Ed. 1202 (1927); *Texas v. Brown,* 460 U.S. 730, 103 S.Ct. 1535, 75 L.Ed.2d 502 (1983). Lower federal courts have even approved miniaturized television camera surveillance. *United States v. Torres,* 751 F. 2d 875 (7th Cir. 1984). The question is whether the police use methods that infringe on a person's reasonable expectations of privacy.

Wiretapping

Responding to growing concern over electronic eavesdropping, Congress enacted Title III of the Omnibus Crime Control and Safe Streets Act of 1968, 18 U.S.C.A. §§ 2510–20. The act prohibits interception of electronic communications without a court order unless one party to the conversation consents. Interception is defined as "aural or other acquisition of the contents of any wire, electronic or oral communication through the use of any electronic, mechanical, or other device." 18 U.S.C.A. § 2510(4). In 1986 wire communications was broadened to include conversations through "switching stations." 18 U.S.C.A. § 2510(1). Therefore, the statute now covers cellular telephones.

The act permits issuance of court orders by federal and state courts on sworn application authorized by the United States Attorney General, a specially designated assistant, or a state official at a similar level. The act expressly preempts state law. Therefore, to permit the use of electronic surveillance, a state must adopt legislation along the lines of the federal act, and many states have done so. See, for example, the New Jersey Wiretapping and Electronic Surveillance Control Act of 1968, N.J. Stat. Ann. § 2A: 156A–(1), et seq.

An application for what is commonly known as a **wiretap order** must contain considerable detailed information along with an explanation of why less intrusive means of investigation will not suffice. 18 U.S.C.A. § 2518(1)(c). The statute requires that normal investigative procedures be employed first. But it does not require an officer to exhaust all possible investigative methods before applying for a wiretap order. Before a court may issue a wiretap order, it must find probable cause that the subject of the wiretap has committed or is committing one of a series of enumerated crimes for which wiretapping is authorized and that conventional modes of investigation will not suffice. 18 U.S.C.A. § 2518(3). Originally these offenses included narcotics, organized crime, and national security violations. In 1986 the act was amended to include numerous other serious crimes, including interstate transportation of stolen vehicles, mail fraud, and money laundering. 18 U.S.C.A. § 2516(1)(c).

Court orders permit surveillance for a thirty-day period. 18 U.S.C.A. § 2518(5). At the period's expiration, the recordings made of intercepted communications must be delivered to the judge who issued the order. They are then sealed under the judge's direction. 18 U.S.C.A. § 2518(8)(a).

Critics of electronic surveillance by police argue that it is too drastic an invasion of individual privacy to be countenanced under any circumstances. Law enforcement officials insist that it is an essential investigative tool where other less intrusive means prove nonproductive. Despite the controversy, it is clear that electronic surveillance will continue to be employed by law enforcement agencies.

Pen Registers

A **pen register** is a device that allows the police to learn every number dialed from a specifically targeted telephone. Arguments have been advanced that the use of a pen register by the police without a warrant violates the Fourth Amendment. The Supreme Court has rejected such arguments, saying that using a pen register to obtain numbers dialed from a telephone does not constitute a search and therefore does not require a warrant. *Smith v. Maryland,* 442 U.S. 735, 99 S.Ct. 2577, 61 L.Ed.2d 220 (1979). Would this principle prevail under a state constitution that proscribes the "unreasonable interception of private communications"?

Cordless and Cellular Telephones

Cordless and cellular telephones use radio waves that can be received by anyone operating a receiver tuned to the proper frequency. Certainly, police have no difficulty in intercepting cordless phone calls using electronic scanners. The federal courts have ruled that police may use randomly intercepted cordless telephone conversations as a basis for obtaining a search warrant. *Tyler v. Berodt,* 877 F. 2d 705 (8th Cir. 1989); *United States v. Smith,* 978 F.2d 171, 177 (5th Cir. 1992). The assumption underlying this position is that cordless phones are essentially broadcast transmitters and that, accordingly, users have no reasonable expectation of privacy.

The state courts differ about whether people using cordless phones have privacy rights under the law. For example, in *State v. Mozo,* 655 So.2d 1115 (Fla. 1995), the Florida Supreme Court held that nonconsensual interception of cordless phone calls without prior judicial approval violates a state statute protecting the privacy of communications. That court declined to reach the constitutional issues in the case, preferring to base its decision on statutory grounds.

Digital Display Pagers

Digital display pagers present a problem similar to that posed by cordless telephones. It is common knowledge that drug dealers often use pagers, or "beepers," to conduct their business. Increasingly, police are intercepting signals directed to the pagers of suspected drug dealers to get the telephone numbers of their clients. But at least one state supreme court has said that police must follow the procedures and standards applicable to wiretapping before they may intercept pager signals. See *State v. Jackson,* 650 So. 2d 24 (Fla. 1995). Undoubtedly, other state and federal courts will be called to address this issue in the near future.

Thermal Imagers

Law enforcement officers often resort to various technological means of detecting illicit activities that are obscured from public view. One increasingly common device used in the war on illegal drugs is the infrared thermal imaging device, which detects heat waves emanating from inside homes, greenhouses, and other structures. Such a device can provide a strong indication of whether marijuana is being grown inside the closed structure. Is the use of such a device a "search," even if the officers using it are not physically positioned on a suspect's property? If so, officers normally must have probable cause and, if possible, must obtain a search warrant before employing the heat detector. The majority of federal courts that have considered this issue have ruled that using thermal imaging devices is not a search within the meaning of the Fourth Amendment. See, for example, *United States v. Pinson,* 24 F.3d 1056 (8th Cir. 1994); *United States v. Ford,* 34 F.3d 992 (11th Cir. 1994); and *United States v. Penny-Feeney,* 773 F. Supp. 220 (DC Hawaii 1991). The federal courts have analogized the use of the thermal imager to the high-altitude aerial photography approved by the Supreme Court in *Dow Chemical Company v. United States,* 476 U.S. 227, 106 S.Ct. 1819, 90 L.Ed.2d 226 (1986). There, the Supreme Court noted that high-altitude photography was incapable of revealing intimate activities that would give rise to constitutional concerns.

As we have frequently noted, state courts are free to provide more protection for individual rights under their respective state constitutions than is provided by prevailing federal court interpretations of the U.S. Constitution. Thus, in *State v. Young,* 867 P.2d 593 (Wash. 1994), the Washington Supreme Court held that the use of a thermal imaging device is a search within the meaning of the Washington state constitution.

Note that in *Kyllo v. U.S.,* 190 F.3d 1041 (9th Cir. 1998), the court held that thermal imaging was not a search within the meaning of the Fourth Amendment. Subsequently, the U.S. Supreme Court granted certiorari. ___ U.S. ___, 121 S.Ct 29, 147 L.Ed.2d 1052 (2000). The case was argued in February 2001 but had not been decided when this book went to print.

•••

The Exclusionary Rule

An excerpt from the Supreme Court's opinion in *Mapp v. Ohio* appears at the end of the chapter.

The **exclusionary rule** is a judicially announced rule that prohibits the use of illegally obtained evidence in a criminal prosecution of the person whose rights were violated by the police in obtaining that evidence. In 1914 the U.S. Supreme Court first held that evidence obtained through an unlawful search and seizure could not be used to convict a person of a federal crime. *Weeks v. United States,* supra. In 1949, in *Wolf v. Colorado,* supra, the Supreme Court had refused to require the states to follow the exclusionary rule, saying that it was not an essential element of Fourth Amendment protection. But in *Mapp v. Ohio,* supra, the Court held that there was no other effective means of enforcing the protections of the Fourth Amendment. The Court reasoned that if the Fourth Amendment was applicable to the states under the Fourteenth Amendment, then the exclusionary rule was also because it was the only effective means of enforcing the Fourth Amendment against overzealous police officers. The *Mapp* decision had an immediate impact. In New York City, for example, in the year preceding *Mapp,* police officers had not bothered to obtain a single search warrant. In the year following *Mapp,* they obtained more than eight hundred!

The Fruit of the Poisonous Tree Doctrine

The **fruit of the poisonous tree doctrine** holds that evidence derived from other evidence that is obtained through an illegal search or seizure is itself inadmissible. *Wong Sun v. United States,* 371 U.S. 471, 83 S.Ct. 407, 9 L.Ed.2d 441 (1963). The general rule is that where there has been an illegal seizure of property, such property cannot be introduced into evidence and no testimony may be given relative to any facts surrounding the seizure. However, the Fourth Amendment does not require evidence to be excluded even if it was initially discovered during an illegal search of private property if that evidence is later discovered during a valid search that is wholly independent of the initial illegal activity. *Murray v. United States,* 487 U.S. 533, 108 S.Ct. 2529, 101 L.Ed.2d 472 (1988).

The Erosion of the Exclusionary Rule

The exclusionary rule is justified by the need to deter police misconduct, but it exacts a high price to society in that "the criminal is to go free because the constable has blundered." As crime rates rose dramatically during the 1960s and 1970s, the exclusionary rule came under attack from critics who argued that the social cost of allowing guilty persons to avoid prosecution outweighed the benefit of deterring police from violating the Fourth Amendment. During the 1970s the Supreme Court used this sort of cost/benefit analysis in curtailing the scope of the exclusionary rule in a series of controversial decisions. In *United States v. Calandra,* 414 U.S. 338, 94 S.Ct. 613, 38 L.Ed.2d 561 (1974), the Court held that illegally obtained evidence could be used to obtain grand jury indictments. In *Michigan v. DeFillippo,* 443 U.S. 31, 99 S.Ct. 2627, 61 L.Ed.2d 343 (1979), the Court allowed the use of evidence obtained through a search incident to arrest pursuant to a law that was later ruled unconstitutional. But the most significant erosions of the rule came in the 1980s.

The Good-Faith Exception

An excerpt from the Supreme Court's decision in *United States v. Leon* appears at the end of the chapter.

In the most significant exclusionary rule cases decided in the 1980s, the Supreme Court held that evidence obtained on the basis of a search warrant that is later held to be invalid may be admitted in evidence at trial if the police officer who conducted the search relied on the warrant in "good faith." *United States v. Leon,* 468 U.S. 897, 104 S.Ct. 3405, 82 L.Ed.2d 677 (1984); *Massachusetts v. Sheppard,* 468 U.S. 981, 104 S.Ct. 3424, 82 L.Ed.2d 737 (1984). It must be noted that the **good-faith exception** to the exclusionary rule applies only in cases where police officers rely on warrants that are later held to be invalid; it does not apply to warrantless searches.

There are four situations in which the good-faith exception to the exclusionary rule does not apply:

1. If the magistrate was misled by an affidavit that the affiant knew was false or would have known was false except for reckless disregard for the truth.
2. If the magistrate wholly abandons his or her judicial role.
3. If the affidavit is so lacking in indicia of probable cause as to render belief in its existence unreasonable.
4. If the warrant is so facially deficient that the executing officer cannot reasonably presume its validity.

CASE-IN-POINT

The Good-Faith Exception Under State Constitutional Law

Acting on the basis of an informant's tip, police obtained a warrant to search a building owned by the defendant. Inside the building they discovered seventeen growing marijuana plants, as well as cultivating equipment. After a suppression hearing, the trial judge determined that the warrant upon which the search was based was defective in that it had not been adequately supported by probable cause. Nevertheless, the judge refused to suppress the evidence, citing the good-faith exception to the exclusionary rule created by the U.S. Supreme Court's decision in *United States v. Leon*. On appeal, the Pennsylvania Supreme Court interpreted its state constitution as affording more protection to a defendant against unreasonable searches and seizures than the federal constitution as interpreted in *Leon*. Thus, the court concluded that the Pennsylvania Constitution does not permit a *Leon*-style good-faith exception to the exclusionary rule.

Commonwealth v. Edmunds, 586 A.2d 887 (Pa. 1991).

THE GOOD-FAITH EXCEPTION UNDER STATE CONSTITUTIONAL LAW

As previously noted, the Fourth Amendment sets a minimal national standard. Most states have adopted the good-faith exception. As pointed out, state courts are free to provide greater levels of protection under the search and seizure sections of state constitutions. This latter approach was followed by the New Jersey Supreme Court in *State v. Novembrino*, 519 A.2d 820 (N.J. 1987), where it refused to follow the good-faith exception to the exclusionary rule as a matter of state law. The court observed that the exclusionary rule was firmly embedded in its own jurisprudence and that a good-faith exception would "ultimately reduce respect for and compliance with the probable cause standard." 519 A.2d 854.

Standing to Invoke the Exclusionary Rule

A person who seeks the benefits of the exclusionary rule must have **standing** to invoke the rule. The concept of standing limits the class of defendants who may challenge an allegedly illegal search and seizure. In *Jones v. United States*, 362 U.S. 257, 80 S.Ct. 725, 4 L.Ed.2d 697 (1960), the Supreme Court granted automatic standing to anyone who was legitimately on the premises searched. In *Rakas v. Illinois*, 439 U.S. 128, 99 S.Ct. 421, 58 L.Ed.2d 387 (1978), however, the Court restricted the *Jones* doctrine by refusing to allow passengers of an automobile to challenge the search of the vehicle in which they were riding.

In *United States v. Salvucci*, 448 U.S. 83, 100 S.Ct. 2547, 65 L.Ed.2d 619 (1980), the Court took the final step in overruling the automatic-standing rule of *Jones v. United States*. Salvucci was charged with possession of stolen mail. The evidence was recovered by police in a search of an apartment that belonged to the mother of Salvucci's accomplice. The federal district court granted Salvucci's motion to suppress the evidence, relying on the automatic-standing doctrine. The Supreme Court reversed, holding that Salvucci was not automatically entitled to challenge the search of another person's apartment. Justice Rehnquist explained the Court's more conservative stance on the issue of standing:

> We are convinced that the automatic standing rule . . . has outlived its usefulness in this Court's Fourth Amendment jurisprudence. The doctrine now serves only

to afford a windfall to defendants whose Fourth Amendment rights have not been violated. 448 U.S. at 95, 100 S.Ct. at 2554, 65 L.Ed.2d at 630.

The Court's current approach is to grant standing only to those persons who have a possessory or legitimate privacy interest in the place that was searched. Thus, a casual visitor to an apartment has no legitimate expectation of privacy in an apartment hallway that would grant standing to contest a search of those premises. *United States v. Burnett*, 890 F.2d 1233 (D.C. Cir. 1989). To successfully invoke the exclusionary rule now, a defendant must show that a legitimate expectation of privacy was violated.

Of course, states may still grant automatic standing to challenge seized evidence. In *Commonwealth v. Amendola*, 550 N.E. 2d 121 (Mass. 1990), the court rejected the Supreme Court's abandonment of the automatic-standing rule:

When a defendant is charged with a crime in which possession of the seized evidence at the time of the contested search is an essential element of guilt, the defendant shall be deemed to have standing to contest the legality of the search and the seizure of that evidence.

The Massachusetts court observed that courts in Louisiana, Michigan, New Hampshire, New Jersey, Pennsylvania, and Vermont have reached similar conclusions.

Conclusion

The constitutional protection against unreasonable searches and seizures is a fundamental right, yet determining the precise scope and meaning of the right is not easy. The constitutional law governing search and seizure is extremely complex. Moreover, it is highly dynamic, as courts decide countless cases in this area each year.

The threshold question in evaluating a given search or seizure is whether the Fourth Amendment is applicable. Certain searches, including those conducted by private individuals where the government does not take part and searches of open fields or abandoned property, are beyond the pale of the Fourth Amendment. In a nutshell, the Fourth Amendment protects persons from unreasonable intrusions where they have a reasonable expectation of privacy. To guard against unreasonable intrusions of privacy, police are normally required to obtain a warrant before engaging in a search and seizure. Courts rigorously enforce the Fourth Amendment requirement that search warrants be issued only "upon probable cause, supported by Oath or affirmation," and are specific as to "the place to be searched and the persons or things to be seized," U.S. Const., Amend. 4. In addition to searches based on consent or conducted incident to a lawful arrest, a number of exceptions to the warrant requirement are based on the doctrine of exigent circumstances. Hot pursuit, evanescent evidence, and certain emergencies qualify as exigent circumstances allowing warrantless searches.

Normally, police must have probable cause before conducting a search. Here, too, there are exceptions—the so-called stop-and-frisk situation, the airport search, and the school search—where police may conduct searches on the basis of a less stringent standard of reasonableness.

One of the most controversial Fourth Amendment issues is how to deter law enforcement officials from conducting improper searches and seizures. The Supreme Court has fashioned a rule excluding illegally obtained evidence from criminal trials.

Here again, there are exceptions to the rule, such as the limited good-faith exception announced in the *Leon* case.

Although technological advances have afforded law enforcement new means to ferret out crime, the use of helicopters and such high-tech devices as infrared sensors, super-sensitive microphones, and miniature radio transmitters challenges the traditional right of privacy enjoyed by citizens in a free country.

The Fourth Amendment has applicability beyond the seizure of evidence. Because the arrest of a suspect is considered a "seizure," the Fourth Amendment applies to arrests and various lesser police–citizen encounters, as well as to the use of force by police in making arrests. We examine these issues, along with police interrogation and identification procedures, in the next chapter.

Key Terms

search
seizure
warrant
probable cause
reasonable suspicion
general warrant
doctrine of incorporation
border searches
curtilage
open fields doctrine
administrative searches
abandoned property
inventory search
consent to a search
implied consent
third-party consent
exigent circumstances
wiretapping
electronic eavesdropping
reasonable expectation of privacy
sobriety checkpoints
strip searches

totality of circumstances
affidavit
affiant
confidential informants
anticipatory search warrant
knock and announce
Franks hearing
warrantless searches
plain-view doctrine
emergency searches
evanescent evidence
automobile exception
search incident to a lawful arrest
hot pursuit
stop-and-frisk
drug courier profiles
wiretap order
pen register
exclusionary rule
fruit of the poisonous tree doctrine
good-faith exception
standing

 # Web-Based Research Activity

1. Go to the web. Log on to **www.findlaw.com.**
2. Go to the following page: **http://www.findlaw.com/casecode/supreme.html**. Use this page to locate the Supreme Court's decision in *United States v. Ramirez*, decided March 4, 1998.
3. Read the decision. Write a brief summary of the decision in which you describe the key facts, the issue before the Supreme Court, the Court's holding, and the rationale for its decision.
4. In your opinion, did the Court make the correct decision?

Questions for Thought and Discussion

1. Today many security personnel are "private police," yet Fourth Amendment protection has been extended only to those searches conducted by government officials. What arguments can be made for and against expanding the prohibitions of the Fourth Amendment to include security personnel?

2. What rationale supports the "search incident to arrest" exception to the warrant requirement? What limitations do the courts impose on such searches?

3. Should one have a reasonable expectation of privacy from infrared detectors and other high-tech devices that enable law enforcement officers to "see" heat emanating from a person's home? Why or why not?

4. Does a person using a public restroom in a government office building have a reasonable expectation of privacy from television security surveillance?

5. In *New Jersey v. T.L.O.* (1985), the Supreme Court adopted a reasonableness standard for public school searches. Should this standard be applied to searches of students in public colleges and universities? What about private colleges? Does it make a difference if the search is conducted in a public setting or in the student's dormitory room?

6. What is the rationale for excluding from trial evidence obtained in violation of the Fourth Amendment? Is this a compelling justification for the exclusion of criminal evidence from the trial of a defendant accused of a serious felony such as aggravated battery?

7. What alternatives to the exclusionary rule might be adopted to enforce the protections of the Fourth Amendment? How effective are such alternatives likely to be?

8. The Supreme Court has created a "good-faith" exception to the exclusionary rule where police rely on a search warrant that is later held to be invalid because the magistrate erred in finding probable cause for a search. Should the good-faith exception be extended to cases where police acting "in good faith" conduct warrantless searches that are later held to be unlawful?

9. What is meant by the "fruit of the poisonous tree doctrine" in relation to searches and seizures?

10. What is the "standing" requirement in the law of search and seizure? What is its purpose?

Problems for Discussion and Solution

1. Police observed an automobile traveling at a high rate of speed and swerving on the road. They gave pursuit and stopped the vehicle after a five-minute chase. The driver, later identified as Jerome Johnson, emerged from the car and began to verbally abuse and threaten the officers. Johnson appeared intoxicated but refused to take any of the standard field sobriety tests. Under state law, refusal to perform a sobriety test results in loss of a driver's license for a period of one year. The law does not authorize police to force suspects to perform any sobriety tests against their will. Johnson was arrested and transported to a local hospital, where he was forcibly restrained and asked to submit to a blood-alcohol test. Johnson refused, saying "I'd

rather lose my license than let you stick me with that needle." The test was administered over Johnson's objection, and the results indicated that Johnson's blood-alcohol level was substantially above the legal limit. Johnson was charged with driving under the influence of alcohol. Before trial, Johnson's attorney moved to suppress the results of the blood-alcohol test, arguing that it was taken without Johnson's consent, without probable cause, and in violation of the state's implied consent law. If you were the judge in this case, how would you be inclined to rule on the admissibility of this evidence? What additional information would you need to render your decision?

2. Acting without a search warrant, police arrive at a home after receiving an anonymous tip that a man has been making illegal explosives in his workshop. The officers find that the man is not at home. Can the man's wife consent to a warrantless search of her husband's workshop, or must police wait until the husband returns to obtain his consent?

● ● ● ● ● ● ● ● ● ● ● ● ●

EXCERPTS FROM JUDICIAL DECISIONS

Katz v. United States

Supreme Court of the United States, 1967.
389 U.S. 347, 88 S.Ct. 507, 19 L.Ed.2d 576.

[In this seminal case, the Supreme Court addresses the scope of protection afforded by the Fourth Amendment.]

Mr. Justice STEWART delivered the opinion of the Court.

At trial the Government was permitted, over the petitioner's objection, to introduce evidence of the petitioner's end of telephone conversations, overheard by FBI agents who had attached an electronic listening and recording device to the outside of the public telephone booth from which he had placed his calls. In affirming his conviction, the Court of Appeals rejected the contention that the recordings had been obtained in violation of the Fourth Amendment, because "[t]here was no physical entrance into the area occupied by [the petitioner]." We granted certiorari in order to consider the constitutional questions thus presented. . . .

The question . . . is whether the search and seizure conducted in this case complied with constitutional standards. In that regard, the Government's position is that its agents acted in an entirely defensible manner: They did not begin their electronic surveillance until investigation of the petitioner's activities had established a strong probability that he was using the telephone in question to transmit gambling information to persons in other States, in vio-

lation of federal law. Moreover, the surveillance was limited, both in scope and in duration, to the specific purpose of establishing the contents of the petitioner's unlawful telephonic communications. The agents confined their surveillance to the brief periods during which he used the telephone booth, and they took great care to overhear only the conversations of the petitioner himself.

Accepting this account of the Government's actions as accurate, it is clear that this surveillance was so narrowly circumscribed that a duly authorized magistrate, properly notified of the need for such investigation, specifically informed of the basis on which it was to proceed, and clearly apprised of the precise intrusion it would entail, could constitutionally have authorized, with appropriate safeguards, the very limited search and seizure that the Government asserts in fact took place.

The Government urges that, because its agents . . . did no more here than they might properly have done with prior judicial sanction, we should retroactively validate their conduct. That we cannot do. It is apparent that the agents in this case acted with restraint. Yet the inescapable fact is that this restraint was imposed by the agents themselves, not by a judicial officer. They were not required, before commencing the search, to present their estimate of probable cause for detached scrutiny by a neutral magistrate. They were not compelled, during the conduct of the search itself, to observe precise limits established in advance by a specific court order. Nor were they directed, after the search had been completed, to notify the authorizing magistrate in detail of all that had been seized. In the absence of such safeguards, this Court has never sustained a search upon the sole ground that officers reasonably expected to find evidence of a particular crime and voluntarily confined their activities to the least intrusive means consistent with that end. Searches conducted without warrants have been held unlawful "notwithstanding facts unquestionably showing probable cause," for the Constitution requires "that the deliberate, impartial judgment of a judicial officer . . . be interposed between the citizen and the police. . . ." "Over and again this Court has emphasized that the mandate of the [Fourth] Amendment requires adherence to judicial processes," and that searches conducted outside the judicial process, without prior approval by judge or magistrate, are per se unreasonable under the Fourth Amendment—subject only to a few specifically established and well-delineated exceptions.

It is difficult to imagine how any of those exceptions could ever apply to the sort of search and seizure involved in this case. Even electronic surveillance substantially contemporaneous with an individual's arrest could hardly be deemed an "incident" of that arrest. Nor could the use of electronic surveillance without prior authorization be justified on grounds of "hot pursuit." And, of course, the very nature of electronic surveillance precludes its use pursuant to the suspect's consent.

The Government does not question these basic principles. Rather, it urges the creation of a new exception to cover this case. It argues that surveillance of a telephone booth should be exempted from the usual requirement of advance authorization by a magistrate upon a showing of probable cause. We cannot agree. Omission of such authorization bypasses the safeguards provided by an objective predetermination of probable cause, and substitutes instead the far less reliable procedure of an after-the-event justification for the . . . search, too likely to be subtly influenced by the familiar shortcomings of hindsight judgment. . . .

And bypassing a neutral predetermination of the scope of a search leaves individuals secure from Fourth Amendment violations "only in the discretion of the police." . . .

These considerations do not vanish when the search in question is transferred from the setting of a home, an office, or a hotel room to that of a telephone booth. Wherever a man may be, he is entitled to know that he will remain free from unreasonable searches and seizures. The government agents here ignored "the procedure of antecedent justification . . . that is central to the Fourth Amendment," . . . a procedure that we hold to be a constitutional precondition of the kind of electronic surveillance involved in this case. Because the surveillance here failed to meet that condition, and because it led to the petitioner's conviction, the judgment must be reversed.

Mr. Justice MARSHALL took no part in the consideration or decision of this case.

Mr. Justice DOUGLAS, with whom Mr. Justice BRENNAN joins, concurring. . . .

Mr. Justice HARLAN, concurring.

. . . "[T]he Fourth Amendment protects people, not places." The question, however, is what protection it affords to those people. Generally, as here, the answer to that question requires reference to a "place." My understanding of the rule that has emerged from prior decisions is that there is a twofold requirement, first that a person have exhibited an actual (subjective) expectation of privacy and, second, that the expectation be one that society is prepared to recognize as "reasonable." Thus a man's home is, for most purposes, a place where he expects privacy, but objects, activities, or statements that he exposes to the "plain view" of outsiders are not "protected" because no intention to keep them to himself has been exhibited. On the other hand, conversations in the open would not be protected against being overheard, for the expectation of privacy under the circumstances would be unreasonable.

The critical fact in this case is that "[o]ne who occupies it [a telephone booth], shuts the door behind him, and pays the toll that permits him to place a call is surely entitled to assume" that his conversation is not being intercepted. The point is not that the booth is "accessible to the public" at other times, but that it is a temporarily private place whose momentary occupants' expectations of freedom from intrusion are recognized as reasonable. . . .

Mr. Justice WHITE, concurring. . . .

Mr. Justice BLACK, dissenting. . . .

Illinois v. Gates

Supreme Court of the United States, 1983.
462 U.S. 213, 103 S.Ct. 2317, 76 L.Ed.2d 527.

[In this case the Supreme Court considers the appropriate standard that magistrates should apply in deciding whether there is probable cause to justify the issuance of a search warrant.]

Justice REHNQUIST delivered the opinion of the Court.

Respondents Lance and Susan Gates were indicted for violation of state drug laws after police officers, executing a search warrant, discovered marijuana and other contraband in their automobile and home. Prior to trial the Gates' moved to suppress evidence seized during this search. The Illinois Supreme Court affirmed the decisions of lower state courts granting the motion. It held that the affidavit submitted in support of the State's application for a warrant to search the Gates' property was inadequate under this Court's decisions in *Aguilar v. Texas* . . . (1964) and *Spinelli v. United States* . . . (1969). . . .

We now turn to the question presented in the State's original petition for certiorari, which requires us to decide whether respondents' rights under the Fourth and Fourteenth Amendments were violated by the search of their car and house. A chronological statement of events usefully introduces the issues at stake. Bloomingdale, Ill., is a suburb of Chicago located in DuPage County. On May 3, 1978, the Bloomingdale Police Department received by mail an anonymous handwritten letter which read as follows:

This letter is to inform you that you have a couple in your town who strictly make their living on selling drugs. They are Sue and Lance Gates, they live on Greenway, off Bloomingdale Rd. in the condominiums. Most of their buys are done in Florida. Sue, his wife drives their car to Florida, where she leaves it to be loaded up with drugs, then Lance flys down and drives it back. Sue flys back after she drops the car off in Florida. May 3 she is driving down there again and Lance will be flying down in a few days to drive it back. At the time Lance drives the car back he has the trunk loaded with over $100,000.00 in drugs. Presently, they have over $100,000.00 worth of drugs in their basement. They brag about the fact they never have to work, and make their entire living on pushers.

I guarantee if you watch them carefully you will make a big catch. They are friends with some big drug dealers, who visit their house often. . . .

The letter was referred by the Chief of Police of the Bloomingdale Police Department to Detective Mader, who decided to pursue the tip. Mader learned from the office of the Illinois Secretary of State, that an Illinois driver's license had been issued to one Lance Gates, residing at a stated address in Bloomingdale. He contacted a confidential informant, whose examination of certain financial records revealed a more recent address for the Gateses, and he also learned from a police officer assigned to O'Hare Airport that "L. Gates" had made a reservation on Eastern Airlines flight 245 to West Palm Beach, Fla., scheduled to depart from Chicago on May 5 at 4:15 P.M.

Mader then made arrangements with an agent of the Drug Enforcement Administration for surveillance of the May 5 Eastern Airlines flight. The agent later reported to Mader that Gates had boarded the flight, and that federal agents in Florida had observed him arrive in West Palm Beach and take a taxi to the nearby Holiday Inn. They also reported that Gates went to a room registered to one Susan Gates and that, at 7:00 A.M. the next morning, Gates and an unidentified woman left the motel in a Mercury bearing Illinois license plates and drove northbound on an interstate frequently used by travelers to the Chicago area. In addition, the DEA agent informed Mader that the license plate number on the Mercury was registered to a Hornet station wagon owned by Gates.

Mader signed an affidavit setting forth the foregoing facts, and submitted it to a judge of the Circuit Court of DuPage County, together with a copy of the anonymous letter. The judge of that court thereupon issued a search warrant for the Gates' residence and for their automobile. The judge, in deciding to issue the warrant, could have determined that the modus operandi of the Gateses had been substantially corroborated.

At 5:15 A.M. on March 7th, only 36 hours after he had flown out of Chicago, Lance Gates, and his wife, returned to their home in Bloomingdale, driving the car in which they had left West Palm Beach some 22 hours earlier. The Bloomingdale police were awaiting them, searched the trunk of the Mercury, and uncovered approximately 350 pounds of marijuana. A search of the Gateses' home revealed marijuana, weapons, and other contraband. The Illinois Circuit Court ordered suppression of all these items, on the ground that the affidavit submitted to the Circuit Judge failed to support the necessary determination of probable cause to believe that the Gateses' automobile and home contained the contraband in question. This decision was affirmed in turn by the Illinois Appellate Court and by a divided vote of the Supreme Court of Illinois. . . .

We agree with the Illinois Supreme Court that an informant's "veracity," "reliability" and "basis of knowledge" are all highly relevant in determining the value of his report. We do not agree, however, that these elements should be understood as entirely separate and independent requirements to be rigidly exacted in every case, which the opinion of the Supreme Court of Illinois would imply. Rather, as detailed below, they should be understood simply as closely intertwined issues that may usefully illuminate the commonsense, practical question whether there is "probable cause" to believe that contraband or evidence is located in a particular place.

This totality of the circumstances approach is far more consistent with our prior treatment of probable cause than is any rigid demand that specific "tests" be satisfied by every informant's tip. Perhaps the central teaching of our decisions bearing on the probable cause standard is that it is a "practical, nontechnical conception." . . . "In dealing with probable cause, . . . as the very name implies, we deal with probabilities. These are not technical, they are the factual and practical considerations of everyday life on which reasonable and prudent men, not legal technicians, act." . . .

. . . [P]robable cause is a fluid concept—turning on the assessment of probabilities in particular factual contexts—not readily, or even usefully, reduced to a neat set of legal rules. Informants' tips doubtless come in many shapes and sizes from many different types of persons. "Informants' tips, like all other clues and evidence coming to a policeman on the scene, may vary greatly in their value and reliability." Rigid legal rules are ill-suited to an area of such diversity. "One simple rule will not cover every situation." . . .

Moreover, the "two-pronged test" directs analysis into two largely independent channels—the informant's "veracity" or "reliability" and his "basis of knowledge." There are persuasive arguments against according these two elements such independent status. Instead, they are better understood as relevant considerations in the totality of circumstances analysis that traditionally has guided probable cause determinations: a deficiency in one may be compensated for, in determining the overall reliability of a tip, by a strong showing as to the other, or by some other indicia of reliability. . . .

If the affidavits submitted by police officers are subjected to the type of scrutiny some courts have deemed appropriate, police might well resort to warrantless searches, with the hope of relying on consent or some other exception to the warrant clause that might develop at the time of the search. In addition, the possession of a warrant by officers conducting an arrest or search greatly reduces the perception of unlawful or intrusive police conduct, by assuring "the individual whose property is searched or seized of the lawful authority of the executing office, his need to search, and the limits of his power to search." . . . Reflecting this preference for the warrant process, the traditional standard for review of an issuing magistrate's probable cause determination has been that so long as the magistrate had a "substantial basis for . . . conclud[ing]" that a search would uncover evidence of wrongdoing, the Fourth Amendment requires no more. . . . We think reaffirmation of this standard better serves the purpose of encouraging recourse to the warrant procedure and is more consistent with our traditional deference to the probable cause determinations of magistrates than is the "two-pronged test."

Finally, the direction taken by decisions following *Spinelli* poorly serves "the most basic function of any government": "to provide for the security of the individual and of his property." . . . The structures that inevitably accompany the "two-pronged test" cannot avoid seriously impeding the task of law enforcement. . . . Ordinary citizens, like ordinary witnesses, generally do not provide extensive recitations of the basis of their everyday observations. Likewise, as the Illinois Supreme Court observed in this case, the veracity of persons supplying anonymous tips is by hypothesis largely unknown and unknowable. As a result, anonymous tips seldom could survive a rigorous application of either of the *Spinelli* prongs. Yet, such tips, particularly when supplemented by independent police investigation, frequently contribute to the solution of otherwise "perfect crimes." While a conscientious assessment of the basis for crediting such tips is required by the Fourth Amendment, a standard that leaves virtually no place for anonymous citizen informants is not.

For all these reasons, we conclude that it is wiser to abandon the "two-pronged test" established by our decisions in *Aguilar* and *Spinelli*. In its place we reaffirm the totality of the circumstances analysis that traditionally has informed probable cause determinations. . . . We are convinced that this flexi-

ble, easily applied standard will better achieve the accommodation of public and private interests that the Fourth Amendment requires than does the approach that has developed from *Aguilar* and *Spinelli*. . . .

Justice WHITE, concurring in the judgment. . . .

Justice BRENNAN, with whom Justice MARSHALL joins, dissenting.

Justice STEVENS, with whom Justice BRENNAN joins, dissenting. . . .

● ● ● ● ● ● ●   ● ● ● ● ● ● ●

United States v. Ross

Supreme Court of the United States, 1982.
456 U.S. 798, 102 S.Ct. 2157, 72 L.Ed.2d 572.

[In Carroll v. United States, 267 U.S. 132 (1925), the Supreme Court upheld a warrantless search of a motor vehicle that was harboring contraband. Thus began the so-called automobile exception to the Fourth Amendment warrant requirement. In the instant case, the Court considers the scope of the automobile exception.]

Justice STEVENS delivered the opinion of the Court.
. . . In this case, we consider the extent to which police officers—who have legitimately stopped an automobile and who have probable cause to believe that contraband is concealed somewhere within it— may conduct a probing search of compartments and containers within the vehicle whose contents are not in plain view. We hold that they may conduct a search of the vehicle that is as thorough as a magistrate could authorize in a warrant "particularly describing the place to be searched."

In the evening of November 27, 1978, an informant who had previously proved to be reliable telephoned Detective Marcum of the District of Columbia Police Department and told him that an individual known as "Bandit" was selling narcotics kept in the trunk of a car parked at 439 Ridge Street. The informant stated that he had just observed "Bandit" complete a sale and that "Bandit" had told him that additional narcotics were in the trunk. The informant gave Marcum a detailed description of "Bandit" and stated that the car was a "purplish ma-

roon" Chevrolet Malibu with District of Columbia license plates.

Accompanied by Detective Cassidy and Sergeant Gonzales, Marcum immediately drove to the area and found a maroon Malibu parked in front of 439 Ridge Street. . . . They pulled alongside the Malibu, noticed that the driver matched the informant's description, and stopped the car. Marcum and Cassidy told the driver—later identified as Albert Ross, the respondent in this action—to get out of the vehicle. While they searched Ross, Sergeant Gonzales discovered a bullet on the car's front seat. He searched the interior of the car and found a pistol in the glove compartment. Ross then was arrested and handcuffed. Detective Cassidy took Ross' keys and opened the trunk, where he found a closed brown paper bag. He opened the bag and discovered a number of glassine bags containing a white powder. Cassidy replaced the bag, closed the trunk, and drove the car to headquarters.

At the police station Cassidy thoroughly searched the car. In addition to the "lunch-type" brown paper bag, Cassidy found in the trunk a zippered red leather pouch. He unzipped the pouch and discovered $3,200 in cash. The police laboratory later determined that the powder in the bag was heroin. No warrant was obtained.

Ross was charged with possession of heroin with intent to distribute. . . . Prior to trial, he moved to suppress the heroin found in the paper bag and the currency found in the leather pouch. After an evidentiary hearing, the District Court denied the motion to suppress. The heroin and currency were introduced in evidence at trial and Ross was convicted. . . .

[On appeal, Ross' conviction was reversed on the grounds that the warrantless search of the containers in the trunk was unreasonable.]

. . . [T]he exception to the warrant requirement established in *Carroll* [*v. United States* (1925)]—the scope of which we consider in this case—applied only to searches of vehicles that are supported by probable cause. In this class of cases, a search is not unreasonable if based on facts that would justify the issuance of a warrant, even though a warrant has not actually been obtained.

The rationale justifying a warrantless search of an automobile that is believed to be transporting contraband arguably applies with equal force to any movable container that is believed to be carrying an illicit substance. . . .

. . . [T]he decision in *Carroll* was based on the Court's appraisal of practical considerations viewed in the perspective of history. It is therefore significant that the practical consequences of the *Carroll* decision would be largely nullified if the permissible scope of a warrantless search of an automobile did not include containers and packages found inside the vehicle. Contraband goods are rarely strewn across the trunk or floor of a car; since by their very nature such goods must be withheld from public view, they rarely can be placed in an automobile unless they are enclosed within some form of container. . . .

A lawful search of fixed premises generally extends to the entire area in which the object of the search may be found and is not limited by the possibility that separate acts of entry or opening may be required to complete the search. . . . A warrant to open a footlocker to search for marihuana would also authorize the opening of packages found inside. A warrant to search a vehicle would support a search of every part of the vehicle that might contain the object of the search. When a legitimate search is under way, and when its purpose and its limits have been precisely defined, nice distinctions between closets, drawers and containers, in the case of a home, or between glove compartments, upholstered seats, trunks and wrapped packages, in the case of a vehicle, must give way to the interest in the prompt and efficient completion of the task at hand.

This rule applies equally to all containers, as indeed we believe it must. . . .

The scope of a warrantless search of an automobile thus is not defined by the nature of the container in which the contraband is secreted. Rather, it is defined by the object of the search and the places where there is probable cause to believe it may be found. . . . Probable cause to believe that a container placed in the trunk of a taxi contains contraband or evidence does not justify search of the entire cab. . . .

The [automobile] exception recognized in *Carroll* is unquestionably one that is "specifically established and well delineated." . . . We hold that the scope of a warrantless search authorized by that exception is no broader and no narrower than a magistrate could legitimately authorize by warrant. If probable cause justifies the search of a lawfully stopped vehicle, it justifies the search of every part of the vehicle that may contain the object of the search. . . .

Justice BLACKMUN, concurring. . . .

Justice POWELL, concurring. . . .

Justice WHITE, dissenting. . . .

Justice MARSHALL, with whom Justice BRENNAN joins, dissenting.

The majority today not only repeals all realistic limits on warrantless automobile searches, it repeals the Fourth Amendment warrant requirement itself. By equating a police officer's estimation of probable cause with a magistrate's, the Court utterly disregards the value of a neutral and detached magistrate. . . .

This case will have profound implications for the privacy of citizens traveling in automobiles. . . .

Mapp v. Ohio

Supreme Court of the United States, 1961.
367 U.S. 643, 81 S.Ct. 1684, 6 L.Ed.2d 1081.

[In this landmark decision, the Supreme Court applies the Fourth Amendment exclusionary rule to the state courts by way of the Fourteenth Amendment.]

Mr. Justice CLARK delivered the opinion of the Court.

Appellant stands convicted of knowingly having had in her possession and under her control certain lewd and lascivious books, pictures, and photographs in violation of . . . Ohio's Revised Code. The Supreme Court of Ohio found that her conviction was valid though "based primarily upon the introduction in evidence of lewd and lascivious books and pictures unlawfully seized during an unlawful search of defendant's home." . . .

On May 23, 1957, three Cleveland police officers arrived at appellant's residence in that city pursuant to information that "a person [was] hiding out in the home, who was wanted for questioning in connection with a recent bombing, and that there was a large amount of policy paraphernalia being hidden in the home." Miss Mapp and her daughter by a former marriage lived on the top floor of the two family dwelling. Upon their arrival at that house, the officers knocked on the door and demanded entrance but appellant, after telephoning her attorney, refused to admit them without a search warrant. They advised their headquarters of the situation and undertook a surveillance of the house.

The officers again sought entrance some three hours later when four or more additional officers arrived on the scene. When Miss Mapp did not come to the door immediately at least one of the several doors to the house was forcibly opened and the policemen gained admittance. Meanwhile Miss Mapp's attorney arrived, but the officers, having secured their own entry, and continuing in their defiance of the law, would permit him neither to see Miss Mapp nor to enter the house. It appears that Miss Mapp was halfway down the stairs from the upper floor to the front door when the officers, in this highhanded manner, broke into the hall. She demanded to see the search warrant. A paper, claimed to be a warrant, was held up by one of the officers. She grabbed the

"warrant" and placed it in her bosom. A struggle ensued in which the officers recovered the piece of paper and as a result of which they handcuffed appellant because she had been "belligerent" in resisting their official rescue of the "warrant" from her person. Running roughshod over appellant, a policeman "grabbed" her, "twisting" [her] hand, and she "yelled [and] pleaded with him" because "it was hurting." Appellant, in handcuffs, was then forcibly taken upstairs to her bedroom where the officers searched a dresser, a chest of drawers, a closet and some suitcases. They also looked into a photo album and through personal papers belonging to the appellant. The search spread to the rest of the second floor including the child's bedroom, the living room, the kitchen and a dinette. The basement of the building and a trunk found therein were also searched. The obscene materials for possession of which she was ultimately convicted were discovered in the course of that widespread search.

At the trial no search warrant was produced by the prosecution, nor was the failure to produce one explained or accounted for. At best, "There is, in the record, considerable doubt as to whether there ever was any warrant for the search of defendant's home." . . . The Ohio Supreme Court believed a "reasonable argument" could be made that the conviction should be reversed "because the methods employed to obtain the [evidence] . . . were such to offend a sense of justice," but the court found determinative the fact that the evidence had not been taken "from defendant's person by the use of brutal or offensive physical force." . . .

Since the Fourth Amendment's right of privacy has been declared enforceable against the States through the Due Process Clause of the Fourteenth, it is enforceable against them by the same sanction of exclusion as is used against the Federal Government. . . .

Moreover, our holding that the exclusionary rule is an essential part of both the Fourth and Fourteenth Amendments is not only the logical dictate of prior cases, but it also makes very good sense. . . .

There are those who say, as did Justice (then Judge) Cardozo, that under our constitutional exclusionary doctrine, "The criminal is to go free because the constable has blundered." . . . In some cases this will undoubtedly be the result. But, . . . "There is another consideration—the imperative of judicial integrity." . . . The criminal goes free, if he must, but it is the law that sets him free. Nothing can destroy a government more quickly than its failure to observe its own laws, or worse, its disregard of the charter of its own existence. . . .

The federal courts themselves have operated under the exclusionary rule . . . for almost half a century; yet it has not been suggested either that the Federal Bureau of Investigation has thereby been rendered ineffective, or that the administration of criminal justice in the federal courts has thereby been disrupted. Moreover, the experience of the states is impressive. . . .

The ignoble shortcut to conviction left open to the State tends to destroy the entire system of constitutional restraints on which the liberties of the people rest. Having once recognized that the right to privacy embodied in the Fourth Amendment is enforceable against the States, and that the right to be secure against rude invasions of privacy by state officers is, therefore, constitutional in origin, we can no longer permit that right to remain an empty promise . . . .

The judgment of the Supreme Court of Ohio is reversed and the cause remanded for further proceedings not inconsistent with this opinion.

Mr. Justice BLACK, concurring. . . .

Mr. Justice DOUGLAS, concurring. . . .

Mr. Justice HARLAN, whom Mr. Justice FRANKFURTER and Mr. Justice WHITTAKER join, dissenting. . . .

● ● ● ● ● ● ● ● ● ● ● ● ● ●

United States v. Leon

Supreme Court of the United States, 1984.
468 U.S. 897, 104 S.Ct. 3405, 82 L.Ed.2d 677.

[Here the Supreme Court considers a limited good-faith exception to the Fourth Amendment exclusionary rule.]

Justice WHITE delivered the opinion of the Court.
. . . In August 1981, a confidential informant of unproven reliability informed an officer of the Burbank Police Department that two persons known to him as "Armando" and "Patsy" were selling large quantities of cocaine and methaqualone from their residence at 620 Price Drive in Burbank, Cal. The informant also indicated that he had witnessed a sale of methaqualone by "Patsy" at the residence approximately five months earlier and had observed at that time a shoebox containing a large amount of cash that belonged to "Patsy." He further declared that "Armando" and "Patsy" generally kept only small quantities of drugs at their residence and stored the remainder at another location in Burbank.

On the basis of this information, the Burbank police initiated an extensive investigation focusing first on the Price Drive residence and later on two other residences as well. Cars parked at the Price Drive residence were determined to belong to respondents Armando Sanchez, who had previously been arrested for possession of marihuana, and Patsy Stewart, who had no criminal record. During the course of the investigation, officers observed an automobile belonging to respondent Ricardo Del Castillo, who had previously been arrested for possession of 50 pounds of marihuana, arrive at the Price Drive residence. The driver of that car entered the house, exited shortly thereafter carrying a small paper sack, and drove away. A check of Del Castillo's probation records led the officers to respondent Alberto Leon, whose telephone number Del Castillo had listed as his employer's. Leon had been arrested in 1980 on drug charges, and a companion had informed the police at that time that Leon was heavily involved in the importation of drugs into this country. Before the current investigation began, the Burbank officers had learned that an informant had told a Glendale police officer that Leon stored a large quantity of methaqualone at his residence in Glendale. During the course of this investigation, the Burbank officers learned that Leon was living at 716 South Sunset Canyon in Burbank.

Subsequently, the officers observed several persons, at least one of whom had prior drug involvement, arriving at the Price Drive residence and leaving with small packages; observed a variety of other material activity at the two residences as well as at a condominium at 7902 Via Magdalena; and witnessed a variety of relevant activity involving respondents' automobiles. The officers also observed respondents Sanchez and Stewart board separate flights for Miami. The pair later returned to Los Angeles together, consented to a search of their luggage that revealed only a small amount of marihuana, and left the airport. Based on these and other observations summarized in the affidavit, Officer Cyril Rombach of the Burbank Police Department, an experienced and well-trained narcotics investigator, prepared an application for a warrant to search 620 Price Drive, 716 South Sunset Canyon, 7902 Via Magdalena, and automobiles registered to each of the respondents for an extensive list of items believed to be related to respondents' drug-trafficking activities. Officer Rombach's extensive application was reviewed by several Deputy District Attorneys.

A facially valid search warrant was issued in September 1981 by a state superior court judge. The ensuing searches produced large quantities of drugs at the Via Magdalena and Sunset Canyon addresses and a small quantity at the Price Drive residence. Other evidence was discovered at each of the residences and in Stewart's and Del Castillo's automobiles. Respondents were indicted by a [federal] grand jury . . . and charged with conspiracy to possess and distribute cocaine and a variety of substantive counts.

The respondents then filed motions to suppress the evidence seized pursuant to the warrant. The District Court . . . concluded that the affidavit was insufficient to establish probable cause, but did not suppress all of the evidence as to all of the respondents because none of the respondents had standing to challenge all of the searches. In response to a request from the Government, the court made clear that Officer Rombach had acted in good faith, but it rejected the Government's suggestion that the Fourth Amendment exclusionary rule should not apply where evidence is seized in reasonable, good-faith reliance on a search warrant. . . .

[The Court of Appeals held that the evidence was inadmissible because the search warrant was not based on probable cause. The Court of Appeals refused to recognize any "good-faith exception" to the exclusionary rule.]

The Fourth Amendment contains no provision expressly precluding the use of evidence obtained in violation of its commands, and an examination of its origin and purposes makes clear that the use of fruits of a past unlawful search or seizure "work[s] no new Fourth Amendment wrong." . . . The wrong condemned by the Amendment is "fully accomplished" by the unlawful search or seizure itself, and the exclusionary rule is neither intended nor able to "cure the invasion of the defendant's rights which he has already suffered." . . . The rule thus operates as "a judicially created remedy designed to safeguard Fourth Amendment rights generally through its deterrent effect, rather than a personal constitutional right of the person aggrieved." . . .

The substantial social costs exacted by the exclusionary rule for the vindication of Fourth Amendment rights have long been a source of concern. "Our cases have consistently recognized that unbending application of the exclusionary sanction to enforce ideals of government rectitude would impede unacceptably the truth-finding functions of judge and jury." . . . [T]he exclusionary rule is designed to deter police misconduct rather than to punish the errors of judges and magistrates. . . . [T]here exists no evidence suggesting that judges and magistrates are inclined to ignore or subvert the Fourth Amendment or that lawlessness among those actors requires application of the extreme sanction of exclusion. . . .

We conclude that the marginal or nonexistent benefits produced by suppressing evidence obtained in objectively reasonable reliance on a subsequently invalidated search warrant cannot justify the substantial costs of exclusion. We do not suggest, however, that exclusion is always inappropriate in cases where an officer has obtained a warrant and abided by its terms. "[S]earches pursuant to a warrant will rarely require any deep inquiry into reasonableness," for "a warrant issued by a magistrate normally suffices to establish" that a law enforcement officer has "acted in good faith in conducting the search." . . . Nevertheless, the officer's reliance on the magistrate's probable-cause determination and on the technical sufficiency of the warrant he issues must be objectively reasonable, and it is clear that in some circumstances the officer will have no reasonable grounds for believing that the warrant was properly issued.

Suppression therefore remains an appropriate remedy if the magistrate or judge in issuing a warrant was misled by information in an affidavit that the affiant knew was false or would have known was false except for his reckless disregard of the truth. The exception we recognize today will also not apply in cases where the issuing magistrate wholly abandoned his judicial role. . . . Nor would an officer manifest objective good faith in relying on a warrant based on an affidavit "so lacking in indicia of probable cause as to render official belief in its existence entirely unreasonable." . . . Finally, depending on the circumstances of the particular case, a warrant may be so facially deficient—i.e., in failing to particularize the place to be searched or the things to be seized—that the executing officers cannot reasonably presume it to be valid. . . .

Nor are we persuaded that application of a good-faith exception to searches conducted pursuant to warrants will preclude review of the constitutionality of the search or seizure, deny needed guidance from the courts, or freeze Fourth Amendment law in its present state . . . .

When the principles we have enunciated today are applied to the facts of this case, it is apparent that the judgment of the Court of Appeals cannot stand. The Court of Appeals applied the prevailing legal standards to Officer Rombach's warrant application and concluded that the application could not support the magistrate's probable-cause determination. In so doing, the court clearly informed the magistrate that he had erred in issuing the challenged warrant. . . .

Having determined that the warrant should not have been issued, the Court of Appeals understand-ably declined to adopt a modification of the Fourth Amendment exclusionary rule that this Court had not previously sanctioned. Although the modification finds strong support in our previous cases, the Court of Appeals' commendable self-restraint is not to be criticized. We have now re-examined the purposes of the exclusionary rule and the propriety of its application in cases where officers have relied on a subsequently invalidated search warrant. Our conclusion is that the rule's purposes will only rarely be served by applying it in such circumstances. . . .

Accordingly, the judgment of the Court of Appeals is reversed.

Justice BLACKMUN, concurring. . . .

Justice BRENNAN, with whom Justice MARSHALL joins, dissenting.

. . . The Court seeks to justify this result on the ground that the "costs" of adhering to the exclusionary rule in cases like those before us exceed the "benefits." But the language of deterrence and of cost/benefit analysis, if used indiscriminately, can have a narcotic effect. It creates an illusion of technical precision and ineluctability. It suggests that not only constitutional principle but also empirical data support the majority's result. When the Court's analysis is examined carefully, however, it is clear that we have not been treated to an honest assessment of the merits of the exclusionary rule, but have instead been drawn into a curious world where the "costs" of excluding illegally obtained evidence loom to exaggerated heights and where the "benefits" of such exclusion are made to disappear with a mere wave of the hand. . . .

Justice STEVENS, dissenting. . . .

CHAPTER 16

Arrest, Interrogation, and Identification Procedures

Introduction

In its most general sense, the term **arrest** refers to the deprivation of a person's liberty by someone with legal authority. In contemporary criminal procedure, an arrest occurs when police take an individual into custody and charge that person with the commission of a crime. Generally, an arrest is made by a police officer, although there are some circumstances in which an arrest can be effected by a private individual.

As a form of "seizure," an arrest is governed by requirements of the Fourth Amendment. However, the formal arrest is not the only type of encounter between police and citizens that implicates the Fourth Amendment. A seizure, for Fourth Amendment purposes, occurs when a police officer, "by means of physical force or show of authority, has in some way restrained the liberty of a citizen." *Terry v. Ohio,* 392 U.S. 1, 19 n. 16, 88 S.Ct. 1868, 1879 n. 16, 20 L.Ed.2d 889, 905 n. 16 (1968). The traditional full-blown arrest clearly constitutes a seizure. So too does a police officer's fatal shooting of a fleeing suspect. *Tennessee v. Garner,* 471 U.S. 1, 105 S.Ct. 1694, 85 L.Ed.2d 1 (1985). Other instances may not be so clear, however. In 1988 the Supreme Court declined to formulate a "bright line" rule delineating what constitutes a seizure; rather, the Court asserted that the test requires an assessment of whether in view of all the circumstances surrounding an incident, "a reasonable person would have believed that he was not free to leave." *Michigan v. Chesternut,* 486 U.S. 567, 108 S.Ct. 1975, 100 L.Ed.2d 565 (1988). The following year, the Court ruled that stopping a motorist at a police roadblock is a seizure for Fourth Amendment purposes. *Brower v. County of Inyo,* 489 U.S. 593, 109 S.Ct. 1378, 103 L.Ed.2d 628 (1989).

Encounters between citizens and police range from formal arrests to situations in which police approach an individual and ask questions. Police–citizen encounters can be placed in four categories:

1. Arrest
2. **Investigatory detention** (also referred to as **stop-and-frisk,** as discussed in Chapter 15)
3. The use of **roadblocks** and **sobriety checkpoints**
4. The **request for information or identification**

Each type of encounter is unique from the standpoint of the Fourth Amendment. Accordingly, we examine each of these separately in this chapter.

Interrogation refers to the questioning of a suspect by law enforcement officers to elicit a confession, an admission, or information that otherwise assists them in solving a crime. Typically, interrogation takes place behind closed doors in a law enforcement facility, although today a suspect being questioned is often accompanied by an attorney. Because interrogation of a suspect carries with it a risk of coercion, confessions obtained by police are subject to constitutional attack under the Self-Incrimination Clause of the Fifth Amendment.

Identification procedures are techniques employed by law enforcement agencies to identify suspects. These fall into two basic categories: scientific means to match physical evidence taken from a suspect with that found at a crime scene and procedures to determine if victims or witnesses can identify perpetrators. Both types of identification procedure are extremely important in building cases against defendants, and both present unique legal problems.

Arrest

Because arrest is the most serious type of police–citizen encounter, it is subject to the most stringent constitutional requirements. Specifically, arrest is subject to the probable cause and warrant requirements of the Fourth Amendment, although there are exceptions to the latter. The Supreme Court has said that the legality of arrests by state and local officers is to be judged by the same constitutional standards applicable to federal agents. *Ker v. California,* 374 U.S. 23, 83 S.Ct. 1623, 10 L.Ed.2d 726 (1963).

The Probable Cause Requirement

For any arrest or significant deprivation of liberty to occur, police officers must have **probable cause.** Although not easy to define, probable cause in the context of arrest means the same thing as in the context of search and seizure (see Chapter 15). The Supreme Court has said that probable cause exists

> where the facts and circumstances within . . . [the officers'] knowledge, and of which they had reasonably trustworthy information, . . . [are] sufficient in themselves to warrant a man of reasonable caution in the belief . . . [that a particular crime had been or was being committed]. *Carroll v. United States,* 267 U.S. 132, 162, 45 S.Ct. 280, 288, 69 L.Ed. 543, 555 (1925).

Police can establish probable cause without personally observing the commission of a crime as long as they have sufficient information to conclude that the suspect probably committed it. Officers often obtain their information from crime victims, eyewitnesses, official reports, and confidential or even anonymous informants.

Search Incident to Arrest

Normally, a search incident to arrest follows the arrest. In *Rawlings v. Kentucky,* 448 U.S. 98, 100 S.Ct. 2556, 65 L.Ed.2d 633 (1980), however, the Supreme Court upheld a search incident to arrest even though the search briefly preceded the arrest. The key point is that probable cause to make the arrest must precede the search;

CASE-IN-POINT   **Arrest and Interrogation**

On March 26, 1971, the owner of a pizza parlor in Rochester, New York, was killed during an attempted armed robbery. Acting without a warrant, police took Irving Dunaway into custody and interrogated him in connection with the attempted robbery and murder. Dunaway was not told that he was under arrest, but he was interrogated, he confessed, and he was ultimately convicted. On appeal, the state ar-

gued that although the police did not have probable cause to make an arrest, the "station-house detention" and interrogation of the suspect could be allowed on the lesser standard of reasonable suspicion. The Supreme Court reversed the conviction, saying that probable cause was necessary to justify a station-house detention and interrogation, irrespective of whether it is termed an "arrest."

Dunaway v. New York, 442 U.S. 200, 99 S.Ct. 2248, 60 L.Ed.2d 824 (1979).

```
┌─────────────────────────────────────────────────────────────────────┐
│                    WARRANT   OF   ARREST                            │
│                                                                     │
│   County of _____. State of _____.                 │
│                                                                     │
│   To any peace officer of said State:                               │
│                                                                     │
│   Complaint on oath having this day been laid before me that the    │
│   crime of                                                          │
│   _____ (designating it generally) has been      │
│   committed and                                                     │
│   accusing _____ (naming defendant) thereof,   │
│   you are therefore                                                 │
│   commanded forthwith to arrest the above named defendant and       │
│   bring him/her before                                              │
│   me at _____ (naming the place), or in case of     │
│   my absence or                                                     │
│   inability to act, before the nearest or most accessible magistrate│
│   in this county.                                                   │
│   Dated at (place) this _____ day of _____, 20__.     │
│                                                                     │
│         _____                │
│            (signature and full official title of magistrate)        │
│                                                                     │
└─────────────────────────────────────────────────────────────────────┘
```

FIGURE 16.1   The Typical Form of an Arrest Warrant

police may not use the search as a means to justify the arrest. (Search and seizure issues are discussed in Chapter 15.)

The Warrant Requirement

An **arrest warrant** (see Figure 16.1) is routine in cases where an arrest is to be made based on an indictment by a grand jury. When a prosecutor files an accusatorial document known as an information, the court issues a **capias,** a document directing the arrest of the defendant. In such cases, suspects are often not aware that they are under investigation, and police officers have ample time to obtain an arrest warrant without fear that suspects will flee. However, most arrests are not made pursuant to secret investigations, but are made by police officers who observe a criminal act, respond to a complaint filed by a crime victim, or have probable cause to arrest after completing an investigation. In such cases it is often unnecessary for police to obtain an arrest warrant, but it is always essential that they have probable cause to make the arrest.

Warrantless Arrests

At common law, police had the right to make a **warrantless arrest** if they observed someone in the commission of a felony or they had probable cause to believe that a person had committed or was committing a felony. To make a warrantless arrest for a misdemeanor, an officer had to observe someone in the commission of the act. Otherwise, to make an arrest, a warrant was required. Many states adopted common-law rules of arrest in statutes allowing police officers broad discretion to make warrantless arrests. As with warrantless searches and seizures, the Supreme Court has approved warrantless arrests (1) where crimes are committed in **plain view** of police officers or (2) where officers possess probable cause to make an arrest, but **exigent circumstances** prohibit them from obtaining a warrant. Absent plain view or compelling exigencies, the need to obtain an arrest warrant is unclear. As a matter of policy, it makes sense for police officers to obtain arrest warrants when possible. However, given the time that it takes to obtain an arrest warrant and the fact that magistrates are not always available around the clock, it is not always feasible for police to obtain warrants before making arrests.

The Supreme Court has upheld the authority of police officers to make warrantless arrests in public, assuming probable cause to do so. *United States v. Watson,* 423 U.S. 411, 96 S.Ct. 820, 46 L.Ed.2d 598 (1976). More problematic are warrantless arrests involving forcible entry of a dwelling. Here we encounter the classic Fourth Amendment concern for the sanctity of the home. For example, in *Payton v. New York,* 445 U.S. 573, 100 S.Ct. 1371, 63 L.Ed.2d 639 (1980), the Supreme Court held that, absent exigent circumstances, a warrantless, nonconsensual entry into a suspect's home to make a routine felony arrest violates the Fourth Amendment. In a footnote, the Court pointed out that at that time, twenty-three states had laws permitting a warrantless entry into the home for the purpose of making an arrest, even in the absence of exigent circumstances. 445 U.S. at 598, n. 46, 100 S.Ct. at 1386, n. 46, 63 L.Ed.2d at 658, n. 46. Courts are generally inclined to uphold warrantless entries into homes for the purpose of arrest if the following conditions are met:

1. There is probable cause to arrest the suspect.

2. The police have good reason to believe the suspect is on the premises.

3. There is good reason to believe the suspect is armed and dangerous.

4. There is a strong probability that the suspect will escape or evidence will be destroyed if the suspect is not soon apprehended.

5. The entry can be effected peaceably.

6. The offense under investigation is a serious felony.

The Right of an Arrestee to a Prompt Appearance Before a Magistrate

Although the Supreme Court has recognized the practical necessity of permitting police to make warrantless arrests, it has stressed the need for immediate *ex post facto* judicial review of detention of a suspect. Writing for the Supreme Court in *Gerstein v. Pugh,* 420 U.S. 103, 95 S.Ct. 854, 43 L.Ed.2d 54 (1975), Justice Stewart observed that "once the suspect is in custody, . . . the reasons that justify dispensing with the magistrate's neutral judgment evaporate." 420 U.S. at 114, 95 S.Ct. at 863, 43 L.Ed.2d at 65. When a suspect is in custody pursuant to a warrantless arrest, "the detached judgment of a neutral magistrate is essential if the Fourth Amendment is to furnish meaningful protection from unfounded interference with liberty." 420 U.S. at 114, 95 S.Ct. at 863, 43 L.Ed.2d at 65. In *County of Riverside v. McLaughlin,* 500 U.S. 44, 111 S.Ct. 1661, 114 L.Ed.2d 49 (1991), the Supreme Court ruled that if an arrested person is brought before a magistrate within forty-eight hours, the requirements of the Fourth Amendment are satisfied.

Actually, any person who is arrested, regardless of whether the arrest was based on a warrant, must be brought promptly before a court of law. Although this is not a federal constitutional right in instances where arrests are made pursuant to warrants, all states now have rules that require the police to promptly bring an arrestee before a magistrate. Similarly, as Fed. R. Crim. P. 5(a) states,

> An officer making an arrest under a warrant issued upon a complaint or any person making an arrest without a warrant shall take the arrested person without unnecessary delay before the nearest available federal magistrate or, in the event that a federal magistrate is not reasonably available, before a state or local judicial officer. . . .

Use of Force by Police Making Arrests

Because suspects frequently resist attempts to take them into custody, police officers often must use force in making arrests. Sometimes, the use of force by police is challenged in civil suits for damages. Typically, in such cases, the courts have said that in making a lawful arrest, police officers may use such force as necessary to effect the arrest and prevent the escape of the suspect. See, for example, *Martyn v. Donlin,* 198 A.2d 700 (Conn. 1964). Generally, a police officer has less discretion to use force in apprehending suspected misdemeanants than suspected felons. See, for example, *City of Mason v. Banks,* 581 S.W.2d 621 (Tenn. 1979). Most states have statutes providing that police officers have the right to require bystanders to assist them in making arrests. See, for example, West's Ann. Cal. Penal Code § 839. Nearly every state has a law governing the use of force by police attempting to make arrests. The Illinois statute is typical:

> (a) A peace officer, or any person he has summoned or directed to assist him, need not retreat or desist from efforts to make a lawful arrest because of resistance or threatened resistance to the arrest. He is justified in the use of any force which he reasonably believes to be necessary to effect the arrest and of any force which he reasonably believes to be necessary to defend himself or another from bodily harm while making the arrest. However, he is justified in using force likely to cause death or great bodily harm only when he reasonably believes that such force is necessary to prevent death or great bodily harm to himself or other such person, or when he reasonably believes both that:
>
> 1. Such force is necessary to prevent the arrest from being defeated by resistance or escape; and
>
> 2. The person to be arrested has committed or attempted a forcible felony which involves the infliction or threatened infliction of great bodily harm or is attempting to escape by use of a deadly weapon, or otherwise indicates that he will endanger human life or inflict great bodily harm unless arrested without delay.
>
> (b) A peace officer making an arrest pursuant to an invalid warrant is justified in the use of any force which he would be justified in using if the warrant were valid, unless he knows that the warrant is invalid. S.H.A. 720 ILCS 5/7–5(a).

An excerpt from the Supreme Court's decision in *Tennessee v. Garner* appears at the end of the chapter.

In *Tennessee v. Garner,* supra, the Supreme Court struck down a statute that permitted police to use **deadly force** against fleeing suspects even when there was no threat to the safety of the officer or the public. This ruling effectively narrowed the discretion of police officers in using force to make arrests and broadened the possibility for civil actions against police for using excessive force.

Concern over police brutality took center stage in 1991, when the nation viewed on television a videotape of what appeared to be the unnecessarily brutal beating of motorist Rodney King by Los Angeles police officers. In response to public outrage, four police officers involved in the incident were prosecuted by state authorities for assault and battery and related crimes. On the motion of the defense, the trial was moved from Los Angeles to a suburban community. No one can forget the riot that ensued in Los Angeles in April 1992 after the jury returned its verdict of "not guilty." In response to the widespread perception that a miscarriage of justice had occurred, the U.S. Justice Department launched its own investigation of the case. In the summer of 1992, a federal grand jury indicted the four officers for violating Rodney King's Fourth Amendment rights. In April 1993, a trial jury returned verdicts of guilty against two of the officers; the other two were acquitted. See *Koon v. United States,* 518 U.S. 81, 116 S.Ct. 2035, 135 L.Ed.2d 392 (1996).

Citizen's Arrest

At common law, a private individual could make a **citizen's arrest** without a warrant for a felony or breach of the peace committed in the presence of that individual. The common-law rule prevails in some states; in others, it has been revised by statute. A California law enacted in 1872 broadens the common law in that it permits a private person to make a warrantless arrest in any of three situations:

A private person may arrest another:

1. For a public offense committed or attempted in his presence.

2. When the person arrested has committed a felony, although not in his presence.

3. When a felony has been in fact committed, and he has reasonable cause for believing the person arrested to have committed it. West's Ann. Cal. Penal Code § 837.

Arrests for Minor Traffic Offenses

In most states, a police officer may either make an arrest or issue a summons or citation to a person who commits a minor traffic violation. Generally, police exercise their discretion by giving the motorist a "ticket," yet there is little judicial guidance for the proper action to be taken.

The Supreme Court has never ruled whether an arrest for a minor traffic offense violates any constitutional protection. However, the Court has limited the ability of police to conduct a search incident to arrest of an automobile when issuing a **traffic citation.** See *Knowles v. Iowa,* 525 U.S. 113, 119 S.Ct. 484, 142 L.Ed.2d 492 (1998). In some instances, police may opt to make an arrest rather than issue a citation so that they can conduct a search of the automobile. See *Gustafson v. Florida,* 414 U.S. 260, 94 S.Ct. 488, 38 L.Ed.2d 456 (1973).

That this area of broad police discretion is subject to abuse was recognized in *State v. Hehman,* 578 P.2d 527 (Wash. 1978), where the Washington Supreme Court ruled that arrests for minor traffic offenses are unjustified if the defendant signs a promise to appear in court as provided by statute. By contrast, an Illinois appellate court upheld the arrest and jailing of a motorist for lacking a front license plate and being unable to produce a driver's license. *People v. Pendleton,* 433 N.E.2d 1076 (Ill. App. 1982).

As an alternative, states can decriminalize certain traffic violations and permit persons cited for such infractions to accept citations and agree to pay a stipulated civil fine or appear in court on schedule. Florida adopted such a statutory scheme in 1974, exempting certain offenses. As now revised, fleeing a police officer, reckless driving, operating a vehicle without valid license plates, leaving the scene of an accident, obstructing an officer, and driving under the influence of drugs or alcohol are excepted offenses. In some instances, a court appearance is waived or the fine for some decriminalized infractions is reduced when the offender elects to attend a state-approved driving improvement course. West's Fla. Stat. Ann. § 318.14(9).

As pointed out above, an arrest allows an officer to make a search incident to the arrest. There has been a conflict among the lower federal courts as to whether it is a constitutional violation for an officer to make a custodial arrest of a person who simply violates a traffic ordinance. In 2000 the U.S. Supreme Court granted review of the issue. See *Atwater v. City of Lago Vista,* No. 99–1408. The Fifth Circuit's decision under review can be found at 195 F.3d 242 (1999).

Investigatory Detention

The second major category of police–citizen encounters involves the so-called stop-and-frisk, discussed in Chapter 15. A more descriptive term for this type of encounter is investigatory detention. Police are permitted to detain persons temporarily for questioning as long as they have **reasonable suspicion** that criminal activity is afoot. If they have reasonable suspicion that the detained person is armed, police may perform a **pat-down search** of the suspect's outer clothing to locate weapons. *Terry v. Ohio,* supra. In conducting the "frisk," police may seize items that plainly feel like contraband. *Minnesota v. Dickerson,* 508 U.S. 366, 113 S.Ct. 2130, 124 L.Ed.2d 334 (1993).

What Constitutes Reasonable Suspicion?

After the U.S. Supreme Court's 1968 decision in *Terry v. Ohio,* supra, the concept of what constitutes "reasonable suspicion" became extremely important both in law enforcement and in criminal procedure in the courts. The concept does not lend itself to a precise definition; however, in *United States v. Cortez,* 449 U.S. 411, 101 S.Ct. 690, 66 L.Ed.2d 621 (1981), after defining it in a rather technical way, the late Chief Justice Warren Burger offered a practical explanation. He said that a trained officer develops a reasonable suspicion that a person is, or is about to be, engaged in criminal activity from the officer's objective observations and from inference and deductions.

Thousands of federal and state judicial decisions have applied the standard of reasonable suspicion, often with degrees of variation. However, courts generally agree that the totality of the circumstances of any given scenario must be examined to determine whether a law officer had a reasonable suspicion as a basis for making an investigatory stop. The difference in application is illustrated by a very recent case. William Wardlow was standing in front of a building around noon in a high-crime area in Chicago known for narcotics trafficking. When he saw a caravan of four police cars pass by, he ran through an alley. Officers in one of the patrol cars pursued and eventually stopped him, patted him down in a protective search for weapons, and searched an opaque bag he was holding. They found him in possession of a handgun and arrested him. Wardlow sought to suppress the weapon on the ground that the officers had no reasonable suspicion to stop and frisk him. Therefore, he argued the seizure of the handgun was in violation of the Fourth Amendment. His motion was denied, and he was convicted. The Illinois Supreme Court reversed, holding the stop illegal. On review, the U.S. Supreme Court, in a 5–4 decision, reversed the Illinois Supreme Court. The justices agreed that the "totality of the circumstances" governs in determining if there is reasonable suspicion for the stop, but they disagreed on the application of that test to the factual situation here. Writing for the majority, Chief Justice Rehnquist found that the officers had a reasonable suspicion based on Wardlow's presence in a high-crime area coupled with his headlong, unprovoked flight from the police. Four justices, in an opinion written by Justice Stevens, disagreed with the majority's conclusion that the Chicago police were justified in stopping Wardlow. *Illinois v. Wardlow,* 528 U.S. 119, 120 S.Ct. 673, 145 L.Ed.2d 570 (2000).

The Length of an Investigatory Detention

The Supreme Court has said that investigatory detentions must be brief (unless, that is, they confirm police suspicions of criminal conduct). *Dunaway v. New York,* 442 U.S. 200, 99 S.Ct. 2248, 60 L.Ed.2d 824 (1979). Nevertheless, the Supreme Court has been disinclined to place an arbitrary time limit on detention. Instead, the Court has considered the purpose of the stop and the reasonableness of the time required for the police to obtain any additional required information. This approach looks at the totality of the circumstances to determine whether there has been an infringement of the suspect's Fourth Amendment rights. In *Florida v. Royer,* 460 U.S. 491, 103 S.Ct. 1319, 75 L.Ed.2d 229 (1983), the Court held that a fifteen-minute detention of a suspect in a police room was unreasonable when the police detained the suspect while they brought his luggage to him. Yet a twenty-minute detention of a truck driver stopped on suspicion of transporting marijuana was found to be reasonable because the time was used by police in pursuing a second, related vehicle necessary to the investigation, and the suspect's actions contributed to the delay. *United States v. Sharpe,* 470 U.S. 675, 105 S.Ct. 1568, 84 L.Ed.2d 605 (1985). Consequently, although detention must be brief in stop-and-frisk situations, the time span must be evaluated in light of the totality of circumstances. In *State v. Merklein,* 388 So. 2d 218 (Fla. App. 1980), a Florida appellate court said it was reasonable for officers to detain suspects for twenty to forty minutes pending arrival of another officer, witnesses, and the victim of a robbery. The key is whether the police are diligently investigating to confirm or dispel the suspicions that led to the stop. *State v. Werner,* 848 P.2d 11 (N.M. App. 1992).

When May Police Conduct a Frisk?

A valid ***Terry*-stop** (a synonym for investigatory detention) does not necessarily permit an officer to conduct a frisk. Rather, the need for protecting the police justifies a frisk. Therefore, an officer who undertakes to frisk a suspect must be able to point to specific facts and reasonable inferences to believe that the individual is armed. Initially, a frisk is limited to a pat-down search of an individual's outer garments. If during the pat-down search the officer feels an object that may be a weapon, the officer may seize it. If it turns out that the object is other than a weapon, it may still be seized if it is contraband. As we have noted, a stop-and-frisk may be based on reasonable suspicion, but absent probable cause, an officer is not justified in simply searching a suspect for contraband when a pat-down does not reveal any weapon-like objects. *Terry v. Ohio,* supra.

In *Ybarra v. Illinois,* 444 U.S. 85, 100 S.Ct. 338, 62 L.Ed.2d 238 (1979), the Supreme Court ruled that because police could not point to any specific facts to support their belief that the suspect was armed and dangerous, they had no grounds for frisking him. The Court has made it amply clear that a frisk must be based on an officer's reasonable suspicion that the suspect is armed, rather than on a desire to locate incriminating evidence. *Sibron v. New York,* 392 U.S. 40, 88 S.Ct. 1889, 20 L.Ed.2d 917 (1968). Under the doctrine of plain view (discussed in Chapter 15), however, contraband that is discovered during a legitimate pat-down for weapons may be admissible in evidence. For example, if during the course of a lawful frisk, a police officer feels what the officer suspects is a knife concealed in the suspect's pocket, the officer may retrieve the object. If the object turns out to be a metal smoking pipe wrapped inside a plastic bag containing "crack" cocaine, the crack would most likely be admissible as evidence of crime under the plain-view doctrine.

Investigatory Automobile Stops

Lower federal and state courts have routinely applied the stop-and-frisk doctrine to stops of vehicles as well as individuals. In many instances, this was stipulated in state statutes codifying the *Terry* standard; otherwise, it was based on the *Terry* rationale. Of course, as in the case of the individual on the street, police must have reasonable suspicion that criminal activity is afoot before they can stop a single motor vehicle. *Delaware v. Prouse*, 440 U.S. 648, 99 S.Ct. 1391, 59 L.Ed.2d 660 (1979).

Normal police practice is for the officer who makes an automobile stop to examine the suspect's driver's license, vehicle registration, and license plate. A rapid computer check can reveal whether there are any outstanding warrants on the driver, whether the license has been suspended or revoked, or whether the automobile has been reported stolen. During the stop the officer also visually scans the driver, any passengers, and any objects in plain view. Such visual scans sometimes provide probable cause to make an arrest or conduct a warrantless automobile search.

Even without probable cause, a police officer may perform a limited automobile search based on reasonable suspicion. In 1983 the Supreme Court held that when police stop an automobile based on reasonable suspicion, they may search the passenger compartment for weapons, assuming they have reason to believe—based on specific and articulable factors, together with rational inferences—that a suspect is dangerous. The search, of course, must be limited to those areas in which a weapon may be placed or hidden. *Michigan v. Long*, 463 U.S. 1032, 103 S.Ct. 3469, 77 L.Ed.2d 1201 (1983). In determining whether an officer possessed such a reasonable suspicion, courts look at many factors. Among these are the knowledge, expertise, and experience of the officer; the physical appearance of a person or vehicle as fitting the description of a person or vehicle wanted for a crime; the item and place where the suspect or vehicle is seen; and their nearness to the scene of a crime. In addition, the suspect's demeanor and any furtive gestures or attempts to flee are relevant considerations. See Chapter 15 for more discussion of automobile searches.

Automobile Stops Based on Anonymous Tips

An issue that often comes before appellate courts is whether reasonable suspicion can be developed on the basis of an anonymous tip. In *Alabama v. White*, 496 U.S. 325, 110 S.Ct. 2412, 110 L.Ed.2d 621 (1990), the U.S. Supreme Court reviewed a case where the police stopped a vehicle based on an anonymous phone tip. The Court held that an anonymous tip corroborated by independent police work was sufficient to establish a reasonable suspicion to make an investigatory stop of the vehicle described by the one who gave police the tip.

Since the Supreme Court's decision in *Alabama v. White*, state courts have been addressing cases where police have made an investigatory stop based on an anonymous tip. State courts have been disinclined to approve an investigatory stop where the anonymous tip lacks indicia of credibility and is not sufficiently verified by independent evidence. See, for example, *State v. Hjelmstad*, 535 N.W.2d 663 (Minn. App. 1995). Nevertheless, many state courts now agree that information supplied by an anonymous source can warrant an investigatory stop if verified by sufficient independent evidence of criminal activity. See, for example, *People v. George*, 914 P.2d 367 (Colo. 1996). In 2000 the Supreme Court of Pennsylvania held that an uncorroborated anonymous tip alleging a defendant was selling marijuana did not create a reasonable suspicion that would justify an investigatory stop of the defendant's car. *Commonwealth v. Goodwin*, 750 A.2d 795 (2000).

Pretextual Automobile Stops

Police have been known to use a minor or technical motor vehicle infraction as a pretext for stopping a vehicle and conducting an investigatory detention. In the past, most federal courts ruled that the police may not use minor traffic violations to justify **pretextual stops.** For example, in *United States v. Smith,* 799 F.2d 704 (11th Cir. 1986), the court said the appropriate analysis was whether a reasonable officer would have stopped the car absent an additional invalid purpose. Many state courts followed this approach. In *Alejandre v. State,* 903 P.2d 794 (Nev. 1995), the Nevada Supreme Court held that a stop of a vehicle for crossing a fog line twice by "about a tire width" was merely a pretext for search for drugs. The court reasoned that a violation of that type would not have caused a reasonable officer to stop the defendant's vehicle.

An excerpt from the Supreme Court's decision in *Whren v. United States* appears at the end of the chapter.

In *Whren v. United States,* 517 U.S. 806, 116 S.Ct. 1769, 135 L.Ed.2d 89 (1996), the U.S. Supreme Court ruled that the motives of an officer in stopping a vehicle are irrelevant as long as there is an objective basis for the stop. Thus, the Court held there is no violation of the Fourth Amendment as long as there is probable cause to believe that even a minor violation has taken place. It remains to be seen whether the states, which may apply a stricter standard under their constitutions, will follow the federal standard.

Can Police Require Drivers and Passengers to Exit Their Vehicles?

During automobile stops, police routinely request that drivers exit their cars. Sometimes they also request that passengers exit. These practices are justified by the need to protect police officers from weapons that might be concealed inside the passenger compartment of a stopped vehicle. In a recent decision upholding these practices, the U.S. Supreme Court noted that in 1994 eleven police officers were killed and more than five thousand officers assaulted during traffic stops. *Maryland v. Wilson,* 519 U.S. 408, 117 S.Ct. 882, 137 L.Ed.2d 41 (1997). Of course, when drivers and passengers are required to exit their automobiles, police often discover contraband or observe behavior indicative of intoxication. Such was the case in *Maryland v. Wilson,* where a passenger who had been ordered to exit a vehicle dropped a quantity of crack cocaine onto the ground. This evidence was used to secure a conviction for possession with intent to distribute; ultimately, the conviction was sustained by the Supreme Court.

Use of Drug Courier Profiles

In recent years, police have developed **drug courier profiles** based on typical characteristics and behaviors of drug smugglers. The profiles include such factors as paying cash for airline tickets, taking short trips to drug-source cities, not checking luggage, and appearing nervous. Police often use these profiles to identify and detain suspected drug couriers, a controversial practice that has resulted in disparate court decisions.

In 1989 the Supreme Court upheld an investigative stop of an air passenger for which a number of circumstances, including the use of the profile, furnished the police a reasonable suspicion of criminal activity. Although the Court found that any one of the several factors relied on by the police may have been consistent with innocent travel, it observed that the evaluation of the stop requires a consideration of the "totality of the circumstances." *United States v. Sokolow,* 490 U.S. 1, 109 S.Ct. 1581, 104 L.Ed.2d 1 (1989).

Although the Supreme Court has upheld the use of profiles in locating suspicious persons, courts must remain on guard against abuse of the practice. In 1990 a Minnesota appellate court reversed a conviction in which the defendant's automobile had been stopped not on the basis of a particular suspicion, but because the driver's behavior loosely fit the police profile of a person looking for prostitutes. In rejecting the use of the profile, the court distinguished the case from *Sokolow,* supra, saying that "the observable facts taken together do not approach the composite bundle available to the DEA in *Sokolow.*" *City of St. Paul v. Uber,* 450 N.W. 2d 623, 626 (Minn. App. 1990). The court concluded that "we cannot sustain what was, in effect, a random stop." 450 N.W.2d at 629.

Racial Profiling

In recent years, a controversy has emerged over whether law enforcement officers stop motorists for traffic violations because they are members of minority groups. This practice became known as **racial profiling,** and it was an issue in the 2000 presidential election. Critics of the practice noted that police made traffic stops when their real purpose was to search vehicles for drugs. In footnote 10 to its opinion in *Illinois v. Wardlow,* supra, the Supreme Court noted the following:

> New Jersey's Attorney General, in a recent investigation into allegations of racial profiling on the New Jersey Turnpike, concluded that minority motorists have been treated differently [by New Jersey State Troopers] than non-minority motorists during the course of traffic stops on the New Jersey Turnpike. The problem of disparate treatment is real—this disparate treatment "engenders feelings of fear, resentment, hostility, and mistrust by minority citizens." . . . Recently, the United States Department of Justice, citing this very evidence, announced that it would appoint an outside monitor to oversee the actions of the New Jersey State Police. . . .

The movement to halt racial profiling has taken both legislative and judicial directions. Several state legislatures have considered bills to require data collection for police stops, while defendants who contend they were stopped on the basis of racial profiling have sought to dismiss charges arising out of police stops, arguing they were denied due process and equal protections of the laws. Others have sought relief through civil litigation. See, for example, *National Congress of Puerto Rican Rights v. City of New York,* 191 F.R.D. 52 (S.D.N.Y. 1999).

Roadblocks and Sobriety Checkpoints

The third major category of police–citizen encounters includes roadblocks and sobriety checkpoints. Police often set up roadblocks for apprehending fleeing suspects or conducting field sobriety tests, or even for merely performing safety checks on automobiles. In addition to locating drunk drivers, roadblocks often lead to the discovery of illegal weapons, drugs, and other contraband.

Because roadblocks do constitute a restraint on the liberty of the motorist, courts have held that they are susceptible to challenge under the Fourth Amendment. Therefore, police agencies must take care that roadblocks are established and operated according to guidelines that minimize the inconvenience to motorists and constrain the exercise of discretion by police officers.

CASE-IN-POINT

The Use of Roadblocks

The Heard County, Georgia, sheriff's department received an anonymous call alleging that a party was going on at a certain address and that teenagers there were drinking alcohol and using drugs. Similar calls had been received in the past regarding this address. Police immediately set up a roadblock on the road between the house and the state highway. The roadblock was designed to stop vehicles going in either direction. Appellant's van was stopped. Police smelled alcohol on appellant and instructed him to exit the car for a field sobriety test. While the test was being administered, an officer leaned into the car and, according to his later testimony, looked over the driver's seat to look for weapons. On the floor of the van, the officer found a small plastic bag containing a white powder. Appellant was arrested and later convicted for possession of cocaine. On appeal, the Georgia Court of Appeals upheld the conviction against appellant's challenge to the use of the roadblock. In upholding the trial court's finding that the roadblock was founded on a legitimate concern for public safety, the appellate court noted that the roadblock had been ordered and conducted by an experienced senior officer.

Brimer v. State, 411 S.E.2d 128 (Ga. App. 1991).

In *Michigan Dept. of State Police v. Sitz,* 496 U.S. 444, 110 S.Ct. 2481, 110 L.Ed.2d 412 (1990), the Supreme Court upheld the use of roadblocks for conducting field sobriety tests. In *Sitz,* the Michigan State Police operated a pilot roadblock program under guidelines drafted by an advisory committee. The sobriety checkpoints operated essentially as follows: Police set up roadblocks at predetermined points along state highways. All vehicles passing through the checkpoints were stopped, and drivers were briefly observed for signs of intoxication. The average length of the stop was less than thirty seconds, except where drivers appeared to be intoxicated. These drivers were instructed to pull their vehicles over to the side of the road for a license and registration check and, if indicated, a **field sobriety test.** Those who failed the test were placed under arrest. At one checkpoint, which was in operation for 75 minutes, 126 vehicles were stopped. Two drivers were given field sobriety tests, and one was arrested for driving under the influence of alcohol. One vehicle failed to stop at the roadblock, but was apprehended and its driver arrested for driving under the influence (DUI).

Decoy Drug Checkpoints

An interesting (and often productive) police tactic is to place a sign on an interstate highway indicating "Notice: Drug Checkpoint Ahead." The sign is placed just before an exit, tempting drivers who wish to avoid the checkpoint to take the exit. Of course, there really is no drug checkpoint on the interstate highway. Rather, police are waiting at the bottom of the exit ramp to see who takes the exit. Typically, the exit chosen is one where there is little or no commercial activity and no connection to a major road. When a van with out-of-state plates takes the exit, is this inherently suspicious? Can police assume that the only reason the driver took the exit was to avoid the spurious drug checkpoint? Can police stop this vehicle, order the driver and passengers to exit the vehicle, and bring out a drug-sniffing canine? Federal courts have reached different conclusions on this issue, suggesting the need for the Supreme Court to get involved. Compare *United States v. Huguenin,* 154 F.3d 547 (6th Cir. 1998), and *United States v. Brugal,* 209 F.3d 353 (4th Cir. 2000).

Requests for Information or Identification

The lowest level of police–citizen encounter takes place when a police officer approaches an individual in public and asks questions or requests identification. Is there a legal duty to cooperate with the police in such instances? In a concurring opinion in *Terry v. Ohio,* supra, Justice Byron White observed the following:

> There is nothing in the Constitution which prevents a policeman from addressing questions to anyone on the streets. Absent special circumstances, the person approached may not be detained or frisked but may refuse to cooperate and go on his way. However, given the proper circumstances . . . , the person may be briefly detained against his will while pertinent questions are directed to him. Of course, the person stopped is not obliged to answer, answers may not be compelled, and refusal to answer furnishes no basis for an arrest, although it may alert the officer to the need for continued observation. 392 U.S. at 34, 88 S.Ct. at 1886, 20 L.Ed.2d at 913.

Historically, many states had laws making it a misdemeanor for persons to refuse to identify themselves when asked to do so by police. In *Brown v. Texas,* 443 U.S. 47, 99 S.Ct. 2637, 61 L.Ed.2d 357 (1979), the Supreme Court reviewed the constitutionality of this Texas statute: "A person commits an offense if he intentionally refuses to report or gives a false report of his name and residence address to a peace officer who has lawfully stopped him and requested the information." The Court held that the statute could not be constitutionally applied in the absence of reasonable suspicion that the individual who was asked for identification was engaged in or had engaged in criminal conduct.

In *Kolender v. Lawson,* 461 U.S. 352, 103 S.Ct. 1855, 75 L.Ed.2d 903 (1983), the Supreme Court reviewed a California statute that required persons who were loitering or wandering on the streets to provide a "credible and reliable" identification and to account for their presence when requested to do so by a police officer. The Court found that the statute was "unconstitutionally vague on its face because it

CASE-IN-POINT

Validity of an Ordinance Requiring Self-Identification

Section 17–13 of the Arlington, Virginia, County Code provides that "[i]t shall be unlawful for any person at a public place . . . to refuse to identify himself by name and address at the request of a uniformed police officer . . . if the surrounding circumstances are such as to indicate to a reasonable man that the public safety requires such identification." The defendant was convicted of failing to identify himself at the request of a police officer, and appealed. The Virginia Supreme Court held that the police

validly stopped the defendant under a *Terry v. Ohio* standard and that the "stop and identify" provision in the county code did not violate the Fourth Amendment. The court distinguished the case from the statute the U.S. Supreme Court struck down in *Kolender,* saying that the California statute at issue there required an individual to provide a credible and reliable identification and required a person to account for his or her presence.

Jones v. Commonwealth of Virginia, 334 S.E.2d 536 (Va. 1985).

CASE-IN-POINT

Coerced Confessions

As an example of psychological coercion, a confession was ruled involuntary where a defendant was incarcerated and subjected to questioning over a four-day period. The defendant's relatives were denied permission to see him, and he was unable to communicate with anyone outside the jail. At one point during the interrogation, defendant was forced to hold for twenty-five minutes a gory picture of the deceased lying in a pool of blood.

Davis v. State, 308 S.W.2d 880, 882 (Tex. Crim. App. 1957).

encourages arbitrary enforcement by failing to describe with sufficient particularity what a suspect must do in order to satisfy the statute." 461 U.S. at 361, 103 S.Ct. at 1860, 75 L.Ed.2d at 911.

Interrogation and Confessions

Although the courts have long recognized the need for police interrogation of suspects, they have also recognized the potential for abuse inherent in the practice of incommunicado interrogation. At early common law, any confession was admissible even if extracted from the accused by torture. As the common law progressed, judges came to insist on proof that a confession was made voluntarily before it could be admitted in evidence.

In 1897 the Supreme Court held that to force a suspect to confess violates the Self-Incrimination Clause of the Fifth Amendment. *Bram v. United States,* 168 U.S. 532, 18 S.Ct. 183, 42 L.Ed. 568. In 1936 the Court held that a **coerced confession** deprived a defendant in a state criminal case of due process of law as guaranteed by the Fourteenth Amendment. *Brown v. Mississippi,* 297 U.S. 278, 56 S.Ct. 461, 80 L.Ed. 682. In 1964 the self-incrimination clause was made applicable to state criminal prosecutions. *Malloy v. Hogan,* 378 U.S. 1, 84 S.Ct. 1489, 12 L.Ed.2d 653 (1964). As a result, federal and state police are held to the same standards in evaluating the voluntariness of confessions of guilt. In *Malloy,* the Court said that the Fifth Amendment prohibits the extraction of a confession by "exertion of any improper influence." 378 U.S. at 7, 84 S.Ct. at 1493, 12 L.Ed.2d at 659. A confession is voluntary when it is made with knowledge of its nature and consequences and without duress or inducement. *United States v. Carignan,* 342 U.S. 36, 72 S.Ct. 97, 96 L.Ed. 48 (1951).

In *Escobedo v. Illinois,* 378 U.S. 478, 84 S.Ct. 1758, 12 L.Ed.2d 977 (1964), the Supreme Court recognized the right of suspects to have counsel present during interrogation. Anticipating the criticism that the Court's decision would hamper law enforcement, Justice Arthur Goldberg observed the following: "If the exercise of constitutional rights will thwart the effectiveness of a system of law enforcement, then there is something very wrong with that system." However, the Court's work in this area was not finished. Two years later, in its landmark decision in *Miranda v. Arizona,* 384 U.S. 436, 86 S.Ct. 1602, 16 L.Ed.2d 694 (1966), the Supreme Court held that before interrogating suspects who are in custody, police must warn them of their right

SUPREME COURT PERSPECTIVE

United States v. Dickerson, 530 U.S. 428, 120 S.Ct. 2326, 147 L.Ed.2d 405 (2000)

In 2000 the Supreme Court reconsidered its landmark 1966 decision in *Miranda v. Arizona.* Chief Justice Rehnquist delivered the opinion of the Court, saying in part:

"In *Miranda* . . . we held that certain warnings must be given before a suspect's statement made during custodial interrogation could be admitted in evidence. In the wake of that decision, Congress enacted 18 U.S.C. § 3501, which in essence laid down a rule that the admissibility of such statements should turn only on whether or not they were voluntarily made. . . .

"Petitioner Dickerson was indicted for bank robbery, conspiracy to commit bank robbery, and using a firearm in the course of committing a crime of violence. . . . Before trial, Dickerson moved to suppress a statement he had made at a Federal Bureau of Investigation field office, on the grounds that he had not received 'Miranda warnings' before being interrogated. The District Court granted his motion to suppress, and the Government took an interlocutory appeal to the United States Court of Appeals for the Fourth Circuit. That court, by a divided vote, reversed . . . [, holding] that our decision in *Miranda* was not a constitutional holding, and that therefore Congress

could by statute have the final say on the question of admissibility.

"We do not think there is . . . justification for overruling *Miranda. Miranda* has become embedded in routine police practice to the point where the warnings have become part of our national culture. . . . While we have overruled our precedents when subsequent cases have undermined their doctrinal underpinnings, . . . we do not believe that this has happened to the *Miranda* decision. If anything, our subsequent cases have reduced the impact of the *Miranda* rule on legitimate law enforcement while reaffirming the decision's core ruling that unwarned statements may not be used as evidence in the prosecution's case in chief."

Justice Scalia, joined by Justice Thomas, dissented, concluding:

"I am not convinced by petitioner's argument that *Miranda* should be preserved because the decision occupies a special place in the 'public's consciousness.' As far as I am aware, the public is not under the illusion that we are infallible. I see little harm in admitting that we made a mistake in taking away from the people the ability to decide for themselves what protections (beyond those required by the Constitution) are reasonably affordable in the criminal investigatory process."

An excerpt from the Supreme Court's decision in Miranda v. Arizona appears at the end of the chapter.

to remain silent and their right to have counsel present during questioning. The typical form of the ***Miranda* warnings** used by law enforcement is as follows:

> You are under arrest. You have the right to remain silent. Anything you say can and will be used against you in a court of law. You are entitled to have an attorney present during questioning. If you cannot afford an attorney, one will be appointed to represent you.

Unless these warnings have been given, no statement made by the suspect may be used in evidence, subject to certain narrow exceptions. The *Miranda* decision was severely criticized by law enforcement interests when it was handed down in 1966. But now it is accepted, even supported, by most law enforcement agencies and has been integrated into routine police procedure. It is also firmly established in the Supreme Court's jurisprudence, as evidenced by the Court's recent decision in *United States v. Dickerson* (2000) (see the Supreme Court Perspective above).

The Fruit of the Poisonous Tree Doctrine

The *Miranda* decision essentially established an **exclusionary rule** applicable to statements made by suspects during custodial interrogation. But the loss of a confession or statement may have consequences for other evidence gathered by the police. Under the **fruit of the poisonous tree doctrine,** evidence that is derived from inadmissible evidence is likewise inadmissible. *Wong Sun v. United States,* 371 U.S. 471, 83 S.Ct. 407, 9 L.Ed.2d 441 (1963). For example, if police learn of the location of a weapon used in the commission of a crime by interrogating a suspect who is in custody, that weapon is considered **derivative evidence.** If the police failed to provide the *Miranda* warnings, not only the suspect's responses to their questions but also the weapon discovered as the fruit of the interrogation is tainted. On the other hand, if the physical evidence was located on the basis of independently and lawfully obtained information, it may be admissible under the independent source doctrine. *Segurra v. United States,* 468 U.S. 796, 104 S.Ct. 3380, 82 L.Ed.2d 599 (1984). Thus, in our hypothetical case, if police learned of the location of the weapon from an informant, the weapon might well be admissible in court, even though the suspect's admissions are still inadmissible.

A variation on the **independent source doctrine** is what is termed the **inevitable discovery doctrine.** A grisly case that illustrates this doctrine is *Nix v. Williams,* 467 U.S. 431, 104 S.Ct. 2501, 81 L.Ed.2d 377 (1984). In this case, a jury in a murder defendant's retrial was not permitted to learn of the defendant's incriminating statements because the police had violated *Miranda.* He was convicted nevertheless, largely on evidence derived from the girl's corpse. The body was discovered when Williams, before meeting with his attorney, led police to the place where he had dumped it. On appeal, Williams argued that evidence of the body was improperly admitted at trial because its discovery was based on inadmissible statements and thus constituted the fruit of the poisonous tree. In reviewing the case, the U.S. Supreme Court held that the evidence of the body was properly admissible at trial because a search party operating in the area where the body was discovered would eventually have located the body, even without assistance from the defendant.

The Public Safety Exception to *Miranda*

Police generally provide the *Miranda* warnings immediately on arrest or as soon as is practicable to preserve as evidence any statements that the suspect might make, as well as any other evidence that might be derived from these statements. In some situations, however, the *Miranda* warnings are delayed because police are preoccupied with apprehending other individuals or taking actions to protect themselves or others on the scene. In *New York v. Quarles,* 467 U.S. 649, 104 S.Ct. 2626, 81 L.Ed.2d 550 (1984), the Supreme Court recognized a **public safety exception** to the *Miranda* exclusionary rule. Under *Quarles,* police may ask suspects questions designed to locate weapons that might be used to harm the police or other persons before providing the *Miranda* warnings. If this interaction produces incriminating statements or physical evidence, the evidence need not be suppressed.

An excerpt from the Supreme Court's decision in New York v. Quarles appears at the end of the chapter.

What Constitutes an Interrogation?

Although interrogation normally occurs at the station house after arrest, it may occur anywhere. For the purpose of determining when the *Miranda* warnings must be given, the Supreme Court has defined interrogation as "express questioning or its functional equivalent," including "any words or actions on the part of the police that the police should know are reasonably likely to elicit an incriminating response from the suspect." *Rhode Island v. Innis,* 446 U.S. 291, 301, 100 S.Ct. 1682, 1693, 64 L.Ed.2d 297, 308 (1980). Before police may engage in such interaction, they must provide the *Miranda* warnings or risk the likelihood that useful **incriminating statements** will be suppressed as illegally obtained evidence.

Waiver of *Miranda* Rights

It is axiomatic that all constitutional rights may be waived. A suspect may elect to waive the right to remain silent or the right to have counsel present during questioning as long as he or she does so knowingly and voluntarily. Courts are apt to strictly scrutinize a **waiver of *Miranda* rights** to make sure it is not the product of some coercion or deception by police. In *United States v. Carra,* 604 F.2d 1271 (10th Cir. 1979), the court observed that "[v]oluntary waiver of the right to remain silent is not mechanically to be determined but is to be determined from the totality of circumstances as a matter of fact." For example, in *United States v. Blocker,* 354 F. Supp. 1195 (D. D.C. 1973), a federal district court observed that a written waiver signed by the accused is not in itself conclusive evidence: "The court must still decide whether, in view of all the circumstances, defendant's subsequent decision to speak was a product of his free will." 354 F. Supp. at 1198 n. 11.

Although they must honor a suspect's refusal to cooperate, police are under no duty to inform a suspect who is considering whether to cooperate that arrangements have been made to provide counsel. In *Moran v. Burbine,* 475 U.S. 412, 106 S.Ct. 1135, 89 L.Ed.2d 410 (1986), police arrested a man on a burglary charge and subsequently linked him to an unsolved murder. The suspect's sister, not aware that a murder charge was about to be filed against her brother, arranged for a lawyer to represent her brother on the burglary charge. The attorney contacted the police to arrange a meeting with her client. The police did not mention the possible murder charge and told the attorney that her client was not going to be questioned until the next day. The police then began to interrogate Burbine, failing to tell him that a lawyer had been arranged for him and had attempted to contact him. Burbine waived his rights and eventually confessed to the murder. The Supreme Court upheld the use of the confession in evidence.

Coerced Confessions

Even where police officers provide the *Miranda* warnings and the suspect agrees to talk to police without having counsel present, a confession elicited from the suspect is inadmissible if it is obtained through coercion, whether physical intimidation or psychological pressure. *United States v. Tingle,* 658 F.2d 1332 (9th Cir. 1981). A classic example of psychological coercion is the so-called Mutt-and-Jeff strategy. Under this tactic, one police officer, the "bad guy," is harsh, rude, and aggressive, while another police officer, the "good guy," is friendly and sympathetic to the suspect. Obviously the objective of the strategy is to get the accused to confess to the "good guy," and there is reason to believe that it is an effective technique. There is controversy about whether the Mutt-and-Jeff tactic is a constitutional means of eliciting a confession from a suspect who has waived his or her *Miranda* rights and agreed to talk to police without the presence of counsel. In *Miranda,* the Supreme Court alluded to the Mutt-and-Jeff routine as a possible example of impermissible psychological coercion. 384 U.S. at 452, 86 S.Ct. at 1614 16 L.Ed.2d at 711. Yet, absent other indications of coercion, courts have generally acquiesced in the practice.

Police Deception

The use of tricks or factual misstatements by police in an effort to induce a defendant to confess does not automatically invalidate a confession. A misstatement by police may affect the **voluntariness of a confession,** but the effect of any misstatements must be considered in light of the totality of surrounding circumstances. In *Frazier v. Cupp*, 394 U.S. 731, 89 S.Ct. 1420, 22 L.Ed.2d 684 (1969), the Supreme Court reversed a conviction where the police had falsely informed a suspect that his codefendant had confessed. Although the Supreme Court found the misstatement relevant to the issue of whether the confession had been given voluntarily, it did not find that the misstatement per se made the confession inadmissible. The Nebraska Supreme Court has held that even deceptive statements referring to nonexistent autopsies of victims will not automatically render a confession involuntary. *State v. Norfolk*, 381 N.W.2d 120 (Neb. 1986).

How far may police go in their use of deception? In 1989 a Florida appellate court affirmed a trial judge's order holding a confession involuntary where police had presented fabricated laboratory reports to the defendant to secure a confession. The "reports," which were on the stationery of a law enforcement agency and a DNA testing firm, indicated that traces of the defendant's semen had been found on the victim's underwear. Among the factors cited by the appellate court in support of the exclusion of the confession were the indefinite life span of manufactured documents, their self-authenticating character, and the ease of duplication. The court expressed concern that false documents could find their way into police files or the courtroom and be accepted as genuine. *State v. Cayward*, 552 So.2d 971 (Fla. App. 1989).

Police deception must be distinguished from cases where the police use or threaten force or promise leniency to elicit a confession. In instances where force is used or leniency is promised, courts will suppress confessions obtained. See *Spano v. New York*, 360 U.S. 315, 79 S.Ct. 1202, 3 L.Ed.2d 1265 (1959). Moreover, when the police furnish a suspect an incorrect or incomplete advisory statement of the penalties provided by law for a particular crime, courts will generally suppress the suspect's confession. See, for example, *People v. Lytle*, 704 P.2d 331 (Colo. App. 1985).

Factors Considered by Judges in Evaluating Confessions

Judges consider several variables in determining whether a challenged confession was voluntary. These include the duration and methods of the interrogation, the length of the delay between arrest and appearance before a magistrate, the conditions of detention, the attitudes of the police toward the defendant, the defendant's physical and psychological state, and anything else that might bear on the defendant's resistance. *Commonwealth v. Kichline*, 361 A.2d 282, 290 (Pa. 1976). Courts are particularly cautious in receiving confessions by juveniles. See, for example, *Haley v. Ohio*, 332 U.S. 596, 68 S.Ct. 302, 92 L.Ed. 224 (1948).

In a landmark ruling, *Arizona v. Fulminante*, 499 U.S. 279, 111 S.Ct. 1246, 113 L.Ed.2d 302 (1991), the Supreme Court said that the use of a confession that should have been suppressed does not automatically require reversal of a defendant's conviction. Rather, the appellate court must determine whether the defendant would have been convicted in the absence of the confession. If so, the admission of the confession is deemed to be a harmless error that does not require reversal. See, for example, *State v. Tart*, 672 So.2d 116 (La. 1996).

Identification Procedures

Police identification procedures include those in which victims and witnesses are asked to identify perpetrators, such as **lineups, showups,** and **photo packs.** They also encompass scientific techniques comparing **forensic evidence** taken from a suspect with that found at a crime scene. All of these procedures are extremely important in police work, but each poses unique legal problems.

Forensic Methods

Forensic methods involve the application of scientific principles to legal issues. In the context of police work, forensic methods commonly include fingerprint identification, comparison of blood samples, matching of clothing fibers, head and body hair comparisons, identification of semen, and, more recently, **DNA tests.** When these methods are conducted by qualified persons, the results are usually admissible in evidence. Indeed, the courts have ruled that obtaining such physical evidence from suspects does not violate the constitutional prohibition of compulsory self-incrimination. *Schmerber v. California,* 384 U.S. 757, 86 S.Ct. 1826, 16 L.Ed.2d 908 (1966).

In *Gilbert v. California,* 388 U.S. 263, 87 S.Ct. 1951, 18 L.Ed.2d 1178 (1967), the U.S. Supreme Court held that a suspect could be compelled to provide a **handwriting exemplar,** explaining that it is not testimony but an identifying physical characteristic. Similarly, in *United States v. Dionisio,* 410 U.S. 1, 93 S.Ct. 764, 35 L.Ed.2d 67 (1973), the Court held that a suspect could be compelled to provide a **voice exemplar** on the ground that the recording is being used only to measure the physical properties of the suspect's voice, as distinct from the content of what the suspect has said.

Of course, police may not use methods that "shock the conscience" in obtaining physical evidence from suspects. *Rochin v. California,* 342 U.S. 165, 72 S.Ct. 205, 96 L.Ed. 183 (1952). Courts will scrutinize closely procedures that subject the suspect to major bodily intrusions. For example, in *Winston v. Lee,* 470 U.S. 753, 105 S.Ct. 1611, 84 L.Ed.2d 662 (1985), the prosecution sought a court order requiring a suspect to have surgery to remove a bullet lodged in his chest. The prosecution believed that ballistics tests on the bullet would show that the suspect had been wounded during the course of a robbery. The Supreme Court, weighing the risks to the suspect against the government's need for evidence, and noting that the prosecution had other evidence against the suspect, disallowed the procedure. The Court declined to formulate a broad rule to govern such cases. Rather, courts must consider such matters on a case-by-case basis, carefully weighing the interests on both sides.

As the 1995 O. J. Simpson murder trial demonstrates, defense lawyers can attack the methodology of forensic procedures as well as the qualifications of those administering them. If the evidence is inherently unreliable, it is inadmissible regardless of whether there were violations of the suspect's constitutional rights. In 1996 the FBI crime laboratory was criticized for allegedly sloppy procedures in the conduct of DNA and other forensic tests. This encouraged defense lawyers to challenge the reliability of the evidence in several cases where prosecutors were using evidence analyzed by the FBI crime lab.

With the rapid progress of science and technology, forensic procedures are constantly evolving and new procedures becoming available to the police. Evidence obtained through scientific and technological innovations can be both relevant and probative in a criminal case. Yet care must be taken to ensure that a new method is clearly supported by research.

Until recently, federal and state courts followed the test articulated in *Frye v. United States,* 293 F. 1013 (D.C. Cir. 1923), and admitted scientific evidence only if it was based on principles or theories generally accepted in the scientific community. In *Daubert v. Merrell Dow Pharmaceuticals, Inc.,* 509 U.S. 579, 113 S.Ct. 2786, 125 L.Ed.2d 469 (1993), the Supreme Court held that the Federal Rules of Evidence supersede *Frye* and govern the admissibility of scientific evidence in the federal courts. This approach causes admissibility of scientific evidence to hinge on such factors as whether the evidence can be tested and whether it has been subjected to peer review. It remains to be seen whether state courts will continue to follow the *Frye* test. (This topic is discussed further in Chapter 18.)

Lineups

An excerpt from the Supreme Court's decision in *United States v. Wade* appears at the end of the chapter.

Eyewitness identification may be more persuasive to juries than forensic evidence, but it can also present problems. One of the most common nonscientific methods of identification is the lineup. In a lineup, a group of individuals, one of whom is the suspect in custody, appears before a victim or witness, who is usually shielded from the suspect's view. Often, the individuals in the lineup are asked to walk, turn sideways, wear certain items of clothing, or speak to assist the victim or eyewitness in making a positive identification. The Supreme Court has held that there is no Fifth Amendment immunity against being placed in a lineup as an identification procedure. *United States v. Wade,* 388 U.S. 218, 87 S.Ct. 1926, 18 L.Ed.2d 1149 (1967). However, courts must guard against the possibility that identification procedures, especially lineups, are unfair when a victim or witness is prompted to identify a particular suspect as the perpetrator. See, for example, *Foster v. California,* 394 U.S. 440, 89 S.Ct. 1127, 22 L.Ed.2d 402 (1969). Obviously, if the perpetrator is known to be black, it is impermissibly suggestive for police to place one African American suspect in a lineup with five white individuals. In practice, however, the more subtle suggestiveness of lineups causes problems for the courts. To avoid such problems, police should place several persons with similar physical characteristics in a lineup.

To further protect the rights of the accused, the Supreme Court has said that after formal charges have been made against a defendant, the defendant has the right to have counsel present at a lineup. *Kirby v. Illinois,* 406 U.S. 682, 92 S.Ct. 1877, 32 L.Ed.2d 411 (1972). To ensure that police and prosecutors honor that right, the Supreme Court has said that a pretrial identification obtained in violation of the right to counsel is per se inadmissible at trial. *Gilbert v. California,* supra. A per se exclusionary rule was deemed necessary to ensure that the police and the prosecution would respect the defendant's right to have counsel present at a lineup. On the other hand, a pretrial identification obtained through impermissibly suggestive identification procedures is not per se inadmissible. Instead, such an identification may be introduced into evidence if the trial judge first finds that the witness's in-court identification is reliable and based on independent recall. In making this determination, the trial judge must consider (1) the opportunity of the witness to view the accused at the time of the crime, (2) the witness's degree of attention, (3) the accuracy of the witness's prior description of the accused, (4) the level of certainty demonstrated at the confrontation, and (5) the time that elapsed between the crime and the confrontation. *Neil v. Biggers,* 409 U.S. 188, 93 S.Ct. 375, 34 L.Ed.2d 401 (1972); see also *Wethington v. State,* 560 N.E.2d 496 (Ind. 1990).

Showups

In a showup, the police take the victim to the suspect to see if the former can make an identification. Although this method has been subject to criticism, when it occurs shortly after the crime has been committed and the showup is conducted near the scene of the crime, it is considered an acceptable method of securing an identification.

People v. Love, 443 N.E.2d 948 (N.Y. 1982). The Supreme Court of Illinois has held that police may transport a person stopped for an investigatory stop a short distance for purposes of a showup. *People v. Lippert,* 432 N.E.2d 605 (1982).

An on-the-scene confrontation between eyewitness and suspect is inherently suggestive because it is apparent that law enforcement officials believe they have caught the offender. However, such a confrontation may be justified by countervailing policy considerations. For example, a victim's or eyewitness's on-the-scene identification is likely to be more reliable than a later identification because the memory is fresher. In addition, prompt identifications exonerate innocent people more expeditiously. *Jones v. State,* 600 P.2d 247, 250 (Nev. 1979).

Photo Packs

A photo pack is simply a set of "mug shots" that are shown individually to the victim or eyewitness in the hope of being able to identify the perpetrator. To produce a reliable, hence admissible, identification, the presentation of the photo pack should not emphasize one photo over the others. The words and actions of the officers making the presentation must manifest an attitude of disinterest. *State v. Thamer,* 777 P.2d 432 (Utah 1989). In analyzing a defendant's claim of being the victim of an impermissibly suggestive photo pack identification, courts generally apply a two-part test. First, did the photo array present the defendant in an impermissibly suggestive posture? Second, if so, under the totality of circumstances, did the procedure give rise to a substantial likelihood of misidentification? *State v. Bedwell,* 417 N.W.2d 66 (Iowa 1987).

Conclusion

Police are permitted broad discretion in their interactions with the public. There are no legal prerequisites to the many consensual encounters through which police routinely perform their investigative and preventive duties. Nonconsensual encounters are subject to legal requirements. To stop and frisk a person requires reasonable suspicion; to make an arrest, police must have probable cause to believe that a crime has been committed. When practicable, it is desirable that police obtain an arrest warrant, but this is not always essential to legitimize an arrest based on probable cause.

Even without probable cause, police are permitted to stop and frisk persons where there is reasonable suspicion that a crime is about to take place. Courts are still struggling with the permissible length and scope of such field detentions.

Persons who are detained or arrested by police possess a constitutional right to remain silent. Under normal circumstances, police may not compel even a suspicious person to identify himself or herself.

When police make an arrest, they must inform the suspect of the constitutional rights to remain silent and consult with counsel. Failure to do so jeopardizes the admissibility of incriminating statements that the suspect might make even voluntarily. It also jeopardizes the use of physical evidence discovered as a result of statements that are later held to be inadmissible. Although the courts are willing to recognize certain exceptional situations, the prudent police officer will "Mirandize" the suspect immediately on arrest.

There is no constitutional prohibition against police taking fingerprints, voice samples, handwriting exemplars, and the like from suspects. Nor is there any prohibition against forcing suspects to appear in lineups for identification by a witness or victim, as long as police avoid suggesting the person to be identified.

Despite the increased scrutiny of courts over the last several decades, law enforcement officers retain considerable discretion in making arrests, conducting investigations, and interviewing suspects. As long as certain essential safeguards are observed, police are not seriously hampered in their efforts to ferret out crime.

Key Terms

arrest
investigatory detention
stop-and-frisk
roadblocks
sobriety checkpoints
request for information or
     identification
interrogation
identification procedures
probable cause
arrest warrant
capias
warrantless arrest
plain view
exigent circumstances
deadly force
citizen's arrest
traffic citation
reasonable suspicion
pat-down search
Terry-stop
pretextual stops

drug courier profiles
racial profiling
field sobriety test
coerced confession
Miranda warnings
exclusionary rule
fruit of the poisonous tree doctrine
derivative evidence
independent source doctrine
inevitable discovery doctrine
public safety exception
incriminating statements
waiver of *Miranda* rights
voluntariness of a confession
police deception
lineups
showups
photo packs
forensic evidence
DNA tests
handwriting exemplar
voice exemplar

Web-Based Research Activity

1. Use **www.findlaw.com** or some other Internet resource to locate the United States Supreme Court's most recent decisions in the areas of arrest and interrogation.
2. Try to determine whether the Court has agreed to hear new cases in these areas and, if so, what issues these cases present.

Questions for Thought and Discussion

1. Practically speaking, what is the difference between "probable cause" and "reasonable suspicion"? How long can police detain a suspect based on reasonable suspicion?
2. What are the practical arguments for and against allowing private citizens to make arrests when they observe criminal activity taking place? What is the law in your state governing "citizen's arrests"?

3. Does your state make any distinction between minor and serious traffic offenses in permitting arrests? Is the use of arrest procedures for relatively minor traffic offenses unnecessary? Is it better to give the individual police officer discretion in these matters, or to adopt laws decriminalizing such infractions?

4. In the *Miranda* case, the Supreme Court released a convicted rapist to impose a requirement that police advise suspects of their constitutional rights before conducting interrogations. Was the Court's decision a wise one? What has been the impact of the *Miranda* decision on law enforcement?

5. What factors do courts consider in determining whether an individual is "in custody" when a police interrogation takes place?

6. How might police coerce a suspect into waiving the right to counsel and to remain silent during interrogation? How can courts ensure that cooperation with police was voluntary?

7. Are the courts correct in limiting the scope of the Fifth Amendment Self-Incrimination Clause to verbal statements so that there is no constitutional protection against compulsory police identification procedures? What would be the implications for law enforcement if the courts included physical evidence like fingerprints or handwriting samples within the scope of the Fifth Amendment privilege?

8. Describe the methods of nonscientific identification used by law enforcement in their attempts to identify suspects. Which do you think is the most reliable?

9. Would it be permissible for police to construct a lineup including four visibly overweight persons along with a slim suspect where the victim told police that her assailant was "very thin"?

10. Discuss racial profiling, which results in a disproportionate number of minorities being stopped for disobeying traffic laws. Should this problem be addressed by (a) courts dismissing charges or suppressing evidence seized as a result of racial profiling based on denial of due process and equal protection of the law, (b) civil litigation seeking financial redress, (c) disciplinary action against law enforcement officers responsible for racial profiling, or (d) some other proposed remedy?

Problems for Discussion and Solution

1. Police obtained a warrant to search a single-family residence for "illegal amphetamines and equipment used in the manufacture of same." The warrant also authorized the search of the person of Harry Hampton, described in the warrant as a white male, 32 years of age, 6 ft. 2 in., and 225 lbs. When they arrived at the scene, one officer began to search Hampton. When that search yielded contraband, another officer detained a second man sitting on the porch (he was later identified as Jimmy Jaffers). The officer subjected Jaffers to a pat-down search. No weapons were discovered on Jaffers's person, but the officer, having felt a "suspicious lump" in Jaffers's front pants pocket, retrieved a plastic bag of capsules that later proved to be illegal amphetamines. In a pretrial motion, Jaffers's counsel moves to suppress the contraband, arguing that his client was the victim of an unreasonable search. Is Jaffers likely to prevail in this contention? Why or why not?

2. A police officer on night patrol saw a car parked off a dirt road in an area known to be a "lovers' lane." As his cruiser approached the car, he observed a male

and a female sitting inside. He noticed the male occupant make a movement that the officer interpreted as an attempt to hide something under the seat. The officer approached the vehicle and directed the occupants to get out. As they did, he observed a marijuana "roach" in the open ashtray. The officer then reached under the front seat and retrieved a small quantity of marijuana. The officer placed both individuals under arrest. In court, the officer admitted that he was not concerned for his safety but simply had a "hunch" that the couple could be "doing drugs." Did the officer make a legal arrest? Why or why not?

EXCERPTS FROM JUDICIAL DECISIONS

Tennessee v. Garner

Supreme Court of the United States, 1985.
471 U.S. 1, 105 S.Ct. 1694, 85 L.Ed.2d 1.

[In this case the Supreme Court holds that use of deadly force by police to prevent the escape of an unarmed felony suspect who does not pose a threat of serious harm is an unreasonable seizure under the Fourth Amendment.]

Justice WHITE delivered the opinion of the court.
    . . . At about 10:45 P.M. on October 3, 1974, Memphis Police Officers Elton Hymon and Leslie Wright were dispatched to answer a "prowler inside call." Upon arriving at the scene they saw a woman standing on her porch and gesturing toward the adjacent house. She told them she had heard glass breaking and that "they" or "someone" was breaking in next door. While Wright radioed the dispatcher to say that they were on the scene, Hymon went behind the house. He heard a door slam and saw someone run across the backyard. The fleeing suspect, . . . Edward Garner, stopped at a 6-feet-high chain link fence at the edge of the yard. With the aid of a flashlight, Hymon was able to see Garner's face and hands. He saw no sign of a weapon, and, though not certain, was "reasonably sure" and "figured" that Garner was unarmed. . . . He thought Garner was 17 or 18 years old and about 5'5" or 5'7" tall. While Garner was crouched at the base of the fence, Hymon called out "police, halt" and took a few steps toward him. Garner then began to climb over the fence. Convinced that if Garner made it over the fence he would elude capture, Hymon shot him. The bullet hit Garner in the back of the head. Garner was taken by ambulance to a hospital, where he died on the operating table. Ten dollars and a purse taken from the house were found on his body.

In using deadly force to prevent the escape, Hymon was acting under the authority of a Tennessee statute and pursuant to Police Department policy. The statute provides that "[i]f, after notice of the intention to arrest the defendant, he either flees or forcibly resists, the officer may use all the necessary means to effect the arrest." Tenn. Code Ann. Sec. 40–7–108 (1982). The Department policy was slightly more restrictive than the statute, but still allowed the use of deadly force in cases of burglary. . . . The incident was reviewed by the Memphis Police Firearm's Review Board and presented to a grand jury. Neither took any action. . . .

Garner's father then brought this action in the Federal District Court for the Western District of Tennessee, seeking damages under 42 USC Sec. 1983 for asserted violations of Garner's constitutional rights. The complaint alleged that the shooting violated the Fourth, Fifth, Sixth, Eighth, and Fourteenth Amendments of the United States Constitution. It named as defendants Officer Hymon, the Police Department, its Director, and the Mayor and city of Memphis. After a 3-day bench trial, the District Court entered judgment for all defendants. It dismissed the claims against the Mayor and the Director for lack of evidence. It then concluded that Hymon's actions were authorized by the Tennessee statute, which in turn was constitutional. Hymon had employed the only reasonable and practicable means of preventing Garner's escape. Garner had "recklessly and heedlessly attempted to vault over the fence to escape, thereby assuming the risk of being fired upon." . . .

The Court of Appeals reversed and remanded. . . . It reasoned that the killing of a fleeing suspect is a "seizure" under the Fourth Amendment, and is therefore constitutional only if "reasonable." The Tennessee statute failed as applied to this case because it did not adequately limit the use of deadly force by distinguishing between felonies of different magnitudes—"the facts, as found, did not justify the use of deadly force under the Fourth Amendment." . . . Officers cannot resort to deadly force unless they "have probable cause . . . to believe that the suspect [has committed a felony and] poses a threat to the safety of the officers or a danger to the community if left at large." . . .

The State of Tennessee, which had intervened to defend the statute . . . appealed to this Court. The city filed a petition for certiorari. We noted probable jurisdiction in the appeal and granted the petition. . . .

Whenever an officer restrains the freedom of a person to walk away, he has seized that person. . . . While it is not always clear just when minimal police interference becomes a seizure, . . . there can be no question that apprehension by the use of deadly force is a seizure subject to the reasonableness requirement of the Fourth Amendment.

A police officer may arrest a person if he has probable cause to believe that person committed a crime. . . . Petitioners and appellant argue that if this requirement is satisfied the Fourth Amendment has nothing to say about how that seizure is made. This submission ignores the many cases in which this Court, by balancing the extent of the intrusion against the need for it, has examined the reasonableness of the manner in which a search or seizure is conducted. . . .

. . . Petitioners and appellant have not persuaded us that shooting nondangerous fleeing suspects is so vital as to outweigh the suspect's interest in his own life.

The use of deadly force to prevent the escape of all felony suspects, whatever the circumstances, is constitutionally unreasonable. It is not better that all felony suspects die than that they escape. Where the suspect poses no immediate threat to the officer and no threat to others, the harm resulting from failing to apprehend him does not justify the use of deadly force to do so. It is no doubt unfortunate when a suspect who is in sight escapes, but the fact that the police arrive a little late or are a little slower afoot does not always justify killing the suspect. A police officer may not seize an unarmed, nondangerous suspect by shooting him dead. The Tennessee statute is uncon-

stitutional insofar as it authorizes the use of deadly force against such fleeing suspects.

It is not, however, unconstitutional on its face. Where the officer has probable cause to believe that the suspect poses a threat of serious physical harm, either to the officer or to others, it is not constitutionally unreasonable to prevent escape by using deadly force. Thus, if the suspect threatens the officer with a weapon or there is probable cause to believe that he has committed a crime involving the infliction or threatened infliction of serious physical harm, deadly force may be used if necessary to prevent escape, and if, where feasible, some warning has been given. As applied in such circumstances, the Tennessee statute would pass constitutional muster. . . .

The District Court concluded that Hymon was justified in shooting Garner because state law allows, and the Federal Constitution does not forbid, the use of deadly force to prevent the escape of a fleeing felony suspect if no alternative means of apprehension is available. . . . This conclusion made a determination of Garner's apparent dangerousness unnecessary. The court did find, however, that Garner appeared to be unarmed, though Hymon could not be certain that was the case. . . . Restated in Fourth Amendment terms, this means Hymon had no articulable basis to think Garner was armed.

In reversing, the Court of Appeals accepted the District Court's factual conclusions and held that "the facts, as found, did not justify the use of deadly force." . . . We agree. . . .

We hold that the statute is invalid insofar as it purported to give Hymon the authority to act as he did. As for the policy of the Police Department, the absence of any discussion of this issue by the courts below, and the uncertain state of the record, preclude any consideration of its validity. The judgment of the Court of Appeals is affirmed, and the case is remanded for further proceedings consistent with this opinion.

Justice O'CONNOR, with whom The CHIEF JUSTICE and Justice REHNQUIST join, dissenting.

. . . Notwithstanding the venerable common-law rule authorizing the use of deadly force if necessary to apprehend a fleeing felon, and continued acceptance of this rule by nearly half the States, . . . the majority concludes that Tennessee's statute is unconstitutional inasmuch as it allows the use of such force to apprehend a burglary suspect who is not obviously armed or otherwise dangerous. Although the circumstances of this case are unquestionably tragic and unfortunate, our constitutional holdings must be sensitive both to the history of the Fourth Amendment and to the general implications of the Court's reasoning. By disregarding the serious and dangerous nature of residential burglaries and the long-standing practice of many States, the Court effectively creates a Fourth Amendment right allowing a burglary suspect to flee unimpeded from a police officer who has probable cause to arrest, who has ordered the suspect to halt, and who has no means short of firing his weapon to prevent escape. I do not believe that the Fourth Amendment supports such a right, and I accordingly dissent. . . .

● ● ● ● ● ● ● ● ● ● ● ● ● ● ●

Whren v. United States

Supreme Court of the United States, 1996.
517 U.S. 806, 116 S.Ct. 1769, 135 L.Ed.2d 89.

[In this case the Supreme Court considers the constitutionality of pretextual automobile stops.]

Justice SCALIA delivered the opinion of the Court.
. . . On the evening of June 10, 1993, plainclothes vice-squad officers of the District of Columbia Metropolitan Police Department were patrolling a "high drug area" of the city in an unmarked car. Their suspicions were aroused when they passed a dark Pathfinder truck with temporary license plates and youthful occupants waiting at a stop sign, the driver looking down into the lap of the passenger at his right. The truck remained stopped at the intersection for what seemed an unusually long time—more than 20 seconds. When the police car executed a U-turn in order to head back toward the truck, the Pathfinder turned suddenly to its right, without signaling, and sped off at an "unreasonable" speed. The policemen followed, and in a short while overtook the Pathfinder when it stopped behind other traffic at a red light. They pulled up alongside, and Officer Ephraim Soto stepped out and approached the driver's door, identifying himself as a police officer and directing the driver, petitioner Brown, to put the vehicle in park. When Soto drew up to the driver's window, he immediately observed two large plastic bags of what appeared to be crack cocaine in petitioner Whren's hands. Petitioners were arrested, and quantities of several types of illegal drugs were retrieved from the vehicle.
Petitioners were charged in a four-count indictment with violating various federal drug laws. . . . At a pretrial suppression hearing, they challenged the legality of the stop and the resulting seizure of the drugs. They argued that the stop had not been justified by probable cause to believe, or even reasonable suspicion, that petitioners were engaged in illegal drug-dealing activity; and that Officer Soto's asserted ground for approaching the vehicle—to give the driver a warning concerning traffic violations—was pretextual. The District Court denied the suppression motion. . . .
Petitioners were convicted of the counts at issue here. The Court of Appeals affirmed the convictions. . . .
The Fourth Amendment guarantees "[t]he right of the people to be secure in their persons, houses, papers, and effects, against unreasonable searches and seizures." Temporary detention of individuals during the stop of an automobile by the police, even if only for a brief period and for a limited purpose, constitutes a "seizure" of "persons" within the meaning of this provision. . . .
Petitioners accept that Officer Soto had probable cause to believe that various provisions of the District of Columbia traffic code had been violated. . . . They argue, however, that "in the unique context of civil traffic regulations" probable cause is not enough. Since, they contend, the use of automobiles is so heavily and minutely regulated that total compliance with traffic and safety rules is nearly impossible, a police officer will almost invariably be able to catch any given motorist in a technical violation. This creates the temptation to use traffic stops as a means of investigating other law violations, as to which no probable cause or even articulable suspicion exists. Petitioners, who are both black, further contend that police officers might decide which motorists to stop

based on decidedly impermissible factors, such as the race of the car's occupants. To avoid this danger, they say, the Fourth Amendment test for traffic stops should be, not the normal one (applied by the Court of Appeals) of whether probable cause existed to justify the stop; but rather, whether a police officer, acting reasonably, would have made the stop for the reason given.

Petitioners contend that the standard they propose is consistent with our past cases' disapproval of police attempts to use valid bases of action against citizens as pretexts for pursuing other investigatory agendas. . . .

. . . But only an undiscerning reader would regard these cases as endorsing the principle that ulterior motives can invalidate police conduct that is justifiable on the basis of probable cause to believe that a violation of law has occurred. In each case we were addressing the validity of a search conducted in the absence of probable cause. Our quoted statements simply explain that the exemption from the need for probable cause (and warrant), which is accorded to searches made for the purpose of inventory or administrative regulation, is not accorded to searches that are not made for those purposes. . . .

We think these cases foreclose any argument that the constitutional reasonableness of traffic stops depends on the actual motivations of the individual officers involved. We of course agree with petitioners that the Constitution prohibits selective enforcement of the law based on considerations such as race. But the constitutional basis for objecting to intentionally discriminatory application of laws is the Equal Protection Clause, not the Fourth Amendment. Subjective intentions play no role in ordinary, probable-cause Fourth Amendment analysis.

Recognizing that we have been unwilling to entertain Fourth Amendment challenges based on the actual motivations of individual officers, petitioners disavow any intention to make the individual officer's subjective good faith the touchstone of "reasonableness." They insist that the standard they have put forward—whether the officer's conduct deviated materially from usual police practices, so that a reasonable officer in the same circumstances would not have made the stop for the reasons given—is an "objective" one.

But although framed in empirical terms, this approach is plainly and indisputably driven by subjective considerations. Its whole purpose is to prevent the police from doing under the guise of enforcing the traffic code what they would like to do for different reasons. Petitioners' proposed standard may not use the word "pretext," but it is designed to combat nothing other than the perceived "danger" of the pretextual stop, albeit only indirectly and over the run of cases. Instead of asking whether the individual officer had the proper state of mind, the petitioners would have us ask, in effect, whether (based on general police practices) it is plausible to believe that the officer had the proper state of mind. . . .

It is of course true that in principle every Fourth Amendment case, since it turns upon a "reasonableness" determination, involves a balancing of all relevant factors. With rare exceptions not applicable here, however, the result of that balancing is not in doubt where the search or seizure is based upon probable cause. That is why petitioners must rely upon cases like [*Delaware v.*] *Prouse* [1979] to provide examples of actual "balancing" analysis. There, the police action in question was a random traffic stop for the purpose of checking a motorist's license and vehicle registration, a practice that—like the practices at issue in the inventory search and administrative inspection cases upon which petitioners rely in making their "pretext" claim—involves police intrusion without the probable cause that is its traditional justification. Our opinion in *Prouse* expressly distinguished the case from a stop based on precisely what is at issue here: "probable cause to believe that a driver is violating any one of the multitude of applicable traffic and equipment regulations." It noted approvingly that "[t]he foremost method of enforcing traffic and vehicle safety regulations . . . is acting upon observed violations," which afford the "quantum of individualized suspicion" necessary to ensure that police discretion is sufficiently constrained. . . . What is true of *Prouse* is also true of other cases that engaged in detailed "balancing" to decide the constitutionality of automobile stops—the detailed "balancing" analysis was necessary because they involved seizures without probable cause. . . .

Petitioners urge as an extraordinary factor in this case that the "multitude of applicable traffic and equipment regulations" is so large and so difficult to obey perfectly that virtually everyone is guilty of violation, permitting the police to single out almost whomever they wish for a stop. But we are aware of no principle that would allow us to decide at what point a code of law becomes so expansive and so commonly violated that infraction itself can no longer be the ordinary measure of the lawfulness of enforcement. And even if we could identify such exorbitant codes, we do not know by what standard (or what right) we would decide, as petitioners would have us do, which particular provisions are sufficiently important to merit enforcement.

For the run-of-the-mine case, which this surely is, we think there is no realistic alternative to the traditional common-law rule that probable cause justifies a search and seizure.

Here the District Court found that the officers had probable cause to believe that petitioners had violated the traffic code. That rendered the stop reasonable under the Fourth Amendment, the evidence thereby discovered admissible, and the upholding of the convictions by the Court of Appeals for the District of Columbia Circuit correct. . . .

● ● ● ● ● ● ● ● ● ● ● ● ● ● ●

Miranda v. Arizona

Supreme Court of the United States, 1966.
384 U.S. 436, 86 S.Ct. 1602, 16 L.Ed.2d 694.

[In this landmark decision, the Supreme Court declares that the police must inform suspects of their constitutional rights before commencing custodial interrogation.]

Mr. Chief Justice WARREN delivered the opinion of the Court.

The cases before us raise questions which go to the roots of our concepts of American criminal jurisprudence: the restraints society must observe consistent with the Federal Constitution in prosecuting individuals for crime. More specifically, we deal with the admissibility of statements obtained from an individual who is subjected to custodial police interrogation and the necessity for procedures which assure that the individual is accorded his privilege under the Fifth Amendment to the Constitution not to be compelled to incriminate himself.

We dealt with certain phases of this problem recently in *Escobedo v. Illinois* . . . (1964).

We start here, as we did in *Escobedo*, with the premise that our holding is not an innovation in our jurisprudence, but is an application of principles long recognized and applied in other settings. We have undertaken a thorough reexamination of the *Escobedo* decision and the principles it announced, and we reaffirm it. That case was but an explication of basic rights that are enshrined in our Constitution—that "No person . . . shall be compelled in any criminal case to be a witness against himself," and that "the accused shall . . . have the Assistance of Counsel"— rights which were put in jeopardy in that case through official overbearing. These precious rights were fixed in our Constitution only after centuries of

persecution and struggle. And in the words of Chief Justice Marshall, they were secured "for ages to come, and . . . designed to approach immortality as nearly as human institutions can approach it." . . .

Our holding will be spelled out with some specificity in the pages which follow but briefly stated it is this: the prosecution may not use statements, whether exculpatory or inculpatory, stemming from custodial interrogation of the defendant unless it demonstrates the use of procedural safeguards effective to secure the privilege against self-incrimination. By custodial interrogation, we mean questioning initiated by law enforcement officers after a person has been taken into custody or otherwise deprived of his freedom of action in any significant way. As for the procedural safeguards to be employed, unless other fully effective means are devised to inform accused persons of their right of silence and to assure a continuous opportunity to exercise it, the following measures are required. Prior to any questioning, the person must be warned that he has a right to remain silent, that any statement he does make may be used as evidence against him, and that he has a right to the presence of an attorney, either retained or appointed. The defendant may waive effectuation of these rights, provided the waiver is made voluntarily, knowingly and intelligently. If, however, he indicates in any manner and at any stage of the process that he wishes to consult with an attorney before speaking there can be no questioning. Likewise, if the individual is alone and indicates in any manner that he does not wish to be interrogated, the police may not question him. The mere fact that he may have answered some questions or volunteered some statements on his own does not deprive him of the right to refrain from answering any further inquiries until he has consulted with an attorney and thereafter consents to be questioned.

The constitutional issue we decide . . . is the admissibility of statements obtained from a defendant questioned while in custody or otherwise deprived of his freedom of action in any significant way. In each, the defendant was questioned by police officers, detectives, or a prosecuting attorney in a room in which he was cut off from the outside world. In none of these cases was the defendant given a full and effective warning of his rights at the outset of the interrogation process. In all the cases, the questioning elicited oral admissions, and in three of them, signed statements as well which were admitted at their trials. They all thus share salient features—incommunicado interrogation of individuals in a police-dominated atmosphere, resulting in self-incriminating statements without full warnings of constitutional rights.

An understanding of the nature and setting of this in-custody interrogation is essential to our decisions today. The difficulty in depicting what transpires at such interrogations stems from the fact that in this country they have largely taken place incommunicado. From extensive factual studies undertaken in the early 1930s, including the famous Wickersham Report to Congress by a Presidential Commission, it is clear that police violence and the "third degree" flourished at that time. In a series of cases decided by this Court long after these studies, the police resorted to physical brutality—beating, hanging, slapping—and to sustained and protracted questioning incommunicado in order to extort confessions. The Commission on Civil Rights in 1961 found much evidence to indicate that "some policemen still resort to physical force to obtain confessions." The use of physical brutality and violence is not, unfortunately, relegated to the past or to any part of the country. Only recently in Kings County, New York, the police brutally beat, kicked and placed lighted cigarette butts on the back of a potential witness under interrogation for the purpose of securing a statement incriminating a third party. . . .

The examples given above are undoubtedly the exception now, but they are sufficiently widespread to be the object of concern. Unless a proper limitation upon custodial interrogation is achieved—such as these decisions will advance—there can be no assurance that practices of this nature will be eradicated in the foreseeable future.

Again we stress that the modern practice of in-custody interrogation is psychologically rather than physically oriented. Interrogation still takes place in privacy. Privacy results in secrecy and this in turn results in a gap in our knowledge as to what in fact goes on in the interrogation rooms. A valuable source of information about present police practices, however, may be found in various police manuals and texts which document procedures employed with success in the past, and which recommended various other effective tactics. These texts are used by law enforcement agencies themselves as guides. It should be noted that these texts professedly present the most enlightened and effective means presently used to obtain statements through custodial interrogation. By considering these texts and other data, it is possible to describe procedures observed and noted around the country. . . .

Even without employing brutality, the "third degree" or the specific stratagems described above, the very fact of custodial interrogation exacts a heavy toll on individual liberty and trades on the weakness of individuals.

In the cases before us today, given this background, we concern ourselves primarily with this interrogation atmosphere and the evils it can bring.

In these cases, we might not find the defendants' statements to have been involuntary in traditional terms. Our concern for adequate safeguards to protect precious Fifth Amendment rights is, of course, not lessened in the slightest. In each of the cases, the defendant was thrust into an unfamiliar atmosphere and run through menacing police interrogation procedures. The potentiality for compulsion is forcefully apparent, for example, in *Miranda,* when the indigent Mexican defendant was a seriously disturbed individual with pronounced sexual fantasies. . . .

It is obvious that such an interrogation environment is created for no purpose other than to subjugate the individual to the will of his examiner. This atmosphere carries its own badge of intimidation. . . . The current practice of incommunicado interrogation is at odds with one of our Nation's most cherished principles—that the individual may not be compelled to incriminate himself. Unless adequate protective devices are employed to dispel the compulsion inherent in custodial surroundings, no statement obtained from the defendant can truly be the product of his free choice. . . .

. . . An individual swept from familiar surroundings into police custody, surrounded by antagonistic forces, and subjected to the techniques of persuasion described above cannot be otherwise than under compulsion to speak. As a practical matter, the compulsion to speak in the isolated setting of the police station may well be greater than in courts or other official investigations, where there are often impartial observers to guard against intimidation or trickery.

The presence of counsel, in all the cases before us today, would be the adequate protective device necessary to make the process of police interrogation conform to the dictates of the privilege. His presence would insure that statements made in the government-established atmosphere are not the product of compulsion.

It is impossible for us to foresee the potential alternatives for protecting the privilege which might be devised by Congress or the States in the exercise of their creative rulemaking capacities. Therefore we cannot say that the Constitution necessarily requires adherence to any particular solution for the inherent compulsions of the interrogation process as it is presently conducted. Our decision in no way creates a constitutional straitjacket which will handicap sound efforts at reform, nor is it intended to have this effect. We encourage Congress and the States to continue their laudable search for increasingly effective ways of protecting the rights of the individual while promoting efficient enforcement of our criminal laws.

A recurrent argument made in these cases is that society's need for interrogation outweighs the privilege. This argument is not unfamiliar to this Court. . . .

In announcing these principles, we are not unmindful of the burdens which law enforcement officials must bear, often under trying circumstances. We also fully recognize the obligation of all citizens to aid in enforcing the criminal laws. This Court, while protecting individual rights, has always given ample latitude to law enforcement agencies in the legitimate exercise of their duties. The limits we have placed on the interrogation process should not constitute an undue interference with a proper system of law enforcement. As we have noted, our decision does not in any way preclude police from carrying out their traditional investigatory functions. Although confessions may play an important role in some convictions, the cases before us present graphic examples of the overstatement of the "need" for confessions.

Therefore, in accordance with the foregoing, the judgments of the Supreme Court of Arizona . . . [are] reversed. . . .

Mr. Justice HARLAN, whom Mr. Justice STEWART and Mr. Justice WHITE join, dissenting. . . .

Mr. Justice WHITE, with whom Mr. Justice HARLAN and Mr. Justice STEWART join, dissenting.

. . . The most basic function of any government is to provide for the security of the individual and of his property. These ends of society are served by the criminal laws which for the most part are aimed at the prevention of crime. Without the reasonably effective performance of the task of preventing private violence and retaliation, it is idle to talk about human dignity and civilized values.

The rule announced today will measurably weaken the ability of the criminal law to perform these tasks. It is a deliberate calculus to prevent interrogations, to reduce the incidence of confessions and pleas of guilty and to increase the number of trials.

There is, in my view, every reason to believe that a good many criminal defendants who otherwise would have been convicted on what this Court has previously thought to be the most satisfactory kind of evidence will now, under this new version of the Fifth Amendment, either not be tried at all or will be acquitted if the State's evidence, minus the confession, is put to the test of litigation.

I have no desire whatsoever to share the responsibility for any such impact on the present criminal process. . . .

New York v. Quarles

Supreme Court of the United States, 1984.
467 U.S. 649, 104 S.Ct. 2626, 81 L.Ed.2d 550.

[In this case the Supreme Court declares a "public safety exception" to the requirements of Miranda v. Arizona.*]*

Justice REHNQUIST delivered the opinion of the Court.

Respondent Benjamin Quarles was charged in New York trial court with criminal possession of a weapon. The trial court suppressed the gun in question, and a statement made by respondent, because the statement was obtained by police before they read respondent his *"Miranda* rights." That ruling was affirmed on appeal through the New York Court of Appeals. We granted certiorari, . . . and we now reverse. We conclude that under the circumstances involved in this case, overriding considerations of public safety justify the officer's failure to provide *Miranda* warnings before he asked questions devoted to locating the abandoned weapon.

On September 11, 1980, at approximately 12:30 A.M., Officer Frank Kraft and Officer Sal Scarring were on road patrol in Queens, New York, when a young woman approached their car. She told them that she had just been raped by a black male, approximately six feet tall, who was wearing a black jacket with the name "Big Ben" printed in yellow letters on the back. She told the officers that the man had just entered the A & P supermarket located nearby and that the man was carrying a gun.

The officers drove the woman to the supermarket, and Officer Kraft entered the store while Officer Scarring radioed for assistance. Officer Kraft quickly spotted respondent, who matched the description given by the woman, approaching a check out counter. Apparently upon seeing the officer, respondent turned and ran toward the rear of the store, and Officer Kraft pursued him with a drawn gun. When respondent turned the corner at the end of an aisle, Officer Kraft lost sight of him for several seconds, and upon regaining sight of respondent, ordered him to stop and put his hands over his head.

Although more than three officers had arrived on the scene by that time, Officer Kraft was the first to reach respondent. He frisked him and discovered that he was wearing a shoulder holster which was then empty. After handcuffing him, Officer Kraft asked him where the gun was. Respondent nodded in the direction of some empty cartons and responded, "the gun is over there." Officer Kraft thereafter retrieved a loaded .38 caliber revolver from one of the cartons, formally placed respondent under arrest, and read him his *Miranda* rights from a printed card. Respondent indicated that he would be willing to answer questions without an attorney present. Officer Kraft then asked respondent if he owned the gun and where he had purchased it. Respondent answered that he did own it and that he had purchased it in Miami, Florida. . . .

We hold that on these facts there is a "public safety" exception to the requirement that *Miranda* warnings be given before a suspect's answers may be admitted into evidence, and the availability of that exception does not depend upon the motivation of the individual officers involved. In a kaleidoscopic situation such as the one confronting these officers, where spontaneity rather than adherence to a police manual is necessarily the order of the day, the application of the exception which we recognize today should not be made to depend on post hoc findings at a suppression hearing concerning the subjective motivation of the arresting officer. Undoubtedly most police officers, if placed in Officer Kraft's position, would act out of a host of different, instinctive, and largely unverifiable motives—their own safety, the safety of others, and perhaps as well the desire to obtain incriminating evidence from the suspect.

Whatever the motivation of individual officers in such a situation, we do not believe that the doctrinal underpinnings of *Miranda* required that it be applied in all its rigor to a situation in which police officers ask questions reasonably prompted by a concern for the public safety. . . .

The police in this case, in the very act of apprehending a suspect, were confronted with the necessity of ascertaining the whereabouts of a gun which they had every reason to believe the suspect had just removed from his empty holster and discarded in the supermarket. So long as the gun was concealed somewhere in the supermarket, with its actual whereabouts unknown, it obviously posed more than one danger to the public safety: an accomplice might make use of it, a customer or employee might later come upon it.

In such a situation, if the police are required to recite the familiar *Miranda* warnings before asking the whereabouts of the gun, suspects in Quarles' position might well be deterred from responding. Procedural safeguards which deter a suspect from responding were deemed acceptable in *Miranda* in order to protect the Fifth Amendment privilege; when the primary social cost of those added protections is the possibility of fewer convictions, the *Miranda* majority was willing to bear that cost. Here, had *Miranda* warnings deterred Quarles from responding to Officer Kraft's question about the whereabouts of the gun, the cost would have been something more than merely the failure to obtain evidence useful in convicting Quarles. Officer Kraft needed an answer to his question not simply to make his case against Quarles but to insure that further danger to the public did not result from the concealment of the gun in a public area.

We conclude that the need for answers to questions in a situation posing a threat to the public safety outweighs the need for the prophylactic rule protecting the Fifth Amendment's privilege against self-incrimination. We decline to place officers such as Officer Kraft in the untenable position of having to consider, often in a matter of seconds, whether it best serves society for them to ask the necessary questions without the *Miranda* warnings and render whatever probative evidence they uncover inadmissible, or for them to give the warnings in order to preserve the admissibility of evidence they might uncover but possibly damage or destroy their ability to obtain that evidence and neutralize the volatile situation confronting them. . . .

The facts of this case clearly demonstrate that distinction and an officer's ability to recognize it. Officer Kraft asked only the question necessary to locate the missing gun before advising respondent of his rights. It was only after securing the loaded re-

volver and giving the warnings that he continued with investigatory questions about the ownership and place of purchase of the gun. The exception which we recognize today, far from complicating the thought processes and the on-the-scene judgments of police officers, will simply free them to follow their legitimate instincts when confronting situations presenting a danger to the public safety.

We hold that the Court of Appeals in this case erred in excluding the statement, "the gun is over there," and the gun because of the officer's failure to read respondent his *Miranda* rights before attempting to locate the weapon. Accordingly we hold that it also erred in excluding the subsequent statements as illegal fruits of a *Miranda* violation. We therefore reverse and remand for further proceedings not inconsistent with this opinion. . . .

Justice O'CONNOR, concurring in part in the judgment and dissenting in part. . . .

Justice MARSHALL, with whom Justice BRENNAN and Justice STEVENS join, dissenting.

The police in this case arrested a man suspected of possessing a firearm in violation of New York law. Once the suspect was in custody and found to be unarmed, the arresting officer initiated an interrogation. Without being advised of his right not to respond, the suspect incriminated himself by locating the gun. The majority concludes that the State may rely on this incriminating statement to convict the suspect of possessing a weapon. I disagree. The arresting officers had no legitimate reason to interrogate the suspect without advising him of his rights to remain silent and to obtain assistance of counsel. By finding on these facts justification for unconsented interrogation, the majority abandons the clear guidelines enunciated in *Miranda v. Arizona* . . . and condemns the American judiciary to a new era of post hoc inquiry into the propriety of custodial interrogations. More significantly and in direct conflict with this Court's long-standing interpretation of the Fifth Amendment, the majority has endorsed the introduction of coerced self-incriminating statements in criminal prosecutions. I dissent. . . .

● ● ● ● ● ● ● ● ● ● ● ● ●

United States v. Wade

Supreme Court of the United States, 1967.
388 U.S. 218, 87 S.Ct. 1926, 18 L.Ed.2d 1149.

[Here the Court considers a suspect's constitutional right to counsel in the context of a post-indictment lineup.]

Mr. Justice BRENNAN delivered the opinion of the court.

The question here is whether courtroom identifications of an accused at trial are to be excluded from evidence because the accused was exhibited to the witnesses before trial at a post-indictment lineup conducted for identification purposes without notice to and in the absence of the accused's appointed counsel.

The federally insured bank in Eustace, Texas, was robbed on September 21, 1964. A man with a small strip of tape on each side of his face entered the bank, pointed a pistol at the female cashier and the vice president, the only persons in the bank at the time, and forced them to fill a pillowcase with the bank's money. The man then drove away with an accomplice who had been waiting in a stolen car outside the bank. On March 23, 1965, an indictment was returned against respondent, Wade, and two others for conspiring to rob the bank, and against Wade and the accomplice for the robbery itself. Wade was arrested on April 2, and counsel was appointed to represent him on April 26. Fifteen days later an FBI agent, without notice to Wade's lawyer, arranged to have the two bank employees observe a lineup made up of Wade and five or six other prisoners and conducted in a courtroom of the local county courthouse. Each person in the line wore strips of tape such as allegedly worn by the robber and upon direction each said something like "put the money in the bag," the words allegedly uttered by the robber. Both bank employees identified Wade in the lineup as the bank robber.

At trial, the two employees, when asked on direct examination if the robber was in the courtroom, pointed to Wade. The prior lineup identification was then elicited from both employees on cross examination. At the close of testimony, Wade's counsel moved for a judgment of acquittal or, alternatively, to strike the bank officials' courtroom identifications on the ground that conduct of the lineup, without notice to and in the absence of his appointed counsel, violated his Fifth Amendment privilege against self-incrimination and his Sixth Amendment right to the assistance of counsel. The motion was denied, and Wade was convicted. The Court of Appeals for the Fifth Circuit reversed the conviction and ordered a new trial at which the in-court identification evidence was to be excluded, holding that, though the lineup did not violate Wade's Fifth Amendment rights, "the lineup, held as it was, in the absence of counsel, already chosen to represent appellant, was a violation of his sixth amendment rights. . . ." We granted certiorari. . . . We reverse the judgment of the court of appeals and remand to that court with direction to enter a new judgment vacating the conviction and remanding the case to the district court for further proceedings consistent with this opinion. . . .

Moreover, it deserves emphasis that this case presents no question of the admissibility in evidence of anything Wade said or did at the lineup which implicates his privilege. The government offered no such evidence as part of its case, and what came out about the lineup proceedings on Wade's cross-examination of the bank employees involved no violation of Wade's privilege. . . .

The fact that the lineup involved no violation of Wade's privilege against self-incrimination does not, however, dispose of his contention that the courtroom identifications should have been excluded because the lineup was conducted without notice to and in the absence of his counsel. . . .

. . . [T]oday's law enforcement machinery involves critical confrontations of the accused by the prosecution at pretrial proceedings where the results might well settle the accused's fate and reduce the trial itself to a mere formality. In recognition of these realities of modern criminal prosecution, our cases have construed the Sixth Amendment guarantee to apply to "critical" stages of the proceedings. The guarantee reads "in all criminal prosecutions, the accused shall enjoy the right . . . to have the assistance of counsel for his defence." The plain wording of this guarantee thus encompasses counsel's assistance whenever necessary to assure a meaningful "defence." . . .

The government characterizes the lineup as a mere preparatory step in the gathering of the prosecution's evidence, not different—for Sixth Amendment purposes—from various other preparatory steps, such as systematized or scientific analyzing of the accused's fingerprints, blood sample, clothing, hair, and the like. We think there are differences which preclude such stages being characterized as critical stages at which the accused has the right to the presence of his counsel. Knowledge of the techniques of science and technology is sufficiently available, and the variables in techniques few enough, that the accused has the opportunity for a meaningful confrontation of the government's case at trial through the ordinary processes of cross examination of the government's expert witnesses and the presentation of the evidence of his own experts. The denial of a right to have his counsel present at such analyses does not therefore violate the Sixth Amendment; they are not critical stages since there is minimal risk that his counsel's absence at such stages might derogate from his right to a fair trial.

. . . [T]he confrontation compelled by the state between the accused and the victim or witnesses to a crime to elicit identification evidence is peculiarly riddled with innumerable dangers and variable factors which might seriously, even crucially, derogate from a fair trial. The vagaries of eyewitness identification are well-known; the annals of criminal law are rife with instances of mistaken identification. . . . A major factor contributing to the high incidence of miscarriage of justice from mistaken identification has been the degree of suggestion inherent in the manner in which the prosecution presents the suspect to witnesses for pretrial identification. . . . Suggestion can be created intentionally or unintentionally in many subtle ways and the dangers for the suspect are particularly grave when the witness' opportunity for observation was insubstantial, and thus his susceptibility to suggestion the greatest.

Moreover, "it is a matter of common experience that, once a witness has picked out the accused at the line-up, he is not likely to go back on his word later on, so that in practice the issue of identity may (in the absence of other relevant evidence) for all practical purposes be determined there and then, before the trial." . . .

Since it appears that there is grave potential for prejudice, intentional or not, in the pretrial lineup, which may not be capable of reconstruction at trial, and since presence of counsel itself can often avert prejudice and assure a meaningful confrontation at trial, there can be little doubt that for Wade the post-indictment lineup was a critical stage of the prosecution at which he was "as much entitled to such aid of counsel . . . as at the trial itself." . . . Thus both Wade and his counsel should have been notified of the impending lineup, and counsel's presence should have been a requisite to conduct of the lineup, absent an "intelligent waiver." . . . No substantial countervailing policy considerations have been advanced against the requirement of the presence of counsel. . . .

We come now to the question whether the denial of Wade's motion to strike the courtroom identification by the bank witnesses at trial because of the absence of his counsel at the lineup required, as the court of appeals held, the grant of a new trial at which such evidence is to be excluded. We do not think this disposition can be justified without first giving the government the opportunity to establish by clear and convincing evidence that the in-court identifications were based upon observations of the suspect other than the lineup identification. . . . Where, as here, the admissibility of evidence of the lineup identification itself is not involved, a per se rule of exclusion of courtroom identification would be unjustified. . . . A rule limited solely to the exclusion of testimony concerning identification at the lineup itself, without regard to admissibility of the courtroom identification, would render the right to counsel an empty one. The lineup is most often used, as in the present case, to crystallize the witnesses' identification of the defendant for future reference. We have already noted that the lineup identification will have that effect. The state may then rest upon the witnesses' unequivocal courtroom identification, and not mention the pretrial identification as part of the state's case at trial. Counsel is then in the predicament in which Wade's counsel found himself—realizing that possible unfairness at the lineup may be the sole means of attack upon the unequivocal courtroom identification, and having to probe in the dark in an attempt to discover and reveal unfairness, while bolstering the government witness' courtroom identification by bringing out and dwelling upon his prior identification. Since counsel's presence at the lineup would equip him to attack not only the lineup identification but the courtroom identification as well, limiting the impact of violation of the right to counsel to exclusion of evidence only of identification at the lineup itself disregards a critical element of that right.

We think it follows that the proper test to be applied in these situations is that quoted in *Wong Sun v. United States*, 371 U.S. 471, 488, "whether, granting establishment of the primary illegality, the evidence to which instant objection is made has been come at by exploitation of that illegality or instead by means sufficiently distinguishable to be purged of the primary taint." . . . Application of this test in the present context requires consideration of various factors; for example, the prior opportunity to observe the alleged criminal act, the existence of any discrepancy between any pre-lineup description and the defendant's actual description, any identification prior to lineup of another person, the identification by picture of the defendant prior to the lineup, failure to identify the defendant on a prior occasion, and the lapse of time between the alleged act and the lineup identification. It is also relevant to consider those facts which, despite the absence of counsel, are disclosed concerning the conduct of the lineup.

We doubt that the court of appeals applied the proper test for exclusion of the in-court identification of the two witnesses. The court stated that "it cannot be said with any certainty that they would have recognized appellant at the time of trial if this intervening lineup had not occurred," and that the testimony of the two witnesses "may well have been colored by the illegal procedure and was prejudicial." . . . Moreover, the court was persuaded, in part, by the "compulsory verbal responses made by Wade at the instance of the special agent." . . . This implies the erroneous holding that Wade's privilege against self-incrimination was violated so that the denial of counsel required exclusion.

On the record now before us we cannot make the determination whether the in-court identifications had an independent origin. This was not an issue at trial, although there is some evidence relevant to a determination. That inquiry is most properly made in the district court. We therefore think the appropriate procedure to be followed is to vacate the conviction pending a hearing to determine whether the in court identifications had an independent source, or whether, in any event, the introduction of the evidence was harmless error . . . and for the district court to reinstate the conviction or order a new trial, as may be proper. . . .

The judgment of the court of appeals is vacated and the case is remanded to that court with direction to enter a new judgment vacating the conviction and remanding the case to the district court for further proceedings consistent with this opinion.

It is so ordered.

The CHIEF JUSTICE joins the opinion of the court [in part]. . . .

Mr. Justice DOUGLAS joins the opinion of the court [in part]. . . .

Mr. Justice CLARK, concurring. . . .

Mr. Justice BLACK, dissenting in part and concurring in part. . . .

Mr. Justice WHITE, whom Mr. Justice HARLAN and Mr. Justice STEWART join, dissenting in part and concurring in part. . . .

The Pretrial Process

Introduction

The United States Constitution and the constitutions of all fifty states guarantee due process of law to all persons accused of criminal wrongdoing. Due process requires that persons accused of crimes be given **fair notice** of criminal charges and an adequate opportunity to contest them. As the Supreme Court has said,

> No principle of procedural due process is more clearly established than that of notice of the specific charge, and a chance to be heard in a trial of the issues raised by that charge, if desired, are among the constitutional rights of every accused in a criminal proceeding, in all courts, state or federal. *Cole v. Arkansas,* 333 U.S. 196, 201, 68 S.Ct. 514, 517, 92 L.Ed. 644, 647 (1948).

For **petty offenses** (minor misdemeanors), due process may require no more than the opportunity for the accused to contest the charge before a magistrate in a single, summary proceeding. For more serious offenses (treason, felonies, and major misdemeanors), the federal and state constitutions impose more elaborate procedural requirements.

As a practical matter, judicial decisions interpreting the generalities of the federal and state constitutions have greatly expanded the procedural rights that must be observed in criminal prosecutions. One result of this judicial activity is that the area of law known as criminal procedure has developed substantially over the past several decades.

Although many people equate the term **criminal procedure** with the criminal trial, the former term is actually much broader. Criminal procedure includes search and seizure, arrest, and interrogation (see Chapters 15 and 16), as well as a variety of other procedures that must occur before a trial can take place. The main components of the pretrial process are the **initial appearance** before a magistrate, the **preliminary hearing,** the **grand jury proceeding,** and the **arraignment.** In addition, judges consider various motions made by the defense and prosecution at pretrial hearings. These pretrial procedures are designed to eliminate from the system those cases for which there is insufficient evidence of criminal wrongdoing and to set the stage for a fair and orderly resolution of cases for which the evidence is sufficiently strong to proceed to trial.

The American public was made aware of the importance of the pretrial process during the latter months of 1994, when the media provided extensive coverage of pretrial procedures in the O. J. Simpson case. What happens during the pretrial process often determines the outcome of a criminal case. Indeed, the overwhelming majority of criminal cases never make it to trial. Some cases are dropped or dismissed for lack of sufficient evidence; many others result in convictions pursuant to guilty pleas. A substantial number of these guilty pleas result from negotiations between prosecutors and defense counsel. In such cases, trials are unnecessary. Where a defendant pleads guilty or no contest to an offense, there is a factual basis for the plea, and the court is satisfied that the plea has been entered voluntarily, guilt is pronounced and the process moves along to the sentencing stage. Given the relative infrequency of trials, pretrial procedures have great importance in the day-to-day operation of the criminal justice system.

The Right to Counsel

Before undertaking a detailed examination of pretrial procedures, we must consider the contours of the **right to counsel,** which is essential to preserving the fundamental fairness of all criminal procedures. The defense attorney not only represents the accused in pretrial court proceedings but also advises on strategy and often serves as the negotiator between the defendant and the prosecutor. Thus, the attorney for the defense plays an essential role in the criminal process. Indeed, in our adversarial legal system, the right to counsel may be the single most important right possessed by persons accused of serious crimes. As the Supreme Court has observed, "[T]he right of one charged with crime to counsel may not be deemed fundamental and essential in some countries, but it is in ours." *Gideon v. Wainwright,* 372 U.S. 335, 344, 83 S.Ct. 792, 796, 9 L.Ed.2d 799, 805 (1963).

Common-Law Background of the Right to Counsel

Under the early English common law, there was no right to counsel for persons accused of treason or felonies. Somewhat ironically, by modern standards, the common law did recognize a right to counsel in misdemeanor cases. See *Argersinger v. Hamlin,* 407 U.S. 25, 92 S.Ct. 2006, 32 L.Ed.2d 530 (1972). In 1698 Parliament enacted a law recognizing a right to counsel in cases of treason. 7 & 8 Will. 3, ch. 3, sec. 1. By the late eighteenth century, the common law recognized a limited right to counsel in felony cases, and in 1836 Parliament passed legislation recognizing the right to counsel for all criminal defendants. 6 & 7 Will. 4, ch. 114, sec. 1. Under the common law and the aforementioned acts of Parliament, the right to counsel meant the right to hire a barrister (a lawyer admitted to trial practice) at a person's own expense. It was not until 1903 that Parliament passed the Poor Prisoner's Defense Act, 3 Edw. 7, ch. 38, sec. 1, requiring that indigent defendants be provided counsel at public expense.

The Modern American Approach

In the United States, the right to counsel has likewise evolved through both judicial decisions and legislation. As the Sixth Amendment to the United States Constitution provides, "In all criminal prosecutions, the accused shall enjoy the right . . . to have the Assistance of Counsel for his defense."

The Sixth Amendment has been consistently interpreted to allow defendants to employ counsel in all federal prosecutions, including treason, felony, and misdemeanor cases. Similar provisions in the fifty state constitutions have been interpreted to allow defendants to retain counsel in state criminal prosecutions. Irrespective of state constitutional protection, the accused is protected by the federal Constitution. In 1963 the Supreme Court held that the Sixth Amendment right to counsel applies to prosecutions in the state courts by way of the Due Process Clause of the Fourteenth Amendment. *Gideon v. Wainwright,* supra. Today, criminal defendants have the right to retain attorneys to represent them in all types of criminal prosecutions, whether in state court, federal court, or before military tribunals.

Indigency and the Right to Counsel

Although criminal defendants have the right to employ attorneys to represent them, many defendants are too poor to afford private counsel. To what extent does the law mandate that they be provided counsel at public expense?

In 1790 Congress first addressed the issue of **indigency** in the context of federal criminal prosecutions for capital crimes. The Judiciary Act of 1790 required federal judges to assign counsel to indigent defendants in capital cases, at least where defendants requested representation. 1 Stat. 118, § 29 (1790). Some states emulated the act of Congress by providing for appointed counsel in capital cases, but most did not.

The Scottsboro Case

In a highly publicized case in the early 1930s, the Supreme Court held that the Fourteenth Amendment required states to observe the requirement long since imposed on federal courts by Congress. *Powell v. Alabama,* 287 U.S. 45, 53 S.Ct. 55, 77 L.Ed. 158 (1932). In the "Scottsboro case," as it has become known, several black youths were charged with raping two white women. Within a week of being arrested, the defendants were tried, convicted, and sentenced to death, all without meaningful assistance of counsel. The Supreme Court reversed their convictions:

> In light of the . . . ignorance and illiteracy of the defendants, their youth, the circumstances of public hostility, the imprisonment and the close surveillance of the defendants by the military forces, the fact that their friends and families were all in other states and communication with them necessarily difficult, and above all that they stood in deadly peril of their lives . . . we think that . . . the failure of the trial court to make an effective appointment of counsel was . . . a denial of due process within the meaning of the Fourteenth Amendment. 287 U.S. at 71, 53 S.Ct. at 65, 77 L.Ed. at 171 (1932).

Relying heavily on its reasoning in *Powell v. Alabama,* the Supreme Court held four years later that the Sixth Amendment requires federal courts to appoint counsel for indigent defendants in all felony cases. *Johnson v. Zerbst,* 304 U.S. 458, 58 S.Ct. 1019, 82 L.Ed. 1461 (1938). Subsequently, Congress enacted the Criminal Justice Act of 1964, 18 U.S.C.A. § 3006A, which provided that all indigent defendants in federal criminal cases are entitled to appointed counsel.

In the wake of *Powell v. Alabama,* many states adopted laws creating a right to counsel at state expense, at least in capital cases. Some states went further by providing counsel for all indigent defendants in felony prosecutions. In states where appointed counsel was not a legal requirement, it was not uncommon for trial judges to appoint new members of the bar to represent indigent felony defendants *pro bono* (free of charge). In so doing, these judges may have anticipated a landmark court decision that was to have a tremendous impact on the criminal justice system.

The *Gideon* Decision

In 1963 the Supreme Court decided that the Fourteenth Amendment requires states to provide counsel to indigent defendants in all felony cases, observing that "any person haled into court, who is too poor to hire a lawyer, cannot be assured a fair trial unless counsel is provided for him." *Gideon v. Wainwright,* supra. The impact of the *Gideon* decision was amplified because it was made retroactive. In Florida, where the *Gideon* case originated, the state was forced to release or retry hundreds of convicted criminals. Other states experienced similar problems. Today, the *Gideon* decision has come to be widely accepted by state officials who recognize that representation by counsel is essential to the fair and effective functioning of the adversary system of justice.

Misdemeanor Defendants

In 1972 the Supreme Court extended the *Gideon* decision to encompass defendants who were sentenced to jail terms for misdemeanors. *Argersinger v. Hamlin,* supra. However, the Court's decision left unresolved the question whether counsel had to be provided to misdemeanor defendants who face possible jail terms, as distinct from those who are actually sentenced to jail. In 1979 the Court opted for the actual imprisonment standard. *Scott v. Illinois,* 440 U.S. 367, 99 S.Ct. 1158, 59 L.Ed.2d 383 (1979). The **actual imprisonment standard** poses a problem for judges, for if an indigent defendant to a misdemeanor charge is denied counsel and is subsequently found guilty, the judge is barred from imposing a jail term. To do so would be a constitutional violation likely to result in a reversal of the defendant's conviction. This places the judge in the anomalous position of having to consider the sentence before determining the guilt of the accused. As a result, several states have gone beyond the federal constitutional requirement announced in *Scott v. Illinois* by providing counsel to indigent defendants in all misdemeanor cases where defendants face possible jail terms.

An excerpt from the U.S. Supreme Court's decision in *Scott v. Illinois* appears at the end of the chapter.

Representation of Indigent Persons at Pretrial Proceedings

Most people think of the right to counsel in terms of a defendant being represented at trial. Although this might be the most important stage of the criminal process for a defendant who pleads not guilty, most criminal cases do not go to trial. For the defendant who elects to plead guilty, the pretrial procedures are critically important. The right of indigent persons to be provided counsel extends to many pretrial procedures. The United States Supreme Court has specifically identified a number of critical stages where counsel must be provided to indigent persons. Such **critical pretrial stages** include preliminary hearings, *White v. Maryland,* 373 U.S. 59, 83 S.Ct. 1050, 10 L.Ed.2d 193 (1963); lineups after charges have been filed against the accused, *United States v. Wade,* 388 U.S. 218, 87 S.Ct. 1926, 18 L.Ed.2d 1149 (1967); post-indictment interrogations, *Massiah v. United States,* 377 U.S. 201, 84 S.Ct. 1199, 12 L.Ed.2d 246 (1964); and arraignments, *Hamilton v. Alabama,* 368 U.S. 52, 82 S.Ct. 157, 7 L.Ed.2d 114 (1961).

Alternative Means of Providing Counsel to Indigent Persons

The representation provided to indigent defendants may take the form of a **public defender** or an attorney appointed ad hoc by the court. Many states have established successful public defender systems. In most states that use this system, the public defender is an elected official provided with funds to hire a staff of lawyers, much like the public prosecutor. In other states, indigent defendants still depend largely on ad hoc appointment of counsel. Very often the attorneys appointed to represent indigent defendants in noncapital cases are new members of the bar with little trial experience. Remuneration for appointed counsel tends to be modest.

There remains considerable controversy over which method of providing counsel is more cost effective and which method more effectively meets a state's constitutional responsibilities. Proponents of the public defender systems note that public defenders are full-time specialists in criminal law, whereas appointed counsel may be relatively inexperienced in the field. Critics of the public defender system express concern about the constant contact between public defenders and prosecutors. They argue that this undermines the adversary system, resulting in a routinization of the criminal process, in which the interests of the accused become subordinated to a bureaucratic effort to maximize efficiency in the processing of cases.

Sometimes the public defender's office has a conflict in which codefendants want to pursue inconsistent defenses. In such instances, an outside attorney should be appointed. If trial counsel representing multiple defendants brings a conflict of interest to the judge's attention, separate counsel must be appointed unless the judge determines that the risk of conflict is remote. *Holloway v. Arkansas,* 435 U.S. 475, 98 S.Ct. 1173, 55 L.Ed.2d 426 (1978). Most states have statutes providing for the appointment of private counsel in instances where public defenders have conflicts, but even in the absence of such statutes, courts generally take the position that they have the inherent authority to make such appointments.

Determining Who Is Indigent

Federal law leaves the determination of indigency to the discretion of the courts. This is also the case in most states. See, for example, Vernon's Ann. Tex. Code Crim. P. art. 26.04(a). Courts tend to be liberal in this regard, refusing to equate indigency with destitution, and are generally inclined to appoint counsel if the cost of hiring a lawyer would prevent the defendant from making **bail** (posting a bond to secure pretrial release).

After arrest, the accused is asked to complete a form to elicit information about employment, income, assets, and liabilities. Before the defendant's first appearance in court, judicial staff persons will attempt to verify the accuracy of the defendant's statement. This information is then passed along to assist the magistrate in determining whether the defendant is entitled to appointed counsel. In most jurisdictions, more than 75 percent of felony defendants are classified as indigent. Some state statutes provide for an assessment of an attorney's fee against a defendant who is represented by the public defender's office. See, for example, *Valdez v. State,* 632 So.2d 655 (Fla. App. 1994). An indigent defendant may be assessed the costs of appointed counsel, and these costs may be collected at some later time if the defendant becomes solvent. See *Fuller v. Oregon,* 417 U.S. 40, 94 S.Ct. 2116, 40 L.Ed.2d 642 (1974).

Self-Representation

The Supreme Court has held that there is a constitutional right to represent oneself in a criminal prosecution. *Faretta v. California,* 422 U.S. 806, 95 S.Ct. 2525, 45 L.Ed.2d 562 (1975). In *Faretta,* the Court said that the defendant's legal knowledge or skill has no bearing on the right to **self-representation.** However, the Court stressed that the defendant who waives the right to counsel and proceeds *pro se* must do so "knowingly and intelligently." Critics of the *Faretta* decision believe that criminal law and procedure have become too complex and technical to permit the nonlawyer defendant to engage in effective self-representation. They argue that due process requires that defendants be represented by trained counsel, lest fundamental fairness be denied. As the Supreme Court recognized in *Powell v. Alabama,*

> Even the intelligent and educated layman has small and sometimes no skill in the science of the law. If charged with a crime, he is incapable, generally, of determining for himself whether the indictment is good or bad. He is unfamiliar with the rules of evidence. Left without the aid of counsel he may be put on trial without a proper charge, and convicted upon incompetent evidence, or evidence irrelevant to the issue or otherwise inadmissible. He lacks both the skill and knowledge adequately to prepare his defense, even though he may have a perfect one. He requires the guiding hand of counsel at every step in the proceedings against him. Without it, though he be not guilty, he faces a danger of conviction because he does not know how to establish his innocence. 287 U.S. 45, 69, 53 S.Ct. 55, 64, 77 L.Ed. 158, 170 (1932).

Despite the potential dangers of the *pro se* defense, the Supreme Court held in *Faretta* that the Constitution places the defendant's "free choice" above the need for effective representation in a criminal trial. The constitutional issue aside, many lawyers have said that "the defendant who chooses to represent himself has a fool for a client!"

In 1984 the Supreme Court ruled that a defendant "does not have a constitutional right to receive personal instruction from the trial judge on courtroom procedure. Nor does the Constitution require the judge to take over chores for a *pro se* defendant that would normally be attended to by trained counsel as a matter of course." *McKaskle v. Wiggins,* 465 U.S. 168, 183–184, 104 S.Ct. 944, 954, 79 L.Ed.2d 122, 136–137 (1984). Moreover, the constitutional right to self-representation does not imply a right to obstruct the workings of the criminal process. A trial judge may terminate self-representation by a defendant who engages in obstructionist conduct. *Illinois v. Allen,* 397 U.S. 337, 90 S.Ct. 1057, 25 L.Ed.2d 353 (1970).

Judges sometimes appoint standby counsel to assist defendants who choose self-representation. There are two principal advantages: (1) standby counsel can be available to answer questions by a *pro se* defendant, and (2) if it is necessary to terminate the *pro se* defense because of misconduct, standby counsel is available to complete the case.

Although a defendant has the right to self-representation, he or she may not be represented by another person who is not a member of the bar. Nor may a defendant force an unwilling attorney to represent him or her. *Wheat v. United States,* 486 U.S. 153, 108 S.Ct. 1692, 100 L.Ed.2d 140 (1988). By the same token, a trial judge does have the discretion to deny an attorney's motion to withdraw from representation—after, of course, examining counsel's reasons for wanting to withdraw.

Disposition of Petty Offenses

Minor misdemeanors are often disposed through **summary justice.** In such cases, the accused is usually not placed under arrest, but is simply issued a **summons** to appear in court to answer the charges. In many cases, such as motor vehicle infractions, the individual who is charged may simply elect to waive this court appearance and satisfy the charge by paying a predetermined fine. If the individual appears in court to contest the charges, the entire matter is typically resolved in one proceeding. The accused enters a plea ("not guilty," "guilty," or "no contest"), evidence is taken, and a verdict is rendered by the judge. If the defendant is found guilty, sentence is generally pronounced immediately. Although defendants clearly have a right to hire attorneys to represent them in minor misdemeanor cases, few exercise this right. Most people would rather go it alone before the magistrate. If they lose, which is highly probable, they typically pay a fine, which tends to be substantially less expensive than hiring an attorney. As noted earlier, the Supreme Court has said that there is no constitutional right for indigent persons to have counsel appointed in such minor cases, except where defendants are actually sentenced to jail terms. *Scott v. Illinois,* supra.

The Initial Court Appearance

In major misdemeanor and felony cases, the procedure is much more complex and protracted. Typically, individuals charged with felonies are placed under arrest before any appearance in court. However, all persons placed under arrest must promptly be taken before a court of law. The purpose of the initial appearance is to begin the formal charging process. Essentially, the magistrate must perform three important functions at the initial appearance: (1) the charges must be read so that the accused knows exactly what he or she is being charged with; (2) the accused must be informed of relevant constitutional rights, including the right to remain silent and the right to counsel; and (3) a determination must be made of whether the accused should be released pending trial or remanded to custody to await the disposition of the case. As we shall discuss, the court may order the defendant to post bond in order to ensure future court appearances. If so, the amount of bail is determined at this time.

All jurisdictions require the prompt appearance of an arrestee before a court of law, but what constitutes "prompt"? Many jurisdictions require a suspect to be brought before a magistrate for an initial appearance within twenty-four hours after arrest. See, for example, Fla. R. Crim. P. Rule 3.130 (a). However, the U.S. Supreme Court has ruled that suspects may be detained for as long as forty-eight hours before being taken before a magistrate. *County of Riverside v. McLaughlin,* 500 U.S. 44, 111 S.Ct. 1661, 114 L.Ed.2d 49 (1991).

Rule 5(a) of the Federal Rules of Criminal Procedure provides that a person arrested for a federal offense shall be taken before a magistrate "without unnecessary delay" for a first appearance. Under the so-called *McNabb–Mallory* rule (see *McNabb v. United States,* 318 U.S. 332, 63 S.Ct. 608, 87 L.Ed. 819 [1943], and *Mallory v. United States,* 354 U.S. 449, 77 S.Ct. 1356, 1 L.Ed.2d 1479 [1957]), confessions made during periods of detention that violate the prompt presentment requirement of Rule 5(a) are inadmissible at trial. Under 18 U.S.C.A. § 3501(c), however, Congress provided that a confession made within six hours after arrest is not rendered inadmissible solely because of delay in bringing the accused before the magistrate.

In *Alvarez-Sanchez v. United States,* 975 F.2d 1396 (9th Cir. 1992), the U.S. Court of Appeals for the Ninth Circuit reversed a federal counterfeiting conviction based on the delay in the pretrial process. The defendant was originally arrested on a Friday by state authorities on state charges. A search of his home turned up evidence of counterfeit U.S. currency. On Monday, federal agents took the defendant into custody and obtained a confession. Because of congestion in court, the defendant was not taken before a federal magistrate until Tuesday. The Ninth Circuit held that the confession could not be used as evidence because of the delay in the first appearance. In reversing the Court of Appeals, the Supreme Court held that the promptness requirement is inapplicable where an accused person is first arrested on state charges and then later turned over to federal authorities on related charges. *United States v. Alvarez-Sanchez,* 511 U.S. 350, 114 S.Ct. 1599, 128 L.Ed.2d 319 (1994). The Court said that the duty to bring an accused person before a federal magistrate does not arise until that person has been arrested for a federal offense.

Pretrial Release and Pretrial Detention

The most important thing to a person who has been arrested and confined to jail is to secure release as soon as possible. Beyond the obvious desirability of freedom, an accused who remains at liberty can be of considerable assistance to defense counsel in locating witnesses and by being able to confer with counsel outside the jail setting. In addition, a person who remains at liberty can usually pursue gainful employment and discharge family responsibilities pending the disposition of the criminal charges.

Granting an accused **pretrial release** is commonly referred to as granting bail. The authority to grant a defendant bail has a common-law origin. *State v. Konigsberg,* 164 A.2d 740 (N.J. 1960). Today the authority is commonly granted by statutes or court rules. In determining whether a defendant is entitled to pretrial release, the court usually considers the accused's prior convictions (if any), character, employment history, and ties to family and the community, as well as the nature and scope of the current charges. In making these determinations, judges rely on reports prepared by court personnel. In the federal system, these reports are prepared by an agency called Pretrial Services. Increasingly, courts are requiring that arrested persons be drug tested. Although not used as evidence, the results of the drug test help inform the judge whether to grant pretrial release and whether to impose conditions upon that release. As with probation and parole, pretrial release may be contingent on a defendant's willingness to abide by certain conditions, such as avoiding certain places or activities, or remaining at home after dark.

Modes of Pretrial Release

Pretrial release can take several forms. The four most common are **release on personal recognizance,** release to the custody of another, posting an individual bond, and posting a **surety bond:**

- *Personal recognizance.* A recognizance is a person's promise to appear in court as required. The defendant signs a guarantee to appear at all required proceedings and, in some cases, acknowledges certain restrictions on his or her activities.

- *Release to the custody of another.* The magistrate may release the defendant to the custody of some responsible person, often the defendant's attorney, who agrees to exercise custodial supervision and to assume responsibility for the defendant's required court appearances.

- *Posting an individual bond.* The defendant posts a bond agreeing to appear in court as required. The defendant may or may not be required to post an amount of cash or other security to guarantee the undertaking.

- *Posting a surety bond.* This is the historic bail-bond method of securing pretrial release. The magistrate sets the amount of a bond for the particular offense. Often, this is based on a schedule of bonds set by the judge of the court having jurisdiction over the offense. The defendant signs the bond, agreeing to appear as required. The bond is guaranteed by the defendant's surety, which means that should the defendant default, the surety, usually an insurance company, is bound to pay the court the amount of the bond (called the "penal sum"). A defendant usually pays a premium of about 10 percent of the amount of the bond and in most instances provides the surety with collateral to induce the surety to sign the bond. Sureties bonding a defendant are responsible for ensuring the defendant's appearance; therefore, they are commonly given the statutory authority to arrest an absconding defendant. To this end, sureties often employ **skip tracers,** who are, in effect, modern bounty hunters who seek out and return an absconding defendant. When a surety promptly produces a defendant, it can usually recover any money forfeited to the court because of the defendant's failure to appear.

The Issue of Excessive Bail

Recognizing the common-law practice of allowing pretrial release on bail, the Eighth Amendment to the federal Constitution states that "excessive bail shall not be required." The Supreme Court has made it clear that the purpose of bail is to ensure the appearance of the accused in court, not to inflict punishment: "Bail set at a figure higher than an amount reasonably calculated to fulfill this purpose is 'excessive' under the Eighth Amendment." *Stack v. Boyle,* 342 U.S. 1, 5, 72 S.Ct. 1, 3, 96 L.Ed.

3, 6 (1951). However, the Supreme Court has never held that the Excessive Bail Clause of the Eighth Amendment is enforceable against the states via the Fourteenth Amendment, leaving the matter of **excessive bail** in state criminal cases to the state constitutions, state legislatures, and state courts.

The Illinois Code of Criminal Procedure provides that "the amount of bail shall be: (1) Sufficient to assure compliance with the conditions set forth in the bail bond; (2) Not oppressive; (3) Considerate of the financial ability of the accused." S.H.A. 725 ILCS 5/110–5. Similarly, the Texas Code of Criminal Procedure states that "the power to require bail is not to be so used as to make it an instrument of oppression." Vernon's Ann. Tex. Code Crim. P. art. 17.15(2).

Pretrial Detention

The constitutional prohibition of "excessive bail" is vague regarding the existence of a constitutional right to pretrial release. However, the Supreme Court has ruled that there is no right to bail under the Eighth Amendment. *United States v. Salerno*, 481 U.S. 739, 107 S.Ct. 2095, 95 L.Ed.2d 697 (1987). The **Federal Bail Reform Act of 1984**, 18 U.S.C.A. § 3141 et seq., allows federal courts to detain arrestees without bail on the ground of the arrestee's danger to the community, as well as the need to ensure future court appearances.

First, the court must determine whether the government has established "by a preponderance of the evidence that the defendant either has been charged with one of the crimes enumerated in Section 3142(f)(1) or that the defendant presents a risk of flight or obstruction of justice." *United States v. Friedman*, 837 F.2d 48, 49 (2d Cir. 1988). If the government satisfies that burden, the court must determine if there are "conditions or a combination of conditions which reasonably will assure the presence of the defendant at trial." *United States v. Shakur*, 817 F.2d 189 (2d Cir. 1987). Congress has set forth various factors that a court must consider in weighing the appropriateness of **pretrial detention.** Among these are the nature of the offense, the weight of the evidence against the suspect, the history and character of the person charged, and the nature and seriousness of the risk to the community. 18 U.S.C.A. § 3142(g). The statute provides for an adversary hearing on the issue of detention. The government must show by clear and convincing evidence that pretrial release will not reasonably ensure the appearance of the accused and the safety of other persons and the community. *United States v. Orta*, 760 F.2d 877 (8th Cir. 1985).

The judge or magistrate who denies pretrial release must prepare a written statement justifying the decision to detain the accused and direct that the detainee be afforded a reasonable opportunity for private consultation with counsel. 18 U.S.C.A. § 3142(i). Finally, the law provides for immediate appellate review of the detention decision. 18 U.S.C.A. § 3145(c). In upholding the Bail Reform Act of 1984 against an Eighth Amendment challenge, the Supreme Court in *United States v. Salerno* said that "when Congress has mandated detention on the basis of a compelling interest other than prevention of flight, as it has here, the Eighth Amendment does not require release on bail." 481 U.S. at 754–755, 107 S.Ct. at 2105, 95 L.Ed.2d at 713–714.

The *Salerno* decision, although technically limited to the constitutionality of federal pretrial detention, suggests the validity of state laws or court decisions that deny bail to persons accused of violent crimes, especially where arrestees have a record of violent crime.

In many states, a defendant is ineligible for pretrial release if charged with a crime punishable by death or life imprisonment and if the "proof is evident or the presumption [of guilt] is great." See, for example, *State v. Arthur*, 390 So.2d 717, 718 (Fla. 1980).

The Supreme Court's decision in *United States v. Salerno* is excerpted at the end of this chapter.

In the majority of these states, before denying pretrial release, courts must determine whether the facts, viewed in the light most favorable to the state, are legally sufficient to sustain a verdict of guilty. See *Fountaine v. Mullen,* 366 A.2d 1138 (R.I. 1976).

The Formal Charging Process

Prosecutors occupy a uniquely important role in the criminal justice system. The prosecutor decides whether to proceed with a criminal case and whether to negotiate charges with the defense, and must, at various stages of the process, demonstrate the veracity of the government's case to the satisfaction of the court. The prosecutor causes the court to issue subpoenas to compel the attendance of witnesses to testify, to bring in documents, and to provide nontestimonial physical evidence such as handwriting specimens, *United States v. Mara,* 410 U.S. 19, 93 S.Ct. 774, 35 L.Ed.2d 99 (1973), and voice exemplars, *United States v. Dionisio,* 410 U.S. 1, 93 S.Ct. 764, 35 L.Ed.2d 67 (1973).

State and federal prosecutors have broad discretion in deciding whether to proceed with criminal charges initiated by a complainant or the police. The prosecutor may decide to drop a case for a variety of reasons, ranging from insufficient evidence to a judgment that the criminal sanction is inappropriate in a given situation. Alternatively, the prosecutor may decide to proceed on a lesser charge.

The American Bar Association's Standards Relating to the Prosecution and Defense Function offers prosecutors guidelines for the exercise of their discretion in making the decision to charge. The standards admonish prosecutors not to be influenced by personal or political motivations and not to bring more charges, in number or degree, than can reasonably be supported at trial.

Prosecutorial discretion facilitates the widespread yet controversial practice of **plea bargaining,** which we discuss later in the chapter. Although very broad, prosecutorial discretion is not unlimited. The Equal Protection Clause of the Fourteenth

CASE-IN-POINT

Racially Motivated Prosecution

One of the long-standing controversies in the criminal justice field is whether police and prosecutors unfairly target people on the basis of race in the enforcement of certain types of criminal prohibitions. In 1996 the United States Supreme Court made it more difficult for criminal defendants to make prosecutors respond to claims that they are engaging in racially motivated selective prosecution. Five African Americans charged with selling crack cocaine persuaded lower courts to dismiss the charges against them because prosecutors refused to explain how they chose which crack cocaine cases to pursue. Dividing 8–1, with only Justice Stevens in dissent, the Court held that defendants who make selective-prosecution claims must show that people of other races were not prosecuted for the same crimes. "To establish a discriminatory effect in a race case, the claimant must show that similarly situated individuals of a different race were not prosecuted," Chief Justice William H. Rehnquist wrote for the court. Because the defendants did not make such a showing, the prosecutors were not required to respond to their allegation of discrimination. In his solo dissent, Justice Stevens stressed "the need for judicial vigilance over certain types of drug prosecutions," referring to the fact that the overwhelming majority of individuals charged with offenses involving crack cocaine are black.

United States v. Armstrong, 517 U.S. 456, 116 S.Ct. 1480, 134 L.Ed.2d 687 (1996).

CASE-IN-POINT

Limitations on Prosecutorial Conduct

E. J. Reagan was charged with torturing a child and assault with intent to do great bodily harm. The prosecutor agreed to drop the charges if Reagan could pass a lie detector test. The defendant agreed and passed the test. Pursuant to the agreement, the prosecutor filed a *nolle prosequi*, and the charges were dismissed. Subsequently, the prosecutor be-came convinced that the polygraph examination was flawed. He then filed a new complaint on the same charges. The defendant was tried and convicted. The Michigan Supreme Court reversed the conviction and discharged the defendant. The court said that "a pledge of public faith in this instance gave force to an unwise agreement."

People v. Reagan, 235 N.W.2d 581, 587 (Mich. 1975).

Amendment is offended by **selective prosecution.** Prosecutors may not single out defendants for prosecution on the basis of race, religion, or other impermissible classifications. *Oyler v. Boles,* 368 U.S. 448, 82 S.Ct. 501, 7 L.Ed.2d 446 (1962).

Courts have not only cloaked prosecutors with broad discretion in determining whether to prosecute, but they have also long held prosecutors immune from civil actions for malicious prosecution, as long as they are acting within the scope of their offices. *Griffith v. Slinkard,* 44 N.E. 1001 (Ind. 1896). More recently, the United States Supreme Court has ruled that the same considerations that underlie **prosecutorial immunity** in tort actions require that prosecutors be immune from damages for deprivation of defendants' constitutional rights under 42 U.S.C.A. § 1983. See *Imbler v. Pachtman,* 424 U.S. 409, 96 S.Ct. 984, 47 L.Ed.2d 128 (1976).

Determining the Sufficiency of the Government's Case

Assuming that the prosecutor decides to proceed with criminal charges, an examination of the sufficiency of the evidence generally follows. The purpose of this procedure is to ensure that there is probable cause for trial. This determination is made by a magistrate, a grand jury, or both. In some jurisdictions, the prosecutor files a document called an **information** in the appropriate court of law. An information is a formal accusatorial document detailing the specific charges against a defendant. After the filing of the information, a **preliminary hearing** may be requested to determine the sufficiency of the evidence in support of the information. In other jurisdictions, the prosecutor must obtain an indictment from a grand jury. Some jurisdictions employ a combination of both mechanisms. In Tennessee, for example, a person accused of a felony must be indicted by a grand jury; a preliminary examination before the grand jury proceeding is available at the option of the accused. Tenn. R. Crim. P., Rule 5.1.

The Preliminary Hearing

In a preliminary hearing (not to be confused with the initial appearance discussed above), a judge or magistrate examines the state's case to determine whether there is probable cause to bind the accused over to the grand jury or (in the absence of a grand jury requirement) hold the accused for trial. The Supreme Court has said that when an arrest is made without a warrant, a preliminary hearing is constitutionally required in the absence of grand jury review to determine the sufficiency of an information.

Gerstein v. Pugh, 420 U.S. 103, 95 S.Ct. 854, 43 L.Ed.2d 54 (1975). However, *Gerstein* does not require preliminary hearings to be full-blown adversarial proceedings. Nevertheless, most states do provide for open hearings with both parties represented. Typically, in a preliminary hearing the defense has the privilege of cross-examining witnesses for the prosecution and can learn the details and strengths of the state's case. The state can preserve testimony of witnesses who may balk at testifying at the trial. Thus, the preliminary hearing serves the interests of both the prosecution and the defense by providing an inquiry into probable cause for arrest and detention, a screening device for prosecutors, and an opportunity for the defense to discover the prosecutor's case.

The Grand Jury

In many jurisdictions, prosecutors must obtain an indictment or "true bill" from the grand jury in addition to, or instead of, the preliminary hearing. The Fifth Amendment to the United States Constitution states that "[n]o person shall be held to answer for a capital, or otherwise infamous crime, unless on a presentment or indictment of a grand jury."

The Supreme Court has held that states are not bound by the Fourteenth Amendment to abide by the grand jury requirement imposed on the federal courts by the Fifth Amendment. *Hurtado v. California,* 110 U.S. 516, 4 S.Ct. 111, 28 L.Ed. 232 (1884). Nevertheless, about half the states have constitutional provisions or statutes requiring the use of grand juries in certain types of criminal cases. Other states use the grand jury primarily in an investigatory or supervisory capacity.

The grand jury is an institution deeply rooted in the common law. For detailed discussion, see *Costello v. United States,* 350 U.S. 359, 362, 76 S.Ct. 406, 408, 100 L.Ed. 397, 401 (1956). At common law, the grand jury comprised twenty-three persons, at least twelve of whom had to agree to hand down an indictment. Today, federal grand juries comprise sixteen to twenty-three persons, Fed. R. Crim. P. 6(a), but the "12-votes for indictment" rule applies in every case, Fed. R. Crim. P. 6(f). States vary in the size of grand juries, but in every state at least a majority of grand jurors must agree that there is probable cause for trial to hand down an **indictment** against the accused. In Texas, for example, the grand jury consists of twelve jurors. Texas Const., Art. V, § 13. At least nine grand jurors must agree to hand down an indictment. Vernon's Ann. Tex. Code Crim. P. Art. 20.19.

Exclusion of Minorities from Grand Juries

As with trial jurors, the selection of grand jurors must not systematically exclude certain groups in the community. A defendant may be able to obtain a reversal of a conviction on this basis. For example, in *Castaneda v. Partida,* 430 U.S. 482, 97 S.Ct. 1272, 51 L.Ed.2d 498 (1977), the Supreme Court reversed a conviction after finding that Mexican Americans had been grossly underrepresented on a grand jury that indicted a Mexican American defendant. In his opinion for the Court, Justice Harry Blackmun outlined the necessary steps to make a case that such a violation has occurred:

> . . . [I]n order to show that an equal protection violation has occurred in the context of grand jury selection, the defendant must show that the procedure employed resulted in substantial underrepresentation of his race or of the identifiable group to which he belongs. The first step is to establish that the group is one that is a recognizable, distinct class, singled out for different treatment under the laws, as written or as applied. . . . Next, the degree of underrepresentation must be proved, by

comparing the proportion of the group in the total population to the proportion called to serve as grand jurors, over a significant period of time. . . . This method of proof, sometimes called the "rule of exclusion," has been held to be available as a method of proving discrimination in jury selection against a delineated class. . . . Finally, . . . a selection procedure that is susceptible of abuse or is not racially neutral supports the presumption of discrimination raised by the statistical showing. . . . Once the defendant has shown substantial underrepresentation of his group, he has made out a *prima facie* case of discriminatory purpose, and the burden then shifts to the State to rebut that case. 430 U.S. at 494, 97 S.Ct. at 1280, 51 L.Ed.2d at 510–511 (1977).

Functions and Powers of the Grand Jury

Historically, the grand jury acted as a shield to prevent unfounded charges and arbitrary and overzealous prosecution. Today, grand juries seldom refuse to hand down indictments sought by prosecutors, causing some critics to question the institution's use as a safeguard for the rights of the accused. Perhaps this perception has led several states to adopt the information or preliminary hearing mechanism in lieu of the grand jury. In most midwestern and western states, the grand jury is seldom used to charge persons with crimes.

The grand jury, like the magistrate presiding over the preliminary hearing, examines testimony and other evidence the prosecution has collected against the accused. Unlike the preliminary hearing, the grand jury proceeding is normally closed: The defendant is generally not represented by counsel or even present at the proceeding. Testimony before the grand jury is not always transcribed, and if it is, access to transcripts is either limited or nonexistent. Although controversial, grand jury secrecy encourages uninhibited testimony by witnesses and prevents the circulation of derogatory statements about persons who are ultimately not indicted. *Pittsburgh Plate Glass Co. v. United States,* 360 U.S. 395, 79 S.Ct. 1237, 3 L.Ed.2d 1323 (1959). As noted in *United States v. Procter & Gamble Co.,* 356 U.S. 677, 78 S.Ct. 983, 2 L.Ed.2d 1077 (1958), grand jury secrecy also protects grand jurors from intimidation and possible reprisals.

After the prosecutor has presented testimony and physical evidence, the members of the grand jury vote whether to hand down an indictment. Rules that determine grand jury indictments vary among jurisdictions, but in no case can a grand jury return a true bill unless a majority of grand jurors vote to indict.

Grand juries possess the authority to compel the appearance of witnesses, to **subpoena** documents, to hold individuals in contempt, and to grant **immunity** from prosecution in exchange for testimony. Immunity is of two kinds. **Transactional immunity** bars any further prosecution of the witness for the specific transaction to which the witness testified. **Use immunity** is more limited, barring only the use of the witness's testimony against the witness in a subsequent prosecution. Federal grand juries are authorized to grant use immunity. 18 U.S.C.A. § 6002. Many states follow the federal statute; some states go further and permit grand juries to grant transactional immunity. The federal statutory bar against the use of immunized testimony applies equally to federal and state proceedings. *In re Grand Jury Proceedings,* 860 F.2d 11 (2d Cir. 1988).

Rights of Witnesses and Suspects

The Supreme Court has held that grand jury witnesses retain their Fifth Amendment privileges against compulsory self-incrimination. *Lefkowitz v. Turley,* 414 U.S. 70, 94 S.Ct. 316, 38 L.Ed.2d 274 (1973). Nevertheless, through a limited grant of immunity, a grand jury can override a witness's refusal to answer questions on Fifth Amendment grounds. The Supreme Court has also held that a grand jury's grant of immunity must be coextensive with the privilege against self-incrimination. Use immunity satisfies this requirement; transactional immunity is not required by the Constitution. *Kastigar v. United States,* 406 U.S. 441, 92 S.Ct. 1653, 32 L.Ed.2d 212 (1972).

Witnesses testifying before grand juries have no right to be represented by counsel, *In re Groban's Petition,* 352 U.S. 330, 77 S.Ct. 510, 1 L.Ed.2d 376 (1957), although some jurisdictions allow witnesses to consult with counsel outside the grand jury room. An attorney's appearance before a grand jury on behalf of a witness is generally thought to cause unnecessary delays and violate the secrecy of the proceeding.

A suspect is not afforded the same degree of legal protection against the grand jury as in a criminal trial. In only a few states does the defendant have a right to appear before the grand jury to confront his or her accusers. Like witnesses, a suspect has no federal constitutional right to be represented by counsel inside the grand jury room. *United States v. Mandujano,* 425 U.S. 564, 96 S.Ct. 1768, 48 L.Ed.2d 212 (1976).

Evidence Before the Grand Jury

Many rules of evidence that apply to the criminal trial do not apply to the grand jury. *Costello v. United States,* 350 U.S. 359, 76 S.Ct. 406, 100 L.Ed. 397 (1956). For example, hearsay evidence is generally admissible, whereas at trial, it is not admitted over the defendant's objection. Moreover, evidence excluded from trial on Fourth or Fifth Amendment grounds is admissible before the grand jury. *United States v. Calandra,* 414 U.S. 338, 94 S.Ct. 613, 38 L.Ed.2d 561 (1974). The theory is, of course, that the grand jury is an investigative body and that any infringement of the rights of the accused can be corrected in subsequent adversary court proceedings. Notwithstanding that a grand jury may consider evidence that is inadmissible at trial, it may not violate a valid evidentiary privilege (see Chapter 18), whether established by the Constitution, statutes, or the common law. *Branzburg v. Hayes,* 408 U.S. 665, 92 S.Ct. 2646, 33 L.Ed.2d 626 (1972).

> The Supreme Court's decision in *United States v. Calandra* is excerpted at the end of the chapter.

Right to a Prompt Indictment

Both federal and state courts have ruled that constitutional due process standards require dismissal of an indictment, even if it is brought within the applicable statute of limitations period, if the defendant can prove that the prosecution's delay in bringing the indictment was a deliberate device to gain an advantage over the defendant and that it caused the defendant actual prejudice in presenting a defense. See, for example, *United States v. Rein,* 848 F.2d 777 (7th Cir. 1988); *State v. Smith,* 699 P.2d 711 (Utah 1985).

Extradition

Extradition is the surrender, on demand, of an individual accused or convicted of an offense within the territorial jurisdiction of the demanding government and outside the territory of the ceding government. See *Terlinden v. Ames,* 184 U.S. 270, 22 S.Ct. 484, 46 L.Ed. 534 (1902). The objective is to prevent escape of persons who stand accused or convicted of crimes and to secure their return to the jurisdiction from which they fled.

In a mobile society such as ours, it is not uncommon for persons accused of crimes to flee across state lines to avoid prosecution. Anticipating this problem, Article IV, Section 2 of the Constitution provides that

> [a] Person charged in any State with Treason, Felony or any other crime, who shall flee from Justice, and be found in another state, shall on demand of the executive Authority of the State from which he fled, be delivered up, to be removed to the State having Jurisdiction of the crime.

To effectuate the constitutional provision, Congress has enacted statutes governing interstate extradition. 18 U.S.C.A. § 3182. Interstate extradition is a summary executive proceeding designed to enable each state to bring offenders to trial swiftly in the state where the alleged crime was committed. *Michigan v. Doran*, 439 U.S. 282, 99 S.Ct. 530, 58 L.Ed.2d 521 (1978). Every offense punishable by law of a jurisdiction where it was committed can be subject to extradition, but extradition is usually sought only in serious offenses. Frequently it is used to regain custody of parole violators, prison escapees, or those persons who have "jumped bail."

Most states have adopted the Uniform Criminal Extradition Law, which sets out procedural rules for handling interstate extradition. The governor of the "demanding" state issues a requisition warrant seeking return of the fugitive. This is presented to the governor of the "asylum" state (that is, the state in which the fugitive is located). After investigation, the governor of the asylum state issues a warrant for the fugitive's arrest. An opportunity exists for the person sought as a fugitive to contest the extradition in a court of law in the asylum state. Often this challenge takes the form of a petition for a writ of habeas corpus challenging whether the petitioner is in fact the person charged or attacking the regularity of the proceedings. See, for example, N.J. Stat. Ann. § 2A: 160–18. Such proceedings seek the release of the prisoner who is to be extradited but do not focus on the issue of the prisoner's guilt or innocence.

Jurisdiction and Venue

Before it may hear and adjudicate a case, a court must possess **jurisdiction** over the subject matter and the parties to the case. State courts have jurisdiction only over persons who commit crimes in their particular states. Of course, it is necessary for a court to acquire jurisdiction over a person before that individual can be tried for an offense. This is generally accomplished through an arrest warrant or a **capias.** The former is issued by a court following an indictment; the latter is issued after a prosecutor has filed an information.

The term **venue** is sometimes confused with the concept of jurisdiction, but it is a distinct concept. Venue refers to the place of the trial, and its importance is underscored by the fact that it is twice mentioned in the U.S. Constitution. As Article III, Section 2 provides, in part,

> Trial shall be held in the State where the said crimes shall have been committed; but when not committed within the State, the Trial shall be at such Place or Places as the Congress may by law have directed.

As the Sixth Amendment provides, "In all criminal prosecutions, the accused shall enjoy the right to a . . . public trial, by an impartial jury of the State and district wherein the crime shall have been committed."

The Sixth Amendment applies to state criminal trials via the Fourteenth Amendment. *Duncan v. Louisiana*, 391 U.S. 145, 88 S.Ct. 1444, 20 L.Ed.2d 491 (1968).

State constitutions, statutes, or court rules usually mirror the provisions of the Sixth Amendment.

Federal courts sit in all fifty states, as well as in federal territories. In some states, federal court jurisdiction is divided into two or more districts. A federal offense is normally tried in the particular federal district where the crime was committed. State courts are usually organized by districts of one or more counties. Likewise, a state criminal case is tried in the particular jurisdiction (district, county, circuit, and so forth) where the offense was committed.

Although venue lies in the district where the offense was committed, there are unique situations in which the nature of the crime makes it difficult to determine in which of two districts the crime occurred. For example, consider the situation where a person fires a rifle across a county or state line, killing a victim in the adjoining county or state. A more probable scenario is a kidnapping in which the perpetrator takes the victim across county or state lines. Courts must resolve these jurisdictional quandaries according to the relevant statutes and precedents.

Defendants commonly seek a **change of venue** if they believe it is impossible to obtain a fair trial in the venue in which the crime occurred. Rule 21(a) of the Federal Rules of Criminal Procedure stipulates the following:

> The court upon motion of the defendant shall transfer the proceeding as to that defendant to another district . . . if the court is satisfied that there exists in the district where the prosecution is pending so great a prejudice against the defendant that the defendant cannot obtain a fair and impartial trial at any place fixed for holding court in that district.

State statutes and court rules generally contain similar provisions. Indeed, some states permit prosecutors to seek a change of venue. See, for example, Fla. R. Crim. P. 3.240. In determining whether to grant a change of venue, courts consider a variety of factors, including (1) the nature of the pretrial publicity and the degree to which it has circulated in the community, (2) the connection of government officials with the release of the publicity, (3) the length of time elapsing between the dissemination of the publicity and the trial, (4) the severity and notoriety of the offense, (5) the area from which the jury is to be drawn, (6) other events occurring in the community that either affect or reflect the attitude of the community or individual jurors toward the defendants, and (7) any factor likely to affect the candor and veracity of the prospective jurors. See, for example, *State v. Bell,* 315 So.2d 307 (La. 1975).

A defendant seeking a change of venue bears the burden of showing the necessity for the change. Changing venue can offend the community sense of justice in not having a trial take place within the community. In addition, it can create hardships and inefficiencies because of the need to transport witnesses and court personnel to sometimes distant locations. Because a decision to change venue depends on many factors that can best be determined by the local judge, trial courts are accorded considerable discretion in determining whether to grant a motion to change venue in a criminal case.

Joinder and Severance

Very often, a defendant stands accused of several distinct offenses arising from one set of related facts. Conceivably, each offense could be prosecuted separately, but it would be more efficient, in most instances, to prosecute such offenses jointly.

Most state rules of criminal procedure follow the federal rule on **joinder of offenses:**

> Two or more offenses may be charged in the same indictment or information in a separate count for each offense if the offenses charged, whether felonies or misdemeanors or both, are of the same or similar character or are based on the same act or transaction or on two or more acts or transactions connected together or constituting parts of a common scheme or plan. Fed. R. Crim. Proc. 8(a).

In determining whether to proceed on multiple criminal charges jointly or separately, a prosecutor must consider the Double Jeopardy Clause of the Fifth Amendment. This clause bars successive prosecutions for the "same offense." A particular set of actions by the defendant may constitute distinct violations of criminal law and yet be considered part of the same offense under the Double Jeopardy Clause. For example, in *Harris v. Oklahoma*, 433 U.S. 682, 97 S.Ct. 2912, 53 L.Ed.2d 1054 (1977), the Supreme Court held that a defendant could not be prosecuted for armed robbery after being convicted of felony murder for a homicide committed during an armed robbery.

The basic test laid down by the Supreme Court for determining whether there are two separate offenses is "whether each provision [of the criminal law] requires proof of an additional fact that the other does not." *Blockburger v. United States*, 284 U.S. 299, 304, 52 S.Ct. 180, 182, 76 L.Ed. 306, 309 (1932). Separate statutory crimes need not be identical—either in constituent elements or in actual proof—to be the "same offense" within the meaning of the Double Jeopardy Clause of the Fifth Amendment. Thus, a defendant cannot be convicted of an offense and a lesser included offense. *Brown v. Ohio*, 432 U.S. 161, 97 S.Ct. 2221, 53 L.Ed.2d 187 (1977). State courts have held that a person cannot be convicted of two separate homicide charges where there is only one victim. See, for example, *Wilcox v. Leapley*, 488 N.W.2d 654 (S.D. 1992).

Severance of Charges

Where two or more related offenses are charged in a single indictment or information, the trial judge ordinarily grants a **severance of the charges** on the motion of either the defense or prosecution, if it is necessary to achieve a fair determination of the defendant's guilt or innocence on each offense. A defendant seeking severance bears the burden of showing that a joint trial would be so unfairly prejudicial that it would result in a miscarriage of justice. *United States v. Williams*, 10 F.3d 1070 (4th Cir. 1993).

Trial judges have considerable discretion in this area, but there are certain situations in which severance seems mandatory. For example, a defendant charged with two offenses might want to testify in one case but decline to testify in the other. Or a defendant might be charged in one case with possession of a firearm by a convicted felon, and in another case with robbery. To sustain the charge in the firearm case, the prosecution would have to show the defendant's prior conviction of a felony. Such a showing would obviously be prejudicial to defense of the robbery charge being heard by the same jury.

Joinder and Severance of Parties

As with multiple offenses, prosecutors generally have broad discretion in deciding whether to prosecute multiple defendants separately or jointly. However, here too there are constitutional considerations. For example, it has been held that separate trials are required where the prosecution plans to use against one defendant evidence that has no relevance to the other defendants. *Kotteakos v. United States*, 328 U.S. 750, 66 S.Ct. 1239, 90 L.Ed. 1557 (1946).

Rule 8(b) of the Federal Rules of Criminal Procedure authorizes joinder of two or more defendants in the same indictment "if they are alleged to have participated in the same act or transaction or the same series of acts or transactions constituting an offense or offenses." However, Rule 14 states that the court "may grant" a severance "if it appears that a defendant or the government is prejudiced by a joinder of offenses or of defendants." Thus, federal judges try to determine whether the failure to sever prevents the moving party from getting a fair trial. Denial of a motion for severance is generally held to be an abuse of discretion if the defendants present conflicting and irreconcilable defenses, and if there is a danger that the jury will infer that such conflict demonstrates that both are guilty. *United States v. Tarantino*, 846 F.2d 1384 (D.C. Cir. 1988).

Rules governing **joinder and severance of parties** are usually spelled out in the rules of criminal procedure in each jurisdiction. The purpose of such rules is to ensure that when two or more persons are charged jointly, each will receive a fair determination of guilt or innocence. The Tennessee Rules of Criminal Procedure are fairly typical in this respect:

> The Court, on motion of the State or on motion of the defendant . . . shall grant a severance of defendants if:
>
> I. before trial, it is deemed necessary to protect a defendant's right to a speedy trial or it is deemed appropriate to promote a fair determination of the guilt or innocence of one or more defendants; or
>
> II. during trial, with the consent of the defendant to be severed, it is deemed necessary to promote a fair determination of the guilt or innocence of one or more defendants. Tenn. R. Crim. Proc., Rule 14(c)(2).

Severance of defendants is almost always granted when jointly charged defendants pursue inconsistent defenses or their interests are otherwise antagonistic, or when one defendant chooses to testify and the other does not. Severance can be crucial when a codefendant's confession implicates another nontestifying codefendant. The Supreme Court addressed the problem in *Bruton v. United States*, 391 U.S. 123, 88 S.Ct. 1620, 20 L.Ed.2d 476 (1968). Bruton and Evans were charged with the same robbery and were tried jointly before the same jury. Evans had confessed that he and Bruton had committed the robbery. Although Evans did not testify, his confession incriminating Bruton was read to the jury. The trial judge instructed the jury to consider the confession as evidence only against Evans. The Supreme Court reversed, finding that introduction of Evans's confession at the joint trial violated Bruton's rights under the Confrontation Clause of the Sixth Amendment.

After *Bruton*, prosecutors devised various methods of redacting (editing) a defendant's confession so that a confession by one defendant could be used at a joint trial without implicating any other defendant. Federal and state appellate courts arrived at varying decisions concerning the methods of redaction employed in the trial courts. Finally, on March 9, 1998, in *Gray v. Maryland*, 523 U.S. 185, 118 S.Ct. 1151, 140 L.Ed.2d. 294 (1998), the Supreme Court reviewed a decision of the Maryland Court of Appeals that addressed the redaction problem in a case that resulted in Kevin Gray's conviction for involuntary manslaughter. Gray's codefendant, Bell, had given a confession to the police in which he said that Bell, Gray, and Vanlandingham had participated in a beating that resulted in the victim's death. Vanlandingham later died, and Bell and Gray were tried jointly for murder. The trial judge, after denying Gray's motion for a separate trial, permitted a police detective to read Bell's redacted confession into evidence. The detective said the word "deleted" or "deletion" whenever Gray's name or Vanlandingham's name appeared. The state then introduced into evidence a written copy of Bell's confession with Gray's and Vanlandingham's names omitted, leaving in their place blank white spaces separated by commas. The Maryland Court of Appeals upheld Gray's conviction. The Supreme Court granted certiorari. In a 5–4 decision, the Court vacated the decision and stated that "redactions that replace a proper name with an obvious blank, the word 'delete,' a symbol, or similarly notify the jury that a name has been deleted are similar enough to *Bruton's* unredacted confession as to warrant the same legal results." Writing for the Court's four dissenting justices, Justice Scalia contended that allowing the confession to be admitted with limiting instructions would be the most "reasonable practical accommodation of the interests of the state and the defendant in the criminal justice process."

Lower federal courts have generally taken the position that Rule 14 entitles defendants to separate trials if their defenses are mutually contradictory. See, for example, *United States v. Tarantino, supra.* In 1993 the U.S. Supreme Court addressed the issue. Writing for the Court, Justice O'Connor made it clear that severance of defendants is not required, as a matter of law, when defendants present mutually antagonistic defenses. Rather, severance is required only if the trial court finds a serious risk that a joint trial would compromise a specific trial right of a properly joined defendant or prevent the jury from making a reliable judgment about guilt or innocence. Circumstances that may require a severance include a case in which joinder results in the admission of evidence that the jury could consider against one defendant but not another, or a case in which evidence exculpating one defendant would have to be excluded at a joint trial. But in federal courts, reliance simply on antagonistic defenses without articulating any specific prejudice is not sufficient to require that a trial court sever the trial of a codefendant. *Zafiro v. United States,* 506 U.S. 534, 113 S.Ct. 933, 122 L.Ed.2d 317 (1993).

Pretrial Motions

Pretrial motions are written requests to the court on behalf of the government or the defendant. They are the means by which defense counsel and prosecutors seek to attain certain objectives before trial. Typically, many motions are available to both the defense and prosecution during the pretrial phase of a criminal case. One common set of motions deals with joinder and severance of offenses and defendants, as previously discussed. Other common pretrial motions include the following:

1. *Motion to dismiss.* Frequently the defense files a motion to dismiss the indictment or information, alleging (a) that the government's allegations, assuming the truth thereof, do not allege a crime, or that the accusatorial document is not correct in form; or (b) that the undisputed facts do not establish a case of *prima facie* guilt against the defendant. Often the court's determination on a motion to dismiss is not final, as the government may be given an opportunity to amend its documentation. In addition, a defendant may file a motion to dismiss on grounds of double jeopardy or having been granted immunity.

2. *Motion to determine the competency of the accused to stand trial.* In cases where the defendant is mentally disturbed, the defendant may be declared incompetent to stand trial on the motion of the defense. In federal cases the trial judge must determine whether the defendant has (1) a rational and factual understanding of the pending proceedings and (2) the ability to consult with his or her lawyer with a reasonable degree of rational understanding. *Dusky v. United States,* 362 U.S. 402, 80 S.Ct. 788, 4 L.Ed.2d 824 (1960). State courts

use varying standards to determine whether an accused person is competent to stand trial. The differences are largely semantic. Some state courts apply the federal standard, with the additional requirement that the accused must understand the range of penalties that would attend conviction and be able to perceive the adversarial nature of the trial process. A person restored to competency may then be tried for the criminal offense originally charged.

3. *Motion to suppress evidence obtained through unlawful search or seizure.* Evidence obtained in violation of a defendant's Fourth Amendment rights cannot be used against the defendant in a criminal trial. *Weeks v. United States,* 232 U.S. 383, 34 S.Ct. 341, 58 L.Ed. 652 (1914); *Mapp v. Ohio,* 367 U.S. 643, 81 S.Ct. 1684, 6 L.Ed.2d 1081 (1961). When the defense moves to suppress evidence on Fourth Amendment grounds, the court generally holds an evidentiary hearing. If the defense is successful in causing the **suppression of evidence,** it may undermine the government's case, leading to a favorable ruling on a subsequent defense motion to dismiss. When the state's case depends solely on the evidence sought to be suppressed, the defense's attempt is often referred to as a **dispositive motion.**

4. *Motion to suppress confessions, admissions, or other statements made to the police.* A defendant is constitutionally entitled to a determination by the court whether a confession is voluntary before the confession is made known to the jury. *Jackson v. Denno,* 378 U.S. 368, 84 S.Ct. 1774, 12 L.Ed.2d 908 (1964). The motion to suppress the confession is the means of bringing this issue before the court. The motion can initiate a number of related inquiries, such as whether the confession was obtained in violation of the *Miranda* rules. Generally, before ruling on a motion to suppress a confession, the court holds an evidentiary hearing. Again, the disposition of such a motion can have a significant impact on the prosecution of a criminal case. If the confession is crucial to the prosecution's case, a favorable ruling on the motion to suppress may lead to a dismissal of the charges.

5. *Motion to suppress a pretrial identification of the accused.* This motion by the defendant is designed to determine whether the pretrial identification procedures employed by the police in having an eyewitness identify the accused violated the due process standards outlined in *Neil v. Biggers,* 409 U.S. 188, 93 S.Ct. 375, 34 L.Ed.2d 401 (1972). The court's inquiry here focuses on whether the identification procedures were impermissibly suggestive to the witness (see Chapter 16).

6. *Motion to require the prosecution to disclose the identity of a confidential informant.* The prosecution is not ordinarily required to disclose the identity of a confidential informant who merely furnishes the probable cause on which an arrest or search is predicated. Nevertheless, if the informant was an "active participant" in the offense, the prosecution may be required to disclose the informant's identity. The test calls for balancing the public interest in protecting the free flow of information to the police against the individual's right to prepare a defense. See *Roviaro v. United States,* 353 U.S. 53, 77 S.Ct. 623, 1 L.Ed.2d 639 (1957). Trial judges have considerable discretion in ruling on this motion.

7. *Motion for change of venue.* The defendant, and in some instances the government, may move for a change of venue (that is, place of trial) on the ground that a fair and impartial trial cannot be had where the case is pending. In recent years, heightened media coverage of crime and criminal prosecutions has generated tremendous concern over the ability of defendants to receive a fair trial.

The concern usually focuses on the difficulty of selecting an impartial jury when potential jurors have been exposed to intensive newspaper, radio, and television coverage of a crime. The Supreme Court, in *Sheppard v. Maxwell*, 384 U.S. 333, 86 S.Ct. 1507, 16 L.Ed.2d 600 (1966), established some guidelines for dealing with the effects of pretrial publicity (see Chapter 18). Since then, an increasing number of defendants have filed motions seeking a change of venue.

8. *Motion for a* **continuance.** Either the government or the defendant may seek a continuance, or postponement, of the trial. A variety of grounds may be asserted, including illness or emergency that makes it difficult or impossible for the defendant, prosecutor, defense counsel, or an important witness to be present as scheduled; the unavailability of a significant witness or piece of documentary evidence; or the lack of adequate time to prepare for trial. Appellate courts consistently hold that there is no abuse of discretion unless a party can show that specific prejudice has resulted to the defendant as a result of the denial of the requested continuance.

9. *Other pretrial motions.* Other common pretrial motions include motions to take a **deposition** to preserve the testimony of an infirm witness or one who might not be available for trial; to inspect the minutes of the grand jury proceeding; to compel the prosecutor to disclose evidence that might be favorable to the accused; and to disqualify the trial judge on grounds of bias, close relationship to parties, or that the judge will be a material witness.

Arraignment

The arraignment is the accused's first appearance before a court of law with the authority to conduct a criminal trial. At this stage of the process, the accused must enter a plea to the charges contained in the indictment or information. There are several options. The accused may choose to enter a **plea of not guilty,** in which case the plea is noted and a trial date is set. The accused may enter a **plea of guilty,** in which case no trial is necessary. Instead, guilt is simply pronounced and sentencing follows, either immediately or at some future court appearance, after a presentence investigation has been completed (see Chapter 19). A plea of guilty containing a protestation of innocence, sometimes called an *Alford* **plea,** can be made when a defendant intelligently concludes that his or her interests require entry of a guilty plea. *North Carolina v. Alford,* 400 U.S. 25, 91 S.Ct. 160, 27 L.Ed.2d 162 (1970). In some jurisdictions, the accused has the option of pleading *nolo contendere* (no contest). The **no contest plea,** although functionally equivalent to a guilty plea in a criminal trial, provides the accused the advantage that it generally cannot be construed as an admission of guilt in a related civil suit. Although a judgment is entered on a no-contest plea, the defendant neither admits nor denies anything.

Because a plea of guilty or *nolo contendere* represents a waiver of constitutional rights, it is essential that the plea be made knowingly and voluntarily. The Federal Rules of Criminal Procedure preclude trial judges from accepting such a plea unless the court determines the plea is "voluntary and not the result of force or threats or of promises apart from a plea agreement." Fed. R. Crim. P. 11(d). In addition to determining voluntariness, a judge must decide whether a factual basis exists for a plea of guilty or *nolo contendere.* A factual basis is necessary to ensure that the accused does not admit to an offense when his or her conduct does not fall within the bounds of the government's accusations. See, for example, *United States v. Montoya-Camacho,* 644 F.2d 480 (5th Cir. 1981).

Most states have adopted similar rules of procedure to ensure that pleas are voluntary and comply with constitutional requirements. For example, Rule 3.170(k) of the Florida Rules of Criminal Procedure specifies that "[n]o plea of guilty or *nolo contendere* shall be accepted by a court without first determining . . . that the circumstances surrounding the plea reflect . . . its voluntariness and that there is a factual basis for the plea."

Rules concerning voluntariness and factual basis generally do not specify any precise method to be followed by the court. Judges employ various methods to determine voluntariness. Often these methods include interrogation of the defendant by the judge, and sometimes by the prosecutor and defense counsel. The extent of questioning often depends on the defendant's educational level and maturity. Frequently, judges ask indigent defendants about their satisfaction with court-appointed counsel. The objective is to establish that no improper inducements have been made to secure a plea, that the defendant understands the basic constitutional rights incident to a trial, that these rights are being waived, and that he or she comprehends the consequences of the plea. *Boykin v. Alabama,* 395 U.S. 238, 89 S.Ct. 1709, 23 L.Ed.2d 274 (1969).

An excerpt from *Boykin v. Alabama* appears at the end of the chapter.

In determining that a factual basis exists for the defendant's plea, judges often have the prosecutor briefly outline available proof to establish a *prima facie* case of the defendant's guilt. A more extensive inquiry may be necessary for specific-intent crimes. The thoroughness of the court's determination of voluntariness and factual basis becomes important if a defendant later moves to withdraw a plea and enter a plea of not guilty.

Plea Bargaining

In most jurisdictions, more than 90 percent of felony suspects arraigned plead guilty or no contest. Very often the guilty plea is the result of a bargain struck between the defense and the prosecution. In a **plea bargain,** the accused agrees to plead guilty in exchange for a reduction in the number or severity of charges or a promise by the prosecutor not to seek the maximum penalty allowed by law. Plea negotiations are subject to the approval of the trial court. In most instances, the bargain is arranged by experienced and knowledgeable counsel on both sides and is readily approved by the court. If, however, the court is unwilling to approve the plea bargain, the defendant must choose between withdrawing the guilty plea (and thus going to trial) and accepting the plea bargain with such modifications as the judge may approve. Once the court has accepted a guilty plea pursuant to a plea bargain, the court cannot unilaterally alter it without permitting the defendant the opportunity to withdraw the plea.

In some jurisdictions, judges participate directly in plea-bargaining discussions. The justification for this practice is that a judge can guide the parties to an equitable and expeditious resolution of the case. On the other hand, some courts disfavor the participation of a trial judge in plea-bargaining discussions on the basis that the power and position of the judge may improperly influence the defendant to enter a guilty plea. See, for example, *Perkins v. Court of Appeals,* 738 S.W.2d 276, 282 (Tex. Crim. App. 1987).

CASE-IN-POINT

Plea Bargaining

Paul LaVallee was charged in a New Hampshire court with the crime of aggravated assault. He elected to plead not guilty, was convicted at trial, and was sentenced to ten to thirty years in prison. LaVallee brought a habeas corpus action challenging his sentence, arguing that it was disproportionate to the sentences given defendants who agreed to plead guilty. He claimed that it was impermissible for the courts to give harsher sentences to defendants who insist on their constitutional right to a trial. The state supreme court rejected LaVallee's challenge. The court said that the defendant's argument ignored "the realities of the plea bargaining process." Further, it noted that "[i]n this state, we have rejected the notion that it is impermissible to compensate one who pleads guilty by extending him a proper degree of leniency."

LaVallee v. Perrin, 466 A.2d 932 (N.H. 1983).

Plea bargaining has been sharply criticized by observers with different perspectives on the criminal process. Some critics fault plea bargaining for reducing the severity of criminal penalties. Others view plea bargaining as an unconstitutional effort to deprive defendants of their right to a fair trial. Plea bargaining has never been popular, but few stop to consider the tremendous costs and delays that would result if the numerous cases currently resolved through plea bargaining were to go to trial.

Despite frequent criticism, the practice of plea bargaining is widespread among American jurisdictions today. In addition to permitting a substantial conservation of prosecutorial and judicial resources, plea bargaining provides a means by which, through mutual concession, the parties can obtain a prompt resolution of criminal proceedings with the benefits that flow from final disposition of a case. The plea bargain, or negotiated sentence, enables the parties to avoid the delay and uncertainties of trial and appeal and permits swift and certain punishment of law violators with a sentence tailored to the circumstances of the case at hand.

Despite constitutional attacks, the Supreme Court has upheld the practice of plea bargaining. In *Brady v. United States,* 397 U.S. 742, 90 S.Ct. 1463, 1471, 25 L.Ed.2d 747, 759 (1970), the Court said that "we cannot hold that it is unconstitutional for the State to extend a benefit to a defendant who in turn extends a substantial benefit to the State." In a subsequent case, the Court was even more sanguine about plea bargaining:

> The disposition of criminal charges by agreement between the prosecutor and the accused, sometimes loosely called "plea bargaining," is an essential component of the administration of justice. Properly administered, it is to be encouraged. *Santobello v. New York,* 404 U.S. 257, 260, 92 S.Ct. 495, 498, 30 L.Ed.2d 427, 432 (1971).

The plea bargain necessarily entails a waiver of the constitutional right to trial, so it must be examined by the trial court to determine whether the accused has knowingly waived his or her rights and agreed to plead guilty without coercion by the state. *Boykin v. Alabama,* supra. Despite such procedural protections, cases still arise challenging the fundamental fairness of certain plea-bargaining tactics. See, for example, *Bordenkircher v. Hayes,* 434 U.S. 357, 98 S.Ct. 663, 54 L.Ed.2d 604 (1978), where a prosecutor threatened a defendant with a more serious indictment to induce him to plead guilty to an indictment already pending against him.

An excerpt from *Bordenkircher v. Hayes* appears at the end of the chapter.

Availability of Compulsory Process

The Sixth Amendment to the Constitution guarantees a defendant in a criminal case the right to "have the **compulsory process** of the law to obtain witnesses in his favor." The "compulsory process" clause was applied to the states in *Washington v. Texas*, 388 U.S. 14, 87 S.Ct. 1920, 18 L.Ed.2d 1019 (1967), although the right previously existed in state constitutions and laws. The method of securing this right is through use of a subpoena, a formal written demand available in all federal and state jurisdictions. Subpoenas are available to both the prosecution and defense.

Rule 17 of the Federal Rules of Criminal Procedure implements this right at the federal level by allowing a defendant to have the court issue a subpoena for witnesses, documents, and objects, and providing for services of such subpoenas. Court clerks, and sometimes judges, issue subpoenas. They are usually served by a marshal in the federal system and a sheriff or process server in the state system. There are costs associated with subpoenas, but the federal rule provides for issuance without cost when a defendant is financially unable to pay costs as long as the witness is "necessary to an adequate defense." States generally have statutes or court rules closely paralleling the federal rule.

In the pretrial stages, challenges may be made to the right to subpoena a witness, document, or object. Challenges are usually based on the contention that such witnesses or items are not material to issues in the case. Judges have considerable discretion in ruling on these challenges.

Pretrial Discovery

The courts have long recognized a prosecutorial duty to disclose to the defense exculpatory information (that is, information that tends to vindicate the accused). This duty is based on the fundamental concept of our system of justice—that individuals accused of crimes must be treated fairly. The Supreme Court has stated that "the suppression by the prosecution of evidence favorable to the accused upon request violates due process where the evidence is material either to guilt or punishment, irrespective of the good faith or bad faith of the prosecution." *Brady v. Maryland,* 373 U.S. 83, 87, 83 S.Ct. 1194, 1996, 10 L.Ed.2d 215, 218 (1963).

The Court has held that, in addition to substantive exculpatory evidence, evidence tending to impeach the credibility of prosecution witnesses falls within *Brady's* definition of evidence favorable to an accused. Therefore, under *Brady* a defendant is entitled to disclosure of information that might be used to impeach government witnesses. See *United States v. Bagley*, 473 U.S. 667, 105 S.Ct. 3375, 87 L.Ed.2d 481 (1985).

Generally, the defense must request the disclosure of the **exculpatory evidence.** If the defense is unaware of the existence of the evidence, however, such a request is impossible. The Supreme Court has held that failure to request disclosure is not necessarily fatal to a later challenge based on *Brady v. Maryland,* but it may significantly affect the standard for determining materiality. *United States v. Agurs,* 427 U.S. 97, 96 S.Ct. 2392, 49 L.Ed.2d 342 (1976).

In a similar vein, it has been held to be a denial of due process if a prosecutor knowingly allows perjured testimony to be used against the accused. *Mooney v. Holohan,* 294 U.S. 103, 55 S.Ct. 340, 79 L.Ed. 791 (1935); *Alcorta v. Texas,* 355 U.S. 28, 78 S.Ct. 103, 2 L.Ed.2d 9 (1957).

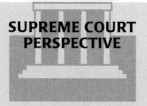

Strickler v. Greene, 527 U.S. 263, 119 S.Ct. 1936, 144 L.Ed.2d 286 (1999)

In this 1999 decision, the Supreme Court refused to overturn a murder conviction and concomitant death sentence that the petitioner challenged on the basis of the Sixth Amendment right to counsel. The petitioner argued that his trial lawyer was less than reasonably effective for failing to file a motion to require the prosecutor to turn over certain potentially exculpatory evidence. The prosecutor had denied withholding the evidence, stating that the office maintained an "open file policy." The Supreme Court held that the petitioner had failed to show a reasonable probability that disclosure of the evidence in question would have changed the outcome of the trial. In his opinion for the Court, Justice Stevens discussed the *Brady* decision, the obligation it imposes on prosecutors, and the benefits it confers on defendants:

"In *Brady* this Court held 'that the suppression by the prosecution of evidence favorable to an accused upon request violates due process where the evidence is material either to guilt or to punishment, irrespective of the good faith or bad faith of the prosecution.' . . . We have since held that the duty to disclose such evidence is applicable even though there has been no request by the accused, . . . and that the duty encompasses impeachment evidence as well as exculpatory evidence. . . . Such evidence is material 'if there is a reasonable probability that, had the evidence been disclosed to the defense, the result of the proceeding would have been different.' . . . Moreover, the rule encompasses evidence 'known only to police investigators and not to the prosecutor.' . . . In order to comply with

Brady, therefore, 'the individual prosecutor has a duty to learn of any favorable evidence known to the others acting on the government's behalf in this case, including the police.'

"These cases, together with earlier cases condemning the knowing use of perjured testimony, illustrate the special role played by the American prosecutor in the search for truth in criminal trials. Within the federal system, for example, we have said that the United States Attorney is 'the representative not of an ordinary party to a controversy, but of a sovereignty whose obligation to govern impartially is as compelling as its obligation to govern at all; and whose interest, therefore, in a criminal prosecution is not that it shall win a case, but that justice shall be done.'

"This special status explains both the basis for the prosecution's broad duty of disclosure and our conclusion that not every violation of that duty necessarily establishes that the outcome was unjust. Thus the term '*Brady* violation' is sometimes used to refer to any breach of the broad obligation to disclose exculpatory evidence—that is, to any suppression of so-called '*Brady* material'—although, strictly speaking, there is never a real '*Brady* violation' unless the nondisclosure was so serious that there is a reasonable probability that the suppressed evidence would have produced a different verdict. There are three components of a true *Brady* violation: The evidence at issue must be favorable to the accused, either because it is exculpatory, or because it is impeaching; that evidence must have been suppressed by the State, either willfully or inadvertently; and prejudice must have ensued. . . ."

Evidence that impeaches the credibility of a prosecution witness is considered to be exculpatory. The Supreme Court of Virginia in 1993 held that before the prosecution is obliged to produce evidence, it must be established that the undisclosed evidence is exculpatory and material to the defendant's guilt or punishment. Accordingly, where the record did not establish that there was any exculpatory evidence in the defendant's accomplices' polygraph tests, the state supreme court said that the trial did not err in denying the defendant's motion seeking to discover the results of the tests. *Ramdass v. Commonwealth,* 473 S.E.2d 566 (Va. 1993).

Most states have now adopted liberal rules pertaining to **pretrial discovery,** rules designed to avoid unfairness to the defense resulting from abdications of prosecutorial

Illinois Discovery Rules

Under statutory authority, Ill. S.H.A. 725 ILCS 5/114–3, the Illinois Supreme Court has promulgated rules governing discovery procedures in criminal cases. In part, those rules are as follows:

Supreme Court Rule 412. Disclosure to Accused

(a) Except as is otherwise provided in these rules . . . , the State shall, upon written motion of defense counsel, disclose . . . the following information or material within its possession or control:

   (i) the names and last known addresses of persons whom the State intends to call as witnesses, together with their relevant written or recorded statements . . . ;

   (ii) any written or recorded statements and the substance of any oral statements made by the accused or by a codefendant, and a list of witnesses to the making and acknowledgment of such statements;

   (iii) a transcript of those portions of grand jury minutes containing testimony of the accused and relevant testimony of persons whom the prosecuting attorney intends to call as witnesses at the hearing or trial;

   (iv) any reports or statements of experts, made in connection with the particular case, including results of physical or mental examinations and of scientific tests, experiments, or comparisons, and a statement of the qualifications of the expert;

   (v) any books, papers, documents, photographs or tangible objects which the prosecuting attorney intends to use in the hearing or trial or which were obtained from or belong to the accused; and

   (vi) any record of prior criminal convictions, which may be used for impeachment, of persons whom the State intends to call as witnesses at the hearing or trial. . . .

Supreme Court Rule 413. Disclosure to Prosecution

(a) The person of the accused. Notwithstanding the initiation of judicial proceedings, and subject to constitutional limitations, a judicial officer may require the accused, among other things, to:

   (i) appear in a line-up;

   (ii) speak for identification by witnesses to an offense;

   (iii) be fingerprinted;

   (iv) pose for photographs not involving reenactment of a scene;

   (v) try on articles of clothing;

   (vi) permit the taking of specimens material under his fingernails;

   (vii) permit the taking of samples of his blood, hair and other materials of his body which involve no unreasonable intrusion thereof;

   (viii) provide a sample of his handwriting; and

   (ix) submit to a reasonable physical or medical inspection of his body.

(b) [provision for appearance of accused and counsel at foregoing]

(c) Medical and scientific reports. . . .

(d) Defenses. Subject to constitutional limitations and within reasonable time after the filing of a written motion by the State, defense counsel shall inform the State of any defenses which he intends to make at a hearing or trial and shall furnish the state with the following material and information within his possession or control:

   (i) the names and last known addresses of persons he intends to call as witnesses together with their relevant written or recorded statements. . . .

   (ii) any books, papers, documents, photographs, or tangible objects he intends to use as evidence or for impeachment at a hearing or trial;

   (iii) and if the defendant intends to prove an alibi, specific information as to the place where he maintains he was at the time of the alleged offense.

(e) Additional disclosure. Upon a showing of materiality, and if the request is reasonable, the court in its discretion may require disclosure to the State of relevant material and information not covered by this rule.

Pretrial Discovery

Police obtained a warrant to search Barton's home based on an officer's affidavit that he had smelled marijuana during a prior consensual entry of the home. At a pretrial suppression hearing, Barton claimed that the officer could not have smelled the marijuana plants that were seized because they had no odor. But by the time of the suppression hearing, the plants had rotted because the police had not ventilated the bag in which they stashed the plants. The court recognized that the destruction by the government of evidence that tends to impeach allegations in an affidavit demonstrating probable cause for a search warrant may violate due process principles. Nevertheless, the defendant did not prevail. Rather, the *Barton* court relied upon the principle declared by the U.S. Supreme Court in *Arizona v. Youngblood*, 488 U.S. 51, 109 S.Ct. 333, 102 L.Ed. 2d 281 (1988). There, the Court held that the failure of law enforcement officers through mere negligence and not in bad faith to preserve evidence that might have been helpful to the defendant does not violate a defendant's right to due process of law.

United States v. Barton, 995 F.2d 931 (9th Cir. 1993).

duty. Using appropriate pretrial motions, the defense and prosecution can gain access to the evidence possessed by the opposing party. Thus, pretrial discovery not only enhances the fairness of the criminal process but also militates against surprises at trial.

Discovery in the Federal Courts

Discovery in a criminal case is somewhat more limited in federal courts than in state courts. Under the provisions of 18 U.S.C.A. § 3500, a federal criminal defendant is not entitled to inspect a statement or report prepared by a government witness "until said witness has testified on direct examination in the trial of the case." After a witness testifies, the government, on proper request of the defense, must then produce that portion of any statement or report that relates to the subject matter on which the witness has testified. The federal statute is commonly referred to as the **Jencks Act** because its effect was first recognized in *Jencks v. United States*, 353 U.S. 657, 77 S.Ct. 1007, 1 L.Ed.2d 1103 (1957). In *Jencks,* a defendant was allowed to obtain for impeachment purposes previous statements made to government agents by prosecution witnesses. Courts have indicated that the principal purpose of the *Jencks* Act is to aid a defendant's right to cross-examination. In some instances the trial judge must make an *in camera* **inspection** of documents where the government asserts that the documents contain statements not relevant to the subject matter to which the witness has testified. The government is not required under the *Jencks* Act to turn over victims' statements to defendants during a pretrial suppression hearing. *United States v. Williams,* 10 F.3d 1070 (4th Cir. 1993).

The Right to a Speedy Trial

The Sixth Amendment to the Constitution guarantees the defendant the **right to a speedy trial.** In *Barker v. Wingo,* 407 U.S. 514, 92 S.Ct. 2182, 33 L.Ed.2d 101 (1972), the Supreme Court refused to mandate a specific time limit between the filing of charges and the commencement of trial, but adopted a balancing test to determine whether a defendant was denied the right to a speedy trial. Under this test, courts must consider (1) the length of the delay, (2) the reasons for the delay, (3) the defendant's assertion of the right, and (4) prejudice to the defendant.

In response to the Court's decision in *Barker v. Wingo,* Congress enacted the **Speedy Trial Act of 1974,** 18 U.S.C.A. § 3161. The act provides specific time limits for pretrial and trial procedures in the federal courts. For example, an indictment must be filed within thirty days of arrest, and trial must commence within seventy days after the indictment. Violations of the time limitations are remedied by dismissal of charges. There are a number of exceptions to the time limits, however, especially where delays are caused by defendants' motions.

Under federal law, the indictment of the accused activates the clock governing the right to a speedy trial. *United States v. Marion,* 404 U.S. 307, 92 S.Ct. 455, 30 L.Ed.2d 468 (1971). Apart from the right to a speedy trial, a defendant who can establish that the prosecutor intentionally delayed indicting him or her to gain a tactical advantage and that the defendant incurred actual prejudice as a result of the delay can assert a claim of denial of due process. *United States v. Lovasco,* 431 U.S. 783, 97 S.Ct. 2044, 52 L.Ed.2d 752 (1977); *United States v. Amuny,* 767 F.2d 1113, 1119 (5th Cir. 1985).

The speedy trial clause of the Sixth Amendment applies to the states through the Fourteenth Amendment. *Klopfer v. North Carolina,* 386 U.S. 213, 87 S.Ct. 988, 18 L.Ed.2d 1 (1967). Most states have adopted legislation or court rules similar to the federal speedy trial law. See, for example, Ill. S.H.A. § 725 ILCS 5/103–5. State laws frequently provide that the right to a speedy trial is activated either on the date of the filing of an indictment, information, or other formal accusatorial document, or on the date that the accused is taken into custody.

Conclusion

The rights afforded by the Fourth, Fifth, Sixth, and Eighth amendments to the United States Constitution (and similar provisions in the state constitutions) vitally affect the procedures used in criminal cases. Many of these rights were redefined or enlarged by the courts during the 1960s and 1970s, and they become important long before a criminal prosecution reaches the trial stage. Of particular importance is the right to counsel guaranteed by the Sixth Amendment.

Because most criminal cases never reach the trial stage, it is essential that the student of criminal justice have a good grasp of the various pretrial procedures that often influence—and frequently determine—the outcome of a criminal case. It is equally important to understand the substantial discretion vested in key actors in the pretrial process, especially in the prosecutor. The prosecutor's discretion is manifested not only in the charging process but also in the pervasive and highly controversial practice of plea bargaining. When the exercise of prosecutorial discretion and the efforts of defense counsel fail to achieve a negotiated guilty plea, then a trial must be held. In the next chapter, we discuss procedures pertaining to the criminal trial.

Key Terms

fair notice
petty offenses
criminal procedure
initial appearance

preliminary hearing
grand jury proceeding
arraignment
right to counsel

indigency
actual imprisonment standard
critical pretrial stages
public defender
bail
self-representation
summary justice
summons
pretrial release
release on personal recognizance
surety bond
skip tracers
excessive bail
Federal Bail Reform Act of 1984
pretrial detention
prosecutorial discretion
plea bargaining
selective prosecution
prosecutorial immunity
information
preliminary hearing
indictment
subpoena
immunity
transactional immunity
use immunity

extradition
jurisdiction
capias
venue
change of venue
joinder of offenses
severance of the charges
joinder and severance of parties
pretrial motions
motion to dismiss
suppression of evidence
dispositive motion
continuance
deposition
plea of not guilty
plea of guilty
Alford plea
no contest plea
plea bargain
compulsory process
exculpatory evidence
pretrial discovery
Jencks Act
in camera inspection
right to a speedy trial
Speedy Trial Act of 1974

Web-Based Research Activity

1. Using the Internet, determine the role of grand juries in your state's criminal justice system.

2. How are grand jurors selected? How long do they serve?

3. What powers does the grand jury possess?

4. Have there been calls for the reform of the grand jury in your state?

Questions for Thought and Discussion

1. Have the courts gone too far or not far enough in requiring that indigent defendants be represented by counsel at public expense?

2. What are the arguments for and against allowing defendants without any legal training to represent themselves in felony prosecutions?

3. In your opinion, does the Eighth Amendment guarantee the right to pretrial release on bail in a felony case? What about a misdemeanor case? Did the Supreme Court decide the *Salerno* case correctly? Why or why not?

4. How does a magistrate determine how much bail is appropriate and how much is "excessive"? What alternatives, if any, do you see to the traditional bail-bond system to ensure the appearance of the defendant in court?

5. Can you imagine a situation in which a prosecutor would run afoul of the Constitution by engaging in selective prosecution? In your state, can a prosecutor be sued for malicious prosecution? How is this proved?

6. Do the courts in your state permit the *nolo contendere* plea? If so, what tactical advantage does the defendant gain by pleading *nolo contendere* rather than guilty?

7. How might a prosecutor persuade a defendant to plead guilty to a criminal charge without running afoul of due process? What prosecutorial tactics are likely to be viewed as fundamentally unfair?

8. Compare the advantages and disadvantages to the defendant of insisting on the right to a speedy trial.

9. Why do you think the United States Supreme Court has never held that the Fifth Amendment requirement of indictment by a grand jury applies to the states as well as to the federal government? Does the grand jury still play a viable role in the criminal justice system? Are the criticisms of the grand jury valid? Why or why not?

10. Should plea bargaining be abolished? If not, what modifications might be necessary to protect (a) the defendant and (b) the public?

Problems for Discussion and Solution

1. Samuel Penurio was president of a community bank in a small town. He was well thought of in the community, but he was known to drink to excess occasionally. One June evening his bank hosted a cocktail party. About 10:00 P.M., after the party was over, Penurio offered to drive his secretary home. Each had drunk several cocktails. En route to her home, Penurio drove through an intersection controlled by a signal light. His car crashed into a car of four students who had just left their high school football game. One student, the popular head female cheerleader, died as a result of the injuries she received from the accident. Penurio's blood-alcohol rate was 1.0. He was charged with vehicular homicide, which carries a maximum punishment of life imprisonment. Penurio and his secretary claim that he drove through the intersection just as the light was changing and that the car occupied by the students drove through the intersection at an excessive rate of speed. The driver of the students' car had not been drinking, and the surviving students all say Penurio drove through the red light. The local newspaper ran a front-page story with pictures of the students holding a school-wide memorial service for the deceased cheerleader, describing the students' version of the accident, and pointing out that Penurio had been convicted of DWI just a year earlier. Over the next several days, the newspaper and the local radio station carried adverse comments from their readers and listeners about Penurio's conduct. Do you think Penurio's counsel should seek a change of venue? What, if any, additional information should be sought to support such a motion?

2. Willy Doolittle, age thirty-eight, is an unemployed male construction worker. He is married with two children in middle school. He has been unable to support his family for the past few weeks because of lack of work. His wife takes care of their rented home, but, in addition to being a high school dropout, she receives Medicaid assistance for a series of physical problems. One night after having a few beers, Doolittle, using a key he possessed from when he had worked in a warehouse, entered the warehouse without authority. The state charged Doolittle with burglary. His bail was set under a standard schedule that calls for $10,000 cash or bond. Doolittle has no means to post

cash or a bond. The public defender (PD) was appointed to represent him. Doolittle has no prior criminal record and has lived in the community for three years. He wants to be released, and the PD thinks he may be able to represent him more effectively if Doolittle is released and obtains employment. A social worker reports that the family is need of support and has offered to assist Doolittle in obtaining employment at a new construction site. The PD asks you to prepare a memorandum to support an application for pretrial release without posting cash or bond. What additional information should you seek? In seeking to obtain Doolittle's release without posting cash or bond, what conditions of release should the PD propose to the court?

EXCERPTS FROM JUDICIAL DECISIONS

Scott v. Illinois

Supreme Court of the United States, 1979.
440 U.S. 367, 99 S.Ct. 1158, 59 L.Ed.2d 383.

[In Gideon v. Wainwright *(1963), the Supreme Court held that indigent defendants facing felony charges in state court are entitled to court-appointed counsel at public expense. In 1972, in* Argersinger v. Hamlin, *the Court extended the* Gideon *decision to encompass misdemeanors punishable by jail terms. However, left unsettled was the question of whether the right to appointed counsel applies in a case where an indigent defendant is accused of a misdemeanor that, although punishable by incarceration, is actually punished only by a fine. In the instant case, the Court addresses this issue.]*

Mr. Justice REHNQUIST delivered the opinion of the Court.

. . . Petitioner Scott was convicted of theft and fined $50 after a bench trial in the Circuit Court of Cook County, Ill. His conviction was affirmed by the state intermediate appellate court and then by the Supreme Court of Illinois, over Scott's contention that the Sixth and Fourteenth Amendments to the United States Constitution required that Illinois provide trial counsel to him at its expense.

Petitioner Scott was convicted of shoplifting merchandise valued at less than $150. The applicable Illinois statute set the maximum penalty for such an offense at a $500 fine or one year in jail, or both. The petitioner argues that a line of this Court's cases culminating in *Argersinger v. Hamlin* . . . requires State provision of counsel whenever imprisonment is an authorized penalty.

The Supreme Court of Illinois rejected this contention. . . .

There is considerable doubt that the Sixth Amendment itself, as originally drafted by the Framers of the Bill of Rights, contemplated any guarantee other than the right of an accused in a criminal prosecution in a federal court to employ a lawyer to assist in his defense. In *Powell v. Alabama*, 287 U.S. 45, 53 S.Ct. 55, 77 L.Ed. 158 (1932), the Court held that Alabama was obligated to appoint counsel for the Scottsboro defendants, phrasing the inquiry as "whether the defendants were in substance denied the right of counsel, and if so, whether such denial infringes the due process clause of the Fourteenth Amendment."

Betts v. Brady, 316 U.S. 455, 62 S.Ct. 1252, 86 L.Ed. 1595 (1942), held that not every indigent defendant accused in a state criminal prosecution was entitled to appointment of counsel. A determination had to be made in each individual case whether failure to appoint counsel was a denial of fundamental fairness. *Betts* was in turn overruled in *Gideon v. Wainwright*, 372 U.S. 335, 83 S.Ct. 792, 9 L.Ed.2d 799 (1963). . . . In *Gideon*, *Betts* was described as holding "that a refusal to appoint counsel for an indigent defendant charged with a felony did not necessarily violate the Due Process Clause of the Fourteenth Amendment. . . ."

Several terms later the Court held in *Duncan v. Louisiana*, 391 U.S. 145, 88 S.Ct. 1444, 20 L.Ed.2d 491 (1968), that the right to jury trial in federal court guaranteed by the Sixth Amendment was applicable to the States by virtue of the Fourteenth Amendment. The Court held, however: "It is doubtless true that there is a category of petty crimes or offenses which is not subject to the Sixth Amendment jury trial provision and should not be subject to the Fourteenth Amendment jury trial requirement here applied to the States. Crimes carrying possible penalties up to six months do not require a jury trial if they otherwise qualify as petty offenses. . . ." In *Baldwin v. New York,* 399 U.S. 66, 69, 26 L.Ed.2d 437, 90 S.Ct. 1886 (1970), the controlling opinion of Mr. Justice White concluded that "no offense can be deemed 'petty' for purposes of the right to trial by jury where imprisonment for more than six months is authorized."

In *Argersinger* the State of Florida urged that a similar dichotomy be employed in the right-to-counsel area: Any offense punishable by less than six months in jail should not require appointment of counsel for an indigent defendant. The *Argersinger* Court rejected this analogy, however, observing that "the right to trial by jury has a different genealogy and is brigaded with a system of trial to a judge alone."

The number of separate opinions in *Gideon, Duncan, Baldwin,* and *Argersinger,* suggests that constitutional line drawing becomes more difficult as the reach of the Constitution is extended further, and as efforts are made to transpose lines from one area of Sixth Amendment jurisprudence to another. The process of incorporation creates special difficulties, for the state and federal contexts are often different and application of the same principle may have ramifications distinct in degree and kind. The range of human conduct regulated by state criminal laws is much broader than that of the federal criminal laws, particularly on the "petty" offense part of the spectrum. As a matter of constitutional adjudication, we are, therefore, less willing to extrapolate an already extended line when, although the general nature of the principle sought to be applied is clear, its precise limits and their ramifications become less so. We have now in our decided cases departed from the literal meaning of the Sixth Amendment. And we cannot fall back on the common law as it existed prior to the enactment of that Amendment, since it perversely gave less in the way of right to counsel to accused felons than to those accused of misdemeanors.

In *Argersinger* the Court rejected arguments that social cost or a lack of available lawyers militated against its holding, in some part because it thought these arguments were factually incorrect. But they were rejected in much larger part because of the Court's conclusion that incarceration was so severe a sanction that it should not be imposed as a result of a criminal trial unless an indigent defendant had been offered appointed counsel to assist in his defense, regardless of the cost to the States implicit in such a rule. The Court in its opinion repeatedly referred to trials "where an accused is deprived of his liberty," and to "a case that actually leads to imprisonment even for a brief period." The Chief Justice in his opinion concurring in the result also observed that "any deprivation of liberty is a serious matter."

Although the intentions of the *Argersinger* Court are not unmistakably clear from its opinion, we conclude today that *Argersinger* did indeed delimit the constitutional right to appointed counsel in state criminal proceedings. Even were the matter *res nova,* we believe that the central premise of *Argersinger*—that actual imprisonment is a penalty different in kind from fines or the mere threat of imprisonment—is eminently sound and warrants adoption of actual imprisonment as the line defining the constitutional right to appointment of counsel. *Argersinger* has proved reasonably workable, whereas any extension would create confusion and impose unpredictable, but necessarily substantial, costs on 50 quite diverse States. We therefore hold that the Sixth and Fourteenth Amendments to the United States Constitution require only that no indigent criminal defendant be sentenced to a term of imprisonment unless the State has afforded him the right to assistance of appointed counsel in his defense. The judgment of the Supreme Court of Illinois is accordingly affirmed.

Mr. Justice POWELL concurring. . . .

Mr. Justice BRENNAN, with whom Mr. Justice MARSHALL and Mr. Justice STEVENS join, dissenting.

. . . The Court in an opinion that at best ignores the basic principles of prior decisions, affirms Scott's conviction without counsel because he was sentenced only to pay a fine. In my view, the plain wording of the Sixth Amendment and the Court's precedents compel the conclusion that Scott's uncounseled conviction violated the Sixth and Fourteenth Amendments and should be reversed. . . .

The apparent reason for the Court's adoption of the "actual imprisonment" standard for all misdemeanors is concern for the economic burden that an "authorized imprisonment" standard might place on the States. But, with all respect, that concern is both irrelevant and speculative. The Court's opinion turns the reasoning of *Argersinger* on its head. It restricts the right to counsel, perhaps the most fundamental Sixth Amendment right, more narrowly than the admittedly less fundamental right to jury trial. The abstract pretext that "constitutional line drawing becomes more difficult as the reach of the Constitution is extended further, and as efforts are made to transpose lines from one area of Sixth Amendment jurisprudence to another," cannot camouflage the anomalous result the Court reaches. Today's decision reminds one of Mr. Justice Black's description of *Betts v. Brady:* "an anachronism when handed down" that "ma[kes] an abrupt break with its own well-considered precedents."

Mr. Justice BLACKMUN, dissenting. . . .

● ● ● ● ● ● ● ● ● ● ● ● ● ● ●

United States v. Salerno

Supreme Court of the United States, 1987.
481 U.S. 739, 107 S.Ct. 2095, 95 L.Ed.2d 697.

[This case stems from the prosecution of two alleged organized crime figures under the federal Racketeer Influenced and Corrupt Organizations (RICO) Act. Here the Supreme Court upholds the constitutionality of a federal statute permitting denial of bail in cases where the pretrial release of a defendant threatens the safety of other persons or the community.]

Chief Justice REHNQUIST delivered the opinion of the Court.

The Bail Reform Act of 1984 allows a federal court to detain an arrestee pending trial if the government demonstrates by clear and convincing evidence after an adversary hearing that no release conditions "will reasonably assure . . . the safety of any other person and the community." The United States Court of Appeals for the Second Circuit struck down this provision of the Act as facially unconstitutional, because, in that court's words, this type of pretrial detention violates "substantive due process." We granted certiorari because of a conflict among the Courts of Appeals regarding the validity of the Act. . . . We hold that, as against the facial attack mounted by these respondents, the Act fully comports with constitutional requirements. We therefore reverse.

Responding to "the alarming problem of crimes committed by persons on release," . . . Congress formulated the Bail Reform Act of 1984 . . . as the solution to a bail crisis in the federal courts. The Act represents the National Legislature's considered response to numerous perceived deficiencies in the federal bail process. By providing for sweeping changes in both the way federal courts consider bail applications and the circumstances under which bail is granted, Congress hoped to "give the courts adequate authority to make release decisions that give appropriate recognition to the danger a person may pose to others if released." . . .

To this end, Sec. 314(a) of the Act requires a judicial officer to determine whether an arrestee shall be detained. Section 3142(e) provides that "[i]f, after a hearing pursuant to the provisions of subsection (f), the judicial officer finds that no condition or combination of conditions will reasonably assure the appearance of the person as required and the safety of any other person and the community, he shall order the detention of the person prior to trial." Section 3142(f) provides the arrestee with a number of procedural safeguards. He may request the presence of counsel at the detention hearing, he may testify and present witnesses in his behalf, as well as proffer evidence, and he may cross-examine other witnesses appearing at the hearing. If the judicial officer finds that no conditions of pretrial release can reasonably assure the safety of other persons and the community, he must state his findings of fact in writing, § 3142(i), and support his conclusion with "clear and convincing evidence." § 3142(f).

The judicial officer is not given unbridled discretion in making the detention determination. Congress has specified the considerations relevant to that decision. These factors include the nature and seriousness of the charges, the substantiality of the government's evidence against the arrestee, the arrestee's background and characteristics, and the nature and seriousness of the danger posed by the suspect's release. § 3142(g). Should a judicial officer order detention, the detainee is entitled to expedited appellate review of the detention order. § 3145(b), (c).

Respondents Anthony Salerno and Vincent Cafaro were arrested on March 21, 1986, after being charged in a 29-count indictment alleging various Racketeer

Influenced and Corrupt Organizations Act (RICO) violations, mail and wire fraud offenses, extortion, and various criminal gambling violations. The RICO counts alleged 35 acts of racketeering activity, including fraud, extortion, gambling, and conspiracy to commit murder. At respondents' arraignment, the Government moved to have Salerno and Cafaro detained pursuant to § 3142(e), on the ground that no condition of release would assure the safety of the community or any person. The District Court held a hearing at which the Government made a detailed proffer of evidence. The Government's case showed that Salerno was the "boss" of the Genovese Crime Family of La Cosa Nostra and that Cafaro was a "captain" in the Genovese Family. Accordingly, to the Government's proffer, based in large part on conversations intercepted by a court-ordered wiretap, the two respondents had participated in wide-ranging conspiracies to aid their illegitimate enterprises through violent means. The Government also offered the testimony of two of its trial witnesses, who would assert that Salerno personally participated in two murder conspiracies. Salerno opposed the motion for detention, challenging the credibility of the Government's witnesses. He offered the testimony of several character witnesses as well as a letter from his doctor stating that he was suffering from a serious medical condition. Cafaro presented no evidence at the hearing, but instead characterized the wiretap conversations as merely "tough talk."

The District Court granted the Government's detention motion, concluding that the Government had established by clear and convincing evidence that no condition or combination of conditions of release would ensure the safety of the community or any person.

Respondents appealed, contending that to the extent that the Bail Reform Act permits pretrial detention on the ground that the arrestee is likely to commit future crimes, it is unconstitutional on its face. Over a dissent, the United States Court of Appeals for the Second Circuit agreed. . . .

Respondents . . . contend that the Bail Reform Act violates the Excessive Bail Clause of the Eighth Amendment. The Court of Appeals did not address this issue because it found that the Act violates the Due Process Clause. We think that the Act survives a challenge founded upon the Eighth Amendment.

The Eighth Amendment addresses pretrial release by providing merely that "Excessive bail shall not be required." The Clause, of course, says nothing about whether bail shall be available at all. Re-

spondents nevertheless contend that this Clause grants them a right to bail calculated solely upon considerations of flight. They rely on *Stack v. Boyle* . . . (1951), in which the Court stated that "bail set at a figure higher than an amount reasonably calculated [to ensure the defendant's presence at trial] is 'excessive' under the Eighth Amendment." In respondents' view, since the Bail Reform Act allows a court essentially to set bail at an infinite amount for reasons not related to the risk of flight, it violates the Excessive Bail Clause. Respondents concede that the right to bail they have discovered in the Eighth Amendment is not absolute. A court may, for example, refuse bail in capital cases. And, as the Court of Appeals noted and respondents admit, a court may refuse bail when the defendant presents a threat to the judicial process by intimidating witnesses. . . . Respondents characterize these exceptions as consistent with what they claim to be the sole purpose of bail—to ensure integrity of the judicial process.

While we agree that a primary function of bail is to safeguard the courts' role in adjudicating the guilt or innocence of defendants, we reject the proposition that the Eighth Amendment categorically prohibits the government from pursuing other admittedly compelling interests through regulation of pretrial release. The above-quoted dicta in *Stack v. Boyle* is far too slender a reed on which to rest this argument. The Court in *Stack* had no occasion to consider whether the Excessive Bail Clause requires courts to admit all defendants to bail, because the statute before the Court in that case in fact allowed the defendants to be bailed. Thus, the Court had to determine only whether bail, admittedly available in that case, was excessive if set at a sum greater than that necessary to ensure the arrestees' presence at trial. . . .

In our society liberty is the norm, and detention prior to trial or without trial is the carefully limited exception. We hold that the provisions for pretrial detention in the Bail Reform Act of 1984 fall within that carefully limited exception. The Act authorizes the detention prior to trial of arrestees charged with serious felonies who are found after an adversary hearing to pose a threat to the safety of individuals or to the community which no condition of release can dispel. The numerous procedural safeguards detailed above must attend this adversary hearing. We are unwilling to say that this congressional determination, based as it is upon the primary concern of every government—a concern for the safety and indeed the lives of its citizens—on its face violates . . . the Excessive Bail Clause of the Eighth Amendment.

The judgment of the Court of Appeals is therefore reversed.

Justice MARSHALL, with whom Justice BRENNAN joins, dissenting.

This case brings before the Court for the first time a statute in which Congress declares that a person innocent of any crime may be jailed indefinitely, pending the trial of allegations which are legally presumed to be untrue, if the Government shows to the satisfaction of a judge that the accused is likely to commit crimes, unrelated to the pending charges, at any time in the future. Such statutes, consistent with the usages of tyranny and the excesses of what bitter experience teaches us to call the police state, have long been thought incompatible with the fundamental human rights protected by our Constitution. Today a majority of this Court holds otherwise. Its decision disregards basic principles of justice established centuries ago and enshrined beyond the reach of governmental interference in the Bill of Rights. . . .

Justice STEVENS, dissenting. . . .

● ● ● ● ● ● ● ● ● ● ● ● ● ●

United States v. Calandra

Supreme Court of the United States, 1974.
414 U.S. 338, 94 S.Ct. 613, 38 L.Ed.2d 561.

[In this case the Supreme Court considers whether a witness summoned to appear and testify before a grand jury may refuse to answer questions on the ground that they are based on evidence obtained from an unlawful search and seizure. In his opinion for the Court, Justice Powell discusses the role and function of the grand jury.]

Mr. Justice POWELL delivered the opinion of the court.

. . . The institution of the grand jury is deeply rooted in Anglo-American history. In England, the grand jury served for centuries both as a body of accusers sworn to discover and present for trial persons suspected of criminal wrongdoing and as a protector of citizens against arbitrary and oppressive governmental action. In this country the Founders thought the grand jury so essential to basic liberties that they provided in the Fifth Amendment that federal prosecution for serious crimes can only be instituted by "a presentment or indictment of a Grand Jury." . . . The grand jury's historic functions survive to this day. Its responsibilities continue to include both the determination whether there is probable cause to believe a crime has been committed and the protection of citizens against unfounded criminal prosecutions. . . .

Traditionally the grand jury has been accorded wide latitude to inquire into violations of criminal law. No judge presides to monitor its proceedings. It deliberates in secret and may determine alone the course of its inquiry. The grand jury may compel the production of evidence or the testimony of witnesses as it considers appropriate, and its operation generally is unrestrained by the technical procedural and evidentiary rules governing the conduct of criminal trials. "It is a grand inquest, a body with powers of investigation and inquisition, the scope of whose inquiries is not to be limited narrowly by questions of propriety or forecasts of the probable result of the investigation, or by doubts whether any particular individual will be found properly subject to an accusation of crime." . . .

The scope of the grand jury's powers reflects its special role in insuring fair and effective law enforcement. A grand jury proceeding is not an adversary hearing in which the guilt or innocence of the accused is adjudicated. Rather, it is an *ex parte* investigation to determine whether a crime has been committed and whether criminal proceedings should be instituted against any person. The grand jury's investigative power must be broad if its public responsibility is adequately to be discharged. . . .

The grand jury's sources of information are widely drawn, and the validity of an indictment is not affected by the character of the evidence considered. Thus, an indictment valid on its face is not subject to challenge on the ground that the grand jury acted on the basis of inadequate or incompetent evidence, . . . or even on the basis of information obtained in violation of a defendant's Fifth Amendment privilege against self-incrimination. . . .

The power of a federal court to compel persons to appear and testify before a grand jury is also firmly established. . . . The duty to testify has long been recognized as a basic obligation that every citizen owes his Government. . . . The duty to testify may on occasion be burdensome and even embarrassing. It may cause injury to a witness' social and economic status. Yet the duty to testify has been regarded as "so necessary to the administration of justice" that the witness' personal interest in privacy must yield to the public's overriding interest in full disclosure. . . . Furthermore, a witness may not interfere with the course of the grand jury's inquiry. He "is not entitled to urge objections of incompetency or irrelevancy, such as a party might raise, for this is no concern of his." . . . Nor is he entitled "to challenge the authority of the court or of the grand jury" or "to set limits to the investigation that the grand jury may conduct." . . .

Of course, the grand jury's subpoena power is not unlimited. It may consider incompetent evidence, but it may not itself violate a valid privilege, whether established by the Constitution, statutes, or the common law. . . . Although, for example, an indictment based on evidence obtained in violation of a defendant's Fifth Amendment privilege is nevertheless valid, . . . the grand jury may not force a witness to answer questions in violation of that constitutional guarantee. Rather, the grand jury may override a Fifth Amendment claim only if the witness is granted immunity co-extensive with the privilege against self-incrimination. . . . Similarly, a grand jury may not compel a person to produce books and papers that would incriminate him. . . . The grand jury is also without power to invade a legitimate privacy interest protected by the Fourth Amendment. A grand jury's subpoena *duces tecum* will be disallowed if it is "far too sweeping in its terms to be regarded as reasonable" under the Fourth Amendment. . . . Judicial supervision is properly exercised in such cases to prevent the wrong before it occurs. . . .

In the instant case, the Court of Appeals held that the exclusionary rule of the Fourth Amendment limits the grand jury's power to compel a witness to answer questions based on evidence obtained from a prior unlawful search and seizure. The exclusionary rule was adopted to effectuate the Fourth Amendment right of all citizens "to be secure in their persons, houses, papers, and effects, against unreasonable searches and seizures. . . ." Under this rule, evidence obtained in violation of the Fourth Amendment cannot be used in a criminal proceeding against the victim of the illegal

search and seizure. . . . This prohibition applies as well to the fruits of the illegally seized evidence. . . .

The purpose of the exclusionary rule is not to redress the injury to the privacy of the search victim. . . . Instead, the rule's prime purpose is to deter future unlawful police conduct and thereby effectuate the guarantee of the Fourth Amendment against unreasonable search and seizures. . . . In sum, the rule is a judicially created remedy designed to safeguard Fourth Amendment rights generally through its deterrent effect, rather than a personal constitutional right of the party aggrieved.

Despite its broad deterrent purpose, the exclusionary rule has never been interpreted to proscribe the use of illegally seized evidence in all proceedings or against all persons. As with any remedial device, the application of the rule has been restricted to those areas where its remedial objectives are thought most efficaciously served. . . .

In deciding whether to extend the exclusionary rule to grand jury proceedings, we must weigh the potential injury to the historic role and functions of the grand jury against the potential benefits of the rule as applied in this context. It is evident that this extension of the exclusionary rule would seriously impede the grand jury. Because the grand jury does not finally adjudicate guilt or innocence, it has traditionally been allowed to pursue its investigative and accusatorial functions unimpeded by the evidentiary and procedural restrictions applicable to a criminal trial. Permitting witnesses to invoke the exclusionary rule before a grand jury would precipitate adjudication of issues hitherto reserved for the trial on the merits and would delay and disrupt grand jury proceedings. Suppression hearings would halt the orderly progress of an investigation and might necessitate extended litigation of issues only tangentially related to the grand jury's primary objective. The probable result would be "protracted interruption of grand jury proceedings," . . . effectively transforming them into preliminary trials on the merits. In some cases the delay might be fatal to the enforcement of the criminal law. . . . [W]e believe that allowing a grand jury witness to invoke the exclusionary rule would unduly interfere with the effective and expeditious discharge of the grand jury's duties.

Against this potential damage to the role and functions of the grand jury, we must weigh the benefits to be derived from this proposed extension of the exclusionary rule. Suppression of the use of illegally seized evidence against the search victim in a criminal trial is thought to be an important method of effectuating the Fourth Amendment. But it does not follow that the Fourth Amendment requires adoption of every proposal that might deter police misconduct. . . .

Any incremental deterrent effect which might be achieved by extending the rule to grand jury proceedings is uncertain at best. Whatever deterrence of police misconduct may result from the exclusion of illegally seized evidence from criminal trials, it is unrealistic to assume that application of the rule to grand jury proceedings would significantly further that goal. Such an extension would deter only police investigation consciously directed toward the discovery of evidence solely for use in a grand jury investigation. The incentive to disregard the requirement of the Fourth Amendment solely to obtain an indictment from a grand jury is substantially negated by the inadmissibility of the illegally seized evidence in a subsequent criminal prosecution of the search victim. For the most part, a prosecutor would be unlikely to request an indictment where a conviction could not be obtained. We therefore decline to embrace a view that would achieve a speculative and undoubtedly minimal advance in the deterrence of police misconduct at the expense of substantially impeding the role of the grand jury. . . .

Mr. Justice BRENNAN, with whom Mr. Justice DOUGLAS and Mr. Justice MARSHALL join, dissenting.

The Court holds that the exclusionary rule in search-and-seizure cases does not apply to grand jury proceedings because the principal objective of the rule is "to deter future unlawful police conduct" . . .

and "it is unrealistic to assume that application of the rule to grand jury proceedings would significantly further that goal." . . .

This downgrading of the exclusionary rule to a determination whether its application in a particular type of proceeding furthers deterrence of future police misconduct reflects a startling misconception, unless it is a purposeful rejection, of the historical objective and purpose of the rule.

The commands of the Fourth Amendment are, of course, directed solely to public officials. Necessarily, therefore, only official violations of those commands could have created the evil that threatened to make the Amendment a dead letter. But curtailment of the evil, if a consideration at all, was at best only a hoped-for effect of the exclusionary rule, not its ultimate objective. Indeed, there is no evidence that the possible deterrent effect of the rule was given any attention by the judges chiefly responsible for its formulation. Their concern as guardians of the Bill of Rights was to fashion an enforcement tool to give content and meaning to the Fourth Amendment's guarantees. . . . Since, however, those judges were without power to direct or control the conduct of law enforcement officers, the enforcement tool had necessarily to be one capable of administration by judges. The exclusionary rule, if not perfect, accomplished the twin goals of enabling the judiciary to avoid the taint of partnership in official lawlessness and of assuring the people—all potential victims of unlawful government conduct—that the government would not profit from its lawless behavior, thus minimizing the risk of seriously undermining popular trust in government. . . .

● ● ● ● ● ● ●   ● ● ● ● ● ● ●

Boykin v. Alabama

Supreme Court of the United States, 1969.
395 U.S. 238, 89 S.Ct. 1709, 23 L.Ed.2d 274.

[Here the Supreme Court holds that because a plea of guilty constitutes a waiver of the right to trial, the trial judge must determine that a defendant's guilty plea is being entered knowingly and intelligently before accepting the plea.]

Mr. Justice DOUGLAS delivered the opinion of the Court.

In the spring of 1966, within the period of a fortnight, a series of armed robberies occurred in Mobile, Alabama. The victims, in each case, were local shopkeepers open at night who were forced by a gunman to hand over money. While robbing one grocery store, the assailant fired his gun once, sending a bullet through a door into the ceiling. A few days earlier in a drugstore, the robber had allowed his gun to discharge in such a way that the bullet, on ricochet from the floor, struck a customer in the leg. Shortly thereafter a local grand jury returned five indictments against petitioner, a 27-year-old Negro, for common-law robbery—an offense punishable in Alabama by death.

Before the matter came to trial, the court determined that petitioner was indigent and appointed counsel to represent him. Three days later, at his arraignment, petitioner pleaded guilty to all five indictments. So far as the record shows, the judge asked no questions of petitioner concerning his plea, and petitioner did not address the court. . . .

A plea of guilty is more than a confession which admits that the accused did various acts; it is itself a conviction; nothing remains but to give judgment and determine punishment. . . . Admissibility of a confession must be based on a "reliable determination on the voluntariness issue which satisfies the constitutional rights of the defendant." . . . The requirement that the prosecution spread on the record the prerequisites of a valid waiver is no constitutional innovation. . . . "The record must show, or there must be an allegation and evidence which show, that an accused was offered counsel but intelligently and understandingly rejected the offer. Anything less is not waiver."

We think that the same standard must be applied to determining whether a guilty plea is voluntarily made. For, as we have said, a plea of guilty is more than an admission of conduct; it is a conviction. Ignorance, incomprehension, coercion, terror, in-

ducements, subtle or blatant threats might be a perfect cover-up of unconstitutionality. The question of an effective waiver of a federal constitutional right in a proceeding is of course governed by federal standards. . . .

Several federal constitutional rights are involved in a waiver that takes place when a plea of guilty is entered in a state criminal trial. First, is the privilege against compulsory self-incrimination guaranteed by the Fifth Amendment and applicable to the States by reason of the Fourteenth. . . . Second, is the right to trial by jury. . . . Third, is the right to confront one's accusers. . . . We cannot presume a waiver of these three important federal rights from a silent record.

What is at stake for an accused facing death or imprisonment demands the utmost solicitude of which courts are capable in canvassing the matter with the accused to make sure he has a full understanding of what the plea connotes and of its consequence. When the judge discharges that function, he leaves a record adequate for any review that may be later sought . . . and forestalls the spin-off of collateral proceedings that seek to probe murky memories.

The three dissenting justices in the Alabama Supreme Court stated the law accurately when they concluded that there was reversible error "because the record does not disclose that the defendant voluntarily and understandingly entered his pleas of guilty." . . .

Mr. Justice HARLAN, whom Mr. Justice BLACK joins, dissenting. . . .

● ● ● ● ● ● ● ● ● ● ● ● ● ●

Bordenkircher v. Hayes

Supreme Court of the United States, 1978.
434 U.S. 357, 98 S.Ct. 663, 54 L.Ed.2d 604.

[In this case the Supreme Court evaluates a particular exercise of prosecutorial discretion associated with the plea-bargaining process.]

Mr. Justice STEWART delivered the opinion of the Court.

The question in this case is whether the Due Process Clause of the Fourteenth Amendment is violated when a state prosecutor carries out a threat made during plea negotiations to reindict the accused

on more serious charges if he does not plead guilty to the offense with which he was originally charged.

The respondent, Paul Lewis Hayes, was indicted by a Fayette County, Ky., grand jury on a charge of uttering a forged instrument in the amount of $88.30, an offense then punishable by a term of two to 10 years in prison. After arraignment, Hayes, his retained counsel, and the Commonwealth's attorney met in the presence of the clerk of the court to discuss a possible plea agreement. During these conferences the prosecutor offered to recommend a sentence of five years in prison if Hayes would plead guilty to the indictment. He also said that if Hayes did not plead guilty and "save the court the inconvenience of a trial," he would return to the grand jury to seek an indictment under the Kentucky Habitual Criminal Act, which would subject Hayes to a mandatory sentence of life imprisonment by reason of his two prior felony convictions. Hayes chose not to plead guilty, and the prosecutor did obtain an indictment charging him under the Habitual Criminal Act. It is not disputed that the recidivist charge was fully justified by the evidence, that the prosecutor was in possession of this evidence at the time of the original indictment, and that Hayes' refusal to plead guilty to the original charge was what led to his indictment under the habitual criminal statute.

A jury found Hayes guilty on the principal charge of uttering a forged instrument and, in a separate proceeding, further found that he had twice before been convicted of felonies. As required by the habitual offender statute, he was sentenced to a life term in the penitentiary. The Kentucky Court of Appeals rejected Hayes' constitutional objections to the enhanced sentence, holding in an unpublished opinion that imprisonment for life with the possibility of parole was constitutionally permissible in light of the previous felonies of which Hayes had been convicted, and that the prosecutor's decision to indict him as an habitual offender was a legitimate use of available leverage in the plea bargaining process.

On Hayes' petition for a federal writ of habeas corpus, the United States District Court for the Eastern District of Kentucky agreed that there had been no constitutional violation in the sentence or the indictment procedure and denied the writ. The Court of Appeals for the Sixth Circuit reversed the District Court's judgment. While recognizing "that plea bargaining now plays an important role in our criminal justice system," the appellate court thought that the prosecutor's conduct during the bargaining negotiations had violated the principles . . . which "protect[ed] defendants from the vindictive exercise of a prosecutor's discretion." . . . We granted certiorari to consider a constitutional question of importance in the administration of criminal justice.

It may be helpful to clarify at the outset the nature of the issue in this case. While the prosecutor did not actually obtain the recidivist indictment until after the plea conferences had ended, his intention to do so was clearly put forth at the outset of the plea negotiations. Hayes was thus fully informed of the true terms of the offer when he made his decision to plead not guilty. This is not a situation, therefore, where the prosecutor without notice brought an additional and more serious charge after plea negotiations relating only to the original indictment had ended with the defendant's insistence on pleading not guilty. As a practical matter, in short, this case would be no different if the grand jury had indicted Hayes as a recidivist from the outset, and the prosecutor had offered to drop that charge as part of the plea bargain.

We have recently had occasion to observe that "whatever might be the situation in an ideal world, the fact is that the guilty plea and the often concomitant plea bargain are important components of this country's criminal justice system. Properly administered, they can benefit all concerned." The open acknowledgment of this previously clandestine practice has led this Court to recognize the importance of counsel during plea negotiations, *Brady v. United States*, 397 U.S. 742, 758, the need for a public record indicating that a plea was knowingly and voluntarily made, *Boykin v. Alabama*, 395 U.S. 238, 242, and the requirement that a prosecutor's plea bargaining promise must be kept, *Santobello v. New York*, 404 U.S. 257, 262. . . .

To punish a person because he has done what the law plainly allows him to do is a due process violation of the most basic sort, . . . and for an agent of the State to pursue a course of action whose objective is to penalize a person's reliance on his legal rights is "patently unconstitutional. . . ." But in the "give-and-take" of plea bargaining, there is no such element of punishment or retaliation so long as the accused is free to accept or reject the prosecution's offer.

Plea bargaining flows from "the mutuality of advantage" to defendants and prosecutors, each with his own reasons for wanting to avoid trial. . . . Defendants advised by competent counsel and protected by other procedural safeguards are presumptively capable of intelligent choice in response to prosecutorial persuasion, and unlikely to be driven to false self-condemnation. Indeed, acceptance of the basic legitimacy of plea bargaining necessarily implies rejection of any notion that a guilty plea is involuntary in a constitutional sense simply because it is the end result of the bargaining process. By hypothesis, the plea may have been induced by promises of a recommendation of a lenient sentence or a reduction of charges, and thus by fear of the possibility of a greater penalty upon conviction after a trial.

While confronting a defendant with the risk of more severe punishment clearly may have a "discouraging effect on the defendant's assertion of his trial rights, the imposition of these difficult choices [is] an inevitable"—and permissible—"attribute of any legitimate system which tolerates and encourages the negotiation of pleas." . . . It follows that, by tolerating and encouraging the negotiation of pleas, this Court has necessarily accepted as constitutionally legitimate the simple reality that the prosecutor's interest at the bargaining table is to persuade the defendant to forego his right to plead not guilty.

It is not disputed here that Hayes was properly chargeable under the recidivist statute, since he had in fact been convicted of two previous felonies. In our system, so long as the prosecutor has probable cause to believe that the accused committed an offense defined by statute, the decision whether or not to prosecute, and what charge to file or bring before a grand jury, generally rests entirely in his discretion. Within the limits set by the legislature's constitutionally valid definition of chargeable offenses, "the conscious exercise of some selectivity in enforcement is not in itself a federal constitutional violation" so long as "the selection was [not] deliberately based upon an unjustifiable standard such as race, religion, or other arbitrary classification. . . ." To hold that the prosecutor's desire to induce a guilty plea is an "unjustifiable standard," which, like race or religion, may play no part in his charging decision, would contradict the very premises that underlie the concept of plea bargaining itself. Moreover, a rigid constitutional rule that would prohibit a prosecutor from acting forthrightly in his dealings with the defense could only invite unhealthy subterfuge that would drive the practice of plea bargaining back into the shadows from which it has so recently emerged.

There is no doubt that the breadth of discretion that our country's legal system vests in prosecuting attorneys carries with it the potential for both individual and institutional abuse. And broad though that discretion may be, there are undoubtedly constitutional limits upon its exercise. We hold only that the course of conduct engaged in by the prosecutor in this case, which no more than openly presented the defendant with the unpleasant alternatives of foregoing trial or facing charges on which he was plainly subject to prosecution, did not violate the Due Process Clause of the Fourteenth Amendment.

Accordingly, the judgment of the Court of Appeals is reversed.

Mr. Justice POWELL, dissenting.

Although I agree with much of the Court's opinion, I am not satisfied that the result in this case is just or that the conduct of the plea bargaining met the requirements of due process. . . .

The plea-bargaining process, as recognized by this Court, is essential to the functioning of the criminal-justice system. It normally affords genuine benefits to defendants as well as to society. And if the system is to work effectively, prosecutors must be accorded the widest discretion, within constitutional limits, in conducting bargaining. . . . This is especially true when a defendant is represented by counsel and presumably is fully advised of his rights. Only in the most exceptional case should a court conclude that the scales of the bargaining are so unevenly balanced as to arouse suspicion. In this case, the prosecutor's actions denied respondent due process because their admitted purpose was to discourage and then to penalize with unique severity his exercise of constitutional rights. Implementation of a strategy calculated solely to deter the exercise of constitutional rights is not a constitutionally permissible exercise of discretion. I would affirm the opinion of the Court of Appeals on the facts of this case.

[Justices BLACKMUN, BRENNAN and MARSHALL also dissented.]

CHAPTER

18

The Criminal Trial

Introduction

More than 90 percent of felony charges and an even higher percentage of misdemeanor offenses are disposed of before trial. Nevertheless, the criminal trial is the centerpiece of the criminal justice system for several reasons. First, trials are generally held before juries drawn from the community. Second, trials are the most visible aspect of the justice system and often attract widespread media coverage. Finally, cases disposed of by trial often have an important impact on the administration of the criminal law.

Before the arrival of William the Conqueror in England in 1066, criminal trials took the forms of compurgation or ordeal. In a trial by compurgation, a defendant who had denied guilt under oath attempted to recruit a body of men to attest to his or her honor. If a group would swear to the defendant's innocence, the law considered the defendant to be innocent. In a trial by ordeal, the defendant was tortured by fire or water. If the defendant survived the ordeal, God had intervened to prove the defendant's innocence before the law.

Jury trials as we know them today originated with the Magna Charta, which the English nobles forced King John to sign at Runnymede in 1215. The Magna Charta granted freemen the right of trial by their peers. Early juries comprised persons who had knowledge of the facts of a case—it was centuries before trial juries functioned in the role they now perform. The jury became characteristic of the English common law, a feature that distinguished it from the law of the European continent, which was based on Roman law.

Constitutional Rights Pertaining to the Criminal Trial

Despite the protections of the common law, English subjects accused of crime were not always afforded fair trials. The notorious Star Chamber was established in the fifteenth century to punish offenses outside the common law. Its real purpose was to punish opponents of the monarch. It met in secret, dispensed with jury trials, and offered no legal protections to the accused. Before the Star Chamber, accusation was tantamount to conviction. Its punishments were unduly harsh, often involving torture and disfigurement. Although the Star Chamber was abolished by Parliament in 1641, the Framers of the American Bill of Rights wanted to make sure that no such institution would ever be established in this country. Thus, as the Sixth Amendment provides,

> In all criminal prosecutions, the accused shall enjoy the right to a speedy and public trial, by an impartial jury of the State and district wherein the crime shall have been committed, which district shall have been previously ascertained by law, and to be informed of the nature and cause of the accusation; to be confronted with the witnesses against him; to have compulsory process for obtaining witnesses in his favor, and to have the Assistance of Counsel for his defence.

Because they are deemed to be fundamentally important in securing liberty and ensuring fairness, the various rights protected by the Sixth Amendment are made applicable to state criminal trials by the Fourteenth Amendment. See, e.g., *Gideon v. Wainwright*, 372 U.S. 335, 344, 83 S.Ct. 792, 796, 9 L.Ed.2d 799, 805 (1963); *Pointer v. Texas*, 380 U.S. 400, 85 S.Ct. 1065, 13 L.Ed.2d 923 (1965); *Duncan v. Louisiana*, 391 U.S. 145, 88 S.Ct. 1444, 20 L.Ed.2d 491 (1968).

The Right to Compulsory Process

The Sixth Amendment guarantees a defendant the right "to have **compulsory process** for obtaining witnesses in his favor." This affords the defendant the right to obtain court process (a **subpoena**) to compel witnesses to appear in court. There are some restrictions (for example, a defendant cannot cause numerous witnesses to be subpoenaed simply to give cumulative testimony), but courts allow defendants a fair degree of liberality in causing witnesses to be subpoenaed. Of course, the prosecution can also compel the attendance of witnesses.

The Right to a Public Trial

The Sixth Amendment guarantees "the right to a speedy and public trial." Although the right to an **open public trial** is central to our system of justice, that right is not absolute. After pointing out that a public trial is for the benefit of the accused and to ensure that the judge and prosecutor carry out their duties responsibly, the Supreme Court in *Waller v. Georgia,* 467 U.S. 39, 45, 104 S.Ct. 2210, 2215, 81 L.Ed.2d 31, 38 (1984), explained that

> the right to an open trial may give way in certain cases to other rights or interests, such as the defendant's right to a fair trial or the government's interest in inhibiting disclosure of sensitive information. Such circumstances will be rare, however, and the balance of interest must be struck with special care.

The Supreme Court has ruled that the requirement for openness extends to all phases of the trial. Consequently, in 1982 it declared invalid a state statute requiring mandatory closing of the courtroom during the testimony of victims of sexual offenses. The Court said the issue of closing should be left to the discretion of the trial judge to determine on a case-by-case basis when the state's legitimate interests for the minor's well-being necessitate closing the courtroom. *Globe Newspaper Company v. Superior Court,* 457 U.S. 596, 102 S.Ct. 2613, 73 L.Ed.2d 248 (1982). Two years later, the Court held that *voir dire* proceedings (discussed later in this chapter) in criminal trials can be closed only by overcoming the presumption of openness. Accordingly, before a trial court orders the closing of court proceedings, it must make specific findings that such closing is essential and explain why available alternatives are inadequate. *Press-Enterprise Company v. Superior Court of California,* 464 U.S. 501, 104 S.Ct. 819, 78 L.Ed.2d 629 (1984).

Among the reasons frequently cited by courts for limiting public access to criminal proceedings are the need to protect rape victims or children who have been molested and the need to protect witnesses and jurors from embarrassment, trauma, or intimidation.

The Sixth Amendment right to a public trial, even if waived by the defendant, does not allow a defendant to invoke the converse of that right—that is, there is no right to a private trial. *Singer v. United States,* 380 U.S. 24, 34–35, 85 S.Ct. 1783, 790, 13 L.Ed.2d 630, 638 (1965).

The Right to Trial by Jury

The Sixth Amendment also ensures the right to trial by jury. However, the amendment leaves unanswered questions concerning the qualifications of jurors, the method of their selection, and the requirements for a jury to convict a person accused of a crime.

An accused may waive the right to a **jury trial.** Indeed, many persons who plead not guilty to misdemeanor charges elect a **bench trial.** On the other hand, most defendants who plead not guilty to felony charges choose to be tried by jury. The

United States Supreme Court has ruled that the constitutional right to a jury trial extends to the class of cases for which an accused was entitled to a jury trial when the Constitution was adopted. This did not include juvenile cases; hence, there is no right to a jury trial for juveniles under the federal constitution. *McKeiver v. Pennsylvania*, 403 U.S. 528, 91 S.Ct. 1976, 29 L.Ed.2d 647 (1971). Furthermore, the right to trial by jury is not applicable to military tribunals. *Ex parte Quirin*, 317 U.S. 1, 63 S.Ct. 1, 87 L.Ed. 3 (1942).

As now interpreted, the Sixth Amendment guarantees an accused the right to a jury trial in criminal cases where a penalty of more than six months' imprisonment can be imposed. *Codispoti v. Pennsylvania*, 418 U.S. 506, 94 S.Ct. 2687, 41 L.Ed.2d 912 (1974). Offenses that carry a possible penalty of no more than six months' imprisonment are generally termed "petty offenses," and a jury trial is not required under the Constitution. *Baldwin v. New York*, 399 U.S. 66, 90 S.Ct. 1886, 26 L.Ed.2d 437 (1970). In 1996, in a 5–4 decision, the Supreme Court ruled that a defendant charged with multiple petty offenses is not entitled to a jury trial under the federal constitution even though the possible sentence may add up to more than six months in prison. *Lewis v. United States*, 518 U.S. 322, 116 S.Ct. 2163, 135 L.Ed.2d 590 (1996).

Notwithstanding the federal constitutional requirements, in some states, under the state constitution or statutory law, an accused has the right to a jury trial for certain offenses even though they may be classified as "petty offenses" from a federal constitutional standpoint. In Florida, for example, a defendant is entitled to a jury trial under the state constitution for any offense that was a *malum in se* and indictable at common law even though the maximum punishment is less than six months. *Reed v. State*, 470 So.2d 1382 (Fla. 1985).

The constitutional requirement of a jury trial applies to the states, thereby guaranteeing a defendant a right to a jury trial in a state criminal prosecution if such a right would exist in a federal prosecution. *Duncan v. Louisiana*, supra. Interestingly, the Sixth Amendment right to a jury trial does not afford a defendant the corresponding right to be tried before a judge without a jury. *Singer v. United States*, 380 U.S. 24, 85 S.Ct. 783, 13 L.Ed.2d 630 (1965).

ANONYMOUS JURIES

Ordinarily, the identities of members of a jury are known. But can the court impanel an anonymous jury? In a recent case the defendants were convicted in a federal district court of participating in a continuing criminal enterprise of murder, drug distribution, and firearms offenses. One ground assigned in their appeal was that they were denied a fair trial because the identities of the jurors who found them guilty were not publicly revealed. The U.S. Court of Appeals for the Fifth Circuit rejected their challenge and held that the trial court did not abuse its discretion in impaneling an anonymous jury. The appellate court mentioned that one of the objectives of the defendants' criminal organization was to interfere with potential witnesses. *United States v. Krout*, 66 F.3d 1420 (5th Cir. 1995).

COMPOSITION OF THE JURY TRIAL

At common law, a jury consisted of twelve men. Rule 23(b), Federal Rules of Criminal Procedure, requires a twelve-member jury in criminal cases in federal courts unless the defendant stipulates to fewer in writing. If the court finds it necessary to excuse a juror after the jury has retired to consider its verdict, in the discretion of the court, a valid verdict may be returned by the remaining eleven jurors. All states require twelve-member juries in capital cases. Most require the same number for all felony prosecutions. However, many now use fewer than twelve jurors in misdemeanor cases. Florida

CASE-IN-POINT

What Happens When a Juror Becomes Emotionally Disabled?

Fred Mills was convicted of aggravated robbery in Dallas County, Texas. On the morning of his trial, one of the jurors impaneled to hear the case requested permission to attend a memorial service for his grandfather, who had died the previous evening. The trial judge found the juror was "emotionally disabled" and would not be able to concentrate if not allowed to attend the memorial service. Attempts to postpone the trial disclosed conflicts for other jurors and schedules for other docketed cases, so over Mills's objection, the judge proceeded with the trial with the remaining eleven jurors. On federal habeas cor-

pus review, the U.S. Court of Appeals for the Fifth Circuit noted that Article 36.29 of the Texas Code of Criminal Procedure specifies a norm of twelve jurors in felony cases, yet it provides that if one juror becomes "disabled," the remaining eleven can render a verdict. Citing *Williams v. Florida,* 399 U.S. 78, 90 S.Ct. 1893, 26 L.Ed.2d 446 (1970), the court denied Mills's petition. The court observed that "since Texas provided Mills with a jury possessing the fundamental attributes of the jury guaranteed by the Sixth and Fourteenth Amendments, Mills has no claim for relief."

Mills v. Collins, 924 F.2d 89 (5th Cir. 1991).

An excerpt from the Supreme Court's decision in *Williams v. Florida* appears at the end of the chapter.

uses six-person juries for all but capital felonies. Fla. R. Crim. P. 3.270. In *Williams v. Florida,* 399 U.S. 78, 90 S.Ct. 1893, 26 L.Ed.2d 446 (1970), the Supreme Court upheld the use of six-person juries in the trial of felony offenses in Florida. Subsequently, in *Ballew v. Georgia,* 435 U.S. 223, 98 S.Ct. 1029, 55 L.Ed.2d 234 (1978), the Court held that a jury of only five persons was not acceptable under the Sixth Amendment.

In federal courts and in the great majority of state courts, a jury verdict in a criminal trial must be unanimous. However, a few states accept less than unanimous verdicts. The Supreme Court has approved nonunanimous verdicts rendered by twelve-person juries. *Johnson v. Louisiana,* 406 U.S. 356, 92 S.Ct. 1620, 32 L.Ed.2d 152 (1972); *Apodaca v. Oregon,* 406 U.S. 404, 92 S.Ct. 1628, 32 L.Ed.2d 184 (1972). But the Court held that a conviction by a nonunanimous six-person jury in a state trial for a nonpetty offense violates the right to trial by jury guaranteed by the Sixth and Fourteenth amendments to the U.S. Constitution. *Burch v. Louisiana,* 441 U.S. 130, 99 S.Ct. 1623, 60 L.Ed.2d 96 (1979).

The Right to Counsel

The Sixth Amendment right to counsel at a criminal trial is well established. But a defendant also has a constitutional right of self-representation, and at times the defendant does not exercise that right until the trial. If the defendant does choose **self-representation,** the trial judge must determine whether the defendant has made a voluntary and intelligent decision. If a careful inquiry by the judge indicates that the defendant's election is voluntary and intelligent, then it is incumbent on the court to allow self-representation. Any such waiver of counsel must be carefully documented in the court records, and the court, at its option, may appoint **standby counsel** to assist the defendant. *Faretta v. California,* 422 U.S. 806, 95 S.Ct. 2525, 45 L.Ed.2d 562 (1975). In *State v. Bakalov,* 862 P.2d 1354 (Utah 1993), the Supreme Court of Utah cautioned trial judges to advise a defendant who elects to proceed *pro se* of the risks of presenting a *pro se* defense. In April 2000, a Pennsylvania appellate court ruled that before the right to counsel may be waived, the trial court is required "to make searching and formal on-the-record inquiry to ascertain (1) whether the defendant is aware of his right to counsel and (2) whether the defendant is aware of the consequences of waiving that right or not." *Commonwealth v. Owens,* 750 A.2d 872, 875 (Pa. Super. 2000).

At trial, a defense counsel who represents multiple defendants might discover a possible conflict in his or her representation of the defendants. In such an instance, it is the trial court's duty "either to appoint separate counsel or to take adequate steps to ascertain whether the risk was too remote to warrant separate counsel." *Holloway v. Arkansas,* 435 U.S. 475, 484, 98 S.Ct. 1173, 1178, 55 L.Ed.2d 426, 434 (1978).

In 1976 the Supreme Court ruled that it is a violation of a defendant's Sixth Amendment right to counsel for a trial judge to bar the defendant from conferring with defense counsel during an overnight recess of a trial. *Geders v. United States,* 425 U.S. 80, 96 S.Ct. 1330, 47 L.Ed.2d 592 (1976). More than a decade later, the Court held it was not a denial of the right to counsel for a trial judge to bar a defendant from conferring with counsel during a brief trial recess that occurred after the defendant testified on direct examination, but before cross-examination by the prosecutor. *Perry v. Leeke,* 488 U.S. 272, 109 S.Ct. 594, 102 L.Ed.2d 624 (1989). The Court's holdings in these cases acknowledge the importance of a close relationship between attorney and client during a trial, but also they recognize that the pursuit of truth is the purpose of the in-court examination of witnesses. Thus, there are valid reasons not to allow any witness to confer with counsel between the direct examination and the cross-examination.

Selection of the Jury

State and federal laws prescribe certain basic qualifications for jurors. Statutes commonly require that jurors be at least eighteen years of age and registered voters in the state or district from which they are to be selected. In contrast with past practices, laws prescribing qualifications cannot discriminate to prevent women as a class from serving as jurors. *Taylor v. Louisiana,* 419 U.S. 522, 95 S.Ct. 692, 42 L.Ed.2d 690 (1975). Convicted felons whose civil rights have not been restored are usually excluded from serving on juries. Beyond this, statutes frequently carve out exemptions for expectant mothers and mothers with young children, persons over seventy years of age, and for physicians, dentists, attorneys, judges, teachers, elected officials, police, firefighters, and emergency personnel. The trend has been for states to restrict exemptions from jury duty so that the pool of prospective jurors reflects a representative cross-section of the community.

The Jury Selection and Service Act of 1968, 28 U.S.C.A. § 1861ff, was enacted to ensure that jury panels in federal courts are selected at random from a fair cross-section of the community. States also have statutes prescribing the process of selection. Local officials compile a list of persons qualified to serve as jurors, generally from the rolls of registered voters, driver's license lists, or some combination thereof. From this list, prospective jurors are randomly selected and summoned to court. Compensation paid to trial jurors ranges from meager to modest amounts for their travel and per diem expenses. Most states prohibit an employer from discharging an employee who has been summoned for jury duty.

The body of persons summoned to be jurors is referred to as the **venire.** After outlining the case to be tried and reciting the names of those expected to participate, the judge may excuse those whose physical disabilities or obvious conflicts of interest based on family relationships or business connections disqualify them from serving. After excusing those who do not qualify, the judge swears in the remaining members of the venire to answer questions put to them by the court and counsel. Then six or twelve of these prospective jurors are called at random to take their seats in the jury box, where the judge or counsel for each side may ask further questions in a process called the ***voir dire.***

The *Voir Dire*

Lawyers for the prosecution and the defense are permitted to challenge prospective jurors either for cause or peremptorily. A challenge is a request that a juror be excused from serving. Challenges are customarily asserted at the *voir dire* (from the French, meaning "to tell the truth"). The function of the *voir dire* is to enable the court and counsel to obtain the information necessary to ensure the selection of a fair and impartial jury. To assist in obtaining background information and thereby expedite the *voir dire* process, it is not uncommon for courts to submit a series of written questions to be answered by prospective jurors in advance of their appearance in court. In some courts, the *voir dire* examination is conducted by the trial judge, who may invite the lawyers to suggest questions to ask the prospective jurors. In others, lawyers for each side conduct the *voir dire*. In either event, the presiding judge exercises broad discretion to keep the questioning within proper bounds. A *voir dire* examination is generally conducted before the six or twelve prospective jurors initially selected; however, under certain circumstances some courts have allowed examination of individual jurors apart from the collective group.

The objective of the *voir dire* examination is to select jurors who can render a verdict fairly and impartially. However, it would be naive to expect that the prosecutor and defense counsel are both striving to seat a wholly objective panel of jurors. Obviously, each trial lawyer wants jurors who will be sympathetic to the cause he or she advocates. To accomplish this, trial lawyers must be well versed in the facts of the case and the relevant law. They must also display ingenuity in questioning the prospective jurors to determine whether to exercise their right to challenge jurors' qualifications to serve. Lawyers must be conversant with local court practices because judges have broad discretion in conducting the *voir dire*. Trial lawyers have their own theories on how to conduct a *voir dire* examination, but most would agree that a practical knowledge of psychology is helpful. In recent years, some have even retained social scientists for advice and assistance in the jury selection process. The process of excusing prospective jurors is accomplished by counsel exercising challenges, either "for cause" or "peremptorily"—that is, without assigning a reason.

Challenges for Cause

Challenges for cause may be directed to the venire on the basis of the panel having been improperly selected. An example is when the defense counsel contends that the selection procedures exclude minority members. More commonly, challenges for cause are directed to a prospective juror individually concerning some fact that would disqualify that person from serving on the particular case. Among the more common reasons for disqualification are having a close relationship with counsel, being significantly involved in the case as a witness or in some other capacity, or having formed a definite opinion about the case. However, it is not expected that the jurors be totally ignorant of the facts and issues involved in the case. Forty years ago, Justice Clark, writing for the Supreme Court, observed the following:

> In these days of swift, widespread and diverse methods of communication, an important case can be expected to arouse the interest of the public in the vicinity,

CASE-IN-POINT

When Should a Juror Be Excused for Cause?

The defendant was tried by jury for rape, sodomy, and some weapons offenses. Prospective jurors were not asked during the *voir dire* if they had ever been raped or had a family member or friend who had been raped. After the jury had been selected, a female juror suggested to the court that she should be excused because her daughter had been raped five years earlier. After being closely questioned by the judge and defense lawyer, she expressed convincingly that she and her daughter had effectively recovered from the trauma of the rape and that she could be a fair and impartial juror. The court refused to excuse her from the jury panel. The defendant was convicted and appealed.

The Georgia Court of Appeals affirmed the defendant's conviction. In rejecting the defendant's argument that the trial court erred in not excusing the juror for cause, the court said that the court had an ample basis upon which to believe the juror would perform her duty justly.

Jamison v. State, 295 S.E.2d 203 (Ga. App. 1982).

and scarcely any of those best qualified to serve as jurors will not have formed some impression or opinion as to the merits of the case. *Irvin v. Dowd,* 366 U.S. 717, 722, 81 S.Ct. 1639, 1642, 6 L.Ed.2d 751, 756 (1961).

With our widespread access to television and the Internet, Justice Clark's observation is even more compelling today than in 1961. Nevertheless, prospective jurors who acknowledge that they have formed an opinion on the merits of the case and cannot disregard this opinion are generally excused for cause. Absent unusual circumstances concerning the parties involved in a case, a person would not be excused for cause because of religious or political affiliations.

The Problem of "Death-Qualified" Juries

In 1970 the Supreme Court expressed concern about some courts automatically excluding from juries trying capital cases persons who oppose or who have conscientious scruples against capital punishment. The Court held that opponents of capital punishment could not be excluded from juries impaneled to hear cases where the death penalty could be imposed unless the prospective jurors indicated that they could not make an impartial decision on the issue of guilt or could never vote to impose the death penalty. *Witherspoon v. Illinois,* 391 U.S. 510, 88 S.Ct. 1770, 20 L.Ed.2d 776 (1968).

In *Wainwright v. Witt,* 469 U.S. 412, 424, 105 S.Ct. 844, 852, 83 L.Ed.2d 841, 851–852 (1985), the Court said that the proper standard for determining when a prospective juror may be excluded for cause because of views on capital punishment is whether the juror's views would "prevent or substantially impair the performance of his duties as a juror in accordance with his instructions and oath." Justice Brennan, with whom Justice Marshall joined in dissent, observed that "basic justice demands that juries with the power to decide whether a capital defendant lives or dies not be poisoned against the defendant." 469 U.S. at 439, 105 S.Ct. at 860, 83 L.Ed.2d at 861.

In capital cases, the jury first hears the evidence bearing on the defendant's guilt or innocence; then, only if a guilty verdict is rendered, the jury receives evidence on whether the death penalty should be imposed. This practice is referred to as a **bifurcated trial** (see Chapter 19). The Supreme Court has said that the **death qualification of a jury** (that is, the exclusion of prospective jurors who will not under any circumstances vote for imposition of the death penalty) is designed to obtain a jury that can properly and impartially apply the law to the facts at both the guilt and sentencing phases of a capital trial. On this rationale, the Court held that removal before the guilt phase in a capital trial of prospective jurors whose opposition to the death penalty would impair or prevent performance of their duties at the sentencing phase is not unconstitutional. *Lockhart v. McCree,* 476 U.S. 162, 106 S.Ct. 1758, 90 L.Ed.2d 137 (1986).

Peremptory Challenges of Jurors

It is not always possible to articulate a basis for dismissing a juror who appears to be biased. Therefore, each side in a criminal trial is also allowed a limited number of **peremptory challenges** that may be exercised on *voir dire* to excuse prospective jurors without stating any reason. The number of peremptory challenges is usually provided by statute or court rules.

In federal courts, each party in a criminal case is allowed twenty peremptory challenges where the offense is punishable by death. If the offense is punishable by more than one year in prison, the government is allowed six and the defendant is allowed ten. Each side is allowed three peremptory challenges where the offense carries a punishment of less than one year in prison. Fed. R. Crim. P. 24(b).

States vary in the number of peremptory challenges allowed in criminal trials. Rather typical is Article 35.15 of the Vernon's Annotated Texas Code of Criminal Procedure, which allows the state and defendant fifteen peremptory challenges in capital cases where the state seeks the death penalty. Where two or more defendants are tried together, the state is entitled to eight peremptory challenges for each defendant, and each defendant is entitled to eight. In noncapital felony cases, and in capital cases where the state does not seek the death penalty, the state and defendant are each entitled to ten peremptory challenges. Where two or more defendants are tried together, each defendant is entitled to six peremptory challenges, and the state is likewise entitled to six for each defendant. In misdemeanor cases, each side is allowed either three or five peremptory challenges, depending on the level of court where the defendant is tried.

To determine whether to exercise a peremptory challenge, an attorney conducting a *voir dire* examination attempts to determine the attitudes, background, and personalities of prospective jurors. Trial courts limit the questions that may be asked of prospective jurors, depending on the nature of the case. Some areas of questioning are considered very delicate and usually will not be permitted. For example, in *Alderman v. State,* 327 S.E.2d 168 (Ga. 1985), the Supreme Court of Georgia upheld a trial judge's refusal to allow a defendant to ask prospective jurors questions concerning the kinds of books and magazines they read, whether they were members of any political organizations, and what kinds of bumper stickers they had on their vehicles.

RACIALLY BASED PEREMPTORY CHALLENGES

To reduce the potential for racial discrimination in the exercise of **racially based peremptory challenges,** courts have recently reassessed the historic freedom accorded counsel in exercising peremptory challenges. In 1965, in *Swain v. Alabama,* 380 U.S. 202, 85 S.Ct. 824, 13 L.Ed.2d 759, the Supreme Court said that it was a violation of the Equal Protection Clause of the Fifth Amendment to systematically exclude someone from serving on a jury because of the person's race. To make a *prima facie* case of purposeful discrimination, the defendant faced the formidable task of proving that the peremptory challenge system as a whole was being perverted. There was considerable criticism of the Court's ruling in *Swain v. Alabama,* and the Court again addressed the problem in *Batson v. Kentucky,* 476 U.S. 79, 106 S.Ct. 1712, 90 L.Ed.2d 69 (1986).

An excerpt from the Supreme Court's decision in *Batson v. Kentucky* appears at the end of the chapter.

In *Batson,* the Supreme Court held that a prosecutor's peremptory challenges to exclude African Americans from a jury trying African American defendants was ground for a defendant to claim discrimination under the Equal Protection Clause of the Fourteenth Amendment to the Constitution. *Batson* became the basis for trial courts to deny the prosecution's use of a peremptory challenge for exclusion of an African American juror from a trial of a person of that race, if the court was persuaded the challenge was racially motivated. In 1991 the Supreme Court broadened the rule so that the racial motivation of the prosecutor became subject to challenge irrespective of the defendant and prospective juror being of the same race. *Powers v. Ohio,* 499 U.S. 400, 111 S.Ct. 1364, 113 L.Ed.2d 411 (1991).

In 1992 the Court revisited this area of the law and extended the *Batson* rule by holding that a defendant's exercise of peremptory challenges was state action, and that the Equal Protection Clause also prohibits defendants from engaging in purposeful discrimination on the ground of race. *Georgia v. McCollum,* 505 U.S. 42, 112 S.Ct. 2348, 120 L.Ed.2d 33 (1992).

As a result of the pronouncements in *Batson, Powers,* and *McCollum,* federal and state courts have reevaluated their views on the exercise of peremptory challenges. In general, trial judges are still vested with broad discretion to determine whether peremptory challenges are racially intended, but many trial lawyers have expressed concern that peremptory challenges could become relics in the American system of jurisprudence.

GENDER-BASED PEREMPTORY CHALLENGES

The views of trial lawyers who predicted that peremptory challenges would become relics of the past were reinforced by a trend in the late 1980s and early 1990s to restrict **gender-based peremptory challenges.** By 1993, federal appellate courts had issued disparate rulings on the issue. Finally, in *J.E.B. v. Alabama ex rel. T.B.,* 511 U.S. 127, 114 S.Ct. 1419, 128 L.Ed.2d 89 (1994), the United States Supreme Court resolved that conflict and held that the Equal Protection Clause of the Fourteenth Amendment prohibits gender-based peremptory challenges. Writing for the majority, Justice Blackmun emphasized the relationship between racially based and gender-based peremptory challenges: "Failing to provide jurors the same protection against gender discrimination as race discrimination could frustrate the purpose of *Batson* itself." 511 U.S. at 148, 114 S.Ct. at 1430, 128 L.Ed.2d at 107.

Impaneling of the Jury

If the court anticipates that a trial might be protracted, it may have one or more alternate jurors selected to serve should any juror become ill or have to respond to an emergency. An alternate juror sits with the jury, but unless substituted for a regular juror, the alternate is excused just before the jury retires to deliberate. After selection of the jury is complete, it is sworn as a body by the judge or the clerk of the court to carry out its duties and is advised not to discuss the case until instructed by the court to deliberate.

Proposals for Jury Reform

On the nationally televised O. J. Simpson case in 1995, the public witnessed considerable bickering between counsel and long delays in impaneling a jury. A protracted jury trial with many delays ensued. Thus, the Simpson trial became a catalyst for reform in the jury processes. Polls taken after that trial revealed a great decline in interest in serving on juries. Many who have been called to serve complain of "just sitting around the courthouse and wasting time" with no explanation for the delay. They are demanding that court officials show them more concern and respect. Although some progress has been made in allowing jurors to remain on call until needed, there remains room for improvement in many jurisdictions.

Many who have served on juries feel that the jury selection process has become too competitive, with little focus on the goal of obtaining a fair and impartial jury. Others emphasize the need not only to expedite the process of impaneling a jury, but also for jurors to be given a greater role during the trial.

Suggestions by jurors who have served include limiting the number of peremptory challenges by counsel, allowing jurors to take written notes as a trial proceeds, and permitting questioning of witnesses by jurors.

Free Press Versus Fair Trial

First Amendment guarantees of freedom of the press often collide with a defendant's right to a fair trial before an impartial jury. This is particularly true when heightened public interest results in mass media coverage of a trial, with potential prejudicial effects on witnesses and jurors. When this occurs, the trial court must protect the defendant's right to a fair trial by taking steps to prevent these influences from affecting the rights of a defendant. Failure to do so can result in a verdict of guilty being overturned by an appellate tribunal.

In a high-profile homicide case, a jury found Dr. Sam Sheppard guilty of the 1954 murder of his wife, Marilyn. His conviction was affirmed on appeal. But in *Sheppard v. Maxwell,* 384 U.S. 333, 86 S.Ct. 1507, 16 L.Ed.2d 600 (1966), the Supreme Court reversed a federal appeals court's denial of Dr. Sheppard's petition for habeas corpus. Observing that jurors at Dr. Sheppard's trial were constantly exposed to intense media coverage until their deliberations and that the "newsmen took over practically the entire courtroom," 384 U.S. at 355, 86 S.Ct. at 1518, 16 L.Ed.2d at 616, the Court found that the highly prejudicial publicity contributed to the denial of due process of law to the defendant. Acknowledging that nothing proscribes the press from reporting events in the courtroom, the Court suggested trial courts can combat the problem through such measures as (1) proscribing out-of-court statements by lawyers, parties, witnesses, or court officials concerning matters that could be prejudicial to the accused and (2) insulating the witnesses and sequestering the jury to prevent exposure to reports by the media. The prosecution was given a reasonable time to retry Dr. Sheppard. On retrial in 1966, he was acquitted. Dr. Sheppard died in 1970, but his son, Sam Reese Sheppard, brought a civil suit against the state of Ohio claiming that his father was wrongfully imprisoned for the crime for which he was later acquitted. In an attempt to clear Dr. Sheppard's reputation, counsel attempted to establish that the DNA of a third person—not Dr. Sheppard or his wife—was present at the crime scene. On April 10, 2000, a jury in Cuyahoga County, Ohio, unanimously rejected the claim.

Although the media cannot "take over" the courtroom, it is equally clear that because of First Amendment rights, the public and the press cannot ordinarily be excluded from criminal trials. In 1980 Chief Justice Burger, writing for the Supreme Court, traced the history of criminal trials in Anglo-American jurisprudence and concluded that public access is an indispensable element of criminal trials. Therefore, the Court concluded that trials may not be closed without findings sufficient to overcome the presumption of openness. *Richmond Newspapers, Inc. v. Virginia,* 448 U.S. 555, 100 S.Ct. 2814, 65 L.Ed.2d 973 (1980).

Cameras in the Courtroom

In 1965, in a 5–4 decision, the Supreme Court held that the defendant, Billy Sol Estes, was denied due process of law because the proceedings of his criminal trial were televised over his objection. *Estes v. Texas,* 381 U.S. 532, 85 S.Ct. 1628, 14 L.Ed.2d 543 (1965). This was consistent with the longtime ban that courts had imposed on allowing cameras in the courtroom. During the 1970s, many state courts began to allow radio, television, and still-camera coverage of court proceedings subject to limitations necessary to preserve the essential dignity of a trial (for example, equipment must be noiseless, and strong lights are not permitted). Also, judges may limit coverage by requiring pooling of media equipment. Nevertheless, Rule 53 of the Federal Rules of Criminal Procedure still prohibits the taking of photographs in the courtroom during the progress of judicial proceedings in federal courts.

Florida is among the states that began permitting televising of trials in the late 1970s. *In re Post-Newsweek Stations, Florida, Inc.,* 370 So.2d 764 (Fla. 1979). Thereafter, Noel Chandler and another defendant, who were charged with several offenses, requested the trial court to exclude live television coverage from their jury trial. The court denied their request, and they were found guilty. A state appellate court affirmed their convictions. *Chandler v. State,* 366 So.2d 64 (Fla. App. 1978). The U.S. Supreme Court granted review. At the outset, the Court acknowledged that it had no supervisory jurisdiction over state courts. Therefore, it confined its review to evaluating the constitutionality of Florida's program permitting radio, television, and photographic coverage of criminal proceedings over an accused's objection. The Court declined to prohibit television cameras from state courts but said that defendants have a right to show that such use prejudiced them in obtaining a fair trial. Finding that Chandler and his codefendant had not shown they were prejudiced in any way by the televising of their trials, the Court denied them any relief. *Chandler v. Florida,* 449 U.S. 560, 101 S.Ct. 802, 66 L.Ed.2d 740 (1981).

By 1993, cameras were allowed in the courtrooms of almost all state courts. And although there has been some backlash following the O. J. Simpson case, most still feel that cameras in the courtroom have enhanced the public's awareness of the judicial processes. However, it is probably a fair generalization to conclude that, depending on the particular case, judges should be more assertive in exercising control over the televising of criminal proceedings.

The federal ban on cameras in the courtroom came to the forefront in March and April 1993, when four police officers, previously acquitted of criminal charges in a state court trial, were tried in a federal district court in Los Angeles on charges of violating the Fourth Amendment rights of Rodney King. Because this trial attracted widespread interest, the media voiced displeasure at their inability to bring to the public live camera coverage. Nevertheless, in 1994 the Judicial Conference of the United States voted to maintain the ban on television cameras in federal courts. There is less resistance to allowing television and still photography coverage of appellate proceedings. In March 1996, the United States Judicial Conference voted 14–12 to allow federal appeals courts to permit television, radio, and still photography in civil, but not criminal, appeals.

With the exception of Indiana, Mississippi, and South Dakota, state courts now permit television and photographic coverage of court proceedings. In most states, the consent of the presiding judge is required, and judges generally have considerable discretion to control the coverage. Coverage of jurors is either prohibited or restricted, and most states prohibit coverage of cases involving juveniles and victims of sex crimes. Some states have such restrictive policies that television coverage of trials almost never takes place. In many states, television cameras that are permanent fixtures of the courtroom record court proceedings. Television stations and networks can simply pick up the signals, which they can edit or present live to their viewers.

The O. J. Simpson case, tried in California in 1995, shows how a sensational criminal trial can draw the mass media's attention. In that case, CNN and Court TV featured live coverage of many of the courtroom activities; other television networks carried daily "O. J. Updates" in their evening news programs.

"Order in the Court"

Occasionally a trial judge is confronted with a defendant or others in attendance at a trial whose disruptive behavior impedes the court from conducting a trial in a proper judicial atmosphere. As Justice Hugo Black observed, "The flagrant disregard in the courtroom of elementary standards of proper conduct should not and cannot be tolerated." *Illinois v. Allen,* 397 U.S. 337, 343, 90 S.Ct. 1057, 1061, 25 L.Ed.2d 353, 359 (1970).

This problem is more likely encountered in a so-called "political trial," where there may be support for the cause the defendant claims to represent. One such highly publicized instance of courtroom disruption occurred in the 1969–1970 "Chicago Seven" conspiracy trial in federal court in Chicago. The seven defendants, including antiwar activist David T. Dellinger, were prosecuted under the Federal Anti-Riot Statute (18 U.S.C.A. §§ 2101–2102) for their actions at the August 1968 Democratic National Convention in Chicago. An eighth defendant, Black Panther party leader Bobby G. Seale, was tried separately on similar charges. Considerable antagonism developed between the trial judge and the defendants and their counsel. As a result of their actions during their trials, all defendants and two of their attorneys were found guilty of contempt of court. Despite the number of unruly and disrespectful actions that took place, the contempt convictions were reversed because of procedural irregularities. *United States v. Seale,* 461 F.2d 345 (7th Cir. 1972); *In re Dellinger,* 461 F.2d 389 (7th Cir. 1972). Subsequently, the defendants' convictions were also reversed by the same federal court of appeals on basis of judicial error. In this latter opinion the appellate court criticized the trial judge for his own antagonistic behavior during the trial. *United States v. Dellinger,* 472 F.2d 340 (7th Cir. 1972).

Unruly Defendants

It is not too difficult for judges to exercise control over members of the public who attend court trials. The problem that confronts judges is when a defendant becomes unruly. In most instances, judges control disruption and defiance by defendants and others through exercise of the **power of contempt.** Yet in recent years, some courts have had to go further. In *Illinois v. Allen,* supra, the Supreme Court recognized that there is no one formula for maintaining the appropriate courtroom atmosphere, but indicated that

> there are at least three constitutionally permissible ways for a trial judge to handle an obstreperous defendant . . . : (1) bind and gag him, thereby keeping him present; (2) cite him for contempt; (3) take him out of the courtroom until he promises to conduct himself properly. 397 U.S. at 343–344, 90 S.Ct. at 1061, 25 L.Ed.2d at 359.

The Sixth Amendment protects the defendant's right to be present at every critical stage of criminal proceedings. *Snyder v. Massachusetts,* 291 U.S. 97, 54 S.Ct. 330, 78 L.Ed. 674 (1934). The right to be present at trial is fundamental; however, it may be forfeited if the defendant is disruptive or fails to comply with reasonable standards of the court. For example, in New York a defendant repeatedly insisted on appearing in court while wearing only his underwear covered by a sheet. After warning him of the consequences of not wearing proper attire to court, the trial court allowed the trial to proceed in the defendant's absence. On appeal, the trial court's action was affirmed. *People v. Hinton,* 550 N.Y.S.2d 438 (N.Y. App. Div. 1990).

Courts insist that a defendant not disrupt courtroom proceedings. Thus, if there is a real threat of serious disruption by a defendant, or where threats of escape or danger to those in and around the courtroom exist, a defendant may be shackled. Federal and state courts are reluctant to shackle a defendant unless it becomes imperative, because in addition to concerns over the appearance of the defendant, shackling may have a prejudicial effect on a defendant's decision to testify at trial. *People v. Duran,* 545 P.2d 1322 (Cal. 1976). Moreover, in some cases such restraints "may . . . impair [the defendant's] ability to confer with counsel, and significantly affect the trial strategy he chooses to follow." *Zygadlo v. Wainwright,* 720 F.2d 1221, 1223 (11th Cir. 1983).

Most state courts probably take the view of the Missouri Supreme Court. In 1996 that court observed that the use of restraints for courtroom security purposes is a matter within the discretion of the trial court. *State v. Kinder,* 942 S.W.2d 313 (Mo. 1996). In 1999 the Illinois Supreme Court, citing one of its earlier decisions, enumerated the following factors a trial judge should consider in determining whether to shackle a defendant: "the seriousness of the present charge against the defendant; defendant's temperament and character; his age and physical attributes; his past record; past escapes or attempted escapes, and evidence of a present plan to escape; threats to harm others or cause a disturbance; self-destructive tendencies; the risk of mob violence or of attempted revenge by others; the possibility of rescue by other offenders still at large; the size and mood of the audience; the nature and physical security of the courtroom; and the adequacy and availability of alternative remedies." *People v. Buss,* 718 N.E.2d 1, 40 (Ill. 1999).

Behavior of Counsel

Dramatic, fictional presentations of courtroom proceedings now occupy a considerable part of television entertainment. A viewer is quite likely to gain an erroneous impression of courtroom proceedings, particularly in respect to the standards of conduct enforced against lawyers in criminal trials. Lawyers are seen asking inflammatory questions of a witness and expressing personal opinions concerning facts in issue. Others persist in interrogating a witness after the court has sustained an objection to such a line of questioning. It is not uncommon to see a lawyer continuing to press a point of law after the trial judge has made a ruling. Some actually appear to practice deceptive tactics on behalf of a client, justifying the means by the ultimate goal of helping a client. A prospective criminal justice professional could misapprehend the true role of a prosecutor or defense lawyer. Moreover, a prospective client who sees lawyers on television dramatically pursue such flagrant tactics may gain a false expectation of what a lawyer's role is in the courtroom and as a result may someday expect his or her own lawyer to pursue such tactics.

In reality, in federal and state courts lawyers are subject to rather strict legal and ethical rules in presenting evidence, following trial procedures, and in courtroom decorum. When making an opening statement, a lawyer must not express personal knowledge or opinion concerning facts in issue. Lawyers must avoid misstating a fact or point of law; must address their arguments to the court, not to opposing counsel; and must avoid disparaging remarks toward opposing counsel. They are expected to refer to adult witnesses by their surnames and refrain from any gestures of approval or disapproval during a witness's testimony. A lawyer is not permitted to express a personal opinion as to the guilt or innocence of a defendant, but may argue whether the evidence shows guilt or innocence. Finally, a lawyer should abstain from flattery or other comments designed to curry favor with a juror. And it goes without saying that a trial judge must maintain a position of dignity and neutrality during the course of a trial.

It is understandable that emotions can run high during a trial, but trial judges generally insist on proper decorum in the courtroom. The court may discipline a lawyer who fails to abide by these rules. An offending lawyer may be found in contempt of court and fined, or even jailed in instances of egregious misconduct. However, because of the possible adverse effect on a case, trial judges are hesitant to reprimand a lawyer, particularly defense counsel, in the presence of a jury. Other forms of disciplinary action may be initiated by a bar association and can range from public reprimands to suspension or even disbarment where a lawyer intentionally deceives the court, knowingly makes a false statement or submits a false document, or improperly withholds material information that causes serious injury to a party or a significant adverse effect on a legal proceeding.

The Rules of Evidence

In our adversary system, the purpose of a trial is to search for the truth. Guilt or innocence is determined based on the evidence produced at a trial. Evidence consists of verbal statements, writings, documents, photographs, and tangible items that tend to prove or disprove some fact in issue. Certain rules govern the introduction of evidence in a court of law. Sometimes a judge will tend to relax these rules in a nonjury trial because the judge is trained to "sort out" the probative evidence from the nonprobative. However, in a jury trial in a criminal case, the rules of evidence are strictly enforced.

The subject of evidence is complex. The rules of evidence prescribed by Congress for use in federal courts are known as the Federal Rules of Evidence and are found in Title 28 of the United States Code Annotated. Some states have legislatively or judicially adopted codes of evidence; in other states, the rules of evidence must be gleaned from a study of the decisional law of the state. Volumes have been written on the subject, and thousands of court decisions address its various aspects and refinements of general rules. From a basic text on criminal law and procedure, the reader can only expect to gain a very basic grasp of the principles involved.

Judicial Notice

Facts commonly known are accepted by courts without formal proof, a process known as the court taking **judicial notice** of certain established facts. Usually there is a request by counsel; however, in some instances courts take judicial notice without request. The rationale for the doctrine of judicial notice is that courts should not exclude consideration of matters of general knowledge that are well known to informed members of the public. To illustrate, courts take judicial notice of who is president of the United States, that a particular date in a given month was on a certain day of the week, or that whiskey is an intoxicating liquor. In some instances it may be necessary to bring such commonly accepted facts to the court's attention by presentation of a calendar or an almanac. Courts in a particular area may be asked to take judicial notice of certain facts within the geographic area of the court's jurisdiction. However, judicial notice of a fact must never be used as a substitute for proof of an essential element of a crime. *State v. Welch,* 363 A.2d 1356 (R.I. 1976). Taking judicial notice is not conclusive because a party can always offer proof to the contrary.

Courts also take judicial notice of the law. All courts take judicial notice of the United States Constitution and general acts of Congress, and federal courts take judicial notice of the federal laws and the laws of each state. State courts take judicial notice of their own state constitution and state laws. Municipal ordinances and the laws of other states generally must be established by formal proof; however, attorneys frequently stipulate as to the text of these laws.

Proof Beyond a Reasonable Doubt

Historically, the requirement for **proof beyond a reasonable doubt** in a criminal trial has required proof whereby the fact finder would have "an abiding conviction, to a moral certainty, of the truth of the charge." *Commonwealth v. Webster,* 59 Mass. (5 Cush.) 295, 320 (1850). The historical requirement was elevated to a constitutional mandate in *In re Winship,* 397 U.S. 358, 90 S.Ct. 1068, 25 L.Ed.2d 368 (1970). There, the Supreme Court held that the Due Process Clause of the Fourteenth Amendment requires the prosecution to establish the elements of a charged crime beyond a reasonable doubt. Judges have defined "beyond a reasonable doubt" in a variety of ways. In *Victor v. Nebraska,* 511 U.S. 1, 114 S.Ct. 1239, 127 L.Ed.2d 583 (1994), the Supreme Court held that the Constitution does not require that any one particular form of words be employed. Rather, judges have wide discretion in instructing juries on the meaning of the reasonable doubt standard. In evaluating jury instructions on this issue, the question is whether the court's instruction, taken as a whole, conveys a correct sense of the concept of reasonable doubt. In *Victor,* the Court avoided defining "reasonable doubt" directly but said that trial courts must avoid definitions of reasonable doubt that permit juries to convict a person on a standard that is less than what is required by due process of law.

Evidentiary Presumptions

This standard of requiring proof beyond a reasonable doubt is central to judicial consideration of the validity of **evidentiary presumptions.** At common law, a child younger than seven years old was conclusively presumed to be incapable of committing a crime. A legal presumption of this type is called an irrebuttable presumption. In other words, no evidence can be introduced in court to overcome it. In criminal law, an irrebuttable presumption which provides that, based on proof of one fact, the fact finder (judge or jury) must conclusively find the existence of another fact is troublesome because it encroaches on a defendant's due process right to have the prosecution prove the defendant guilty beyond a reasonable doubt.

Today, most presumptions in criminal law are permissive. These are evidentiary devices designed to aid a party who has the burden of proof. For example, under this type of presumption, once evidence establishes a fact, the jury may infer that something else is true, provided there is a rational connection between the basic fact and the presumed fact.

In *County Court of Ulster County, New York v. Allen,* 442 U.S. 140, 99 S.Ct. 2213, 60 L.Ed.2d 777 (1979), the Supreme Court upheld the application of a New York statutory presumption that occupants of a car in which firearms were present were in illegal possession of them, as applied to a case in which three adults and a juvenile were tried for illegal possession of handguns. When the police stopped the vehicle in which the suspects were riding, they saw the handguns located crosswise in an open handbag. The juvenile admitted ownership of the bag. At the conclusion of the trial, the judge instructed the jury, in part, that "you may infer and draw a conclusion that such prohibited weapon was possessed by each of the defendants who occupied the automobile at the time when such instruments were found. The presumption, or presumptions, is effective only so long as there is no substantial evidence contradicting the conclusion flowing from the presumption, and the presumption is said to disappear when such contradictory evidence is adduced." The Supreme Court pointed out that "the presumption was merely a part of the prosecution's case, that it gave rise to a permissive inference available only in certain circumstances, rather than a mandatory conclusion of possession, and that it could be ignored by the jury even if there was no affirmative proof offered by defendants in rebuttal." 442 U.S. at 160–161, 99 S.Ct. at 2213, 60 L.Ed.2d at 794.

Shortly thereafter, in *Sandstrom v. Montana*, 442 U.S. 510, 99 S.Ct. 2450, 61 L.Ed.2d 39 (1979), the Court reviewed a case in which the state of Montana charged the defendant, David Sandstrom, with a homicidal crime where intent was a necessary element of the offense. The trial court instructed the jury that "the law presumes that a person intends the ordinary consequences of his voluntary act." Historically, many trial courts commonly instructed juries substantially as quoted. But in *Sandstrom*, the Supreme Court noted that since the jury was not told that the presumption could be rebutted, it may have interpreted the presumption as being conclusive or as shifting to the defendant the burden of persuasion on the element of intent. Thus, the Court viewed the issue to be whether such an instruction relieved the state of its burden to prove the defendant guilty beyond any reasonable doubt. The Court found that the instruction mandated a conclusive presumption that removed the need to prove the essential element of intent and ruled that such a presumption violated the defendant's due process rights under the Fourteenth Amendment.

A decade later, the Court reiterated the principle announced in *Sandstrom*. A defendant had been prosecuted for violating a statute that provided as follows:

> Whenever any person who has . . . rented a vehicle willfully and intentionally fails to return the vehicle to its owner within 5 days after the . . . rental agreement has expired, . . . shall be presumed to have embezzled the vehicle.

The Court held that the jury instruction that included the mandatory presumption of the statute violated the defendant's due process rights. *Carella v. California*, 491 U.S. 263, 109 S.Ct. 2419, 105 L.Ed.2d 218 (1989).

Requirements of Admissibility

As we pointed out in Chapter 16, a defendant has certain constitutional protections concerning the prosecution's use of forced admissions and confessions and of other evidence that has been illegally obtained. In addition, before evidence may be admitted in court, whether real or testimonial and whether direct or circumstantial, it must meet certain legal requirements. First, all evidence must be relevant (that is, it must tend to prove or disprove a material fact in issue). For example, assume that a defendant is charged with armed robbery. It would be relevant to show where the defendant and victim were located when the offense occurred, the money or other articles stolen, the force applied by the victim's assailant, details of any weapon used, the victim's resistance, and the defendant's fingerprints. Flight by the defendant when the police sought to make an arrest and, of course, any admissions or confessions of the defendant material to the crime would also be relevant. But offenses committed by the defendant completely unrelated to the crime of robbery would be irrelevant, as would be the defendant's individual likes, dislikes, and lifestyle.

Similar Fact Evidence

So-called **similar fact evidence** consists of facts similar to the facts in the crime charged. Such evidence might reveal the commission of a collateral crime. The test of admissibility is whether such evidence is relevant and has a probative value in establishing a material issue. Thus, under some limited circumstances, evidence of other crimes or conduct similar to that charged against the defendant may be admitted in evidence in a criminal prosecution. Although such evidence cannot be admitted to prove the defendant's bad character or propensity to commit a crime, in some instances it may be admitted to show motive, identity, or absence of mistake or accident. See, for example, *Williams v. State,* 110 So.2d 654 (Fla. 1959). This is a very technical area of the law of evidence.

The trend is to admit similar fact evidence in cases involving prosecutions for sexual abuse of children. In these cases, it often becomes important to establish opportunity, motive, intent, identity, or the absence of a mistake or accident, or even to establish a child's credibility as a witness if such credibility is attacked by the defendant. This last point is illustrated by *Gezzi v. State,* 780 P.2d 972 (Wyo. 1989). There, the Wyoming Supreme Court reviewed a defendant's conviction on two counts of committing indecent acts with the younger of his two daughters. During the defendant's trial, the older sister testified to a course of sexual misconduct occurring between her and the defendant similar to the molestation occurring between the defendant and the younger sister. Admission of this testimony was upheld, since the younger sister's credibility was attacked and the evidence admitted at trial was inconclusive as to the cause of the younger sister's physical symptoms. In affirming the defendant's conviction, the court included an exhaustive footnote showing that about half of the state courts now liberally recognize the admissibility of prior bad acts (similar acts) as evidence in sexual offenses for various purposes.

Classifications of Evidence

There are several classifications of evidence. First, evidence may be real or testimonial. **Real evidence** consists of maps, blood samples, X-rays, photographs, stolen goods, fingerprints, knives, guns, and other tangible items. **Testimonial evidence** consists of sworn statements of witnesses. Watching a television drama might give the impression that a criminal trial consists largely of real evidence, but the great majority of evidence presented in criminal trials comes from the mouths of the witnesses, both lay and expert.

Next, evidence may be direct or indirect. **Direct evidence** includes **eyewitness testimony,** whereas **indirect evidence** usually consists of circumstantial evidence— that is, attendant facts from which inferences can be drawn to establish other facts in issue at the trial. To illustrate, a person who testifies to having seen the defendant enter the victim's house is giving direct evidence. Testimony that reveals that the defendant's fingerprints were found on a windowpane of that house shortly after it was broken into is **circumstantial evidence** from which, depending on the circumstances, it may be inferred that the defendant entered the house through that window. The admissibility of circumstantial evidence in criminal trials is well established in American law. *Tot v. United States,* 319 U.S. 463, 63 S.Ct. 1241, 87 L.Ed. 1519 (1943).

The same evidence can be direct regarding one fact and circumstantial regarding another. The witness who testifies that the defendant had possession of a pistol is giving direct evidence of that fact. Depending on other circumstances, it may be inferable from proof of that fact that the defendant attacked the victim.

Actually, there is no real difference in the weight given circumstantial as opposed to real evidence. Circumstantial evidence may once have been suspect, yet lawyers and judges can point to many instances where circumstantial evidence has proven to be more reliable than testimonial evidence. As the Supreme Court has observed,

> [C]ircumstantial evidence may in some cases point to a wholly incorrect result. Yet this is equally true of testimonial evidence. In both instances, a jury is asked to weigh the chances that the evidence correctly points to guilt against the possibility of inaccuracy or ambiguous inference. In both the jury must use its experience with people and events in weighing the probabilities. *Holland v. United States*, 348 U.S. 121, 140, 75 S.Ct. 127, 137–138, 99 L.Ed. 150, 166–167 (1954).

In *Jackson v. State,* a Florida appellate court finds the circumstantial evidence of the defendant's guilt insufficient to uphold the defendant's conviction for first-degree murder and armed burglary. The court's opinion is reprinted at the end of the chapter.

The Requirement of Competency

To be admissible in court, evidence must also be competent. In determining whether a witness is **competent to testify,** the trial judge must consider the ability of the witness to receive and recollect impressions, to understand questions, and to appreciate the moral duty to tell the truth. A very young child may or may not be competent to testify. This depends on the court's finding regarding the child's ability to understand the meaning of telling the truth. No precise rule can be set forth about when a young child may be competent to testify. Rather, it is a matter for determination in the sound discretion of the trial judge, and considerations include the child's age, intelligence, and capacity to appreciate the requirement to tell the truth. See *Wheeler v. United States*, 159 U.S. 523, 16 S.Ct. 93, 40 L.Ed. 244 (1895). A determination that a child is competent to testify will generally not be overturned by an appellate court unless the trial court's judgment is clearly erroneous. *Trujillo v. State*, 880 P.2d 575 (Wyo. 1994). Persons of unsound mind may not be competent to testify, but again, a judge must determine this. The presiding judge and members of the jury would not be competent to testify at a trial where they serve.

Expert Witnesses

Today, **forensic experts** in nearly every field make a specialty of testifying in court. To qualify as an expert, a witness must present proper credentials and be received by the trial court as an expert. A court may call experts on its own motion, but usually the prosecution or defense produces experts. After one side offers a witness as an expert, opposing counsel may cross-examine the prospective witness about his or her qualifications. For example, a physician who is to give evidence as to the cause of death of someone is first asked to relate his or her educational background and experience in the specialized area of medical practice in question. In many cases, attorneys for the prosecution and defense will stipulate that a particular witness is an expert in the field. The trial judge has considerable discretion in determining whether a witness is to be received as an expert.

Unlike lay witnesses, an expert witness may respond to **hypothetical questions** and may express opinions within the realm of his or her expertise. Fingerprint identification, ballistics tests, handwriting exemplars, and medical tests have been prominent among areas where expert evidence is commonly received in criminal cases. More recently, evidence of speed-detection devices, Intoximeters, and other devices to test blood-alcohol content has become commonplace. Judges and jurors are not necessarily scientists. Indeed, it is unlikely that many of them have more than a basic knowledge of scientific principles. Yet courts must make rational judgments about new scientific advances to determine their admissibility in court. To accomplish this, courts must depend on experts in the field.

An expert who has knowledge from personal observation may testify on that basis. For example, a psychiatrist who has examined the accused may offer an opinion as to the accused's sanity. If the expert is not acquainted with the person or subject from personal observation, the expert's opinion can be based on hypothetical questions that assume the existence of facts the evidence tends to establish. Medical experts and handwriting experts frequently are asked hypothetical questions in court, and experts on the subject of accident reconstruction frequently offer testimony about speed, braking, and other factors relevant to determining fault in cases involving auto accidents.

Scientific Evidence in the Courtroom

Evidence obtained through scientific and technological innovations can be both relevant and probative in a criminal case. Yet care must be taken to ensure that a new principle or technique is well supported by research and is generally accepted by the scientific community. The basic issue the courts face is whether the expert **scientific evidence** is reliable. In *Frye v. United States*, 293 F. 1013 (D.C. Cir. 1923), the court said that

> in admitting expert testimony deduced from a well-recognized scientific principle or discovery, the thing from which the deduction is made must be sufficiently established to have gained general acceptance in the particular field in which it belongs. 293 F. at 1014.

For seventy years the *Frye,* or the **general acceptance test,** was commonly applied in federal and most state courts faced with the issue of whether new scientific tests should be admitted into evidence in criminal trials. In 1993, however, in *Daubert v. Merrell Dow Pharmaceuticals, Inc.,* 509 U.S. 579, 113 S.Ct. 2786, 125 L.Ed.2d 469, the U.S. Supreme Court rejected the "general acceptance" test. Rather, the Court ruled that the federal rules of evidence supersede *Frye*. The Court held that admissibility of scientific evidence must be based on several factors, including whether the evidence can be tested and whether it can be subjected to peer review. Under *Daubert,* the trial judge must make a preliminary assessment of whether the reasoning or methodology underlying the expert's testimony is scientifically valid and whether that reasoning or methodology can be applied to the facts in issue. Once the court determines admissibility, the jury then determines the weight to give to such evidence. Because the Court's ruling in *Daubert* is not one of constitutional dimension, state courts are not required to follow it. Indeed, many state courts still follow the *Frye* test as a standard for admitting scientific evidence.

Hypnotically Enhanced Testimony

One controversial area of expert testimony concerns whether **hypnotically enhanced testimony** is admissible in a criminal trial. After examining extensive scientific literature, research, and testimony on the reliability of hypnotically refreshed memory and determining that the scientific community was divided on the subject, the California Supreme Court determined that hypnotically refreshed memory should not be admitted in judicial proceedings. *People v. Shirley,* 723 P.2d 1354 (Cal. 1982). In earlier years, some courts tended to admit such evidence—see, for example, *Harding v. State,* 246 A.2d 302 (Md. App. 1968)—however, the trend seems to have moved in the direction of not allowing such evidence. The majority of courts in the last decade have held that hypnotically enhanced testimony is not sufficiently reliable to be admissible. In *State v. Tuttle,* 780 P.2d 1203 (Utah 1989), the Utah Supreme Court published an exhaustive opinion analyzing the status of the law in this area and held that hypnotically enhanced testimony, as well as testimony regarding anything first recalled from the time of a hypnotic session forward, is inadmissible as evidence.

In *Rock v. Arkansas,* 483 U.S. 44, 107 S.Ct. 2704, 97 L.Ed.2d 37 (1987), the United States Supreme Court held that excluding hypnotically enhanced testimony, when applied to prevent an accused from testifying to her own posthypnotic recall, violated her constitutional right to testify on her own behalf. Accordingly, the position of the majority of courts to exclude all hypnotically induced testimony should not prevent an accused from testifying to his or her own posthypnotic recall.

Polygraph Evidence

Known in the vernacular as a "lie detector," a polygraph records a subject's respiration, blood pressure, and heartbeat as the subject is questioned by an examiner. The examiner poses certain questions and records the subject's responses. The premise of the polygraph is that deception is accompanied by stress that is manifested in increased respiration, pulse, and blood pressure. The use of a polygraph is controversial. Polygraph operators argue that a properly administered polygraph test is effective in detecting deception, and they cite impressive figures attesting to the accuracy of results. However, some critics argue that an individual can so control physiological responses as to distort the findings.

Historically, federal and state courts have declined to admit **polygraph evidence.** As late as 1989, the Minnesota Supreme Court held that the results of polygraph tests, as well as any direct or indirect references to the taking of or refusal to take such tests, are inadmissible. *State v. Fenney,* 448 N.W.2d 54 (Minn. 1989). Most state courts agree and hold that the reliability of polygraph testing has not been scientifically demonstrated to such a degree of certainty as to permit its use in evidence. However, some courts allow the results of polygraph testing to be admitted in court on the stipulation of the prosecution and the defense. See, for example, *State v. Valdez,* 371 P.2d 894 (Ariz. 1962).

The South Carolina Supreme Court has held that evidence that the defendant confessed immediately after taking a polygraph examination is inadmissible. The court said that the court's instruction for the jury to disregard the polygraph results could not cure the prejudice suffered by the defendant. *State v. Pressley,* 349 S.E.2d 403 (S.C. 1986).

The prognosis for use of polygraph evidence remains uncertain. Advocates of polygraph evidence were heartened in 1989 when the Eleventh Circuit Court of Appeals observed that polygraph testing has gained increasingly widespread acceptance as a useful and reliable scientific tool: "We agree with those courts which have found that a per se rule disallowing polygraph evidence is no longer warranted." *United States v. Piccinonna,* 885 F.2d 1529, 1535 (11th Cir. 1989). But on March 31, 1998, the U.S. Supreme Court upheld a ban on the use of polygraph evidence in military courts. *United States v. Scheffer,* 523 U.S. 303, 118 S.Ct. 1261, 140 L.Ed.2d 413 (1998). A military appeals court had ruled that an airman should not have been barred from introducing lie-detector evidence during his court-martial on charges of using drugs and writing bad checks. In reversing that decision, the Court, in an opinion by Justice Thomas,

United States v. Scheffer, 523 U.S. 303, 118 S.Ct. 1261, 140 L.Ed.2d 413 (1998)

In this case the Supreme Court upheld a ban on the use of polygraph evidence in military courts. Justice Clarence Thomas delivered the opinion of the Court, saying in part:

"State and federal governments unquestionably have a legitimate interest in ensuring that reliable evidence is presented to the trier of fact in a criminal trial. Indeed, the exclusion of unreliable evidence is a principal objective of many evidentiary rules. . . .

". . . [T]here is simply no consensus that polygraph evidence is reliable. To this day, the scientific community remains extremely polarized about the reliability of polygraph techniques. . . . Some studies have concluded that polygraph tests overall are accurate and reliable. . . . Others have found that polygraph tests assess truthfulness significantly less accurately—that scientific field studies suggest the accuracy rate of the 'control question technique' polygraph is 'little better than could be obtained by the toss of a coin,' that is, 50 percent. . . . This lack of scientific consensus is reflected in the disagreement among state and federal courts concerning both the admissibility and the reliability of polygraph evidence.

"Although some Federal Courts of Appeal have abandoned the per se rule excluding polygraph evidence, . . . at least one Federal Circuit has recently reaffirmed its per se ban, . . . and another recently noted that it has 'not decided whether polygraphy has reached a sufficient state of reliability to be admissible.' . . . Most States maintain per se rules excluding polygraph evidence. . . .

"Whatever their approach, state and federal courts continue to express doubt about whether such evidence is reliable.

"[E]xcluding polygraph evidence in all military trials is a rational and proportional means of advancing the legitimate interest in barring unreliable evidence. Although the degree of reliability of polygraph evidence may depend upon a variety of identifiable factors, there is simply no way to know in a particular case whether a polygraph examiner's conclusion is accurate, because certain doubts and uncertainties plague even the best polygraph exams. Individual jurisdictions therefore may reasonably reach differing conclusions as to whether polygraph evidence should be admitted."

observed that there was no consensus that such evidence is reliable and ruled that the military ban on the use of such evidence did not unconstitutionally abridge the airman's right to present a defense. However, four of the justices in the court's eight-member majority recognized that in some future case, the polygraph test might be so crucial that its results should be allowed (see the Supreme Court Perspective above).

Battered Woman Syndrome

Expert testimony concerning the **battered woman syndrome** has gained substantial scientific acceptance, and in the past several years such testimony has been received in many courts in cases where women claim to have acted in self-defense. In 1989 the Ohio Supreme Court receded from its 1981 decision declaring such evidence inadmissible. The court took a fresh look at the literature published in this area since 1981 and said that "expert testimony on the battered woman syndrome would help dispel the ordinary lay person's perception that a woman in a battering relationship is free to leave at any time. Popular misconceptions about battered women should be put to rest, including beliefs that the women are masochistic." *State v. Koss*, 551 N.E.2d 970, 971 (Ohio 1990). To some extent, a woman's reliance on evidence of the battered woman's syndrome depends on whether state law imposes a duty to retreat before defending oneself with deadly force. We discuss this subject in Chapter 14 concerning defenses.

DNA Evidence

A new scientific procedure that has proved to be valuable to law enforcement in identifying those who perpetrate homicidal and sexual assault offenses is called DNA printing. DNA is an abbreviation of deoxyribonucleic acid, the chemical that carries an individual's genetic information. DNA is extracted from a biological specimen (for example, white blood cells, semen, body hair, and tissue). Through sophisticated testing results, **DNA printing tests** compare DNA molecules extracted from a suspect's specimen with DNA molecules extracted from specimens found at a crime scene to determine whether the samples match. Scientists and law enforcement attempt to develop what a layperson might call **genetic fingerprints.** Evidence of the reliability of DNA typing analysis is now generally accepted when such a test is properly conducted by qualified personnel. *State v. Woodall,* 385 S.E.2d 253 (W.Va. 1989).

Shortly after being introduced judicially in 1987, DNA profiling was widely heralded by prosecutors. Defense counsel usually accepted the validity of the evidence without presenting their own experts to challenge it. Courts, too, were extremely impressed with this new form of evidence. One federal court referred to the reliability and accuracy of DNA profiling as justifying "an aura of amazement." See *United States v. Jakobetz,* 747 F. Supp. 250, 258 (D.Vt. 1990). More recently, however, false positive and false negative entries by DNA laboratories have been documented, leading some courts to express skepticism about the use of DNA results. Questions are now frequently raised about the quality of the laboratory methods and the statistical estimations on the frequency or rarity of matching profiles. See, for example, *State v. Cauthron,* 846 P.2d 502 (Wash. 1993); *People v. Barney,* 10 Cal. Rptr. 2d 731 (Cal. App. 1992).

"Your Honor, I Object"

Anyone who has observed a criminal trial, or even a television drama depicting one, is familiar with the advocates frequently addressing the court: "Your honor, I object. . . ." To this, the objecting lawyer might add "on the ground that the testimony is irrelevant." This is called a **general objection.** Or the lawyer might make a **specific objection** and add "because the testimony sought would be hearsay," "because the answer calls for an opinion of the witness which the witness is not qualified to give," or for another specific reason. There are numerous other grounds for specific objections. We consider some of the more common objections in the following sections.

ON THE GROUND OF HEARSAY

Hearsay evidence refers to an oral or written statement by a person other than the one testifying in court. The general rule is often stated as follows: A witness may not testify as to a statement made by another if that statement is offered as proof of the matter asserted. Thus, a witness who testifies that "I know the defendant was home on the night of the offense because my sister told me so" would be giving hearsay testimony.

The hearsay rule has many exceptions. Sometimes a hearsay statement is admissible to prove something other than the truth of the statement itself. Spontaneous or excited utterances, a person's dying declaration, evidence of a person's reputation, matters contained in old family records, and certain business and public records are among the most common exceptions recognized by courts. Likewise, a defendant's out-of-court statement generally may be used if it is an admission, confession, or some other statement against the defendant's interest.

ON THE GROUND OF THE BEST EVIDENCE RULE

Ordinarily, the **best evidence** of a transaction must be offered in court. This rule applies to writings and means that an original document must be offered unless the party who offers a copy can present a plausible explanation of why the original is not available. For example, the original check allegedly forged by the defendant should be produced rather than a photocopy of it.

ON THE GROUND THAT THE QUESTION
CALLS FOR AN OPINION OF THE WITNESS

A lay witness is supposed to testify regarding facts of which he or she has personal knowledge. In addition, lay witnesses are generally permitted to testify about such matters perceived through their physical senses and matters that are within the common knowledge of most people, such as the speed of a vehicle, sizes, distances, or the appearance of a person. They cannot give opinions on matters beyond the common experience and understanding of laypersons. To illustrate, a driver can give an estimate of the speed of a vehicle he or she observed traveling on the street, but a witness must be qualified as an expert to be permitted to testify as to the speed of a car based on observation of the car's skid marks on the pavement. Such an opinion must generally be based on facts perceived by the witness and not on hearsay statements. Rule 701 of the Federal Rules of Evidence limits lay witnesses to testifying to those opinions rationally based on the perception of the witness and helpful to an understanding of the testimony or determination of a fact in issue. States have similar rules.

A trial judge has considerable discretion to determine whether to admit **opinion evidence** from a lay witness. Although it is difficult to formulate precise rules, two illustrations shed light on the views of appellate courts. In *State v. Anderson,* 390 So.2d 878 (La. 1980), the Louisiana Supreme Court held that it was an error for the trial court to have allowed a police detective to give his opinion regarding the reasons why he received an anonymous call in a homicide case; however, the court found the error harmless under the circumstances of the case. In *State v. Lagasse,* 410 A.2d 537 (Me. 1980), the court held that a lay witness's opinion testimony that a girl "looked like she had been slapped" was admissible.

Privileged Communications

The rules of evidence also recognize certain **privileges** that limit testifying. Privileges raise difficult issues by requiring the law, in the search for truth, to choose between protecting a person's confidentiality and allowing testimony that can result in full disclosure of all relevant evidence.

At common law, individuals who were in certain close relationships were privileged not to testify about certain matters. Today, statutes, court rules of evidence, and judicial decisions protect parties in certain relationships from being required to testify. These protections are known as privileges, and a person who asserts a privilege must establish the existence of the required relationship. We discuss the most common evidentiary privileges, which protect communications between attorney and client, husband and wife, and clergy and penitent.

ATTORNEY–CLIENT PRIVILEGE

The **attorney–client privilege** can be claimed either by the client or by the attorney on behalf of the client regarding communications between them in the course of the attorney's legal representation. The privilege belongs to the client, and if the client waives that privilege, the attorney can be required to disclose the communication.

Hunt v. Blackburn, 128 U.S. 464, 9 S.Ct. 125, 32 L.Ed. 488 (1888). Several state supreme courts have ruled that the privilege survives the client's death. There was doubt as to whether this prevailed at the federal level; however, in a 1998 case involving activities of the Independent Counsel, the U.S. Supreme Court in a 7–2 decision ruled that the attorney–client privilege does survive the client's death. *Swidler & Berlin v. United States,* 524 U.S. 399, 118 S.Ct. 2081, 1421 L.Ed.2ds 379 (1998).

MARITAL PRIVILEGE

Confidential communications between married persons are generally privileged from disclosure. Therefore, married persons generally have the privilege not to testify against each other. The **marital privilege** emanates from the common law and is based on the policy of promoting and preserving domestic harmony and the repugnance against convicting one person through the testimony of another who shares intimate secrets of domestic life. Either spouse may assert the privilege to prevent disclosing privileged matters; either may assert it to prevent the other spouse from testifying about privileged matters. Some courts have held that even after divorce, a spouse has the privilege not to testify against his or her former spouse concerning confidential communications made between them during their marriage. See, for example, *State v. Richards,* 391 S.E.2d 354 (W.Va. 1990).

CLERGY–PENITENT PRIVILEGE

Generally priests, ministers, and rabbis are prohibited from testifying about matters related to them by the penitent in confidence. This is known as the **clergy–penitent privilege,** and the clergyperson can assert the privilege on behalf of the penitent.

OTHER PRIVILEGES

Some jurisdictions also recognize testimonial privileges between a physician and a patient, between a psychotherapist and a patient, and between an accountant and a client. These expand the common-law concept of testimonial privilege, so the statutes and judicial decisions of a particular jurisdiction must be consulted.

....

The Trial Process

A trial is the centerpiece of the criminal justice system, and in American courts the trial judge is the person most responsible for ensuring that the system operates in a fair, efficient, and impartial manner. Trial judges come into office through election or appointment. Ideally, they are selected because of their scholarship and integrity and the patience and compassion the public associates with the fair and impartial administration of justice. To those appearing before the court, and to the jurors and court personnel, the black-robed judge stands as a symbol of justice. In previous chapters, we have pointed out that judges perform numerous functions in the pretrial phases of the criminal justice system, but the most visible aspects of the judge's work are presiding at trials and, when convictions result, setting punishments.

During a trial, the judge serves as an umpire in many respects. The judge rules on the questions that may be asked of potential jurors, determines whether witnesses are competent to testify, controls the scope of interrogation of lay and expert witnesses, and instructs the jury on the law applicable to the particular case. The judge also determines all important judicial and administrative matters concerning the trial.

Trial judges are held accountable by appellate courts sitting to review judgments and sentences and to correct harmful errors. Yet in numerous administrative and procedural areas (for example, whether to grant a postponement of a trial or to limit the number of expert witnesses), a judge's actions are discretionary, and appellate review in such areas is limited to determining whether the trial judge abused that discretion.

Trial judges must be very cautious of being critical of attorneys, especially in a jury trial, because jurors place great importance on the judge's attitudes. A trial judge who is critical of a defendant's attorney might hold that attorney up to ridicule in the eyes of the jury and thereby impede the fairness of the trial. *People v. Kelley,* 449 N.W.2d 109 (Mich. App. 1989). In *State v. Jenkins,* 445 S.E.2d 622 (N.C. App. 1994), the court reversed a defendant's convictions because the judge turned his back to the defendant and the jury during the defendant's testimony. The appellate court was concerned that the jury may have interpreted the judge's action to mean that he did not believe the defendant's testimony to be credible.

Usually, either or both sides in a criminal trial request the court to invoke the traditional rule that requires all witnesses except the defendant to remain outside the courtroom except when testifying. The purpose of **putting witnesses under the rule,** as lawyers commonly refer to it, is to prevent witnesses from matching narratives. Whether witnesses should be excluded from the courtroom is a matter within the sound discretion of the trial court, *Witt v. United States,* 196 F.2d 285 (9th Cir. 1952); however, the request is generally granted.

Witnesses are interrogated by counsel in the adversary system of American justice; however, it is the right, and sometimes becomes the duty, of a judge to interrogate a witness. This is another delicate area, and appellate courts have emphasized that questioning from the bench should not show bias or feeling and should not be protracted. *Commonwealth v. Hammer,* 494 A.2d 1054, 1060 (Pa. 1985).

The Opening Statements

Once the jury is in place, the trial is ready to begin. The prosecution and the defense are each allowed to make an **opening statement** outlining their respective theories of the case and the evidence to be presented. These opening statements must not be argumentative, nor may counsel make disparaging remarks against one another. Often a defense lawyer defers making an opening statement until the prosecution rests its case. Opening statements are designed to orient the jury; therefore, if the defendant elects a bench trial, they are frequently waived. If not waived, opening statements of counsel are usually very brief in bench trials. After the opening statements have been presented, the prosecution calls its first witness to take the stand.

The Case for the Prosecution

Prosecutors are ever mindful that when a defendant pleads not guilty, the government must establish the defendant's guilt beyond any reasonable doubt. In presenting the government's case, the prosecuting attorney usually calls as witnesses police officers, the victim, and any other available witnesses whose testimony can support the charge against the defendant. The government's witnesses may also include experts. For example, in a homicide prosecution the prosecutor usually calls a physician; in a drug trafficking case, a chemist; in a forgery prosecution, a handwriting expert. A scientist who has conducted laboratory tests on DNA samples in homicide and sexual battery cases is often called to testify.

The Right to Confrontation and Cross-Examination

The Sixth Amendment to the Constitution guarantees the defendant the right to be confronted with the witnesses who offer evidence against the defendant. This means that the defendant has the right to be present at trial, *Illinois v. Allen,* supra, and to cross-examine each witness. As explained in *California v. Green,* this right of confrontation

1. insures that the witness will give his statements under oath . . .

2. forces the witness to submit to cross examination, the "greatest legal engine ever invented for the discovery of truth" [and]

3. permits the jury . . . to observe the demeanor of the witness . . . thus aiding the jury in assessing his credibility. 399 U.S. 149, 158, 90 S.Ct. 1930, 1935, 26 L.Ed.2d 489, 497 (1970).

The **right of cross-examination** of an adversary's witness is absolute. *Alford v. United States,* 282 U.S. 687, 51 S.Ct. 218, 75 L.Ed. 624 (1931). However, the permissible scope of cross-examination varies somewhat in different jurisdictions and is a matter largely within the discretion of the trial court. *Smith v. Illinois,* 390 U.S. 129, 88 S.Ct. 748, 19 L.Ed.2d 956 (1968). Courts generally agree that the right of cross-examination is limited to (1) questioning the witness about matters he or she testified to on direct examination and (2) asking any questions that might tend to impeach the witness's credibility or demonstrate any bias, interest, or hostility of the witness.

The right of cross-examination is available to both the prosecutor and the defense counsel and is extremely valuable in criminal trials. Although in most instances it is objectionable for a lawyer who is examining a witness to ask **leading questions** on direct examination, the rules of evidence permit a cross-examiner to ask leading questions. When skillfully employed, cross-examination often develops facts favorable to the cross-examiner's side of the case. Frequently, a cross-examiner is successful in bringing out inconsistencies and contradictions and any bias or hostility of the witness. A witness may also be subject to **impeachment**—that is, having his or her credibility attacked on cross-examination. A witness's credibility may be attacked in the following ways:

- Showing the witness's inability to have viewed or heard the matters the witness has testified to, or inability to recall the event testified to

- Demonstrating that the witness has made prior conflicting statements on an important point

- Showing the witness has been convicted of a crime

- Establishing that the witness bears a bad reputation for truthfulness in the community

- Showing bias, prejudice, or motive to misrepresent the facts, or that the witness has a definite interest in the result of the trial

The defendant's **right of confrontation** guaranteeing a face-to-face meeting with witnesses appearing before the judge or jury is not absolute. It must occasionally give way to considerations of public policy and the necessities of the case. *Thomas v. People,* 803 P.2d 144 (Colo. 1990).

The constitutional right of confrontation came into sharp focus in 1988, when the Supreme Court held that a defendant's Sixth Amendment right to confront witnesses was violated in a sexual abuse case in which the trial judge, pursuant to an Iowa law, allowed a screen to be erected between the defendant and the two thirteen-year-old girls that he was accused of assaulting. The two children were situated so they could not see the defendant during their testimony. *Coy v. Iowa,* 487 U.S. 1012, 108 S.Ct. 2798, 101 L.Ed.2d 857 (1988). The Court left open the question of whether a procedure that shields a child sex abuse victim may be constitutionally acceptable if there is an individualized finding that the witness is in need of such protection. Two years later, in *Maryland v. Craig,* 497 U.S. 836, 110 S.Ct. 3157, 111 L.Ed.2d 666 (1990), the Court held that the Confrontation Clause of the Sixth Amendment does not absolutely prohibit states from using one-way closed circuit television to receive a child's testimony in a case involving child abuse.

Since the Supreme Court's decision in *Coy,* several states have refined their **child shield statutes** affecting children who are victims of sexual abuse. These revised statutes have met with varying reactions from state appellate courts. However, one thing seems clear: To avoid the constitutional requirements of the Confrontation Clause, the prosecution must show and the trial judge must make particularized findings that a child victim of sexual abuse would suffer unreasonable and unnecessary mental or emotional harm if the child were to testify in the presence of the defendant.

It must be remembered that all evidence, whether from the prosecution or defense, must comport with the rules of evidence as previously outlined. When the prosecution rests its case, the next move is up to the defense.

The Defense Strategy in Moving for a Judgment of Acquittal

At the close of the prosecution's evidence, the defense counsel will frequently move the court to grant a **directed verdict** or, as it is called in federal courts and some state courts, a **judgment of acquittal.** The purpose of such a motion is to have the trial judge determine whether the evidence presented by the prosecution is legally sufficient to support a verdict of guilty. For the purpose of ruling on the motion, the trial judge must view the prosecution's evidence in the light most favorable to the government. The trial judge's authority to direct a verdict has long been recognized. *France v. United States,* 164 U.S. 676, 17 S.Ct. 219, 41 L.Ed. 595 (1897).

Should the motion be granted, the defendant is discharged. If, as in most cases, the motion is denied, defense counsel proceeds with the case on behalf of the defendant, and if additional evidence is offered, defense counsel may renew the motion at the close of the evidence. Federal appellate courts will not review the sufficiency of the evidence to support a verdict unless a motion for a judgment of acquittal was made at the close of all the evidence in the trial court. See, for example, *Corbin v. United States,* 253 F.2d 646 (10th Cir. 1958). This principle also prevails in many state appellate courts.

The Defense Case—Will the Defendant Take the Stand?

Under the Fifth Amendment, the defendant does not have to testify in a criminal case, and often defendants choose to rely simply on cross-examination of the government's witnesses in an effort to obtain an acquittal. Or the defendant may present witnesses in support of an alibi, to contradict the prosecution's witnesses, or to establish an affirmative defense.

Perhaps the major tactical decision a defendant and defense counsel must make at trial is whether the defendant will take the stand and testify on his or her behalf. The Fifth Amendment privilege against self-incrimination that applies to the states through the Fourteenth Amendment, *Malloy v. Hogan,* 378 U.S. 1, 84 S.Ct. 1489, 12 L.Ed.2d 653 (1964), protects the defendant from being required to testify, absent a grant of immunity. Moreover, it also forbids any direct or indirect comment by the prosecution on the accused's failure to testify. *Griffin v. California,* 380 U.S. 609, 85 S.Ct. 1229, 14 L.Ed.2d 106 (1965).

When an accused chooses to testify on his or her behalf, the prosecution may cross-examine the accused about his or her testimony with the same latitude as with any other witness. *Fitzpatrick v. United States,* 178 U.S. 304, 20 S.Ct. 944, 44 L.Ed. 1078 (1900). Moreover, even though illegally obtained evidence cannot be used to prove the government's case, in recent years it has been held that there is no federal constitutional prohibition that prevents the prosecution from using such evidence to impeach statements made by the defendant on cross-examination. *United States v. Havens,* 446 U.S. 620, 100 S.Ct. 1912, 64 L.Ed.2d 559 (1980); *Harris v. New York,* 401 U.S. 222, 91 S.Ct. 643, 28 L.Ed.2d 1 (1971). These realities must weigh heavily in a defendant's decision whether to testify because the threat of contradiction and impeachment always exists in cross-examination. Regardless of whether the defendant testifies, any witnesses presented by the defendant are subject to cross-examination by the prosecution.

The Rebuttals

At the conclusion of the defendant's case, the prosecution is entitled to present **rebuttal witnesses** to dispute the testimony of the defendant's witnesses. After examination by the prosecution and cross-examination by the defense counsel, the defense may then present its rebuttal witnesses. They, in turn, are subject to examination by the defense counsel and to cross-examination by the prosecutor. This usually concludes the evidentiary phase of the trial.

Conduct of the Jury During the Trial

The traditional role of the juror has been to attentively listen to the evidence as presented by the prosecution and defense, to avoid any outside influences, and to withhold judgment until all the evidence has been presented and the jury retires to deliberate. In recent years, many trial judges have allowed jurors to take notes. But is a juror privileged to ask questions of a witness? In *United States v. Land,* 877 F.2d 17, 19 (8th Cir. 1989), the court noted that the practice is "fraught with dangers which can undermine the orderly progress of the trial to verdict." Some courts have suggested that the trial judge should require jurors to submit questions in writing, whereupon the court may pose the question in its original or restated form. Nevertheless, trial judges have substantial latitude in overseeing the conduct of the jury, and appellate courts are not prone to reverse their decisions on allowing questions from a juror where the evidence is clearly sufficient to support the jury's verdict. See, for example, *United States v. Gray,* 897 F.2d 1428 (8th Cir. 1990).

The Jury Instructions Conference

After all evidence has been presented in a jury trial, the trial judge customarily confers with counsel outside the presence of the jury concerning the instructions on the law that the judge will give to the jury. The prosecutor and defense counsel may be asked to present proposed instructions for the court to consider. More commonly, the trial judge announces that the court will give certain standard instructions and offers to supplement them with specific instructions to be chosen from those submitted by counsel. A defendant is entitled to have the jury instructed on the law applicable to any legitimate theory of defense that is supported by the evidence presented. See *United States v. Creamer,* 555 F.2d 612 (7th Cir. 1977). **Jury instructions** are settled in advance of closing arguments by counsel so that the prosecutor and defense counsel can present their arguments knowing how the judge will instruct the jury.

The Closing Arguments of Counsel

The Sixth Amendment guarantee of the right to assistance of counsel has been interpreted to include the right to present **closing arguments** in a criminal case, whether the case is tried before a jury or before a judge. *Herring v. New York,* 422 U.S. 853, 95 S.Ct. 2550, 45 L.Ed.2d 593 (1975). A defendant represented by counsel has no right to share the closing argument with his or her counsel, but if the defendant is *pro se*—that is, representing self—the court must allow the defendant to make a closing argument. *State v. Plaskonka,* 577 A.2d 729 (Conn. App. 1990). Although the constitutional guarantee accords the right of closing argument to the defendant, by statute or rules of court the government and the defendant are each accorded the right for counsel to make closing arguments. The order of the arguments may be set by statute or court rule, but the trial judge retains control of the extent of the argument. The prosecutor usually argues first, followed by the defense counsel, with the prosecutor having an opportunity for a brief rebuttal.

Closing arguments are designed to assist the jury in recalling and evaluating the evidence and in drawing inferences therefrom. Many lawyers begin by recapitulating the evidence in the light most favorable to their client. After that, the arguments frequently become emotional, with each side entreating the jury to "do its duty" by either convicting or acquitting the defendant, arguing why the jury should by its interpretation of the evidence thereby either convict or acquit.

In closing arguments, counsel may comment on the weight of the evidence and the credibility of the witnesses, but it is improper for either the prosecutor or defense counsel to state a personal belief about the guilt or innocence of the accused. Likewise, it is improper for counsel to refer to any matters—other than those of common, everyday knowledge—that have not been introduced in evidence. Because a judge is trained in evaluating evidence, counsel in nonjury cases frequently waive their right to make closing arguments; otherwise, the arguments are generally quite brief.

Although prosecutors may use every legitimate method to obtain a conviction, a legion of appellate court opinions admonishes them to be fair and objective in their presentations to a jury. Characteristically, the Wisconsin Supreme Court observed that the prosecutor's role should be "to analyze the evidence and present facts with a reasonable interpretation to aid the jury in calmly and reasonably drawing just inferences and arriving at a just conclusion. . . ." *State v. Genova,* 8 N.W.2d 260, 263 (Wis. 1943).

Prosecutors are prohibited from making inflammatory remarks to the jury. If a prosecutor does make inflammatory remarks or statements that have no basis in the evidence or that can be interpreted as a comment on the defendant's failure to testify, the judge may admonish the prosecutor. Usually this is followed by a cautionary instruction directing the jury to disregard such remarks. If the defendant objects and the trial judge fails to take appropriate action, or if the prosecutor's remarks are so prejudicial that they cannot be erased from the minds of the jurors, the defendant may be able to obtain a mistrial or, if convicted, win a new trial from an appellate court.

Perhaps because the government cannot ordinarily appeal on basis of improper comments by a defense counsel, the law seems to indulge a defendant in a somewhat wider latitude in jury arguments. Nevertheless, there are restraints, and sanctions for violations may take the form of an admonition by the trial judge or even disciplinary action where a defense lawyer's performance is egregious. Despite the fact that counsel must strive for acquittal of a client in our adversary system of justice, courts

Improper Argument by a Prosecutor

Defendant Larry Witted was charged with attempted murder and armed robbery. At his jury trial, the chief issue was whether the victim had correctly identified the defendant as the person who robbed him. While the victim's testimony was positive, it was uncorroborated by any other evidence. During closing argument, the defense counsel argued that the process used to identify the defendant as the perpetrator was unduly suggestive. In rebuttal, the prosecutor implied that witnesses for the defense had perjured themselves at the request of defense counsel and that the defendant had a criminal background that the defense was hiding from the jury. Since the prosecutor's remarks were made during his closing argument, the defense had no opportunity to challenge the inferences that were made. Witted was convicted, but the Illinois Court of Appeals awarded him a new trial.

People v. Witted, 398 N.E.2d 68 (Ill. App. 1979).

frequently remind defense lawyers that they, too, are officers of the court. Accordingly, they must aid in the administration of justice and to the end that the lawful rights and privileges of the defendant are not violated. See, for example, *State v. Leaks,* 10 A.2d 281 (N.J. 1940).

The Judge Instructs the Jury

Typically, at the conclusion of the closing arguments the judge either reads the indictment or information or explains the charges against the defendant to the jury. This is followed by an admonition that the defendant is presumed innocent unless and until the government proves the defendant guilty of each element of the crime beyond a reasonable doubt. The judge defines the elements of any crime charged and explains any technical legal terms. Where applicable, the court generally instructs on an attempt to commit the crime charged as well. Where the jury may convict the defendant of a lesser offense, the judge must go further than merely defining the crime charged. For example, if the defendant is charged with first-degree murder, the judge must describe the lesser degrees of murder as well as manslaughter and excusable and justifiable homicide.

These instructions on the crimes may be followed by an explanation of any defenses pled by the defendant and the burden of proof, if any, on the defendant to sustain such defenses. A defendant is entitled to an instruction about any defense sustained by the evidence. On the request of the defendant, the judge usually informs the jury that it should not consider any inference of guilt because the defendant exercised the right not to testify. However, many defense lawyers prefer not to have the judge give this instruction.

The trial judge always explains to the jury that its role is to be the sole judge of the facts and advises the jury about some of the things it should consider in evaluating the credibility of the evidence presented. If expert witnesses have testified, the judge explains their role and informs the jury that it is free to accept or reject their opinions. In America, in contrast with the English practice, the trial judge generally is not permitted to summarize the evidence or express an opinion on the weight of that evidence or the credibility of the witnesses.

Rule 31(c) of the Federal Rules of Criminal Procedure provides that "a defendant may be found guilty of an offense necessarily included in the offense charged."

A defendant is entitled to have the jury instructed on any lesser included offense whenever (1) the elements of the lesser offense are a subset of elements of the charged offense, and (2) the evidence at trial is such that a jury could rationally find the defendant guilty of the lesser offense yet acquit the defendant of the greater offense. *Schmuck v. United States,* 489 U.S. 705, 109 S.Ct. 1443, 103 L.Ed.2d 734 (1989).

Practices in state courts vary in the extent to which the trial judge must instruct a jury on offenses that are lesser than the offense charged against a defendant. Some courts distinguish between those offenses that are necessarily included in the offense charged and those that may be included based on the allegations of the offense charged and the evidence presented at trial. In state courts, a defendant is generally entitled to an instruction of an offense of a less serious nature than the one charged if the elements of the charged offense can constitute the lesser crime. If the evidence is such that no rational jury could conclude the lesser offense was proper, however, then the trial court's refusal to give the lesser offense instruction is not necessarily considered reversible error by most appellate courts. See, for example, *People v. Tucker,* 542 N.E.2d 804 (Ill. App. 1989).

In a few states, juries determine sentences. In these jurisdictions, the judge must also instruct the jury on the range of sentences permitted. In most states that have the death penalty, a jury trial in a capital case is bifurcated, with the jury first determining guilt or innocence. If the jury finds the defendant guilty, a second phase ensues, during which the jury hears evidence of aggravating and mitigating circumstances and determines whether the death penalty should be imposed (see Chapter 19).

The judge's instructions are given orally, and in some instances the jury is given a copy of the instructions. The clerk furnishes the jury forms of verdicts so they may find the defendant not guilty, guilty as charged, or guilty of some degree of the offense charged or of a lesser included offense. In federal criminal trials and in most state courts, the judge explains the requirement for a unanimous verdict. In some states, the judge is required to inform the jury of the penalties that can be imposed for the offense charged. Finally, the jury is directed to retire, select one of its members as **foreperson,** and deliberate on its verdict. Usually a jury is allowed to take with it to the jury room all exhibits received in evidence.

The Jury Deliberates and Returns Its Verdict

When directed to deliberate, the jurors are escorted to their quarters by a court bailiff. In some cases, the judge orders the jury sequestered, which means the jury must remain together until it reaches its verdict. **Sequestration** often requires the bailiff to escort the jurors to a hotel and to be present with them during meals to ensure that no outside influences are brought to bear on their judgment. Once in the jury room, the jurors' first order of business is to elect a foreperson. Then they are ready to commence their deliberations.

Because jury deliberations are secret, we can only speculate about the reasoning processes of jurors. However, we do know that juries usually take a preliminary vote shortly after electing a foreperson. In most cases, the jury probably arrives at its verdict without much discussion. In the famous "Monkey Trial" of John Scopes in Dayton, Tennessee, in 1925, the jury deliberated only eight minutes before convicting Scopes of unlawfully teaching the theory of evolution in his high school biology class. More recently, in the O. J. Simpson case the jury returned its verdict of not guilty after only four hours. In other instances, jurors may deliberate for hours or days, and many votes may be taken. In the murder trial of Charles Manson in 1971, the jury deliberated about 42 hours.

The Deadlocked Jury

Sometimes juries become "hung"—that is, they cannot agree on a verdict. This was illustrated in 1988, when a young man was tried in New York City for allegedly strangling a young woman in Central Park. The so-called "yuppie murder case" drew national attention, partly because the testimony revealed that the victim's death resulted from "a rough sexual encounter" between the defendant and the victim. After a twelve-week trial, a panel of eight men and four women deliberated for nine days. They then sent a note to the judge saying they had reached an impasse. At that point, in a desire to conclude the proceedings—and perhaps rather than risk another trial—the defendant entered a negotiated plea of guilty to manslaughter, a lesser offense than that charged.

If a jury reports that it is a **deadlocked jury,** the trial judge can either declare a mistrial or urge the jury to make further attempts to arrive at a verdict. One tool that both federal and state trial judges sometimes employ is to give the jury a supplemental instruction called an **_Allen_ charge**. The instruction takes its name from an opinion issued by the Supreme Court at the turn of the century, _Allen v. United States,_ 164 U.S. 492, 17 S.Ct. 154, 41 L.Ed. 528 (1896). A number of modifications have been made to the original _Allen_ charge, but the basic thrust remains to urge

> that if much the larger number were for conviction, a dissenting juror should consider whether his doubt was a reasonable one. . . . If, upon the other hand, the majority were for acquittal, the minority ought to ask themselves whether they might not reasonably doubt the correctness of a judgment that was not concurred in by the majority. 164 U.S. at 501, 17 S.Ct. at 157, 41 L.Ed. at 531.

In Colorado the _Allen_ charge is called "the third-degree instruction," and New Mexico courts have referred to it as the "shotgun instruction." _Leech v. People,_ 146 P.2d 346, 347 (Colo. 1944); _State v. Nelson,_ 321 P.2d 202, 204 (N.M. 1958).

The use of the _Allen_ charge in its original or in its many modified forms has been criticized as having a coercive effect for implying that the majority view is the correct one and for importuning the minority to change their views. In a few states, the state

CASE-IN-POINT

Factors Considered in Approving Trial Court's Use of _Allen_ Charge Where Jury Is Deadlocked

Defendants Lindel and others were charged in United States District Court with thirty-five counts of various crimes stemming from a marijuana importation scheme. They were convicted on several counts and then appealed. Among their points on appeal, the defendants contended that when the jury sent notes that it was hopelessly deadlocked, the trial court should have declared a mistrial instead of giving an _Allen_ charge to the jury. In rejecting the defendants' challenge, the United States Court of Appeals for the Fifth Circuit first noted that the language in the judge's charge to the jury comported with the modified _Allen_ charge language repeatedly approved. Then the court pointed out that the trial lasted for three weeks, that the verdict was a discriminating one returning both guilty and not guilty verdicts on the various counts, that in giving the _Allen_ charge the judge did not set a deadline on deliberations, and that the verdict was not returned until two days after the _Allen_ charge was given. Considering these factors, the court found no abuse of discretion in the trial judge having given the charge, and after rejecting other points raised by the defendants, the court of appeals affirmed the defendants' convictions.

United States v. Lindel, 881 F.2d 1313 (5th Cir. 1989).

supreme court has banned its use. See, for example, *State v. Randall,* 353 P.2d 1054 (Mont. 1960). Nevertheless, federal and most state courts have generally approved the use of some version of the instruction when it has been cautiously given. See, for example, *Benscoter v. United States,* 376 F.2d 49 (10th Cir. 1967).

Jury Pardons

At times, juries disregard the evidence and the judge's instructions on the law and acquit a defendant or convict the defendant for a lesser offense than charged. This is referred to as **jury nullification** or as granting the defendant a **jury pardon.** Jurors, of course, take an oath to follow the law as charged by the judge and are expected to do so. *United States v. Powell,* 469 U.S. 57, 105 S.Ct. 471, 83 L.Ed.2d 461 (1984). But it is also recognized that a jury has the prerogative to exercise its judgment and bring in a verdict of not guilty or guilty of a lesser offense.

In death penalty cases, there has been explicit recognition of the principle. For instance, in *Beck v. Alabama,* 447 U.S. 625, 100 S.Ct. 2382, 65 L.Ed.2d 392 (1980), the Supreme Court held that the death penalty may not be imposed if the jury is not permitted to consider a verdict of guilt of a lesser included noncapital offense when the evidence would have supported such a verdict. The Court explained that "the nearly universal acceptance of the rule in state and federal courts establishes the value to the defendant of this procedural safeguard." 447 U.S. at 637, 100 S.Ct. at 2389, 65 L.Ed.2d at 402.

In trials for noncapital offenses, the reality of jury nullification exists, but there is no requirement for a judge to inform the jury of that power. See, for example, *United States v. Dougherty,* 473 F.2d 1113 (D.C. Cir. 1972). Acquittals by juries are not subject to appeal, so it is difficult to know when jury nullification occurs, but undoubtedly some defendants are acquitted or convicted of lesser offenses as a result of a jury pardon. In *United States v. Dougherty,* the court in footnote 33 cites a number of examples taken from a study undertaken at the University of Chicago Law School of the types of cases in which a jury voted to acquit because of its empathy with the defendant. The examples mentioned include statutory rape of a promiscuous female, sale of liquor to a minor who is a member of the armed forces, and violence erupting after domestic strife.

The Verdict

As we pointed out earlier in this chapter, the Sixth Amendment to the United States Constitution requires a unanimous **verdict** in federal cases. *Andres v. United States,* 333 U.S. 740, 68 S.Ct. 880, 92 L.Ed. 1055 (1948); see also Fed. R. Crim. P. 31(a). A few states permit a less than unanimous verdict in criminal cases. State constitutional and statutory provisions that authorize a less than unanimous verdict by a twelve-person jury have been held not to violate the federal constitution, *Johnson v. Louisiana,* supra, although verdicts by six-person juries must be unanimous, *Burch v. Louisiana,* supra.

When a jury has concluded its deliberations, it returns to the courtroom and delivers its written verdict. The verdict is usually first handed to the judge, who reviews it to determine whether it is in proper form. If it is, the judge hands the verdict to the clerk or jury foreperson to be read aloud in open court. A defendant who is acquitted by a jury is immediately discharged. If a jury finds the defendant guilty, the defendant is generally taken into custody to await sentencing. In some instances, the defendant may be continued on bail, pending application for a new trial or an appeal. We discuss sentencing and appellate procedures in chapters 19 and 20, respectively.

Polling the Jury

After a verdict has been read, the court or any party may have the jury polled individually. The clerk or judge handles **polling the jury** by asking each juror, "Is this your verdict?" or words to that effect. In most cases, each juror responds affirmatively and the jury is discharged. If, on the other hand, a juror expresses dissent from the verdict, the trial judge may either direct the jury to retire for further deliberation or discharge the jury. See *People v. Kellogg*, 397 N.E.2d 835 (Ill. 1979).

Posttrial Motions

A convicted defendant may, and frequently does, file a **motion for a new trial,** alleging that errors were committed at trial. This type of motion affords the trial judge an opportunity to rectify errors by awarding the defendant a new trial. In most instances, however, it is a *pro forma* prelude to an appeal and is denied by the trial court. A defendant may also seek bail pending appeal (see Chapter 20). When the trial court disposes of these motions, the defendant is sentenced (see Chapter 19).

....

Conclusion

Despite the relatively small percentage of criminal cases that go to trial, the criminal trial remains a vital part of the criminal justice system. Adjudications at trial set the overall tone for the administration of the criminal law in the community. Jury verdicts become "weather vanes" of the public's attitude on the enforcement of the law.

Criminal trials also have an important bearing on the reshaping of both the statutory and decisional law in light of contemporary community values. With counsel now readily available to indigent defendants for handling their appeals as well as for representation at trial, appellate courts have the opportunity to update precedents and refine trial court procedures based on present constitutional standards.

Courts are slow to change, but change will occur. Scientific evidence now plays a more important role in criminal trials, especially in sexual assaults, homicide offenses, and offenses involving intoxication. With the emphasis on DNA testing, that role will become very significant. Increasingly, videotapes and other photographic means will present evidence at trials. With the increased emphasis on efficiency, state legislative bodies and courts may soon find it advisable to reexamine the need for a jury of twelve persons as well as the traditional requirement for a unanimous verdict.

The increased criminal caseload in the federal and state courts can be alleviated to a considerable extent by decriminalization of most traffic offenses, further institution of drug courts, and resort to pretrial diversionary programs for first offenders charged with misdemeanor or, in some instances, nonviolent felony offenses.

In contrast with our earlier history, most jurors today are well educated. They respond favorably when the trial judge, at the inception of a trial, gives a basic orientation on the standard of proof and definition of crimes and an explanation of the trial procedures that are about to take place. This initial orientation is especially useful because the trial judge's jury instructions given just before the jury retires to deliberate on the verdict are often lengthy and complex. Modern technology makes it feasible for the trial judge's instructions on the law to be recorded and copies handed to the jury before it commences deliberations.

Despite changes, the basic function of the criminal trial by a jury of one's peers will remain. It must because it is not only each citizen's protection against overzealous law enforcement and prosecutions; it also ensures the public that no defendant will gain preferred status by virtue of prominence or be dealt with unfairly because of lowly status.

Key Terms

compulsory process	battered woman syndrome
subpoena	DNA printing tests
open public trial	genetic fingerprints
jury trial	general objection
bench trial	specific objection
self-representation	hearsay evidence
standby counsel	best evidence
venire	opinion evidence
voir dire	privileges
challenges for cause	attorney–client privilege
bifurcated trial	marital privilege
death qualification of a jury	clergy–penitent privilege
peremptory challenges	putting witnesses under the rule
racially based peremptory challenges	opening statement
gender-based peremptory challenges	right of cross-examination
power of contempt	leading questions
judicial notice	impeachment
proof beyond a reasonable doubt	right of confrontation
evidentiary presumptions	child shield statutes
similar fact evidence	directed verdict
real evidence	judgment of acquittal
testimonial evidence	rebuttal witnesses
direct evidence	jury instructions
eyewitness testimony	closing arguments
indirect evidence	foreperson
circumstantial evidence	sequestration
competent to testify	deadlocked jury
forensic experts	*Allen* charge
hypothetical questions	jury nullification
scientific evidence	jury pardon
general acceptance test	verdict
hypnotically enhanced testimony	polling the jury
polygraph evidence	motion for a new trial

Web-Based Research Activity

1. Go to the Court TV web site (**http://www.courtv.com**).
2. Follow Court TV's coverage of a current trial.
3. Write a memorandum to your instructor summarizing the major factual and legal issues before the court.

Questions for Thought and Discussion

1. Jurors are generally selected from among those citizens who have registered to vote or who have registered motor vehicles. Do these methods of selection produce jurors drawn from a "representative cross-section of the community"? Can you suggest a better way of selecting jurors?

2. In England, the *voir dire* process is conducted by the trial judge and is extremely limited. Do you think the American system of criminal justice would have more credibility if the *voir dire* were conducted exclusively by the judge, with only challenges for cause permitted?

3. What factors do you think a defense attorney considers in deciding whether to advise a client to testify in his or her own behalf at trial?

4. In 1965 Justice Tom Clark, writing for the Supreme Court in *Estes v. Texas,* observed that "[t]rial by television is . . . foreign to our system." Evaluate Justice Clark's statement in view of contemporary attitudes toward communications technology.

5. Many rules of evidence applied in jury trials are derived from the early common law, when jurors were largely uneducated. These rules were designed to prevent jurors from hearing evidence that might prejudice their judgment in the case. Given the educational standards in the United States, should these rules be made less restrictive regarding evidence that can be presented in courts? What constitutional problems would arise by allowing hearsay evidence to be presented against a defendant?

6. What testimonial privileges are available to witnesses in your state? What is the rationale for each?

7. Do you think a trial judge should be allowed to summarize the evidence for the jury's benefit before the jurors retire to deliberate? What advantages and disadvantages can you see in such a practice? Would it be constitutional?

8. In some jurisdictions, a judge instructs the jury regarding its general duties and responsibilities at the beginning of the trial rather than waiting until the evidence has been presented. Do you favor this approach? Why or why not?

9. Do you think that the trial judge should inform a jury that it has the power to issue a "jury pardon" despite the evidence of the defendant's guilt when the jury feels that in "good conscience" the defendant should not be convicted of the crime charged or any lesser crime supported by the evidence at trial? Give reasons for your view.

10. The Supreme Court has said that state criminal trial juries need not observe the unanimity principle that obtains in the federal courts. Could it not be argued that the reasonable doubt standard necessarily entails the unanimity principle, as the doubt of one juror is sufficient to suggest a reasonable doubt about the guilt of the accused?

Problems for Discussion and Solution

1. A defendant is tried before a jury on a DWI charge. At the conclusion of the trial the judge instructs the jury: "If you find from the evidence that the defendant had a blood-alcohol content of .10, you may presume she was intoxicated." Should the defendant's attorney object to this instruction? On what basis?

2. A defendant is being tried for first-degree murder. The prosecutor presents an eyewitness to the victim's being shot. After asking the witness some preliminary questions, the prosecutor asks, "When the defendant shot and killed the victim. . . ." Would the defense attorney pose an objection to this question? On what ground?

3. In response to the prosecutor's questions to a state's witness, Jerry Sixpack, a layman who is a high school graduate, testifies as follows: "I measured the defendant's skid marks, and I believe he was driving at a speed of at least 65 miles per hour." "In my opinion, anyone who drinks two beers becomes intoxicated." "When I saw the defendant right after the accident, his face appeared flushed and he staggered as he walked." "My sister told me that the defendant did a lot of drinking at the nearby bar." What objections, if any, should the defense make to the witness's statements?

4. Luke Lumberjack is being tried for raping a woman he has known for a year. The state's evidence disclosed that Lumberjack, age twenty-three, had spent an evening with the female complainant, age twenty-one. Afterward, at his invitation, they went to his apartment and had a few beers. The complainant testified that Lumberjack, a large, husky male, forced her to have sex with him, despite her stated unwillingness. During cross-examination, the complainant admitted having once before had a consensual sexual relationship with the defendant. During the state's closing argument, in referring to the defendant, the prosecutor told the jury, "This big hunk of cruelty is an animal, one who must be put away to protect the young women of this community. It's important to do your duty by convicting him to send a message to the community.". Defense counsel objected on the ground that the prosecutor's comments were inflammatory, prejudicial, and unfair. He requested that the trial judge strike the prosecutor's comments, inform the jury that they should be disregarded, and admonish the prosecutor for having made such statements. What do you think the trial judge's ruling should be?

● ● ● ● ● ● ● ● ● ● ● ● ●

EXCERPTS FROM JUDICIAL DECISIONS

Williams v. Florida

Supreme Court of the United States, 1970.
399 U.S. 78, 90 S.Ct. 1893, 26 L.Ed.2d 446.

[In this case the U.S. Supreme Court considers whether six-person juries may be used in noncapital felony trials.]

Mr. Justice WHITE delivered the opinion of the Court.

. . . [Williams] filed a pretrial motion to impanel a 12-man jury instead of the six-man jury provided by Florida law in all but capital cases. That motion . . . was denied. Petitioner was convicted [of robbery] as charged and was sentenced to life imprisonment. The District Court of Appeal affirmed, rejecting petitioner's claims that his Fifth and Sixth Amendment rights had been violated. We granted certiorari. . . .

The question in this case then is whether the constitutional guarantee of a trial by "jury" necessarily requires trial by exactly 12 persons, rather than some lesser number—in this case six. We hold that the 12-man panel is not a necessary ingredient of "trial by jury," and that respondent's refusal to impanel more than the six members provided for by Florida law did not violate petitioner's Sixth Amendment rights as applied to the States through the Fourteenth.

While "the intent of the Framers" is often an elusive quarry, the relevant constitutional history casts considerable doubt on the easy assumption in our past decisions that if a given feature existed in jury at common law in 1789, then it was necessarily preserved in the Constitution. Provisions for jury trial were first placed in the Constitution in Article III's provision that "the Trial of all Crimes . . . shall be by Jury; and such Trial shall be held in the State where the said Crimes shall have been committed." The "very scanty history [of this provision] in the records of the Constitution Convention" sheds little light either way on the intended correlation between Article III's "jury" and the features of the jury at common law. . . .

We do not pretend to be able to divine precisely what the word "jury" imported to the Framers, the First Congress, or the States in 1789. It may well be that the usual expectation was the jury would consist of 12, and that hence, the most likely conclusion to be drawn is simply that little thought was actually given to the specific question we face today. But there is absolutely no indication in "the intent of the Framers" of an explicit decision to equate the constitutional and common-law characteristics of the jury. Nothing in this history suggests, then, that we do violence to the letter of the Constitution by turning to other than purely historical considerations to determine which features of the jury system, as it existed at common law, were preserved in the Constitution. The relevant inquiry, as we see it, must be the function that the particular feature performs and its relation to the purposes of the jury trial. Measured by this standard, the 12-man requirement cannot be regarded as an indispensable component of the Sixth Amendment.

The purpose of the jury trial . . . is to prevent oppression by the Government. "Providing an accused with the right to be tried by a jury of his peers gave him an inestimable safeguard against the corrupt or overzealous prosecutor and against the compliant, biased, or eccentric judge." . . . Given this purpose, the essential feature of a jury obviously lies in the interposition between the accused and his accuser of the commonsense judgment of a group of laymen, and in the community participation and shared responsibility that results from that group's determination of guilt or innocence. The performance of this role is not a function of the particular number of the body that makes up the jury. To be sure, the number should probably be large enough to promote group deliberation, free from outside attempts at intimidation, and to provide a fair possibility for obtaining a representative cross-section of the community. But we find little reason to think that these goals are in any meaningful sense less likely to be achieved when the jury

numbers six, than when it numbers 12—particularly if the requirement of unanimity is retained. And, certainly the reliability of the jury as a factfinder hardly seems likely to be a function of its size.

It might be suggested that the 12-man jury gives a defendant a greater advantage since he has more "chances" of finding a juror who will insist on acquittal and thus prevent conviction. But the advantage might just as easily belong to the State, which also needs only one juror out of twelve insisting on guilt to prevent acquittal. What few experiments have occurred—usually in the civil area—indicate that there is no discernible difference between the results reached by the two different-sized juries. In short, neither currently available evidence nor theory suggests that the 12-man jury is necessarily more advantageous to the defendant than a jury composed of fewer members.

Similarly, while in theory the number of viewpoints represented on a randomly selected jury ought to increase as the size of the jury increases, in practice the difference between the 12-man and the six-man jury in terms of the cross-section of the community represented seems likely to be negligible. Even the 12-man jury cannot insure representation of every distinct voice in the community, particularly given the use of the peremptory challenge. As long as arbitrary exclusions of a particular class from the jury rolls are forbidden, . . . the concern that the cross-section will be significantly diminished if the jury is decreased in size from 12 to six seems an unrealistic one.

We conclude, in short, as we began: the fact that the jury at common law was composed of precisely 12 is a historical accident, unnecessary to effect the purposes of the jury system and wholly without significance "except to mystics." . . . To read the Sixth Amendment as forever codifying a feature so incidental to the real purpose of the Amendment is to ascribe a blind formalism to the Framers which would require considerably more evidence than we have been able to discover in the history and language of the Constitution or in the reasoning of our past decisions. We do not mean to intimate that legislatures can never have good reasons for concluding that the 12-man jury is preferable to the smaller jury, or that such conclusions—reflected in the provisions of most States and in our federal system—are in any sense unwise. Legislatures may well have their own views about the relative value of the larger and smaller juries, and may conclude that, wholly apart from the jury's primary function, it is desirable to spread the collective responsibility for the determination of guilt among the larger group. In capital cases, for example, it appears that no State provides for less than 12 jurors—a fact that suggests implicit recognition of the value of the larger body as a means of legitimating society's decision to impose the death penalty. Our holding does no more than leave these considerations to Congress and the States, unrestrained by an interpretation of the Sixth Amendment that would forever dictate the precise number that can constitute a jury. Consistent with this holding, we conclude that petitioner's Sixth Amendment rights, as applied

to the States through the Fourteenth Amendment, were not violated by Florida's decision to provide a six-man rather than a 12-man jury. The judgment of the Florida District Court of Appeal is Affirmed.

Mr. Justice BLACKMUN took no part in the consideration or decision of this case.

Mr. Chief Justice BURGER, concurring. . . .

Mr. Justice BLACK, with whom Mr. Justice DOUGLAS joins, concurring in part and dissenting in part. . . .

Mr. Justice MARSHALL, dissenting in part. . . .

● ● ● ● ● ● ● ● ● ● ● ● ● ●

Batson v. Kentucky

Supreme Court of the United States, 1986.
476 U.S. 79, 106 S.Ct. 1712, 90 L.Ed.2d 69.

[In this case the Supreme Court considers the use of peremptory challenges to exclude persons of the defendant's race from the trial jury.]

Justice POWELL delivered the opinion of the Court.

This case requires us to reexamine that portion of *Swain v. Alabama*, 380 U.S. 202, 13 L.Ed.2d 759, 85 S.Ct. 824 (1965), concerning the evidentiary burden placed on a criminal defendant who claims that he has been denied equal protection through the State's use of peremptory challenges to exclude members of his race from the petit jury.

Petitioner, a black man, was indicted in Kentucky on charges of second-degree burglary and receipt of stolen goods. On the first day of trial in Jefferson Circuit Court, the judge conducted *voir dire* examination of the venire, excused certain jurors for cause, and permitted the parties to exercise peremptory challenges. The prosecutor used his peremptory challenges to strike all four black persons on the venire, and a jury composed only of white persons was selected. Defense counsel moved to discharge the jury before it was sworn on the ground that the prosecutor's removal of the black veniremen violated petitioner's rights under the Sixth and Fourteenth Amendments to a jury drawn from a cross-section of the community, and under the Fourteenth Amendment to equal protection of the laws. Counsel requested a hearing on his motion. Without expressly

ruling on the request for a hearing, the trial judge observed that the parties were entitled to use their peremptory challenges to "strike anybody they want to." The judge then denied petitioner's motion, reasoning that the cross-section requirement applies only to selection of the venire and not to selection of the petit jury itself.

The jury convicted petitioner on both counts. . . .

The Supreme Court of Kentucky affirmed. . . . We granted certiorari . . . and now reverse.

In *Swain v. Alabama,* this Court recognized that a "State's purposeful or deliberate denial to Negroes on account of race of participation as jurors in the administration of justice violates the Equal Protection Clause." . . . This principle has been "consistently and repeatedly" reaffirmed, . . . in numerous decisions of this Court both preceding and following *Swain.* We reaffirm the principle today.

More than a century ago, the Court decided that the State denies a black defendant equal protection of the laws when it puts him on trial before a jury from which members of his race have been purposefully excluded. *Strauder v. West Virginia,* 100 U.S. 303, 25 L.Ed. 664 (1880). That decision laid the foundation for the Court's unceasing efforts to eradicate racial discrimination in the procedures used to select the venire from which individual jurors are drawn. In *Strauder,* the Court explained that the central concern of the recently ratified Fourteenth

Amendment was to put an end to governmental discrimination on account of race.... Exclusion of black citizens from service as jurors constitutes a primary example of the evil the Fourteenth Amendment was designed to cure.

In holding that racial discrimination in jury selection offends the Equal Protection Clause, the Court in *Strauder* recognized, however, that a defendant has no right to a "petit jury composed in whole or in part of persons of his own race."... "The number of our races and nationalities stands in the way of evolution of such a conception" of the demand of equal protection.... But the defendant does have the right to be tried by a jury whose members are selected pursuant to nondiscriminatory criteria.... The Equal Protection Clause guarantees the defendant that the State will not exclude members of his race from the jury venire on account of race, ... or on the false assumption that members of his race as a group are not qualified to serve as jurors....

Purposeful racial discrimination in selection of the venire violates a defendant's right to equal protection because it denies him the protection that a trial by jury is intended to secure. "The very idea of a jury is a body ... composed of the peers or equals of the person whose rights it is selected or summoned to determine; that is, of his neighbors, fellows, associates, persons having the same legal status in society as that which he holds."... The petit jury has occupied a central position in our system of justice by safeguarding a person accused of crime against the arbitrary exercise of power by prosecutor or judge.... Those on the venire must be "indifferently chosen" to secure the defendant's right under the Fourteenth Amendment to "protection of life and liberty against race or color prejudice."...

Racial discrimination in selection of jurors harms not only the accused whose life or liberty they are summoned to try. Competence to serve as a juror ultimately depends on an assessment of individual qualifications and ability impartially to consider evidence presented at a trial.... A person's race simply "is unrelated to his fitness as a juror."... As long ago as *Strauder*, therefore, the Court recognized that by denying a person participation in jury service on account of his race, the State unconstitutionally discriminated against the excluded juror....

The harm from discriminatory jury selection extends beyond that inflicted on the defendant and the excluded juror to touch the entire community. Selection procedures that purposefully exclude black persons from juries undermine public confidence in the fairness of our system of justice.... Discrimination within the judicial system is most pernicious because it is "a stimulant to that race prejudice which is an impediment to securing to [black citizens] that equal justice which the law aims to secure to all others."...

As in any equal protection case, the "burden is, of course," on the defendant who alleges discriminatory selection of the venire "to prove the existence of purposeful discrimination."... In deciding if the defendant has carried his burden of persuasion, a court must undertake "a sensitive inquiry into such circumstantial and direct evidence of intent as may be available."... Circumstantial evidence of invidious intent may include proof of disproportionate impact.... We have observed that under some circumstances proof of discriminatory impact "may for all practical purposes demonstrate unconstitutionality because in various circumstances the discrimination is very difficult to explain on nonracial grounds."... For example, "total or seriously disproportionate exclusion of Negroes from jury venires is itself such an 'unequal application of the law ... as to show intentional discrimination.'"...

Moreover, since *Swain*, we have recognized that a black defendant alleging that members of his race have been impermissibly excluded from the venire may make out a *prima facie* case of purposeful discrimination by showing that the totality of the relevant facts gives rise to an inference of discriminatory purpose.... Once the defendant makes the requisite showing, the burden shifts to the State to explain adequately the racial exclusion.... The State cannot meet this burden on mere general assertions that its officials did not discriminate or that they properly performed their official duties.... Rather, the State must demonstrate that "permissible racially neutral selection criteria and procedures have produced the monochromatic result."...

The standards for assessing a *prima facie* case in the context of discriminatory selection of the venire have been fully articulated since *Swain*.... These principles support our conclusion that a defendant may establish a *prima facie* case of purposeful discrimination in selection of the petit jury solely on evidence concerning the prosecutor's exercise of peremptory challenges at the defendant's trial. To establish such a case, the defendant first must show that he is a member of a cognizable racial group, ... and that the prosecutor has exercised peremptory challenges to remove from the venire members of the defendant's race. Second, the defendant is entitled to rely on the fact, as to which there can be no dispute, that peremptory challenges constitute a jury selection practice that permits "those to discriminate who are of a mind to discriminate." . . . Finally, the defendant must show that these facts and any other relevant circumstances raise an inference that the prosecutor used that practice to exclude the veniremen from the petit jury on account of their race. This combination of factors in the empanelling of the petit jury, as in the selection of the venire, raises the necessary inference of purposeful discrimination.

In deciding whether the defendant has made the requisite showing, the trial court should consider all relevant circumstances. For example, a "pattern" of strikes against black jurors included in the particular venire might give rise to an inference of discrimination. Similarly, the prosecutor's questions and statements during *voir dire* examination and in exercising his challenges may support or refute an inference of discriminatory purpose. These examples are merely illustrative. We have confidence that trial judges, experienced in supervising *voir dire*, will be able to decide if the circumstances concerning the prosecutor's use of peremptory challenges creates a *prima facie* case of discrimination against black jurors.

Once the defendant makes a *prima facie* showing, the burden shifts to the State to come forward with a neutral explanation for challenging black jurors. Though this requirement imposes a limitation in some cases on the full peremptory character of the historic challenge, we emphasize that the prosecutor's explanation need not rise to the level justifying exercise of a challenge for cause. But the prosecutor may not rebut the defendant's *prima facie* case of discrimination by stating merely that he challenged jurors of the defendant's race on the assumption—or his intuitive judgment—that they would be partial to the defendant because of their shared race. . . . Just as the Equal Protection Clause forbids the States to exclude black persons from the venire on the assumption that blacks as a group are unqualified to serve as jurors, . . . so it forbids the States to strike black veniremen on the assumption that they will be biased in a particular case simply because the defendant is black. The core guarantee of equal protection, ensuring citizens that their State will not discriminate on account of race, would be meaningless were we to approve the exclusion of jurors on the basis of such assumptions, which arise solely from the jurors' race.

Nor may the prosecutor rebut the defendant's case merely by denying that he had a discriminatory motive or "affirming his good faith in individual selections." . . . If these general assertions were accepted as rebutting a defendant's *prima facie* case, the Equal Protection Clause "would be but a vain and illusory requirement." . . . The prosecutor therefore must articulate a neutral explanation related to the particular case to be tried. The trial court then will have the duty to determine if the defendant has established purposeful discrimination.

The State contends that our holding will eviscerate the fair trial values served by the peremptory challenge. Conceding that the Constitution does not guarantee a right to peremptory challenges and that *Swain* did state that their use ultimately is subject to the strictures of equal protection, the State argues that the privilege of unfettered exercise of the challenge is of vital importance to the criminal justice system.

While we recognize, of course, that the peremptory challenge occupies an important position in our trial procedures, we do not agree that our decision today will undermine the contribution the challenge generally makes to the administration of justice. The reality of practice, amply reflected in many state and federal court opinions, shows that the challenge may be, and unfortunately at times has been, used to discriminate against black jurors. By requiring trial courts to be sensitive to the racially discriminatory use of peremptory challenges, our decision enforces the mandate of equal protection and furthers the ends of justice. In view of the heterogeneous population of our nation, public respect for our criminal justice system and the rule of law will be strengthened if we ensure that no citizen is disqualified from jury service because of his race.

Nor are we persuaded by the State's suggestion that our holding will create serious administrative difficulties. In those states applying a version of the evidentiary standard we recognize today, courts have not experienced serious administrative burdens, and the peremptory challenge system has survived. We decline, however, to formulate particular procedures to be followed upon a defendant's timely objection to a prosecutor's challenges.

In this case, petitioner made a timely objection to the prosecutor's removal of all black persons on the venire. Because the trial court flatly rejected the objection without requiring the prosecutor to give an explanation for his action, we remand this case for further proceedings. If the trial court decides that the facts establish, *prima facie,* purposeful discrimination and the prosecutor does not come forward with a neutral explanation for his action, our precedents require that petitioner's conviction be reversed. . . .

Justice WHITE, concurring. . . .

Justice MARSHALL, concurring. . . .

Justice STEVENS, with whom Justice BRENNAN joins, concurring. . . .

Justice REHNQUIST, with whom The CHIEF JUSTICE joins, dissenting.

. . . I cannot subscribe to the Court's unprecedented use of the Equal Protection Clause to restrict the historic scope of the peremptory challenge, which has been described as "a necessary part of trial by jury." . . . In my view, there is simply nothing "un-equal" about the State using its peremptory challenges to strike blacks from the jury in cases involving black defendants, so long as such challenges are also used to exclude whites in cases involving white defendants, Hispanics in cases involving Hispanic defendants, Asians in cases involving Asian defendants, and so on. This case-specific use of peremptory challenges by the State does not single out blacks, or members of any other race for that matter, for discriminatory treatment. Such use of preemptories is at best based upon seat-of-the-pants instincts, which are undoubtedly crudely stereotypical and may in many cases be hopelessly mistaken. But as long as they are applied across the board to jurors of all races and nationalities, I do not see—and the Court most certainly has not explained—how their use violates the Equal Protection Clause. . . .

• • • • • • • •   • • • • • • • •

Jackson v. State

District Court of Appeal of Florida, 1987.
511 So.2d 1047.

[Here, a Florida appellate court explains an appellate court's standard of review when a criminal conviction is based on circumstantial evidence, as it considers whether the trial judge erred in denying the defendant's motion for a directed verdict of acquittal.]

SCHEB, Acting Chief Judge.

The state charged John William Jackson with first degree murder and armed burglary. Jackson was tried by jury and found guilty of both offenses. The trial court sentenced him to life imprisonment with a minimum mandatory term of twenty-five years. In this appeal we focus on the one meritorious point presented by Jackson that the trial court erred in denying his motion for judgment of acquittal.

At Jackson's trial, the state's evidence revealed that on December 19, 1983, around 4:30 A.M. Marie Felver Porter was raped and stabbed in her house trailer on Drawdy Road, Plant City. She went to a neighbor's door for help and told him that "an orange picker, Michigan tag" had done it. She died shortly thereafter from multiple stab wounds to her neck. An autopsy revealed a bruise on her right wrist which was later determined to be a bite mark. At ap-proximately 7:30 A.M. on the day of the crime the police arrived at the scene, where they obtained blood, semen and saliva stains, fingerprints, and hair samples.

Jackson, a 31-year-old, Caucasian male, had lived in the vicinity of the victim's trailer from approximately July 1983 until a few days before the crime, when he moved a few miles away. He lived in the yards of various neighbors, either in a tent or in his car.

On January 13, 1984, Jackson was questioned by the police. He appeared voluntarily and denied knowing the victim or her husband. He told the police he had spent the night of the murder at a rest area on Interstate 4, some fifteen to twenty miles from Marie Porter's trailer. He said that on December 19, 1983, at around 5:15 A.M. he went to the Minute Man Labor Pool in Tampa, where he remembered seeing a Mr. Abe Abdu. The Minute Man Labor Pool records did not reveal that he had worked on that day. Mr. Abdu did not see Jackson at the labor pool in the early morning; he saw him only at the time he was leaving. With Jackson's consent he was fingerprinted. Also with his consent, the police took impressions of his teeth and collected samples of his pubic and head hair and his blood.

On January 31, 1984, Jackson had a conversation with Charles and Patricia Fuller, on whose property he had lived during the latter part of 1983. Jackson told them that when the police had interrogated him he learned that the victim had been raped, stabbed and bitten. This was before the police had released the information that the victim had been bitten. Mrs. Fuller acknowledged that Jackson had told her that he had been picking oranges. She also stated that she had seen the defendant carrying a knife. Mr. Fuller testified that during the time he knew him, the defendant had worked as a heavy equipment operator out of a labor pool in Tampa.

The state presented a number of expert witnesses. Dr. Richard Souviron, a forensic odontologist, concluded that the bite mark on the victim's wrist was consistent with Jackson's teeth impressions. FBI Agent Michael Malone, an expert in hair and fibers analysis, identified two head hairs found on the victim's pajama top as being indistinguishable from Jackson's hair sample. These hairs on the victim's pajamas were identified as having been forcibly removed. Negroid hairs found in a window screen and a Negroid pubic hair found in the combed pubic hair of the victim plus several other strands of Caucasian hair, were not identified.

At the conclusion of the state's case, Jackson moved for a judgment of acquittal under Florida Rule of Criminal Procedure 3.380. He argued that the state's case was based entirely on circumstantial evidence and did not exclude any reasonable hypothesis consistent with innocence. The trial court denied his motion. The defendant then introduced evidence on his own behalf, none of which tended to incriminate him. At the conclusion of all evidence, the defendant again moved for judgment of acquittal. Again, the trial court denied the motion.

When, as here, the state's evidence against the defendant is circumstantial, this court's role is to determine whether the jury might have reasonably concluded that the evidence excluded every reasonable hypothesis but that of guilt. . . . The weight of the evidence is a matter for the trier of fact, and a jury verdict should not be reversed when there is substantial, competent evidence to support it. . . . Nevertheless, in criminal convictions based solely on circumstantial evidence, it is our duty to reverse the conviction when that evidence, although strongly suggesting guilt, fails to eliminate any reasonable hypothesis of

innocence. . . . Here, we conclude that the state did not present substantial, competent evidence to support the jury's verdict; hence, we must vacate the defendant's convictions.

There were three items of crucial evidence presented by the state: first, the consistent bite mark; second, Jackson's statement to the Fullers that the victim had been bitten; and the third, the strands of hair found on the victim matching Jackson's hair. We now examine the probative effect of each of these items of evidence.

Dr. Souviron was qualified as an expert in forensic odontology and bite-mark analysis. He testified that the bite mark on the victim's wrist was made through clothing. In his own words, it was a tough bite: "It's tough because it's a bite through the cloth . . . a difficult bite to diagnose." Dr. Souviron matched the impressions of Jackson's teeth to pictures of the bite and found similarities such as a left tooth sticking out, space between front teeth, and unique characteristics of the curvature of the arch. However, Dr. Souviron stated that this was not a positive bite . . . and said "I certainly hope he [Detective Baker] didn't arrest John Jackson on this bite." Moreover, testimony for the defense of another forensic odontologist cast considerable doubt on the reliability of Dr. Souviron's conclusions.

In *Bradford v. State*, 460 So.2d 926 (Fla. 2d DCA 1984), . . . this court affirmed the defendant's conviction of murder where bite-mark evidence was introduced by the state. In *Bradford*, Dr. Souviron, again the state's expert witness, testified that, to a reasonable degree of dental certainty or probability, the two abrasion patterns on the index finger of the appellant had been made by the victim's teeth. However, in *Bradford*, the state presented substantial evidence that the defendant had been in the victim's apartment at or about the time the crime had been committed. It also introduced other circumstantial evidence tending to show the defendant's guilt.

The fact that Jackson knew that the victim had been bitten is not probative of his guilt. Prior to defendant's conversation with the Fullers, the police had taken impressions of his teeth. This would certainly be a strong indication to anyone that a bite mark was involved.

The only other significant evidence presented against Jackson was Agent Malone's testimony that two strands of hair found on the victim's pajamas matched the defendant's hair samples. Agent Malone explained that he was trained to recognize the unique microscopic characteristics of hair. He testified that he has to come up with at least fifteen matching characteristics before he can say that two hair samples are consistent with having originated from the same person. Malone identified twenty characteristics present in Jackson's hair samples and in the hair found on the victim's pajamas. He concluded that the hairs were indistinguishable. Despite his conclusion, Agent Malone testified that "hair will never get unique enough to be like a fingerprint." He also agreed that hair comparisons do not constitute a basis for positive personal identification and stated that "it's not a fingerprint, no. I cannot say that hair came from John Jackson and nobody else."

Given the quality of the state's evidence, it is clear that Jackson's conviction hinges on two hairs found on the victim's clothing which match his hair sample. Hair comparison testimony, while admissible, does not result in identifications of absolute certainty. . . . There was no evidence placing the defendant at the scene of the crime, no indication of a relationship of any kind between the defendant and the victim, or that they even knew each other. The victim's dying words pointed to an "orange picker, Michigan tag." Jackson's car, however, had a Florida tag. None of the fingerprints found at the scene of the crime matched Jackson's. This, plus the presence of Negroid pubic hair in the victim's pubic hair comb-

ings, adds support to a reasonable hypothesis that someone else committed the crime.

Even if the hair evidence were as positive as a fingerprint, the state would have to show that the hair could only have been placed on the victim's pajamas during the commission of the crime. . . . This the state failed to show. Furthermore, although a defendant's motive is not an element of a crime, where, as here, the evidence is entirely circumstantial, the lack of any motive on the part of the defendant becomes a significant consideration. . . .

The Supreme Court of Florida has repeatedly said that "[w]here the only proof of guilt is circumstantial, no matter how strongly the evidence may suggest guilt a conviction cannot be sustained unless the evidence is inconsistent with any reasonable hypothesis of innocence." . . .

Viewing all the evidence presented in a light most favorable to the state, as we must do on appellate review, we find that the state failed to present substantial, competent evidence sufficient to enable the jury to exclude every reasonable hypothesis of defendant's innocence.

Accordingly, we reverse the trial court's denial of the defendant's motion for a judgment of acquittal and vacate the defendant's convictions and sentence.

CAMPBELL and SCHOONOVER, JJ., concur.

CHAPTER 19

Sentencing and Punishment

Introduction

The concept of criminal punishment is an ancient one. The Code of Hammurabi, promulgated in Babylonia nearly two thousand years before the birth of Christ, contained a detailed schedule of crimes and punishments and first codified the notion of "an eye for an eye." In a similar vein, the Old Testament mandated severe but proportionate punishment based on this principle of **retribution.**

While it is sometimes equated with legalized vengeance, the concept of retribution was a great leap forward in the evolution of criminal punishment. It replaced the personal or familial (and often excessive) acts of vengeance that frequently followed injuries to persons or property. Moreover, retribution carried with it a sense of **proportionality,** which continues to have relevance in criminal sentencing today.

Most ancient legal systems prescribed severe punishments for those who committed the kinds of acts we now consider *mala in se.* Execution, torture, mutilation, and banishment from the community were not uncommon. But ancient legal systems also employed economic sanctions such as forfeiture of property, especially when members of the upper classes committed transgressions against members of the lower classes.

The Common-Law Background

By contemporary standards, the English common law was quite severe—the death penalty was prescribed for most felonies. In the early days of the common law, nobles who committed **capital crimes** were shown mercy by simply being beheaded. Commoners who were sentenced to death were often subjected to more grisly forms of punishment—they were broken on the wheel, burned at the stake, or drawn and quartered. Eventually, the comparatively humane method of hanging was adopted as the principal means of execution in England.

Persons convicted of misdemeanors were generally subjected to nonlethal **corporal punishment** such as flogging. The misdemeanant was taken into the public square, bound to the whipping post, and administered as many lashes as were prescribed by law for the offense.

In England—indeed, throughout Europe—the administration of punishment was intentionally a matter of public spectacle. The idea was that public display of painful and humiliating punishment would deter others from engaging in criminal acts. This theory, known as **general deterrence,** is still prevalent today.

During the colonization of the New World, English subjects convicted of misdemeanors were often sent to penal colonies in America to do hard labor. After the American Revolution, they were sent to Australia.

The American Experience

In colonial America, criminal punishment followed common-law practice, although the Massachusetts Code of 1648 mandated capital punishment in cases of idolatry, witchcraft, blasphemy, sodomy, adultery, and "man stealing," as well as for the common-law capital crimes. At the time of the American Revolution, the death penalty was in wide use for a variety of felonies. And corporal punishment, primarily flogging, was widely used for a variety of crimes, including many misdemeanors.

The American Bill of Rights, ratified in 1791, prohibited the imposition of "cruel and unusual punishments." The Framers of the Bill of Rights sought to prevent the use of torture, which had been common in Europe as late as the eighteenth century.

However, they did not intend to outlaw the death penalty, nor did they intend to abolish all forms of corporal punishment.

During the nineteenth century, reformers introduced the concept of the **penitentiary**—literally, "a place to do penance." The idea was that criminals could be reformed through isolation, Bible study, and hard labor. This gave rise to the notion of **rehabilitation,** the idea that the criminal justice system could reform criminals and reintegrate them into society. Many of the educational, occupational training, and psychological programs found in modern prisons are based on this theory.

By the twentieth century, **incarceration** replaced corporal punishment as the mainstay of criminal sentencing. All states, as well as the federal government, constructed prisons to house persons convicted of felonies. Even cities and counties constructed jails to confine persons convicted of misdemeanors. However, the **death penalty** remained in wide use for the most serious violent felonies. But it was rendered more "humane" as the gallows were replaced by the firing squad, the gas chamber, the electric chair, and, eventually, lethal injection. The death penalty remains in effect today in more than half the states, although its use is now limited to the most aggravated cases of murder. Yet it remains one of the most intensely controversial aspects of the American system of criminal justice.

Today, the focus of criminal punishment is on the goal of **incapacitation.** Incapacitation means that offenders are prevented from committing further criminal acts. In ancient societies, banishment was sometimes used to protect the community from those whose presence was regarded as unduly threatening. Contemporary American society resorts to imprisonment or, in extreme cases, execution to rid itself of seriously threatening behavior. Although nearly everyone favors incapacitation of violent offenders, in practice incapacitation extends beyond execution or incarceration. When a state revokes a person's driver's license for driving while intoxicated, the purpose is primarily incapacitation. Similarly, some states have laws offering convicted rapists the option of taking a drug to render them incapable of committing rape. Other forms of incapacitation can be extremely controversial. For example, may a judge order a convicted child abuser to refrain from having any more children to prevent future child abuse?

Those who favor incapacitation to the exclusion of the other purposes of punishment are likely to favor harsh sentences, even for relatively minor crimes. They prefer to "lock 'em up and throw away the key." Again, we must consider the issue of proportionality: Crime control is not the only goal of the criminal justice system—dispensing justice is equally important.

Legal Constraints on Sentencing and Punishment

There are procedural as well as substantive issues in the area of sentencing and punishment. Sharp disagreements exist regarding the roles that legislatures, judges, and corrections officials should play in determining punishments. Generally, judges are required to impose sentences that fall within the parameters of appropriate punishment specified by statute, yet within these parameters, courts exercise substantial discretion. Recent concern about sentencing disparities has resulted in a variety of measures aimed at reducing the range of judicial discretion in sentencing.

Just as judges' sentencing decisions are constrained by statutes, statutory penalties must comport with substantive and procedural requirements imposed by the federal and state constitutions. Specifically, criminal punishment is limited by the Eighth Amendment prohibition of "cruel and unusual punishments," the due process clauses of the Fifth and Fourteenth amendments, and by similar provisions in all fifty state constitutions. Recent judicial activity in the areas of sentencing and punishment has focused on the need for procedural regularity in sentencing and proportionality in punishment.

··

Contemporary Forms of Criminal Punishment

Today the criminal law provides for a variety of criminal punishments, including monetary fines, incarceration, probation, community service, and, of course, the death penalty. Although most people agree about the propriety of punishing criminal behavior, they disagree about the legality, morality, and efficacy of specific modes of criminal punishment. The death penalty in particular remains a hotly debated issue.

Fines

By far the most common form of criminal punishment today is the **monetary fine.** Most misdemeanors carry monetary fines, especially for first offenses. Some felonies, especially serious economic crimes defined by federal law, carry heavy monetary fines as penalties. For example, offenses against federal banking laws and securities and exchange laws are punishable by fines reaching into the millions of dollars. Increasingly, drug trafficking offenders are being punished by large fines.

In many states, a court can sentence a defendant to pay a fine in addition to a sentence of imprisonment or probation (see Table 19.1). In New Jersey, for example, such fines may range from $500 to $200,000, depending on the nature and degree of the offense. N.J. Stat. Ann. 2C: 43–3. Fines might be appropriate devices of retribution and deterrence for economic crimes, but they hardly seem suitable as punishments for criminal acts of violence. And many have questioned the fairness and effectiveness of established minimum and maximum fines that do not consider the economic circumstances of individual defendants.

Forfeiture of Property

Federal law provides for forfeiture of the proceeds of a variety of criminal activities. See, generally, 18 U.S.C.A. §§ 981–982. More controversial are the federal law provisions allowing **forfeiture of property** used in illicit drug activity. Under federal law a "conveyance," which includes aircraft, motor vehicles, and vessels, is subject to forfeiture if it is used to transport controlled substances. 21 U.S.C.A. § 881(a)(4). Real estate may be forfeited if it is used to commit or facilitate commission of a drug-related felony. 21 U.S.C.A. § 881(a)(7). Many states have similar statutes. See, for example, Oklahoma's Uniform Controlled Dangerous Substances Act, 63 Okl.St.Ann. § 2–503. State courts dealing with forfeiture under state law have generally found that homesteads are exempt from forfeiture. See, for example, *Butterworth v. Caggiano*, 605 So.2d 56 (Fla. 1992). However, a federal appeals court has ruled that federal law preempts—that is, overrides—state homestead exemptions when federal crimes have been committed. *United States v. Lot 5, Fox Grove, Alachua County, Fla.*, 23 F.3d 359 (11th Cir. 1994).

Though technically this kind of forfeiture is a civil, rather than a criminal sanction, the U.S. Supreme Court has recognized that forfeiture constitutes significant punishment and is thus subject to constitutional limitations under the Eighth Amendment. *Austin v. United States*, 509 U.S. 602, 113 S.Ct. 2801, 125 L.Ed.2d 488 (1993). The

Table 19.1 A Sample of Crimes and Punishments Under Texas Law

Classification	Punishment	Examples of Offenses
Felonies		
Capital	Death or life imprisonment	Capital murder
First degree	Life imprisonment or 5–99 years and maximum fine of $10,000	Felony murder Aggravated sexual assault Armed robbery Arson (injury or death) Theft ($200,000 or more)
Second degree	Two–twenty years and maximum fine of $10,000	Aggravated kidnapping Aggravated assault Theft ($100,000 or more) Robbery
Third degree	Two–ten years and maximum fine of $10,000	Involuntary manslaughter Kidnapping Theft (under $20,000) (or certain number of head of livestock) Tampering with evidence Aggravated perjury
Misdemeanors		
Class A	Maximum jail term of one year and/or maximum fine of $4,000	Theft (under $1,500) Resisting arrest Perjury Cruelty to animals
Class B	Maximum jail term of 180 days and/or maximum fine of $2,000	Theft (under $500) Prostitution Enticing child from custody of parent False report to police
Class C	No jail term and maximum fine of $500	Theft (under $50) (or less than $20 if theft results from issuing or passing check) Public intoxication Gambling Reckless destruction of property

Source: Vernon's Texas Penal Code Annotated §§ 12.01–12.34.

Court said that forfeiture "constitutes 'payment to a sovereign as punishment for some offense' . . . and, as such, is subject to the limitations of the Eighth Amendment's Excessive Fines Clause." 509 U.S. at 622, 113 S.Ct. at 2812, 125 L.Ed.2d at 505. However, the Court left it to state and lower federal courts to determine the tests of "excessiveness" in the context of forfeiture. In 1994 the Illinois Supreme Court said that three factors should be considered in this regard: (1) the gravity of the offense relative to the value of the forfeiture, (2) whether the property was an integral part of the illicit activity, and (3) whether illicit activity involving the property was extensive. *Waller v. 1989 Ford F350 Truck (Kusumoto)*, 642 N.E.2d 460 (Ill. 1994).

Incarceration

Confinement is generally regarded as the only effective way to deal with violent offenders. Although some question the efficacy of the prison, regarding it as little more than a factory for producing future criminals, incarceration does protect society from dangerous offenders. Prison is an effective incapacitator; it is rarely an effective rehabilitator. In fact, serving time in prison often reinforces criminal tendencies.

Today, more than one million inmates are in federal and state penal institutions, an all-time high. Consequently, many prisons are overcrowded. This problem has led to judicial intervention in many instances, yet society appears reluctant to provide additional resources to expand prison capacity. Imprisonment is expensive, costing taxpayers nearly $20 billion per year.

As criminologists have become increasingly dissatisfied with the effects of the prison system, judges have responded by imposing limits on prison populations and scrutinizing the conditions of confinement. Meanwhile, fiscal pressures prevent legislatures from appropriating the funds necessary to construct more prisons. Accordingly, attention has shifted to alternatives to incarceration, especially for less dangerous offenders. One of the most serious criticisms of all such alternatives emphasizes the difficulty of determining who should be eligible for an alternative form of punishment. In an age of overcrowded prisons, alternative punishments carry the real possibility that truly dangerous offenders will not be sufficiently controlled.

The Boot Camp: An Alternative to Prison?

In recent years, one alternative to the traditional prison setting has been the **boot camp,** a program designed to employ a system of discipline much like the one the military uses to instill discipline in its recruits. In early 1993, the American Correctional Association counted sixty-five adult boot camps in twenty-seven states and nineteen juvenile camps in eight states. The inmates are generally young, nonviolent offenders who have committed theft, burglary, forgery, and other nonviolent offenses, often brought about by their drug abuse. In lieu of a prison sentence, they elect to undergo three to six months of training that often includes drug rehabilitation and repairing roads and other public facilities. Ideally, their stint in boot camp is followed by a period of supervised probation. In addition to boot camps being less costly than traditional methods of incarceration, communities gain from the labor performed by the inmates, and their early release conserves financial resources essential to operating regular prisons.

Probation

Of the various alternatives to incarceration, **probation** is by far the most common. Probation is the conditional release of a convicted offender by a trial court. If prisons are little more than factories for producing future criminals, then probation seems to be a reasonable response to many first offenses punishable by prison terms. The offender is released under the supervision of a probation officer, who is responsible for making sure that the offender abides by the **conditions of probation.**

Probation is usually granted on the conditions that the probationer will not commit further crimes, will avoid certain persons or places, will maintain gainful employment and support any dependents, will not travel without permission of the court or probation officer, and often other conditions related to the probationer's rehabilitation. Typically, courts have broad discretion in imposing conditions of probation. Thus, constitutional rights may be limited by conditions that are related to the goal of rehabilitation. Even the highly protected First Amendment rights of free speech and association may be severely restricted by probation conditions. *Malone v. United States,* 502 F.2d 554 (9th Cir. 1974); *Porth v. Templar,* 453 F.2d 330 (10th Cir. 1971).

Nevertheless, there are limits to probation conditions. For example, a Florida appellate court held that a condition prohibiting custody of children had a clear

Conditions of Probation

In 1990 the Supreme Court of Ohio reviewed the conviction of a defendant on a charge of contributing to the delinquency of a child by furnishing alcohol to three young boys. The court focused on a single point: whether the trial court abused its discretion in imposing a condition of probation stipulating that the defendant "have no association or communication, direct or indirect, with anyone under the age of 18 years not a member of his immediate family." The court noted that while a trial judge is granted broad discretion in setting conditions of probation, that discretion is not limitless, and courts must guard against overly broad conditions that impinge upon the probationer's liberty. Nevertheless, the court found the restriction imposed against the defendant "reasonably related to rehabilitating [the defendant] without being unduly restrictive." Citing various state and federal authorities, the court said that in setting conditions of probation, trial judges should consider whether a condition to be imposed (1) is reasonably related to rehabilitating the offender, (2) has some relationship to the crime for which the offender was convicted, and (3) relates to conduct that is criminal or reasonably related to future criminality.

State v. Jones, 550 N.E.2d 469 (Ohio 1990).

relationship to the crime of child abuse and was valid, but that conditions prohibiting marriage and pregnancy added nothing to decrease the possibility of further child abuse and were accordingly invalid. *Rodriguez v. State,* 378 So.2d 7 (Fla. App. 1979). Three years later, the same court struck down a condition of probation that required that the defendant "must not father any children during [the] probation period." *Burchell v. State,* 419 So.2d 358 (Fla. App. 1982). Similarly, in *Biller v. State,* 618 So.2d 734 (Fla. 1993), the Florida Supreme Court invalidated a probation order that required the probationer to refrain from using or possessing alcoholic beverages. The court pointed out that nothing in the record showed any connection between alcohol consumption and the weapons violation of which the probationer had been convicted.

Community Service

Another alternative to incarceration, **community service** is growing in popularity. Community service refers to sentences whereby offenders are required to perform a specified number of hours of service to the community, doing specified tasks. Often, community service is required as one of several conditions of probation.

Community service has the virtues of keeping the offender out of the undesirable prison environment and exacting a penalty that is useful to the community. Ideally, it seems like an excellent way to instill in the offender a sense of responsibility to the community for having committed criminal actions, but community service also has its drawbacks. It is difficult for the community to reap any real benefit without providing a degree of training for and supervision of the offender. Training and supervision can be costly and can, in many instances, exceed the value of the community service to be performed.

Community Control

Another alternative to incarceration is **community control,** a neologism for an ancient practice known as **house arrest.** Under this alternative, an offender is allowed to leave home only for employment and approved community service activities. Increasingly, house arrest is monitored electronically by requiring persons to wear bracelets that permit officials to track their whereabouts. Community control is generally employed when incarceration is not warranted, but probation is not considered sufficiently restrictive. Community control requires intensive surveillance and supervision, and might not be practical in many cases. For example, consider a convicted rapist whose occupation is plumbing. To allow this offender to carry on his trade may pose a significant risk to householders. Comparable risks often militate against placing offenders under community control.

Creative Alternatives to Confinement

Judges seeking alternatives to jail or prison have been increasingly creative recently. One judge in Houston, Texas, has been known to require offenders to clean out the police department stables as part of their "community service." Some juvenile courts require offenders to make public apologies to their victims. In a few cities, billboards have been erected bearing the names of persons convicted for driving while under the influence of intoxicating substances. Some jurisdictions even publish the names of persons who patronize prostitutes. These actions are intended to shame offenders by drawing public attention to their misconduct. In seventeenth-century Massachusetts, women found guilty of adultery were required to wear a scarlet "A." This idea that offenders need to experience shame appears to be making a comeback.

In 1987 a convicted child molester was sentenced by an Oregon court to five years' probation on the condition that he display on his front door and automobile a warning sign: "Dangerous Sex Offender: No Children Allowed." Although the unusual sentence drew praise from prosecutors and many citizens' groups, civil libertarians objected.

One county judge in Sarasota, Florida, made national news in 1986 by requiring that DWI offenders—as a condition of probation—place bumper stickers on their cars to alert the driving public to their convictions! On appeal, the practice was upheld against an Eighth Amendment attack. As the appellate court said, "The mere requirement that a defendant display a 'scarlet letter' as part of his punishment is not necessarily offensive to the Constitution." *Goldschmitt v. State,* 490 So.2d 123, 125 (Fla. App. 1986). On the other hand, the New York Court of Appeals has invalidated a similar condition of probation on the ground that it bears no relationship to the goal of rehabilitation. *People v. Letterlough,* 655 N.E.2d 146 (N.Y. 1995). Obviously, there is room for judicial disagreement on such matters.

The Death Penalty

The death penalty remains the single most controversial issue in the realm of criminal punishment. Although the death penalty has deep roots in religious and legal traditions, the twentieth century witnessed widespread abolition of **capital punishment.** At present, the United States is the only Western democracy that retains the death penalty. Thirty-nine states currently authorize capital punishment for first-degree murder or other types of aggravated homicide.

Historical Background

The Framers of the Bill of Rights did not intend for the Cruel and Unusual Punishments Clause of the Eighth Amendment to abolish the death penalty. The Bill of Rights assumes the existence of capital punishment. Indeed, the Fifth Amendment refers specifically to "capital" crimes and the deprivation of life. A reform movement in the nineteenth century succeeded in limiting public executions and reducing the range of capital offenses. The movement to eliminate the death penalty achieved its first victory in 1847, when Michigan abolished capital punishment. This movement grew steadily throughout the twentieth century. By the 1960s, it appeared that the death penalty was on the way out. Public opinion no longer favored it; many states abolished it. In those that did not, the courts began to impose restrictions on its use. In 1967 two persons were executed in the United States. Ten years passed before another person was put to death. When the Supreme Court declared Georgia's death penalty law unconstitutional in *Furman v. Georgia*, 408 U.S. 238, 92 S.Ct. 2726, 33 L.Ed.2d 346 (1972), many observers thought it signaled the demise of the death penalty.

An excerpt from the U.S. Supreme Court's decision in *Furman v. Georgia* appears at the end of the chapter.

The Supreme Court Invalidates a Death Penalty Statute

The Supreme Court's 1972 decision striking the Georgia death penalty concentrated on the virtually unlimited discretion the state placed in trial juries empowered to impose death sentences. According to Justice Stewart's concurring opinion in *Furman,* Georgia's administration of the death penalty was unpredictable to the point of being "freakishly imposed." 408 U.S. 238, 310, 92 S.Ct. 2726, 2763, 33 L.Ed.2d 346, 390 (1972). In the wake of the *Furman* decision, Georgia and most other states revised their death penalty laws to address the concerns raised by the Court.

The Revised Georgia Statute

Under the revised Georgia statute, a **bifurcated trial** is held in cases where the state seeks the death penalty. In the first stage, guilt is determined according to the usual procedures, rules of evidence, and standard of proof. If the jury finds the defendant guilty, the same jury considers the appropriateness of the death sentence in a separate proceeding where additional evidence is received to determine aggravation or mitigation of the punishment. To impose the death penalty, the jury must find at least one of several **aggravating factors** specified in the statute. The purpose of requiring aggravating factors before imposing the death penalty is to narrow the cases and persons eligible for capital punishment and make the imposition of the death penalty more predictable.

Under Georgia law, the specific aggravating factors to be considered by the jury are whether

1. The offense . . . was committed by a person with a prior record of conviction for a capital felony;

2. The offense . . . was committed while the offender was engaged in . . . another capital felony or aggravated battery, or the offense of murder was committed while the offender was engaged in the commission of another capital felony or aggravated battery or . . . burglary or arson in the first degree;

3. The offender . . . knowingly created a great risk of death to more than one person in a public place by means of a weapon or device which would normally be hazardous to the lives of more than one person;

4. The offender committed the offense of murder for himself or another for the purpose of receiving money or any other thing of monetary value;

5. The murder of a judicial officer, former judicial officer, a district attorney or solicitor-general, or former district attorney, solicitor or solicitor-general was committed during or because of the exercise of his or her official duties;

6. The offender caused or directed another to commit murder or committed murder as an agent or employee of another person;

7. The offense . . . was outrageously or wantonly vile, horrible or inhuman in that it involved torture, depravity of mind or an aggravated battery to the victim;

8. The offense of murder was committed against any peace officer, corrections employee, or fireman while engaged in the performance of his official duties;

9. The offense of murder was committed by a person in, or who has escaped from, the lawful custody of a peace officer or place of lawful confinement; or

10. The murder was committed for the purpose of avoiding, interfering with, or preventing a lawful arrest or custody in a place of lawful confinement, of himself or another. Official Ga. Code Ann. § 17–10–30(b).

To hand down a death sentence, a Georgia jury must find that at least one of these aggravating circumstances was present in the crime. The jury must then weigh the aggravating factors against any **mitigating factors** presented by the defense. See Official Ga. Code Ann. § 17–10–30(b). Should the jury make this finding and opt for the death penalty, the statute provides for automatic appeal to the state supreme court. That court is required to consider

1. Whether the sentence of death was imposed under the influence of passion, prejudice or any other arbitrary factor; and

2. Whether . . . the evidence supports the jury's or judge's finding of a statutory aggravating circumstance . . . , and

3. Whether the sentence of death is excessive or disproportionate to the penalty imposed in similar cases, considering both the crime and the defendant. Official Code Ga. Ann. § 17–10–35(c).

Reinstatement of the Death Penalty

In *Gregg v. Georgia*, 428 U.S. 153, 96 S.Ct. 2909, 49 L.Ed.2d 859 (1976), the Supreme Court upheld Georgia's revised death penalty statute by a vote of 7–2. Apparently, the Court was satisfied that this scheme had sufficiently addressed the evils identified in *Furman*. Thirty-eight states now have death penalty statutes modeled along the lines of the law upheld in *Gregg*.

An excerpt from the U.S. Supreme Court's decision in *Gregg v. Georgia* appears at the end of the chapter.

Shortly after the death penalty was effectively reinstated by the Supreme Court's *Gregg* decision, executions in the United States began anew. On January 17, 1977, the state of Utah executed convicted murderer Gary Gilmore by firing squad. Between the date of the Gilmore execution and July 26, 2000, 654 prisoners were executed in the United States. As of April 1, 1999, there were 3,565 persons under sentence of death in thirty-six jurisdictions (thirty-four states, the U.S. military, and the federal government) (see Table 19.2).

The Federal Death Penalty

In August 1997, Timothy McVeigh was sentenced to death by lethal injection for his role in the bombing of the federal office building in Oklahoma City in 1995. In his federal trial, McVeigh was convicted of twenty-eight counts of murder of a federal law enforcement agent on active duty. See 18 U.S.C.A. § 1114. Under federal law, executions are carried out in the state where the defendant was sentenced, unless that state has no death penalty, in which case the prisoner is transferred to another state for execution. 18 U.S.C.A. § 3596. Prior to May 2001, the federal government

Table 19.2 Persons Under Sentence of Death in the U.S., by Jurisdiction, as of April 1, 1999

Jurisdiction	Number of Persons Sentenced to Death	Jurisdiction	Number of Persons Sentenced to Death
Federal	21	Missouri	84
U.S. Military	8	Montana	6
Alabama	178	Nebraska	9
Alaska	0	Nevada	86
Arizona	120	New Hampshire	0
Arkansas	42	New Jersey	16
California	536	New Mexico	4
Colorado	3	New York	2
Connecticut	5	North Carolina	212
Delaware	19	North Dakota	0
Florida	390	Ohio	192
Georgia	123	Oklahoma	151
Hawaii	0	Oregon	26
Idaho	22	Pennsylvania	225
Illinois	156	Rhode Island	0
Indiana	45	South Carolina	69
Iowa	0	South Dakota	2
Kansas	2	Tennessee	104
Kentucky	39	Texas	437
Louisiana	82	Utah	11
Maine	0	Vermont	0
Maryland	17	Virginia	37
Massachusetts	0	Washington	17
Michigan	0	West Virginia	0
Minnesota	0	Wisconsin	0
Mississippi	65	Wyoming	2

Source: NAACP Legal Defense and Educational Fund, Inc., *Death Row U.S.A. Spring 1999.*

had not executed anyone since 1963, but many observers expect the McVeigh conviction to spur the federal government to renew executions.

The Anti-Drug Abuse Act of 1988, 21 U.S.C.A. § 848(e), allows the death penalty for so-called "drug kingpins" who control "continuing criminal enterprises" whose members intentionally kill or procure others to kill in furtherance of the enterprise. In 1993 Juan Raul Garza was sentenced to death under this statute for three murders committed as head of a Texas-based drug trafficking organization. *United States v. Juan Raul Garza,* No. CR 93–0009 (S.D. Tex.). *United States v. Juan Raul Garza* was affirmed by the Fifth U.S. Court of Appeals in *United States v. Flores & Garza,* 53 F.3d 1342 (5th Cir. 1995). A federal district judge set Garza's execution for August 5, 2000, but in late July of that year President Bill Clinton ordered the execution delayed to allow Garza to request executive clemency under new rules promulgated by the Justice Department.

Aggravating and Mitigating Circumstances in Death Penalty Cases

A Texas death penalty statute provided that the jury was to be instructed to consider three "special issues": (1) whether the defendant acted deliberately or with reasonable expectation that death would result; (2) whether the defendant would be a continuing violent threat to society; and (3) if applicable, whether the killing was an unreasonable response to any provocation by the deceased. If the jury answered all three questions in the affirmative, the judge was required to enter a death sentence. The Supreme Court found that although the application of the Texas statute permitted the jury to consider evidence of the defendant's mental retardation and abuse as a child as mitigation, the special issues prevented the jury from giving effect to that evidence.

Penry v. Lynaugh, 492 U.S. 302, 109 S.Ct. 2934, 106 L.Ed.2d 256 (1989).

The **Violent Crime Control and Law Enforcement Act of 1994** (see Title 42 U.S.C.A.), better known as the Federal Crime Bill, dramatically increased the number of federal crimes eligible for the death penalty. Capital punishment is now authorized for dozens of federal crimes, including treason, murder of a federal law enforcement official, and kidnapping, carjacking, child abuse, or bank robbery that results in death. It remains to be seen whether the federal courts will permit the death penalty for nonhomicidal crimes. *Coker v. Georgia,* 433 U.S. 584, 97 S.Ct. 2861, 53 L.Ed.2d 982 (1977), would suggest otherwise. There, the Supreme Court prohibited capital punishment for the crime of rape. Although the decision lacked a majority opinion, it suggests that the death penalty is an inappropriate punishment for any crime that does not involve the taking of a human life.

Is the Death Penalty Racially Discriminatory?

Whether the Court achieved the evenhandedness in the administration of capital punishment it sought through its decisions in *Furman* and *Gregg* is questionable. Evidence indicates that the death penalty remains racially discriminatory, as regards both the race of the offender and the race of the murder victim. Criminologist David Baldus collected data on more than one thousand murder cases in Georgia during the 1970s and found significant disparities in the imposition of the death penalty, based primarily on the race of the murder victims and, to a lesser extent, on the race of the defendants. The data reveal that blacks who killed whites were more than seven times more likely to receive the death sentence than were whites who killed blacks.

In April 1987, the Supreme Court reviewed the death sentence of a black man convicted of killing a white police officer in Georgia. The Court refused to accept statistical evidence derived from the Baldus study as a basis for reversing the death. In the Court's view, even if there is statistical evidence of race discrimination, a defendant sentenced to death cannot prevail on appeal unless the defendant can show that the death sentence was imposed because of race discrimination in this case. *McCleskey v. Kemp,* 481 U.S. 279, 107 S.Ct. 1756, 95 L.Ed.2d 262 (1987). Obviously, this would be difficult, although certainly not impossible, for a defendant to demonstrate.

In a 1990 report, the U.S. General Accounting Office concluded that available research demonstrated "a pattern of evidence indicating racial disparities in the charging, sentencing, and imposition of the death penalty. . . ." Similarly, in 1994 the U.S.

House of Representatives Subcommittee on Civil and Constitutional Rights concluded that members of racial minorities were being disproportionately prosecuted under the federal death penalty law. According to the Death Penalty Information Center, of the 133 defendants authorized for death penalty prosecution from 1988 to 1998, 76 percent were members of racial minorities. Certainly the debate over the discriminatory impact of the death penalty is bound to continue. Still, for a particular defendant to succeed in challenging a death sentence, the defendant must show discrimination in his or her particular case.

Death, Deterrence, Retribution, and Incapacitation

One of the most intense battles among academicians in the field of criminal justice has been waged over the alleged deterrent value of the death penalty. At this point, the evidence appears to be mixed, making firm conclusions impossible. Whatever the possible deterrent value of the death penalty, its actual deterrent effect is reduced by the years of delay between sentencing and execution.

Obviously, the death penalty has no value as a means of rehabilitation. Therefore, if the death penalty is to be justified, it must be primarily on grounds of retribution and incapacitation. Supporters of the death penalty argue, perhaps ironically, that the value of human life is underscored by imposing the severest of sanctions on those who commit murder. Certainly the death penalty is proportionate to the crime of murder. Indeed, the Supreme Court has made it clear that murder is the only crime for which the death penalty is permissible. *Coker v. Georgia,* supra.

Advocates of capital punishment also stress the incapacitation of the offender, and it is difficult to argue that death is not a complete incapacitator. But are retribution and incapacitation sufficient justifications for the death penalty?

When Can a Juvenile Be Executed?

One very difficult issue that the Supreme Court faced during the 1980s was whether, and under what circumstances, a juvenile may be executed when convicted of a capital crime. The Court responded in three decisions. In *Thompson v. Oklahoma,* 487 U.S. 815, 108 S.Ct. 2687, 101 L.Ed.2d 702 (1988), the Court ruled in a 6–3 decision that the Constitution forbids executing a juvenile who was fifteen years of age or younger at the time of commission of a capital crime. The following year, in *Stanford v. Kentucky,* 492 U.S. 361, 109 S.Ct. 2969, 106 L.Ed.2d 306 (1989), the Supreme Court split five to four in holding that a juvenile sixteen or older at the time of the crime may be sentenced to death. Concurring in *Stanford,* Justice O'Connor commented that "it is sufficiently clear that no national consensus forbids the imposition of capital punishment on 16- or 17-year-old capital murderers." 492 U.S. at 381, 109 S.Ct. at 2981, 106 L.Ed.2d at 325. In both *Thompson* and *Stanford,* the Court referred to "evolving standards of decency" as the proper test for judging the constitutionality of whether a juvenile may be executed. Given this standard and with the sharp disagreement on the Supreme Court, the present judicial consensus might change with changing membership on the Court.

Methods of Execution

Currently, five methods of execution exist in the United States: electric chair, lethal injection, gas chamber, firing squad, and hanging. Hanging is by far the least common and, with the possible exception of the gas chamber, is also the least humane mode of

Does the Eighth Amendment Prohibit the Execution of a Prisoner Who Has Become Insane?

In 1974 Alvin Ford was convicted of murder and sentenced to death by a Florida court. There was no indication that he was mentally incompetent at the time of the trial. However, while in prison awaiting execution, Ford began to exhibit profound changes in behavior and to experience bizarre delusions. In 1983 a prison psychiatrist diagnosed Ford as suffering from a severe and uncontrollable mental disease closely resembling paranoid schizophrenia. Ford's attorney then invoked procedures under Florida law governing the determination of competency of a condemned prisoner. A panel of psychiatrists examined Ford, and although they differed in their specific diagnoses, all agreed that Ford was not insane under Florida law.

On April 30, 1984, Governor Bob Graham signed Alvin Ford's death warrant. Ford's attorney then filed a petition for habeas corpus in the United States District Court, seeking an evidentiary hearing on his client's sanity. The district court denied relief, and the court of appeals affirmed. The United States Supreme Court agreed to review the case to resolve the issue of whether the Eighth Amendment prohibits the execution of a person who is insane. On June 26, 1986, the Supreme Court announced its decision in *Ford v. Wainwright*, 477 U.S. 399, 106 S.Ct. 2595, 91 L.Ed.2d 335 (1986). The Court held that the Eighth Amendment bars the execution of a person who is insane. Writing for a plurality of justices, Justice Thurgood Marshall declared that "[i]t is no less abhorrent today than it has been for centuries to exact in penance the life of one whose mental illness prevents him from comprehending the reasons for the penalty or its implications."

477 U.S. at 417, 106 S.Ct. at 2606, 91 L.Ed.2d at 351.

capital punishment. Nevertheless, a federal appeals court ruled in 1994 that hanging, as it is administered by the state of Washington, is not cruel and unusual punishment. *Campbell v. Wood,* 978 F.2d 1502 (9th Cir. 1994). The court discussed at some length the grisly mechanics of hanging and concluded that hanging, as practiced in Washington, is likely to produce a quick and painless death. In a subsequent decision, however, a federal district court in Washington forbade the hanging of a 409-pound man, saying that there was a significant risk that hanging a person of that weight would result in decapitation. The court said that such an execution would be akin to beheading by ax or guillotine and would be inconsistent with the concept of human dignity underlying the Eighth Amendment. *Rupe v. Wood,* 863 F. Supp. 1315 (D.C. W.Wash. 1994).

THE GAS CHAMBER CONTROVERSY

In a related case, a federal district court in California ruled that execution by means of the gas chamber is unconstitutional. The court found that the gas chamber produces a lingering death accompanied by intense pain, anxiety, and muscle spasms. *Fierro v. Gomez,* 865 F. Supp. 1387, 1389 (N.D. Cal. 1994). Interestingly, the district court relied on the Ninth Circuit's decision in *Campbell v. Wood,* supra, which the district court interpreted to forbid unnecessarily cruel means of execution. In 1996 the Ninth Circuit Court of Appeals upheld the prohibition on the gas chamber. *Fierro v. Gomez,* 77 F.3d 301 (9th Cir. 1996). Later that year, however, the Supreme Court granted certiorari and remanded the case to the Ninth Circuit for reconsideration in light of an amended California statute. *Gomez v. Fierro,* 519 U.S. 918, 117 S.Ct. 285, 136 L.Ed.2d 204 (1996). On remand, the Ninth Circuit held that Gomez lacked standing to challenge the constitutionality of execution by lethal gas, because the amended

California death penalty statute affords the choice of either lethal gas or lethal injection, with lethal injection being the default method in absence of an election. Because Gomez did not elect the lethal gas option, he had no standing to challenge that method of execution. *Fierro v. Tehune,* 147 F.3d 1158 (9th Cir. 1998).

THE ELECTRIC CHAIR DEBATE

The electric chair was introduced in the 1890s as a "humanitarian" alternative to the gallows. The "chair" is now employed in only six states: Alabama, Florida, Georgia, Kentucky, Nebraska, and Tennessee. This method of execution subjects the inmate to approximately 2,000 volts of electricity conducted through copper electrodes attached to the head. Usually, the first jolt of electricity causes death by cardiac arrest and respiratory paralysis, although there have been several instances where multiple jolts have had to be applied. In some cases, the administration of electricity produces smoke and even fire. In March 1997, some observers were shocked when white smoke and flames nearly a foot high issued from the head of Pedro Medina when he was executed in "Old Sparky," Florida's seventy-four-year-old electric chair. Later that year a Florida trial judge rejected a death row inmate's constitutional challenge to the use of the electric chair. And in *Jones v. State,* 701 So.2d 76 (Fla. 1997), the Florida Supreme Court in a 4–3 decision upheld the constitutionality of using the electric chair. Three dissenting justices described its use as archaic and barbaric.

The *Jones* decision prompted the Florida legislature to revise the law to provide persons under sentence of death with the option of being executed by lethal injection. As amended in 2000, Section 922.105, Florida Statutes now provides the following:

(1) A death sentence shall be executed by lethal injection, unless the person sentenced to death affirmatively elects to be executed by electrocution. . . .

(2) A person convicted and sentenced to death for a capital crime at any time shall have one opportunity to elect that his or her death sentence be executed by electrocution. The election for death by electrocution is waived unless it is personally made by the person in writing and delivered to the warden of the correctional facility within 30 days after the issuance of mandate pursuant to a decision by the Florida Supreme Court affirming the sentence of death.

(3) If electrocution or lethal injection is held to be unconstitutional by the Florida Supreme Court under the State Constitution, or held to be unconstitutional by the United States Supreme Court under the United States Constitution, or if the United States Supreme Court declines to review any judgment holding a method of execution to be unconstitutional under the United Sates Constitution made by the Florida Supreme Court or the United States Court of Appeals that has jurisdiction over Florida, all persons sentenced to death for a capital crime shall be executed by any constitutional method of execution.

Other Recent Death Penalty Concerns

In 1994 the U.S. Supreme Court rendered several important decisions dealing with capital punishment. In *Tuilaepa v. California,* 512 U.S. 967, 114 S.Ct. 2630, 129 L.Ed.2d 750 (1994), the Court upheld California's death penalty statute against a Fourteenth Amendment challenge asserting that the statute was void for vagueness. The challenge was brought by a man who was sentenced to death in 1982 for the murder of a woman whom he also robbed and raped. At the time of the crime, the perpetrator was only twenty and had just been released from a youth-rehabilitation program. The challenged statute directed juries to consider the defendant's age, record of criminal violence, and the circumstances of the crime. But the law failed to indicate whether these factors could be considered as aggravating, mitigating, or both. Dividing 8–1, the Court held that the law gives sentencing juries adequate guidance. In rejecting the challenge, the Court found that the law had a "common-sense core of meaning that criminal juries should be capable of understanding." 114 S.Ct. at 2636. Although this ruling seemed to represent a retreat from earlier decisions applying the vagueness doctrine, had the Court's decision been otherwise, nearly 400 inmates currently under sentence of death in California could have challenged their death sentences.

In 1994 the Supreme Court also decided two important cases dealing with the information that juries may consider in deciding whether to impose the death penalty. In *Romano v. Oklahoma*, 512 U.S. 1, 114 S.Ct. 2004, 129 L.Ed.2d 1 (1994), the Court held that neither the Eighth Amendment nor the Due Process Clause of the Fourteenth Amendment prohibits capital-sentencing juries from being informed that the defendant is already under sentence of death for another crime. Petitioner John Romano had already been sentenced to death for robbing and murdering one man when he was tried for another robbery-murder. During the sentencing phase, the prosecution sought to introduce evidence of the former crime and sentence. Romano's attorney objected, claiming that for the jury to know of the previous death sentence would diminish its sense of responsibility in imposing another death sentence. The trial judge overruled the objection, and Romano was sentenced to death. Writing for the Supreme Court, Chief Justice Rehnquist observed that although the prior death sentence was irrelevant, the Constitution "does not establish a federal code of evidence to supersede state evidentiary rules in capital sentencing proceedings." 114 S.Ct. at 2011.

Chief Justice Rehnquist's observation in *Romano* notwithstanding, the Court in *Simmons v. South Carolina,* 512 U.S. 154, 114 S.Ct. 2187, 129 L.Ed.2d 133 (1994), held that defendants facing the death penalty have a right to tell juries if the only alternative to a death sentence is life imprisonment without the possibility of parole. Jonathan Simmons was convicted of murdering a seventy-nine-year-old woman in her home. Because Simmons had been convicted twice before of sexually assaulting elderly women, South Carolina law provided that he would be ineligible for parole if sentenced to prison. Over defense counsel's objection, the trial judge granted the prosecution's motion to exclude any mention of parole during the trial. During the sentencing phase, the court denied defense counsel's request to explain to the jury that a life sentence carried no possibility of parole. Finally, during deliberations the judge told the jury not to consider whether Simmons could be paroled if he was sentenced to life imprisonment. Simmons was sentenced to death. The Supreme Court remanded the case for resentencing, saying that the trial judge's refusal to provide the requested instruction constituted a denial of due process. In dissent, Justice Scalia accused the Court of trying to impose on the states a "Federal Rules of Death Penalty Evidence." 114 S.Ct. at 2205.

The Sentencing Stage of the Criminal Process

Every jurisdiction requires that criminal sentences for adults be imposed in open court, although in many instances juvenile offenders may be sentenced *in camera.* In misdemeanor cases, sentencing usually occurs immediately on conviction. In felony cases, where penalties are greater, sentencing may be postponed to allow the court to conduct a **presentence investigation.**

The Presentence Report

In many states as well as in the federal system, the court is required to order a **presentence report** when the offender to be sentenced is a first offender or is under a certain age. In other state jurisdictions, the sentencing judge is accorded discretion in this area. For example, Rule 1403 of the Pennsylvania Rules of Criminal Procedure provides as follows:

A. Presentence Investigation Report.

1. The sentencing judge may, in his discretion, order a presentence investigation report in any case.

2. The sentencing judge shall place on the record his reasons for dispensing with the presentence investigation report if the court fails to order a presentence report in any of the following instances;

(a) where incarceration for one year or more is a possible disposition under the applicable sentencing statutes; or

(b) where the defendant is less than twenty-one years old at the time of conviction or entry of a plea of guilty; or

(c) where a defendant is a first offender in that he has not heretofore been sentenced as an adult.

Rule 1404 makes the reports confidential and available only to the sentencing judge, counsel for the state and the defense, and experts appointed by the court to assist the court in sentencing.

In some states, statutes, court rules, or judicial interpretations mandate that courts release a presentence report to the defendant or defendant's counsel, usually allowing some exemptions for sensitive material. In other states, courts have ruled that this is a matter within the discretion of the sentencing judge. In some instances, courts will reveal factual material such as police reports but decline to disclose statements made in confidence to investigators. Often the judicial interpretation depends on the language of the statute or court rule. The Supreme Court requires release of presentence reports to defendants who may be sentenced to death.

The presentence report sets forth the defendant's history of delinquency or criminality, medical history, family background, economic status, education, employment history, and so forth. Much of this information is obtained by probation officers, who interview defendants' families, friends, employers, and so on. In addition, most

CASE-IN-POINT **Presentence Reports**

Daniel Gardner was found guilty of first-degree murder, and the jury recommended a sentence of life imprisonment. The jury's recommendation was based on its finding that mitigating factors outweighed the aggravating circumstances of the crime. However, the trial judge sentenced Gardner to death, relying on a confidential portion of a presentence report that had not been made available to the defense. The United States Supreme Court vacated the sentence and directed the trial court to conduct another sentencing proceeding in which the defendant would have an opportunity to deny or explain the contents of the presentence report.

Gardner v. Florida, 430 U.S. 349, 97 S.Ct. 1197, 51 L.Ed.2d 393 (1977).

jurisdictions allow courts to order physical or mental examinations of defendants. This information can be very useful to a judge who must determine a sentence that is at once fair, humane, and meaningful.

The Sentencing Hearing

After the presentence report is completed, a **sentencing hearing** is held. At this hearing, the court considers the evidence received at trial, the presentence report, any evidence offered by either party in aggravation or mitigation of sentence, and any statement the defendant wishes to make. In addition, most jurisdictions require judges to hear arguments concerning various sentencing alternatives. Sentencing is a critical stage of the criminal process, and counsel must be supplied to indigent defendants. *Mempa v. Rhay*, 389 U.S. 128, 88 S.Ct. 254, 19 L.Ed.2d 336 (1967).

Pronouncement of Sentence

After the judge has digested the sentencing report, heard arguments from counsel and the defendant's statement, and considered the relevant provisions of law, the sentence is pronounced in open court. The **pronouncement of sentence** is the stage when the trial court imposes a penalty on a defendant for the offense of which the defendant has been adjudged guilty. Sentences are usually pronounced by the judge who presided at the defendant's trial or the entry of plea. In misdemeanor cases, sentencing often occurs immediately after the entry of a plea or a finding of guilty by the judge or jury. In felony cases, the pronouncement is often delayed until the court has received a presentence investigation report or until the prosecutor and defense counsel have had an opportunity to prepare a presentation.

The rules of evidence are relaxed during a sentencing proceeding. Traditionally, a defendant has been afforded an opportunity to make a statement on his or her own behalf, a procedure often referred to as the **right of allocution.** Generally, special rules govern the sentencing of a defendant who is insane, and often sentencing must be deferred for a female defendant who is pregnant.

The procedure at the pronouncement stage is generally outlined in the criminal procedure rules of each jurisdiction. Typically, Rule 1405, Pennsylvania Rules of Criminal Procedure, provides the following:

C. Sentencing Proceeding

(1) At the time of sentencing, the judge shall afford the defendant the opportunity to make a statement in his or her behalf and shall afford counsel for both parties the opportunity to present information and argument relative to sentencing.

(2) The judge shall state on the record the reasons for the sentence imposed.

(3) The judge shall determine on the record that the defendant has been advised of the following:

(a) of the right to file a post-sentence motion and to appeal, of the time within which the defendant must exercise those rights, and of the right to assistance of counsel in the preparation of the motion and appeal;

(b) of the rights, if the defendant is indigent, to proceed *in forma pauperis* and to proceed with assigned counsel as provided in Rule 316;

(c) of the time limits within which post-sentence motions must be decided;

(d) that issues raised before or during trial shall be deemed preserved for appeal whether or not the defendant elects to file a post-sentence motion; and

(e) of the defendant's qualified right to bail under Rule 4009(B).

(4) The judge shall require that a record of the sentencing proceeding be made and preserved so that it can be transcribed as needed. The record shall include:

(a) the record of any stipulation made at a pre-sentence conference; and

(b) a verbatim account of the entire sentencing proceeding.

CREDIT FOR TIME SERVED

When the trial court sentences a defendant to incarceration, it generally allows the defendant credit against any term of incarceration for all time spent in custody as a result of the charge for which sentence is imposed. See, for example, 42 Pa. Stat. Ann. § 9760.

SUSPENDED SENTENCES

In most instances where defendants are convicted of **noncapital crimes,** courts are authorized to suspend the imposition of sentence and place defendants on probation or under community control for some determinate period. Statutes often require courts to impose certain conditions (similar to probation conditions) on a defendant whose sentence is suspended. See, for example, N.J. Stat. Ann. 2C: 45–1. Of course, if the defendant violates conditions set by the court, the original sentence may be imposed. A **suspended sentence** is most often used for first offenses or nonviolent offenses. In fact, some state statutes specifically prohibit judges from suspending sentences in cases involving the most serious violent felonies. See, for example, Annotated Laws of Massachusetts, C. 279, § 1A.

CONCURRENT AND CONSECUTIVE SENTENCES

A defendant who is convicted of multiple crimes must be given separate sentences for each offense. These sentences may run consecutively or concurrently, usually at the

---

CASE-IN-POINT | **Involuntary Confinement Not a Criminal Proceeding**

In 1994 Kansas enacted the Sexually Violent Predator Act. The act establishes procedures for the civil commitment of persons who, because of mental abnormality or personality disorder, are likely to engage in "predatory acts of sexual violence." Leroy Hendricks, an inmate with a history of sexually molesting children, was scheduled for release from prison soon after the act became effective. The State invoked the act to commit him to custody. After hearing testimony, which included Hendricks' own testimony that when he gets "stressed" he continues to be unable to control his sexual desires for children, a jury determined he was a sexually violent predator. The court ordered him confined. On appeal, the Kansas Supreme Court invalidated the act, and the state of Kansas sought review in the U.S. Supreme Court.

In a 5–4 decision, the United States Supreme Court rejected Hendricks' arguments. The Court held that the act does not offend the constitutional prohibitions against *ex post facto* laws and double jeopardy because it does not criminalize conduct that was legal before its enactment and because it does not constitute punishment.

Writing for the majority, Justice Thomas stated that "[t]he State may take measures to restrict the freedom of the dangerously mentally ill. This is a legitimate nonpunitive governmental objective." Dissenting justices argued that the act was not simply an effort to commit Hendricks civilly, but rather an effort to inflict further punishment upon him for crimes committed prior to enactment of the act.

Kansas v. Hendricks, 521 U.S. 346, 117 S.Ct. 2072, 138 L.Ed.2d 501 (1997).

discretion of the sentencing judge. See, for example, Pa. R. Crim. P. 1406. **Concurrent sentencing** in a given case may simply reflect the court's view that **consecutive sentencing** would result in a punishment that is too harsh for the crime.

Sentencing in Capital Cases

In those cases where the prosecution is permitted by law to seek the death penalty, the sentencing procedure is considerably more complex. As we noted in the discussion of the death penalty, a bifurcated trial is employed. Following the conviction of a defendant for a capital crime, the jury hears testimony in aggravation or mitigation of the sentence. For the jury to hand down the death penalty, it must find beyond a reasonable doubt that the aggravating factors outweigh the mitigating ones. The aggravating factors are specified by law; the mitigating factors are those characteristics of the defendant or the crime that suggest that leniency might be appropriate. Quite often the defense attorney will put the defendant's relatives on the stand to testify about the defendant's redeeming qualities or to generally plead for mercy.

VICTIM IMPACT EVIDENCE

Prosecutors counter emotional pleas on the defendant's behalf by presenting **victim impact evidence.** This evidence takes the form of testimony addressing the impact of the murder on the victim and the victim's family, including the physical, economic, and psychological effects of the crime. For example, the victim's surviving spouse might be called to testify to the toll the homicide has taken on the family. Needless to say, such testimony is often fraught with emotion and can have a powerful impact on the jury.

In 1987 the United States Supreme Court struck down a Maryland statute requiring that a **victim impact statement** be considered during the penalty phase of capital cases. *Booth v. Maryland,* 482 U.S. 496, 107 S.Ct. 2529, 96 L.Ed.2d 440 (1987). The Court said that such statements raised the real possibility that death sentences would be based on irrelevant considerations. Four years later, however, in *Payne v. Tennessee,* 501 U.S. 808, 111 S.Ct. 2597, 115 L.Ed.2d 720 (1991), the Court overruled its decision in *Booth.* According to Chief Justice Rehnquist, who wrote the majority opinion in *Payne,* the *Booth* decision "deprives the State of the full moral force of its evidence and may prevent the jury from having before it all the information necessary to determine the proper punishment for a first-degree murder." 501 U.S. at 825, 111 S.Ct. at 2608, 115 L.Ed.2d at 735. Notwithstanding the Supreme Court's decision in *Payne v. Tennessee,* appellate courts may still find that a particular victim impact statement has impermissibly injected too much emotionalism into the jury's sentencing deliberations.

THE ROLE OF THE JUDGE IN CAPITAL SENTENCING

Under the capital sentencing procedures in Georgia, where a statutory aggravating circumstance is found and a recommendation of death is made, the trial judge must sentence the defendant to death. Official Ga. Code Ann. § 17–10–31. In other states, a different method is employed. For example, in Florida the trial court decides whether to accept a jury's recommendation of death or life imprisonment. See *Spaziano v. Florida,* 468 U.S. 447, 104 S.Ct. 3154, 82 L.Ed.2d 340 (1984). Where a jury recommends life imprisonment and the trial court overrides that recommendation and imposes the death penalty, the decision is carefully scrutinized by the Florida Supreme Court. For the trial court's override to be sustained, the life imprisonment recommendation by the jury must have been unreasonable. If the supreme court's review finds there was a reasonable basis for the jury's recommendation, it reverses

An excerpt from the U.S. Supreme Court's decision in *Payne v. Tennessee* appears at the end of the chapter.

Jones v. United States, 527 U.S. 373, 119 S.Ct. 2090, 144 L.Ed.2d 370 (1999)

In this case the Supreme Court considered a number of issues relative to the Federal Death Penalty Act. In his opinion for the Court, Justice Clarence Thomas made the following observations about the process of capital sentencing:

"To be sure, we have said that the Eighth Amendment requires that a sentence of death not be imposed arbitrarily. . . . In order for a capital sentencing scheme to pass constitutional muster, it must perform a narrowing function with respect to the class of persons eligible for the death penalty and must also ensure that capital sentencing deci-

sions rest upon an individualized inquiry. Our cases have held that in order to satisfy the requirement that capital sentencing decisions rest upon an individualized inquiry, a scheme must allow a 'broad inquiry' into all 'constitutionally relevant mitigating evidence.'"

"Ensuring that a sentence of death is not so infected with bias or caprice is our 'controlling objective when we examine eligibility and selection factors for vagueness.' . . . Our vagueness review, however, is 'quite deferential.' As long as an aggravating factor has a core meaning that criminal juries should be capable of understanding, it will pass constitutional muster."

the court's imposition of the death penalty and remands the case for a sentence as recommended by the jury. *Buford v. State*, 570 So. 2d 923 (Fla. 1990).

WHAT HAPPENS WHEN THE CAPITAL JURY IS DEADLOCKED ON THE SENTENCE?

When the jury in a capital case cannot agree on the appropriate sentence, sentencing normally reverts to the judge. As we have seen, in some jurisdictions, the judge is barred from imposing the death penalty without a jury recommendation. In such instances, the judge must sentence the defendant to any lesser sentence authorized by law. The judge is not required to instruct the jury with regard to the consequences of deadlock, however. *Jones v. United States*, 527 U.S. 373, 119 S.Ct. 2090, 144 L.Ed.2d 370 (1999).

Granting and Revoking Probation

Probation is a sentencing option in the federal courts and in most state courts. Under federal law, a defendant who has been found guilty of an offense may be sentenced to a term of probation unless (1) the offense is a felony where the maximum term of imprisonment authorized is twenty-five years or more, life imprisonment, or death; (2) the offense is one for which probation has been expressly precluded; or (3) the defendant is sentenced at the same time to a term of imprisonment for the same or a different offense. A defendant who has been convicted for the first time of a domestic violence crime must be sentenced to a term of probation if not sentenced to a term of imprisonment. 18 U.S.C.A. § 3561.

Probation terms for a felony must not be less than one nor more than five years and for a misdemeanor not more than five years. 18 U.S.C.A. § 3561. Certain conditions of probation are mandatory, and others are discretionary with the federal judge who imposes probation. 18 U.S.C.A. § 3563. In most states, the term of probation is limited to the maximum statutory term of confinement for the particular offense. Probation is granted on the condition that the defendant abide by various stipulations. In some instances, mandatory conditions are imposed by statute, but the trial court may impose additional conditions. Probation is often combined with a fine, restitution to the victim, or a short term of incarceration to give the probationer "a taste of jail." Because the procedures in state courts vary widely, it is difficult to generalize; however, it is important for the probationer to receive a written order incorporating the terms of probation and outlining his or her responsibilities to the probation officer and the court. Courts must guard against imposing vague conditions of probation or delegating overly broad authorities to probation officers.

Revocation of Probation

In every jurisdiction, the commission of a felony while on probation is grounds for revocation. In many jurisdictions, certain misdemeanors qualify as grounds for revocation. As well, the violation of any substantive condition of probation is grounds for revocation. Typically, a probation officer is vested with broad discretion in determining when to seek revocation of probation. A probationer facing the loss of freedom is entitled to a fair hearing. At this hearing the probationer has the right to call favorable witnesses, to confront hostile witnesses, and to be represented by counsel. *Gagnon v. Scarpelli*, 411 U.S. 778, 93 S.Ct. 1756, 36 L.Ed.2d 656 (1973). In *Gagnon*, the Supreme Court said that indigent probationers may have a constitutional right to have counsel appointed at revocation hearings, depending on the complexity of the issues involved, and that if counsel is not provided, the judge must state the reason. In practice, counsel is usually provided. There is a statutory right to appointment of counsel for those financially unable to obtain counsel in federal probation revocation proceedings. 18 U.S.C.A. § 3006A.

The Federal Rules of Criminal Procedure requires a two-step process before probation can be revoked:

1. Preliminary Hearing. Whenever a person is held in custody on the ground that the person has violated a condition of probation, . . . the person shall be afforded a prompt hearing . . . in order to determine whether there is probable cause to hold the person for a revocation hearing. The person shall be given

   (A) notice of the preliminary hearing and of its purpose and of the alleged violation;

   (B) an opportunity to appear at the hearing and present evidence in the person's own behalf;

   (C) upon request, the opportunity to question witnesses against the person unless, for good cause, the federal magistrate decides that justice does not require the appearance of the witness; and

   (D) notice of the person's right to be represented by counsel.

   The proceedings shall be recorded stenographically or by an electronic recording device. If probable cause is found to exist, the person shall be held for a revocation hearing. . . .

2. Revocation Hearing. The revocation hearing, unless waived by the person, shall be held within a reasonable time in the district of jurisdiction. The person shall be given

   (A) written notice of the alleged violation . . . ;

   (B) disclosure of the evidence against the person;

   (C) an opportunity to appear and to present evidence in the person's own behalf;

   (D) the opportunity to question adverse witnesses; and

   (E) notice of the person's right to be represented by counsel. Fed. R. Crim. Proc. 32.1(a).

CASE-IN-POINT

Revocation of Probation Requires a Willful Violation

Danny Bearden pled guilty to charges of burglary and theft. Pursuant to Georgia's First Offenders Act, Official Code Ga. Ann. § 27–2727 et seq., current version at § 42–8–60, he was placed on three years' probation. As a condition of his probation, Bearden was required to pay a $500 fine and make restitution of $250, according to a court-imposed payment schedule. After making some payments, Bearden was laid off from work and became unable to continue making payments. As a result, the trial court revoked his probation and sentenced him to serve the remaining portion of his term of probation in prison. The United States Supreme Court reversed the revocation of probation because the trial court had made no finding that Bearden was responsible for his failure to make the required payments. Nevertheless, the Court said, "If the probationer willfully refused to pay or failed to make sufficient bona fide efforts legally to acquire the resources to pay, the court may revoke probation."

Bearden v. Georgia, 461 U.S. 660, 672, 103 S.Ct. 2064, 2073, 76 L.Ed.2d 221, 233 (1983).

The rules of evidence applicable at criminal trials are relaxed at probation revocation hearings. For example, hearsay evidence may be received over a probationer's objection because a probation revocation hearing is not a criminal trial. *United States v. Miller,* 514 F.2d 41 (9th Cir. 1975). However, a legion of appellate court decisions holds that probation cannot be revoked solely on the basis of hearsay evidence. *Turner v. State,* 293 So.2d 771 (Fla. App. 1974). Courts have frequently articulated that the standard to be applied at revocation hearings is not "reasonable doubt" or "preponderance of evidence," but whether from the evidence presented the court is reasonably satisfied of the probationer's violation. Nor is there any requirement that a probationer be granted a jury trial in revocation proceedings, even when those proceedings are predicated on a violation of a criminal law. *United States v. Czajak,* 909 F.2d 20 (1st Cir. 1990). Often a court will modify rather than revoke a defendant's probation, but if the court does revoke probation, statutory and decisional law generally permit it to sentence the defendant to any term that would have been appropriate for the underlying offense. And although a probationer may not be sentenced on revocation for the conduct that constituted the probation violation, it is proper for the trial court to consider the probationer's conduct while on probation to assess a potential for rehabilitation. See, for example, *People v. Vilces,* 542 N.E.2d 1269 (Ill. App. 1989).

The violation of any valid substantive condition is grounds for revocation of probation. Although the rules of evidence applicable at criminal trials are relaxed at probation revocation hearings, appellate courts have been diligent in ensuring that such hearings meet the basic requirements of due process. For example, in 1993 the Tennessee Supreme Court held that probation could not be revoked based solely on a lab test indicating that the probationer had used illicit drugs where the technician who performed the drug test was not available to be cross-examined at the revocation hearing. *State v. Wade,* 863 S.W.2d 406 (Tenn. 1993).

Statutory Approaches to Incarceration

Once it has been determined that a defendant is to be incarcerated, several variations of the type and extent of the defendant's sentence may be available. The legislative trend has been to limit judicial discretion in imposing incarceration by statutorily providing whether the defendant is subject to an indeterminate or determinate sentence and whether a minimum mandatory term is to be imposed. In recent years, in an attempt to cope with the problem of recidivism, legislatures have enacted laws providing for enhanced terms of incarceration.

Indeterminate Sentencing

For much of the twentieth century, legislatures commonly allowed judges to sentence criminals to imprisonment for indeterminate periods. This was designed to assist corrections officials in rehabilitating offenders. Officials were permitted to hold the criminal in custody until they determined that he or she was rehabilitated. Under this system, release from prison took the form of parole. Abuses of the system, combined with the decline of popular support for rehabilitation, have led most jurisdictions to abandon the concept of **indeterminate sentencing.**

Notwithstanding the trend away from indeterminate sentencing, a number of state laws retain indeterminate sentencing for youthful offenders. For example, New Jersey law specifies the following:

> Any person who, at time of sentencing, is less than 26 years of age and who has been convicted of a crime may be sentenced to an indeterminate term at the Youth Correctional Institution Complex, . . . in the case of men, and to the Correctional Institute for Women, . . . in the case of women, instead of the sentences otherwise authorized by the code. N.J. Stat. Ann. 2C: 43–5.

Definite and Determinate Sentencing

At the opposite extreme from indeterminate sentencing is **definite sentencing.** The concept here is to eliminate discretion and ensure that offenders who commit the same crimes are punished equally. The definite sentence is set by the legislature, with no leeway for judges or corrections officials to individualize punishment. Under **determinate sentencing,** a variation of the definite sentence, the judge sets a fixed term of years within statutory parameters, and the offender is required to serve that term without the possibility of early release.

Indefinite Sentencing

The most common statutory approach to sentencing is referred to as **indefinite sentencing.** Here, there is judicial discretion to impose sentences within a range of prescribed minimum and maximum penalties for specific offenses. What distinguishes indefinite from determinate sentencing is that indefinite sentencing allows early release from prison on parole. An example of a statute that permits indefinite sentencing can be drawn from the New Jersey Code:

> Except as otherwise provided, a person who has been convicted of a crime may be sentenced to imprisonment, as follows: (1) In the case of a crime of the first degree, for a specific term of years which shall be fixed by the court and shall be between 10 years and 20 years; (2) In the case of a crime of the second degree, for a specific term of years which shall be fixed by the court and shall be between 5 years and 10 years; (3) In the case of a crime of the third degree, for a specific term of years which shall be fixed by the court and shall be between 3 years and 5 years; (4) In the case of a crime of the fourth degree, for a specific term which shall be fixed by the court and shall not exceed 18 months. N.J. Stat. Ann. 2C: 43–6(a).

Table 19.3 Statutory Approaches to Sentencing				
Approach to Sentencing	**Indeterminate Sentencing**	**Indefinite Sentencing**	**Determinate Sentencing**	**Definite Sentencing**
How it works	Judges sentence criminals to imprisonment for indeterminate periods. Corrections officials determine how long criminal is held.	Judges impose sentences within a range of prescribed minimum and maximum penalties. Early release from prison possible.	Judges impose sentences within a range of prescribed minimum and maximum penalties. No possibility of early release from prison.	Sentence set by the legislature, with no leeway for judges or corrections officials to individualize punishment.

Except for certain offenses where a mandatory minimum sentence applies, New Jersey judges retain discretion to impose probation, fines, or other alternatives to incarceration. N.J. Stat. Ann. 2C: 43–2. If the judge opts for imprisonment, the judge's discretion is channeled as indicated earlier. The New Jersey scheme qualifies as indefinite sentencing because in most cases the law allows offenders to be released on parole before the completion of their prison terms.

Mandatory Minimum Sentencing

Mandatory sentences result from legislative mandates that offenders who commit certain crimes must be sentenced to prison terms for minimum periods. Under **mandatory minimum sentencing,** judges have no option to place offenders on probation. Most often, mandatory sentences are required for violent crimes, especially those involving the use of firearms. For example, Iowa law mandates that persons who use firearms in the commission of "forcible felonies" must be sentenced to a five-year minimum prison term with no eligibility for parole until the person has served the minimum sentence of confinement. Iowa Code Ann. § 902.7.

As a result of the "war on drugs" launched in the 1980s, federal law now mandates minimum prison terms for serious drug crimes. For example, a person charged with possession with the intent to distribute more than five kilograms of cocaine is subject to a mandatory minimum sentence of ten years in prison. See 21 U.S.C.A. § 841(b)(1)(A). In *Melendez v. United States*, 518 U.S. 120, 116 S.Ct. 2057, 135 L.Ed.2d 427 (1996), the U.S. Supreme Court made it clear in a unanimous decision that federal courts have no authority to impose lesser sentences than those mandated by Congress unless prosecutors specifically request such departures. This, of course, provides federal prosecutors substantial leverage in persuading defendants to provide evidence against other suspects, which is particularly useful in prosecuting drug distribution conspiracies.

Habitual Offender Statutes

In an effort to incapacitate habitual offenders, the laws of many states require automatic increased penalties for persons convicted of repeated felonies. For example, as Iowa law states:

An habitual offender is any person convicted of a class "C" or a class "D" felony, who has twice before been convicted of any felony in a court of this or any other state, or of the United States. An offense is a felony if, by the law under which the person was convicted, it is so classified at the time of the person's conviction. A person sentenced as an habitual offender shall not be eligible for parole until he or she has served the minimum sentence of confinement of three years. Iowa Code Ann. § 902.8.

Most courts hold that habitual offender status is not established if a defendant committed the present offense before having been convicted of a prior offense. Courts have struggled with the issue of whether multiple convictions entered on one day are to be treated as separate or as one conviction, but usually treat these multiple convictions as one irrespective of whether they arise from one or multiple criminal transactions.

In *Rummel v. Estelle,* 445 U.S. 263, 100 S.Ct. 1133, 63 L.Ed.2d 382 (1980), the United States Supreme Court upheld a life sentence imposed under the Texas habitual offender statute mandating life terms for persons convicted of three felonies. Rummel was convicted of obtaining $120.75 under false pretenses after previously being convicted of the fraudulent use of a credit card to obtain $80 worth of goods and passing a forged check for $28.36. After his third felony conviction, Rummel was sentenced to life imprisonment.

In *Solem v. Helm,* 463 U.S. 277, 103 S.Ct. 3001, 77 L.Ed.2d 637 (1983), the Court vacated a life sentence without parole under a South Dakota **habitual offender statute.** Because the defendant's convictions involved nonviolent felonies, the Court found the life sentence to be "significantly disproportionate" and thus invalid under the Eighth Amendment.

"Three Strikes and You're Out"

A variation on the habitual offender law is known colloquially as **three strikes and you're out.** In 1994 California voters overwhelmingly approved a ballot initiative under which persons convicted of a third violent or "serious" felony would be incarcerated for twenty-five years to life. Prosecutors immediately availed themselves of this new weapon, but in many instances the new law led to controversial results. In one well-known case, a man received twenty-five years to life after being convicted of robbery stemming from an incident where he stole a slice of pizza. *People v. Romero,* 917 P.2d 628 (Cal. 1996). In reversing the sentence, the California Supreme Court said that judges must retain the power to set sentences in furtherance of justice.

The 1994 Federal Crime Bill provided for mandatory life sentences for persons convicted in federal court of a "serious violent felony" after having been previously convicted, in federal or state court, of two "serious violent felonies." 18 U.S.C.A. § 3559. Currently, the federal government and most states have some form of habitual offender or "three strikes" statute. In most states, prosecutions under these statutes are relatively infrequent.

Truth in Sentencing

Truth in sentencing refers to a movement that began in the 1980s to close the gap between the sentences imposed by courts and the time actually served in prison. Prior to the enactment of truth in sentencing laws, the average prisoner served less than half the sentence in prison before being paroled. The **Federal Sentencing Reform Act of 1984** dramatically toughened federal sentencing policies by abolishing parole, ending **good time credit** (time off for good behavior in prison), and prohibiting judges from imposing suspended sentences. Of course, these reforms applied only to the federal justice system. In 1994 Congress provided a strong financial incentive to the states to change their sentencing laws. The Violent Crime Control and Law Enforcement Act of 1994 provides federal grants to states that conform to the federal truth in sentencing guideline, which mandates actual confinement for at least 85 percent of the court-imposed prison sentence. As of summer 2000, about two-thirds of the states had adopted truth in sentencing laws to comply with the federal guideline.

Penalty Enhancement

Another approach to sentencing that has gained popularity in recent years is enhancing or extending penalties based on characteristics of the crime or the victim. For example, in an effort to strengthen law enforcement in the war on drugs, the Violent Crime Control and Law Enforcement Act of 1994 included several provisions for enhanced penalties. Drug trafficking in prisons and "drug-free" zones, and illegal drug use in or smuggling drugs into federal prisons are now subject to enhanced penalties. See 42 U.S.C.A. §§ 14051, 14052.

ENHANCED PENALTIES FOR HATE CRIMES

As we noted in Chapter 6, recent years have seen growing concern over "hate crimes," crimes where victims are targeted on the basis of race, gender, or other characteristics. The federal government and many states currently have laws increasing the severity of punishment in hate crime cases. In 1993 the U.S. Supreme Court upheld a Wisconsin statute of this type. *Wisconsin v. Mitchell*, 508 U.S. 476, 113 S.Ct. 2194, 124 L.Ed.2d 436 (1993). Stressing that the statute was aimed at conduct rather than belief, the Court held that increasing punishment because the defendant targeted the victim on the basis of his race does not infringe the defendant's freedom of conscience as protected by the First Amendment.

Typically, **penalty enhancement statutes** require that a judge find by a preponderance of the evidence that a crime was racially motivated before applying penalty enhancement during sentencing. In a decision with far-reaching implications, the U.S. Supreme Court in June 2000 ruled that any fact that increases criminal punishment beyond the statutory maximum (other than a prior conviction) must be submitted to a jury and proved beyond a reasonable doubt. *Apprendi v. New Jersey*, 530 U.S. 466, 120 S.Ct. 2348, 147 L.Ed.2d 435 (2000). This 5–4 decision raises questions about numerous statutory sentencing schemes under which particular sentencing determinations are based on facts found by judges during sentencing rather than by juries as part of the trial.

The Supreme Court's *Apprendi* decision is excerpted at the end of the chapter.

Sentencing Guidelines

Facing considerable criticism of judicial discretion, which often resulted in great disparities in sentences, Congress and a number of state legislatures adopted **sentencing guidelines.** Some states have adopted voluntary guidelines; others have mandated that sentencing conform to guidelines absent a compelling reason for departing from them.

THE SENTENCING REFORM ACT OF 1984

The federal guidelines came into being with the enactment of the Sentencing Reform Act of 1984, now codified at 18 U.S.C.A. §§ 3551–3586, 28 U.S.C.A. §§ 991–998. The new act applies to all crimes committed after November 1, 1987. The stated purpose of the act was "to establish sentencing policies and practices for the federal criminal justice system that will assure the ends of justice by promulgating detailed guidelines prescribing the appropriate sentences for offenders convicted of federal crimes." To accomplish this, the act created the **United States Sentencing Commission** to establish sentencing guidelines. The commission promulgated guidelines that drastically reduced the discretion of federal judges by establishing a narrow sentencing range, with the requirement that judges who depart from these ranges state in writing their reasons for doing so. In addition, the new act provides for appellate review for sentences and abolishes the United States Parole Commission.

In *United States v. Scroggins,* 880 F.2d 1204 (11th Cir. 1989), the Eleventh Circuit Court of Appeals discussed the mechanics of sentencing under the new federal guidelines:

> [T]he district court begins the guidelines sentencing process by determining the circumstances of the defendant's offense conduct, the defendant's criminal history, and any other facts deemed relevant by the guidelines. The court then proceeds to assess the severity of the defendant's offense by applying the guidelines to the facts and circumstances of the defendant's offense conduct. . . . This process yields a numeric "total offense level" that consists of three elements: a "base offense level," which reflects the seriousness of the average offense sentenced under that particular guideline; "specific offense characteristics," which increase or decrease the base offense level in light of various factors considered relevant to the defendant's offense conduct; and "adjustments," which increase or decrease the offense level in light of certain factors considered generally relevant for sentencing purposes. The resulting total offense level can range from 1 (least serious) to 43 (most serious).
>
> Having determined the total offense level, the court next surveys the criminal history of the offender. . . . This inquiry places the defendant within a "criminal history category" that evaluates the need to increase his sentence incrementally to deter him from further criminal activity. By correlating the offense level with the offender's criminal history category on the sentencing table developed by the Sentencing Commission, the court then identifies the "guideline range" for the offender's sentence. . . . In general, the district court must sentence the offender within this range.

DEPARTURE FROM THE GUIDELINES

The sentence prescribed by the guidelines is not absolute. The sentencing court may depart from the guidelines if it "finds that there exists an aggravating or mitigating circumstance of a kind, or to a degree, not adequately taken into consideration . . . in formulating the guidelines that should result in a sentence different from that described." *United States v. Aguilar-Pena,* 887 F.2d 347, 349 (1st Cir. 1989). Of course, it is impermissible to depart from the guidelines on the basis of the defendant's race, sex, national origin, religion, or socioeconomic status. *United States v. Burch,* 873 F.2d 765 (5th Cir. 1989). Other factors not ordinarily deemed relevant in determining whether to depart include the defendant's age, education, mental and physical condition, employment history, and family and community ties. *United States v. Lira-Barraza,* 897 F.2d 981 (9th Cir. 1990), n. 5.

In *Nichols v. United States,* 511 U.S. 738, 114 S.Ct. 1921, 128 L.Ed.2d 745 (1994), the Supreme Court overruled precedent and held that a prior misdemeanor conviction in which the defendant was not represented by counsel could form the basis for a two-year sentence enhancement under the federal sentencing guidelines. Acting without counsel, Kenneth Nichols had pleaded no contest to a DUI charge in 1983. In 1990, then represented by counsel, Nichols was convicted of a federal drug conspiracy offense. The judge gave Nichols an enhanced sentence based on the prior DUI conviction. The Supreme Court upheld the enhanced sentence, saying that the sentencing process is a broad inquiry that may bring in information regarding the defendant's past misconduct even if it had not resulted in a criminal conviction. The Court thus went well beyond the facts of the case to permit federal judges broad dis-

In *Koon v. United States* (1996), a case that stemmed from the Rodney King beating episode, the U.S. Supreme Court discusses the standards for downward departures from the federal sentencing guidelines. An excerpt from *Koon* appears at the end of the chapter.

cretion in handing down enhanced sentences under the sentencing guidelines. Critics of the Court's decision in *Nichols* pointed out that the reason the guidelines were adopted was to reduce judicial discretion in sentencing.

THE STATE EXPERIENCE

States have experimented with sentencing guidelines with varying results. Minnesota, the first state to adopt presumptive sentencing guidelines, in 1970, has a relatively simple system that has proven to be workable, although it has resulted in a higher incarceration rate. Washington's sentencing guidelines worked reasonably well until the state legislature began to mandate increased penalties overall as well as harsher minimum sentences for particular crimes. This has necessitated that the guidelines be revised. In Tennessee, the commission that established sentencing guidelines was terminated, although the guidelines themselves remain in effect. In Wisconsin, one of the early states to adopt sentencing guidelines, the sentencing commission as well as the guidelines it promulgated have been abolished by the state legislature because of political forces and fiscal pressures.

In 1990 the North Carolina legislature created the Sentencing and Policy Advisory Commission to study and repair a system of sentencing that had become dysfunctional. Due to prison overcrowding, felons were being paroled to the point that the system had become a revolving door. Thus, sentencing guidelines in North Carolina originated not so much from concern for sentencing disparity but from a desire to rationalize a system that had become chaotic. The commission followed the example of states such as Washington and Minnesota in adopting a simplified model of sentencing guidelines. Whereas the federal sentencing guidelines contain forty-three levels of felony offenses, the North Carolina guidelines contain ten levels. Thus far, the system seems to have worked reasonably well. However, it should be noted that North Carolina has eased pressure on the prison system by adopting intermediate measures such as house arrest and electronic monitoring for less serious offenders.

There is still considerable uncertainty about the efficacy of sentencing guidelines. There is evidence that they have reduced sentencing disparities, but they clearly have not eliminated this problem altogether. There is also concern that sentencing guidelines have generally promoted higher incarceration rates and have thus contributed to the problem of prison overcrowding. It is fair to say that to be successful, sentencing guidelines must be accompanied by policies designed to effectively manage prison populations.

The Rights of Prisoners

Contrary to popular mythology, America's prisons are not country clubs. Although some **minimum security facilities** (like the military base where the Watergate conspirators were confined) are reasonably comfortable, **maximum security prisons** are another story. They are sometimes unsanitary; they are almost all overcrowded. All are violent, dangerous places to live.

The federal courts have made it clear that the Eighth Amendment's prohibition of cruel and unusual punishments imposes obligations on prison administrators to maintain certain standards of confinement. A sizable number of state prison systems have been or are currently under court orders to improve conditions of confinement or reduce overcrowding. Recently, some state courts have begun to focus their attention on the deplorable conditions existing in many city and county jails.

Historically, courts were quite unreceptive to claims brought by prisoners. They essentially adopted a "hands-off" policy, allowing prison officials free rein. In the late 1960s, that began to change as federal and state tribunals examined prison conditions and policies. As the courts signaled their willingness to scrutinize the prisons, litigation in this area mushroomed.

In one dramatic case involving prison conditions, Federal District Judge Frank M. Johnson Jr., found that the **conditions of confinement** in the Alabama system were barbarous and inhumane, thus violating the Eighth Amendment. Judge Johnson issued a detailed set of requirements to remedy the situation and appointed a special committee to oversee implementation of the order. Moreover, he threatened to close down the prison system unless his requirements were met. *Pugh v. Locke*, 406 F. Supp. 318 (M.D. Ala. 1976), aff'd sub nom. *Newman v. Alabama*, 559 F.2d 283 (5th Cir. 1977).

Perhaps the most notorious story of prison conditions is that of the Arkansas prison system, which was scrutinized in a series of federal lawsuits beginning in 1969. *Holt v. Sarver*, 309 F. Supp. 362 (E.D. Ark. 1970), aff'd., 442 F.2d 304 (8th Cir. 1971). The most egregious conditions occurred at prison farms run largely by "trusties," senior prisoners entrusted with the job of controlling their fellow inmates. It should be noted that the trusty system is widely condemned by penologists. Under the Arkansas system, trusties smuggled in weapons, liquor, and drugs and sold them to the other inmates. Trusties hoarded food purchased with taxpayers' money and forced the other inmates to pay for their meals. Violence and even torture were commonly used by the trusties in maintaining their grip over the other prisoners. Medical care was almost totally lacking, and conditions of sanitation were miserable. Some prisoners were held in punitive isolation cells for months at a time. Overall, the penal farms were characterized by pervasive filth, disease, and violence.

In a series of decisions handed down during the 1970s, the federal district court issued detailed orders aimed at remedying the conditions in the Arkansas prison system. Especially controversial was an order placing a maximum limit of thirty days on the use of punitive isolation. The Supreme Court had little difficulty upholding this measure on appeal. *Hutto v. Finney*, 437 U.S. 678, 98 S.Ct. 2565, 57 L.Ed.2d 522 (1978).

As currently interpreted, the Eighth Amendment requires that prisoners must be provided with reasonably adequate food, clothing, shelter, medical care, and sanitation. There must also be a reasonable assurance of their personal safety. In 1992 the Supreme Court held that a prisoner who is beaten maliciously by guards may bring a civil action for damages based on a claim of cruel and unusual punishment, even if the prisoner does not suffer "significant injuries." *Hudson v. McMillian*, 503 U.S., 112 S.Ct. 995, 1004, 117 L.Ed.2d 156 (1992).

During the 1990s, prisoners began litigating the question of whether being subjected to environmental tobacco smoke (ETS) amounts to a violation of a prisoner's rights to due process of law and to protection from a deliberate indifference to the prisoner's health. Lower federal courts have recognized that the state has a duty to provide a safe environment for those incarcerated in its institutions. Recently, one United States court of appeals held that exposing a prisoner to ETS in a small cell by involuntary double-celling with smokers raises an issue of fact as to whether such exposure creates an unreasonable risk to the prisoner's health. *Clemmons v. Bohannon*, 918 F.2d 858 (10th Cir. 1990). Litigation of this type in the lower federal courts may lead to revisions in prison policies to protect the nonsmokers from ETS in instances where inmates are closely confined. In 1993 the Supreme Court ruled that involuntary exposure of prisoners to secondhand tobacco smoke is grounds for them to sue their custodians on the basis of an Eighth Amendment violation. *Helling v. McKinney*, 509 U.S. 25, 113 S.Ct. 2475, 125 L.Ed.2d 22 (1993).

The Eighth Amendment does not require that prisoners must be provided every amenity they deem essential to their physical or psychological well-being. *Newman v. Alabama*, supra. Air conditioning, television, weightlifting equipment, and other nonessential items can be provided or removed at the discretion of prison authorities.

The Overcrowding Issue

Much of the current litigation challenging conditions of criminal confinement focuses on the problem of prison overcrowding. During the 1980s, the prison population in the United States nearly doubled. Rising crime rates and an increasingly punitive posture adopted by legislatures and courts, combined with fiscal stress, led to an overcrowding crisis in many prison systems. As mandatory sentence laws and sentencing guidelines have required judges to imprison larger numbers of convicted criminals, the number of prisoners has far outstripped the capacity of prisons in the United States. For example, California prisons are designed to hold approximately 78,000 persons. As of June 30, 1998, 158,742 were incarcerated in California institutions. Likewise, the federal prison system, which is designed to accommodate roughly 72,000 persons, actually housed 118,908. Only a handful of states are below capacity; most are filled well beyond design capacity. (See U.S. Department of Justice, Bureau of Justice Statistics, *Sourcebook of Criminal Justice Statistics 1998*, Table 6.38, p. 492.)

Throughout the 1980s, litigation in the federal courts by prisoners increased dramatically. Although the Supreme Court has said that "the Constitution does not mandate comfortable prisons," *Rhodes v. Chapman*, 452 U.S. 337, 101 S.Ct. 2392, 69 L.Ed.2d 59 (1981), lower federal courts have intervened to limit the number of inmates who can be housed in some prisons. The public is relatively unconcerned about prison overcrowding, but prison officials often welcome judicial intervention. Prison overcrowding makes it considerably more difficult to control inmate populations.

Other Rights of Prisoners

In addition to Eighth Amendment challenges to prison conditions, numerous lawsuits have sought to persuade the courts to recognize other **constitutional rights of prison inmates.** Traditionally, convicted felons were viewed as having forfeited most, if not all, of their constitutional rights. Thus, even reform-minded judges have been cautious in this area. For the most part they have deferred to prison officials, stressing the traditional view that "lawful incarceration brings about the necessary withdrawal or limitation of many privileges and rights, a retraction justified by the considerations underlying our penal system." *Price v. Johnston*, 334 U.S. 266, 285, 68 S.Ct. 1049, 92 L.Ed. 1356, 1369 (1948). Nevertheless, certain constitutional rights have been recognized. The Supreme Court has held that a prison inmate retains those First Amendment rights "that are not inconsistent with his status as a prisoner or with the legitimate penological objectives of the corrections system." *Pell v. Procunier*, 417 U.S. 817, 822, 94 S.Ct. 2800, 2804, 41 L.Ed.2d 495, 501 (1974).

For example, consider rights arising under the free exercise of religion clause of the First Amendment. Courts are generally receptive to prisoners' rights to possess bibles, prayer books, and other religious materials, as well as inmates' rights to be visited by the clergy. On the other hand, courts have generally upheld restrictions on religious exercises if they disrupt prison order or routine. See, for example, *O'Lone v.*

Estate of Shabazz, 482 U.S. 342, 107 S.Ct. 2400, 96 L.Ed.2d 282 (1987). If prison officials allow inmates who belong to mainstream religious denominations to attend worship services, however, then members of other religious sects must be given a reasonable opportunity to exercise their religious beliefs as well. *Cruz v. Beto,* 405 U.S. 319, 92 S.Ct. 1079, 31 L.Ed.2d 263 (1972).

One of the most firmly established rights of prisoners is the right of access to the courts. The Supreme Court made it clear decades ago that prison officials may not deny inmates access to the courts or penalize them for using that access. *Ex parte Hull,* 312 U.S. 546, 61 S.Ct. 640, 85 L.Ed. 1034 (1941). Similarly, courts have held that indigent inmates must be furnished writing materials and notarial services to assist them in filing petitions and seeking writs from courts. Courts have generally upheld the right of prisoners to meet with counsel in privacy and, in the absence of other forms of legal assistance, to have access to law libraries. See *Bounds v. Smith,* 430 U.S. 817, 97 S.Ct. 1491, 52 L.Ed.2d 72 (1977).

The courts have also recognized that prisoners are entitled to limited rights of expression. For example, prisoners retain a limited right to communicate with the outside world via the mails, although prison officials may limit and censor the mail prisoners send and receive, provided there is no interference with attorney–client relationships. *Lee v. Tahash,* 352 F.2d 970 (8th Cir. 1965).

Prison officials also have broad latitude to restrict visitation privileges if there is reason to believe that an inmate is receiving contraband being smuggled into the prison by visitors. *Kentucky Department of Corrections v. Thompson,* 490 U.S. 454, 109 S.Ct. 1904, 104 L.Ed.2d 506 (1989).

Likewise, prison regulations impinging on inmates' interests in free assembly and association have been consistently upheld. See, for example, *Jones v. North Carolina Prisoners' Labor Union, Inc.,* 433 U.S. 119, 97 S.Ct. 2532, 53 L.Ed.2d 629 (1977), where the Supreme Court refused to extend First Amendment protection to an effort to organize a labor union among prisoners. Obviously, prison is by definition antithetical to the ideas of freedom of assembly and freedom of association.

Prison Disciplinary Measures

The federal courts have imposed limits on **prison disciplinary measures** such as corporal punishment and the extended use of **punitive isolation.** Today, prison discipline is largely accomplished by granting and removing good-time credit—that is, early release for good behavior. If officials pursue this policy, then due process demands that certain procedural requirements be observed before good time is removed for disciplinary purposes. Specifically, there must be written notice of the disciplinary action, and the inmate has the right to an administrative hearing with a written record. The inmate must be accorded the right to produce evidence refuting the charges of misconduct and may even call witnesses on his or her behalf. *Wolff v. McDonnell,* 418 U.S. 539, 94 S.Ct. 2963, 41 L.Ed.2d 935 (1974). These rights have not been extended to allow an inmate to have counsel present at such a hearing. *Baxter v. Palmigiano,* 425 U.S. 308, 96 S.Ct. 1551, 47 L.Ed.2d 810 (1976).

Parole and Its Revocation

Historically, the federal government and most states provided for early release from prison on **parole** for those inmates who could demonstrate to the parole board's satisfaction their willingness to conform their conduct to the requirements of the law.

In recent years, parole has been abolished or restricted greatly in many jurisdictions. This generally corresponds to the "truth in sentencing" movement described above.

Naturally, there are also provisions by which parole can be revoked if the offender violates the conditions of release. As with internal prison disciplinary actions, the revocation of parole is affected by due process considerations. Essentially, before parole can be revoked, the parolee has the right to a hearing within a reasonable time after being retaken into custody. *Morrissey v. Brewer,* 408 U.S. 471, 92 S.Ct. 2593, 33 L.Ed.2d 484 (1972). However, the Supreme Court has stressed the informality of this hearing, saying that "the process should be flexible enough to consider evidence including letters, affidavits, and other material that would not be admissible in an adversary criminal trial." 408 U.S. at 489, 92 S.Ct. at 2604, 33 L.Ed.2d at 499. In practice, courts generally admit any relevant evidence not privileged, but generally do not allow revocation based solely on hearsay evidence. See, for example, *Grello v. Commonwealth,* 477 A.2d 45 (Pa. Cmwlth. 1984).

A year after its decision in *Morrissey v. Brewer,* the Supreme Court held that the right to counsel may apply to **parole revocation hearings,** depending on the complexity of the issues involved. *Gagnon v. Scarpelli,* supra. In federal parole revocation hearings, there is a statutory right to appointment of counsel for those financially unable to obtain counsel. 18 U.S.C.A. § 3006A; *Baldwin v. Benson,* 584 F.2d 953 (10th Cir. 1978).

The Rights of Crime Victims

Although crime is by definition an injury against society as a whole, we must not forget that most serious crimes injure individual victims, often quite severely. The injury may transcend physical or economic injury to include emotional hardship. During the 1960s the dominant concern of the criminal law was for the rights of the accused. In the 1990s the trend was to recognize the rights of crime victims. Several states—including Arizona, California, Florida, Michigan, New Jersey, Rhode Island, Texas, and Washington—have adopted constitutional amendments specifically recognizing **victims' rights.** Other states have adopted statutes along these lines. See, for example, West's Annotated Cal. Penal Code § 679. Recently, a proposal to add a victims' rights amendment to the U.S. Constitution surfaced in Congress. Clearly, substantial public support exists for efforts to recognize and enhance victims' rights.

The Uniform Victims of Crime Act

The **Uniform Victims of Crime Act** (UVCA) is an attempt to lend uniformity to the patchwork of victims' rights laws that now exists at the state level. The UVCA was developed by the Uniform Law Commission, a voluntary association representing the legal profession. Like the Model Penal Code developed by the American Law Institute, the UVCA has no status as law unless and until it is adopted by a state legislature.

Under the UVCA, prosecutors or court personnel must notify victims of their rights under the act, as well as the times of any court proceedings involving the person or persons who allegedly victimized them. A crime victim has the right to be present at any court proceeding that the defendant has the right to attend. If the defendant is convicted, the victim has the right to make an impact statement during the sentencing hearing and assert an opinion as to the proper sentence. Finally, the UVCA provides for victims to be compensated by the state, up to $25,000, for any physical or emotional injuries suffered as the result of the victimization. However, this amount may be denied or reduced if the victim receives compensation through insurance or restitution from the defendant.

Restitution

Restitution is a time-honored means of protecting the interests of crime victims. Restitution refers to "the return of a sum of money, an object, or the value of an object that the defendant wrongfully obtained in the course of committing the crime." *State v. Stalheim,* 552 P.2d 829, 832 (Or. 1976). Although restitution was practiced under the early common law, it was eventually abandoned as a remedy in criminal cases in favor of fines payable to the Crown. In modern America, however, restitution is making a comeback in the criminal law. Several states have enacted laws allowing trial courts to require restitution as a condition of probation, in lieu of sentencing offenders to prison. In states that have adopted restitution laws, courts have held that (1) restitution is not necessarily incompatible with incarceration, *State v. Murray,* 621 P.2d 334 (Hawaii 1980); (2) restitution may be ordered for damages caused by the defendant during a criminal episode, irrespective of whether the loss is directly related to a specific conviction, *People v. Gallagher,* 223 N.W.2d 92 (Mich. App. 1974); and (3) a defendant may be ordered to pay restitution to a party other than the victim, *Shenah v. Henderson,* 476 P.2d 854 (Ariz. 1970).

Restitution is not practical in many criminal cases. Many offenders are not suited to probation, and even among those who are, there is no guarantee that they will be able to make payments to the victim. Recognizing this problem, several states have established victims' compensation commissions. For example, the Florida Crimes Compensation Act of 1977 makes victims and certain relatives eligible for compensation from a state commission where a crime results in injuries and is reported within 72 hours. Awards are limited to meeting the victims' actual needs. West's Fla. Stat. Ann. §§ 960.001–960.298.

Conclusion

The various forms of punishment meted out to convicted criminals rest on differing assumptions about crime and human nature. These assumptions lead to differing philosophies of punishment that stress retribution, deterrence, incapacitation, or rehabilitation. A great debate continues regarding both the propriety of these goals and the efficacy of the measures designed to achieve them. In particular, the deterrent value of the death penalty and the rehabilitative value of incarceration have been seriously questioned.

Courts of law tend to avoid the philosophical, theoretical, and empirical questions that surround the various forms of criminal punishment. Rather, they focus on the substantive and procedural limitations that the federal and state constitutions impose on the criminal justice system. In so doing, they tend to reflect the dominant values of the society. Thus, courts have not hesitated to invalidate torture and flogging as cruel and unusual punishments forbidden by the Eighth Amendment, yet they have been extremely reluctant to reach similar conclusions regarding the death penalty.

One current issue in criminal justice is the problem of sentencing disparity. The death penalty has been challenged, albeit unsuccessfully, as being racially discriminatory. But the allegations of disparity extend well beyond the death penalty to encompass the entire regime of criminal punishment. One approach to reducing sentencing disparity is to limit judicial discretion through more determinate sentencing. Another is the development of sentencing guidelines.

Over the last several decades, courts have become more active in the area of prisoners' rights. Decisions have protected inmates' access to counsel and the courts, invalidated extreme conditions of confinement, and recognized limited First Amendment freedoms. Courts have imposed minimal due process requirements on prison disciplinary proceedings, and on parole and probation revocation decisions as well. On the other hand, courts have tended to defer to corrections officials regarding most substantive restrictions on inmate behavior.

There is profound dissatisfaction with the nation's prison system. Little evidence exists that prisons provide any sort of meaningful rehabilitation. Yet few observers have proposed viable alternatives for dealing with violent criminals. As crime rates soared over the last three decades, the public began to demand stiffer sentences, especially for repeat offenders. The result is a prison system that is grossly overcrowded. In truth, our nation's correctional system is in a state of crisis. As the crisis worsens, policy makers face three choices: (1) change the criminal laws to make sentencing more lenient, (2) appropriate more revenues to construct new prison facilities, or (3) develop effective alternatives to confinement. Society appears reluctant to follow either of the first two courses, so exploring meaningful alternatives to incarceration is essential.

Key Terms

retribution
proportionality
capital crimes
corporal punishment
general deterrence
penitentiary
rehabilitation
incarceration
death penalty
incapacitation
monetary fine
forfeiture of property
boot camp
probation
conditions of probation
community service
community control
house arrest
capital punishment
bifurcated trial
aggravating factors
mitigating factors
Violent Crime Control and Law
    Enforcement Act of 1994

presentence investigation
presentence report
sentencing hearing
pronouncement of sentence
right of allocution
noncapital crimes
suspended sentence
concurrent sentencing
consecutive sentencing
victim impact evidence
victim impact statement
indeterminate sentencing
definite sentencing
determinate sentencing
indefinite sentencing
mandatory minimum sentencing
habitual offender statute
three strikes and you're out
truth in sentencing
Federal Sentencing Reform Act
    of 1984
good time credit
penalty enhancement statutes
sentencing guidelines

United States Sentencing Commission   punitive isolation
minimum security facilities   parole
maximum security prisons   parole revocation hearings
conditions of confinement   victims' rights
constitutional rights of prison inmates   Uniform Victims of Crime Act
prison disciplinary measures   restitution

Web-Based Research Activity

1. Go to the web. Locate your state's statutes pertaining to criminal procedure.
2. Does your state impose a mandatory minimum sentence for a defendant who is convicted of carrying a firearm during the commission of any offense?
3. What sentence must be imposed?

Questions for Thought and Discussion

1. Why have the courts generally viewed corporal punishment as "cruel and unusual," yet been unwilling to take the same view of capital punishment?

2. How could a prisoner on death row establish that his or her death sentence was the result of racial discrimination?

3. Does your state impose the death penalty? If so, what does the state law provide with respect to juries considering aggravating and mitigating factors? Do you think your state's law governing the death penalty should be amended? If so, explain why and how.

4. What alternatives to imprisonment exist to deal with violent criminals who are repeat offenders? What alternatives, if any, would you propose? What legal problems are implicit in these alternatives to incarceration?

5. Suppose you were a probation officer and a judge asked you to recommend probation conditions for a first-time offender convicted of the sale and possession of cocaine. What specific conditions would you propose?

6. Should a defendant always be permitted to view the contents of a presentence report? What are the arguments pro and con?

7. What is meant by "truth in sentencing"?

8. What implications, if any, does the U.S. Supreme Court's recent decision in *Apprendi v. New Jersey* (2000) have for sentencing guidelines?

9. What is the rationale for granting only minimal due process rights to parolees and probationers and to prisoners in disciplinary proceedings?

10. How have the legal rights of prisoners been expanded since the 1960s? Have the courts been unduly solicitous in entertaining lawsuits brought by prison inmates?

11. Do you think that the introduction of a victim impact statement during the sentencing phase of a capital trial is appropriate, or do you think it might inject too much emotionalism into the process?

Problems for Discussion and Solution

1. Inmate Jay Leburd has brought suit in federal court challenging the conditions of his confinement in the Intensive Management Unit (IMU) of a maximum security state prison. Specifically, Leburd argues that the lack of any opportunity for outdoor exercise, total lack of reading materials, and absence of radio and television amount to "cruel and unusual punishment" in violation of the Eighth Amendment. Responding to the suit, the state prison system has conceded that the conditions in the IMU are "substantially as described by plaintiff." Nevertheless, the state has asked the court to dismiss the suit on the ground that "the Eighth Amendment does not guarantee fresh air and sunshine to inmates in solitary confinement, nor does it require that they be entertained." What is the federal judge likely to do? What should the judge do?

2. In 1987 Douglas Deville was convicted in a state court for felonious possession of cocaine. He received probation for that offense. Three years later, Deville was found guilty of another drug-related felony in the same state. For that offense, he served five years in state prison. Three months after being released from prison, Deville was arrested for possession of 100 grams of cocaine base and 400 grams of marijuana. This time the case was prosecuted in federal court, where Deville was convicted of felony possession with intent to distribute. Because this was his third drug-related felony, Deville was sentenced to life imprisonment without parole under 21 U.S.C.A. § 841(b)(1)(A) (1994). On appeal, Deville claims that this sentence is "utterly disproportionate to his offense" and that, accordingly, it constitutes a violation of the Eighth Amendment's Cruel and Unusual Punishment Clause. Deville is relying on the U.S. Supreme Court's opinion in *Solem v. Helm*, 463 U.S. 277 (1983). Does Deville have a case? Is he likely to prevail? In your opinion, is Deville's sentence fair and just? Is it constitutional?

EXCERPTS FROM JUDICIAL DECISIONS

Furman v. Georgia

Supreme Court of the United States, 1972.
408 U.S. 238, 92 S.Ct. 2726, 33 L.Ed.2d 346.

[In this landmark decision, the U.S. Supreme Court invalidates Georgia's death penalty statute. This decision represents three death penalty cases that were consolidated on appeal. All three defendants were African American. One of them was convicted for murder; two were found guilty of rape. All three were sentenced by juries to death.]

PER CURIAM.

The Court holds that the imposition and carrying out of the death penalty in these cases constitutes cruel and unusual punishment in violation of the Eighth and Fourteenth Amendments. The judgment in each case is therefore reversed insofar as it leaves undisturbed the death sentence imposed, and the cases are remanded for further proceedings.

Mr. Justice Douglas, Mr. Justice Brennan, Mr. Justice Stewart, Mr. Justice White, and Mr. Justice Marshall have filed separate opinions in support of the judgments. The Chief Justice, Mr. Justice Blackmun, Mr. Justice Powell, and Mr. Justice Rehnquist have filed separate dissenting opinions.

Mr. Justice DOUGLAS concurring.

. . . In each [of these cases] the determination of whether the penalty should be death or a lighter punishment was left by the State to the discretion of the judge or of the jury. . . . I vote to vacate each judgment, believing that the exaction of the death penalty does violate the Eighth and Fourteenth Amendments. . . .

The words "cruel and unusual" certainly include penalties that are barbaric. But the words, at least when read in light of the English proscription against selective and irregular use of penalties, suggest that it is "cruel and unusual" to apply the death penalty— or any other penalty selectively to minorities whose numbers are few, who are outcasts of society, and who are unpopular, but whom society is willing to see suffer though it would not countenance general application of the same penalty across the board. . . .

. . . [W]e deal with a system of law and of justice that leaves to the uncontrolled discretion of judges or juries the determination whether defendants committing these crimes should die or be imprisoned. Under these laws no standards govern the selection of the penalty. People live or die, dependent on the whim of one man or of 12. In a Nation committed to equal protection of the laws there is no permissible "caste" aspect of law enforcement. Yet we know that the discretion of judges and juries in imposing the death penalty enables the penalty to be selectively applied, feeding prejudices against the accused if he is poor and despised, lacking political clout, or if he is a member of a suspect or unpopular minority, and saving those who by social position may be in a more protected position. . . .

The high service rendered by the "cruel and unusual" punishment clause of the Eighth Amendment is to require legislatures to write penal laws that are evenhanded, nonselective, and nonarbitrary, and to require judges to see to it that general laws are not applied sparsely, selectively, and spottily to unpopular groups.

. . . [T]these discretionary statutes are unconstitutional in their operation. They are pregnant with discrimination and discrimination is an ingredient not compatible with the idea of equal protection of the laws that is implicit in the ban on "cruel and unusual" punishments.

Mr. Justice BRENNAN, concurring.

Ours would indeed be a simple task were we required merely to measure a challenged punishment against those that history has long condemned. That narrow and unwarranted view of the Clause, however, was left behind with the 19th century. Our task today is more complex. We know "that the words of the [Clause] are not precise and that their scope is not static." We know, therefore, that the Clause "must draw its meaning from the evolving standards of decency that mark the progress of a maturing society." That knowledge, of course, is but the beginning of the inquiry.

. . . [T]he question is whether [a] penalty subjects the individual to a fate forbidden by the principle of civilized treatment guaranteed by the [Clause]. It was also said that a challenged punishment must be examined "in light of the basic prohibition against inhuman treatment" embodied in the Clause.

. . . "The basic concept underlying the [Clause] is nothing less than the dignity of man. While the State has the power to punish, the [Clause] stands to assure that this power be exercised within the limits of civilized standards." At bottom, then, the Cruel and Unusual Punishment Clause prohibits the infliction of uncivilized and inhuman punishments. The State, even as it punishes, must treat its members with respect for their intrinsic worth as human beings. A punishment is "cruel and unusual," therefore, if it does not comport with human dignity. . . .

. . . [T]he punishment of death is inconsistent with . . . four principles: Death is an unusually severe and degrading punishment; there is a strong probability that it is inflicted arbitrarily; its rejection by contemporary society is virtually total; and there is no reason to believe that it serves any penal purpose more effectively than the less severe punishment of imprisonment. The function of these principles is to enable a court to determine whether a punishment comports with human dignity. Death, quite simply, does not. . . .

Mr. Justice STEWART, concurring.

. . . The instinct for retribution is part of the nature of man, and channeling that instinct in the administration of criminal justice serves an important purpose in promoting the stability of a society governed by law. When people begin to believe that organized society is unwilling or unable to impose upon criminal offenders the punishment they "deserve," then there are sown the seeds of anarchy—of self-help, vigilante justice and lynch law.

The constitutionality of capital punishment in the abstract is not, however, before us in these cases.

For the Georgia and Texas Legislatures have not provided that the death penalty shall be imposed upon all those who are found guilty of forcible rape. And the Georgia Legislature has not ordained that death shall be the automatic punishment for murder.

Instead, the death sentences now before us are the product of a legal system that brings them, I believe, within the very core of the Eighth Amendment's guarantee against cruel and unusual punishments, a guarantee applicable against the States through the Fourteenth Amendment. In the first place, it is clear that these sentences are "cruel" in the sense that they excessively go beyond, not in degree but in kind, the punishments that the state legislatures have determined to be necessary. In the second place, it is equally clear that these sentences are "unusual" in the sense that the penalty of death is infrequently imposed for murder, and that its imposition for rape is extraordinarily rare. But I do not rest my conclusion upon these two propositions alone.

These death sentences are cruel and unusual in the same way that being struck by lightning is cruel and unusual. For, of all the people convicted of rapes and murders in 1967 and 1968, many just as reprehensible as these, the petitioners are among a capriciously selected random handful upon whom the sentence of death has in fact been imposed. My concurring Brothers have demonstrated that, if any basis can be discerned for the selection of these few to be sentenced to die, it is the constitutionally impermissible basis of race. But racial discrimination has not been proved, and I put it to one side. I simply conclude that the Eighth and Fourteenth Amendments cannot tolerate the infliction of a sentence of death under legal systems that permit this unique penalty to be so wantonly and so freakishly imposed.

Mr. Justice WHITE, concurring.

. . . [L]ike my Brethren, I must arrive at judgment; and I can do no more than state a conclusion based on 10 years of almost daily exposure to the facts and circumstances of hundreds and hundreds of federal and state criminal cases involving crimes for which death is the authorized penalty. That conclusion, as I have said, is that the death penalty is exacted with great infrequency even for the most atrocious crimes and that there is no meaningful basis for distinguishing the few cases in which it is imposed from the many cases in which it is not. The short of it is that the policy of vesting sentencing authority primarily in juries—a decision largely motivated by the desire to mitigate the harshness of the law and to bring community judgment to bear on the sentence as well as guilt or innocence—has so effectively achieved its aims that capital punishment within the confines of the statutes now before us has for all practical purposes run its course. . . .

Mr. Justice MARSHALL, concurring.

. . . Perhaps the most important principle in analyzing "cruel and unusual" punishment questions is one that is reiterated again and again in the prior opinions of the Court: i.e., the cruel and unusual language "must draw its meaning from the evolving standards of decency that mark the progress of a maturing society." Thus, a penalty that was permissible at one time in our Nation's history is not necessarily permissible today. . . .

In judging whether or not a given penalty is morally acceptable, most courts have said that the punishment is valid unless "it shocks the conscience and sense of justice of the people."

While a public opinion poll obviously is of some assistance in indicating public acceptance or rejection of a specific penalty, its utility cannot be very great. This is because whether or not a punishment is cruel and unusual depends, not on whether its mere mention "shocks the conscience and sense of justice of the people," but on whether people who were fully informed as to the purposes of the penalty and its liabilities would find the penalty shocking, unjust, and unacceptable.

In other words, the question with which we must deal is not whether a substantial proportion of American citizens would today, if polled, opine that capital punishment is barbarously cruel, but whether they would find it to be so in the light of all information presently available.

This information would almost surely convince the average citizen that the penalty was unwise, but a problem arises as to whether, it would convince him that the penalty was morally reprehensible. This problem arises from the fact that the public's desire for retribution, even though this is a goal that the legislature cannot constitutionally pursue as its sole justification for capital punishment, might influence the citizenry's view of the morality of capital punishment. The solution to the problem lies in the fact that no one has ever seriously advanced retribution as a legitimate goal of our society. Defenses of capital punishment are always mounted on deterrent or other similar theories. This should not be surprising. It is the people of this country who have urged in the past that prisons rehabilitate as well as isolate offenders, and it is the people who have injected a sense of purpose into our penology. I cannot believe that at this stage in our history, the American people would ever knowingly support purposeless vengeance. Thus, I believe that the great mass of citizens would conclude on the basis of the material already considered that the death penalty is immoral therefore unconstitutional.

In striking down capital punishment, this Court does not malign our system of government. On the contrary, it pays homage to it. Only in a free society could right triumph in difficult times, and could civilization record its magnificent advancement. In recognizing the humanity of our fellow beings, we pay ourselves the highest tribute. We achieve "a major milestone in the long road up from barbarism" and join the approximately 70 other jurisdictions in the world which celebrate their regard for civilization and humanity by shunning capital punishment.

Mr. Chief Justice BURGER, with whom Mr. Justice BLACKMUN, and Mr. Justice REHNQUIST, join, dissenting.

. . . Although the Eighth Amendment literally reads as prohibiting only those punishments that are both "cruel" and "unusual," history compels the conclusion that the Constitution prohibits all punishments of extreme and barbarous cruelty, regardless of how frequently or infrequently imposed.

But where, as here, we consider a punishment well known to history, and clearly authorized by legislative enactment, it disregards the history of the Eighth Amendment and all the judicial comment that has followed to rely on the term "unusual" as affecting the outcome of these cases. Instead, I view these cases as turning on the single question whether capital punishment is "cruel" in the constitutional sense. The term "unusual" cannot be read as limiting the ban on "cruel" punishments or as somehow expanding the meaning of the term "cruel." For this reason I am unpersuaded by the facile argument that since capital punishment has always been cruel in the everyday sense of the word, and has become unusual due to decreased use, it is, therefore, now "cruel and unusual." . . .

Mr. Justice BLACKMUN, dissenting.

. . . Were I a legislator, I would vote against the death penalty for the policy reasons argued by counsel for the respective petitioners and expressed and adopted in the several opinions filed by the Justices who vote to reverse these convictions.

Although personally I may rejoice at the Court's result, I find it difficult to accept or to justify as a matter of history, of law, or of constitutional pronouncement. I fear the Court has overstepped. It has sought and has achieved an end.

Mr. Justice POWELL, with whom The CHIEF JUSTICE, Mr. Justice BLACKMUN, and Mr. Justice REHNQUIST join, dissenting.

. . . The Court granted certiorari in these cases to consider whether the death penalty is any longer a permissible form of punishment. It is the judgment of five Justices that the death penalty, as customarily prescribed and implemented in this country today, offends the constitutional prohibition against cruel and unusual punishments. The reasons for that judgment are stated in five separate opinions, expressing as many separate rationales. In my view, none of these opinions provides a constitutionally adequate foundation for the Court's decision. . . .

Mr. Justice REHNQUIST, with whom The CHIEF JUSTICE, Mr. Justice BLACKMUN, and Mr. Justice POWELL join, dissenting.

. . . Whatever its precise rationale, today's holding necessarily brings into sharp relief the fundamental question of the role of judicial review in a democratic society. How can government by the elected representatives of the people co-exist with the power of the federal judiciary, whose members are constitutionally insulated from responsiveness to the popular will, to declare invalid laws duly enacted by the popular branches of government?

Sovereignty resides ultimately in the people as a whole and, by adopting through their States a written Constitution for the Nation and subsequently adding amendments to that instrument, they have both granted certain powers to the National Government, and denied other powers to the National and the State Governments. Courts are exercising no more than the judicial function conferred upon them by Art. III of the Constitution when they assess, in a case before them, whether or not a particular legislative enactment is within the authority granted by the Constitution to the enacting body, and whether it runs afoul of some limitation placed by the Constitution on the authority of that body. For the theory is that the people themselves have spoken in the

Constitution, and therefore its commands are superior to the commands of the legislature, which is merely an agent of the people.

The Founding Fathers thus wisely sought to have the best of both worlds, the undeniable benefits of both democratic self-government and individual rights protected against possible excesses of that form of government.

The very nature of judicial review, as pointed out by Justice Stone in his dissent in the *Butler* case,

makes the courts the least subject to Madisonian check in the event that they shall, for the best of motives, expand judicial authority beyond the limits contemplated by the Framers. It is for this reason that judicial self-restraint is surely an implied, if not an expressed, condition of the grant of authority of judicial review. The Court's holding in these cases has been reached, I believe, in complete disregard of that implied condition.

● ● ● ● ● ● ● ● ● ● ● ● ● ●

Gregg v. Georgia

Supreme Court of the United States, 1976.
428 U.S. 153, 96 S.Ct. 2909, 49 L.Ed.2d 859.

[Here the Supreme Court effectively reinstates the death penalty by sustaining a revised Georgia death penalty law. The petitioner, Troy Gregg, was convicted of armed robbery and murder and was sentenced to death. In accordance with Georgia's death penalty law, revised after Furman v. Georgia, the trial was in two stages, a guilt stage and a sentencing stage.]

Judgment of the Court, and opinion of Mr. Justice STEWART, Mr. Justice POWELL, and Mr. Justice STEVENS, announced by Mr. Justice STEWART.

. . . There is no question that death as a punishment is unique in its severity and irrevocability. When defendant's life is at stake, the Court has been particularly sensitive to insure that every safeguard is observed. But we are concerned here only with the imposition of capital punishment for the crime of murder, and when a life has been taken deliberately by the offender, we cannot say that the punishment is invariably disproportionate to the crime. It is an extreme sanction, suitable to the most extreme of crimes.

We hold that the death penalty is not a form of punishment that may never be imposed, regardless of the circumstances of the offense, regardless of the character of the offender, and regardless of the procedure followed in reaching the decision to impose it.

We now turn to consideration of the constitutionality of Georgia's capital-sentencing procedures. In the wake of *Furman*, Georgia amended its capital punishment statute, but chose not to narrow the scope of its murder provisions. Thus, now as before

Furman, in Georgia "[a] person commits murder when he unlawfully and with malice aforethought, either express or implied, causes the death of another human being." All persons convicted of murder "shall be punished by death or by imprisonment for life."

Georgia did act, however, to narrow the class of murderers subject to capital punishment by specifying 10 statutory aggravating circumstances, one of which must be found by the jury to exist beyond a reasonable doubt before a death sentence can ever be imposed. In addition, the jury is authorized to consider any other appropriate aggravating or mitigating circumstances. The jury is not required to find any mitigating circumstance in order to make a recommendation of mercy that is binding on the trial court, but it must find a statutory aggravating circumstance before recommending a sentence of death.

These procedures require the jury to consider the circumstances of the crime and the criminal before it recommends sentence. No longer can a Georgia jury do as Furman's jury did: reach a finding of the defendant's guilt and then, without guidance or direction, decide whether he should live or die. Instead, the jury's attention is directed to the specific circumstances of the crime: Was it committed in the course of another capital felony? Was it committed for money? Was it committed upon a peace officer or judicial officer? Was it committed in a particularly heinous way or in a manner that endangered the lives of many persons? In addition, the jury's attention is focused on the characteristics of the person who committed the crime: Does he have a record of prior convictions for capital offenses? Are there any special facts about this defendant that mitigate against imposing capital punishment (e.g., his youth, the extent of his cooperation with the police, his emotional state at the time of the crime). As a result, while some jury discretion still exists, "the discretion to be exercised is controlled by clear and objective standards so as to produce non-discriminatory application."

As an important additional safeguard against arbitrariness and caprice, the Georgia statutory scheme provides for automatic appeal of all death sentences to the State's Supreme Court. That court is required by statute to review each sentence of death and determine whether it was imposed under the influence of passion or prejudice, whether the evidence supports the jury's finding of a statutory aggravating circumstance, and whether the sentence is disproportionate compared to those sentences imposed in similar cases.

In short, Georgia's new sentencing procedures require as a prerequisite to the imposition of the death penalty, specific jury findings as to the circumstances of the crime or the character of the defendant. Moreover to guard further against a situation comparable to that presented in *Furman,* the Supreme Court of Georgia compares each death sentence with the sentences imposed on similarly situated defendants to ensure that the sentence of death in a particular case is not disproportionate. On their face these procedures seem to satisfy the concerns of *Furman.* No longer should there be "no meaningful basis for distinguishing the few cases in which [the death penalty] is imposed from the many cases in which it is not."

The basic concern of *Furman* centered on those defendants who were being condemned to death capriciously and arbitrarily. Under the procedures before the Court in that case, sentencing authorities were not directed to give attention to the nature or circumstances of the crime committed or to the character or record of the defendant. Left unguided, juries imposed the death sentence in a way that could only be called freakish. The new Georgia sentencing procedures, by contrast, focus the jury's attention on the particularized nature of the crime and the particularized characteristics of the individual defendant. While the jury is permitted to consider any

aggravating or mitigating circumstances, it must find and identify at least one statutory aggravating factor before it may impose a penalty of death. In this way the jury's discretion is channeled. No longer can a jury wantonly and freakishly impose the death sentence; it is always circumscribed by the legislative guidelines. In addition, the review function of the Supreme Court of Georgia affords additional assurance that the concerns that prompted our decision in *Furman* are not present to any significant degree in the Georgia procedure applied here.

Mr. Justice WHITE, with whom The CHIEF JUSTICE and Mr. Justice REHNQUIST join, concurring in the judgment. . . .

Mr. Justice BLACKMUN, concurring in the judgment. . . .

Mr. Justice MARSHALL, dissenting.

In *Furman v. Georgia,* I set forth at some length my views on the basic issue presented to the Court in these cases. The death penalty, I concluded, is a cruel and unusual punishment prohibited by the Eighth and Fourteenth Amendments. That continues to be my view.

The mere fact that the community demands the murderer's life in return for the evil he has done cannot sustain the death penalty, for as the plurality reminds us, "the Eighth Amendment demands more than that a challenged punishment be acceptable to contemporary society." To be sustained under the Eighth Amendment, the death penalty must "[comport] with the basic concept of human dignity at the core of the Amendment." . . . Under these standards, the taking of life "because the wrongdoer deserves it" surely must fall, for such a punishment has as its very basis the total denial of the wrongdoer's dignity and worth.

The death penalty, unnecessary to promote the goal of deterrence or to further any legitimate notion of retribution, is an excessive penalty forbidden by the Eighth and Fourteenth Amendments. I respectfully dissent from the Court's judgment upholding the sentences of death imposed upon the petitioners in these cases.

Mr. Justice BRENNAN, dissenting. . . .

Payne v. Tennessee

Supreme Court of the United States, 1991.
501 U.S. 808, 111 S.Ct. 2597, 115 L.Ed.2d 720.

[In this case the Supreme Court overturns its decisions in Booth v. Maryland, 482 U.S. 496, 107 S.Ct. 2529, 96 L.Ed.2d 440 (1987), and South Carolina v. Gathers, 490 U.S. 805, 109 S.Ct. 2207, 104 L.Ed.2d 876 (1989), barring the admission of victim impact evidence during the sentencing phase of a capital trial.]

Chief Justice REHNQUIST delivered the opinion of the Court.

. . . The petitioner, Pervis Tyrone Payne, was convicted by a jury on two counts of first-degree murder and one count of assault with intent to commit murder in the first degree. He was sentenced to death for each of the murders, and to 30 years in prison for the assault.

The victims of Payne's offenses were 28-year-old Charisse Christopher, her 2-year-old daughter Lacie, and her 3-year-old son Nicholas. The three lived together in an apartment in Millington, Tennessee, across the hall from Payne's girlfriend, Bobbie Thomas. On Saturday, June 27, 1987, Payne visited Thomas' apartment several times in expectation of her return from her mother's house in Arkansas, but found no one at home. On one visit, he left his overnight bag, containing clothes and other items for his weekend stay, in the hallway outside Thomas' apartment. With the bag were three cans of malt liquor.

Payne passed the morning and early afternoon injecting cocaine and drinking beer. Later, he drove around the town with a friend in the friend's car, each of them taking turns reading a pornographic magazine. Sometime around 3 P.M., Payne returned to the apartment complex, entered the Christophers' apartment, and began making sexual advances towards Charisse. Charisse resisted and Payne became violent. A neighbor who resided in the apartment directly beneath the Christophers, heard Charisse screaming, "'Get out, get out' as if she were telling the children to leave." The noise briefly subsided and then began "horribly loud." The neighbor called the police after she heard a "blood curdling scream" from the Christopher apartment. . . .

When the first police officer arrived at the scene, he immediately encountered Payne who was leaving the apartment building, so covered with blood that he appeared to be "sweating blood." The officer confronted Payne, who responded, "I'm the complainant." . . . When the officer asked, "What's going on up there?" Payne struck the officer with the overnight bag, dropped his tennis shoes, and fled.

Inside the apartment, the police encountered a horrifying scene. Blood covered the walls and floor throughout the unit. Charisse and her children were lying on the floor in the kitchen. Nicholas, despite several wounds inflicted by a butcher knife that completely penetrated through his body from front to back, was still breathing. Miraculously, he survived, but not until after undergoing seven hours of surgery and a transfusion of 1700 cc's of blood—400 to 500 cc's more than his estimated normal blood volume. Charisse and Lacie were dead.

Charisse's body was found on the kitchen floor on her back, her legs fully extended. She had sustained 42 direct knife wounds and 42 defensive wounds on her arms and hands. The wounds were caused by 41 separate thrusts of a butcher knife. None of the 84 wounds inflicted by Payne were individually fatal; rather, the cause of death was most likely bleeding from all of the wounds.

Lacie's body was on the kitchen floor near her mother. She had suffered stab wounds to the chest, abdomen, back, and head. The murder weapon, a butcher knife, was found at her feet. Payne's baseball cap was snapped on her arm near her elbow. Three cans of malt liquor bearing Payne's fingerprints were found on a table near her body, and a fourth empty one was on the landing outside the apartment door.

Payne was apprehended later that day hiding in the attic of the home of a former girlfriend. As he descended the stairs of the attic, he stated to the arresting officers, "Man, I ain't killed no woman." According to one of the officers, Payne had "a wild look about him. His pupils were contracted. He was foaming at the mouth, saliva. He appeared to be very nervous. He was breathing real rapid." He had blood on his body and clothes and several scratches across his chest. It was later determined that the blood stains matched the victims' blood types. A search of his pockets revealed a packet containing cocaine residue, a hypodermic syringe wrapper, and a cap from a hypodermic syringe. His overnight bag, containing a bloody white shirt, was found in a nearby dumpster.

At trial, Payne took the stand and, despite the overwhelming and relatively uncontroverted evidence against him, testified that he had not harmed any of the Christophers. Rather, he asserted that another man had raced by him as he was walking up the stairs to the floor where the Christophers lived. He stated that he had gotten blood on himself when, after hearing moans from the Christopher's apartment, he had tried to help the victims. According to his testimony, he panicked and fled when he heard police sirens and noticed the blood on his clothes. The jury returned guilty verdicts against Payne on all counts.

During the sentencing phase of the trial, Payne presented the testimony of four witnesses: his mother and father, Bobbie Thomas, and Dr. John T. Huston, a clinical psychologist specializing in criminal court evaluation work. Bobbie Thomas testified that she met Payne at church, during a time when she was being abused by her husband. She stated that Payne was a very caring person, and that he devoted much time and attention to her three children, who were being affected by her marital difficulties. She said that the children had come to love him very much and would miss him and that he "behaved just like a father that loved his kids." She asserted that he did not drink, nor did he use drugs, and that it was generally inconsistent with Payne's character to have committed these crimes.

Dr. Huston testified that based on Payne's low score on an IQ test, Payne was "mentally handicapped." Huston also said that Payne was neither psychotic nor schizophrenic, and that Payne was the most polite prisoner he had ever met. Payne's parents testified that their son had no prior criminal record and had never been arrested. They also stated that Payne had no history of alcohol or drug abuse, he worked with his father as a painter, he was good with children, and that he was a good son.

The State presented the testimony of Charisse's mother, Mary Zvolanek. When asked how Nicholas had been affected by the murders of his mother and sister, she responded:

"He cries for his mom. He doesn't seem to understand why she doesn't come home. And he cries

for his sister Lacie. He comes to me many times during the week and asks me, Grandmama, do you miss my Lacie. And I tell him yes. He says, I'm worried about my Lacie." . . .

In arguing for the death penalty during closing argument, the prosecutor commented on the continuing effects of Nicholas' experience, stating:

"But we do know that Nicholas was alive. And Nicholas was in the same room. Nicholas was still conscious. His eyes were open. He responded to the paramedics. He was able to follow their directions. He was able to hold his intestines in as he was carried to the ambulance. So he knew what happened to his mother and baby sister. . . .

"There is nothing you can do to ease the pain of any of the families involved in this case. There is nothing you can do to ease the pain of Bernice or Carl Payne, and that's a tragedy. There is nothing you can do basically to ease the pain of Mr. and Mrs. Zvolanek, and that's a tragedy. They will have to live with it the rest of their lives. There is obviously nothing you can do for Charisse and Lacie Jo. But there is something that you can do for Nicholas.

"Somewhere down the road Nicholas is going to grow up, hopefully. He's going to want to know what happened. And he is going to know what happened to his baby sister and his mother. He is going to want to know what type of justice was done. He is going to want to know what happened. With your verdict, you will provide the answer." . . .

In the rebuttal to Payne's closing argument, the prosecutor stated:

"You saw the videotape this morning. You saw what Nicholas Christopher will carry in his mind forever. When you talk about cruel, when you talk about atrocious, and when you talk about heinous, that picture will always come into your mind, probably throughout the rest of your lives.

". . . No one will ever know about Lacie Jo because she never had the chance to grow up. Her life was taken from her at the age of two years old. So, no, there won't be a high school principal to talk about Lacie Jo Christopher, and there won't be anybody to take her to her high school prom. And there won't be anybody there—there won't be her mother there or Nicholas' mother there to kiss him at night. His mother will never kiss him good night or pat him as he goes off to bed, or hold him and sing him a lullaby.

"[Petitioner's attorney] wants you to think about a good reputation, people who love the defendant and things about him. He doesn't want you to think about the people who love Charisse Christopher, her mother and daddy who loved her. The people who loved little Lacie Jo, the grandparents who are still here. The brother who mourns for her every single day and wants to know where his best little playmate is. He doesn't have anybody to watch cartoons with him, a little one. These are the things that go into why it is especially cruel, heinous, and atrocious, the burden that that child will carry forever." . . .

The jury sentenced Payne to death on each of the murder counts.

The Supreme Court of Tennessee affirmed the convictions and sentence. The court rejected Payne's contention that the admission of the grandmother's testimony and the State's closing argument constituted prejudicial violations of his rights under the Eighth Amendment. . . .

We granted certiorari . . . to reconsider our holdings in *Booth* [*v. Maryland*] and [*South Carolina v.*] *Gathers*. . . .

We are now of the view that a State may properly conclude that for the jury to assess meaningfully the defendant's moral culpability and blameworthiness, it should have before it at the sentencing phase evidence of the specific harm caused by the defendant. "[T]he State has a legitimate interest in counteracting the mitigating evidence which the defendant is entitled to put in, by reminding the sentencer that just as the murderer should be considered as an individual, so too the victim is an individual whose death represents a unique loss to society and in particular to his family." . . . *Booth* deprives the State of the full moral force of its evidence and may prevent the jury from having before it all the information necessary to determine the proper punishment for a first-degree murder.

The present case is an example of the potential for such unfairness. The capital sentencing jury heard testimony from Payne's girlfriend that they met at church, that he was affectionate, caring, kind to her children, that he was not an abuser of drugs or alcohol, and that it was inconsistent with his character to have committed the murder. Payne's parents testified that he was a good son, and a clinical psychologist testified that Payne was an extremely polite prisoner and suffered from a low IQ. None of this testimony was related to the circumstances of Payne's brutal crimes. In contrast, the only evidence of the impact of Payne's offenses during the sentencing phase was Nicholas' grandmother's description—in response to a single question—that the child misses

his mother and baby sister. Payne argues that the Eighth Amendment commands that the jury's death sentence must be set aside because the jury heard this testimony. But the testimony illustrated quite poignantly some of the harm that Payne's killing had caused; there is nothing unfair about allowing the jury to bear in mind that harm at the same time as it considers the mitigating evidence introduced by the defendant. The Supreme Court of Tennessee in this case obviously felt the unfairness of the rule pronounced by *Booth* when it said "[i]t is an affront to the civilized members of the human race to say that at sentencing in a capital case, a parade of witnesses may praise the background, character and good deeds of Defendant (as was done in this case) without limitation as to relevancy, but nothing may be said that bears upon the character of, or the harm imposed, upon the victims." . . .

We thus hold that if the State chooses to permit the admission of victim impact evidence and prosecutorial argument on that subject, the Eighth Amendment erects no per se bar. A State may legitimately conclude that evidence about the victim and about the impact of the murder on the victim's family is relevant to the jury's decision as to whether or not the death penalty should be imposed. There is no reason to treat such evidence differently than other relevant evidence is treated. . . . Reconsidering these decisions now, we conclude for the reasons heretofore stated, that they were wrongly decided and should be, and now are, overruled. We accordingly affirm the judgment of the Supreme Court of Tennessee.

Justice O'CONNOR, with whom Justice WHITE and Justice KENNEDY join, concurring. . . .

Justice SCALIA, with whom Justice O'CONNOR and Justice KENNEDY join [in part], concurring. . . .

Justice SOUTER, with whom Justice KENNEDY joins, concurring. . . .

Justice MARSHALL, with whom Justice BLACKMUN joins, dissenting. . . .

Justice STEVENS, with whom Justice BLACKMUN joins, dissenting.

. . . Until today our capital punishment jurisprudence has required that any decision to impose the death penalty be based solely on evidence that tends to inform the jury about the character of the offense and the character of the defendant. Evidence that serves no purpose other than to appeal to the sympathies or emotions of the jurors has never been considered admissible. Thus, if a defendant, who had murdered a convenience store clerk in cold blood in the course of an armed robbery, offered evidence unknown to him at the time of the crime about the immoral character of his victim, all would recognize immediately that the evidence was irrelevant and inadmissible. Even-handed justice requires that the same constraint be imposed on the advocate of the death penalty. . . .

● ● ● ● ● ● ● ● ● ● ● ● ● ● ●

Apprendi v. New Jersey

United States Supreme Court, 2000.
530 U.S. 466, 120 S.Ct. 2348, 147 L.Ed.2d 435.

[In this case the Court considers the constitutionality of a New Jersey hate crime statute that provides for a greater period of incarceration if the trial judge determines, based on a preponderance of the evidence, that the defendant "acted with a purpose to intimidate an individual or group of individuals because of race, color, gender, handicap, religion, sexual orientation or ethnicity."]

Justice STEVENS delivered the opinion of the Court.

. . . The question presented is whether the Due Process Clause of the Fourteenth Amendment requires that a factual determination authorizing an increase in the maximum prison sentence for an offense from 10 to 20 years be made by a jury on the basis of proof beyond a reasonable doubt. . . .

At 2:04 A.M. on December 22, 1994, petitioner Charles C. Apprendi, Jr., fired several .22-caliber bullets into the home of an African-American family that had recently moved into a previously all-white neighborhood in Vineland, New Jersey. Apprendi was promptly arrested and, at 3:05 A.M., admitted that he was the shooter. After further questioning, at 6:04 A.M., he made a statement—which he later retracted—that even though he did not know the occupants of the house personally, "because they are black in color he does not want them in the neighborhood." . . .

A New Jersey grand jury returned a 23-count indictment charging Apprendi with four first-degree, eight second-degree, six third-degree, and five fourth-degree offenses. The charges alleged shootings on four different dates, as well as the unlawful possession of various weapons. None of the counts referred to the hate crime statute, and none alleged that Apprendi acted with a racially biased purpose.

The parties entered into a plea agreement, pursuant to which Apprendi pleaded guilty to two counts (3 and 18) of second-degree possession of a firearm for an unlawful purpose, N.J. Stat. Ann. § 2C:39–4a (West 1995), and one count (22) of the third-degree offense of unlawful possession of an antipersonnel bomb, § 2C:39–3a; the prosecutor dismissed the other 20 counts. Under state law, a second-degree offense carries a penalty range of 5 to 10 years, § 2C:43–6(a)(2); a third-degree offense carries a penalty range of between 3 and 5 years, § 2C:43–6(a)(3). As part of the plea agreement, however, the State reserved the right to request the court to impose a higher "enhanced" sentence on count 18 (which was based on the December 22 shooting) on the ground that that offense was committed with a biased purpose, as described in § 2C:44–3(e). Apprendi, correspondingly, reserved the right to challenge the hate crime sentence enhancement on the ground that it violates the United States Constitution. . . .

After the trial judge accepted the three guilty pleas, the prosecutor filed a formal motion for an extended term. The trial judge thereafter held an evidentiary hearing on the issue of Apprendi's "purpose" for the shooting on December 22. Apprendi adduced evidence from a psychologist and from seven character witnesses who testified that he did not have a reputation for racial bias. He also took the stand himself, explaining that the incident was an unintended consequence of overindulgence in alcohol, denying that he was in any way biased against African-Americans, and denying that his statement to the police had been accurately described. The judge, however, found the police officer's testimony credible, and concluded that the evidence supported a finding "that the crime was motivated by racial bias." . . . Having found "by a preponderance of the evidence" that Apprendi's actions were taken "with a purpose to intimidate" as provided by the statute, . . . the trial judge held that the hate crime enhancement applied. Rejecting Apprendi's constitutional challenge to the statute, the judge sentenced him to a 12-year term of imprisonment on count 18, and to shorter concurrent sentences on the other two counts.

Apprendi appealed, arguing, *inter alia,* that the Due Process Clause of the United States Constitution requires that the finding of bias upon which his hate crime sentence was based must be proved to a jury beyond a reasonable doubt. . . .

A divided New Jersey Supreme Court affirmed. . . .

At stake in this case are constitutional protections of surpassing importance: the proscription of any deprivation of liberty without "due process of law," . . . and the guarantee that "[i]n all criminal prosecutions, the accused shall enjoy the right to a speedy and public trial, by an impartial jury." . . . Taken together, these rights indisputably entitle a criminal defendant to "a jury determination that [he] is guilty of every element of the crime with which he is charged, beyond a reasonable doubt." . . .

Equally well founded is the companion right to have the jury verdict based on proof beyond a reasonable doubt. "The 'demand for a higher degree of persuasion' in criminal cases was recurrently expressed from ancient times, [though] its crystallization into the formula 'beyond a reasonable doubt' seems to have occurred as late as 1798. It is now accepted in common law jurisdictions as the measure of persuasion by which the prosecution must convince the trier of all the essential elements of guilt." . . .

Any possible distinction between an "element" of a felony offense and a "sentencing factor" was unknown to the practice of criminal indictment, trial by jury, and judgment by court as it existed during the years surrounding our Nation's founding. As a general rule, criminal proceedings were submitted to a jury after being initiated by an indictment containing "all the facts and circumstances which constitute the offence, . . . stated with such certainty and precision, that the defendant . . . may be enabled to determine the species of offence they constitute, in order that he may prepare his defence accordingly . . . and *that there may be no doubt as to the judgment which should be given,* if the defendant be convicted." . . . The defendant's ability to predict with certainty the judgment from the face of the felony indictment flowed from the invariable linkage of punishment with crime. . . .

Thus, with respect to the criminal law of felonious conduct, "the English trial judge of the later eighteenth century had very little explicit discretion in sentencing. The substantive criminal law tended to be sanction-specific; it prescribed a particular sentence for each offense. The judge was meant simply to impose that sentence (unless he thought in the circumstances that the sentence was so inappropriate that he should invoke the pardon process to commute it)." . . .

This practice at common law held true when indictments were issued pursuant to statute. Just as the circumstances of the crime and the intent of the defendant at the time of commission were often essential elements to be alleged in the indictment, so too were the circumstances mandating a particular punishment. "Where a statute annexes a higher degree of punishment to a common-law felony, if committed under particular circumstances, an indictment for the offence, in order to bring the defendant within that higher degree of punishment, must expressly charge it to have been committed under those circumstances, and must state the circumstances with certainty and precision." . . . If, then, "upon an indictment under the statute, the prosecutor proves the felony to have been committed, but fail in proving it to have been committed under the circumstances specified in the statute, the defendant shall be convicted of the common-law felony only." . . .

We should be clear that nothing in this history suggests that it is impermissible for judges to exercise discretion—taking into consideration various factors relating both to offense and offender—in imposing a judgment *within the range* prescribed by statute. We have often noted that judges in this country have long exercised discretion of this nature in imposing sentence *within statutory limits* in the individual case. . . .

The historic link between verdict and judgment and the consistent limitation on judges' discretion to operate within the limits of the legal penalties provided highlight the novelty of a legislative scheme that removes the jury from the determination of a fact that, if found, exposes the criminal defendant to a penalty *exceeding* the maximum he would receive if punished according to the facts reflected in the jury verdict alone.

We do not suggest that trial practices cannot change in the course of centuries and still remain true to the principles that emerged from the Framers' fears "that the jury right could be lost not only by gross denial, but by erosion." . . . But practice must at least adhere to the basic principles undergirding the requirements of trying to a jury all facts necessary to constitute a statutory offense, and proving those facts beyond reasonable doubt. . . . If a defendant faces punishment beyond that provided by statute when an offense is committed under certain circumstances but not others, it is obvious that both the loss of liberty and the stigma attaching to the offense are heightened; it necessarily follows that the defendant should not—at the moment the State is put to proof of those circumstances—be deprived of protections that have, until that point, unquestionably attached. . . .

In sum, our reexamination of our cases in this area, and of the history upon which they rely, confirms the opinion that we expressed in *Jones* [*v. United States* (1999)]. Other than the fact of a prior conviction, any fact that increases the penalty for a crime beyond the prescribed statutory maximum must be submitted to a jury, and proved beyond a reasonable doubt. With that exception, we endorse the statement of the rule set forth in the concurring opinions in that case: "[I]t is unconstitutional for a legislature to remove from the jury the assessment of facts that increase the prescribed range of penalties to which a criminal defendant is exposed. It is equally clear that such facts must be established by proof beyond a reasonable doubt." . . .

The New Jersey statutory scheme that Apprendi asks us to invalidate allows a jury to convict a defendant of a second-degree offense based on its finding beyond a reasonable doubt that he unlawfully possessed a prohibited weapon; after a subsequent and separate proceeding, it then allows a judge to impose punishment identical to that New Jersey provides for crimes of the first degree, . . . based upon the judge's finding, by a preponderance of the evidence, that the defendant's "purpose" for unlawfully possessing the weapon was "to intimidate" his victim on the basis of a particular characteristic the victim possessed. In light of the constitutional rule explained above, and all of the cases supporting it, this practice cannot stand. . . .

The New Jersey procedure challenged in this case is an unacceptable departure from the jury tradition that is an indispensable part of our criminal justice system. Accordingly, the judgment of the Supreme Court of New Jersey is reversed. . . .

Justice SCALIA, concurring. . . .

Justice THOMAS, . . . concurring. . . .

Justice O'CONNOR, with whom the Chief Justice, Justice KENNEDY, and Justice BREYER join, dissenting.

Last Term, in *Jones v. United States* (1999), this Court found that our prior cases suggested the following principle: "[U]nder the Due Process Clause of the Fifth Amendment and the notice and jury trial guarantees of the Sixth Amendment, any fact (other than prior conviction) that increases the maximum penalty for a crime must be charged in an indictment, submitted to a jury, and proven beyond a reasonable doubt." . . . At the time, Justice Kennedy rightly criticized the Court for its failure to explain the origins, contours, or consequences of its purported constitutional principle; for the inconsistency of that principle with our prior cases; and for the serious doubt that the holding cast on sentencing systems employed by the Federal Government and States alike. . . . Today, in what will surely be remembered as a watershed change in constitutional law, the Court imposes as a constitutional rule the principle it first identified in *Jones*. . . .

Justice BREYER, with whom Chief Justice REHNQUIST joins, dissenting.

The majority holds that the Constitution contains the following requirement: "any fact [other than recidivism] that increases the penalty for a crime beyond the prescribed statutory maximum must be submitted to a jury, and proved beyond a reasonable doubt." . . . This rule would seem to promote a procedural ideal—that of juries, not judges, determining the existence of those facts upon which increased punishment turns. But the real world of criminal justice cannot hope to meet any such ideal. It can function only with the help of procedural compromises, particularly in respect to sentencing. And those compromises, which are themselves necessary for the fair functioning of the criminal justice system, preclude implementation of the procedural model that today's decision reflects. At the very least, the impractical nature of the requirement that the majority now recognizes supports the proposition that the Constitution was not intended to embody it. . . .

Koon v. United States

Supreme Court of the United States, 1996.
518 U.S. 81, 116 S.Ct. 2035, 135 L.Ed.2d 392.

[In this case the U.S. Supreme Court reviews the sentence imposed on two police officers who were convicted of violating Rodney King's civil rights by subjecting him to police brutality during an arrest for a traffic offense in 1991. The legal question in this highly publicized case is whether the trial judge was correct in his downward departure from the federal sentencing guidelines.]

Justice KENNEDY delivered the opinion of the Court.

The petitioners' guilt has been established, and we are concerned here only with the sentencing determinations made by the District Court and Court of Appeals. . . .

. . . Koon, Powell, Briseno, and Wind were tried in state court on charges of assault with a deadly weapon and excessive use of force by a police officer. The officers were acquitted of all charges, with the exception of one assault charge against Powell that resulted in a hung jury. The verdicts touched off widespread rioting in Los Angeles. More than 40 people were killed in the riots, more than 2,000 were injured, and nearly $1 billion in property was destroyed. . . .

On August 4, 1992, a federal grand jury indicted the four officers under 18 U.S.C. § 242 charging them with violating King's constitutional rights under color of law. Powell, Briseno, and Wind were charged with willful use of unreasonable force in arresting King. Koon was charged with willfully permitting the other officers to use unreasonable force during the arrest. After a trial in United States District Court for the Central District of California, the jury convicted Koon and Powell but acquitted Wind and Briseno.

We now consider the District Court's sentencing determinations. Under the Sentencing Guidelines, a district court identifies the base offense level assigned to the crime in question, adjusts the level as the Guidelines instruct, and determines the defendant's criminal history category. . . . Coordinating the adjusted offense level and criminal history category yields the appropriate sentencing range. . . .

The court granted a five level departure because "the victim's wrongful conduct contributed significantly to provoking the offense behavior." . . . The court also granted a three level departure, based on a combination of four factors. First, as a result of the "widespread publicity and emotional outrage which have surrounded this case," petitioners were "particularly likely to be targets of abuse" in prison. . . . Second, petitioners would face job termination proceedings, after which they would lose their positions as police officers, be disqualified from prospective employment in the field of law enforcement, and suffer the "anguish and disgrace these deprivations entail." . . . Third, petitioners had been "significantly burden[ed]" by having been subjected to successive state and federal prosecutions. . . . Fourth, petitioners were not "violent, dangerous, or likely to engage in future criminal conduct," so there was "no reason to impose a sentence that reflects a need to protect the public from [them]." . . . The court concluded these factors justified a departure when taken together, although none would have been sufficient standing alone. . . .

The departures yielded an offense level of 19 and a sentencing range of 30 to 37 months' imprisonment. The court sentenced each petitioner to 30 months' imprisonment. The petitioners appealed their convictions, and the Government appealed the sentences, arguing that the District Court erred in granting the downward departures and in failing to adjust the offense level upward for serious bodily injury. The Court of Appeals affirmed petitioners' convictions, and affirmed the District Court's refusal to adjust the offense level, but it reversed the District Court's departure determinations. Only the last ruling is before us. . . .

We granted certiorari to determine the standard of review governing appeals from a district court's decision to depart from the sentencing ranges in the Guidelines. The appellate court should not review the departure decision *de novo,* but instead should ask whether the sentencing court abused its discretion. Having invoked the wrong standard, the Court of Appeals erred further in rejecting certain of the downward departure factors relied upon by the District Judge. . . .

The Sentencing Reform Act of 1984, as amended, 18 U.S.C. § 3551 et seq., 28 U.S.C. §§ 991–998, made far reaching changes in federal sentencing. Before the Act, sentencing judges enjoyed broad discretion in determining whether and how long an offender should be incarcerated. *Mistretta v. United States,* 488 U.S. 361, 363 (1989). The discretion led to perceptions that "federal judges mete out an unjustifiably wide range of sentences to offenders with similar histories, convicted of similar crimes, committed under similar circumstances." . . . In response, Congress created the United States Sentencing Commission and charged it with developing a comprehensive set of sentencing guidelines, 28 U.S.C. § 994. The Commission promulgated the United States Sentencing Guidelines, which "specify an appropriate [sentencing range] for each class of convicted persons" based on various factors related to the offense and the offender. . . . A district judge now must impose on a defendant a sentence falling within the range of the applicable Guideline, if the case is an ordinary one.

The Act did not eliminate all of the district court's discretion, however. Acknowledging the wisdom, even the necessity, of sentencing procedures that take into account individual circumstances, . . . Congress allows district courts to depart from the applicable Guideline range if "the court finds that there exists an aggravating or mitigating circumstance of a kind, or to a degree, not adequately taken into consideration by the Sentencing Commission in formulating the guidelines that should result in a sentence different from that described." . . .

. . . As an initial matter, the Government urges us to hold each of the factors relied upon by the District Court to be impermissible departure factors under all circumstances. A defendant's loss of career opportunities must always be an improper consideration, the Government argues, because "persons convicted of crimes suffer a wide range of consequences in addition to the sentence." . . . Susceptibility to prison abuse, continues the Government, likewise never should be considered because the "degree of vulnerability to assault is an entirely 'subjective' judgment, and the number of defendants who may qualify for that departure is 'virtually unlimited.'" . . .

Those arguments, however persuasive as a matter of sentencing policy, should be directed to the Commission. Congress did not grant federal courts authority to decide what sorts of sentencing consid-

erations are inappropriate in every circumstance. Rather, 18 U.S.C. § 3553(b) instructs a court that, in determining whether there exists an aggravating or mitigating circumstance of a kind or to a degree not adequately considered by the Commission, it should consider "only the sentencing guidelines, policy statements, and official commentary of the Sentencing Commission." The Guidelines, however, "place essentially no limit on the number of potential factors that may warrant departure." . . . The Commission set forth factors courts may not consider under any circumstances but made clear that with those exceptions, it "does not intend to limit the kinds of factors, whether or not mentioned anywhere else in the guidelines, that could constitute grounds for departure in an unusual case." . . . Thus, for the courts to conclude a factor must not be considered under any circumstances would be to transgress the policymaking authority vested in the Commission. . . .

We conclude, then, that a federal court's examination of whether a factor can ever be an appropriate basis for departure is limited to determining whether the Commission has proscribed, as a categorical matter, consideration of the factor. If the answer to the question is no—as it will be most of the time—the sentencing court must determine whether the factor, as occurring in the particular circumstances, takes the case outside the heartland of the applicable Guideline. We now turn to the four factors underlying the District Court's three level departure. . . .

The goal of the Sentencing Guidelines is, of course, to reduce unjustified disparities and so reach towards the evenhandedness and neutrality that are the distinguishing marks of any principled system of justice. In this respect, the Guidelines provide uniformity, predictability, and a degree of detachment lacking in our earlier system. This too must be remembered, however. It has been uniform and constant in the federal judicial tradition for the sentencing judge to consider every convicted person as an individual and every case as a unique study in the human failings that sometimes mitigate, sometimes magnify, the crime and the punishment to ensue. We do not understand it to have been the congressional purpose to withdraw all sentencing discretion from the United States District Judge. Discretion is reserved within the Sentencing Guidelines, and reflected by the standard of appellate review we adopt. . . .

The Court of Appeals identified the wrong standard of review. It erred as well in finding that victim misconduct did not justify the five level departure and that susceptibility to prison abuse and the burdens of successive prosecutions could not be relied upon for the three level departure. Those sentencing determinations were well within the sound discretion of the District Court. The District Court did abuse its discretion in relying on the other two factors forming the three level departure: career loss and low recidivism risk. When a reviewing court concludes that a district court based a departure on both valid and invalid factors, a remand is required unless it determines the district court would have imposed the same sentence absent reliance on the invalid factors. . . . As the District Court here stated that none of the four factors standing alone would justify the three level departure, it is not evident that the court would have imposed the same sentence if it had relied only on susceptibility to abuse in prison and the hardship of successive prosecutions. The Court of Appeals should therefore remand the case to the District Court.

The judgment of the Court of Appeals is affirmed in part and reversed in part, and the case is remanded for further proceedings consistent with this opinion.

It is so ordered.

Justice STEVENS, concurring in part and dissenting in part. . . .

Justice SOUTER, with whom Justice GINSBURG joins, concurring in part and dissenting in part.

I believe that it was . . . an abuse of discretion for the District Court to depart downward because of the successive prosecutions. In these cases, there were facial showings that the state court system had malfunctioned when the petitioners were acquitted (or, in the case of one charge, had received no verdict), and without something more one cannot accept the District Court's conclusion that there was no demonstration that a "clear miscarriage of justice" caused the result in the state trial. . . . This is so simply because the federal prosecutors, in proving their cases, proved conduct constituting the crimes for which petitioners had been prosecuted unsuccess-

fully in the state court. . . . While such a facial showing resulting from the identity of factual predicates for the state and federal prosecutions might in some cases be overcome (by demonstrating, say, that a crucial witness for the State was unavailable in the state trial through no one's fault), there was no evidence to overcome it here. . . .

This is not, of course, to say that a succession of state and federal prosecutions may never justify a downward departure. If a comparison of state and federal verdicts in relation to their factual predicates indicates no incongruity, a downward departure at federal sentencing could well be consistent with an application of a rational heartland concept. But these are not such cases.

Justice BREYER, with whom Justice GINSBURG joins, concurring in part and dissenting in part. . . .

In my view, the relevant Guideline . . . encompasses the possibility of a double prosecution. That Guideline applies to various civil rights statutes, which Congress enacted, in part, to provide a federal forum for the protection of constitutional rights where state law enforcement efforts had proved inadequate. . . . Before promulgating the Guidelines, the Commission "examined the many hundreds of criminal statutes in the United States Code," . . . and it would likely have been aware of this well known legislative purpose. The centrality of this purpose, the Commission's likely awareness of it, and other considerations that Justice Souter mentions . . . lead me to conclude on the basis of the statute and Guideline itself, that the Commission would have considered a "double prosecution" case as one ordinarily within, not outside, the "civil rights" Guideline's "heartland." For that reason, a simple double prosecution, without more, does not support a departure. . . .

. . . I cannot find in this record anything sufficiently unusual, compared, say, with other policemen imprisoned for civil rights violations, as to justify departure.

CHAPTER

20

Appeal and Postconviction Relief

Introduction

Society's commitment to standards of fairness and procedural regularity is reflected in the opportunities that exist for defendants in criminal cases to seek judicial review of adverse court decisions. These opportunities have increased in recent decades, largely through judicial interpretation of various constitutional and statutory provisions.

Forms of review in criminal cases include **trial *de novo*, appeal of right, discretionary review,** and **postconviction relief.** Trial *de novo* occurs when a trial court of general jurisdiction reviews a conviction rendered by a court of limited jurisdiction. Appeal of right, the most common form of appeal, refers to an appellate court's review of a criminal conviction rendered by a trial court of general jurisdiction. A defendant whose conviction is affirmed on appeal may seek further review by a higher court by petitioning for discretionary review. Finally, a defendant confined to prison may seek additional review of his or her conviction or sentence by applying for a **writ of habeas corpus.** The writ of habeas corpus allows a court of competent jurisdiction to review the legality of a prisoner's confinement. This device permits prisoners to raise a variety of legal issues in attacking their convictions and/or sentences. Each mechanism plays an important part in determining cases that move beyond the trial stage of the criminal process. In addition to correcting errors made by lower courts, appeals allow higher courts to refine and standardize both the substantive and procedural law.

The Common-Law Background

Before the eighteenth century, there was no common-law right to appeal from a criminal conviction. On rare occasions, the Crown issued a writ of error to require a new trial, but there was no appeal in the modern sense. Indeed, the term "appeal" at common law had a very different usage from ours. At common law, appeal referred to an effort by a person convicted of treason to obtain a pardon from the Crown by accusing others of being accomplices to the treasonable act.

In a landmark decision, the Court of King's Bench ruled in 1705 that a **writ of error** had to be issued where a person convicted of a misdemeanor made proper application for the writ. *Paty's Case,* 91 Eng. Rep. 431 (K.B. 1705). In cases of felony and treason, the writ of error continued to be discretionary, although after 1700 the courts became more liberal in their issuance of the writ. The writ of error was finally abolished when Parliament enacted the Criminal Appeal Act of 1907, giving defendants the right to appeal their convictions.

Appeal of Right

The federal constitution makes no mention of the right to appeal from a criminal conviction, although some might argue that the right to appeal is implicit in the due process clauses of the Fifth and Fourteenth amendments. In 1894 the United States Supreme Court held that the federal constitution provides no right to appeal from a criminal conviction. *McKane v. Durston,* 153 U.S. 684, 14 S.Ct. 913, 38 L.Ed. 867 (1894). Given the recent expansion of the concept of due process, it is likely that the Court would reconsider this holding but for the fact that federal and state statutes allow criminal defendants to appeal their convictions and seek other forms of postconviction relief. Defendants convicted after entering a plea of not guilty are entitled under federal and state law to one appeal as a matter of right.

Appeals of right in federal criminal cases are heard by United States courts of appeals (circuit courts). State criminal appeals are heard by state supreme courts, by intermediate appellate courts, and—in Alabama, Oklahoma, Tennessee, and Texas—by specialized appellate courts that hear only criminal appeals. Beyond these appeals of right, opportunities exist for defendants to have their cases reviewed by the highest state courts and the United States Supreme Court, which may review convictions by issuing **writs of certiorari.** Many states provide automatic appeal of death sentences to their highest court (see Chapter 19).

A party who takes an appeal of right is called the **appellant;** the party against whom the appeal is taken is the **appellee.** A party who seeks further review is referred to as the **petitioner;** the other party is designated the **respondent.**

What Defendants May Challenge on Appeal

In a direct appeal from a criminal conviction, a defendant may challenge any act of the trial court objected to by the defendant during the pretrial, trial, or posttrial phases of the defendant's case. Irrespective of whether an objection was made in the trial court, a defendant may challenge the trial court's jurisdiction and those trial court actions or rulings considered to be **fundamental errors.** Appellate courts take different approaches to how serious an error must be to be classified as fundamental. When the defendant has been convicted of a capital crime, courts are more liberal in reviewing errors first challenged at the appellate stage. Indeed, the United States Supreme Court has said that those fundamental errors not specifically challenged by the appellant should be corrected when a person's life is at stake. *Fisher v. United States,* 328 U.S. 463, 66 S.Ct. 1318, 90 L.Ed. 1382 (1946).

In practice, a defendant usually raises from one to six major points on appeal as a basis for reversal of the trial court's judgment or sentence. Often these points are referred to as **assignments of error.** The most common assignments of error on direct appeal are claims that the trial court erred in rulings in one or more of the following areas:

1. Pretrial violations of the defendant's rights, particularly those rights guaranteed by the Fourth, Fifth, and Sixth amendments to the federal constitution
2. Procedural matters, especially trial court rulings admitting or excluding evidence
3. Irregularities in the impaneling or conduct of the jury
4. Failure to give jury instructions requested by the defendant or giving instructions objected to by the defendant
5. Prosecutorial misconduct such as improper remarks or arguments
6. Sufficiency of the evidence to support a finding of the defendant's guilt beyond a reasonable doubt
7. Interpretations of statutes or ordinances
8. The legality and, in some jurisdictions, the reasonableness of the sentence imposed
9. Jury selection, deliberation, and misconduct
10. The voluntariness of a guilty plea

A 1989 study conducted for the National Center for State Courts looked at the distribution of outcomes in five representative appellate courts across the country. Nearly 80 percent of all judgments were affirmed in these courts during the period under study. Of the reversals, the most frequent outcome was a remand for resentencing. In less than 10 percent of these reversals did defendants win outright acquittal. The most frequent claims of error in criminal appeals in these five appellate courts involved the admissibility of challenged evidence. Yet less than 8 percent of these claims resulted in reversals. The second-most commonly raised issue involved the trial judge's instructions to the jury. Roughly 10 percent of these claims resulted in reversals. (See Joy A. Chapper and Roger A. Hanson, "Understanding Reversible Error in Criminal Appeals," Final Report Submitted to the State Justice Institute, National Center for State Courts, October 1989, p. 5.)

The Doctrine of Harmless Error

Although appellate review is designed to correct errors that occur before, during, or after trial, not all errors necessitate reversal. To obtain reversal of a judgment, the appellant must show that some prejudice resulted from the error and that the outcome of the trial or the sentence imposed would probably have been different in the absence of the error. Although specific standards vary among jurisdictions, all appellate courts operate on the principle that reversal is required only when substantial, as distinct from merely technical, errors are found in the record. This approach is illustrated by a provision of the California Constitution that permits reversal on appeal only to prevent a **miscarriage of justice.** The California Supreme Court has interpreted this standard as follows:

> [A] "miscarriage of justice" should be declared only when the court, after an examination of the entire cause, including the evidence, is of the opinion that it is reasonably probable that a result more favorable to the appealing party would have been reached in the absence of the error. *People v. Watson,* 299 P.2d 243, 254 (Cal. 1956).

Appellate courts frequently find that technical errors cited by appellants are harmless and do not merit a reversal; however, the United States Supreme Court has imposed a strict standard on the finding of harmless error. Where an error at trial involves provisions of the federal constitution, the Supreme Court has said that appellate courts must find beyond a reasonable doubt that the error was harmless if they are to affirm the trial court. *Chapman v. California,* 386 U.S. 18, 87 S.Ct. 824, 17 L.Ed.2d 705 (1967).

The **doctrine of harmless error** is subject to certain qualifications. For example, appellate courts generally do not consider each error at trial in isolation. Rather, they often consider the cumulative effect of a series of errors. Thus, an appellant may secure reversal of a conviction where the trial was replete with error, even though each particular error might be considered harmless by itself.

When an Appeal May Be Taken by a Defendant

Generally, only a defendant who has pled not guilty has the right to appeal, and that appeal must wait until the defendant has been convicted and sentenced. However, there are some instances in which courts permit other appeals by defendants. For example, an order modifying or revoking probation is usually appealable.

Typically, a defendant who pleads guilty may raise on appeal only those issues relating to the trial court jurisdiction, the voluntariness of the guilty plea, and the legality of the sentence imposed. Even then, an appellate court may refuse to review these aspects of a case, other than the issue of jurisdiction, unless the trial court has refused the defendant's request to withdraw the plea of guilty.

Some jurisdictions permit a defendant to plead *nolo contendere* and reserve the right to appeal a specific ruling of the trial court. See, for example, *Cooksey v. State,*

524 P.2d 1251 (Alaska 1974). Defendants who unsuccessfully urge a constitutional defense frequently rely on this procedure. For instance, a defendant may file a pretrial motion to suppress certain evidence on the ground that it was obtained in violation of the Fourth Amendment. If the trial judge denies the motion, the defendant can plead *nolo contendere,* reserving the right to appeal that specific point of law.

Appeals by the Prosecution

Early rulings by American state courts uniformly denied state governments the right to appeal acquittals of criminal defendants. The United States Supreme Court adopted this position in 1892, when it ruled that the federal government had no right to appeal an acquittal. *United States v. Sanges,* 144 U.S. 310, 12 S.Ct. 609, 36 L.Ed. 445 (1892). This prohibition is sensible inasmuch as the Double Jeopardy Clause of the Fifth Amendment (applicable to the states through the Fourteenth Amendment) prohibits a defendant who has been acquitted from being tried again for the same offense.

Notwithstanding the general prohibition on appeals by the prosecution, the prosecution has limited opportunities provided by statute to appeal certain trial court decisions before acquittal, such as unfavorable rulings on pretrial motions. For example, Virginia law provides as follows:

> A petition or appeal from a circuit court appeal may be taken by the Commonwealth only in felony cases, before a jury is impaneled and sworn in a jury trial, or before the court begins to hear or receive evidence or the first witness is sworn, whichever occurs first, in a nonjury trial. The appeal may be taken from:
>
> 1. An order of a circuit court dismissing a warrant, information or indictment, or any count or charge thereof on the ground that a statute upon which it was based is unconstitutional; or
>
> 2. An order of a circuit court prohibiting the use of certain evidence at trial on the grounds that such evidence was obtained in violation of the provisions of the Fourth, Fifth, or Sixth Amendments to the Constitution of the United States or Article I, Sections 8, 10, or 11 of the Constitution of Virginia prohibiting illegal searches and seizures and protecting rights against self-incrimination, provided that the Commonwealth certifies the evidence is essential to the prosecution. Va. Code Ann. § 19.2–398.

The statute adds that the appeal "shall be taken within 30 days after the decision, judgment, or order has been rendered and shall be diligently prosecuted."

Either by statute or rule of court, most states afford similar opportunities for appeals by the prosecution. Similarly, 18 U.S.C.A. § 3731 permits the federal government to appeal an order of a federal district court (a) dismissing an indictment, (b) granting a new trial after judgment or verdict, (c) releasing a defendant before trial or after conviction, or (d) suppressing evidence before the time that the defendant is put in jeopardy. Both the government and the defendant have the right to appeal from a sentence imposed in violation of law, or one that results from an erroneous application of a sentencing guideline or is imposed by the court in violation of the terms of a plea agreement. Appeals by the prosecution from sentencing require prior approval by the office of the Attorney General or Solicitor General. 18 U.S.C.A. § 3742(b).

The constitutional proscription of double jeopardy does not prevent appeals by the prosecutor of pretrial orders because jeopardy does not apply before the impaneling of a jury or the taking of evidence in a nonjury trial. *Crist v. Bretz,* 437 U.S. 28, 98 S.Ct. 2156, 57 L.Ed.2d 24 (1978); *Serfass v. United States,* 420 U.S. 377, 95 S.Ct. 1055; 43 L.Ed.2d 265 (1975).

Trial *de Novo* in Minor Misdemeanor Cases

Most criminal appeals are heard "on the record." This means that the appellate court is asked to scrutinize the official record of the trial for procedural errors that would require reversal of the judgment. Many misdemeanor cases are tried in local courts that are not courts of record; therefore, no record of the proceedings is available for review. Most of these involve summary justice. Trial is before a judge or magistrate without a jury, in what is commonly called a bench trial. Counsel is rarely present, and frequently the only witnesses for the prosecution are police officers. The defendant may or may not choose to testify. Yet persons convicted of misdemeanors are generally entitled to an appeal by law. Where no record has been made of the proceedings, a trial *de novo* (literally, a "new trial") is held in a trial court of superior jurisdiction. In some instances, persons convicted at trial *de novo* may take an appeal to a higher court, but further review of such cases is generally discretionary.

Error Correction and Lawmaking Functions of Appellate Courts

Appellate courts perform dual functions in the criminal process: **error correction** and **lawmaking.** Most criminal appeals are reviewed by intermediate federal or state appellate courts, although in the less populous states, routine appeals are handled by the highest court of the state (see Figure 20.1). In these routine appeals, the primary function of appellate courts is correcting errors made by trial courts. Appellate review

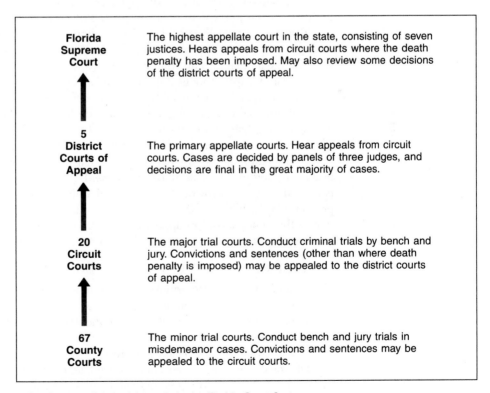

Florida Supreme Court
The highest appellate court in the state, consisting of seven justices. Hears appeals from circuit courts where the death penalty has been imposed. May also review some decisions of the district courts of appeal.

5 District Courts of Appeal
The primary appellate courts. Hear appeals from circuit courts. Cases are decided by panels of three judges, and decisions are final in the great majority of cases.

20 Circuit Courts
The major trial courts. Conduct criminal trials by bench and jury. Convictions and sentences (other than where death penalty is imposed) may be appealed to the district courts of appeal.

67 County Courts
The minor trial courts. Conduct bench and jury trials in misdemeanor cases. Convictions and sentences may be appealed to the circuit courts.

FIGURE 20.1   Criminal Appeals in the Florida Court System.

Sources: West's Fla. Stat. Ann. Const. art. V, §§ 1–6; West's Fla. Stat. Ann. chs. 26, 34, 35.

is designed to ensure that substantive justice has been accomplished under constitutional standards of due process of law. Because of gaps in the statutory law and the inevitable need to interpret both statutory and constitutional provisions, appellate courts in effect must "make law." This lawmaking function is more characteristic of the highest levels of courts than of intermediate appellate tribunals.

The Appellate Process

To the layperson, the jurisdictional requirements and procedures of appellate courts appear complex. Although these procedures vary in detail, they essentially follow the same basic path. In some instances the defendant must first file a motion for a new trial before making an appeal. This is often a *pro forma* measure, but it affords the trial judge an opportunity to review the defendant's claim of error and award a new trial if necessary.

Release of Defendant on Bail Pending Appeal

Federal and state statutes and rules of court usually specify criteria for the release of a convicted defendant pending appeal. Admission to bail after conviction is not a matter of right but is at the discretion of the trial court. A defendant wanting to appeal is not aided by a presumption in favor of release on bail. Principally, the trial judge attempts to determine whether an appeal is taken in good faith and whether it presents a debatable point of law for appellate review. An appeal must not be frivolous or taken for the purpose of delay. *Birge v. State,* 230 S.E.2d 895 (Ga. 1976).

Trial judges typically consider several factors in exercising their discretion to grant or deny bail pending appeal. Among those factors are the defendant's habits and respect for the law, family and community ties, and the severity of punishment imposed. If the term of imprisonment imposed is relatively short, the court may also consider whether the denial of bail would render the defendant's right to appeal meaningless. Rules of criminal procedure generally provide for prompt appellate review of a decision denying bail to a convicted defendant or setting that bail unreasonably high. Absent such procedures, a defendant may seek a writ of habeas corpus.

If the State takes an appeal, the defendant is often released on personal recognizance during the **pendency of the appeal**—that is, while the appeal is being decided. Most states provide for release of defendants pending an appeal by the prosecution. In Illinois, for example, "a defendant shall not be held in jail or to bail during the pendency of an appeal by the State . . . unless there are compelling reasons for his continued detention or being held to bail." Ill. Sup. Ct. Rule 604(a) (3).

RELEASE OF THE DEFENDANT IN FEDERAL APPEALS

Under the Federal Bail Reform Act of 1966 (repealed in 1984), the defendant in a federal court was entitled to bail unless there was "reason to believe that no one or more conditions of release will reasonably assure that the person will not flee, or pose a danger to any other person or any other community." The **Bail Reform Act of 1984,** 18 U.S.C.A. §§ 3141–3150, reversed that presumption of entitlement. Under the 1984 act, the defendant now has the burden of proving an entitlement to bail based on criteria specified in the law. Before granting bail pending appeal, the court must find

1. that the defendant is not likely to flee or pose a danger to the safety of any other person or the community if released;

2. that the appeal is not for the purpose of delay;

3. that the appeal raises a substantial question of law or fact; and

4. that if that substantial question is determined favorably to defendant on appeal, that decision is likely to result in reversal or an order for a new trial of all counts on which imprisonment has been imposed. *United States v. Miller,* 753 F.2d 19, 24 (3d Cir. 1985).

In an earlier topic, we pointed out that the federal government can take an appeal from certain pretrial orders under 18 U.S.C.A. § 3731 or from sentencing or plea agreement violations under 18 U.S.C.A. § 3742(b). Where an appeal is taken under § 3731, the Bail Reform Act ordinarily governs release of the defendant pending the appeal. If the government's appeal is taken under § 3742 and the defendant has been sentenced to imprisonment, the defendant is ordinarily not released pending the appeal.

Right to Counsel on Appeal

An excerpt from *Douglas v. California* appears at the end of the chapter.

As we pointed out in Chapter 17, the United States Supreme Court has interpreted the Constitution to require that indigent defendants be furnished assistance of counsel in criminal prosecutions. To what extent does the Constitution require appointment of counsel for indigent defendants who appeal their convictions to higher courts? In *Douglas v. California,* 372 U.S. 353, 83 S.Ct. 814, 9 L.Ed.2d 811 (1963), the Supreme Court said that states must provide counsel to indigent persons convicted of felonies who exercise their statutory right to appeal. In *Ross v. Moffitt,* 417 U.S. 600, 94 S.Ct. 2437, 41 L.Ed.2d 341 (1974), however, the Supreme Court held that a state's failure to provide counsel to an indigent defendant seeking discretionary review in the state and federal supreme courts did not violate due process or equal protection. Thus, government must provide counsel as a matter of course when defendants have a statutory right to be heard in an appellate court. At later stages of the appeals process, there is no such requirement.

The Supreme Court's decision in *Douglas v. California* produced a tremendous increase in appellate caseloads. Providing counsel at public expense aggravated the problem of **frivolous appeals** (that is, appeals lacking any arguable basis for reversal). In such cases, appointed counsel will often attempt to withdraw.

In *Anders v. California,* 386 U.S. 738, 87 S.Ct. 1396, 18 L.Ed.2d 493 (1967), the Supreme Court invalidated a state rule that allowed appointed counsel to withdraw by merely stating that an appeal had no merit. Reasoning that the right to counsel meant the right to have an effective advocate on appeal, the Court held that appointed counsel could withdraw only after submitting a brief claiming that the appeal was wholly frivolous and referring to any arguable issues. Recently, California developed a new procedure for handling criminal appeals by indigents. An appointed attorney may now write a "no merit brief" summarizing the procedural and factual history of the case. The court orders briefing by counsel only if it finds arguable issues. Therefore, before rejecting the appeal, both counsel and the court have to find the appeal lacking in arguable issues. In January 2000, in *Smith v. Robbins,* 528 U.S. 259, 120 S.Ct. 746, 145 L.Ed.2d 756, the U.S. Supreme Court ruled that such "no-merit brief" procedure satisfies the requirements of *Anders v. California.* The basic *Anders* approach is followed in most jurisdictions, and when an appellate court accepts an ***Anders* brief**, it usually notifies the defendant of the appointed counsel's withdrawal and permits the defendant to file a memorandum pointing to any claim of error. With the proliferation of criminal appeals by indigent defendants, the *Anders* brief has become a commonplace element of appellate procedure.

SELF-REPRESENTATION ON APPEAL

In Chapter 18, we pointed out that it is incumbent on a trial judge to allow self-representation by a defendant who voluntarily and intelligently elects to proceed in the trial court without counsel. *Faretta v. California*, 422 U.S. 806, 95 S.Ct. 2525, 45 L.Ed.2d 562 (1975). Many appellate courts allow convicted defendants to file *pro se* petitions for habeas corpus but generally do not allow defendants to handle direct appeals on a *pro se* basis. After he represented himself before a trial court, the California courts denied Salvador Martinez the right to represent himself in the California Court of Appeal. He obtained review in the U.S. Supreme Court, and on January 12, 2000, the Court upheld California's denial of his right to handle his appeal without counsel. The Court observed that although the Sixth Amendment to the Constitution provides a basis for self-representation at the trial level, it does not include any right to appeal. The Court pointed to significant differences between the trial and appellate stages of a criminal proceeding and emphasized the need for a defendant to have counsel when attempting to overturn a criminal conviction. The Court recognized that states are free to determine whether to allow a defendant to proceed in an appellate court without counsel; nevertheless, it held that a criminal defendant does not have the right under the U.S. Constitution to elect self-representation on a direct appeal from a judgment of conviction. *Martinez v. California Court of Appeal*, 528 U.S. 152, 120 S.Ct. 684, 145 L.Ed.2d 597 (2000).

Filing the Appeal

Once the appellant has determined the correct forum for an appeal or a petition for discretionary review, the process is governed by federal or state rules of appellate procedure. The notice of appeal or petition for review must be filed in the appropriate court within a specified period of time. The time requirement tends to be strictly enforced because this notice or petition confers jurisdiction for the appellate court to act on the case.

Rule 4(b) of the **Federal Rules of Appellate Procedure** provides that an appeal by a defendant from a judgment and sentence in a federal district court must be filed within ten days after the entry of the judgment. Under certain circumstances, the time period may be extended but cannot exceed an additional thirty days. If a defendant makes a timely motion for judgment of acquittal, for a new trial, or for arrest of a judgment, then the **notice of appeal** must be filed within ten days after the trial court enters an order disposing of such motion(s). When an appeal by the government is authorized by statute, the notice of appeal must be filed within thirty days after the entry of judgment.

In state courts, an aggrieved party usually has thirty days after entry of judgment and sentence to file an appeal. For example, Maryland requires that the notice of appeal must be filed within thirty days after the trial court has entered its judgment or denied a motion for a new trial. Md. R. 8–202. The filing of a notice of appeal must be accompanied by the payment of a required filing fee. Indigent defendants may move to proceed *in forma pauperis* ("in the manner of a pauper") to avoid filing fees and other costs associated with the appeal. (Figure 20.2 details the procedures associated with appeals in South Carolina.)

Filing Petitions for Discretionary Review

A defendant whose conviction has been sustained by an intermediate appellate court may petition a court of last resort for discretionary review. In the United States Supreme

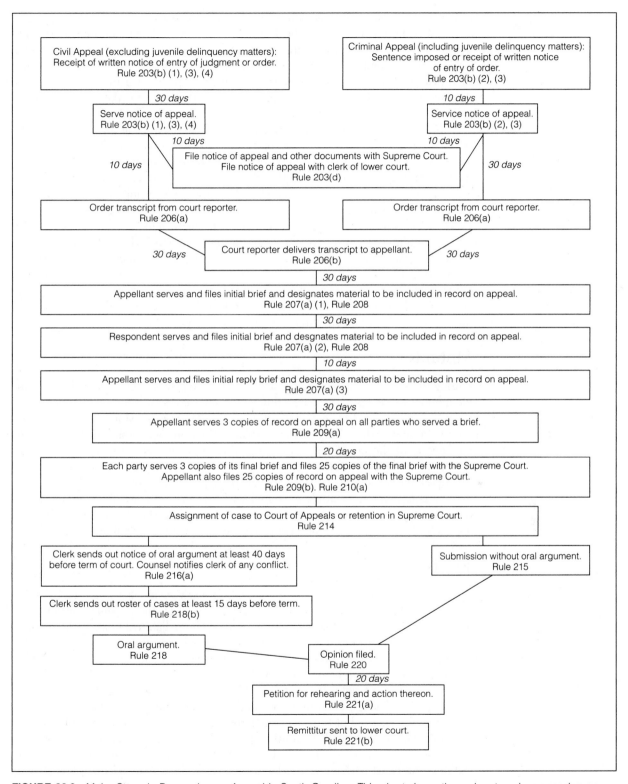

FIGURE 20.2 Major Steps in Processing an Appeal in South Carolina. This chart shows the major steps in processing an appeal under the South Carolina Appellate Court Rules and is intended to provide an overview of the appeals process. Source: Court Rules, Supreme Court of South Carolina, *West's Southeastern Reporter,* August 30, 1990, pages CXXI–CXXII.

Court and most state supreme courts, discretionary review occurs through the grant of a writ of certiorari. Rule 13 of the Rules of the United States Supreme Court states that a "petition for a writ of certiorari . . . shall be in time when it is filed . . . within 90 days after the entry of the judgment" of the lower court. The highest court in each state (usually the state supreme court) may entertain petitions if they are filed within the time prescribed by the court's rules, usually thirty days after the intermediate appellate court enters its decision.

"**Cert petitions,**" as they are commonly called, are granted at the discretion of the reviewing court. In deciding whether to exercise its discretion, the United States Supreme Court evaluates whether a **substantial federal question** is involved. If so, the Court is then interested in whether the petitioner has exhausted all other remedies available. In deciding whether to grant certiorari, the Court follows the rule of four, meaning that at least four of the nine justices must vote to place a case on the docket.

In determining whether to grant review, the high state appellate tribunals usually have unlimited discretion. The U.S. Supreme Court's **rule of four** serves as a model for some state supreme courts; however, others are guided by formal or informal rules in determining whether to "grant cert." Among the criteria frequently employed are whether the intermediate appellate court's decision conflicts with a decision of another intermediate court or the supreme court, is without authoritative precedent, or departs from the essential requirements of the law.

Motions

During the early stages of the appellate process, counsel for both parties frequently file motions in the appellate court. Some motions address substantive issues—for example, a motion asserting legal grounds to dismiss the appeal. More commonly, counsel use motions to draw the court's immediate attention to procedural matters outside the routine of the appellate process. For example, counsel may request additional time to meet deadlines for filing petitions and briefs. Occasionally, counsel will move for expedited consideration of an appeal. By appropriate motions, separate appeals may be consolidated; multiple appeals may be severed. Ordinarily, filing an appeal does not stay the judgment or sentence. However, on a showing of good cause, an appellate court may stay a judgment or sentence pending resolution of the appeal.

Briefs

After a notice of appeal or a petition for discretionary review has been filed, a series of procedural steps are set in motion. It is incumbent on the appellant or petitioner to have the clerk of the trial court forward to the appellate tribunal certified copies of pertinent records and transcripts of testimony relevant to the issues to be raised on appeal. Beyond this, procedures vary somewhat, depending largely on whether the appeal is one of right or whether the defendant is seeking discretionary relief.

In an appeal of right, the appellant files a **brief** summarizing the legal posture and the factual background of the case in the lower tribunal and the legal authorities that support a reversal of the trial court's ruling. Briefs are the principal instruments used to persuade the appellate court to reverse, affirm, or modify the decision being appealed. They are usually heavily laden with citations to constitutional provisions, statutes, and court decisions regarded as persuasive by the advocates. The extent of background information contained in the briefs depends on the points to be presented to the appellate court. The appellee is permitted to respond to the appellant's contentions by filing an **answer brief,** and the appellant is usually permitted a **reply**

brief. The whole process resembles the order of a classroom debate, where the affirmative presents its case, followed by the negative and a rebuttal by the affirmative.

Where a petitioner seeks discretionary review, the appellate court must first decide whether to accept or deny the request to take jurisdiction. If the court determines to proceed on the petition, it will order all affected parties to furnish the court a written response. As in an appeal of right, often the petitioner is permitted to file a reply to that response. The petition and response may be supplemented by such briefs as the court requires.

The format and submission of briefs must adhere closely to the requirements of the particular jurisdiction. Counsel must always furnish copies of briefs and other materials to their adversaries.

Oral Argument

After briefs have been submitted and reviewed by the appellate court, an **oral argument** may be held where counsel for both parties appear. Typically, appellate courts conduct oral arguments in about half the cases they decide. During oral argument, counsel for both parties summarize their positions orally and then respond to questions from the bench.

The appellate rules of courts in many jurisdictions set out the time allowed for oral argument. For example, as Rule 24 of the Rhode Island Rules of Appellate Procedure stipulates, "Counsel on each side will be allowed a period not in excess of thirty minutes for presentation of argument, and a period not in excess of ten minutes will be allowed the moving party for reply." As Rule 28 of the U.S. Supreme Court provides, "Unless the Court directs otherwise, each side is allowed one-half hour for argument." Rule 34(d) of the U.S. Court of Appeals for the Fourth Circuit allows either 15 or 20 minutes, depending on the type of appeal. Rather than stipulating a specific time, rules in some federal and state jurisdictions provide that the appellate court will specify the times for oral argument on the court calendar.

The Judicial Conference

Appellate judges customarily confer about disposition of appeals. The **judicial conference** is regarded as an essential part of the collegial process that distinguishes the appellate role from that of the trial court. If there has been oral argument, it is common for the panel of judges who heard the case to confer shortly thereafter. At that time the panel frequently attempts to determine the disposition of the appeal but, in some instances, finds it necessary to further canvass the record or call on counsel or the court's own staff lawyers for additional legal research. Where there has been no oral argument, the panel of judges assigned to the case usually confers after each judge has reviewed the briefs, pertinent records, and the results of any research assignments given to the court's legal staff.

Judgment of the Court

Essentially, an appellate court has three options in addressing a case before it. First, it may dismiss the appeal. This is uncommon in appeals of right, unless the appeal is untimely. Dismissal is more common in cases of discretionary review. For example, the United States Supreme Court will sometimes dismiss a petition for certiorari as having been improvidently granted, even after the case has been fully argued. When an appeal or cert petition is dismissed, the judgment of the lower court remains undisturbed.

The second option of the appellate court is to **affirm** the decision being reviewed, which preserves the judgment of the lower court. The third option is to **reverse** the judgment of the lower court. A reversal is usually accompanied by an order to **remand** the case to the lower court for further proceedings consistent with the higher court's opinion. In the criminal context, this may mean the defendant receives a new trial or new sentencing hearing. When a court of last resort remands a case to an intermediate appellate court, the latter must reconsider the case based on the higher court's decision.

Appellate Court Opinions

After an appellate court has arrived at a decision, the court will issue an opinion announcing its decision. Some opinions simply announce the court's decision; others are quite lengthy in considering the arguments of counsel and articulating the reasons for the court's decision. Opinions are generally prepared by an individual judge or justice. If responsibility for preparation of an opinion has not been previously given to one judge, that responsibility is usually assigned at conference by the senior judge or the senior judge voting with the majority of the panel.

There are two basic types of appellate court opinions: *per curiam* and signed. A *per curiam* **opinion** represents the appellate court as a whole; it is not attributed to any individual judge or group of judges on the court. More commonly the decision of the appellate court is announced in an **opinion of the court** authored by one judge and joined by other judges constituting a majority. A judge who disagrees with the decision of the court may write a **dissenting opinion.** A judge who agrees with the court's decision but wants to address or emphasize certain arguments not addressed or emphasized in the opinion of the court may write a separate **concurring opinion.** Sometimes, a separate opinion is listed as **concurring in the judgment** only, meaning that it supports the decision of the court but for reasons other than those articulated in the court's opinion.

Publication of Appellate Decisions

Most decisions of appellate courts in America are published in books known as **reporters.** Access to published opinions is discussed in some detail in Appendix A. The publication of appellate decisions plays an important role in developing the law because judges and lawyers regularly consult the case reporters for guidance in pending cases.

Motions for Rehearing

Rules of appellate procedure uniformly permit the filing of a motion asking the appellate court to reconsider its decision in a given case. A **motion for rehearing** is designed to address some misstatement of material fact or to direct the court's attention to an overlooked or misapprehended proposition of law. In the United States courts of appeals and in many state appellate courts, where cases are decided by panels of judges, a party may request that all judges of the court participate in an *en banc* **rehearing.** The likelihood of an appellate court granting a motion for *en banc* rehearing is greater when there are conflicting opinions between or among panels of judges within the court. Appellate courts view many motions for rehearing as little more than attempts by dissatisfied parties to have another chance to persuade the court of their position. Accordingly, motions for rehearing are seldom granted.

Postconviction Relief

Normally, an appeal of a lower court decision must be made in a timely manner, usually within thirty days after that court's judgment or sentence. Petitions for certiorari (or other forms of discretionary review) are also subject to time limits. Yet incarcerated criminals may seek review of their convictions long after their rights to appeal have been exhausted or expired by means of a mechanism known as the writ of habeas corpus. It is available in the federal courts and in all fifty state judicial systems.

Habeas corpus is a Latin term meaning "you have the body." In law, it refers to a writ issued by a court to a person who is holding another in custody, requiring that the former show cause for holding the latter. Habeas corpus has roots deep in the common law. Blackstone called it "the most celebrated writ in the English law." 3 W. Blackstone, *Commentaries* 129. The framers of the American Constitution explicitly recognized habeas corpus as a fundamental right of citizens by declaring that "[t]he Privilege of the Writ of Habeas Corpus shall not be suspended unless when in Cases of Rebellion or Invasion the public Safety may require it." U.S. Const., Art. 1, Sec. 9. Only once in our history, during the Civil War, was the writ of habeas corpus suspended throughout the federal courts. This thoroughgoing suspension was subsequently declared unconstitutional. *Ex parte Milligan*, 71 U.S. (4 Wall.) 2, 18 L.Ed. 281 (1866).

Challenging State Court Convictions in Federal Court

The United States Supreme Court can review only a minute proportion of the thousands of petitions for certiorari through which persons convicted in state courts challenge their convictions on federal constitutional grounds. In recent decades, **federal habeas corpus review** of state criminal convictions has become a common form of appellate procedure. It has also greatly multiplied the opportunities for persons convicted of state offenses to obtain relief. Consequently, it has become the focus of considerable controversy.

The Judiciary Act of 1789, 1 Stat. 82 (1789), recognized the power of federal courts to issue writs of habeas corpus only for federal prisoners. In 1867 federal law was amended, 14 Stat. 385, 386, to allow federal courts to entertain habeas petitions from state prisoners who allege that their incarceration violates provisions of the U.S. Constitution or federal statutes or treaties. The federal law on habeas corpus currently provides the following:

> The Supreme Court, a Justice thereof, a circuit judge, or a district court shall entertain an application for a writ of habeas corpus in behalf of a person in custody pursuant to the judgment of a State court only on the ground that he is in custody in violation of the Constitution or laws or treaties of the United States. 28 U.S.C.A. § 2254(a).

Before the twentieth century, the federal habeas corpus jurisdiction was seldom used to review state criminal convictions. When habeas corpus was granted, it was merely to ascertain that the state trial court had jurisdiction over the person being tried. In *Frank v. Mangum*, 237 U.S. 309, 35 S.Ct. 582, 59 L.Ed. 969 (1915), the Supreme Court broadened federal habeas corpus review to ensure that states supplied some "corrective process" whereby criminal defendants could seek to vindicate their federal constitutional rights. In 1953 the Court held that federal courts could use habeas corpus review to readjudicate federal constitutional issues that had been addressed in state court proceedings. *Brown v. Allen*, 344 U.S. 443, 73 S.Ct. 397, 97 L.Ed. 469 (1953).

Federal law had long provided that federal habeas corpus relief was available only to state prisoners who had exhausted all available remedies in the state courts. In 1963 the Supreme Court held that a state prisoner did not have to take a direct appeal to the state supreme court to seek federal habeas corpus review. Nor was the prisoner barred from raising constitutional issues in federal court merely because the issues had not been raised on direct appeal in state courts. *Fay v. Noia,* 372 U.S. 391, 83 S.Ct. 822, 9 L.Ed.2d 837 (1963).

The Supreme Court's efforts to broaden the availability of federal habeas corpus review coincided with its expansion of the constitutional rights of the accused. No doubt, the Court was initially reluctant to depend on state courts to implement these expanded rights, so it broadened the power of the federal district courts to review state criminal convictions. This resulted in numerous state convictions being overturned by the federal courts, often on Fourth or Fifth Amendment grounds. Indeed, many observers came to see state criminal trials merely as precursors to inevitable federal intervention.

Supreme Court Restrictions of Federal Habeas Corpus Relief

A growing criticism of federal court intervention, coupled with the increasing professionalism of the state judiciaries, persuaded the Supreme Court to restrict access to federal habeas corpus relief. During the 1970s, a more conservative Supreme Court began to narrow access to federal habeas corpus relief. In a seminal case, *Stone v. Powell,* 428 U.S. 465, 96 S.Ct. 3037, 49 L.Ed.2d 1067 (1976), the Court held that state prisoners could not use federal habeas corpus hearings to challenge searches and seizures where they had been provided an opportunity for full and fair litigation of a Fourth Amendment claim in the state courts.

Despite *Stone v. Powell,* federal habeas corpus review remains available to state prisoners seeking to challenge their convictions on a variety of constitutional grounds. For instance, the Supreme Court has said that federal habeas corpus review must remain available to state prisoners alleging racial discrimination in their indictments or convictions, regardless of their opportunity to raise such objections in the state courts. *Rose v. Mitchell,* 443 U.S. 545, 99 S.Ct. 2993, 61 L.Ed.2d 739 (1979). In another significant decision in 1979, *Jackson v. Virginia,* 443 U.S. 307, 99 S.Ct. 2781, 61 L.Ed.2d 560, the Court held that a federal court reviewing a state conviction on habeas corpus must consider whether any reasonable trier of fact could have found a defendant guilty beyond a reasonable doubt. Before *Jackson,* federal courts would not reverse state convictions for insufficient evidence if there was "any evidence" of the defendant's guilt.

In *Engle v. Isaac,* 456 U.S. 107, 102 S.Ct. 1558, 71 L.Ed.2d 783 (1982), the Supreme Court refused to allow a state prisoner to use federal habeas corpus to challenge a questionable jury instruction to which he failed to object during trial. Other decisions of the Court during the 1980s chipped away at the Court's earlier expansive interpretations of federal habeas corpus relief. See, for example, *Kuhlmann v. Wilson,* 477 U.S. 436, 106 S.Ct. 2616, 91 L.Ed.2d 364 (1986); *Straight v. Wainwright,* 476 U.S. 1132, 106 S.Ct. 2004, 90 L.Ed.2d 683 (1986).

During the early 1990s, the Supreme Court continued the trend toward limiting access to federal habeas corpus. In 1991 the Court said that Warren McCleskey, a prisoner on death row in Georgia, had abused the writ of habeas corpus when he filed a second federal habeas corpus petition. *McCleskey v. Zant,* 499 U.S. 467, 111 S.Ct. 1454, 113 L.Ed.2d 517 (1991). In the *McCleskey* case, the Court held that a state need not prove that a petitioner deliberately abandoned a constitutional claim in his or her first habeas corpus petition for the petitioner to be barred from raising the claim in a subsequent petition. The Court thus moved away from the "deliberate abandonment" standard it had previously articulated in *Sanders v. United States,* 373 U.S. 1, 83 S.Ct. 1068, 10 L.Ed.2d 148 (1963).

Similarly, in *Keeney v. Tamayo-Reyes,* 504 U.S. 1, 112 S.Ct. 1715, 118 L.Ed.2d 318 (1992), the Court overruled another earlier habeas corpus decision, *Townsend v. Sain,* 372 U.S. 293, 83 S.Ct. 745, 9 L.Ed.2d 770 (1963). In *Townsend,* the Court had held that a petitioner could challenge a state conviction despite a failure to develop a material fact in state proceedings unless it was determined that the petitioner deliberately bypassed the opportunity to develop the fact in the state courts. In *Keeney v. Tamayo-Reyes,* supra, the Court held that a petitioner's failure to develop a claim in state court proceedings should be excused only if he or she can show that a fundamental miscarriage of justice would result from failure to hold a federal evidentiary hearing.

The Supreme Court's decisions in *McCleskey v. Zant* and *Keeney v. Tamayo-Reyes* came when many in Congress were calling for legislative restrictions on federal habeas corpus. Both the Supreme Court and Congress were responding to a widespread perception that state prisoners were being afforded excessive opportunities to challenge their convictions in federal courts. Indeed, some conservative commentators questioned the need for federal postconviction review of state criminal cases altogether. Although federal habeas corpus has been subject to abuse by state prisoners, eliminating this aspect of federal jurisdiction altogether would remove some of the pressure that has led to an increased awareness of and appreciation for defendants' rights in the state courts. Indeed, in the *McCleskey* case, the Supreme Court expressed a commitment to the continued efficacy of habeas corpus to prevent miscarriages of justice in the state courts.

In 1993 the Supreme Court handed down two decisions restricting federal habeas corpus review of state criminal convictions. In *Herrera v. Collins,* 506 U.S. 390, 113 S.Ct. 853, 122 L.Ed.2d 203 (1993), the Court held that a belated claim of innocence does not entitle a state prisoner on death row to a federal district court hearing before being executed. In *Brecht v. Abrahamson,* 507 U.S. 619, 113 S.Ct. 1710, 123 L.Ed.2d 353 (1993), the Court ruled that federal district courts may not overturn state criminal convictions unless the petitioner can show that he or she suffered "actual prejudice" from the errors cited in the habeas corpus petition. Previously, the state carried the burden of proving beyond a reasonable doubt that any constitutional error committed during or before trial was "harmless"—that is, not prejudicial to the defendant. *Brecht v. Abrahamson* had the effect of shifting the burden of proof from the state to the petitioner in a federal habeas corpus hearing.

Congressional Modifications of the Federal Habeas Corpus Procedure

On April 24, 1996, President Clinton signed into law the **Antiterrorism and Effective Death Penalty Act of 1996.** One provision of this statute curtails second habeas corpus petitions by state prisoners who have already filed such petitions in federal court. Under the new statute, any second or subsequent habeas petition must meet a particularly high standard and must pass through a "gatekeeping" function exercised by the U.S. Courts of Appeals. The appellate court must grant a motion giving the inmate permission to file the petition in a district court; denial of this motion is not appealable to the Supreme Court. 18 U.S.C.A. § 2244(b)(3)

An excerpt from *Felker v. Turpin* appears at the end of the chapter.

In *Felker v. Turpin,* 518 U.S. 651, 116 S.Ct. 2333, 135 L.Ed.2d 827 (1996), an inmate awaiting execution in Georgia challenged the constitutionality of this provision, posing two constitutional objections: (1) that the new law amounted to an unconstitutional "suspension" of the writ of habeas corpus and (2) that the prohibition against Supreme Court review of a circuit court's denial of permission to file a subsequent habeas petition is an unconstitutional interference with the Supreme Court's jurisdiction as defined in Article III of the Constitution.

In a unanimous decision rendered less than one month after the case was argued, the Supreme Court rejected these challenges and upheld the statute. In a "saving construction" of the statute, the Court interpreted the law in such a way as to preserve the right of state prisoners to file habeas petitions directly in the Supreme Court. However, the Court stated that it would exercise this jurisdiction only in "exceptional circumstances."

It should be noted that the provision at issue in *Felker* was but one of several restrictions on habeas corpus petitions embodied in the Antiterrorism Act. Indeed, other challenges to various sections of the law are working their way through the lower federal courts. The Supreme Court will likely address these issues in the near future. The enactment of "habeas corpus reform," and the Court's refusal to invalidate it, indicate the existence of a clear consensus in the national government that "abuse of the writ" of habeas corpus must be curtailed.

SUPREME COURT PERSPECTIVE

O'Sullivan v. Boerckel, 526 U.S. 838, 119 S.Ct. 1728, 144 L.Ed.2d 1 (1999)

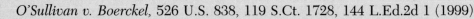

In 1977 Darren Boerckel was convicted in an Illinois court of rape, burglary, and aggravated battery. The Illinois Appellate Court affirmed the conviction, and the Illinois Supreme Court denied Boerckel's petition for discretionary review. Boerckel then initiated a federal habeas corpus action in which he raised six federal constitutional claims. Under 28 U.S.C. § 2254(c), federal habeas corpus relief is available to state prisoners only after they have exhausted their remedies in state court. The federal district court denied the petition, finding that Boerckel had "procedurally defaulted" his first three claims by failing to include them in his petition for discretionary review to the Illinois Supreme Court. On appeal, the Seventh Circuit reversed, holding that filing for discretionary review by the state's highest court is not necessary to exhaust one's state court remedies for purposes of the federal habeas corpus statute. Reviewing the case on certiorari, the Supreme Court reversed again, holding that a state prisoner must present his claims to a state supreme court in a petition for discretionary review when such review is part of the State's "ordinary appellate review procedure." Failure to do so constitutes procedural default and precludes these issues being raised on federal habeas review.

Justice O'Connor delivered the opinion of the Court, saying in part:

"Because the exhaustion doctrine is designed to give the state courts a full and fair opportunity to resolve federal constitutional claims before those claims are presented to the federal courts, we conclude that state prisoners must give the state courts one full opportunity to resolve any constitutional issues by invoking one complete round of the State's established appellate review process. Here, Illinois's established, normal appellate review procedure is a two-tiered system. Comity, in these circumstances, dictates that Boerckel use the State's established appellate review procedures before he presents his claims to a federal court. . . . [A] petition for discretionary review in Illinois's Supreme Court is a normal, simple, and established part of the State's appellate review process. In the words of the statute, state prisoners have 'the right . . . to raise' their claims through a petition for discretionary review in the state's highest court. . . . Granted, as Boerckel contends, he has no right to *review* in the Illinois Supreme Court, but he does have a 'right . . . to raise' his claims before that court. That is all § 2254(c) requires."

Right to Counsel in Federal Habeas Corpus Cases

Nearly half of federal habeas corpus petitions allege some deprivation of the right to counsel. The Supreme Court has shown greater receptivity to habeas corpus cases where right to counsel is at issue. A good recent example is *McFarland v. Scott*, 512 U.S. 849, 114 S.Ct. 2568, 129 L.Ed.2d 666 (1994). This case involved a convicted murderer on death row in Texas who asked a federal judge to issue a stay of execution so that he could obtain a lawyer to prepare a federal habeas corpus petition. The judge denied the stay, ruling that because the inmate had not yet filed a habeas corpus petition, the federal courts had no jurisdiction over his case. But the Supreme Court stayed the execution and ruled that an indigent inmate must be provided counsel if the inmate wants to file a habeas corpus petition. The Court also said that lower federal courts are empowered to delay executions until inmates have had an opportunity to file their federal habeas corpus petitions.

Collateral Attack in State Court

The constitutional rights of criminal defendants were greatly expanded in the 1960s as a result of the Supreme Court's decisions "nationalizing" criminal procedure. During those years the states began to review the efficacy of the writ of habeas corpus as a basis for permitting challenges to judgments and sentences subsequent to conclusion of a direct appeal. As a result, most states adopted statutes or court rules that permit a postappeal challenge to an illegal conviction or sentence. These procedures, known as **collateral attack** or collateral relief, provide a mechanism to permit review of judgments and sentences imposed in violation of the federal or state constitutions.

North Carolina statutes that provide opportunities for collateral relief to convicted defendants appear typical of the grounds for postconviction relief available to defendants convicted in state courts. The grounds that a defendant may assert by a motion for collateral relief include the following:

- the trial court lacked jurisdiction over the defendant;
- the defendant's conviction was obtained in violation of the United States or North Carolina Constitutions;
- that a significant change has occurred in the law applied in the proceedings leading to the defendant's conviction or sentence and such changed law must be applied retroactively;
- the defendant's sentence is illegal; or the defendant is entitled to release for having fully served the sentence imposed.

In addition, within a reasonable time after discovery, a defendant may assert that evidence is available which was unknown or unavailable to the defendant at trial and which has a direct and material bearing on the defendant's eligibility for the death penalty or the defendant's guilt or innocence. West's N.C.G.S.A. § 15A–1415.

Ineffective Counsel as a Basis for Postconviction Relief

The Supreme Court has recognized that the right to counsel means little unless counsel provides a defendant effective representation. *McMann v. Richardson*, 397 U.S. 759, 90 S.Ct. 1441, 25 L.Ed.2d 763 (1970). Failure of counsel, whether appointed or retained, to be an effective advocate for the defendant constitutes a basis to award a defendant a new trial. *Cuyler v. Sullivan*, 446 U.S. 335, 100 S.Ct. 1708, 64 L.Ed.2d

333 (1980). Some examples of ineffective representation where relief might well be afforded include failure of counsel to present evidence favorable to the accused, failure to challenge the admissibility of evidence presented by the prosecution, and failure to challenge prosecutorial misconduct.

The requirement to furnish counsel to indigent defendants has probably contributed to a rise in claims of **ineffective assistance of counsel.** Indigent defendants are sometimes distrustful of public defenders and other appointed counsel. If convicted, these defendants may be more likely to feel that their representation was ineffective compared with that provided by privately retained attorneys.

A defendant's claim of error or deficiency in counsel's performance is rarely challenged in the trial court, so it is not generally subject to being raised on direct appeal. But in some instances where the record of the trial shows on its face that counsel was ineffective, an appellate court will consider the issue on direct appeal. For example, in *Eure v. State,* 764 So.2d 798 (Fla. App. 2000), on a direct appeal from the defendant's conviction for possession and sale of cocaine, a Florida appellate court reversed the defendant's conviction because it found the defendant's counsel was ineffective for failing to object to a series of improper arguments by the prosecutor.

In *Strickland v. Washington,* 466 U.S. 668, 104 S.Ct. 2052, 80 L.Ed.2d 674 (1984), the Supreme Court articulated a uniform constitutional standard for determining the issue of ineffective counsel:

> First, the defendant must show that counsel's performance was deficient. This requires showing that counsel made errors so serious that counsel was not functioning as the "counsel" guaranteed the defendant by the Sixth Amendment. Second, the defendant must show that the deficient performance prejudiced the defense. This requires showing that counsel's errors were so serious as to deprive the defendant of a fair trial, a trial whose result is reliable. Unless a defendant makes both showings, it cannot be said that the conviction . . . resulted from a breakdown in the adversary process that renders the result unreliable. 466 U.S. at 687, 104 S.Ct. at 2063, 80 L.Ed.2d at 693.

THE LAWYER'S FAILURE TO FILE NOTICE OF APPEAL: INEFFECTIVE ASSISTANCE OF COUNSEL?

A question sometimes arises whether the failure of a defendant's lawyer to file a notice of appeal constitutes ineffective counsel. In *Roe v. Flores-Ortega,* 528 U.S. 470, 120 S.Ct. 1029, 145 L.Ed.2d 985 (2000), the U.S. Supreme Court rejected any bright line rule that counsel must always consult with a defendant regarding an appeal. Rather, the Court held that counsel has a constitutionally imposed duty to consult with the defendant about taking an appeal where there is either a rational basis for an appeal or the defendant has demonstrated to counsel an interest in appealing.

Nonjudicial Remedies Available to Persons Convicted of Crimes

Under the English common law, appeal to the Crown predated appeal to higher courts as the remedy for an unjust conviction or unreasonable sentence. In addition, because a crime was viewed as an offense against the Crown, the monarch possessed the authority to forgive the wrongdoer or grant **clemency.** In contemporary America, the appeal to executive authority remains as a carryover from the common law and a supplement to judicial review.

Article 2, Section 2, Clause 1 of the United States Constitution states that the president "shall have Power to grant Reprieves and Pardons for Offences against the United States, except in Cases of Impeachment." This broad power includes the right to commute sentences, remit fines and penalties, and even grant conditional pardons. Indeed, the presidential **pardon** may be issued before conviction, as was amply demonstrated in 1974, when President Gerald Ford pardoned former President Richard Nixon for his role in the Watergate scandal. It was demonstrated again in December 1992, when President George Bush granted a pardon to Caspar Weinberger, the former Secretary of Defense, and five others who allegedly were involved in the much-publicized controversy concerning the trading of arms for hostages. However, the controversies that followed President Ford's pardon of Richard Nixon and President Bush's pardon of Caspar Weinberger paled in comparison to President Clinton's last-minute pardon of Marc Rich, a fugitive from a 1983 indictment for federal income tax evasion. The Rich pardon, which was given without the normal consultation with the Department of Justice, prompted congressional hearings and an investigation by federal prosecutors. Investigators looked into the possibility that Rich purchased a presidential pardon by passing money through his former wife, who made large contributions both to the Clinton presidential library foundation and to Hillary Clinton's 2000 Senate campaign.

The Supreme Court has said that

> [t]he plain purpose of the broad power conferred . . . was to allow . . . the President to "forgive" the convicted person in part or entirely, to reduce a penalty in terms of a specified number of years, or to alter it with conditions which are in themselves constitutionally unobjectionable. *Schick v. Reed*, 419 U.S. 256, 266, 95 S.Ct. 379, 385, 42 L.Ed.2d 430, 438–439 (1974).

A full presidential pardon totally restores any civil rights the recipient may have lost as a result of conviction. In effect, the full pardon makes an individual as innocent as if the crime had never been committed. *Ex parte Garland*, 71 U.S. (4 Wall.) 333, 18 L.Ed. 366 (1866).

Either by constitutional or statutory provisions, executive authorities in all fifty states are likewise granted broad powers to pardon and commute sentences of persons convicted of violations of state criminal law. In many states, the pardoning power is vested exclusively in the governor. In a few states, the governor is limited to granting pardons approved by a state commission. In some states, the pardoning power is vested entirely in a state commission. One high-profile case of clemency was that of Jean Harris, former headmistress of a girls' school who was convicted in 1980 of killing Dr. Herman Tarnower, creator of the Scarsdale Diet. After serving about twelve years of a fifteen-years-to-life sentence, Ms. Harris was granted clemency by Governor Mario Cuomo of New York in December 1992.

Conclusion

Under the early English common law, the right to appeal was nonexistent. Eventually, through court decisions and statutes, defendants gained the right to appeal criminal convictions. In America, statutes and judicial decisions have created numerous opportunities for appeal in criminal cases. Federal and state statutes guarantee at least one appeal of right to defendants who are convicted after entering a plea of not guilty. Beyond these appeals of right, defendants may seek review from higher courts by filing petitions for certiorari or discretionary review. Finally, the historic writ of habeas corpus provides an avenue of postconviction relief in state and federal tribunals. In many states, postconviction relief has become structured under criteria specified by statute or rules of court.

Recently, there has been much criticism of the seemingly inexhaustible routes of appellate review. Some would argue that the numerous opportunities for defendants to obtain review of their convictions by higher courts result in unnecessary delays in dispensing justice. On the premise that "justice is due the accuser as well as the accused," critics would cite the old aphorism that "justice delayed is justice denied."

Certainly, an abundance of cases supports the criticism. Many involve the controversial issue of capital punishment. Such cases attract the media's attention and arouse the public. There is an unfortunate tendency to assume that such cases are typical and that the appellate process is incapable of moving expeditiously. The public is generally unaware of the thousands of appeals that are resolved in a timely manner for each one that becomes a case study in delay.

Perhaps as a response to such criticism, the United States Supreme Court has narrowed the access of state prisoners to federal postconviction relief. Today, federal habeas corpus review tends to focus largely on capital cases. Yet substantial opportunities remain for prisoners to seek postconviction review by state and federal tribunals. One of the most common issues raised on postconviction review is whether defendants received effective assistance of counsel at trial.

Although it must be conceded that the appellate process does often delay the imposition of criminal punishments, such delay must be weighed against our society's deep and historic commitment to fundamental fairness. In America, criminal law and criminal procedure are guided by due process values as well as by society's need for crime control.

Key Terms

trial *de novo*	notice of appeal
appeal of right	*in forma pauperis*
discretionary review	"cert petitions"
postconviction relief	substantial federal question
writ of habeas corpus	rule of four
writ of error	brief
writs of certiorari	answer brief
appellant	reply brief
appellee	oral argument
petitioner	judicial conference
respondent	affirm
fundamental errors	reverse
assignments of error	remand
miscarriage of justice	*per curiam* opinion
doctrine of harmless error	opinion of the court
error correction	dissenting opinion
lawmaking	concurring opinion
pendency of the appeal	concurring in the judgment
Bail Reform Act of 1984	reporters
frivolous appeals	motion for rehearing
Anders brief	*en banc* rehearing
Federal Rules of Appellate Procedure	federal habeas corpus review

Antiterrorism and Effective Death
     Penalty Act of 1996
collateral attack

ineffective assistance of counsel
clemency
pardon

Web-Based Research Activity

1. Locate your state's on-line resources on the web. Find the opinions of the appellate court or courts that review routine criminal appeals.
2. Determine whether that court's opinions are posted online. If so, examine the ten or twenty most recent posted decisions. Categorize these decisions by the issue(s) presented on appeal.
3. From this sample, what kinds of issues are being raised in criminal appeals in your state? How do they compare with the kinds of issues discussed in this chapter?

Questions for Thought and Discussion

1. What court or courts in your state have jurisdiction to hear appeals from felony convictions? What changes, if any, would you propose for your state's system of appellate courts?
2. Is the right to appeal a necessary concomitant of due process of law? In the absence of statutory rights to appeal, would the current Supreme Court find a constitutional right to appeal implicit in the due process requirements of the Constitution?
3. What new or revised procedures would expedite the resolution of criminal appeals? Would such procedures detract from the fair and deliberative review essential to determine whether the decision of the trial court in a criminal case was arrived at fairly and accurately?
4. In addition to determining whether a sentence imposed on a convicted defendant is within the statutory bounds, do you think an appellate court is an appropriate forum to reconsider the reasonableness of the sentence imposed by the trial court?
5. How has the "nationalization" of the criminal law that occurred through decisions of the U.S. Supreme Court during the 1960s and 1970s affected the appellate process?
6. The U.S. Supreme Court has recognized a constitutional right to represent oneself in a criminal trial. Could a person who insisted on self-representation at trial later challenge his or her conviction by claiming ineffective assistance of counsel?
7. Where a defendant has had an opportunity for a full and fair review of his or her trial through an appeal, what justifies the availability of additional avenues of review through collateral attack?
8. After studying briefs submitted by counsel and hearing oral arguments in a proceeding open to the public, appellate judges retire to privately discuss and decide the merits of criminal appeals. Should these deliberations be open to the public? Why or why not?

Problems for Discussion and Solution

1. John Dunnit was convicted of aggravated sexual battery and was sentenced to state prison. After exhausting his appellate remedies in the state courts, Dunnit filed a federal habeas corpus application, which was denied. Dunnit appealed the denial of relief to the federal circuit court and was denied relief. Dunnit filed a second federal habeas corpus petition after President Clinton signed the Antiterrorism and Effective Death Penalty Act of 1996 amending the federal habeas corpus statute. How does this new law affect Dunnit's case?

2. Culp Able was convicted of murder in state court. Central to the state's case was a confession that Able uttered before being given his *Miranda* warnings. The trial judge received the confession in evidence over the defendant's objection, and Able was convicted. On appeal, the state intermediate appellate court and state supreme court considered and rejected Able's challenge to the admissibility of the confession. Then Able filed an application for federal habeas corpus relief, citing only the alleged *Miranda* violation as a basis for the reversal of his conviction. Relying on *Stone v. Powell* (1976), the state argues that the petition should be dismissed because Able was afforded "a full and fair opportunity to litigate his Fifth Amendment claim in the state courts." If you were the federal district judge, how would you rule? Should Able get his day in federal court?

EXCERPTS FROM JUDICIAL DECISIONS

Douglas v. California

Supreme Court of the United States, 1963.
372 U.S. 353, 83 S.Ct. 814, 9 L.Ed.2d 811.

[This case deals with the right of an indigent defendant to have appointed counsel to assist in an appeal.]

Mr. Justice DOUGLAS delivered the opinion of the Court.

Petitioners, Bennie Will Meyes and William Douglas, were jointly tried and convicted in a California court on an information charging them with thirteen felonies. A single public defender was appointed to represent them. At the commencement of the trial, the defender moved for a continuance, stating that the case was very complicated, that he was not as prepared as he felt he should be because he was handling a different defense every day, and that there was a conflict of interest between the petitioners requiring the appointment of separate counsel for each of them. This motion was denied. Thereafter, petitioners dismissed the defender, claim-

ing he was unprepared, and again renewed motions for separate counsel and for a continuance. These motions also were denied, and petitioners were ultimately convicted by a jury of all 13 felonies, which included robbery, assault with a deadly weapon, and assault with intent to commit murder. Both were given prison terms. Both appealed as of right to the California District Court of Appeal. That court affirmed their convictions. Both Meyes and Douglas then petitioned for further discretionary review in the California Supreme Court, but their petitions were denied without a hearing.

Although several questions are presented in the petition for certiorari, we addressed ourselves to only one of them. The record shows that petitioners requested, and were denied, the assistance of counsel on appeal, even though it plainly appeared they were indigents. In denying petitioners' requests, the

California District Court of Appeal stated that it had "gone through" the record and had come to the conclusion that "no good whatever could be served by appointment of counsel." . . . The District Court of Appeal was acting in accordance with a California rule of criminal procedure which provides that state appellate courts, upon the request of an indigent for counsel, may make "an independent investigation of the record and determine whether it would be of advantage to the defendant or helpful to the appellate court to have counsel appointed. . . . After such investigation, appellate courts should appoint counsel if in their opinion it would be helpful to the defendant or the court, and should deny the appointment of counsel only if in their judgment such appointment would be of no value to either the defendant or the court."

. . . [U]nder [California's] present practice the type of an appeal a person is afforded in the District Court of Appeal hinges upon whether or not he can pay for the assistance of counsel. If he can, the appellate court passes on the merits of his case only after having the full benefit of written briefs and oral argument by counsel. If he cannot, the appellate court is forced to prejudge the merits before it can even determine whether counsel should be provided. At this stage in the proceedings only the barren record speaks for the indigent, and, unless the printed pages show that an injustice has been committed, he is forced to go without a champion on appeal. Any real chance he may have had of showing that his appeal has hidden merit is deprived him when the court decides on an *ex parte* examination of the record that the assistance of counsel is not required.

We are not here concerned with problems that might arise from the denial of counsel for the preparation of a petition for discretionary or mandatory review beyond the stage in the appellate process at which the claims have once been presented by a lawyer and passed upon by an appellate court. We are dealing only with the first appeal, granted as a matter of right to rich and poor alike . . . from a criminal conviction. We need not now decide whether California would have to provide counsel for an indigent seeking a discretionary hearing from the California Supreme Court after the District Court of Appeal had sustained his conviction . . . or whether counsel must be appointed for an indigent seeking review of an appellate affirmance of his conviction in this Court by appeal as of right or by petition for a writ of certiorari which lies within the Court's discretion. But it is appropriate to observe that a State can, consistently with the Fourteenth Amendment, provide for differences so long as the result does not amount to a denial of due process or an "invidious discrimination." . . . Absolute equality is not required; lines can be and are drawn and we often sustain them. . . . But where the merits of the one and only appeal an indigent has as of right are decided without benefit of counsel, we think an unconstitutional line has been drawn between rich and poor.

When an indigent is forced to run this gauntlet of a preliminary showing of merit, the right to appeal does not comport with fair procedure. In the federal courts, on the other hand, an indigent must be afforded counsel on appeal whenever he challenges a certification that the appeal is not taken in good faith. . . . The federal courts must honor his request for counsel regardless of what they think the merits of the case may be; and "representation in the role of an advocate is required." . . . In California, however, once the court has "gone through" the record and denied counsel, the indigent has no recourse but to prosecute his appeal on his own, as best he can, no matter how meritorious his case may turn out to be. The present case, where counsel was denied petitioners on appeal, shows that the discrimination is not between "possibly good and obviously bad cases," but between cases where the rich man can require the court to listen to argument of counsel before deciding on the merits, but a poor man cannot. There is lacking that equality demanded by the Fourteenth Amendment where the rich man, who appeals as of right, enjoys the benefit of counsel's examination into the record, research of the law, and marshalling of arguments on his behalf, while the indigent, already burdened by a preliminary determination that his case is without merit, is forced to shift for himself. The indigent, where the record is unclear or the errors are hidden, has only the right to a meaningless ritual, while the rich man has a meaningful appeal.

We vacate the judgment of the District Court of appeal and remand the case to that court for further proceedings not inconsistent with this opinion. It is so ordered. . . .

Mr. Justice CLARK, dissenting. . . .

Mr. Justice HARLAN, whom Mr. Justice STEWART joins, dissenting. . . .

Felker v. Turpin

Supreme Court of the United States, 1996.
518 U.S. 651, 116 S.Ct. 2333, 135 L.Ed.2d 827.

[In this case the U.S. Supreme Court reviews legislation adopted by Congress in 1996 that further restricts state prisoners' access to federal habeas corpus review.]

Chief Justice REHNQUIST delivered the opinion of the Court.

Title I of the Antiterrorism and Effective Death Penalty Act of 1996 (Act) works substantial changes to chapter 153 of Title 28 of the United States Code, which authorizes federal courts to grant the writ of habeas corpus. . . . We hold that the Act does not preclude this Court from entertaining an application for habeas corpus relief, although it does affect the standards governing the granting of such relief. We also conclude that the availability of such relief in this Court obviates any claim by petitioner under the Exceptions Clause of Article III, Section 2, of the Constitution, and that the operative provisions of the Act do not violate the Suspension Clause of the Constitution, Article I, Section 9.

On a night in 1976, petitioner approached Jane W. in his car as she got out of hers. Claiming to be lost and looking for a party nearby, he used a series of deceptions to induce Jane to accompany him to his trailer home in town. Petitioner forcibly subdued her, raped her, and sodomized her. Jane pleaded with petitioner to let her go, but he said he could not because she would notify the police. She escaped later, when petitioner fell asleep. Jane notified the police, and petitioner was eventually convicted of aggravated sodomy and sentenced to 12 years' imprisonment.

Petitioner was paroled four years later. On November 23, 1981, he met Joy Ludlam, a cocktail waitress, at the lounge where she worked. She was interested in changing jobs, and petitioner used a series of deceptions involving offering her a job at "The Leather Shoppe," a business he owned, to induce her to visit him the next day. The last time Joy was seen alive was the evening of the next day. Her dead body was discovered two weeks later in a creek. Forensic analysis established that she had been beaten, raped, and sodomized, and that she had been strangled to death before being left in the creek. Investigators dis-

covered hair resembling petitioner's on Joy's body and clothes, hair resembling Joy's in petitioner's bedroom, and clothing fibers like those in Joy's coat in the hatchback of petitioner's car. One of petitioner's neighbors reported seeing Joy's car at petitioner's house the day she disappeared.

A jury convicted petitioner of murder, rape, aggravated sodomy, and false imprisonment. Petitioner was sentenced to death on the murder charge. The Georgia Supreme Court affirmed petitioner's conviction and death sentence . . . and we denied certiorari. . . . A state trial court denied collateral relief, the Georgia Supreme Court declined to issue a certificate of probable cause to appeal the denial, and we again denied certiorari. . . .

Petitioner then filed a petition for a writ of habeas corpus in the United States District Court for the Middle District of Georgia, alleging that (1) the State's evidence was insufficient to convict him; (2) the State withheld exculpatory evidence, in violation of *Brady v. Maryland* . . . (1963); (3) petitioner's counsel rendered ineffective assistance at sentencing; (4) the State improperly used hypnosis to refresh a witness' memory; and (5) the State violated double jeopardy and collateral estoppel principles by using petitioner's crime against Jane W. as evidence at petitioner's trial for crimes against Joy Ludlam. The District Court denied the petition. The United States Court of Appeals for the Eleventh Circuit affirmed, . . . [denied a] petition for rehearing, . . . and we denied certiorari. . . .

The State scheduled petitioner's execution for the period May 2–9, 1996. On April 29, 1996, petitioner filed a second petition for state collateral relief. The state trial court denied this petition May 1, and the Georgia Supreme Court denied certiorari May 2.

On April 24, 1996, the President signed the Act into law. Title I of this Act contained a series of amendments to existing federal habeas corpus law. The provisions of the Act pertinent to this case concern second or successive habeas corpus applications by state prisoners. Subsections 106(b)(1) and (b)(2) specify the conditions under which claims in second or successive applications must be dismissed, amending 28 U.S.C. Section 2244(b) to read:

"(1) A claim presented in a second or successive habeas corpus application under section 2254 that was presented in a prior application shall be dismissed.

"(2) A claim presented in a second or successive habeas corpus application under section 2254 that was not presented in a prior application shall be dismissed unless—

"(A) the applicant shows that the claim relies on a new rule of constitutional law, made retroactive to cases on collateral review by the Supreme Court, that was previously unavailable; or

"(B)(i) the factual predicate for the claim could not have been discovered previously through the exercise of due diligence; and

"(ii) the facts underlying the claim, if proven and viewed in light of the evidence as a whole, would be sufficient to establish by clear and convincing evidence that, but for constitutional error, no reasonable factfinder would have found the applicant guilty of the underlying offense." . . .

Subsection 106(b)(3) creates a "gatekeeping" mechanism for the consideration of second or successive applications in district court. The prospective applicant must file in the court of appeals a motion for leave to file a second or successive habeas application in the district court. Section 106(b)(3)(A). A three-judge panel has 30 days to determine whether "the application makes a *prima facie* showing that the application satisfies the requirements of" Section 106(b). . . . Section 106(b)(3)(E) specifies that "[t]he grant or denial of an authorization by a court of appeals to file a second or successive application shall not be appealable and shall not be the subject of a petition for rehearing or for a writ of certiorari."

On May 2, 1996, petitioner filed in the United States Court of Appeals for the Eleventh Circuit a motion for stay of execution and a motion for leave to file a second or successive federal habeas corpus petition under Section 2254. Petitioner sought to raise two claims in his second petition, the first being that the state trial court violated due process by equating guilt "beyond a reasonable doubt" with "moral certainty" of guilt in *voir dire* and jury instructions. . . . He also alleged that qualified experts, reviewing the forensic evidence after his conviction, had established that Joy must have died during a period when petitioner was under police surveillance for Joy's dis-

appearance and thus had a valid alibi. He claimed that the testimony of the State's forensic expert at trial was suspect because he is not a licensed physician, and that the new expert testimony so discredited the State's testimony at trial that petitioner had a colorable claim of factual innocence.

The Court of Appeals denied both motions the day they were filed, concluding that petitioner's claims had not been presented in his first habeas petition, that they did not meet the standards of Section 106(b)(2) of the Act, and that they would not have satisfied pre-Act standards for obtaining review on the merits of second or successive claims. . . . Petitioner filed in this Court a pleading styled a "Petition for Writ of Habeas Corpus, for Appellate or Certiorari Review of the Decision of the United States Circuit Court for the Eleventh Circuit, and for Stay of Execution." On May 3, we granted petitioner's stay application and petition for certiorari. We ordered briefing on the extent to which the provisions of Title I of the Act apply to a petition for habeas corpus filed in this Court, whether application of the Act suspended the writ of habeas corpus in this case, and whether Title I of the Act, especially Section 106(b)(3)(E), constitutes an unconstitutional restriction on the jurisdiction of this Court. . . .

We first consider to what extent the provisions of Title I of the Act apply to petitions for habeas corpus filed as original matters in this Court pursuant to 28 U.S.C. Sections 2241 and 2254. We conclude that although the Act does impose new conditions on our authority to grant relief, it does not deprive this Court of jurisdiction to entertain original habeas petitions.

Section 106(b)(3)(E) of the Act prevents this Court from reviewing a court of appeals order denying leave to file a second habeas petition by appeal or by writ of certiorari. More than a century ago, we considered whether a statute barring review by appeal of the judgment of a circuit court in a habeas case also deprived this Court of power to entertain an original habeas petition. *Ex parte Yerger* . . . (1869). We consider the same question here with respect to Section 106(b)(3)(E).

Yerger's holding is best understood in the light of the availability of habeas corpus review at that time. Section 14 of the Judiciary Act of 1789 authorized all federal courts, including this Court, to grant the writ of habeas corpus, when prisoners were "in custody, under or by colour of the authority of the United States, or [were] committed for trial before some court of the same." . . . Congress greatly expanded the scope of federal habeas corpus in 1867, authorizing federal courts to grant the writ, "in addition to the authority already conferred by law," "in all cases where any person may be restrained of his or her liberty in violation of the constitution, or of any treaty or law of the United States." . . . Before the Act of 1867, the only instances in which a federal court could issue the writ to produce a state prisoner were if the prisoner was "necessary to be brought into court to testify," . . . was "committed . . . for any act done . . . in pursuance of a law of the United States," . . . or was a "subjec[t] or citize[n] of a foreign State, and domiciled therein," and held under state law. . . .

The Act of 1867 also expanded our statutory appellate jurisdiction to authorize appeals to this Court from the final decision of any circuit court on a habeas petition. . . . This enactment changed the result of *Barry v. Mercein* . . . (1847), in which we had held that the Judiciary Act of 1789 did not authorize this Court to conduct appellate review of circuit court habeas decisions. However, in 1868, Congress revoked the appellate jurisdiction it had given in 1867, repealing "so much of the [Act of 1867] as authorizes an appeal from the judgment of the circuit court to the Supreme Court of the United States." . . .

In *Yerger*, we considered whether the Act of 1868 deprived us not only of power to hear an appeal from an inferior court's decision on a habeas petition, but also of power to entertain a habeas petition to this Court under Section 14 of the Act of 1789. We concluded that the 1868 Act did not affect our power to entertain such habeas petitions. We explained that the 1868 Act's text addressed only jurisdiction over appeals conferred under the Act of 1867, not habeas jurisdiction conferred under the Acts of 1789 and 1867. We rejected the suggestion that the Act of 1867 had repealed our habeas power by implication. . . . Repeals by implication are not favored, we said, and the continued exercise of original habeas jurisdiction was not "repugnant" to a prohibition on review by appeal of circuit court habeas judgments. . . .

Turning to the present case, we conclude that Title I of the Act has not repealed our authority to entertain original habeas petitions, for reasons similar to those stated in *Yerger*. No provision of Title I mentions our authority to entertain original habeas petitions; in contrast, Section 103 amends the Federal Rules of Appellate Procedure to bar consideration of original habeas petitions in the courts of appeals. Although

Section 106(b) (3)(E) precludes us from reviewing, by appeal or petition for certiorari, a judgment on an application for leave to file a second habeas petition in district court, it makes no mention of our authority to hear habeas petitions filed as original matters in this Court. As we declined to find a repeal of Section 14 of the Judiciary Act of 1789 as applied to this Court by implication then, we decline to find a similar repeal of Section 2241 of Title 28—its descendant—by implication now.

This conclusion obviates one of the constitutional challenges raised. The critical language of Article III, Section 2, of the Constitution provides that, apart from several classes of cases specifically enumerated in this Court's original jurisdiction, "[i]n all the other Cases . . . the supreme Court shall have appellate Jurisdiction, both as to Law and Fact, with such Exceptions, and under such Regulations as the Congress shall make." Previous decisions construing this clause have said that while our appellate powers "are given by the constitution," "they are limited and regulated by the [Judiciary Act of 1789], and by such other acts as have been passed on the subject." . . . The Act does remove our authority to entertain an appeal or a petition for a writ of certiorari to review a decision of a court of appeals exercising its "gatekeeping" function over a second petition. But since it does not repeal our authority to entertain a petition for habeas corpus, there can be no plausible argument that the Act has deprived this Court of appellate jurisdiction in violation of Article III, Section 2.

We consider next how Title I affects the requirements a state prisoner must satisfy to show he is entitled to a writ of habeas corpus from this Court. Title I of the Act has changed the standards governing our consideration of habeas petitions by imposing new requirements for the granting of relief to state prisoners. Our authority to grant habeas relief to state prisoners is limited by Section 2254, which specifies the conditions under which such relief may be granted to "a person in custody pursuant to the judgment of a State court." . . . Several sections of the Act impose new requirements for the granting of relief under this section, and they therefore inform our authority to grant such relief as well.

Section 106(b) of the Act addresses second or successive habeas petitions. Section 106(b)(3)'s "gatekeeping" system for second petitions does not apply to our consideration of habeas petitions because it applies to applications "filed in the district court." . . .

There is no such limitation, however, on the restrictions on repetitive and new claims imposed by subsections 106(b)(1) and (2). These restrictions apply without qualification to any "second or successive habeas corpus application under section 2254." . . . Whether or not we are bound by these restrictions, they certainly inform our consideration of original habeas petitions.

Next, we consider whether the Act suspends the writ of habeas corpus in violation of Article I, Section 9, clause 2, of the Constitution. This clause provides that "[t]he Privilege of the Writ of Habeas Corpus shall not be suspended, unless when in Cases of Rebellion or Invasion the public Safety may require it."

The writ of habeas corpus known to the Framers was quite different from that which exists today. As we explained previously, the first Congress made the writ of habeas corpus available only to prisoners confined under the authority of the United States, not under state authority . . . The class of judicial actions reviewable by the writ was more restricted as well. . . .

It was not until 1867 that Congress made the writ generally available in "all cases where any person may be restrained of his or her liberty in violation of the constitution, or of any treaty or law of the United States." . . . And it was not until well into this century that this Court interpreted that provision to allow a final judgment of conviction in a state court to be collaterally attacked on habeas. . . . But we assume, for purposes of decision here, that the Suspension Clause of the Constitution refers to the writ as it exists today, rather than as it existed in 1789. . . .

The Act requires a habeas petitioner to obtain leave from the court of appeals before filing a second habeas petition in the district court. But this requirement simply transfers from the district court to the court of appeals a screening function which would previously have been performed by the district court. . . . The Act also codifies some of the pre-existing limits on successive petitions, and further restricts the availability of relief to habeas petitioners. But we have long recognized that "the power to award the writ by any of the courts of the United States, must be given by written law," . . . and we have likewise recognized that judgments about the proper scope of the writ are "normally for Congress to make." . . .

The new restrictions on successive petitions constitute a . . . restraint on what is called in habeas corpus practice "abuse of the writ." In *McCleskey v. Zant* . . . (1991), we said that "the doctrine of abuse of the writ refers to a complex and evolving body of equitable principles informed and controlled by historical usage, statutory developments, and judicial decisions." . . . The added restrictions which the Act places on second habeas petitions are well within the compass of this evolutionary process, and we hold that they do not amount to a "suspension" of the writ contrary to Article I, Section 9.

We have answered the questions presented by the petition for certiorari in this case, and we now dispose of the petition for an original writ of habeas corpus. Our Rule 20.4(a) delineates the standards under which we grant such writs:

A petition seeking the issuance of a writ of habeas corpus shall comply with the requirements of 28 U.S.C. Sections 2241 and 2242, and in particular with the provision in the last paragraph of Section 2242 requiring a statement of the "reasons for not making application to the district court of the district in which the applicant is held." If the relief sought is from the judgment of a state court, the petition shall set forth specifically how and wherein the petitioner has exhausted available remedies in the state courts or otherwise comes within the provisions of 28 U.S.C. Section 2254(b). To justify the granting of a writ of habeas corpus, the petitioner must show exceptional circumstances warranting the exercise of the Court's discretionary powers and must show that adequate relief cannot be obtained in any other form or from any other court. These writs are rarely granted.

Reviewing petitioner's claims here, they do not materially differ from numerous other claims made by successive habeas petitioners which we have had occasion to review on stay applications to this Court. Neither of them satisfies the requirements of the relevant provisions of the Act, let alone the requirement that there be "exceptional circumstances" justifying the issuance of the writ.

The petition for writ of certiorari is dismissed for want of jurisdiction. The petition for an original writ of habeas corpus is denied. . . .

Justice STEVENS, joined by Justice SOUTER and Justice BREYER, concurring.

Justice SOUTER, joined by Justice STEVENS and Justice BREYER, concurring.

Access to the Law Through Legal Research

The Nature of Legal Research

Successful legal research requires a systematic method of finding the law applicable to a particular problem or set of facts. Before beginning research it is helpful, if not essential, for the criminal justice professional or student to have a basic understanding of the law and the legal system.

After assembling the relevant facts and completing a preliminary analysis of the problem, the researcher must find the applicable constitutional and statutory materials, then search for authoritative interpretations of the law. Interpretations are usually found in appellate court decisions construing the particular constitutional provision or statute in analogous situations. These judicial decisions are referred to as "cases in point." Legislative and judicial sources of the law are referred to as "primary sources" because they are authoritative.

A variety of other legal materials, called "secondary sources," are available to the researcher. These consist of legal encyclopedias, textbooks by scholars and practitioners, law reviews published by law schools, and journals and periodicals published by various legal organizations. These secondary sources are extremely helpful to the researcher, especially to one unfamiliar with the law in a given area.

Primary Legal Sources

Federal and state constitutions are often the beginning points in legal research in the criminal justice area because they provide the framework for our government and guarantee certain basic rights to the accused. As explained in this text, the rights of an accused are protected by several provisions of the federal constitution and the Bill of Rights. Most state constitutions afford criminal defendants similar protections. For instance, a person concerned about the legality of an arrest, search, or seizure would examine the relevant constitutional provisions and then seek to determine how the courts have construed the law in analogous situations.

Federal offenses are defined in statutes enacted by the United States Congress, and state offenses are defined in statutes enacted by state legislatures. Federal statutes (in sequence of their adoption) are published annually in the *United States Statutes at Large*. Most states have similar volumes, called session laws, that incorporate the laws enacted during a given session of the legislature. These federal and state laws are initially compiled in sequence of their adoption. Later they are merged into legal codes that systematically arrange the statutes by subject and provide an index. Of far greater assistance to the criminal justice researcher are commercially prepared codes that classify all federal and state laws of a general and permanent nature by subject and include reference materials and exhaustive indexes. These volumes are kept current by periodic supplements and revised volumes.

The *United States Code Annotated*

One popular compilation of the federal law widely used by lawyers, judges, and criminal justice professionals is the *United States Code Annotated*. "U.S.C.A.," as it is known, is published by the West Group of St. Paul, Minnesota. The U.S.C.A. consists of fifty separate titles that conform to the text of the Official Code of the Laws of the United States. For instance, Title 18 is entitled "Crimes and Criminal Procedure" and is of particular interest to the criminal justice researcher. Each section of statutory law in U.S.C.A. is followed by a series of annotations consisting of court decisions interpreting the particular statute along with historical notes, cross-references, and other editorial features. If the researcher knows only the popular name of a federal statute, the corresponding U.S. Code title and section number can be found in the Popular Name Table. A sample page from the U.S.C.A. is included as Exhibit 1. A sample page from the Popular Name Table is included as Exhibit 2.

Annotated State Codes

Most states have annotated statutes published by either the state or a private publisher. For example, *West's Annotated California Codes* follows the same general format as the *United States Code Annotated*. A sample page is included as Exhibit 3. Annotated statutes are popular aids to legal research and can save the researcher valuable time in locating cases in point. They are especially effective tools for locating interpretations of criminal statutes.

The National Reporter System

Volumes containing appellate court decisions are referred to as "reporters." The National Reporter System includes decisions from the United States Supreme Court, the lower federal courts, and the state appellate courts. Back reporters are now available both in bound-volumes editions and on CD-ROM.

Decisions of the United States Supreme Court are officially published in the *United States Reports* (abbreviated U.S.). Two private organizations also report these decisions in hard-cover volumes. The *Supreme Court Reporter* (abbreviated S.Ct.) is published by West, and *Lawyers Edition*, now in its second series (abbreviated L.Ed.2d), is published by the Lawyers Cooperative Publishing Company. Although the three reporters have somewhat different editorial features, the opinions of the Supreme Court are reproduced identically in all three reporters.

CHAPTER 87—PRISONS

Sec.
1791. Traffic in contraband articles.
1792. Mutiny, riot, dangerous instrumentalities prohibited.

Cross References

Escape and rescue, see section 751 et seq. of this title.

§ 1791. Traffic in contraband articles

Whoever, contrary to any rule or regulation promulgated by the Attorney General, introduces or attempts to introduce into or upon the grounds of any Federal penal or correctional institution or takes or attempts to take or send therefrom anything whatsoever, shall be imprisoned not more than ten years.

(June 25, 1948, c. 645, 62 Stat. 786.)

Historical and Revision Notes

Reviser's Note. Based on Title 18, U.S.C., 1940 ed., §§ 753j, 908 (May 14, 1930, c. 274, § 11, 46 Stat. 327; May 27, 1930, c. 339, § 8, 46 Stat. 390).

Section consolidates sections 753j and 908 of Title 18, U.S.C., 1940 ed. The section was broadened to include the taking or sending out of contraband from the institution. This was suggested by representatives of the Federal Bureau of Prisons and the Criminal Division of the Department of Justice. In other respects the section was rewritten without change of substance.

The words "narcotic", "drug", "weapon" and "contraband" were omitted, since the insertion of the words "contrary to any rule or regulation promulgated by the attorney general" preserves the intent of the original statutes.

Words "guilty of a felony" were deleted as unnecessary in view of definitive section 1 of this title. (See also reviser's note under section 550 of this title.)

Minor verbal changes also were made.

Cross References

Bureau of Prisons employees, power to arrest without warrant for violations of this section, see section 3050 of this title.

West's Federal Forms

Sentence and fine, see § 7531 et seq.

Code of Federal Regulations

Federal penal and correctional institutions, traffic in contraband articles, see 28 CFR 6.1.

Library References

Prisons ☜17½.
C.J.S. Prisons § 22.

Notes of Decisions

Aiding and abetting 7
Admissibility of evidence 13

Articles prohibited 3
Assistance of counsel 11

585

EXHIBIT 1 United States Code Annotated.

Source: Reprinted with permission from 18 U.S.C.A. § 1791. Copyright 1984 by West Publishing Co., 1-800-328-9352.

Crimes and Criminal Procedure—Continued

Oct. 28, 1992, Pub.L. 102–550, Title XIII, Subtitle A, § 1353, Title XV, Subtitle A, §§ 1504(c), 1512(a), (c), 1522(a), 1523(a), 1524, 1525(c)(1), 1526, 1527, 1528, 1530, 1531, 1533, 1534, 1536, Subtitle D, § 1543, Subtitle E, §§ 1552, 1553, 1554, 106 Stat. 3970, 4055, 4057, 4063, 4064, 4065, 4066, 4067, 4069, 4070, 4071 (Title 18, §§ 474, 474A, 504, 981, 982, 984, 986, 1510, 1905, 1956, 1957, 1960, 6001)

Oct. 28, 1992, Pub.L. 102–561, 106 Stat. 4233 (Title 18, § 2319)

Oct. 29, 1992, Pub.L. 102–572, Title I, § 103, Title VII, §§ 701, 703, 106 Stat. 4507, 4514, 4515 (Title 18, §§ 3143, 3154, 3401, 3603)

Criminal Appeals Act

Mar. 2, 1907, ch. 2564, 34 Stat. 1246 (See Title 18, § 3731)

Criminal Code

Mar. 4, 1909, ch. 321, 35 Stat. 1088 (See Title 18, chapters 1–15)

June 25, 1910, ch. 431, § 6, 36 Stat. 857 (See Title 18, §§ 1853, 1856)

Mar. 4, 1921, ch. 172, 41 Stat. 1444 (See Title 18, §§ 831–835)

Mar. 28, 1940, ch. 73, 54 Stat. 80 (See Title 18, § 1382)

Apr. 30, 1940, ch. 164, 54 Stat. 171 (See Title 18, § 1024)

June 6, 1940, ch. 241, 54 Stat. 234 (See Title 18, § 13)

June 11, 1940, ch. 323, 54 Stat. 304 (See Title 18, § 7)

Apr. 1, 1944, ch. 151, 58 Stat. 149 (See Title 18, § 491)

Sept. 27, 1944, ch. 425, 58 Stat. 752 (See Title 18, § 371)

June 8, 1945, ch. 178, 59 Stat. 234 (See Title 18, §§ 371, 1503, 1505)

Criminal Fine Enforcement Act of 1984

Pub.L. 98–596, Oct. 30, 1984, 98 Stat. 3134 (Title 18, §§ 1, 1 note, 3565, 3565 note, 3569, 3579, 3591 to 3599, 3611 note, 3621 to 3624, 3651, 3655, 4209, 4214; Title 18, F.R.Crim.Proc. Rules 12.2, 12.2 note)

Criminal Fine Improvements Act of 1987

Pub.L. 100–185, Dec. 11, 1987, 101 Stat. 1279 (Title 18, §§ 1 note, 18, 19, 3013, 3559, 3571, 3572, 3573, 3611, 3611 note, 3612, 3663; Title 28, § 604)

Criminal Justice Act Revision of 1984

Pub.L. 98–473, Title II, § 1901, Oct. 12, 1984, 98 Stat. 2185 (Title 18, § 3006A)

Criminal Justice Act Revision of 1986

Pub.L. 99–651, Title I, Nov. 14, 1986, 100 Stat. 3642 (Title 18, § 3006A)

Criminal Justice Act of 1964

Pub. L. 88–455, Aug. 20, 1964, 78 Stat. 552 (Title 18, § 3006A)

Criminal Law and Procedure Technical Amendments Act of 1986

Pub.L. 99–646, Nov. 10, 1986, 100 Stat. 3592 (Title 18, §§ 1 note, 3, 17, 18, 113, 115, 201, 201 note, 203, 203 note, 209, 219, 351, 373, 513, 524, 666, 1028, 1029, 1111, 1153, 1201, 1366, 1512, 1515, 1791, 1791 note, 1793, 1961, 1963, 2031, 2032, 2113, 2232, 2241, 2241 notes, 2242, 2243, 2244, 2245, 2315, 2320, 3050, 3076, 3141, 3142, 3143, 3143 note, 3144, 3146, 3147, 3148, 3150a, 3156, 3156 note, 3185, 3522, 3551 note, 3552, 3552 note, 3553, 3553 notes, 3556, 3561, 3561 note, 3563, 3563 notes, 3579, 3579 notes, 3583, 3583 note, 3603, 3603 note, 3624, 3624 note, 3671, 3671 note, 3672, 3672 note, 3673, 3673 note, 3681, 3682, 3731, 3742, 4044, 4045, 4082, 4203, 4204, 4208, 4209, 4210, 4214, 4217, 5003, 5037, 5037 note; Title 18, F.R.Crim.Proc. Rules 12.2, 29, 29 note, 32, 32 note, 32.1, 32.1 note; Title 21, §§ 802, 812, 845a, 875, 878, 881; Title 28, §§ 546, 992, 993, 994, 1921, 1921 note; Title 42, §§ 257, 300w–3, 300w–4, 9511, 10601, 10603, 10604)

Pub.L. 100–185, § 4(c), Dec. 11, 1987, 101 Stat. 1279 (Title 18, § 18)

Pub.L. 100–690, Title VII, §§ 7012 to 7014, Nov. 18, 1988, 102 Stat. 4395 (Title 18, §§ 18, 1961, 4217)

Criminal Victims Protection Act of 1990

Pub.L. 101–581, Nov. 15, 1990, 104 Stat. 2865 (Title 11, §§ 101 note, 523, 523 note, 1328)

Pub.L. 101–647, Title XXXI, Nov. 29, 1990, 104 Stat. 4916 (Title 11, §§ 101 note, 523, 523 note, 1328)

Critical Agricultural Materials Act

Pub.L. 95–592, Nov. 4, 1978, 92 Stat. 2529 (Title 7, §§ 178, 178a to 178n, 1314f); Pub.L. 98–284, May 16, 1984, 98 Stat. 184 (Title 7, §§ 178, 178 note, 178a to 178i, 178k to 178n)

Pub.L. 99–198, Title XIV, § 1439, Dec. 23, 1985, 99 Stat. 1559 (Title 7, § 178c)

Pub.L. 101–624, Title XVI, § 1601(e), Nov. 28, 1990, 104 Stat. 3704 (Title 7, § 178n)

EXHIBIT 2 Popular Name Table (from U.S.C.A.).

Source: Reprinted with permission from U.S.C.A. Copyright 1992 by West Publishing Co., 1-800-328-9352.

warrant. People v. Golden (1971) 97 Cal.Rptr. 476, 20 C.A.3d 211.

4. Affidavits

"Oral" procedure is permitted only as to affidavit in support of search and warrant itself must be in writing. Bowyer v. Superior Court of Santa Cruz County (1974) 111 Cal.Rptr. 628, 37 C.A.3d 151, rehearing denied 112 Cal.Rptr. 266, 37 C. A.3d 151.

For an affidavit based on informant's hearsay statement to be legally sufficient to support issuance of a search warrant, two requirements must be met: (1) affidavit must allege the informant's statement in language that is factual rather than conclusionary and must establish that informant spoke with personal knowledge of the matters contained in such statement, and (2) the affidavit must contain some underlying factual information from which magistrate issuing the warrant can reasonably conclude that informant was credible or his information reliable. People v. Hamilton (1969) 77 Cal.Rptr. 785, 454 P.2d 681, 71 C.2d 176.

5. Arrest

An arrest without a warrant may not be made on a belief, founded on information received from a third person, that a misdemeanor is being committed. Ware v. Dunn (1947) 183 P.2d 128, 80 C.A.2d 936.

Arrest under warrant issued by justice of peace directed to any sheriff "in the state," where proper sheriff did receive warrant and executed it, and person arrested was not prejudiced, and was not ground for complaint by person arrested, notwithstanding under statutes warrant should have been directed to any sheriff "in the county". Elliott v. Haskins (1937) 67 P.2d 698, 20 C.A.2d 591.

6. Unreasonable searches

Alleged action of city police on specified occasions in blocking off designated portions of city and stopping all persons and automobiles entering or leaving the blocked off area and searching them with-

out first obtaining a search warrant and without having probable cause for believing the searched individuals to have violated some law or that automobiles were carrying contraband, would be unconstitutional as being "unreasonable searches and seizures". Wirin v. Horrall (1948) 193 P.2d 470, 85 C.A.2d 497.

7. Admissibility of evidence

Rule excluding in criminal prosecutions evidence obtained through unlawful searches and seizures by police and governmental officers does not apply to evidence obtained by a private person, not employed by nor associated with a governmental unit. People v. Johnson (1957) 315 P.2d 468, 153 C.A.2d 870.

Evidence obtained in violation of constitutional guarantees against unreasonable searches and seizures is inadmissible. People v. Cahan (1955) 282 P.2d 905, 44 C.2d 434, 50 A.L.R.2d 513.

In a prosecution for burglary in the second degree, the fact that articles claimed to have been taken were seized from the person of accused without warrant in violation of Const.Art. 1, § 19 (repealed; see, now, Const.Art. 1, § 13) did not render their introduction in evidence error, although the court overruled the motion of accused to have the articles returned to him. People v. Watson (1922) 206 P. 648, 57 C.A. 85.

8. Federal and state warrants distinguished

Although a California municipal court judge is a "judge of a court of record" and thus authorized to issue federal warrants, the search warrant in question was clearly issued under state, not federal, authority, where it was issued by a California municipal judge on a California form, on the application of a California narcotics agent, and where there was no attempt to comply with the requirements of Fed. Rules of Cr.Proc. rule 41, 18 U.S.C. A. U. S. v. Radlick (C.A.1978) 581 F.2d 225.

§ **1524.**   Issuance; grounds; special master

(a) A search warrant may be issued upon any of the following grounds:

(1) When the property was stolen or embezzled.

(2) When the property or things were used as the means of committing a felony.

(3) When the property or things are in the possession of any person with the intent to use it as a means of committing a public of-

EXHIBIT 3   West's Annotated California Code.

Source: Reprinted with permission from *West's Annotated California Codes*, Vol. 51A, § 1524. Copyright 1982 by West Publishing Co., 1-800-328-9352.

References to judicial decisions found in the reporters are called "citations." United States Supreme Court decisions are often cited to all three publications—for example, *Miranda v. Arizona,* 384 U.S. 436, 86 S.Ct. 1602, 16 L.Ed.2d 694 (1966). A sample page from *West's Supreme Court Reporter* is included as Exhibit 4.

Since 1889, the decisions of the United States Courts of Appeals have been published in *West's Federal Reporter,* now in its third series (abbreviated F.3d). Decisions of federal district (trial) courts are published in *West's Federal Supplement,* which is now in its second series (abbreviated F. Supp. 2d). A citation to a case in *Federal Reporter* will read, for example, *Newman v. United States,* 817 F.2d 635 (10th Cir. 1987). This refers to a 1987 case reported in volume 817, page 635 of the *Federal Reporter,* second series, decided by the United States Court of Appeals for the Tenth Circuit. A citation to *United States v. Klopfenstine,* 673 F. Supp. 356 (W.D. Mo. 1987), refers to a 1987 federal district court decision from the western district of Missouri reported in volume 673, page 356 of the *Federal Supplement.*

Additional federal reporters publish the decisions from other federal courts (for example, bankruptcy and military appeals), but the federal reporters referred to earlier are those most frequently used by criminal justice professionals.

The Regional Reporters

The decisions of the highest state courts (usually but not always called supreme courts) and the decisions of other state appellate courts (usually referred to as intermediate appellate courts) are found in seven regional reporters, *West's California Reporter,* and the *New York Supplement.* Regional reporters, with their abbreviation in parentheses, include decisions from the following states:

- *Atlantic Reporter* (A. and A.2d): Maine, Vermont, New Hampshire, Connecticut, Rhode Island, Pennsylvania, New Jersey, Maryland, Delaware, and the District of Columbia
- *North Eastern Reporter* (N.E. and N.E.2d): Illinois, Indiana, Massachusetts, New York (court of last resort only), and Ohio
- *North Western Reporter* (N.W. and N.W.2d): North Dakota, South Dakota, Nebraska, Minnesota, Iowa, Michigan, and Wisconsin
- *Pacific Reporter* (P. and P.2d): Washington, Oregon, California, Montana, Idaho, Nevada, Utah, Arizona, Wyoming, Colorado, New Mexico, Kansas, Oklahoma, Alaska, and Hawaii
- *Southern Reporter* (So. and So.2d): Florida, Alabama, Mississippi, and Louisiana
- *South Eastern Reporter* (S.E. and S.E.2d): Virginia, West Virginia, North Carolina, South Carolina, and Georgia
- *South Western Reporter* (S.W. and S.W.2d): Texas, Missouri, Arkansas, Kentucky, and Tennessee

For many states (in addition to New York and California), West publishes separate volumes reporting the decisions as they appear in the regional reporters. *Pennsylvania Reporter* and *Texas Cases* are examples of this.

The following examples of citation forms appear in some of the regional reporters:

- *State v. Hogan,* 480 So.2d 288 (La. 1985). This refers to a 1985 decision of the Louisiana Supreme Court found in volume 480, page 288 of the *Southern Reporter,* second series.

384 U.S. 436
Ernesto A. MIRANDA, Petitioner,

v.

STATE OF ARIZONA.

Michael VIGNERA, Petitioner,

v.

STATE OF NEW YORK.

Carl Calvin WESTOVER, Petitioner,

v.

UNITED STATES.

STATE OF CALIFORNIA, Petitioner,

v.

Roy Allen STEWART.

Nos. 759–761, 584.

Argued Feb. 28, March 1 and 2, 1966.

Decided June 13, 1966.

Rehearing Denied No. 584
Oct. 10, 1966.

See 87 S.Ct. 11.

Criminal prosecutions. The Superior Court, Maricopa County, Arizona, rendered judgment, and the Supreme Court of Arizona, 98 Ariz. 18, 401 P.2d 721, affirmed. The Supreme Court, Kings County, New York, rendered judgment, and the Supreme Court, Appellate Division, Second Department, 21 A.D.2d 752, 252 N.Y.S.2d 19, affirmed, as did the Court of Appeals of the State of New York at 15 N.Y.2d 970, 259 N.Y.S.2d 857, 207 N.E.2d 527. The United States District Court for the Northern District of California, Northern Division, rendered judgment, and the United States Court of Appeals for the Ninth Circuit, 342 F.2d 684, affirmed. The Superior Court, Los Angeles County, California, rendered judgment and the Supreme Court of California, 62 Cal.2d 571, 43 Cal. Rptr. 201, 400 P.2d 97, reversed. In the first three cases, defendants obtained certiorari, and the State of California obtained certiorari in the fourth case. The Supreme Court, Mr. Chief Justice Warren, held that statements obtained from defendants during incommunicado interrogation in police-dominated atmosphere, without full warning of constitu-

tional rights, were inadmissible as having been obtained in violation of Fifth Amendment privilege against self-incrimination.

Judgments in first three cases reversed and judgment in fourth case affirmed.

Mr. Justice Harlan, Mr. Justice Stewart, and Mr. Justice White dissented; Mr. Justice Clark dissented in part.

1. Courts ⬅️397½

Certiorari was granted in cases involving admissibility of defendants' statements to police to explore some facets of problems of applying privilege against self-incrimination to in-custody interrogation and to give concrete constitutional guidelines for law enforcement agencies and courts to follow.

2. Criminal Law ⬅️393(1), 641.1

Constitutional rights to assistance of counsel and protection against self-incrimination were secured for ages to come and designed to approach immortality as nearly as human institutions can approach it. U.S.C.A.Const. Amends. 5, 6.

3. Criminal Law ⬅️412.1(4)

Prosecution may not use statements, whether exculpatory or inculpatory, stemming from custodial interrogation of defendant unless it demonstrates use of procedural safeguards effective to secure privilege against self-incrimination. U.S.C.A.Const. Amend. 5.

4. Criminal Law ⬅️412.1(4)

"Custodial interrogation", within rule limiting admissibility of statements stemming from such interrogation, means questioning initiated by law enforcement officers after person has been taken into custody or otherwise deprived of his freedom of action in any significant way. U.S.C.A.Const. Amend. 5.

See publication Words and Phrases for other judicial constructions and definitions.

EXHIBIT 4 *Supreme Court Reporter.*

- *State v. Nungesser*, 269 N.W.2d 449 (Iowa 1978). This refers to a 1978 decision of the Iowa Supreme Court found in volume 269, page 449 of the *North Western Reporter*, second series.
- *Henry v. State*, 567 S.W.2d 7 (Tex. Cr. App. 1978). This refers to a 1978 decision of the Texas Court of Criminal Appeals found in volume 567, page 7 of the *South Western Reporter*, second series.

A sample page from *Southern Reporter*, second series, is included as Exhibit 5.

Syllabi, Headnotes, and Key Numbers

The National Reporter System and the regional reporters contain not only the official text of each reported decision but also a brief summary of the decision, called the "syllabus," and one or more topically indexed "headnotes." These headnotes briefly describe the principles of law expounded by the court and are indexed by a series of topic "key numbers." West assigns these key numbers to specific points of decisional law. For instance, decisions dealing with first-degree murder are classified under the topic "homicide" and assigned a key number for each particular aspect of that crime. Thus, a homicide case dealing with the intent requirement in first-degree murder may be classified as: "Homicide 9—Intent and design to effect death." Using this key number system, a researcher can locate headnotes of various appellate decisions on this aspect of homicide and is, in turn, led to relevant decisional law.

In addition, each of these volumes contains a table of statutes construed in the cases reported in that volume, with reference to the American Bar Association's Standards for Criminal Justice.

United States Law Week

United States Law Week, published by the Bureau of National Affairs, Inc., Washington, D.C., presents a weekly survey of American law. *Law Week* includes all the latest decisions from the United States Supreme Court as well as significant current decisions from other federal and state courts.

Criminal Law Reporter

Published by the Bureau of National Affairs, Inc., Washington, D.C., the weekly *Criminal Law Reporter* reviews contemporary developments in the criminal law. It is an excellent source of commentaries on current state and federal court decisions in the criminal law area.

The Digests

West also publishes *Decennial Digests,* which topically index all the appellate court decisions from the state and federal courts. Digests are tools that enable the researcher to locate cases in point through topics and key numbers. Ten *Decennial Digests* have been published as of 1999, the most recent being the *Tenth Decennial Digest* (Part 2) that embraces federal and state appellate decisions from 1991 to 1996. Later cases are contained in a set called the *General Digests*. A series of federal digests contains key number headnotes for decisions of the federal courts. The current series published by

288 La.   **480 SOUTHERN REPORTER, 2d SERIES**

imprisonment. It is indeed unlikely that the enactment of art. 893.1 was designed to punish more severely those who commit negligent homicide than perpetrators of second degree murder, manslaughter, aggravated battery, etc.

In summary, therefore, we find as regards defendant's second assignment of error that the art. 893.1 enhancement is not constitutionally infirm as cruel, unusual and excessive punishment; that the absence of art. 894.1 sentence articulation in this case was harmless, there existing in this record sufficient factors to support this penalty which is well within the statutory range; that the two year penalty imposed in this case under § 14:95.2 is illegal; that art. 893.1 is applicable to all felonies, including those specially enumerated in § 14:95.2 and that therefore the art. 893.1 enhancement in this case is valid.

Decree

Accordingly, defendant's conviction is affirmed; his sentence is reversed and the case remanded for resentencing in accordance with the views expressed herein and according to law.

CONVICTION AFFIRMED; SENTENCE REVERSED; CASE REMANDED.

DIXON, C.J., and DENNIS, J., concur.

WATSON, J., dissents as to requiring notice.

STATE of Louisiana

v.

Patrick HOGAN.

No. 84–K–1847.

Supreme Court of Louisiana.

Dec. 2, 1985.

Defendant was convicted in the First Judicial District Court, Parish of Caddo, Charles R. Lindsay, J., of aggravated battery, and he appealed. The Court of Appeal, 454 So.2d 1235, affirmed, and defendant's petition for writ of review was granted. The Supreme Court, Calogero, J., held that: (1) sentence enhancement by reason of use of a firearm in commission of a felony was not constitutionally infirm as cruel, unusual and excessive; (2) existence of some mitigating factors did not preclude enhancement; (3) imposition of an additional two-year penalty for use of a gun while attempting commission of a specified felony was impermissible when not preceded by an appropriate notice; and (4) enhancement was not invalid, however, since minimum sentence mandated by use of firearm was applicable to all felonies.

Conviction affirmed, sentence reversed, and case remanded.

Dennis, J., concurred.

Watson, J., dissented as to requiring notice.

1. Criminal Law ☞1206.1(1), 1213.2(1)

General sentencing enhancement statute [LSA-R.S. 14:34, 14:95; LSA-C.Cr.P. art. 893.1] applicable when a firearm is used in commission of a felony, does not impose cruel, unusual, and excessive punishment and is not constitutionally infirm on its face or as applied. U.S.C.A. Const. Amend. 8.

2. Criminal Law ☞1213.8(7)

Imposition of mandatory minimum sentence under enhancement statute [LSA-R.S. 14:34, 14:95; LSA-C.Cr.P. art. 893.1]

EXHIBIT 5 *Southern Reporter.*

Source: Reprinted with permission from 480 So.2d 288. Copyright 1986 by West Publishing Co., 1-800-328-9352.

West is *Federal Practice Digest 4th*. In addition, separate digests are published for some states as well as for the Atlantic, North Western, Pacific, and South Eastern reporters.

The index at the beginning of each topic identifies the various points of law by numerically arranged key numbers. In addition to the basic topic of criminal law, many topics in the field of criminal law are listed by specific crimes (such as homicide, forgery, and bribery). Procedural topics such as arrest and search and seizure are also included. The digests contain a descriptive word index and a table of cases sorted by name, listing the key numbers corresponding to the decisions. Thus, the researcher can find, by key number, reference topics that relate to the principles set out in the headnotes prepared for each judicial decision. A researcher who locates a topic and key number has access to all reported decisions on this point of law. A sample page from the *Texas Digest*, second series, is reprinted as Exhibit 6.

Shepard's Citations

Shepard's Citations is a series published by Shepard's/McGraw-Hill, Inc., of Colorado Springs, Colorado, that provides the judicial history of cases by reference to the volume and page number of the cases in the particular reporters. By using the symbols explained in this work, the researcher can determine whether a particular decision has been affirmed, followed, distinguished, modified, or reversed by subsequent court decisions. Most attorneys "Shepardize" the cases they cite in their law briefs to support various principles of law. There is a separate set of *Shepard's Citations* for the United States Supreme Court reports, for the federal appellate and district courts, for each regional reporter, and for each state that has an official reporter.

Secondary Sources

Legal authorities other than constitutions, statutes, ordinances, regulations, and court decisions are called "secondary sources," yet they are essential tools in legal research. A basic necessity for any legal researcher's work is a good law dictionary. Several are published, and *Black's Law Dictionary* (6th ed.) is one of the best known. *Black's* is available both in print and computer disk media.

Legal Encyclopedias

Beyond dictionaries, the most common secondary legal authorities are legal encyclopedias. These are arranged alphabetically by subject and are used much like any standard encyclopedia. There are two principal national encyclopedias of the law: *Corpus Juris Secundum* (C.J.S.), published by West, and *American Jurisprudence*, second edition (Am.Jur.2d), published by Lawyers Cooperative. A sample page from C.J.S. appears as Exhibit 7. Appellate courts frequently document propositions of law contained in their opinions by citations to these encyclopedias, as well as to cases in the reporters. Each of these encyclopedias is an excellent set of reference books; one significant difference is that *Corpus Juris Secundum* cites more court decisions, whereas *American Jurisprudence 2d* limits footnote references to the leading cases pertinent to the principles of law in the text. *Corpus Juris Secundum* includes valuable cross-references to West topic key numbers and other secondary sources, including forms. *American Jurisprudence 2d* includes valuable footnote references to another of the company's publications, *American Law Reports,* now in its fifth series.

6 Tex D 2d—155

ARREST ☞**63.3**

For references to other topics, see Descriptive-Word Index

was observed in act of smoking a marihuana cigarette, for violation of narcotics laws, was legal. Code Cr.Proc.Tex.1925, arts. 212, 215; 26 U.S.C.A. §§ 2557(b) (1), 2593(a).

Rent v. U. S., 209 F.2d 893.

D.C.Tex. 1975. Arrest and subsequent detention of husband plaintiff by deputies without warrant was not unlawful where husband plaintiff appeared to be intoxicated in public place. 28 U.S.C.A. § 1343; 42 U.S.C.A. §§ 1983, 1985; U.S.C.A.Const. Amend. 4; Vernon's Ann.Tex.C.C.P. art. 14.01.

Lamb v. Cartwright, 393 F.Supp. 1081, affirmed 524 F.2d 238.

D.C.Tex. 1972. The "presence" of the officer, under Texas statute providing that a police officer may arrest an offender without a warrant for any offense committed in his "presence" or within his view, is satisfied if the violation occurs within reach of the officer's senses. Vernon's Ann.Tex.C.C.P. art. 14.01(b).

Taylor v. McDonald, 346 F.Supp. 390.

D.C.Tex. 1967. It is not the case that officer may arrest person committing felony in his presence irrespective of whose privacy officer must violate in order to place commission of felony in his presence.

Gonzales v. Beto, 266 F.Supp. 751, affirmed State of Tex. v. Gonzales, 388 F.2d 145.

Tex.Cr.App. 1981. Observation by police officer of the exchange of money between defendant and another person for tinfoil bindles coupled with officer's knowledge that heroin is normally packaged in tinfoil bindles was sufficient to provide probable cause to believe that an offense had been committed and, thus, defendant's warrantless arrest was valid under statute which allows peace officer to arrest an offender without a warrant "for any offense committed in his presence or within his view." Vernon's Ann.C.C.P. art. 14.01(b).

Boyd v. State, 621 S.W.2d 616.

Tex.Cr.App. 1981. Where defendant was observed in supermarket placing a steak and bottle of bath oil in her purse and observed leaving the store without paying for such items and was apprehended and placed in custody of city police officer who had been summoned by the manager, defendant's arrest was lawful. Vernon's Ann.C.C.P. art. 18.16.

Stewart v. State, 611 S.W.2d 434.

Tex.Cr.App. 1980. Peace officer need not determine whether material in question is in fact obscene in order to make a valid arrest for offense of commercially distributing obscene material; warrantless arrest is proper if there is probable cause to believe the publication commercially distributed in officer's pres-

see Vernon's Annotated Texas Statutes

ence or within his view was obscene. Vernon's Ann.C.C.P. art. 14.01(b); V.T.C.A., Penal Code § 43.21(1).

Carlock v. State, 609 S.W.2d 787.

Tex.Cr.App. 1980. Fact that defendants were in possession of a stolen gun several hours prior to their arrest was not a sufficient basis for the officers' conclusion that defendants were committing an offense within their presence so as to justify a warrantless arrest.

Green v. State, 594 S.W.2d 72.

Tex.Cr.App. 1979. Defendant had no reasonable expectation of privacy while sitting in a restaurant, so that, upon observing drug transaction in plain view from public vantage point outside the restaurant and recognizing it as offense, officers were authorized to make warrantless arrest. Vernon's Ann.C.C.P. art. 14.01.

Hamilton v. State, 590 S.W.2d 503.

Tex.Cr.App. 1979. Where defendants' vehicle was not stopped by any overt action on the part of off-duty police officers, who simply turned around and began to follow defendants' vehicle after spotting it traveling in the opposite direction and noting that defendants appeared to be smoking a marihuana cigarette, where it was only after defendants stopped at a traffic light that one officer was able to approach the vehicle and then noticed the odor of marihuana, and where it was at that point that the officer directed defendants to pull over to the side of the street and get out of their car, the arrest and subsequent search were reasonable under the circumstances. Vernon's Ann.C.C.P. art. 14.01(b).

Isam v. State, 582 S.W.2d 441.

Tex.Cr.App. 1979. Although detective did not view any of the reading matter of the magazine before making warrantless arrest of seller, the magazine's front and back covers, depicting an act of fellatio on a nude male and an act of cunnilingus on a nude female, gave the officer sufficient probable cause to reasonably believe that a violation of the obscenity statute had occurred in his presence and within his view justifying a warrantless arrest. V.T.C.A., Penal Code § 43.21(1); Vernon's Ann.C.C.P. art. 14.01(b).

Price v. State, 579 S.W.2d 492.

Tex.Cr.App. 1979. Though the scope of an investigation cannot exceed the purposes which justify initiating the investigation, if, while questioning a motorist regarding the operation of his vehicle, an officer sees evidence of a criminal violation in open view or in some other manner acquires probable cause with respect to a more serious charge, the officer may arrest for that offense and, incident thereto, conduct an additional search for physical evidence. Vernon's Ann.Civ.St. art.

EXHIBIT 6   *Texas Digest 2d.*

These volumes (cited as A.L.R.) include annotations to the decisional law on selected topics. For example, a 1987 annotation from A.L.R. entitled "Snowmobile Operation as D.W.I. or D.U.I." appears in 56 A.L.R. 4th 1092. Both *Corpus Juris Secundum* and *American Jurisprudence 2d* are supplemented annually by cumulative pocket parts and are exceptionally well indexed. They serve as an excellent starting point for a researcher because they provide a general overview of topics.

For example, a person researching the defenses available to a defendant charged with forgery would find a good discussion of the law in this area in either of these encyclopedias. A citation to the text on defenses to forgery found in *Corpus Juris Secundum* would read as follows: 37 C.J.S. Forgery § 41; in *American Jurisprudence 2d* it would read like this: 36 Am. Jur. 2d Forgery § 42. In addition to these major national encyclopedias, some states have encyclopedias for the jurisprudence of their state—for example, *Pennsylvania Law Encyclopedia* and *Texas Jurisprudence*. Like the volumes of *Corpus Juris Secundum* and *American Jurisprudence 2d*, most encyclopedias of state law are annually supplemented with cumulative pocket parts.

Textbooks

Textbooks and other treatises on legal subjects often read much like encyclopedias; however, most address specific subjects in great depth. Two of the better-known textbooks on law are *Wharton's Criminal Evidence*, published by Lawyers Cooperative; and LaFave and Scott, *Criminal Law*, published by West.

Law Reviews

In addition, most leading law schools publish law reviews that contain articles, commentaries, and notes by academics, judges, lawyers, and law students who exhaustively research topics. A recent law review article in the criminal justice field, "Running Rampant: The Imposition of Sanctions and the Use of Force Against Fleeing Criminal Suspects," 80 Geo. L.J. 2175 (August 1992), refers to a scholarly article published in volume 80 at page 2175 of the *Georgetown Law Journal*.

Professional Publications and Other Useful Secondary Sources

An example of a professional publication is the *Criminal Law Bulletin*, published bimonthly by Warren, Gorham and Lamont, of Boston. It contains many valuable articles of contemporary interest. For instance, "Stop and Frisk: The Triumph of Law Enforcement Over Private Rights" was published in the January–February 1988 issue. The American Bar Association and most state bar associations publish numerous professional articles in their journals and reports. Some of these present contemporary views on the administration of justice.

The *Index to Legal Periodicals*, published by H. W. Wilson Company of the Bronx, New York, indexes articles from leading legal publications by subject and author. This valuable research tool is found in many law libraries and is kept current by periodic supplements.

Words and Phrases, another West publication, consists of numerous volumes alphabetically arranged in dictionary form. Hundreds of thousands of legal terms are defined with citations to appellate court decisions. The volumes are kept current by annual pocket part supplements. A sample page from *Words and Phrases* is reprinted as Exhibit 8. Periodicals published by law schools, bar associations, and other religious beliefs.[38] The burden falls on prison officials to prove that the food available to a religious inmate is consistent with his dietary laws and provides adequate nourishment.[39] Thus, a prisoner who strictly adheres to Jewish dietary laws may be entitled to prepare his own meals during the Passover holiday,[40] and Muslim inmates may be entitled to a diet that provides them with adequate nourishment without requiring them to eat pork.[41]

However, where Muslim inmates are able to practice their religion conscientiously and still receive a sufficiently nutritious diet, the prison is not obligated to provide them with a special diet.[42]

Prison authorities are not required to supply a prisoner with a special religious diet where the prisoner's beliefs are not religious in nature.[43]

§ 95. Religious Names

Although under some authorities prisoners lose the right to change their names for religious purposes, other authorities generally preclude a categorical refusal to accord legal recognition to religious names adopted by incarcerated persons.

Library References

Prisons ☜4(14).

Although it has been held that a common-law name change, even for religious purposes, is among the rights that inmates lose as inconsistent with their status as prisoners,[44] it has also been held that a state's categorical refusal to accord legal recognition to religious names adopted by incarcerated persons is not reasonably and substantially justified by considerations of prison discipline and order.[45]

Thus, the inmates' free exercise of religion may be burdened by prison officials who continue for all purposes to use the names under which the inmates were committed,[46] and it may be unlawful for the state to refuse to deliver mail addressed to the prisoner under his legal religious name.[47]

On the other hand, inmates are not entitled to have prison officials use their new names for all purposes.[48] For example, correctional authorities generally do not have to reorganize institutional records to reflect prisoners' legally adopted religious names.[49]

E. COMMUNICATIONS AND VISITING RIGHTS AND RESTRICTIONS

§ 96. Communications in General

Prison inmates have a right to communicate with people living in free society, but this right is not unfettered and may be limited by prison officials in order to promote legitimate institutional interests.

Library References

Prisons ☜4(5, 6).

Prison inmates have a constitutional right to communicate with people living in free society.[50] However, this right is not absolute, and is subject

---

38. U.S.—Prushinowski v. Hambrick, D.C.N.C., 570 F.Supp. 863.

39. U.S.—Prushinowski v. Hambrick, D.C.N.C., 570 F.Supp. 863.

40. U.S.—Schlesinger v. Carlson, D.C.Pa., 489 F.Supp. 612.

41. U.S.—Masjid Muhammad-D.C.C. v. Keve, D.C.Del., 479 F.Supp. 1311.

42. U.S.—Masjid Muhammad-D.C.C. v. Keve, D.C.Del., 479 F.Supp. 1311.

43. U.S.—Africa v. Commonwealth of Pennsylvania, C.A.Pa., 662 F.2d 1025, certiorari denied 102 S.Ct. 1756, 456 U.S. 908, 72 L.Ed.2d 165.

44. U.S.—Salahuddin v. Coughlin, D.C.N.Y., 591 F.Supp. 353.

45. U.S.—Barrett v. Commonwealth of Virginia, C.A.Va., 689 F.2d 498.

46. U.S.——Masjid Muhammad-D.C.C. v. Keve, D.C.Del., 479 F.Supp. 1311.

47. U.S.—Barrett v. Commonwealth of Virginia, C.A.Va., 689 F.2d 498.

Masjid Muhammad-D.C.C. v. Keve, D.C.Del. 479 F.Supp. 1311.

48. U.S.—Azeez v. Fairman, D.C.Ill., 604 F.Supp. 357—Masjid Muhammad-D.C.C. v. Keve, D.C.Del., 479 F.Supp. 1311.

49. U.S.—Barrett v. Commonwealth of Virginia, C.A.Va., 689 F.2d 498.

Azeez v. Fairman, D.C.Ill., 604 F.Supp. 357.

Failure to follow statutory mechanism

Inmates' constitutional rights were not violated by failure of prison officials to recognize their use of Muslim names in records of department of correctional services, where inmates had not followed statutory mechanism for name change.

U.S.—Salahuddin v. Coughlin, D.C.N.Y., 591 F.Supp. 353.

50. U.S.—Pell v. Procunier, Cal., 94 S.Ct. 2800, 417 U.S. 817, 41 L.Ed.2d 495.

Inmates of Allegheny County Jail v. Wecht, D.C.Pa., 565 F.Supp. 1278.

Friends and relatives

U.S.—Hutchings v. Corum, D.C.Mo., 501 F.Supp. 1276.

501

EXHIBIT 7 *Corpus Juris Secundum.*

Source: Reprinted with permission from *Corpus uris Secundum,* Vol. 72, Prisons § 96, p. 501.
Copyright 1987 by West Publishing Co., 1-800-328-9352.

RESISTANCE

RESISTANCE—Cont'd

Where a contract for the purchase of defendant's stock in plaintiff corporation provided that defendant should not concern himself in the manufacture or sale of resistance or steel armature binding wire, sheet, or strip, such manufactures must be understood as some alloy of copper used in the manufacture of electric apparatus which does not conduct electricity as freely as pure copper, which is the best conductor, and hence is called "resistance, wire, sheet, or strip." Driver-Harris Wire Co. v. Driver, 62 A. 461, 463, 70 N.J.Eq. 34.

Breaking of glass bottles on roadway over which pneumatic-tired trucks, which were loaded with goods being removed from building by United States Marshal under writ of replevin, were required to pass, held criminal contempt of court, since "resistance" as used in contempt statute includes willful purpose and intent to prevent execution of process of court. Russell v. United States, C.C.A.Minn., 86 F.2d 389, 394, 109 A.L.R. 297.

RESIST HORSES, CATTLE AND LIVE STOCK

Under the statute which requires railroad companies to maintain fences sufficient to "resist horses, cattle and live stock," an instruction that a company was required to maintain one sufficient to "turn stock" was not improper; the quoted terms being synonmous. Deal v. St. Louis, I. M. & S. Ry. Co., 129 S.W. 50, 52, 144 Mo.App. 684.

Under Rev.St.1899, § 1105, Mo.St.Ann. § 4761, p. 2144, requiring a railroad company to construct and maintain fences sufficient to prevent stock getting on the track, an instruction in an action under such section for injuries to stock, which defined a lawful fence as one sufficient "to resist horses, cattle, swine, and like stock," was not erroneous for using the phrase "to resist"; such phrase not being as strong as the phrase "to prevent" in the statute. Hax v. Quincy, O. & K. C. R. Co., 100 S.W. 693, 695, 123 Mo.App. 172.

RESISTING AN OFFICER

To constitute the offense of "resisting an officer," under Act March 8, 1831, § 9, it is not necessary that the officer should be assaulted, beaten, or bruised. Woodworth v. State, 26 Ohio St. 196, 200.

RESISTING AN OFFICER—Cont'd

A justice of the peace being a conservator of the peace, under Const. art. 7, § 40, and being, under Crawford & Moses' Dig. § 2906, without authority to make an arrest himself, act of one in resisting an arrest by a justice does not constitute offense of "resisting an officer," in violation of section 2585 et seq. Herdison v. State, 265 S.W. 84, 86, 166 Ark. 33.

"Resist," as used in Code, § 4476, providing for the punishment of any person who shall knowingly and willfully obstruct, resist, or oppose any officer or other person duly authorized in serving or executing any lawful process, imports force. The words "obstruct," "resist," or "oppose" mean the same thing, and the word "oppose" would cover the meaning of the word "resist" or "obstruct." It does not mean to oppose or impede the process with which the officer is armed, or to defeat its execution, but that the officer himself shall be obstructed. Davis v. State, 76 Ga. 721, 722.

RESISTING AN OFFICER IN DISCHARGE OF HIS DUTY

Where police officers investigated defendant's premises to determine whether he was killing sheep or cattle in alleged violation of an ordinance and after failing to discover indications of such killing one of officers informed defendant that he was under arrest and attempted to put upon his hand a wrist chain and defendant resisted such action for three or four minutes and then submitted quietly, defendant's actions did not constitute "resisting an officer in discharge of his duty" since officers had no right to arrest defendant. City of Chicago v. Delich, 1st Dist. No. 20,686, 193 Ill.App. 72.

Where police officers investigated defendant's premises to determine whether he was killing sheep or cattle in alleged violation of an ordinance and after failing to discover indications of such killing one of officers informed defendant that he was under arrest and attempted to put upon his hand a wrist chain and defendant resisted such action for three or four minutes and then submitted quietly, action of wife who took some part in the altercation with the officers did not constitute "resisting an officer in discharge of his duty," since officers had no right to arrest defendant. City of Chicago v. Delich, 1st Dist., No. 20,687, 193 Ill. App. 74.

612

EXHIBIT 8 *Words and Phrases.*

professional organizations can be valuable both in doing research and in gaining a perspective on many contemporary problems in the criminal justice field. The federal government also publishes numerous studies of value to the criminal justice professional and student.

Computerized Legal Research

Increasingly, legal research is being done electronically using computerized legal databases and retrieval systems like WESTLAW. WESTLAW operates from a central computer system at the West headquarters in St. Paul, Minnesota. Stored there are the databases for state and federal statutes, appellate decisions, attorney general opinions, and certain legal periodicals. For example, the law review article referred to earlier, "Running Rampant: The Imposition of Sanctions and the Use of Force Against Fleeing Criminal Suspects," 80 Geo. L.J. 2175 (August 1992), is available on WESTLAW in the GEOLJ database and can be retrieved using the query ci (80 +5 2175). Subscribers can access WESTLAW via specialized terminals or from their own personal computers using WESTLAW software or through the Internet. WESTLAW users enter "queries" into the system to begin research. A properly formulated query pinpoints the legal issue to be researched and instructs WESTLAW to retrieve all data relevant to the query.

WESTLAW has a searching method that uses natural language, called WIN, that allows queries to be entered in plain English. The statutes, cases, and other research results found on WESTLAW can be printed on paper or downloaded onto computer disks, allowing the material to be incorporated into word processing documents. Computer-assisted legal research (CALR) is an increasingly useful supplement to traditional methods of legal research. One of the most useful features of WESTLAW is the ability to check the history of cases using a service called KeyCite. When the researcher needs to update a large number of cases, WESTLAW can save a tremendous amount of time and substantially reduce the possibility of error.

Legal Research Using the Internet

The newest avenue for finding legal materials is the Internet. The phenomenal growth of the Internet makes it impossible to firmly state what might be available because new things are being added constantly. The federal and state governments are among those rapidly adding data to the Internet, and for that reason a person looking for government information, or statutes and codes, is likely to find it on the Net. Among the best ways to search for legal information is to use a comprehensive legal site, such as Findlaw (**http://www.findlaw.com**), which uses categories to neatly divide legal information so that a user can search for the appropriate category and then find the information available on that topic or issue. Among Findlaw's categories are state law (further divided into categories for each individual state) and international law (indeed, the Internet is currently the best source for locating law from other countries). Another excellent source for federal information is Thomas (**http://thomas.loc.gov**), the Congressional web site, which contains pending bills, federal laws, and links to other federal sites.

Findlaw's Supreme Court category offers United States Supreme Court opinions dating back to 1893, in a searchable format. In addition, the Legal Information

Institute at Cornell University (**http://supct.law.cornell.edu/supct/**) offers downloadable Supreme Court opinions under the auspices of Project Hermes, the Court's electronic dissemination project. The LII archive now contains all opinions of the Court issued since May of 1990 as well as hundreds of the most important historical decisions of the Court. The Supreme Court itself now has its own web site, useful for finding information about pending or recently decided cases, at **http://www.supremecourtus.gov.**

More and more lower courts, both at the federal and state levels, are putting up their own web sites, and often very recently decided cases can be found at these. Findlaw is a good place to begin in trying to locate these sites. Findlaw can help the researcher find the statutes, court decisions, and court rules of most states, almost all of which are now on the Internet. Also, regular search engines such as Google, AltaVista, Lycos, Webcrawler, and Excite can be very helpful in locating court sites and other legal information. When using one of these search engines to locate a particular court decision, it is important to be very specific. One might try a docket number or an obscure or unique term that is found in the case.

Although the Internet is convenient and low in cost, there are limitations to consider in doing research there. The Internet is a solid source for finding up-to-date information, such as current state statutes and some recent court decisions, but usually a researcher will need to locate older materials that may not be posted on the Net. When that is the case, the researcher will need to fall back on traditional methods of research.

The Internet is also a good source for finding factual material, such as statistics and background information. Because most legal research involves finding more than just the latest cases and laws, however, a researcher will usually need to use other written or computer resources in addition to the Internet.

How to Research a Specific Point of Law

The following example demonstrates how a legal researcher might employ the research tools discussed earlier to find the law applicable to a given set of facts. Consider this hypothetical scenario:

> Mary Jones, a student at a Florida college, filed a complaint accusing Jay Grabbo for taking her purse while she was walking across campus on November 20, 1999. In her statement to the police, Ms. Jones was vague on whether Grabbo had used any force in taking the purse and whether she had offered any resistance. She stated that she had recently purchased the purse for $29 and that it contained $12 in cash plus a few loose coins and personal articles of little value. Further inquiry by the police revealed that Grabbo was unarmed.

A researcher who needs to gain a general background on the offense of robbery and how it differs from theft can profitably consult one of the legal encyclopedias mentioned earlier. Someone with a general knowledge of criminal offenses might still need to review the offense of robbery from the standpoint of state law. If so, *Florida Jurisprudence 2d* or some similar text should be consulted.

Given a general knowledge of the crimes of theft and robbery, a likely starting point would be the state statutes. In this instance, reference could be made to the official Florida Statutes. But from a research standpoint, it might be more productive to locate the statutes proscribing theft and robbery in the index to *West's Florida Statutes Annotated* and review the statutes and pertinent annotations in both the principal volume and the pocket part. The researcher would quickly find the offense of theft defined in Section 812.014 and the offense of robbery defined in Section 812.13.

Research of the statutory law would disclose that under Florida law, theft of Jones's purse would be petit theft in the second degree if the total value was less than $100. West's Fla. Stat. Ann. § 812.014. This offense is a misdemeanor for which the maximum penalty is sixty days in jail and a $500 fine. West's Fla. Stats. Ann. § 775.082 and § 775.083. Unarmed robbery, on the other hand, is defined as

> the taking of money or other property which may be the subject of larceny from the person or custody of another, with intent to either permanently or temporarily deprive the person or the owner of the money or other property, when in the course of the taking there is the use of force, violence, assault, or putting in fear and where the perpetrator is unarmed.

It is a second-degree felony that subjects the offender to a maximum fifteen years' imprisonment and a maximum fine of $10,000. West's Fla. Stats. Ann. § 812.13; § 775.082 and § 775.083. Therefore, it is very important to determine whether Grabbo should be charged with petit theft or robbery.

The researcher would then proceed to references noted under the topics of "force" and "resistance" following the text of the robbery statute. The annotated statutes would identify pertinent Florida appellate decisions on these points. For example, the researcher would find a headnote to *Mims v. State,* 342 So.2d 116 (Fla. App. 1977), indicating that purse snatching is not robbery if no more force is used than is necessary to physically remove the property from a person who does not resist. If the victim does resist and that resistance is overcome by the force of the perpetrator, however, the crime of robbery is complete. Another reference points the researcher to *Goldsmith v. State,* 573 So.2d 445 (Fla. App. 1991), which held that the slight force used in snatching a $10 bill from a person's hand without touching the person was insufficient to constitute robbery, and instead constituted petit theft. Additional decisions refer to these and related points of law. For example, *Robinson v. State,* 680 So.2d 481 (Fla. App. 1999), indicates that while a stealthful taking may be petit theft, the force required to take someone's purse can make the offense robbery.

As a final check on statutes, the researcher finds that the 1999 Session Laws reveal that the 1999 Florida Legislature enacted a new law concerning robbery by sudden snatching. That act became effective on October 1, 1999:

> (1) "Robbery by sudden snatching" means the taking of money or other property from the victim's person, with intent to permanently or temporarily deprive the victim or the owner of the money or other property, when, in the course of the taking, the victim was or became aware of the taking. In order to satisfy this definition, it is not necessary to show that:
>
> > (a) The offender used any amount of force beyond that effort necessary to obtain possession of the money or other property; or
> >
> > (b) There was any resistance offered by the victim to the offender or that there was injury to the victim's person.

The new offense is a third-degree felony, which is punishable by a maximum of five years' imprisonment and a fine of $5,000. West's Fla. Stats. Ann. § 775.082 and § 775.083.

After locating these and other pertinent references, the researcher should go to the *Southern Reporter 2d* and read the located cases. After concluding the search, the researcher should "Shepardize" the decisions to determine if they have been subsequently commented on, distinguished, or even reversed.

If the research is undertaken for the prosecutor or the police, once it is completed they can determine whether any further factual investigation is necessary. They can decide the charge to place against Grabbo and the proof required to sustain that charge. On the other hand, if the research was undertaken for a defense counsel, the results would assist the counsel in advising a defendant how to plead and what defense may be available.

The steps outlined here are basic and are designed to illustrate rudimentary principles of gaining access to the criminal law on a particular subject. As previously indicated, another method might involve using digests with the key number system of research. Moreover, there will often be issues of interest still undecided by courts in a particular state. If so, then research into the statutes and court decisions of other states may be undertaken. The methodology and level of research pursued will often depend on the researcher's objective, knowledge of the subject, and experience in conducting legal research.

Conclusion

Understanding how to gain access to the primary and secondary sources of the criminal law is tremendously important. The ability to assemble relevant facts, analyze a problem, and conduct a systematic search for applicable authoritative statements of constitutional, statutory, and decisional law is a skill to be acquired by both the criminal justice student and the working professional. Professionally trained lawyers, who must make the critical judgments concerning the prosecution and defense of criminal actions, increasingly assign basic legal research to paralegal and criminal justice staff personnel. The ability to access the law through traditional as well as through the new computerized methods will assist the student and professional in becoming better acquainted with the dynamics of the criminal law. Moreover, the honing of such skill will enhance a person's ability to carry out specific research assignments and to support his or her recommendations with relevant legal authorities.

The Constitution of the United States of America

We the People of the United States, in Order to form a more perfect Union, establish Justice, insure domestic Tranquility, provide for the common defence, promote the general Welfare, and secure the Blessings of Liberty to ourselves and our Posterity, do ordain and establish this Constitution for the United States of America.

Article I

Section 1. All legislative Powers herein granted shall be vested in a Congress of the United States, which shall consist of a Senate and House of Representatives.

Section 2. (1) The House of Representatives shall be composed of Members chosen every second Year by the People of the several States, and the Electors in each State shall have the Qualifications requisite for Electors of the most numerous Branch of the State Legislature.

(2) No Person shall be a Representative who shall not have attained to the age of twenty-five Years, and been seven Years a Citizen of the United States, and who shall not, when elected, be an Inhabitant of that State in which he shall be chosen.

(3) Representatives and direct Taxes shall be apportioned among the several States which may be included within this Union, according to their respective Numbers, which shall be determined by adding to the whole Number of free Persons, including those bound to Service for a Term of Years, and excluding Indians not taxed, three fifths of all other Persons. The actual Enumeration shall be made within three Years after the first Meeting of the Congress of the United States, and within every subsequent Term of ten Years, in such Manner as they shall by Law direct. The Number of Representatives shall not exceed one for every thirty Thousand, but each State shall have at Least one Representative; and until such enumeration shall be made, the State of New Hampshire shall be entitled to chuse three, Massachusetts eight, Rhode Island and Providence Plantations one, Connecticut five, New York six, New Jersey four, Pennsylvania eight, Delaware one, Maryland six, Virginia ten, North Carolina five, South Carolina five, and Georgia three.

(4) When vacancies happen in the Representation from any State, the Executive Authority thereof shall issue Writs of Election to fill such Vacancies.

(5) The House of Representatives shall chuse their Speaker and other Officers; and shall have the sole Power of Impeachment.

Section 3. (1) The Senate of the United States shall be composed of two Senators from each State, chosen by the Legislature thereof, for six Years; and each Senator shall have one Vote.

(2) Immediately after they shall be assembled in Consequence of the first Election, they shall be divided as equally as may be into three Classes. The Seats of the Senators of the first Class shall be vacated at the Expiration of the second Year, of the second Class at the Expiration of the fourth Year, and of the third Class at the Expiration of the sixth Year, so that one third may be chosen every second Year; and if Vacancies happen by Resignation, or otherwise, during the Recess of the Legislature of any State, the Executive thereof may make temporary Appointments until the next Meeting of the Legislature, which shall then fill such Vacancies.

(3) No Person shall be a Senator who shall not have attained, to the Age of thirty Years, and been nine Years a Citizen of the United States, and who shall not, when elected, be an Inhabitant of that State for which he shall be chosen.

(4) The Vice President of the United States shall be President of the Senate, but shall have no Vote, unless they be equally divided.

(5) The Senate shall chuse their other Officers, and also a President pro tempore, in the Absence of the Vice President, or when he shall exercise the Office of the President of the United States.

(6) The Senate shall have the sole Power to try all Impeachments. When sitting for that Purpose, they shall be on Oath or Affirmation. When the President of the United States is tried, the Chief Justice shall preside: And no Person shall be convicted without the Concurrence of two thirds of the Members present.

(7) Judgment in Cases of Impeachment shall not extend further than to removal from Office, and disqualification to hold and enjoy any Office of honor, Trust or Profit under the United States: but the Party convicted shall nevertheless be liable and subject to Indictment, Trial, Judgment and Punishment, according to Law.

Section 4. (1) The Times, Places and Manner of holding Elections for Senators and Representatives, shall be prescribed in each State by the Legislature thereof; but the Congress may at any time by Law make or alter such Regulations, except as to the Places of chusing Senators.

(2) The Congress shall assemble at least once in every Year, and such Meeting shall be on the first Monday in December, unless they shall by Law appoint a different Day.

Section 5. (1) Each House shall be the Judge of the Elections, Returns and Qualifications of its own Members, and a Majority of each shall constitute a Quorum to do Business; but a smaller Number may adjourn from day to day, and may be authorized to compel the Attendance of absent Members, in such Manner, and under such Penalties as each House may provide.

(2) Each House may determine the Rules of its Proceedings, punish its Members for disorderly Behaviour, and, with the Concurrence of two thirds, expel a Member.

(3) Each House shall keep a Journal of its Proceedings, and from time to time publish the same, excepting such Parts as may in their Judgment require Secrecy; and the Yeas and Nays of the Members of either House on any question shall, at the Desire of one fifth of those Present, be entered on the Journal.

(4) Neither House, during the Session of Congress, shall, without the Consent of the other, adjourn for more than three days, nor to any other Place than that in which the two Houses shall be sitting.

Section 6. (1) The Senators and Representatives shall receive a Compensation for their Services, to be ascertained by Law, and paid out of the Treasury of the United

States. They shall in all Cases, except Treason, Felony and Breach of the Peace, be privileged from Arrest during their Attendance at the Session of their respective Houses, and in going to and returning from the same; and for any Speech or Debate in either House, they shall not be questioned in any other Place.

(2) No Senator or Representative shall, during the Time for which he was elected, be appointed to any civil Office under the Authority of the United States, which shall have been created, or the Emoluments whereof shall have been increased during such time; and no Person holding any Office under the United States, shall be a Member of either House during his Continuance in Office.

Section 7. (1) All Bills for raising Revenue shall originate in the House of Representatives; but the Senate may propose or concur with Amendments as on other Bills.

(2) Every Bill which shall have passed the House of Representatives and the Senate, shall, before it become a Law, be presented to the President of the United States; If he approve he shall sign it, but if not he shall return it, with his Objections to that House in which it shall have originated, who shall enter the Objections at large on their Journal, and proceed to reconsider it. If after such Reconsideration two thirds of that House shall agree to pass the Bill, it shall be sent, together with the Objections, to the other House, by which it shall likewise be reconsidered, and if approved by two thirds of that House, it shall become a Law. But in all such Cases the Votes of both Houses shall be determined by Yeas and Nays, and the Names of the Persons voting for and against the Bill shall be entered on the Journal of each House respectively. If any Bill shall not be returned by the President within ten Days (Sunday excepted) after it shall have been presented to him, the Same shall be a Law, in like Manner as if he had signed it, unless the Congress by their Adjournment prevent its Return, in which Case it shall not be a Law.

(3) Every Order, Resolution, or Vote to which the Concurrence of the Senate and House of Representatives may be necessary (except on a question of Adjournment) shall be presented to the President of the United States; and before the Same shall take Effect, shall be approved by him, or being disapproved by him, shall be repassed by two thirds of the Senate and House of Representatives, according to the Rules and Limitations prescribed in the Case of a Bill.

Section 8. (1) The Congress shall have Power To lay and collect Taxes, Duties, Imposts and Excises, to pay the Debts and provide for the common Defence and general Welfare of the United States; but all Duties, Imposts and Excises shall be uniform throughout the United States;

(2) To borrow Money on the credit of the United States;

(3) To regulate Commerce with foreign Nations, and among the several States, and with the Indian Tribes;

(4) To establish an uniform Rule of Naturalization, and uniform Laws on the subject of Bankruptcies throughout the United States;

(5) To coin Money, regulate the Value thereof, and of foreign Coin, and to fix the Standard of Weights and Measures;

(6) To provide for the Punishment of counterfeiting the Securities and current Coin of the United States;

(7) To establish Post Offices and post Roads;

(8) To promote the Progress of Science and useful Arts, by securing for limited Times to Authors and Inventors the exclusive Right to their respective Writings and Discoveries;

(9) To constitute Tribunals inferior to the supreme Court;

(10) To define and punish Piracies and Felonies committed on the high Seas, and Offenses against the Law of Nations;

(11) To declare War, grant Letters of Marque and Reprisal, and make Rules concerning Captures on Land and Water;

(12) To raise and support Armies, but no Appropriation of Money to that Use shall be for a longer Term than two Years;

(13) To provide and maintain a Navy;

(14) To make Rules for the Government and Regulation of the land and naval Forces;

(15) To provide for calling forth the Militia to execute the Laws of the Union, suppress Insurrections and repel Invasions;

(16) To provide for organizing, arming, and disciplining, the Militia, and for governing such Part of them as may be employed in the Service of the United States, reserving to the States respectively, the Appointment of the Officers, and the Authority of training the Militia according to the discipline prescribed by Congress;

(17) To exercise exclusive Legislation in all Cases whatsoever, over such District (not exceeding ten Miles square) as may, by Cession of particular States, and the Acceptance of Congress, become the Seat of the Government of the United States, and to exercise like Authority over all Places purchased by the Consent of the Legislature of the State in which the Same shall be, for the Erection of Forts, Magazines, Arsenals, dock-Yards, and other needful Buildings;—And

(18) To make all Laws which shall be necessary and proper for carrying into Execution the foregoing Powers, and all other Powers vested by this Constitution in the Government of the United States, or in any Department or Officer thereof.

Section 9. (1) The Migration or Importation of such Persons as any of the States now existing shall think proper to admit, shall not be prohibited by the Congress prior to the Year one thousand eight hundred and eight, but a Tax or Duty may be imposed on such Importation, not exceeding ten dollars for each Person.

(2) The Privilege of the Writ of Habeas Corpus shall not be suspended unless when in Cases of Rebellion or Invasion the public Safety may require it.

(3) No Bill of Attainder or ex post facto Law shall be passed.

(4) No Capitation, or other direct, Tax shall be laid, unless in Proportion to the Census or Enumeration herein before directed to be taken.

(5) No Tax or Duty shall be laid on Articles exported from any State.

(6) No Preference shall be given by any Regulation of Commerce or Revenue to the Ports of one State over those of another; nor shall Vessels bound to, or from, one State, be obliged to enter, clear or pay Duties in another.

(7) No Money shall be drawn from the Treasury, but in Consequence of Appropriations made by Law; and a regular Statement and Account of the Receipts and Expenditures of all public Money shall be published from time to time.

(8) No Title of Nobility shall be granted by the United States: And no Person holding any Office of Profit or Trust under them, shall, without the Consent of the Congress, accept of any present, Emolument, Office, or Title, of any kind whatever, from any King, Prince or foreign State.

Section 10. (1) No State shall enter into any Treaty, Alliance, or Confederation; grant Letters of Marque and Reprisal; coin Money; emit Bills of Credit; make any Thing but gold and silver Coin a Tender in Payment of Debts; pass any Bill of Attainder, ex post facto Law, or Law impairing the Obligation of Contracts, or grant any Title of Nobility.

(2) No State shall, without the Consent of Congress, lay any Imposts or Duties on Imports or Exports, except what may be absolutely necessary for executing its inspection Laws: and the net Produce of all Duties and Imposts, laid by any State on Imports or Exports, shall be for the Use of the Treasury of the United States; and all such Laws shall be subject to the Revision and Control of the Congress.

(3) No State shall, without the Consent of Congress, lay any Duty of Tonnage, keep Troops, or Ships of War in time of Peace, enter into any Agreement or Compact with another State, or with a foreign Power, or engage in War, unless actually invaded, or in such imminent Danger as will not admit of Delay.

Article II

Section 1. (1) The executive Power shall be vested in a President of the United States of America. He shall hold his Office during the Term of four Years, and, together with the Vice President, chosen for the same Term, be elected, as follows:

(2) Each State shall appoint, in such Manner as the Legislature thereof may direct, a Number of Electors, equal to the whole Number of Senators and Representatives to which the State may be entitled in the Congress: but no Senator or Representative, or Person holding an Office of Trust or Profit under the United States, shall be appointed an Elector.

The Electors shall meet in their respective States, and vote by Ballot for two Persons, of whom one at least shall not be an Inhabitant of the same State with themselves. And they shall make a List of all the Persons voted for, and of the Number of Votes for each; which List they shall sign and certify, and transmit sealed to the Seat of the Government of the United States, directed to the President of the Senate. The President of the Senate shall, in the presence of the Senate and House of Representatives, open all the Certificates, and the Votes shall then be counted. The Person having the greatest Number of Votes shall be the President, if such Number be a Majority of the whole Number of Electors appointed; and if there be more than one who have such Majority, and have an equal Number of Votes, then the House of Representatives shall immediately chuse by Ballot one of them for President; and if no Person have a Majority, then from the five highest on the List the said House shall in like Manner chuse the President. But in chusing the President, the Votes shall be taken by States, the Representation from each State having one Vote; a quorum for this Purpose shall consist of a Member or Members from two thirds of the States, and a Majority of all the States shall be necessary to a Choice. In every Case, after the Choice of the President, the Person having the greatest Number of Votes of the Electors shall be the Vice President. But if there should remain two or more who have equal Votes, the Senate shall chuse from them by Ballot the Vice President.

(3) The Congress may determine the Time of chusing the Electors, and the Day on which they shall give their Votes; which Day shall be the same throughout the United States.

(4) No Person except a natural born Citizen, or a Citizen of the United States, at the time of the Adoption of this Constitution, shall be eligible to the Office of President; neither shall any Person be eligible to that Office who shall not have attained to the Age of thirty five Years, and been fourteen Years a Resident within the United States.

(5) In Case of the Removal of the President from Office, or of his Death, Resignation, or Inability to discharge the Powers and Duties of the said Office, the Same shall devolve on the Vice President, and the Congress may by Law provide for the Case of Removal, Death, Resignation or Inability, both of the President and Vice President, declaring what Officer shall then act as President, and such Officer shall act accordingly, until the Disability be removed, or a President shall be elected.

(6) The President shall, at stated Times, receive for his Services, a Compensation, which shall neither be increased nor diminished during the Period for which he shall

have been elected, and he shall not receive within that Period any other Emolument from the United States, or any of them.

(7) Before he enter on the Execution of his Office, he shall take the following Oath or Affirmation:—"I do solemnly swear (or affirm) that I will faithfully execute the Office of President of the United States, and will to the best of my Ability, preserve, protect and defend the Constitution of the United States."

Section 2. (1) The President shall be Commander in Chief of the Army and Navy of the United States, and of the Militia of the several States, when called into the actual Service of the United States; he may require the Opinion, in writing, of the principal Officer in each of the executive Departments, upon any Subject relating to the Duties of their respective Offices, and he shall have Power to grant Reprieves and Pardons for Offenses against the United States, except in Cases of Impeachment.

(2) He shall have Power, by and with the Advice and Consent of the Senate, to make Treaties, provided two thirds of the Senators present concur; and he shall nominate, and by and with the Advice and Consent of the Senate, shall appoint Ambassadors, other public Ministers and Consuls, Judges of the supreme Court, and all other Officers of the United States, whose Appointments are not herein otherwise provided for, and which shall be established by Law: but the Congress may by Law vest the Appointment of such inferior Officers, as they think proper, in the President alone, in the Courts of Law, or in the Heads of Departments.

(3) The President shall have Power to fill up all Vacancies that may happen during the Recess of the Senate, by granting Commissions which shall expire at the End of their next Session.

Section 3. He shall from time to time give to the Congress Information of the State of the Union, and recommend to their Consideration such Measures as he shall judge necessary and expedient; he may, on extraordinary Occasions, convene both Houses, or either of them, and in Case of Disagreement between them, with Respect to the Time of Adjournment, he may adjourn them to such Time as he shall think proper; he shall receive Ambassadors and other public Ministers; he shall take Care that the Laws be faithfully executed, and shall Commission all the Officers of the United States.

Section 4. The President, Vice President and all Civil Officers of the United States, shall be removed from Office on Impeachment for, and Conviction of, Treason, Bribery, or other high Crimes and Misdemeanors.

Article III

Section 1. The judicial Power of the United States, shall be vested in one supreme Court, and in such inferior Courts as the Congress may from time to time ordain and establish. The Judges, both of the supreme and inferior Courts, shall hold their Offices during good Behaviour, and shall, at stated Times, receive for their Services, a Compensation, which shall not be diminished during their Continuance in Office.

Section 2. (1) The judicial Power shall extend to all Cases, in Law and Equity, arising under this Constitution, the Laws of the United States, and Treaties made, or which shall be made, under their Authority;—to all Cases affecting Ambassadors, other public Ministers and Consuls;—to all Cases of admiralty and maritime Jurisdiction;—to Controversies to which the United States shall be a party;—to Controversies between two or more States;—between a State and Citizens of another State;—between Citizens of different States;—between Citizens of the same State claiming Lands under Grants of different States, and between a State, or the Citizens thereof, and foreign States, Citizens or Subjects.

(2) In all Cases affecting Ambassadors, other public Ministers and Consuls, and those in which a State shall be Party, the supreme Court shall have original Jurisdiction. In all the other Cases before mentioned, the supreme Court shall have appellate Jurisdiction, both as to Law and Fact, with such Exceptions, and under such Regulations as the Congress shall make.

(3) The Trial of all Crimes, except in Cases of Impeachment, shall be by Jury; and such Trial shall be held in the State where the said Crimes shall have been committed; but when not committed within any State, the Trial shall be at such Place or Places as the Congress may by Law have directed.

Section 3. (1) Treason against the United States, shall consist only in levying War against them, or in adhering to their Enemies, giving them Aid and Comfort. No Person shall be convicted of Treason unless on the Testimony of two Witnesses to the same overt Act, or on Confession in open Court.

(2) The Congress shall have Power to declare the Punishment of Treason, but no Attainder of Treason shall work Corruption of Blood, or Forfeiture except during the Life of the Person attainted.

Article IV

Section 1. Full Faith and Credit shall be given in each State to the public Acts, Records, and judicial Proceedings of every other State. And the Congress may by general Laws prescribe the Manner in which such Acts, Records and Proceedings shall be proved, and the Effect thereof.

Section 2. (1) The Citizens of each State shall be entitled to all privileges and Immunities of Citizens in the several States.

(2) A Person charged in any State with Treason, Felony, or other Crime, who shall flee from Justice, and be found in another State, shall on Demand of the executive Authority of the State from which he fled, be delivered up, to be removed to the State having Jurisdiction of the Crime.

(3) No Person held to Service of Labour in one State, under the Laws thereof, escaping into another, shall, in Consequence of any Law or Regulation therein, be discharged from such Service or Labour, but shall be delivered up on Claim of the Party to whom such Service or Labour may be due.

Section 3. (1) New States may be admitted by the Congress into this Union; but no new State shall be formed or erected within the Jurisdiction of any other State; nor any State be formed by the Junction of two or more States, or Parts of States, without the Consent of the Legislatures of the States concerned as well as of the Congress.

(2) The Congress shall have power to dispose of and make all needful Rules and Regulations respecting the Territory or other Property belonging to the United States; and nothing in this Constitution shall be so construed as to Prejudice any Claims of the United States, or of any particular State.

Section 4. The United States shall guarantee to every State in this Union a Republican Form of Government, and shall protect each of them against Invasion; and on Application of the Legislature, or of the Executive (when the Legislature cannot be convened) against domestic Violence.

Article V

The Congress, whenever two thirds of both Houses shall deem it necessary, shall propose Amendments to this Constitution, or, on the Application of the Legislatures of two thirds of the several States, shall call a Convention for proposing Amendments, which, in either Case, shall be valid to all Intents and Purposes, as Part of this Constitution, when ratified by the Legislatures of three fourths of the several States, or by Conventions in three fourths thereof, as the one or the other Mode of Ratification may be proposed by the Congress; Provided that no Amendment which may be made prior to the Year One thousand eight hundred and eight shall in any Manner affect the first and fourth Clauses in the Ninth Section of the first Article; and that no State, without its Consent, shall be deprived of its equal Suffrage in the Senate.

Article VI

(1) All Debts contracted and Engagements entered into, before the Adoption of this Constitution, shall be as valid against the United States under this Constitution, as under the Confederation.

(2) This Constitution, and the Laws of the United States which shall be made in Pursuance thereof; and all Treaties made, or which shall be made, under the Authority of the United States, shall be the supreme Law of the Land; and the Judges in every State shall be bound thereby, any Thing in the Constitution or Laws of any State to the Contrary notwithstanding.

(3) The Senators and Representatives before mentioned, and the Members of the several State Legislatures, and all executive and judicial Officers, both of the United States and of the several States, shall be bound by Oath or Affirmation, to support this Constitution; but no religious Test shall ever be required as a Qualification to any Office or public Trust under the United States.

Article VII

The Ratification of the Conventions of nine States, shall be sufficient for the Establishment of this Constitution between the States so ratifying the Same.

Articles in Addition to, and Amendment of, the Constitution of the United States of America, Proposed by Congress, and Ratified by the Several States, Pursuant to the Fifth Article of the Original Constitution

Amendment I (1791)

Congress shall make no law respecting an establishment of religion, or prohibiting the free exercise thereof; or abridging the freedom of speech, or of the press; or the right of the people peaceably to assemble, and to petition the Government for a redress of grievances.

Amendment II (1791)

A well regulated Militia, being necessary to the security of a free state, the right of the people to keep and bear Arms, shall not be infringed.

Amendment III (1791)

No Soldier shall, in time of peace be quartered in any house, without the consent of the Owner, nor in time of war, but in a manner to be prescribed by law.

Amendment IV (1791)

The right of the people to be secure in their persons, houses, papers, and effects, against unreasonable searches and seizures, shall not be violated, and no Warrants shall issue, but upon probable cause, supported by Oath or affirmation, and particularly describing the place to be searched, and the persons or things to be seized.

Amendment V (1791)

No person shall be held to answer for a capital, or otherwise infamous crime, unless on a presentment or indictment of a Grand Jury, except in cases arising in the land or naval forces, or in the Militia, when in actual service in time of War or public danger; nor shall any person be subject for the same offence to be twice put in jeopardy of life or limb; nor shall be compelled in any criminal case to be a witness against himself, nor be deprived of life, liberty, or property, without due process of law; nor shall private property be taken for public use, without just compensation.

Amendment VI (1791)

In all criminal prosecutions, the accused shall enjoy the right to a speedy and public trial, by an impartial jury of the State and district wherein the crime shall have been committed, which district shall have been previously ascertained by law, and to be informed of the nature and cause of the accusation; to be confronted with the witnesses against him; to have compulsory process for obtaining witnesses in his favor, and to have the Assistance of Counsel for his defence.

Amendment VII (1791)

In Suits at common law, where the value in controversy shall exceed twenty dollars, the right of trial by jury shall be preserved, and no fact tried by a jury, shall be otherwise re-examined in any Court of the United States, than according to the rules of the common law.

Amendment VIII (1791)

Excessive bail shall not be required, nor excessive fines imposed, nor cruel and unusual punishments inflicted.

Amendment IX (1791)

The enumeration in the Constitution, of certain rights, shall not be construed to deny or disparage others retained by the people.

Amendment X (1791)

The powers not delegated to the United States by the Constitution, nor prohibited by it to the States, are reserved to the States respectively, or to the people.

Amendment XI (1798)

The Judicial power of the United States shall not be construed to extend to any suit in law or equity, commenced or prosecuted against one of the United States by Citizens of another State, or by Citizens or Subjects of any Foreign State.

Amendment XII (1804)

The Electors shall meet in their respective states and vote by ballot for President and Vice-President, one of whom, at least, shall not be an inhabitant of the same state with themselves; they shall name in their ballots the person voted for as President, and in distinct ballots the person voted for as Vice-President, and they shall make distinct lists of all persons voted for as President, and of all persons voted for as Vice-President, and of the number of votes for each, which lists they shall sign and certify, and transmit sealed to the seat of the government of the United States, directed to the President of the Senate;—The President of the Senate shall, in the presence of the Senate and House of Representatives, open all the certificates and the votes shall then be counted;—The person having the greatest number of votes for President, shall be the President, if such number be a majority of the whole number of Electors appointed; and if no person have such majority, then from the persons having the highest numbers not exceeding three on the list of those voted for as President, the House of Representatives shall choose immediately, by ballot, the President. But in choosing the President, the votes shall be taken by states, the representation from each state having one vote; a quorum for this purpose shall consist of a member or members from two-thirds of the states, and a majority of all the states shall be necessary to a choice. And if the House of Representatives shall not choose a President whenever the right of choice shall devolve upon them, before the fourth day of March next following, then the Vice-President shall act as President, as in the case of the death or other constitutional disability of the President—The person having the greatest number of votes as Vice-President, shall be the Vice-President, if such number be a majority of the whole number of Electors appointed, and if no person have a majority, then from the two highest numbers on the list, the Senate shall choose the Vice-President; A quorum for the purpose shall consist of two-thirds of the whole number of Senators, and a majority of the whole number shall be necessary to a choice. But no person constitutionally ineligible to the office of President shall be eligible to that of Vice-President of the United States.

Amendment XIII (1865)

Section 1. Neither slavery nor involuntary servitude, except as a punishment for crime whereof the party shall have been duly convicted, shall exist within the United States, or any place subject to their jurisdiction.

Section 2. Congress shall have power to enforce this article by appropriate legislation.

Amendment XIV (1868)

Section 1. All persons born or naturalized in the United States and subject to the jurisdiction thereof, are citizens of the United States and of the State wherein they reside. No State shall make or enforce any law which shall abridge the privileges or immunities of citizens of the United States; nor shall any State deprive any person of life, liberty, or property, without due process of law; nor deny to any person within its jurisdiction the equal protection of the laws.

Section 2. Representatives shall be apportioned among the several States according to their respective numbers, counting the whole number of persons in each State, excluding Indians not taxed. But when the right to vote at any election for the choice of electors for President and Vice-President of the United States, Representatives in Congress, the Executive and Judicial officers of a State, or the members of the Legislature thereof, is denied to any of the male inhabitants of such State, being twenty-one years of age, and citizens of the United States, or in any way abridged, except for participation in rebellion, or other crime, the basis of representation therein shall be reduced in the proportion which the number of such male citizens shall bear to the whole number of male citizens twenty-one years of age in such State.

Section 3. No person shall be a Senator or Representative in Congress, or elector of President and Vice-President, or hold any office, civil or military, under the United States, or under any State, who, having previously taken an oath, as a member of Congress, or as an officer of the United States, or as a member of any State legislature, or as an executive or judicial officer of any State, to support the Constitution of the United States, shall have engaged in insurrection or rebellion against the same, or given aid or comfort to the enemies thereof. But Congress may by a vote of two-thirds of each House, remove such disability.

Section 4. The validity of the public debt of the United States, authorized by law, including debts incurred for payment of pensions and bounties for services in suppressing insurrection or rebellion, shall not be questioned. But neither the United States nor any State shall assume or pay any debt or obligation incurred in aid of insurrection or rebellion against the United States, or any claim for the loss or emancipation of any slave; but all such debts, obligations and claims shall be held illegal and void.

Section 5. The Congress shall have power to enforce, by appropriate legislation, the provisions of this article.

Amendment XV (1870)

Section 1. The right of citizens of the United States to vote shall not be denied or abridged by the United States or by any State on account of race, color, or previous condition of servitude.

Section 2. The Congress shall have power to enforce this article by appropriate legislation.

Amendment XVI (1913)

The Congress shall have power to lay and collect taxes on incomes, from whatever source derived, without apportionment among the several States, and without regard to any census or enumeration.

Amendment XVII (1913)

The Senate of the United States shall be composed of two Senators from each State, elected by the people thereof, for six years; and each Senator shall have one vote. The electors in each State shall have the qualifications requisite for electors of the most numerous branch of the State legislatures.

When vacancies happen in the representation of any State in the Senate, the executive authority of such State shall issue writs of election to fill such vacancies: Provided, That the legislature of any State may empower the executive thereof to make temporary appointments until the people fill the vacancies by election as the legislature may direct.

This amendment shall not be so construed as to affect the election or term of any Senator chosen before it becomes valid as part of the Constitution.

Amendment XVIII (1919)

Section 1. After one year from the ratification of this article the manufacture, sale, or transportation of intoxicating liquors within, the importation thereof into, or the exportation thereof from the United States and all territory subject to the jurisdiction thereof for beverage purposes is hereby prohibited.

Section 2. The Congress and the several States shall have concurrent power to enforce this article by appropriate legislation.

Section 3. This article shall be inoperative unless it shall have been ratified as an amendment to the Constitution by the legislatures of the several States, as provided in the Constitution, within seven years from the date of the submission hereof to the States by the Congress.

Amendment XIX (1920)

The right of citizens of the United States to vote shall not be denied or abridged by the United States or by any State on account of sex.

Congress shall have power to enforce this article by appropriate legislation.

Amendment XX (1933)

Section 1. The terms of the President and Vice President shall end at noon on the 20th day of January, and the terms of Senators and Representatives at noon on the 3d day of January, of the years in which such terms would have ended if this article had not been ratified; and the terms of their successors shall then begin.

Section 2. The Congress shall assemble at least once in every year, and such meeting shall begin at noon on the 3d day of January, unless they shall by law appoint a different day.

Section 3. If, at the time fixed for the beginning of the term of the President, the President elect shall have died, the Vice President elect shall become President. If a President shall not have been chosen before the time fixed for the beginning of his term, or if the President elect shall have failed to qualify, then the Vice President elect shall act as President until a President shall have qualified; and the Congress may by law provide for the case wherein neither a President elect nor a Vice President elect shall have qualified, declaring who shall then act as President, or the manner in which one who is to act shall be selected, and such person shall act accordingly until a President or Vice President shall have qualified.

Section 4. The Congress may by law provide for the case of the death of any of the persons from whom the House of Representatives may choose a President whenever the right of choice shall have devolved upon them, and for the case of the death of any of the persons from whom the Senate may choose a Vice President whenever the right of choice shall have devolved upon them.

Section 5. Sections 1 and 2 shall take effect on the 15th day of October following the ratification of this article.

Section 6. This article shall be inoperative unless it shall have been ratified as an amendment to the Constitution by the legislatures of three-fourths of the several States within seven years from the date of its submission.

Amendment XXI (1933)

Section 1. The eighteenth article of amendment to the Constitution of the United States is hereby repealed.

Section 2. The transportation or importation into any State, Territory or possession of the United States for delivery or use therein of intoxicating liquors, in violation of the laws thereof, is hereby prohibited.

Section 3. This article shall be inoperative unless it shall have been ratified as an amendment to the Constitution by conventions in the several States, as provided in the Constitution, within seven years from the date of the submission hereof to the States by the Congress.

Amendment XXII (1951)

Section 1. No person shall be elected to the office of the President more than twice, and no person who has held the office of President, or acted as President, for more than two years of a term to which some other person was elected President shall be elected to the office of the President more than once. But this Article shall not apply to any person holding the office of President when this Article was proposed by the Congress, and shall not prevent any person who may be holding the office of President, or acting as President, during the term within which this Article becomes operative from holding the office of President or acting as President during the remainder of such term.

Section 2. This Article shall be inoperative unless it shall have been ratified as an amendment to the Constitution by the legislatures of three-fourths of the several States within seven years from the date of its submission to the States by the Congress.

Amendment XXIII (1961)

Section 1. The District constituting the seat of Government of the United States shall appoint in such manner as the Congress may direct:

A number of electors of President and Vice President equal to the whole number of Senators and Representatives in Congress to which the District would be entitled if it were a State, but in no event more than the least populous State; they shall be in addition to those appointed by the States, but they shall be considered, for the purposes of the election of President and Vice President, to be electors appointed by a State; and they shall meet in the District and perform such duties as provided by the twelfth article of amendment.

Section 2. The Congress shall have power to enforce this article by appropriate legislation.

Amendment XXIV (1964)

Section 1. The right of citizens of the United States to vote in any primary or other election for President or Vice President, for electors for President or Vice President, or for Senator or Representative in Congress, shall not be denied or abridged by the United States or any State by reason of failure to pay any poll tax or other tax.

Section 2. The Congress shall have power to enforce this article by appropriate legislation.

Amendment XXV (1967)

Section 1. In case of the removal of the President from office or of his death or resignation, the Vice President shall become President.

Section 2. Whenever there is a vacancy in the office of the Vice President, the President shall nominate a Vice President who shall take office upon confirmation by a majority vote of both Houses of Congress.

Section 3. Whenever the President transmits to the President pro tempore of the Senate and the Speaker of the House of Representatives his written declaration that he is unable to discharge the powers and duties of his office, and until he transmits to them a written declaration to the contrary, such powers and duties shall be discharged by the Vice President as Acting President.

Section 4. Whenever the Vice President and a majority of either the principal officers of the executive departments or of such other body as Congress may by law provide, transmit to the President pro tempore of the Senate and the Speaker of the House of Representatives their written declaration that the President is unable to discharge the powers and duties of his office, the Vice President shall immediately assume the powers and duties of the office as Acting President.

Thereafter, when the President transmits to the President pro tempore of the Senate and the Speaker of the House of Representatives his written declaration that no inability exists, he shall resume the powers and duties of his office unless the Vice President and a majority of either the principal officers of the executive department or of such other body as Congress may by law provide, transmit within four days to the President pro tempore of the Senate and the Speaker of the House of Representatives their written declaration that the President is unable to discharge the powers and duties of his office. Thereupon Congress shall decide the issue, assembling within forty-eight hours for that purpose if not in session. If the Congress, within twenty-one days after receipt of the latter written declaration, or, if Congress is not in session, within twenty-one days after Congress is required to assemble, determines by two-thirds vote of both Houses that the President is unable to discharge the powers and duties of his office, the Vice President shall continue to discharge the same as Acting President; otherwise, the President shall resume the powers and duties of his office.

Amendment XXVI (1971)

Section 1. The right of citizens of the United States, who are eighteen years of age or older, to vote shall not be denied or abridged by the United States or by any State on account of age.

Section 2. The Congress shall have power to enforce this article by appropriate legislation.

Amendment XXVII (1992)

No law, varying the compensation for the services of the Senators and Representatives, shall take effect, until an election of Representatives shall have intervened.

Glossary

abandoned property   Property over which the former owner has relinquished any claim of ownership.

abortion   The intentional termination of a pregnancy.

abuse of the elderly   Infliction of physical or mental harm on elderly persons.

access devices   Cards, plates, codes, electronic serial numbers, mobile identification numbers, personal identification numbers, and telecommunications services, equipment, or instrument identifiers or other means that can be used to obtain goods or services.

accessory   A person who aids in the commission of a crime.

accessory after the fact   A person who with knowledge that a crime has been committed conceals or protects the offender.

accessory before the fact   A person who aids or assists another in commission of an offense.

accomplice   A person who voluntarily unites with another in commission of an offense.

accusatorial system   A system of criminal justice where the prosecution bears the burden of proving the guilt of the accused.

act of omission   The failure to perform an act required by law.

actual imprisonment standard   The standard governing the applicability of the federal constitutional right of an indigent person to have counsel appointed in a misdemeanor case. For the right to be violated, the indigent defendant must actually be sentenced to jail or prison after having been tried without appointed counsel.

actual possession   Possession of something with the possessor having immediate control.

actus reus   A "wrongful act" that, combined with other necessary elements of crime, constitutes criminal liability.

adjudication   The formal process by which courts decide cases.

adjudicatory hearing   A proceeding in juvenile court to determine whether a juvenile has committed an act of delinquency.

administrative demotion actions   Administrative means of demoting a military service member based on reasons specified in regulations in that member's branch of military service—for example, failure to perform duties at a minimum level of competence.

administrative discharge actions   Administrative means of discharging a military service member for reasons set out in regulations in that member's branch of military service—for example, fraudulent enlistment.

administrative searches   Searches of premises by a government official to determine compliance with health and safety regulations.

administrative-type acts   Ministerial acts performed by executive officers in carrying out duties assigned by law.

adultery   Voluntary sexual intercourse where at least one of the parties is married to someone other than the sexual partner.

adversary system   A system of justice involving conflicting parties where the role of the judge is to remain neutral.

adverse administrative actions   Actions taken against military service members by commanders—for example, reprimands and admonitions.

affiant   A person who makes an affidavit.

affidavit   A written document attesting to specific facts of which the affiant has knowledge, and sworn to or affirmed by the affiant.

affirm   To uphold, ratify, or approve.

affirmative defense Defense to a criminal charge where the defendant bears the burden of proof. Examples include automatism, intoxication, coercion, and duress.

aggravated assault An assault committed with a dangerous weapon or with intent to commit a felony.

aggravated battery A battery committed by use of an instrument designed to inflict great bodily harm on the victim.

aggravated mayhem The act of willfully inflicting injuries that cause great bodily harm to another.

aggravated robbery A robbery committed by a person armed with a dangerous weapon.

aggravating circumstances Factors attending the commission of a crime that make the crime or its consequences worse.

aggravating factors See aggravating circumstances.

aiding and abetting Assisting in or otherwise facilitating the commission of a crime.

Alford **plea** A plea of guilty with a protestation of innocence.

ALI standard A test proposed by American Law Institute to determine if a defendant is legally insane. See substantial capacity test.

alibi Defense to a criminal charge that places the defendant at some place other than the scene of the crime at the time the crime occurred.

allegation Assertion or claim made by a party to a legal action.

Allen **charge** A judge's instruction to jurors who are deadlocked, encouraging them to listen to one another's arguments and reappraise their own positions in an effort to arrive at a verdict.

amendment A modification, addition, or deletion.

Anders **brief** A law brief submitted to an appellate court by publicly appointed defense counsel in which counsel explains that the defendant's appeal is nonmeritorious and requests release from further representation of the defendant.

animus furundi Intent to steal or otherwise deprive an owner of property.

anonymous tip Information from an unknown source concerning alleged criminal activity.

answer brief The appellee's written response to the appellant's law brief filed in an appellate court.

anticipatory search warrant A search warrant issued based on an affidavit that at a future time evidence of a crime will be at a specific place.

antismoking laws Statutes or ordinances prohibiting or restricting smoking in all or specified public places.

Antiterrorism and Effective Death Penalty Act of 1996 A federal statute designed to effectuate reforms in administration of the death penalty by curtailing successive petitions for habeas corpus by prisoners sentenced to death.

antitrust violations Violations of laws designed to protect the public from price fixing, price discrimination, and monopolistic practices in trade and commerce.

appeal Review by a higher court of a lower court decision.

appeal of right An appeal that a defendant is entitled to make as a matter of law.

appellant A person who takes an appeal to a higher court.

appellate courts Judicial tribunals that review decisions from lower tribunals.

appellate jurisdiction The authority of a court to hear appeals from decisions of lower courts.

appellee A person against whom an appeal is taken.

arraignment An appearance before a court of law for the purpose of pleading to a criminal charge.

arrest To take someone into custody or otherwise deprive that person of freedom of movement.

arrest warrant A document issued by a magistrate or judge directing that a named person be taken into custody for allegedly having committed an offense.

arrestee A person who is arrested.

arson The crime of intentionally burning someone else's house or building—now commonly extended to other property as well.

asportation The carrying away of something: in kidnapping, the carrying away of the victim; in larceny, the carrying away of the victim's property.

assault The attempt or threat to inflict bodily injury upon another person.

assignments of error A written presentation to an appellate court identifying the points that the appellant claims constitute errors made by the lower tribunal.

assisted suicide An offense (in some jurisdictions) of aiding or assisting a person to take his or her life.

asylum Sanctuary; a place of refuge.

attempt An intent to commit a crime coupled with an act taken toward committing the offense.

Attorney General The highest legal officer of a state or of the United States.

attorney–client privilege The right of a person (client) not to testify about matters discussed in confidence with an attorney in the course of the attorney's representation.

automatism The condition under which a person performs a set of actions during a state of unconsciousness.

automobile exception Exception to the Fourth Amendment warrant requirement. The exception allows the warrantless search of a vehicle by police who have probable cause to search but because of exigent circumstances are unable to secure a warrant.

bail The conditional release of a person charged with a crime.

Bail Reform Act of 1984 See Federal Bail Reform Act of 1984.

bankruptcy fraud Dishonest or deceitful acts committed by one who seeks relief under laws designed to protect honest debtors from their creditors.

battered child syndrome A group of symptoms typically manifested by a child who has suffered continued physical or mental abuse, often from a parent or person having custody of the child.

battered woman syndrome A group of symptoms typically manifested by a woman who has suffered continued physical or mental abuse, usually from a male with whom she lives.

battery The unlawful use of force against another person that entails some injury or offensive touching.

bench trial A trial held before a judge without a jury present.

bench warrant An arrest warrant issued by a judge.

best evidence Primary evidence used to prove a fact—usually an original written document that evidences a communication or transaction.

best evidence rule The requirement that the original document or best facsimile must be produced to prove the content of a writing.

beyond a reasonable doubt The standard of proof that is constitutionally required to be introduced before a defendant can be found guilty of a crime or before a juvenile can be adjudicated a delinquent.

bid rigging An illegal manipulation in submitting bids to obtain a contract, usually from a public body.

bifurcated trial A capital trial with separate phases for determining guilt and punishment.

bigamy The crime of being married to more than one person at the same time.

bill of attainder A legislative act imposing punishment without trial upon persons deemed guilty of treason or felonies (prohibited by the U.S. Constitution).

Bill of Rights A written enumeration of basic rights, usually annexed to a written constitution—for example, the first ten amendments to the U.S. Constitution.

Blackstone's *Commentaries* A massive treatise on the English common law published in 1769 by Sir William Blackstone, a professor at Oxford University. In America, Blackstone's *Commentaries* became something of a "legal bible."

***Blockburger* test** A test applied by courts to determine if the charges against a defendant would constitute a violation of the constitutional prohibition against double jeopardy—that is, being tried twice for the same offense. The *Blockburger* test holds that it is not double jeopardy for a defendant to be tried for two offenses if each offense includes an element that the other offense does not.

bona fide "In good faith"; without the attempt to defraud or deceive.

boot camp An institution that provides systematic discipline in a military-like environment designed to rehabilitate an offender; employed as a sentencing alternative.

border search A search of persons entering the borders of the United States.

bounty hunter A person paid a fee or commission to capture a defendant who has fled a jurisdiction to escape punishment.

Brady Bill Legislation passed by Congress in 1993 requiring a five-day waiting period before the purchase of a handgun, during which time a background check is conducted of the buyer.

brain death The cessation of activity of the central nervous system.

breach of contract The violation of a provision in a legally enforceable agreement that gives the damaged party the right to recourse in a court of law.

breach of the peace The crime of disturbing the public tranquility and order; a generic term encompassing disorderly conduct, riot, etc.

breaking See breaking and entering.

breaking and entering Forceful, unlawful entry into a building or conveyance.

Breathalyzer A device that detects the amount of alcohol in a sample of a person's breath.

bribery The crime of offering, giving, requesting, soliciting, or receiving something of value to influence a decision of a public official.

brief A document filed by a party to a lawsuit to convince the court of the merits of that party's case.

burden of persuasion The legal responsibility of a party to convince a court of the correctness of a position asserted.

burden of production of evidence The obligation of a party to produce some evidence in support of a proposition asserted.

burden of proof The requirement to introduce evidence to prove an alleged fact or set of facts.

burglar's tools Special tools for lock picking and other means of forced entry into a building.

burglary At common law, the crime of breaking and entering a house at night with the intent to commit a felony therein. Under modern statutes, burglary frequently consists of breaking and entering a structure or conveyance at any time with the intent to commit any offense therein.

canonical Pertaining to the canons or laws of a church.

canons of construction Rules governing the judicial interpretation of constitutions, statutes, and other written instruments.

capias "That you take." A general term for various court orders requiring that some named person be taken into custody.

capital crime A crime for which death is a permissible punishment.

capital punishment The death penalty.

caption At common law, a taking or seizure.

carjacking Taking a motor vehicle from someone by force and violence or by intimidation.

carnal knowledge Sexual intercourse.

case law Law derived from judicial decisions, also known as decisional law.

castle doctrine "A man's home is his castle." At common law, the right to use whatever force is necessary to protect one's dwelling and its inhabitants from an unlawful entry or attack.

causation An act that produces an event or an effect.

caveat emptor "Let the buyer beware." Common-law maxim requiring the consumer to judge the quality of a product before making a purchase.

cert petition A petition to a higher court asking the court to review a lower court decision.

certiorari Writ issued by an appellate court to grant discretionary review of a case decided by a lower court.

challenge for cause Objection to a prospective juror on some specified ground (for example, a close relationship to a party in the case).

change of venue The removal of a legal proceeding, usually a trial, to a new location.

child abuse Actions that physically, mentally, or morally endanger the welfare of a child.

child pornography Material depicting persons under the age of legal majority in sexual poses or acts.

child shield statutes Laws that allow a screen to be placed between a child victim of sexual abuse and a defendant while the child testifies in court.

child snatching Action by one parent in deliberately retaining or concealing a child from the other parent.

chilling effect A law or policy that discourages persons from exercising their rights.

churning Making purchases and sales of securities in a client's account simply to generate commissions for the broker.

circumstantial evidence Indirect evidence from which the existence of certain facts may be inferred.

citation (1) A summons to appear in court, often used in traffic violations. (2) A reference to a statute or court decision, often designating a publication where the law or decision appears.

citizen's arrest An arrest made by a person who is not a law enforcement officer.

civil action A lawsuit brought to enforce private rights and to remedy violations thereof.

civil infractions Noncriminal violation of a law, often referring to minor traffic violations.

civil law (1) The law relating to rights and obligations of parties. (2) The body of law, based essentially on Roman law, that prevails in most non-English-speaking nations.

civil rights Rights protected by the federal and state constitutions and statutes. The term is often used to denote the right to be free from unlawful discrimination.

claim of right A contention that an item was taken in a good-faith belief that it belonged to the taker; sometimes asserted as a defense to a charge of larceny or theft.

Clean Air Act A federal statute designed to deter polluters and thereby enhance the quality of the air.

Clean Water Act A federal statute designed to deter polluters and thereby enhance the quality of bodies of public water.

clear and convincing evidence standard An evidentiary standard that is higher than the standard of "preponderance of the evidence" applied in civil cases, but lower than the standard of "beyond a reasonable doubt" applied in criminal cases. For example, under the new federal standard for the affirmative defense of insanity, the defendant must establish the defense of insanity by "clear and convincing evidence."

clear and present danger doctrine In constitutional law, the doctrine that the First Amendment does not protect those forms of expression that pose a "clear and present danger" of bringing about some substantive evil that government has a right to prevent.

clemency A grant of mercy by an executive official commuting a sentence or pardoning a criminal.

clergy–penitent privilege The exemption of a clergyperson and a penitent from disclosing communications made in confidence by the penitent.

closing arguments Arguments presented at trial by counsel at the conclusion of the presentation of evidence.

code   A systematic collection of laws.

coerced confession   A confession or other incriminating statements obtained from a suspect by police through force, violence, threats, intimidation, or undue psychological pressure.

collateral attack   The attempt to defeat the outcome of a judicial proceeding by challenging it in a different proceeding or court.

commercial bribery   Offering, soliciting, or accepting a benefit or consideration in respect to a business or professional matter in violation of a person's duty of fidelity.

common law   A body of law that develops through judicial decisions, as distinct from legislative enactments. Originally developed by English courts of law.

common-law rape   Sexual intercourse by a male with a female, other than his wife, by force and against the will of the female.

community control   A sentence imposed on a person found guilty of a crime that requires that the offender be placed in an individualized program of noninstitutional confinement.

community policing   Style of police work that stresses development of close ties between police officers and the communities they serve.

community service   A sentence requiring that the criminal perform some specific service to the community for some specified period of time.

commutation   A form of clemency that lessens the punishment for a person convicted of a crime.

compelling government interest   A government interest sufficiently strong that it overrides the fundamental rights of persons adversely affected by government action or policy.

competency   The state of being legally qualified to give testimony or stand trial.

competent to testify   A person who has the legal capacity to offer evidence under oath in court.

complicity   A person's voluntary participation with another person in commission of a crime or wrongful act.

compounding a crime   The acceptance of money or something else of value in exchange for an agreement not to prosecute a person for committing a crime.

Comprehensive Environmental Response, Compensation and Liability Act   A Congressional enactment commonly known as the Superfund Law. Its purpose is to finance cleanup and provide for civil suits by citizens. The act also imposes reporting requirements for collection and disposal of solid wastes.

comprehensive planning   A guide for the orderly development of a community, usually to be implemented by enactment of zoning ordinances.

compulsory process   See subpoena.

compurgation   A method of trial used before the thirteenth century whereby a person charged with a crime could be absolved by swearing to innocence and producing a number of other persons willing to swear that they believed the accused's declaration of innocence.

Computer Abuse Amendments Act   Enacted in 1994, this federal act makes it a crime to "knowingly cause the transmission of a program, information, code, or command" in interstate commerce with an intent to cause damage to a computer exclusively for the use of a financial institution or the U.S. government.

computer fraud   An offense consisting of obtaining property or services by false pretenses through use of a computer or computer network.

computer trespass   An offense consisting of the unauthorized copying, alteration, or removal of computer data, programs, or software.

concealed weapon   A weapon carried on or about a person in such a manner as to hide it from the ordinary sight of another person.

concurrent sentencing   The practice in which a trial court imposes separate sentences to be served at the same time.

concurring in the judgment   An opinion by a judge or justice agreeing with the judgment of an appellate court without agreeing with the court's reasoning process.

concurring opinion   Opinion handed down by a judge that supports the judgment of the court but often based on different reasoning.

conditions of confinement   The conditions under which inmates are held in jails and prisons. These conditions are subject to challenge under the Eighth Amendment's cruel and unusual punishments clause.

conditions of probation   A set of rules that must be observed by a person placed on probation.

confidential informant (CI)   An informant known to the police but whose identity is held in confidence.

consanguinity   Kinship; the state of being related by blood.

consecutive sentencing   The practice in which a trial court imposes a sentence or sentences to be served following completion of a prior sentence or sentences.

consent   Voluntarily yielding to the will or desire of another person.

consent to a search   The act of a person voluntarily permitting police to conduct a search of person or property.

consideration, prize, and chance   The legal elements that constitute gambling under most statutes that make it an offense to gamble.

conspiracy The crime of two or more persons agreeing or planning to commit a crime. The crime of conspiracy is distinct from the crime contemplated by the conspirators (the "target crime").

constitutional rights of prison inmates Under modern interpretation of the federal and state constitutions, prisoners retain those constitutional rights that are not inconsistent with the fact that they are confined in a secure environment.

constitutional supremacy The doctrine that the Constitution is the supreme law of the land and that all actions and policies of government must be consistent with it.

construction Interpretation.

constructive breaking Where the law implies a breaking. For example, a person who gains entry into someone's house through fraud or deception may be said to have made a constructive breaking.

constructive intent Intent inferred by law as a result of circumstances surrounding a party's actions.

constructive possession Being in the position to effectively control something, even if it is not actually in one's possession.

contemnor A person found to be in contempt of court.

contempt of court Any action that embarrasses, hinders, obstructs, or is calculated to lessen the dignity of a court of law.

continuance Delay of a judicial proceeding on the motion of one of the parties.

contraband Any property that is inherently illegal to produce or possess.

contractual immunity A grant by a prosecutor with approval of a court that makes a witness immune from prosecution in exchange for the witness's testimony.

controlled substance A drug designated by law as contraband.

Controlled Substance Act A federal law listing controlled substances according to their potential for abuse. States have similar statutes.

convening authorities The military authorities with jurisdiction to convene a court-martial for trial of persons subject to the Uniform Code of Military Justice.

conversion The unlawful assumption of the rights of ownership to someone else's property.

corporal punishment Punishment that inflicts pain or injury to a person's body.

corpus delicti "The body of the crime." The material thing upon which a crime has been committed (for example, a burned-out building in a case of arson).

corrections system The system of prisons, jails, and other penal and correctional institutions.

corroboration Evidence that strengthens or validates evidence already given.

counsel A lawyer who represents a party.

counterfeiting Making an imitation of something with the intent to deceive—for example, the offense of making imitations of U.S. coins and currency.

Court of Appeals for the Armed Forces The court (formerly known as the court of Military Appeals) consisting of five civilian judges that reviews sentences affecting a general or flag officer or imposing the death penalty as well as cases certified for review by the judge advocate general of a branch of service. May grant review of convictions and sentences on petitions by service members.

courts of general jurisdiction Courts that conduct trials in felony and major misdemeanor cases. Also refers to courts that have jurisdiction to hear civil as well as criminal cases.

courts of limited jurisdiction Courts that handle pretrial matters and conduct trials in minor misdemeanor cases.

court-martial A military tribunal convened by a commander of a military unit to try a person subject to the Uniform Code of Military Justice who is accused of violating a provision of that code.

credit card fraud The offense of using a credit card to obtain goods or services by a person who knows that the card has been stolen, forged, or canceled.

crime syndicates An association or group of persons that carries out organized crime activities.

criminal Pertaining to crime; a person convicted of a crime.

criminal contempt Punishment imposed by a judge against a person who violates a court order or otherwise intentionally interferes with the administration of the court.

criminal intent A necessary element of a crime— the evil design associated with the criminal act.

criminal negligence Conduct involving the reckless and flagrant disregard of the life or safety of another.

criminal procedure The rules of law governing the procedures by which crimes are investigated, prosecuted, adjudicated, and punished.

criminal responsibility Refers to the set of doctrines under which individuals are held accountable for criminal conduct.

criminal syndicalism The crime of advocating violence as a means to accomplish political change.

criminal trial A trial in a court of law to determine the guilt or innocence of a person charged with a crime.

criminology The study of the nature of, causes of, and means of dealing with crime.

critical pretrial stages Significant procedural steps that occur preliminary to a criminal trial. A defendant has the right to counsel at these critical stages.

cross-examination The process of interrogating a witness who has testified on direct examination by asking the witness questions concerning his or her testimony. Cross-examination is designed to bring out any bias or inconsistencies in the witness's testimony.

cruel and unusual punishment Punishment that shocks the moral conscience of the community—for example, torturing or physically beating a prisoner.

culpability Guilt.

curfew ordinances Ordinances typically requiring minors to be off the streets by a certain time of night.

curtilage At common law, the enclosed space surrounding a dwelling house; in modern codes, this space has been extended to encompass other buildings.

damages Monetary compensation awarded by a court to a person who has suffered injuries or losses to person or property as a result of someone else's conduct.

de facto "In fact"; as a matter of fact"

de jure "In law"; as a matter of law.

de minimis "Minimal."

deadlocked jury A jury where the jurors cannot agree on a verdict.

deadly force The degree of force that may result in the death of the person against whom the force is applied.

death penalty Capital punishment; a sentence to death for the commission of a crime.

death-qualified jury A trial jury composed of persons who do not entertain scruples against imposing a death sentence.

decisional law Law declared by appellate courts in their written decisions and opinions.

decriminalization of routine traffic offenses The recent trend toward treating minor motor vehicle offenses—for example, speeding—as civil infractions rather than crimes.

defendant A person charged with a crime or against whom a civil action has been initiated.

defense A defendant's stated reasons of law or fact as to why the prosecution or plaintiff should not prevail.

defense attorneys Lawyers who represent defendants in criminal cases.

defense of habitation and other property The right of a defendant charged with an offense to assert that he or she used reasonable force to protect his or her home or property.

defense of others The defense asserted by one who claims the right to use reasonable force to prevent commission of a felony against another person.

definite sentence Criminal penalty set by law with no discretion for the judge or correctional officials to individualize punishment.

definite sentencing Legislatively determined sentencing with no discretion given to judges or corrections officials to individualize punishment.

delinquency petition A written document alleging that a juvenile has committed an offense and asking the court to hold an adjudicatory hearing to determine the merits of the petition.

demurrer A document challenging the legal sufficiency of a complaint or indictment.

Department of Justice The department of the federal government that is headed by the Attorney General and staffed by United States Attorneys.

deposition The recorded sworn testimony of a witness; not given in open court.

depraved mind or heart A serious moral deficiency; a high level of malice often linked to second-degree murder.

derivative evidence Evidence that is derived from or obtained only as a result of other evidence.

desertion In military law, the voluntary departure from military assignment with no intent to return to the military service.

detention Holding someone in custody.

detention hearing A proceeding held to determine whether a juvenile charged with an offense should be detained pending an adjudicatory hearing.

determinate sentence Variation on definite sentencing whereby a judge fixes the term of incarceration within statutory limits.

determinate sentencing The process of sentencing whereby the judge sets a fixed term of years within statutory parameters and the offender must serve that term without possibility of early release.

deterrence Prevention of criminal activity by punishing criminals so that others will not engage in such activity.

dicta Statements contained in a judicial opinion that are not essential to the resolution of the case and do not become legal precedents.

diminished capacity See substantial capacity test.

diplomatic immunity A privilege to be free from arrest and prosecution granted under international law to diplomats, their staffs, and household members.

direct contempt An obstructive or insulting act committed by a person in the immediate presence of the court.

direct evidence   Evidence that applies directly to proof of a fact or proposition. For example, a witness who testifies to having seen an act done or heard a statement made is giving direct evidence.

direct filing   A term often used in reference to a prosecutor filing an information charging a juvenile with an offense rather than filing a petition in juvenile court to declare the juvenile delinquent for having committed an offense.

directed verdict   A verdict rendered by a jury by direction of the presiding judge.

discretion   The power of public officials to act in certain situations according to their own judgment rather than relying on set rules or procedures.

discretionary review   Form of appellate court review of lower court decisions that is not mandatory but occurs at the discretion of the appellate court. See also certiorari.

dismissal   A judicial order terminating a case.

disorderly conduct   Illegal behavior that disturbs the public peace or order.

disorderly intoxication   An offense consisting of misbehavior by a person who is drunk that results in disturbing the public peace or safety.

disposition   The final settlement of a case.

dispositive motion   A motion made to a court where the ruling on the motion will determine the outcome of the case.

dissenting opinion   An opinion rendered by a judge disavowing or disagreeing with the decision of a collegial court.

DNA printing tests   Laboratory tests that compare DNA molecules extracted from a suspect's specimen with DNA molecules extracted from specimens found at a crime scene to determine whether the samples match.

docket   The set of cases pending before a court of law.

doctrine of harmless error   The doctrine that holds that an error committed by a lower tribunal shall be deemed harmless and thus no ground for reversal of the lower tribunal's judgment. To be considered harmless, an error of constitutional magnitude must be found by the appellate court to be "harmless beyond any reasonable doubt."

doctrine of incorporation   The doctrine under which provisions of the Bill of Rights are held to be incorporated within the Due Process Clause of the Fourteenth Amendment and are thereby made applicable to actions of the state and local governments.

doctrine of overbreadth   This doctrine enables a person to make a facial challenge to a law on the ground that the law might be applied in the future against activities protected by the First Amendment.

doctrine of transferred intent   Where a person intends to commit a criminal act against one person but the act is accomplished against a different person, the actor's original intent is said to be transferred to the second person. For example, if A fires a pistol intending to kill B, but the bullet strikes C, A's criminal intent to kill B is said to be transferred to C.

double jeopardy   The condition of being tried twice for the same criminal offense.

drug courier profile   A set of characteristics thought to typify persons engaged in drug smuggling.

drug court   A specialized court or division of a court designed to deal specifically with defendants charged with violating laws proscribing the possession and use of controlled substances. Drug courts emphasize rehabilitation of offenders.

drug paraphernalia   Items closely associated with the use of illegal drugs.

DUBAL   Driving with an unlawful blood alcohol level.

Due Process Clause   The clause of the Fifth Amendment to the U.S. Constitution that prohibits the federal government from depriving persons within its jurisdiction of life, liberty, or property without due process of law. A similar provision in the Fourteenth Amendment imposes the same prohibition on state governments.

due process of law   Procedural and substantive rights of citizens against government actions that threaten the denial of life, liberty, or property.

DUI   The crime of driving under the influence of alcohol or drugs.

duress   The use of illegal confinement or threats of harm to coerce someone to do something he or she would not do otherwise.

Durham test   A test for determining insanity developed by the United States Court of Appeals for the District of Columbia Circuit in the case of *Durham v. United States* (1954). Under this test, a person is not criminally responsible for an unlawful act if it was the product of a mental disease or defect.

duty   An obligation that a person has by law or contract.

DWI   The crime of driving while intoxicated.

early delinquency intervention   A form of pretrial diversion adapted to the juvenile justice system.

ecclesiastical   Pertaining to religious laws or institutions.

electronic eavesdropping   Covert listening to or recording of a person's conversations by electronic means.

element of a crime   Any one of the elements of a criminal offense—for example, *actus reus*.

embezzlement   The crime of using a position of trust or authority to transfer or convert the money or property of another to oneself.

emergency searches A search by law enforcement officers in response to an emergency. In such an instance, police can seize evidence in plain view despite not having a search warrant.

en banc "In the bench." Refers to a session of a court, usually an appellate court, in which all judges assigned to the court participate.

en banc **rehearing** A rehearing in an appellate court in which all or a majority of the judges participate.

Endangered Species Act A 1973 act of Congress designed to conserve ecosystems by preserving wildlife, fish, and plants. The act imposes criminal penalties against any person who knowingly violates regulations issued under the act.

endangering the welfare of a child Knowingly acting in a manner likely to be injurious to the physical, mental, or moral welfare of a child.

English common law The body of decisional law based largely on custom as declared by English judges after the Norman Conquest of 1066. See also *stare decisis*.

enterprise An individual, partnership, corporation, association, or other legal entity; a union or group of individuals although not a legal entity.

entrapment The act of government agents in inducing someone to commit a crime that the person would not otherwise be disposed to commit.

enumerated powers Powers explicitly granted governments by their constitutions.

equal protection of the laws Constitutional requirement that the government afford the same legal protection to all persons.

error correction The function of appellate courts in reviewing routine appeals and correcting the errors of trial courts.

error correction function One of the principal functions of an appellate court—that is, to correct errors of a lower tribunal.

escape Unlawfully fleeing to avoid arrest or confinement.

evanescent evidence Evidence that tends to disappear or be destroyed. Often, police seek to justify a warrantless search on the ground that destruction of the evidence is imminent.

evidence Testimony, writings, or material objects offered in proof of an alleged fact or proposition.

evidentiary Pertaining to the rules of evidence or the evidence in a particular case.

evidentiary presumption Establishment of one fact allows inference of another fact or circumstance.

ex parte Refers to a proceeding in which only one party is involved or represented.

ex post facto **law** A retroactive law that criminalizes actions that were innocent at the time they were taken or increases punishment for a criminal act after it was committed.

excessive bail Where a court requires a defendant to post an unreasonably large amount or imposes unreasonable conditions as a prerequisite for a defendant to be released before trial. The Eighth Amendment to the U.S. Constitution prohibits courts from requiring "excessive bail."

excessive noise Unnecessarily loud sounds that interfere with the public peace and endanger the public peace, health, and welfare; sounds emitted that exceed the levels permitted by law or ordinance.

exclusionary rule Judicial doctrine forbidding the use of evidence in a criminal trial where the evidence was obtained in violation of the defendant's constitutional rights.

exculpatory Tending to exonerate a person of allegations of wrongdoing.

exculpatory evidence That which exonerates or tends to exonerate a person from fault or guilt.

excusable homicide A death caused by accident or misfortune.

exigent circumstances Unforeseen situations that demand unusual or immediate action.

expert witness A witness with specialized knowledge or training called to testify in his or her field of expertise.

extortion The crime of obtaining money or property by threats of force or the inducement of fear.

extradition The surrender of a person by one jurisdiction to another for the purpose of criminal prosecution.

eyewitness testimony Testimony given by a person based on personal observation of an event.

factual impossibility That which is in fact impossible to achieve.

fair hearing A hearing in which both parties have a reasonable opportunity to be heard—to present evidence and make arguments.

fair notice The requirement, stemming from due process, that government provide adequate notice to a person before it deprives that person of life, liberty, or property.

false arrest The tort or crime of unlawfully restraining a person.

False Claims Act A federal statute that makes it unlawful for a person to knowingly present a false or fraudulent claim to the U.S. government.

false imprisonment See false arrest.

false pretenses The crime of obtaining money or property through misrepresentation.

False Statements Act A federal statute making it a crime for a person to knowingly make a false and material statement to a U.S. government agency to obtain a government benefit or in connection with performing work for the government.

Federal Anti-Riot Act of 1968 A law making it a crime to travel or use interstate or foreign commerce facilities in connection with inciting, participating in, or aiding acts of violence.

Federal Bail Reform Act of 1984 An act that provides that a defendant charged with a federal crime may be denied bail if the prosecution can show a threat to public safety.

Federal Bureau of Investigation (FBI) The primary federal agency charged with investigating violations of federal criminal laws.

Federal Gun Control Act of 1968 This statute prohibits firearms dealers from transferring handguns to persons who are younger than 21, nonresidents of the dealer's state, and those who are otherwise prohibited by state or local laws from purchasing or possessing firearms. It also forbids possession of a firearm by, and transfer of a firearm to, persons in a number of categories, including convicted felons, users of controlled substances, persons adjudicated as incompetent or committed to mental institutions, illegal aliens, persons dishonorably discharged from the military, persons who have renounced their citizenship, and fugitives from justice.

federal habeas corpus review Review of a state criminal trial by a federal district court on a writ of habeas corpus after the defendant has been convicted, has been incarcerated, and has exhausted appellate remedies in the state courts.

Federal Rules of Appellate Procedure Rules governing the practice of law in the U.S. Courts of Appeals.

federalism The constitutional distribution of government power and responsibility between the national government and the states.

felony A serious crime for which a person may be imprisoned for more than one year.

felony murder A homicide committed during the course of committing another felony other than murder (for example, armed robbery). The felonious act substitutes for the malice aforethought ordinarily required in murder.

field sobriety test A test administered by police to persons suspected of driving while intoxicated. Usually consists of requiring the suspect to demonstrate the ability to perform such physical acts as touching one's finger to nose or walking backwards.

fighting words Utterances that are inherently likely to provoke a violent response from the audience.

fighting words doctrine The First Amendment doctrine which holds that certain utterances are not constitutionally protected as free speech if they are inherently likely to provoke a violent response from the audience.

fines See monetary fines.

first appearance An initial judicial proceeding at which the defendant is informed of the charges and of the right to counsel, and a determination is made as to bail.

first-degree murder The highest degree of unlawful homicide, usually defined as "an unlawful act committed with the premeditated intent to take the life of a human being."

flogging Whipping with a lash as a form of corporal punishment.

force The element of compulsion in such crimes against persons as rape and robbery.

forcible rape Sexual intercourse by force and against the will of the victim.

forensic evidence Evidence obtained through scientific techniques of analyzing physical evidence.

forensic experts Persons qualified in the application of scientific knowledge to legal principles, usually applied to those who participate in discourse or who testify in court.

forensic methods The application of scientific knowledge to legal principles.

foreperson The person selected by fellow jurors to chair deliberations and report the jury's verdict.

forfeiture Sacrifice of ownership or some right (usually property) as a penalty.

forgery The crime of making a false written instrument or materially altering a written instrument (such as a check, promissory note, or college transcript) with the intent to defraud.

fornication Sexual intercourse between unmarried persons; an offense in some jurisdictions.

***Franks* hearing** A pretrial proceeding that allows a defendant to challenge the veracity of an affiant's statements in the affidavit that supports issuance of a search warrant.

fraud Intentional deception or distortion in order to gain something of value.

freedom of expression The right of the individual to express thoughts and feelings through speech, writing, and other media of expression; protected by the First Amendment to the U.S. Constitution.

freedom of religion The First Amendment right to free exercise of one's religion.

frivolous appeals Appeals wholly lacking in legal merit.

fruit of the poisonous tree doctrine A doctrine based on judicial interpretation of the Fourth Amendment which holds that evidence that is derived from illegally seized evidence cannot be used by the prosecution.

***Frye* test** See general acceptance test.

fundamental constitutional rights Those constitutional rights that have been declared to be fundamental by the courts. Includes First Amendment freedoms, the right to vote, and the right to privacy.

fundamental error An error in a judicial proceeding that adversely affects the substantial rights of the accused.

fundamental rights See fundamental constitutional rights.

gambling Operating or playing a game for money in the expectation of gaining more than the amount played.

gender-based peremptory challenges A challenge to a prospective juror's competency to serve based solely on the prospective juror's gender.

gender-neutral A law or practice that applies equally to males and females—that is, nondiscriminatory. For example, rape laws traditionally proscribed acts by a male against a female whereas newer sexual battery laws proscribe acts by or against a person of either gender. Thus, they are gender-neutral.

general acceptance test Also known as the *Frye* test, this test is used by many state courts to determine whether to admit expert testimony in scientific matters. It must be established that the scientific principle from which the expert's deduction is made has gained general acceptance in its field.

General Article Article 134 of the Uniform Code of Military Justice, which covers offenses not expressly made punishable by specific articles of the UCMJ.

general court-martial A court-martial composed of three or more military members and a military judge or a military judge alone with jurisdiction to try the most serious offenses under the Uniform Code of Military Justice.

general deterrence The theory that punishment serves to deter others from committing crimes.

general intent The state of mind to do something prohibited by law without necessarily intending to accomplish the harm that results from the illegal act.

general objection An objection raised against a witness's testimony or introduction of evidence when the objecting party does not recite a specific ground for the objection.

general warrant A search or arrest warrant that is not particular as to the person to be arrested, place to be searched, or the property to be seized.

general-intent statutes Statutes defining crimes that require only general intent, as distinct from specific intent, on the part of the violator.

genetic fingerprints A nonscientific term referring to comparing the DNA molecules from a suspect's specimen with those from specimens found at a crime scene.

good-faith exception An exception to the exclusionary rule (which bars use of evidence obtained by a search warrant found to be invalid). The exception allows use of the evidence if the police relied in good faith on the search warrant, even though the warrant is subsequently held to be invalid.

good-time credit Credit toward early release from prison based on good behavior during confinement (often referred to as "gain time").

grand jury A group of citizens convened either to conduct an investigation or to determine if there is sufficient evidence to warrant prosecution of an accused.

grand jury proceeding A group of citizens designated by law to make an investigation or to determine if there is sufficient evidence to prosecute someone for a crime.

grand theft Theft of a sufficient value of property to make the crime a felony.

guilty but mentally ill A form of verdict that may be rendered in some states where the jury finds that the defendant's mental illness does not deprive the defendant of substantial capacity sufficient to satisfy the insanity test but warrants the defendant's treatment in addition to incarceration.

gun control laws Laws regulating the manufacture, importation, sale, distribution, possession, or use of firearms.

Gun-Free School Zones Act Federal statute making it a crime "for any individual knowingly to possess a firearm at a place that the individual knows, or has reasonable cause to believe, is a school zone." This law was declared unconstitutional by the U.S. Supreme Court in *United States v. Lopez* (1995).

habeas corpus "You have the body." A judicial writ requiring that a party be brought before a court. The primary function of habeas corpus is to release a person from unlawful confinement.

habitation Residence or dwelling place.

habitual offender One who has been repeatedly convicted of crimes.

habitual offender statute A law that imposes an additional punishment on a criminal who has previously been convicted of crimes.

Hale's Rule English common law credited to Sir Matthew Hale, Lord Chief Justice in the seventeenth century, holding that a husband could not be charged with the rape of his wife.

handwriting exemplar A sample of a suspect's handwriting.

hard-core pornography Pornography that is extremely graphic in its depiction of sexual conduct.

harmless error doctrine   The doctrine that minor or harmless errors during a trial do not require reversal of the lower court's judgment by an appellate court.

harmless errors   Errors that occur in a judicial proceeding that do not materially affect the court's decision. To be harmless, a constitutional error must be harmless beyond any reasonable doubt.

hate crimes   Crimes in which the victim is selected on the basis of race, religion, sexual orientation, or ethnicity.

hate speech   Offensive speech directed at members of racial, religious, sexual orientation or ethnic minorities.

hearing   A proceeding, usually less formal than a trial, held to determine procedural or substantive issues of fact or law.

hearsay evidence   Statements made by someone other than a witness offered in evidence at a trial or hearing to prove the truth of the matter asserted.

heat of passion   A violent and uncontrollable rage resulting from a provocation that would cause such a response by a reasonable person—for example, a person who views his or her spouse in an act of committing adultery.

Hobbs Act   A 1946 act of Congress authorizing criminal penalties for whoever in any way or degree obstructs, delays, or affects commerce or the movement of any article or commodity in commerce, by robbery or extortion or attempts or conspires so to do, or commits or threatens physical violence to any person or property in furtherance of a plan or purpose to do anything in violation of this section.

holding   The legal determination made by a court in a particular case.

homicide   The killing of a human being.

hostage taking   The act in which the perpetrator of a robbery or some other crime forcibly detains innocent bystanders.

hot pursuit   (1) The right of police to cross jurisdictional lines to apprehend a suspect or criminal; (2) the Fourth Amendment doctrine allowing warrantless searches and arrests where police pursue a fleeing suspect into a protected area.

house arrest   A sentencing alternative to incarceration where the offender is allowed to leave home only for employment and approved community service activities.

hung jury   A trial jury unable to reach a verdict.

hypnotically enhanced testimony   Testimony offered by a witness whose memory has been refreshed through hypnosis.

hypothetical question   A question based on an assumed set of facts. Hypothetical questions may be asked of expert witnesses in criminal trials.

identification procedures   Scientific and nonscientific procedures employed by police to assist in the identification of suspects.

illegitimacy   Condition of a child being born out of wedlock.

imminent lawless action   Unlawful conduct that is about to take place and which is inevitable unless there is intervention by the authorities.

imminently dangerous or outrageous conduct   The type of action that, when resulting in someone's death, usually characterizes second-degree murder.

immunity   Exemption from civil suit or prosecution. See also use immunity and transactional immunity.

impeachment   (1) A legislative act bringing a charge against a public official that, if proven in a legislative trial, will cause his or her removal from public office; (2) impugning the credibility of a witness by introducing contradictory evidence or proving his or her bad character.

implied consent   An agreement or acquiescence manifested by a person's actions or inaction.

implied consent statutes   Laws providing that by accepting a license a driver arrested for a traffic offense consents to urine, blood, and breath tests to determine blood alcohol content.

implied exception   An exclusion that can reasonably be inferred or assumed based on the purpose and intent of an ordinance, statute, or contract.

implied powers   Powers not expressly granted to government by a constitution but fairly implied by the document.

imposition of restraint   Arrest, custody, incarceration, or detention.

impotency   Lacking in power; in reference to a male, the inability to copulate.

in camera   In a judge's chambers.

in forma pauperis   "In the manner of a pauper." Waiver of filing costs and other fees associated with judicial proceedings to allow an indigent person to proceed.

in loco parentis   "In the place of the parents."

in re   "In the matter of."

incapacitation   Punishment making it impossible for an offender to re-offend.

incapacity   An inability, legal or actual, to act.

incarceration   Imprisonment.

incest   Sexual intercourse with a close blood relative or, in some cases, a person related by affinity.

inchoate offenses   Offenses preparatory to committing other crimes. Inchoate offenses include attempt, conspiracy, and solicitation.

incite   To provoke or set in motion.

inciting a riot The crime of instigating or provoking a riot.

incriminating statements Statements typically made to police that increase the likelihood that one will be found guilty of a crime.

inculpatory Tending to incriminate.

indecent exposure The intentional exposure in public of private areas of a person's body.

indefinite sentence Form of criminal sentencing whereby a judge imposes a term of incarceration within statutory parameters, and corrections officials determine actual time served through parole or other means.

independent counsel A special prosecutor appointed to investigate and, if warranted, prosecute official misconduct.

independent source doctrine The doctrine that permits evidence to be admitted at trial as long as it was obtained independently from illegally obtained evidence.

indeterminate sentence A prison sentence for an indefinite time, but within stipulated parameters, that allows correction officials to determine the prisoner's release date.

indeterminate sentencing Form of criminal sentencing where criminals are sentenced to prison for indeterminate periods until corrections officials determine that rehabilitation has been accomplished.

index crimes Offenses included in the FBI Uniform Crime Reports: willful homicide, forcible rape, robbery, burglary, aggravated assault, grand larceny, and motor vehicle theft.

indictment A formal document handed down by a grand jury accusing one or more persons of the commission of a crime or crimes.

indigent Poor; unable to afford legal representation.

indigent defendants Defendants who cannot afford to retain private legal counsel and are therefore entitled to be represented by a public defender or a court-appointed lawyer.

indirect contempt An act committed outside the presence of the court that insults the court or obstructs a judicial proceeding.

indirect evidence Inferences and presumptions that are probative of various facts in issue.

ineffective assistance of counsel Deficient performance by a lawyer representing a defendant that results in serious errors that prejudice the right of a defendant to a fair trial.

inevitable discovery doctrine The doctrine that holds that evidence derived from inadmissible evidence is admissible if it inevitably would have been discovered independently by lawful means.

infancy The condition of being below the age of legal majority.

inflammatory remarks Remarks by counsel during a trial designed to excite the passions of the jury.

information A document filed by a prosecutor under oath charging one or more persons with commission of a crime.

infra "Below."

initial appearance After arrest, the first appearance of the accused before a judge or magistrate.

injunction A court order prohibiting someone from doing some specified act or commanding someone to undo some wrong or injury.

inmate One who is confined in a jail or prison.

insanity A degree of mental illness that negates the legal capacity or responsibility of the affected person.

insanity defense A defense that seeks to exonerate the accused by showing that he or she was insane at the time of the crime and thus not legally responsible.

Insanity Defense Reform Act of 1984 An act of Congress that specifies that insanity is an affirmative defense to a prosecution under a federal statute and details the requirements for establishing such a defense.

insider trading Transactions in securities by a person who operates "inside" a corporation and, by using material nonpublic information, trades to his or her advantage without first disclosing that information to the public.

insufficient evidence Evidence that falls short of establishing that required by law, usually referring to evidence that does not legally establish an offense or a defense.

intangible property Property with no tangible value, such as bonds, promissory notes, and stock certificates.

intent A state of mind in which a person seeks to accomplish a given result through a course of action.

intent to deprive The willful design to take goods or services from another without permission or authority of law.

intentionally Willfully; with a mental purpose to act.

inter alia "Among other things."

intermediate appellate courts Judicial tribunals consisting of three or more judges that review decisions of trial courts but that are subordinate to the final appellate tribunals.

interrogation Questioning of a suspect by police or questioning of a witness by counsel.

interrogatories Written questions put to a witness.

interstate commerce Economic activity between or among states.

intoxication Condition in which a person has impaired physical and/or mental capacities due to ingestion of drugs or alcohol.

invalidate Annul, negate, set aside.

inventory search An exception to the warrant requirement that allows police who legally impound a vehicle to conduct a routine inventory of the contents of the vehicle.

investigatory detention Brief detention of suspects by a police officer who has reasonable suspicion that criminal activity is afoot. See also stop-and-frisk.

involuntary intoxication Intoxication that is not the result of a person's intentional ingestion of an intoxicating substance. A person may become involuntarily intoxicated through the trickery or fraud of another person or through the inadvertent ingestion of medicine.

involuntary manslaughter The unintentional killing of another person as the result of gross or wanton negligence.

ipso facto "By the mere fact"; by the fact itself.

irresistible impulse A desire that cannot be resisted due to impairment of the will by mental disease.

Jencks **Act** The common name for a federal statute that permits a defendant to review a witness's prior written or recorded statement, but only after the witness has testified on direct examination for the government.

joinder and severance of parties The uniting or severing of two or more parties charged with a crime or crimes.

joinder of offenses The uniting for trial in one case of different charges or counts alleged in an information or indictment.

joyriding The temporary taking of an automobile without intent to permanently deprive the owner of same.

judge advocates (JAGs) Attorneys designated by the Judge Advocate General of their branch of service to serve as prosecutors (trial counsel), defense counsel, military judges, appellate counsel, appellate judges, and staff officers who give legal advice to commanders.

judgment The final and official decision of a court of law in a given case.

judgment of acquittal In a nonjury trial, a judge's order exonerating a defendant based on a finding that the defendant is not guilty. In a case heard by a jury finding a defendant guilty, a judge's order exonerating a defendant on the ground that the evidence was not legally sufficient to support the jury's finding of guilt.

judicial conference A meeting of judges to deliberate on disposition of a case.

judicial notice The act of a court recognizing, without proof, the existence of certain facts that are commonly known. Such facts are often brought to the court's attention through the use of a calendar or almanac.

judicial review The power of courts of law to review governmental acts and declare them null and void if they are found to be unconstitutional.

jurisdiction The authority of a court to hear and decide certain categories of legal disputes. Jurisdiction relates to the authority of a court over the person, subject matter, and geographical area.

jurist A person who is skilled or well versed in the law; a term often applied to lawyers and judges.

jury A group of citizens convened for the purpose of deciding factual questions relevant to a civil or criminal case.

jury instructions A judge's explanation of the law applicable to a case being heard by a jury.

jury nullification The fact of a jury disregarding the court's instructions and rendering a verdict on the basis of the consciences of the jurors.

jury pardon An action taken by a jury, despite the quality of the evidence, acquitting a defendant or convicting the defendant of a lesser crime than charged.

jury selection The process of selecting prospective jurors at random from lists of persons representative of the community.

Jury Selection and Service Act of 1968 A federal statute enacted to ensure that jury panels in federal courts are selected at random from a fair cross-section of the community.

jury trial A judicial proceeding to determine a defendant's guilt or innocence conducted before a body of persons sworn to render a verdict based on the law and the evidence presented.

justifiable homicide Killing another in self-defense or defense of others when there is serious danger of death or great bodily harm to self or others, or when authorized by law.

justifiable use of force The necessary and reasonable use of force by a person in self-defense, defense of another, or defense of property.

justification A valid reason for one's actions.

juvenile A person who has not yet attained the age of legal majority.

juvenile court A judicial tribunal having jurisdiction over minors defined as juveniles who are alleged to be status offenders or to have committed acts of delinquency.

juvenile delinquency Actions of a juvenile in violation of the criminal law.

juvenile delinquency hearing Hearing in which a juvenile court determines whether a juvenile should be found to be delinquent. Analogous to a criminal trial in the adult justice system.

kidnapping   The forcible abduction and carrying away of a person against that person's will.

kidnapping for ransom   The offense of unlawfully taking and confining a person until a specified payment is made to the offender.

kinship   Relationship by blood.

knock and announce rule   The provision under federal and most state laws that requires a law enforcement officer to first knock and announce his or her presence and purpose before entering a person's home to serve a search or arrest warrant.

knowingly   Consciously and willfully—i.e., with knowledge.

larceny   At common law, the unlawful taking of property with the intent of permanently depriving the owner of same.

lawmaking function   One of the principal functions of an appellate court, often referred to as the law development function.

leading questions   A question that suggests an answer. Leading questions are permitted at a criminal trial on cross-examination of witnesses and in other limited instances.

legal impossibility   A defense allowed in some jurisdictions when although the defendant intended to commit a crime, it was impossible to do so because the completed act is not a crime.

legislation   Law enacted by a lawmaking body.

legislative intent   The purpose the legislature sought to achieve in enacting a particular provision of law.

legislature   An elected lawmaking body such as the Congress of the United States or a state assembly.

lewd and lascivious conduct   Indecent exposure of a person's private parts in public; indecent touching or fondling of a child.

lex non scripta   "The unwritten law" or common law.

libel   The tort of defamation through published writing or pictures.

lineup   A police identification procedure where a suspect is included in a group with other persons and the group is exhibited to a victim.

loansharking   The practice of lending money at illegal rates of interest.

loitering   Standing around idly; "hanging around."

loss of civil rights   Forfeiture of certain rights, such as voting, as a result of a criminal conviction.

lottery   A drawing in which prizes are distributed to winners selected by lot from among those who have participated by paying a consideration.

***M'Naghten* Rule**   Under this rule, for a defendant to be found not guilty by reason of insanity, it must be clearly proved that, at the time of committing the act, the defendant was suffering such a defect of reason, from disease of the mind, as not to know the nature and quality of the act he was doing; or, if he did know it, that he did not know what he was doing was wrong.

magistrate   A judge with minor or limited authority.

Magna Charta   The "Great Charter" signed by King John in 1215 guaranteeing the legal rights of English subjects. Generally considered the foundation of Anglo-American constitutionalism.

mail fraud   A scheme devised or intended to defraud or to obtain money or property by fraudulent means, and/or the use or causing to use the mails in furtherance of the fraudulent scheme.

majority opinion   An appellate court opinion joined in by a majority of the judges who heard the appeal.

mala in se   "Evil in itself." Refers to crimes such as murder that are universally condemned.

mala prohibita   "Prohibited evil." Refers to crimes that are wrong primarily because the law declares them to be wrong.

malice aforethought   The mental predetermination to commit an illegal act.

malicious mischief   The crime of willful destruction of the personal property of another.

mandate   A command or order.

mandatory minimum sentence   A sentence in which the minimum duration of incarceration is specified by law.

mandatory sentencing   Sentencing practice in which trial courts are constrained by law to impose prison terms of certain minimum duration.

manifest necessity   That which is clearly or obviously necessary or essential.

manslaughter   The crime of unlawful killing of another person without malice.

marital exception   The traditional common-law principle that a husband could not be guilty of raping his wife.

marital privilege   The privilege of married persons not to be compelled to testify against each other.

marital rape   Rape committed against one's spouse.

material   Important, relevant, necessary.

maximum security prisons   Prisons designed to minimize the movement and maximize the surveillance and control of inmates.

mayhem   At common law, the crime of injuring some-one so as to render that person less able to fight.

Megan's law   Name applied to statutes that require convicted sex offenders, upon release from prison, to register with local law enforcement agencies (named in memory of Megan Kanka, who died in 1994 at the hands of a released offender).

mens rea   "Guilty mind"; criminal intent.

Migratory Bird Conservation Act   Act of Congress protecting certain species of migratory birds from hunt-ing within the United States and its territories.

military judges   Judges of courts-martial selected from the ranks of military attorneys (judge advocates).

Military Rules of Evidence (MREs)   The rules of evi-dence contained in the Manual for Courts-Martial.

minimum security facilities   Prisons and jails that offer inmates the most freedom of movement within the least secure environment.

Miranda **warning**   Based on the Supreme Court's deci-sion in *Miranda v. Arizona* (1966), this warning is given by police to individuals who are taken into custody be-fore they are interrogated. The warning informs persons in custody that they have the right to remain silent and to have a lawyer present during questioning, and that anything they say can and will be used against them in a court of law.

misappropriation   Wrongful taking or diversion of funds or other property.

miscarriage of justice   Decision of a court that is incon-sistent with the substantial rights of a party to the case.

misdemeanor   A minor offense usually punishable by fine or imprisonment for less than one year.

misprision of felony   The crime of concealing a felony committed by another.

misrepresentation   An untrue statement of fact made to induce action.

mistake of fact   Unconscious ignorance of a fact or be-lief in the existence of something that does not exist.

mistake of law   An erroneous opinion of legal princi-ples applied to a set of facts.

mitigating circumstances   Circumstances or factors that tend to lessen culpability.

mitigating factors   See mitigating circumstances.

mitigation   Reduction or alleviation, usually of punishment.

Model Penal Code (MPC)   Published by the American Law Institute (ALI), the MPC consists of general provi-sions concerning criminal liability, sentences, defenses, and definitions of specific crimes. The MPC is not law; rather, it is designed to serve as a model code of criminal law for all states.

monetary fines   Sums of money that offenders are re-quired to pay as punishment for the commission of crimes.

money laundering   The offense of disguising illegal in-come to make it appear legitimate.

Money Laundering Control Act   A 1986 act of Congress providing criminal penalties for a person who, knowing that the property involved in a financial trans-action represents the proceeds of some form of unlawful activity, conducts or attempts to conduct such a financial transaction that in fact involves the proceeds of specified unlawful activity.

monogamy   The practice of having only one spouse, as distinct from bigamy or polygamy.

moot   A point that no longer has any practical signifi-cance; academic.

motion   An application to a court of law for the pur-pose of obtaining some particular order or ruling.

motion for a new trial   A formal request made to a trial court to hold a new trial in a particular case that has already been adjudicated.

motion for rehearing   A formal request made to a court of law to convene another hearing in a case in which the court has already ruled.

motion to dismiss   A formal request to a trial court to dismiss the criminal charges against the defendant.

motive   A person's conscious reason for acting.

motor vehicle offense   Minor crime involving the op-eration of motor vehicles; see rules of the road.

murder   The unlawful killing of a person by another with malice aforethought or premeditation, or through outrageous conduct.

necessity   A condition that compels or requires a cer-tain course of action.

negative defense   Any criminal defense not required to be specifically pled.

negligence   The failure to exercise ordinary care or caution.

neutral and detached magistrate   A judicial officer without an interest in the outcome of a case.

no bill   "Not found"; conclusion of a grand jury that de-clines to return an indictment.

no contest plea   A plea to a criminal charge that, al-though it is not an admission of guilt, generally has the same effect as a plea of guilty.

noise ordinances   Local laws restricting the making of noise.

nolle prosequi   A formal entry by a prosecutor who de-clines to proceed further in the prosecution of an of-fense; commonly called a "nol pros."

nolo contendere "I will not contest it." Refers to a plea of no contest in a criminal case.

noncapital crimes Crimes that do not carry the ultimate penalty, whether death or life in prison with no possibility of parole.

nondeadly force Force that does not result in death.

not guilty by reason of insanity A plea that admits criminal conduct but raises the insanity defense.

notice of appeal Document filed notifying an appellate court of an appeal from a judgment of a lower court.

novel and innovative defenses New defenses based on heretofore unaccepted principles of criminal responsibility.

nuisance An unlawful or unreasonable use of a person's property that results in an injury to another or to the public.

nullen crimen, nulla poena, sine lege "There is no crime, there is no punishment, without law." Refers to the doctrine that one cannot be found guilty of a crime unless there is a violation of an existing provision of law defining the applicable criminal conduct.

numbers racket A common form of illegal gambling in which one places a bet on a number with the hope that it will correspond to a preselected number.

obiter dicta See dicta.

objective test A legal test based on external circumstances rather than the perceptions or intentions of an individual actor.

objective test for use of deadly force Under this test, the judge or jury place themselves in the shoes of a hypothetical reasonable and prudent person to determine if a defendant's use of deadly force was permissible.

objective test of entrapment Under this approach to determining whether police engaged in entrapment, a court inquires whether the police methods were so improper as likely to induce or ensnare a reasonable person into committing a crime.

obscenity Explicit sexual material that is patently offensive, appeals to a prurient or unnatural interest in sex, and lacks serious scientific, artistic, or literary content.

obstruction of justice The crime of impeding or preventing law enforcement or the administration of justice.

omission The failure to do what the law requires a person to do.

one year and a day rule See year-and-a-day rule.

open fields doctrine The doctrine that the Fourth Amendment does not apply to the open fields around a home, even if these open fields are private property.

open public trial A trial that is held in public and is open to spectators.

opening statement A prosecutor's or defense lawyer's initial statement to the judge or jury in a trial.

opinion evidence Testimony in which the witness expresses an opinion, as distinct from knowledge of specific facts.

opinion of the court The opinion expressing the views of the majority of judges participating in a judicial decision.

oral argument Verbal presentation made to an appellate court in an attempt to persuade the court to affirm, reverse, or modify a lower court decision.

order maintenance The police officer's function of keeping the peace, as distinct from enforcement of the law.

ordinance An enactment of a local governing body such as a city council or commission.

organized crime Syndicates involved in racketeering and other criminal activities.

Organized Crime Control Act A 1970 federal law dealing with organized crime. Title IX of the act is entitled "Racketeer Influenced and Corrupt Organizations" and is commonly referred to by the acronym RICO.

original jurisdiction The authority of a court of law to hear a case in the first instance.

overbreadth doctrine First Amendment doctrine that holds that a law is invalid if it can be applied to punish people for engaging in constitutionally protected expression.

overrule To reverse or annul by subsequent action.

overt act A visible act by an individual.

panel A set of jurors or judges assigned to hear a case.

pardon An executive action that mitigates or sets aside punishment for a crime.

parens patriae "The parent of the country." Refers to the role of the state as guardian of minors or other legally disabled persons.

Parental Kidnapping Prevention Act (PKPA) A federal act adopted in 1980 designed to prevent jurisdictional conflicts over child custody matters. The primary goal of the statute is to reduce any incentive for parental child snatching.

parole Conditional release from jail or prison of a person who has served part of his or her sentence.

parole revocation hearing An administrative hearing held for the purpose of determining whether an offender's parole should be revoked.

partial birth abortion A method of abortion in which the fetus is partially delivered before its life is terminated and it is removed from the mother's body.

pat-down search A manual search by a police officer of the exterior of a suspect's outer garments.

patently offensive   That which is obviously offensive or disgusting.

pattern of racketeering   To obtain a conviction under the federal RICO statute, the government must establish the defendant's involvement in a "pattern of racketeering" that requires proof of at least two predicate acts of racketeering having occurred within a period of ten years, excluding any period of imprisonment.

pen register   Device that enables law enforcement to obtain the numbers that have been dialed by use of a specific telephone instrument.

penal   Of or pertaining to punishment.

penalty enhancement statutes   Sentencing laws that provide for increased penalties when certain conditions were present in crimes—for example, the racial motivations of the perpetrator.

pendency of the appeal   The period after an appeal is filed but before the appeal is adjudicated.

penitentiary   A prison.

penology   The study or practice of prison management.

per curiam   "By the court." A term used to distinguish an opinion rendered by the whole court rather than by an individual judge.

per curiam **opinion**   An opinion rendered "by the court" as distinct from one attributed to one or more judges.

per se   "By itself"; in itself.

peremptory challenge   An objection to the selection of a prospective juror in which the attorney making the challenge is not required to state the reason for the objection.

perjury   The crime of making a material false statement under oath.

perjury by contradictory statements   Commission of the offense of perjury by a witness who makes conflicting statements under oath.

petit (trial) jury   A trial jury, usually composed of either six or twelve persons.

petit theft   Minor form of larceny; theft of property of sufficiently small value that the offense is classified as a misdemeanor.

petition   A formal written request addressed to a court of law.

petitioner   A person who brings a petition before a court of law.

petty (petit) offenses   Minor crimes for which fines or short jail terms are the only prescribed modes of punishment.

photo pack   A collection of "mug shots" to be exhibited to a victim or witness in an attempt to identify the perpetrator of a crime.

Pinkerton **Rule**   Rule enunciated by the Supreme Court in *Pinkerton v. United States* (1946) holding that a member of a conspiracy is liable for all offenses committed in furtherance of the conspiracy.

plain view   Readily visible to the naked eye.

plain view doctrine   The Fourth Amendment doctrine under which a police officer may seize evidence of crime that is readily visible to the officer's naked eye as long as the officer is legally in the place where the evidence becomes visible.

plaintiff   A person who initiates a civil suit.

plea bargain   An agreement between a defendant and a prosecutor whereby the defendant agrees to plead guilty in exchange for some concession (such as a reduction in the number of charges brought).

plea of guilty   A formal answer to a criminal charge in which the accused acknowledges guilt and waives the right to trial.

plea of not guilty   A formal answer to a criminal charge in which the accused denies guilt and thus exercises the right to a trial.

plurality opinion   An opinion of an appellate court that is joined by more judges than have joined any concurring opinion, although not by a majority of judges in the court.

police deception   Intentional deception by police in order to elicit incriminating statements from a suspect.

police departments   Organizations established by municipalities and sometimes states whose function is to enforce the criminal laws within their respective jurisdictions.

police interrogation   Questioning by the police of a suspect in custody.

police power   The power of government to legislate to protect public health, safety, welfare, and morality.

police requests for information or identification   Police questions asking persons for information or proof of their identity.

polling the jury   Practice in which trial judge asks each member of the jury whether he or she supports the jury's verdict.

polygamy   Plural marriage; having more than one spouse.

polygraph evidence   Results of lie detector tests (generally inadmissible into evidence).

pornography   Material that appeals to the sexual impulse or appetite.

possession   The actual or constructive control or occupancy of real or personal property. See also actual possession; constructive possession.

possession of burglar's tools   The knowing control of instruments, machines, or substances designed to enable one to forcefully break into buildings or vaults in order to carry out the intent to steal or destroy property.

postconviction relief   Term applied to various mechanisms a defendant may use to challenge a conviction after other routes of appeal have been exhausted.

power of contempt   The authority of a court of law to punish someone who insults the court or flouts its authority.

precedent   A judicial decision cited as authority controlling or influencing the outcome of a similar case.

predicate acts   Prior acts of racketeering used to demonstrate a pattern of racketeering in a RICO prosecution.

preferral of charges   Refers to charges being brought against a person in the military, usually by the individual's commander.

prejudicial error   An error at trial that substantially affects the interests of the accused.

preliminary hearing   A hearing held to determine whether there is sufficient evidence to hold an accused for trial.

premeditation   Deliberate decision or plan to commit a crime.

premenstrual syndrome (PMS)   Physiological changes that occur in some women prior to onset of menstruation. This results from hormonal imbalance and may cause serious depression and irritability.

preparatory conduct   Actions taken to prepare to commit a crime.

preponderance of evidence   Evidence that has greater weight than countervailing evidence.

presentence investigation   An investigation held to aid the court in determining the appropriate punishment before sentencing a convicted criminal.

presentence report   A report containing the results of a presentence investigation.

presumption   An inference about the existence of some fact drawn from the existence of some other fact.

presumption of innocence   In a criminal trial, the accused is presumed innocent until proven guilty.

presumption of validity   In constitutional law, a statute is generally presumed to be valid until it is demonstrated otherwise.

pretextual stop   An incident in which police stop a suspicious vehicle on the pretext of a motor vehicle infraction.

pretrial confinement   See pretrial detention.

pretrial detention   Holding a defendant in jail pending trial.

pretrial discovery   The process by which the defense and prosecution interrogate witnesses for the opposing party and gain access to the evidence possessed by the opposing party prior to trial.

pretrial diversion program   A program in which a first-time offender is afforded the opportunity to avoid criminal prosecution by participating in some specified treatment, counseling, or community service.

pretrial motion   A request for a ruling or order before the commencement of a trial.

pretrial release   Release of a defendant on bail or personal recognizance pending adjudication of criminal charges.

preventive detention   Holding a suspect in custody before trial to prevent escape or other wrongdoing.

price fixing   Sellers unlawfully entering into agreements as to the price of products or services.

prima facie   "On its face"; at first glance.

principal   A perpetrator of or aider and abettor in the commission of a crime (as distinguished from an accessory).

principals   Persons whose conduct involves direct participation in a crime.

prison disciplinary measures   Steps taken by prison officials to punish prisoners for misconduct, largely accomplished by removing good-time credits that prisoners earn for exemplary behavior in prison.

privileges   Rights extended to persons by virtue of law—for example, the right accorded a spouse in not being required to testify against the other spouse.

pro bono   "For the good." Performing service without compensation.

pro se   On one's own behalf.

***pro se* defense**   Representing oneself in a criminal case.

probable cause   A reasonable ground for belief in certain alleged facts.

probation   Conditional release of a convicted criminal in lieu of incarceration.

probative   Tending to prove the truth or falsehood of a proposition.

procedural criminal law   The branch of the criminal law that deals with the processes by which crimes are investigated, prosecuted, and punished.

procedural due process   Set of procedures designed to ensure fairness in a judicial or administrative proceeding.

procedural law   The law regulating governmental procedure (for example, rules of criminal procedure).

profanity   Irreverence toward sacred things; foul language.

pronouncement of sentence Formal announcement of a criminal punishment by a trial judge.

proof beyond a reasonable doubt The standard of proof in a criminal trial or a juvenile delinquency hearing.

proportionality The degree to which a particular punishment matches the seriousness of a crime or matches the penalty other offenders have received for the same crime.

proscribe To forbid; prohibit.

prosecution Initiation and conduct of a criminal case.

prosecutor A public official empowered to initiate criminal charges and conduct prosecutions.

prosecutor's information An accusatorial document filed under oath by a prosecutor charging a person with one or more violations of the criminal law; similar to an indictment issued by a grand jury.

prosecutorial discretion The leeway afforded prosecutors in deciding whether or not to bring charges and to engage in plea bargaining.

prosecutorial immunity A prosecutor's legal shield against civil suits stemming from his or her official actions.

prosecutrix A female victim who makes a criminal complaint.

prostitution The act of selling sexual favors.

provocation Refers to conduct that prompts another person to react through criminal conduct.

proximate cause The cause that is nearest a given effect in a causal relationship.

prurient interest An excessive or unnatural interest in sex.

public defender An attorney responsible for defending indigent persons charged with crimes.

public drunkenness The offense of appearing in public while intoxicated.

public forum A public space generally acknowledged as appropriate for public assemblies or expressions of views.

public indecency Vulgar, lewd, immoral, or obscene acts committed in public that are defined as offensive by law in accordance with constitutional standards.

public law General classification of law consisting of constitutional law, administrative law, international law, and criminal law.

public safety exception Exception to the requirement that police officers promptly inform suspects taken into custody of their rights to remain silent and have an attorney present during questioning. Under the public safety exception, police may ask suspects questions motivated by a desire to protect public safety without jeopardizing the admissibility of suspects' answers to those questions or subsequent statements.

punitive isolation Solitary confinement of a person who is incarcerated.

Pure Food, Drug, and Cosmetic Act Federal law that prohibits traffic in food, drugs, and cosmetics being prepared or handled under unsanitary circumstances or under conditions that render them injurious to health.

putting witnesses under the rule Placing witnesses under the traditional rule that requires them to remain outside the courtroom except when testifying.

quash To vacate or annul.

Quiet Communities Act Federal law enacted in 1978 to protect the environment against noise pollution.

racial profiling Practice of making traffic stops of members of minority groups by law enforcement officers.

racially based peremptory challenges Peremptory challenges to prospective jurors that are based solely on racial animus or racial stereotypes.

rape shield law A law that protects the identity of a rape victim or prevents disclosure of a victim's sexual history.

rape trauma syndrome A recurring pattern of physical and emotional symptoms experienced by rape victims.

rational basis test The judicial requirement that legislation must be rationally related to a legitimate government objective in order to survive constitutional challenge.

real evidence Refers to maps, blood samples, X-rays, photographs, stolen goods, fingerprints, knives, guns, and other tangible items introduced into evidence.

real property Land and buildings permanently attached thereto.

reasonable doubt The doubt that a reasonable person might entertain in regard to the veracity of a proposition after hearing the evidence.

reasonable expectation of privacy A person's expectations of privacy that society is prepared to recognize as reasonable and legitimate.

reasonable force The maximum degree of force that is necessary to accomplish a lawful purpose.

reasonable suspicion A police officer's belief based on all relevant circumstances that criminal activity is afoot.

reasoning The logic of a legal argument or judicial opinion.

rebuttal witnesses Witnesses called to dispute the testimony of the opposing party's witnesses.

recantation The withdrawal or repudiation of previous statements. In some instances, a person who has lied under oath is permitted to recant to avoid being guilty of perjury.

receiving stolen property Knowingly receiving possession and control of personal property belonging to another with the intent to permanently deprive the owner of possession of such property.

recidivism Repetitive criminal activity.

recklessly Without regard to consequences.

recklessness Wanton conduct in violation of law.

recognizance An obligation to appear in a court of law at a given time.

recusal A decision of a judge to withdraw from a given case, usually because of bias or personal interest.

regulation A rule or order prescribed by controlling authority.

regulatory offenses Strict-liability criminal offenses dealing with public health and the environment.

rehabilitation Restoring someone or something to its former status—a justification for punishment emphasizing reform rather than retribution.

release on personal recognizance Pretrial release of a defendant based solely on the defendant's promise to appear for future court dates.

relevant evidence Evidence tending to prove or disprove an alleged fact.

remand To send back, usually with instructions.

remedy The means by which a right is enforced or a wrong is redressed.

repeal A legislative act removing a law from the statute books.

reply brief A brief submitted by appellant in response to an appellee's answer brief.

reporters Books containing judicial decisions and accompanying opinions.

request for information or identification A police–citizen encounter in which the police officer requests the citizen to provide identification or provide certain information.

res judicata "Things judged." Matters already decided by courts, not subject to relitigation.

res nova "A new matter." A question not previously decided.

resentencing Refers to a new sentencing hearing ordered by an appellate court.

resisting arrest The crime of obstructing or opposing a police officer making an arrest.

Resource Conservation and Recovery Act (RCRA) Enacted in 1976, RCRA is the major federal law dealing with transportation, storage, and disposal of hazardous waste.

respondent A person asked to respond to a lawsuit or writ.

responsible corporate officer A person holding a supervisory position in an organization who may be subject to criminal liability for regulatory offenses committed by subordinates.

restitution The act of compensating someone for losses suffered.

retreat rule The common-law requirement that a person being attacked "retreat to the wall" before using deadly force in self-defense.

retribution Something demanded as payment; the theory of punishment that stresses just deserts.

retroactive Having an effect on things or actions in the past.

reverse To set aside a decision on appeal.

revocation The withdrawal of some right or power (such as the revocation of parole).

RICO The Racketeer Influenced Corrupt Organizations Act.

right from wrong test See *M'Naghten* Rule.

right of allocution The right of a criminal defendant to make a statement on his or her own behalf before sentence is pronounced.

right of confrontation The right to face one's accusers in a criminal case.

right of cross-examination The right to question witnesses for the opposing side in a criminal trial.

right of privacy Constitutional right to engage in intimate personal conduct or make fundamental life decisions without interference by the government.

right to a speedy trial Constitutional right to have an open public trial conducted without unreasonable delay.

right to appeal Statutory right to appeal decisions of lower courts in certain circumstances.

right to counsel (1) The right to retain an attorney to represent oneself in court; (2) the right of an indigent person to have an attorney provided at public expense.

right to die Controversial "right" to terminate one's own life under certain circumstances.

right to keep and bear arms Right to possess certain weapons, protected against federal infringement by the Second Amendment to the U.S. Constitution.

right to refuse medical treatment The right of a patient—or patient's surrogate in some instances—to refuse to allow doctors to administer medical treatment.

riot A public disturbance involving acts of violence, usually by three or more persons.

Rivers and Harbors Act An 1899 act of Congress making it a misdemeanor to discharge refuse into the navigable waters of the United States.

roadblocks Barriers set up by police to stop motorists.

robbery The crime of taking money or property from a person against that person's will by means of force.

rout At common law, disturbance of the peace similar to riot but without carrying out the intended purpose.

rule of four U.S. Supreme Court rule whereby the Court grants certiorari only on the agreement of at least four justices.

rule of law The idea that law, not the discretion of officials, should govern public affairs.

rules of evidence Legal rules governing the admissibility of evidence at trial.

rules of procedure Rules promulgated by courts of law under constitutional or statutory authority governing procedures for trials and other judicial proceedings.

rules of statutory interpretation Rules developed by courts to determine the meaning of legislative acts.

rules of the road Rules for the operation of motor vehicles on the public streets.

same elements test Test that bars separate punishment for offenses that have the same elements, or when one offense includes or is included in another offense.

same evidence test A test applicable to the Double Jeopardy Clause of the Fifth Amendment. If to establish an essential element of an offense charged, the government will prove conduct that constitutes an offense for which the defendant has already been prosecuted, a second prosecution is barred.

sanction Penalty or other mechanism of enforcement.

scientific evidence Evidence obtained through scientific and technological innovations.

scope of authority In white-collar crime cases, the scope of an agent's authority depends on whether the commission of the offense was authorized, requested, commanded, performed, or recklessly tolerated by the board of directors or by a high managerial agent acting in behalf of the corporation within the scope of his or her office or employment.

search and seizure Refers to the police search for and/or seizure of contraband or other evidence of crime.

search incident to a lawful arrest Search of a person placed under arrest and the area within the arrestee's grasp and control.

second-degree murder Typically refers to a killing perpetrated by any act imminently dangerous to another and evincing a depraved mind regardless of human life, although without any premeditated design to effect the death of any particular individual.

Securities and Exchange Act The 1934 act of Congress regulating the sale of securities in interstate commerce.

seduction The common-law crime of inducing a woman to have sexual intercourse outside of wedlock on the promise of marriage.

seizure Action of police in taking possession or control of property or persons.

selective prosecution Singling out defendants for prosecution on the basis of race, religion, or other impermissible classifications.

self-defense The protection of one's person against an attack.

self-representation See *pro se* defense.

sentence The official pronouncement of punishment in a criminal case.

sentencing guidelines Legislative guidelines mandating that sentencing conform to guidelines absent a compelling reason for departing from them.

sentencing hearing A hearing held by a trial court before the sentence is pronounced.

Sentencing Reform Act of 1984 A federal act directing the promulgation of sentencing guidelines.

separation of powers Constitutional assignment of legislative, executive, and judicial powers to different branches of government.

sequestration Holding jurors incommunicado during trial and deliberations.

severance Separation of cases so that they can be tried separately.

severance of charges Conducting multiple trials for multiple charges, as distinct from joinder, which refers to trying all charged offenses at once. Where two or more related offenses are charged in a single indictment or information, the trial judge often grants a severance of the charges on the motion of either the defense or the prosecution.

sexual assault See sexual battery.

sexual battery In modern statutes, the unlawful oral, anal, or vaginal penetration by or union with the sexual organ of another.

sexual contact The intentional touching of the victim's intimate parts or the intentional touching of the clothing covering the immediate area of the victim's intimate parts, if that intentional touching can reasonably be construed as being for the purpose of sexual arousal or gratification.

sexual penetration Sexual intercourse, cunnilingus, fellatio, anal intercourse, or any other intrusion, however slight, of any part of a person's body or by any object into the genital or anal openings of another person's body.

sheriff The chief law enforcement officer of the county.

Sherman Antitrust Act A federal statute prohibiting any contract, combination, or conspiracy in restraint of trade. The act is designed to protect and preserve a system of free and open competition. Its scope is broad and reaches individuals and entities in profit and nonprofit activities as well as local governments and educational institutions.

showup An event in which a crime victim is taken to see a suspect to make an identification.

similar fact evidence Refers to evidence of facts similar to the facts in the crime charged. The test of admissibility is whether such evidence is relevant and has a probative value in establishing a material issue. Under some limited circumstances, evidence of other crimes or conduct similar to that charged against the defendant may be admitted in evidence in a criminal prosecution.

simple kidnapping The abduction of another person without a demand for ransom.

skip tracer A person who tracks down alleged offenders who have fled to avoid prosecution. See bounty hunter.

slander The tort of defaming someone's character through verbal statements.

sobriety checkpoints Roadblocks set up for the purpose of administering field sobriety tests to motorists who appear to be intoxicated.

sodomy Oral or anal sex between persons, or sex between a person and an animal, the latter commonly referred to as bestiality.

solicitation The inchoate offense of requesting or encouraging someone to engage in illegal conduct.

special agents Officers of the Federal Bureau of Investigation with the power to make arrests and use force in the enforcement of federal law.

specific intent The mental purpose to accomplish a specific act prohibited by law.

specific objection Counsel's objection to a question posed to a witness by opposing trial counsel where a specific reason is given for the objection—for example, that the question calls for hearsay evidence.

specific-intent statute A statute defining criminal conduct in which the offender must harbor a specific intent to accomplish a prohibited result.

speedy and public trial An open and public criminal trial held without unreasonable delay.

Speedy Trial Act of 1974 This federal statute act provides specific time limits for pretrial and trial procedures in the federal courts. For example, an indictment must be filed within thirty days of arrest, and trial must commence within seventy days after the indictment.

sports bribery Offering anything of value to a participant or official in an amateur or professional athletic contest to vary his or her performance.

spousal abuse Physical, emotional, or sexual abuse of one's husband or wife.

spousal rape See marital rape.

stalking Following or placing a person under surveillance and threatening that person with bodily harm, sexual assault, confinement, or restraint, or placing that person in reasonable fear of bodily harm, sexual assault, confinement, or restraint.

standby counsel An attorney appointed to assist an indigent defendant who elects to represent himself or herself at trial.

standing The right to initiate a legal action or challenge based on the fact that one has suffered or is likely to suffer a real and substantial injury.

stare decisis The doctrine of deciding cases based on precedent.

state supreme court The highest appellate court of a state.

state's attorney A state prosecutor.

status offenses Noncriminal conduct on the part of juveniles that may subject juveniles to the authority of a juvenile court.

statute A generally applicable law enacted by a legislature.

statute of limitations A law proscribing prosecutions for specific crimes after specified periods of time.

statutory rape The strict liability offense of having sexual intercourse with a minor, irrespective of the minor's consent.

stay of execution An order suspending the enforcement of a judgment of a court.

stop-and-frisk An encounter between a police officer and a suspect during which the latter is temporarily detained and subjected to a "pat-down" search for weapons.

strict judicial scrutiny Judicial review of government action or policy in which the ordinary presumption of constitutionality is reversed.

strict liability Criminal responsibility based solely on the commission of a prohibited act.

strict liability offenses Offenses that do not require proof of the defendant's intent.

strip searches Searches of suspects' or prisoners' private parts.

structuring Engaging in multiple smaller transactions to avoid currency reporting requirements.

subjective standard of reasonableness A test used by courts to determine whether it was appropriate for a defendant to use deadly force in self-defense. Under this approach, the jury is asked to place itself in the shoes of the defendant.

subjective test A legal test based on the perceptions or intentions of an individual actor, rather than external circumstances.

subjective test of entrapment Whether the defendant's criminal intent originated in the mind of the police officer or whether the defendant was predisposed to commit the offense.

subornation of perjury The crime of procuring someone to lie under oath.

subpoena A judicial order to appear at a certain place and time to give testimony.

substantial capacity test The doctrine that a person is not responsible for criminal conduct if at the time of such conduct, as a result of mental disease or defect, the person lacks substantial capacity either to appreciate the wrongfulness of his or her conduct or to conform his or her conduct to the requirements of the law.

substantial federal question A significant legal question pertaining to the U.S. Constitution, a federal statute, treaty, regulation, or judicial interpretation of any of the foregoing.

substantial step A significant step toward completion of an intended result.

substantive criminal law That branch of the criminal law that defines criminal offenses and defenses, and specifies criminal punishments.

substantive due process Doctrine that due process clauses of the Fifth and Fourteenth amendments to the United States Constitution require legislation to be fair and reasonable in content as well as application.

substantive law That part of the law that creates rights and proscribes wrongs.

suicide The intentional taking of a person's own life.

summary court-martial Court-martial composed of only one officer with jurisdiction only over enlisted personnel and with limited authority to impose punishments.

summary justice Trial held by court of limited jurisdiction without benefit of a jury.

summary trial A bench trial of a minor misdemeanor.

summons A court order requiring a person to appear in court to answer a criminal charge.

suppression doctrine See exclusionary rule.

suppression of evidence See exclusionary rule.

supra "Above."

surety bond A sum of money or property that is posted or guaranteed by a party, usually an insurer, to ensure the future court appearance of another person.

suspended sentence Trial court's decision to place a defendant on probation or under community control instead of imposing an announced sentence on the condition that the original sentence may be imposed if the defendant violates the conditions of the suspended sentence.

sustain To uphold.

sworn officers Law enforcement officers sworn to uphold the Constitution and laws of the United States and of their own states.

symbolic speech Expression by symbols, gestures, and so forth.

tangible property Property that has physical form, substance, and value in itself.

target crime A crime that is the object of a conspiracy. For example, in conspiracy to traffic in illegal drugs, the offense of trafficking in illegal drugs is the target crime.

tax fraud False or deceptive conduct performed with the intent of violating revenue laws, especially the Internal Revenue Code.

***Terry*-stop** See stop-and-frisk.

testimonial evidence Evidence received by a court from witnesses who have testified under oath.

testimony Evidence given by a witness who has sworn to tell the truth.

theft Taking someone's tangible or intangible property with intent to temporarily or permanently deprive the person of the property or some benefit therefrom.

theft of computer services Stealing software, data, computer access codes, computer time, and so on.

third-party consent Consent, usually to a search, given by a person on behalf of another—for example, a college roommate who allows the police to search his or her roommate's effects.

three strikes and you're out Popular term for a statute that provides for mandatory life imprisonment for a convicted felon who has been previously convicted of two or more serious felonies.

time, place, and manner doctrine First Amendment doctrine holding that government may impose reasonable limitations on the time, place, and manner of expressive activities.

time, place, and manner regulations Government limitations on the time, place, and manner of expressive activities.

tolling Ceasing. For example, one who conceals himself or herself from the authorities generally causes a "tolling" of the statutes of limitation on prosecution of a crime.

tort A wrong or injury other than a breach of contract for which the remedy is a civil suit for damages.

totality of circumstances Circumstances considered in the aggregate as opposed to individually.

Toxic Substances Control Act A federal statute authorizing the Environmental Protection Agency to prohibit manufacture, distribution, or use of chemicals that present unreasonable risks to the environment and to regulate the disposal of such chemicals.

traffic courts Courts of limited jurisdiction whose main function is the adjudication of traffic offenses and other minor misdemeanors.

traffic violations Violations of laws and ordinances regulating motor vehicle traffic.

transactional immunity A grant of immunity applying to offenses that a witness's testimony relates to.

transcript A written record of a trial or hearing.

transferred intent Doctrine holding that if A intends to injure B but instead injures C, then A's intent to injure B supplies the requisite intent to injure C.

treason The crime of attempting by overt acts to overthrow the government, or of betraying the government to a foreign power.

trespass An unlawful interference with one's person or property.

trial A judicial proceeding held for the purpose of making factual and legal determinations.

trial courts Judicial tribunals usually presided over by one judge who conducts proceedings and trials in civil and criminal cases with or without a jury.

trial de novo "A new trial." Refers to trial court review of convictions for minor offenses by courts of limited jurisdiction by conducting a new trial instead of merely reviewing the record of the initial trial.

trial jury A fixed number of citizens, usually six or twelve, selected according to law and sworn to hear the evidence presented at a trial and to render a verdict based on the law and the evidence.

tribunal A court of law.

truancy Staying away from required school attendance without permission.

true bill An indictment handed down by a grand jury.

trustee A person entrusted to handle the affairs of another.

trusty A prisoner entrusted with authority to supervise other prisoners in exchange for certain privileges and status.

truth in sentencing Laws requiring that persons sentenced to prison serve a specified proportion of their sentences.

two-witness rule A requirement that to prove a defendant guilty of perjury, the prosecution must prove the falsity of the defendant's statements either by two witnesses or by one witness and corroborating documents or circumstances.

UCMJ The Uniform Code of Military Justice, adopted by the U.S. Congress.

UCR The Uniform Crime Reports, compiled by the Federal Bureau of Investigation.

ultra vires Beyond the scope of a prescribed authority.

unconstitutional as applied Declaration by a court of law that a statute is invalid insofar as it is enforced in some particular context.

unconstitutional *per se* A statute that is unconstitutional under any given circumstances.

Uniform Child Custody Jurisdiction Act (UCCJA) A law in force in all fifty states that generally continues jurisdiction for custody of children in the home or resident state of the child.

Uniform Code of Military Justice (UCMJ) A code of laws enacted by Congress that governs military service persons and defines the procedural and evidentiary requirements in military law and the substantive criminal offenses and punishments.

Uniform Victims of Crime Act A law proposed by the Uniform Law Commission designed to provide uniform rights and procedures concerning crime victims.

United States Attorneys Attorneys appointed by the president with consent of the U.S. Senate to prosecute federal crimes in a specific geographical area of the United States.

United States Court of Appeals for the Armed Forces See Court of Appeals for the Armed Forces.

United States Courts of Appeals The twelve intermediate appellate courts of appeals in the federal system that sit in specified geographical areas of the United States and in which panels of appellate judges hear appeals in civil and criminal cases primarily from the U.S. District Courts.

United States District Courts The principal trial courts in the federal system that sit in 94 districts—usually, one judge hears proceedings and trials in civil and criminal cases.

United States Marshals Law enforcement officers of the United States Department of Justice who are responsible for enforcing federal laws, enforcing federal court decisions, and effecting the transfer of federal prisoners.

United States Sentencing Commission A federal body that proposes guideline sentences for defendants convicted of federal crimes.

United States Supreme Court The highest court in the United States, consisting of nine justices, that has jurisdiction to review, by appeal or writ of certiorari, the decisions of lower federal courts and many decisions of the highest courts of each state.

unlawful assembly A group of individuals, usually five or more, assembled to commit an unlawful act or to commit a lawful act in an unlawful manner.

use immunity   A grant of immunity that forbids prosecutors from using immunized testimony as evidence in criminal prosecutions.

uttering a forged instrument   The crime of passing a false or worthless instrument, such as a check, with the intent to defraud or injure the recipient.

vacate   To annul, set aside, or rescind.

vagrancy   The offense of going about without any visible means of support.

vagueness doctrine   Doctrine of constitutional law holding unconstitutional (as a violation of due process) legislation that fails to clearly inform the person what is required or proscribed.

valuable consideration   Money or something else of value offered as an inducement for someone to enter into a contract.

vandalism   The willful destruction of the property of another person.

vehicular homicide   Homicide resulting from the unlawful and negligent operation of a motor vehicle.

venire   The group of citizens from whom a jury is chosen in a given case.

venue   The location of a trial or hearing.

verdict   The formal decision rendered by a jury in a civil or criminal trial.

vicarious liability   Liability of one party for acts committed by another person.

vice crimes   Crimes of immoral conduct, such as prostitution, gambling, and the use of narcotics.

victim   A person who is the object of a crime or tort.

victim impact evidence   Evidence relating to the physical, economic, and psychological impact that a crime has on the victim or victim's family.

victim impact statement   Statement read into the record during the sentencing phase of a criminal trial to inform the court about the impact of the crime on the victim or victim's family.

victimless crimes   Crimes in which no particular person appears or claims to be injured, such as prostitution or gambling.

victims' rights   Refers to the various rights possessed by victims of crimes. See Uniform Victims of Crime Act.

Violent Crime Act   See Violent Crime Control and Law Enforcement Act of 1994.

Violent Crime Control and Law Enforcement Act of 1994   Known generally as the "Crime Bill," this federal statute dramatically increased the number of federal crimes eligible for the death penalty, authorized federal grants for drug court programs that include court-supervised drug treatment, and created the offense of "interstate domestic violence."

voice exemplar   A sample of a person's voice, usually taken by police for the purpose of identifying a suspect.

void-for-vagueness   See vagueness doctrine.

voir dire   "To speak the truth." The process by which prospective jurors are questioned by counsel and/or the court before being selected to serve on a jury.

voluntariness of a confession   The quality of a confession having been freely given.

voluntary intoxication   The state of becoming drunk or intoxicated on one's own free will.

voluntary manslaughter   The intentional killing of a human without malice or premeditation and usually occurring during a sudden quarrel or in the heat of passion.

waiver   The intentional and voluntary relinquishment of a right, or conduct from which such relinquishment may be inferred.

waiver of juvenile court jurisdiction   A relinquishment by a juvenile court to allow prosecution of a juvenile in an adult court.

waiver of _Miranda_ rights   A known relinquishment of the right against self-incrimination provided by the Fifth Amendment to the U.S. Constitution.

warrant   A judicial writ or order directed to a law enforcement officer authorizing the doing of a specified act, such as arrest or search.

warrantless arrest   An arrest made by police who do not possess an arrest warrant.

warrantless searches   Searches made by police who do not possess search warrants.

weapons offenses   Violations of laws restricting or prohibiting the manufacture, sale, transfer, possession, or use of certain firearms.

weight of the evidence   The balance or preponderance of the evidence. Weight of the evidence is to be distinguished from "legal sufficiency of the evidence," which is the concern of an appellate court.

well-regulated Militia   This phrase, from the Second Amendment to the U.S. Constitution, refers to a citizen army subject to government regulations. In the early history of the United States, the militia was the set of able-bodied men who could be pressed into military service by the governor of the state. The National Guard is the modern counterpart.

Wharton's Rule   Named after Francis Wharton, a well-known commentator on criminal law, this rule holds that two people cannot conspire to commit a crime such as adultery, incest, or bigamy inasmuch as these offenses involve only two participants.

white-collar crimes   Various criminal offenses committed by persons in the upper socioeconomic strata of society, often in the course of the occupation or profession of such persons.

wire fraud   A fraudulent scheme that uses interstate television, radio, or wire communications.

wiretap order   A court order permitting electronic surveillance for a limited period.

wiretapping   The use of highly sensitive electronic devices designed to intercept electronic communications.

worthless check statutes   Laws making it an offense to knowingly pass a worthless check.

writ   An order issued by a court of law requiring the performance of some specific act.

writ of certiorari   See certiorari.

writ of error   A writ issued by an appellate court for the purpose of correcting an error revealed in the record of a lower court proceeding.

writ of habeas corpus   See habeas corpus.

writ of prohibition   A court order that prevents another court from exercising jurisdiction in a particular case.

writs of assistance   Ancient writs issuing from the Court of Exchequer ordering sheriffs to assist in collecting debts owed the Crown. Prior to the American Revolution, the writs of assistance gave agents of the Crown in the American colonies the unlimited right to search for smuggled goods. In modern practice, judicial orders to put someone in possession of property.

year-and-a-day rule   A common-law rule that to convict a defendant of homicide, not more than a year and a day can intervene from defendant's criminal act to the death of the victim.

zoning ordinance   A local law regulating the use of land.

Table of Cases

The excerpted cases are in **bold** type. Cases cited or discussed are in roman type. References are to pages.

Index